Information Centre
Bristows LLP
100 Victoria Embankment
London
EC4Y 0DH

TERRELL

ON THE

LAW OF PATENTS

TERRELL

ON THE

LAW OF PATENTS

EIGHTEENTH EDITION

Published in 2016 by Sweet & Maxwell, Thomson Reuters (Professional) UK Limited trading as Sweet & Maxwell, Friars House, 160 Blackfriars Road, London, SE1 8EZ (Registered in England & Wales, Company No 1679046. Registered Office and address for service: 2nd Floor, 1 Mark Square, Leonard Street, London EC2A 4EG.)

For further information on our products and services, visit
www.sweetandmaxwell.co.uk

Printed and bound in Great Britain by CPI Group (UK) Ltd, Croydon, CR0 4YY. No natural forests were destroyed to make this product; only farmed timber was used and re-planted. A CIP catalogue record of this book is available for the British Library.

ISBN: 9780414052659

PREVIOUS EDITIONS

First Edition (1884) by Thomas Terrell

Second Edition (1889) by Thomas Terrell

Third Edition (1895) by W.P. Rylands

Fourth Edition (1906) by Courtney Terrell

Fifth Edition (1909) by Courtney Terrell

Sixth Edition (1921) by Courtney Terrell and A.D. Jaffe

Seventh Edition (1927) by Courtney Terrell and D.H. Corsellis

Eighth Edition (1934) by J.R. Jones

Ninth Edition (1951) by K.E. Shelley KC

Tenth Edition (1961) by K.E. Shelley QC

Eleventh Edition (1965) by Guy Aldous QC, Douglas Falconer and William Aldous

Twelfth Edition (1971) by Douglas Falconer QC William Aldous and David Young

Thirteenth Edition (1982) by William Aldous QC, David Young QC, A. Watson and S. Thorley

Fourteenth Edition (1994) by David Young QC, Antony Watson QC, Simon Thorley QC and Richard Miller

Fifteenth Edition (2000) by Simon Thorley QC, Richard Miller QC, Guy Burkill and Colin Birss

Sixteenth Edition (2006) by Simon Thorley QC, Richard Miller QC, Guy Burkill QC, Colin Birss and Douglas Campbell

Seventeenth Edition (2011) by Richard Miller QC, Guy Burkill QC, Colin Birss QC, and Douglas Campbell

PREFACE

This edition marks major changes in the editorial team. After many years' long service, both Richard Miller QC and Guy Burkill QC have stepped down and a new group of editors have come forward, appointing me as the general editor. Richard and Guy put so much into *Terrell* for so many years that their influence remains throughout.

The Supreme Court has been active in patents since the last edition, with important decisions in *HGS v Eli Lilly*, *Schutz v Werit*, *Servier v Apotex* and *Virgin v Zodiac*. Whether this is an indication that the Supreme Court will tend to hear more patent appeals than the House of Lords did remains to be seen.

The judgments in *HGS* refer to plausibility. The emergence of that concept (or rather arguments about an alleged lack of it) in relation to each of inventive step, sufficiency and industrial applicability represents a significant recent legal development in the life sciences. The other contender for this crown is the nature of infringement in second medical use cases, where a previously known product is sold for a patented new use, as seen in the ongoing *Warner-Lambert* (*Lyrica*) litigation. In information technology, arguments about standards essential patents and FRAND licences continue. Since the last edition the successful reforms to the Patents County Court were completed with the creation of its successor, the Intellectual Property Enterprise Court, or IPEC. The name change more accurately reflects the existing workload of that court, rather than indicating any reduced role for patent cases. That court continues to go from strength to strength. The Jackson reforms to civil procedure which were introduced in April 2013 have also had an impact on litigation in the Patents Court (i.e. the High Court).

As well as new chapters focussing on FRAND and the IPEC, in this edition we have included a new chapter on the Unified Patent Court. Although the UPC is not yet in operation, it is likely to start during the currency of this edition.

The appendices have been pruned down to relevant UK primary legislation and European legislation.

The whole team would like to thank Georgina Messenger for all her hard work marshalling and indexing relevant cases.

With the exception of the chapter on the UPC, we have tried to state the law as at 1 January 2016.

This edition is dedicated to RM and GB.

C.B.

Middle Temple
3 February 2016

TABLE OF CONTENTS

CHAPTERS

APPENDICES

TABLE OF CASES

TABLE OF EPO DECISIONS

(References are to Paragraph numbers)

TABLE OF EPO DECISIONS

DECISIONS OF THE OPPOSITION DIVISION

TABLE OF STATUTES

(References are to Paragraph numbers)

TABLE OF STATUTORY INSTRUMENTS

(References are to Paragraph numbers)

TABLE OF CIVIL PROCEDURE RULES

(References are to Paragraph numbers)

TABLE OF CIVIL PROCEDURE RULES – PRACTICE DIRECTIONS

(References are to Paragraph numbers)

TABLE OF EUROPEAN AND INTERNATIONAL TREATIES AND CONVENTIONS

(References are to Paragraph numbers)

TABLE OF EU LEGISLATION

(References are to Paragraph numbers)

CHAPTER 1

PATENTS

CONTENTS

1. INTRODUCTION

What is a patent?

The grant of a patent for an invention is the grant to the patentee for a limited period of a monopoly right in respect of that invention, i.e. the right to exclude others from using that invention. The patentee is required to disclose the invention, and following expiry of the patent term it may be freely used. In this way innovation is encouraged and knowledge is disseminated.

1-01

Origin of the term "Patent": Letters Patent

The term "patent" is derived from "Letters Patent" and indeed in statutes prior to the Patents Act 1977 "patent" was defined as meaning "Letters Patent for an invention". "Letters Patent," that is, open letters, *literae patentes*, are documents which are so called "because they are not sealed up, but exposed to view, with the Great Seal pendant at the bottom, and are usually addressed by the Sovereign to all the subjects of the Realm".[1] They derive their authority from the fact that they are issued under the Great Seal, "for all the King's subjects are bound to take notice of the King's Great Seal".[2] They are the common form of making grants of dignities, appointments to certain offices of state and grants of privilege of various kinds, including, until the coming into operation of the Patents Act 1977 on 1 June 1978, monopoly rights in inventions.

1-02

Prior to the Patents, Designs and Trade Marks Act 1883, letters patent for inventions were issued under the Great Seal and consequently by the Lord Chancellor as Keeper of the Great Seal. The process of sealing a patent was attended with all the formalities and expense which surround an important act of State.[3] From 1883 until the coming into operation of the Patents Act 1977 the seal of the Patent Office was substituted for the Great Seal, successive Statutes providing[4]:

1-03

"A patent sealed with the seal of the Patent Office shall have the same effect as if it were sealed with

---

[1] Blackstone's Commentaries, Vol.II, c.21, s.2.
[2] *East India Co v Sandys* (1684) Skin. 224.
[3] The short story by Charles Dickens, "A poor man's tale of a patent", describes the various steps (and costs) involved in securing grant of a patent.
[4] Patents, Designs and Trade Marks Act 1883 s.12; Patents Act 1907 s.14; Patents Act 1949 s.21.

[1]

the Great Seal of the United Kingdom, and shall have effect throughout the United Kingdom[5] and the Isle of Man".

1-04   The language of the grant itself preserved the royal prerogative to grant or to withhold a patent. After the royal greeting and a recital of the application the formal wording proceeded[6]:

"AND WHEREAS We, being willing to encourage all inventions which may be for the public good, are graciously pleased to condescend to the request:
    KNOW YE, THEREFORE, that We, of our especial grace, certain knowledge, and mere motion do by these presents, for Us, our heirs and successors, give and grant unto the person(s) above named ... our especial licence, full power, sole privilege, and authority, that the patentee or any agent or licensee of the patentees and no others, may subject to the conditions and provisions prescribed by any statute or order for the time being in force at all times hereafter during the term of years herein mentioned, make, use, exercise and vend the said invention within our United Kingdom of Great Britain and Northern Ireland, and the Isle of Man, and that the patentee shall have and enjoy the whole profit and advantage from time to time accruing by reason of the said invention during the term of sixteen years from the date hereunder written of these presents ..."

1-05   Statutes prior to the 1977 Act contained no further definition of infringement: this was unnecessary, for infringement was simply the doing of that which was prohibited by the words of the royal command which immediately followed:

"AND to the end that the patentee may have and enjoy the sole use and exercise and the full benefit of the said invention, We do by these presents for Us, our heirs and successors, strictly command all our subjects whatsoever within our United Kingdom of Great Britain and Northern Ireland, and the Isle of Man, that they do not at any time during the continuance of the said term either directly or indirectly make use of or put in practice the said invention, nor in anywise imitate the same, without the written consent, licence or agreement of the patentee, on pain of incurring such penalties as may be justly inflicted on such offenders for their contempt of this our Royal Command, and of being answerable to this patentee according to law for damages thereby occasioned."

1-06   The meaning and scope of the granted monopoly to "make use exercise and vend" the invention was the subject of debate in many authorities: the interested reader is referred to previous editions of this work.

Modern form of patent

1-07   Since the coming into operation (on 1 June 1978) of the Patents Act 1977, Letters Patent are no longer issued to patentees on the grant of a patent for an invention. Indeed, under the 1977 Act, a patent for an invention is not granted under the royal prerogative at all but instead is a purely statute-based right. The word "patent" has been retained but there is no other connection with Letters Patent. Thus, on grant of a patent under the 1977 Act, the Comptroller sends to the proprietor a certificate in the prescribed form stating that the patent has been granted to him.[7] In the case of a European patent, the European Patent Office issues a similar certificate as soon as the specifications of the European patent has been published.[8]

---

5   This includes Northern Ireland, but not the Channel Islands.
6   As set out in Rules made under the 1949 Patents Act.
7   PA 1977 s.24(2); Patents Rules 2007 r.34.
8   EPC Rules r.74.

2. HISTORY OF THE DEVELOPMENT OF UK PATENT LAW

The following short outline of the history of the development of the patent system   **1-08**
and of patent law and practice in the UK may perhaps be helpful as an introduction to, and explanation of the origins of, present practice and legislation.

Early industrial grants

In early times, the regulation of trade lay within the prerogative of the Crown.   **1-09**
The charters and patents granted to the mediaeval trade guilds and corporations
exemplified this. Grants of special privileges were, however, also made to individuals from time to time. Thus, between 1331 and 1452, various letters of protection
were issued to foreign weavers and other craftsmen.[9] In 1347, there was a complaint
in Parliament that an alien merchant had a monopoly of exporting Cornish tin[10];
while in 1376 John Peeche, Alderman of Walbrook Ward, was impeached in respect
of a patent giving him the right to sell sweet wines in the City of London contrary
to an ordinance of Parliament.[11]

A grant by Henry VI in 1449 gave a 20-year monopoly to John Utynam of   **1-10**
Flanders, who had "come to make glass of all colours for the windows of Eton College and the college of S.Mary and S.Nicholas, Cambridge [King's College]",
because "the said art has never been used in England" and he intended to instruct
apprentices in that and in "many other arts never used in the realm beside the said
art of making glass".[12] This appears to be the earliest instance in which a monopoly
for a limited period of time (20 years) was granted in relation to a novel art in return
for disclosure of its method of implementation.

However the practice of the Crown granting monopolies was open to abuse, and   **1-11**
while the system may originally have been intended to encourage the setting up of
new industries,[13] it in fact became a method of rewarding favourites and raising
revenue, particularly as a result of the "Monopoly System" inaugurated by Cecil
during the reign of Queen Elizabeth I (1558-1603). In 1571 a complaint was made
in Parliament because coal, oil, salt, vinegar, starch, iron, glass, were the subjects
of monopoly. However, despite that complaint, the Queen insisted on exercising her
prerogative powers and continued to do so. In 1601, in the last parliament of the
reign, two Bills were introduced with the object of reforming the system, but were
not proceeded with[14] as the Queen promised to recall some of the patents
complained of and, as to the others, proclaimed that none "should be put in execution but such as should first have a trial according to law".[15]

---

[9]   See, e.g. Cal. Pat. Rolls (1330-34) 161; (1367-70) 105; Rymer, x, 761; xi, 317.
[10] Tydman of Lynnburgh, who had liberty to export tin without paying the customary tax: see Rot. Parl.
      ii, 168; Cal. Close Rolls (1346-49) 328.
[11] The facts are obscure: see Rot. Parl. ii, 328; Cal. Pat. Rolls (1374-77) 448, 457; Cal. Fine Rolls, viii,
      225, 227. The case was cited in *Darcy v Allin* (1602) 1 W.P.C. 1, 4.
[12] Cal. Pat. Rolls, Hen. VI, v. 255, dated 3 April 1449.
[13] For the provisions of the early patents see E.Wyndham Hulme, "The History of the Patent System
      under the Prerogative and at Common Law" (1896) 12 L.Q.R. 141.
[14] There is no record of their provisions.
[15] A fuller discussion of this episode may be found in Frederic Jesup Stimson, *Popular law-making :
      a study of the origin, history, and present tendencies of law-making by statute,* (London: Chapman
      & Hall, 1911).

The Case of Monopolies

1-12   Such a trial soon came before the Common Law court in the famous Case of Monopolies[16] concerning Darcy's patent for the monopoly of importing, manufacturing and selling playing cards. Although the case began in 1602, judgment was not delivered until after the Queen's death in 1603 and the accession of King James I (1603-1625). The patent was held invalid as being a monopoly illegal at common law, and also as being a licence for importation of playing cards contrary to certain statutes. The Court of King's Bench (Popham CJ) considered that the grant was a monopoly in restraint of trade and tending to raise prices and lower quality. The court reasoned that the Crown, having recited in the preamble of the patent that the grant was intended for the public good, could not have intended such abuse and must therefore have been deceived, and the grant was accordingly void. Although it was not contended that Darcy's patent was a patent for a new trade or an invention, the court reviewed how the Common Law treated such patents and stated:

> "…where any man, by his own charge and industry, or by his own wit or invention, doth bring any new trade into the realm, or any engine tending to the furtherance of a trade that never was used before, and that for the good of the realm, that in such cases the king may grant to him a monopoly patent, for some reasonable time, until the subjects may learn the same, in consideration of the good that he doth bring by his invention to the commonwealth, otherwise not."[17]

1-13   The court went on to note three earlier cases in which actions had been brought on patents for inventions granted to one Hastings (fine cloths known as frisadoes), Matthey (knives), and Humphrey (sieves). In the third case it appears that Humphrey himself claimed to be the inventor, whereas the first two cases involved an introduction from abroad. The cases had each turned on the question of whether the subject of the patent had been used in England before the date of the grant.

The Book of Bounty

1-14   In 1610, the proclamation usually known as "St James's Book of Bounty" or "The Book of Bounty" was issued. The proclamation was drafted some two years earlier, reputedly by Cecil. As a practical matter it was intended to curb the King's largess towards those he favoured, particularly by the exercise of the Royal Prerogative.

1-15   The proclamation set forth "monopolies" as the first of the "special things for which We expressly command that no suitor presume to move Us". However "projects of new inventions" were excepted from this prohibition, provided they were not contrary to law or "mischievous to the State, by raising prices of commodities at home, or hurt of trade, or otherwise inconvenient".

---

16 Otherwise, *Darcy v Allin* (1602) 1 W.P.C. 1 and 5; Noy 173 (74 ER 1131); Moore K.B. 671; 11 Co.Rep. 85. See the composite report in J.W. Gordon, K.C., *Monopolies by Patents and the Statutable Remedies Available to the Public* (London: Stevens and Sons, 1897). There had been a previous action on the patent before the Privy Council: see E.W. Hulme, 16 L.Q.R., xvi, 51.

17 1 W.P.C. 5 at 6; Noy 173 at 182 (74 ER 1131 at 1139).

Clothworkers of Ipswich Case

A further judicial pronouncement on the legality of patents for inventions appeared in 1614 in the report of the *Clothworkers of Ipswich Case*[18]:

> "But if a man hath brought in a new invention and a new trade within the kingdom in peril of his life and consumption of his estate or stock, etc., or if a man hath made a new discovery of anything, in such cases the King of his grace and favour in recompense of his costs and travail may grant by charter unto him that he shall only use such a trade or trafique for a certain time, because at first people of the kingdom are ignorant, and have not the knowledge and skill to use it. But when the patent is expired the King cannot make a new grant thereof".

1-16

Statute of Monopolies 1623

The abuses of the monopoly system finally became so scandalous that the agents most concerned in enforcing certain patents were impeached. Some 20 patents were thereupon revoked by proclamation, and others left for trial in the courts. At the same time a joint committee of both Houses of Parliament agreed a Bill which finally received Royal Assent on 25 May 1624.[19]

1-17

This Act is the Statute of Monopolies.[20] It recited the publication and effect of the Book of Bounty and declared all monopolies, dispensations, and grants to compound penalties void. All such grants were to be tried at common law; and by s.6 the foundations of modern patent law were laid down in the following terms:

1-18

> "Provided also (and be it declared and enacted)[21] that any declaration before mentioned shall not extend to any letters patent and grants of privilege for the term of fourteen years or under, hereafter to be made, of the sole working or making of any manner of new manufactures within this realm, to the true and first inventor and inventors of such manufactures which others at the time of making such letters patent and grants shall not use, so as also they be not contrary to the law or mischievous to the state, by raising prices of commodities at home, or hurt of trade, or generally inconvenient".

The Statute was intended to be declaratory of the common law.[22] It did not create a new statutory right but saved and merely limited the prerogative of the Crown to grant monopolies. Thus Letters Patent for inventions continued (until the coming into force of the 1977 Act) to be granted under the Crown's prerogative and indeed s.102 of the Patents Act 1949 (and corresponding sections in earlier statutes) contained an express saving for such prerogative in relation to "the granting of letters patent or to the withholding of a grant thereof". Consequently an application for a patent could be refused where the grant would have been withheld under the royal prerogative, and applications e.g. for contraceptive devices were commonly refused under this power.[23]

1-19

For various reasons, but probably mainly on account of the exception in favour of corporations made by section 9, the Act had little practical effect for many years, and the Age of Monopolies did not finally come to an end until the outbreak of the Civil War in 1642. Patents for inventions continued to be granted under the Com-

1-20

---

[18] Godbolt 252 (78 ER 147).
[19] 21 Jac. 1, c.3.
[20] It is generally known as the Statute of Monopolies 1623, although in fact enacted in the following year.
[21] Words in brackets repealed by the Statute Law Revision Act 1888 s.1 Sch. Pt 1.
[22] See Co.Inst. III, c.85; *Feather v R.* (1865) 6B.&S.257 at 285; *Australian Gold, etc., Co v Lake View, etc., Ltd* [1901] 18 R.P.C. 105, 114.
[23] See *A&H's Application* (1927) 44 R.P.C. 298.

monwealth; and the law and practice remained almost unchanged until long after
the Restoration of the Monarchy in 1660. For example, in the early days of the patent system all patents contained a proviso for revocation by the Privy Council and
questions of validity were normally tried before it.[24] It was not until about 1753
onwards that patent litigation (with the exception of petitions for extension
introduced by the Patent Act 1835)[25] was conducted in the Court of Chancery and
Queen's Bench. Likewise, prior to 1795, there were practically no reported cases
on the construction of the words "any manner of new manufacture" in the Statute
of Monopolies.[26] The development of modern patent law can be said to date, for
practical purposes, from this period.

Local novelty under the Statute: imported inventions

1-21   The Statute of Monopolies sanctioned the then-existing practice of granting
patents not only to original inventors, but also to the first importers of new
manufactures, which as illustrated above had been regarded as beneficial under the
common law. As stated in *Edgeberry v Stephens*:

> "A grant of a monopoly may be to the first inventor, by the 21 Jac. 1, and if the invention be new in
> England, a patent may be granted though the thing was practised beyond sea before; for the statute
> speaks of new manufactures within this realm; so that if it be new here, it is within the statute; for
> the act intended to encourage new devices useful to the kingdom, and whether learned by travel or
> by study it is the same thing."[27]

1-22   Thus the words "true and first inventor" in s.6 of the Statute of Monopolies were
construed as covering the first introducer. They therefore included both original
inventors in the modern sense, and also true and first importers into the realm. The
effect of the earlier decisions was summed up in 1876 by Jessel MR in *Plimpton v
Malcolmson*:

> "What is the meaning of a first and true inventor? To ascertain its meaning you must have recourse,
> no doubt, to various decisions given on the statute. ... As I understand shortly after the passing of
> the statute, the question arose whether a man could be called a first and true inventor who, in the
> popular sense, had never invented anything, but who, having learned abroad (that is out of the realm,
> in a foreign country, because it has been decided that *Scotland* is within the realm for this purpose)
> that somebody else had invented something, quietly copied the invention, and brought it over to this
> country, and then took out a patent. As I said before, in the popular sense he had invented nothing.
> But it was decided, and now, therefore, is the legal sense and meaning of the statute, that he was a
> first and true inventor within the statute. ..."[28]

1-23   To similar effect, Lindley LJ in *Moser v Marsden*[29] said:

> "The patentee is the true and first inventor within the meaning of the patent laws, whether he invents
> himself or whether he simply imports a foreign invention".

1-24   The law therefore required only local novelty: in other words, a patent was valid

---

[24] For an account of the practice at this date, see E.W. Hulme, "Privy Council Law and Practice of Letters Patent for Invention from the Restoration to 1794" 33 L.Q.R. 65.
[25] 5 & 6 Will. 4, c.83.
[26] See Eyre L.C.J. in Boulton and *Watt v Bull* (1795) 2 H.Bl. 463 (126 ER 651, 663). The notable
exception is *Edgeberry v Stephens* (1691) 1 WPC 35; 2 Salk 447 (91 ER 387) referred to in the next
paragraph.
[27] (1691) 1 W.P.C. 35; 2 Salk 447 (91 ER 387).
[28] (1876) LR 3 Ch D. 531, 555; and see also Jessel MR in *Marsden v Saville Street Foundry and
Engineering Co* (1878) 3 Ex.D. 203.
[29] (1893) 10 R.P.C. 350, 359.

if the invention was new in the United Kingdom, even if had been published or was otherwise known elsewhere. Indeed when the grounds for revocation of a patent were codified in s.32(1) of the Patents Act 1949, it was expressly provided that prior art relating to novelty or obviousness was confined to what was "known or used ... in the United Kingdom". This position continued to apply until the coming into force of the Patents Act 1977 on 1 June 1978. The definition of the "state of the art", in s.2(1) of the 1977 Act, expressly incorporates the words "whether in the United Kingdom or elsewhere" thereby underlining the change in the law. The word "inventor" is also now defined in s.7(3) of the 1977 Act as "the actual deviser of the invention" thereby excluding the importer of an invention as an inventor.[30]

The development of the patent specifications and of the claims

In the early days of the patent system, the working of the invention was part of the consideration for the grant; and in many cases provisions were inserted in the patent requiring the instruction of apprentices.[31] In the case of one invention only was the grantee required to publish a description of his invention[32]; and there is some reason for supposing that this was done at the instance of the patentee himself.[33]

1-25

The original practice was merely to state the subject-matter of the invention in very general terms in the patent itself.[34] It was thus open to the patentee to allege that anything which fell within this general description or title was an infringement of the patent. The difficulties caused by this practice were met to a limited extent by introducing into the recitals technical details of the invention.[35] In 1711, however, we find it stated in Naismith's Patent No.387 that the patentee "has proposed to ascertain" the details of his invention "in writing under his hand and seal to be enrolled in our Court of Chancery" within six months after the date of the patent. And after 1716, a proviso requiring this to be done was inserted in every patent.

1-26

In *British United Shoe Machinery Co Ltd v A. Fussell & Sons Ltd*,[36] Fletcher Moulton LJ dealt with the history of distinct claims as part of specifications. After mentioning the proviso (formerly inserted in the patent itself), which required the patentee to state in writing the nature of his invention and the method of performing the same, he said:

1-27

"These two things—the delimitation of the invention and full practical directions how to use it— are in their nature almost antagonistic. As it is the duty of the inventor to give the fullest practical information to the public, he is bound to put in, if, for instance, the invention is a process, quantities and times which are the best he knows. But it would be very cruel to hold him to the invention when carried out only with those best quantities and times, because a person could then take his invention in substance if he did not take it in quite the best way, and the value of the grant would be practi-

---

[30]   cf. Patents Act 1949 s.16(2). And see *Stanelco Fibre Optic Ltd's Application* [2005] R.P.C. 15, [10].

[31]   See E.W. Hulme, "Consideration of the Patent Grant" 12, 13 L.Q.R.; Co.Inst. 3.

[32]   Sturtevant and Rovinson's Patents (1611-12); see Supplement to Patent Office Series of Specifications.

[33]   See E.W. Hulme, "The history of the patent system under the prerogative and at ... system under the prerogative at common law: A sequel" (1900) 16 L.Q.R. 44.

[34]   e.g. 1 W.P.C. 9; J.W. Gordon, K.C., *"Monopolies by Patents and the Statutable Remedies Available to the. Public"* (London: Stevens and Son, 1897), p.240 (Gilbert's "Water Plough" Patent) .

[35]   e.g. Pownall's Patent No.391 (1712).

[36]   (1908) 25 R.P.C. 631, 650, cited in *Assidoman Multipack Ltd v The Mead Corporation* [1995] R.P.C. 321.

cally nothing. Hence inventors, in their own protection, took to introducing into their specifications language intended to distinguish between that which was there for the practical information of the public, and that which was there for delimitation of the invention. Out of that has arisen the practice, which originally was perfectly optional, of having a separate part of the specifications primarily designed for delimitation. That is what we call the claim."

Patent Legislation 1852 to 1949

1-28   Until 1852, patents were granted in all cases upon applications which specified the "title" only of the invention, and no obligation to file specifications arose until the patent was sealed. As mentioned above, a period of six months was then allowed for furnishing the description in order to ensure that the inventor should not be forestalled before he could complete the invention and bring it to a practical form. It was, however, necessary that the specifications should not be inconsistent with or wider than the "title" (which still continued to form the basis of the grant), and patents were frequently held invalid on the ground of variance between the title and the specifications as constituting a "fraud on the Crown".[37]

1-29   The Patent Law Amendment Act 1852[38] effected a change in the procedure on application, and an inventor had thereafter to file either "provisional" or "complete" specifications at the time he made his application.[39] The practice of filing provisional and complete specifications continued up to the 1977 Act, with the 1949 Act providing that every non-convention application had to be accompanied by either a complete specifications or a provisional specifications (followed by a complete specifications within a period of 15 months) and every convention application had to be accompanied by a complete specifications.[40] The object of the legislature in providing for the filing of a provisional specifications was to enable the inventor to improve and perfect the invention during the period of "provisional protection" and at the same time maintain as the priority date of the later filed "complete specifications " the date of the earlier filed provisional specifications .[41]

1-30   Other important changes in the procedure for obtaining the grant (including provisional protection) were introduced by the 1852 Act,[42] and by the Acts of 1883 to 1888[43] there came into being the system that existed until June 1, 1978, when the Patents Act 1977 came into operation. The law and practice under that system was amended and developed from time to time in various statutes. Thus, until the Patents and Designs Act 1932[44] the grounds upon which a patent could be revoked (i.e. the grounds of invalidity) had remained those available at common law, but that Act, while retaining the grounds at common law, introduced a number of specific statu-

---

[37] See *Brunton v Hawkes* (1821) 4 Barn. & Ald. 541; see also *Cochrane v Smethurst* (1816) Dav. P.C. 354; *R. v Else* (1785) 1 W.P.C. 76; *Bloxam v Elsee* (1827) 6 Barn. & Cress. 169; *Croll v Edge* (1850) 9 C.B. 479.

[38] 15 & 16 Vict. c.83.

[39] In *Stoner v Todd* (1876) 4 Ch D. 58, Jessel MR said: "A provisional specification was never intended to be more than a mode of protecting an inventor until the time of filing a final specification; it was not intended to contain a complete description of the thing so as to enable any workman of ordinary skill to make it, but only to disclose the invention, fairly no doubt, but in its rough state."

[40] PA 1949 s.3(1). For the meaning of a "convention application", see para.1-60.

[41] Lloyd-Jacob J explained in *Glaxo Group Ltd's Application* [1968] R.P.C. 473 at 480 that "The interval of time between the filing of the two specifications [i.e. the provisional and the complete] is intended to provide an opportunity for the development and precise expression of the invention foreshadowed in the provisional ...". See also *ICI (Clark's Application)* [1969] R.P.C. 574, 583.

[42] 15 & 16 Vict. c.83.

[43] 46 & 47 Vict. c.57; 48 & 49 Vict. c.63; 49 & 50 Vict. c.37; 51 & 52 Vict. c.50.

[44] 22 & 23 Geo. 5, c.32.

tory grounds. The Patents Act 1949 abolished the grounds available at common law leaving the statutory grounds specified in that Act[45] as constituting the complete code of grounds upon which a patent could be revoked.[46] The 1949 Act was also noteworthy as providing, for the first time, for the appointment of specialist patent judges to hear patent matters.[47] Notwithstanding the enactment of the 1977 Act, certain provisions of the 1949 Act continued to apply to existing patents and patent applications,[48] i.e. patents granted and applications for patents in being before 1 June 1978, the last of which did not expire until 1998.

3. The Modern Law

Patents Act 1977

The 1977 Act effected far-reaching changes in our patent system and law.[49] The statute is divided into three parts: **1-31**

> Part I, sub-titled "New Domestic Law", enacts a code of domestic patent law changed in many significant respects from that developed and existing under previous legislation.
> Part II of the Act enacts provisions intended to meet the United Kingdom's obligations under three international Conventions: the Patent Co-operation Treaty of 1970,[50] the European Patent Convention of 1973[51] and the Community Patent Convention of 1975.[52]
> Part III deals with miscellaneous and general matters including provisions as to legal proceedings and the creation of the Patents Court.

Many of the changes to the law contained in Pt I of the 1977 Act are intended to assimilate UK domestic patent law to that of the European patent system established by the European Patent Convention signed in Munich on 5 October 1973 ("the EPC") and also, at least in some respects, to that of the Community Patent Convention signed in December 1975 ("the CPC").[53] Thus, as will be developed more fully in the next chapter, a statutory definition of patentability has been introduced and its language closely parallels that of the definition in the EPC.[54] The new statutory definition replaces the law which had been developed as to what constituted patentable inventions. Again, while it has long been a requirement of English law that to be patentable an invention should be new and should have involved an inventive step (i.e. should not have been obvious), the 1977 Act now contains provisions as to novelty and inventive step which follow corresponding provisions in the EPC.[55] Further, whereas previously the law as to what constituted infringement of a patent had been built up around the language contained in the form of Letters Patent **1-32**

---

[45] PA 1949 s.32.
[46] *American Cyanamid Co (Dann's Patent)* [1971] R.P.C. 425.
[47] PA 1949 s.84(1), thereby giving effect to the Second Interim Report of the Departmental Committee of 18 February 1946 (Cmnd.6789), paras 99-111 (the Swan Report).
[48] PA 1977 s.127 and Schs 1, 2, 3 and 4.
[49] Most of the Act came into operation on 1 June 1978. See SI 1978/586.
[50] Cmnd.4530.
[51] Cmnd.5656.
[52] Cmnd.6553.
[53] PA 1977 s.130(7).
[54] PA 1977 s.1; and cf. EPC arts 52 and 53; and see Ch.2.
[55] PA 1977 s.2(1), (2) and (3); cf. EPC arts 54-56, and see Chs 10-12.

granted for inventions, in the 1977 Act there is a statutory definition of infringement which follows, with some differences of wording, the corresponding provisions as to infringement in the CPC.[56] The term of the national patent has been
increased from 16 years from the date of filing of the complete specifications to 20
years from the date of filing of the application—in line with the term of a European
patent.[57]

1-33   The 1977 Act also introduces changes in the procedure for obtaining the grant
of a patent,[58] including changes in the rules of priority.[59] Whereas, under the 1949
Act, the system of filing a provisional and then a complete specification allowed
inventors a period of time within which to perfect their invention,[60] the effect of the
1977 Act is that there is only one specification per application and, in general, it cannot be amended after the date of filing so as to add subject matter.[61] Later developments of the invention can be included in a subsequent application, but the later
developments themselves will not be entitled to claim priority from the earlier
application.

Copyright, Designs and Patents Act 1988

1-34   Prior to the 1988 Act, actions for infringement of patents could not be brought
in the county court.[62] Whilst there was a provision for infringement issues to be
determined by agreement in the Patent Office, the procedure was seldom invoked.[63]
Due to concern about the high cost of patent litigation in the High Court, provision was made for patent infringement and revocation actions to be brought in a
county court having "special jurisdiction".[64] The Act also preserved the "ordinary
jurisdiction" which the same court had by virtue of being a county court.[65] The first
county court to be so nominated was Edmonton County Court, based at Wood
Green in North London.[66] This designation was subsequently revoked in favour of
Central London County Court in the West End of London.[67] In 2002 the PCC
moved to Field House, Breams Buildings, and it moved again to St Dunstan's
House, Fetter Lane in 2008.

1-35   A particular feature of the court, as originally constituted, was that a registered
patent agent[68] could act in Patents County Court proceedings falling within its

[56]   PA 1977 s.60; cf. CPC arts 29, 30, 31, and see Ch.14.
[57]   PA 1977 s.25(1); cf. EPC art.63(1), and see Ch.5.
[58]   See Ch.3, "The Application".
[59]   See Ch.7, "Priority Date".
[60]   See, e.g. *Glaxo Group Ltd's Application* [1968] R.P.C. 473; and para.1-29.
[61]   PA 1977 s.76; and see Ch.15, "Amendment".
[62]   PA 1977 ss.61(1) and 130(1), as originally enacted.
[63]   PA 1977 s.61(3).
[64]   Copyright, Designs and Patents Act 1988 (CDPA 1988) ss.287 and 291. The "special jurisdiction"
       referred to proceedings relating to patents or designs, or ancillary to, or arising out of the same
       subject matters as, proceedings relating to patents or designs: see s.287(1)(a), (b).
[65]   Copyright Designs and Patents Act 1988 s 287(5). The "ordinary jurisdiction" grew to include UK
       trade mark, passing off and copyright cases: see *National Guild of Removers & Storers Ltd v Silveria*
       [2011] F.S.R. 9, [7]-[11]; *Suh v Ryu* [2012] F.S.R. 31.
[66]   SI 1990/1496.
[67]   SI 1994/1609.
[68]   CDPA 1988 s.275, as originally enacted. Following amendment of this section by the Legal Services
       Act 2007 the term "registered patent attorney" is now used instead: see s.275(2).

special jurisdiction without the intervention of a solicitor.[69] Since 1999, patent attorneys to whom Litigator Certificates have been granted have additionally had wider rights of audience, including the right to conduct all types of intellectual property litigation (i.e. not just cases falling within the special jurisdiction) in the Patents County Court and indeed in the High Court.[70] The term "intellectual property litigation" is broad enough to cover a dispute as to whether products fall within the scope of a granted patent.[71]

The designated Patents County Court had jurisdiction throughout England and Wales and until 2011 (see paras 1-37 and 1-38) had no financial limitation.[72] Special provisions were made with regard to transfer between the High Court and the Patents County Court.[73] The Patents County Court was subsequently also designated to hear Community trade mark and Community design cases.[74]

1-36

Reform of the Patents County Court

In 2009 extensive reforms were proposed for the Patents County Court[75] including:

(1) a financial limit on the Court's jurisdiction,
(2) repeal of the special provisions on transfer by the High Court from the Patents County Court contained in s.289(1) of the Copyright, Designs and Patents Act 1988,
(3) a new procedural regime aimed at reducing costs and speeding up the court process,
(4) scale costs, and
(5) a cap on the maximum amount of costs which may be recovered.

1-37

These proposals were adopted in the Jackson Review.[76] The new procedural regime and the new provisions as to costs came into effect on October 1, 2010 by amendments made to CPR Pts 45 and 63[77] and to the Costs Practice Direction and PD63. In 2011 the PCC moved to the Rolls Building along with the Chancery Division of the High Court. A financial limit of £500 000 was implemented with effect from 14 June 2011 in relation to claims within the special jurisdiction of the court,[78] and the same limit was implemented with effect from 1 October 2011 in relation to claims which within the ordinary jurisdiction.[79]

1-38

In response to proposals originally made in the Jackson Review and further

1-39

---

[69] CDPA 1988 s.292, as originally enacted. CDPA 1988 s.292 was repealed by the Legal Services Act 2007 s.208, Sch.21 para.80 and s.210 Sch.23 with effect from 1 January 2010.
[70] The current regulations are the CIPA Higher Court Qualification Regulations 2007, issued by the Chartered Institute of Patent Attorneys as an authorised body under s.29 of the Courts and Legal Services Act 1990.
[71] See *Atrium Medical Corporation v DSB Invest Holdings* [2011] R.P.C. 24.
[72] CDPA 1988 ss.287(2) and 288. Patents County Court (Designation and Jurisdiction) Order 1994, see SI 1994/1609.
[73] CDPA 1988 s.289 and paras 20-07 to 20-11.
[74] See SI 2006/1027, SI 2005/696 respectively.
[75] See the Final Report on Proposals for Reform of the Patents County Court by the Working Group of the Intellectual Property Court Users Committee, dated 31 July 2009.
[76] See also the Final Report of the Review of Civil Litigation Costs by Jackson LJ (the Jackson Report), dated 21 December 2009.
[77] The Civil Procedure (Amendment No.2) Rules 2010 (SI 2010/1953).
[78] The Patents County Court (Financial Limits) Order 2011 (SI 2011/1402).
[79] The Patents County Court (Financial Limits) (No. 2) Order 2011 (SI 2011/2222).

recommended by the Hargreaves Review, a small claims track was introduced into the Patents County Court with effect from 1 October 2012.[80] Its primary focus was to provide a low cost forum for copyright disputes (e.g. those brought by photographers) and it had no jurisdiction for patent or registered design cases.[81] Originally the value of the claim had to be not more than £5,000 but this was subsequently increased to £10 000 on 1 April 2013.

Reorganisation of the Patents County Court into the Intellectual Property Enterprise Court (IPEC)

1-40   The complicated basis of the Patents County Court's jurisdiction was increasingly subjected to criticism.[82] For instance, it was doubted whether the court had jurisdiction to deal with free-standing claims for breach of confidence (i.e. those which were not ancillary to, or arising out of the same subject matter as, a case within the court's designated jurisdiction).[83] As a result the court was reconstituted as a specialist list within the Chancery Division of the High Court on 1 October 2013.[84] Its name was changed to the Intellectual Property Enterprise Court both to reflect the fact that its remit had grown beyond patents, and to acknowledge that it was particularly directed at small to medium-sized enterprises ("SMEs"). The judges of the court are now referred to as enterprise judges.[85] The relationship of the IPEC to the Patents Court of the Chancery Division is similar to the position of the Mercantile Courts with respect to the Commercial Court of the Queen's Bench Division.

1-41   The new rules included revised provision for transfer between the general Chancery Division and the new court[86] and as regards appeals[87] but otherwise generally preserved the existing rules of the Patents County Court. This included, in particular, the financial limit of £500 000.[88] All proceedings that had been started in the PCC were effectively transferred to the IPEC.[89] An independent review of the PCC/IPEC covering the years 2010-2013 concluded that the reforms had substantially increased the number of cases brought for all IP rights and that access to justice for SMEs and individuals had been greatly improved.[90]

Supplementary Protection Certificates

1-42   A patent proprietor cannot lawfully market a new pharmaceutical product until all the regulatory hurdles have been cleared. Typically this can take several years. Meanwhile the proprietor's 20-year period of patent protection is eroded. In broad terms, the Supplementary Protection Certificate regime is intended to compensate the patent proprietor for this loss of patent protection.

---

[80] Effected by the Civil Procedure (Amendment No. 2) Rules 2012 (SI 2012/2208) r.10(c).
[81] See Pt 63.27(1)(a).
[82] *Suh v Ryu* [2012] F.S.R. 31.
[83] See *Ningbo v Wang* [2013] F.S.R. 40.
[84] See the Civil Procedure (Amendment No. 7) Rules 2013 (SI 2013/1974) r.26. The relevant sections of the Copyright, Designs, and Patents Act 1988 were repealed, and the Patents County Court abolished, by reason of s.17(5) and Sch.9 Pt II para.30 of the Crime and Courts Act 2013.
[85] Pt 63.1(2)(h).
[86] See Pt 63.18, as amended by SI 2013/1974 r.26(k).
[87] See Pt 63.19, as amended by SI 2013/1974 r.26(l).
[88] See Pt 63.17A, as introduced by SI 2013/1974 r.26(j).
[89] See the Civil Procedure (Amendment No. 7) Rules 2013 (SI 2013/1974) r.30.
[90] Dr. C. Helmers, Dr. Y. Lefouili, Dr. L. McDonagh, "*Evaluation of the Reforms of the Intellectual Property Enterprise Court 2010-2013*", 22 June 2015.

Supplementary Protection Certificates were first created by Council Regulation **1-43** (EEC) Nos 1768/92[91] and 1610/96. To assist in the implementation of these Regulations, the Patents (Supplementary Protection Certificate for Medicinal Products) Regulations 1992[92] and the Patents (Supplementary Protection Certificate for Plant Protection Products) Regulations 1996[93] extended and applied the provisions of the Patents Act 1977 to certificates and applications for certificates as they applied to patents and applications for patents.

The two UK Regulations were revoked from 17 December 2007, by the Patents **1-44** (Compulsory Licensing and Supplementary Protection Certificates) Regulations 2007[94] which amends the Patents Act 1977 by inserting a new s.128B and Sch.4A in order to set out the provisions of the Act which now apply to Supplementary Protection Certificates and applications for certificates and to give effect to changes made to the supplementary protection certificate regime by Regulation (EC) No.1901/2006 of the European Parliament and of the Council of 12 December 2006 on medicinal products for paediatric use (see Ch.6).[95]

The Patents and Trade Marks (World Trade Organisation) Regulations 1999

The Patents and Trade Marks (World Trade Organisation) Regulations 1999[96] **1-45** amend s.48 of the Patents Act 1977 and insert new ss.48A and 48B in order to implement the UK's obligations arising under the TRIPS Agreement,[97] particularly in relation to the application and grant of compulsory licences. A new s.52 is also substituted. The Regulations came into force on 29 July 1999 (see Ch.17).

The Patents Regulations 2000

The Patents Regulations 2000[98] amend the Patents Act 1977 in order to make **1-46** provision for the implementation of arts 1-11 of Directive 98/44/EC of the European Parliament and of the Council of 5 July 1998, on the legal protection of biotechnological inventions ("the Biotech Directive") and to implement art.27(2) of the TRIPS Agreement.[99] The Regulations amend s.1 of the Act (patentable inventions), s.60 (meaning of infringement) and ss.125A and 130 ("biological material" and "biological invention"), and insert a new s.76A and new Schs A1 and A2. The Regulations came into force on 28 July 2000.

---

[91] To consolidate various amendments, Council Regulation (EEC) No.1768/92 was repealed and codified by Regulation (EC) No.469/2009 of the European Parliament and of the Council of 6 May 2009. The new Regulation came into force on 6 July 2009.

[92] SI 1992/3091.

[93] SI 1996/3120.

[94] SI 2007/3293. See also paras 1-47 and 1-53.

[95] s.128B and Sch.4A of the 1977 Act were subsequently amended to refer to Regulation (EC) No.469/2009 with effect from 1 October 2014, pursuant to the Patents (Supplementary Protection Certificates) Regulations 2014 (SI 2014/2411).

[96] SI 1999/1899.

[97] See para.1-72.

[98] SI 2000/2037.

[99] See para.1-72.

The Patents and Plant Variety Rights (Compulsory Licensing) Regulations 2002

1-47   The Patents and Plant Variety Rights (Compulsory Licensing) Regulations 2002[100] (as amended by Reg.3 of the Patents (Compulsory Licensing and Supplementary Protection Certificates) Regulations 2007[101]) implement art.12 of the Biotech Directive (see para.1-46). The Regulations enable the Comptroller of Patents and the Controller of Plant Variety Rights, acting jointly, to grant non-exclusive compulsory licences and cross-licences where the exploitation of a plant variety right would infringe a patent and vice versa (see Ch.17).

The Regulatory Reform (Patents) Order 2004

1-48   The Regulatory Reform (Patents) Order 2004[102] amends the 1977 Act in order to enable it to be administered in conformity with the Patent Law Treaty ("the PLT")[103] adopted at Geneva on 1 June 2000 and so as to make a number of other deregulatory changes. In general, the changes to the 1977 Act involve the removal or reduction of a number of the burdens placed upon the applicant for a patent. The Order was made by the Secretary of State for Trade and Industry in exercise of the powers conferred by s.1 of the Regulatory Reform Act 2001 and came into force on 1 January 2005. The Order contains a large number of amendments to the 1977 Act and includes transitional provisions (see arts 20-23 of the Order).

Patents Act 2004

1-49   The Patents Act 2004 further amends the 1977 Act. One of the main purposes of the 2004 Act is to bring UK domestic patent law into line with the revisions to the EPC agreed by Diplomatic Conference in November 2000 ("the EPC 2000", see para.1-66). In addition the 2004 Act introduces measures designed to assist in the enforcement of patent rights and in the resolution of patent disputes between patent proprietors and third parties. The 2004 Act also includes a number of measures intended to update the 1977 Act.

1-50   Part of the 2004 Act was brought into force on 22 September 2004[104] and further parts on 1 January 2005[105] and 1 October 2005.[106] The provisions of the Act concerned with the implementation of the EPC 2000 came into force on 13 December 2007[107] at the same time as that Convention (see para.1-66).

---

[100] SI 2002/247.

[101] SI 2007/3293. See also para.1-44 and para.1-53.

[102] SI 2004/2357.

[103] See para.1-80.

[104] The Patents Act 2004 (Commencement No.1 and Consequential, etc. and Transitional Provisions) Order 2004 (SI 2004/2177).

[105] The Patents Act 2004 (Commencement No.2 and Consequential, etc. and Transitional Provisions) Order 2004 (SI 2004/3205).

[106] The Patents Act 2004 (Commencement No.3 and Transitional Provisions) Order 2005 (SI 2005/2471).

[107] The Patents Act 2004 (Commencement No.4 and Transitional Provisions) Order 2007 (SI 2007/3396).

The Medicines (Marketing Authorisations Etc.) Amendment Regulations 2005

The Medicines (Marketing Authorisations Etc.) Amendment Regulations 2005[108] implement art.10(6) of Directive 2001/83/EC of the European Parliament and of the Council on the Community code relating to medicinal products for human use (substituted by art.1(8) of Directive 2004/27/EC), and art.13(6) of Directive 2001/82/EC on the Community code relating to veterinary medicinal products (substituted by art.1(6) of Directive 2004/28/EC). The Regulations amend s.60 of the 1977 Act so as to provide that an act done in conducting a study, test or trial which is necessary for and is conducted with a view to the application of art.10(1)-(4) of Directive 2001/83/EC (applications for generic medicinal products) or art.13(1)-(5) of Directive 2001/82/EC, and the consequential practical requirements, shall not constitute an infringement of a patent.[109] The Regulations came into force on 30 October 2005.

1-51

The Intellectual Property (Enforcement, etc) Regulations 2006

The Intellectual Property (Enforcement, etc) Regulations 2006[110] implement Directive 2004/48/EC of the European Parliament and of the Council of 29 April 2004 on the enforcement of intellectual property rights (the IP Enforcement Directive).[111] The Regulations amend the Patents Act 1977[112] and, by Regulation 3, give effect to art.13 of the IP Enforcement Directive on the assessment of damages. The Regulations came into force on 29 April 2006.

1-52

The Patents (Compulsory Licensing and Supplementary Protection Certificates) Regulations 2007

In addition to other matters,[113] the Patents (Compulsory Licensing and Supplementary Protection Certificates) Regulations 2007[114] also assist in the implementation of Regulation (EC) No.816/2006 of the European Parliament and of the Council of 17 May 2006 on compulsory licensing of patents relating to the manufacture of pharmaceutical products for export to countries with public health problems.[115] The EC Regulation itself implemented a Decision of 30 August 2003 of the General Council of the World Trade Organisation on the implementation of para.6 of the Doha Declaration of 14 November 2001 on the Agreement on Trade-Related Aspects of Intellectual Property Rights (TRIPS) and Public Health.[116]

1-53

The UK Regulations amend the Patents Act 1977 by inserting a new s.128A which gives effect under national law to a compulsory licence granted under Regulation (EC) No.816/2006. The UK Regulations came into effect on 17 December 2007 (see Ch.17).

1-54

---

108 SI 2005/2759.
109 See para.14-196.
110 SI 2006/1028.
111 [2004] O.J. L195/16.
112 Principally ss.62, 63, and 68. See Sch.2 paras 2-4.
113 See also para.1-43.
114 SI 2007/3293.
115 [2006] O.J. L157/1.
116 See para.1-75, et seq.

Legal Services Act 2007

1-55   The Legal Services Act 2007 amended those sections of the Copyright, Designs and Patents Act 1988 relating to patent attorneys, notably as regards registration, regulation, and privilege for communications[117] and came into force on 1 January 2010. As required by the 2007 Act, the Chartered Institute of Patent Agents set up an independent Board known as the Intellectual Property Regulation Board ("IPReg") to set standards for patent attorneys and to police them.

Intellectual Property Act 2014

1-56   The Intellectual Property Act 2014 introduced a number of amendments to the Patents Act 1977 as previously amended by the Patents Act 2004.[118] The 2004 Act had given the comptroller (i.e. the UK Intellectual Property Office) the power to issue opinions on infringement and validity under a new s.74A of the 1977 Act, but in the latter case only having regard to novelty and obviousness. The 2014 Act[119] extended the scope of the latter to include nearly all statutory objections to validity[120] and also conferred a new power on the controller under s.73A to revoke patents following an adverse opinion on validity under s.74A. In addition the 2014 Act made provision for the implementation of the Agreement on a Unified Patent Court made in Brussels on 19 February 2013. The above measures came into force on 1 October 2014.[121]

Legislative Reform (Patents) Order 2014

1-57   The Legislative Reform (Patents) Order 2014[122] amends s.60 of the 1977 Act so as to provide a wider exemption for infringement in relation to acts done for experimental purposes relating to the subject-matter of the invention. In particular, new subs.60(6D) provided that anything done in or for the purposes of a "medicinal product assessment" which would otherwise constitute an infringement was to be regarded as done for lawful experimental purposes under s.60(5)(b). The term "medicinal product assessment" was in turn defined in new subss.60(6E) and 60(6F) to include various acts connected with obtaining marketing authorisations and/or compliance with regulatory requirements for medicinal products. The Order came into force on 1 October 2014.

Practice and procedure

1-58   At the present time the substantive practice and procedure as to patents in this country is regulated by:

---

[117] See ss.275, 275A, and 280 of the 1988 Act as amended.
[118] The majority of the provisions in the 2014 Act related to designs. Other provisions relating to patents included the introduction of "webmarking", i.e. allowing a proprietor to put a relevant internet link instead of a patent number for purposes of s.62 of the 1977 Act.
[119] In conjunction with r.93(6) of the Patent Rules 2007 as amended.
[120] Not including, for instance, s.72(1)(b) of the 1977 Act.
[121] See The Intellectual Property Act 2014 (Commencement No. 3 and Transitional Provisions) Order 2014.
[122] SI 2014/1997.

(a)   the Patents Rules 2007[123] (as amended), being rules made pursuant to powers in the 1977 Act[124];

(b)   the Civil Procedure Rules and, in particular, Pt 63 and the Practice Direction to Pt 63, namely the Practice Direction—Intellectual Property Claims;

(c)   the Patents Court Guide, and

(d)   the Intellectual Property Enterprise Court Guide.

4.   INTERNATIONAL CONVENTIONS

Some brief reference should be made at this point to international conventions relevant to UK patent law and practice, including those international conventions referred to above.   **1-59**

Paris Convention

The International Convention for the Protection of Industrial Property (signed in   **1-60**
Paris in 1883 and revised on a number of occasions, the last revision being in 1967)
provides that, as regards the protection of industrial property, each member country
shall afford to nationals of other member countries the same protection as it affords to its own nationals and that the filing of an application for a patent in one
member country gives a right of priority to the date of that filing in respect of corresponding applications filed in other member countries within 12 months of that
date. Since the Act of 1883,[125] United Kingdom patent legislation has provided for
such "convention applications" from nationals of other convention countries and
the 1977 Act retains such provision.[126]

Patent Co-operation Treaty

The PCT (signed in Washington in 1970) has as one of its objects "to simplify   **1-61**
and render more economical the obtaining of protection for inventions where
protection is sought in several countries", but is not intended to diminish rights
under the Paris Convention.[127] Under the Treaty, where patent protection for an
invention is sought in a member of the contracting states, a single "international application" may be filed at one of the "receiving offices" (which will usually be the
applicant's local national office) and the application will have a right of priority
from the date of such filing. An application for a European patent may also be made
by the international application. The Treaty, which is more fully considered later
in this work,[128] also makes provision for an international search for prior art to be
made in respect of each such international application.

To meet the United Kingdom's obligations under this Treaty the 1977 Act   **1-62**
provides that such an international application which designates the United
Kingdom as a country for which patent protection is sought is to be treated as an
application for a patent under the Act, with the date of its international filing as its

---

[123] SI 2007/3291, as amended by SI 2009/546, SI 2010/33, SI 2011/2052, SI 2014/578, and SI 2014/
       2401. See also the Patents (Fees) Rules 2007, SI 2007/3292, as amended by SI 2009/2089, and SI
       2010/33.
[124] PA 1977 ss.14(6), 25(5), 32, 74B, 77(9), 92, 123, 125A and 130(2).
[125] Patents, Designs and Trade Marks Act 1883 s.103.
[126] PA 1977 ss.5 and 90.
[127] PCT art.1(2).
[128] See para.3-80.

filing date under the Act and, if published in accordance with the Treaty, is to be treated as published under the Act provided certain conditions are fulfilled.[129]

European Patent Convention

1-63   The EPC was signed in Munich on 5 October 1973. The Convention established a European Patent Organisation, the constituent bodies of which are the European Patent Office and the Administrative Council. The European Patent Office, situated in Munich, is responsible for the granting of European patents under the system of law set out in the Convention. The EPC is expressed to be a special agreement within the Paris Convention,[130] (as indeed is the CPC) and it incorporates the requirements of the Strasbourg Convention.[131] The EPC is governed by conventional international law and does not form part of the Community legal order.

1-64   Under the system of the EPC, a patent application must designate in which of the Contracting States of the Convention patent protection is desired and if, after the examination by the EPO, the application is accepted, a European patent is granted for each of the designated states, the patents having the same specifications and normally the same claims. Any such European patent is to be treated in the state for which it is granted as having "the effect of and be subject to the same conditions as a national patent granted by that state".[132]

1-65   The 1977 Act meets that obligation by providing that any European patent granted for the United Kingdom (a "European patent (UK)") shall be treated as if it were a patent granted under the Act,[133] so that questions of infringement and validity of European patents (UK) will be for United Kingdom courts and the Comptroller in cases where his jurisdiction under the 1977 Act is invoked. The validity of the patent in all designated states can additionally be challenged in opposition proceedings at the EPO for a limited period after grant.[134]

EPC 2000

1-66   An Act revising the EPC was adopted on 29 November 2000 by Diplomatic Conference held in Munich. One of the main objectives of the revisions was to bring the EPC into line with the TRIPS Agreement of 1994,[135] the Patent Law Treaty 2000[136] and European Union legislation.[137] The revised Convention (originally known as the EPC 2000 but now referred to as "the EPC") came into force on 13 December 2007, and the corresponding provisions of the Patents Act 2004 implementing the revised Convention came into effect on the same date.[138] One of

[129] PA 1977 s.89.
[130] Paris Convention art.19.
[131] The Council of Europe Convention on the Unification of Certain Points of Substantive Law on Patents for Invention (the Strasbourg Convention) 1963; Cmnd.2362.
[132] EPC art.2(2).
[133] PA 1977 s.77(1).
[134] EPC art.99. See para.5-12.
[135] See para.1-72.
[136] See para.1-80.
[137] See para.1-81, et seq.
[138] The Patents Act 2004 (Commencement No.4 and Transitional Provisions) Order 2007 (SI 2007/3396).

the changes introduced was a new procedure for centrally limiting or revoking a European patent at the request of the proprietor.[139]

The London Agreement

The London Agreement (or the Agreement on the Application of Article 65 of the Convention on the Grant of European Patents) was signed in London on 17 October 2000.[140] The Agreement is aimed at reducing the translation costs of European patents by relaxing the translation requirements contained in art.65 of the EPC which allow any Contracting State of the EPC to prescribe that if a translation of a European patent is not filed with the national patent office of that state within the time allowed, then "the European patent shall be deemed to be void ab initio in that State". These requirements were originally implemented in the United Kingdom in the case of European patents published in French or German (and any amendments thereto) by s.77(6) of the Patents Act 1977.   **1-67**

The London Agreement stemmed from the Paris Intergovernmental Conference held on 25 June 1999. At that Conference, two Working Parties were set up. The first led to the London Agreement and the second to the European Patent Litigation Agreement.[141]   **1-68**

The London Agreement came into force on 1 May 2008 and applies to all European patents granted on or after that date. However it should be noted that the Agreement is optional and that it has not been ratified by all the Contracting States of the EPC. Thus there is no relaxation of the translation requirements in those States that have not ratified it. Nevertheless the United Kingdom, Germany, France and the Netherlands (amongst others[142]) have ratified the Agreement. So far as concerns the implementation of the London Agreement in the United Kingdom, s.77(6) of the 1977 Act ceased to have effect on the day of the coming into force of the Agreement.[143]   **1-69**

Community Patent Convention

The CPC, was signed in December 1975 and was intended to create a Community-wide patent system for the EC. The Convention was not sufficiently ratified and did not come into force. The section of the 1977 Act which was going to make the CPC part of our law was never brought into force and was repealed by the 2004 Act.   **1-70**

The CPC remains of relevance to patents in the UK because it was the main source of the law of infringement found in s.60 of the Patents Act 1977. The CPC also forms part of the background to the new Unified Patent Court, and is considered in a more detail in the chapter dedicated to that court.   **1-71**

---

[139] See art 105a. The request can be filed at any time during the term of the European patent, save while opposition proceedings are pending.
[140] Cmnd.5247.
[141] See para.26-11.
[142] At time of writing these are Albania, Croatia, Denmark, Hungary, Iceland, Latvia, Lithuania, Slovenia, and Switzerland.
[143] Patents Rules 2007 r.56(9) and (10). However s.78(7) still requires filing of a translation into English of the claims of a European patent application in French or German in the circumstances set out in that subsection.

The TRIPS Agreement

1-72   The Agreement on Trade-Related Aspects of Intellectual Property Rights (the TRIPS Agreement) formed part of the final agreement establishing the World Trade Organisation made at the Uruguay Round of the GATT talks in April 1994. The TRIPS Agreement builds on the Paris Convention but goes much further in laying down minimum standards for judicial and administrative procedures and for the enforcement of intellectual property rights. Such minimum standards are likely to have a major impact on developing countries and other countries where the local law either does not recognise intellectual property rights or fails to provide an effective means for their enforcement. It is this aspect of the TRIPS Agreement in particular which has led to it being hailed as "perhaps the most far-reaching international instrument ever subscribed on intellectual property rights".[144]

1-73   The TRIPS Agreement was signed by the UK and by the Council of the EU on which all Member States of the EU are represented. It has also been ratified by the Council of the EU (see Council Decision 94/800/EEC) and, under UK national law, it is to be regarded as a Community Treaty as defined in s.1(2) of the European Communities Act 1972.[145] However, it is clear that the TRIPS Agreement is not directly applicable in Member States of the EU.[146] Nevertheless the ECJ has held that, in a field to which TRIPS applies and in respect of which the Community has already legislated, the judicial authorities of the Member States are required by virtue of Community law, when called upon to apply national rules falling within that field, to do so as far as possible in the light of the wording and purpose of TRIPS.[147]

1-74   Many of the minimum standards required by the TRIPS Agreement already form part of UK intellectual property law. But in order to comply with the UK's obligations under the Agreement, UK national law has been modified by the Patents and Trade Marks (World Trade Organisation) Regulations 1999.[148] Amongst other things, the Regulations amend the provisions of the Patents Act 1977 relating to the application and grant of compulsory licences. The 1977 Act has also been amended by the Patents Regulations 2000[149] in order to implement, inter alia, art.27(2) of TRIPS relating to the protection of biotechnological inventions.

---

[144] C.M. Correa, "The GATT Agreement on Trade-Related Aspects of Intellectual Property Rights: New Standards for Patent Protection" [1994] 8 E.I.P.R. 327.

[145] The European Communities (Definition of Treaties) (The Agreement Establishing the World Trade Organisation) Order 1995 (SI 1995/265).

[146] *Parfums Christian Dior SA v Tuk Consultancy BV* (C-300-/98 and C-392/98) [2000] E.C.R. I-11307; [2001] E.T.M.R. 26, [44]; *Monsanto Technology LLC v Cefetra BV* (C-428/08) (Grand Chamber, 6 July 2010), [71]. See also *Azrak-Hamway International Inc's Licence of Right (Design Right and Copyright) Application* [1997] R.P.C. 134; *C-G Lenzing A.G.'s European Patent* [1997] R.P.C. 245.

[147] *Hermès International v FHT Marketing Choice BV* (C-53/96) [1998] E.C.R. I-3603, [1998] E.T.M.R. 425; *Parfums Christian Dior SA v Tuk Consultancy BV* (C-300-/98 and C-392/98) [2000] E.C.R. I-11307, [2001] E.T.M.R. 26; *Schieving-Nijstad VOF v Groeneveld* (C-89/99) [2001] E.C.R. I-5851, [2002] F.S.R. 22; *Merck Genéricos—Produtos Farmacêuticos* (C-431/05) [2007] E.C.R. I-7001, [35]; *Monsanto Technology LLC v Cefetra BV* (C-428/08) (Grand Chamber, 6 July 2010), [77]. And see also *Nova Productions Ltd v Mazooma Games Ltd* [2007] E.M.L.R. 14, [37]; *Experience Hendrix LLC v Purple Haze Records Ltd* [2008] E.M.L.R. 10, [27]-[28]; *Supreme Petfoods v Henry Bell & Co* [2015] E.T.M.R. 20, [48]-[49]. See also para.1-86.

[148] SI 1999/1899.

[149] SI 2000/2037.

The Doha Declaration

The Doha Declaration was adopted by the WTO Ministerial Conference in Doha on 14 November 2001. The Declaration concerns the scope of the TRIPS Agreement and, in particular, the extent to which the government of a WTO Member can legitimately use the subject matter of a patent, without the authorisation of the right holder, in order to protect public health.　　1-75

The problem addressed by the Declaration stems from art.31 of the TRIPS Agreement which sets out certain minimum provisions which must be respected where the law of a WTO Member allows for use of the subject matter of a patent without the authorisation of the right holder, including use of that subject matter by the government or third parties authorised by the government. In particular, art.31(b) provides that such use:　　1-76

"… may only be permitted if, prior to such use, the proposed user has made efforts to obtain authorization from the right holder on reasonable commercial terms and conditions and that such efforts have not been successful within a reasonable period of time. This requirement may be waived by a Member in the case of a national emergency or other circumstances of extreme urgency or in cases of public non-commercial use. In situations of national emergency or other circumstances of extreme urgency, the right holder shall nevertheless be notified as soon as reasonably practicable …"

So is the protection of public health capable of amounting to "a national emergency or other circumstances of extreme urgency" within the meaning of art.31(b)? And, if so, who decides whether the particular circumstances relating to the protection of public health are such that the provisions relating to "national emergency or other circumstances of extreme urgency" can be legitimately invoked? In response to these issues, para.5(c) of the Doha Declaration provides, by way of interpretation of the TRIPS Agreement, that:　　1-77

"Each Member has the right to determine what constitutes a national emergency or other circumstances of extreme urgency, it being understood that public health crises, including those relating to HIV/AIDS, tuberculosis, malaria and other epidemics, can represent a national emergency or other circumstances of extreme urgency."

Further it was recognised that WTO Members with insufficient or no manufacturing capacities in the pharmaceutical sector could face difficulties in making effective use of compulsory licensing under the TRIPS Agreement. Accordingly, by para.6 of the Doha Declaration, the Council for TRIPS was instructed "to find an expeditious solution to this problem and to report to the General Council before the end of 2002." This led to the Decision of the General Council of 30 August 2003,[150] which created a temporary waiver whereby WTO Members could issue compulsory licenses to permit the manufacture and export of generic versions of patented medicines to countries with insufficient manufacturing capacity themselves.　　1-78

Amendment of TRIPS

Subsequent to the creation of the temporary waiver, a permanent amendment to the TRIPS Agreement was approved by the General Council on 6 December 2005 introducing a new art.31bis. The proposed amendment to the Agreement was circulated to WTO Members for formal adoption. However, ratification is required　　1-79

---

[150] See *https://www.wto.org/english/tratop_e/trips_e/implem_para6_e.htm* [Accessed 18 February 2016].

by at least two-thirds of the WTO's 161 Members which has not yet been achieved. At time of writing, only 59 countries had ratified the amendment.[151]

The Patent Law Treaty

1-80   The Patent Law Treaty ("the PLT") was adopted at Geneva on 1 June 2000. The Treaty seeks to harmonise the procedural requirements associated with the filing and prosecution of a patent application. The Regulatory Reform (Patents) Order (see para.1-48) amends the 1977 Act in order to give effect to the PLT.

The European Union

1-81   The United Kingdom joined the European Economic Community (as it was then known) on 1 January 1973. The European Communities Act 1972 gives effect to the United Kingdom's obligations as a member of the European Community.[152] The Act has been amended several times, most recently by the European Union (Amendment) Act 2008 in order to implement the Treaty of Lisbon which came into effect on 1 December 2009.[153]

1-82   The European Union (as it is now known) is currently founded upon two principal treaties: (1) the Treaty on European Union ("the TEU") which entered into force on 1 November 1993, as part of the Treaty of Maastricht; and (2) the Treaty on the Functioning of the European Union ("the TFEU") which is the original Treaty establishing the European Economic Community of 1957 ("the EEC Treaty")[154] as amended over the years. It was re-named the Treaty establishing the European Community ("the EC Treaty") by the Treaty of Maastricht in 1993 and given its current name by the Treaty of Lisbon in 2009. The TFEU "organises the functioning of the Union and determines the areas of, delimitation of, and arrangements for exercising its competences".[155]

1-83   The Articles of both the TEU and the EC Treaty were re-numbered by the Treaty of Amsterdam which came into force on 1 May 1999. Despite the inconvenience and confusion that the re-numbering exercise has caused, the Treaty of Lisbon has re-numbered the Articles of both Treaties for a second time.

EU competition law

1-84   Articles 34, 35 and 36 of the TFEU[156] relate to the free movement of goods within the EU, art.101[157] relates to agreements which may affect trade between Member States and which have as their object or effect the prevention, restriction or distortion of competition within the internal market, and art.102[158] relates to any abuse by one or more undertakings of a dominant position. These Articles form the

---

[151] See *https://www.wto.org/english/tratop_e/trips_e/amendment_e.htm* [Accessed 18 February 2016].
[152] European Communities Act 1972 s.2(1).
[153] The European Act 2011 subsequently introduced a requirement that a referendum be held on amendments of the Treaty of the European Union, in response to the fact that the 2008 Act had been passed without such a referendum.
[154] Also commonly known as the Treaty of Rome.
[155] TFEU art.1(1).
[156] ex-arts 28, 29 and 30 of the EC Treaty and, prior to the Treaty of Amsterdam arts 30, 34 and 36.
[157] Ex-art.81 of the EC Treaty and, prior to the Treaty of Amsterdam art.85.
[158] Ex-art.82 of the EC Treaty and, prior to the Treaty of Amsterdam art.86.

cornerstone of EU competition law and are of particular significance in relation to patents and patentees. Specific instances are dealt with later in this work.[159]

Implementing Community obligations in the UK

The European Communities Act also provides that any designated Minister may **1-85** by regulations make provision for, inter alia, the purpose of implementing any Community obligation of the United Kingdom.[160] By this means Council Regulations, Directives, and other Community obligations may be given effect in the United Kingdom (or their implementation assisted) by Statutory Instrument. To date this power has been exercised in relation to patents as follows[161]:

(1) To assist in the implementation of Supplementary Protection Certificates in accordance with various Council Regulations, see the Patents (Supplementary Protection Certificate for Medicinal Products) Regulations 1992,[162] the Patents (Supplementary Protection Certificate for Plant Protection Products) Regulations 1996,[163] the Patents (Compulsory Licensing and Supplementary Protection Certificates) Regulations 2007,[164] and the Patents (Supplementary Protection Certificates) Regulations 2014 (paras 1-42 to 1-44).

(2) To implement the UK's obligations arising under TRIPS particularly in relation to the application and grant of compulsory licences, see the Patents and Trade Marks (World Trade Organisation) Regulations 1999[165] (para.1-72).

(3) To implement arts 1-11 of the Biotech Directive and art.27(2) of TRIPS, see the Patents Regulations 2000[166] (para.1-46).

(4) To implement art.12 of the Biotech Directive, see the Patents and Plant Variety Rights (Compulsory Licensing) Regulations 2002,[167] as amended, (para.1-47).

(5) To implement art.10(6) of Directive 2001/83/EC of the European Parliament and of the Council on the Community code relating to medicinal products for human use (substituted by art.1(8) of Directive 2004/27/EC), and art.13(6) of Directive 2001/82/EC on the Community code relating to veterinary medicinal products (substituted by art.1(6) of Directive 2004/28/EC), see the Medicines (Marketing Authorisations etc.) Amendment Regulations 2005[168] and the Legislative Reform (Patents) Order 2014[169] (para.1-57).

(6) To implement Directive 2004/48/EC of the European Parliament and of the

---

[159] See, for example, para.14-240, et seq. and para.16-123, et seq.

[160] European Communities Act 1972 s.2(2). And see *Oakley Inc v Animal Ltd* [2005] R.P.C. 30; [2006] R.P.C. 9 (CA) where the scope of s.2(2) was considered.

[161] The Patents Act 1977 (Amendment) Regulations 2011 had also introduced a new s.118A to the 1977 Act with effect from 1 October 2011 in order to give effect to the Information Society Directive, 2001/29/EC, but that was subsequently repealed by the Copyright (Public Administration) Regulations 2014 with effect from 1 June 2014.

[162] SI 1992/3091, now revoked.

[163] SI 1996/3120, now revoked.

[164] SI 2007/3293.

[165] SI 1999/1899.

[166] SI 2000/2037.

[167] SI 2002/247.

[168] SI 2005/2759.

[169] SI 2014/1997.

Council of 29 April 2004 on the enforcement of intellectual property rights (the IP Enforcement Directive), see the Intellectual Property (Enforcement, etc) Regulations 2006[170] (para.1-52).

(7) To assist in the implementation Regulation (EC) No.816/2006 of the European Parliament and of the Council of 17 May 2006 on compulsory licensing of patents relating to the manufacture of pharmaceutical products for export to countries with public health problems, see the Patents (Compulsory Licensing and Supplementary Protection Certificates) Regulations 2007[171] (paras 1-53 to 1-54).

The effect of a directive: interpretation of national law

1-86   Article 288 (third paragraph) of the Treaty on the Functioning of the European Union[172] provides that a directive is "binding, as to the result to be achieved, upon each Member State to which it is addressed ...".[173] Further art.4 of the Treaty on European Union[174] provides that Member States "shall take any appropriate measure, general or particular, to ensure fulfilment of the obligations arising out of the Treaties ...". In *Von Colson and Karman v Land Nordhein-Westfalen*,[175] the ECJ held that a Member State's obligation arising from a directive to achieve the result envisaged by the directive and its duty to take all appropriate measures to ensure fulfilment of that obligation is binding on all the authorities of the Member State including the courts. Consequently, the ECJ held that, in applying national law and in particular the provisions of a national law specifically introduced in order to implement a directive, the national court was required to interpret its national law in the light of the wording and the purpose of the directive in order to achieve that result.[176] Moreover, EU directives themselves have to be construed by reference not only to their wording but also the context in which they occur and the objectives pursued by the rules of which they are part.[177]

1-87   Although *Von Colson* concerned a directive where the Member State in question had specifically introduced national legislation in order to implement that directive, the ECJ subsequently held that the same approach must apply to the interpretation of national law even where there has been no implementing legislation and irrespective of whether the national law in question was enacted before or after the issue of the directive in question. In particular, in *Marleasing SA v La Comercial Internacional de Alimentación SA*[178], the ECJ held:

"... in applying national law, whether the provisions in question were adopted before or after the directive, the national court called upon to interpret it is required to do so, as far as possible, in the light of the wording and the purpose of the directive in order to achieve the result pursued by the lat-

---

[170]   SI 2006/1028.
[171]   SI 2007/3293.
[172]   Ex-art.249 (third paragraph) of the EC Treaty and, prior to the Treaty of Amsterdam art.189 (third paragraph).
[173]   It follows that a directive does not of itself impose obligations on an individual and cannot therefore be relied upon before a national court for that purpose, see *Marshall v Southampton and South-West Hampshire Area Health Authority* (152/84) [1986] E.C.R. 723.
[174]   Ex-art.10 of the EC Treaty and, prior to the Treaty of Amsterdam art.5.
[175]   [1984] E.C.R. 1891.
[176]   *Von Colson and Karman v Land Nordhein-Westfalen* (14/83) [1984] E.C.R. 1891, [26].
[177]   See *Sociedad General de Autores y Editores de Espana v Rafael Hoteles SA* (C-306/05) [2006] E.C.R. I-11519, [34].
[178]   (C-106/89) [1990] E.C.R. I-4135.

ter and thereby comply with the third paragraph of Article 189 [now the third paragraph of Article 288 of the TFEU]."[179]

It follows from the decision of the ECJ in *Marleasing* that the issue of a directive can cause the proper interpretation of pre-existing national law to change.

Consequences of failure to implement a directive: Francovich damages

Where it is not possible for the national court to interpret national law in conformity with a directive, then EU law may require the Member State in question to make good the damage caused to individuals through the failure to implement the directive.[180] In *Faccini Dori v Recreb Srl*[181] the ECJ referred to the national court's obligation and duty when applying national law to interpret that law, so far as possible, in the light of the wording and purpose of the directive and went on to say: **1-88**

"If the result prescribed by the directive cannot be achieved by way of interpretation, it should also be borne in mind that, in terms of the judgment in Joined Cases C-6/90 and C-9/90 *Francovich and Others v Italy* [1991] E.C.R. I-5357, paragraph 39, Community law requires the Member States to make good damage caused to individuals through failure to transpose a directive, provided that three conditions are fulfilled. First, the purpose of the directive must be to grant rights to individuals. Second, it must be possible to identify the content of those rights on the basis of the provisions of the directive. Finally, there must be a causal link between the breach of the State's obligation and the damage suffered."

Agreement on a Unified Patent Court

The Agreement on a Unified Patent Court was signed on 19 February 2013. The court and the agreement itself, are both discussed in more detail in Ch.26. **1-89**

5. REQUIREMENTS OF A VALID PATENT

The primary requirements of a valid patent effective in the United Kingdom at the present time may be summarised as follows: **1-90**

Any person may apply for a patent but a patent may only be granted to the inventor, or a person entitled to the whole property in the invention by operation of law or prior agreement, or the successor in title to the inventor or such person. **1-91**

The applicant must make a proper disclosure of their invention and must clearly specify the limits of the monopoly claimed. The invention must be "patentable", i.e. be new, not obvious to those skilled in the art to which it relates, and be capable of industrial application. Further, it must not be one the publication or exploitation of which would be generally expected to encourage offensive, immoral or antisocial behaviour. **1-92**

The patent may be granted by the UK Patent Office following an application made in accordance with procedure laid down in the 1977 Act, and the 2007 Rules.[182] Alternatively, the application may be prosecuted pursuant to the EPC by an application made to the EPO designating the United Kingdom.[183] In either case **1-93**

---

[179] See [8]. See also *Wagner Miret v Fondo de Garantia Salarial* (C-334/92) [1993] E.C.R. I-6911, [20].
[180] *Francovich v Italy* (C-6/90 and C-9/10) [1991] E.C.R. I-5357, [39].
[181] (C-91/92) [1994] E.C.R. I-3325.
[182] PA 1977 ss.14-21; Patents Rules 2007 rr.19-33.
[183] EPC arts 75-85 and 90-98; EPC Rules rr.35-50 and 55-74.

the application may be initiated by an international application under the PCT. Once granted, a European Patent (UK) has the same effect in this country as though it had been granted by the UK Patent Office.[184] Prior to grant, an European patent application equates with an application made under the 1977 Act.[185] Section 88A of the Patents Act 1977 (as introduced by s.17 of the Intellectual Property Act 2014) confers upon the Secretary of State the power to make an order giving effect in the United Kingdom to the provisions of the UPC Agreement. However, at the time of writing although a draft statutory instrument has been laid before Parliament, no such order had yet been made.

[184] PA 1977 s.77(1).
[185] PA 1977, s.78.

CHAPTER 2

THE NATURE OF PATENTABLE INVENTIONS

CONTENTS

1.   PATENTABLE INVENTIONS

The requirements of patentability are set out in in s.1(1)-1(4) of the 1977 Act. **2-01**
They are based upon and intended to have the same effect as[1] the corresponding
provisions of arts 52-57 of the EPC, with the amendments to s.1(3) and (4)[2] giving
effect to art.27(2) of TRIPS.[3]

With effect from 13 December 2007 s.1(1)(d) has been amended by the Patents **2-02**
Act 2004[4] to include a reference to new s.4A (which, in turn, was introduced by s.1
of the 2004 Act).

Article 27(1) of TRIPS makes clear that patents shall be available for "any inven- **2-03**
tions, whether products or processes, in all fields of technology provided they are
new, involve an inventive step and are capable of industrial application". Further,
"patents shall be available and patent rights enjoyable without discrimination as to
the place of invention, the field of technology and whether products are imported
or locally produced". Nevertheless there are certain categories of technology which,
for policy reasons, are not deemed patentable and which are discussed further
below. These policies are disparate and as there is no evident underlying purpose
lying behind the provisions as a group to guide their construction, caution should
be exercised before applying automatically the approach under one exclusion to any
other.[5]

It has frequently been observed in the English Courts that it is a pity that the **2-04**
parliamentary draughtsman sought to paraphrase the Articles of the EPC and then
seek to ensure a uniformity of approach by providing in s.130(7) of the Act that the
paraphrase was "so framed as to have, as nearly as practicable, the same effects in
the United Kingdom as the corresponding provisions of the European Patent
Convention".[6] To date, there has been no occasion on which the courts of this
country have identified a change in the language between the wording of the EPC

---

[1]   PA 1977 s.130(7). Note that s.1(5), the Secretary of State's power to vary the provisions of s.1(2), is not mentioned in s.130(7).

[2]   Made by the Patent Regulations 2000 (SI 2000/2037).

[3]   See paras 1-45 and 1-85. See also paras 1-72 to 1-79.

[4]   PA 2004 s.16, Sch.2 para.2.

[5]   *Aerotel* [2007] R.P.C. 7 per Jacob LJ at [9].

[6]   See, e.g. Pumfrey J in *Halliburton Energy Services Inc v Smith International (North Sea) Ltd* [2006] R.P.C. 2, [210]. Such observations have, however, been criticised for failing to take into account the

and that of the Statute which has rendered it impractical to give the two the same effect.[7] In *Aerotel*[8] the Court of Appeal ignored the UK Act in favour of working directly from the source, and pointed out the advantages of doing so in terms of European consistency.

2-05   The effective law is, however, that of the 1977 Act and s.1(1) requires consideration of four matters:

(a)   Is the invention new?
(b)   Does it involve an inventive step?
(c)   Is it capable of industrial application?
(d)   Is it excluded from patentability by subs.(2), or (3) or s.4A?

2-06   The first two, that the invention be novel and that it involve an inventive step, are explained in ss.2 and 3 of the Act. They are more fully discussed in Chs 11 and 12. The meaning of "invention" and the third and fourth conditions are discussed in this chapter.

Standard of proof in relation to questions of patentability

2-07   In *Aerotel*[9] the court held that that any pure question of law involved should be decided during prosecution and that it is not sufficient for the patentee to show that as a matter of law it merely arguably covers patentable subject-matter. In relation to questions of fact that court held as follows:

"… if a debatable question of pure fact is or may be involved at the application stage, things are different—one cannot then say that the decision at that point must be the last word on the subject. Then the applicant must be given the benefit of any reasonable doubt."

2-08   In *Blacklight Power Inc's Application*[10] Floyd J elaborated on the passage set out above as follows:

"It is not the law that any doubt, however small, on an issue of fact would force the Comptroller to allow the application to proceed to grant. Rather he should examine the material before him and attempt to come to a conclusion on the balance of probabilities. If he considers that there is a substantial doubt about an issue of fact which could lead to patentability at that stage, he should consider whether there is a reasonable prospect that matters will turn out differently if the matter is fully investigated at a trial. If so he should allow the application to proceed."[11]

Comptroller allowed to take fresh points on appeal to the Court

2-09   In *Raytheon Co's Application*[12] Kitchin J considered whether the Comptroller was allowed to take fresh points on appeal to the Court. He held that the Comptrol-

context in which the Act was drafted in the 1970s—see P. Johnson, "Mr Skemp's preposterous provision: the drafting of the Patents Act 1977 and harmonization in the 1970s", *Queen Mary Journal of Intellectual Property* (2015) 5(4), 367-388.

7   A challenge was rejected in *Beloit Technologies Inc v Valmet Paper Machines Inc (No.2)* [1995] R.P.C. 705. See also *Bristol Myers Squibb v Baker Norton* [1999] R.P.C. 253, 259.
8   [2007] R.P.C. 7.
9   [2007] R.P.C. 7.
10   [2009] R.P.C. 6.
11   Floyd J also criticised the Comptroller for failing to serve a Respondent's Notice, as a result of which the case had to be remitted back to the Comptroller for further consideration. He intimated that had such a Notice been served, it may have been possible to determine that the application should be refused outright.
12   [2008] R.P.C. 3.

ler has an obligation to seek to raise proper objections on appeal even if not taken before, consistent with his duty to refuse applications which did not comply with the requirements of the Act; and that whether the Comptroller would be allowed to do so depended on the nature of the proceedings, the nature of the new objections, and the extent of notice given to the applicant.

2.   WHAT IS AN INVENTION?

The first consideration is the meaning to be given to the word "invention". Whilst the expression "patentable invention" is defined by s.1(1), there is no definition of "invention" as such. An initial consideration of the language of s.1 might properly lead to the conclusion that anything could be an invention provided:

2-10

(a)   it satisfied the requirements of subss.(1)(a)-(c); and

(b)   it was not excluded from being patented by virtue of subs.(1)(d).

However, subs.(1)(d) is a non-exhaustive list since subs.(2) refers to "the following (among other things)" and subs.(5) expressly gives the Secretary of State the power to alter subs.(2). A submission that the list was exhaustive unless and until the Secretary of State altered it would not be in conformity with art.52 of the EPC which has no provision equivalent to s.1(5) of the Act. However, art.52(2) is likewise non-exhaustive—"the following in particular shall not be regarded as inventions".

2-11

This question was considered in the Court of Appeal by Mustill LJ in *Genentech Inc's Patent*.[13] He said (at 262):

2-12

"This suggestion of a need to identify the invention leads me to a part of the case which I have found most perplexing. Most of the arguments have been concentrated on the three conditions precedent to the grant of a patent set out in paragraphs (a) to (c) of section 1(1)—and understandably so, given the shape of the old law. But this approach tends to mask a more fundamental requirement which must be satisfied before a patent can properly be granted, namely that the applicant has made an 'invention'.

In my judgment, this requirement emerges clearly from the opening words of s.1(1):

'A patent may be granted only for an invention in respect of which the following conditions are satisfied ...'.

Compliance with these four conditions turns an invention into a 'patentable invention' (see the concluding words of s.1(1)). Section 1(2) then goes on to exclude certain matters from the scope of 'invention'—not 'patentable invention'. To my mind, this shows that the question whether the claim discloses anything which can be described as an invention must be answered in the affirmative before compliance with paras (a)-(d) becomes relevant; and the wording of art.52 in all three languages is even more plainly to the same effect."

Mustill LJ continued (at 263):

2-13

"Thus, although the objection to a patent on the ground that it monopolises something which is not an invention will very often overlap another potential objection—and such an element of overlapping is nothing new in patent law—it is none the less a separate element which, in the appropriate case, ought to be separately investigated.

Turning to the specific question of a naturally occurring substance such as t-PA, there are several quite distinct types of new steps forward which may be taken by an ingenious researcher. Thus—

1.   he may for the first time find out that the substance exists;

2.   he may find out that it exists in a hitherto unsuspected place or form;

3.   he may find out some of its properties, such as its molecular composition or physical structure;

---

[13]   [1989] R.P.C. 147, 261-266.

4.   he may find a new use for it;

5.   he may devise a new way of extracting the natural substance from other natural substances, or purifying it from harmful admixtures;

6.   he may devise a new way of giving the natural substance a new form;

7.   he may devise a new method by which the substance is synthesised from other substances.

Now it seems to me clear that quite apart from section 1(2)(a), and quite apart also from section 60(1), which inferentially confines 'inventions' to those relating to either a product or a process, the first three activities, unlike the last three, do not in ordinary speech amount to an invention. You cannot invent water, although you certainly can invent ways in which it may be distilled or synthesised. I prefer to say nothing in respect of the fourth activity, since it does not arise for consideration here, and may prove to be a source of difficulty in the future, except within the limited compass of section 2(6), for at present I do not see how the ascription of a hitherto unknown property to a known substance can be either the invention of that 'product' or the invention of a 'process'—although some authorities seem to assume that it can."

2-14   The question was reconsidered in the House of Lords in *Biogen Inc v Medeva Plc*[14] but an answer to it was unnecessary. Lord Mustill (as he had by then become) expressly declined to express any opinion on the correctness of his reasoning in *Genentech*[15] and Lord Hoffmann thought the question would almost invariably be academic.[16]

2-15   It cannot therefore be concluded that every disclosure which satisfies the requirements of s.1(1)(a)-(c) and is not excluded by s.1(1)(d) will qualify for the grant of a patent. There may remain scope for debate as to whether certain types of disclosure are not "inventions" at all. In a majority of cases, however, a disclosure which complies with s.1(1)(a)-(d) will qualify for the grant of a patent.

3. INDUSTRIAL APPLICABILITY

2-16   "Industrial Applicability" is defined in s.4(1) of the Act[17] in the following terms:

"An invention shall be taken to be capable of industrial application if it can be made or used in any kind of industry, including agriculture."

This is based upon and intended to have the same effect as the corresponding provision of the EPC,[18] art.57, which provides:

"An invention shall be considered susceptible of industrial application if it can be made or used in any kind of industry, including agriculture."

2-17   It has become clear that "industry" is to be construed in the widest possible sense,[19] as including almost any commercial enterprise.

2-18   The Guidelines[20] suggest the following considerations:

"'Industry' should be understood in its broad sense as including any physical activity of 'technical character' (see G-I, 2), i.e. an activity which belongs to the useful or practical arts as distinct from the aesthetic arts; it does not necessarily imply the use of a machine or the manufacture of an article and could cover e.g. a process for dispersing fog or for converting energy from one form to another. Thus, Art. 57 excludes from patentability very few 'inventions' which are not already excluded by

---

14   [1997] R.P.C. 1.

15   [1997] R.P.C. 1, 32.

16   [1997] R.P.C. 1, 41.

17   As amended by the Patents Act 2004 with effect from 13 December 2007, SI 2007/3396.

18   s.130(7) PA 1977.

19   See para.2-23.

20   Guidelines for Examination in the EPO, November 2015 edn, G-III, 1.

the list in Art. 52(2) (see F-II, 1). One further class of "invention" which would be excluded, however, would be articles or processes alleged to operate in a manner clearly contrary to well-established physical laws, e.g. a perpetual motion machine. Objection could arise under Art. 57 only insofar as the claim specifies the intended function or purpose of the invention, but if, say, a perpetual motion machine is claimed merely as an article having a particular specified construction then objection should be made under Art. 83 (see F-III, 3)."

The Supreme Court reviewed the UK, US and European authorities relating to industrial applicability in *Human Genome Sciences v Eli Lilly*.[21] Much of the reasoning in the main judgment (delivered by Lord Neuberger) is expressed as relating to the application of art.57 to patents of the kind in suit, namely patents for biological material. However, as Lord Hope noted at [142], the standard to be met under art.57 must in principle be the same in all fields of industry.

2-19

Lord Neuberger emphasised the importance of UK patent law aligning itself with the jurisprudence of the EPO (particularly decisions of the EBA)[22] and, whilst noting that circumstances may exist where this approach should not be adopted,[23] concluded that he should take the law to be that laid down in the EPO's jurisprudence. He summarised this jurisprudence at [107]:

2-20

"The essence of the Board's approach in relation to the requirements of Art.57 in relation to biological material may, I think, be summarised in the following points:
The general principles are:

(i)   The patent must disclose 'a practical application' and 'some profitable use' for the claimed substance, so that the ensuing monopoly 'can be expected [to lead to] some ... commercial benefit' (T 0870/04, para.4; T 0898/05, paras.2 and 4);

(ii)   A 'concrete benefit', namely the invention's 'use ... in industrial practice' must be 'derivable directly from the description', coupled with common general knowledge (T 0898/05, para.6; T 0604/04, para.15);

(iii)   A merely 'speculative' use will not suffice, so 'a vague and speculative indication of possible objectives that might or might not be achievable' will not do (T 0870/04, para.21; T 0898/05, paras.6 and 21);

(iv)   The patent and common general knowledge must enable the skilled person 'to reproduce' or 'exploit' the claimed invention without 'undue burden', or having to carry out 'a research programme' (T 0604/04, para.22; T 0898/05, para.6);

Where a patent discloses a new protein and its encoding gene:

(v)   The patent, when taken with common general knowledge, must demonstrate 'a real as opposed to a purely theoretical possibility of exploitation' (T 0604/04, para.15; T 0898/05, paras.6, 22 and 31);

(vi)   Merely identifying the structure of a protein, without attributing to it a 'clear role', or 'suggest[ing]' any 'practical use' for it, or suggesting 'a vague and speculative indication of possible objectives that might be achieved', is not enough (T 0870/04, paras.6-7, 11 and 21; T 0898/05, paras.7, 10 and 31);

(vii)   The absence of any experimental or wet lab evidence of activity of the claimed protein is not fatal (T 0898/05, paras.21 and 31; T 1452/06, para.5);

(viii) A 'plausible' or 'reasonably credible' claimed use, or an 'educated guess', can suffice (T 1329/04, paras.6 and 11; T 0604/04, para.6; T 0898/05, paras.8, 21, 27 and 31; T 1452/06, para.6; T 1165/06 para.25);

(ix)   Such plausibility can be assisted by being confirmed by 'later evidence', although later evidence on its own will not do (T 1329/04, para.12; T 0898/05, para.24; T 1452/06, para.6; T 1165/06, para.25);

(x)   The requirements of a plausible and specific possibility of exploitation can be at the biochemical, the cellular or the biological level (T 0898/05, paras.29-30);

---

21 [2011] UKSC 51; [2012] R.P.C. 6.
22 [2012] R.P.C. 6, [84].
23 [2012] R.P.C. 6, [87].

Where the protein is said to be a family or superfamily member:

(xi) If all known members have a 'role in the proliferation, differentiation and/or activation of immune cells' or 'function in controlling physiology, development and differentiation of mammalian cells', assigning a similar role to the protein may suffice (T 1329/04, para.13; T 0898/85, para.21; T 1165/06, paras.14 and 16; T 0870/04, para.12);

(xii) So 'the problem to be solved' in such a case can be 'isolating a further member of the [family]' (T 1329/04, para.4; T 0604/04, para.22; T 1165/06, paras.14 and 16);

(xiii) If the disclosure is 'important to the pharmaceutical industry', the disclosure of the sequences of the protein and its gene may suffice, even though its role has not 'been clearly defined' (T 0604/04, para.18);

(xiv) The position may be different if there is evidence, either in the patent or elsewhere, which calls the claimed role or membership of the family into question (T 0898/05 para.24; T 1452/06, para.5);

(xv) The position may also be different if the known members have different activities, although they need not always be 'precisely interchangeable in terms of their biological action', and it may be acceptable if 'most' of them have a common role (T 0870/04, para.12; T 0604/04, para.16; T 0898/05, para.27)."

2-21 Lord Neuberger acknowledged that the dividing line between "plausibility"/ "educated guess" and "speculation" could be difficult to discern but concluded that the EPO's approach to the question was sufficiently clear.[24] Regarding the meaning of "plausible" Lord Hope observed as follows at [149]:

"I would not quarrel with Jacob LJ's comment [in the decision under appeal], after consulting the Shorter Oxford English Dictionary, that the sense the word conveys is that there must be some real reason for supposing that the statement is true: para 111. The important point, however, is that the standard is not any higher than that."

2-22 The issue of plausibility has also recently gained prominence in the contexts of obviousness and insufficiency. See paras 12-39 to 12-51 and 13-54 to 13-64 for a discussion of plausibility as it has developed in those contexts.

2-23 At first instance in *Eli Lilly & Co v Human Genome Sciences Inc*,[25] Kitchin J considered the meaning of the term "industry" at [226(i)]:[26]

"The notion of industry must be construed broadly. It includes all manufacturing, extracting and processing activities of enterprises that are carried out continuously, independently and for commercial gain (*BDPI Phosphatase/Max-Planck*). However, it need not necessarily be conducted for profit (*Chiron*) and a product which is shown to be useful to cure a rare or orphan disease may be considered capable of industrial application even if it is not intended for use in any trade at all (*Hematopoietic cytokine receptor/Zymogenetics*)."

Methods of treatment of humans and animals

2-24 Section 4A provides as follows:

"(1) A patent shall not be granted for the invention of—
    (a) a method of treatment of the human or animal body by surgery or therapy, or
    (b) a method of diagnosis practised on the human or animal body.
(2) Subsection (1) above does not apply to an invention consisting of a substance or composition for use in any such method."

2-25 Section 4A is one of the sections referred to in s.130(7) of the Act and thus is to

---

24 [2012] R.P.C. 6, [123].

25 [2008] EWHC 1903 (Pat); [2008] R.P.C. 29.

26 This passage was not challenged on appeal and the Supreme Court cited similar observations in TBA decisions with apparent approval at [45] and [58].

be interpreted, if possible, in the same way as the corresponding article of the EPC, art.53(c). This Article provides:

> "European patents shall not be granted in respect of ... (c) methods for treatment of the human or animal body by surgery or therapy and diagnostic methods practised on the human or animal body; this provision shall not apply to products, in particular substances or compositions, for use in any of these methods."

The exclusion in s.4A(1) is a public policy exclusion. Doctors and vets should **2-26** be free to perform diagnoses and give the most appropriate treatment without fear of patent litigation.[27] The original proposal at the Diplomatic Conference in Munich which led to the EPC was that not only methods of treatment but also that therapeutic products themselves should be excluded. However, the rival public interest of stimulating research and development by providing a reward by way of patent protection led to the compromise which now forms section 4A(2). The caveat of s.4A(2) is a significant exception and is considered in more detail at paras 2-47 to 2-62.

The exclusion of subs.4A(1) covers methods of treatment involving surgery, **2-27** methods of treatment involving therapy and methods of diagnosis. It is, however, only claims to methods that are exempted, not claims to, for example, surgical instruments or therapeutic or diagnostic apparatus. It has been argued on the basis of the Enlarged Board of Appeal decision in G 3/83[28] that the corresponding provision of the EPC must be narrowly interpreted merely because it is an exclusion from patentability but this argument was rejected in G 1/07.[29]

Although the exclusion relates to methods that would in many cases be **2-28** performed by medical or veterinary professionals its application is not dependent upon the characteristics of the person who carries out the method.[30]

The EPO's Guidelines for Examination[31] identify three broad limitations to the **2-29** scope of the exclusion.

First, "methods for treatment of the human or animal body by surgery or therapy" **2-30** does not cover methods for treatment by non-surgical and non-therapeutic means. So, for example, treatment of animals to promote growth or to increase the yield or quality of products derived from those animals is patentable.[32] Similarly, "diagnostic methods practised on the human or animal body" does not cover measuring or recording characteristics of the human or animal body for reasons other than diagnosis.

Secondly, claims to a purely cosmetic treatment by administration of a chemi- **2-31** cal product are considered patentable[33] but a cosmetic treatment by means of surgery or therapy would not be patentable.

Thirdly, the exclusion is confined to acts carried out on the living human or **2-32** animal body and does not cover treatments or diagnostic methods performed upon

---

27 See G 1/04 point 4 of the Reasons; G 1/07 point 3.3.6 of the Reasons.
28 *EISAI/Second medical indication* (G 5/83) [1985] O.J. EPO 64; [1979-85] E.P.O.R. B241.
29 *MEDI-PHYSICS/Treatment by surgery* (G1/07), point 3.1 of the Reasons.
30 See G 1/04, point 6.3 of the Reasons; G 1/07, point 3.4.1 of the Reasons.
31 Guidelines for Examination (November 2015), G-II, 4.2.1.
32 This distinction between veterinary and farming techniques is not necessarily an easy one to draw. See, for example, *WELLCOME/Pigs I* (T116/85) [1989] O.J. EPO 13; [1988] E.P.O.R. 1 where a claim to a method of controlling parasites on pigs was rejected on the ground that, although it was carried out on a large scale by farmers, it was no different from the same treatment by a vet.
33 See T 144/83.

a dead human or animal body or tissues or fluids removed from the human or animal body provided they are not returned to the same body.

Methods for treatment of the human or animal body by surgery or therapy

2-33   The Enlarged Board considered the scope of the treatment by surgery exclusion in *MEDI-PHYSICS/Treatment by surgery* (G1/07). A number of principles emerge from its decision.

2-34   First, the exclusion applies to any method claim that comprises or encompasses at least one feature defining a physical activity or action that constitutes a method step for treatment of a human or animal body by surgery or therapy.[34] This contrasts with the exclusions under art.52(2) EPC which only apply when the excluded subject matter is claimed *as such*.[35]

2-35   Secondly, the term "treatment by surgery" is not confined to surgical methods pursuing a therapeutic purpose.[36]

2-36   Thirdly, although the EPO had previously relied upon a broad construction of "surgery" which covered any non-insignificant intervention performed on the structure of an organism by conservative ("closed, non-invasive") procedures such as repositioning or by operative (invasive) procedures using instruments including endoscopy, puncture, injection, excision, opening of the bodily cavities and catheterisation, such a construction was over-broad. Similarly, it held that the definition given in opinion G 1/04[37] of a method of surgery as "any physical intervention on the human or animal body" was too broad.[38] Its reasoning was as follows:

"The advances in safety and the now routine character of certain, albeit invasive techniques, at least when performed on uncritical parts of the body, have entailed that many such techniques are nowadays generally carried out in a non-medical, commercial environment like in cosmetic salons and in beauty parlours and it appears, hence, hardly still justified to exclude such methods from patentability. This applies as a rule to treatments such as tattooing, piercing, hair removal by optical radiation, micro abrasion of the skin.

If so, that can also not be ignored when it comes to the application of routine interventions in the medical field.

Today, numerous and advanced technologies do exist in the medical field concerning the use of devices which in order to operate must in some way be connected to the patient. Methods for retrieving patient data useful for diagnosis may require administering an agent to the patient, potentially by an invasive step like by injection, in order to yield results or at least they yield better results when using such a step.

Considering this technical reality, excluding from patentability also such methods as make use of in principle safe routine techniques, even when of invasive nature, appears to go beyond the purpose of the exclusion of treatments by surgery from patentability in the interest of public health."

2-37   Fourthly, the Board declined to give a revised definition of the term "treatment by surgery"[39], instead choosing to articulate certain "elements of a narrower understanding":[40]

"Hence, a narrower understanding of what constitutes by its nature a 'treatment by surgery' within the meaning of Article 53(c) EPC is required. It must allow the purpose of the exclusion to be effec-

---

[34]   See G 1/07, point 3.2.5 of the Reasons.
[35]   art.52(3) EPC. See also para.2-65.
[36]   See G 1/07, point 3.3.10 of the Reasons.
[37]   G 1/04, point 6.2.1 of the Reasons.
[38]   G1/07, point 3.4.2.2 of the Reasons.
[39]   G1/07, point 3.4.2.4 of the Reasons.
[40]   G1/07, point 3.4.2.3 of the Reasons.

tive but it must also not go beyond it. The exclusion serves the purpose of, in the interests of public health and of patients, specifically freeing the medical profession from constraints which would be imposed on them by patents granted on methods for surgical or therapeutic treatment, thus any definition of the term 'treatment by surgery' must cover the kind of interventions which represent the core of the medical profession's activities, i.e. the kind of interventions for which their members are specifically trained and for which they assume a particular responsibility.

These are the physical interventions on the body which require professional medical skills to be carried out and which involve health risks even when carried out with the required medical professional care and expertise. It is in this area that the ratio legis of the provision to free the medical profession from constraints by patents comes into play. Such a narrower understanding rules out from the scope of the application of the exclusion clause uncritical methods involving only a minor intervention and no substantial health risks, when carried out with the required care and skill, while still adequately protecting the medical profession.

One amicus curiae observed that the administration of diagnostic agents often causes negative side effects. It is therefore convenient to clarify that there is an exclusion from patentability as a surgical method only if the health risk is associated with the mode of administration and not solely with the agent as such.

It was also remarked that it would be absurd if administering a diagnostic agent by an injection was excluded from patentability but administering by inhalation was not. It is not for the Enlarged Board to decide whether a method involving the injection of a contrast agent is in fact excluded from patentability under the definition of 'treatment by surgery' given here. As a matter of patent law, however, this argument does not hold good, since, by contrast to one early draft version of Article 52(4) EPC 1973, neither its final version nor Article 53(c) EPC stipulate an overall exclusion of medical methods from patentability. Both provisions only exclude the therapeutic, diagnostic and surgical methods listed in the Articles. Hence, where a step is neither a therapeutic nor a diagnostic nor a surgical method the legal situation was and is that it is not excluded from patentability."

In light of the above, the Guidelines[41] provide the following examples of excluded treatments by surgery: injection of a contrast agent into the heart, catheterisation and endoscopy. Tattooing, piercing, hair removal by optical radiation and micro-abrasion of the skin are given as examples of invasive techniques of a routine character which are performed on uncritical body parts and are generally carried out in a non-medical, commercial environment and are therefore not excluded from patentability.   **2-38**

Treatment by therapy has received less attention but a number of principles should be noted.   **2-39**

A suggestion that "therapy" was limited to curative medical treatment as opposed to prophylactic treatment was rejected in *Unilever Limited (Davis's) Application*[42] where it was held that "therapy" included any medical treatment of disease whether preventative or curative. The EPO adopts the same approach.[43]   **2-40**

The Technical Boards of Appeal have held that (non-surgical) contraceptive methods are not excluded as pregnancy is not an illness and therefore its prevention does not constitute therapy.[44] A claim will, however, be excluded if it includes administration of a contraceptive agent and a second agent intended to counteract adverse effects of the contraceptive agent, as the administration of the second agent is a treatment by therapy.[45] In any case it will be necessary to show that the method   **2-41**

---

41 Guidelines for Examination (November 2015), G-II 4.2.1.1.
42 [1983] R.P.C. 219.
43 See T 19/86, point 7 of the Reasons.
44 See *BRITISH TECHNOLOGY GROUP/Contraceptive method* (T 74/93) [1995] O.J. EPO 712; [1995] E.P.O.R. 279 at point 2.2.4 of the Reasons.
45 *GENERAL HOSPITAL/Contraceptive method* (T 820/92) [1995] O.J. EPO 113; [1995] E.P.O.R. 446, points 5.1 and 5.2 of the Reasons.

is capable of industrial application which may not be straightforward where the method is self-administered as a personal and private matter.[46]

2-42   Two further considerations are identified in the Guidelines:[47]

"A method for therapeutic purposes concerning the functioning of an apparatus associated with a living human or animal body is not excluded from patentability if no functional relationship exists between the steps related to the apparatus and the therapeutic effect of the apparatus on the body (see T 245/87).

     As clinical trials have a therapeutic aspect for the human subjects undergoing them, an objection under Art. 53(c) should be raised if a claim includes a step relating to a method of treatment of the human body by therapy (see G-II, 4.2.2)."

Diagnostic methods

2-43   The Enlarged Board of Appeal considered the scope of the diagnostic methods exclusion in *Diagnostic methods* (G 1/04). It defined "diagnosis" as "the determination of the nature of a medical or veterinary medicinal condition intended to identify or uncover a pathology" and held that a negative finding that a particular condition can be ruled out is included within the definition.[48]

2-44   However, the exclusion does not relate to all acts related to diagnosis. Instead it must be established whether each of the following features is present in the claim:[49]

     (i)   the examination phase, involving the collection of data;
     (ii)   the comparison of these data with standard values;
     (iii)   the finding of any significant deviation, i.e. a symptom, during the comparison; and
     (iv)   the attribution of the deviation to a particular clinical picture, i.e. the deductive medical or veterinary decision phase.

2-45   It should be noted that it is not necessarily possible to avoid including one or more of these features in a claim. If the deductive decision phase is a purely intellectual exercise (i.e. of a non-technical nature) it will be necessary to include preceding technical steps to comply with art.52(1) EPC.[50]

2-46   The Guidelines[51] give the following examples of methods for merely obtaining information from the human or animal body which are not excluded as diagnostic methods under art.53(c): X-ray investigations, MRI studies, and blood pressure measurements.

Medical use

2-47   Historically, the first inventor of a new product suitable for use in medical treatment was entitled to a claim to the product per se. This remains the case. Difficulties arise where the product is already known and the invention resides in the discovery of a novel medical use (first medical use), or where, although known for medical use, the invention resides in the discovery of a novel second medical use.

---

46   T 74/93 at points 2.2.5-2.2.6
47   Guidelines for Examination (November 2015), G-II, 4.2.1.2.
48   G 1/04, point 5.1 of the Reasons.
49   G 1/04, points 5-8 of the Reasons.
50   G 1/04, point 5.3 of the Reasons.
51   Guidelines for Examination (November 2015) G-II 4.2.1.3

First medical use

First medical use is covered by s.4A(3) of the Act[52] which corresponds to art.54(4) of the EPC. The fact that a substance or composition forms part of the state of the art does not prevent the invention from being taken to be new if any medical use of the product does not form part of the state of art.[53] Provided that the use is otherwise inventive, a claim to the product for use in the medical application is permissible. Moreover, both the EPO and the UK IPO will allow a general claim to the medical use of the product (e.g. "substance X for use as a medicament") even if only one indication is identified in the application.[54]

2-48

Second medical use

The permissibility of second medical use claims has been considered both in the EPO[55] and in the national courts.[56] In summary, such claims were held allowable under the original (1973) version of the EPC and remain allowable, albeit on a different basis, under the EPC 2000.

2-49

In the EPO, in the *EISAI* case, it was held that, whilst a claim to the method of use could not be permitted under the 1973 version of the convention, a claim to the use of a product for the manufacture of a medicament for a specified new and inventive medical use could be permitted (the so-called Swiss type of claim), the Swiss national patent office having instituted a practice of allowing such claims [1984] O.J. EPO 581 (contrary to the established practice in the German national patent office). The EPO in *EISAI* concluded that there was no discernible intention in the EPC or in the *travaux préparatoires* to exclude such claims. This reasoning was approved in *Wyeth's Application*[57] where the Patents Court sat *en banc*.

2-50

In *Actavis v Merck*[58] the Court of Appeal held that second medical use claims were allowable even where the novelty resided solely in a new dosage regime or other form of administration of a substance. It noted that such claims were allowed in the EPO, Germany, and New Zealand and concluded that there was no clear ratio to the contrary in *Bristol Myers Squibb Co v Baker Norton Pharmaceuticals Inc.*[59] Furthermore, even if there had been a clear ratio to the contrary in one of its own previous decisions, the Court of Appeal should follow clear European Patent Office authority, as an exception to the rule in *Young v Bristol Aeroplane Co Ltd*[60] given the importance of a common European approach to patentability.

2-51

---

[52] Note that s.4A(3) was introduced by the Patents Act 2004 and SI 2007/3396 with effect from 13 December 2007, whereby s.2(6) of the Act was also repealed.

[53] *Sopharma S.A.'s Application* [1983] R.P.C. 195. See also *ABBOTT RESPIRATORY/dosage regime* (G2/08) at [5.8], concluding that new art.54(4) EPC 2000 has the same effect as art.54(5) EPC 1973.

[54] See (T 128/82) [1984] O.J. EPO 164; (T 36/83) [1986] O.J. EPO 295; Guidelines for Examination (November 2015) G-VI 7.1; *Manual of Patents Practice* (July 2015 edn), para.4A.17.

[55] *EISAI/Second medical indication* (G 5/83) [1985] O.J. EPO 64; [1979-85] E.P.O.R. B241. See also *ABBOTT RESPIRATORY/dosage regimen claims* (G2/08).

[56] *Wyeth's Application* [1985] R.P.C. 545; *Bristol Myers Squibb v Baker Norton* [1999] R.P.C. 253 and [2001] R.P.C. 1, CA; *Actavis v Merck* [2008] R.P.C. 26.

[57] [1985] R.P.C. 545.

[58] [2008] R.P.C. 26.

[59] [2001] R.P.C. 1.

[60] [1944] KB 718.

2-52   In the subsequent European case of *ABBOTT RESPIRATORY/dosage regime* (G2/08), in which the *Actavis v Merck* decision was cited,[61] the Enlarged Board of Appeal of the EPO considered the allow ability of second medical use claims under the EPC 2000. It began by noting the new art.54(5), which provides as follows[62]:

> "(5) Paragraphs 2 and 3 shall also not exclude the patentability of any substance or composition referred to in paragraph 4 for any specific use in a method referred to in Article 53(c), provided that such use is not comprised in the state of the art."

2-53   It pointed out that this stood in contrast to the absence of any such provision in the EPC 1973, and explained that:

> "Thus, under the new law the lacuna in the former provisions, which had been filled in a praetorian way by the Enlarged Board of Appeal with decision G 5/83 and the case law based on that decision, no longer exists."[63]

2-54   The Enlarged Board then went on to confirm that the words "any specific use" should be construed broadly. In particular such words should be interpreted merely as contrasting with the generic broad protection conferred by the first claimed medical application of a substance or composition, and need not be the treatment of another disease. It could for instance relate to a novel group of subjects treated, to a new route or mode of administration, or to a different technical effect: see G2/08 at para.5.10.7. However, any such new use must of course satisfy the requirement for an inventive step.

2-55   In conclusion the Enlarged Board noted that since the reason for Swiss-type claims had ceased, applications for such claims should likewise cease.[64] The UK IPO has followed suit.[65]

2-56   It has been pointed out that a more logical approach, though leading to the same result, would be to permit claims to extend to the method of treatment using the compound or composition but to require from the patentee a disclaimer of any right to sue the practitioner.[66] However the Enlarged Board explained that "in view of the clear provisions of art.53(c), second sentence, and art.54(5) EPC and the intention of the legislator, the Enlarged Board has no power to broaden or reduce in a praetorian way the scope of these provisions. If deemed necessary, the freedom of medical practitioners may be protected by other means on the national level": see G2/08, para.6.5.

2-57   Second medical use claims can therefore be obtained providing they are drafted appropriately. However, it is necessary that the claim should, on a proper examination, be for a second medical use and not be for a mere discovery about an old use. In *Bristol Myers Squibb v Baker Norton*,[67] Jacob J identified this important distinction[68] and quoted from the Dutch Court of Appeal in the corresponding case in Holland, *Bristol-Myers Squibb v Yew Tree*:

> "It must be assumed that there is not a single expert/doctor in the present field of science, who would

---

[61] See III.9.3.
[62] Which corresponds to s.4A(4) of the 1977 Act as amended by the Patents Act 2004.
[63] See paras 5.9, 5.10.2, and 6.4.
[64] With effect from three months after publication of G2/08 in the Official Journal.
[65] See Practice Note on Patents Act 1977: Second medical use claims, 26 May 2010. This practice note came into effect immediately on publication.
[66] *Pharmaceutical Management Agency v Commissioner of Patents* [2000] R.P.C. 857, Court of Appeal of New Zealand.
[67] [1999] R.P.C. 253.
[68] See [57]-[60] at 277-278.

believe that what is involved here is a second medical indication in the sense of an application of a substance for a different therapeutic purpose (for example, to fight another illness or for prevention instead of as a cure)."

Jacob J's decision in *Bristol Myers Squibb* was upheld in the Court of Appeal,[69] where the reasoning in the above passage from the *Wyeth* case was approved, and it was confirmed that the novelty in a Swiss-type claim resided in "the new second (or subsequent) therapeutic use".[70] **2-58**

In *Bristol-Myers Squibb* the claim included the words "for treating cancer", in relation to which Aldous LJ held as follows: **2-59**

"The words 'for treating cancer' have to be construed in context. The skilled addressee would realise that drugs which were suitable for treatment would not always be successful. However, drugs which had no effect were not suitable. The phrase means 'suitable for trying to treat cancer'. What is suitable is a question of fact, not one of perception. If the drug has a beneficial effect in the treatment of cancer it will be suitable. If not, it will not be."

Accordingly a second medical use claim only survives because the compound is effective to achieve a new treatment. If it is not effective, or not discernibly so, it is not suitable for that treatment. If administration of the compound results in some patients getting better, but the same improvement would be achieved by the administration of any placebo, that is not enough: the patient benefit is in that situation achieved simply because the patient believes he is being treated, not because of any peculiar feature or efficacy of the patented compound.[71] **2-60**

It is possible, but not necessary, for a claim to specify the means by which the clinical benefit is to be measured. In *Hospira v Genentech*[72] the claim required that the treatment "provide clinical benefit as measured by increased time to disease progression ['TTP']", TTP being one of a number of clinical endpoints used in the field.[73] An argument that a skilled reader would not consider it essential that there be an increase in TTP provided that there was some increase in clinical efficacy was rejected and it was held that the clinical benefit must be manifested by increased TTP.[74] There may, however, be a distinction to be drawn between defining the beneficial effects of the subject matter of the claim and claiming the absence of harmful effects of subject matter outside the claim but whilst this point arose in *Hospira v Genentech* it was left undecided.[75] **2-61**

Although it is now clear that second medical use claims are not excluded from patentability, they do give rise to a number of potentially difficult issues which are considered elsewhere in this work. Particular attention is drawn to the issues arising as to the construction of such claims,[76] the requirements for a prior art disclosure to anticipate such a claim,[77] the disclosure required to support such a claim for the purposes of sufficiency[78] and the circumstances in which such claims are infringed.[79] **2-62**

---

[69] [2001] R.P.C. 1, [36]-[37].
[70] See also *Laboratorios Almirall SA v Boehringer Ingelheim Int GmbH* [2009] F.S.R. 12, where *Bristol-Myers Squibb* was cited and the claim in question was held to be excluded under s.4A(1)(a).
[71] *Pfizer Ltd's Patent* [2001] F.S.R. 16, 201, not considered on appeal.
[72] [2015] EWHC 1796 (Pat).
[73] See [47].
[74] See [53]–[56].
[75] See [57].
[76] See paras 9-268 to 9-298.
[77] See para.11-97 and paras 11-142 to 11-146.
[78] See paras 13-54 to 13-64.

4. EXCLUDED INVENTIONS

2-63   Section 1(2) sets out a list of items which are declared not to be inventions for the purposes of the Act:

> "It is hereby declared that the following (among other things) are not inventions for the purposes of this Act, that is to say, anything which consists of—
>
> (a)   a discovery, scientific theory or mathematical method;
> (b)   a literary, dramatic, musical or artistic work or any other aesthetic creation whatsoever;
> (c)   a scheme, rule or method for performing a mental act, playing a game or doing business, or a program for a computer;
> (d)   the presentation of information;
>
> but the foregoing provision shall prevent anything from being treated as an invention for the purposes of this Act only to the extent that a patent or application for a patent relates to that thing as such."

"The following (among other things)"

2-64   First, it is to be noted that the list is not an exhaustive one, for "other things" may still be included.[80] In particular, power to vary s.1(2) is given to the Secretary of State by s.1(5). This power is yet to be exercised however.

"Relates to that thing as such"

2-65   Secondly, it is necessary to consider the effect of the words "only to the extent that a patent or application for a patent relates to that thing as such", which have given rise to considerable difficulties. Furthermore, notwithstanding the English Court of Appeal's judgment in *Symbian* (discussed below in relation to computer programs) it seems clear that there is a divergence between UK and EPO practice. As pointed out in *Halliburton Energy Services Inc's Patent Application*,[81] the EPO's approach to patentability goes hand-in-hand with its special approach to inventive step in such cases, which means that there is no reason why there should be a different outcome overall. However, care should be taken not to create an illegitimate combination of approaches. Arden LJ concluded in *Lantana Ltd v Comptroller General of Patents, Designs and Trade Marks*[82] that EPO decisions can provide only limited assistance in determining the same issue in this jurisdiction.

2-66   In the EPO, it seems clear that very few instances of claims to business methods or computer programs will be held merely to *"relate to that thing as such"* following the EPO decisions in *Pensions Benefit System*,[83] *Hitachi*,[84] *MICROSOFT/data transfer*,[85] *DUNS LICENSING ASSOCIATES/Estimating sales activity*,[86] and the Enlarged Board of Appeal decision in G3/08.[87]

---

[79]   See paras 14-20 to 14-24, 14.38 and 14-119 to 14-123.
[80]   See para.2–11.
[81]   *Halliburton Energy Services Inc's Patent Application* [2011] EWHC 2508 (Pat); [2012] R.P.C. 12, [79].
[82]   [2014] EWCA Civ 1463; [2015] R.P.C. 16, [52].
[83]   T 931/95.
[84]   T 258/03.
[85]   *MICROSOFT/Data transfer* (T 424/03) with expanded clipboard formats, 23 February 2006, Board of Appeal, EPO.
[86]   (T 154/04) [2007] E.P.O.R. 38.
[87]   Opinion of the Enlarged Board of Appeal of the EPO in G3/08 (10 May 2010).

In the UK, the matter was considered in *Gale's Patent Application*[88] when 2-67
Nicholls LJ stated the law to be:

"Section 1(2) comprises a non-exhaustive catalogue of matters or things, starting with 'a discovery',
which as such are declared not to be inventions. Thus, a discovery as such is not patentable as an
invention under the Act. But when applied to a product or process which, in the language of the 1977
Act, is capable of industrial application, the matter stands differently. This was so held in *Genentech
Inc's Patent* [1989] R.P.C. 147. There, this court by a majority decision held that section 1(2) did
not depart from the established principle mentioned above. Purchas L.J., at page 208, and also Dillon L.J., at page 240, decided that the quotation from Whitford J. set out above[89] still represented the
law. Dillon LJ said:

'In so far as a patent claims as an invention the practical application of a discovery, the patent does
not, in my judgment, relate only to the discovery as such, even if the practical application may
be obvious once the discovery has been made, even though unachievable in the absence of the
discovery'."

Subsequent UK cases, culminating in *Symbian*,[90] have refined the UK approach 2-68
but it is not the same as that of the EPO. The majority of the cases dealing with
"relates to that thing as such" have considered computer programs, and this topic
will be explored under that heading.

The excluded categories

Thirdly, it is necessary to consider the ambit of the excluded categories under 2-69
s.1(2) of the Act (which occur also in art.52(2) of the EPC).[91] These are all abstract
matters which are thought to be better protected under other areas of industrial
property law, particularly copyright. However, it has been pointed out on several
occasions that these exceptions need to be considered separately, and it can be
confusing to take principles in relation to one category and apply them to other
categories.[92]

Discovery, scientific theory, mathematical method

Section 1(2)(a) excludes any discovery, scientific theory or mathematical method. 2-70
This follows the old law, which distinguished between an invention and a mere
disclosure of a principle. The distinction was stated by Whitford J in *Genentech
Inc's Patent* at first instance[93] in a passage approved by the majority in the Court
of Appeal[94] in the following terms:

"It is trite law that you cannot patent a discovery, but if on the basis of that discovery you can tell
people how it can be usefully employed, then a patentable invention may result. This in my view
would be the case, even though once you have made the discovery, the way in which it can be usefully employed is obvious enough."

---

[88] [1991] R.P.C. 305, 324.
[89] See *Genentech Inc's Patent* [1987] R.P.C. 533, 566.
[90] [2009] R.P.C. 1.
[91] s.130(7) of PA 1977 applies to s.1(2) of PA 1977.
[92] See *Aerotel* [2007] R.P.C. 7, Court of Appeal; *CFPH LLC's Application* [2006] R.P.C. 5; *Halliburton Energy Services Inc v Smith International (North Sea) Ltd* [2006] R.P.C. 2; *Shopalotto.com
Ltd's Application* [2006] R.P.C. 7.
[93] [1987] R.P.C. 553, 566.
[94] [1989] R.P.C. 147, 208 and 240. Subsequently applied in, e.g. *DSM NV's Patent* [2001] R.P.C. 35,
709 at [155].

2-71   In *Kirin-Amgen Inc v Hoechst Marion Roussel Ltd*,[95] Lord Hoffmann cited the above passage and then explained (at [77]):

"In such a case, while it may be true to say, as the Court of Appeal did ([2003] R.P.C. 31, 62) that Table VI lay 'at the heart of the invention', it was not the invention. An invention is a practical product or process, not information about the natural world. That seems to me to accord with the social contract between the state and the inventor which underlies patent law. The state gives the inventor a monopoly in return for an immediate disclosure of all the information necessary to enable performance of the invention. That disclosure is not only to enable other people to perform the invention after the patent has expired. If that were all, the inventor might as well be allowed to keep it secret during the life of the patent. It is also to enable anyone to make immediate use of the information for any purpose which does not infringe the claims. The specifications of valid and subsisting patents are an important source of information for further research, as is abundantly shown by a reading of the sources cited in the specification for the patent in suit. Of course a patentee may in some cases be able to frame his claim to a product or process so broadly that in practice it will be impossible to use the information he has disclosed, even to develop important improvements, in a way which does not infringe. But it cannot be right to give him a monopoly of the use of the information as such."

2-72   In *Tate & Lyle Technology Ltd v Roquette Frères*[96] the claim in question was for "The use of maltotriitol to modify or control the form of maltitol crystals." Lewison J held as follows:

"Roquette have explained *why* maltitol crystals take the habit that they do, but have not added anything else to the sum of human knowledge. The claim is not saved from unpatentability simply by the addition of the phrase 'the use of'. What matters is the substance of the claim rather than its form. It would have been possible to claim particular processes or products that took advantage of the discovery, for instance by claiming certain levels of concentration of maltotriitol within the syrup, or crystals produced with the aid of the discovery. Indeed that is what Roquette did, but all their claimed products and processes have been declared invalid (or have been abandoned)."

Literary, dramatic, musical or artistic work, etc.

2-73   Section 1(2)(b) excludes any literary, dramatic, musical or artistic work or any other aesthetic creation whatsoever. Again, there is no change from the old law.[97] Such things are regarded as more properly the subject of copyright protection, which protects only the form of expression and not the underlying idea.

Scheme, rule or method for performing a mental act

2-74   In *Halliburton Energy Services Inc's Patent Application*[98] the court considered the patentability of a method of designing a drill bit which involved computer simulation of the interaction of the bit with the material being drilled to optimise various design features of the bit.[99] HHJ Birss QC (sitting as a judge of the High Court) identified two possible approaches to interpreting this exclusion (at [42] and [43]):

"... The wide construction is that a method is "a scheme, rule or method for performing a mental act" if it is capable of being performed mentally regardless of whether, as claimed, it is in fact

---

[95] [2005] R.P.C. 9, 169.
[96] [2010] F.S.R. 1, [75]. Affirmed on appeal [2010] EWCA Civ 1049; [2011] F.S.R. 3.
[97] *Nelson's Application* [1980] R.P.C. 173.
[98] *Halliburton Energy Services Inc's Patent Application* [2011] EWHC 2508 (Pat); [2012] R.P.C. 12.
[99] *Halliburton Energy Services Inc's Patent Application* [2011] EWHC 2508 (Pat); [2012] R.P.C. 12, [15]–[17].

performed mentally. Read this way the exclusion excludes methods of the type performed mentally regardless of how they are claimed. So a claim to a computer programmed to carry out a method of performing a calculation (say a square root), would not only be caught by the computer program and mathematical method exclusions but would also be excluded by the mental act exclusion because calculations are the kind of thing which are capable of being performed mentally…

… The narrow construction is that the exclusion only excludes acts carried out mentally. On the narrow construction a claim to a calculation carried out on a computer could never be caught by the mental act exclusion because the claim does not encompass carrying out the calculation mentally…"

Having reviewed the case law and noted that the wide construction had been provisionally favoured by Aldous LJ in *Fujitsu*[100] and that this had been doubted by Jacob LJ in *Aerotel*,[101] the judge held that the narrow construction of the mental act exclusion was the correct one to adopt.[102]   **2-75**

This finding had the consequence that it was not necessary for the claim to include an additional "tethering" step requiring the manufacture of the drill bit designed in accordance with the claim.[103] This was in marked contrast to the result in *Halliburton Energy Services Inc v Smith International (North Sea) Ltd*.[104] In that case a claim to a method of designing a drill bit (which did not contain any express reference to the method being carried out on a computer) was held invalid as being "directed purely to the intellectual content of a design process". However, following the EPO's decision in *IBM/Method for physical VLSI-chip design*,[105] it was held that this defect could be cured by amendment by the addition of a further limitation to the claim of the form "and materially producing the [item] so designed".   **2-76**

Games

Warren J considered the meaning of the word "game" for the purposes of s.1(2) in *IGT v The Comptroller General of Patents*[106]:   **2-77**

"… In the physical world, it is (usually) possible to describe a game in words and to set out its rules in writing. The rules of a game are not restricted to what a player may or may not do; some rules may set the physical constraints of a game. Thus the rules of most sports will set out the rules about physical location (e.g. size of pitch or court, size of ball or racket) as well as the rules of play (e.g. permitted interactions with a ball, offside rules, scoring and the like). There may be schemes or methods of play which do not form part of the rules (e.g. methods of card play designed to enhance the player's chances of success). In these cases, it is straightforward to identify the rules of the game, for the game is really defined by its rules. And, once the rules of the game have been set, players may be able to develop successful stratagems—methods of play—for playing the game better than others."

The judge went on to consider the position in the virtual world at [23], et seq. This issue involves a considerable overlap with the computer program exclusion and is therefore addressed at para.2–86.   **2-78**

---

[100] *Fujitsu Ltd's Application* [1997] R.P.C. 608.
[101] *Aerotel Ltd v Telco Holding Ltd; Macrossan's Application* [2007] R.P.C. 7.
[102] *Halliburton Energy Services Inc's Patent Application* [2011] EWHC 2508 (Pat); [2012] R.P.C. 12, [63].
[103] *Halliburton Energy Services Inc's Patent Application* [2011] EWHC 2508 (Pat); [2012] R.P.C. 12, [68]–[70].
[104] [2006] R.P.C. 2, [217].
[105] T0453/91.
[106] [2007] EWHC 1341 (Pat).

Business methods

2-79   As observed in *CFPH LLC's Application*,[107] this exclusion will quite often overlap with that relating to computer programs although the policy reasons for the exclusion are not the same in each case.[108]

2-80   In the *Hitachi* case[109] it was held by the EPO that method steps consisting of modifications to a business scheme and aimed at circumventing a technical problem rather than solving it by technical means cannot contribute to the technical character of the subject-matter claimed. Since this was what was claimed (in particular, a modification of the rules of a Dutch auction to avoid data transmission delays), the application was refused.

2-81   In *CFPH LLC's Application*[110] the result was similar. It was held that both patents involved altering business schemes to overcome technical problems (shortage of bandwidth and data transmission delays), rather than solving such problems by technical means. Thus, even assuming novelty and inventive step, the alleged inventions could only be innovations in business methods.

2-82   In *Shopalotto.Com's Application*[111] the claim was to a computer configured to provide a lottery playable via the internet. It was held that there was no contribution to the art outside the provision of the various pages to any person suitably equipped to view the pages provided by the server; furthermore, any element of reinforcing the message of the brand or brands selected by the player was a method of doing business and so lay in a forbidden subject-matter.[112]

2-83   In *Crawford's Application*,[113] which was heard after *CFPH*, the court identified a "consistent principle that an inventor must make a contribution to the art (that is to say the invention must be new and not obvious) and that contribution must be of a technical nature (susceptible of industrial application and not within one of the areas excluded by Art.52(2))" and applied this approach to a display system for buses. The only advance in the art which was said to be new and inventive was the nature of the information to be displayed on the outside of a bus and the method of operating a bus in so-called "exit mode"[114] but these were not, individually or collectively, of a technical nature. The information to be displayed was the presentation of information, whereas the method of operating a bus in exit mode was a method of doing business.

2-84   In *Raytheon's Application*[115] the patent related to a method of stock control. It was submitted that the technical contribution was threefold: first, the replacement of textual descriptions by visual representations; secondly, the representations were synthesised from individual images of the components of the rack stored in digital form in the database, so reducing the usage of memory and the load on the proces-

---

[107] [2005] EWHC 1589 (Pat).
[108] See also *Merrill Lynch's Application* [1989] R.P.C. 561, another case of business methods.
[109] T258/03. This was cited with approval by Lewison J in *AT&T Knowledge Ventures/Cvon Innovations* [2009] F.S.R. 19.
[110] [2006] R.P.C. 5.
[111] [2006] R.P.C. 7.
[112] As a result of this case, the Patent Office changed its approach to examining games: see *Patent Office Practice Note (Patentability of Games)* [2006] R.P.C. 8.
[113] [2006] R.P.C. 11.
[114] "Exit mode" meant that the bus would only drop off passengers and not allow any to board, which was said to alleviate "bus bunching".
[115] [2008] R.P.C. 3.

sor; and thirdly, the system was navigable by the user who started with a high level interactive graphical representation and could "drill down" to the particular rack or component of interest by, for example, clicking on the representation of the rack or equipment in question. It was held that the second and third contributions fell within the computer program exclusion whereas the first fell under the business method exclusion.

In *Halliburton Energy Services Inc's Patent Application*[116] HHJ Birss QC (sit- **2-85**
ting as a judge of the High Court) identified the difficulties that can arise from the combination of the computer program and business method exclusions (at [35]):

> "The business method cases can be tricky to analyse by just asking whether the invention has a techni-
> cal effect or makes a technical contribution. The reason is that computers are self evidently techni-
> cal in nature. Thus when a business method is implemented on a computer, the patentee has a rich
> vein of arguments to deploy in seeking to contend that his invention gives rise to a technical effect
> or makes a technical contribution. For example the computer is said to be a faster, more efficient
> computerized book keeper than before and surely, says the patentee, that is a technical effect or techni-
> cal advance. And so it is, in a way, but the law has resolutely sought to hold the line at excluding
> such things from patents. That means that some apparently technical effects do not always count. So
> a computer programmed to be a better computer is patentable (*Symbian*) but as Fox LJ pointed out
> in relation to the business method exclusion in *Merrill Lynch*, the fact that the method of doing busi-
> ness may be an improvement on previous methods is immaterial because the business method exclu-
> sion is generic."

Computer programs

The 1977 Act declares in s.1(2)(c) that computer programs as such are not inven- **2-86**
tions and in consequence not patentable. Considerable difficulties have arisen in the course of determining the precise scope of this exception, which has been considered four times by the Court of Appeal[117] and once by the Enlarged Board of Appeal of the EPO[118] in the last decade. In order to render the most recent case law intelligible, it is useful to explore the way in which the case law has developed. A summary of the law as it now stands is provided at para.2-113. This section should also be read in conjunction with the "business methods" exclusion, since experience has shown that the two often overlap.

Early UK cases

In *Merrill Lynch Inc's Application*,[119] Falconer J held that if anything in the **2-87**
excluded categories constituted the inventive step then no patent could be granted regardless of how the claim was drafted. This reasoning was rejected in the Court of Appeal (see below),[120] although it was subsequently applied by Pumfrey J in *Shopalotto*.[121]

---

[116] *Halliburton Energy Services Inc's Patent Application* [2011] EWHC 2508 (Pat); [2012] R.P.C. 12.
[117] *Aerotel v Telco; Macrossan's Application* [2007] R.P.C. 7; *Symbian Ltd v Comptroller-General of Patents* [2009] R.P.C. 1; *HTC v Apple* [2013 EWCA Civ 451, [2013] R.P.C. 30; *Lantana Ltd v Comptroller General of Patents, Designs and Trade Marks* [2014] EWCA Civ 1463, [2015] R.P.C. 16.
[118] Opinion of the Enlarged Board of Appeal of the EPO in G3/08 (10 May 2010).
[119] [1988] R.P.C. 1.
[120] [1989] R.P.C. 561 following *Genentech Inc's Patent* [1989] R.P.C. 553, 563–569, see Fox LJ.
[121] *Shopalotto.com Ltd's Application* [2006] R.P.C. 7.

The VICOM case introduces the requirement for a "technical contribution"

2-88   In the *VICOM* case,[122] the Board of Appeal of the EPO allowed a claim to a technical process carried out under the control of a computer program. The Board reasoned:

> "The Board is of the opinion that a claim directed to a technical process which process is carried out under the control of a program (be this implemented in hardware or in software), cannot be regarded as relating to a computer program as such *within the meaning of* Article 52(3) EPC, as it is the application of the program for determining the sequence of steps in the process for which in effect protection is sought. Consequently, such a claim is allowable under Article 52(2)(c) and (3) EPC."

The Board then continued:

> "Generally speaking, an invention which would be patentable in accordance with conventional patentability criteria should not be excluded from protection by the mere fact that for its implementation modern technical means in the form of a computer program are used. Decisive is what technical contribution the invention as defined in the claim when considered as a whole makes to the known art."

2-89   It was this last sentence which gave rise to difficulty since, as was later pointed out in *CFPH LLC's Application*,[123] because: (a) it introduces the inherently uncertain test of what is "technical", and (b) the word "technical" is not used in art.52 at all.[124]

2-90   Nevertheless the decision in the *VICOM* case was approved by the Court of Appeal in *Merrill Lynch Inc's Application*,[125] where Fox LJ observed:

> "It seems to me to be clear … that it cannot be permissible to patent an item excluded by section 1(2) under the guise of an article which contains that item—that is to say, in the case of a computer program, the patenting of a conventional computer containing that program. Something further is necessary.
> The nature of the addition is I think to be found in the *Vicom* case where it is stated: 'Decisive is what technical contribution the invention makes to the known art.'"[126]

2-91   In *Fujitsu Limited's Application*[127] the Court of Appeal found difficulty in identifying the boundary line between what was and what was not a technical contribution and emphasised that each case must be decided on its own facts. In that case, on full analysis, the only technical advance was in the computer program which enabled a quicker result and the claim was therefore not allowed.[128]

2-92   The *VICOM* case was followed by further EPO decisions including two IBM

---

122 *VICOM/Computer-related invention* (T208/84) [1987] O.J. EPO 14; [1987] E.P.O.R. 74.
123 [2005] EWHC 1589 (Pat).
124 It is used in r.29, but this was said to be "little more than a procedural rule" and not a substantive provision.
125 [1989] R.P.C. 561.
126 It will be noted that in *VICOM* the EPO had in fact said "Decisive is what technical contribution the invention as defined in the claim when considered as a whole makes to the known art.'
127 [1997] R.P.C. 608.
128 The correctness of the actual result has subsequently been doubted. See *Symbian*, [42], where the Court of Appeal held "It is fair to add that we can see a powerful case for saying that, while the test applied by the court in Fujitsu was ostensibly consistent with that in *Vicom* and *Gale*, the outcome is a little hard to reconcile with the view taken in those two cases to the question of what constitutes a 'technical' contribution. This is, we think, supported by the difficulty Aldous LJ said that he had with the reasoning in *Vicom*. However, even if that is right, the actual decision in Fujitsu may well have been justified on the alternative ground tentatively relied on by Aldous LJ, namely that the alleged invention was a 'method for performing mental acts'".

applications.[129] The Board concluded that protection could be given to a computer program claimed by itself if the program when running on a computer was capable of bringing about a technical effect which went beyond the normal physical interactions between the program and the computer on which it was run. The Board felt unable to draw any logical distinction in these circumstances between claim to the program itself or to the program as a record on a carrier. An objection to patentability will however be maintained when, on analysis, the real basis for protection was the patenting of a mental act dressed up as a computer program. The Board reached this conclusion by giving an even narrower meaning to the words "as such" than that given in the *VICOM* case.[130] In reaching its decisions, the Board was plainly influenced by the language of TRIPS[131] although it held that TRIPS was not at that time binding on the EPO.

The EPO retreats from the "technical contribution" approach in favour of the "any hardware" approach

2-93
The EPO later began to encounter problems with the "technical contribution" approach and began to move away from it in *Pensions Benefit System Partnership*[132] where the patent concerned the operation of a pension scheme on a computer. There were claims both to the method and to computer apparatus used for carrying out the method. The Board held that the new method involved no more than a method of doing business, and was to be rejected for that reason. However it also held that the claim to the computer apparatus could not be rejected even if it were entirely conventional. Its conventional nature went to whether the claim was new and non-obvious, and not to whether it was excluded from protection under art.52(2)(c).[133] The Board went on to hold[134] that because the regime of patentable subject-matter was only entered as the result of the programming of a computer system for carrying out the invention, the assessment of inventive step had to be carried out from the point of view of a software developer having the knowledge of the concept and structure of the improved pension benefits system and of the underlying schemes of information processing. Thus the non-patentable subject matter was ignored for the purposes of assessing inventive step.

2-94
The EPO in the *Hitachi* case[135] went one step further in rejecting the contribution approach entirely. It expressed its agreement with the view that:

"There is no basis in the EPC for distinguishing between 'new features' of an invention and features of that invention which are known from the prior art when examining whether the invention

[129] *IBM/Computer program product* (T1173/97) [1999] O.J. EPO 609; and *IBM/Computer programs* (T935/97) [1999] R.P.C. 861; [1999] E.P.O.R. 301. These prompted an almost immediate change in UK Patent Office procedure: see *Patent Office Practice Note* [1999] R.P.C. 563.
[130] [1997] O.J. E.P.O. 14; [1997] E.P.O.R. 74; and see para.2–88.
[131] GATT Agreement in Trade-Related Aspects of Intellectual Property Rights, February 1994, art.27 of which does not exclude computer programs from patentability. See paras 1–72 to 1–79.
[132] T931/95.
[133] It should be noted that in *Hutchins' Application* [2002] R.P.C. 8, and also in *Pintos Global Services* (SRIS O/171/01), the UK Patent Office had expressly rejected submissions that it should adopt the *Pension Benefit System Partnership* approach.
[134] At para.8 of the Reasons.
[135] T258/03.

concerned may be considered to be an invention within the meaning of Article 52(1) EPC. Thus there is no basis in the EPC for applying this so-called contribution approach for this purpose."[136]

2-95   In particular the Board held that a claim containing a mixture of technical and non-technical features would generally be regarded as an invention within the meaning of the Article. The definition of technical features was extremely broad: it included not only items such as a "server computer", "client computers" and a "network" but also "the act of writing using pen and paper". This definition would only exclude, e.g. "purely abstract concepts devoid of any technical implications". However the Board went on to stress that:

> "Needless to say, however, this does not imply that all methods involving the use of technical means are patentable. They still have to be new, represent a non-obvious technical solution to a technical problem, and be susceptible of industrial application."

2-96   The final EPO decision in this field was *MICROSOFT/Data transfer*.[137] This held that any program on a carrier has a technical character and so escapes the prohibition in art.52 following *Hitachi*. The Board then proceeded to consider inventive step. However, in doing so, and in contrast to *Pension Benefit* and *Hitachi*, there is no express indication it put to one side non-patentable subject matter.[138]

2-97   Thus only claims to "purely abstract concepts devoid of any technical implications" or the like will now be refused by the EPO as being excluded from protection, though any such claims will still have to satisfy the other substantive requirements of patentability.

The UK court rejects the "any hardware" approach

2-98   In *Aerotel v Telco; Macrossan's Application ("Aerotel")*[139] the Court of Appeal considered the previous UK and EPO case law, which it summarised as follows:

> "(1) *The contribution approach* Ask whether the inventive step resides *only* in the contribution of excluded matter—if yes, Art.52(2) applies. This approach was supported by Falconer J. in *Merrill Lynch* but expressly rejected by this Court.
>
> (2) *The technical effect approach* Ask whether the invention as defined in the claim makes a technical contribution to the known art—if no, Art.52(2) applies. A possible clarification (at least by way of exclusion) of this approach is to add the rider that novel or inventive purely excluded matter does not count as a 'technical contribution'. This is the approach (with the rider) adopted by this Court in *Merrill Lynch*. It has been followed in the subsequent decisions of this Court, *Gale* and *Fujitsu*. The approach (without the rider as an express caution) was that first adopted by the EPO Boards of Appeal, see *Vicom*, *IBM/Text processing* and *IBM/Data processor network*.
>
> (3) *The 'any hardware' approach* Ask whether the claim involves the use of or is to a piece of physical hardware, however mundane (whether a computer or a pencil and paper). If yes, Art.52(2) does not apply. This approach was adopted in three cases, *Pension Benefits*, *Hitachi* and *MICROSOFT/Data transfer* (the 'trio'). It was specifically rejected by this Court in *Gale*."

2-99   The Court of Appeal expressly rejected the third approach; indeed, it suggested that the "trio" of cases were not even consistent with each other. It expressed a preference for the first approach, but held that it was bound by its own previous decisions to follow the second. It then laid down the following four-step test to

---

[136] *Pensions Benefit System Partnership* (T931/95), headnote IV.
[137] *MICROSOFT/Data transfer* (T424/03) 23 February 2006, Board of Appeal, EPO.
[138] As pointed out by Kitchin J in *Astron Clinica* [2008] R.P.C. 14, at [37]–[39].
[139] [2007] R.P.C. 7. See also the Patent Office Practice Note of 2 November 2006.

decide whether a claimed invention is patentable under that approach:

(i)   properly construe the claim;

(ii)   identify the actual contribution;

(iii) ask whether the identified contribution falls solely within the excluded subject matter; and

(iv) check whether the actual or alleged contribution is actually technical in nature.

It held that the fourth step may not in fact be necessary since it should have been considered during the third step but was formally necessary in order to follow *Merrill Lynch*. The Court also rejected a suggestion, based on comments made by Pumfrey J in *Inpro Licensing v RIM*,[140] that there should be a policy bias towards patentability in the case of computer programs.[141]   **2-100**

Aerotel was followed by a number of domestic first instance decisions which sought to apply it, namely *Cappellini's Application; Bloomberg LLP's Application*,[142] *Oneida Indian Nation's Application*,[143] *Raytheon Co's Application*,[144] *AstronClinica v Comptroller General*,[145] and *Autonomy Corp Ltd's Patent Application*.[146]   **2-101**

The most individually significant of these decisions is that of Kitchin J in *Astron Clinica v Comptroller General*.[147] He concluded that where, as a result of applying the test formulated in *Aerotel*, claims to a method performed by running a suitably programmed computer or to a computer programmed to carry out the method are allowable then, in principle, a claim to the program itself should also be allowable. Hence it was wrong to say that patent claims could never be granted for computer programs. However, mere inclusion of a computer program on a disk is not enough.[148] Finally Kitchin J made it clear that the claim to the computer program must be drawn to reflect the features of the invention which would ensure the patentability of the method which the program is intended to carry out when it is run.   **2-102**

In *Autonomy*, Lewison J extracted the following propositions from the existing law. It is submitted that they continue to provide useful guidance on the UK approach following *Symbian*:   **2-103**

> "29. Where does all this leave us? From these authorities I think that the following can be deduced:
>
> (i)   A computer program is not merely a set of instructions to a computer, but can include the medium (e.g. floppy disc or CD ROM) which causes the computer to execute the program (*Aerotel*) or a programmed computer (*Cappellini*);
>
> (ii) However what is excluded from patentability is not a computer program but a computer program "as such". Accordingly the mere fact that a claim relates to a computer program does not necessarily disqualify it from patentability (*Astron Clinica*);
>
> (iii) In order to decide whether a computer program is excluded from patentability because it is a computer program 'as such' one must consider the substance of the claimed invention (*Cappellini*);

---

[140] [2006] R.P.C. 20.
[141] See *Aerotel*, at [22].
[142] [2007] F.S.R. 26.
[143] [2007] EWHC 954 (Pat).
[144] [2008] R.P.C. 3.
[145] [2008] R.P.C. 14.
[146] [2008] R.P.C. 16.
[147] [2008] R.P.C. 14.
[148] [2008] R.P.C. 14, explaining the decision of Mr Christopher Floyd QC (as he then was) in *Oneida Indian Nation's Application* [2007] EWHC 954 (Pat).

(iv) If the claimed contribution exists independently of whether it is implemented by a computer, in the sense of embodying a technical process lying outside the computer, then the contribution will not be a computer program as such (*Gale*; *Raytheon*);

(v) This will be the case even though the only practicable way of implementing the contribution is by means of a computer (*Raytheon*);

(vi) If the contribution requires new hardware or a new combination of hardware, or consists of a better computer or solves a technical problem in the functionality of a computer it is unlikely to be a computer program as such (*Aerotel*; *Raytheon*);

(vii) On the other hand, a mere new hardware test is not enough if the newness consists of a computer program on a known medium (*Aerotel* commenting on *Gale*);

(viii) The mere fact that a computer program reduces the load on the processor or makes economical use of the computer's memory or makes more efficient use of the computer's resources does not amount to making a better computer, and thus does not take it outside the category of computer program as such (*Aerotel* commenting on *Gale*; *Raytheon*);

(ix) An effect caused merely by the running of the program will not take a program outside the exclusion (*Aerotel*);

(x) The manipulation of data stored on a computer (whether on the computer in use or on a remote computer) is unlikely to give rise to a contribution that exists independently of whether it is implemented by a computer (*Bloomberg*);

(xi) Even if the claimed invention is not a computer program as such, it is still necessary to ask whether the contribution lies solely in some other field of excluded matter. If it does, then the contribution will not be patentable (*Oneida*);

(xii) In such a case, although the contribution may well be described as having a technical effect, it is not the right kind of technical effect, and so does not count (*Shoppalotto*; *Aerotel*; *Oneida*)."

The EPO rejects the criticisms of its "any hardware" approach

2-104   The *Aerotel* judgment was then considered by the EPO Technical Board of Appeal in *DUNS LICENSING ASSOCIATES/Estimating sales activity*.[149] The Board carried out a review of the previous EPO decisions and concluded that no referral to the Enlarged Board of Appeal was required in order to ensure uniform application of the law. It was no more complimentary of the UK Court's approach than the UK Court had been of its approach, stating as follows:

"41. The 'technical effect approach' endorsed by Jacob LJ in the *Aerotel/Macrossan* judgement (see paras 26(2) and 38) ... is not consistent with a good-faith interpretation of the European Patent Convention in accordance with Art.31 of the Vienna Convention on the Law of Treaties of 1969.

42. Actually, any reference to the prior art in the context of Art.52(2) and (3) EPC would lead to insurmountable difficulties; the prior art, the 'state of the art' in the terminology of the Convention, is a complex concept finely tuned by a combination of provisions, Arts 54 to 56 EPC, and depending on the filing and priority dates of the application or patent as well as on the patentability requirement involved. There is, however, no rule whatsoever defining the prior art which should be applied in the context of Art.52(2) EPC. It is simply inconceivable that the contracting states missed such an important point in the conclusion of the Convention. Hence, there are convincing reasons why the 'contribution' or 'technical effect' approach should be abandoned, which the boards did some ten years ago."

2-105   Thus the Board in *Duns* endorsed the "any hardware" approach. However, it did go on to explain that on this approach "only technical features and aspects of the claimed invention should be taken into account in assessing inventive step, i.e. the innovation must be on the technical side, not in a non-patentable field".[150] *Duns* was

---

149 (T154/04) [2007] E.P.O.R. 38.
150 (T154/04) [2007] E.P.O.R. 38, [48].

then followed by another European case, *Gameaccount*,[151] in which a differently constituted Technical Board of Appeal again acknowledged the criticisms made in *Aerotel* and took the opportunity to reformulate its approach.

The UK Court attempts to reconcile the UK and European approaches

The stage was thus set for a return to the English Court of Appeal in *Symbian Ltd v Comptroller-General of Patents ("Symbian")*.[152] In *Symbian*, the Court of Appeal noted the apparent conflict between *Aerotel* and *Duns* and stated that (unlike in *Actavis v Merck*) it would follow its own previous case law unless inconsistent with clear guidance from the EPO, in which case it would follow the latter unless satisfied it was wrong. However it also concluded that the two approaches could in any event be largely reconciled:

> "However, at least as a matter of broad principle, it seems to us that the approaches in the two cases and indeed in the great majority of cases in this jurisdiction and in the EPO, are, on a fair analysis, capable of reconciliation. The third stage mandated in Aerotel, which we would have thought normally raises the crucial issue, is whether the alleged contribution is excluded by Art.52(2), as limited by Art.52(3). So far as we can see, there is no reason, at least in principle, why that test should not amount to the same as that identified in *Duns*, namely whether the contribution cannot be characterised as 'technical'. In effect, this can be said to involve conflating the third and fourth stages in *Aerotel*, a conflation which is easy to accept bearing in mind that it was said in *Aerotel* that the fourth stage, while required by *Merrill Lynch*, was unlikely to add anything to the third stage (a view supported by Kitchin J. in *AstronClinica Ltd v Comptroller-General* [2008] R.P.C. 14, [49] and by Patten J. in this case at [44]).
> ...
> We are fortified in reaching this view by a more recent decision of the Board given on 29 June 2007, *Game account Ltd* T1543/06. In that case, at para.2.5, after expressly considering *Aerotel* and *Duns*, and in words reminiscent of those used in both those decisions, the Board said this:
>
> > '[A]n invention which as a whole falls outside the exclusion zone of [Art.52(2)] (i.e. is technical in character) cannot rely on excluded subject matter alone, even if it is novel and non-obvious (in the colloquial sense...), for it to be considered to meet the requirement of inventive step... [I]t cannot have been the legislator's purpose and intent on the one hand to exclude from patent protection such subject matter, while on the other hand awarding protection to a technical implementation thereof, where the only identifiable contribution of the claimed technical implementation to the state of the art is the excluded subject-matter itself. It is noted that here the term "contribution" encompasses both means (i.e. tangible features of the implementation) and effects resulting from implementation.'
>
> In our opinion, that approach is consistent with that of this court in *Aerotel* as well as with that of the Board in *Duns*. It plainly requires one to identify 'the contribution' (which equates to stage 2 in *Aerotel*) in order to decide whether that contribution is solely 'the excluded subject-matter' itself (equating to stage 3 in *Aerotel*), while emphasising that the contribution must be 'technical' (effectively stage 4 in *Aerotel*). The order in which the stages are dealt with is different, but that should affect neither the applicable principles nor the outcome in any particular case."

The Court of Appeal's belief that the UK and European approaches can be reconciled is not shared by the UK IPO, which follows the UK approach.[153] In *Really Virtual Company Limited v Comptroller-General of Patents*[154] John Baldwin QC (sitting as a Deputy Judge of the High Court) declined an invitation to assess the case using both the UK and EPO approaches with a view to checking they do lead to the same result and proceeded on the approach set out in *Aerotel* only.

2-106

2-107

---

[151] T1543/06, Technical Board of Appeal, 29 June 2007.
[152] [2009] R.P.C. 1.
[153] See the UK IPO's Practice Note on Patentability of Computer Programs dated 8 December 2008 (i.e. post-*Symbian*) at *http://www.ipo.gov.uk/pro-types/pro-patent/p-law/p-pn/p-pn-computer.htm*, para.6.
[154] [2012] EWHC 1086 (Pat); [2013] R.P.C. 3.

2-108   In *Symbian* itself, the claim before the Court was to a computer program which enabled devices such as computers, cameras, and mobile phones to work faster and more reliably—in particular, working faster and more reliably than a similar prior art computer. The Court of Appeal said:

> "To say 'oh but that is only because it is a better program—the computer itself is unchanged' gives no credit to the practical reality of what is achieved by the program. As a matter of such reality there is more than just a 'better program', there is a faster and more reliable computer."[155]

2-109   The Court went on to accept that two types of technical advantage which are attributable to computer programs may suffice for patentability. The first is where the program solves a problem within the computer itself. The second is where the effect of the program is not merely within the computer but where the beneficial consequences feed into other devices. It concluded:

> "Indeed, it appears to us that upholding the conclusion of the Comptroller in this case, would involve the English courts departing from all the decisions of the Board to which we have referred. In particular ... we consider that it would be inconsistent with the reasoning of the Board in *Game account*, if we allowed this appeal. In [2.7], the Board said that there must be 'further technical advantages or effects associated with specific features of implementation over and above the effects and advantages inherent in the excluded subject-matter'. That cannot mean that any technical advantage attributable to a computer program is excluded, as it would make a nonsense of art 52(3) and of all the previous Board decisions. Therefore, it must mean, consistently with *Vicom* and the two *IBM Corp.* cases, that a technical innovation, whether within (as in the last-mentioned cases) or outside the computer will normally suffice to ensure patentability (subject of course to the claimed invention not falling foul of the other exclusions in art 52(2))."

The Enlarged Board of Appeal of the EPO declines jurisdiction

2-110   Meanwhile, and as envisaged in *Aerotel*, the issue had been referred to the Enlarged Board of the EPO as G3/08. However in its Opinion dated 10 May 2010 the Board took a notably narrow view of what constituted different decisions of Boards of Appeal giving rise to an admissible reference. It said that "even a radical shift in jurisprudence need not necessarily be construed as a different decision ... provided that the Board corrects itself and—mostly in explicit fashion—declares its earlier practices to be no longer relevant".[156] Perhaps unsurprisingly given this approach, it held that it could not identify any inconsistencies between the decisions of the Boards and the referral was therefore inadmissible. Furthermore, and again perhaps unsurprisingly, the Enlarged Board also declined to define the term *"technical"*.[157]

2-111   However, the Enlarged Board did at least confirm that the *"contribution approach"* had been abandoned, from which it followed: (a) that the question of patentability was considered independently of the state of the art, and (b) that determining the technical contribution an invention achieves with respect to the prior art was to be done in the context of examining novelty and inventive step.[158] Finally it implicitly endorsed the current EPO approach including the *"further technical effect"* requirement, i.e. that there be a technical effect going beyond those effects which occur inevitably when any program is run. In particular it should be noted that under EPO practice, only claimed features which contribute to that

---

[155] See also Pumfrey J in *Inpro Licensing v RIM* [2006] R.P.C. 20, [186].
[156] At para.7.3.5.
[157] See para.9.2.
[158] See paras 10.4–10.5.

technical character should be taken into account for the assessment of whether there is an inventive step.[159]

The Court of Appeal maintains the Aerotel approach

The Court of Appeal once again considered the computer program exclusion in *HTC Europe v Apple*.[160] Kitchin LJ reviewed the history of the UK and EPO case law on the subject and concluded that (as was common ground between the parties) the *Aerotel* approach should not be abandoned.[161]   **2-112**

It seems unlikely that the above discussion represents the last word on this subject but in the absence of any admissible referral to the Enlarged Board of Appeal and/or any consideration by the Supreme Court, the law under the 1977 Act is as set out in *HTC v Apple*. The principles set out in the decision are summarised below.   **2-113**

The Court must "consider whether the invention made a technical contribution to the known art, with the rider that novel or inventive purely excluded subject matter does not count as a technical contribution."[162]   **2-114**

It is helpful, but not strictly necessary, to follow the four-stage approach adopted in *Aerotel*:[163]   **2-115**

(i)   to properly construe the claim;
(ii)   to identify the actual contribution;
(iii)   to ask whether it falls solely within the excluded subject matter; and
(iv)   to check whether the actual or alleged contribution is actually technical in nature.

At first instance in *HTC v Apple*, Floyd J (as he then was) held that the appropriate baseline for the purposes of determining what the contribution is is any item of prior art admissible for novelty, not merely the common general knowledge.[164]   **2-116**

There is no clear rule to determine whether or not a program is excluded—each case must be determined on its own facts bearing in mind the guidance given by the Court of Appeal in *Merrill Lynch* and *Gale* and by the Boards of Appeal in *Vicom, IBM Corporation/Data processing network* and *IBM Corporation/ Computer-related invention*.[165]   **2-117**

The fact that improvements are made to the software programmed into the computer rather than hardware forming part of the computer does not make a difference. The analysis must be carried out as a matter of substance not form.[166]   **2-118**

The computer program exclusion operates cumulatively with the other exclusions. Thus, neither a computer program incorporating a mathematical method (as in *Gale*) nor a computer program for carrying out a method for doing business (as in *Macrossan*) is patentable.[167] As a result it is helpful to ask: what does the invention contribute to the art as a matter of practical reality over and above the fact   **2-119**

---

[159] See para.13.5; see also paras 10.13–10.13.2.
[160] [2013] EWCA Civ 451; [2013] R.P.C. 30.
[161] [2013] EWCA Civ 451; [2013] R.P.C. 30. [44].
[162] [2013] EWCA Civ 451; [2013] R.P.C. 30, [44].
[163] [2013] EWCA Civ 451; [2013] R.P.C. 30, [44].
[164] [2012] EWHC 1789 (Pat), [15]; not challenged on appeal.
[165] [2013] EWCA Civ 451; [2013] R.P.C. 30, [45].
[166] [2013] EWCA Civ 451; [2013] R.P.C. 30, [46].
[167] [2013] EWCA Civ 451; [2013] R.P.C. 30, [47].

that it relates to a program for a computer? If the only contribution lies in excluded matter then it is not patentable.[168]

2-120   Another useful approach is to consider whether the invention may be regarded as solving a problem (whether inside or outside the computer) which is essentially technical. An invention which solves a technical problem within the computer will have a relevant technical effect in that it will make the computer, as a computer, an improved device, for example by increasing its speed. An invention which solves a technical problem outside the computer will also have a relevant technical effect, for example by controlling an improved technical process. In either case it will not be excluded as relating to a computer program as such.

2-121   Five "signposts" derived from the judgment of Lewison J (as he then was) in *AT&T Knowledge Ventures LP's Patent Application*[169] are useful but not necessarily determinative indications of the necessary technical contribution:[170]

    (i)   whether the claimed technical effect has a technical effect on a process which is carried on outside the computer;

    (ii)   whether the claimed technical effect operates at the level of the architecture of the computer; that is to say whether the effect is produced irrespective of the data being processed or the applications being run;

    (iii)   whether the claimed technical effect results in the computer being made to operate in a new way;

    (iv)   whether a program makes a computer a better computer in the sense of running more efficiently and effectively as a computer; and

    (v)   whether the perceived problem is overcome by the claimed invention as opposed to being merely circumvented.

2-122   It should be noted that the scope of this exclusion was considered by the European Union on 6 July 2005, but the proposed directive[171] was defeated by the European Parliament (by 648 votes to 14 with 18 abstentions) and it will not be reintroduced.

Presentation of information

2-123   Section 1(2)(d) excludes from the class of inventions anything which consists of the presentation of information. It seems clear that where the presentation of information has new "technical features", the claim amounts to more than presentation as such, and should be allowed.[172] This was confirmed by Mann J in *Gemstar—TV Guide International v Virgin Media*,[173] as follows:

"... if the presentation of information has some technical features over and above the information and its delivery, then it might be patentable. So the contrast is between the content or its mere delivery, on the one hand, and that material plus some additional technical aspect of its delivery, on the other. That approach is consistent with the law on computer programs, discussed above."

2-124   Mann J went on to reject a submission that the wording of the subsection is

---

168 [2013] EWCA Civ 451; [2013] R.P.C. 30, [48].
169 [2009] EWHC 343 (Pat), [2009] F.S.R. 19.
170 [2013] EWCA Civ 451; [2013] R.P.C. 30, [50]–[51].
171 See the Draft Directive on the Patentability of Computer-Implemented Inventions; COM(2002) 92 final: 2002/0047 (COD): C151E/05; 2005/C144E/02, C144E, p.9.
172 Compare *Pitman's Application* [1969] R.P.C. 646; *Gever's Application* [1970] R.P.C. 91. Contrast *BBC/Colour television signal* (T163/85) [1990] O.J. EPO 379; [1990] E.P.O.R. 599 and *FUJI/ Coloured disk jacket* (T119/88) [1990] O.J. EPO 395; [1990] E.P.O.R. 615.
173 [2010] R.P.C. 10.

intended only to exclude those inventions which are defined solely by the content of the information presented. However, it is submitted that there is no reason why a novel and inventive method of presenting information should be excluded from patentability, provided that the information content itself is not claimed. The Guidelines for Examination support this view:[174]

"A feature relating to a presentation of information defined solely by the content of the information does not have a technical character. This applies whether the feature is claimed as a presentation of the information per se (e.g. by acoustical signals, spoken words, visual displays, books defined by their subject, gramophone records defined by the musical piece recorded, traffic signs defined by the warning thereon) or as relating to processes and apparatus for presenting information (e.g. features of indicators or recorders defined solely by the information indicated or recorded would not be technical features).

A feature which relates to the manner in which cognitive content is conveyed to the user on a screen normally does not contribute to a technical solution to a technical problem. An exception would be if the arrangement or manner of presentation can be shown to have a credible technical effect (T 1741/08, T 1143/06).

Examples in which such a technical feature may be present are: a telegraph apparatus or communication system using a particular code to represent the characters (e.g. pulse code modulation); a measuring instrument designed to produce a particular form of graph for representing the measured information; a gramophone record having a particular groove form to allow stereo recordings; a computer data structure (see T 1194/97) defined in terms which inherently comprise the technical features of the program which operates on said data structure (assuming the program itself, in the particular case, to be patentable); and a diapositive with a soundtrack arranged at the side of it."

Gemstar was distinguished in *HTC Corporation v Yozmot 33 Ltd*[175]:　　　　**2-125**

"HTC says that the contribution made by the claimed invention is no more than the presentation of information in an audible way. Accordingly, HTC contends that this is not a technical contribution, but one which falls solely within excluded subject matter. In support of this argument, HTC relies upon the decision of Mann J in *Gemstar*. I do not accept this argument. While the invention of claim 7 involves the audible presentation of information, in my judgment the contribution made by the invention does not lie solely in that area, but on the contrary has a technical character. The invention provides a technical solution to the problem of identifying unlisted or unknown callers."

See also *Crawford's Application*,[176] where the only advance in the art which was　　**2-126**
said to be new and inventive was the nature of the information to be displayed on the outside of a bus (in particular, whether the bus was allowing passengers to board and exit, or merely to exit). Consistently with the above analysis, this was held to be the presentation of information.

5.　EXCEPTIONS TO PATENTABILITY

Offensive, immoral, and antisocial inventions

Section 1(3) of the 1977 Act[177] provides that a patent should not be granted for　**2-127**
an invention the commercial exploitation of which would be contrary to public policy or morality. This is qualified by s.1(4), which provides that behaviour shall not be regarded as contrary to public policy or morality only because it is prohibited by domestic law.

The provisions of s.1(3) and 1(4) are based upon art.53(a) of the EPC which in　**2-128**

---

[174] Guidelines for Examination (November 2015) G-II 3.7.
[175] [2010] EWHC 786 (Pat).
[176] [2006] R.P.C. 11.
[177] As amended by the Patents Regulations 2000 (SI 2000/2037) reg.3, with effect from 28 July 2000.

turn is based on art.4*quater* of the Paris Convention.[178] Article 53(a) refers expressly to "*ordre public* or morality" so that the appropriate test laid down in the Guidelines[179] is "to deny protection to inventions likely to induce riot or public disorder, or to lead to criminal or other generally offensive behaviour."

2-129 The purpose of s.1(4) is to ensure that differences in national laws do not lead to anomalies in the patentability of inventions as between different states.[180]

2-130 It is thus only in a plain case that the exclusion will apply. The EPO considered the scope of art.53(a) in the *Onco-mouse* case[181] and in T356/93,[182] the Technical Board of Appeal stated:

"5. It is generally accepted that the concept of *'ordre public'* covers the protection of public security and the physical integrity of individuals as part of society. This concept encompasses also the protection of the environment. Accordingly, under Article 53(a) EPC, inventions the exploitation of which is likely to breach public peace or social order (for example, through acts of terrorism) or to seriously prejudice the environment are to be excluded from patentability as being contrary to *'ordre public'*.

6. The concept of *morality* is related to the belief that some behaviour is right and acceptable whereas other behaviour is wrong, this belief being founded on the totality of the accepted norms which are deeply rooted in a particular culture. For the purposes of the EPC, the culture in question is the culture inherent in European society and civilisation. Accordingly, under Article 53(a) EPC, inventions the exploitation of which is *not* in conformity with the conventionally-accepted standards of conduct pertaining to this culture are to be excluded from patentability as being contrary to morality."

Biotechnological inventions

2-131 Articles 1–11 of the European Directive 98/44/EC on the legal protection of biotechnological inventions were incorporated into United Kingdom law with effect from 28 July 2000 by the Patents Regulations 2000,[183] and the 1977 Act amended accordingly.

2-132 Section 76A of the 1977 Act, as amended, provides that any patents or patent applications which concern a biotechnological invention are subject to the provisions of Sch.A2. The more important paragraphs of Sch.A2 (which mirror arts 4–6 of the Biotechnology Directive) are:

"(1) An invention shall not be considered unpatentable solely on the ground that it concerns—
(a) a product consisting of or containing biological material; or
(b) a process by which biological material is produced, processed or used.

(2) Biological material which is isolated from its natural environment or produced by means of a technical process may be the subject of an invention even if it previously occurred in nature.

(3) The following are not patentable inventions—
(a) the human body, at the various stages of its formation and development, and the simple discovery of one of its elements, including the sequence or partial sequence of a gene;
(b) processes for cloning human beings;
(c) processes for modifying the germ line genetic identity of human beings;
(d) uses of human embryos for industrial or commercial purposes;

---

[178] It also corresponds to art.27(2) of TRIPs.
[179] Guidelines for Examination (November 2015) G-II 4.1.
[180] Indeed, note that art.53(a) contains the proviso that exploitation shall not be deemed to be contrary to order public or morality merely because it is prohibited by law or regulation in some *or all* of the Contracting States.
[181] *HARVARD/Onco-mouse* (T19/90) [1990] O.J. EPO 476; [1990] E.P.O.R. 501 11 (Technical Board of Appeal); and [1992] O.J. EPO 588 (Examining Board).
[182] *PLANT GENETIC SYSTEMS/Glutamine synthetase inhibitors* (T356/93) [1995] O.J. EPO 545; [1995] E.P.O.R. 357.
[183] SI 2000/2037.

(e) processes for modifying the genetic identity of animals which are likely to cause them suffering without any substantial medical benefit to man or animal, and also animals resulting from such processes;

(f) any variety of animal or plant or any essentially biological process for the production of animals or plants, not being a micro-biological or other technical process or the product of such a process.

(4) Inventions which concern plants or animals may be patentable if the technical feasibility of the invention is not confined to a particular plant or animal variety.

(5) An element isolated from the human body or otherwise produced by means of a technical process, including the sequence or partial sequence of a gene, may constitute a patentable invention, even if the structure of that element is identical to that of a natural element.

(6) The industrial application of a sequence or partial sequence of a gene must be disclosed in the patent application as led."

The Netherlands brought an action for annulment of the Biotechnology Directive. **2-133** This was dismissed by the European Court of Justice, noting that there was nothing to prevent the Community legislature from having recourse to harmonisation by means of a Directive in preference to the more indirect and unpredictable approach of seeking to amend the wording of the European Patent Convention.[184]

Human embryos

The CJEU considered the exclusion from patentability of "uses of human **2-134** embryos for industrial or commercial purposes" under art.6(2)(c) of the Biotechnology Directive in *Brüstle*.[185] It held that the term "human embryo" must be given a broad definition and includes any human ovum after fertilisation, any non-fertilised human ovum into which the cell nucleus from a mature human cell has been transplanted and any non-fertilised human ovum whose division and further development have been stimulated by parthenogenesis.[186] More generally it concluded that any cell "capable of commencing the process of development of a human being" was included within the meaning of "human embryo".[187] The question of whether a stem cell obtained from a human embryo at the blastocyst stage satisfied this definition was left as a matter for the referring court to determine.[188]

The court also held that the exclusion from patentability concerning the use of **2-135** human embryos "for industrial or commercial purposes" covers the use of human embryos for purposes of scientific research.[189] The only exception to this rule was that identified in Recital (42) of the Biotechnology Directive, namely that use for therapeutic or diagnostic purposes which are applied to the human embryo and are useful to it being patentable.[190]

Finally, the CJEU held that art.6(2)(c) should be broadly construed to exclude **2-136** an invention from patentability where the technical teaching which is the subject-matter of the patent application requires the prior destruction of human embryos or their use as base material, whatever the stage at which that takes place and even if

---

[184] *Netherlands v European Parliament* (C-377/98) [2002] F.S.R. 36, ECJ.
[185] *Brüstle v Greenpeace eV* (C-34/10) [2011] E.C.R. I-9821; [2012] 1 C.M.L.R. 41.
[186] *Brüstle v Greenpeace eV* (C-34/10) [2011] E.C.R. I-9821; [2012] 1 C.M.L.R. 41, [35]–[36].
[187] *Brüstle v Greenpeace eV* (C-34/10) [2011] E.C.R. I-9821; [2012] 1 C.M.L.R. 41, [36]–[37].
[188] *Brüstle v Greenpeace eV* (C-34/10) [2011] E.C.R. I-9821; [2012] 1 C.M.L.R. 41, [37].
[189] *Brüstle v Greenpeace eV* (C-34/10) [2011] E.C.R. I-9821; [2012] 1 C.M.L.R. 41, [39]–[46].
[190] *Brüstle v Greenpeace eV* (C-34/10) [2011] E.C.R. I-9821; [2012] 1 C.M.L.R. 41, [44], [46].

the description of the technical teaching claimed does not refer to the use of human embryos.[191]

2-137   On a reference from the Chancery Division in *International Stem Cell Corporation*[192] the CJEU clarified the position regarding non-fertilised human ova stimulated by parthenogenesis as a result of technical information which was not before it in *Brüstle*. The Court accepted an observation made by the Advocate General that such ova must necessarily have the inherent capacity of developing into a human being in order to be classified as a "human embryo"; it is not sufficient that they undergo some process of development if such capacity is lacking.[193] Thus non-fertilised human ova stimulated by parthenogenesis which commenced the process of development of a human being but were, according to current scientific knowledge, not capable of completing it, were held to be patentable.

2-138   Rules 26–29 EPC were introduced to bring the provisions of the EPC into line with those of the Biotech Directive and all Contracting States to the EPC, regardless of whether they are members of the EU or not, have thereby indicated that these rules should be used to interpret the EPC.[194] Although the Enlarged Board has held that the jurisprudence of the CJEU is not binding upon the Boards of Appeal[195] and no power exists for the Boards of Appeal to refer questions on the interpretation of these provisions to the CJEU,[196] the Technical Board of appeal has relied upon *Brüstle* as persuasive.[197] In particular the Technical Board of Appeal has held that, consistent with *Brüstle*, an invention that was entirely dependent upon the use of human embryonic stem cells, either obtained by de novo destruction of human embryos or by using established human embryonic stem cell lines which initially were obtained by methods involving the destruction of human embryos, was excluded from patentability under Rule 28(c) EPC.[198]

2-139   The UKIPO's practice in this area follows the jurisprudence of the CJEU.[199]

Plant and animal varieties

2-140   Article 53(b) EPC (which corresponds to para.3(f) of Sch.A2 of the Act) provides that:

> "European patents shall not be granted in respect of … plant or animal varieties or essentially biological processes for the production of plants or animals; this provision shall not apply to microbiological processes or the products thereof".

2-141   The term plant variety is defined in Rule 26(4) EPC:

> "(4)   "Plant variety" means any plant grouping within a single botanical taxon of the lowest known rank, which grouping, irrespective of whether the conditions for the grant of a plant variety right are fully met, can be:
> (a)   defined by the expression of the characteristics that results from a given genotype or combination of genotypes,

[191]   *Brüstle v Greenpeace eV* (C-34/10) [2011] E.C.R. I-9821; [2012] 1 C.M.L.R. 41, [47]–[52].
[192]   *International Stem Cell Corporation v Comptroller-General of Patents, Designs and Trade Marks* (C-364/13) [2015] R.P.C. 19.
[193]   *International Stem Cell Corporation v Comptroller-General of Patents, Designs and Trade Marks* (C-364/13) [2015] R.P.C. 19, [27]–[35].
[194]   *Use of embryos/WARF* (G 2/06) at point 5 of the Reasons.
[195]   *Use of embryos/WARF* (G 2/06), [7].
[196]   *Use of embryos/WARF* (G 2/06), [10].
[197]   *TECHNION/Culturing stem cells* (T2221/10) at point 39 of the Reasons.
[198]   *TECHNION/Culturing stem cells (T2221/10)*, [36] and [44].
[199]   Practice Notice: Inventions involving human stem cells: 25 March 2015.

(b)   distinguished from any other plant grouping by the expression of at least one of the said
      characteristics, and
(c)   considered as a unit with regard to its suitability for being propagated unchanged."

Recital (26) of the Biotechnology Directive[200] states that "inventions which **2-142** concern plants or animals are patentable provided that the application of the invention is not technically confined to a single plant or animal variety". Furthermore, the expression "plant varieties" is limited by the EPO to lowest rank plant groupings and does not extend to plant cells.[201]

The exclusion contained in para.3(f) of Sch.A2 does not apply to microbiologi- **2-143** cal processes or the products thereof. Paragraph 36 of the decision in *PLANT GENETIC SYSTEMS*[202] defined the scope of a similar provision under the previous law as follows:

> "In the Board's judgment, the concept of 'microbiological processes' under Article 53(b) EPC, second half-sentence, refers to processes in which micro-organisms as defined above (see point 34, supra), or their parts, are used to make or to modify products or in which new micro-organisms are developed for specific uses. Consequently, the concept of 'the products thereof' under Article 53(b) EPC, second half-sentence, encompasses products which are made or modified by micro-organisms as well as new micro-organisms as such."

In a decision on consolidated referrals *BROCCOLI I* (G 2/07) and *TOMATO I* **2-144** (G 1/08), the Enlarged Board of Appeal considered the meaning of "essentially biological processes for the production of plants". It held that the exclusion covered any process for the production of plants based on the sexual crossing of whole genomes and subsequent selection of plants including processes where technical means are provided to enable or assist the performance of the process. However, the exclusion does not apply to such a process if it includes a "step of a technical nature, which step by itself introduces a trait into the genome or modifies a trait in the genome of the plant produced, so that the introduction or modification of that trait is not the result of the mixing of the genes of the plants chosen for sexual crossing". Such a process would be outside the realm of plant breeding and therefore outside the area intended to be excluded.

The Enlarged Board held in a subsequent decision that the art.53(b) exclusion of **2-145** essentially biological processes for the production of plants did not have an effect on the allowability of product claims directed at plants or plant material (e.g. fruit), even where the only method available at the filing date of the patent is an essentially biological process for the production of plants.[203]

It can thus be seen that in the field of plants the exclusion under art.53(b) is of **2-146** narrow scope, applying only to plant varieties (narrowly construed) and essentially biological processes for the production of plants (but not plants produced by such processes). Under the legal systems of most contracting states, plant varieties are protected otherwise than by patents. In the United Kingdom, plant varieties may be protected by the provisions of the Plant Varieties and Seeds Act 1964 and the Plant Varieties Act 1997. Council Regulation (EC) 2100/94 of 27 July 1994

---

[200] The Biotechnology Directive is to be used as a supplementary means of interpretation of the EPC pursuant to Rule 26(1) EPC.
[201] See *CIBA-GEIGY/Propagating Material* (T 49/83) [1984] O.J. EPO 112; [1979–85] E.P.O.R. C758 and *PLANT GENETIC SYSTEMS/Glutamine synthetase inhibitors* (T 356/93) [1995] O.J. EPO 545; [1995] E.P.O.R. 501.
[202] T 356/93.
[203] See the decision in consolidated referrals *TOMATO II (G 2/12)* and *BROCCOLI II* (G 2/13).

on Community plant variety rights also establishes a Community regime which, although co-existing with national regimes, allows for the grant of industrial property rights valid throughout the Community by the Community Plant Variety Office.

2-147   Animal varieties are not protectable although the EPO has interpreted the expression "animal varieties" narrowly, specifically as not extending to animals per se,[204] it being limited to a sub-unit of a species.

---

[204] *HARVARD/Onco-mouse* (T 19/90) [1990] O.J. EPO 476; [1990] E.P.O.R. 501; [1992] O.J.EPO 588.

CHAPTER 3

THE APPLICATION

CONTENTS

1. INTRODUCTION

The types of patent available

Currently, two types of United Kingdom patent may be applied for, namely: **3-01**

(a) a national patent granted by the UK Patent Office and restricted in territory to the United Kingdom; or
(b) a European patent granted by the European Patent Office which so far as it designates the United Kingdom is from the date of grant (when published in the *European Patent Bulletin*) to be treated as if it were a national patent under the Patents Act 1977, and as if notice of the grant of the patent had, on the date of that publication, been published under s.24 of the 1977 Act in the journal.[1]

These patents may be applied for either by application made directly to the UK **3-02**
Patent Office under the 1977 Act or to the European Patent Office under the EPC, or indirectly by means of the PCT.[2] To comply with national security requirements a resident of the United Kingdom must file a European application or a PCT application to which s.23(1A) of the 1977 Act applies[3] at the UK Patent Office unless certain conditions are met or permission to do otherwise is obtained in advance from the Patent Office.[4]

However, a likely third option in the near future will be a European patent with **3-03**
unitary effect. A proprietor of a European Patent can request that unitary effect shall be registered by the European Patent Office in the Register. Unitary effect shall be registered only if the European patent has been granted with the same set of claims

---

[1] PA 1977 s.77(1).
[2] See paras 3-80 to 3-89.
[3] s.23(1A) applies to an application if: (a) the application contains information which relates to military technology or for any other reason publication of the information might be prejudicial to national security; or (b) the application contains information the publication of which might be prejudicial to the safety of the public. See also para.3-91.
[4] PA 1977 s.23. See para.3-91.

in respect of all the participating Member States.[5] This is irrespective of whether those states have ratified the UPC Agreement or not.[6]

Choosing between the national and European routes

3-04   The choice between the national patent office route and the EPO route may depend to some extent on the number of countries in Europe in which the applicant wishes to seek protection. Clearly, if protection is only desired for the United Kingdom a national patent should be applied for as it will be cheaper to obtain than a European patent (UK) and once granted will have the same effect.[7] If protection is desired for a number of European countries, the European route will become more attractive from a cost point of view but the decision to use the EPO (as opposed to national patent offices) may then depend on weighing up the probability of obtaining the patent in the desired form via the EPO as opposed to via the various national patent offices, including the UK Patent Office. Another factor which may influence the choice of route is whether the patent is likely to be opposed. The EPC provides that any person may oppose the grant of a European patent retrospectively provided opposition is entered within nine months from the publication of the grant in the *European Patent Bulletin*.[8] Opposition will apply to all the contracting states in which the European patent has effect[9] and such oppositions may therefore be attractive to a third party as a convenient way of seeking to challenge the patentee's patent. Opposition proceedings in the EPO can take a number of years to be resolved and this factor alone can lead to the national route being favoured.

Applying for both a UK national patent and a European patent

3-05   An applicant may apply for both a UK national patent and a European patent (UK) in respect of the same invention in order to safeguard the possibility of not obtaining a patent by one of the two methods. A consequence of this approach is that, assuming both the national patent and the European patent (UK) are granted for the same invention, the Comptroller must revoke the national patent.[10] Revocation will be ordered if a claim in the national patent and a claim in the European patent (UK) cover the same subject matter, regardless of whether the claims may cover other things.[11] The mechanism under which the Comptroller will revoke the national patent does not come into effect until either the end of the period for filing an opposition, or if later, the date on which opposition proceedings in the EPO (including appeals) are concluded. Before the Comptroller revokes the national pat-

5   Rule 5 (1) and (2) of Part II "Procedures to be carried out by the European Patent Office under Regulations (EU) No 1257/2012 and No 1260/2012)" see the decision of the Select Committee of the Administrative Council of the European Patent Organisation of 15 December 2015, adopting the Rules relating to Unitary Patent Protection.
6   This is explained in para.2 of the official commentary which forms part of the rules, p.17/83.
7   One difference between a UK national patent and a European patent (UK) is the ability to register it in other countries. See Registration of European patents (UK) in overseas states or territories O.J. EPO 2004; 179.
8   See EPC art. 99. See also para.5-12, et seq.
9   EPC art.99(2).
10   PA 1977 s.73(2) and (3) (as amended).
11   *Marley Roof Tile Co Ltd's Patent* [1994] R.P.C. 231, CA. See also *Maag Gear Wheel and Machine Co Ltd's Patent* [1985] R.P.C. 572.

ent, the patentee is given the opportunity of making observations and of amending the specification of the patent.

Conversion

An application for a European patent (UK) may be converted into a UK national **3-06** application in accordance with the provisions of s.81 of the 1977 Act if the European patent application is deemed to be withdrawn under the EPC. See para.3-73.

2. APPLICATION FOR UK NATIONAL PATENT

In accordance with s.14(1) of the 1977 Act, every application for a patent shall **3-07** be made in the prescribed form[12] and shall be filed at the Patent Office in the prescribed manner,[13] and the application fee must be paid within the prescribed period.[14] Furthermore, every application shall contain a request for the grant of a patent, a specification containing a description of the invention, a claim or claims and any drawing referred to in the description or claims and an abstract.[15] The purpose of the abstract is to give technical information, and it may be re-framed by the Comptroller if the abstract is determined not to fulfil its purpose adequately.[16] The abstract does not form part of the state of the art on a date prior to the date of its actual publication.[17] In view of the power to revoke a patent if the matter disclosed in the specification of the patent extends beyond that disclosed in the application for the patent as filed,[18] it is of great importance that the description of the invention included with the application is correct.

Date of filing

If a declaration of priority pursuant to s.5(2) of the 1977 Act is made, it must be **3-08** made at the time of filing the application[19] or within the time allowed by the Rules.[20] The declaration must state the date of filing of any application specified in the declaration and the country in or for which it was made.[21] Section 15(1) of the 1977 Act defines the date of filing the application as the earliest date on which the following conditions are satisfied, namely:

(a)   the documents filed at the Patent Office indicate that a patent is sought;
(b)   the documents identify the person applying for a patent or contain information sufficient to enable that person to be contacted by the Patent Office; and
(c)   the documents contain either something which appears to be a description of the invention for which a patent is sought, or a reference, complying with

---

12   Patents Form No.1; see Patents Rules 2007 r.12(1).
13   Patents Rules 2007 rr.12–18.
14   PA 1977 s.14(1A) and s.15(1)(c) and see Patents Rules 2007 r.22.
15   PA 1977 s.14(2) and cf. EPC art.78(1). See also PA 1977 s.15 for putting an application in order.
16   PA 1977 s.14(7).
17   PA 1977 s.14(7).
18   PA 1977 s.72(1)(d). See also Ch.15.
19   Patents Rules 2007 r.6(1).
20   Patents Rules 2007 rr.6(2) and 7(9). See also PA 1977 s.5(2B) and (2C).
21   Patents Rules 2007 r.6(4).

the relevant requirement of rules, to an earlier relevant application made by the applicant or a predecessor in title of his.[22]

3-09   It is immaterial whether the "something" referred to in (c) is in, or is accompanied by a translation into, a language accepted by the Patent Office in accordance with rules[23]; and it is also immaterial whether that "something" otherwise complies with the other provisions of this Act and with any relevant rules.[24]

Delays in communication services

3-10   Rule 111 of the Patents Rules 2007 provides for extensions of time as a result of delay or failure of a "communication service". This rule is the modern successor of what used to be called the "postal rules".[25] The Comptroller has power to extend any period of time specified by the Act or the Rules if he is satisfied that the failure to do something was wholly or mainly attributable to a delay in or failure of a communication service. In this rule a communication service means a service by which documents may be sent and delivered and includes post, electronic communications, and courier.[26] The provisions apply to patent applications under the 1977 Act as much as to any other document sent to the Patent Office but they do not apply to international applications, since in that case the Patent Office is acting as a receiving office under the PCT and the Patents Rules are irrelevant. This was the outcome of *Archibald Kenrick's International Application*[27] which although related to the prior form of the rule, still applies.

The specification

3-11   In accordance with s.14(3) of the 1977 Act the specification must disclose the invention in a manner "which is clear enough and complete enough for the invention to be performed by a person skilled in the art."[28] In accordance with s.14(5) the claim or claims must:

(a)   define the matter for which the applicant seeks protection;
(b)   be clear and concise;
(c)   be supported by the description; and
(d)   relate to one invention or to a group of inventions which are so linked as to form a single inventive concept.[29]

3-12   The specification must be preceded by the title of the invention, continue with the description and the claims and the drawings (if any) in that order.[30] There are special provisions dealing with the order where the application is delivered in electronic form or using electronic communications.[31] The title must be short and

---

[22]   PA 1977 s.15(1).
[23]   PA 1977 s.15(2)(a).
[24]   PA 1977 s.15(2)(b).
[25]   See *Terrell on the Law of Patents* 16th edn (London: Sweet & Maxwell, 2006). para.3–19.
[26]   Patents Rules 2007 r.111(3).
[27]   [1994] R.P.C. 635.
[28]   See PA 1977 s.72(1)(c) where the same test is to be applied for revocation of the granted patent, and see Ch.13.
[29]   See "Single Invention", para.3–23.
[30]   Patents Rules 2007 r.12(4).
[31]   Patents Rules 2007 r.12(5).

indicate the matter to which the invention relates[32] The description must also include a list briefly describing the figures in the drawings (if any).[33] A consistory clause in the specification is not the same as a claim.[34]

The claims

The requirements that the claim(s) must be "clear and concise" and "supported by" the description are to be found only in s.14 of the 1977 Act and are not expressed as such in the grounds on which a patent may be revoked once granted.[35] However, in relation to the requirement for clarity, the courts have expressed the view that although ambiguity is not a ground of invalidity, no infringement could be established of a claim which was so unclear as to have no meaning at all.[36] Further in *Biogen Inc v Medeva Plc*,[37] the House of Lords held that s.72(1)(c) gives effect to the requirement that the claim be "supported by" the description because both provisions amounted to a requirement that the specification should constitute an enabling disclosure.[38] In any event, the test of clarity is whether it is clear to a skilled person in the art, and it does not matter whether something clearer and shorter could have been drafted.[39]   **3-13**

In relation to the test to be applied in assessing whether claims are "supported by" the description, in *Schering Biotech Corp's Application* Aldous J said[40]:   **3-14**

> "The correct approach under the 1977 Act is to consider the description and claims in the specification through the eyes of the skilled man in the Art. Under section 125(1) the invention is that specified in the claims. Thus to decide whether the claims are supported by the description it is necessary to ascertain what is the invention which is specified in the claims and then compare that with the invention which has been described in the specification. Thereafter the [tribunal's] task is to decide whether the invention in the claims is supported by the description. I do not believe that the mere mention in the specification of features appearing in the claim will necessarily be sufficient support. The word 'support' means more than that and requires the description to be the base which can fairly entitle the patentee to a monopoly of the width claimed."

The principle is that the extent of the monopoly, as defined by the claims, should correspond to the technical contribution to the art in order for it to be supported or justified.[41]   **3-15**

The requirement for support is also related to the prohibition against adding mat-   **3-16**

---

[32] Patents Rules 2007 r.12(6).
[33] Patents Rules 2007 r.12(7).
[34] *R. (On the application of Penife International Ltd) v Comptroller-General of Patents* [2004] R.P.C. 37, 737.
[35] And see *Schering Biotech Corp's Application* [1993] R.P.C. 249, referring to *Genentech Inc's Patent* [1989] R.P.C. 147.
[36] *Milliken v Walk-off Mats* [1996] F.S.R. 292; approved by the Court of Appeal in *Scanvaegt v Pelcombe* [1998] F.S.R. 786.
[37] [1997] R.P.C. 1.
[38] per Lord Hoffmann at 47.
[39] *Strix v Otter* [1995] R.P.C. 607. The EPO view is that art.84 EPC requires that claims are clear in themselves when being read with the normal skills including the knowledge about the prior art, but not including any knowledge derived from the description of the patent application or the amended patent: *ICI/Optical sensing apparatus* (T454/89).
[40] [1993] R.P.C. 249, 252.
[41] *EXXON/Fuel Oils* (T409/91) [1994] O.J. EPO 641; [1994] E.P.O.R 149 cited with approval on this point by Lord Hoffmann in *Biogen Inc v Medeva Plc* [1997] R.P.C. 1, 49; and see also the related European decisions *AGREVO/Triazoles* (T939/92) [1996] O.J. EPO 309; [1996] E.P.O.R. 171 and *MYCOGEN/Plant modifying cells* (T694/92) [1997] O.J. EPO 408; [1998] E.P.O.R. 114.

ter which arises in other contexts such that in *Protoned BV's Application*[42] when an amendment which sought to delete from the claim the word "compression" in the expression "mechanical compression spring" was considered. Whitford J held that not only would such an amendment result in "added matter" of other types of spring contrary to s.76(2)(a) but also that such a claim would not be supported by the description and therefore would be contrary to s.14(5)(c). In *Environmental Recycling Technologies Plc v Upcycle Holdings Limited*[43] the court considered the claimant's argument that a *Protoned* widening amendment arose but rejected the argument on the facts of the case.

Claims to the further use of a known medicament

3-17   For claims to the further medical use of a known medicament a clear indication that such a treatment has been tried and tested is essential to provide the necessary support.[44] In *American Home Products v Novartis*[45] the claim was construed as being limited to a second medical use of rapamycin; had it been construed so widely as to include derivatives of rapamycin, the claim would have been insufficient since there was no sufficient disclosure that such derivatives would work. *American Home Products* was considered in *Merck v Ono*[46] where the court further commented that "leaving the skilled person to ascertain by research what would work is not sufficient … . [*American Home Products*] shows that the quality of any work required may well matter as well as its quantity." See also para.2-49, et seq.

The disclosure of the invention

3-18   The disclosure of the invention must be in a manner which is clear enough and complete enough for the invention to be performed by a person skilled in the art.[47] There is a difference between on the one hand a specification which requires the skilled person to use his skill and application to perform the invention and, on the other, a specification which requires the skilled person to go to the expense and labour of trying to ascertain whether some product has the required properties. When carrying out the former the skilled person is trying to perform the invention, whereas the latter requires him to go further and to carry out research to ascertain how the invention is to be performed. If the latter is required the specification would appear to be insufficient. The duty upon the patentee is to provide a description which enables the skilled person to perform the invention across the breadth of the claim, not to supply a starting point for a research programme.[48] Nor will a claim to a class of new compounds be supported by the description if, on analysis, the claim is merely a generalised description of a large number of chemical compounds rather than a class as such.[49]

---

[42] [1983] F.S.R. 110 and see Ch.15.
[43] [2013] EWPCC 4.
[44] *McManus's Application* [1994] F.S.R. 558 (per Aldous J approving the decision of the principal examiner), followed in *Consultants Suppliers Ltd's Application* [1996] R.P.C. 348 and see *Hoerrmann's Application* [1996] R.P.C. 341.
[45] [2001] R.P.C. 8, 159. And see also on construction of such claims, para.9-268, et seq.
[46] *Merck Sharp & Dohme Ltd v Ono Pharmaceutical Co Ltd* [2015] EWHC 2973 (Pat), [130].
[47] PA 1977 s.14(3).
[48] *American Home Products v Novartis* [2001] R.P.C. 8, 159, [40]–[43], CA.
[49] *Monsanto Co v Merck & Co Inc* [2000] R.P.C. 709.

The drawings

The detailed requirements for the drawings forming part of the application are set out in Sch.2 Pt 3 of the Patents Rules 2007.[50]

3-19

Late filed material

There are special provisions in relation to late filed material (drawings or part of the description). Material of that kind cannot be filed after the date which is treated as being the date of filing without altering that date to the date on which the drawing is filed.[51] However, the severity of this provision is mitigated both by s.15(7) of the Act, whereby priority may be claimed for the missing part, and also by s.15(8) which confirms that both ss.15(6) and 15(7) are without prejudice to the Comptroller's power to correct errors or mistakes under s.117(1) of the Act. Where, therefore, the failure to file the right drawings is due to a clerical error, or mistake, the discretion to correct the error arises. In this respect the decision in *Antiphon A.B.'s Application*[52] from 1984 is not good law.

3-20

Biological material

Biological material is defined as any material containing genetic information and capable of reproducing itself or being reproduced in a biological system.[53] In accordance with s.125A of the 1977 Act, r.13 of the Patents Rules 2007, and Sch.1 thereto, lay down the detailed requirements for making available to the public biological material for inventions, which involve the use of or concern the same. These requirements include the deposit of the biological material in a depository institution which is able to furnish a sample of the biological material not later than the date of filing the application, and the supplying, either in the specification as filed, or within a prescribed period thereafter,[54] of the name of such depository institution, the accession number of the deposit and, where the biological material has been deposited by a person other than the applicant, the name and address of the depositor. Where the biological material has been deposited by a person other than the applicant, a document must also be filed satisfying the Comptroller that the depositor has authorised the applicant to refer to the deposited material in the specification and has given his irrevocable consent to the deposited material being made available to the public in accordance with Sch.1.

3-21

In *Chinoin's Application*,[55] which considered the phrase "micro-organism" appearing in a previous version of the rules, Falconer J held that the rule did not require the deposit of every strain of a new species to support a claim relating to

3-22

---

50   Patents Rules 2007 r.14(3).
51   PA 1977 s.15(5) and (6); Patents Rules 2007 r.18. and see *Antiphon A.B.'s Application* [1984] R.P.C. 1; *VEB Kombinat Walzlager's Application* [1987] R.P.C. 405.
52   [1984] R.P.C. 1.
53   The definition originates in the European Directive on the Legal Protection of Biotechnological Inventions, Directive 98/44 art.2(1)(a) [1998] O.J. L213; see EPC Rules r.26(1). The Directive was implemented in the United Kingdom by the Patents Regulations 2000 (SI 2000/2037) which came into force on 28 July 2000, although in *Monsanto Technology LLC v Cefetra BV* (C-428/08) the Court of Justice held that the Directive applies to all patents whether originating before or after the date when the Directive came into effect.
54   Patents Rules 2007 Sch.1 para.3(1).
55   [1986] R.P.C. 39; see also *Genentech Inc's Patent* [1989] R.P.C. 147, where Chinoin's Application is considered.

that species but that the deposit of one strain would only support that strain and strains derived therefrom. It is submitted that a similar principle would apply in relation to biological materials.[56]

Unity of invention

3-23   An application must relate to one invention or to a group of inventions so linked as to form a single inventive concept.[57] Although no precise definition can be given as to what constitutes a single invention, if a novel and inventive general principle is disclosed, any machine or process which embodies that general principle can be regarded as an embodiment of a single invention,[58] notwithstanding that there may also be disclosed additional optional details or non-fundamental variants which are claimed in subsidiary claims.

3-24   Guidance as to what constitutes a group of inventions so linked as to form a single inventive concept can be obtained from Patents Rules 2007 r.16 which provides that if a technical relationship exists between inventions (whether claimed separately or not) and the technical relationship involves the same or corresponding "special technical features" then those inventions shall be treated as being so linked as to form a single inventive concept. "Special technical features" are technical features which define a contribution which each claimed invention makes over the prior art. The purpose of this somewhat elaborate provision was to bring the Patents Rules into conformity with the corresponding rules under the EPC[59] and PCT.[60]

Divisional applications

3-25   To avoid the objection of multiplicity of inventions, an applicant may divide the inventions to form separate applications and the new application(s) may be entitled to the original filing date.[61] A divisional application of this nature is, however, only permitted to retain the original filing date if there is no new matter added in the new application.[62] The test for new matter is the test laid down in s.76(1). It should be noted that the contents of the claims form part of the disclosure in addition to the material in the body of the specification.[63] If the divisional application does contain new matter, it can be amended, prior to grant, to exclude that matter. In this respect *Hydroacoustics Inc's Application* is not good law.[64]

3-26   In *Ratiopharm v Napp* the question of the test for added matter in the context of divisional applications arose. The patentee argued that the more generous "undisclosed disclaimer" rules permitted in certain cases by the EPO[65] (G1/03) were

---

[56] See, however, *American Home Products v Novartis* [2000] R.P.C. 547.
[57] PA 1977 s.14(5)(d) and EPC art.82.
[58] cf. W06/90 *DRAENERT/Single General Concept* [1991] O.J. EPO 438.
[59] EPC Rules r.44.
[60] PCT Rules r.13.2.
[61] The practice is described by Jacob LJ in *Ratiopharm v Napp* [2009] EWCA Civ 252, [2009] R.P.C. 18, [7]–[13].
[62] PA 1977 s.15(9).
[63] PA 1977 s.130(3); and see *Van der Lely's Application* [1987] R.P.C. 61.
[64] [1981] F.S.R. 538.
[65] EPO Enlarged Board of Appeal Decision *PPG Industries*.

applicable to divisional applications as well. This was rejected on the ground that
the test for added matter was always the same.[66]

There is a time limit within which a divisional application can be made. The
definition of the time limit is in Patents Rules 2007 r.19. In effect a divisional application can only be made while the earlier application is still live. The time limit
expires when an application is withdrawn or terminated, within two months of
notification that the patent will be granted or within three months of the overall time
limit for putting an application in order for grant.[67]

3-27

The Patent Office operates an informal practice of warning applicants who had
indicated that they might wish to file a divisional application that grant was
impending.[68] The sending of such a warning letter is an obligation publicly assumed by the Office and therefore constitutes part of the safety net provided by the
Comptroller to the advantage of careless applicants. Accordingly in a case in which
such a letter was not sent when it should have been, and as a result an applicant
missed an opportunity to file a divisional application the Comptroller should have
exercised his discretion to allow the applicant to file a divisional application.[69]

3-28

Once granted no objection can be taken to the validity of the patent on grounds
of lack of unity of invention.[70]

3-29

In the EPO the examiner may raise a double patenting objection and refuse
amendments to the claims of a later divisional patent application.[71] This can arise
where the amended claims of the divisional application claim the same subject-
matters as a pending parent application or a granted parent patent, and the applicant has no legitimate interest in proceedings leading to the granting of a second
patent with the same scope and subject matter as a first granted patent which the
applicant already possesses.[72] An applicant may have such a legitimate interest
where the claims of the divisional patent application are broader than but encompass
the scope of those of the parent.[73]

3-30

Preliminary examination

Section 15A(1) provides that the Comptroller must refer an application for a patent to an examiner for a preliminary examination if the application has a date of filing, it has not been treated as withdrawn, and the application fee has been paid. This
preliminary examination is to determine whether the application complies with the
formal requirements of the Act.[74]

3-31

---

[66] *Ratiopharm v Napp* [2009] EWCA Civ 252, [68]–[85].
[67] Patents Rules 2007 r.19(1) and 19(3).
[68] See *Luk Lamellan und Kupplungsbau GmbH's Application* [1997] R.P.C. 104.
[69] *Howmet Research Corp's Application* [2006] EWHC 725 (Pat), [2006] R.P.C. 27.
[70] PA 1977 s.26.
[71] Although double patenting is not a ground of revocation of a patent either under the 1977 Act or
the EPC.
[72] *Koninklijke Philips Electronics NV v Nintendo of Europe GmbH* [2014] EWHC 1959 (Pat), [296]
citing *Divisional/ASTROPOWER* (G1/05) and *Sequences of Divisionals/SEIKO* (G1/06), para.13.4.
[73] *Koninklijke Philips*, [308].
[74] PA 1977 ss.15A(2); Patents Rules 2007 r.23.

Search

3-32   After preliminary examination the next step is search, which the applicant must request and pay for within a period set by the rules.[75] Failure to make such a request will mean that application is taken to be withdrawn.[76]

3-33   The Comptroller is obliged to inform the applicant of the examiner's search report.[77]

Withdrawal of application

3-34   An application may be withdrawn at any time before a patent is granted.[78] Any withdrawal of an application may not be revoked.[79] Nevertheless the Comptroller retains power under s.117(1) to correct an error or mistake in the withdrawal of an application.[80] In *Siemens Medical Systems Inc's Application*[81] the UK Patent Office held that the withdrawal takes effect as of the date the request to withdraw is filed, provided it is clear and unambiguous, and not on the date that the Register is updated showing that the withdrawal has taken place.

Abandoned applications

3-35   In the event of an application being abandoned or becoming void before publication the application, specification, drawings, specimens and samples left in connection with the application are not thereafter published nor are they open to public inspection.[82] This general position is subject to certain exceptions,[83] one of which is where the applicant later applies for a new application relating to the subject-matter of the earlier abandoned application, if the later application is published.

Publication of application

3-36   Except for those applications containing matter which might be prejudicial to national security or the safety of the public,[84] the Comptroller shall publish the application as soon as possible after a period of 18 months from the declared priority date or, where there is no declared priority date, the date of filing the application.[85] Preparations for publication are normally completed when the specification has been allocated to a printing contractor.[86] After this time, publication cannot be avoided by seeking to withdraw the application.

Rights on publication of application

3-37   From the date of publication of the application until the grant of the patent, an applicant has the same right as he would have had if the patent had been granted

75   PA 1977 s.17(1); Patents Rules 2007 r.17.
76   PA 1977 s.15(10)(d).
77   PA 1977 s.17(5).
78   PA 1977 s.14(9).
79   PA 1977 s.14(9); applied in *Spectra-Tech Inc's Application* [1999] R.P.C. 187.
80   PA 1977 s.14(10).
81   BL O/063/00, para.21.
82   PA 1977 s.118(2).
83   PA 1977 s.118(3)–(5).
84   PA 1977 s.22.
85   PA 1977 s.16; Patents Rules 2007 r.26.
86   *Intera Corp's Application* [1986] R.P.C. 459; and see *Peabody International's Application* [1986] R.P.C. 521.

on the date of publication of the application, except that he cannot institute proceedings for infringement until the patent has been granted.[87] However, in order to obtain relief for infringement in respect of acts committed prior to grant it must be established that the allegedly infringing act infringes the claims of the application (in the form they were just prior to publication of the application) as well as the claims of the patent as granted.[88]

Substantive examination

Either at the time of requesting a search or no later than six months from the date of publication of the application an applicant must request a substantive examination.[89] The application is examined to ensure that it complies with all the requirements of the 1977 Act and the Patent Rules 2007.[90] This includes a consideration as to whether the invention is new and involves an inventive step in the light of the documents resulting from the search.[91] The approach to the consideration of inventive step at this stage, involving as it does an assessment by a Patent Office examiner with technical skills and extensive knowledge in their particular field, was reviewed in *Degussa-Huls v Comptroller*.[92]

3-38

If the examiner reports that any of the requirements are not complied with, the Comptroller must give the applicant an opportunity "within a specified period" to make observations on the report and to amend the application so as to comply with those requirements.[93] The specified period may be extended; however the fact that other patent offices have not yet reported on foreign parallel patents is not a good reason for such an extension since otherwise UK patent prosecution would be slowed to the pace of the slowest patent office in the world.[94] Once a favourable report is provided, it is not open to the Patent Office to rescind it even if the examiner subsequently becomes aware of further relevant prior art.[95]

3-39

Amendment prior to grant

On receipt of the examiner's search report under s.17(5) or the examiner's report after substantive examination under s.18(3), an applicant has the opportunity to amend the specification of his own volition and without the consent of the Comptroller.[96] Any further amendment requires the consent of the Comptroller.[97] No amendment is permissible which results in the application or specification disclosing matter which extends beyond that disclosed in the application as it is

3-40

---

[87] PA 1977 s.69(1)–(2); corresponding provisions apply to European patent applications see EPC art.67. See also PCT art.29 for international applications.
[88] PA 1977 s.69(2)(b).
[89] PA 1977 s.18(1); Patents Rules 2007 r.28. Note there are exceptions to the time limit mentioned in r.28—see rr.28(3) and 28(4) and rr.60 and 68(4).
[90] PA 1977 s.18(2).
[91] PA 1977 s.17(4).
[92] [2004] EWHC 3213 (Pat), [2005] R.P.C. 29.
[93] PA 1977 s.18(3).
[94] *Smart Card Solutions Ltd's Application* [2004] R.P.C. 12, 273.
[95] *Nokia Mobile Phones (UK) Ltd's Application* [1996] R.P.C. 733.
[96] Patents Rules 2007 rr.31(3)–(4).
[97] Patents Rules 2007 r.31(5).

filed.[98] It appears that the general power to amend under s.19 of the 1977 Act cannot be used to circumvent the specific requirements of other sections of the Act.[99]

Grant

3-41   If the examiner reports that the application complies with the requirements of the Act and the rules the Comptroller will notify the applicant and, subject to certain other provisions,[100] the Comptroller shall grant the patent.[101] In practice the letter to the applicant will state that the requirements have been complied with and will state when the grant is expected to be published in the journal. The grant is published in the Official Journal and that date of publication is deemed by s.25(1) to be the date the patent is granted and takes effect for the purposes of the "following" provisions of the Act. For the purposes of the preceding sections (ss.1–23 of the Act) the date the grant is the date of the letter informing the applicant of that fact.[102] The Comptroller's practice includes "rescission of grant" under s.18(4) under the power to correct irregularities in procedure provided by the rules.[103]

Failures in the course of prosecution

3-42   The 1977 Act, and the Patents Rules 2007, lay down a number of specific time limits which have to be met and other requirements which have to be fulfilled in order for a patent to be granted. Inevitably there will be failures in meeting those time limits and requirements and the different ways in which various mistakes might be corrected are considered below.

Corrections of errors in documents

3-43   Section 117(1) of the Act provides that:

"The comptroller may, subject to any provision of rules, correct any error of translation or transcription, clerical error or mistake in any specification of a patent or application for a patent or any document filed in connection with a patent or such an application".

3-44   The breadth of this discretion is, however, limited in two ways. First, the subsection cannot be invoked to circumvent other mandatory statutory requirements. This is illustrated by the problem of a drawing referred to in an application but which by mistake has not been filed with the application. Section 15 of the Act provides a mandatory regime which deals with this situation (and other similar ones concerning drawings). If, on preliminary examination, it is found that there is a reference to a drawing in the application but the drawing has not been filed then provided the

---

[98]   PA 1977 ss.19(1), 76 and 72(1)(d).

[99]   *Payne's Application* [1985] R.P.C. 193.

[100] The provision is subject to s.18(5) (two applications for the same invention), s.19(amendment) and s.22 (national security).

[101] PA 1977 s.18(4).

[102] Since although there is provision in s.18(4) for a fee to be paid, no fee has been prescribed, *Howmet Research Corp's Application* [2006] EWHC 725 (Pat), [2006] R.P.C. 27, [8]. On the state of the rules at that time, the period for divisional applications expired on that date and the applicant lost the right to file a divisional application as a result. This problem has been addressed by a change in the rules so that under Patents Rules 2007 r.19(3) the period is now two months after the notification. See also *ITT Industries Inc's Application* [1984] R.P.C. 23 and *Ogawa Chemical Industries Ltd's Applications* [1986] R.P.C. 63.

[103] Patents Rules 2007 r.107.

drawing is filed within a period specified by the Patent Office the only consequence is that the date of filing of the drawing is treated as the date on which the application itself was filed.[104] However, the effective re-dating of the application might very well pose serious problems for an applicant since, for example, it might lead to a loss of priority if the new date on which the application is deemed to be made is more than 12 months from the priority date. Accordingly, when a situation like this arose in *Antiphon's Application*[105] the applicant sought to invoke the Comptroller's discretion under s.117 to correct an obvious error. The absence of a drawing was obviously a mistake since the drawing was referred to in the application expressly and furthermore the priority document itself also contained a copy of the drawing.[106] However, the court held that, although absent the provisions of s.15 (at that time), the mistake could have been corrected by allowing the drawing to be included in the application under s.117 without leading to a re-dating of the deemed date of filing the application, the provisions of s.15 as they then were precluded that result. Consequently, s.15 was amended by the CDPA 1988[107] so as to preserve the power to correct errors under s.117 thereby reversing the effect of *Antiphon's Application*. Following the amendment of s.15 by the Regulatory Reform (Patents) Order 2004,[108] the preservation of the power to correct errors under s.117 is now contained in s.15(8) (see para.3-20).

Secondly, in so far as the correction is a correction to the specification, it can only be made if the correction is obvious in the sense that it is immediately evident that nothing else would have been intended than what was offered as the correction.[109] However, this restriction does not apply where the error in the specification is connected to the electronic delivery of the application.[110] The Comptroller is entitled to require the proposed correction to be advertised and opposition can be entered to the correction.[111] No advertisement is required if the Comptroller determines that no person could reasonably object.[112]

3-45

The Comptroller's power under s.117 to correct errors or mistakes extends to correcting an error or mistake in the withdrawal of an application for a patent.[113] This can result in the resuscitation of a withdrawn application. Consequently s.117A[114] provides protection for a person who has begun to use the invention after withdrawal but before publication of notice of the request to correct the error or mistake in the withdrawal.[115] The right given to such a person is similar to that under s.64 of the 1977 Act.[116]

3-46

---

[104] PA 1977 s.15(6)(b).
[105] [1984] R.P.C. 1.
[106] But note that the priority document does not form part of the application. See *Mitsui* [1984] R.P.C. 471 and *VEB Kombinat Walzlager's Application* [1987] R.P.C. 405.
[107] CDPA 1988 Sch.5 para.2, inserting a new s.15(3A).
[108] SI 2004/2357.
[109] Patents Rules 2007 r.105(3); see *Antiphon A.B.'s Application* [1984] R.P.C. 1; *Dukhovskoi's Application* [1985] R.P.C. 8; and *CELTRIX/Correction of errors* (G11/91) [1993] O.J. EPO 125.
[110] Patents Rules 2007 r.105(4).
[111] Patents Rules 2007 r.105(5)–(6).
[112] Patents Rules 2007 r.105(5).
[113] PA 1977 s.117(3)–(4).
[114] Inserted by the Regulatory Reform (Patents) Order 2004 (SI 2004/2357).
[115] See para.14-214.
[116] See paras 14-199 to 14-213.

Alteration of time limits

3-47   The degree of flexibility to extend time limits depends upon the nature of the time limit which has been missed. These are dealt with by rule 108 of the Patents Rules 2007 and by s.117B of the 1977 Act.[117] An automatic extension of two months is available in many cases.[118] Further extensions are available in the exercise of the Comptroller's discretion.[119] The basic principle applied by the Patent Office in these cases is that an applicant should not suffer loss of rights through unforeseen circumstances.[120] However, in order to secure more time to undertake an action, an applicant must show that he intended to carry out that action in the first place. Otherwise the grant of an extension would effectively allow the applicant to change his mind after the time for taking the action has expired.[121] In other cases no extension is permitted.[122] The Comptroller's power to extend time under s.117B applies to periods set by the Comptroller in connection with a patent or application.[123] Under the previous Patents Rules 1995 the Comptroller had power to shorten some time limits but that power has been abolished.[124]

Correction of irregularities

3-48   In addition to the above, the Comptroller has a general discretion under r.107 of the Patents Rules 2007 to allow any irregularity in procedure to be rectified on such terms as he shall direct.[125] In the case of time limits specified in the 1977 Act or listed in Pts 1 to 3 of Sch.4 of the 2007 Rules, alteration is only permissible if the irregularity is attributable wholly or in part to an error, default, or omission on the part of the Patent Office and it appears to the Comptroller that the irregularity should be rectified.[126]

Reinstatement of application

3-49   The Regulatory Reform (Patents) Order 2004[127] has amended the 1977 Act so as to empower the Comptroller to reinstate an application for a patent which is refused or treated as having been refused or withdrawn as a direct consequence of a failure by the applicant to comply with a requirement of the Act or the rules within a period which is either set out in the Act or rules or specified by the Comptroller.[128]

3-50   The power to reinstate an application will be exercised by the Comptroller if, but only if, the applicant requests him to do so, the request complies with the relevant requirements of the rules,[129] and the Comptroller is satisfied that the original failure

---

[117] See also Patents Rules 2007 r.109.
[118] Patents Rules 2007 r.108(2), and see *Aisin Seiki K.K.'s Application* [1984] R.P.C. 191.
[119] Patents Rules 2007 r.108(3).
[120] *Heatex* [1995] R.P.C. 546, 550.
[121] See *Pilat's Application* [2003] R.P.C. 13, 253.
[122] Patents Rules 2007 r.108(1).
[123] Patents Act 1977 s.117B(1).
[124] Patents Rules 1995 r.110(2). This rule has no counterpart in the Patents Rule 2007.
[125] See *EDF's Patents* [1992] R.P.C. 205.
[126] Patents Rules 2007 r.107(3) and *E's Application* [1983] R.P.C. 231. See also *Mill's Application* [1985] R.P.C. 339; *Mitsubishi Jidosha Kogyo K.K.'s Application* [1988] R.P.C. 449.
[127] SI 2004/2357 art.8.
[128] PA 1977 s.20A(1).
[129] See, in particular, Patents Rules 2007 r.32.

by the applicant to comply with a requirement of the Act or the rules was unintentional.[130]

The request to reinstate must be made before the end of the period of 12 months starting on the date on which the application was terminated, or the period of two months starting on the date on which the removal of the cause of non-compliance occurred, whichever is the earlier.[131]   **3-51**

The Comptroller will not reinstate the application if an extension remains available under this Act or rules for the period which the applicant has failed to comply with. Nor will he reinstate the application if such period is set out or specified in relation to any proceedings before the Comptroller, or for the purposes of s.5(2A)(b) (late filing for priority), or for the purposes of a request under s.20A (request for reinstatement) or s.117B.[132]   **3-52**

If an application is reinstated, the applicant must comply with the requirement giving rise to his original failure within the further period specified by the Comptroller in the order reinstating the application.[133] That period will not be less than two months.[134] If the applicant still fails to comply within the period specified, the application will be treated as withdrawn on expiry of the period.[135]   **3-53**

Where the application was published before termination (i.e. it was published before it was refused or treated as having been refused or withdrawn, see s.20B(7)), there are special provisions for the protection of a person who, after termination and before publication of notice of the request for reinstatement, began in good faith to do an act which would have constituted an infringement of the rights conferred by publication of the application if the termination had not taken place, or made in good faith effective and serious preparations to do such an act. Such a person has a right to continue to do, or do, the act notwithstanding the reinstatement of the application and the grant of the patent.[136] The right is similar to that under s.64 of the 1977 Act.[137] On the other hand, a person who was infringing after publication of the application but before termination gets no protection.[138] Nor does a person who infringes at a time when it was possible for the period which the applicant originally failed to comply with to be extended.[139]   **3-54**

Hearing and appeal

If the applicant and Comptroller disagree on any matter, the Comptroller must give the applicant an opportunity of a hearing.[140] An appeal lies from the Comptroller's decision to the Patents Court.[141] If a question of EU law were to arise (for   **3-55**

---

[130] PA 1977 s.20A(2). The same test of a remedy being available if a failure was unintentional was introduced into PA 1977 s.5(2C) [priority] and s.28(3) [renewal fees].
[131] Patents Rules 2007 r.32(1) and (2).
[132] PA 1977 s.20A(3).
[133] PA 1977 s.20A(7).
[134] PA 1977 s.20A(8).
[135] PA 1977 s.20A(9).
[136] PA 1977 s.20B(4). And see para.14-216.
[137] See paras 14-199 to 14-213.
[138] PA 1977 s.20B(3)(b).
[139] PA 1977 s.20B(3)(a).
[140] PA 1977 s.101.
[141] PA 1977 s.97.

example arising under the Biotechnology Directive[142]) it is submitted that the Comptroller would be able refer questions directly to the Court of Justice.[143]

Period for putting application in order—compliance period

3-56   The time for putting an application in order is called the compliance period.[144] Subject to any appeal, the compliance period is the later of: (a) four and a half years from the declared priority date or, where there is no declared priority date, from the date of filing of the application[145]; or (b) 12 months from the date of the first substantive examination report.[146]

Third party objections

3-57   Between publication and grant a third party may make observations in writing to the Comptroller on the question whether the invention is a patentable invention, stating reasons for the observations, and the Comptroller shall consider the observations in accordance with rules.[147] There is no mechanism by which a third party can oppose the grant of a UK national patent. In this respect the procedure for obtaining a UK national patent differs significantly from a European patent (UK). Making observations under s.21 is thus the only way by which a third party can seek to influence the grant, or refusal, of a UK national patent. The third party's rights are limited to making written observations. He has no right to be heard, or to be informed of the examiner's, or applicant's reaction to the observations.

Grant of patent

3-58   The Comptroller must publish a notice of the grant of the patent in the *Official Journal* as soon as is practicable after grant[148] and a patent takes effect on the date on which such notice is published.[149]

3.   APPLICATION FOR EUROPEAN PATENT (UK)

3-59   The procedure for applying, and the manner in which European patents are prosecuted to grant, are covered in detail in the publication Guidelines for Examination in the European Patent Office published by the EPO. There follows a very brief

---

[142] Directive 98/44/EC.

[143] In *Azrak-Hamway International Inc.'s Licence of Right (Design Right and Copyright) Application* [1997] R.P.C. 134 the Comptroller's Hearing Officer (Mr Dennehey) held that at least in proceedings such as those before him, the Comptroller was a "court or tribunal" within what was then the relevant article of the Treaty of Rome art.117. This is now art.267 of the Treaty on the Functioning of the European Union. See also para.9 of the *Information Note on references from national courts for a preliminary ruling* O.J. EU C/297/1, 5 December 2009.

[144] Patents Rules 2007 r.30(1).

[145] PA 1977 s.20; Patents Rules 2007 r.30(2)(a).

[146] PA 1977 s.20; Patents Rules 2007 r.30(2)(b).

[147] PA 1977 s.21(1); Patents Rules 2007 r.33.

[148] PA 1977 s.24(1).

[149] PA 1977 s.25(1). Strictly the section provides that the date of publication amounts to the date of grant only for the purposes of the provisions of the 1977 Act following s.25. These provisions include all the relevant ones from the point of view of the effect of the patent (infringement, licensing, property in patents, revocation, etc.). The purpose of the provision is to distinguish between the process of applying for a patent, which is catered for by the provisions in the Act up to s.25.

discussion on the procedure designed primarily to contrast that procedure with the procedure for obtaining a UK national patent.

Language

There are three official languages of the EPO, English, French and German, and European patent applications must be filed in one of these languages, or if filed in any other language, be translated into one of the official languages.[150] The selected official language is used in all subsequent proceedings[151] subject to certain exceptions.[152] The authentic text of a European patent or patent application, is the language used in the proceedings before the EPO.[153] Where the language of the proceedings is French or German, a translation into English of the specification or the claims is to be treated as the authentic text for the purposes of domestic proceedings in the UK other than proceedings for revocation if as translated the scope is narrower than that of the original language.[154] Subject to safeguarding provisions, a proprietor or applicant may file a corrected translation.[155]

3-60

Where to apply

An application for a European patent (UK) can either be made at the UK Patent Office or with the EPO in Munich or The Hague. United Kingdom residents must normally file through the Patent Office[156] for security reasons where s.23(1A) of the 1977 Act applies.[157] A European divisional application must, however, be filed with the EPO.[158] Where a European application (UK) is made at the Patent Office, the Patent Office must forward all applications, other than for secret patents, to the EPO in the shortest time compatible with the secrecy provisions of s.22 of the 1977 Act.[159] An application which does not reach the EPO before the end of the fourteenth month after filing (or if priority is claimed, after the date of priority) shall be deemed to be withdrawn. Any fees paid in respect of this application shall be refunded.[160] However, such an application can be converted to a national application.[161]

3-61

How to apply

The requirements for a European patent application are set out by the EPC and the EPC Rules and are analogous to the corresponding requirements of the 1977

3-62

---

[150] EPC art.14(1) and (2).
[151] EPC art.14(3).
[152] EPC Rules rr.3 and 4.
[153] EPC art.70; PA 1977 s.80(1).
[154] PA 1977 s.80(2).
[155] PA 1977 s.80(3)–(4); and see *Rhône-Poulenc-Santé's European Patent (UK)* [1996] R.P.C. 125.
[156] PA 1977 s.23; EPC art.75(1).
[157] s.23(1A) applies to an application if: (a) the application contains information which relates to military technology or for any other reason publication of the information might be prejudicial to national security; or (b) the application contains information the publication of which might be prejudicial to the safety of the public. See also para.3-91.
[158] EPC art.76.
[159] EPC art.77 and EPC Rules r.37(1): within six weeks where clearly no secrecy problems, within four months (or 14 months if priority claimed from priority date) where further examination required.
[160] EPC art.77(3) and EPC Rules r.37(2).
[161] PA 1977 s.81; EPC art.135(1)(a).

Act.[162] All contracting states are deemed to be designated in the request for the grant,[163] however the designation of a contracting state may be withdrawn at any time up to the grant of the European patent.[164] The formalities required to secure a date of filing documents are analogous to the corresponding provisions of the 1977 Act.[165]

3-63 Particular features of EPO practice which differ from UK practice are:

(a) Where appropriate the claims should first define the subject-matter by reference to features which are part of the closest prior art followed by a characterising portion.[166]

(b) The EPO frequently requires the insertion of reference numerals into the claim.

(c) Claims shall not rely on references to the drawings or description except where absolutely necessary[167] and the practice of providing "omnibus claims" is strongly discouraged.[168] An application to the UK Patent Office to amend a European patent (UK) after grant in order to add an omnibus claim (amongst other things), has been allowed.[169]

Biological material

3-64 Special requirements for deposit of biological material are laid down in the EPC Rules.[170]

Formal examination of application and search

3-65 The Receiving Section[171] examines the application to make sure the correct fee has been paid and the application is generally in order[172] so that a date of filing may be accorded the application. Once a date of filing has been accorded, the Receiving Section further examines the application to make sure the detailed formal requirements of the EPC have been complied with.[173] Deficiencies may be corrected within specified time limits which vary according to the nature of the deficiency.[174] At the same time, the Search Division draws up a European search report.[175] The search report shall mention those documents which may be taken into consideration in deciding novelty and inventive step. In all these aspects the procedure at the EPO is analogous to the procedure at the UK Patent Office.

---

[162] EPC arts 78, 82, 83 and 84 and cf. PA 1977 s.14.
[163] EPC art.79(1). This represents a change in EPC 2000 from the previous form of art.79. In effect the old "opt in" system has been reversed so that all states are automatically designated and an applicant who wishes to do so has to withdraw the designation of a state under art.79(3) before grant of the patent.
[164] EPC art.79(3).
[165] EPC art.80 and EPC Rules r.40 and cf. PA 1977 s.15.
[166] EPC Rules r.29(1).
[167] EPC Rules r.29(6).
[168] EPC Rules r.29(6); and see *IFF/Claim categories* (T150/82) [1984] O.J. EPO 309.
[169] *Philips Electronic and Associated Industries Ltd's Patent* [1987] R.P.C. 244.
[170] EPC Rules rr.28 and 28a.
[171] EPC art.16.
[172] EPC art.90; EPC Rules r.55.
[173] EPC art.90; EPC Rules rr.57 and 56.
[174] See, e.g. EPC Rules rr.45, 56, 58 and 133.
[175] EPC art.92; EPC Rules rr.61 and 62.

Inspection of files

Before publication of an application the files relating to the application are not available for public inspection without the applicant's consent,[176] although this is subject to an exception in the case of a person who can prove that the applicant has invoked rights under the application against them.[177] After publication of an application the files relating to the application are available for public inspection subject to certain exceptions.[178] Thus if an application is withdrawn (see below) before technical preparations for publication have been completed, the files relating to it will not normally be available for inspection.

3-66

Publication of application

A European application must be published as soon as possible after the expiry of the period of 18 months from the date of filing or from the date of priority (if priority has been claimed) whichever is the appropriate date.[179] It is contemplated that the European search report and the abstract will generally be published at the same time. An application can be withdrawn at any time up to the date when the technical preparations for publication have been completed.[180]

3-67

Rights on publication of application

From the date of publication of the application until the grant of the patent, an applicant has the same right as he would have had if the patent had been granted on the date of publication of the application.[181] In order to take effect in the United Kingdom, a European patent (UK) is treated for the purpose of parts of the Patents Act 1977 as if it were a patent under that Act.[182] Thus, the patentee cannot institute proceedings for infringement until the patent has been granted.[183]

3-68

Substantive examination

A request for examination must be filed not later than six months from when the *European Patent Bulletin* has mentioned the publication of the European search report. The request may not be withdrawn.[184] For an international application under the PCT, the six months is taken from the publication of the PCT search report.[185] An Examining Division consisting of three technically qualified examiners[186] is responsible for the examination of each European patent application. Examination prior to a final decision will, as a general rule, be entrusted to one member of the division (the substantive examiner) but oral proceedings will be before the Divi-

3-69

---

[176] EPC art.128(1).
[177] EPC art.128(2); PA 1977 s.118(4) enacts a corresponding provision in relation to the UK Patent Office. And see para.16–183.
[178] EPC art.128(4); EPC Rules r.144.
[179] European Patent Convention art.93; EPC Rules rr.67 and 69.
[180] EPC Rules r.67.
[181] EPC art.67.
[182] PA 1977 s.77(1).
[183] PA 1977 s.69(1), (2). And see para.14–12.
[184] EPC Rules r.70(1).
[185] EPC art.153(6).
[186] EPC art.18.

sion itself which may be enlarged by the addition of a legally qualified examiner.[187] Besides considering the application for novelty and inventive step, the examiner will be concerned with the sufficiency of description, clarity of claims and whether there is unity of invention. The examiner must invite the applicant to file his observations to any objections that the examiner may have[188] and such objections shall be contained in a reasoned statement.[189]

Amendment before grant

3-70   An applicant can freely amend the description, claims and drawings of his own volition after receiving the European search report and before receipt of the first communication from the Examining Division.[190] After receipt of such communication the applicant may only amend once without the consent of the Examining Division.[191] No amendment is permissible by which an application in its amended form contains subject-matter which extends beyond the content of the application as filed.[192] Where there is more than one invention an applicant may file a divisional application in respect of subject-matter that does not extend beyond the content of the earlier application[193] thereby retaining for the divisional application the filing date of the earlier application. Again these provisions are analogous to the procedure at the UK Patent Office. Historically the major difference between the UK Patent Office and the EPO concerning divisional applications was that in the EPO there was no time limit within which divisionals had to be filed whereas there was a time limit in the UK system but on 1 April 2010 the EPC Rules were changed to implement a time limit.[194] Divisionals must be filed within two years of the earliest communication of the Examining Division or two years from the first objection of lack of unity under art.82 EPC.[195] This was then in turn changed to repeal the 24-month time limits for the filing of divisional applications on 18 October 2013. This decision has been in force since 1 April 2014 and applies to all divisional applications filed on or after that date. This enables the filing of divisional applications as long as the parent application is still pending.[196]

Observations by third parties

3-71   Following publication of the European patent application any person may present observations to the EPO concerning the patentability of the invention. However, such a person does not become a party to the proceedings before the EPO.[197] As with the position under the 1977 Act, this procedure suffers from the disadvantage

---

[187] EPC art.18.
[188] EPC art.94(3).
[189] EPC Rules r.72(2).
[190] EPC Rules r.137(2).
[191] EPC art.123; EPC Rules r.137(3).
[192] EPC art.123(2).
[193] EPC art.76.
[194] EPC Rules r.36 (1) as amended by the decision of the EPO Administrative Council CA/D 2/09 of 25 March 2009 (O.J. EPO 2009, 296).
[195] EPC Rules r.36(1)(a) and (b).
[196] Decision of the Administrative Council of 16 October 2013 amending rr.36, 38 and 135 of the Implementing Regulations to the European Patent Convention (CA/D 15/13).
[197] EPC art.115.

that whilst observations can be made, the person making them does not know what effect the observations have on the examiner or the applicant.

Grant of the patent

If the Examining Division decides to grant the European patent, it will inform the applicant of the text in which the Examining Division intends to grant the patent and seek the applicant's approval of that text within a four-month period.[198] If the applicant proposes amendments to the application then the matter will be dealt with.[199] If the applicant pays all fees due and files translations of the claims into the two other official languages of the EPO then the text is deemed to be approved and the patent will be granted.[200] The grant will not take effect until mention of the fact has been made in the *European Patent Bulletin*.[201] At the time of such mention the EPO must publish a specification of the European patent.[202] As from the publication of such mention, a European patent (UK) shall be treated for the purposes of Pts I and III of the 1977 Act as if it were a patent granted under the 1977 Act.[203] Before the London Agreement[204] came into force on 1 May 2008, it was also necessary to file translations into English of European patents (UK) in French or German.[205]

3-72

Conversion of a European patent application (UK) to an application under the 1977 Act

The Comptroller may direct that an application for a European patent (UK) be treated as an application under the 1977 Act where the application is deemed to be withdrawn under the provisions of the EPC relating to the time for forwarding the applications to the EPO.[206]

3-73

Effect of filing an application for a European patent (UK)

An application for a European patent (UK) having a date of filing under the EPC shall be treated for the purposes of certain provisions of the 1977 Act as an application under the 1977 Act.[207]

3-74

Representation

Natural or legal persons having either a residence or their principal place of business within the territory of one of the contracting states do not have to be

3-75

---

198 EPC Rules r.73(1).
199 See Guidelines for Examination in the EPO C-VI. 4.9.
200 EPC Rules r.73(1) and EPC art.97(1).
201 EPC art.97(3).
202 EPC art.98; and see EPC Rules r.53.
203 PA 1977 s.77(1); EPC art.64.
204 The Agreement on the Application of art.65 of the Convention on the Grant of European Patents signed in London on 17 October 2000, Cmnd.5247. And see para.1–67.
205 s.77(6) of the 1977 Act ceased to have effect from the date when the London Agreement came into force, see Patents Rules 2007 rr.56(9) and 56(10). But s.78(7) still requires the filing of a translation into English of the claims of a European patent application in French or German in the circumstances set out in that subsection.
206 PA 1977 s.81.
207 PA 1977 s.78(1) as amended by the CDPA 1988 Sch.5 para.22; and see *L'Oréal's Application* [1986] R.P.C. 19; the same provisions apply to an international application for a European Patent (UK), see PA 1977 s.79; cf. PA 1977 s.89 for an international application for a patent.

represented by a professional representative but other persons, except for filing an application, must be represented professionally.[208] There is a list of professional representatives.[209] In addition, professional representation may also be undertaken by any legal practitioner qualified in one of the contracting states and having his place of business within such state to the extent that he is entitled, within the state, to act as a professional representative in patent matters.[210] The EPO maintains a register of legal practitioners who indicate their intention to undertake representation in proceedings before the EPO. This register is not the same as the list of professional representatives.[211]

Oral hearings

3-76   Oral proceedings may take place either at the instance of the EPO if it considers this to be expedient or at the request of any party to the proceedings.[212] However, oral proceedings before the Receiving Section will only take place at the request of the applicant where the Receiving Section considers this to be expedient or where it envisages refusing the application.[213] Further requests for oral proceedings by the same parties on the same subject will generally not be allowed.[214] Such proceedings are not in public except when before the Board of Appeal and the Enlarged Board of Appeal after publication of the application.[215] At the pre-grant stage, the hearing will usually be an informal discussion with the Receiving Section or Examining Division. Written evidence and documents will normally be used and only in exceptional cases will oral evidence be adduced. The rules, however, require that minutes be kept and be provided to the parties.[216]

Appeals

3-77   Certain decisions of the Receiving Section and Examining Divisions are appealable to a Board of Appeal.[217] However, unless the decision indicates an appeal is permissible therefrom, it may only be appealed either if it is a final decision or together with a final decision.[218] Notice of appeal must be filed at the EPO within two months of the date of notification of the decision.[219] A statement of grounds must be filed within four months.[220] In ex parte proceedings the notice of appeal is first considered by the Receiving Section or Examining Division who may in clear cases allow the appeal.[221] This procedure is called an interlocutory revision. If the appeal is not allowed within three months it must be remitted to the Board of Ap-

[208] EPC art.133; Authorisation of representatives is covered by EPC Rules r.157.
[209] EPC art.134.
[210] EPC art.134(8).
[211] See *Decision of the President EPO dated March 10, 1989* [1989] O.J. EPO 177; and see also *Professional representation by legal practitioners* (J27/95).
[212] EPC art.116(1); EPC rr.115 and 116.
[213] EPC art.116(2).
[214] EPC art.116(1).
[215] EPC art.116(3) and (4).
[216] EPC Rules r.124.
[217] EPC art.106(1).
[218] EPC art.106(2).
[219] EPC art.108; see EPC r.99 for content of the notice of appeal.
[220] EPC art.108.
[221] EPC art.109.

peal[222] without delay and without comment. On appeal the Board of Appeal must invite the party or parties to file observations on points raised by another party or by the Board itself.[223] As a result of such exchange of views it may be necessary or desirable to request an oral hearing.

4. APPLICATION FOR UNITARY PATENT

The unitary patent will sit alongside the European patents granted by the European Patent Office, and can be applied for via the same existing procedure as that for European Patent Applications. The process will be the same up to the point of grant. If the applicant wishes to obtain unitary effect for the territory of the participating states, procedurally, this is obtained by a formal request to the EPO.[224]   **3-78**

The request for unitary effect shall be filed with the European Patent Office no later than one month after publication of the mention of the grant of the European patent in the European Patent Bulletin.[225] This request shall be filed in writing in the language of the proceedings and shall contain[226]:   **3-79**

(a) particulars of the proprietor of the European patent making the request (hereinafter "the requester") as provided for in r.41 para.2(c) of the EPC;

(b) the number of the European patent to which unitary effect shall be attributed;

(c) where the requester has appointed a representative, particulars as provided for in r.41 para.2(d) of the EPC;

(d) a translation of the European patent as required under art.6 para.1 Reg.(EU) No 1260/2012, as follows:
- where the language of the proceedings is French or German, a full translation of the specification of the European patent into English; or
- where the language of the proceedings is English, a full translation of the specification of the European patent into any other official language of the European Union.

5. THE PATENT CO-OPERATION TREATY

International application

In addition to a national application or a European Patent (UK) application in the manner mentioned above, ss.89, 89A and 89B of the 1977 Act[227] give effect to the PCT under which, on the basis of a single application called an international application, an applicant may seek patents in the contracting states of the PCT. An international application includes applications for patents via the national route and also application via regional patent offices such as the EPO.   **3-80**

The PCT was ratified by this country on 24 October 1977, and the starting date   **3-81**

---

[222] See EPC art.21 for constitution of Board of Appeal.
[223] EPC Rules r.100(2).
[224] See para.3–03 and the EPO Rules relating to Unitary Patent Protection (SC/D 1/15 e) adopted by the decision of the Select Committee of the Administrative Council of the European Patent Organisation of 15 December 2015.
[225] r.6(1) of the EPO Rules relating to Unitary Patent Protection (SC/D 1/15 e).
[226] rr.6(2)(a)–(d) of the EPO Rules relating to Unitary Patent Protection (SC/D 1/15 e).
[227] As amended by the CDPA 1988 Sch.5 para.25 and by art.16 of the Regulatory Reform (Patents) Order 2004 (SI 2004/2357).

for filing international applications was 1 June 1978. The manner of operation of the PCT is laid down in the Treaty itself and in the Regulations under the PCT (PCT rules).[228] The benefit of an application made under the PCT is that a single application can be made seeking protection in a number of convention countries. From 1 January 2004 an application under the PCT is automatically deemed to designate all states and regions.[229]

The way the PCT works

3-82   In outline, the Treaty works in the following way: an applicant (who must either be a national or resident of a PCT contracting state) may make his international application either to its local patent office or, in those contracting states that have also ratified the EPC, to the EPO. Where s.23(1A) of the 1977 Act applies,[230] then, in order to comply with national security requirements a resident of the United Kingdom must file a PCT application at the UK Patent Office unless permission to do otherwise is obtained in advance from the Patent Office.[231] The local patent office is referred to as the Receiving Office. The Receiving Office will check the application for formalities and provide the application with its international filing date.[232] The Receiving Office will then forward a copy of the application to the International Bureau and to the International Searching Authority[233] which may either be a national office (if of sufficient size) or an intergovernmental organisation such as the International Patent Institute.[234] Such Searching Authority will carry out an international search which is sent to the International Bureau. The international application and the international search[235] are published by the International Bureau. They are also communicated to the patent offices of each of the Contacting States designated in the application—"a designated office". If the applicant wishes to proceed further he must ensure that the application has been sent to the designated offices and the required fees paid in general within 20 months of the priority date of the application.[236] The remainder of the prosecution to grant is carried out in the designated offices.

---

[228] PCT art.58. The Regulations can be and are amended by the Assembly and serve as the means for regulating the manner of operation of the Treaty.
[229] PCT Rules r.4.9(a).
[230] s.23(1A) applies to an application if: (a) the application contains information which relates to military technology or for any other reason publication of the information might be prejudicial to national security; or (b) the application contains information the publication of which might be prejudicial to the safety of the public. See also paras 3–88 to 3-94.
[231] PA 1977 s.23.
[232] PCT art.11; and see *Archibald Kenrick & Sons Ltd's International Application* [1994] R.P.C. 635; and below at para.3–83. A failure to file claims is contrary to art.11 such that no filing date can be given, see *R. v Comptroller-General of Patents* [2004] R.P.C. 37, 737.
[233] PCT art.12; the International Bureau is the International Bureau of the World Intellectual Property Organisation (WIPO), the International Searching Authority for PCT applications filed at the UK or European Patent Offices is the EPO.
[234] PCT art.16.
[235] PCT arts 20 and 21.
[236] PCT arts 20, 22 and 39(1)(a)—or if applicable up to 25 months if there is an international preliminary examination.

The PCT is a complete code

The PCT (together with its rules) contain a complete code for filing international **3-83** applications.[237] It follows that a PCT application cannot be an application under the 1977 Act except to the extent that the Act says it is and the circumstances in which a PCT application can be treated as an application for a patent under the 1977 Act are dealt with in ss.89, 89A and 89B of the Act (per Lewison J in *Abaco Machines (Australasia) Pty Ltd's Application*[238]). The UK Patent Office's jurisdiction to act as a receiving office under the PCT comes from the PCT and when acting in that manner it must apply the rules, regulations and conditions laid down by the PCT.[239] Thus, for example, the provision of the Patents Rules which relates to service by post of documents on the Patent Office does not apply to applications for priority filed under the PCT.[240] The procedures and time limits for making an application under the PCT are complex. They are supervised by the International Bureau who publish a *Gazette* and other advisory material relating to the operation of the PCT.[241]

International preliminary examination

Chapter II of the PCT additionally provides for an international preliminary **3-84** examination on the demand of the applicant—the objective of such provisions being to formulate a "preliminary and non-binding opinion of the questions whether the claimed invention appears to be novel, to involve any inventive step (to be non-obvious) and to be industrially applicable".[242] Chapter II is not applicable to all contracting states.

International application for a UK national patent

The relationship between an international application and the grant of a UK **3-85** national patent is regulated by ss.89, 89A and 89B of the 1977 Act as amended.[243] Up until the expiry of the prescribed period, the application is deemed to be in the international phase.[244] Thereafter, it is deemed to be in the national phase.[245] The

---

[237] *Archibald Kenrick & Sons Ltd's International Application* [1994] R.P.C. 635; which was applied in *Intelligence Quotient International Ltd's International Application* [1996] R.P.C. 245 and in *Abaco Machines (Australasia) Pty Ltd's Application* [2007] EWHC 347 (Pat). However, see also the observations in a further decision—*Intelligence Quotient International Ltd's International Application* [1996] R.P.C. 258, 268.

[238] [2007] EWHC 347 (Pat).

[239] *Archibald Kenrick & Sons Ltd's International Application* [1994] R.P.C. 635. Accordingly, review of decisions by the Patent Office when acting as a receiving office are not conducted by way of an appeal direct to the Patents Court but by way of the judicial review procedure to the Divisional Court of the Queens Bench Division in which a judge assigned to the Patents Court will sit. See, e.g. *R. v The Comptroller-General of Patents, Ex p. Celltech Ltd* [1991] R.P.C. 475.

[240] *Archibald Kenrick & Sons Ltd's International Application* [1994] R.P.C. 635. See also *Brossmann's Application* [1983] R.P.C. 109 and *Matsushita Electric Work's Application* [1983] R.P.C. 105 —both concerning whether a failure to comply with the PCT could be mitigated by invoking the provisions in the Patents Rules.

[241] PCT art.55.

[242] PCT art.33.

[243] CDPA Sch.5 para.25 and art.16 of the Regulatory Reform (Patents) Order 2004 (SI 2004/2357).

[244] PA 1977 s.89A(2).

[245] PA 1977 s.89A(3).

prescribed period is, in general, 31 months from the priority date.[246] In order to enter the national phase all necessary fees must be paid and translations filed at the Patent Office,[247] and provided copies of any amendment effected during the international phase (and any translation) are filed at the Patent Office, the amendment is treated as though made under the 1977 Act.[248] Whilst in the international phase, the provisions of the PCT relating to publication, search, examination and amendment apply and not those of the Act.[249] In all other respects the Act applies.[250] Once in the national phase, the provisions of the Act apply subject to certain exceptions.[251] Further, during the international phase, the application is treated as a foreign or convention application for the purpose of determining questions about entitlement. Section 12 of the 1977 Act thus applies. Once the national phase is entered, s.8, rather than s.12, applies.[252]

3-86   When the national phase begins, the Comptroller considers the international search report and refers the application for so much of the examination and search required in the case of a national application under ss.17 and 18 of the 1977 Act as he sees fit.[253] Thereafter, the application proceeds in the same way as a national application.

International application for a European patent (UK)

3-87   An international application can be made for a European patent (UK) and as such is not treated as an application for a UK national patent.[254] The EPO acts as the Receiving Office,[255] International Searching Authority[256] and International Preliminary Examining Authority.[257] The EPO may also act as a designated office to receive the international search report and process the application to grant if an international application seeks a European patent designating one or more contracting states which have also ratified the EPC.[258] In such cases the EPO will adopt the international search report in lieu of the European search report subject to any supplementary European search reports deemed necessary by the Administrative Council.[259] In addition, the EPO may act as an elected office for the purposes of using an international preliminary examination.[260]

---

[246] Patent Rules 2007 r.66(1).
[247] PA 1977 s.89A(3).
[248] PA 1977 s.89A(5).
[249] PA 1977 s.89A(1); and see, e.g. *Prangley's Application* [1988] R.P.C. 187; and *Vapocure Technologies Application* [1990] R.P.C. 1 (both relating to old s.89(1) to which the present s.89A(1) and s.89(1) now correspond) and the discussion of those cases in *Intelligence Quotient International Ltd's International Application* [1996] R.P.C. 258.
[250] PA 1977 s.89(1).
[251] PA 1977 s.89(1).
[252] PA 1977 s.89B(4).
[253] PA 1977 s.89B(5).
[254] PA 1977 s.130(4A). This provision replaced PA 1977 s.89(4) when the PCT system was changed so that international applications automatically designated all states and regions.
[255] EPC Rules r.157.
[256] EPC Rules r.158.
[257] EPC art.152.
[258] EPC art.153.
[259] EPC art.153(6) and (7).
[260] EPC art.153(1)(b).

6. NATIONAL SECURITY AND PUBLIC SAFETY

Restrictions on publication

There are circumstances in which directions may be given for keeping secret any information contained in a patent application. Two types of case exist, one concerned with security, i.e. information which might be prejudicial to national security[261] and the other concerned with public safety, i.e. information which might be prejudicial to the safety of the public.[262]

3-88

In the case of national security, the Comptroller must decide whether information in the application is of a description notified to him by the Secretary of State as being information the publication of which might prejudice the defence of the realm and if so then directions prohibiting or restricting publication may be given.[263]

3-89

In the case of public safety, the Comptroller must decide whether publication of the information might prejudice the safety of the public and if so then similar directions may be given. In the latter case the directions may only run until three months after what would have been the date for publication,[264] however, that time can be extended by the Secretary of State if he considers the safety of the public to be at risk.[265] If the application is a European application or international application then, while directions are in force, it may not be sent to the appropriate international processing institution.[266] If the application is a national application under the 1977 Act then it may proceed up to the stage where it is in order for grant but it is not published and no patent is granted thereon.[267] The position must be reviewed within the first nine months from the date of filing of the application and thereafter at least once in every period of 12 months.[268] Once secrecy directions are revoked, the Comptroller may extend the time for doing anything required to be done in connection with the application.[269] If any use of a secret invention is made by a government department after the application has been brought in order for grant (and after the period for publication has expired) or if the applicant suffers hardship by reason of the secrecy directions, compensation may be claimed.[270] Compensation for use by a government department is dealt with under the Crown use provisions[271] which are deemed to apply.[272] Compensation in the case of hardship is by way of a payment (if any) which appears to be reasonable to the Secretary of State and the

3-90

---

[261] PA 1977 s.22(1), as amended by PA 2004 s.16 and Sch.2 para.8 with effect from 1 January 2005 (SI 2004/3205).

[262] PA 1977 s.22(2).

[263] PA 1977 s.22(1).

[264] PA 1977 s.22(2) and the reference therein to s.16.

[265] PA 1977 s.22(5).

[266] In the case of a European application, the EPO; and in the case of an international application, the International Bureau.

[267] PA 1977 s.22(3)(a).

[268] PA 1977 s.22(5).

[269] PA 1977 s.22(5).

[270] PA 1977 s.22(7).

[271] i.e. PA 1977 ss.55–59.

[272] PA 1977 s.22(7)(a).

Treasury.[273] No renewal fees are payable during the period of secrecy.[274] A person who fails to comply with any secrecy directions will commit an offence.[275]

Restrictions on filing applications abroad

3-91   Persons resident in the United Kingdom are not entitled to file[276] outside the UK an application for a patent to which s.23(1A) of the 1977 Act applies unless certain conditions are satisfied.[277] Section 23(1A) applies to an application if:

(a)   the application contains information which relates to military technology or for any other reason publication of the information might be prejudicial to national security; or

(b)   the application contains information the publication of which might be prejudicial to the safety of the public.[278]

3-92   The exempting conditions are either that written authority has been granted by the Comptroller[279] or else that an application for a patent for the same invention must have already been filed in the UK Patent Office no less than six weeks beforehand,[280] and in the meantime no secrecy directions must have been made by the Comptroller or, if they had been made, they must have been revoked[281] (as to which, see paras 3–88 to 3–90).

3-93   The prohibition of s.23 of the Act applies to all applications whether they are national applications under the 1977 Act, European applications (which can be filed at the Patent Office) or international applications (in which case the Patent Office can act as the receiving office).[282]

Offence

3-94   A person who files or causes an application to be filed knowing that filing the application, or causing it to be filed, would contravene these provisions (or who is reckless as to whether filing the application, or causing it to be filed, would contravene these provisions) commits an offence.[283]

---

273 PA 1977 s.22(7)(b).
274 PA 1977 s.22(8).
275 PA 1977 s.22(9).
276 Or "cause to be filed".
277 PA 1977 s.23. See also EPC art.75.
278 PA 1977 s.23(1A), as amended by PA 2004 s.7.
279 PA 1977 s.23(1).
280 PA 1977 s.23(1)(a).
281 PA 1977 s.23(1)(b).
282 PA 1977 s.23(4)(b).
283 PA 1977 s.23(3) and (3A).

CHAPTER 4

ENTITLEMENT

CONTENTS

1. INTRODUCTION

This chapter deals with the right to apply for and be granted a patent and the way **4-01**
in which disputes about entitlement are resolved. A notable development in this area
of law relates to the decision of the Court of Appeal in March 2005, *Markem v
Zipher*.[1] This held that any claim to entitlement required reliance on some rule of
law besides the statute. The proposition was disapproved by the House of Lords in
October 2007 in *Yeda v Rhône-Poulenc Rorer*.[2] Thus the law today on the authority of *Yeda* is that the relevant parts of the Patents Act 1977 are an exhaustive code
for determining who is entitled to a patent.

2. WHO MAY APPLY?

Any person, either alone or jointly with another, may make an application for a **4-02**
patent—whether for a national patent under the 1977 Act,[3] or a European patent
under the EPC.[4] An international application under the PCT may be made by a
resident or national of a contracting state to the PCT.[5] The UK Patent Office is
competent to receive international applications provided at least one applicant is a
resident or national of the UK.[6]

An application for a European patent is likely to designate more than one **4-03**
Contracting State in which it is intended to have effect once granted and a single
European application may be filed by more than one person designating different
Contracting States.[7]

---

[1] *Markem Corporation v Zipher Ltd* (CA) [2005] EWCA (Civ) 267, [2005] R.P.C. 31. See also
University of Southampton's Applications (CA) [2006] R.P.C. 21, [8].

[2] *Yeda Research and Development Co Ltd v Rhône-Poulenc Rorer International Holdings Inc* (HL)
[2007] UKHL 43, [2008] R.P.C. 1.

[3] PA 1977 s.7(1).

[4] EPC art.58 and see art.59 for joint applications.

[5] PCT art.9.

[6] PCT Rules r.19.1 and 19.2; Note that r.19.4 provides for transmission to the International Bureau
of an international application made to an office which is not competent to receive it because of the
applicant's nationality or residence.

[7] EPC art.59; see art.79 as to the need to designate the contracting state or states in which protection
is desired, and see art.118 as to the requirement for unity of application where applicants are not the
same.

Applicant may act by agent

4-04   An agent may sign Patents Form No.1 (Request for grant of a patent) on behalf of the applicant and any notice or other documents under the 1977 Act.[8] When an agent is appointed when a person starts or joins any proceedings the appointment must simply be in writing.[9] Where an agent is appointed after a person has started or joined any proceedings, Form 51 (Appointment or change of agent) is required.[10] For international applications under the PCT an express authorisation has to be submitted to the Patent Office (as the receiving office) or the International Bureau.[11] There is no requirement that agents must be entered on the Register of Patent Agents.[12] Nevertheless, the Comptroller has power to refuse to recognise an agent in circumstances in which misconduct has taken place.[13] In practice, an applicant would be well advised to employ the services of a Registered Patent Agent (or a person on the European list or firm or company entitled to describe themselves as European patent attorneys), not least because of the provisions about patent agents privilege which only apply to communications relating to such persons.[14] The EPC restricts the persons who may act on behalf of another for any purpose connected with European patents.[15]

3. WHO MAY BE GRANTED A PATENT?

4-05   The freedom to make an application should be contrasted with the requirements as to who is entitled to be granted a patent. A patent may only be granted to a person entitled to that grant. Section 7(2) of the 1977 Act is structured so that "primarily" the right to be granted a patent belongs to the inventor (s.7(2)(a))[16]; in preference to the inventor a patent may be granted to a person who was entitled to the whole property in the patent at the time the invention was made (s.7(2)(b))[17]; and finally to a successor in title to either of those (s.7(2)(c)). The section ends with the words "and to no other person" and this, coupled with the word "primarily" at the outset shows that the section is an exhaustive code for determining entitlement and emphasises that a patent may be granted only to the inventor or someone claiming through them.[18]

4-06   In the case of joint inventors, the 1977 Act provides for them[19] but the position of joint inventors is not catered for expressly in the EPC.[20] Lord Hoffmann held in

---

[8]   Patents Rules 2007 r.101.
[9]   Patents Rules 2007 r.101(1)(a).
[10] Patents Rules 2007 r.101(1)(b).
[11] PCT Rules Part F r.90.4.
[12] CDPA 1988 ss.274 and 275.
[13] CDPA 1988 s.281 (power to makes rules) and The Patent Agents (Non-Recognition of Certain Agents by Comptroller) Rules 1990 (SI 1990/1454).
[14] CDPA 1988 s.280.
[15] See EPC art.134 and para.3-75. This is unaffected by UK law—CDPA 1988 s.274(2).
[16] See also EPC art.60(1).
[17] By virtue of rules or law (including foreign law and international treaties) or by an enforceable term of any prior agreement.
[18] See the speech of Lord Hoffman in *Yeda Research and Development Co Ltd v Rhône-Poulenc Rorer International Holdings Inc* (HL) [2007] UKHL 43, [2008] R.P.C. 1, at [18].
[19] PA 1977 s.7(2)(a).
[20] EPC art.60 does not refer to joint inventors.

Yeda that the convention "leaves it to be assumed that the singular includes the plural".[21]

Presumption that applicant is entitled

Although the rules of entitlement to grant are mandatory, there is also a presump-   **4-07**
tion that the person who makes an application for a patent is entitled to be granted
the patent.[22] This is a useful presumption from a practical point of view since it
means that entitlement does not need to be investigated before grant. However,
despite the presumption, it is important for the correct person(s) to apply for the patent in view of: (a) the power to revoke the patent if such persons are not granted
the patent,[23] and also (b) the potential loss of priority if the person making an application did not have the right to claim priority at the right time. In *Edwards
Lifesciences v Cook Biotech*[24] Kitchin J held that the fact that under PA 1977 s.7
Cook Biotech was entitled to make the patent application and, since they were the
successor in title to all the inventors, entitled to be granted the patent, did not mean
their priority claim was a good one. The problem was that the assignment from
which Cook Biotech derived title from certain of the original inventors post dated
the patent application and therefore did not give them the right to claim priority
from a priority document filed by the inventors personally. Note that in *HTC v
Gemalto*,[25] Birss J held that if a person had acquired the whole beneficial interest
in the invention at the relevant time, than that was enough to claim priority from
the application relied upon.

Machinery exists both before the grant and after the grant of a patent for   **4-08**
determination as to whether any other person is entitled to the patent either alone
or jointly.[26]

The inventor

In order to determine who is the inventor, the following aspects have been   **4-09**
considered:

(1) The meaning of "inventor".
(2) The meaning of "invention" and the relevance of the claims.
(3) The relevance of an enabling disclosure.
(4) The relevance of validity.

(1) The meaning of "inventor" The 1977 Act defines the inventor as "the   **4-10**
actual deviser of the invention"[27] although no such definition exists in the EPC. The
relevant parts of the Patents Act 1977 (subss.7(2), 7(3) and 7(4)) are an exhaustive code for determining who is entitled to the grant of a patent.[28] Entitlement does
not depend on anything other than being the inventor (or then if necessary deriv-

---

[21] Per Lord Hoffmann, *Yeda Research and Development Co Ltd v Rhône-Poulenc Rorer International
Holdings Inc* (HL) [2007] UKHL 43, [2008] R.P.C. 1, at [33].
[22] EPC art.60(3) and PA 1977 s.7(4).
[23] See PA 1977 s.72(1)(b) and 72(2), as amended by the CDPA 1988 Sch.5 para.18.
[24] *Edwards Lifesciences v Cook Biotech* [2009] EWHC 1304, [2009] F.S.R. 27 (Pat) and see also *KCI
Licensing v Smith & Nephew* [2010] EWHC 1487, [2010] F.S.R. 31 (Pat). See also para.7-06, et seq.
[25] [2013] EWCH 1876 (Pat); [2014] R.P.C. 9, [134].
[26] See paras 4-35 to 4-58.
[27] PA 1977 s.7(3).
[28] *Yeda Research and Development Co Ltd v Rhône-Poulenc Rorer International Holdings Inc* (HL)

ing entitlement from the inventor). There is no justification, in a dispute over who was the inventor, to import questions of whether one claimant has some personal cause of action against the other.[29]

4-11   **(2) The meaning of "invention" and the relevance of the claims** Section 125 of the 1977 Act provides that an invention is to be taken as that specified in a claim (as purposively interpreted) unless the context otherwise requires. However the question of entitlement can arise before any application for a patent has been made or on the basis of an application which has been filed without any claims. Further, where there is an application, the scope of the claims may change during prosecution. The Court of Appeal considered this point in *Markem Corporation v Zipher Ltd*[30] where Jacob LJ concluded that s.125 did not apply and stated[31]:

> "100. So what then about s.8? Does "invention" there mean what is claimed or does the context otherwise require? We think it must have some more general meaning than what is in the claims. The most obvious reason for that is that s.8 applies to situations where there are no claims at all—indeed even prior to a patent application. And applications themselves are not required to have claims. The question of entitlement can therefore arise before any claims exist—and in principle must remain the same whatever claims later emerge. Moreover, as the Deputy Judge observed, it is often the practice of patent agents to put in first drafts of claims which are wider than they expect to end up with so as to draw a wide search. As for the final claims in the patent as granted, their form and content will depend upon a number of individual factors—what has turned up in the prior art forcing reduction in scope, what subsidiary claims the patent agent has formulated based on the description and what monopoly is actually thought to be valuable (there is no point in claiming wider).
>
> 101. Accordingly we think one is driven to the conclusion that s.8 is referring essentially to information in the specification rather than the form of the claims. It would be handy if one could go by the claims, but one cannot. S.8 calls for identification of information and their rights in it. Who contributed what and what rights if any they had in it lies at the heart of the inquiry, not what monopolies were actually claimed."

4-12   The House of Lords in *Yeda*[32] disapproved of a different aspect of the reasoning in *Markem*,[33] the reasoning above was not doubted and stands as good law. It is thus necessary to determine what the heart of the invention disclosed is and this is frequently referred to as the inventive concept. Earlier, in *Henry Brothers (Magherafelt) Ltd v Ministry of Defence*,[34] the Court of Appeal had held that the inventive concept had to be identified and this reasoning has been developed in subsequent cases.[35] As Lord Hoffmann said in *Yeda*, "it is not enough that someone contributed to the claims, because they may include non-patentable integers derived from prior art."[36] No doubt, particularly in the case of a granted patent, the claims will assist in determining (if not be determinative of) the inventive concept but the existence of claims cannot serve to restrict the enquiry. In some cases there may

[2007] UKHL 43, [2008] R.P.C. 1.
[29] *Yeda Research and Development Co Ltd v Rhône-Poulenc Rorer International Holdings Inc* (HL) [2007] UKHL 43, [2008] R.P.C. 1, [21].
[30] [2005] EWCA (Civ) 267, [2005] R.P.C. 31.
[31] At [100] and [101].
[32] *Yeda Research and Development Co Ltd v Rhône-Poulenc Rorer International Holdings Inc* (HL) [2007] UKHL 43; [2008] R.P.C. 1.
[33] [2005] EWCA (Civ) 267; [2005] R.P.C. 31.
[34] [1999] R.P.C. 442.
[35] See *Collag Corp v Merck & Co Inc* [2003] F.S.R. 16, 263, *University of Southampton's Applications* [2005] R.P.C. 11, 220, *Stanelco Fibre Optics Ltd's Applications* [2005] R.P.C. 15, 319.
[36] *Yeda Research and Development Co Ltd v Rhône-Poulenc Rorer International Holdings Inc* (HL) [2007] UKHL 43, [2008] R.P.C. 1, [20].

be more than one inventive concept, and care must be taken in considering subsidiary claims to determine whether the added features constitute part of the same inventive concept or whether a separate inventive concept is disclosed.[37]

(3) The relevance of an enabling disclosure Difficult questions can arise when   **4-13**
the subject matter of a patent derives from more than one source. Those who contribute enough information by way of necessary enablement to make an otherwise non-enabling idea patentable would count as "actual devisors" of an invention and therefore as joint inventors.[38] However, by contrast in a case in which devisor of the idea was not a person acquainted with the art and the contribution from a second person was no more than the common general knowledge in that art, the second person's contribution did not make them an "actual devisor".[39] There is a distinction between devising an invention and providing an enabling disclosure:

> "In my view, devising an invention and providing an enabling disclosure are two quite different things. Although both may be necessary to secure valid protection, as s.14 of the Act shows, they relate to different aspects of the law of patents. It is very possible to make a good invention but to lose one's patent for failure to make an enabling disclosure. The requirement to include an enabling disclosure is concerned with teaching the public how the invention works, not with devising the invention in the first place."[40]

Hence, determination of who are the devisers of an invention for the purposes   **4-14**
of s.7 does not involve a purely mechanistic approach. In some cases the sole deviser will be the person having the original idea with the embodiment of the idea, once had, being purely routine.[41] In other cases it will not be clear until the idea has been reduced to practice whether it is feasible.[42]

(4) The relevance of validity In determining what are the inventive concepts   **4-15**
embodied within a disclosure, whether it be before an application is made or as a result of considering an application or a patent, no full scale enquiry into the validity of a patent granted in respect of such concepts should be undertaken. However, the Comptroller is given a wide discretion as to the relief which can be granted in entitlement proceedings and it would be wrong for relief to be granted naming a party as the inventor in circumstances where it is plain that no patent for that invention could validly be granted.

Jacob LJ in *Markem* expressed the matter thus[43]:   **4-16**

> "87. This brings us to the next point. Mr Watson [Counsel for Markem] submits that under s.8 the

---

[37] See *Stanelco Fibre Optics Ltd's Applications* [2005] R.P.C. 15, 319, [83]–[84].
[38] *University of Southampton's Application* (CA) [2006] EWCA Civ 145, [2006] R.P.C. 21 see [37]–[39] of the judgment of Jacob LJ.
[39] *University of Southampton's Application* (CA) [2006] EWCA Civ 145, [2006] R.P.C. 21 see [37]–[39] of the judgment of Jacob LJ.
[40] This was [46] of the judgment of Laddie J in *University of Southampton's Application* [2004] EWHC 2107 (Pat), [2005] R.P.C. 11. Although an appeal to the Court of Appeal was allowed in that case, this passage was approved in *Synthon BV v SmithKline Beecham Plc* [2005] UKHL 59 at [28] and see also *University of Southampton's Application* (CA) [2006] EWCA Civ 145, [2006] R.P.C. 21, [38].
[41] See, e.g. *Stanelco Fibre Optics Ltd's Applications* [2005] R.P.C. 15, [14]–[18] and [71]–[82].
[42] See, e.g. *Markem Corp v Zipher Ltd* [2005] EWCA (Civ) 267, [2005] R.P.C. 31, [36]–[38].
[43] *Markem Corp v Zipher Ltd* [2005] EWCA (Civ) 267, [2005] R.P.C. 31, [82] and [88]. This reasoning was not affected by the House of Lords in *Yeda Research and Development Co Ltd v Rhône-Poulenc Rorer International Holdings Inc* (HL) [2007] UKHL 43, [2008] R.P.C. 1. As confirmed by Floyd J in *Welland v Hadley* [2011] EWHC 1994 (Pat).

validity of the patent is completely irrelevant. The only question is: who is entitled? Mr Thorley [Counsel for Zipher] accepted that s.8 proceedings cannot turn into a full-scale inquiry into validity in a difficult case but that where an unanswerable case of validity was raised, the Comptroller can act upon it. He drew an analogy with proceedings for amendment of a patent where a roving inquiry into validity is not permitted but one can inquire as to whether a proposed amendment dealt with the reason advanced for making it. *Great Lakes Carbon's Patent* [1971] R.P.C. 117.

88.   We have no doubt that Mr Thorley is right. If the patent or part of it is clearly and unarguably invalid, then we see no reason why as a matter of convenience, the Comptroller should not take it into account in exercising his wide discretion. The sooner an obviously invalid monopoly is removed the better from the public point of view. But we emphasise that the attack on validity should be clear and unarguable. Only when there is self-evidently no bone should the dogs be prevented from fighting over it."

4-17   These considerations are practical in nature and do not go to the underlying jurisdiction under the Act. For example in *LIFFE v Pinkava* the dispute concerned entitlement to US patents for inventions which were unpatentable under the Act under s.1(2)(c).[44]

Persons claiming through the inventor (s.7(2)(b) and (c))

The requirement of causation

4-18   A person claiming to be entitled to an invention devised by another (the inventor) must demonstrate a relevant connection between him and the inventor. There must be relevant "causation" or nexus.[45] Accordingly person claiming to be entitled to an invention devised by another cannot succeed merely on the basis that he devised the invention first.

4-19   Since English law, in common with the laws of most other countries except the USA proceeds on a "first to file" rather than a "first to invent" basis, it is possible for a person who actually devises an invention first to be refused a patent because a third party, who devised the same invention later, applied for a patent first. In these circumstances, the earlier deviser is left to the limited protection provided by s.64 of the Act.[46] No question of entitlement arises in that case.[47]

Assignment of right to a patent

4-20   The inventor's right to a patent is subject to any assignment before[48] or after[49] making the invention or to any other enactment, rule of law, treaty or international

---

44   [2007] EWCA Civ 217; [2007] R.P.C. 30. See [2] and [88]–[89]. At [89] Jacob LJ records that the parties had agreed that for the purposes of the relevant provisions of the Act (the employer/ employee provisions in PA 1977 ss.39–43) the innovations in question were "inventions" and holds that the parties were probably right to do so.

45   See *Stanelco Fibre Optics Ltd's Applications* [2005] R.P.C. 15, 319, [21]; *Markem Corp v Zipher Ltd* [2005] EWCA (Civ) 267, [2005] R.P.C. 31, [31] and [77]; and *Yeda Research and Development Co Ltd v Rhône-Poulenc Rorer International Holdings Inc* (HL) [2007] UKHL 43, [2008] R.P.C. 1, [28].

46   See para.14-199.

47   *Yeda Research and Development Co Ltd v Rhône-Poulenc Rorer International Holdings Inc* (HL) [2007] UKHL 43, [2008] R.P.C. 1, [28].

48   PA 1977 s.7(2)(b).

49   PA 1977 s.7(2)(c).

convention.[50] In *KCI Licensing v Smith & Nephew*[51] Arnold J considered PA 1977 s.7(2)(b) and held that it is possible to assign the legal title (and not just the beneficial interest) in an invention before it is made, rejecting the submission that a purported assignment of a future invention only took effect as an agreement to assign.

The successors in title of an inventor or assignee or person otherwise entitled to the patent are themselves entitled to the grant of the patent.[52] If the inventor is an employee then the right to the grant of a European patent shall be determined in accordance with the law in the state in which the employee is mainly employed or, if not known, then the law of the state in which the employer has their place of business.[53] In the United Kingdom, the position of employees is governed by s.39 of the 1977 Act (see para.4-22). **4-21**

Employees' inventions

Section 39 of the 1977 Act governs the entitlement as between employer and employee to inventions made by an employee. The section only applies if the employee was mainly employed in the UK when he made the invention,[54] or else if the employer had a place of business in the UK to which the employee was attached and the employee was not mainly employers anywhere or his place of employment could not be determined.[55] The section applies to foreign patents as well as UK patents.[56] **4-22**

An invention made by an employee shall be taken to belong to the employer if, but only if: **4-23**

(a) it was made in the course of the normal duties of the employee or in the course of duties specifically assigned to him (but outside his normal duties) and the circumstances in either case were such that an invention might reasonably be expected to result therefrom[57];

(b) it was made in the course of the duties of the employee which duties were such as to give rise to a special obligation to further the interests of the employer's undertaking.[58]

Where s.39(1) applies, there can be no question of the employee retaining beneficial ownership against the employer.[59] Ownership as between employer and employee is governed by the Act and not by contract.[60] **4-24**

---

50 PA 1977 s.7(2)(b).
51 [2010] EWHC 1487 (Pat), see [67]. And see *HTC v Gemalto* [2013] EWCH 1876 (Pat); [2014] R.P.C. 9.
52 PA 1977 s.7(2)(c); and EPC art.60(1).
53 EPC art.60.
54 PA 1977 s.43(2)(a). The same provisions apply to employee's compensation, see below para.5-50.
55 PA 1977 s.43(2)(b). The same provisions apply to employee's compensation, see below para.5-50.
56 PA 1977 s.43(4). The same provisions apply to employee's compensation, see below para.5-50.
57 PA 1977 s.39(1)(a).
58 PA 1977 s.39(1)(b).
59 *French v Mason* [1999] F.S.R. 597.
60 *LIFFE v Pinkava* [2007] EWCA Civ 217; [2007] R.P.C. 30.

Normal and specifically assigned duties—s.39(1)(a)

4-25   Section 39(1)(a) was reviewed in detail by the Court of Appeal in *LIFFE v Pinkava*.[61] In that case the trial judge had found on the facts that the employee (Pinkava) had been employed by LIFFE to devise new products of a certain type (but not of the type in question), that on December 2003 LIFFE had assigned to Pinkava a further task to consider how to develop products of the relevant kind and in July 2004 Pinkava had made the inventions. Pinkava claimed that the inventions belong to him and not his employer. The judge held that the inventions had not been made in the course of Pinkava's normal duties but had been made in the course of duties specifically assigned to him.[62] The trial judge also held that the circumstances were such that an invention might reasonably be expected to result and thus found for LIFFE. Both sides appealed. The Court of Appeal held unanimously that the inventions were made in the course of Pinkava's normal duties and otherwise upheld the trial judge. On one point Jacob LJ gave a dissenting judgment which did not affect the overall outcome. The following propositions on s.39(1)(a) emerge from the Court of Appeal:

(a)   The collection of sections in the 1977 Act dealing with employees' inventions are more favourable to the employee than the previous common law rules and there is no reason to interpret s.39(1)(a) by reference to those rules.[63]

(b)   "Normal" and "specifically assigned" duties are mutually exclusive. Unless the invention was made under a duty falling within one or other description, s.39(1)(a) cannot apply and the invention will belong to the employee.[64]

(c)   The key question was what was it that the employee was employed to do? The section focuses on the employee's "duties", i.e. obligations. The primary source of a duty is the contract of employment.[65]

(d)   However, the contract is not the sole arbiter of the duty. The contract and the general nature of the job call for examination. Contracts evolve and the actions of employer and employee over time can give rise to an expansion or contraction. In the end, one is asking whether an employee is employed to innovate and if so what general sort of area its innovation duties cover.[66]

(e)   The argument that normal duties meant "day to day" or "primary" duties was rejected. The test was not so limited.[67]

(f)   The relevant date was the date on which the invention was made and thus on the facts of the case the relevant date was July 2004. Accordingly given that the task of considering the relevant products had been assigned specifi-

---

[61]   [2007] EWCA Civ 217; [2007] R.P.C. 30.

[62]   [2006] EWHC 595 (Pat).

[63]   Per Chancellor Morritt, [74]–[77] [2007] EWCA Civ 217; [2007] R.P.C. 30, see also Jacob LJ, [92]. As a result Falconer J's decision in *Harris' Patent* [1985] R.P.C. 19 was disapproved.

[64]   Per Chancellor Morritt, [2007] EWCA Civ 217; [2007] R.P.C. 30, [56].

[65]   Per Chancellor Morritt, [2007] EWCA Civ 217, [56] and Jacob LJ, [2007] EWCA Civ 217; [2007] R.P.C. 30, [97].

[66]   Per Chancellor Morritt, [56] and Jacob LJ [2007] EWCA Civ 217; [2007] R.P.C. 30, [98]–[99]. Cf. *Greater Glasgow Health Board's Application* [1996] R.P.C. 207 in which the court considered what the employee did as well as what his contract said he ought to do.

[67]   Per Chancellor Morritt, [57] and Jacob LJ, [2007] EWCA Civ 217; [2007] R.P.C. 30, [97].

cally to Pinkava in December 2003, by July 2004 it had become part of his normal duties.[68]

(g) For the section to apply the reasonable expectation test must also be satisfied.[69] This was not concerned with whether the particular invention was foreseeable but was addressed to whether "an invention" in general terms might result from the work.[70]

The majority in *Pinkava v LIFFE* (Chancellor Morritt and Longmore LJ) also held that the particular attributes of the employee in question were relevant to the reasonable expectation limb of s.39(1)(a).[71] The issue did not matter on the facts but Jacob LJ dissented on the point, questioning whether there can be a difference (all other things being equal) depending on whether the employee was thick or brilliant.[72]

4-26

Special obligation—s.39(1)(b)

Section 39(1)(b) was addressed by Falconer J in *Harris' Patent*.[73] This decision remains the only case on the point but it needs to be considered with care following *Pinkava v LIFFE*.[74] Falconer J held that two conditions had to be satisfied in relation to the special obligation limb of s.39(1), namely: (i) that the invention was made in the course of the duties of the employee; and (ii) that because of the nature of those duties and the particular responsibilities arising from the nature of those duties, a special obligation to further an employer's interests existed. With regard to condition (ii) Falconer J said, at 37:

4-27

"Under paragraph (b), the question is whether Mr Harris's duties were such as to place him under such 'a special obligation to further the interests of this employer's undertaking', in this case the valve business of Reiss Engineering. The wording of the paragraph, under condition (ii), clearly envisages that the extent and nature of the 'special obligation to further the interests of the employer's undertaking' will depend upon the status of the employee and the attendant duties and responsibilities of that status. Thus, plainly the position in this regard of a managing director whose obligation to further the interests of his employer's undertaking of which he is the managing director will, no doubt, extend across the whole spectrum of the activities of the undertaking, will differ from that of, say, a sales manager."

Where invention belongs to employer

Where the invention belongs to the employer, the employer should normally apply for the grant of the patent in his own name, the employee inventor having a right to be mentioned in any patent granted thereon.[75] Such an application must be accompanied by a statement of the employer's right to the grant of a patent and the name of the inventor(s).[76]

4-28

If the employee applies for the patent in his own name, he will hold it on trust

4-29

---

[68]   Per Chancellor Morritt, [2007] EWCA Civ 217; [2007] R.P.C. 30, [60].
[69]   Chancellor Morritt, [2007] EWCA Civ 217; [2007] R.P.C. 30, [71].
[70]   Chancellor Morritt, [73] and Jacob LJ, [2007] EWCA Civ 217; [2007] R.P.C. 30, [102].
[71]   Chancellor Morritt, [78] and Longmore LJ, [2007] EWCA Civ 217; [2007] R.P.C. 30, [86].
[72]   Jacob LJ, [2007] EWCA Civ 217; [2007] R.P.C. 30, [103].
[73]   [1985] R.P.C. 19. See *Staeng Ltd's Patents* [1996] R.P.C. 183 for a case before the Comptroller in which a special obligation was found to exist.
[74]   [2007] EWCA Civ 217; [2007] R.P.C. 30 see para.4–25.
[75]   PA 1977 s.13(1).
[76]   PA 1977 s.13(2); Patents Form Nos 1 and 7.

for the employer and can be ordered to transfer the same to the employer.[77] Alternatively, the employer may within two years[78] of the grant of the patent apply to revoke the same and make a fresh application for a patent which will be treated as having been filed on the date of filing of the earlier patent. Application may be made in the joint names of inventor and employee; however, this may encourage employees to seek compensation.[79]

Where the invention belongs to the employee—employee's immunity

4-30   By s.39(2)[80] of the 1977 Act where an invention belongs to an employee, any exploitation of that invention by the employee enjoys immunity from suit by the employer in respect of infringement of any copyright, or design right vested in the employer.

Convention application

4-31   A patent may also be applied for under the 1977 Act by a person resident abroad who has made an application in a convention country[81] for protection in respect of an invention equivalent to such application, and if such application is made within a period of 12 months from the date of the application in the convention country, the priority date of that invention will be the date of filing of the convention application provided it is supported by matter disclosed in the earlier convention application.[82] However, the persons entitled to the grant of such a patent are the same as a non-convention application under the 1977 Act.

Mention of inventor

4-32   The inventor(s) have the right to be mentioned as such in any granted patent or published application for a patent.[83] The counterpart of this is that an applicant who is not the sole/joint inventor(s) must make a statement on Patents Form No.7 identifying the inventor(s) and the derivation of the applicant's right to be granted the patent.[84] Such a statement must be made within 16 months after the declared priority date or, where there is no declared priority date, the date of filing the application.[85] Failure to make such a statement within the 16-month period will mean that the application will be taken to be withdrawn.[86]

4-33   An inventor may waive his right to be mentioned as inventor and, in those

---

[77] *Amplaudio Ltd v Snell* (1938) 55 R.P.C. 237; *Forte v Martinex* (1947) 64 R.P.C. 26.
[78] The period of two years does not apply if the person registered as proprietor of the patent knew he was not entitled to the patent: s.37(5) of the 1977 Act. PA 1977 ss.37(5) and 72(1)(b). Note that para.3(b) of the Schedule to the Intellectual Property Act 2014 (which came in to force on 1 October 2014) varies s.37(5) and changes the relevant period to the two-year anniversary of the date of grant, rather than one day prior to that, thereby adding a day.
[79] As to compensation of employees see ss.40 and 41 of the 1977 Act and para.5-50.
[80] Introduced by CDPA 1988 Sch.5 para.11.
[81] A convention country is one declared as such by Order Council (see s.90 of the 1977 Act). See also para.1-60.
[82] PA 1977 s.5(2), (4), (5).
[83] PA 1977 s.13(1).
[84] PA 1977 s.13(2); Patents Rules 2007 r.10(4).
[85] Patents Rules 2007 r.10(3).
[86] PA 1977 s.13(2).

circumstances, the Comptroller is not required to identify that inventor under s.24(3) of the Act.[87]

Machinery exists for disputing inventorship and the Comptroller has power to certify that any person was wrongly named as an inventor on an application by the true inventor or joint inventor.[88]   **4-34**

4. ENTITLEMENT PROCEEDINGS

Disputes often arise which relate to the ownership of rights in and under patents and related matters. The Comptroller and the courts may be called upon to decide such questions whether the subject-matter is a patent under the 1977 Act or otherwise. The questions may involve deciding the identity of the true inventors and determining the persons to whom a patent should be or should have been granted. The questions may also involve resolving as between co-applicants the manner in which a patent application should be handled; and resolving as between co-owners whether a licence should be granted to a third party. The jurisdictions as they relate to different types of question and different forms of patent and application are set out below. The Comptroller has a broad jurisdiction to resolve these matters and to grant appropriate relief. Nevertheless, the details of the jurisdiction are complex, especially in relation to European patent applications where the Comptroller and court exercise a jurisdiction provided for by the Protocol on Recognition[89] under the EPC.   **4-35**

In *Hughes v Paxman*[90] the Court of Appeal rejected a submission that the Comptroller's jurisdiction did not extend to determine whether a licence should be granted to a third party in a dispute between co-proprietors. Parliament could not have intended it to be possible that exploitation of an invention could be frustrated by a deadlock and the Comptroller did have the power to do so, acting rationally, fairly and proportionately.[91] The Comptroller's powers in such a case include ordering the sale of a patent as well.[92]   **4-36**

Entitlement jurisdiction

Jurisdiction concerning patents applied for under the 1977 Act

The Comptroller's power to decide questions of entitlement at any time before a UK national patent has been granted arises under s.8. This power exists whether or not an application has been made for a patent. By s.8(1)(a), the Comptroller may determine questions as to whether any person is entitled to be granted a patent or has, or would have, any right in or under any such patent or application.[93] Similarly, under s.8(1)(b), the Comptroller may decide on a reference by a co-proprietor   **4-37**

---

[87] PA 1977 s.24(3), as amended by PA 2004 s.16 Sch.2 para.9. PA 1977 s.13(3); Patents Rules 2007 r.10(2).

[88] PA 1977 s.24(3), as amended by PA 2004 s.16 Sch.2 para.9. PA 1977 s.13(3); Patents Rules 2007 r.10(2).

[89] Protocol on Jurisdiction and the Recognition of Decisions in Respect of the Right to the Grant of a European Patent, see App.E-142.

[90] [2006] EWCA (Civ) 818; [2007] R.P.C. 2.

[91] *Hughes v Paxman* [2006] EWCA (Civ) 818; [2007] R.P.C 2, [13] and [25].

[92] *Hughes v Paxman* [2006] EWCA (Civ) 818; [2007] R.P.C 2 para.17 and see *Florey's Patent* [1962] R.P.C. 186 for a case in which the same jurisdiction under the 1949 Patents Act.

[93] PA 1977 s.8(1)(a).

whether any right in or under the application should be transferred or granted to any person.[94]

4-38   Granting of a patent is not prevented by an application to decide questions of entitlement. The procedure under s.9 is that in the event that the entitlement proceedings are not determined before grant then the patent will be granted and the person referring the entitlement question will be treated as having done so under s.37 (see para.4-54). Alternatively, in an appropriate case the Comptroller may exercise the power under s.10 to delay grant until the matter is resolved.[95]

4-39   As a related matter, under s.13, the Comptroller has power to issue a certificate to correct any mention of a person as an inventor of an invention.[96] This will include a certificate to the effect that a person mentioned as inventor in a patent or published application ought not to have been so mentioned as well as a certificate to the effect that a person not mentioned as inventor ought to have been. The power relates to patents applied for under the 1977 Act and also applications for a European patent (UK)[97] and it arises once any person has been mentioned as inventor.[98]

Jurisdiction concerning other patents and applications

4-40   By s.12, the Comptroller has the power to hear and determine questions as to the entitlement[99] to patents applied for under the law of any country other than the United Kingdom or any treaty or international convention.[100] Broadly this includes both applications for European patents, international applications for UK national patents and other applications. But as regards European applications see paras 4-43 to 4-51, and as regards international applications see para.4-53. The limitation to s.12 to deciding questions "before a patent is granted" is important because there is no equivalent statutory power under the 1977 Act to decide entitlement after grant (though note that if a patent proceeds to grant during entitlement proceedings this does not extinguish the jurisdiction).[101] The Patents Court has an inherent jurisdiction to make declarations of right but the circumstances in which it might do so in relation to foreign intellectual property rights are limited.[102]

4-41   A recent example of the exercise of the s.12 jurisdiction was *LIFFE v Pinkava*[103] in which the court heard an entitlement case relating to certain US applications. Notably by s.43(4) of the 1977 Act, s.39 governed the question of whether the invention belonged to the employer or the employee and notably also the invention would have been unpatentable in the UK.

---

94   PA 1977 s.8(1)(b) and see *Hughes v Paxman* [2006] EWCA (Civ) 818; [2007] R.P.C. 2.
95   *Goddin and Rennie's Application* [1996] R.P.C. 141, 144.
96   PA 1977 s.13(3).
97   PA 1977 s.78(2).
98   PA 1977 s.13(3).
99   As with s.8, under s.12 a distinction is drawn between a determination whether any person is entitled to be granted a patent or has or would have any right in or under any such patent or application (s.12(1)(a)) and a reference by a co-proprietor whether any right in or under the application should be transferred or granted to any person (s.12(1)(b)).
100   See, e.g. *Canning's U.S. Application* [1992] R.P.C. 459.
101   *Innovia Films Ltd v Frito-Lay* [2012] EWHC; [2012] R.P.C. 24, [94]–[98].
102   In *Tyburn Productions v Conan Doyle* [1990] R.P.C. 185, Vinelott J held that the issue of entitlement to American copyright was not justiciable in the English courts but in *Pearce (Gareth) v Ove Arup* [1999] F.S.R. 525, CA, that decision was distinguished at least in relation to claims covered by the Brussels Convention. See also para.19-71. Note that s.12(2) confers a specific jurisdiction on the court to determine a question arising under s.12 which is referred to the court by the Comptroller.
103   [2007] EWCA Civ 217; [2007] R.P.C. 30. And see *Innovia Films v Frito-Lay* [2012] EWHC [2012] R.P.C. 24.

Arnold J considered the court's jurisdiction under s.12 in *Innovia v Frito-Lay*.[104] That case concerned, inter alia, pending US applications. The judge found that s.12 conferred subject-matter jurisdiction but not of itself personal jurisdiction over a defendant. Furthermore, even if personal jurisdiction could be established, the court could still decline that jurisdiction on forum non conveniens grounds. Considering the latter point, the judge accepted that the fact that international priority was claimed from filings in a non-EPC country (i.e. the USA) might be a factor pointing away from the court exercising its jurisdiction. However, it was not a determinative factor and on the facts did not prevail.[105] The court was therefore prepared to determine entitlement in relation to the US applications. However, as the court also found that there was a substantive rule of US law preventing a challenge to inventorship until grant, there could be no claim to entitlement until grant.[106]

Jurisdiction concerning European patents

The EPO does not decide who is entitled to the grant of a European patent. Once a dispute has arisen as to the person entitled to the grant of a European patent, the EPO has power to stay the prosecution of the European application until the matter is resolved.[107] If before grant by a final decision it is adjudged that a person other than the applicant is entitled to the grant, the EPO has power to substitute the successful claimant as applicant, or allow them to file a new application or refuse the existing application.[108]

The UK jurisdiction to determine entitlement in relation to European patents before grant is governed by the provisions of s.82 of the 1977 Act, a provision which is framed so as to have as nearly as practicable the same effect as the EPC itself[109] and the Protocol on Recognition.[110] The purpose of the Protocol on Recognition is to provide a scheme amongst the contracting states of the EPC under which questions of entitlement can be determined by national authorities.

This is required because the EPO itself has no means for determining such disputes and the Protocol is also intended to avoid conflicts of jurisdiction between authorities of different contracting states.

The jurisdiction conferred on the Comptroller and the court does not depend on whether or not the European application in question designates the United Kingdom. The provisions of s.82 are exclusive and oust any other power the court or the Comptroller might have had to decide such questions in relation to European patents before grant.[111] The issues to which s.82 applies are questions as to whether a person has the right to be granted a European patent or a share in it.[112]

The jurisdiction under art.82 is exclusive. Thus if the UK court has jurisdiction (for example under art.82(4)(b), by reason of the residences/places of business of

4-42

4-43

4-44

4-45

4-46

4-47

---

104 *Innovia Films Ltd v Frito-Lay*, at [87]–[98].
105 *Innovia Films Ltd v Frito-Lay*, at [90].
106 *Innovia Films Ltd v Frito-Lay*, at [93].
107 EPC Rules r.14.
108 EPC art.61.
109 PA 1977 s.130(7). And see Arnold J's analysis in *Innovia v Frito-Lay* [2012] EWHC 790 (Pat); [2012] R.P.C. 24, at [33]–[36].
110 PA 1977 s.130(6) includes protocols—such as the Protocol on Recognition—within the definition of the EPC used in s.130(7).
111 PA 1977 s.82(1)—the court; and s.82(2)—the Comptroller.
112 PA 1977 s.82(3).

the parties) it is to the exclusion of all other courts (regardless of whether they are in convention or non-convention countries).[113] A consequence of this is that where jurisdiction is is founded on arts 3 or 4 of Brussels I, the court can not decline jurisdiction and/or grant a stay so far as it relates to European applications on forum non conveniens grounds.[114] Whilst the court has, in principle, the ability to grant a stay on case management grounds, it is clear that it is unlikely to do so, particularly if this would achieve no more than a forum non conveniens stay by the backdoor.[115]

4-48   Jurisdiction on the court or Comptroller can be conferred by agreement. Furthermore, it is possible for the parties to agree to submit to the jurisdiction of a contracting state other than the UK.[116] The question of submission to the jurisdiction of the UKIPO was considered by HHJ Hacon in *Future New Developments v B&S*.[117] Here a German domiciled registered proprietor challenged the jurisdiction of the UKIPO to hear an entitlement dispute concerning a European Patent. Rejecting the challenge on the facts, HHJ Hacon found that the UKIPO was a court for the purposes of Brussels I and a party by putting in an appearance at the UKIPO could (per art.24 of Brussels I) therefore submit to its jurisdiction.[118] However, when considering jurisdiction in an entitlement dispute, art.5(3) of Brussels I (and therefore the relevance of the country of domicile of the party) was not engaged.

4-49   In the absence of agreement, if the question to be decided is one between an employer and employee, arising out of an application for a European patent for an invention made by an employee,[119] then the Comptroller has jurisdiction in the following circumstances:

(a)   if the employee is mainly employed in the United Kingdom[120]; or

(b)   if the employer has a place of business in the United Kingdom and the employee is not mainly employed anywhere or his main place of employment cannot be determined.[121]

4-50   In the absence of agreement, if the question is not an "employer-employee question"[122] then the Comptroller has jurisdiction in the following circumstances:

(a)   if the applicant for the European patent has his residence or principal place of business in the United Kingdom[123]; or

(b)   if the applicant for the European patent does not have his residence nor principal place of business in any Contracting State of the EPC, but the party

---

[113] *Innovia v Frito-Lay* [2012] EWHC 790 (Pat); [2012] R.P.C. 24, [48]–[76].*Conductive Inkjet Technology v Uni-Pixel* [2013] EWHC 2968 (Ch) [2014] F.S.R. 22, 78–83

[114] *Innovia v Frito-Lay* [2012] EWHC 790 (Pat); [2012] R.P.C. 24, at [77]–[85]. *Conductive Injet v Uni-Pixel* [2013] EWHC 2968 (Ch); [2014] F.S.R. 22, [78]–[88].

[115] *Conductive Injet v Uni-Pixel* [2013] EWHC 2968 (Ch); [2014] F.S.R. 22, [90]–[94]. *Innovia v Frito-Lay* [2012] EWHC 790 (Pat); [2012] R.P.C. 24, [86] and [127]–[134].

[116] PA 1977 s.82(6) and see Protocol on Recognition art.5. This provision is subject to a proviso that there is "written evidence" of the agreement. Further in the case of an employee, the law of the employment contract must recognise the validity of the agreement (Protocol on Recognition art.5(2)). See also *Kakkar v Szelke* [1988] F.S.R. 97 and [1989] F.S.R. 225; and also *Duijnstee v Lodeewijk Goderbauer* [1985] F.S.R. 221, ECJ; [1985] 1 C.M.L.R. 220. The two decisions cannot be easily reconciled.

[117] [2014] EWHC 1874 (IPEC); [2015] F.S.R. 15.

[118] Council Regulation (EC) 44/2001.

[119] Referred to as an "employer-employee" question, PA 1977 s.82(3) and (5).

[120] PA 1977 s.82(5)(a) and see the Protocol on Recognition art.4 and EPC art.60(1).

[121] PA 1977 s.82(5)(b); and see Protocol on Recognition art.4; and EPC art.60(1).

[122] Defined in PA 1977 s.82(3).

[123] PA 1977 s.82(4)(a); and see Protocol on Recognition art.2.

claiming that the patent should be granted to him has his residence or principal place of business in the United Kingdom.[124]

The Protocol on Recognition provides that the courts of the Federal Republic of Germany shall have exclusive jurisdiction in cases where none of the above provisions apply.[125] Provisions also exist to deal with the possibility of a reference of a question of entitlement to the Comptroller or the court in the United Kingdom at a time when the same question has already been referred to the competent authority of another relevant contracting state.[126] Essentially the Comptroller or the court must stay the proceedings before them until the foreign authority has either decided the matter or declined jurisdiction.[127] Once the foreign authority has decided the matter the stay will be lifted if the foreign court's determination is one which the English court or Comptroller refuses to recognise under s.83.[128] If the foreign court's determination is one which the English court or Comptroller will recognise under s.83 then that decision will be binding in the UK.[129]

4-51

Stay procedure adopted by EPO

The procedure the EPO adopts when a dispute arises is to stay proceedings ex officio if a third party provides proof that entitlement proceedings have been started. The patentee will not be heard at this stage but may ask the EPO Legal Division to lift the stay.[130] Since a decision by the Examining Division to grant a patent does not take effect until the grant is published in the European Patent Bulletin, a request for suspension in that interim period is admissible and the EPO has in such cases suspended the grant of the patent.[131]

4-52

Jurisdiction concerning international applications

During the international phase of an international application made under the PCT, an application is treated as a foreign or convention application (regardless of whether it is or includes a designation of the UK and regardless of whether the UK Patent Office has received the application as the receiving office) such that s.12 ap-

4-53

---

[124] PA 1977 s.82(4)(b); and see Protocol on Recognition art.3.
[125] Protocol on Recognition art.6.
[126] Defined as a Contracting State to the EPC which has not exercised the right to exclude the application of the Protocol on Recognition (PA 1977 s.82(9)).
[127] PA 1977 s.82(7). This provision is intended to mirror art.8 of the Protocol on Recognition but the scheme is not quite the same. The Protocol (art.8) always requires the court to decline jurisdiction of its own motion in the event that the same question between the same parties has already been referred to another court unless that other court declines jurisdiction. There is no analogue to s.82(7)(b) which provides for a stay even if the other court has not declined jurisdiction.
[128] PA 1977 s.83(2) sets out the grounds on which recognition may be refused. Recognition may be refused if the applicant did not contest the proceedings either because he was not notified of them properly or at all or not in sufficient time to allow him to contest them (s.83(2)(a)). Recognition may also be refused if the determination conflicts with an earlier determination between the same parties in a relevant court (s.83(2)(b)). See arts 9 and 10 of the Protocol on Recognition.
[129] PA 1977 s.83(1).
[130] EPC Rules r.14 and see J28/94 O.J. EPO 1997, 400.
[131] EPC Rules r.14 and see J7/96 *Instance/Labels* O.J. EPO 1999, 443.

plies to any entitlement dispute and s.8 does not.[132] Conversely, after the end of the international phase, s.8 applies but s.12 does not.[133]

Jurisdiction concerning granted patents

4-54
After a patent has been granted, s.37 provides the power by which the Comptroller may decide who is or are the true proprietor(s)[134]; whether the patent should have been granted to the person(s) to whom it was granted[135]; and whether any right in or under the patent should be transferred or granted to a third party.[136] This jurisdiction applies to patents granted under the 1977 Act[137] and also to granted European patents (UK).[138]

4-55
In *Cinpres Gas Injection Ltd v Melea*,[139] the Court of Appeal held that the jurisdiction under s.8 (pre-grant) and s.37 (post-grant) concerning the corresponding applications and patents related to the same cause of action. The significance of this decision was that it formed part of a judgment to set aside an earlier judgment in entitlement proceedings as having been obtained by fraud.

Comptroller declining to deal with a case

4-56
Sections 8, 12 and 37 of the 1977 Act all provide that the Comptroller may decline to deal with a question referred to him under these provisions if the question would more properly be dealt with by the Patents Court. There is a difference in the provision in s.37(8) as compared to ss.8(7) and 12(2) and care is needed to approach the provisions correctly although there is no reported case in which the distinction made a difference.[140] The Comptroller is the arbiter of which forum was more appropriate.[141] A decision of the Comptroller's not to decline to deal with an entitlement case of some complexity was overturned on appeal to the Patents Court in *Luxim v Ceravision*[142] although in its application of the law to the facts the case was decided at a time when the rather complex approach to entitlement in *Markem v Zipher*[143] was thought to be good law, before *Yeda*[144] in the House of Lords.

The court's jurisdiction

4-57
The court has its own jurisdiction to make binding declarations of right[145] but in the case of granted patents this jurisdiction is ousted by s.37(9) in proceedings com-

---

132 PA 1977 s.89B(4).
133 PA 1977 s.89B(4).
134 PA 1977 s.37(1)(a).
135 PA 1977 s.37(1)(b).
136 PA 1977 s.37(1)(c) and see *Hughes v Paxman* [2006] EWCA (Civ) 818; [2007] R.P.C. 2.
137 PA 1977 s.37(1).
138 PA 1977 s.77(1).
139 [2008] EWCA Civ 9, [2008] R.P.C. 17.
140 See *Luxim v Ceravision* [2007] EWHC 1624 (Ch), [2007] R.P.C. 33, [5] and [18].
141 *Luxim v Ceravision* [2007] EWHC 1624 (Ch), [2007] R.P.C. 33, [63]. Note also that the approach to this issue in *Baldwin's Patent* [1998] R.P.C. 415 was disapproved at [14]–[20].
142 [2007] EWHC 1624 (Ch), [2007] R.P.C. 33.
143 *Markem Corp v Zipher Ltd* [2005] EWCA (Civ) 267, [2005] R.P.C. 31.
144 *Yeda Research and Development Co Ltd v Rhône-Poulenc Rorer International Holdings Inc* (HL) [2007] UKHL 43, [2008] R.P.C. 1.
145 CPR r.40.20.

menced after two years from the date of grant.[146] Section 82 confers on the court a parallel jurisdiction in relation to applications for European patents as is conferred on the Comptroller.[147] Note also that a party cannot challenge ownership in a patent action after judgment is given and an enquiry ordered (because the court is functus).[148]

Handling joint applications

4-58   The Comptroller also has power to give such directions as he thinks fit for enabling an application to proceed if a dispute arises between joint applicants for a patent. The power relates both to patents applied for under the 1977 Act[149] and also any other applications.[150]

Burden of proof in entitlement proceedings

4-59   The 1977 Act provides that "except so far as the contrary is established" a person who makes an application for a patent shall be taken to be the person entitled.[151] The effect of this provision is that the person who seeks to be added as joint inventor bears the burden of proving that he contributed to the inventive concept while a person seeking to be substituted as the sole inventor bears the additional burden of proving that the named inventor did not make such a contribution.[152]

Procedure

4-60   The procedure concerning references to the Comptroller under ss.8, 12 and 37 follows the normal Patent Office scheme.[153] The proceedings are commenced by a form and a statement of grounds.[154] The statement of grounds must include a concise statement of the facts and grounds relied on and specify the remedy sought.[155] A copy of the form and statement are sent to all other persons concerned.[156] In doing so the Comptroller will specify a period within which a counterstatement may be filed.[157] The Comptroller will send a copy of the counter-statement to the appropriate persons.[158] If the counter-statement has been filed the

---

[146] Unless it is shown that the person registered as proprietor knew he was not entitled to the patent (PA 1977 s.37(9)). See also *Christopher French v Paul Mason* [1999] F.S.R. 597, an action for a declaration of trust in relation to certain patents.

[147] PA 1977 s.82(4), (5) and (6).

[148] *KCI Licensing v Smith & Nephew*, unreported, 1 March 2012.

[149] PA 1977 s.10.

[150] PA 1977 s.12(4). Note that this provision excludes the power to regulate the manner in which such an application to proceed and is therefore in effect limited to deciding only whether an application should proceed.

[151] PA 1977 s.7(4).

[152] Per Lord Hoffmann at [21] in *Yeda Research and Development Co Ltd v Rhône-Poulenc Rorer International Holdings Inc* (HL) [2007] UKHL 43, [2008] R.P.C. 1.

[153] See Patents Rules 2007 r.76. And see the *Patent Hearings Manual* available on the Patent Office website.

[154] Patents Rules 2007 r.76(1). The relevant form is Patents Form 2, see Patents Rules 2007 r.76(3)(b) and Sch.3 Pt. 1.

[155] Patents Rules 2007 r.76(4)(a) and (d).

[156] Patents Rules 2007 r.77.

[157] Patents Rules 2007 r.77(5).

[158] Patents Rules 2007 r.80(1)(a).

Comptroller will specify dates by which any evidence is to be filed.[159] Also once the counter-statement has been filed, the claimant must decide whether to continue the proceedings and if he wishes to do so filed Patents Form 4.[160]

4-61   The Comptroller has power to extend or shorten the above time periods if he thinks fit upon such notice to the parties and upon such terms as he may direct.[161]

4-62   The Comptroller will give the parties an opportunity to be heard[162] and if a hearing is requested the Comptroller will give notice of the date to the parties.[163]

4-63   The status of hearsay evidence in Patent Office proceedings[164] is governed by the Civil Evidence Act 1995. Accordingly, no separate hearsay notice is required in relation to witness statements, statutory declarations or affidavits filed as evidence before the Comptroller,[165] however if hearsay evidence is contained within such a statement it should be filed in sufficient time and should contain sufficient particulars to enable the other party to deal with it.

4-64   The Comptroller may exercise all the powers of a judge of the High Court in relation to the attendance of witnesses and the disclosure and production of documents,[166] save for the power to punish summarily for contempt of court.[167] The Comptroller also has power to order security for costs in certain circumstances.[168] By the amended provisions the Comptroller can now order security for costs against a company where there is reason to believe that it will be unable to pay another party's costs.[169]

4-65   Contemporaneous documentary evidence is of the highest importance in cases of this kind and parties should make every effort to present such material in their evidence.

The hearing

4-66   Entitlement proceedings are usually decided after an oral hearing before a Divisional Director or Deputy Director acting for the Comptroller. The Hearing Officer will generally expect Skeleton Arguments to be lodged at least two days before the date of the hearing, together with authorities.[170] The hearing will consist of submissions by the parties' representatives and may involve hearing oral evidence from live witnesses. When, as is often the case in entitlement proceedings, the written evidence contains testimony as to matters of primary fact which are in dispute, the only proper means by which these disputes can be resolved is by cross-examination of the witnesses on their statements. The policy of the Patent Office in relation to cross-examination is that in the absence of a request for cross-examination, it will not take place. However, if cross-examination is requested it

---

[159] Patents Rules 2007 r.80(1)(b).
[160] Patents Rules 2007 r.80(1A).
[161] Patents Rules 2007 r.81.
[162] Patents Rules 2007 r.80(4).
[163] Patents Rules 2007 r.80(5).
[164] Except in Scotland.
[165] *Patent Office Practice Note on Evidence* [1999] R.P.C. 294. And see the *Patent Hearings Manual*, paras 3.87–3.90.
[166] Patents Rules 2007 r.86.
[167] Patents Rules 2007 r.86.
[168] PA 1977 s.107(4), as amended by PA 2004 s.15 in respect of proceedings commenced on or after 1 October 2005. See also Patent Rules 2007 r.85.
[169] See Patent Rules 2007 r.85(1)(b), reversing *Abdulhayoglu's Application* [2000] R.P.C. 18.
[170] *Patent Hearings Manual*, para.4.65.

will be allowed save in exceptional cases.[171] Reasonable notice of a desire to cross-examine in advance of a hearing ought to be given, with four weeks' notice being regarded as the minimum.[172]

The decision

A written decision is usually handed down within a few weeks of the hearing. In order to avoid the need for a further hearing, the parties should, if possible, indicate what orders and other relief they are seeking at the conclusion of the main hearing and make any submissions as to costs. However, the question of what relief should be granted, particularly in cases where the decision concludes that some inventive concepts belong to one party and others to another, may be exceedingly complicated and a further hearing may be necessary.[173]

4-67

Relief

Under ss.8, 12 and 37 of the 1977 Act, the Comptroller is given the widest possible discretion as to the order he may make to give effect to his determination. Sections 8(1), 12(1) and 37(1) each empower the Comptroller to make "such order as he shall see fit". Subsection (2) of each of those sections go on to give examples of the type of order which may be made but this is expressly said to be "without prejudice to the generality" of subs.(1). The correct relief therefore must depend upon the facts of each particular case. In an appropriate case, the Comptroller may substitute one name of an applicant for another, refuse the application, require appropriate amendments or make an order transferring or granting any licence or other right in or under the application.[174] In addition to such powers, in accordance with ss.8(3), 12(6) and 37(4) and subject to the limitations imposed therein, the Comptroller may by order permit the person who is held to be entitled to a part or the whole of the patent when granted to make a new application in respect thereof within three months from the expiry of time for appealing from the Comptroller's order or where appeal is brought from the day on which it is finally disposed of.[175] Furthermore, there are provisions for safeguarding those original applicants (and licensees of the original applicants) who are held not to be entitled to the grant of the patent, but who before registration of a reference under ss.8, 12 or 37 in good faith worked the invention in this country or made effective and serious preparations to do so.[176] These provisions correspond in part to those of s.64[177] and other sections of the 1977 Act[178] and provide protection for acts carried out in good faith prior to the commencement of the entitlement proceedings. Equivalent protection is available to those granted licences under patents or patent applications prior to

4-68

[171] *Peckitt's Application* [1999] R.P.C. 337.
[172] See the *Patents Hearings Manual*, paras 4.72–4.73.
[173] See, for example, *Markem Corp v Zipher Ltd (No.3)* [2005] R.P.C. 3; see also the editor's note at the conclusion of *Norris' Patent* [1988] R.P.C. 159, 176.
[174] See *Norris' Patent* [1988] R.P.C. 159; *Viziball's Application* [1988] R.P.C. 213; and *Markem Corp v Zipher Ltd (No.3)* [2005] R.P.C. 3.
[175] Patents Rules 2007 r.20; and see *Amateur Athletic Association's Application* [1989] R.P.C. 717.
[176] PA 1977 ss.11(3) and (3A), 12(5) and 38(3).
[177] See para.14-199, et seq.
[178] See para.14-214, et seq.

registration of the reference.[179] Note that adding a joint proprietor has somewhat different consequences for third parties compared to replacing a sole proprietor but the difference was not regarded as sufficient to lead to the conclusion that part entitlement and sole entitlement were different rights.[180]

4-69 Costs before the Comptroller usually follow the event and an order in relation to them will usually award a contribution to be paid.[181] The contribution is not intended to reflect the parties' actual legal costs of the hearing; the Comptroller's policy is to make an award based on a published scale.[182] The Comptroller may depart from an order based on the published scale in an appropriate case.[183]

Appeal

4-70 Any appeal from a decision of the Comptroller will be to the Patents Court[184] and CPR Pt 52 will apply to any such appeal.[185] Permission to appeal is not required, but the appeal must be made within 21 days unless the Comptroller indicates otherwise. The UK Litigation Manual indicates that the appeal period set by the Comptroller will normally be 28 days (unless the decision document indicates otherwise).[186] If an extension of time for appeal is desired, permission must be sought from the Patents Court as the Comptroller has no such discretion nor can this be agreed between the parties.[187] Part 52 lays down a comprehensive code for the hearing of appeals and the only additional requirement is that where Pt 52 requires a document to be served, it must also be served on the Comptroller.[188] The appeal from the Hearing Officer to the judge will normally be by way of review.[189] Where the decision is given under ss.8, 12 or 37 of the Act, a further appeal lies from the Patents Court to the Court of Appeal with permission of either the Patents Court or the Court of Appeal.[190] CPR r.52.13 generally requires the permission of the Court of Appeal in the case of a second tier appeal (which permission will not be given unless the criteria set out in r.52.13(2) are met), but the Court of Appeal held in *Smith International Inc v Specialised Petroleum Services*[191] that s.55 of the Access to Justice Act 1999—and thus CPR r.52.13—do not apply to appeals under s.97(3) of the Patents Act 1977.

---

[179] PA 1977 ss.11(1)–(5), 12(5) and 38(1)–(5).

[180] *Yeda Research and Development Co Ltd v Rhône-Poulenc Rorer International Holdings Inc* (HL) [2007] UKHL 43, [2008] R.P.C. 1, [35].

[181] *Patent Hearings Manual*, paras 5.35–5.51.

[182] *Patent Office Practice Note* TPN 4/2007. And see, e.g. *Goddin and Rennie's Application* [1996] R.P.C. 141.

[183] *Patent Hearings Manual*, para.5.49. The older practice based on *Rizla's Application* [1993] R.P.C. 365 that the scale would only be departed from in cases of abuse of process is no longer followed by the Comptroller.

[184] PA 1977 s.97(1).

[185] CPR r.63.16.

[186] See CPR 52.4(2)(a) and (b) and the UKIPO Litigation Manual, January 2015, section 6.02.

[187] CPR PD52D paras 13.1.

[188] CPR r.63.17(3).

[189] CPR r.52.11; and see *Reef T.M.* [2003] R.P.C. 5, 101, [17]–[30].

[190] PA 1977 s.97(3)(a).

[191] [2005] EWCA (Civ) 1357, [2006] F.S.R. 36, following *Henry Boot (UK) Ltd v Malmaison Hotel* [2001] Q.B. 388, CA.

CHAPTER 5

THE GRANTED PATENT

CONTENTS

1. PERIOD OF PROTECTION

Term of patent

Under the Patents Act 1977 the maximum term of a patent is 20 years from the date of filing the application.[1] For the special case of medicinal products and plant protection products Supplementary Protection Certificates have been introduced in order to extend the period of protection initially conferred by a patent, once that patent has expired. Supplementary Protection Certificates for medicinal products may also be extended when the medicinal product is approved for paediatric use. These provisions are considered elsewhere.[2]   **5-01**

Once granted, a patent may cease to have effect in a number of different ways: **5-02**

(a) the patent may run to its full 20-year term and expire at that point by operation of law[3];

(b) the renewal fees which have to be paid to maintain the patent in force, and which increase over time, may stop being paid either deliberately or by mistake. The effect will be that the patent lapses at the end of the period during which the fee was due to be paid.[4] In certain circumstances it may be possible to reinstate a patent which lapsed for that reason[5];

(c) the patent may be surrendered by the patentee[6]; and

(d) the patent may be revoked by the court, Comptroller, or the EPO,[7] essentially on the basis that it is invalid.[8]

---

[1] PA 1977 s.25(1).
[2] See Ch.6.
[3] PA 1977 s.25(1).
[4] PA 1977 s.25(3), provided the fee is not paid within the six months' grace period (s.25(4)).
[5] See paras 5-04 to 5-10.
[6] See paras 22-78 to 22-88.
[7] See Ch.22.
[8] The grounds for revocation are dealt with in Ch.10.

Expiry compared to revocation

5-03   If the patent expires, lapses or is surrendered then, as from the date on which the event occurs, the patent is no longer in effect and thus, subject to any application to restore in the case of a lapsed patent,[9] cannot be infringed in future. However, prior to that date the patent was in full force and effect and the fact that the patent is no longer in force makes no difference to the state of affairs beforehand except that, in the case of surrender, no action lies in respect of any act done before the date of surrender.[10] In contrast, an order for revocation takes effect ab initio[11] and accordingly (for example) an act which might have fallen within the claims of a patent before revocation is not an infringement at all if the patent has been revoked. This distinction in effect may be important with regard to the position of licensees of the patent and their ability to claw back paid licence fees either as provided for by the licence agreement or by a potential restitutionary claim.

2. RESTORATION OF LAPSED PATENTS

5-04   From the fourth anniversary of the date of filing renewal fees have to be paid annually to maintain a patent in force, so that failure to pay the appropriate renewal fees on time will lead to the patent ceasing to have effect at the end of the period prescribed for payment.[12] Provided that the fees are paid as required, then a failure by the Patent Office to record such payment does not mean that the patent in fact ceases to have effect: any incorrect entry on the register of patents can be rectified under s.34 of the Act.[13]

5-05   By s.25(4), a period of grace of six months is allowed providing the renewal fee and a supplementary fee is paid within that period. Thereafter, restoration of the patent for failure to pay the renewal fees can only be obtained if the requirements of s.28 of the 1977 Act, as amended, are met.[14] As amended, the section provides:

"**28.**—(1)   Where a patent has ceased to have effect by reason of a failure to pay any renewal fee, an application for the restoration of the patent may be made to the comptroller within the prescribed period.

(1A)   Rules prescribing that period may contain such transitional provisions and savings as appear to the Secretary of State to be necessary or expedient.

(2)   An application under this section may be made by the person who was the proprietor of the patent or by any other person who would have been entitled to the patent if it had not ceased to have effect; and where the patent was held by two or more persons jointly, the application may, with the leave of the comptroller, be made by one or more of them without joining the others.

(2A)   Notice of the application shall be published by the comptroller in the prescribed manner.

(3)   If the comptroller is satisfied that the failure of the proprietor of the patent

(a)   to pay the renewal fee within the prescribed period; or

(b)   to pay that fee and any prescribed additional fee within the period ending with the sixth month after the month in which the prescribed period ended,

---

[9]   See paras 5-04 to 5-10.
[10]   PA 1977 s.29(3). And see para.22-78.
[11]   EPC art.68. Although no corresponding express provision to this effect exists in the Patents Act 1977, it must follow from the meaning of "revocation" as used in PA 1977 s.72, which is a provision listed in PA 1977 s.130(7) as having the same effect in the UK as corresponding provisions of the EPC.
[12]   PA 1977 s.25(3); Patent Rules 2007 rr.37 and 38. Under the Rules the renewal period is three months ending with the last day of the month in which the renewal date falls.
[13]   *Eveready Battery Co Inc's Patent* [2000] R.P.C. 852. In that case the register wrongly recorded that the patent had ceased to have effect.
[14]   PA 1977 s.28, as amended by CDPA 1988 Sch.5 para.6. Subsection (3) was further amended with effect from 1 January 2005 by the Regulatory Reform (Patents) Order (SI 2004/2357) art.9 and then still further amended by PA 2004 s.8.

was unintentional, the comptroller shall by order restore the patent on payment of any unpaid renewal fee and any prescribed additional fee.

(4) An order under this section may be made subject to such conditions as the comptroller thinks fit (including a condition requiring compliance with any provisions of the rules relating to registration which have not been complied with), and if the proprietor of the patent does not comply with any condition of such an order the comptroller may revoke the order and give such directions consequential on the revocation as he thinks fit."

Rule 40 of the Patents Rules 2007 provides a period of 13 months after the end of the period specified in s.25(4) as being the prescribed period for the purposes of s.28(1).[15] Thus, a proprietor can overlook two annuity payments and still be able to apply to restore the patent. In order to obtain restoration the proprietor must show that the failure to pay the renewal fee (and any additional fee) was unintentional. Evidence must be filed.[16]

5-06

The importance of the evidence can be seen from *Matsushita Electric Industrial Co v Comptroller-General of Patents*.[17] In that case the Patents Court upheld the Comptroller's refusal of restoration on the basis that the requirement in s.28(3) is for the Comptroller to be satisfied that the failure was unintentional. A mere assertion that the failure was unintentional was not sufficient. The applicant bore the burden to satisfy the Comptroller. In all likelihood an applicant for restoration will need to explain the circumstances surrounding the failure in order to do so.

5-07

Section 28(3) is a relaxation of the previous law, whereby the proprietor had to prove that he took reasonable care to see such fees were paid. That in turn had been a relaxation of the original version of s.28(3) which had required also that he should show that the fees were not paid due to circumstances beyond his control. It would now appear that even negligence on the part of the proprietor should no longer defeat an application for restoration providing at all times he intended that it should be paid. However, once a decision not to pay a renewal fee is reached by the patentee or his authorised agent then s.28(3) is no longer applicable.[18]

5-08

Section 28A of the 1977 Act[19] makes provision for regulating acts done during the period of lapse where a patent is subsequently restored. Anything done in relation to the patent in that period (e.g. assignments or licensing) is valid.[20] An infringing act is actionable providing it took place during the six-month period of grace or was the continuation or repetition of an earlier infringing act.[21] Further, there are provisions for safeguarding those persons who began in the lapsed period in good faith to do or make effective and serious preparations to do an act which would otherwise have been an infringing act had the patent not lapsed.[22] These provisions equate to the protection given by s.64 of the Act to a person who has secretly prior used an invention.[23]

5-09

---

[15] Patents Rules 2007 r.40(1).
[16] Patents Rules 2007 r.40(4).
[17] [2008] EWHC 2071 (Pat), [2008] R.P.C. 35. Note that at [4] of the judgment refers to s.20 of the Patents Act 1977 by mistake and para.H4 of the headnote in the R.P.C. repeats the mistake. The relevant section is s.28.
[18] *Atlas Powder Co's Patent* [1995] R.P.C. 666. This was a decision under the previous version of s.28 but the result must follow.
[19] Inserted by CDPA 1988 Sch.5 para.7.
[20] PA 1977 s.28A(2).
[21] PA 1977 s.28A(3).
[22] PA 1977 s.28A(4), (7) and s.77(5).
[23] See paras 14-199 to 14-213.

European patents (UK)

5-10   The provisions concerning restoration apply to granted European patents (UK)
as well as to national patents.[24] The EPO has its own body of laws governing "re-
establishment of rights"[25] but these apply to proceedings in the EPO and not in the
UK.[26] These principles include provision for protection for third parties who in good
faith have used, or made effective and serious preparations for using, an invention
during an interim period.[27]

Supplementary protection certificates

5-11   The fee payable for a supplementary protection certificate is not an annual
renewal fee but is payable as a single cumulative amount as a condition of the
certificate taking effect.[28] Accordingly there are no provisions for restoration of
lapsed supplementary protection certificates because the situation will not arise.

3. OPPOSITION TO THE GRANT OF A EUROPEAN PATENT

Introduction

5-12   As from the publication of the mention of its grant in the *European Patent Bulletin*, a European Patent (UK) is treated as if it were a patent granted by the UK Patent Office.[29] As a result of the London Agreement[30] coming into effect on 1 May
2008, s.77(6) of the 1977 Act (which required translations to be filed if the patent
was published in French or German) is no longer in force.[31] However, a European
Patent (UK) remains subject to the EPC and in particular to that part of the Convention providing for opposition proceedings in the EPO[32] and the centralised revocation and limitation procedure[33] after grant.

Grounds of opposition

5-13   Once granted, the validity of grant in all designated States can be opposed by an
opposition lodged at the EPO. The term "opposition" may be seen as a misnomer
since the procedure is in substance a post-grant revocation action conducted at the
EPO using the centralised European procedure. Opposition may only be filed on the
grounds that[34]:

---

[24] PA 1977 s.77(1). Section 28 is within Pt I of the Act.
[25] EPC art.122.
[26] See *Ament's Application* [1994] R.P.C. 647.
[27] EPC art.122(5).
[28] See para.6-14 and the Patents (Fees) Rules 2007 (SI 2007/3292) for the fees payable.
[29] PA 1977 s.77(1).
[30] The Agreement on the Application of art.65 of the Convention on the Grant of European Patents
made in London on 17 October 2000 (Cmnd.5247). See paras 1-67 to 1-69, et seq.
[31] Patents Rules 2007 rr.56(9) and (10).
[32] EPC Pt V.
[33] EPC art.105a–105c.
[34] EPC art.100.

(a) the subject-matter of the European patent is not patentable within the terms of arts 52–57[35];

(b) the European patent does not disclose the invention in a manner sufficiently clear and complete for it to be carried out by a person skilled in the art[36]; and

(c) the subject-matter of the European patent extends beyond the content of the application as filed or, if the patent was granted on a divisional application or on a new application filed in accordance with art.61, beyond the content of the earlier application as filed.[37]

Time for opposition

Notice must be given to the EPO within nine months from the publication of the mention of the grant of the European patent in the *European Patent Bulletin*,[38] and the opposition fee must be paid within the same period. As a matter of practice the EPO does not start dealing with any opposition filed until the end of the period so as to deal with all oppositions filed against the same patent together. An opposition may be filed even if the European patent has been surrendered or has lapsed for all designated states.[39]

5-14

The opponent

Any person may oppose a European patent.[40] "Any person" is to be construed in line with art.58 of the EPC as meaning any natural person (private individual, self-employed persons, etc.), any legal person or any body treated as a legal person under the law governing it.[41] In particular, the fact that an opposition has been filed by a person acting on behalf of another (undisclosed) person does not per se affect the admissibility of the opposition.[42] However, an opposition may not be filed by a proprietor against its own patent[43] although a patentee may now apply to revoke their own patent at any time after the opposition procedure is finished under art.105a–105c of the EPC.

5-15

A professional representative may not file an opposition in its own name (other than on its own behalf), unless the party whom it represents is identified before the end of the opposition period.[44] Thus, if an opposition has been filed by a "man of

5-16

---

35 EPC art.100(a). Equivalent to PA 1977 ss.1–3. See Chs 2, 11–13.

36 EPC art.100(b). Equivalent to PA 1977 s.72(1)(c). See Ch.13.

37 EPC art.100(c), which mirrors the prohibition on added matter set out in art.123(2). Equivalent to PA 1977 s.72(1)(d). See para.15-29, et seq.

38 EPC art.99(1).

39 The provision providing for this was originally EPC art.99(3) but, following the EPC 2000, it is now EPC Rules r.75.

40 EPC art.99(1).

41 Guidelines for Examination in the EPO D-I. 4. The Guidelines refer to "any body assimilated to a legal person" which appears to mean bodies treated as legal persons.

42 *INDUPACK & GENENTECH/Opposition on behalf of third party* (G03/97 and G04/97) [1999] O.J. EPO 245, 270.

43 *PEUGEOT AND CITROËN II/Opposition by patent proprietor* (G09/93) [1994] O.J. EPO 891; [1995] E.P.O.R. 260; reversing *MOBIL OIL/Opposition by proprietor* (G01/84) [1985] O.J. EPO 299; [1986] E.P.O.R. 39, although oppositions by the proprietor filed before that decision was reversed, are unaffected by it EPO Guidelines D-I. 4.

44 *BAYER/Admissibility of opposition* (T10/82) [1983] O.J. EPO 407; [1979–85] E.P.O.R., B:381;

straw" so as to circumvent such prohibitions by way of an abuse of process, then
the opposition would be inadmissible.[45]

Intervention

5-17   If an opposition has been filed and has not been concluded (including any appeals),[46] any third party who proves that proceedings for infringement of the same
patent have been instituted against them may intervene in the proceedings.[47] Notice
of the intervention must be given within three months of the date on which the
infringement proceedings were instituted.[48] Intervention may take place during appeal proceedings but only where one of the parties adversely affected by the decision appealed against remains a party to the appeal and an intervention on that basis
cannot continue if the only appeal is withdrawn.[49]

5-18   Similarly, any third party may also intervene if they prove:

(a)   that the proprietor of the patent has requested that he cease alleged infringement of the patent; and

(b)   that they have instituted proceedings for a court ruling that he is not infringing the patent.[50]

Territorial effect of opposition

5-19   Article 99(2) of the EPC provides that the opposition shall apply to the patent
in all contracting states in which the patent has effect. Where the opposition is filed
in respect of only some of the designated states it will be treated as if it were in
respect of all the designated states.[51] If the patent contains different claims for different contracting states, then the effect of the opposition may accordingly differ and
the patent may be revoked in certain states and not in others.[52]

Procedure

Notice of opposition

5-20   The notice of opposition must contain[53]:

DEUTSCHE GELATINE-FABRIKEN, STOESS & Co/Opponent-identifyability (T25/85) [1986] O.J.
EPO 81; [1986] E.P.O.R. 158.

[45] *INDUPACK & GENENTECH/Opposition on behalf of third party* (G03/97 and G04/97) [1999] O.J.
EPO 245, 270.

[46] *ALLIED COLLOIDS/Intervention* (G01/94) [1994] O.J. EPO 787; [1994] E.P.O.R. 491; but see
DOLEZYCH II/Intervention (G04/91) [1993] O.J. EPO 707; [1993] E.P.O.R. 361 in which it was
held that an intervention filed during the two-month appeal period had no effect if none of the existing parties (opponent or patentee) appealed.

[47] EPC art.105(1).

[48] EPC Rules r.89. It remains to be decided whether, in relation to English proceedings, the date of issue or the date of service on the other party represents "institution" of proceedings for the purpose
of EPC art.105.

[49] *EOS/Intervention* (G03/04) [2006] O.J. EPO 118.

[50] EPC art.105(1).

[51] Guidelines for Examination in the EPO D-I. 3.

[52] Although such circumstances are rare, different claims are permitted and envisaged by EPC Rules
rr.18 and 138.

[53] EPC Rules r.76(2).

(a)   the particulars of the opponent[54];
(b)   the number of the patent against which opposition is led, and the name of the proprietor and title of the invention;
(c)   a statement of the extent to which the patent is opposed and of the grounds on which the opposition is based as well as an indication of the facts, evidence and arguments presented in support of these grounds; and
(d)   if the opponent has appointed a representative, the particulars of the representative.[55]

If the notice is defective, the opponent will be invited to remedy the deficiency. Where the notice fails to comply with EPC art.99(1), EPC Rules r.76(2)(c), or does not provide sufficient identification of the patent against which opposition has been led, the deficiency must be remedied before expiry of the opposition period.[56] In other cases, the opposition division shall specify an appropriate period (usually two months) for remedying the deficiency.[57] If the opponent fails to remedy the deficiency, the opposition will be rejected as inadmissible.[58]   **5-21**

The "grounds on which the opposition is based" are the legal bases on which an opposition can be based[59] (novelty, inventive step, etc.); in effect they correspond to the relevant articles of the EPC which govern substantive patentability (e.g. novelty as required by art.54 of the EPC, etc.).   **5-22**

The requirement of r.76(2)(c) for the notice of opposition to contain "an indication of the facts, evidence and arguments presented in support of" the opposition is fulfilled only if the contents of the notice are sufficient to enable the opponent's case to be properly understood by both the opposition division and the proprietor.[60] Merely citing a prior art document, without identifying the relevant passage within it, may not be adequate.[61]   **5-23**

Substantive examination of the opposition

Examination is conducted by an Opposition Division in accordance with the provision of the implementing regulations.[62] An Opposition Division is made up of three technical examiners at least two of whom shall not have taken part in the proceedings for grant of the patent to which the opposition relates.[63] Normally, an Opposition Division will entrust one of its members with examination of the opposition (but not with the conduct of oral proceedings) up to the time of the final decision of the opposition.[64]   **5-24**

---

[54]   See EPC Rules r.41(2)(c) which sets out detailed rules about the manner in which such information is to be provided.
[55]   EPC Rules r.41(2)(d).
[56]   EPC Rules r.77(1).
[57]   EPC Rules r.77(2).
[58]   EPC Rules r.77(2).
[59]   *DE LA RUE/Fresh grounds of opposition* (G01/95) [1995] O.J. EPO 615; [1995] E.P.O.R. 601; and *ETHICON/Fresh grounds of opposition* (G07/95) [1995] O.J. EPO 626.
[60]   *PPG/Ungelled polyesters* (T222/85) [1988] O.J. EPO 128; [1987] E.P.O.R. 99.
[61]   *PPG/Ungelled polyesters* (T222/85) [1988] O.J. EPO 128; [1987] E.P.O.R. 99.
[62]   EPC art.101; the Implementing Regulations are rr.75–89 of the EPC.
[63]   EPC art.19(2).
[64]   EPC art.19(2); and see EPO Guidelines D-II. 5.

5-25   As a general rule, the Opposition Division confines its examination to those grounds of opposition relied upon by the opponent.[65] However, the Opposition Division is not restricted to those grounds and may, of its own motion, broaden the inquiry.[66] Like the examination procedure, opposition proceedings are based on the investigative principle, but they are not to be treated as a continuation of the examination proceedings.[67] In particular, it is not open to the Opposition Division to consider whether a claim is "clear" and supported by the description, as required by art.84, since this is not a ground of opposition, unless an amendment to the claims is offered during opposition proceedings.[68] Even then, the ambit of the objection under art.84 is confined to the question whether the amendment itself causes the claim to be unclear or lacking in support.[69] However, in a case in which the lack of clarity causes a problem of insufficiency, then the objection is admissible.[70]

5-26   In preparation of the examination of the opposition, the proprietor of the patent is invited to file their observations on the opposition and to file any amendments he may wish to make.[71] The observations and amendments are communicated to the other parties to the opposition and, if the Opposition Division considers it expedient, they will be invited to reply.[72] The process of filing observations may be dispensed with in the case of an intervention.[73]

5-27   In order to overcome objections raised in an opposition, amendments to the description, claims and drawings may be offered. However, an amendment may only be made which is occasioned by any ground for opposition specified in art.100 of the EPC, even if that ground has not been invoked by the opponent.[74] Thus, the proprietor does not have a completely free hand to improve the specification by making amendments of the kind which might have been made in the course of application. This issue is an important one in practice but is rarely reflected in the formal decisions of the EPO Boards of Appeal and Opposition Division because the objection leads to the amendments not being admitted into the proceedings for substantive consideration at all.

5-28   Amended claims may be put forward in the form of one or more "auxiliary requests", which will be considered only if the Opposition Division finds the "main request" not to be valid. Normally a patentee's "main request" will be for the patent to be upheld in an unamended form, i.e. as granted.

5-29   In exceptional cases (e.g. where the scope of the main claim is narrowed by amendment to a dependent claim originally thought to be of minor importance) the Opposition Division may carry out an additional search and cite new material.[75] However, as the grant of the patent will have been preceded by a search by the search division, cases involving additional searches are very rare.

5-30   The parties may submit evidence in support of alleged facts.[76] Evidence may be given or obtained by:

---

[65] Guidelines for Examination in the EPO D-V. 2.2.
[66] EPC art.114(1).
[67] *NAIMER/Computer-controlled switch* (T23/86) [1987] O.J. EPO 316; [1987] E.P.O.R. 383.
[68] *NAIMER/Computer-controlled switch* (T23/86) [1987] O.J. EPO 316; [1987] E.P.O.R. 383.
[69] *BIOGEN/Recombinant DNA* (T301/87) [1990] O.J. EPO 335; [1990] E.P.O.R. 190.
[70] *MAGNETI MARELLI CLIMATIZZAZIONE/Condenser for air conditioning systems* (T5/99).
[71] EPC Rules r.79(1).
[72] EPC Rules r.79(3).
[73] EPC Rules r.79(4).
[74] EPC Rules r.80.
[75] Guidelines for Examination in the EPO D-VI. 5.
[76] Guidelines for Examination in the EPO E-III. 1.2 and see EPC art.117.

(1) requests for information;
(2) production of documents;
(3) opinions by experts;
(4) inspection;
(5) sworn statements in writing; or
(6) hearing the parties or witnesses.[77]

Although evidence may be submitted at any time, this should be done at the earli-   **5-31**
est opportunity. If oral proceedings have been requested, the parties will usually be
invited by the Opposition Division to submit any further observations or evidence
no later than four weeks before the oral proceedings are scheduled to take place.

Matters filed late

Late filed grounds of opposition, or facts, evidence and argument filed late that   **5-32**
are relevant to a ground of opposition which is already current in the opposition,
may be disregarded by the EPO.[78] A ground of opposition which had not been raised
in the notice of opposition does not have to be considered by the Opposition Division but in exceptional cases the Opposition Division can, of its own motion, raise
a ground of opposition which had not been put forward in the notice provided that
there are clear reasons to believe that the ground would be determinative of the
outcome of the opposition.[79] Equally, facts, evidence and argument which have been
filed late and which relate to an existing ground of opposition will normally be
admitted only if they are considered to be determinative of the outcome of the
opposition. The lateness of any material is also relevant such that, for example,
experimental results will not be admitted if they are filed so late that the other party
could not counter them with tests of their own.[80] However, experimental data held
to be rightly not admitted before the opposition division as being too late was admitted on appeal since the respondent now had had ample time and opportunity to carry
out its own experiments and had in fact done so.[81]

The decision

In theory the Opposition Division will first of all endeavour to reach a decision   **5-33**
in written proceedings.[82] However, if the division considers it expedient or if any
party requests it, oral proceedings will be held.[83] Since oral proceedings are
routinely requested, oral proceedings are more or less inevitable. At the oral
proceedings the parties may state their cases and put forward and argue
submissions. Members of the Opposition Division may put questions to the parties.
If the Opposition Division considers it necessary, the oral proceedings will include
the taking of oral evidence.[84] However, there is no obligation upon the division to
take oral evidence, even if a party has requested it. The decision of the Opposition
Division may be:

---

[77] Guidelines for Examination in the EPO E-III. 1.2. and see EPC art.117.
[78] EPC art.114(2); and see *PETTERSSON/Queueing system* (T1002/92) [1995] O.J. EPO 605; [1996]
      E.P.O.R. 1 (concerning grounds of opposition).
[79] *ROHM AND HAAS/Power to examine* (G10/91) [1993] O.J. EPO 420; [1993] E.P.O.R. 485.
[80] e.g. *ASAHI/Polyphenylene ether compositions* (T270/90) [1992] E.P.O.R. 365.
[81] *ARCO/Miscible polyblend* (T685/91) [1999] E.P.O.R. 237.
[82] Guidelines for Examination in the EPO D-VI. 1.
[83] EPC art.116.
[84] EPC Rules r.117.

(a) to revoke the patent;
(b) to reject the opposition; or
(c) to maintain the patent as amended.[85]

5-34   The decision may only be based on the grounds or evidence on which the parties have had an opportunity to present their comments.[86]

5-35   Before deciding to maintain the patent in amended form, the Opposition Division must inform the parties of its intention and invite them to state their observations within two months if they disapprove of the text in which it is intended to maintain the patent.[87] However, the practice of the EPO is to regard this requirement as fulfilled if the amendment is requested during oral proceedings, and the opponent has been given a reasonable opportunity during the oral proceedings to comment on the amendment.[88] The Opposition Division will then deliver an interlocutory decision, against which an appeal may be lodged.

Costs

5-36   The general rule is that each party pays its own costs. In cases where there have been oral proceedings or evidence has been taken orally, the Opposition Division may "for reasons of equity" order a different apportionment.[89] In 1987 there was an example of costs being awarded against a party who requested oral proceedings but presented no new arguments during the oral proceedings[90] but since then that practice has not been followed.[91] Costs have been awarded against a party who failed to inform the EPO of facts which would have rendered oral proceedings unnecessary if disclosed earlier.[92] Costs may also be awarded against a party who produces new facts or evidence after the end of the opposition period.[93] The apportionment of costs is dealt with in the decision of the Opposition Division.[94] Any final decision of the EPO fixing the amount of costs may be enforced in the UK by the procedure set out in s.93 of the 1977 Act.

Appeal

5-37   An appeal lies from all final decisions of the Opposition Division to the Board of Appeal. Interlocutory decisions may only be appealed together with the final decision, unless the decision allows separate appeal.[95] An appeal has suspensive effect.[96] Notice of appeal must be filed in writing at the EPO within two months after

---

85   EPC art.101.
86   EPC art.113(1).
87   EPC Rules r.82.
88   *BASF/Zeolites* (T219/83) [1986] O.J. EPO 211; [1986] E.P.O.R. 247; and *BASF/Paint line supply system* (T185/84) [1986] O.J. EPO 373; [1987] E.P.O.R. 34; and Guidelines for Examination in the EPO D-VI. 7.2.1.
89   EPC art.104(1).
90   *NISSAN/Fuel injectorvalve* (T167/84) [1987] O.J. EPO 369; [1987] E.P.O.R. 344.
91   See e.g. *SYMBOL/Optical scanning head* (T408/02).
92   *BAYER/Admissibility of opposition* (T10/82) [1983] O.J. EPO 407; [1979–85] E.P.O.R. B381.
93   *FILMTEC/Costs* (T117/86) [1989] O.J. EPO 401; [1989] E.P.O.R. 504.
94   EPC art.104(2). For the procedure, see EPC Rules r.88.
95   EPC art.106(1) and (2).
96   EPC art.106(1).

the date of notification of the decision appealed from.[97] Within four months after the date of notification, a written statement setting out the grounds of appeal must be led.[98]

The departments of the EPO have the power, known as "interlocutory revision", to rectify their decisions if they consider an appeal to be admissible and well-founded but this does not apply where the appeal is opposed by another party to the proceedings and so is unlikely to arise in relation to oppositions.[99]   **5-38**

Following examination as to the allowability of the appeal, the Board may either exercise any power within the competence of the Opposition Division or remit the case for further consideration by the department responsible for the decision under appeal.[100] The remittal can greatly delay the overall resolution of the dispute.   **5-39**

In general, the provisions relating to the proceedings before the Opposition Division apply to the appeal proceedings mutatis mutandis.[101] The Boards of Appeal also have their own Rules of Procedure.[102]   **5-40**

The Enlarged Board of Appeal

Cases may come before the Enlarged Board of Appeal of the EPO by a number of routes. Under art.112(1)(a) of the EPC a Board of Appeal may during proceedings refer a question to the Enlarged Board either of its own motion or at the request of a party. The parties have no right to such a reference. Under art.112(1)(b) EPC the President of the EPO may refer a point of law to the Enlarged Board. However, the President may only do so where two Boards of Appeal have given conflicting decisions[103] and the Enlarged Board will refused such a reference if it decides there is no conflict.[104]   **5-41**

Under a procedure introduced in 2008, by art.112a EPC any party to appeal proceedings adversely affected by the decision may file a petition for review of the decision by the Enlarged Board. The grounds for review are limited in nature and the scheme is not intended to operate simply as a further tier of appeals. The grounds include a fundamental violation of art.113 EPC (right to be heard and for the decision to be based on the material submitted) and other fundamental procedural defects defined in the Implementing Regulations[105] (failing to arrange oral proceedings which were requested and deciding an appeal without deciding on a relevant request). The petition for review does not have suspensive effect[106] and provisions protecting third parties who use the invention in good faith in the interim period or make serious and effective preparations to do so exist.[107]   **5-42**

---

[97] EPC art.108.
[98] EPC art.108.
[99] EPC art.109.
[100] EPC art.111(1).
[101] EPC Rules r.100.
[102] The current version is appended to the Decision of the Administrative Council 25 October 2007 O.J. EPO 11/2007, p.536.
[103] EPC art.112(1)(b).
[104] For example, see (G3/08) Programs for Computers of 12 May 2010.
[105] EPC Rules r.104.
[106] EPC art.112(3).
[107] EPC art.112(6).

Acceleration of EPO proceedings

5-43 Oppositions in the EPO are generally handled in the order of receipt. The EPO recognises a number of exceptional reasons for giving proceedings priority.[108] One ground on which the EPO will accelerate the processing of an opposition or an appeal is that an infringement action is pending before a national court. The EPO will accept a reasoned request for acceleration on that basis from a party to the proceedings or else the EPO can be informed by the national court that infringement actions are pending.[109] Curiously the stated grounds on which the Boards of Appeal will entertain acceleration are wider than the grounds on which the Opposition Division will do so. The ground on which acceleration may be sought for opposition proceedings is limited to pending infringement proceedings before a national court.[110] By contrast Board of Appeal will contemplate acceleration when infringement proceedings are pending or envisaged and when the decision of a potential licensee hinges on the outcome.[111] For examples in which English judges have communicated directly with the EPO to ask for acceleration of EPO proceedings running in parallel to cases before them, see *Eli Lilly v Human Genome Sciences*[112] and *GSK v Novartis*.[113] The provisions for acceleration of opposition and appeal proceedings are distinct from the EPO's PACE programme for acceleration of examination of patent applications, a revised version of which came into force on 1 January 2016.[114]

Status of a European patent (UK) during opposition proceedings

5-44 Oppositions take place after grant, at which point a European patent (UK) is treated under UK law as being a patent granted by the UK Patent Office (subject to the matter of translations).[115] Since an opposition generally takes a number of years to be completed, including an appeal, and since also proceedings before the English courts concerning the infringement and validity of such patents are often not stayed pending the outcome of an opposition,[116] the question arises as to the status of a European patent (UK) in those circumstances.

The form of the specification

5-45 During an opposition the patentee might submit proposed amendments by way of auxiliary requests. If the Opposition Division decides that the patent in its form

---

108 Guidelines for Examination in the EPO D-VII. 1.1 and 1.2.
109 For opposition proceedings, see the Notice from the EPO dated 17 March 2008, O.J. EPO 4/2008, 221; for appeal proceedings, see Notice from the Vice-President Directorate-General 3 dated 17 March 2008 concerning accelerated processing before the boards of appeal, O.J. EPO 4/2008, 220 (and supplementary publication No.1 of 2014).
110 Notice from the EPO dated 17 March 2008, O.J. EPO 4/2008, 221.
111 Notice from the Vice-President Directorate-General 3 dated 17 March 2008 concerning accelerated processing before the boards of appeal, O.J. EPO 4/2008, 220.
112 EPO Decision *HUMAN GENOME SCIENCES* (T18/09), see [1]–[4], *Eli Lilly v Human Genome Sciences* Court of Appeal, 23 February 2009, [2009] EWCA Civ 168 and full judgment on 9 February 2010 [2010] EWCA Civ 33, especially [6]–[10].
113 The only report is the EPO Board of Appeal in *NOVARTIS* (T25/09), [III]–[VII]. An earlier decision of the Patents Court in the same case, refusing a stay pending the EPO proceedings is *GlaxoSmithKline Biologicals SA v Novartis AG* [2009] EWHC 931 (Pat).
114 See Guidelines for Examination in the EPO C-VI.2 and E-VII.3.2.
115 PA 1977 s.77(1).
116 See paras 19-12 to 19-15.

as granted is invalid, they may revoke it or allow the patent to be maintained in an amended form based on the auxiliary requests.[117] An appeal has suspensive effect[118] and so until the conclusion of the appeal, the decision of the Opposition Division is suspended. Thus in these circumstances it is submitted that the proper approach for the UK courts is to consider the European patent (UK) in its form as granted,[119] at least until the conclusion of any appeal even although a patentee might have submitted amendment proposals by way of "auxiliary requests" and although the Opposition Division might have revoked the patent entirely (provided an appeal is pending). In some cases, a patentee has sought leave to make amendments before the English courts which correspond to amendments sought in the EPO.[120] This can be a very convenient course since it is capable of producing a consistent outcome in the sense that the patent might be upheld in the same amended form by both the EPO and the national court. Directions have been given in the Patents Court to provide a period after grounds of appeal were lodged in the EPO which might have filed to amendments in the EPO, for parallel patent amendments to be put forward in the Patents Court.[121] It should be noted that there is nothing which binds the English court to find an amendment allowable simply because it has been allowed by the EPO.[122] Furthermore, a patentee who seeks amendments before the EPO without seeking corresponding amendments before the English court runs the risk that the amendments may not take effect in England in time for the trial of the infringement action.[123]

However, complications will arise if, during an opposition, a patentee unequivocally abandons the claims in their form as granted and only seeks maintenance of the patent in an amended form. For the purposes of the decision by the Opposition Division the "main request" will be something other than maintenance of the patent as granted. A favourable decision by the Opposition Division on the basis of such a "main request" would be to uphold the patent in an amended form and in those circumstances one would not expect to see an appeal by the patentee; indeed it seems that a patentee would have no right to appeal such a decision anyway since only a party adversely affected by a decision may appeal.[124] If the opponent appealed, then dismissal of the appeal (the outcome most favourable to the patentee) would lead to the decision of the Opposition Division being upheld, i.e. the patent would be maintained as amended. Appeals have a suspensive effect[125] and this presumably means that the patent is to be treated as remaining in its form as granted even though it can never again take that form. Accordingly, a court faced with a patent in these circumstances is likely to require a patentee to apply to amend the patent to bring it into the same form as was upheld by the Opposition Division, the

5-46

---

[117] See EPC art.68 for the effect of revocation of a European patent in an opposition.

[118] EPC art.106(1).

[119] This is the approach taken in *Beloit Technologies Inc v Valmet Paper Machinery Inc* [1995] R.P.C. 705, Pat Ct and [1997] R.P.C. 489, CA.

[120] e.g. *Richardson-Vicks Inc's Patent* [1995] R.P.C. 568; and see *Petrolite Holdings Inc v Dyno Oil Field Chemicals UK Ltd* [1998] F.S.R. 190; and *Petrolite Holdings Inc v Dyno Oil Field Chemicals UK Ltd (No.2)* [1998] F.S.R. 646 for a case in which a patentee was forced to apply to amend in these circumstances.

[121] See, e.g. *GlaxoSmithKline Biologicals SA v Novartis AG* [2009] EWHC 931 (Pat), [38].

[122] Indeed, in *Palmaz's European Patents (UK)* [1999] R.P.C. 47, the Patents Court refused to allow an amendment to the claims which had been allowed by the Technical Board of Appeal.

[123] See Aldous LJ in *Beloit Technologies Inc v Valmet Paper Machinery Inc* [1997] R.P.C. 489, 503.

[124] EPC art.107.

[125] EPC art.106(1).

alternative being to stay the court proceedings pending the outcome in the EPO.[126] Continuance of proceedings before the English court on the basis of the patent as granted would be unsatisfactory since it involves the court in an action of a hypothetical nature only. Equally, if an amendment is effected conclusively by the EPO prior to resolution of the UK proceedings, the UK court can only consider the validity of the amended claim, no other claim being in existence.[127] As to retrospective amendment before the EPO, whether by amendments put to the EPO in contested proceedings or by an application for central amendment,[128] the Court of Appeal has been prepared to adjourn its proceedings pending central amendment[129] and conduct its proceedings on the basis of the amended claims.[130]

Effect in an opposition of an English order for revocation

5-47   Since European patents generally designate more than one Contracting State, revocation of a European patent (UK) by an English court (after the conclusion of any appeals) will have no practical effect in the EPO during an opposition because the patent is not thereby revoked for the other designated states. The national decision itself may be regarded by the EPO as setting out compelling reasons to revoke a European patent but the EPO is in no sense bound by the decisions of national courts in this respect and may not follow it.[131] In his judgment in *Eli Lilly v Human Genome Sciences*, Jacob LJ explained at length why the Court of Appeal were differing from the EPO in their judgment on validity concerning the same ground (industrial applicability) on the basis that despite the fact that the law applied in both the national courts and the EPO was the same, the facts and evidence before each were not and the conclusion was different.[132] However, the Supreme Court allowed the appeal from the Court of Appeal[133] and decided to follow the outcome on the EPO, holding that the difference in outcome between the EPO and the lower courts in that case was not due to a difference in evidence and argument but due to a difference in a manner in which the law was being applied. Since the EPO's approach to the law derived form a consistent and carefully considered cases, it should be followed.

5-48   Conversely, since an opposition runs to a different timetable to proceedings before the English courts, there is no reason why a patent might not be finally revoked by the EPO even after an English court had upheld it, granting an injunction to restrain infringement and awarding costs and damages. In those circumstances, the injunction granted by the UK court would cease to have effect upon revocation of the underlying patent.

5-49   As to the award of costs and damages upon final determination of English proceedings, prior to the decision of the Supreme Court in *Virgin Atlantic Airways*

[126] See *Palmaz's European Patents (UK)* [1999] R.P.C. 47, 58, et seq.
[127] See *Palmaz's European Patents (UK)* [2000] R.P.C. 631, CA and see *IPCom GmbH v HTC Europe Co Ltd* [2015] EWHC 1034 (Pat) in which the patentee applied to amend the claims to put them in the same form as allowed by the EPO Board of Appeal.
[128] Under EPC art.105a.
[129] *Samsung Electronics Co Ltd v Apple Retail UK Ltd* [2014] EWCA Civ 250, [2015] R.P.C. 3.
[130] *Eli Lilly v Human Genome Sciences* [2010] EWCA Civ 33, [2010] R.P.C. 14.
[131] For an example of a patent revoked by the English courts but upheld by the EPO, see *BIOGEN/Hepatitis B* (T296/93) [1995] O.J. EPO 627; [1995] E.P.O.R. 1; and *Biogen Inc v Medeva Plc* [1997] R.P.C. 1.
[132] *Eli Lilly v Human Genome Sciences* [2010] EWCA Civ 33, see especially [38]–[41].
[133] *Eli Lilly v Human Genome Sciences* [2011] UKSC 51, see especially [83]–[95].

v Zodiac Seats UK,[134] it was thought that such matters were res judicata as between the parties and the entitlement to damages remained, despite any decision of the EPO to the contrary.[135] This longstanding principle was overturned by the Supreme Court in *Virgin v Zodiac*, which held that the application of cause of action estoppel in *Coflexip* and *Unilin* had been misconceived and that in fact the defendant had only needed to rely on the mere fact of revocation, which was a decision in rem and could not be said to be re-litigating a decided point. The court also held that the position in *Coflexip* had been bad for certainty, since it had depended on the arbitrary matter of which tribunal came to a final decision first. Further, since revocation by the EPO took effect retrospectively, this could be relied on by the world, and it would make no sense to discharge the injunction while maintaining the patentee's right to damages. *Virgin* was decided prior to the hearing of the inquiry, and it was not decided by the Supreme Court whether an infringer could reopen proceedings after payment of damages, indeed many years thereafter, by a restitutionary claim or otherwise. Such circumstances would raise more difficult issues of policy and finality of litigation.

4. EMPLOYEE'S RIGHTS TO COMPENSATION

The Patents Act 1977 enacts a scheme under which employees who have made **5-50** inventions may be entitled to a measure of financial reward or compensation depending upon the benefit the employer has obtained from an invention or a patent for it. The threshold required in order to trigger the jurisdiction depends on whether the invention was one which always belonged to the employer or the employee (see below). Section 39 sets out the provisions which determine whether an invention belongs to the employer or the employee.[136]

As originally enacted, the scheme focused attention on the benefit to the employer **5-51** *of the patent*, rather than *the invention*.[137] However, by s.10 of the Patents Act 2004, the scheme has been amended so that consideration must now be given to the benefit of both the invention and the patent for it. The amended provisions came into force on 1 January 2005[138] but they apply only to an invention the patent for which is applied for on or after that date.[139] So, for example, the most recent cases on the point, *Kelly and Chiu v GE Healthcare*[140] and *Shanks v Unilever*[141] dealt with the unamended version of the legislation.

Common requirements

Compensation can only be awarded in cases where an invention is made by an **5-52** employee who is employed or mainly employed in the United Kingdom or, if not

---

[134] *Virgin Atlantic Airways Limited v Zodiac Seats UK Limited* [2013] UKSC 46.
[135] See *Poulton v Adjustable Cover and Boiler Block Co* (1908) 25 R.P.C. 529 (Parker J) and 661, CA; *Cofiexip SA v Stolt Offshore MS Ltd (No.2)* [2004] F.S.R. 7 (Jacob J), [2004] F.S.R. 34, CA; *Unilin Beheer BV v Berry Floor NV* [2007] EWCA Civ 364, [2007] F.S.R. 25, CA and *Virgin Atlantic v Premium Aircraft* [2009] EWCA Civ 1513, [2010] F.S.R. 15, CA.
[136] See paras 4-22 to 4-30.
[137] See PA 1977 s.40(1) and (2)(c), s.41(1), (4), and (5), and s.43(5) as originally enacted. And see *Memco-Med Ltd's Patent* [1992] R.P.C. 403.
[138] The Patents Act 2004 (Commencement No.2 and Consequential, etc. and Transitional Provisions) Order 2004 (SI 2004/3205).
[139] PA 2004 s.10(8).
[140] [2009] EWHC 181 (Pat); [2009] R.P.C. 12.
[141] [2014] EWHC 1647 (Ch); [2014] R.P.C. 29

mainly employed anywhere and his place of employment cannot be determined, then if their employer has a place of business in the United Kingdom to which the employee is attached.[142] Compensation can only be granted in respect of an invention for which a patent has been granted[143] but, for the purposes of ss.39–42 of the 1977 Act, "patent" is defined as a patent or other protection. The meaning of "other protection" was considered in *Kelly and Chiu v GE Healthcare*.[144] It was held to mean "other monopoly protection" so that it did not include regulatory data exclusivity or "RDE". RDE (also called data protection) makes it more difficult for a competitor to enter certain regulated markets (such as the pharmaceutical market) because to do so they must generate their own safety and efficacy data in order to obtain a marketing authorisation. Floyd J held that RDE protects data and not the invention and is not within the definition.

5-53   References to the patent being "granted" mean references to its being granted whether under the law of the UK or the law in force in any other country or under any treaty or international convention.[145] The provisions only apply to inventions made after 1 June 1978.[146]

5-54   The compensation is available to an inventor in the sense of the actual deviser of the invention as opposed to those who merely contribute to an invention without being a joint inventor.[147]

Inventions belonging to the employer

5-55   Where it can be established that an invention (of which the applicant is an inventor) or the patent for it (or the combination of both) is of "outstanding benefit" to the employer, and that it is just that the employee should be awarded compensation, the court or Comptroller may award such compensation to secure for the employee a fair share of the benefit which the employer has derived or may reasonably be expected to derive from the invention in question, or the patent for it.[148] The benefit derived or expected to be derived by an employer from an invention does not include any benefit derived or expected to be derived after the patent has expired or has been surrendered or revoked.[149]

Outstanding benefit

5-56   The onus is on the employee to show outstanding benefit, and that the benefit was derived from the invention or the patent for it (or the combination of both).[150] The onus may shift to the employer, but this will depend upon the evidence before the

---

[142] PA 1977 s.43(2).

[143] PA 1977 s.40(1)(a) (as amended) and (2)(a).

[144] [2009] EWHC 181 (Pat); [2009] R.P.C. 12.

[145] PA 1977 s.43(4). See also *Memco-Med Ltd's Patent* [1992] R.P.C. 403; *GEC Avionics Ltd's Patent* [1992] R.P.C. 107; *British Steel Plc's Patent* [1992] R.P.C. 117; *Entertainment UK Ltd's Patent* [2002] R.P.C. 11, 291; *Kelly and Chiu v GE Healthcare Ltd* [2009] EWHC 181 (Pat); [2009] R.P.C. 12.

[146] PA 1977 s.43(1): 1 June 1978 being the appointed day.

[147] PA 1977 s.43(3) and see *Kelly and Chiu v GE Healthcare Ltd* [2009] EWHC 181 (Pat); [2009] R.P.C. 12, at [11].

[148] PA 1977 ss.40(1) and 41(1) (as amended).

[149] PA 1977 s.43(5A), inserted by PA 2004 s.10(7).

[150] *Memco-Med Ltd's Patent* [1992] R.P.C. 403; *GEC Avionic Ltd's Patent* [1992] R.P.C. 107; *British Steel Plc's Patent* [1992] R.P.C. 117. These decisions were prior to the amendment of the scheme by the 2004 Act, see para.5-55.

court; there is no presumption that returns obtained from the sales of goods or services, which are the subject of a patent, were due in part to the patent[151] or (under the law as amended) to the invention.[152]

Whether any benefit is outstanding is a question of fact, although the 1977 Act directs that both the size and nature of the employer's undertaking are relevant considerations.[153] However, this is not intended to mean that a larger undertaking is less likely to pay employee compensation but a given monetary benefit might be outstanding for a small undertaking and not for a large one.[154] The word "outstanding" denotes something special and requires the benefit to be more than substantial or good.[155] The benefit must be something more than one would normally expect to arise from the duties for which the employee is paid,[156] although the question of whether the employee had gone beyond their duties was not a relevant matter.[157] "Benefit" is defined as being benefit in money or money's worth.[158] A patent may be of benefit to an employer even when there are multiple causes for the profits under consideration and it is to be assumed that the draftsman of the section understood that a patent for an invention does not earn benefits on its own: a product has to be manufactured and promoted, and if it is a pharmaceutical, licensed.[159]

5-57

Although each case will be decided on its own facts, the difficulty in establishing the existence of an outstanding benefit is illustrated by the fact that since the section came into force in 1978, the only case in which it has been established has been *Kelly v GE Healthcare*[160] in 2009.[161]

5-58

Fair share (inventions belonging to the employer)

In determining the fair share of the benefit, the court or Comptroller shall take the following matters into account[162]:

5-59

(a) the nature of the employee's duties, their remuneration and the other advantages they derive or have derived from their employment or the invention;

(b) the effort and skill which—

   (i) the employee has devoted to making the invention; and

---

[151] *Memco-Med Ltd's Patent* [1992] R.P.C. 403 at 415, not following on this point the decision in *GEC Avionics Patent* [1992] R.P.C. 107.

[152] See para.5-51.

[153] PA 1977 s.40(1).

[154] See Arnold J in *Shanks v Unilever plc* [2014] EWHC 1647 (Ch); [2014] R.P.C. 29 at [67]–[71]. In a reasoned judgment Floyd LJ gave permission to appeal ([2015] EWCA 787). At the time of writing the appeal has not been heard.

[155] See Aldous J in *Memco-Med Ltd's Patent* [1992] R.P.C. 403, 413–414 and Floyd J in *Kelly and Chiu v GE Healthcare Ltd* [2009] EWHC 181 (Pat); [2009] R.P.C. 12, [17]–[25] and [60(iv)–(v)].

[156] *Kelly and Chiu v GE Healthcare Ltd* [2009] EWHC 181 (Pat); [2009] R.P.C. 12; and see also *GEC Avionic's Patent* [1992] R.P.C. 107.

[157] See Arnold J in *Shanks v Unilever plc* [2014] EWHC 1647 (Ch); [2014] R.P.C. 29, [81]. In a reasoned judgment Floyd LJ gave permission to appeal ([2015] EWCA 787). At the time of writing the appeal has not been heard.

[158] PA 1977 s.43(7).

[159] *Kelly and Chiu v GE Healthcare Ltd* [2009] EWHC 181 (Pat); [2009] R.P.C. 12.

[160] *Kelly and Chiu v GE Healthcare Ltd* [2009] EWHC 181 (Pat); [2009] R.P.C. 12.

[161] In all four reported cases in which the issue had been considered other than *Kelly v GE Healthcare*, the applicant failed to establish an outstanding benefit. In *Entertainment UK Ltd's Patent* [2002] R.P.C. 11, 291 a claim survived an application by the employer for summary judgment, but largely because of unpleaded arguments first raised by the employee during the hearing itself.

[162] PA 1977 s.41(4).

(ii) any other person has devoted including advice or other assistance by any other employee not a joint inventor[163]; and

(c) the contribution made by the employer to the making, developing and working of the invention.

Inventions belonging to the employee

5-60   The court or the Comptroller will award compensation where it can be established that:

(a) a patent has been granted for an invention made by and belonging to an employee;

(b) their rights in the invention, application or patent have been assigned to the employer or an exclusive licence has been granted to the employer;

(c) the benefit derived by the employee from the assignment or licence is inadequate in relation to the benefit derived by the employer from the invention or the patent for it (or both); and

(d) it is just that the employee should be awarded compensation in addition to the benefit already received.[164]

Once more, it is the benefit that the employer derives from the invention or the patent for it (or both), not merely the patent as under the old law,[165] that has to be considered and in this case measured against the benefit derived by the employee from the assignment of their rights in the invention.

Fair share (inventions belonging to the employee)

5-61   The court or Comptroller must consider the following matters[166]:

(a) any conditions in any licence granted in respect of the invention or patent for it;

(b) the extent to which the invention was made jointly by the employee with any other person; and

(c) the contribution made by the employer to the making, developing and working of the invention.

5-62   For employees' inventions, the nature of the employee's duties and their remuneration are not to be taken into account, whilst terms in any licences granted by the employer are. In other respects the matters to be taken account of are the same as for employer's inventions.

Claims procedure

5-63   The detailed procedure on an application for compensation by an employee under s.40 to the Court is governed by CPR Pt 63 r.63.12 and para.12.1 of the Practice

163 See PA 1977 s.43(3) which provides that "making an invention" excludes merely contributing advice or other assistance; and see *British Steel Plc's Patent* [1992] R.P.C. 117 and *Kelly and Chiu v GE Healthcare Ltd*.
164 PA 1977 s.40(2) (as amended).
165 See para.5-51.
166 PA 1977 s.41(5) (as amended).

Direction. For an application to the Comptroller, the procedure is governed by Pt 7 of the Patents Rules 2007.[167]

A claim may be made at any time after the patent is granted and prior to the expiration of one year after it ceases to have effect.[168] The claimant will generally be the employee but where they die before an award is made, their personal representatives or their successors in title may exercise their right to make or proceed with an application.[169] The fact that a claimant has made an earlier application for an award (whether successful or not) will not prevent a further application in respect of the same invention.[170] Equally, once an order has been made it can be subsequently varied or discharged, suspended or revised as the case may be.[171]

5-64

Contracting out of the awards provisions

Rights to compensation will be substituted where there is a collective agreement between a trade union to which the employee belongs and the employer or an employers' association.[172] Apart from this, in the case of employees' inventions it is not possible for an employer to compromise the employee's right to compensation.[173] As regards an employers' invention, it is possible to compromise a claim to compensation once the invention has been made; in the case of prospective inventions, however, it is not possible to diminish an employee's right to compensation.[174]

5-65

Dealings in the patent

An employer cannot avoid the claim to compensation where they assign the patent or application for the patent to a person connected with the employer.[175] In such a case, to determine the benefit derived by the employer the court will assess the amount that could reasonably be expected to have been derived if the transaction had been an arm's length one.[176] In *Shanks v Unilever*[177] on appeal from an interim decision of the Comptroller, the Court of Appeal confirmed that the benefit derived by the employer in such a case is assessed as if the assignment had been to a notional non-connected counterparty operating in the appropriate market at the appropriate time. The decision of the Comptroller's Hearing Officer (Dr Elbro) that the approach was to consider the notional counterparty as being the very same assignee but simply without the connection to the employer was rejected.

5-66

5. FALSE MARKING

Falsely representing an article as "patented" or "patent applied for"

If any person falsely represents that anything disposed of by them for value is a

5-67

---

[167] Patents Rules 2007 r.73(1)(a) and Sch.3 Pt 1.
[168] Patents Rules 2007 r.91(1); special provisions apply if a patent has been restored under s.28 of the PA 1977 (r. 91(2)).
[169] PA 1977 s.43(6).
[170] PA 1977 s.41(7).
[171] PA 1977 s.41(8).
[172] PA 1977 s.40(3) and (6).
[173] PA 1977 s.40(4).
[174] PA 1977 s.42(1) and (2).
[175] PA 1977 s.41(1)(c) (as amended).
[176] PA 1977 s.41(2).
[177] [2010] EWCA Civ 1283; [2011] R.P.C. 12.

patented product they are liable on summary conviction to a fine.[178] To dispose of an article for value having stamped, engraved or impressed on it or otherwise applied to it the word "patent" or "patented" or anything expressing or implying that the article is a patented product will be taken to represent that the article is a patented product.[179] "Patent" includes a European patent (UK).[180] "Patented product" is a defined expression in the Act.[181]

5-68   Similar provisions apply to where a person falsely represents that a patent has been applied for or that a patent is pending.[182] Application includes an application for a European patent (UK).[183]

5-69   It is no offence, however, to describe an article as patented or patent applied for after the patent has expired or been revoked or, in the case of an application, after the application has been refused within a period thereafter not reasonably sufficient to enable the accused to take steps to ensure the representation is not made or continued to be made.[184]

5-70   It is a defence for the accused to prove that he used due diligence to prevent the commission of the offence.[185] If there is a patent it is only a defence if it can be established that the claims of the patent relied upon, on a proper construction, cover the article sold as "patented".[186]

Marking article "licensed"

5-71   There is no specific remedy relating to patents to prevent falsely marking an article as "licensed". The issue arose in a number of old cases, mainly interlocutory injunctions, in which the outcome inevitably turned on their particular facts.[187] A marking of that kind must risk being found to fall within the prohibition above as a representation expressing or implying that the article is a patented product.

6.   PATENT OFFICE OPINIONS

Introduction

5-72   A non-binding opinion on the questions of validity or infringement of a UK or European patent or related Supplementary Protection Certificate ("SPC") can be obtained from the Patent Office. The procedure first came into force on 1 October 2005[188] and was expanded on 1 October 2014[189] to encompass opinions on a wider range of issues, namely:

---

[178] PA 1977 s.110(1). The maximum fine is not exceeding level 3 on the standard scale (£1000)—see Criminal Justice Act 1982 s.37(2) as substituted by Criminal Justice Act 1991 s.17.

[179] PA 1977 s.110(2).

[180] PA 1977 s.77(1)(b).

[181] PA 1977 s.130(1).

[182] PA 1977 s.111.

[183] PA 1977 s.78(1).

[184] PA 1977 ss.110(3) and 111(2).

[185] PA 1977 ss.110(4) and 111(4).

[186] *Esco Ltd v Rolo Ltd* (1923) 40 R.P.C. 471.

[187] *Post Card Automatic Supply Co v Samuel* (1889) 6 R.P.C. 560. See *Austin Baldwin, etc. v Greenwood, etc.* (1925) 42 R.P.C. 454; *Ormond Engineering Co v Knopf* (1932) 49 R.P.C. 634; and *British and International Proprietaries Ltd v Selcol Products Ltd* [1957] R.P.C. 3.

[188] The amendments were introduced by s.13 of the Patents Act 2004. See also The Patents Act 2004 (Commencement No.3 and Transitional Provisions) Order 2005 (SI 2005/2471).

[189] The amendments were introduced by the s.16 of the Intellectual Property Act 2014 and by amend-

(a) whether a particular act constitutes (or would constitute) an infringement of the patent;

(b) whether, or to what extent, an invention for which a patent has been granted is new and/or involves an inventive step;

(c) whether the invention in question is capable of industrial application;

(d) whether the invention in question relates to matter excluded by s.1(1)(d) of the Patents Act 1977;

(e) whether the specification of the patent discloses the invention clearly and completely enough for it to be performed by a person skilled in the art;

(f) whether the matter disclosed in the specification of the patent extends beyond that disclosed in the application for the patent as filed;

(g) whether the protection conferred by the patent has been extended by an amendment which should not have been allowed;

(h) whether a particular act constitutes or (if done) would constitute an infringement of a SPC; and

(i) whether a SPC is invalid.

The cost of the opinion is currently set at £200 and opinions can be requested at any time (unlike EPO oppositions, which have a nine-month time limit post-grant). The purpose of such opinions is now several. The Comptroller now has the power to revoke patents which have been the subject of opinions where he has concluded that the patent lacks novelty or inventive step.[190] The opinion may assist in the settlement of patent disputes by alternative dispute resolution. And even if the opinion does not bring about a settlement of the dispute, a favourable opinion may make it easier and cheaper to obtain "after the event" insurance or other funding for litigation. **5-73**

Requesting an opinion

The proprietor of a patent or any other person may request an opinion.[191] The opinion may relate to a prescribed matter in relation to the patent[192] as set out at para.5-72. An opinion may be requested even if the patent has expired or has been surrendered.[193] **5-74**

Procedure

A request is made on Patents Form 17 and must be accompanied by a copy and a statement setting out fully[194]: **5-75**

(a) the question upon which the opinion is sought;

(b) the requester's submissions on that question; and

(c) any matters of fact which are requested to be taken into account.

The statement must be accompanied by: (a) the name and address of any persons, of whom the requester is aware, having an interest in that question, and (b) **5-76**

---

ment to the Patents Rules 2007 r.93(6).

[190] PA 1977 s.73(1A)–(1C), referring to the requirement for novelty under s1(1)(a) and inventive step under s1(1)(b).

[191] PA 1977 s.74A(1).

[192] PA 1977 s.74A(1).

[193] PA 1977 s.74A(2).

[194] Patents Rules 2007 r.93(1).

particulars of any relevant proceedings[195] of which the requester is aware which relate to the patent and which may be relevant to that question.[196] However, if the requester is acting as an agent in making the request, they are not required to identify the person for whom they are acting.[197]

5-77   The request must also be accompanied by a copy of any evidence or other document (except documents published by the Comptroller or kept at the Patent Office) which is referred to in the statement.[198] The statement, evidence or other document must be provided in duplicate.[199]

Refusing the request

5-78   The Comptroller may refuse to issue an opinion if the request appears to them to be frivolous or vexatious or the question upon which the opinion is sought appears to them to have been sufficiently considered in any proceedings.[200] Likewise they may refuse to issue an opinion if for any reason they consider it inappropriate in all the circumstances to do so.[201]

Withdrawing the request

5-79   If the requester of the opinion withdraws their request, then the Comptroller shall not issue an opinion.[202]

Notification of the request

5-80   The Comptroller is required to notify the following persons of the request (except where the person concerned is the requester)[203]:

(a) the patent holder[204];
(b) any holder of a licence or sub-licence under the patent which has been registered under r.47;
(c) any person who has made a request in respect of the patent under r.54 regarding an opinion; and
(d) any person identified in the requester's statement as having an interest in the question.

5-81   The Comptroller may also notify any other person of the request who appears to him to be likely to have an interest in the question upon which the opinion is sought.[205]

5-82   The Comptroller must send a copy of the Patents Form 17 and the requester's

---

[195] "Relevant proceedings" means proceedings whether pending or concluded before the Comptroller, the court of the EPO. Patents Rules 2007 r.92.
[196] Patents Rules 2007 r.93(2).
[197] Patents Rules 2007 r.93(3).
[198] Patents Rules 2007 r.93(4).
[199] Patents Rules 2007 r.93(5).
[200] PA 1977 s.74A(3)(a); Patents Rules 2007 r.94(1).
[201] PA 1977 s.74A(3)(b).
[202] Patents Rules 2007 r.94(2).
[203] Patents Rules 2007 r.95(1).
[204] The "patent holder" means the proprietor of the patent and any exclusive licensee, see Patents Rules 2007 r.92.
[205] Patents Rules 2007 r.95(2).

statement to each person so notified, together with a copy of such other documents as may have been filed by the requester as the Comptroller sees fit.[206]

Withdrawal of the request

If the request is refused or withdrawn before a mandatory notification has been made, the patent holder alone shall be notified of the request (and of the fact that it has been refused or withdrawn).[207] However, the Comptroller is not required to provide a copy of the form or statement, etc. Nor is the Comptroller required to advertise the request in these circumstances.[208]

5-83

Advertisement and submissions of observations

The Comptroller must advertise the request in such manner as he may think fit.[209] Before the end of four weeks beginning with the date of the advertisement,[210] any person may file observations on any issue raised by the request.[211] Within the same time, the person filing the observations must ensure that a copy of such observations is received by the patent holder and the requester.[212] The observations may include reasons why the Comptroller should refuse the request.[213]

5-84

A person to whom observations are sent may, within two weeks, file observations confined strictly to matters in reply.[214] Within the same time, the person filing the observations in reply must ensure that a copy of such observations is received by the patent holder or the requester, as appropriate.[215]

5-85

Preparing the opinion

After the end of the observations procedure, the Comptroller will refer the request to an examiner for preparation of the opinion.[216] The opinion is issued by the Comptroller by sending a copy of it to the requester, the patent holder, and any other person who has filed observations under the observations procedure.[217] The Patent Office has also indicated that the opinion will be published on its website.

5-86

Review of the opinion

The patent holder may before the end of the period of three months beginning with the date on which the opinion is issued apply to the Comptroller for a review of the opinion.[218]

5-87

---

206 Patents Rules 2007 r.95(3).
207 Patents Rules 2007 r.95(5).
208 Patents Rules 2007 r.95(5).
209 Patents Rules 2007 r.95(4).
210 Patents Rules 2007 r.96(7).
211 Patents Rules 2007 r.96(1).
212 Patents Rules 2007 r.96(3).
213 Patents Rules 2007 r.96(2).
214 Patents Rules 2007 r.96(4).
215 Patents Rules 2007 r.96(5).
216 PA 1977 s.74A(5); Patents Rules 2007 r.97(1).
217 Patents Rules 2007 r.97(2).
218 PA 1977 s.74B(1); Patents Rules 2007 r.98(1).

5-88   The application for a review may be made on the following grounds only[219]:

(a) that the opinion wrongly concluded that the patent was invalid, or was invalid to a limited extent; or

(b) that, by reason of its interpretation of the specification of the patent, the opinion wrongly concluded that a particular act did not or would not constitute an infringement of the patent.

Procedure on application for a review

5-89   The application for a review is made on Patents Form 2 and must be accompanied by a copy and a statement in duplicate setting out fully the grounds on which the review is sought.[220] The statement must contain particulars of any proceedings of which the applicant is aware which may be relevant to the question whether the proceedings for a review may be brought or continued.[221]

5-90   Upon receipt of the application for review, the Comptroller is required to send a copy of the form and the statement to the requester and all persons who filed observations under the observations procedure[222] and to advertise the application in such manner as he may think fit.[223]

5-91   Before the end of the period of four weeks beginning with the date that the application for review is advertised (or, if later, two months beginning with the date on which the opinion is issued),[224] any person may file (in duplicate) a statement in support of the application or a counter-statement contesting it and, on so doing, that person becomes a party to the proceedings.[225] The Comptroller is also required to send a copy of each such statement or counter-statement to the other parties.[226]

Outcome of the review

5-92   Upon completion of the review procedure, the Comptroller must either set aside the opinion in whole or in part or decide that no reason has been shown for the opinion to be set aside.[227]

5-93   The nature of the task on a review was explained by Kitchin J in *DLP Ltd's Patent*.[228] It is not the function of a review to express an opinion on the question the subject of the original request. The hearing officer should only decide an opinion is wrong if the examiner has made an error of principle or reached a conclusion which is clearly wrong. An opinion within the range of reasonable opinions cannot be characterised as wrong just because the hearing officer may not agree with it.

[219] Patents Rules 2007 r.98(5).
[220] Patents Rules 2007 r.98(3).
[221] Patents Rules 2007 r.98(4).
[222] Patents Rules 2007 r.99(1).
[223] Patents Rules 2007 r.99(2).
[224] Patents Rules 2007 r.99(3).
[225] Patents Rules 2007 r.99(3).
[226] Patents Rules 2007 r.99(5).
[227] Patents Rules 2007 r.100.
[228] *DLP Ltd's Patent* [2007] EWHC 2669 (Pat); [2008] R.P.C. 11.

The effect of an opinion or a decision on review

A Patent Office opinion is non-binding for any purposes.[229] Likewise, a deci-   **5-94**
sion on review (whether setting aside an opinion or deciding that no reason has been
shown for setting it aside) does not estop any party to proceedings from raising any
issue regarding the validity or the infringement of the patent.[230]

Appeal

A decision not to set aside an opinion is a decision of the Comptroller within   **5-95**
s.97(1) of the 1977 Act and, accordingly, an appeal lies from such a decision to the
Patents Court. The first such appeal to come to the Patents Court was *DLP Ltd's
Patent*.[231] Here Kitchin J considered a number of matters arising relating to the
conduct of such appeals, holding:

(a) There had been a decision which can be appealed. The non-binding nature
     of opinions does preclude an appeal. Although they are non-binding, such
     opinions are potentially of great value to the persons concerned.
(b) Although the Comptroller is entitled to appear on such appeals, the
     Comptroller treats appeals of this kind as inter partes in nature and will not
     appear as a matter of course.
(c) Such appeals in general will consist of a review the hearing officer's
     decision. The decision the subject of the appeal is the review decision itself,
     i.e. the decision of the hearing officer as to whether the opinion of the
     examiner was wrong.
(d) The starting point is only an expression of opinion. There may well be
     opinions which a hearing officer or a court will not agree with but which
     cannot be characterised as wrong. Such opinions merely represent differ-
     ent views within which a range within which reasonable people can differ.
(e) However, it is not the function of the Court (nor the hearing officer) to
     express an opinion on the question the subject of the original request.

On the facts of the case itself in *DLP Ltd's Patent*,[232] Kitchin J held that the   **5-96**
opinion of non-infringement was a reasonable view and was not clearly wrong. The
appeal was dismissed.

There is no appeal under s.97 from a decision to set aside an opinion, except   **5-97**
where the appeal relates to a part of the opinion that is not set aside.[233]

Comptroller's power to revoke

If the Comptroller is of the opinion that the invention for which the patent was   **5-98**
granted lacks novelty or inventive step, the Comptroller has the power to revoke
the patent of its own initiative.[234] This power may not be exercised by the end of
the period in which the proprietor of the patent may apply for a review of the

---

[229] PA 1977 s.74A(4).
[230] Patents Rules 2007 r.100(2).
[231] *DLP Ltd's Patent* [2007] EWHC 2669 (Pat); [2008] R.P.C. 11.
[232] *DLP Ltd's Patent* [2007] EWHC 2669 (Pat); [2008] R.P.C. 11.
[233] PA 1977 s.74B(2)(d) and s.97(1)(d); Patents Rules 2007 r.100(3).
[234] PA 1977 s.73(1A).

opinion, or the determination of any review or appeal[235] and thereby gives the proprietor opportunity to make observations and to amend the specification of the patent.[236] Such a decision to revoke is a decision of the Comptroller within s.97(1) of the 1977 Act and therefore appeal lies to the Patents Court.

5-99   In practice, the Comptroller has indicated that it shall exercise its discretion to revoke patents only in clear-cut cases where the patented invention clearly lacks novelty or an inventive step.[237]

Entries in the register

5-100   The Comptroller is required to cause to be entered in the register[238]:

    (a)   a notice that a request for an opinion has been received;

    (b)   a notice that a request has been refused or withdrawn; and

    (c)   a notice that an opinion has been issued.

---

[235] PA 1977 s.73(1B).

[236] PA 1977 s.73(1C).

[237] See UKIPO guidance dated July 2014 entitled "Expansion of the Patent Opinions Service". At the time of writing there has been only one instance of revocation by the Comptroller following Opinion Number 04/15.

[238] Patents Rules 2007 r.44(5).

CHAPTER 6

SUPPLEMENTARY PROTECTION CERTIFICATES

CONTENTS

1. INTRODUCTION

Background to the introduction of the Regulations

In 1990 the European Commission published a proposal for a Council Regula-   **6-01**
tion concerning the creation of a supplementary protection certificate for medicinal
products.[1] The aim of the proposed Regulation was to improve the protection of innovation in the pharmaceutical sector. The proposal explained that the duration of
a patent in Europe is 20 years from the date of application and once a patent has
been applied for the patent holder may, in principle, immediately make use of the
invention concerned on the market.[2] However, the proposal pointed out that this is
not the case for medicinal products, since the holder of a patented medicinal product
must refrain from using it until he has obtained authorisation from the health
authorities to place the product on the market. The tests required to compile the application for authorisation and the procedure itself for obtaining authorisation
involved elapses of time which were becoming increasingly longer and proportional
to the importance of the innovation, leading to a corresponding loss of a very
substantial part of the period of exclusivity granted by the patent. Accordingly the
Commission proposed a Regulation which would introduce a system of extensions to the duration of patents in the pharmaceutical field.

The proposal was also put forward with an eye on developments in the law   **6-02**
elsewhere in the 1980s which had created patent term extensions in those national
markets. Such systems had been introduced in 1984 in the USA and 1988 in Japan.[3]
The statute in the USA was known as the Hatch-Waxman Act.[4] There was a concern
that doing nothing similar in Europe would risk a decrease in research due to insufficient resources and relocation of research centres away to non-member countries

---

[1]   COM (90) 101 final [1990] O.J. C114/10. This document is often called the "Explanatory
Memorandum".

[2]   See Explanatory Memorandum COM (90) 101 final [1990] O.J. C114/10 at para.2. The paragraph
refers to making use of the invention after the patent being granted but then notes that this use "may
even be made" before grant.

[3]   See para.6 of Explanatory Memorandum COM (90) 101 final [1990] O.J. C114/10.

[4]   Drug Price Competition and Patent Term Restoration Act of 1984, United States of America, Pub.
L. No.98–417, 98 Stat. 1585.

that offered better protection and an environment more conducive to innovation.[5] Such concerns had led certain states of the Community to look into providing supplementary protection for patented medicinal products on a national basis and in the early 1990s France and Italy had introduced supplementary protection certificates of their own.[6] An important reason for the Regulation therefore was to prevent heterogeneous development of pharmaceutical patent extensions in different Member States.[7]

6-03   On 18 June 1992 EEC Regulation 1768/92[8] concerning the creation of a supplementary protection certificate for medicinal products was enacted. This "Medicinal Products Regulation" entered into force on 2 January 1993.[9] The Medicinal Products Regulation provided for an extension of the patent exclusivity in the pharmaceutical field. The period of the extension depended on the time lost before the first authorisation to place the relevant product on the market had been obtained, with a maximum extension of five years. Transitional provisions were included to address products already on the market. The Regulation was intended to represent a simple transparent system which can be easily applied by the parties concerned.[10]

6-04   On 23 July 1996 the Medicinal Products Regulation was followed by EEC Regulation 1610/96 concerning the creation of a supplementary protection certificate for plant protection products.[11] This regulation is known as the Plant Protection Regulation. It operated in the same way as the Medicinal Products Regulation.

6-05   In 2006 the Medicinal Products Regulation 1768/92 was amended to include the possibility of a so called paediatric extension to the duration of the certificate.[12] This allowed for an extension of the duration of up to six months if certain criteria were satisfied. Essentially the paediatric extension is intended to encourage pharmaceutical companies to extend the scope of their authorisations so that the medicines may be used to treat children.

The legislative history of the Regulations

6-06   As stated above, the Medicinal Products Regulation came into force on 2 January 1993.[13]

EEA amendments

6-07   As a result of the process which formed the European Economic Area (EEA), the EEA Agreement[14] came into force on 1 January 1994. The EEA Agreement implemented various adjustments to Community instruments, including the

---

5   See recital 6 to the codified version of the Medicinal Products Regulation (EC) No. 469/2009 and para.7 of Explanatory Memorandum COM (90) 101 final [1990] O.J. C114/10.
6   1990 in France and 1991 in Italy; see paras 5 and 6 of the Opinion of AG Colomer in *Novartis v Comptroller; Ministre De L'Economie v Millenium* (C207/03 and C-252/03) [2005] R.P.C. 33.
7   Recital 7 to the codified version of the Medicinal Products Regulation (EC) No. 469/2009.
8   O.J. L/182, 2.7.1992, p.1.
9   Six months after publication in the Official Journal, see art.23 of Regulation 1768/92.
10   Explanatory Memorandum COM (90) 101 final [1990] O.J. C114/10, para.16.
11   O.J. L/198, 8.8.1996, p.30.
12   O.J. L/378 27.12.2006, p.1.
13   Six months after publication in the Official Journal, see art.23 of Regulation 1768/92.
14   O.J. L1 3.1.1994, p.9.

Medicinal Products Regulation and extended them to operate throughout the EEA. Today the EEA consists of the EU and Norway, Iceland and Lichtenstein. Other states (Austria, Finland and Sweden) were originally in the EEA but not the Community but have since joined the Community.

The way the adjustment to the Medicinal Products Regulation work is as follows: **6-08**

(i)   Article 7 of the EEA Agreement[15] provides that acts referred to in the annexes to the agreement and decisions of the EEA Joint Committee shall be binding on the parties and part of their legal order. The parties include the Community as well as the then EFTA countries.

(ii)   Annex XVII[16] to the EEA Agreement lists acts relevant to intellectual property and by point 5 of annex 15[17] to Decision 7/94 of the EEA Joint Committee,[18] annex XVII concerning intellectual property was amended to include as para.6 a provision including the Medicinal Products Regulation in the annex. Various amendments to the Medicinal Products Regulation are included (to art.3(b) and art.19 as it then was) and the Medicinal Products Regulation is to be read with those amendments for the purposes of the EEA agreement.

(iii)   Protocol 1[19] to the EEA Agreement provides that whenever acts contain references to the territory of the Community the references will in effect be references to the EEA.

These amendments are important even from the point of view of UK supplementary protection certificates not least because the duration of a certificate set by art.13 of the Regulations is governed by the date of the first authorisation anywhere in the EEA. So, for example, although the codified form of art.13 of the Medicinal Products Regulation refers to the first authorisation in the Community, Protocol 1 to the EEA Agreement requires it to be read as a reference to the EEA and if in fact there was an earlier authorisation in an EEA state which is not a member of the Community then that first authorisation is the relevant one for all supplementary protection certificates throughout the Community as well as the EEA. This is what happened in the *Novartis* case.[20] Similarly a marketing authorisation granted in Sweden while it was in the EEA before joining the Community was taken into account under art.13 for a German application for a certificate.[21] **6-09**

Challenge by Spain

After it came into force a challenge to the validity of the Medicinal Products Regulation was brought by Spain. It was rejected in *Kingdom of Spain v Council of the European Union*[22] in 1995. **6-10**

---

[15] O.J. L1/9 3.1.94.
[16] O.J. L1/482 3.1.94.
[17] O.J. L160/138 28.6.94.
[18] O.J. L160/1 28.6.94.
[19] O.J. L1/38 3.1.94.
[20] *Novartis AG, University College London and Institute of Microbiology and Epidemiology v Comptroller* (C-207/03) conjoined with *Ministre de l'économie v Millenium Pharmaceuticals Inc.* (C-252/03).
[21] *Decision X ZB 31/06 of the German Federal Court of Justice*, 27 May 2008, concerning pantoprazole.
[22] *Kingdom of Spain v Council of the European Union* (C-350-92) [1996] F.S.R. 73.

The Plant Protection Regulation

6-11   On 23 July 1996 the Plant Protection Regulation was enacted. The structure of the Plant Protection Regulation is closely based on the Medicinal Products Regulation. However, the Plant Protection Regulation also includes additional recitals and certain further provisions as compared to the Medicinal Products Regulation. Recital 17 of the Plant Protection Regulation expressly cross refers to the Medicinal Products Regulation and states that these further provisions are "valid mutatis mutandis for the interpretation of" the corresponding parts of the Medicinal Products Regulation.

Enlargement of the Community

6-12   In 1994, 2003 and 2005 various amendments were made to the texts taking into account the accession of various states to what is now the European Union.[23]

The codified Medicinal Products Regulation

6-13   In 2006 the amendments to the Medicinal Products Regulation 1768/92 to incorporate paediatric extensions were enacted.[24] On 16 June 2009 a codified version of the Medicinal Products Regulation dated 6 May 2009 was published in the Official Journal[25] which pulled together the various amendments which were still relevant. It was not intended to change the law. The Patents (Supplementary Protection Certificates) Regulations 2014/2411 amended the Patents Act to refer to the codified version. The recitals to the Medicinal Products Regulation were given numbers in the codified version; unhelpfully however the codification process introduced a new first recital which means that those numbers are out of register with the recitals in the original Medicinal Products Regulation and therefore is not the same as the numbering used in the decided cases prior to codification. Notably the provisions in the Plant Protection Regulation which are to apply to the Medicinal Products Regulation by means of recital 17 of the Plant Protection Regulation were not incorporated expressly into the codified version, albeit they are no doubt intended to remain applicable.

The implementation of the Regulations in the UK

6-14   As European Regulations, the Medicinal Products Regulation and Plant Protection Regulation are directly effective. Nonetheless there are elements of UK legislation which have importance in their implementation in the UK. When they first came into force, the relevant UK legislation was the Patents (Supplementary Protection Certificate for Medicinal Products) Regulations 1992 (SI 1992/3091) and the Patents (Supplementary Protection Certificate for Plant Protection Products) Regulations 1996 (SI 1996/3120). These instruments were repealed by the Patents (Compulsory Licensing and Supplementary Protection Certificates) Regulations 2007 (SI 2007/3293) which came into force on 17 December 2007. This instrument introduced a new s.128B into the Patents Act 1977 to deal with sup-

---

[23] O.J. C/241 29.8.1994, p.21; O.J. L/1 1.1995, p.1; O.J. L/236 23.9.2003, p.33; O.J. L/157 21.6.2005, p.203.
[24] O.J. L/378 27.12.2006, p.1.
[25] O.J. L/152 16.6.2009, p.1.

plementary protection certificates and a new Sch.4A to the 1977 Act as well. Rule 116 of the Patents Rules 2007 (SI 2007/3291) deals with applications for supplementary protection certificates. The various fees payable in relation to supplementary protection certificates are set by the Patents (Fees) Rules 2007 (SI 2007/3292).

The importance of supplementary protection certificates

Although a maximum duration of five years and a maximum further paediatric extension of six months may appear to be a modest extension of time having regard to a patent life of 20 years, nevertheless supplementary protection certificates can be very important. Amongst patents generally, the patents in the pharmaceutical sector tend to be the most valuable as compared to other sectors. The certificates are only granted for products which have achieved a marketing authorisation, thereby automatically selecting out from the range of patents filed by researchers only those which have reached the market. Moreover the period of exclusivity granted by the certificate operates at the end of normal patent life, which is often the most valuable time from the point of view of the company in question. The market for the product has been built up over time and is now well established. Thus supplementary protection certificates are of considerable economic significance in the industrial sectors in which they apply.[26]

6-15

Approach to the interpretation of the Regulations

The Regulations are instruments of European Union law and therefore are interpreted on that basis. A full analysis of the European Union approach to legislative interpretation is beyond the scope of this work. However, there are some particular matters to be kept in mind. Whereas the European Patent Convention exists in three language texts, each of which is equally authentic,[27] the Regulations exist in many more equally authentic texts, in all the languages of the EU. The various language versions of provisions of Community law must be uniformly interpreted and, in the case of divergence between those versions, the provision in question must be interpreted by reference to the purpose and general scheme of the rules of which it forms part (per the Court of Justice in *Hässle*[28]). For example in *AHP v BIE*,[29] a case referred from the Netherlands, the Court of Justice relied on the absence of the word "pending" from the Italian version of the relevant article in the Plant Protection Regulation[30] as part of their reasoning to justify a conclusion which in effect construes that word out of existence overall.[31]

6-16

One of the fundamental principles of legislative interpretation in EU law is that a teleological approach is taken rather than one based on historical methods.[32] Thus the purposes set out in the recitals to the Regulations are of paramount importance.

6-17

---

[26] Another way of gauging their significance may be seen from *Astra Zeneca and EFPIA v the European Commission* (T-321/05) (before the General Court) concerning allegations of an abuse of dominant position, the first being an allegation of abuse relating to applications for supplementary protection certificates (see [295], et seq.).

[27] EPC art.177(1).

[28] *Aktiebolaget Hässle v Ratiopharm* (C-127/00).

[29] *A.H.P. v B.I.E.* (C-482/07) [2010] F.S.R. 23.

[30] art.3(2).

[31] *A.H.P. v B.I.E.* (C-482/07) [2010] F.S.R. 23, [25]; and the remainder of the judgment [26] to [43].

[32] Per Lord Diplock in *D.P.P. v Henn & Darby* [1980] 2 C.M.L.R. 229, 233 at [14].

What matters is the spirit, general scheme and wording and the courts look for the general principles of the Regulations in seeking to find the meaning of a specific provision.[33] The Explanatory Memorandum[34] can also be a key aid to construction.[35]

6-18   Other Community instruments are relevant. For example, there is an express cross reference between the Medicinal Products Regulation and the Plant Protection Regulation,[36] some of the definitions used in the Medicinal Products Regulation and Plant Protection Regulation derive from the corresponding legislation concerned with authorisations themselves[37] and some of the rules on paediatric extensions are found in the Regulation on Medicinal Products for Paediatric Use.[38]

Role of the Court of Justice

6-19   Since the Regulations are part of the law of the EU, the Court of Justice of the European Union in Luxembourg plays a pivotal role. However, a number of issues arising in relation to the Regulations have not (yet) been considered by the Court of Justice but are the subject of decisions in courts of the Member States. It is now a regular occurrence before the national courts to cite cases from other Member States in relation to questions arising under the Regulations.[39] The situation also arises in which there are inconsistent decisions between the courts of different Member States on a given point and no clear answer from the Court of Justice.[40] Of course while the courts of one Member State will give due weight to the decisions of the courts of another, such decisions are not binding precedents. One practical reason why some issues remain undecided by the Court of Justice is the reluctance of litigants to seek a reference from the national courts because of the timescale involved. Certificates can be very valuable commercially but they are rarely litigated inter partes until late in the life of the product concerned. At that late stage the time required for a reference to the Court of Justice when added on to the timescale of national proceedings, can make a reference an unattractive option.

Availability of written submissions to the Court of Justice

6-20   As part of the procedure on a reference from the national courts the Court of Justice can receive submissions from the national governments (and the Commission) as well as the parties to the case. Although these written submissions are not readily accessible to third parties, copies of the submissions of the UK government in the *Farmitalia* case[41] have been obtained from the UKIPO under the Freedom of Information Act 2000.

---

[33]   Per Jacob LJ in *Draco A.B.'s SPC Application* [1996] R.P.C. 417, 437, lines 15–17.
[34]   COM (90) 101 final [1990] O.J. C114/10.
[35]   For an example of its use, see *A.H.P. v B.I.E.* (C-482/07) [2010] F.S.R. 23, [28].
[36]   Recital 17 of Plant Protection Regulation.
[37]   For example, the definition of medicinal product and plant protection product.
[38]   1901/2006, see art.36.
[39]   See, e.g. *Synthon B.V. v Merz Pharma GmbH & Co KgaA* [2009] EWHC 656 (Pat); [2009] R.P.C. 20, 674.
[40]   See, e.g. *Synthon B.V. v Merz Pharma GmbH & Co KgaA* [2009] EWHC 656 (Pat); [2009] R.P.C. 20, 674.
[41]   (C-392/97) [1996] R.P.C. 111.

Interface between two systems of law

The Regulations came about as a result of the interaction between two distinct systems of law and practice, the patent system and the system of authorisation of medicinal products. The timing inherent in the authorisation system meant that inventors were obtaining a shorter period of exclusivity for their products than the patent system was designed to give them.[42] As a result the Regulations operate at the interface between patent protection of "products" and authorisation to market "medicinal products". The distinction between these two terms is critical to the working of the Regulation (per Attorney General Jacobs in the *Pharmacia Italia* case[43]).

6-21

In *Generics v Daiichi*[44] Jacob LJ applied an approach from the law of patents and the law controlling the authorising of medicines to support a proposition in the context of supplementary protection certificates (that an enantiomer was not the same product as a racemate). He did so asking the rhetorical question "Why should the law about SPCs, built as it is on those two branches of law, go off in a different direction?"

6-22

The law governing the authorisation of medicinal and plant protection products was already part of EU law when the Regulations were passed but patent law remains a separate matter. As the Court of Justice noted in the *Farmitalia* case[45] provisions concerning patents have not yet been made the subject of harmonisation at Community level or of an approximation of laws and therefore, in the absence of Community harmonisation of patent law, the extent of patent protection can be determined only in the light of non-Community rules which govern patents. It may be that the divergent approaches in the member states relating to cases about combination products (see below) arose in part as a result of this hybrid nature of the Regulations, including as they do both harmonised EU law aspects as well as unharmonised patent law.

6-23

The purposes for which the Regulations were enacted and the basis for them

In the case of *Kingdom of Spain v Council of the European Union* which concerned the validity of the Medicinal Products Regulation itself as an instrument of Community law, one of the questions the Court of Justice had to consider was whether arts 222 and 36 of the EEC Treaty (as it then was) reserved power to regulate substantive patent law for the national legislatures and thereby excluded any Community action in the matter.[46] The Court of Justice held that although it is for the national legislature to determine the conditions and rules regarding the protection conferred by patents,[47] nevertheless neither art.222 or art.36 of the EEC Treaty (as it then was) reserved power to regulate substantive patent law to the national legislature to the exclusion of any Community action in the matter.[48] At the level of internal legislation, the Community is competent in the field of intel-

6-24

---

[42] Explanatory Memorandum COM (90) 101 final [1990] O.J. C114/10, para.2.

[43] *Pharmacia Italia v Deutsches Patentamt* (C-31/03) [2005] R.P.C. 27; Opinion of Attorney General Jacobs at [38].

[44] [2009] EWCA Civ 646; [2009] R.P.C. 23, [63].

[45] *Farmitalia Carlo Erba SRL* (C-392/97) [1996] R.P.C. 111, [26] and [27].

[46] *Kingdom of Spain v Council of the European Union* (C-350-92) [1996] F.S.R. 73, [16].

[47] *Kingdom of Spain v Council of the European Union* (C-350-92) [1996] F.S.R. 73, [17], citing *Commission v United Kingdom* (C-30/90) [1992] E.C.R. I-892.

[48] *Kingdom of Spain v Council of the European Union* (C-350-92) [1996] F.S.R. 73, [22].

lectual property to harmonise national laws pursuant to arts 100 and 100a (of the Treaty as it then was) and may use art.235 of the Treaty (as it then was) as the basis for creating new rights superimposed on national rights.

6-25   Note that, despite any appearance to the contrary, the Regulations have been held not to constitute Community legislation in the sphere of patents. This is the judgment of the Court of Justice in the *Merck Genericos v Merck & Co* case,[49] the upshot of which was that interpretation of the TRIPs Agreement was not a matter for the Court of Justice. However, in *Daiichi Sankyo*[50] the court held that the law had developed since *Merck* and that the TRIPs Agreement did fall within the field of the common commercial policy and accordingly is capable of interpretation by the court.

Free movement of goods and the internal market

6-26   In the *Spain v Council* case a further objection was taken to the Medicinal Products Regulation based on the purposes for which it was enacted and the Court of Justice had to consider and analyse these purposes when dealing with the Spanish objections. The argument was that the legal basis of the Regulation was flawed because the only basis for it was arts 235 and 100 of the Treaty (as it then was) and those provisions would have required unanimity amongst all Member States and therefore did not affect their sovereignty. In rejecting this objection the court accepted the submission of the Council that the relevant basis was art.100a but in order to do that the court had to investigate whether the Regulation did indeed fall within the scope of art.100a. In confirming this, the court emphasised that at the time the Regulation was adopted provisions concerning the creation of a supplementary protection certificate for medicinal products existed in two Member States and were in a draft stage in another state. Thus the Regulation was intended precisely to establish a uniform Community approach by creating a supplementary protection certificate which may be obtained by the holder of a national or European patent under the same conditions in each Member State and providing in particular for a uniform duration of protection.[51] The court referred to the 6th recital (as it then was) and stated that the Regulation thus aimed to prevent heterogeneous development of national laws which would be likely to create obstacles to the free movement of medicinal products within the Community and directly affect the function of the internal market.[52] The court also held that EU law required in this context that a balance be struck between the interests of the undertakings which hold patents and the interests of manufacturers of generic medicines and that, having particular regard to the 9th recital (as it then was) and to art.13(2) which set a maximum duration of five years for the certificate, the Regulation did not disregard the interests of the consumers or of the generic pharmaceutical industry and was validly within the scope of art.100a.[53]

---

[49] *Merck Genericos v Merck & Co* (C-431/05) see [39]–[46].
[50] *Daiichi Sankyo and Sanofi-Aventis Deutschland* (C-414/11).
[51] *Kingdom of Spain v Council of the European Union* (C-350-92) [1996] F.S.R. 73, [34].
[52] *Kingdom of Spain v Council of the European Union* (C-350-92) [1996] F.S.R. 73, [35] and [36].
[53] *Kingdom of Spain v Council of the European Union* (C-350-92) [1996] F.S.R. 73, [37]–[40].

The objective of preventing heterogeneous development of national laws and having a uniform solution at Community level has been employed as an aid to interpretation of the Regulations in other judgments of the Court of Justice.[54]   **6-27**

Ensuring pharmaceutical research was profitable

Although the legal basis for the Medicinal Products Regulation as a matter of EU law was determined in *Spain v Council*[55] as being derived from its effect on free movement of goods and the functioning of the internal market, in the *Novartis* case[56] Advocate-General Colomer noted that analysis of the preamble to the Medicinal Products Regulation shows that the legislature's main motivation in adopting the legislation was not to guarantee the free movement of medicinal products but rather was to create the conditions necessary to ensure that pharmaceutical research is profitable and to deter firms in that industry from leaving the Union.[57] The unimpeded trade in medicinal products was an indirect result of that main objective. Attorney General Colomer noted that while it was true that primary importance was attributed the free movement of goods in order to provide justification for the Community's competence and to situate the Regulation's legal basis in art.100a of the EC Treaty (as it then was) that does not mean that the provisions are to be observed exclusively from the point of view of the functioning of the common market whilst any other reasons which were decisive in adoption of the rules are to be disregarded.[58] The judgment of the Court of Justice in the *Novartis* case[59] does not expressly endorse this element of the Advocate-General's opinion; however it does endorse the conclusion the AG reached based on this reasoning.[60] In any event the 2nd to 6th recitals of the Medicinal Products Regulation (as codified) support the Opinion of A.G. Colomer. The prime purpose of the Regulation is to support research. The Regulation seeks to do so without impeding free movement of goods and without ignoring other interests such as public health, consumers and the generic industry.   **6-28**

The objective of encouraging pharmaceutical research has also been employed as an aid to interpretation of the Regulations in judgments of the Court of Justice.[61]   **6-29**

---

[54] Such as *Aktiebolaget Hässle v Ratiopharm* (C-127/00), [37]; *A.H.P. v B.I.E.* (C-482/07) [2010] F.S.R. 23, [35].

[55] *Kingdom of Spain v Council of the European Union* (C-350-92) [1996] F.S.R. 73.

[56] *Novartis AG, University College London and Institute of Microbiology and Epidemiology v Comptroller* (C-207/03) conjoined with *Ministre de l'économie v Millenium Pharmaceuticals Inc* (C-252/03).

[57] *Novartis AG, University College London and Institute of Microbiology and Epidemiology v Comptroller* (C-207/03) conjoined with *Ministre de l'économie v Millenium Pharmaceuticals Inc* (C-252/03), Attorney General's Opinion at [42].

[58] *Novartis AG, University College London and Institute of Microbiology and Epidemiology v Comptroller* (C-207/03) conjoined with *Ministre de l'économie v Millenium Pharmaceuticals Inc* (C-252/03), Attorney General's Opinion at [42].

[59] *Novartis AG, University College London and Institute of Microbiology and Epidemiology v Comptroller* (C-207/03) conjoined with *Ministre de l'économie v Millenium Pharmaceuticals Inc* (C-252/03).

[60] *Novartis AG, University College London and Institute of Microbiology and Epidemiology v Comptroller* (C-207/03) conjoined with *Ministre de l'économie v Millenium Pharmaceuticals Inc* (C-252/03), [31] and [32].

[61] Such as *Farmitalia* (C-392/97), [19]; *A.H.P. v B.I.E.* (C-482/07) [2010] F.S.R. 23, [30].

What kind of pharmaceutical research is to be encouraged?

6-30   The Explanatory Memorandum states that "all research, whatever the strategy or final result, must be given sufficient protection"[62] and also that "all pharmaceutical research provided it leads to a new invention which can be patented ... must be encouraged, without any discrimination and must be able to be given a supplementary certificate of protection provided that all the conditions ... are fulfilled".[63] Nevertheless, in *Draco's Application*[64] Jacob J stated that the supplementary protection certificate scheme is not for the general protection of the fruits of research and that formulation research (unless it warrants its own patent) was not to be protected by the scheme while in *Generics v Daiichi*[65] in the Court of Appeal Jacob LJ confirmed that this remained his view and was acte claire.

6-31   This raises the question as to whether medical devices are protectable under the Medicinal Products Regulation on the basis that research is required to develop them, they are often covered by patents and their launch may be delayed by the requirement to obtain an EC Design Examination Certificate under Directive 93/42/EEC. So far the UKIPO has rejected attempts by manufacturers of medical devices to obtain supplementary protection certificates for such products per se. In *Cerus Corporation*[66] the Hearing Officer decided that the conformity assessment procedure for a Class III medical device is not the same as or equivalent to the process carried out to authorise a medicinal product for human use and rejected the application under arts 2 and 3(b) of the Medicinal Products Regulation. This reasoning has been followed in *Leibniz-Institut für Neue Materialien Gemeinnützige GmbH*[67] and *Angiotech Pharmaceuticals Inc & University of British Columbia*.[68] In the latter case the applicant sought to rely on the fact that a product may in certain circumstances be classified as both a medical device and a medicinal product in different Member States.[69] However, the Court of Justice had emphasised in *Laboratoires Lyocentre* that only a product which does not achieve its principal intended action in or on the human body by pharmacological, immunological or metabolic means may be classified as a medical device[70] and that, if in doubt, a product must be classified as a medicinal product[71], and so the Hearing Officer rejected the argument that this meant that all medical device approvals met the requirements under art.3(b) of the Medicinal Products Regulation.[72]

Taking account of all interests at stake

6-32   Recital 10 (codified version of Medicinal Products Regulation) provides that all the interests at stake including those of public health should be taken into account. In the original form of the Medicinal Products Regulation this recital was the 9th one and it was followed by a further 10th recital expressed as related to the

62 COM (90) 101 final [1990] O.J. C114/10, para.12.
63 para.29 of the Explanatory Memorandum COM (90) 101 final [1990] O.J. C114/10.
64 [1996] R.P.C. 417, 439.
65 [2009] EWCA Civ 646, [79].
66 O/141/14.
67 O/328/14.
68 O/466/15.
69 *Laboratoires Lyocentre* (C-109/12).
70 *Laboratoires Lyocentre* (C-109/12), at [44].
71 *Laboratoires Lyocentre* (C-109/12), at [40]–[41] and [59].
72 See *Angiotech Pharmaceuticals Inc & University of British Columbia*, at [77].

transitional provisions which referred to making sure health policies pursued both at a national and community level was not compromised. These two recitals were often considered together (see, e.g. Attorney General Jacobs in *Pharmacia Italia*[73]) and were taken to include the interests of the generic pharmaceutical industry as well as that of the research based pharmaceutical industry (see also [31], [32] and [45] of the Opinion of Attorney General Stix-Hackl in *Hässle*[74]). Although the original 10th recital has not been reproduced in the codified Medicinal Products Regulation (presumably since the original transitional provisions have gone), clearly the overall objectives of the Regulation have not changed.

In any case it is clear that the consideration of all interests at stake is a key justification for the overall 15 years maximum exclusivity period.[75]   **6-33**

Providing a simple and straightforward system

Although not mentioned in the recitals, it is clear that one of the objectives of the scheme is for it to be an administratively simple system. The national patent offices were supposed to be able to handle the grant of the certificates in an administratively simple manner. There was not intended to be a need for the kinds of more complex procedures which are a feature of patent granting; the conditions to be fulfilled were intended to involve objective data which was easily verified.[76]   **6-34**

Purposes of the plant protection regulation

The recitals to the Plant Protection Regulation differ in various ways from those in the Medicinal Products Regulation but there is no difference in substance. Objectives expressed as relating to public health and pharmaceutical research in the Medicinal Products Regulation are expressed as relating to the production and procurement of plentiful food, environmental protection and research into plant protection in the Plant Protection Regulation (see Plant Protection Regulation recitals 1–3 and 8). Competition from Japan and North America is referred to in terms (Plant Protection Regulation recital 7) as compared to recital 6 of the codified Medicinal Products Regulation which is a more oblique reference to the same concept.   **6-35**

2.   THE APPLICATION FOR A CERTIFICATE

Date by which an application must be made—art.7

Article 7 of both the Medicinal Products Regulation and Plant Protection Regulation governs the date by which an application for a certificate must be made. The primary rule is that an application for a certificate must be lodged within six months of the date on which marketing authorisation in the relevant Member State has been   **6-36**

---

[73] *Pharmacia Italia v Deutsches Patentamt* (C-31/03) [2005] R.P.C. 27; Opinion of Attorney General Jacobs at [42] and [43], approved by the Court in its judgment at [22].
[74] *Aktiebolaget Hässle v Ratiopharm* (C-127/00), Attorney General Stix-Hackl.
[75] See *Kingdom of Spain v Council of the European Union* (C-350-92) [1996] F.S.R. 73, [38] and *A.H.P. v B.I.E.* (C-482/07) [2010] F.S.R. 23, [39].
[76] See paras 16 and 17 of the Explanatory Memorandum COM (90) 101 final [1990] O.J. C114/10 and see [39] of the judgment of Kitchin J in *Gilead's SPC Application* [2008] EWHC 1902 (Pat).

granted.[77] This rule assumes that the patent was filed and granted before the marketing authorisation. Correspondingly art.3 of both regulations, which governs the conditions for obtaining a certificate, requires that at the date of the application for the certificate the basic patent is in force and a marketing authorisation has been granted.

6-37   The question of what art.7(1) means by the date of grant of a marketing authorisation has arisen a number of contexts. There are two possible kinds of marketing authorisation referred to in the Medicinal Products Regulation which art.7 could be referring to—namely the local authorisation in the Member State in which the application is being made, or the "first authorisation for placing the product on the market in the community", which plays a role in setting the duration of the certificate under art.13 and may have a much earlier date than the local authorisation. It is clear from the fact that art.7(1) refers to the "authorisation referred to in Art 3(b)" that it is the local marketing authorisation which is relevant.

6-38   Thus the time for a UK applicant which runs under art.7(1) does not start even if that applicant has obtained a marketing authorisation elsewhere in the Community. The time under art.7(1) only starts to run once a authorisation applicable to the UK has been granted. This was part of the problem confronted by the applicant in the *Yamanouchi* case.[78] In that case, on the date of its application on 15 January 1993 the applicant had obtained a marketing authorisation in France but its application in the UK had been delayed. It was not ultimately granted until 1995. However, the patent expired on 17 January 1993. Thus if the applicant had waited until 1995 to make the application under art.7(1) within six months of the date of the UK application, then the patent would have expired two years beforehand and art.3(a) would not have been satisfied. The applicant therefore tried to bring its application under the then transitional provisions (art.19) but that attempt failed as well on the basis that the court held that there had to be a local authorisation in place.

6-39   In the *Abbott Laboratories' SPC application*[79] the Comptroller's Hearing Officer (Mr Walker) had to consider whether the date referred to in art.7(1) was the date the grant of the authorisation was notified to the public or the actual date of grant. He held that it was the date of grant.[80] However, this decision now seems doubtful in the light of the decision of the Court of Justice in *Seattle Genetics*[81] whereby the court held that the similar provision of art.13(1) relating to the term of a SPC should be calculated by reference to the date of notification of grant of the relevant MA (which is likely to provide a valuable additional few days' protection to most right holders). See also the preceding decision of the UKIPO on art.13(1) in *Genzyme Corporation*.[82] However, pending clarification from the Court of Justice, a cautious applicant ought to apply within six months of the date of grant.

6-40   In *Kirin-Amgen v Lithuania State Patent Bureau*[83] one of the issues the Court of Justice had to decide was how the provisions of art.7(1) applied in a case in which a centralised Community-wide marketing authorisation had been granted in the then Community before the accession of a state (Lithuania) but then one of the

---

[77] Medicinal Products Regulation art.7(1); Plant Protection Regulation art.7(1).
[78] *Yamanouchi Pharmaceuticals Co Ltd v C-G* (C-110/95) [1997] R.P.C. 844.
[79] See *Abbott Laboratories' SPC application* [2004] R.P.C. 20.
[80] *Abbott Laboratories' SPC application* [2004] R.P.C. 20, 391, at [10]–[31].
[81] (C-471/14).
[82] BL/O/418/13.
[83] *Kirin-Amgen Inc v Lithuania State Patent Bureau* (C-66/09).

consequences of the accession was to extend the effect of the centralised authorisation to that state. The applicant argued that the relevant date for the purposes of art.7(1) was the date the authorisation took effect in the Member State. The Court of Justice held that art.7(1) was not to be interpreted in that way and that the relevant date was the date of the original marketing authorisation, particularly having regard to the transitional provisions. Any other an interpretation would run counter to the outcome of the negotiations leading to accession.[84] See also *Hogan Lovells International LLP*[85] in which the Court of Justice held that a provisional marketing authorisation for a plant protection product was a valid authorisation taking into account the relevant transitional provisions. The EFTA Court (responsible for determining questions under the Medicinal Products Regulation referred by the national courts of Norway, Iceland and Liechtenstein) came to a similar conclusion in the context of veterinary vaccine products in *Pharmaq v Intervet*.[86]

Application if the marketing authorisation precedes the grant of the patent

Article 7(2) of both the Medicinal Products Regulation and Plant Protection Regulation provides notwithstanding art.7(1), that where the authorisation is granted before the basic patent is granted, the application shall be made within six months of the date on which the patent is granted. **6-41**

Transitional provisions

In the original form of the Medicinal Products Regulation, art.19(2) provided that certain applications for a certificate had to be submitted within six months of the date on which the Regulation entered into force (i.e. within six months of 2 January 1993). These provisions related to applications for certificates under the transitional provisions in art.19(1), which were cases in which, on the date the Regulation entered into force, the products were already protected by a patent and for which marketing authorisations had already been granted. Therefore, art.19(2) in the original Regulation operated as a derogation from art.7 in order to allow applications to be made in certain cases which would otherwise have been too late under art.7.[87] Article 19 of the original Regulation is not included in the codified version of the Medicinal Products Regulation because applications can no longer be made under it. However, the importance of this provision remains because a number of the key cases before the Court of Justice relating to supplementary protection certificates related to art.19 (e.g. *Yamanouchi*[88] and *Hässle*[89]) and the modern transitional provisions which are part of the codified Medicinal Products Regulation are based on art.19 at least in part.[90] **6-42**

---

[84] *Kirin-Amgen Inc v Lithuania State Patent Bureau* (C-66/09), [50].
[85] (C-229/09).
[86] (E-16/14).
[87] See *Yamanouchi Pharmaceuticals Co Ltd v C-G* (C-110/95) [1997] R.P.C. 844, [19].
[88] *Yamanouchi Pharmaceuticals Co Ltd v C-G* (C-110/95) [1997] R.P.C. 844.
[89] *Aktiebolaget Hässle v Ratiopharm* (C-127/00).
[90] See Codified Medicinal Products Regulation art.20.

Extensions of time for the application

6-43   In *Abbott Laboratories' SPC application*[91] the applicant for a certificate missed the six months deadline by six days. The Patent Office examiner rejected the application as out of time and the applicant took the matter to an oral hearing before the Comptroller's Hearing Officer (Mr Walker). Mr Walker held that the application was indeed late but that the period under art.7 may be extended at the Comptroller's discretion under r.110(1) of the Patents Rules 1995 (as it then was) as well as art.18 of the Medicinal Products Regulation (now art.19 of the codified Medicinal Products Regulation) which provides that in the absence of procedural provisions in the Regulation, the national procedural provisions applicable to the basic patent shall apply. Mr Walker also noted that the authorities in other Member States had allowed similar extensions of time.[92] The approach applied by the Comptroller under r.110(1) of the Patents Rules 1995 (as it then was) was to grant an extension of time if the application is filed late due to unforeseen circumstances and the applicant acts promptly to rectify the situation, following the decision on r.110 in the *Heatex* case.[93] Today the Comptroller's power to extend time is r.108 of the Patents Rules 2007.[94]

6-44   However, this approach is to be contrasted with that in *Otsuka Pharmaceuticals Company Limited*[95] where an extension of time for further data to be obtained in support of an application for a paediatric extension was refused and the Hearing Officer (Dr Cullen) found that on the balance of probabilities the data would not be obtained before expiry of the SPC.

Form of the application

6-45   Article 8 of both the Medicinal Products Regulation and Plant Protection Regulation provides that the application for a certificate contains the following:

(a)   a request for the grant of a certificate;
(b)   a copy of the marketing authorisation referred to in art.3(b) of the Regulation, in other words the authorisation which is operative for the UK market; and
(c)   if the authorisation for the UK is not the earliest authorisation somewhere in the Community, a copy of the appropriate notice of that first Community authorisation.

6-46   The request itself will contain details of the applicant and any representative as well as details of the basic patent, the number and date of the relevant UK marketing authorisation and, if necessary, the number and date of the earlier first authorisation somewhere in the Community. For the case in which the applicant is unable to provide a copy of the relevant authorisation see *Biogen*.[96]

6-47   Where the application for a certificate includes a request for a paediatric extension, further appropriate information is required as well. This is dealt with below.

6-48   The application is made to the UKIPO, i.e. the competent industrial property of-

[91]   *Abbott Laboratories' SPC application* [2004] R.P.C. 20.
[92]   *Abbott Laboratories' SPC application* [2004] R.P.C. 20, [42].
[93]   *Heatex Group Ltd's Application* [1995] R.P.C. 546.
[94]   SI 2007/3291.
[95]   BL/O/098/15.
[96]   *Biogen v SmithKline Beecham* (C-181/95) [1997] R.P.C. 833.

fice of the Member State: see art.9 of the Medicinal Products Regulation and Plant Protection Regulation.

Duty of candour?

Clearly applications for certificates should contain accurate information. In the **6-49** *Astra Zeneca* case[97] the European Court of Justice (General Court) held that the submission to patent offices of objectively misleading representations by an undertaking in a dominant position which are of such a nature as to lead those offices to grant it supplementary protection certificates to which it is not entitled or to which it is entitled for a shorter period, thus resulting in a restriction or elimination of competition, constituted an abuse of that position.[98] The mere fact that certain public authorities did not let themselves be misled and detected the inaccuracies or that competitors obtained revocation of those certificates after their unlawful grant was not an answer.[99]

Procedure dealing with the application

Article 10 of both the Medicinal Products Regulation and Plant Protection **6-50** Regulation provides that the relevant authority (i.e. the UKIPO in the UK) will grant or reject the certificate on the basis of whether or not it meets the conditions laid down in the Regulations. Articles 10(3)–10(4) allow the UKIPO to ask the applicant to rectify any irregularity in or settle a fee if the application does not meet the formal requirements of art.8, and to reject the application if those requirements are not rectified. Third party observations are admissible during the application process.[100]

The Regulations give the relevant authority the power to grant certificates without **6-51** verifying that certain conditions (arts 3(c) and 3(d)) are met but the UKIPO does not seek to avoid this task.

There is no time limit by which an application must be processed (see *AHP v* **6-52** *BIE*[101]). In some states the local rules require an application to be dealt with as quickly as possible while in others the application is not considered until the relevant basic patent is about to expire.[102] In the UK the applications are dealt with as part of the normal work of the UKIPO.

Fee to be paid for the certificate to take effect

Articles 12 and 14 of both Regulations provide that Member States may require **6-53** the payment of annual fees and that the certificate will lapse if the fee is not paid. In the UK these fees have been implemented as a single fee whose size depends on the duration of the certificate which must be paid as a condition for the certificate

---

[97] *Astra Zeneca and EFPIA v the European Commission* (European Court of Justice, General Court) (T-321/05), see [355]–[368].
[98] *Astra Zeneca and EFPIA v the European Commission* (European Court of Justice, General Court) (T-321/05), [361].
[99] *Astra Zeneca and EFPIA v the European Commission* (European Court of Justice, General Court) (T-321/05), [360].
[100] *Icahn School of Medicine at Mount Sinai's SPC* BL O/552/14 [2015] R.P.C. 21, at [19]–[30].
[101] *A.H.P. v B.I.E.* (C482/07), at [37].
[102] *A.H.P. v B.I.E.* (C482/07), at [37].

to take effect.[103] The fee is due before the end of the prescribed period which is three months ending with the start date of the certificate.[104] There is a six-month grace period afterwards within which the fee may be paid with an additional fee which amounts to an additional sum of half the main fee.[105] Nevertheless the fees are still "annual" fees within the meaning of the Regulations and a challenge brought to declare the UK regime ultra vires was dismissed in *Tulane Education Fund's SPC*.[106]

Publication of the grant of a certificate

6-54   Notification that a certificate has been granted is published pursuant to Article 11 of both Regulations and art.11(1)(a)–(f) sets out the details which must be included in the notification. They include the identity of the holder, details of the patent and relevant authorisations and the duration of the certificate.

6-55   Notable by its absence from this mandatory list is a statement of the nature of the product the subject of the certificate. The reason for this absence is presumably because the Regulations presuppose that the identity of the product is something which could readily be discerned from consideration of the basic patent and marketing authorisations. In any case the UKIPO as a matter of practice includes in its notification a description of the product.

6-56   While of course publication of a description of the product is highly desirable and allows an insight into the basis on which the UKIPO granted a given certificate, the legal status of that description is not clear. There is no procedure for a purported amended of such a description because the description itself is not accorded any status in the scheme of the Regulations. Nevertheless, the correct identification of the "product" for which the certificate has been granted can be vital. This can be seen for example from the *Farmitalia* case[107] in which the dispute was that the German Patent Office was only prepared to grant a certificate for "the medicament Zavedos containing as its active ingredient idarubicin hydrochloride" whereas the applicant wanted a certificate for "idarubicin and salts thereof including idarubicin hydrochloride" or alternatively "idarubicin and idarubicin hydrochloride".[108]

Who may be granted a SPC?

6-57   Article 6 of both the Medicinal Products Regulation and Plant Protection Regulation provides that the certificate shall be granted to the holder of the basic patent or his successor in title. In the light of art.1(c) this has been held to be a reference to the holder of the patent at the time the application was made.[109] Since the basic patent may well not be held by the same undertaking as the marketing authorisation, the question of parties has arisen in a number of contexts.

6-58   It is clear from the decision of the European Court of Justice in *Biogen Inc v*

---

[103] PA 1977 Sch.4A para.5; and see Patents (Fees) Rules 2007 r.6.
[104] PA 1977 Sch.4A para.5(a); and Patents Rules 2007 r.116(2). There is an exception to deal with a case in which the certificate is granted within that three-month period.
[105] PA 1977 Sch.4A para.5(b); and Patents (Fees) Rules 2007 r.6(4).
[106] [2013] EWCA Civ 890, [2014] R.P.C. 10.
[107] *Farmitalia Carlo Erba SRL* (C-392/97) [1996] R.P.C. 111.
[108] *Farmitalia Carlo Erba SRL* (C-392/97) [1996] R.P.C. 111, [9] and [10].
[109] *Teva v Amgen* [2013] EWHC 3711 (Pat), [56].

SmithKline Beecham Biologicals S.A.[110] that the basic patent and the marketing authorisation may be held by different people and this is no bar to the grant of the certificate. Even if the patent holder is unable to provide a copy of the authorisation the application for the certificate must not be refused on that ground alone.[111] The Court of Justice also held that the Regulation does not itself impose an obligation on the holder of the marketing authorisation in those circumstances to provide a copy to the patent holder,[112] although the court observed that the Regulation does not preclude an obligation to provide such a copy from being deemed to be inherent in the relationship between the patent holder and the holder of the authorisation.

The *Biogen* case was one in which the holder of the marketing authorisation (SKB) was a licensee under the patent.[113] The problem arose because SKB understood that the Medicinal Products Regulation only permitted one certificate per product, SKB thought that Biogen's patents were of uncertain validity and SKB were also a licensee under a patent held by Institut Pasteur, to whom they had already provided a copy of the authorisation in order for Institut Pasteur to obtain a certificate for its patent.[114] Inherent in the circumstances facing the Court of Justice in the *Biogen* case was the fact that the holder of the marketing authorisation (SKB) did not want the patent holder (Biogen) to obtain a certificate prolonging the lifetime of Biogen's patent and the court's decision permitting Biogen to obtain a certificate in any event necessarily shows that a patent holder does not need the consent of the holder of the relevant marketing authorisation to obtain a certificate.

6-59

Certificate when authorisation held by infringer

The question which remains and is yet to be decided is whether a patent holder could obtain a certificate in a case in which the holder of the marketing authorisation has no licence and is infringing. Such a person obviously would not want the patent life extended since it would extend their liability for infringement. There is nothing in the terms of the Regulations which requires the holder of the marketing authorisation to be a licensee at all. Clearly the scheme was not set up contemplating that patent holders would seek supplementary protection certificates to cover other people's products but the logic of the *Biogen* case would support such an application. The Patents Court indicated in *Eli Lilly v Human Genome Sciences Inc*[115] that the holder of a basic patent can indeed make an application for a SPC in reliance on an MA held by an unconnected third party. Warren J held that the issue was sufficiently clear at the first instance level for no reference to be made on its own, but that the point was worthy of a reference if made at the same time as another relevant reference arising out of the same facts. In the circumstances of that case a trial was ordered to find the relevant facts but that aspect of the action was compromised before the trial could take place.

6-60

[110] *Biogen Inc v SmithKline Beecham Biologicals S.A.* (C-181/95) [1997] R.P.C. 833.
[111] *Biogen Inc v SmithKline Beecham Biologicals S.A.* (C-181/95) [1997] R.P.C. 833, [39]–[47].
[112] *Biogen Inc v SmithKline Beecham Biologicals S.A.* (C-181/95) [1997] R.P.C. 833, [31]–[38].
[113] *Biogen Inc v SmithKline Beecham Biologicals S.A.* (C-181/95) [1997] R.P.C. 833, [4]–[5].
[114] *Biogen Inc v SmithKline Beecham Biologicals S.A.* (C-181/95) [1997] R.P.C. 833, [10], and see the headnote to the report of the case in the R.P.C.
[115] [2012] EWHC 2290 (Pat).

Invalidity of a certificate and correction of errors after grant

6-61   Article 15 of both Regulations provides that a certificate shall be invalid on various grounds. An application to revoke is brought before the body responsible under national law for the revocation of the corresponding basic patent. Thus an action for revocation can be brought in the UK before the UKIPO, the Patents Court or the Intellectual Property Enterprise Court.

6-62   The grounds of revocation are:

(a) the certificate was granted contrary to art.3;

(b) the basic patent has lapsed before the term of the certificate expires;

(c) the basic patent was been amended so as to no longer protect the product; and

(d) after the basic patent has expired, it would have been invalid.

6-63   Although the Regulations do not provide expressly for it, it is clear that a certificate can be rectified on proper grounds after grant. The most obvious case being one in which the duration has been wrongly calculated and needs to be corrected.[116]

3.   SUBSTANTIVE CONDITIONS FOR THE GRANT OF A CERTIFICATE

Conditions for obtaining a certificate

6-64   Article 3 of both the Medicinal Products Regulation and Plant Protection Regulation provides that a certificate shall be granted if, in the Member State in which the application is submitted and at the date of that application:

(a) the product is protected by a basic patent in force[117];

(b) an appropriate and valid authorisation to place the product on the market has been granted[118];

(c) the product has not already been the subject of a certificate[119]; and

(d) the authorisation referred to in (b) above is the first authorisation to place the product on the market as a medicinal/plant protection product.[120]

6-65   A further condition is that the holder of more than one patent for the same product shall not be granted more than one certificate for that product. This rule is expressly part of the Plant Protection Regulation in art.3(2). Recital 17 of the Plant Protection Regulation states that this is one of the "detailed rules" of the Plant Protection Regulation which is also valid mutatis mutandis for the interpretation of the Medicinal Products Regulation and in particular art.3 thereof.

6-66   The expressions used in these conditions are defined in both regulations in specific and important ways. The definitions are essentially the same in both the Medicinal Products Regulation and Plant Protection Regulation and are set out in

---

[116] See *Aktiebolaget Hässle v Ratiopharm* (C-127/00), at [88] and see also [62]–[75] of the Opinion of Advocate-General Colomer in *Novartis AG, University College London and Institute of Microbiology and Epidemiology v Comptroller* (C-207/03) conjoined with *Ministre de l'économie v Millenium Pharmaceuticals Inc* (C-252/03).

[117] Medicinal Product Regulation art.3(a); Plant Protection Regulation art.3(1)(a).

[118] Medicinal Product Regulation art.3(b); Plant Protection Regulation art.3(1)(b).

[119] Medicinal Product Regulation art.3(c); Plant Protection Regulation art.3(1)(c).

[120] Medicinal Product Regulation art.3(d); Plant Protection Regulation art.3(1)(d).

art.1. Below, the definitions are addressed first followed by consideration of the conditions.

"Product"

The definition of the product in question is central to the scheme of the Regulations. The various conditions for the grant of a certificate depend on that defined concept and the subject matter of protection conferred by the certificate is also defined by reference to the product.[121] In the Medicinal Products Regulation "product" means the active ingredient or combination of active ingredients of a medicinal product[122] and "medicinal product" means the substance or combination of substances presented for treating or preventing disease, etc.[123] (the full definition of medicinal product is addressed below). Thus, at least in a simple case, the medicinal product will be the full pharmaceutical formulation of the drug in question which may, for example, include inert ingredients going to make up a tablet as well as the active ingredient whereas the product is the active ingredient.   **6-67**

Jacob J explained the difference between the "product" and the "medicinal product" in *Draco A.B.'s SPC Application*.[124] He noted that recitals 9 and 10 of the Medicinal Products Regulation[125] use both the phrase *medicinal product* and *product* and that without more there could be ambiguity. The recitals provide that the period of exclusivity should be a maximum of 15 years from the date the *medicinal product* first obtains authorisation but that the scope of protection should be strictly confined to the *product* which obtained authorisation. As Jacob J explained,[126] it is clear the authors of the Regulation have thought about the difference between the active ingredient (product) and actual formulation (medicinal product), and this is because authorisations typically are not for active ingredients as such. They are much more tightly drawn, generally to dosage and formulation or presentation and that has to be so because the actual performance of an active ingredient depends on these matters in addition to the active ingredient itself. So in the *Draco* case itself the argument that the "product" could be defined as micronised particles of budesonide (a dry powder formulation) in order to avoid the problem that there was an earlier authorisation for budesonide formulated in an aerosol, was rejected.[127] The product was simply budesonide. A similar conclusion was reached by the Comptroller's Hearing Officer in a case where there was an existing certificate for the active ingredient sevelamer hydrochloride and the applicant tried to obtain a second certificate for sevelamer carbonate. The active ingredient in each case was sevelamer.[128]   **6-68**

Excipients

A "product" does not include any excipient over and above the active ingredient no matter how important that excipient may be to the functioning of the active   **6-69**

---

121   Medicinal Products Regulation and Plant Protection Regulation art.4.
122   Medicinal Product Regulation art.1(b).
123   Medicinal Product Regulation art.1(a).
124   *Draco A.B.'s SPC Application* [1996] R.P.C. 417.
125   Recitals 8 and 9 in the form of the Medicinal Products Regulation considered by Jacob J in *Draco A.B.'s SPC Application* Patents Court [1996] R.P.C. 417.
126   *Draco A.B.'s SPC Application* Patents Court [1996] R.P.C. 417, 438 lines 5–40.
127   *Draco A.B.'s SPC Application* Patents Court [1996] R.P.C. 417, 439–440.
128   *Genzyme Corporation* BL O/495/12.

ingredient. This was decided by the Court of Justice in *Massachusetts Institute of Technology*.[129] Since there is no definition of "active ingredient" in the Medicinal Products Regulation, the Court decided that the meaning of that term must be determined from its context and from its usual meaning in every day language, and that meant that a substance which had no effect on its own was not an active ingredient.[130] The basic patent covered a combination of two elements, a polymeric biodegradeable excipient and a chemotherapy drug (carmustine). The combination was used in the form of a device implanted into the cranium for the treatment of recurrent brain tumours. Although the excipient in question had no therapeutic effect on its own Advocate-General Leger noted that the combination gave the active ingredient entirely new properties in terms of efficacy and safety of use.[131] The problem from the point of view of a supplementary protection certificate was that the drug alone had been authorised for a long time and no certificate could be granted for it. The applicant therefore argued that the "product" in question was the combination of carmustine and the polymer. Although the opinion of Advocate General Leger was firmly in the applicant's favour, the Court of Justice rejected that approach. The Court held that the definition of product in art.1(b) of the Medicinal Products Regulation must be interpreted such that a "combination of active ingredients of a medicinal product" did not include a combination of two substances when only one of which has therapeutic effects while the other is an excipient. The fact the excipient was one which rendered possible a pharmaceutical form of the medicinal product which was necessary for the therapeutic efficacy of the drug in the indication was irrelevant.

6-70   The Court of Justice addressed this issue by reference to the use of adjuvants in the manufacture of vaccines in *Glaxosmithkline Biologicals, Niederlassung der Smithkline Beecham Pharma GmbH & Co KG, v Comptroller-General of Patents, Designs and Trade Marks*.[132] In its reasoned order, it held that just as an adjuvant does not fall within the definition of "active ingredient" within the meaning of that provision, so a combination of two substances, namely an active ingredient having therapeutic effects on its own, and an adjuvant which, while enhancing those therapeutic effects, has no therapeutic effect on its own, does not fall within the definition of "combination of active ingredients" within the meaning of that provision. However, in contrast to the facts of MIT and GSK, in *Bayer CropScience AG v Deutsches Patent- und Markenamt*[133] the Court of Justice held that, for the purposes of the Plant Protection Regulation,[134] an active substance may include a substance intended to be used as a safener, where that substance has a toxic, phytotoxic or plant protection action of its own.

6-71   This issue was addressed again in *Arne Forsgren v Österreichisches Patentamt*[135] in the context of the use of carrier proteins in pneumococcal vaccines to which are conjugated the relevant pneumococcal polysaccharides. The Protein D carrier proteins in that case acted as adjuvants to increase the effectiveness of the pneumococcal polysaccharides to stimulate an immune response in children.

---

[129] Proceedings initiated by *Massachusetts Institute of Technology* (C-431/04).
[130] *Proceedings initiated by Massachusetts Institute of Technology* (C-431/04), [15]–[18].
[131] *Proceedings initiated by Massachusetts Institute of Technology* (C-431/04), Opinion of Advocate General Leger of 24 November 2005, [51].
[132] (C-210/13).
[133] (C-11/13).
[134] See para.6-11.
[135] (C-631/13).

However, unlike the facts of GSK, they also provided protection themselves against (a different) Haemophilus influenzae bacterium from which they were derived.[136] Following *Massachusetts Institute of Technology* the court held that only a substance which has a pharmacological, immunological or metabolic action of its own, independent of any covalent binding with other active ingredients, could be an active ingredient within the meaning of art.1(b) of the Medicinal Products Regulation.[137] This did not necessarily exclude active ingredients which were covalently bound to other active ingredients.[138] However, under art.3(b) of the Medicinal Products Regulation the active ingredient must also have an effect which falls within the therapeutic indications covered by the wording of the relevant marketing authorisation. This did not apply to Protein D because the marketing authorisation referred only to diseases caused by Streptococcus pneumonia.[139]

Use of a product

The use to which a product is to be put (also known as the "indication") is not part of the definition of product either. This was decided in the *Yissum* case[140] as follows. The same questions as had been referred in *Massachusetts Institute of Technology* were also referred in *Yissum* but once the judgment in *Massachusetts Institute of Technology* was given, those same questions were withdrawn. However a further question had been referred in the *Yissum* case as to whether the use to which the product was being put could be regarded as relevant so that a drug with a new use could be regarded as a different product from the same drug with an old use. The Court of Justice gave its answer by reasoned order and without an oral hearing on the basis that the answer to it could clearly be deduced from existing case law.[141] The court held that the concept of "product" cannot include the therapeutic use of an active ingredient.[142]   **6-72**

This, however, does not preclude the grant of separate SPCs for the same product and a different medical use—see *Neurim*[143] discussed further below.   **6-73**

Plant protection Regulation

In the Plant Protection Regulation, "product" is defined in a manner which closely corresponds to the definition in the Medicinal Products Regulation albeit that the definition is more elaborate (see Plant Protection Products below).   **6-74**

Combinations

The part played by the correct definition of "product" in cases about combinations of active ingredients are addressed below (see para.6–119, et seq.).   **6-75**

---

[136] See [13].
[137] At [27] and [53]–[54].
[138] See [28].
[139] See [37]–[39].
[140] *Yissum Research and Development Company of the Hebrew University of Jerusalem v Comptroller-General of Patents* (202/05) [2007] E.C.R. I-2839.
[141] See also *Neurim Pharmaceuticals (1991) Ltd v Comptroller-General of Patents* [2010] EWHC 976 (Pat)
[142] *Yissum Research and Development Company of the Hebrew University of Jerusalem v Comptroller-General of Patents* (202/05) [2007] E.C.R. I-2839, [18].
[143] *Neurim Pharmaceuticals (1991) Ltd v Comptroller-General of Patents* (C-130/11) [2013] R.P.C. 23.

"Medicinal Product"

6-76   In the Medicinal Products Regulation "medicinal product" is defined as any substance or combination of substances presented for treating or preventing disease in human beings or animals and any substance or combination of substances which may be administered to human beings or animals with a view to making a medical diagnosis or to restoring, correcting or modifying physiological functions in humans or in animals.[144] As Jacob J explained in Draco,[145] this means the actual formulation in question.

6-77   The definition in the Medicinal Products Regulation is precisely the same as the definition of "medicinal product" in Directive 65/65/EEC art.1(2), which was the relevant European legislation concerning the need for authorisations to place proprietary medicinal products on the market when the Medicinal Products Regulation was enacted. It is also the same as the definition in the modern counterpart of Directive 65/65/EEC (i.e. Directives 2001/83/EEC and 2001/82/EEC which relate to medicinal products for human and veterinary use respectively). Accordingly it ought to be possible to identify the "medicinal product" by looking at the authorisation.

"Plant Protection Product"

6-78   In the Plant Protection Regulation, the definitions of "plant protection products" and "product" are more elaborate than the corresponding definitions in the Medicinal Products Regulation but the distinctions do not appear to create any difference in substance. The Plant Protection Regulation definitions clearly track the correspond terms of Directive 91/414/EEC concerning the placing of plant protection products on the market just as the definition of medicinal product in the Medicinal Products Regulation corresponds to Directive 65/65/EEC.

6-79   "Plant protection products" means active substances and preparations containing them put up in the form in which they are intended to be supplied to the user and intended to protect or preserve plants, influence their life processes or destroy undesirable plants or parts of them.[146] In summary, leaving aside combinations, in the Plant Protection Regulation "product" means "active substance" of a "plant protection product"[147]; "active substances" are defined as "substances" or micro-organisms (including viruses) which have general or specific action against plants or plant pathogens[148]; and "substances" means chemical elements and their compounds.[149]

6-80   In the *BASF v BIE* case[150] the Court of Justice decided that in the Plant Protection Regulation, two products which differ only in the proportion of the active chemical compound to the impurity they contain, one having a greater percentage of the impurity than the other, must be regarded as the same "product". This ques-

---

[144] Medicinal Products Regulation art.1(a).
[145] *Draco A.B.'s SPC Application Patents Court* [1996] R.P.C. 417, 438 at lines 5–40.
[146] Plant Protection Regulation art.1(1).
[147] Plant Protection Regulation art.1(8).
[148] Plant Protection Regulation arts 1(3) and 1(7). See also *Bayer CropScience AG v Deutsches Patent- und Markenamt* (C-11/13).
[149] Plant Protection Regulation art.1(2). The definition of "substance" also includes certain impurities.
[150] *BASF AG v Bureau voor de Industriële Eigendom* (C-258/99) [2002] R.P.C. 9. See also *BASF AG's Application (Comptroller)* [2000] R.P.C. 1 in which the same case came before the UKIPO with the same outcome.

tion would probably not have arisen in relation to the Medicinal Products Regulation, but in the Plant Protection Regulation the chain of definitions leading to the definition of "product" does refer to impurities.[151]

"Basic patent"

In the Medicinal Products Regulation "basic patent" means a patent which protects a product as such, a process to obtain a product or an application of a product.[152] This is intended to be a wide definition since "all pharmaceutical research provided it leads to a new invention which can be patented ... must be encouraged, without any discrimination and must be able to be given a supplementary certificate of protection provided that all the conditions ... are fulfilled".[153]

6-81

Thus the basic patent may be a patent claiming the product as a new chemical entity or it may claim a new process for obtaining a product. In the case of the latter, the Comptroller's Hearing Officer has held that the product must be identified in the wording of the claims of the basic patent as the product deriving from the process in question. However, it is not necessary to go further and show that the product approved has actually been manufactured according to the process.[154] The reference to an "application of a product" is intended to include second medical use claims (whether in the Swiss style current at the time the Medicinal Products Regulation was enacted or the new form of use claim under EPC 2000), as can be seen from para.29 of the Explanatory Memorandum which refers in this context to a "new application of a new or known product".[155] This was made explicit by the Court of Justice in *Neurim*[156] at [24]. In that case the patentee sought a SPC for the use of melatonin to treat insomnia in humans in a situation where the same active ingredient had previously been approved for use as a veterinary medicine for regulating the seasonal breeding activity of sheep. The court ruled that the mere existence of an earlier marketing authorisation obtained for a veterinary medicinal product did not preclude the grant of a supplementary protection certificate for a different application of the same product for which a marketing authorisation had also been granted, provided that the application was within the limits of the protection conferred by the new basic patent relied upon.[157] In such circumstances the relevant marketing authorisation for the purposes of art.13(1) was that coming within the limits of protection conferred by the new basic patent.[158]

6-82

"Authorisation to place the product on the market"

The Regulations use the expression "authorisation to place the product on the market" and similar expressions in various places, without a formal definition being included in the Regulation. A number of issues arise which concern the appropriate character of the authorisations referred to.

6-83

---

[151] See Plant Protection Regulation art.1(2).
[152] Medicinal Products Regulation art.1(c).
[153] Explanatory Memorandum COM (90) 101 final [1990] O.J. C114/10, para.29.
[154] *Icahn School of Medicine at Mount Sinai's SPC* BL O/552/14 [2015] R.P.C. 21, [67].
[155] Explanatory Memorandum COM (90) 101 final [1990] O.J. C114/10. See also para.28 thereof which refers to an "application or use" of the medicinal product.
[156] *Neurim Pharmaceuticals (1991) Ltd v Comptroller-General of Patents* (C-130/11) [2013] R.P.C. 23.
[157] See [27].
[158] See [31].

6-84 In its original form art.3(b) of the Medicinal Products Regulation referred to authorisations granted in accordance with Council Directive 65/65/EEC or Directive 81/851/EEC. These directives related to the grant of marketing authorisations for medicinal products for human and veterinary use respectively and laid down the Community rules for procedures. By the time the Medicinal Products Regulation was codified they had been replaced by Directives 2001/83/EC and 2001/82/EC respectively and these are the provisions referred to in the codified Medicinal Products Regulation.[159] The other EU instrument relating to the grant of marketing authorisations is the European Medicines Agency Regulation which set up a centralised procedure for the authorisation of certain medicinal products. The current form of that instrument is Regulation 726/2004.

6-85 Although it is not expressly mentioned in the codified Medicinal Products Regulation, authorisations granted under the European Medicines Agency Regulation 726/2004 are clearly intended to be capable of supporting an application for a supplementary protection certificate in an otherwise appropriate case. Regulation 726/2004 expressly provides[160] that a marketing authorisation granted under the regulation shall confer the same rights and obligations in each member state as a marketing authorisation granted in that Member State in accordance with Directive 2001/83/EC.

6-86 Notably art.13 of the Medicinal Products Regulation also refers to an "authorisation to place the product on the market", this time in the Community. Unlike art.3(b), art.13 does not include an express reference to this authorisation being one granted in accordance with Council Directive 65/65/EEC or its parallel Directives or successors. The relevance of this distinction in wording has been considered in some of the cases discussed below.

6-87 In *BTG's SPC Application*[161] the Comptroller's Hearing Officer (Mr Wood) held that a letter permitting the supply of a product for use in a clinical trial was not to be an authorisation to place a product on the market as required by art.3(b).

Authorisation has same meaning throughout the Regulation

6-88 An authorisation which is required under legislation on pricing or reimbursement laws is not the correct kind of authorisation under the Regulations. This was the issue before the Court of Justice in the *Hässle*[162] case. In that case the applicant for a certificate was seeking to avoid reliance on a marketing authorisation granted pursuant to Directive 65/65/EEC but rather to rely on later authorisations under price control and social security reimbursement schemes in France and Luxembourg. These were said to be the relevant "marketing authorisations" for the purposes of art.19 of the Medicinal Products Regulation (in its original form). The applicant was seeking a supplementary protection certificate in Germany and the problem it faced was that, as it applied to applications in Germany, the transitional provision art.19(1) prevented the grant of such a certificate if the first authorisation anywhere in the Community was before 1 January 1988. The first authorisations under Directive 65/65/EEC had been granted in April 1987 in France and November 1987 in Luxembourg. The applicant argued that the laws in France and Luxembourg were such that it was not allowed to actually sell the product until after

---

[159] See, e.g. art.2.
[160] art.13.
[161] [1997] R.P.C. 118.
[162] *Aktiebolaget Hässle v Ratiopharm* (C-127/00).

the price control/reimbursement authorisations were in place and since they came after 1 January 1988, art.19 was satisfied. In an important judgment the Court of Justice decided that there was nothing to justify interpreting the words "authorisation to place on the market" differently depending on the provision of the Regulation in which they appear.[163] Therefore the reference in art.19 to an authorisation to place the product on the market meant an authorisation under Directive 65/65/EEC and not one concerning pricing or reimbursement.[164]

Authorisation not granted under Directive 65/65/EEC (or equivalent)

A rather different question from the one in *Hässle*[165] is the status of marketing **6-89** authorisations which may not been granted pursuant to Directive 65/65/EEC (or equivalent) but are of the same character. These are sometimes called "technical authorisations" to distinguish them from the sort of pricing or reimbursement authorisations at issue in *Hässle*. The technical authorisations which have arisen for consideration are authorisations to place a product in the market but are either so old that Directive 65/65/EEC did not apply at the time or were in states that did not have to comply with Directive 65/65 for some reason but are still relevant. So, for example, in *Synthon B.V. v Merz Pharma GmbH & Co KgaA*[166] and in *Generics [UK] Ltd v Synaptech Inc*[167] similar facts arose. In each case the drug in question had been authorised on the market somewhere in the Community for many years but these old technical authorisations had arguably not been granted pursuant to Directive 65/65/EEC. Later, when new uses for the drugs were discovered, more recent authorisations were granted unquestionably compliant with Directive 65/65/EEC and the applicants obtained supplementary protection certificates in the UK based on these later authorisations. Generic pharmaceutical companies applied to revoke the certificates or at least to limit their duration, based on submissions concerning the relevance of the earlier authorisations. The holders of the certificates contended that the earlier authorisations were irrelevant.

On a reference made by the High Court, the Court of Justice explained in *Synthon* **6-90** *v Merz*[168] that a product placed on the market without having obtained a marketing authorisation under Directive 65/65/EEC (and without having undergone safety and efficacy testing), is not within the scope of the Medicinal Products Regulation at all and so no supplementary protection certificate can be granted in respect of it. As Floyd J had observed provisionally in making the reference, where there was no need to go through the administrative procedure of the Directive to place the product on the market in the first place, there is no need for compensation for lost time.[169] Floyd J noted that the German Federal Patent Court had reached the same view of art.2 in the parallel case in Germany.[170]

Floyd J also formed the following provisional views on the first and second ques- **6-91** tions referred, neither of which the Court of Justice felt it necessary to answer given the ruling referred to above:

(i)   That an authorisation granted in Luxembourg when Directive 65/65 was in

---

[163] See [57].
[164] See [55]–[61].
[165] *Aktiebolaget Hässle v Ratiopharm* (C-127/00).
[166] [2009] EWHC 656 (Pat); [2009] R.P.C. 20, 674.
[167] [2009] EWHC 659 (Ch) and [2009 EWHC 1163 (Pat).
[168] C-195/09.
[169] [2009] EWHC 656 (Pat); [2009] R.P.C. 20, [76].
[170] [2009] R.P.C. 20, [40]-[41].

force was relevant. The applicant had argued that Luxembourg's law at the time was not in fact compliant with the Directive but Floyd J provisionally preferred the submission that such questions were irrelevant once it was clear the national provision under which the authorisation was granted is one which gives effect of the Directive.[171] The issue was referred to the ECJ as question 1.

(ii) That assuming the earlier authorisations did not comply with Directive 65/65, the question of whether they were relevant to the calculation of the term of the supplementary protection certificate under art.13 and relevant under art.19 should be referred. Floyd J[172] noted that the *Hässle*[173] case appeared to support the proposition that non-65/65 authorisations were irrelevant but also noted that the opinion of the Advocate-General in the *Novartis* case[174] provided some basis for a retreat from that position albeit that the judgment of the ECJ itself did not and noted the existence of parallel conflicting decisions of the Courts in Belgium and Germany.[175] The issue was referred to the ECJ as question 2.

6-92   The *Synaptech* case was conducted as a streamlined trial and the only point taken was the argument that the kind of authorisation relevant to the calculation of duration under art.13 included old non-65/65 authorisations from the 1960s and 1970s in Austria and Germany respectively. This was based on the decision of the Court of Justice in the *Novartis* case which held that a non-65/65 authorisation granted by Switzerland and effective in Lichtenstein was relevant to the calculation of duration of a UK supplementary protection certificate under Article 13. Roger Wyand QC (sitting as a Deputy Judge of the Patents Court) noted the existence of divergent cases in the first instance Belgian and German courts[176] (see also *Synthon* above) and held that the decision in *Novartis* was based on the EEA Agreement, such that in effect the Swiss non-65/65 authorisation was treated as being a Directive 65/65 authorisation for the purposes of the Regulation.[177] On that basis the *Hässle*[178] case stood for the proposition that the authorisations had to be compliant with Directive 65/65.

6-93   By the time the *Synaptech* case reached the English Court of Appeal, the Court of Appeal in Brussels had maintained the view in Belgium that *Hässle* was not determinative, that *Novartis* could not be explained as based only on the EEA Agreement and that therefore *Novartis* decided that a non-65/65 compliant authorisation was relevant for the point of view of art.13 (calculating duration).[179] Therefore in *Synaptech* the English Court of Appeal referred two questions, one dealing with whether a Directive 65/65 authorisation was required for art.13 of the Medicinal Products Regulation and the other dealing with whether the various

[171] *Synthon v Merz* [2009] EWHC 656 (Pat); [2009] R.P.C. 20, [48]–[54].
[172] *Synthon v Merz Patents Court* [2009] EWHC 656 (Pat); [2009] R.P.C. 20, [55]–[66].
[173] *Aktiebolaget Hässle v Ratiopharm* (C-127/00).
[174] *Novartis AG, University College London and Institute of Microbiology and Epidemiology v Comptroller* (C-207/03) conjoined with *Ministre de l'économie v Millenium Pharmaceuticals Inc* (C-252/03).
[175] *Merck v Almirall German Federal Patent Court*, 18 July 2006 Case 14 W (pat) 42/04; and *NV Merck v SA Almirall Prodesfarma Brussels Court of First Instance* (24th Chamber) 15 June 2007.
[176] [2009] EWHC 659 (Ch) and [2009] EWHC 1163 (Pat), [31]–[36].
[177] [2009] EWHC 659 (Ch) and [2009] EWHC 1163 (Pat), [30].
[178] *Aktiebolaget Hässle v Ratiopharm* (C-127/00).
[179] *Laboratorios Almirall v B.V.B.A. Mylan*, Court of Appeal of Brussels, 23 June 2009.

provisions which arose from the accession of Austria operated to treat an old Austrian authorisation as complaint with Directive 65/65 anyway.[180]

In a judgment handed down on the same date, the Court of Justice repeated its ruling in *Synthon v Merz*[181] and did not answer either of the two questions specifically asked.

6-94

Product is protected by a basic patent in force

(art.3(a) Medicinal Products Regulation/art.3(1)(a) Plant Protection Regulation)

As the Court of Justice has now pointed out on a number of occasions,[182] the provisions concerning patents have not yet been made the subject of harmonisation at European Union level. This has created a difficulty of interpretation when the Court of Justice has been asked to opine on certain issues arising for interpretation under art.3(a). Clearly in a simple case a patent which claims a chemical compound can be said to protect that product and no difficulty arises. Equally a patent with a claim to the use of a product for the manufacture of a medicament to treat a disease must be a patent which "protects" the product within the terms of art.3(a) of the Medicinal Products Regulation.[183] However, since a basic patent can be patent for a process to obtain a product, does "protection" extend to a product "obtained directly by means of a process" pursuant to art.64 EPC which provides in terms that "the protection conferred by" a patent for a process "shall extend to the products directly obtained by such a process"[184]?

6-95

As an example of the difficulties which can arise under art.3(a), in *Centocor Inc's SPC Application*[185] a certificate was rejected by the Comptroller's Hearing Officer (Mr Lewis) on the ground that a product the sale of which might infringe a patent under the contributory infringement provisions (PA 1977 s.60(2)) was not a product protected by a patent within the meaning of art.3(a). The Court of Justice agreed when this issue was raised expressly in a reference made in the *Yeda* case,[186] discussed in more detail below.

6-96

In *Farmitalia*[187] the Court of Justice were asked what were the criteria according to art.3(a) for determining whether or not a product is protected by a basic patent. The court decided that in the absence of Community harmonisation of patent law, the extent of patent protection can be determined only in the light of the

6-97

---

[180] *Generics v Synaptech* (Court of Appeal) [2009] EWCA Civ 1119, referral (C-427/09).

[181] (C-195/09).

[182] e.g. in *Medeva BV v Comptroller General of Patents, Designs and Trade Marks* (C-322/10) [2012] R.P.C. 25, [22].

[183] *Neurim Pharmaceuticals (1991) Ltd v Comptroller-General of Patents* (C-130/11) [2013] R.P.C. 23.

[184] As to this, see [37]–[41] of the judgment of the Court of Justice in *University of Queensland, CSL Limited v Comptroller-General of Patents* (C-630/10) where the court explained that a SPC could only be granted for such a product where it was identified in the wording of the claims as a product deriving from that process, but that protection under the SPC granted for the process may extend to the product under relevant national law.

[185] *Centocor Inc's SPC Application (Comptroller)* [1996] R.P.C. 118.

[186] *Yeda Research and Development Company Ltd and Aventis Holdings Inc v Comptroller General of Patents, Designs and Trade Marks* (C-518/10).

[187] *Farmitalia Carlo Erba Srl's Supplementary Protection Certificate Application* (C-392/97) [2000] R.P.C. 580.

non-Community rules which govern patents[188] and therefore that in order to determine whether a product is protected by a basic patent, reference must be made to the rules which govern the patent.[189]

6-98   By 2009 *Farmitalia* had been regarded in both the UK and Germany as deciding that questions under art.3(a) were matters for national patent law[190] but the position remained controversial. In the UK at least two approaches to the application of art.3(a) had been discussed.[191] One is the so called "infringement test" in which the phrase "product protected by the basic patent" is said to extend to anything with respect to which proceedings could be successfully brought in any national court for infringing the patent. The alternative, sometimes called the "identification" or "disclosure" test, is narrower, such that the fact a product might infringe is a necessary but not sufficient condition. In *Astellas*,[192] Arnold J pointed out that a claim may cover a product without disclosing it and held that in the case before him the product in question was covered but not disclosed and did not satisfy art.3(a).

6-99   In 2010 the Court of Appeal in *Medeva's SPC Applications*[193] suggested that *Farmitalia* has been misunderstood. The Chancellor (Sir Andrew Morritt) suggested at [35] of his judgment that even if the Court of Justice intended to leave to the national courts the determination of the precise scope of the protection afforded by the patent, there must be a real question whether it is compatible with EU law to interpret the phrase "product protected by the basic patent" in art.3(a) as extending to any product with respect to which proceedings could be successfully brought in any national court for infringing the patent. The fact that there has been no EU harmonisation of patent law indicates the need for the concept of "protection by a basic patent in force" in relation to a "product" as defined in art.1(b) to reflect a European concept separate from its meaning in any particular system of national law.[194] Accordingly the Court of Appeal referred questions to the Court of Justice, the first being to ask what the criteria are for deciding whether a "product protected by the basic patent" in art.3(a).[195]

6-100   Many of the cases on art.3(a) relate to combinations of active ingredients, a topic which first came before the Patents Court in *Takeda Chemical Industries Ltd's SPC Applications*.[196] The issue is addressed in a separate section below since it cuts across a number of aspects of the Regulation.

6-101   The product may be protected by many patents, in which case it is for the proprietor to choose which one to base the certificate on.[197]

---

[188]   *Farmitalia Carlo Erba Srl's Supplementary Protection Certificate Application* (C-392/97) [2000] R.P.C. 580, [27].

[189]   *Farmitalia Carlo Erba Srl's Supplementary Protection Certificate Application* (C-392/97) [2000] R.P.C. 580, [29].

[190]   In the UK see, e.g. *Gilead's SPC Application Patents Court* [2008] EWHC 1902 (Pat); [2008] EWHC 1902 and in Germany see Decision X ZB 1/08 of the Federal Supreme Court on 8 July 2008 concerning pantoprazole, [5].

[191]   *Gilead's SPC Application Patents Court* [2008] EWHC 1902 (Pat); [2008] EWHC 1902 and *Astellas Pharma Inc Patents Court* [2009] EWHC 1916 (Pat).

[192]   *Astellas Pharma Inc Patents Court* [2009] EWHC 1916 (Pat), [27].

[193]   [2010] EWCA Civ 700.

[194]   [2010] EWCA Civ 700, [35].

[195]   See para.6-129, et seq.

[196]   *Takeda Chemical Industries Ltd's SPC Applications (No.3) Patents Court* [2004] R.P.C. 3.

[197]   Explanatory Memorandum COM (90) 101 final [1990] O.J. C114/10; para.33.

An appropriate and valid authorisation to place the product on the market has been granted

(art.3(b) Medicinal Products Regulation/art.3(1)(b) Plant Protection Regulation)

The appropriate authorisation under art.3(b) is a local one, i.e. an authorisation   **6-102**
in the UK. That can be seen by reading art.3(b) with the preamble in art.3 overall
which states "in the Member State in which the application is submitted". An
authorisation elsewhere in the Community, although potentially relevant for
determining the overall period of validity of any certificate under art.13, is not
relevant under art.3(b) and there must be a valid authorisation in the UK at the date
of the application.[198] The authorisation referred to in art.3(b) must be of the appropriate kind, i.e. one granted in accordance with Directive 65/65 (now Directive
2001/83/EC) since art.3(b) says as much in express terms.

In *Farmitalia*[199] the Court of Justice considered the identity of the product which   **6-103**
the authorisation actually authorises to be placed on the market. In effect the decision holds that the terms of the marketing authorisation itself are not wholly
determinative. The court decided that even though the active ingredient in the
authorisation was in the form of a salt, the certificate was not so limited and was
capable of covering the various derived forms such as salts and esters, as medicinal
products, in so far as they are covered by the protection of the basis patent.[200] The
precise way in which the identity of the active ingredient is to be determined
(whether by reference to the title of the marketing authorisation alone or taking into
account its overall contents) awaits clarification.

In *Georgetown University, University of Rochester, Loyola University of*   **6-104**
Chicago, v Comptroller General of Patents, Designs and Trade Marks[201] the Court
of Justice explained that for the purposes of art.3(b), the medicinal product referred
to in the marketing authorisation could contain additional active ingredients over
and above those specified in the application for the supplementary protection
certificate.[202] This allows for a SPC to be granted under art.3(b) for a new active
ingredient which was first authorised in a medicinal product in combination with
other active ingredients, which is common in the field of, e.g. vaccines where
combination products are routinely used.

The product has not already been the subject of a certificate

(art.3(c) Medicinal Products Regulation/art.3(1)(c) Plant Protection Regulation)

The rule that a certificate may not be granted if the product has already been the   **6-105**
subject of a certificate refers to a certificate in the same Member State (see the
preamble to art.3 in both Regulations). The purpose of the rule is explained in the

---

[198] *Yamanouchi Pharmaceuticals Co Ltd v C-G* (C-110/95) [1997] R.P.C. 844.
[199] *Farmitalia Carlo Erba Srl's Supplementary Protection Certificate Application* (C-392/97) [2000] R.P.C. 580.
[200] *Farmitalia Carlo Erba Srl's Supplementary Protection Certificate Application* (C-392/97) [2000] R.P.C. 580, [21].
[201] (C-422/10).
[202] See also *Medeva BV v Comptroller General of Patents, Designs and Trade Marks* (C-322/10) [2012] R.P.C. 25, [29]–[42] which are to the same effect.

Explanatory Memorandum. The certificate is designed to encourage research into new medicinal products so that the overall duration of protection (maximum 15 years) is sufficient to enable the investment to be recovered. Since there would be a risk that the duration for one and the same medicinal product might be exceeded if the same product were able to be the subject of several successive certificates, only one certificate per product is permitted.[203]

6-106   Although the Medicinal Products Regulation does not say so in terms, it is clear that the rule is not intended to preclude different parties from obtaining a certificate for the same product based on their own distinct patents. That is the thrust of the decision of the Court of Justice on the second question in the *Biogen* case.[204] The prohibition in art.3(c) can only be understood as referring to the same person being prevented from obtaining successive certificates for the same product.

6-107   However, in the *Biogen* case the Court of Justice also stated that "Under Art. 3(c) of the Regulation, however, only one certificate may be granted for each basic patent".[205] That statement needs to be treated with care and not taken out of context for two reasons. First, a patent may protect more than one product and there is no obvious reason based on the purposes of the Regulations why a patent which did cover two products should not be entitled to give rise to two different certificates, one for each product. Secondly, the Court of Justice was not holding that a party who had two patents protecting the same product could obtain two certificates, far from it, as this would be contrary to para.33 of the Explanatory Memorandum.[206] Instead *Biogen* should be interpreted as deciding that the holder of more than one patent for the same product could not be granted more than one certificate for that product: i.e. the limiting factor is the number of products, not the number of patents. This conclusion was reached by Mr Walker, the Hearing Officer for the Comptroller in *Takeda Chemical Industries Ltd's SPC's Applications (No.2)*,[207] following a careful consideration of the interlocking effects of the decision of the Court of Justice in the *Biogen* case,[208] the Medicinal Products Regulation itself and also the further requirements imposed by art.3(2) of the Plant Protection Regulation and applied to the Medicinal Products Regulation by recital 17 of the Plant Protection Regulation. Note that the *Biogen* case was heard on 11 July 1996, prior to the publication of Plant Protection Regulation on 23 July 1996 and takes no account of it. Article 3(2) of the Plant Protection Regulation provides in terms that a certificate may be issued for the same product to two holders of different patents.

6-108   This was confirmed by the Court of Justice in *Georgetown University v Octrooicentrum Nederland* (C-484/12) where it ruled that under art.3(c) a patent holder could obtain more than one SPC based on the same basic patent for different active ingredients or different combinations of active ingredients, so long as each active ingredient or combination is protected as such by the basic patent. In that case the patentee already had a SPC for a combination of four active ingredients and wanted a separate SPC for one of those active ingredients based on the same basic patent. The court held that this was permissible in circumstances where both the combination and the single active ingredient were protected as such by the basic

---

[203] Explanatory Memorandum COM (90) 101 final [1990] O.J. C114/10; para.36.

[204] *Biogen Inc v SmithKline Beecham Biologicals S.A.* (C-181/95) [1997] R.P.C. 833, [20]–[30].

[205] Repeated at [41] of *Medeva BV v Comptroller General of Patents, Designs and Trade Marks* (C-322/10) [2012] R.P.C. 25.

[206] COM (90) 101 final [1990] O.J. C114/10.

[207] [2004] R.P.C. 2, 20.

[208] *Biogen Inc v SmithKline Beecham Biologicals S.A.* (C-181/95) [1997] R.P.C. 833.

patent, and that even if the protection conferred by the two SPCs overlapped, they would in principle expire on the same date.[209]

Co-pending applications

In its English version, art.3(2) of the Plant Protection Regulation uses the word "pending" and appears to allow two certificates to two different holders only if they are co-pending applications. However, in *AHP v BIE*[210] the Court of Justice held that art.3(c) of the Medicinal Products Regulation (in the light of art.3(2) of the Plant Protection Regulation) must be interpreted as not precluding the grant of a certificate to the holder of a patent even if, when the application is submitted, one or more certificates for the same product have already been granted to holders of other basic patents.

6-109

Patents in different hands for the same product

In *Chiron Corp's and Novo Nordisk A/S's SPC Application*[211] the examiner rejected an application for a certificate for the product Moroctocog alfa under art.3(c) of the Medicinal Products Regulation because there were already two certificates in existence for the same product granted to different parties. The Comptroller's Hearing Officer (Mr Walker) overturned that rejection, holding that where there are a number of patents in different hands but protecting the same product, all holders of basic patents may be granted certificate but only one certificate may be granted for that product each.[212]

6-110

The presence of the rule in art.3(c) often explains why applicants have taken a particular approach to the manner in which their application is presented. So in the series of decisions concerning Takeda's application for a certificate relating to lansoprazole which arose from its use as or as part of a treatment for diseases caused by H. pylori,[213] of which *Takeda Chemical Industries Ltd's SPC's Applications (No.2)* is one such, an important element in the background was that lansoprazole itself had already been the subject of a certificate beforehand, arising from its authorisation as a treatment of the upper gastro-intestinal tract.[214] Thus in those cases the applicant submitted that the "product" in question was not lansoprazole itself, because if the "product" was lansoprazole then the applications would have fallen foul of art.3(c).

6-111

The relevant authorisation is the first authorisation to place the product on the market as a medicinal/plant protection product

(art.3(d) Medicinal Products Regulation/art.3(1)(d) Plant Protection Regulation)

The fourth condition for the grant of a certificate is that the local marketing authorisation referred to in art.3(b) is the first authorisation to place the product on

6-112

---

[209] See [35].
[210] 3 September 2009 (C-482/07) [2010] F.S.R. 23.
[211] *Chiron Corp's and Novo Nordisk A/S's SPC Application (Comptroller)* [2005] R.P.C. 24.
[212] *Chiron Corp's and Novo Nordisk A/S's SPC Application (Comptroller)* [2005] R.P.C. 24, [57].
[213] *Takeda Chemical Industries Ltd's SPC's Applications (No.1) (Comptroller)* [2004] R.P.C. 1; *Takeda Chemical Industries Ltd's SPC's Applications (No.2) (Comptroller)* [2004] R.P.C. 1; *Takeda Chemical Industries Ltd's SPC's Applications (No.3) (Patents Court)* [2004] R.P.C. 1.
[214] *Takeda Chemical Industries Ltd's SPC's Applications (No.3) (Patents Court)* [2004] R.P.C. 1, [4].

the market as a medicinal product in the Member State. The Explanatory Memorandum explains that it occurs very often that one and the same product is successfully granted several authorisations, for example when a modification is made affecting the pharmaceutical form, dose composition or indications, in such a case only the first authorisation is taken into account. This is relevant to the calculation of the six-month period for the application itself under art.7 and also may be relevant if the first authorisation is also the first authorisation in the Community since it will then serve as the reference for the duration of the certificates for that product in all states.[215]

6-113   The rule is that the relevant authorisation is the first to place the *product* on the market rather than the first to place the *medicinal product* on the market and this distinction was explained by Jacob J in *Draco A.B.'s SPC Application*[216] in which an application for a certificate based on eligible (1989/1990) market authorisations in respect of a dry powder formulation of a drug was refused under art.3(d) owing to the existence of earlier ineligible (1981/1982) market authorisations for the same active ingredient formulated in a different way.

6-114   However, an earlier authorisation for the same product (active ingredient) may not be relevant under art.3(d) if it is for a different indication and/or to treat disease in a different species and the application for the SPC is limited to a new use of that product within the limits of the protection conferred by the later basic patent. This was the conclusion reached by the Court of Justice in *Neurim Pharmaceuticals (1991) Ltd v Comptroller-General of Patents*.[217]

Plant Protection Regulation art.3(2) and its effect in the Medicinal Products Regulation

6-115   Article 3(2) of the Plant Protection Regulation provides that:

> "The holder of more than one patent for the same product shall not be granted more than one certificate for that product. However, where two or more applications concerning the same product and emanating from two or more holders of different patents are pending, one certificate for this product may be issued to each of these holders."

6-116   This provision is said to apply to the Medicinal Products Regulation by means of recital 17 of the Plant Protection Regulation. Despite that, the provision was not incorporated into the codified Medicinal Products Regulation when that was published in 2009.

6-117   In its effect, art.3(2) of the Plant Protection Regulation is closely related to the condition that the product in question should not already have been the subject of a certificate (art.3(c)/art.3(1)(c)) which is addressed above.

Patents held by companies in the same group

6-118   In order to apply art.3(2), a distinction must be drawn between one holder of two patents and two holders of two patents. The Regulations are silent about the state of affairs in which one overall commercial undertaking may, for perfectly good corporate reasons, have one patent held by one group company and another patent for the same product held by another group company. If a "holder" were interpreted

---

[215] Explanatory Memorandum COM (90) 101 final [1990] O.J. C114/10; para.35.
[216] [1996] R.P.C. 417.
[217] (C-130/11) [2013] R.P.C. 23.

narrowly to refer to an individual company regardless of its status vis a vis other companies in the same group then the prohibition in art.3(2) would be open to being avoided readily. As yet there has been no decision on this point.

Cases which concern combinations of active ingredients

The definitions of product and medicinal product/plant protection product include references to combinations and in various different contexts problems have arisen with the application of the Regulations to combination cases.

6-119

Enantiomers and racemates

In *Generics v Daiichi*[218] the Court of Appeal considered a case about enantiomers. Daiichi had a patent for an enantiomer (levofloxacin) and a corresponding supplementary protection certificate. It was argued by the generic company that in truth the real first authorisation for the enantiomer was an earlier authorisation for the racemic mixture called ofloxacin of which levofloxacin is only one enantiomer. This would have meant that the levofloxacin certificate was contrary to art.3(d). However in answering the question of what was the correct "product" under art.1(b) in relation to the earlier authorisation Jacob LJ held that the answer is clear—it was the racemic mixture:

6-120

> "In the Regulation "product" means 'the active ingredient or combination of active ingredients' (art.1(b)). Clearly that must be read with the words 'as the case may be' at the end. If you have two active ingredients the 'product' is the pair of them. And ofloxacin is a combination of significantly active ingredients. So it is that combination which was the subject of the 1990 and 1985 authorisations. The authorisation for levofloxacin was the first authorisation for that active ingredient alone."[219]

On that basis the existence of the earlier certificate based on an authorisation for the racemate ofloxacin did not prejudice the later certificate based on an authorisation for the enantiomer levofloxacin. Jacob LJ also observed that the position might have been different if the other component in the racemic mixture was inactive biologically and in effect no more than an excipient but that issue was moot and left undecided.[220]

6-121

The Takeda case

In *Takeda Chemical Industries Ltd's SPC Applications (No.3)*[221] the Patents Court had to consider an appeal from a refusal to grant various supplementary protection certificates by the UKIPO. A patent filed in 1985 claimed lansoprazole itself, lansoprazole was first authorised in the Community in France in 1990 and in 1994 an UK authorisation for lansoprazole for the treatment of the upper gastro-intestinal tract was granted. A certificate was granted which would expire in 2005. A second patent was filed in 1990 claiming the use of lansoprazole for preventing or treatment infectious diseases caused by H. pylori. When further research showed that lansoprazole was effective against H. pylori when taken with certain antibiotics, the product licence was amended to include the treatment of H. pylori when in

6-122

---

[218] [2009] EWCA Civ 646; [2009] R.P.C. 23.
[219] [2009] EWCA Civ 646; [2009] R.P.C. 23, [58].
[220] [2009] EWCA Civ 646; [2009] R.P.C. 23, [59].
[221] [2004] R.P.C. 3.

combination with certain antibiotics. Takeda sought six further certificates on a number of alternative bases, three distinct combinations of lansoprazole and certain particular antibiotics based on either of the two patents. These certificates would expire in about 2010–2011. The Comptroller's Hearing Officer (Mr Walker) refused all six inter alia on the basis that art.3(a) was not satisfied. The "product" was not protected by either of the patents.

6-123   In order to avoid the effect of the earlier certificate for lansoprazole under art.3(c), Takeda argued that the "product" in question was the combination of lansoprazole and an antibiotic on the basis of the reference in art.1(b) to product meaning the combination of active ingredients of a medicinal product. Takeda then argued that art.3(a) was satisfied because the combination of lansoprazole with an antibiotic if sold would infringe either patent and so the combination is protected by the basic patent. Jacob J rejected that approached as flawed. He said:

> "The so-called 'combination' of lansoprazole and an antibiotic would only infringe because of the presence of the lansoprazole. In truth, the combination is not as such 'protected by a basic patent in force'. What is protected is only the lansoprazole element of that combination. It is sleight-of-hand to say that the combination is protected by the patent. The sleight-of-hand is exposed when one realises that any patent in Mr Alexander's sense protects the product of the patent with anything else in the world. But the patent is not of course for any such 'combination'.[222]"

Thus the appeal was dismissed.

6-124   It is relevant to note that the *Takeda* case was not about a single composition which comprised two agents A and B and a patent only for A. Although the judgment of Jacob J is clearly expressed in wide terms, *Takeda* was in fact about an authorisation in which lansoprazole and the antibiotic were to be used side by side as distinct compositions (see Jacob J's judgment at [3]–[5] and see, e.g. para.30 of the Comptroller's decision under appeal[223]). This may be why Jacob J referred to the combination as a "so called" combination in the key passage in para.10. The "so called combination of lansoprazole and an antibiotic" is not a reference to a single composition such as a capsule which includes both substances. In *Takeda* the only "product" which could infringe the patent (using the word product in the sense of s.60(1)(a) of the Patents Act 1977) was the lansoprazole capsule. It made no difference whether that capsule would be prescribed or sold with an antibiotic. Sales of the antibiotic could never have been restrained by the patent. This may be different from the situation of a single composition of two active ingredients, where restraining the sale of a pill comprising agent A necessarily prevents sales of agent B because the two are mixed up together on one pill. The cases after *Takeda* have applied the judgment as if it decided that a patent claiming an active compound does not "protect" a product which is a single formulation comprising that active ingredient and another active ingredient. It is submitted that this is not the ratio decidendi of *Takeda*. A product which is a co-formulation of two active ingredients would certainly infringe a patent for one ingredient and, it is submitted, a finding that such a patent "protects" that product from the point of view of art.3(a) of the Medicinal Products Regulation would not be inconsistent with the ratio of *Takeda*.

---

[222] [2004] R.P.C. 3, [10].
[223] [2004] R.P.C. 1, [30].

The Gilead case

The matter next came before the Patents Court in *Gilead's SPC Application*.[224] **6-125**
Here the issue related to a patent claiming a compound (tenofovir) and an authorisation for a composition containing both tenofovir together with emtricitabine.[225] The
Comptroller regarded *Takeda* as authority that the so-called "infringement" test
under art.3(a) was not the law and that not everything which infringes can be said
to be protected under the Regulation and relied on.[226] Thus the application was
rejected. On appeal, although Kitchin J considered that *Takeda* raised difficult questions as to whether it was correct,[227] he dismissed the appeal on that issue. The judge
thought that *Farmitalia*[228] might be said to mandate the infringement test and that
might lead to a different answer since under the Patents Act 1977, a product is
protected by a patent if it falls within the scope of a claim. Kitchin J also stated that
he thought the approach in *Takeda* could produce harsh results[229] and suggested that
the issues may merit consideration by the Court of Justice.

The identification or disclosure test

A second issue arose in *Gilead* because the patent also had a claim to a **6-126**
pharmaceutical composition comprising tenofovir and "optionally other therapeutic
ingredients" (claim 27). Kitchin J held that this claim did protect a combination of
active ingredients and so the Comptroller had been wrong to reject the certificate
on that basis. The UKIPO had applied a test based on asking whether the product
was "identifiable with the invention" of the basic patent or whether there was a
"clear pointer" to the specific combination authorised for use. The Patents Court
rejected those approaches since they were neither precise nor founded on the
Regulation of the Act.[230] The approach taken by Kitchin J was to identify the active ingredients which are relevant and then ask what brings the product within the
claim. So a claim to ingredient A does not protect ingredients A and B since only
A brings the product within the claim. Since Gilead's claim 27 claimed "tenofovir
and optionally other therapeutic ingredients" the combination product fell within
the claim as a result of the presence of both tenofovir and emtricitabine. It may be
noted that the second ingredient emtricitabine was not identified with any
specificity. The Comptroller's submission that it had to be identified as well was
rejected.[231]

The Astellas case

In *Astellas Pharma Inc*[232] the same issue came before Arnold J in the Patents **6-127**
Court on appeal from a refusal to grant a certificate by the UKIPO. Again the
product to be protected was a single composition with two active ingredients

---

[224] [2008] EWHC 1902 (Pat).
[225] [2008] EWHC 1902 (Pat), see [3]–[8].
[226] [2008] EWHC 1902 (Pat), [20].
[227] [2008] EWHC 1902 (Pat), see [23]–[30].
[228] *Farmitalia Carlo Erba Srl's Supplementary Protection Certificate Application* (C-392/97) [2000]
R.P.C. 580.
[229] [2008] EWHC 1902 (Pat), see [28].
[230] [2008] EWHC 1902 (Pat), see [32]–[33].
[231] [2008] EWHC 1902 (Pat), see [35]–[37].
[232] [2009] EWHC 1916 (Pat).

(emodepside and praziquantel) and the *Takeda* case was put to the court on the same basis as in *Gilead*. The appellant argued that *Takeda* was wrong and the correct test to apply was the infringement test. Arnold J was not convinced *Takeda* was wrong but agreed with Kitchin J that there are arguments in favour of the infringement test which merited consideration by a higher court or perhaps the ECJ.[233]

6-128   The patentee also argued that one of the claims satisfied the narrower identification or disclosure test. The claim was to "an agent which comprises …. [emodepside]" and was said to protect the combination of emodepside and praziquantel on the same basis as claim 27 in *Gilead*. This was on the basis that "comprises" means "includes". Arnold J accepted the claim covered the combination but held it did not disclose it and so the test was not satisfied.[234] The appeal was dismissed.

The Medeva case and its progeny—the Court of Justice provides initial guidance on art.3(a)

6-129   The issue of how to deal with combination products under art.3(a) was first referred to the Court of Justice in *Medeva's SPC Applications*[235] in the context of multi-disease vaccines. The patent in that case protected two antigens (pertactin and FHA) useful against one disease (pertussis) but the authorised medicinal products in question were multi-disease combination vaccines comprising many more antigens. The UKIPO refused the applications and on appeal to the Patents Court the appellant did not seek to challenge the *Takeda/Gilead/Astellas* line of authority at that level. The Patents Court did not accept the case could be distinguished from the *Takeda/Gilead/Astellas* line of authority and dismissed the appeal. The Court of Appeal decided to refer questions to the Court of Justice. The questions referred raised head on the general matter of what "the product is protected by a basic patent in force" in art.3(a) means and what are the criteria for deciding the matter (Question 1 of the reference), more specifically in a case about multiple active ingredients in the field of vaccines (Questions 2 to 5). The questions also raised an issue under art.3(b) and its application to multi-disease vaccines.

6-130   Following *Medeva*, a related reference to the Court of Justice was made under art.3(b) in a group of cases concerning vaccines again human papillomavirus (HPV).[236] The ruling in this case[237] was handed down on the same date as *Medeva*. There were also three further related references made by the High Court on combination products which resulted in reasoned orders being handed down on the day after *Medeva/Georgetown I*. These were *Queensland*,[238] *Yeda*[239] and *Daichii*.[240]

6-131   The debate in the *Medeva* case turned on whether the test under art.3(a) should be a broad infringement test or some other narrower identification/disclosure test.

---

[233] [2009] EWHC 1916 (Pat), [31]–[35] and [36]–[49].

[234] [2009] EWHC 1916 (Pat), [22]–[30].

[235] [2010] EWCA Civ 700.

[236] Patents Court (Kitchin J) 19 July 2010 *Georgetown University's SPC Applications* on appeal from the decision of the Comptroller's Hearing Officer (Dr Cullen) BLO/401/09.

[237] *Georgetown University, University of Rochester, Loyola University of Chicago, v Comptroller General of Patents, Designs and Trade Marks* (C-422/10).

[238] *University of Queensland, CSL Limited v Comptroller-General of Patents* (C-630/10) noted at para.6-95.

[239] *Yeda Research and Development Company Ltd and Aventis Holdings Inc v Comptroller General of Patents, Designs and Trade Marks* (C-518/10) discussed in the following section.

[240] *Daiichi Sankyo v Comptroller-General of Patents* (C-6/11) which adds nothing of substance to *Medeva*.

There was a further debate during the written and oral phases before the Court of Justice as to whether the broader test proposed should be by reference to national law provisions of infringement, or to the provisions of art.69 EPC and the Protocol on Interpretation thereof which refer to the "Extent of Protection" of a European Patent. At the same time the court was asked to provide guidance on the scope of art.3(b) and the various participants to the proceedings noted that both provisions needed to be interpreted together within the overall scheme of the Regulation to provide a sensible outcome overall.

Advocate General Trstenjak delivered what it is submitted is a comprehensive and thoughtful Opinion which sought to balance the competing interests of those on all sides of the pharmaceutical industry. She interpreted the provisions of the Regulation both literally and teleologically, and decided first that art.3(b) should not be construed narrowly to preclude the grant of a SPC where the relevant marketing authorisation contained more active ingredients than were identified in the application.[241] Having reached this conclusion, she recognised that a similarly broad interpretation of art.3(a) could over-compensate applicants for SPCs.[242] Accordingly she favoured an interpretation of art.3(a) which limited the meaning of product to be "the same as the product which forms the subject-matter of the basic patent".[243] She noted that this interpretation ought to prevent so-called "evergreening" by applicants by limiting them to only one SPC for each active ingredient or combination of active ingredients which is the subject-matter of a patent, regardless of the number of combinations of active ingredients in which the patented active ingredient or combination of active ingredients has been used.[244]

6-132

As for how to determine whether a product forms the subject-matter of a basic patent, Advocate General Trstenjak explained that that was in principle a matter for the (national) rules governing the basic patent, but that the Regulation precluded combinations of active ingredients which were not the subject-matter of a basic patent, but which nevertheless enjoyed patent protection due to the presence of a patented active ingredient, from being characterised as a product within the meaning of art.3(a).[245] She went on to state expressly in the following paragraph in answer to the first Question referred that "the definition of the basic patent laid down in Article 1(c) of the regulation precludes use of the protective effect of the basic patent from being invoked as a criterion for the purpose of [Article 3(a)]", although care must be taken to understand what she meant by the use of the contrasting terms "extent of protection" and "protective effect".[246]

6-133

Regrettably, the reasoning of the court is neither as comprehensive nor as easy to follow as that of the Advocate-General.[247] Further, the court elected not to answer Question 1 of the reference made, dealing instead with Questions 1–5 compendiously.

6-134

---

[241] See paras 89–90 of her Opinion.
[242] See paras 91–97 of her Opinion.
[243] See para.98 of her Opinion.
[244] See para.100 of her Opinion.
[245] See para.112 of her Opinion.
[246] See *Eli Lilly and Company Ltd v Human Genome Sciences Inc* [2014] EWHC 2404 (Pat); [2015] R.P.C. 8, [14]–[15].
[247] For a critique of the court's judgment in Medeva and the related cases, see the observations of Arnold J in *Novartis v MedImmune* [2012] EWHC 181; [2012] F.S.R. 23, [37]–[49].

6-135   On the issue of the interpretation of art.3(a), the court at [22]–[23] referred back to its statements in *Farmitalia*[248] to the effect that the extent of patent protection can be determined only in the light of the non-European rules governing patents. In [25] it stated that art.5 of the Medicinal Products Regulation provides that any SPC confers the same rights as conferred by the basic patent and is subject to the same limitations and obligations. It continued "It follows that Article 3(a) of the regulation precludes the grant of a SPC relating to active ingredients which are not specified in the wording of the claims of the basic patent."[249] It explained further at [26] in relation to combination products that if a product is composed of two active ingredients, then a SPC cannot be granted under art.3(a) on the basis of a patent for the one active ingredient considered in isolation. In support of this ruling, the court relied at [27] on the fact that the Explanatory Memorandum[250] refers expressly and solely to the wording of the claims of the basic patent. Accordingly it ruled that art.3(a) must be interpreted as precluding the grant of a SPC relating to active ingredients "which are not specified in the wording of the claims of the basic patent".

6-136   In the three reasoned orders handed down the following day,[251] the court used the wording "identified in the wording of the claims" instead of "specified". It appears that the court was using the words interchangeably, as in *Medeva* at [15] it characterised the original patent office decision in that case as refusing the application because more active ingredients were specified in the applications than were "identified in the wording of the claims of the basic patent". Further, pursuant to the first sub-para. of art.104(3) of the Rules of Procedure of the CJEU, a reasoned order can be given where a reference "is identical to a question on which the Court has already ruled, or where the answer to such a question may be clearly deduced from existing case-law".

6-137   When *Medeva* returned to the Court of Appeal[252] following the ruling of the Court of Justice, the applicant sought to persuade the Court of Appeal that the "comprising" wording in the claims of the basic patent relied upon was sufficient to allow for the grant of a SPC based on the application of art.69 EPC, notwithstanding that the relevant active ingredients were not named in the claims. The Court of Appeal rejected this contention, noting that both the Advocate General and the court had rejected the infringement test.[253] The Chancellor, Sir Andrew Morritt, explained at [33] that whilst the ambit of "specified" may range from express naming, through description, necessary implication to reasonable interpretation,[254] the problem for the applicant in that case was that wherever the dividing line is to be drawn, the relevant active ingredients were excluded. However, he specifically

---

[248] *Farmitalia Carlo Erba Srl's Supplementary Protection Certificate Application* (C-392/97) [2000] R.P.C. 580.
[249] This reflects the wording found in s.125 of the Patents Act 1977; whether it is intended to have the same meaning is less clear.
[250] COM (90) 101 final [1990] O.J. C114/10.
[251] *University of Queensland, CSL Limited v Comptroller-General of Patents* (C-630/10); *Yeda Research and Development Company Ltd and Aventis Holdings Inc v Comptroller General of Patents, Designs and Trade Marks* (C-518/10) and *Daiichi Sankyo v Comptroller-General of Patents* (C-6/11).
[252] [2012] R.P.C. 26.
[253] At [32]—although note the debate that had taken place during the reference as to the difference between the so-called infringement test and a test based on art.69 EPC.
[254] And the examples of salts, antibodies and *Markush* claims were put forward as demonstrating the difficulty in interpreting the ruling of the CJEU.

contemplated that further references would be necessary to ascertain precisely where on the scale the dividing line should be drawn.

The Yeda Research case

Shortly after the first instance hearing in *Medeva* the Patents Court heard an appeal from the Comptroller in *Yeda Research and Development v Comptroller*.[255] This case concerned a patent claiming a combination of two agents in a single composition and a marketing authorisation relating to the antibody itself. The agents were cetuximab and irinotecan. The Patents Court upheld the decision of the Comptroller rejecting two parallel applications. One application defined the product as cetuximab in combination with irinotecan and on the interpretation then being applied[256] this failed to satisfy art.3(b) because the authorisation was for cetuximab alone. The other application defined the product as cetuximab and this failed to satisfy art.3(a) because the cetuximab (as opposed to the combination) was held not to be protected by the patent. Only the application refused under art.3(a) was appealed and on 8 October 2010 the Court of Appeal referred a question to the Court of Justice in this case.

6-138

The SPC applied for was for cetuximab but the claims of the basic patent referred to the combination of cetuximab with irinotecan. Yeda argued that under the doctrine of contributory infringement the use of cetuximab could infringe the claims of the basic patent if carried out with irinotecan. In a reasoned order[257] handed down the day after *Medeva*, the Court of Justice did not answer the question directly but instead repeated the observation that patent law had not been harmonised across the European Union and noted that the Medicinal Products Regulation was intended to prevent the heterogeneous development of national laws.[258] In apparently rejecting any reliance on the national rules governing contributory infringement, it amplified the ruling in *Medeva* and held that a SPC should be precluded if it related to a single active ingredient which was not specified in the wording of the claims of the basic patent alone but was only specified in combination with another active ingredient which was not referred to in the SPC applied for.

6-139

Further References

As predicted by the Chancellor in *Medeva*, the courts have felt it necessary to make further references in an attempt to tease out precisely what the Court of Justice meant by "specified in the wording of the claims". These references have arisen in the following cases, with the rulings in *Eli Lilly* and *Actavis I* being handed down on the same day.[259] Regrettably, in spite of being asked to provide clarification in general terms, the court has tended to confine its answers to the specific facts of each case and has not answered all the questions referred.

6-140

---

[255] Patents Court (Lewison J) [2010] EWHC 1733 (Pat).

[256] But later amended following *Medeva* and *Georgetown*.

[257] *Yeda Research and Development Company Ltd and Aventis Holdings Inc v Comptroller General of Patents, Designs and Trade Marks* (C-518/10).

[258] At [36].

[259] 12 December 2013 and on the same day as *Georgetown University v Octrooicentrum Nederland* (C-484/12).

The Eli Lilly[260] case

6-141   This was a case about antibodies. The claim in issue defined an antibody in functional terms, by reference to its binding ability to a polypeptide whose sequence was disclosed for the first time in the basic patent. No sequence information was provided for the antibody. On a reference made by the High Court prior to trial in an action seeking declaratory relief the Court of Justice question 1 was re-asked from *Medeva* together with a more specific question about whether an antibody could be defined by reference to its binding characteristics or whether it was necessary to provide a structural definition.

6-142   In answering the questions together, the court referred at [32] of the judgment to s.125 of the Patents Act 1977 and art.69 EPC as being the relevant rules for determining what is protected by a basic patent. It went on to repeat that the rules governing infringement proceedings were not relevant and that the claims played a key role in assessing whether the conditions of art.3(a) were met.[261] The court noted that the active ingredient relied upon was not expressly named in the claims or specification but that a functional definition in a claim was nevertheless acceptable so long as "the claims relate, implicitly but necessarily and specifically, to the active ingredient in question". The court also commented on the fact that the application had been made based on an active ingredient which had been developed by a party other than the owner of the basic patent, even though the question referred on that topic had been withdrawn prior to the hearing. It stated at [43] that refusal of an application may be justified in circumstances "where the holder of the patent in question has failed to take any steps to carry out more in-depth research and identify his invention specifically, making it possible to ascertain clearly the active ingredient which may be commercially exploited...". Such circumstances would undermine the objective of the Medicinal Products Regulation.

6-143   Upon its return to the High Court, the national judge struggled to obtain clear guidance from the decision and both sides submitted that they had won.[262] The applicant submitted that the test was equivalent to that mandated by art.69 EPC whilst the developer of the active ingredient in question relied upon [43] of the Court of Justice decision as indicating that the court did not think that a certificate should be granted on the facts of that case. The court agreed with the applicant, describing the test under art.3(a) as an elusive concept[263] and held that an active ingredient is "identified" so as to fall within the protection of a basic patent if the active ingredient is within the claims of the basic patent, provided the claims relate implicitly but necessarily and specifically, to the active ingredients.[264]

The Actavis I case[265]

6-144   In this case, the patentee had developed a new antihypertensive active ingredient, irbesartan. It had already obtained a SPC for that product based upon claim 1 of the basic patent. Claim 20 of the basic patent related to the combination of

---

[260] *Eli Lilly and Company Ltd v Human Genome Sciences Inc*, (C-493/12).

[261] At [34].

[262] *Eli Lilly and Company Ltd v Human Genome Sciences Inc* [2014] EWHC 2404 (Pat); [2015] R.P.C. 8, [4].

[263] See [55].

[264] See [68].

[265] *Actavis Group PTC EHF, Actavis UK Ltd v Sanofi* (C-443/12).

irbesartan with an (unnamed) diuretic. The case turned on the availability of a second SPC for the combination of irbesartan and hydrochlorothiazide, a well known diuretic at the priority date of the patent. The High Court referred questions relating to both art.3(a) and art.3(c).

The Court of Justice only answered the question referred under art.3(c) and **6-145** indicated that the applicant should not be able to obtain a second SPC for irbesartan and hydrochlorothiazide. Its reasoning[266] was that even if art.3(a) was satisfied, for the purposes of art.3(c), the holder of a basic patent "should not be able to obtain a new SPC, potentially for a longer period of protection, each time he places on the market in a Member State a medicinal product containing, on the one hand, the principle active ingredient, protected as such by the holder's basic patent and constituting, according to the statements of the referring court, the core inventive advance of that patent, and, on the other, another active ingredient which is not protected as such by that patent". The court recorded that it was common ground that hydrochlorothiazide was not protected "as such" by the basic patent.[267] It went on to note that under the original irbesartan SPC, the holder could have prevented the sale of combinations of irbesartan and hydrochlorothiazide but that upon expiry of the original SPC, third parties ought to be permitted to sell irbesartan in combination with another active ingredient not protected as such by the basic patent or any other patent.[268] The court reiterated at [41] that the basic objective of the Medicinal Products Regulation was to compensate for the delay to the marketing of what constitutes "the core inventive advance" of the basic patent. This was to be contrasted with active ingredients which were "not protected as such by the basic patent but simply referred to in the wording of the claims of the patent in general terms" (e.g. "beta-blocking compound", "diuretic").

The Actavis II case[269]

This was another case about the use of hydrochlorothiazide in combination with **6-146** a new active ingredient called telmisartan. The applicant had already obtained a SPC for telmisartan alone. Following its application for a SPC for the combination, the applicant sought to amend the claims of the basic patent to refer expressly to the combination of telmisartan and hydrochlorothiazide, there being support in the specification for so doing. The High Court referred a series of questions relating to the legitimacy of the amendment process and also aspects arising out of the validity and term of the combination SPC. Some of these questions overlapped with those referred in *Actavis I*, as that decision was not available at the time the later reference was made.

The Court of Justice only addressed issues relating to the validity of the combina- **6-147** tion SPC under arts 1 and 3 of the Medicinal Products Regulation. It emphasised that it was telmisartan that was the innovative active ingredient of the basic patent and the sole subject-matter of the invention. It noted that the applicant did not contribute to the discovery of hydrochlorothiazide, a molecule within the public domain, and that the claim relating to that substance did not constitute the subject-

---

[266] At [30].
[267] At [32].
[268] At [36].
[269] *Actavis Group PTC EHF, Actavis UK Ltd v Boehringer Ingelheim Pharma GmbH & Co KG* (C-577/13).

matter of the invention.[270] It also noted that the effect of arts 1(c) and 3(a)–(b) of the Regulation was that a SPC may be granted only if the product is protected "as such" by the basic patent.

6-148   As to the meaning of "as such" in art.1(c), the Court of Justice reiterated that multiple SPCs could be obtained from the same basic patent where such multiple products were protected "as such", citing *Actavis I* and *Georgetown University v Octrooicentrum Nederland* (C-484/12). Whilst seeking to compensate applicants for the delay in commercial exploitation caused by the regulatory process, the court emphasised that not all such delay was compensable, particularly for the product in all its possible commercial forms, including combinations based on the same active ingredient.[271] Otherwise multiple SPCs would be obtainable for combinations of active ingredients which did not constitute the subject-matter of the invention.[272] Accordingly for a basic patent to protect an active ingredient "as such" within the meaning of arts 1(c) and 3(a), that active ingredient must constitute the subject-matter of the invention covered by that patent.[273]

6-149   Having made these general observations, the court then reached a narrower ruling directed to the specific facts of the case. The ruling determined that where a basic patent includes a claim to a product comprising an active ingredient which constitutes the sole subject-matter of the invention, for which the holder of that patent has already obtained a supplementary protection certificate, as well as a subsequent claim to a product comprising a combination of that active ingredient and another substance, that provision precludes the holder from obtaining a second supplementary protection certificate for that combination.

6-150   In spite of these multiple references it appears likely that yet further references will have to be made by national courts to clarify the approach under art.3(a) and resolve the questions that have thus far remained unanswered. The debate revolves around precisely what, if anything, is required in the wording of the claim beyond the application of art.69 EPC and its Protocol on Interpretation for the active ingredient to be "specified" in the claim and/or for the claim "to relate, implicitly but necessarily and specifically" to the active ingredient. Further guidance may also be required in relation to the task of identifying the subject-matter of the invention and/or the core inventive advance of the basic patent and the relevance thereof to the grant of a SPC.

4.   EFFECTS OF A CERTIFICATE

Subject matter of protection—art.4

6-151   Article 4 of the Medicinal Products Regulation provides that within the limits of protection conferred by the basic patent, the protection conferred by a certificate shall extend only to the product covered by the authorisation to place the corresponding medicinal product on the market and for any use of the product as a medicinal product that has been authorised before expiry of the certificate. Article 4 of the Plant Protection Regulation is in corresponding terms.

6-152   Article 4 contains two elements, the first element refers to the product covered by the authorisation and the second element refers to any use of the product as a

---

[270] See [26].
[271] See [35].
[272] See [36].
[273] See [38].

medicinal product that has been authorised before expiry of the certificate. It is not clear how these two elements are intended to interact. On one view the first element is the key one, functioning to limit the protection only to the relevant product. The second element (any use that has been authorised) is not intended to be a limitation but is simply a statement of the consequences of what happens when the rules are applied. However, the Explanatory Memorandum[274] in the passage from para.38 to para.45, especially paras 41 and 44 supports an alternative view that the two elements of art.4 are conjunctive in nature and therefore in addition to being limited to the product in question, the protection conferred by a certificate extends only to uses of the product as a medicinal product which have been authorised before expiry.

The operation of the first element of art.4 can be seen by considering a basic patent which claims a series of many compounds as a class using a general formula and a marketing authorisation which authorises a tablet made up of one of those compounds formulated with other excipients such as talc, for use in treating a particular disease. The authorised tablet is the medicinal product while the compound is the product. While the patent is in force, the monopoly covers all the compounds of the claimed formula. Once the patent has expired but the supplementary protection certificate is in force, art.4 means that the monopoly extends only to the compound, since that is the product in question.[275] Thus is it is clear that once the patent has expired, if a rival sought to market a different compound which was within the formula of the patent but was not the product the subject of the certificate, then they would be free to do so.[276]   **6-153**

However, more difficult questions arise in relation to art.4 when considering the extent to which the certificate would allow the holder to restrain other goods which include the same "product", i.e. the same active ingredient, but in a different form in some way. The possible different forms include different formulations from the medicinal product which gave rise to the certificate, different salts of the active ingredient, combinations of active ingredients and different uses of the products. Some of these situations have been addressed by the decided cases but some have not and doubt remains.   **6-154**

Formulations

Provided the basic patent itself would cover it, a certificate granted based on a first authorisation for a product in one form (say a tablet) must extend under art.4 to prevent marketing of the same active ingredient in another form (say a solution) at least assuming the different form is intended to treat the same disease.   **6-155**

This follows from a number of considerations of the scheme of the Regulations as a whole. The formulations of medicines and plant protection products are often changed in various ways over time, resulting in multiple authorisations existing for one product.[277] The application process requires the Patent Office to be notified of the *first* authorisation for the product in the UK to be considered under art.3(b) of the Medicinal Products Regulation but there is no need for subsequent authorisations to be notified. Subsequent authorisations relating to the same product but in a different form, i.e. a different medicinal product, do not give rise to a right to a   **6-156**

---

[274] Explanatory Memorandum COM (90) 101 final [1990] O.J. C114/10.
[275] See Explanatory Memorandum COM (90) 101 final [1990] O.J. C114/10, para.39.
[276] See Explanatory Memorandum COM (90) 101 final [1990] O.J. C114/10, para.39.
[277] Explanatory Memorandum COM (90) 101 final [1990] O.J. C114/10, para.35.

further certificate.[278] Also the first authorisation in the Community which determines the duration of the certificate under art.13 may not be for the same "medicinal product" as the authorisation under art.3(b) which gives rise to the right to a UK certificate.[279] For all these reasons it must necessarily follow that the protection conferred by a certificate under art.4 will extend to other formulations of the same product as long as they are within the scope of the basic patent.

Salts and esters

6-157   In the *Farmitalia* case[280] the Court of Justice held that in a case in which the compound was authorised in the form of a salt (as pharmaceuticals often are) then provided the patent would itself cover such things, the subject matter of protection was not limited to the particular salt used in the authorised medicinal product but would extend to other salts or esters of the same compound. The compound authorised was the salt idarubicin hydrochloride. The difficulty was in effect whether to regard the "active ingredient" as the free base idarubicin itself or the compound idarubicin hydrochloride. The court took the view that different salt forms were in principle therapeutically equivalent and so to limit the certificate only to the salt form in the authorisation would frustrate the purpose of the Regulation.[281]

6-158   One of the factors relied on by the Court of Justice in *Farmitalia*[282] was that recital 13 of the Plant Protection Regulation (which is applicable to the interpretation of the Medicinal Products Regulation[283]) states in terms that where a basic patent covers an active substance and its various derivatives (salts and esters) the certificate confers the same protection.

Strain variants

6-159   In *Pharmaq v Intervet*[284] the EFTA Court extended the reasoning under art.3(b) in *Arne Forsgren v Österreichisches Patentamt*[285] to art.4. In essence agreeing with the Commission, who had submitted observations, it ruled that the scope of protection conferred by a SPC extended to a specific strain of a virus covered by the basic patent but not referred to in the relevant marketing authorisation, only if the specific strain constitutes the same active ingredient as the authorised medicinal product and has therapeutic effects falling within the therapeutic indications for which the marketing authorisation was granted. However, it was not relevant whether a medicinal product based on such other strain would require a separate marketing authorisation. The court also ruled that a SPC is invalid to the extent it is granted a wider scope than that set out in the relevant marketing authorisation.

---

[278] *Massachusetts Institute of Technology* (C-431/04).
[279] See, e.g. *Pharmacia Italia v Deutsches Patentamt* (C-31/03) [2005] R.P.C. 27.
[280] *Farmitalia Carlo Erba Srl's Supplementary Protection Certificate Application* (C-392/97) [2000] R.P.C. 580.
[281] *Farmitalia Carlo Erba Srl's Supplementary Protection Certificate Application* (C-392/97) [2000] R.P.C. 580, [18].
[282] *Farmitalia Carlo Erba Srl's Supplementary Protection Certificate Application* (C-392/97) [2000] R.P.C. 580.
[283] By recital 17 of the Plant Protection Regulation.
[284] (E-16/14).
[285] (C-631/13).

Combinations of active ingredients

Consider the case of a basic patent covering a single chemical compound **6-160** (compound A) and then successive authorised medicinal products, first for a tablet comprising A alone, and second for a tablet comprising A and another active ingredient B. Would a supplementary protection certificate granted based on the first authorisation (for A alone) extend to cover the second tablet (A plus B)? Sales of the tablet comprising A and B could be prevented by the basic patent for A and so on one view, since a certificate is primarily an extension of the protection conferred by the patent, the same should be true for the certificate. Support for that can be found in para.39 of the Explanatory Memorandum.[286] If the second compound B had been an excipient rather than an active ingredient, even one as significant and inventive as the polymer in *Massachusetts Institute of Technology*,[287] the logic of the *Massachusetts Institute of Technology* case would mandate a conclusion that the combination of A plus excipient was covered.[288]

On the other hand, the question of whether a tablet comprising A plus B could **6-161** be restrained by a certificate based on compound A might relate to the issue of what "product is protected by a basic patent in force" in art.3(a) means in the context of the combination cases (see above). The "specified in the wording of the claims" test leads to the conclusion that the second combination tablet would not be within the protection conferred by the certificate granted for A alone. On that basis the only way the patent holder could cover the combination of A plus B with a certificate at all would be to obtain a second certificate directed to that combination. However, since the basic patent would not satisfy art.3(a) in such a case, the only way to achieve that would be to have obtained a second patent on A plus B. But that combination may not be patentable at all. It may be wholly obvious.

The Court of Justice answered this question in a reasoned order in *Novartis v* **6-162** *Actavis*, stating that the answer may be clearly deduced from existing case law.[289] It emphasised that a SPC confers the same rights as were conferred by the basic patent relied upon, within the limits of protection conferred by that patent. Accordingly any uses of the product in the form of a medicinal product consisting of such a product or containing it which could have been opposed during the lifetime of the patent could still be opposed under the SPC.[290] In that case the SPC was for the active ingredient valsartan but this could be used to oppose the marketing of the combination of valsartan and hydrochlorothiazide which had been authorised under the relevant MA. See also the discussion in *Actavis I* at [34]–[35].[291]

Other uses of the product

The second element of art.4 of the Medicinal Products Regulation refers to the **6-163** protection conferred by the certificate extending only to any use of the product as a medicinal product that has been authorised before expiry. Thus once the basic patent has expired, even if it claimed the compound per se, the certificate would not

---

[286] Explanatory Memorandum COM (90) 101 final [1990] O.J. C114/10; para.39.
[287] *Massachusetts Institute of Technology* (C-431/04).
[288] In *Generics v Daiichi* [2009] EWCA Civ 646 the Court of Appeal drew precisely this distinction in a slightly different context. The court distinguished between a case when the second compound was an inert excipient and one where it was active, see [59].
[289] C-442/11 at [18].
[290] See [20].
[291] *Actavis Group PTC EHF, Actavis UK Ltd v Sanofi* (C-443/12).

extend to the compound per se but only to its authorised use as a medicinal product, i.e. only to a formulated form presented to treat certain diseases. In *Pharmacia Italia*[292] the Court of Justice held that the protection conferred by art.4 relates to any use of the product as a medicinal product without any distinction between use of the product as a medicinal product for human use and as a veterinary medicinal product.[293]

6-164   If the compound in question was useful to treat a disease and also useful for some non-medical purpose, the basic patent might cover both before expiry but after expiry of the patent the certificate would only cover the compound formulated to treat authorised diseases. As para.41 of the Explanatory Memorandum states in the context of the proposal for the Medicinal Products Regulation "only uses in the pharmaceutical field come under the protection of the certificate, authorised use of the product as a herbicide for example would not be protected under the certificate".[294] This makes sense given that there is no ostensible reason why a system of patent extensions in the medical field should extend monopolies beyond that. However, there are other possible circumstances which may arise, including off label use of the product (i.e. use which may not be "authorised") and coverage of the raw active pharmaceutical ingredient (i.e. use which is not "as a medicinal product"). Both of these are cases in which the basic patent may well have given the patentee the right to restrain the activity but art.4 appears to exclude it. So far there has been no decision on either point.

Effects of a certificate—art.5

6-165   Article 5 of both Regulations provides that subject to art.4 the certificate shall confer the same rights as conferred by the basic patent and shall be subject to the same limitations and the same obligations. Therefore the certificate does not affect the extent of protection conferred by the patent itself, which is still governed by domestic law.[295]

6-166   Conferring the same rights as the basic patent means for example that a certificate based on a process patent will protect the product made directly by means of the process just as the basic patent did.[296] Being subject to the same limitations and obligations means for example that exceptions to infringement in s.60(5) of the Patents Act 1977 will apply as will any provisions on compulsory licensing.

6-167   It also appears that the rules on contributory infringement under s.60(2) of the Patents Act 1977 would continue to apply, even though these are not relevant for the decision under art.3(a).[297] See the discussion at *Actavis I*, [37].[298]

6-168   An endorsement licence of right applying to the basic patent will apply to the certificate.[299]

---

[292] *Pharmacia Italia v Deutsches Patentamt* (C-31/03) [2005] R.P.C. 27.
[293] *Pharmacia Italia v Deutsches Patentamt* Case C-31/03 [2005] RPC 27, paras 17–20.
[294] Explanatory Memorandum COM (90) 101 final [1990] O.J. C114/10.
[295] *Merck Genericos v Merck & Co* 11 September 2007, Court of Justice, (C-431/05), [44]–[45].
[296] Explanatory Memorandum COM (90) 101 final [1990] O.J. C114/10, para.44.
[297] See *Yeda Research and Development Company Ltd and Aventis Holdings Inc v Comptroller General of Patents, Designs and Trade Marks* (C-518/10).
[298] *Actavis Group PTC EHF, Actavis UK Ltd v Sanofi* (C-443/12).
[299] *Research Corp's SPC (Comptroller)* [1994] R.P.C. 667. The licence of right itself was settled in *Research Corp's SPC (No.2.) (Comptroller)* [1996] R.P.C. 320.

Duration of the certificate

Article 13 of both Regulations governs the duration of a supplementary protection certificate. The duration is equal to the patent life lost between patent filing date
and the date of first marketing authorisation in the Community, minus five years,
subject to a long stop of five years.[300] Overall this calculation means a certificate
gives a maximum period of 15 years from the first Community marketing
authorisation. The Court of Justice has emphasised that art.13 must be interpreted
as precluding a certificate holder from obtaining a period of exclusivity of greater
than 15 years.[301]

6-169

The relevant marketing authorisation used for the calculation is the first one to
place the product on the market anywhere in the Community. This may or may not
be the first authorisation in the Member State in which the certificate is sought. The
purpose of this is to further the objective of preventing heterogeneous development of national laws and creating further obstacles to the free movement of goods
by ensuring that patent protection will terminate at the same point in time in all
Member States where the certificate was granted even if the patent application was
made at different times or the local marketing authorisation was granted in different years.[302]

6-170

The first Community authorisation for the purposes of calculating the duration
under art.13 needs to be for the same product but it need not be for the same
formulation, indication or for treating the same species. The term "first authorisation in the Community" is used both in art.13 for the purposes of calculating duration and in art.19 of the Medicinal Products Regulation (as was originally enacted)
for the purposes of the transitional provisions. In *Pharmacia Italia v Deutsches
Patentamt*[303] the applicant sought a certificate in Germany based on a local German marketing authorisation for the product (cabergoline) in 1994. The marketing
authorisation from the point of view of art.3(b) and 3(d) was the local German
authorisation. The dispute arose as to whether the application was precluded by the
transitional provision in art.19 of the Medicinal Products Regulation (as it then was)
owing to the existence of an Italian authorisation from 1987, whereas the cut off
date applicable to applications for a certificate in Germany was 1 January 1988. The
applicant contended that a prior Dutch authorisation in 1992 was the correct "first
authorisation in the Community" both for art.19 and art.13 because it was the first
authorisation for cabergoline for human use. The earlier Italian authorisation was
for the same active ingredient but for veterinary use. The Court of Justice held that
the Italian authorisation was the relevant "first authorisation in the Community" for
all purposes and therefore the application fell foul of art.19. One of the reasons the

6-171

---

[300] Medicinal Product Regulation art.13; Plant Protection Regulation art.13; and see *Farmitalia Carlo Erba SRL (Comptroller)* [1996] R.P.C. 111.

[301] *Merck Canada Inc v Accord Healthcare Ltd* (C-555/13).

[302] See [77] of the judgment of the court in *Aktiebolaget Hässle v Ratiopharm* (C-127/00) and see also para.44 of the Opinion of Advocate-General Jacobs in *Kingdom of Spain v Council of the European Union* (C-350-92); para.85 of the Opinion Advocate-General Stix-Hackl in *Aktiebolaget Hässle v Ratiopharm* (C-127/00); para.44 of the Opinion of Advocate-General Jacobs in *Pharmacia Italia v Deutsches Patentamt* (C-31/03) [2005] R.P.C. 27; and para.47 of the Opinion of Advocate-General Colomer in *Novartis AG, University College London and Institute of Microbiology and Epidemiology v Comptroller* (C-207/03) conjoined with *Ministre de l'Économie v Millenium Pharmaceuticals Inc* (C-252/03).

[303] *Pharmacia Italia v Deutsches Patentamt* (C-31/03) [2005] R.P.C. 27.

court gave was that otherwise the duration of the protection conferred by art.13 could be different for the same product.[304]

6-172   The first Community authorisation for the purposes of calculating the duration under art.13 only has to authorise marketing somewhere within the Community (or EEA), it need not permit free circulation of the product throughout the Community. This issue was decided in *Novartis*.[305] Here the applicant applied for a certificate in the UK. The UKIPO contended that an authorisation granted by Switzerland but effective in Lichtenstein as a result of Lichtenstein law was the relevant first authorisation for the purposes of calculating the duration of the certificate under art.13. Although Switzerland was not part of the EEA, Lichtenstein was. The issue was referred to the Court of Justice and was heard with a similar case referred from the courts in Luxembourg. The Court of Justice decided that the Swiss authorisation which was effective to authorise marketing in Lichtenstein was the relevant first authorisation in one of the states of the EEA within the meaning of art.13. The deciding factor was that this must be correct because otherwise there would be a risk that the period of 15 years of exclusivity would be exceeded in the EEA.[306] The fact that the authorisation effective in part of the EEA (Lichtenstein) did not permit the product to be freely distributed on the market of the other Member States was not relevant since even authorisations granted in one state under the relevant European law (Directive 65/65, etc.) do not permit the product to be freely distributed.[307] The CJEU affirmed its decision in *Novartis* in its reasoned order in *Astrazeneca*.[308]

5. The Paediatric Extension of the Duration of a Certificate

The paediatric extension

6-173   A six-month extension to the duration of a supplementary protection certificate under the Medicinal Products Regulation is available as an incentive to the industry to investigate and develop medicines for children. The provisions came into effect on 26 January 2007. The relevant legislation consists of amendments to the Medicinal Products Regulation made on 27 December 2006 and now part of the codified Medicinal Products Regulation as well as the Regulation on Medicinal Products for Paediatric Use (EC) 1901/2006. The record of the third meeting of national SPC experts on 26 September 2008 addressed the paediatric extension system specifically.[309]

6-174   A summary of the aims and objectives of this system can be found in the judg-

---

[304] *Pharmacia Italia v Deutsches Patentamt* (C-31/03) [2005] R.P.C. 27, [21] and see Advocate General Jacobs, [47].

[305] *Novartis AG, University College London and Institute of Microbiology and Epidemiology v Comptroller* (C-207/03) conjoined with *Ministre de l'économie v Millenium Pharmaceuticals Inc* (C-252/03).

[306] *Novartis AG, University College London and Institute of Microbiology and Epidemiology v Comptroller* (C-207/03) conjoined with *Ministre de l'économie v Millenium Pharmaceuticals Inc* (C-252/03), [31].

[307] *Novartis AG, University College London and Institute of Microbiology and Epidemiology v Comptroller* (C-207/03) conjoined with *Ministre de l'économie v Millenium Pharmaceuticals Inc* (C-252/03), [32].

[308] *Astrazeneca AB v Comptroller General of Patents, Designs and Trade Marks* (617/12).

[309] The first meeting was on 3 February 1995 and the second on 9 October 2006. The minutes of these meetings are available at: *http://thespcblog2.blogspot.co.uk* [Accessed 23 February 2015].

ment of Jacob LJ in *E I Du Pont Nemours & Co v UKIPO*[310] (at [37]–[38]) as follows:

(i)   To facilitate the development and accessibility of medicinal products for use in the paediatric population.

(ii)   To ensure that medicinal products that are used to treat the paediatric population are subject to ethical research of high quality and are appropriately authorised for use in the paediatric population.

(iii) To improve the information available on the use of medicinal products in the various paediatric populations.

Zero term SPCs

The availability of the paediatric extension to a certificate created an incentive on applicants to obtain so called "zero term SPCs". These are certificates which under the normal calculation rules of art.13 of the Medicinal Products Regulation would have had a duration which was mathematically nil or even a negative number. The point being that a six-month extension will still be worth having in such a case. In *Merck & Co's Application*[311] the Comptroller's Hearing Officer (Mr Howard) decided that a supplementary protection certificate could be granted notwithstanding that a positive value for the term of protection does not result when the calculations are made as prescribed by the Medicinal Products Regulation. The Hearing Officer noted the views of the European Commission expressed in the records of the first and second meetings of national experts relating to supplementary protection certificates,[312] which were that a certificate of zero term should not be granted but could find no basis for such an approach in either the Medicinal Products Regulation nor the Regulation on Medicinal Products for Paediatric Use. The decision recognised that the purpose of such a certificate was to keep open the possibility in future of applying for a paediatric extension and determined the duration as minus three months and 14 days (therefore leaving a potential paediatric extension of some three months). He refused to round the term to zero.

6-175

In a reference from the German Patent Office, in *Merck Sharp & Dohme Corp*[313] the Court of Justice subsequently approved the grant of zero term certificates, recognising their utility for those applicants seeking paediatric extensions.

6-176

Choice of extension

In certain cases the applicant has a choice whether to obtain the six-month extension on a supplementary protection certificate or else a one-year extension of the period of marketing protection for a medicinal product (i.e. what is sometimes called data exclusivity) which may be obtained on the ground that a new paediatric indication brings significant clinical benefit in comparison with existing therapies.[314] The legislation is clear that the applicant cannot have both.

6-177

---

[310] [2009] EWCA Civ 996; [2010] R.P.C. 6.

[311] Decision BL O/108/08 of 14 April 2008.

[312] The first meeting was on 3 February 1995 and the second on 9 October 2006. The minutes of these meetings are available at: *http://thespcblog2.blogspot.co.uk* [Accessed 23 February 2015].

[313] (C-125/10).

[314] art.36(1) of Regulation 1901/2006 and see also Regulation 726/2004 and Directive 2001/83/EC.

Application for a paediatric extension

6-178   An application for an extension may be made when lodging the basic application for a supplementary protection certificate in the first place, it may be added to a pending application in appropriate circumstances or it may be made after the certificate is granted, up until two years before expiry of the certificate.[315]

6-179   A transitional provision also permits applications no later than six months before expiry of certificates which have already granted.[316] This transitional provision is in effect for five years from 26 January 2007.[317]

6-180   The application for an extension is required to include a copy of the statement indicating compliance with an agreed completed paediatric investigation plan (PIP).[318] To obtain the extension the applicant will also need to prove that they possess authorisations to place the product on the market of all other Member States. The fundamental marketing authorisation which provides the basis for the supplementary protection certificate in the first place (the one referred to in art.3(b) of the Medicinal Products Regulation) may prove that anyway but if necessary proof is required of possession of authorisations to place the product on the market of all other Member States.[319]

6-181   The process of grant or rejection and of publication is the same as that for supplementary protection certificates generally.[320]

Curing irregularity in the application

6-182   Article 10(3) of the Medicinal Products Regulation gives the Comptroller the power to ask the applicant to rectify irregularities in an application within a stated time. In *E I Du Pont Nemours & Co v UKIPO*[321] the problem facing the applicant was that by the end of the period within which an application could be made, the formal conditions required to grant the extension were not satisfied but they were clearly going to be satisfied soon, albeit probably after the last date on which an application could be made, but nevertheless before the end of the extension (if granted). Therefore, asking for an extension was well worthwhile. The applicant made an application for an extension within the time set by art.7(5) and then sought a period within which to rectify the "irregularity" in its application. The "irregularity" in the application was that neither of the two documents required were or could be provided at the date of the application. The application did not have a copy of the statement required by art.8(1)(d)(i) nor proof that the product was authorised in all Member States as required by art.8(1)(d)(ii); the reason why not being the same in both cases namely that as at the date of application there was no such statement nor was the product authorised across all Member States as required. The UKIPO purported to set a date for the irregularities to be cured but also stated that the defects were incurable. The Court of Appeal ruled that the defects were irregularities within art.10(3), they could be cured and the right thing to do was to

---

[315] Medicinal Products Regulation arts 7(3) and 7(4).
[316] Medicinal Products Regulation art.7(5).
[317] The date of coming into force of Regulation 1901/2006.
[318] Medicinal Products Regulation art.8(1)(d); the paediatric investigation plan is as referred to in art.36(1) of Regulation 1901/2006.
[319] Medicinal Products Regulation art.8(1)(d)(ii).
[320] Medicinal Products Regulation arts 10(6) and 11(3).
[321] [2009] EWCA Civ 966; [2010] R.P.C. 6.

set a date by which the documents had to be provided. By the time the case had reached the Court of Appeal the defects had been cured and the Court's decision was that the UKIPO could extend the supplementary protection certificate.

Date for assessing criteria for grant

The *E I Du Pont Nemours & Co* decision is significant since its effect is that the **6-183** date on which the criteria for grant of an extension have to be satisfied is not the date of the application for the extension and is not limited by requirements in art.7 for the date by which an application must be made. While this is undoubtedly a pragmatic decision in the circumstances it remains to be seen whether the same approach might be extended to applications for basic supplementary protection certificates themselves. The problem in the *Yamanouchi* case[322] was similar to that faced by *E I Du Pont Nemours* —at the last date on which the rules provided that *Yamanouchi* could apply for a supplementary protection certificate they did not and could not satisfy the criteria for grant of a certificate because they had no UK marketing authorisation. They had applied for one and would get it in future before the end of the period which the certificate would have covered if granted. However, *Yamanouchi* did not obtain a certificate. Similarly the Comptroller's Hearing Officer refused a certificate in *Merck Sharp & Dohme Corporation's Application*[323] where an "End of Procedure Communication of Approval" had been received from the Reference Member State at the date of application but not formal approval for marketing authorisation.

Conditions for grant of a paediatric extension

The conditions on which the extension is granted are not set by the Medicinal **6-184** Products Regulation itself but rather are set by art.36(1) of the Regulation for Medicinal Products for Paediatric Use (i.e. Regulation 1901/2006).[324] The conditions are drafted in a somewhat complex manner but in *E I Du Pont Nemours & Co v UKIPO*[325] the Court of Appeal summarised them as follows:

(1) all measures in the agreed paediatric investigation plan (PIP) must have been complied with;
(2) the authorised product information must include relevant information on the results of the studies; and
(3) the product must be authorised in all Member States.[326]

In *Dr Reddy's Laboratories (UK) Ltd v Warner-Lambert Company LLC*[327] the **6-185** High Court held that it had a discretion under art.16 of the Medicinal Products Regulation as to whether to revoke a paediatric extension, but not an obligation to do so, particularly in circumstances where there had been a technical but not a substantive failure to comply with all the requirements of art.36 of the Regulation for Medicinal Products for Paediatric Use.

---

[322] *Yamanouchi Pharmaceuticals Co Ltd v C-G* (C-110/95) [1997] R.P.C. 844.
[323] BL O/117/16.
[324] See, e.g. Medicinal Products Regulation art.16(1).
[325] [2009] EWCA Civ 996; [2010] R.P.C. 6.
[326] [2009] EWCA Civ 996; [2010] R.P.C. 6, Jacob LJ at [38].
[327] [2012] EWHC 3715 (Pat); [2013] R.P.C. 31, [34]–[39].

PIP complied with and information included (conditions (1) and (2))

6-186   Formally art.36(1) Regulation 1901/2006 provides that the right to the extension derives from the inclusion, in the application for a marketing authorisation under arts 7 or 8 of the Regulation 1901/2006, of the results of all studies conducted in compliance with an agreed paediatric investigation plan. Essentially art.7 requires all applications for a marketing authorisation for a medicinal product not already authorised for human use in the Community at the time the Regulation came into force (26 January 2007) to include the results of appropriate paediatric studies.[328] Article 8 applies these rules to applications for authorisations for new indications (including paediatric indications), new pharmaceutical forms and new routes of administration.

6-187   It is not enough for the paediatric investigation itself to have been carried out, it is also necessary for a copy of the marketing authorisation which includes the information gained from the paediatric investigation to be provided as well (*E I Du Pont Nemours & Co v UKIPO*[329]). The issue arose as follows. By arts 36(2) and 28(3) of Regulation 1901/2006, if the application complies with the agreed paediatric investigation plan, etc. the competent authority will include in the marketing authorisation a "statement" indicating compliance with the agreed plan and this statement is used for the purposes of applying the condition set by art.36(1). This "statement" is obviously the statement referred to in the Medicinal Products Regulation at art.8(1)(d)(i).[330] The importance of the "statement" itself over and above the mere fact the investigation has been carried out was addressed by the Court of Appeal in the *E I Du Pont Nemours* case.[331] There the applicant submitted that all that was necessary was to show that the work had in fact been done. The application for a paediatric extension did not need to include a copy of the marketing authorisation which actually an art.28(3) "statement". This submission was rejected[332] on the ground that the extension was only obtained once the final form of the marketing authorisation itself was settled, reflecting the information gained. Thus a copy of the marketing authorisation including the "statement" was necessary. One reason for this was that the objectives of the Regulation included improving the information available on the use of medicinal products in various paediatric populations. The need for dissemination of such information was important and so the requirement for an actual authorisation reflecting the information was necessary. On the other hand, it was lawful for a condition of the investigation plan to be that a study should be commenced, and it was not necessary for the results of the study to have been published in the investigation plan, particularly where the study would have taken some years to complete.[333]

6-188   Note that extension is still granted provided the investigation was carried out even if the investigation fails to lead to the authorisation of a paediatric indication (see Regulation 1901/2006 art.36(1) second part).[334]

---

[328] There is provision for certain waivers of various kinds.

[329] [2009] EWCA Civ 996; [2010] R.P.C. 6.

[330] Albeit that the statement is not referred to in art.36(1) of Regulation 1901/2006 despite art.8(1)(d)(i) of the Medicinal Products Regulation stating that it is.

[331] [2009] EWCA Civ 996; [2010] R.P.C. 6

[332] [2009] EWCA Civ 996; [2010] R.P.C. 6, [26]–[38].

[333] *Dr Reddy's Laboratories (UK) Ltd v Warner-Lambert Company LLC* [2012] EWHC 3715 (Pat); [2013] R.P.C. 31, [40]–[56].

[334] Provided the results of the studies are reflected in the summary of product characteristics and, if ap-

Product authorised in all Member States (condition (3))

The third condition for an extension is set by art.36(3) of Regulation 1901/ **6-189**
2006. Although it states that the "product" must be authorised in all Member States,
the word "product" is not used in the defined sense of the Medicinal Products
Regulation as "active ingredient". On the contrary it means the formulations
presented in accordance with the requirements of the marketing authorisation under
Regulation 1901/2006, such that the presentation of that formulation will include
the information resulting from carrying out the agreed PIP. This point was also
decided by the Court of Appeal in *E I Du Pont Nemours & Co v UKIPO*[335] at [39]–
[44].

---

propriate, the package leaflet; Regulation 1901/2006 art.36, second part.
[335] [2009] EWCA Civ 996; [2010] R.P.C. 6

CHAPTER 7

PRIORITY DATE

CONTENTS

1. INTRODUCTION

The proper assessment of the patentability of an invention will always depend **7-01**
on the date on which the patentability is to be considered. This is because the
comparison is always a relative one in the sense that the invention is considered
relative to the prior art available at a particular date and also relative to the state of
the common general knowledge of those skilled in the art at that date. The priority
system provides for a means by which material filed on one date is to be treated as
having been filed on an earlier "priority" date which may be up to 12 months
beforehand as of right, and up to 14 months where the applicant has requested and
the comptroller has granted a request for permission to make a late declaration.[1]

Under previous legislation, an important function of the analogous system of fil- **7-02**
ing a provisional and then a complete specification was in order to allow inventors
a period of time within which to perfect their invention.[2] However, the effect of the
modern law of priority (as to which see below) and in particular the need for an
enabling disclosure in the priority document is different. The modern system allows an applicant to file an application for a patent and then wait 12 months before
having to decide whether to pursue that application both in this country and
elsewhere.[3] This is useful bearing in mind the investment required in applying for
patents, and allows a patentee time to decide whether the invention is worth patenting at all. Broadly speaking, further developments of the invention in the priority
period can be made the subject of a full consolidated patent application which seeks
to claim priority from the first filing, but the further developments themselves will
not be entitled to claim priority from the first filing.

The determination of a priority date arises in two contexts: **7-03**

---

[1] PA 1977 ss.5(2), 5(2A)(b), and 5(2B). And see Patents Rules 2007 r.7. Note that the provisions relating to making a late declaration do not apply to applications made prior to 1 January 2005.

[2] See, e.g. *Glaxo Group Ltd's Application* [1968] R.P.C. 473.

[3] The Comptroller has power to permit late declarations (i.e. later than the 12 months normally allowed) under s.5(2B) of the PA 1977 where the applicant's failure to file an application within the
normal 12-month period was unintentional. This is analoguous to his power under s.28(3) to permit
restoration of lapsed patents where the failure to pay fees within the relevant period was
unintentional.

(1) An invention has a priority date which must be ascertained in order to assess the patentability of that invention.[4]

(2) Matter contained in an application for a patent also has a priority date which must be determined in order to ascertain the date on which that matter forms part of the state of the art[5] and thus whether the matter in an application can act as a disclosure against other patents.[6]

7-04 For these reasons the declaration required in order to claim priority should be made wherever possible.

2. THE BASIC RULE AND THE RIGHT OF PRIORITY

7-05 The basic rule is that the priority date of an invention to which an application for a patent relates and any matter contained in an application is the date of filing the application.[7] But the basic rule is subject to the right of an applicant to claim, as an earlier priority date, the date of filing of an earlier application.[8] This right to claim priority from another application is known as a right of priority[9] and applies to applications filed under the 1977 Act and also to equivalent applications in convention countries.[10]

Conditions which must be satisfied

7-06 To enable a successful claim to be made to the filing date of an earlier application, the following formal conditions must be satisfied:

(a) the claim (by declaration) must be made by the applicant or a predecessor in title of their;

(b) the declaration must specify one or more earlier relevant applications made by the applicant or a predecessor in title of their;[11] and

(c) the application in suit must have a date of filing which is either;

(i) during the period of 12 months immediately following the date of filing of the earlier specified relevant application or, if there is more than one, of the earliest of them,[12] or

(ii) two months later than such period of 12 months, where the applicant has requested and the comptroller has granted a request for permission to make a late declaration.[13]

7-07 A person who files a patent application for an invention is afforded the privilege

---

4   PA 1977 ss.2 and 3.
5   PA 1977 s.5(1).
6   PA 1977 s.2(3).
7   PA 1977 s.5(1).
8   PA 1977 s.5(2). See also Patent Rules 2007 r.3.
9   See, e.g. EPC art.87(1); and Paris Convention for the Protection of Industrial Property art.4A.
10 PA 1977 s.5(5). A convention country includes a country which is a member of the World Trade Organisation—see s.5(6), as amended by the Patents and Trade Marks (World Trade Organisation) Regulations 1999 (SI 1999/1899).
11 For cases in which the question of whether the applicant was in fact the successor in title to the applicant who filed the earlier relevant application was considered, see *Beloit Technologies Inc v Valmet Paper Machinery Inc* [1995] R.P.C. 705, 732, and *Edwards Lifesciences AG v Cook Biotech Inc* [2009] F.S.R. 27.
12 PA 1977 s.5(2) and 5(2A)(a).
13 PA 1977 ss.5(2), 5(2A)(b), and 5(2B). And see Patents Rules 2007 r.7. Note that the provisions relating to making a late declaration do not apply to applications made prior to 1 January 2005.

of claiming priority only if they themselves filed the earlier relevant application from which priority is claimed or if he is the successor in title to the person who made that earlier application. If they are neither the person who filed the earlier relevant application nor the successor in title, then they are denied the privilege. Moreover, their position is not improved if they subsequently acquires title to the invention after the date of filing of the application.[14]

The Comptroller grants permission to make a late declaration if and only if the request complies with the rules,[15] and the controller is satisfied that the applicant's failure to file the application in suit within the original 12-month period was unintentional.[16] The "application in suit" referred to is the GB national application, such that "the applicant must have intended to file the very same GB national application with the same application papers before the priority period expired", as opposed to intending to file some other application with the same subject matter.[17]   **7-08**

Providing the above formal conditions are satisfied, then any invention to which the application in suit relates, which is supported by matter disclosed in the earlier relevant application or applications, will be entitled to the priority of the earliest relevant application containing such disclosure.[18] Further, the priority date of any matter contained in the application in suit which was disclosed in an earlier application will be the earliest relevant application containing such disclosure.[19]   **7-09**

Where invention or matter is disclosed in two applications

In the case where an invention or other matter was disclosed in two earlier applications by the same applicant, then priority can only be claimed from the first and the second will be disregarded, unless the second application was filed in the same country as the first and before the second was filed the first was withdrawn, abandoned or refused without having been made available to the public, without leaving any rights outstanding and without serving to establish a priority date for any other application.[20] These provisions are to prevent applicants extending the period of 12 months provided in the 1977 Act.[21] Applicants can instead "regenerate" their priority date by withdrawing a first application and then filing a second application in respect of the same invention more than 12 months after the priority date of the withdrawn application. In this case, however, the priority date will be that of the second application and the patentee is at risk as to intervening prior art.[22]   **7-10**

Successor in title

Where the earlier relevant application is made by the inventor, a person is the successor in title of the inventor if, at the time of the making of the invention, that person was entitled to the whole of the property in it in the United Kingdom by   **7-11**

---

[14] *Edwards Lifesciences AG v Cook Biotech Inc* [2009] F.S.R. 27.
[15] Patents Rules 2007 r.7.
[16] PA 1977 s.5(2C). The "unintentional" test is the UK's chosen method of implementing the Patent Law Treaty art.13: see *Sirna Therapeutic Inc's Application* [2006] R.P.C. 12.
[17] See *Sirna Therapeutic Inc's Application* [2006] R.P.C. 12.
[18] PA 1977 s.5(2)(a).
[19] PA 1977 s.5(2)(b).
[20] PA 1977 s.5(3).
[21] PA 1977 s.5(2).
[22] See *Haberman v Comptroller-General* [2004] R.P.C. 21, 414.

virtue of any enforceable term of any agreement entered into with the inventor before the making of the invention.[23]

7-12   With respect to applications for patents filed under the Patent Cooperation Treaty, art.8 of the PCT provides that the conditions for, and the effect of, any priority claim declared in an international application shall be as provided in art.4 of the Paris Convention of 1883, and therefore "successor in title" should be construed in the same manner as for art.87(1) EPC.

7-13   Concerns that a patentee would lose priority for not having executed a formal retrospective assignment in writing have been lessened by the approach taken by Arnold J in *KCI Licensing*[24] in which a future beneficial assignment (in a confidentiality agreement) was held to be sufficient. It was not necessary for the patentee to hold the bare legal title to the patent at the relevant date. Therefore, in *HTC v Gemalto*,[25] Birss J was able to infer from the circumstances that the parties must have agreed by conduct to transfer the entire beneficial interest in the invention without written agreement. Such assessments of assignment of the right to priority will frequently require evidence of foreign law and it cannot be assumed that employers would automatically have a right to employee inventions in other jurisdictions, nor that beneficial title would pass in similar circumstances in other countries.

7-14   A curious aspect of the requirements to assign priority is the extent to which *Edwards v Cook* principles apply to prior art cited against patents and determination of the state of the art under s.2(3) of the Act. It might be said that "the priority date of that matter" in s.2(3) refers only to the disclosure in the priority document and not to whether assignment of the right to priority had been made, since the legal claim to priority by a successor in title would not be necessary in circumstances where the application was merely cited as prior art.[26]

3.   PRIORITY—THE TEST

The position under the European Patents Convention

7-15   The relevant provisions concerning priority in the EPC are arts 87–89.[27] Article 88(3) requires the *elements* of the European application to be included in the application or applications whose priority is claimed. Article 88(4) states that if certain elements of the invention for which priority is claimed do not appear among the claims formulated in the previous application, priority may, nonetheless, be granted provided that the documents of the previous application as a whole specifically disclose such elements. The Guidelines for Examination in the EPO (see F-VI, 2.1–2.4, "Determining Priority Dates") confirm that an element may be a feature disclosed or it may be the combination of certain features. The priority of elements thus corresponds to the requirements under the Patents Act 1977 for the priority of matter.[28]

7-16   The substantive test for priority of inventions applied by the European Patent Of-

---

[23]   *KCI Licensing Inc v Smith & Nephew plc* [2010] EWHC 1487 (Pat). And see PA 1977 s.7(2)(b).
[24]   *KCI Licensing Inc v Smith & Nephew plc* [2010] EWHC 1487 (Pat), [49]–[100].
[25]   *HTC Corp v Gemalto SA* [2014] R.P.C. 9, the judgment of the Court of Appeal in that case is [2014] EWCA 1335 but the issue was not taken to the Court of Appeal.
[26]   See *Idenix Pharmaceuticals v Gilead Sciences* [2014] EWHC 3916 (Pat).
[27]   For consideration of multiple priorities see paras 7-38 to 7-41.
[28]   See paras 7-23 and 7-41.

fice is whether the two applications relate to the same invention (art.87(1)).[29] This was considered in the leading case of G02/98.

Same Invention (G02/98)[30] was a decision of the Enlarged Board of Appeal fol- **7-17** lowing a reference made by the President of the EPO. The principal issue on the reference was as follows:

"Does the requirement of the 'same invention' in Article 87(1) EPC mean that the extent of the right to priority derivable from a priority application for a later application is determined by, and at the same time limited to, what is at least implicitly disclosed in the priority application?"

This issue had arisen due to previous conflicting decisions of the Boards of **7-18** Appeal. The "traditional" line of authority (e.g. T116/84, T184/84, T85/87) had proceeded on the answer to this question was "yes". This was the so-called "novelty test", although it could more accurately be called the "disclosure test". By way of contrast, a less strict approach had developed in parallel following *HOWARD/ Snackfood* (T73/88).[31] That case decided that a feature in a claim which was in effect a disclaimer of some products which would otherwise be within the scope of the claim, was not to be regarded as an essential feature of the invention (for the purposes of determining priority) if the presence of the feature did not change the character and nature of the claimed invention. Thus, the absence from the priority document of features claimed in the patent in question which were not essential features of the invention itself—although they may have been essential limitations in order to ensure that the claim was valid—was not a bar to a successful claim to priority.

It was pointed out that notwithstanding the apparent benefit to the patentee of the **7-19** approach in T73/88 this could in fact be to the patentee's detriment where the patentee had made two previous national filings, the first of which did not disclose (whether expressly or implicitly) the claimed subject matter and the second of which did. In particular a European patent could be granted on the basis of a European patent application A (taking advantage of the first filing), and a later-filed European patent application B (seeking to take advantage of the priority interval of the second filing) claiming the same subject matter could be refused. This could occur in spite of the fact that the second filing had actually been the first application disclosing the claimed subject matter.[32]

The Enlarged Board of Appeal considered the problem identified by the President **7-20** and concluded that the "narrow or strict" interpretation (i.e. as in the "traditional" line of cases) was preferable to the "extensive or broad" interpretation given in T73/88, and that this was "solidly supported by the provisions of the Paris Convention".

It would therefore appear that the following principles established in EPO cases **7-21** decided before G02/98 remain good law. In order to establish a valid claim to priority, the subject-matter of the claim must be clearly identifiable in the priority document but identical wording is not required; all the essential features of the invention must be expressly disclosed in the priority document or clearly and

[29] See Jacob J in *Beloit Technologies Inc v Valmet Paper Machinery Inc* [1995] R.P.C. 705, 733 (although the case went to the Court of Appeal, this point did not arise on appeal).
[30] [2001] O.J. EPO 413; [2002] E.P.O.R. 167.
[31] [1992] O.J. EPO 557; [1990] E.P.O.R. 12.
[32] The problem was more acute when one considered the position of two applicants with overlapping priority documents and applications: see the example considered in G02/98 at [8.1]–[8.2] thereof.

unambiguously derivable from it.[33] An enabling disclosure is required.[34] The disclosure in the priority document as a whole must be considered, so that the fact that a claim in a priority document might be broad enough to cover a particular specific feature does not mean that it discloses that particular feature for the purposes of claiming priority.[35]

Priority in English law

7-22   If a priority date earlier than the date of filing is sought for an invention pursuant to s.5(2)(a), then the earlier priority will be obtained if the invention "is supported by matter disclosed in the earlier relevant application". This provision is to be construed, per s.130(7) as having as nearly as practicable the same effects as art.87(1) of the European Patent Convention. As such, the High Court has been able to apply the respective provisions of the EPC and their corresponding case law directly to questions of priority before it.[36]

7-23   Whereas s.5(2)(a) permits a right of priority if the invention is supported by the matter disclosed, art.87(1) establishes priority if the earlier application is "in respect of the same invention". Further, in *Same Invention* (G02/98),[37] it was held that "the same invention" was equivalent to "the same subject matter, as used in art.87(4) EPC" and that priority was to be acknowledged "only if the skilled person can derive the subject-matter of the claim directly and unambiguously, using common general knowledge, from the previous application as a whole".

7-24   In *Asahi Kasei Kogyo K.K.'s Application*,[38] the House of Lords decided that for the matter to be capable of supporting an invention within the meaning of s.5(2)(a) it must contain an enabling disclosure, that is to say it must disclose the invention in a way which will enable it to be performed by a person skilled in the art.[39]

7-25   In *Evans Medical Ltd's Patent*,[40] Laddie J rejected a submission that for an enabling disclosure to be established it was sufficient to show that it was more likely that a person skilled in the art would go down the enabling route rather than any other. He held that:

> "It is not enough if the instructions in a priority document are such that a number of equally qualified notional addressees can arrive at completely different end points some within the scope of the claimed invention and some not. If reasonable addressees can come to different conclusions there is a conundrum as to which is right. That is not enablement."[41]

7-26   The correct approach, and taking into account that of G02/98, was authoritatively explained by the Court of Appeal in *Unilin Beheer NV v Berry Floor NV*[42] where Jacob LJ (with whom Sir Martin Nourse and Ward LJ agreed) held that:

   (a) Reference should be made to the wording of art.87(1) of the European Pat-

---

33 *COLLABORATIVE RESEARCH/Preprorennin* (T81/87) [1990] O.J. EPO 250; [1990] E.P.O.R. 361.
34 *COLLABORATIVE RESEARCH/Preprorennin* (T81/87) [1990] O.J. EPO 250; [1990] E.P.O.R. 361.
35 *FUJITSU/Avalanche Photo Diodes* (T490/90) [1993] O.J. EPO 40; [1991] E.P.O.R. 423.
36 See, for example, *Unilin Beheer NV v Berry Floor NV* [2005] F.S.R. 6, and *Intervet UK Limited v Merial* [2010] EWHC 294 (Pat).
37 [2001] O.J. EPO 413; [2002] E.P.O.R. 167, a decision of the Enlarged Board of Appeal of the EPO.
38 [1991] R.P.C. 485.
39 See also *Biogen Inc v Medeva Plc* [1997] R.P.C. 1, 46, per Lord Hoffmann, as explained in *SmithKline Beecham Plc's (Paroxetine Methanesulfonate) Patent* [2006] R.P.C. 10.
40 *Evans Medical Ltd's Patent* [1998] R.P.C. 517.
41 [1998] R.P.C. 517, 536–537.
42 [2005] F.S.R. 6.

ent Convention rather than s.5 of the 1977 Act, since the latter is intended to enact the former. Indeed art.87(1) itself seeks to implement the Paris Convention of 1883, an even wider agreement.[43]

(b) The approach is not formulaic: priority is a question about technical disclosure, explicit or implicit. Is there enough in the priority document to give the skilled man essentially the same information as forms the subject of the claim and enables him to work the invention in accordance with that claim?

(c) The main claim and consistory clause of the priority document are just part of its disclosure. For the purposes of priority one looks at the disclosure as a whole. Were the law otherwise, inventors and their advisors would have to start worrying not only about the technical information disclosed in the priority document but how it was to be claimed.[44]

(d) Care should be taken where the priority document discloses combinations of features. Some inventions consist of a combination of features—the invention consists in the very idea of putting them together. In other cases that is simply not so—the features are independent one from the other. Whether, given a disclosure of A-B-C, there is also a disclosure of A or B or C independently depends on substance, not a formula. The ultimate question is simply whether the skilled man can derive the subject-matter of the claim from the priority document as a whole.

(e) *Biogen Inc v Medeva Plc* is consistent with G02/98 even though it was decided before. The law can be summed up pithily in the following sentence: "What is required, as Lord Hoffmann pointed out in *Biogen*, is that the priority document must contain sufficient material for the priority document to constitute the enabling disclosure of [the claim concerned]".[45]

A line must be drawn between what is disclosed, whether explicitly or implicitly and what is obvious. In assessing what is disclosed, it is permissible to take into account the common general knowledge of the skilled addressee as a mental backdrop when deciding what they would understand from a priority document, but not to use that common general knowledge to supplement the disclosure of that document.[46] While it can be difficult to draw such a line, the EPO has held, in the context of assessing added matter, that an implicit disclosure means no more than the clear and unambiguous consequence of what is explicitly mentioned, taking into account the common general knowledge.[47] **7-27**

It also follows that, since the priority document must be read as a whole, its general description is no less a part of the technical content than the examples.[48] Furthermore, the degree of effort required by the skilled addressee when considering enablement for the purposes of priority must be the same as for the requirement of sufficiency of disclosure and accordingly: **7-28**

---

[43] A point made in G02/98 itself—see para.7-17, et seq.

[44] Similarly it is not enough to ask what is enabled by the claims: see *Abbott Laboratories Limited v Evysio Medical Devices ULC* [2008] R.P.C. 23. The question is whether the disclosure as a whole is enabling and effectively gives the skilled person what is in the claim whose priority is in question.

[45] Per Aldous LJ in *Pharmacia Corp v Merck & Co Inc* [2002] R.P.C. 41, cited in *Unilin Beheer*. It is submitted that other previous UK cases are likewise consistent with G02/98: see, e.g. *Balmoral Group Ltd v CRP Marine Ltd* [2000] F.S.R. 860, CA.

[46] *HTC Corporation v Gemalto S.A.* [2014] EWCA 1335, [65] and [70].

[47] *PPG/Coating* (T 823/96) [1999] E.P.O.R. 417. See Ch.15 for further discussion.

[48] Per Laddie J in *Evans Medical Ltd's Patent* [1998] R.P.C. 517, 535.

"even though a reasonable amount of trial and error is permissible when it comes to the sufficiency in an unexplored field or ... where there are many technical difficulties, there must be available adequate instructions in the specification or on the basis of common general knowledge which would lead the skilled person necessarily and directly towards success through the evaluation of initial failures or through an acceptable statistical expectation rate in the case of random experiments."[49]

Priority document must disclose the claimed invention

7-29   Assessment of entitlement to priority must therefore be made not only with the disclosure of the priority document but also with the scope of the invention of the claims in mind. Simply because the patent contains additional information not present in the priority document does not mean that the claims are not entitled to priority. Further, it is frequently the case that a priority document will be filed without claims and in such a specification the various features found in the claim of the granted patent are unlikely to be written out together in a neat paragraph.[50]

7-30   However, asking whether a priority document provides an enabling disclosure—in the narrow sense that it explains how to make the invention of the claims work—is not the only question which falls to be considered when determining whether a claimed invention is supported by matter disclosed in a priority document. For instance, where the priority document discloses certain features but does not suggest they are essential to the invention, a claim lacking such features can properly claim priority,[51] and conversely a priority document which fails to disclose a certain feature forms no basis for a monopoly with such feature.[52]

7-31   Another aspect of the requirement for support arises from the breadth of the claim in question by comparison with the disclosure in the priority document. This was considered by Jacob J in *Beloit v Valmet*[53] and he decided that the test for support set out by Aldous J in *Schering Biotech Corp's Application*[54] in relation to s.14(5)(c) also applied in assessing priority. Jacob J held that priority will only be found if the description in the priority document provides a base which fairly entitles the patentee to priority for a claim of the breadth concerned. In *Intervet v Merial*,[55] Arnold J held that a priority document disclosed three strains of particular viruses and implied that they might be representative of three classes of such viruses. However, as a matter of substance rather than terminology, the priority document did not disclose the existence of such classes, being very broadly and imprecisely defined. In *Unwired Planet v Huawei*[56] Birss J rejected the submission that the added matter test applied in *AC Edwards v Acme*[57] and other cases, which led to a claim of wider scope not amounting to added matter, was enough to satisfy the test

---

49   *UNILEVER/Stable bleaches* (T226/85) [1988] E.P.O.R 336, referred to with approval by both Aldous J and the Court of Appeal in *Mentor v Hollister* [1991] F.S.R. 557 and [1993] R.P.C. 7; and applied by Laddie J in *Evans Medical Ltd's Patent* [1998] R.P.C. 517, 537. See also *SmithKline Beecham Plc's (Paroxetine Methanesulfonate) Patent* [2006] R.P.C. 10.

50   As was the case in *Hospira UK Limited v Genentech Inc* [2014] EWHC 1094 (Pat).

51   See *Rocky Mountain Traders Ltd v Hewlett Packard GmbH* [2000] F.S.R. 411. Although the case went to the Court of Appeal, this point did not arise on appeal.

52   See *Balmoral Group Ltd v CRP Marine Ltd* [2000] F.S.R. 860, CA.

53   [1995] R.P.C. 705, 732–734 (although the case went to the Court of Appeal, this point did not arise on appeal.)

54   [1993] R.P.C. 249, 252. *Schering* has since been followed by the Court of Appeal in *Balmoral Group Ltd v CRP Marine Ltd* [2000] F.S.R. 860 and by Pumfrey J in *Rocky Mountain Traders Ltd v Hewlett Packard GmbH* [2000] F.S.R. 411.

55   *Intervet UK Limited v Merial* [2010] EWHC 294 (Pat), [187].

56   [2015] EWHC 3336 (Pat), [103]–[107].

57   [1992] R.P.C. 131 and see *AP Racing v Alcon* [2014] EWCA 40 (Pat).

for priority. If a claim of wider scope does not disclose any new matter then the added matter test is satisfied, although to maintain priority such a claim must also be supported by the priority document. Priority is primarily a question of construction of the claim and the priority document, and it is submitted that disclosure can be explicit or implicit and will be a matter of construction by the court when properly instructed.[58]

The correspondence between the need for support in order to found a claim for priority and the requirement in s.14(5)(c) of the 1977 Act that, in a patent application, a claim shall be supported by the description was taken into account by Lord Hoffmann in *Biogen Inc v Medeva Plc*[59] when he held, following *Asahi*, that an enabling disclosure is needed to satisfy the requirements of support under s.5(2)(a), to provide a valid patent application under s.14 and for sufficiency under s.72(1)(c).[60] Furthermore, in the *Biogen* case the House of Lords decided that what constitutes a sufficiently enabling disclosure to support a claim will depend on the breadth of the claim itself.[61] Thus a disclosure of a principle capable of general application may support claims in correspondingly general terms, such that a patentee will not need to show that they have proved the application of the principle in every individual instance. However, if the claims include a number of discrete methods or products the patentee must enable the invention to be performed in respect of each of them.[62]

7-32

Selection of sub-class

Another aspect of *Biogen* (as explained in *Pharmacia Corp v Merck & Co Inc*)[63] is the fact that the disclosure of a broad class of compounds in a priority document does not necessarily support the selection of a sub-class having the properties of the invention as claimed in the subsequent patent. Of course it is possible to claim a narrower range of compounds than that disclosed in the priority document. However, the fact that it is a narrower range does not mean that there is support for that range. In the *Pharmacia* case the priority document disclosed neither the class of compounds claimed in the patent, nor the properties which the patent required such class to have (namely that the class had anti-inflammatory activity and was COX II selective).

7-33

A similar difficulty was encountered in *Hospira UK Limited v Novartis AG*[64] where the relevant claim was for around 2 up to about 10 mg of zoledronate for osteoporosis where the period between administrations was about once a year, and in combination with other features of the claim including the method of administration. The priority document disclosed 2–10 mg once a year but said nothing about any method of administration or condition, and disclosed an example with a total dose of 4 mg per annum. As the Court of Appeal noted, the disclosure of the priority document was either too general, in which case the claim was an unsup-

7-34

---

[58] In relation to the test for support generally (i.e. as opposed to support for the claim's breadth) see paras 7-24 to 7-26.

[59] [1997] R.P.C. 1.

[60] See Lord Hoffmann at 47.

[61] [1997] R.P.C. 1, 48.

[62] [1997] R.P.C. 1.

[63] [2002] R.P.C. 41, 775), CA, upholding the first instance decision of Pumfrey J reported as *Monsanto Co v Merck & Co Inc* [2000] R.P.C. 709.

[64] *Hospira UK Limited v Novartis AG* [2013] EWHC 516, [126]-[146], upheld on appeal in *Hospira UK Limited v Novartis AG* [2015] R.P.C. 1.

ported selection of a sub-class, or too specific, being the disclosure of the example. The Court rejected priority on the basis of reading the priority document as a whole, and that the reader was told that it was not merely the 4mg dose that was suitable for the claimed methods of administration and condition.

Priority document need not state the advantages of the invention

7-35   Provided that the priority document supports the claimed invention, it is irrelevant whether it mentions any advantages of that invention. However, if such advantages are neither mentioned nor hinted at, nor could they have been predicted from what is described in the priority document, then the patentee is not entitled to rely on such advantages in support of non-obviousness.[65]

Priority of claims to a therapeutic use

7-36   A divergence of approach has arisen between the English Court and the EPO has been observed with respect to claims to a therapeutic use, where such claims have been held to be sufficiently disclosed if the specification makes such a use plausible (see paras 13-54 to 13-64).

7-37   In *Gemvax*[66] the priority document lacked the experimental results found in the patent. The Technical Board of Appeal held that the priority document disclosed the invention in an enabling way, in that the invention of the claims was disclosed and could be performed and there was no legal basis for imposing additional criteria such as plausibility. This approach was reluctantly but explicitly rejected by Birss J in *Hospira UK Limited v Genentech Inc*,[67] where the judge held that the requirements for sufficiency of disclosure logically applied just as much to priority and the test for priority included a requirement of plausibility.

4. MULTIPLE AND PARTIAL PRIORITIES

7-38   Section 125(2) of the 1977 Act provides that where more than one invention is specified in any claim, each invention may have a different priority date. This provision should be read together with s.14(5)(d) which states that the claim or claims shall relate to one invention or a group of inventions which are so linked to form a single inventive concept. Thus, a single claim can contain more than one invention and each invention may have a different priority date. The scheme of the 1977 Act, read in isolation, makes it impossible to conclude that a single invention could ever have more than one priority date under the Act, since s.5 is concerned with determining *the* priority date of *an* invention.

7-39   However, all the provisions of the 1977 Act concerned with priority[68] are listed in s.130(7) as being provisions which are intended to have the same effect as the corresponding provisions of the European Patent Convention, the Community Patent Convention and the Patent Co-operation Treaty. Furthermore, with particular reference to the EPC—which contains substantive provisions concerned with prior-

---

[65] See Kitchin J in *Generics (UK) Ltd v Daiichi Pharmaceutical Co Ltd* [2009] R.P.C. 4, [116]–[117].

[66] T903/05.

[67] *Hospira UK Limited v Genentech Inc* [2014] EWHC 1094 (Pat), at [149] followed by the same judge in *Merck v Ono* [2015] EWHC 2973 (Pat).

[68] In particular, PA 1977 s.5 and s.125(2), as well as ss.2 and 3, and analogous provisions such as s.14(5).

ity—the wording of the 1977 Act is quite different to the wording of the EPC. The provision of the EPC which corresponds to s.125(2) is art.88(2), which provides that "Multiple priorities may be claimed in respect of a European patent application … Where appropriate, multiple priorities may be claimed for any one claim." Thus unlike s.125(2), the EPC does not impose, as an apparent condition precedent to a claim having multiple priorities, a requirement that more than one invention is specified in the claim.

It is submitted that there is no conflict between the 1977 Act and the European Patent Convention if the reference to "more than one invention" in s.125(2) is seen as declaratory of a consequence of the set of circumstances which make it appropriate, under the EPC, to claim multiple priorities for one claim, rather than as a freestanding requirement in its own right. If the facts are such that a claim is entitled to multiple priorities, then it follows as a consequence that the claim specifies more than one invention.

7-40

When can a claim have multiple priorities?

If a claim is drafted in such a way that it encompasses clear alternatives—for example, a claim which defines a chemical compound by reference to a structure which may take identified alternative forms—then attributing multiple priorities is unlikely to cause difficulty. In effect, the claim can be regarded as being made up of several discrete claims[69] or—in the words of s.125(2)—as specifying more than one invention, each with a different priority date. However, it is difficult to see how a broad claim which does not set out alternatives as such could be regarded as specifying more than one invention, and it is hard to see how such a claim could allow for multiple priorities to be claimed. This is in line with the approach taken by the European Patent Office.[70]

7-41

The priority date of matter

The principles set out above are concerned with establishing the priority date of a claimed invention rather than the priority date of matter. The priority date of matter contained in an application is deemed to be the filing date of an earlier relevant application if it was "disclosed in" that earlier application.[71] Section 130(3) of the 1977 Act—which provides that matter shall be taken to have been disclosed in any relevant application if it was either claimed or disclosed in that application—is no more than a statement that one is entitled to look at the claims as much as any other part of the specification of an application in order to ascertain whether matter is disclosed in an application.[72] Thus, in the *Asahi* case,[73] matter consisting of a formula for a chemical compound claimed in an application cited as prior art in the case under consideration was found to be entitled to an earlier priority because the formula itself was present in the priority document. However, it was also held that this fact did not prejudice the novelty of a claim to the compound which was entitled

7-42

[69] See *Hallen Co v Brabantia* [1990] F.S.R. 134 where Aldous J construed a claim as being divided into a number of discrete claims.

[70] See *Case Law of the Boards of Appeal of the European Patent Office*, 6th edn (Munich: EPO, 2010), Ch.IV-D, 3.

[71] PA 1977 s.5(2)(b).

[72] per Lord Oliver in *Asahi Kasei Kogyo K.K.'s Application* [1991] R.P.C. 485, at 531–535 and see especially 533.

[73] [1991] R.P.C. 485; and see Lord Jauncey at 547. See also para.11-112.

to a later priority date because the formula per se did not amount to an enabling disclosure of the compound.

Partial priority and poisonous priorities

7-43   With art.88(2) EPC in mind, the Enlarged Board in G02/98 held that, with respect to claims where one feature *or* another feature might be adopted, then the claim might have partial priority with respect to each feature. Referring back to arts 87(1) and 87(4), the Enlarged Board held that "the same invention" could be equated with "the same subject matter" and therefore as long as the later claimed matter was indeed the same invention and subject matter as disclosed in an earlier application, it would take priority. This would be particularly pertinent to claims where several possible features were claimed, and as the Enlarged Board stated:

> "The use of a generic term or formula in a claim for which multiple priorities are claimed in accordance with Article 88(2) EPC, second sentence, is perfectly acceptable under Articles 87(1) and 88(3) EPC, provided that it gives rise to the claiming of a limited number of clearly defined alternative subject-matters."[74]

7-44   However, a difficulty arises with the test of partial priority being stated by the Enlarged Board as being limited "clearly defined alternative subject matters". Where features of a claim are clearly set out as possible alternatives, then it is simple for the reader to identify which part of the claim is entitled to priority. If however the granted claim contains a broader range, e.g. 1 to 100mg or a halogen ion, when the priority document discloses, e.g. 10mg or the chloride ion, it might be said that claim was not entitled to priority, being only a generalisation of the priority disclosure and without clearly defined alternative subject matters. One can see that while the claim was not entitled to priority, the priority document, or indeed a divisional application with more specific claims to, e.g. 10mg or chloride, would not only benefit from the priority date but would also destroy the novelty of the parent application with their broader claims. Such priority or divisional applications have been referred to as "poisonous priority" or "poisonous divisionals".

7-45   The consequences of this decision in G02/98 have led to a divergence of approach before the Technical Boards of Appeal of the EPO. In T1496/11,[75] Technical Board 3.2.05 held that the subject matter of the main request was a generalised form of that disclosed in the priority document and that the feature of the priority document, although falling within the scope of the main request, was not part of the subject matter of those claims. Therefore, the patentee's divisional application, which was identical to the priority document, was novelty destroying.

7-46   In T1127/00,[76] Technical Board 3.3.08 confirmed the position with regard to claims to a great number of compounds, in this case nucleic acid sequences, although it would seem to be equally applicable to more traditional *Markush* claims to chemical entities. Since the alternative compounds were not spelled out in the claim, the Board held that "the fact that they might be intellectual envisaged to fall within the scope of the claim [did] not make up for a clear and unambiguous presence of these alternatives, individualized as such, in the claim." Thus the claim was denied partial priority.

---

[74] [2001] O.J. EPO 413; [2002] E.P.O.R. 167, at Reason 6.7.
[75] *SECURENCY INTERNATIONAL/Self-verifying security documents* (T1496/11) at Reason 3.
[76] *GENE SHEARS/Ribozymes* (T1127/00). See also T665/00 and T1877/08 in which a similarly strict approach was taken.

Other decisions of the Technical Boards of Appeal have taken a more liberal approach to partial priority and held that alternative subject matters need not be clearly stated in the claim, but must simply be clearly defined in the sense of being able to be conceptually identified.[77] **7-47**

In *Novartis v Johnson & Johnson*,[78] Kitchin J held that the principle set out in **7-48** G02/98 applied "even if the claim has adopted a generic term to describe and encompass those alternatives". This would seem to imply that a *Markush* claim could still take several priority dates even though the claim was not structurally or linguistically clearly divided into express alternatives, and to follow the liberal approach above. However, in *Nestec v Dualit*,[79] Arnold J held that claim 1 covered embodiments disclosed in the priority document, although they were not clearly defined alternatives to the other arrangements covered and therefore the claim lacked novelty. It seems that the wording of s.5(2)(a) of the Act ("supported by matter disclosed"), rather than art.87(1) EPC, reflects more properly the correct approach that should be adopted in this regard.

T557/13 has now been referred to the Enlarged Board of Appeal, as G01/15.[80] **7-49** The questions referred have been cast both in terms of partial priorities more generally, and specifically as to whether divisional applications may as a matter of procedure be cited against other applications in the same family.[81] It does seem to be odd that priority and divisional applications may anticipate in this way, and it may be that the Enlarged Board will clarify matters so as to bring the phenomenon of toxic priority and divisional applications to an end. Nevertheless, there are difficulties with taking the more liberal approach and treating a generalised claim as an individualised disclosure of each and every sub-class and embodiment falling within that claim, as discussed at paras 7-33 to 7-34, and with regard to the principles of added matter more generally.

---

[77] See *KAO CORPORATION* (T1222/11) [2013] E.P.O.R. 37 and *ASTRAZENECA* (T571/10) [2015] E.P.O.R. 16 of Technical Board of Appeal 3.3.07.

[78] *Novartis AG v Johnson & Johnson Medical Ltd* [2009] EWHC 1671 (Pat), [122].

[79] *Nestec SA v Dualit Limited* [2013] R.P.C. 32, [90]–[104]. Note that in *HTC v Gemalto* [2013] EWHC 1876, [157]–[163] Birss J rejected a submission said to be based on *Nestec* that unless one can establish partial priority for different alternatives within the generic claim, the claim loses priority. It was rejected as being contrary to *Biogen v Medeva* [1997] R.P.C. 1. On appeal in *HTC* at [2014] EWCA 1335 the Court of Appeal upheld the judgment on priority on the facts. This point was not argued.

[80] See *INFINEUM/Partial priority* (T0557/13) [2015] E.P.O.R. 37.

[81] Readers may recall that in G3/93, the Enlarged Board held that a document published during the priority interval, corresponding to that of the priority document, did constitute prior art citable against a European patent application claiming that priority, to the extent that such priority is not validly claimed. Therefore, it would seem inconsistent with G3/93 were the Enlarged Board in G1/15 to hold that there was any special rule for divisional applications in this regard.

CHAPTER 8

THE "PERSON SKILLED IN THE ART" AND COMMON GENERAL KNOWLEDGE

CONTENTS

1. THE "PERSON SKILLED IN THE ART"

The importance of correct identification

A significant issue in many aspects of patent litigation is the identity of the **8-01** notional "person skilled in the art" (often termed the "skilled person" or the "skilled (or notional) addressee" of the patent specification).

The "person skilled in the art" is expressly referred to in the statutory provi- **8-02** sions relating to obviousness and insufficiency. More generally, the correct identification of such a person (or team of persons) may have important conse- quences for the identification of the common general knowledge in the art, the construction of the specification, and therefore for the issues of infringement and/or validity. As Jacob LJ explained in *Technip France SA's Patent*[1]:

> "The 'man skilled in the art' is invoked at many critical points of patent law. The claims of a patent must be understood as if read by that notional man—in the hackneyed but convenient phrase the 'court must don the mantle of the skilled man.' Likewise many questions of validity (obviousness, and sufficiency for instance) depend upon trying to view matters as he would see them. He indeed has statutory recognition—Arts. 56, 83 and 100 of the EPC expressly refer to 'the person skilled in the art.'"

Since the correct identification of such a person may therefore affect a number **8-03** of disparate issues, the overall legal principles involved are discussed separately here, prior to detailed consideration of those specific topics in separate chapters below. This reflects the approach taken in many judgments, in which the identifica- tion of the skilled person and the common general knowledge is reviewed in a self- contained section at an early stage.

The person skilled in the art and construction

The EPC and the 1977 Act contain a number of provisions relating to construc- **8-04** tion, including the Protocol on the Interpretation of art.69 of the EPC (which is expressly stated to apply equally to the 1977 Act in s.125(3) thereof). These do not expressly refer to the skilled person, save in one narrowly defined negative sense in the Protocol, which provides as follows:

> "Article 69 should not be interpreted in the sense that the extent of the protection conferred by a

---

[1] [2004] R.P.C. 46, [6]. Kitchen J similarly commented ("relevant to all aspects of the dispute I have to decide") in *Generics v Lundbeck* [2007] R.P.C. 32, at [37].

European patent is to be understood as that defined by the strict, literal meaning of the wording used in the claims, the description and drawings being employed only for the purpose of resolving an ambiguity found in the claims. Neither should it be interpreted in the sense that the claims serve only as a guideline and that the actual protection conferred may extend to what, from a consideration of the description and drawings by a person skilled in the art, the patentee has contemplated. On the contrary, it is to be interpreted as defining a position between these extremes which combines a fair protection for the patentee with a reasonable degree of certainty for third parties."

8-05   It is however settled at the highest level that the correct, purposive, approach to the construction of patent claims requires the court to give to the language of the claim the meaning which would have been understood by the appropriately skilled and informed audience to which it was actually addressed. The decision of the House of Lords in *Kirin-Amgen*[2] contains a very full explanation of the relevant principles and is discussed further below in the chapter dedicated to construction.[3] For present purposes the following passage from Lord Hoffmann's speech may be noted[4]:

"...Construction is objective in the sense that it is concerned with what a reasonable person to whom the utterance was addressed would have understood the author to be using the words to mean. ... What the author would have been understood to mean by using those words is not simply a matter of rules. It is highly sensitive to the context of and background to the particular utterance. It depends not only upon the words the author has chosen but also upon the identity of the audience he is taken to have been addressing and the knowledge and assumptions which one attributes to that audience."

8-06   Establishing the necessary context, and specifically "the identity of the audience" and "the knowledge and assumptions which one attributes to that audience" is therefore a vital step in construing the document.

8-07   The EPO similarly construes terms in patent documents as they would be read by a person skilled in the art who construes the patent with "a mind willing to understand not a mind desirous of misunderstanding".[5]

8-08   As noted in Ch.9 at para.9–149, et seq., the skilled addressee is also expressly invoked for the purpose of applying the second "Improver" or "Protocol" question.

The person skilled in the art and obviousness

8-09   Section 3 of the 1977 Act provides:

"An invention shall be taken to involve an inventive step if it is not obvious to a person skilled in the art, having regard to any matter which forms part of the state of the art by virtue only of section 2(2) above (and disregarding section 2(3) above)."

The corresponding provision in the EPC, art.56, provides in relevant part:

"An invention shall be considered as involving an inventive step if, having regard to the state of the art, it is not obvious to a person skilled in the art."

8-10   Such persons will be taken to be acquainted with the common general knowledge in the art. Further, it may be pertinent that they also have the "mindset" of those in the art; see further paras 12–35 and 12–54, et seq.

---

2   *Kirin-Amgen v Hoechst Marion Roussel* [2005] R.P.C. 9, [30].
3   See Ch.9, para.9–54, et seq.
4   *Kirin-Amgen v Hoechst Marion Roussel* [2005] R.P.C. 9, [32].
5   See, e.g. *NGK/Engine Exhaust Gas System* (T1321/04) particularly at [2.1]–[2.3] and *YKK/Woven Slide Fastener Stringer* (T190/99) particularly at [2.4], decisions of the Technical Board of Appeal of the EPO. Further cases are set out in Ch.9, "Construction".

The person skilled in the art and (in)sufficiency

Section 14(3) of the 1977 Act provides that:　　　　　　　　　　　　　　8-11

"(3)　The specification of an application shall disclose the invention in a manner which is clear
enough and complete enough for the invention to be performed by a person skilled in the
art.[…]"

This corresponds to EPC art.83, entitled "Disclosure of the invention", which　　8-12
provides that:

"The European patent application must disclose the invention in a manner sufficiently clear and
complete for it to be carried out by a person skilled in the art".

The consequence of non-compliance with s.14(5) is set out in s.72(1)(c) of the　　8-13
1977 Act, which provides that a patent may be revoked if:

"the specification of the patent does not disclose the invention clearly enough and completely enough
for it to be performed by a person skilled in the art".

Again, this corresponds to EPC art.100(b), which provides as one of the grounds　　8-14
of opposition to grant that:

"the European patent does not disclose the invention in a manner sufficiently clear and complete for
it to be carried out by a person skilled in the art".

The identification of the person skilled in the art is therefore an important step　　8-15
in determining whether or not the specification is sufficient. As Lord Hoffmann
explained in *Kirin-Amgen*[6]:

"The first step is to identify the invention and decide what it claims to enable the skilled man to do.
Then one can ask whether the specification enables him to do it".

Overall, the skilled person is taken as lacking in inventive capacity but is deemed　　8-16
to have the common knowledge of those working in the field to which the invention relates, and as further explained in *Kirin-Amgen*[7]:

"… reads the specification on the assumption that its purpose is to both to describe and to demarcate
an invention—a practical idea which the patentee has had for a new product or process—and not to
be a textbook in mathematics or chemistry or a shopping list of chemicals or hardware".

Is the "person skilled in the art" the same for all such purposes?

The correct identification of the level of skill of the skilled person, and the com-　　8-17
mon general knowledge that such a person should be taken to possess, may
therefore be particularly important where a "squeeze" arises between insufficiency and obviousness.[8] The addressee of the patent must have sufficient skill and
knowledge to put the invention into effect, for otherwise the patent will be
insufficient. But the higher the level of skill and knowledge of those in the art, the
greater the risk that the invention may be considered to be obvious.

When considering the issues of construction and sufficiency, the "person skilled　　8-18
in the art" is assumed to have the patent specification in his hands, and the expres-

---

[6]　*Kirin-Amgen v Hoechst Marion Roussel* [2005] R.P.C. 9, [103].
[7]　*Kirin-Amgen v Hoechst Marion Roussel* [2005] R.P.C. 9, [33].
[8]　See e.g. *Omnipharm v Merial* [2013] EWCA Civ 2, [34]–[35], [55], [67]–[74], [92].

sion "skilled addressee" is therefore equivalent. Both the problem and the patentee's solution are in front of him. However, when considering obviousness, the skilled person is deemed only to be considering the prior art, and the issue is whether the claimed invention would have been obvious without hindsight knowledge of it. In *Zipher v Markem*[9], Floyd J noted that:

> "Although the skilled team for the purposes of insufficiency does not possess any greater skill than that for obviousness, the insufficiency team has the advantage that it will have the invention in view. The skilled team is trying to carry out the invention and achieve success[10], ... not searching for a solution in ignorance of it."

8-19   In most cases where the invention addresses a problem in some art and then provides a solution to it, the relevant "art" will be the same, as will the characteristics of a person skilled in it. However, there may be cases where the inventive solution involves bringing in new expertise (and the patent would be sufficient to a team including someone with that expertise) but where the introduction of such expertise into a "prior art team" involves a step towards the invention taken only with hindsight.[11]

8-20   In *Inhale v Quadrant*[12] Laddie J accepted (obiter) that in some cases there could be invention in marrying together concepts from two unrelated arts. In *Schlumberger v EMGS*,[13] the Court of Appeal confirmed that the person skilled in the art for obviousness is not necessarily the same person skilled in the art for performing the invention once it is made. Addressing an argument that the same expression "person skilled in the art" cannot have different meanings in different places in the Act or Treaty, Jacob LJ said[14]:

> "I think the flaw in that is to assume that 'the art' is necessarily the same both before and after the invention is made. The assumption may be correct in most cases, but some inventions are themselves art changing. If a patentee says 'marry the skills of two different arts to solve a problem,' marrying may be obvious or it may not. If it is not, and doing so results in a real technical advance then the patentee deserves and ought to have, a patent. His vision is out of the ordinary."

8-21   This is not because a different construction is being given to the phrase 'person skilled in the art' in the different Articles. It is because the phrase is being applied to different situations. Where the issue is claim construction or sufficiency one is considering a post-patent situation where the person skilled in the art has the patent in hand to tell him how to perform the invention and what the monopoly claimed is. But ex-hypothesi the person skilled in the art does not have the patent when considering obviousness and 'the art' may be different if the invention of the patent itself is art changing.

8-22   In the case of obviousness in view of the state of the art, a key question is generally 'what problem was the patentee trying to solve?' That leads one in turn to consider the art in which the problem in fact lay. It is the notional team in that art

---

9   *Zipher Ltd v Markem Systems Ltd* [2009] F.S.R. 1, [366].

10   That the skilled person is seeking success comes from the statement to that effect by Aldous J in *Mentor Corp v Hollister Inc* [1991] F.S.R. 557, at 162, as approved by the Court of Appeal in the same case, [1993] R.P.C. 7 at 14, as set out in *Zipher* at 364. As a concept, however, it has its limits—as discussed by Lord Hoffmann in *Kirin-Amgen v Hoecsht Marion Roussel* [2005] R.P.C. 9, at [128] and [130]. Ordinarily, it is clear enough. The skilled person is taken to be trying to make the invention work.

11   See, e.g. *JALON/Luminescent Security Fibres* (T422/93).

12   [2002] R.P.C. 21, [42].

13   [2010] EWCA Civ 819, [30]–[70].

14   [2010] EWCA Civ 819, [62]–[64].

which is the relevant team making up the person skilled in the art. If it would be obvious to that team to bring in different expertise, then the invention will nonetheless be obvious. Likewise if the possessor of the 'extra expertise' would himself know of the other team's problem. But if it would not be obvious to either of the notional persons or teams alone and not obvious to either sort of team to bring in the other, then the invention cannot fairly be said to be obvious."

Identifying the "person skilled in the art"

Disputes as to the identity of the person skilled in the art generally involve some or all of the following questions[15]:

8-23

(1) What is the relevant art?
(2) Should the "person skilled in the art" be taken as comprising a team, each member bringing a particular skill, and if so then what is the composition of that notional team?
(3) What are the attributes and qualifications, and in particular the level of skill, of the notional skilled person or team?
(4) What is the common general knowledge to be imputed to such person or team?

Evidence

On all such matters, evidence is admissible. It is of course important to distinguish the notional person skilled in the art from the real witnesses, and in particular the expert witnesses. Jacob LJ explained this in *Technip France SA's Patent*[16] as follows:

8-24

> "I must explain why I think the attempt to approximate real people to the notional man is not helpful. It is to do with the function of expert witnesses in patent actions. Their primary function is to educate the court in the technology—they come as teachers, as makers of the mantle for the court to don. For that purpose it does not matter whether they do or do not approximate to the skilled man. What matters is how good they are at explaining things."

The practice of calling a worker supposedly representative of the skilled addressee, while common in former times, is rare if not extinct today. In *British Celanese Ltd v Courtaulds Ltd*,[17] addressing an argument that evidence-in-chief could not prove common knowledge, Clauson J said:

8-25

> "I have a man properly informed in the art who knows so and so. I can infer that everybody properly informed in the art will have some knowledge because they have exactly the same opportunity as he has ... I must be satisfied that he has not an excess of any peculiar or special sort of knowledge, but that what he is telling me is what he has acquired in his ordinary practice as a man engaged in the art."

Evidence of fact, for example as to the training of, or the textbooks actually available to and consulted by, a person working in the field, may be of some value, but the risks in attempting to extrapolate from a single individual to a notional class are plain.

8-26

---

15 In the IPEC the pleadings should identify the technical field of the person skilled in the art. See *Environmental Defence Systems Ltd v Synergy Health Plc* [2014] EWHC 1306 (IPEC).
16 [2004] R.P.C. 46.
17 (1933) 50 R.P.C. 63, 90.

What is the relevant art?

8-27   The patent specification is addressed, as stated by Lord Diplock in *Catnic v Hill & Smith*,[18] to someone "likely to have a practical interest in the subject matter of his invention (i.e. 'skilled in the art')". The relevant art, at least for the purposes of construction and sufficiency, should therefore usually be apparent from the specification itself. It is not necessarily the case that the same addressee is required for all claims, although the question has not been definitively decided.[19]

8-28   As Pumfrey J pointed out in *Horne Engineering v Reliance Water Controls*[20]:

> "... although it has to be remembered that a specification may fail to provide sufficient details for the addressee to understand and apply the invention, and so be insufficient and invalid, it is often possible to deduce the attributes which the skilled man must possess from the assumptions which the specification clearly makes about his abilities."

8-29   For the purpose of considering obviousness, there can of course be no "addressee" of the specification. The relevant skilled person or composition of the skilled team will in most cases be the same as for construction and sufficiency. Although, as discussed at paras 8-17 to 8-22, this cannot be a fixed rule. The Court of Appeal in *Schlumberger v EMGS*[21] drew specific attention to the words "often possible" in the above passage. There is a risk that working backwards from considerations of sufficiency may improperly build hindsight into the obviousness aspects. As the EPO pointed out in *Two Identities/COMVIK*[22]:

> "The technical problem should not be formulated to refer to matters of which the skilled person would only have become aware by knowledge of the solution now claimed. Such formulation of the problem involving inadmissible hindsight of the solution must be avoided by reformulation of the technical problem to be solved. Thus a problem should not contain pointers to the solution or partially anticipate it."

8-30   The appropriate test in the case of obviousness is therefore to consider the relevant art in which the problem in fact lay (which will usually but not inevitably be the same art as that of the solution). It is the notional team in that art which is the relevant team making up the person skilled in the art.[23] An example of the court independently analysing the identities of the skilled addressee on the one hand and the skilled person for the purposes of obviousness on the other is found in *HTC v Gemalto*.[24]

8-31   It is important not to define the art too narrowly, limited to a small band of persons making the precise products in issue, or this could have the impermissible result that any prior user no matter how obscure could be deemed to be common general knowledge.[25]

8-32   There may be more than one relevant art or skill and therefore more than one person skilled in the art. In such cases, if the invention is obvious to a person skilled in the art of any one of those skills, then the invention is obvious, for it would

---

18   [1982] R.P.C. 183, 242.
19   *Actavis v Eli Lilly* [2015] EWCA Civ 555, 34.
20   [2000] F.S.R. 90, [11].
21   [2010] EWCA Civ 819; [2010] R.P.C. 33, [51].
22   *COMVIK GSM/Mobile Telephone Systems* (T0641/00), [7].
23   *Schlumberger v EMGS* [2010] EWCA Civ 819; [2010] R.P.C. 33, [65].
24   *HTC v Gemalto* [2013] EWHC 1876 (Pat), [2014] R.P.C. 9, [34]–[36], [206], [250]–[262].
25   *Folding Attic Stairs v Loft Stairs* [2009] F.S.R. 24, [33].

otherwise impede a class of person who found it obvious.[26] Such an issue arose in *Inhale Therapeutic Systems v Quadrant Healthcare*,[27] where the invention involved improvements in stability and there were two possible techniques (spray drying and freeze drying) which could be used to put it into effect. It was contended that a single individual would be responsible for stability, it was therefore not appropriate to consider a team, and that individual would be familiar only with one technique, and in particular the more common latter technique. This was rejected on the basis that where the invention is widely claimed and spans several separate fields, the court may consider a worker from either field, this being the necessary consequence of the width.

"Person skilled in the art" may be a team

It has long been settled in general terms, both in English law and in the case law   8-33
of the EPO, that the "person skilled in the art" may, where necessary, be a notional
team of people having different skills.[28] The Court of Appeal so stated in *General
Tire v Firestone*[29]:

> "If the art is one having a highly developed technology, the notional skilled reader to whom the document is addressed [i.e. the cited piece of prior art] may not be a single person but a team, whose combined skills would normally be employed in that art in interpreting and carrying into effect instructions such as those which are contained in the document to be construed."

The purpose of assembling a team of different specialists is, of course, that each   8-34
member should bring his or her individual skill and general knowledge. As Pumfrey
J held in *Halliburton Energy Services, Inc v Smith International*[30]:

> "The skilled person is essentially a legal construct, and not a mere lowest common denominator of all the persons engaged in the art at a particular time. In some cases, it is clear that the specification is addressed to sets of skills that in the real world would be possessed by more than one person, and such a specification can be said to be addressed to a team."

Thus where the skilled addressee was a notional team, a submission that the "common general knowledge was only what is common to persons with all those different backgrounds", the smallest common denominator approach, was rejected as misconceived.[31] In *Generics (UK) v Warner-Lambert*[32] it was accepted that the same approach must be applied to to sufficiency, i.e. it is enough if the invention can be performed by one of the addressees using that addressee's common general knowledge.

Disputes as to the composition of the skilled team frequently arise, in particular   8-35
as to whether a particular specialist should or should not be included as part of the
team. This is a question of fact in each case, and may give rise to "squeeze" arguments between obviousness and insufficiency. In *Schlumberger v EMGS*,[33] Jacob

---

[26] *Schlumberger v EMGS* [2010] EWCA Civ 819; [2010] R.P.C. 33, [52]–[53].
[27] [2002] R.P.C. 21, [35]–[42].
[28] *Schlumberger v EMGS* [2010] EWCA Civ 819; [2010] R.P.C. 33, [33]–[36].
[29] [1972] R.P.C. 457, 485.
[30] [2005] EWHC 1623, [39].
[31] *Inhale Thereapeutic Systems v Quadrant Healthcare* [2002] R.P.C. 21, [39]–[42].
[32] [2015] EWHC 2548 (Pat), [122].
[33] [2010] EWCA Civ 819, [41].

LJ referred to the facts of *Dyson v Hoover*,[34] in which an inventive vacuum cleaner involved the non-obvious introduction of cyclone technology, and stated:

> "I think one can draw from this case that the Court, in considering the skills of the notional 'person skilled in the art' for the purposes of obviousness will have regard to the reality of the position at the time. What the combined skills (and mind-sets) of real research teams in the art is what matters when one is constructing the notional research team to whom the invention must be obvious if the patent is to be found invalid on this ground."

8-36   A submission that one should consider the notional team's reaction to the prior art item by item, but bearing in mind that if the art specifically flags a technology in which they would regard themselves as inadequately skilled, they would consider getting help from someone else, was accepted in *Pfizer Ltd's Patent*.[35]

8-37   It was held in *Halliburton v Smith*[36] that no specialist within the team is regarded as more significant than any other: "If the addressee of a patent is a notional team of persons with differing skills, then it is a team with no boss. Each member of the team is assumed to play his/her own part". However, in *KCI Licensing v Smith & Nephew*[37] the court accepted unchallenged evidence that the skilled team would be led by the clinician, who would make decisions on appropriate treatments but would take advice on details.[38] In the latter situation, however, one cannot ignore the supporting team members when considering the relevant common general knowledge. Arnold J considered *Halliburton* in *Generics (UK) v Warner-Lambert*[39] and said:

> "I do not understand Jacob L.J. to have meant that, as a matter of law, a skilled team can never be led by one member. As he said, each member of the team is assumed to play his (or her) own part. Depending on the facts of the case, that may involve one member taking the lead. Taking the lead is not the same thing as directing the other member as if the other member were a subordinate."

8-38   In a case where the team has a leader, the leader will not necessarily approach and consult other members of the team when considering an item of prior art. *OOO Abbott v Design & Display Ltd*[40] is an example from the Patents County Court (now IPEC) in which it was not obvious for the leader to do so.

8-39   In most cases it is the party attacking a patent on the ground of obviousness who wishes to introduce extra members into the team. Unusually the opposite was the case in *Richardson Vicks' Patent*.[41] In rejecting an argument by the patentee that the skilled team in that case would also have included a regulatory expert, Aldous LJ said:

> "There is no basis in law or in logic for including within the concept of 'a person skilled in the art' a person who is not directly involved in producing the product described in the patent or in carrying out the process of production."

8-40   He therefore rejected (on four separate grounds) an argument that the invention would not have been obvious because it would not have been thought likely to obtain regulatory approval.

---

[34] [2002] R.P.C. 22.
[35] [2001] F.S.R. 16, [67].
[36] *Halliburton Energy Services Inc v Smith International (North Sea) Ltd* [2006] EWCA Civ 1715, CA, [14].
[37] [2010] EWHC 1487 (Pat); [2010] F.S.R. 31, [103]. On appeal it was held that there was no effective challenge to this proposition. See *KCI v Smith & Nephew* [2011] F.S.R. 8, at [70].
[38] For another example see *Actavis v Eli Lilly* [2015] EWHC 3294, at [10].
[39] [2015] EWHC 2548 (Pat), [118].
[40] [2013] EWPCC 27, [44].
[41] [1997] R.P.C. 888, 895.

In a case of a claim in "Swiss-form" (e.g. use of substance X in the manufacture **8-41** of a medicament for treating disease Y), an argument that the skilled team would not include a person whose role related to the manufacture of the medicament because the claim was only framed by reference to "manufacture" because of the legal fiction required to circumvent the restriction on patenting methods of treatment was rejected. The manufacturing step is an essential requirement of the claim. In the absence of evidence that the substance in question is generally available, manufacture of the medicament includes making the active ingredient, such that the skilled team should include an individual capable of making it.[42]

Attributes of the person skilled in the art

The general characteristics of such a person were described in a classic state- **8-42** ment by Lord Reid in *Technograph*,[43] which has been incorporated into the fuller discussion by Jacob LJ in *Technip France SA's Patent*[44] as follows:

> "It is settled that this man, if real, would be very boring—a nerd. Lord Reid put it this way in [*Technograph*]:
>
> '... the hypothetical addressee is a skilled technician who is well acquainted with workshop technique and who has carefully read the relevant literature. He is supposed to have an unlimited capacity to assimilate the contents of, it may be, scores of specifications but to be incapable of scintilla of invention. When dealing with obviousness, unlike novelty, it is permissible to make a "mosaic" out of the relevant documents, but it must be a mosaic which can be put together by an unimaginative man with no inventive capacity.'
>
> The no-mosaic rule makes him also very forgetful. He reads all the prior art, but unless it forms part of his background technical knowledge, having read (or learnt about) one piece of prior art, he forgets it before reading the next unless it can form an uninventive mosaic or there is a sufficient cross-reference that it is justified to read the documents as one.
>
> He does, on the other hand, have a very good background technical knowledge—the so-called common general knowledge. Our courts have long set a standard for this which is set out in the oft-quoted passage from *General Tire v Firestone Tire & Rubber* [1972] R.P.C. 457 at 482 which in turn approves what was said by Luxmoore J. in *British Acoustic Films* 53 R.P.C. 221 at 250. For brevity I do not quote this in full—Luxmoore J.'s happy phrase "common stock of knowledge" conveys the flavour of what this notional man knows. Other countries within the European Patent Convention apply, so far as I understand matters, essentially the same standard.
>
> The man can, in appropriate cases, be a team—an assembly of nerds of different basic skills, all unimaginative. But the skilled man is not a complete android, for it is also settled that he will share the common prejudices or conservatism which prevail in the art concerned."

In the same case, Pill LJ stated[45] in relation to the above passage that "I do **8-43** respectfully prefer, for its clarity, Lord Reid's terminology cited at paragraph 7 of the judgment". But his preference appeared to be confined to the phraseology rather than expressing any reservation as to the substantive points being made by Jacob LJ. Mummery LJ agreed with both judgments, thus further supporting the view that there was no other difference of principle.

Level of skill

The level of skill and training assumed of such a person may differ widely **8-44** depending on the subject matter. There are technologies where no great knowledge

---

[42] *Actavis v Eli Lilly* [2015] EWCA Civ 555, 33.
[43] *Technograph v Mills & Rockley* [1972] R.P.C. 346, 355.
[44] [2004] R.P.C. 46, [7]–[10].
[45] At [135].

is to be attributed to the skilled person and others (such as genetic engineering) where to attribute an unrealistically low level of attainment to the skilled person would prejudice industrial development.[46]

8-45 Finding the appropriate level of skill may significantly affect the outcome: too low, and nothing may be obvious but the patent may appear insufficient: too high and the opposite may be true. Pumfrey J noted in *Conor v Angiotech*[47] that it was "essential to try to reflect, to the extent that the evidence permits, the actual ordinary skills of the real-life contemporaries of the skilled man at the priority date". He went on to observe that:

> "To an inappropriately defined skilled man, nothing may be obvious or everything may be obvious. The most difficult part of any obviousness case is the attribution of the relevant skill and knowledge to the notional addressee of the patent. When the common general knowledge is identified, the height of the bar is set.
> Normally, there are two main inputs. The first is the inference that one can draw from the other allegations that are made in the case. Thus, the agreement by the parties that the specification is sufficient will give a substantial indication of the degree of skill and knowledge to be attributed to the skilled addressee. The other input is the expert evidence as to the common general knowledge. It is perhaps a surprising feature of the passage that I have quoted from *Mölnlycke* that the Vice-Chancellor does not refer expressly to the common general knowledge and to the light that may be thrown on the level of skill and the common general knowledge by the contemporary history."

8-46 In *Laboratorios Almirall v Boehringer Ingelheim*,[48] the court held that the skilled addressee was obviously a team, but also observed that "unlike the expert witnesses who gave evidence, they will not however be at the top of their professions".

8-47 Observations on the skilled person's "mindset" in *Dyson v Hoover*[49] were made in the context of obviousness, though there appears to be no reason in principle why they should not also be relevant to construction in an appropriate case. In *Teva v Leo*[50] Jacob LJ referred to the attribution of the "bagridden" mindset of real vacuum cleaner designers to the person skilled in art when emphasising that the "law of obviousness attributes to the notional person the real prejudices and practices of persons skilled in the art".

Other attributes: knowledge of the law

8-48 It is clear from *Kirin-Amgen* that the notional skilled person is also taken to have sufficient understanding of patent law to appreciate the general nature and function of a patent specification and claims. Lord Hoffmann there observed:

> "But the person skilled in the art (who must, in my opinion, be assumed to know the basic principles of patentability) might well have thought that the claims were restricted to existing technology because of doubts about sufficiency rather than lack of foresight about possible developments."[51]

8-49 In *Virgin v Premium Aircraft Interiors*,[52] the Court of Appeal applied this principle and held that the skilled reader, probably with the benefit of skilled advice, would have in mind the explicit drafting conventions by which a patent and its claims are framed. When considering the claim, the reader would in particular have

[46] *Glaxo Group's Patent* [2004] R.P.C. 43, [24].
[47] [2006] R.P.C. 28, [35]. But note that the overall result was reversed by the House of Lords.
[48] [2009] F.S.R. 12, [132].
[49] [2002] R.P.C. 22, [84]–[97]; see para.12-35 and para.12-54, et seq.
[50] *Teva UK Limited v LEO Pharma A/S* [2015] EWCA Civ 779, [29].
[51] *Kirin-Amgen v Hoechst Marion Roussel* [2005] R.P.C. 9, [78].
[52] [2010] R.P.C. 8, [15].

in mind the fact that reference numerals are not to be used to limit a claim, and the nature of the two-part claim structure in which features found in the prior art are incorporated into the pre-characterising portion. Furthermore, it was said that:

"because the skilled reader knows that the patentee is trying to claim something which he, the patentee, considers to be new, he will be strongly averse to ascribe to the claim a meaning which covers that which the patentee acknowledges is old"[53].

Nevertheless, the question is one of construction and whether what is claimed is **8-50** or is not new will depend on, rather than be determinative of, the construction of the claim. The court also held that the skilled reader would know about the practice of divisional applications and that this might affect their understanding of a claim because they will know that there are or may be aspects of what is described in the patent which are actually claimed in some other patent or patents divided out from the original application.[54]

A further example of the understanding of drafting conventions can be found in **8-51** *Schenck v Universal Balancing*[55] in which it was held that the skilled reader would be aware of the convention that "for" almost always means "suitable for".

In *Virgin v Delta*[56] Arnold J concluded that it followed from the logic of the Court **8-52** of Appeal in the earlier *Virgin v Premium Aircraft Interiors* case that the skilled reader is also deemed to know about, and take into account, that:

"(i)   It is possible to frame claims in a variety of different ways. In particular, claims may be directed, subject to constraints on unity of invention, both to the whole of an inventive product and to its key components separately.

(ii)   It is possible to infringe a patent both directly under s.60(1) of the Patents Act 1977 corresponding to Art.25 of the Community Patent Convention and indirectly under s.60(2) of the 1977 Act corresponding to Art.26 CPC. As discussed in more detail below, the latter type of infringement element involves the supply or offer to supply of 'any of the means, relating to an essential element of the invention' i.e. less than the whole of a claimed product.

(iii)   Patents are territorial in nature. This has two aspects to it. The first is that a UK patent prevents persons other than those 'entitled to work the invention' (to use the language of s.60(2)) from doing things in the UK. The second is that a patentee can in principle obtain, and may well have in fact obtained, parallel patent protection in other countries. In saying this, I am not going so far as to presume that the skilled person will actually carry out a search to locate any corresponding foreign patents, even though a well-advised person would do so and nowadays would be able to locate most such patents quickly and easily using electronic databases."

Ranbaxy v AstraZeneca[57] was a case in which it was held that the skilled person's **8-53** knowledge of the law was such that they would appreciate that claims fall into various sets (e.g. "Swiss-form claims, conventional product claims, etc.).

In *Generics (UK) v Warner-Lambert*[58] Floyd LJ held that the skilled person faced **8-54** with a claim in Swiss-form would understand that it was necessary for the claim to include a manufacturing step to ensure that the claim does not touch the doctor and fall foul of the method of treatment exclusion. However, the skilled person would understand that any manufacturing step is adequate for this purpose, as the doctor does not manufacture the medicament. Furthermore, the skilled person would understand that the claim in question owes its novelty to the discovery of the

---

53   *Virgin v Premium Aircraft Interiors* [2010] R.P.C. 8, [21].
54   [2010] R.P.C. 8, [10].
55   [2012] EWHC 1920 (Pat), [86].
56   [2010] EWHC 3094 (Pat), [2011] R.P.C. 8, [49].
57   [2011] EWHC 1831 (Pat); [2011] F.S.R. 45.
58   [2015] EWCA Civ 556; [2015] R.P.C. 25, [118]–[121].

new therapeutic use of the medicament and accordingly would understand that the technical subject matter of the claim was concerned with the ultimate end use of the medicament, from which it derived its novelty.

8-55   The skilled addressee will assume when reading the patent that the patentee is also skilled in the art.[59]

2. COMMON GENERAL KNOWLEDGE

What is common general knowledge?

8-56   "Common general knowledge" means "the information which, at the date of the patent in question, is common knowledge in the art or science to which the alleged invention relates, so as to be known to duly qualified persons engaged in that art or science"[60]; in other words, it is part of the mental equipment necessary for competency in that art or science concerned, such as every worker in the art may be expected to have as part of his technical equipment.[61] In the context of construction, Aldous LJ explained in *Lubrizol v Esso Petroleum*[62]:

> "Patent specifications are intended to be read by persons skilled in the relevant art, but their construction is for the Court. Thus the court must adopt the mantle of the notional skilled addressee and determine, from the language used, what the notional skilled addressee would understand to be the ambit of the claim. To do that it is often necessary for the Court to be informed as to the meaning of technical words and phrases and what was, at the relevant time, the common general knowledge; the knowledge that the notional skilled man would have."

8-57   More generally, the common general knowledge permeates everything that is required of the skilled person: for example, in reading and understanding the Patent, in understanding and reacting to the cited prior art or in bringing his mind to bear upon any technical problem which arises.[63]

8-58   For the court to take it into account for such purposes, the relevant knowledge must be commonly and generally known. This has been explained in two classic statements of the law. The first is that of Fletcher Moulton LJ in *British Ore Concentrate Syndicate Ltd v Minerals Separation Ltd*[64]:

> "[The court] has to arrive as closely as it can at the mental attitude of a well-instructed representative of the class to whom the Specification is addressed, and no more. In other words, in the performance of this part of its task it has to ask itself what ought fairly to be considered to be the state of knowledge in the trade or profession at the date of the patent with respect to the matters in question, and if any facts or documents are such that in ordinary probability they would not be known to competent members of such trade or profession they ought not to be taken, either for or against the public on the one hand, or the inventor on the other, as forming part of public general knowledge."

8-59   The other classic statement of what constitutes common general knowledge is to be found in the *General Tire* decision, which has often been quoted[65]:

> "The common general knowledge imputed to such an addressee must, of course, be carefully distinguished from what in patent law is regarded as public knowledge. This distinction is well

---

[59] *Merck & Co Inc v Generics (UK) Ltd* [2004] R.P.C. 31, [23].

[60] *British Thomson-Houston Co Ltd v Stonebridge Electrical Co Ltd* (1916) 33 R.P.C. 166, 171.

[61] *Automatic Coil Winder, etc., Co Ltd v Taylor Electrical Instruments Ltd* (1944) 61 R.P.C. 41, 43.

[62] [1998] R.P.C. 727, 738.

[63] *Kavanagh Balloons v Cameron Balloons* [2004] R.P.C. 5, [33].

[64] (1909) 26 R.P.C. 124, 138.

[65] *General Tire & Rubber Co v Firestone Tyre & Rubber Co Ltd* [1972] R.P.C. 457, 482.

explained in *Halsbury's Laws of England*, Vol. 29, para.63. As regards patent specifications it is the somewhat artificial (see per Lord Reid in the *Technograph* case [1971] F.S.R. 188 at 193) concept of patent law that each and every specification, of the last 50 years, however unlikely to be looked at and in whatever language written, is part of the relevant public knowledge if it is resting anywhere in the shelves of the Patent Office. On the other hand, common general knowledge is a different concept derived from a commonsense approach to the practical question of what would in fact be known to an appropriately skilled addressee—the sort of man, good at his job, that could be found in real life.

The two classes of documents which call for consideration in relation to *common general* knowledge in the instant case were individual patent specifications and 'widely read publications'.

As to the former, it is clear that individual patent specifications and their contents do not normally form part of the relevant *common general* knowledge, though there may be specifications which are so well known amongst those versed in the art that upon evidence of that state of affairs they form part of such knowledge, and also there may occasionally be particular industries (such as that of colour photography) in which the evidence may show that all specifications form part of the relevant knowledge.

As regards scientific papers generally, it was said by Luxmoore J. in *British Acoustic Films* (53 R.P.C. 221 at 250):

'In my judgment it is not sufficient to prove common general knowledge that a particular disclosure is made in an article, or series of articles, in a scientific journal, no matter how wide the circulation of that journal may be, in the absence of any evidence that the disclosure is accepted generally by those who are engaged in the art to which the disclosure relates. A piece of particular knowledge as disclosed in a scientific paper does not become common general knowledge merely because it is widely read, and still less because it is widely circulated. Such a piece of knowledge only becomes general knowledge when it is generally known and accepted without question by the bulk of those who are engaged in the particular art; in other words, when it becomes part of their common stock of knowledge relating to the art.'

And a little later, distinguishing between what has been written and what has been used, he said:

'It is certainly difficult to appreciate how the use of something which has in fact never been used in a particular art can ever be held to be common general knowledge in the art.[66]'

Those passages have often been quoted, and there has not been cited to us any case in which they have been criticised. We accept them as correctly stating in general the law on this point, though reserving for further consideration whether the words 'accepted without question' may not be putting the position rather high: for the purposes of this case we are disposed, without wishing to put forward any full definition, to substitute the words 'generally regarded as a good basis for further action'."

As the first part of the above passage makes clear, the common general knowledge is to be distinguished from, and fulfils a quite different function from, the prior art cited against a patent. (The common general knowledge may however also form part of the relevant art used to attack the patent and it is possible that a claim may be held obvious or even anticipated having regard to common general knowledge alone: but this is a separate issue and may give rise to pleading considerations).[67]   **8-60**

A scientific theory does not have to have been generally accepted as correct if it is regarded as a reasonable working hypothesis by the bulk of those skilled in art. Furthermore, a theory may be regarded as a good basis for some forms of action (such as experiments in vitro or in animal models) even if not for others (such as administration to humans).[68]   **8-61**

In *Merck v Ono*[69] Birss J held that an area of scientific doubt was, of itself, capable of forming part of the common general knowledge. He explained (at [24]):   **8-62**

---

[66] But see comments in *Abbott Laboratories v Evysio* [2008] R.P.C. 23, at [54].
[67] For examples, see para.12–37.
[68] *Generics (UK) v Warner-Lambert* [2015] EWHC 2548 (Pat), [125].
[69] [2015] EWHC 2973 (Pat).

"I do not believe the court in General Tire was seeking to address factual circumstances like those said to arise in this case. In principle the common general knowledge of a skilled person must be capable of including contradictory ideas on a topic, always assuming that information reaches the standard for common general knowledge. The existence of a defined area of doubt and uncertainty does not mean that, in principle, such knowledge is not part of the common general knowledge. An example, referred to by Ono, was in the judgment of Floyd J in *Regeneron v Genentech* [2012] EWHC 657 (Pat) e.g. at paragraph 67 and the conclusion at paragraph 88 (upheld by the Court of Appeal at [2013] EWCA Civ 93, paragraph 22). Merck submitted the evidence in Regeneron was much stronger than the evidence in this case. The submission about evidence does not alter the point of principle."

Differentiating what is known from what is common general knowledge

8-63   It is not enough to show that a matter was known to some but not to others and in particular it is not good enough to show that knowledge (or a prejudice) was confined to one or a limited class of skilled exemplars of the skilled person.[70] It is not enough to say that a document was available to be referred to, nor that it has been referred to frequently, but it is not necessary to show that all or a majority of skilled workers in the field knew it in the sense of having memorised it. As Laddie J explained in *Raychem Corp's Patents*[71]:

> "The common general knowledge is the technical background of the notional man in the art against which the prior art must be considered. This is not limited to material he has memorised and has at the front of his mind. It includes all that material in the field he is working in which he knows exists, which he would refer to as a matter of course if he cannot remember it and which he understands is generally regarded as sufficiently reliable to use as a foundation for further work or to help understand the pleaded prior art. This does not mean that everything on the shelf which is capable of being referred to without difficulty is common general knowledge nor does it mean that every word in a common text book is either. In the case of standard textbooks, it is likely that all or most of the main text will be common general knowledge. In many cases common general knowledge will include or be reflected in readily available trade literature which a man in the art would be expected to have at his elbow and regard as basic reliable information."

8-64   On the basis of this passage, a potentially very large stock of information may be part of the common general knowledge. However, whether it would be sought or applied in any given circumstance is a separate question. In *Generics v Daiichi*,[72] Jacob LJ referred to the above passage and stated:

> "Of course material readily and widely to hand can be and may be part of the common general knowledge of the skilled person—stuff he is taken to know in his head and which he will bring to bear on reading or learning of a particular piece of prior art. But there will be other material readily to hand which he will not carry in his head but which he will know he can find *if he needs to do so* (my emphasis). The whole passage is about material which the skilled man would refer to 'as a matter of course.' It by no means follows that the material should be taken to be known to the skilled man if he has no particular reason for referring to it."

8-65   In *KCI Licensing v Smith & Nephew*,[73] Arnold J explained the principle thus:

> "It follows that, even if information is neither disclosed by a specific item of prior art nor common general knowledge, it may nevertheless be taken into account as part of a case of obviousness if it is proved that the skilled person faced with the problem to which the patent is addressed would acquire that information as a matter of routine. For example, if the problem is how to formulate a particular pharmaceutical substance for administration to patients, then it may be shown that the skilled formula-

---

[70]   *Raychem Corp's Patents* [1998] R.P.C. 31, [25].
[71]   [2009] R.P.C. 23, [25].
[72]   [2009] R.P.C. 23, [25].
[73]   [2010] EWHC 1487 (Pat); [2010] F.S.R. 31, [108]–[112].

tor would as a matter of routine start by ascertaining certain physical and chemical properties of that substance (e.g. its aqueous solubility) from the literature or by routine testing. If so, it is legitimate to take that information into account when assessing the obviousness of a particular formulation. But that is because it is obvious for the skilled person to obtain the information, not because it is common general knowledge."

With increasing specialisation, the difficulty has increased of differentiating **8-66** between matter which was merely part of the state of the art, and matter which can properly be regarded as part of the common general knowledge. Aldous LJ explained in *Beloit v Valmet (No.2)*[74]:

"It has never been easy to differentiate between common general knowledge and that which is known by some. It has become particularly difficult with the modern ability to circulate and retrieve information. Employees of some companies, with the use of libraries and patent departments, will become aware of information soon after it is published in a whole variety of documents; whereas others, without such advantages, may never do so until that information is accepted generally and put into practice. The notional skilled addressee is the ordinary man who may not have the advantages that some employees of large companies may have. The information in a patent specification is addressed to such a man and must contain sufficient details for him to understand and apply the invention. It will only lack an inventive step if it is obvious to such a man.

It follows that evidence that a fact is known or even well-known to a witness does not establish that that fact forms part of the common general knowledge. Neither does it follow that it will form part of the common general knowledge if it is recorded in a document."

He then cited the above-quoted passage from *General Tire*,[75] and proceeded to **8-67** apply it. He held that although a concept was well-known to some, it was not part of the common general knowledge because the evidence had not established that it was known to the bulk of those skilled in the art, let alone that it had been accepted without question by them.

At the same time, the skilled person should not be taken to represent some sort **8-68** of lowest common denominator of persons actually engaged in the field, possessed only of the knowledge and prejudices that all of them can be said to possess.[76]

The issue of whether it is sufficient to establish that matter was known in the **8-69** United Kingdom, or whether it is necessary to establish, where the art is an international one, that it was known more widely arose in *Generics (UK) v Warner-Lambert*.[77] Arnold J held that, at minimum, it must be shown that the matter in question was common general knowledge in the UK. Accordingly, in the case of a European Patent (UK) or a UK patent, it does not matter if a fact was common general knowledge in a foreign country if it was not common general knowledge in the UK.

Proof of common general knowledge

Common general knowledge is ordinarily established, where not agreed,[78] by **8-70** expert evidence. This function falls within the more general role of the expert witness in educating the court in the technology.[79]

In order to establish whether something is common general knowledge, the first **8-71**

---

[74] [1997] R.P.C. 489, 494.
[75] *General Tire v Firestone Tire & Rubber* [1972] R.P.C. 457.
[76] *Glaxo Group's Patent* [2004] R.P.C. 43, [32].
[77] [2015] EWHC 2548 (Pat), [124].
[78] See para.8–24.
[79] *Technip France SA's Patent* [2004] R.P.C. 46. And see para.8–24.

and most important step is to look at the sources from which the skilled addressee could acquire his information.[80] The expert evidence is usually supported by reference to textbooks or other reference works to which the skilled person would be expected to have access. Evidence of the typical training and qualifications of those practising in the art may also be significant. In case T890/02, the EPO Technical Board of Appeal held:

"The common general knowledge of the person skilled in the art has been defined by the Boards of Appeal as being normally represented by the content of encyclopaedias, handbooks and dictionaries on the subject in question ... In several cases, however, and by way of exception, patent specifications and scientific publications have also been considered as forming part of the common general knowledge .... In particular, special considerations prevail when a field of research is so new that technical knowledge is not yet available from textbooks."

8-72   The publication at or before the relevant date of other documents such as patent specifications may be to some extent prima facie evidence tending to show that the statements contained in them were part of the common knowledge, but is far from complete proof, as the statements may well have been discredited or forgotten or merely ignored.[81] Evidence may, however, be given to prove that such statements did become part of the common knowledge.[82]

8-73   The method of operation of an actual working machine, rather than a description in a document, is more likely to be accepted as part of the common general knowledge, even on the harder test of "accepted without question" as well as "regarded as a good basis for further action".[83]

8-74   The current Patents Court Guide provides at para.13.6 that where a technical primer has been produced, the parties should identify those parts which are agreed to form part of the common general knowledge.

---

[80]   *Horne Engineering v Reliance Water Controls* [2000] F.S.R. 90, [14].
[81]   *The Solvo Laundry Supply Co Ltd v Mackie* (1893) 10 R.P.C. 68; *Holliday v Heppenstall* (1889) 6 R.P.C. 320, 327; *Metropolitan-Vickers, etc., Co Ltd v British Thomson-Houston Co Ltd* (1925) 42 R.P.C. 76, 93.
[82]   *Sutcliffe v Thomas Abbott* (1903) 20 R.P.C. 50, 55.
[83]   *Bühler v Satake* [1997] R.P.C. 232, 236.

CHAPTER 9

CONSTRUCTION OF THE SPECIFICATION AND CLAIMS

CONTENTS

1. INTRODUCTION

Determination of the true construction of the claims of a patent specification,   **9-01**
which are to be read in the context of the specification, is commonly one of the most
significant issues, if not the single most significant issue, in litigation involving
patents.

Once the scope of the claims is ascertained, the question of whether or not there   **9-02**
has been infringement, and whether or not a cited piece of prior art anticipates the
claim, can often be answered immediately. Similarly, construction is an essential
step in considering other grounds of invalidity.

For the patentee, it is often a case of treading a line between contending that the   **9-03**
scope of a claim is broad enough to cover an alleged infringement, but sufficiently
narrow so as not to cover the prior art. Defendants meanwhile will often run a so-
called "squeeze" argument, namely that if the claim is broad enough to cover their
activities, then it is also broad enough to cover the prior art, or what is obvious from
the prior art.

Subject to what follows, patent specifications are construed like other docu-   **9-04**
ments and the normal rules of construction of documents therefore apply. However,
a number of considerations specific to patents also arise, from the particular nature
and purpose of a patent specification and because the Patents Act 1977 introduced
express statutory principles relating to construction, based on art.69 of the EPC and
incorporating its Protocol.[1]

As will be apparent from what follows (and is to be expected from the require-   **9-05**
ment to strike a fair balance between the interests of the patentee and the public),
tensions inevitably arise from competing principles.

Thus purposive construction must take into account the way in which a skilled   **9-06**
reader would understand the specification; but construction is ultimately a matter
for the court and not the witnesses. There is no doctrine of equivalents; although

---

[1]   PA 1977 s.125; see Section 2 of this chapter at para.9-34, et seq.

equivalence may be taken into account, not because there is a "doctrine of equivalence" as such but because that is the fair way to read the claim in context.[2]

9-07   The claims must be read in the context of the specification as a whole. However, the description and claims fulfil separate roles and it is not permissible to import a "gloss" from the former into the latter. Thus Robert Walker LJ observed in *Carton-neries De Thulin v CTP White Knight*[3] that the following (which was originally said in an earlier authority on statutory construction) may also be apposite to the construction of patent specifications:

> "…it is natural enough that in a matter so complex the guiding principles should be stated in different language and with such varying emphasis on different aspects of the problem that support of high authority may be found for general and apparently irreconcilable propositions."

9-08   This chapter endeavours to gather the principal authorities, but where convenient it lets those authorities speak for themselves rather than attempting to add any different emphasis. It is hoped that the result may at least not aggravate the problem still further, or exacerbate the feelings alluded to by Lord Hoffmann in his speech in *Kirin-Amgen*[4]:

> "No doubt there will be patent lawyers who are dismayed at the notion that the Protocol questions do not provide an answer in every case. They may feel cast adrift on a sea of interpretative uncertainty. But that is the fate of all who have to understand what people mean by using language."

The House of Lords authorities on purposive construction

9-09   Since the landmark decision of the House of Lords in *Catnic v Hill & Smith*,[5] the accepted approach to patent construction has been "purposive construction" as there explained in the speech of Lord Diplock. That case involved a patent granted under the 1949 Act. However, as described below, the principles there laid down thereafter have continued to be applicable to patents granted under the 1977 Act.[6]

9-10   More recently, the House of Lords in *Kirin-Amgen v Hoechst Marion Roussel*[7] has now comprehensively reviewed the principles applicable to patent construction under the Act. In his speech, with which all other members of the House agreed, Lord Hoffmann has confirmed that the principle of purposive construction as articulated in *Catnic* is "precisely in accordance with the Protocol"[8] and is therefore the correct approach under the 1977 Act.

9-11   These authorities are reviewed in detail below in Section 3 of this chapter.

Principles equally applicable to infringement and validity

9-12   Section 125(1) defines an "invention" as (unless the context otherwise requires) that specified in a claim of the specification, and both validity (see ss.1–4 and 72 of the Act) and infringement (see s.60) are to be tested by reference to the "invention".

9-13   It is, of course, a fundamental principle that the construction of a claim is the

---

[2]   See the propositions stated in the judgment of the Court of Appeal in *Virgin Atlantic Airways Ltd v Premium Aircraft Interiors UK Ltd* [2009] EWCA Civ 1062; [2010] R.P.C. 8, at 5.
[3]   [2001] R.P.C. 6, [21].
[4]   *Kirin-Amgen v Hoechst Marion Roussel* [2005] R.P.C. 9, [71].
[5]   [1982] R.P.C. 183.
[6]   See, for example, *Actavis UK v Eli Lilly* [2015] EWCA Civ 555, at [46]–[53].
[7]   [2005] R.P.C. 9.
[8]   At [48].

same whether validity or infringement is to be considered; no patentee is entitled
to the luxury of an "elastic" claim which has a narrow meaning in the former case
but a wide meaning in the latter. Under English procedure, infringement and validity are normally litigated at the same time[9] and therefore the court is astute to avoid
such a result. Thus in *European Central Bank v Document Security Systems*,[10]
Kitchin J at first instance noted that:

"This case therefore seems to me to be a very powerful illustration of why it is desirable to try
infringement and validity issues together, where at all possible. If they are tried separately it is all
too easy for the patentee to argue for a narrow interpretation of his claim when defending it but an
expansive interpretation when asserting infringement."

In the same case in the Court of Appeal, Jacob J made the same point more
graphically: **9-14**

"Professor Mario Franzosi likens a patentee to an Angora cat. When validity is challenged, the
patentee says his patent is very small: the cat with its fur smoothed down, cuddly and sleepy. But
when the patentee goes on the attack, the fur bristles, the cat is twice the size with teeth bared and
eyes ablaze."

The principle that the construction of a claim is the same whether validity or   **9-15**
infringement is to be considered is however subject to one caveat in the context of
product-by-process claims.[11] Specifically, in *Hospira UK v Genentech*,[12] it was held
that the effect of *Kirin-Amgen* was that a new process which produces a product
identical to an old product cannot confer novelty on that product. To be novel, a
product "obtained" or "obtainable by" a process has to have some novel attribute
conferred on it by the process as compared to the known product. Hence a claim
to a product obtained by a claimed process is anticipated by a prior art product with
the same characteristics, whether or not it was obtained by the claimed process.

Although this was held to be a rule of the law of novelty and not a principle of   **9-16**
claim construction, in effect the rule treats "*obtained by*" language the same as
"*obtainable by*" language. Nevertheless, as a matter of claim construction, so far
as infringement and sufficiency are concerned, a claim to a product "*obtained by*"
a process means what it says and the use of the process will be relevant to the scope
of the claim, but not for consideration of novelty.

It is often said that the scope of a claim should be ascertained without reference   **9-17**
to the prior art or the alleged infringement, and its ambit must be the same whatever
case is pleaded against the patent.[13] Although this has been qualified in *Rockwater
v Technip-France SA*[14] as discussed further below, the boundary of the monopoly
nevertheless needs to be defined clearly, in the interests of all parties. Lord
Hoffmann pointed out in *Kirin-Amgen*:

"The need to set clear limits upon the monopoly is not only, as Lord Russell emphasised, in the

---

9   But Pumfrey J ordered separate trials of infringement and validity in *Canady v Erbe Eeectromedizin*
     [2006] F.S.R. 10, noting that there did not appear to be "squeeze" arguments between the two is-
     sues in that particular case.
10   [2007] EWHC 600 (Pat); [2008] EWCA Civ 192. See also Jacob J's discussion in *Beloit v Valmet*
     [1995] R.P.C. 705, 720.
11   See also in the discussion of product-by-process claims at para.9-299.
12   [2014] EWHC 3857 (Pat), [147], discussed further at paras 9-303 to 9-308.
13   *Kastner v Rizla* [1995] R.P.C. 585, 595. See also the Supreme Court of Canada's decision in
     Whirlpool v Camco [2001] F.S.R. 46, at [43] and [49(b)].
14   [2014] EWCA Civ 381; [2004] R.P.C. 46, [42] (see paras 9-68 to 9-70).

interests of others who need to know the area 'within which they will be trespassers' but also in the interests of the patentee, who needs to be able to make it clear that he lays no claim to prior art or insufficiently enabled products or processes which would invalidate the patent".[15]

9-18   After explaining how purposive construction combines fair protection to the patentee with a reasonable degree of protection for third parties, he added:

"Indeed, any other principle would also be unfair to the patentee, because it would unreasonably expose the patent to claims of invalidity on grounds of anticipation or insufficiency."[16]

9-19   It follows that the same principles of construction apply in either case, so that any canon of construction discussed below in the context of considering infringement will apply equally when validity is in issue and vice versa.

Construction and the context of the alleged infringement or prior art

9-20   Strictly speaking, a claim is to be construed without reference to the alleged infringement; it should be construed "*as if we had to construe it before the Defendant was born*".[17] The objective of the exercise is to determine the true scope of the claims as they would have been read and understood at the date of publication of the specification[18] without knowledge of particular allegedly infringing acts. As Neuberger LJ pointed out in *Ultraframe v Eurocell Building Plastics*[19]:

"... one must be careful of being seduced into construing the patent in reference to extraneous circumstances, which cannot fairly be said to be part of the context. In this connection, most patent cases in this jurisdiction (and the present case is no exception) involve the court having to construe the patent and to consider an alleged infringement in the same proceedings. I accept that it may be wrong to divorce the two concepts altogether, but it cannot be right, purely as a matter of principle, that a product or process which, *ex hypothesi*, will have come into existence after the priority date of the patent, to be used as a means for interpreting the patent".

9-21   Once the true scope of the monopoly has been determined, the question of whether the alleged infringement falls within its scope may then be determined and will depend upon the facts proved.

9-22   But application of the principles of purposive construction may involve consideration of the nature of the alleged infringement, because although the meaning of the claim has to be determined without reference to the infringement, in practice the court does and must know what the alleged infringement is before embarking on the exercise of construing it. Only then does it become possible to isolate what are the material points of construction which actually arise for decision. Thus Aldous J considered it convenient to approach questions of construction in *Lux Traffic Controls v Pike Signals*[20] "in the context in which they arise".

9-23   Similarly, in *Technip France SA's Patent*,[21] Jacob LJ stressed the practical advantage of such a course:

"Although it has often been said that the question of construction does not depend on the alleged

---

[15]   *Kirin-Amgen v Hoechst Marion Roussel* [2005] R.P.C. 9, [21].
[16]   *Kirin-Amgen v Hoechst Marion Roussel* [2005] R.P.C. 9, [47].
[17]   *Nobel's Explosives Co Ltd v Anderson* (1894) 11 R.P.C. 519, at 523.
[18]   See para.9-27, et seq.
[19]   [2005] R.P.C. 36, [76]; but note that his was a dissenting judgement on the facts of the case.
[20]   [1993] R.P.C. 107, 126.
[21]   [2004] R.P.C. 46. See also *Taylor v Ishida* [2001] I.P. & T. 1209; *Inpro's Patent* [2006] R.P.C. 20, [37]; *Qualcomm v Nokia* [2008] EWHC 329, [7]–[8].

infringement ('as if we had to construe it before the Defendant was born' per Lord Esher M.R. in *Nobel v Anderson* (1894) 11 R.P.C. 519 at 523), questions of construction seldom arise in the abstract. That is why in most sensible discussions of the meaning of language run on the general lines 'does it mean this, or that, or the other?' rather than the open-ended 'what does it mean?'"

In *Merck & Co Inc v Generics(UK) Ltd*,[22] Laddie J similarly held that it was useful to have in mind the relevant features of the allegedly infringing process, if only to help identify the areas of dispute, but he also went on to point out that:

9-24

"the proper approach is to construe the Patent and its claims in the absence of the infringement and only when this has been done, to look at the infringement. One of the advantages of this is that it allows one to appreciate the full breadth of the monopoly asserted".

Pumfrey J also warned in *Nokia v Interdigital*[23]:

9-25

"Although one construes a claim 'as if the defendant had never been born', in any complex case it is essential to see where the shoe pinches so that one can concentrate on the important points. It is important nevertheless that the opportunity thus presented to construe the document with one eye on the infringement must be rejected, as far as possible".

Construing the claim in context is particularly convenient if the scope is being tested by application of the "Protocol" or "*Improver*" questions,[24] as these require identification of the relevant "variant". Some of the acontextual meanings may be wholly inappropriate and in such case one must realistically consider the alleged infringement in order not to waste time with the inappropriate.[25]

9-26

Date as of which specification is to be construed

In *Biogen v Medeva*,[26] the House of Lords held that the relevant date on which the specification must sufficiently disclose the invention is the filing date, reversing the decision at first instance that it was the date of publication of the application.

9-27

While it might be assumed that this should also be the correct date for construing the specification and claims for all other purposes, this is not yet clearly established in the authorities. Under the pre-1977 law, it was held that a specification was to be construed with reference to the state of knowledge at the time it was published.[27] Lord Esher MR in *Nobel's Explosives Co Ltd v Anderson*[28] said: "Now what is the very first canon of construction of all written business documents? Why, that the court ought to construe them as if it had to construe them the day after they were published."[29]

9-28

Although there are suggestions in some post-1977 authorities that the patent

9-29

---

22 [2004] R.P.C. 31, [21] and [23].
23 [2007] EWHC 3077 (Pat), [25].
24 See Section 3 of this chapter at para.9-41, et seq.
25 *Wesley Jessen v CooperVision* [2003] R.P.C. 20, [39(d)]. See also *Minnesota Mining and Manufacturing's Patent* [1999] R.P.C. 135, 143; *Consafe v Emtunga* [1999] R.P.C. 154, 160.
26 [1997] R.P.C. 1, 53–54.
27 *Badische Anilin und Soda Fabrik v Levinstein* (1887) 4 R.P.C. 449, 463; *Lane-Fox v Kensington and Knightsbridge Electric Lighting Co Ltd* (1892) 9 R.P.C. 413, 417; *Presto Gear Case, etc., Co v Orme, Evans & Co Ltd* (1901) 18 R.P.C. 17, 23; *Marconi's Wireless Telegraph Co v Mullard Radio Valve Co* (1923) 40 R.P.C. 323, 334.
28 (1894) 11 R.P.C. 519, 523.
29 And see *Ore Concentration Co (1905) v Sulphide Corp* (1914) 31 R.P.C. 206, at 224. See *American Cyanamid Co v Upjohn Co* [1970] 1 W.L.R. 1507, per Lord Diplock.

should be construed as of the priority date or the application date,[30] the Court of Appeal held in *Willemijn Houdstermaatschappij B.V. v Madge Networks*[31] in relation to a 1977 Act patent that "a patent specification must be construed as at the date of its publication".

9-30   Nevertheless, as was subsequently pointed out in *Sundstrand v Safe Flight Instrument Corp*,[32] this can give rise to anomalies in that common general knowledge therefore has to be assessed as at the date of publication for the purposes of construction, whereas only the common general knowledge at the priority date is relevant to obviousness. *Willemijn* was nonetheless followed, the court observing that it would be still more anomalous to separate the date of construction from the date for sufficiency (but which was then understood also to be the publication date).

9-31   However, as noted above, the House of Lords subsequently considered the relevant date for the purpose of sufficiency in *Biogen*. Lord Hoffmann reviewed those parts of the 1977 Act that addressed sufficiency, and concluded (though it was not necessary for decision) that the relevant date on which the specification must "disclose the invention clearly enough and completely enough for it to be performed by a person skilled in the art" is the filing date, because matter may not be added and an insufficient application should not become sufficient because of general developments in the state of the art after the filing date.

9-32   Thereafter, in *Dyson v Hoover* at first instance,[33] the deputy judge simply held that "a patent must be construed as of the application date", citing *Biogen* in support without further discussion. *Willemijn* and *Sundstrand* were not referred to and the issue did not arise on the subsequent appeal. But the Supreme Court of Canada has preferred the publication date,[34] not following *Dyson*; the court there accepted that this meant that there was no single critical date for obviousness, sufficiency and claim construction.

9-33   The correct date for construction of the claims therefore still merits further specific review. The leading contender is the date of publication of the granted patent. It is submitted that this is further supported by the consideration that the specification and claims may be amended up until grant, and this would also be consistent with the express provision in s.27(3) that if a patent is subsequently amended, the amendment shall take effect from the grant of the patent. The fact that different dates may be relevant for obviousness (priority), for sufficiency (filing), and for construction (publication) may be inconvenient but it is submitted that it is not so anomalous as to be rejected: it merely reflects the different underlying policies. In most cases it is unlikely to make a material difference, and the parties ordinarily lead evidence of the common general knowledge as of the priority date;

---

[30]   In *Helitune Ltd v Stewart Hughes* [1991] F.S.R. 171, Aldous J considered evidence as to how "memory" would be understood in 1982, the year of priority and of application. In *Glaverbel v British Coal* [1995] R.P.C. 255, Staughton LJ said that the court should consider the surrounding circumstances as at "the date of publication of the specification (or perhaps the priority date)". In *Kastner v Rizla* [1995] R.P.C. 585, the Court of Appeal accepted evidence relating to the *Improver* questions considered as of 1979, the priority date. Mummery J referred to "or possibly at the time of ling of the specification" in *Glaverbel (No.2)* [1993] R.P.C. 90, at 93, citing *Osram v Pope* (1917) 34 R.P.C. 369, at 391.

[31]   [1992] R.P.C. 386, 388.

[32]   [1994] F.S.R. 599, 607.

[33]   [2001] R.P.C. 26, [48(k)].

[34]   *Free World Trust v Electo Santé Inc* [2001] F.S.R. 45, [52]–[54].

it can usually be assumed that by the filing date and/or the date of publication of the granted claims, such matters will not have ceased to be part of it.

2. THE STATUTORY PROVISIONS AS TO CONSTRUCTION IN THE 1977 ACT

The 1977 Act for the first time contains, and incorporates by reference, statu- 9-34
tory principles relating to the scope of protection and in particular to the construction of claims. These had no parallel in earlier legislation and are derived from the
provisions of the EPC, in particular art.69, which provides:

"The extent of the protection conferred by a European patent or a European patent application shall
be determined by the claims. Nevertheless, the description and drawings shall be used to interpret
the claims."

Section 125 of the 1977 Act (which corresponds to art.69 of the EPC, and as 9-35
s.130(7) confirms is intended to do so) provides:

"**125.**—(1) For the purposes of this Act an invention for a patent for which an application has
been made or for which a patent has been granted shall, unless the context otherwise requires, be
taken to be that specified in a claim of the specification of the application or patent, as the case may
be, as interpreted by the description and any drawings contained in that specification, and the extent
of the protection conferred by a patent or application for a patent shall be determined accordingly.
  (2) [...]
  (3) The Protocol on the Interpretation of Article 69 of the European Patent Convention (which
Article contains a proviso corresponding to subsection (1) above) shall, as for the time being in force,
apply for the purposes of subsection (1) above as it applies for the purposes of that Article"

The requirement in art.69 that "the description and drawings shall be used to 9-36
interpret the claims" is further explained by the Protocol to art.69, which by s.125(3)
expressly applies to s.125(1). The Protocol is set out at App.E, para.155, et seq. and
provides as follows:

"**Article 1:**

General Principles

  Article 69 should not be interpreted as meaning that the extent of the protection conferred by a
European patent is to be understood as that defined by the strict, literal meaning of the wording used
in the claims, the description and drawings being employed only for the purpose of resolving an
ambiguity found in the claims. Nor should it be taken to mean that the claims serve only as a guideline
and that the actual protection conferred may extend to what, from a consideration of the description
and drawings by a person skilled in the art, the patent proprietor has contemplated. On the contrary,
it is to be interpreted as defining a position between these extremes which combines a fair protection for the patent proprietor with a reasonable degree of legal certainty for third parties.

Article 2:

Equivalents

  For the purpose of determining the extent of protection conferred by a European patent, due account shall be taken of any element which is equivalent to an element specified in the claims."

Article 1 of the Protocol, as revised in its EPC 2000 version set out above, es- 9-37
sentially tracks the previous version, with minor changes in wording that do not appear to change its meaning. It calls for an approach which takes a middle ground
between a purely literal construction of patent claims, and a free approach using the

claim only as a guideline. As explained by Lord Hoffmann in *Kirin-Amgen*,[35] this gave effect to a compromise between what were perceived by the contracting states to be the different principles previously applied in infringement proceedings in the UK and Germany respectively.[36]

9-38   However, as he went on to explain,[37] the UK's approach had already begun to move on from strict literalism, and the approach known as "purposive construction", described in the next section of this chapter, correctly applies the principles of construction called for by art.69 and its Protocol.

9-39   Article 2 of the Protocol was new in EPC 2000, and requires "due account" to be taken of equivalents, without further elaboration as to how this is to be done.

9-40   For reasons discussed further below,[38] this may not have made any significant change to the way in which the English court already construes patent claims, in particular the approach taken to "variants".

3. PURPOSIVE CONSTRUCTION: THE CATNIC AND KIRIN-AMGEN DECISIONS

The development of purposive construction as applied to patents

9-41   Before the decision of the House of Lords in *Catnic v Hill & Smith*,[39] infringement had been approached in two separate ways. First, if the alleged infringement fell within the strict literal meaning of the claims and embodied every integer there recited, there was said to be "textual infringement". However, the law did not restrict the patentee's monopoly to the strict language of the claims so as to enable a potential infringer to avoid infringement by incorporating immaterial variations. This led to the development of the so-called "Pith and Marrow" doctrine, which was established through the cases and is charted at para.6.52, et seq. of the 13th edn of this work. As was pointed out in *Kirin-Amgen*,[40] the pith and marrow doctrine was "always a bit vague", and indeed it was unclear whether the courts regarded it as a principle of construction of the claims or as an extension of protection outside the claims.

9-42   In *Catnic*, a case involving construction of a patent granted under the 1949 Act, the House of Lords reviewed and disapproved of this dual approach. Lord Diplock said (at 242):

> "My Lords, in their closely reasoned written cases in this House and in the oral argument, both parties to this appeal have tended to treat 'textual infringement' and infringement of the 'pith and marrow' of an invention as if they were separate causes of action, the existence of the former to be determined as a matter of construction only and of the latter upon some broader principle of colourable evasion. There is, in my view, no such dichotomy; there is but a single cause of action and to treat it otherwise, particularly in cases like that which is the subject of the instant appeal, is liable to lead to confusion."

9-43   He then proceeded to describe, in a passage analysed in more detail below, the purposive approach.

---

[35] *Kirin-Amgen v Hoechst Marion Roussel* [2005] R.P.C. 9, [20]–[24].
[36] And maybe even caricaturing them: *Auchincloss v Agricultural and Veterinary Supplies* [1997] R.P.C. 649, 663.
[37] At [30].
[38] See para.9-63, et seq.
[39] [1982] R.P.C. 183.
[40] *Kirin-Amgen v Hoechst Marion Roussel* [2005] R.P.C. 9, [36].

The approach in *Catnic* thereafter supplanted entirely the old "pith and mar-   **9-44**
row" approach.[41] Although doubt was thereafter expressed in one Court of Appeal
decision[42] that *Catnic* was applicable to patents granted under the 1977 Act, these
doubts were obiter and were pointedly not followed by the Patents Court in two
subsequent decisions, which concluded that the *Catnic* decision did accord with the
Protocol.[43] Subsequently a differently constituted Court of Appeal also agreed.[44]

The House of Lords has now authoritatively confirmed in *Kirin-Amgen*[45] that   **9-45**
although *Catnic* was concerned with a patent granted under the 1949 Act, its approach is also the proper one to be adopted in applying the statutory provisions of
the 1977 Act. Lord Hoffmann there unequivocally stated:

"The *Catnic* principle of construction is therefore in my opinion precisely in accordance with the
Protocol. It is intended to give the patentee the full extent, but not more than the full extent, of the
monopoly which a reasonable person skilled in the art, reading the claims in context, would think
he was intending to claim."[46]

Purposive construction: the decision in Catnic

In *Catnic* Lord Diplock laid out the correct approach to construction of patent   **9-46**
claims, the purposive approach, as follows[47]:

"My Lords, a patent specification is a unilateral statement by the patentee, in words of his own choosing, addressed to those likely to have a practical interest in the subject matter of his invention (i.e.
'skilled in the art'), by which he informs them what he claims to be the essential features of the new
product or process for which the letters patent grant him a monopoly. It is those novel features only
that he claims to be essential that constitute the so-called 'pith and marrow' of the claim. A patent
specification should be given a purposive construction rather than a purely literal one derived from
applying to it the kind of meticulous verbal analysis in which lawyers are too often tempted by their
training to indulge. The question in each case is: whether persons with practical knowledge and
experience of the kind of work in which the invention was intended to be used, would understand
that strict compliance with a particular descriptive word or phrase appearing in a claim was intended
by the patentee to be an essential requirement of the invention so that any variant would fall outside
the monopoly claimed, even though it could have no material effect upon the way the invention
worked."

The true question to be asked is thus, in summary, whether strict compliance with   **9-47**
the particular piece of claim language would be understood to be an essential
requirement of this invention. The necessary understanding is that of those skilled
in the art (though ultimately, as explained below,[48] the final determination of the true
construction is a matter for the court, once properly instructed, and not the
witnesses).

Lord Diplock continued: **9-48**

"The question, of course, does not arise where the variant would in fact have a material effect upon

---

[41] *Codex-Corp v Racal-Milgo* [1983] R.P.C. 369, 380. See also, for example, *Improver v Remington*
[1989] R.P.C. 69, CA; *A.C. Edwards v Acme* [1992] R.P.C. 131, 136, CA; *Southco Inc v Dzus
Fastener Europe* [1992] R.P.C. 299, 312, CA.
[42] *PLG v Ardon* [1995] R.P.C. 287, 309.
[43] *Assidoman Multipack v Mead* [1995] R.P.C. 321, 328–337, per Aldous J; *Beloit Technologies Inc
v Valmet Paper Machinery Inc (No.2)* [1995] R.P.C. 705, 719–721, per Jacob J.
[44] *Kastner v Rizla* [1995] R.P.C. 585.
[45] *Kirin-Amgen v Hoechst Marion Roussel* [2005] R.P.C. 9.
[46] *Kirin-Amgen v Hoechst Marion Roussel* [2005] R.P.C. 9, [48].
[47] [1982] R.P.C. 183, [242]–[243].
[48] See para.9-189, et seq.

the way the invention worked. Nor does it arise unless at the date of publication of the specification it would be obvious to the informed reader that this was so. Where it is not obvious, in the light of then-existing knowledge, the reader is entitled to assume that the patentee thought at the time of the specification that he had good reason for limiting his monopoly so strictly and had intended to do so, even though subsequent work by him or others in the field of the invention might show the limitation to have been unnecessary. It is to be answered in the negative only when it would be apparent to any reader skilled in the art that a particular descriptive word or phrase used in a claim cannot have been intended by a patentee, who was also skilled in the art, to exclude minor variants which, to the knowledge of both him and the readers to whom the patent was addressed, could have no material effect upon the way in which the invention worked."

9-49 The above paragraph is the basis of the so-called "*Improver*" or "*Protocol*" questions which provide tests which may assist in obtaining the answer as to whether a given article or method falls within the scope of a claim; these are discussed at para.9-134, et seq. (As is confirmed by the structure of those questions, the word "this" at the end of the second sentence of the paragraph quoted above refers back to the qualification "even though it could have no material effect upon the way the invention works", rather than to its immediately preceding sentence.) The rationale underlying these considerations was explained by Aldous LJ in *Wheatley v Drillsafe*).[49] However the House of Lords in *Kirin-Amgen* regarded the Protocol questions as not necessarily useful in all circumstances, as discussed further para.9-164.[50]

9-50 The facts of *Catnic* exemplify the application of purposive construction with particular clarity, in view of the simple mechanical subject matter of the invention. The patent related to steel lintels, and the claim required a "support member extending vertically". The defendant's products had backplates which were not precisely vertical, extending in one case at 6° and another at 8° from the vertical. The Court of Appeal had regarded "vertically" as a word of precision so that there was no literal infringement: Buckley LJ had considered that the patentee by his choice of words had made precision a requirement even though it would make no difference to the working of the invention. Lord Diplock rejected this approach and went on to analyse the case before him, applying the principles which he had earlier stated, in this way:

"Put in a nutshell the question to be answered is: Would the specification make it obvious to a builder familiar with ordinary building operations that the description of a lintel in the form of a weight-bearing box girder of which the back plate was referred to as 'extending vertically' from one of the two horizontal plates to join the other, could not have been intended to exclude lintels in which the back plate although not positioned at precisely 90° to both horizontal plates was close enough to 90° to make no material difference to the way the lintel worked when used in building operations? No plausible reason has been advanced why any rational patentee should want to place so narrow a limitation on his invention. On the contrary, to do so would render his monopoly for practical purposes worthless, since any imitator could avoid it and take all the benefit of the invention by the simple expedient of positioning the back plate a degree or two from the exact vertical."

9-51 Lord Diplock's "nutshell" question—"would the reader consider that the patentee had intended to exclude the variant in question"—is therefore sometimes posed.[51] In *Catnic* itself, as the rest of the above paragraph makes clear, it received the answer "no". In other cases the answer has been to the contrary, for example

---

[49] [2001] R.P.C. 7, [23]; see para.9-136.

[50] See *Kirin-Amgen v Hoechst Marion Roussel* [2005] R.P.C. 9, per Lord Hoffmann at [51]–[52], [69], [81]–[84], and Lord Walker at [138]–[139].

[51] See, e.g. *Impro Limited's Patent* [1998] F.S.R. 299, at 303; *3M v Plastus Kreativ* [1997] R.P.C. 737, at 747.

because the variant would not work or because the patent would then have been clearly invalid over acknowledged prior art or the common general knowledge.[52]

Lord Diplock went on to demonstrate that the word "vertical" could have different meanings in different contexts, and to explain that the correct meaning depended upon how the relevant addressee would have understood it:

9-52

"It may be that when used by a geometer addressing himself to fellow geometers, such expressions descriptive of relative position as 'horizontal', 'parallel', 'vertical' and 'vertically' are to be understood as words of precision only; but when used in a description of a manufactured product intended to perform the practical function of a weight-bearing box girder in supporting courses of brickwork over window and door spaces in buildings, it seems to me that the expression 'extending vertically' as descriptive of the position of what in use will be the upright member of a trapezoid-shaped box girder, is perfectly capable of meaning positioned near enough to the exact geometrical vertical to enable it in actual use to perform satisfactorily all the functions that it could perform if it were precisely vertical; and having regard to those considerations to which I have just referred that is the sense in which in my opinion 'extending vertically' would be understood by a builder familiar with ordinary building operation. Or, putting the same thing in another way, it would be obvious to him that the patentee did not intend to make exact verticality in the positioning of the back plate an essential feature of the invention claimed."

He regarded the fact that the specification had sometimes expressly referred to a degree of imprecision (two horizontal plates being "substantially" parallel) but with no such qualification to the word "vertically", as inconclusive and of little weight compared to the broader considerations of purpose; this appears to be the "kind of meticulous verbal analysis" which he had earlier criticised as contrary to the proper approach.

9-53

Purposive construction: the decision in Kirin-Amgen

As explained above, the decision in *Catnic* then continued to be applied, not only to patents granted under the 1949 Act but also those under the 1977 Act. The *Catnic* approach was held by the Court of Appeal in a number of decisions to reflect the requirements of the new Act and the EPC, but it was not until 2004 that the House of Lords had an opportunity to consider whether this was correct.

9-54

In *Kirin-Amgen*[53] Lord Hoffmann noted that by the time the Protocol on EPC art.69 was signed, the English courts had already begun to abandon a strict literal approach to construction, not only for patent claims, but for commercial documents generally. He went on to say:

9-55

"It came to be recognised that the author of a document such as a contract or patent specification is using language to make a communication for a practical purpose and that a rule of construction which gives his language a meaning different from the way it would have been understood by the people to whom it was actually addressed is liable to defeat his intentions. It is against that background that one must read the well known passage in the speech of Lord Diplock in *Catnic Components Ltd v Hill & Smith Ltd* [1982] R.P.C. 183, 243 when he said that the new approach should also be applied to the construction of patent claims:

'A patent specification should be given a purposive construction rather than a purely literal one derived from applying to it the kind of meticulous verbal analysis in which lawyers are too often tempted by their training to indulge.'

This was all of a piece with Lord Diplock's approach a few years later in The *Antaios* [1985] A.C. 191, 201 to the construction of a charterparty:

'I take this opportunity of re-stating that if detailed semantic and syntactical analysis of words in

52 See, e.g. *Beloit v Valmet (No.2)* [1995] R.P.C. 705, at 720.
53 *Kirin-Amgen v Hoechst Marion Roussel* [2005] R.P.C. 9, [30].

> a commercial contract is going to lead to a conclusion that flouts business commonsense, it must be made to yield to business commonsense.'"

9-56   The correct principle is therefore to give to the language of the claim the meaning which would have been understood by the audience to which it was actually addressed.

9-57   Lord Hoffmann went on to point out[54] that what the author intended to say, and what he would be understood to be saying, were not necessarily the same thing, and he emphasised that it is the latter which is relevant:

> "Construction, whether of a patent or any other document, is of course not directly concerned with what the author meant to say. There is no window into the mind of the patentee or the author of any other document. Construction is objective in the sense that it is concerned with what a reasonable person to whom the utterance was addressed would have understood the author to be using the words to mean. Notice, however, that it is not, as is sometimes said, 'the meaning of the words the author used', but rather what the notional addressee would have understood the author to mean by using those words. The meaning of words is a matter of convention, governed by rules, which can be found in dictionaries and grammars. What the author would have been understood to mean by using those words is not simply a matter of rules. It is highly sensitive to the context of and background to the particular utterance. It depends not only upon the words the author has chosen but also upon the identity of the audience he is taken to have been addressing and the knowledge and assumptions which one attributes to that audience."

9-58   Establishing the necessary context, namely "the identity of the audience" and "the knowledge and assumptions which one attributes to that audience" is therefore vital; these topics are discussed in Ch.8 of this work. Their importance was further stressed in Lord Hoffmann's speech at [33]:

> "In the case of a patent specification, the notional addressee is the person skilled in the art. He (or, I say once and for all, she) comes to a reading of the specification with common general knowledge of the art. And he reads the specification on the assumption that its purpose is to both to describe and to demarcate an invention—a practical idea which the patentee has had for a new product or process—and not to be a textbook in mathematics or chemistry or a shopping list of chemicals or hardware. It is this insight which lies at the heart of 'purposive construction'. If Lord Diplock did not invent the expression, he certainly gave it wide currency in the law. But there is, I think, a tendency to regard it as a vague description of some kind of divination which mysteriously penetrates beneath the language of the specification. Lord Diplock was in my opinion being much more specific and his intention was to point out that a person may be taken to mean something different when he uses words for one purpose from what he would be taken to mean if he was using them for another. The example in the *Catnic* case was the difference between what a person would reasonably be taken to mean by using the word 'vertical' in a mathematical theorem and by using it in a claimed definition of a lintel for use in the building trade."

9-59   After approving, with one qualification, Jacob LJ's summary of the relevant principles in *Technip France SA's Patent*,[55] Lord Hoffmann went on to stress that (as EPC art.69 and PA 77 s.125 require) it is the claims themselves that must determine the scope of protection:

> "'Purposive construction' does not mean that one is extending or going beyond the definition of the technical matter for which the patentee seeks protection in the claims. The question is always what the person skilled in the art would have understood the patentee to be using the language of the claim to mean. And for this purpose, the language he has chosen is usually of critical importance. The conventions of word meaning and syntax enable us to express our meanings with great accuracy and subtlety and the skilled man will ordinarily assume that the patentee has chosen his language accordingly. As a number of judges have pointed out, the specification is a unilateral document in

---

[54] *Kirin-Amgen v Hoechst Marion Roussel* [2005] R.P.C. 9, [32].
[55] [2004] R.P.C. 46 also known as *Rockwater v Technip*. See paras 9-68 to 9-70.

words of the patentee's own choosing. Furthermore, the words will usually have been chosen upon skilled advice. The specification is not a document *inter rusticos* for which broad allowances must be made. On the other hand, it must be recognised that the patentee is trying to describe something which, at any rate in his opinion, is new; which has not existed before and of which there may be no generally accepted definition. There will be occasions upon which it will be obvious to the skilled man that the patentee must in some respect have departed from conventional use of language or included in his description of the invention some element which he did not mean to be essential. But one would not expect that to happen very often.'

Lord Hoffmann then explained that one reason why it will be unusual for the notional skilled man to conclude that the patentee must nevertheless have meant something different from what he appears to have meant is that there are necessarily gaps in our knowledge as to why the patentee had chosen the words which he had used. This is discussed further at para.9-99. **9-60**

He then confirmed at [47]–[48] that the principles laid down in *Catnic* do indeed satisfy the requirements of the Protocol to art.69: **9-61**

"The claims must be construed in a way which attempts, so far as is possible in an imperfect world, not to disappoint the reasonable expectations of either side. What principle of interpretation would give fair protection to the patentee? Surely, a principle which would give him the full extent of the monopoly which the person skilled in the art would think he was intending to claim. And what principle would provide a reasonable degree of protection for third parties? Surely again, a principle which would not give the patentee more than the full extent of the monopoly which the person skilled in the art would think that he was intending to claim. Indeed, any other principle would also be unfair to the patentee, because it would unreasonably expose the patent to claims of invalidity on grounds of anticipation or insufficiency.

The *Catnic* principle of construction is therefore in my opinion precisely in accordance with the Protocol. It is intended to give the patentee the full extent, but not more than the full extent, of the monopoly which a reasonable person skilled in the art, reading the claims in context, would think he was intending to claim. Of course it is easy to say this and sometimes more difficult to apply it in practice, although the difficulty should not be exaggerated. The vast majority of patent specifications are perfectly clear about the extent of the monopoly they claim. Disputes over them never come to court. In borderline cases, however, it does happen that an interpretation which strikes one person as fair and reasonable will strike another as unfair to the patentee or unreasonable for third parties. That degree of uncertainty is inherent in any rule which involves the construction of any document."

Lord Hoffmann then moved on to consider what assistance can be derived from the application of the "*Improver*" or "Protocol" questions. These are analysed in Section 5 of this chapter at para.9-134, et seq. **9-62**

Equivalents and construction

Article 69 of the EPC makes it clear that the scope of protection is confined to the claims. It is therefore impermissible to extend protection outside their scope, by appeal to any broader principle of "colourable evasion" or the old "pith and marrow" doctrine. Such a broad approach, without more, would be to use the claims only as a guideline, failing to provide a reasonable degree of certainty for third parties, and thus contravene the requirement of art.69 and its Protocol. However, art.2 of the Protocol, in its EPC 2000 version, now provides that: **9-63**

"For the purpose of determining the extent of protection conferred by a European patent, due account shall be taken of any element which is equivalent to an element specified in the claims."

The *Kirin-Amgen* case was decided before that Article came into force, although its terms were already settled and so the House of Lords had an opportunity to consider its effect. Lord Hoffmann there explained how a literal approach to construing the language of claims had given rise to the "pith and marrow" doctrine **9-64** formerly applied in the UK, and the "doctrine of equivalents" in the US, but these approaches respectively did and do give rise to problems of their own.[56] In *Actavis UK v Eli Lilly*[57] Floyd LJ noted that Lord Hoffmann had "firmly rejected the adoption of such an approach into our patent law". However, Lord Hoffmann stated that[58]:

> "Although article 69 prevents equivalence from extending protection outside the claims, there is no reason why it cannot be an important part of the background of facts known to the skilled man which would affect what he understood the claims to mean. That is no more than common sense. It is also expressly provided by the new article 2 added to the Protocol by the Munich Act revising the EPC, dated 29 November 2000 (but which has not yet come into force[59])."

9-65 It therefore seems that the new art.2 may not in practice result in any change to the way in which claims are already construed. Taking "due account" of such elements expressly confirms the "common sense" which was already being applied. While there has been no "doctrine of equivalents" as such under English law, it is nevertheless clear from *Catnic* itself, and in particular the passage on which the first two *Improver*/Protocol questions are based,[60] that whether a "variant" works in an equivalent way as the invention is a relevant consideration when construing the claim. The Protocol questions (discussed further starting at para.9-134) are indeed most useful as a guide to whether simple equivalents fall within the scope of the claim when properly construed. As Floyd LJ put it in *Actavis v Lilly* "English law recognises the impact of equivalents in what became known as the *Improver* and subsequently the Protocol questions".[61]

9-66 The new art.2 of the Protocol clearly does not mean that the claims are reduced in importance or that the scope of protection should now extend beyond the claims themselves so as to cover them, as this would violate the other requirements of art.69 and the Protocol.

4. PURPOSIVE CONSTRUCTION IN PRACTICE

9-67 The Protocol to art.69 requires a balance to be struck between the extreme approaches to construction which it mentions. The importance of striking the right balance was explained concisely by Aldous LJ in *Wheatley v Drillsafe*[62]: "A claim interpreted on the one hand too liberally can render the patent invalid and on the other too literally can allow third parties to avoid the monopoly". Though the aim is easily stated, applying it in practice is not always easy; achieving the balance required by the Protocol has been described as "navigating between Scylla, the rock of literal construction; and Charybdis, the whirlpool of guided freedom".[63] The

---

[56] *Kirin-Amgen v Hoechst Marion Roussel* [2005] R.P.C. 9, [36]–[44]. US construction rules were considered and applied by the Court of Appeal in *Celltech (Adair's) US Patent* [2004] F.S.R. 3 (the Court of Appeal had to apply US construction rules in relation to a US patent licensed under a licence governed by English law); the *Festo* cases relating to the US doctrine of prosecution history estoppel are reported at [2003] F.S.R. 10 and [2004] F.S.R. 11.
[57] [2015] EWCA Civ 555, [44].
[58] *Kirin-Amgen v Hoechst Marion Roussel* [2005] R.P.C. 9, [49].
[59] It has since come into force, and is set out at para.9-136. See also App.E-155, et seq.
[60] See paras 9-46 and 9-48.
[61] [2015] EWCA Civ 555, [46].
[62] [2001] R.P.C. 7, [21].
[63] *Hoechst Celanese v B.P. Chemicals* [1999] F.S.R. 319, 324.

principles which the Court applies in seeking to strike that balance are reviewed below, though it will be seen that here too there are competing considerations.

Technip: A practical working guide

Since construction is such a central topic in many actions, it is not surprising to find that many authorities have set out the principles, or a relevant selection from them, before moving on to apply them to the particular facts in issue.

9-68

In particular, in *Technip France SA's Patent*,[64] Jacob LJ summarised the principles of purposive construction as applicable to patents in a passage described by Lord Hoffmann in *Kirin-Amgen*[65] as an "admirable summary" subject to one reservation. Subsequently in *Mayne Pharma v Pharmacia Italia*,[66] Jacob LJ noted that "As a practical working guide, it will generally be sufficient to use my summary as approved". He there distilled it still further; and subsequently made a minor amendment to the distilled version in *Virgin v Premium Aircraft Interiors*.[67]

9-69

Jacob LJ's fuller summary in *Technip* was adopted, but with the correction required by *Kirin-Amgen* duly made, by Pumfrey J in *Halliburton v Smith*[68] and is set out below.

9-70

"(a) The first, overarching principle, is that contained in Art 69 itself. Sometimes I wonder whether people spend more time on the gloss to Art 69, the Protocol, than to the Article itself, even though it is the Article which is the main governing provision.

(b) Art 69 says that the extent of protection is determined by [the terms of[69]] the claims. It goes on to say that the description and drawings shall be used to interpret the claims. In short the claims are to be construed in context.

(c) It follows that the claims are to be construed purposively—the inventor's purpose being ascertained from the description and drawings.

(d) It further follows that the claims must not be construed as if they stood alone—the drawings and description only being used to resolve any ambiguity. The Protocol expressly eschews such a method of construction but to my mind that would be so without the Protocol. Purpose is vital to the construction of claims.

(e) When ascertaining the inventor's purpose, it must be remembered that he may have several purposes depending on the level of generality of his invention. Typically, for instance, an inventor may have one, generally more than one, specific embodiment as well as a generalised concept. But there is no presumption that the patentee necessarily intended the widest possible meaning consistent with his purpose be given to the words that he used: purpose and meaning are different.

(f) Thus purpose is not the be-all and end-all. One is still at the end of the day concerned with the meaning of the language used. Hence the other extreme of the Protocol—a mere guideline—is also ruled out by Art 69 itself. It is [the terms of] the claims which delineate the patentee's territory.

(g) It follows that if the patentee has included what is obviously a deliberate limitation in his claims, it must have a meaning. One cannot disregard obviously intentional elements. Hoffmann LJ put it this way in *STEP v Emson* [1993] R.P.C. at 522:

'The well known principle that patent claims are given a purposive construction does not mean that an integer can be treated as struck out if it does not appear to make any difference to the inventive concept. It may have some other purpose buried in the prior art and even if this is not discernible, the patentee may have had some reason of his own for introducing it.'

(h) It also follows that where a patentee has used a word or phrase which, acontextually, might"

---

64 [2004] R.P.C. 46; also known as *Rockwater Ltd v Technip France SA* [2004] EWCA Civ 381.
65 *Kirin-Amgen v Hoechst Marion Roussel* [2005] R.P.C. 9, [33].
66 *Mayne Pharma PTY Ltd v Pharmacia Italia SPA* [2005] EWCA Civ 137.
67 [2010] R.P.C. 8, [5].
68 *Halliburton Energy Services, Inc v Smith International (North Sea) Ltd* [2005] EWHC 1623 (Pat).
69 The words "the terms of" no longer appear in art.69 in the EPC 2000.

have a particular meaning (narrow or wide) it does not necessarily have that meaning in context. A good example of this is the Catnic case itself—'vertical' in context did not mean 'geometrically vertical', it meant 'vertical enough to do the job' (of supporting the upper horizontal plate). The so-called 'Protocol questions' (those formulated by Hoffmann J. in *Improver v Remington* [1990] F.S.R. 181 at p.189) are of particular value when considering the difference of meaning between a word or phrase out of context and that word or phrase in context. At that point the first two Protocol questions come into play. But once one focuses on the word in context, the Protocol question approach does not resolve the ultimate question— what does the word or phrase actually mean, when construed purposively? That can only be done on the language used, read in context.

(i) It further follows that there is no general 'doctrine of equivalents.' Any student of patent law knows that various legal systems allow for such a concept, but that none of them can agree what it is or should be. Here is not the place to set forth the myriad versions of such a doctrine. For my part I do not think that Art. 69 itself allows for such a concept—it says the extent of protection shall be determined by [the terms of] the claims. And so far as I can understand, the French and German versions mean the same thing. Nor can I see how the Protocol can create any such doctrine.

(j) On the other hand purposive construction can lead to the conclusion that a technically trivial or minor difference between an element of a claim and the corresponding element of the alleged infringement nonetheless falls within the meaning of the element when read purposively. This is not because there is a doctrine of equivalents: it is because that is the fair way to read the claim in context.

(k) Finally purposive construction leads one to eschew what Lord Diplock in *Catnic* called (at p.243):

'the kind of meticulous verbal analysis which lawyers are too often tempted by their training to indulge.'

Pedantry and patents are incompatible. In *Catnic* the rejected 'meticulous verbal analysis' was the argument that because the word 'horizontal' was qualified by 'substantially' whereas 'vertical' was not, the latter must mean 'geometrically vertical.'"

9-71   Pumfrey J then himself added the following:

"I would diffidently add three observations of my own. The first is merely the trite principle that the addressee of the specification is the person skilled in the art, who approaches the document with the common general knowledge. Second, there may be obscurities and difficulties in a claim that cannot be resolved by an appeal to context. It is very rare that some sensible meaning cannot be attributed to the words used in a patent claim, but where a claim permits alternative interpretations it is possible to be left with no alternative but to take the most straightforward. Finally, and most importantly, over-meticulousness is not to be equated to carefulness. Care in working out what the patentee was aiming at when he chose the words he used is absolutely necessary."

9-72   It has been subsequently stressed, in *Jarden v SEB*[70] that the above-stated rules of construction were not merely to be treated as a mantra:

"In many cases, the rules of construction are stated as something of a mantra without always being given their full and proper effect. This is a case that I have found repays a close study of the principles so often set out. I will try to explain what I mean. The founding principle is in article 69 of the EPC which provides that *'[t]he extent of the protection conferred by a European patent ... shall be determined by the claims. Nevertheless, the description and drawings shall be used to interpret the claims'*. As was said in the oft-cited passage from Virgin Atlantic cited above and by the judge ' *[i]n short the claims are to be construed in context'*, and ' *[i]t follows that the claims are to be construed purposively—the inventor's purpose being ascertained from the description and the drawings'*. The next passage is equally important: ' *[i]t further follows that the claims must not be construed as if they stood alone—the drawings and the description only being used to resolve any ambiguity. Purpose is vital to the construction of claims'*, as is what follows, namely that the *'purpose is not the be-all and end-all. One is still at the end of the day concerned with the meaning of the language*

---

[70]   [2014] EWCA Civ 1629 per Vos LJ, at [36].

used ... if the patentee has included what is obviously a deliberate limitation in his claim, it must have a meaning ... '".

Meticulous verbal analysis

Lord Diplock in *Catnic* stressed that "A patent specification should be given a purposive construction rather than a purely literal one derived from applying to it the kind of meticulous verbal analysis in which lawyers are too often tempted by their training to indulge." This was a reference to the defendant's exercise of combing through the specification and contrasting the use in the claim of the unqualified word "vertically" with other geometrical expressions which had been preceded by the word "substantially"—the argument was that "vertically" must have been intentionally not so qualified and therefore intended to be a word of precision. Such analysis was purely "verbal" in the sense that it was an arid study of the words used (a mere mechanical counting of the uses of the word "substantially"), uninformed by any attention to the underlying technical teaching. Lord Diplock regarded such matters as inconclusive and of little weight compared to the broader considerations of purpose. Pumfrey J put it in this way in *Ranbaxy v Warner-Lambert*[71]:

9-73

> "An over-meticulous analysis is one that is too willing to draw from a detailed analysis of the grammar, the punctuation and the particular words and phrases used inferences as to meaning that the words might support but which the skilled person would not draw, and it is the antithesis of giving to the words chosen in their context the meaning that the skilled person would give them".

The broader approach was further emphasised by Aldous J in *Rediffusion Simulation v Link Miles* as follows[72]:

9-74

> "There is seldom a case where a person, who is asked to look at every word of a specification to try to destroy it, cannot make out a case of potential ambiguity. That is not the correct approach. The specification should be read through the eyes of the skilled addressee, attempting to give it a practical meaning and endeavouring to ascertain the intention of the draftsman. I believe that the defendant's reluctance to accept that the word 'centre' is clear and means the physical centre has been the result of an attempt to take the specification apart word by word and destroy it rather than trying to give it a practical meaning."

This recalls the much earlier statement by Chitty J in *Lister v Norton Brothers*[73] that a patent "must be read by a mind willing to understand, not by a mind desirous of misunderstanding". The Supreme Court of Canada, citing this observation, added in *Whirlpool v Camco*[74] that "a 'mind willing to understand' necessarily pays close attention to the purpose and intent of the author." The concept of the skilled person having the "mind willing to understand" is now widely adopted and applied in the European Patent Office.[75]

9-75

As Pumfrey J noted in the passage from *Halliburton* cited above, "over-

9-76

---

[71] [2006] F.S.R. 14, [10]; quoted with apparent approval on appeal [2007] R.P.C. 4, at [7].
[72] [1993] F.S.R. 369, 388.
[73] (1886) 3 R.P.C. 199 (Ch D.), 203. See also *YKK* (T190/99): the skilled reader "should try, with synthetical propensity, i.e. building up rather than tearing down, to arrive at an interpretation of the claim which is technically sensible".
[74] [2001] F.S.R. 46, [49(c)].
[75] Under the mantra "The patent must be construed by a mind willing to understand, not a mind desirous of mis-understanding" (T 190/99; confirmed in numerous cases including: T 437/98, T 1084/00, T 920/00, T 552/00, T 500/01, T 1023/02, T 749/03, T 859/03, T 1241/03, T 1418/04, T 906/05, T 405/06, T 1537/05, T 1204/06, T 1771/06). However, in T 1408/04 the board emphasised that this is understood to mean only that technically illogical interpretations should be excluded. A mind willing to understand did not require that a broad term needed to be interpreted more narrowly (even

meticulousness is not to be equated to carefulness. Care in working out what the patentee was aiming at when he chose the words he used is absolutely necessary." Care in understanding what is being taught (as a matter of technical purpose) is therefore not misplaced. Likewise, the words of the claim should not be subject to paraphrase and in *Rovi Guides v Virgin Media*[76] Floyd LJ stated that:

"the process of construction is seldom assisted by taking paraphrases of the words of the claim. The judge warned himself about this danger when faced with the use of the word 'pointer' as a paraphrase for what was contended to be the requirement of option (b) of feature C(ii) of claim 3. The word does not appear anywhere in the claims or, I believe, in the body of the specification. The judge was right to maintain his focus on the claim language, which does not descend to this level of detail."

"A purposive construction rather than a purely literal one"

9-77   As Jacob J said in *3M v Plastus Kreativ*,[77] "The words are to be construed having regard to the inventor's purpose as set out in the rest of his patent. That is why the words 'purposive construction' are apt."

9-78   The facts of *Catnic* itself illustrate this principle with particular clarity—the purpose of the vertically extending member was to bear a load, and consideration of this function was the key to finding the relevant meaning. In Lord Diplock's words:

"it seems to me that the expression 'extending vertically' as descriptive of the position of what in use will be the upright member of a trapezoid-shaped box girder, is perfectly capable of meaning positioned near enough to the exact geometrical vertical to enable it in actual use to perform satisfactorily all the functions that it could perform if it were precisely vertical".

9-79   The same approach has been applied in many cases since. Thus in *Dyson v Hoover*,[78] the Court of Appeal had to consider a very similar factual situation and held:

"the words frusto-conical as used in the patent are not to be given the precise mathematical definition. They must be construed purposively so as to encompass a shape, generally frusto-conical, which achieves the desired concentration and separation of fine particles."

Apparently absolute limitations may involve questions of degree

9-80   Thus a claim that includes words which may have an absolute meaning, but are capable of involving a question of degree, will therefore usually be construed to achieve the necessary requirement for practical purposes and not as an absolute. In *Milliken Denmark A/S v Walk Off Mats Ltd*,[79] Jacob J said:

"Moreover, I cannot think of any reason why the skilled man would have wanted to exclude the case of mats which leaked a very small amount. In so holding I believe I am doing very much the same as was done by the House of Lords in, what was perhaps the first of the modern purposive construction cases, *Henriksen v Tallon Ltd* [1965] R.P.C. 434. There the claim was for a ball-point pen having a particular reservoir. Lord Reid said at page 445:

---

if, as in the case at issue, the narrower interpretation would refer to a structure which is very common, but not exclusive, in the technical field concerned); see the Case Law of the EPO at II.6.1.

[76]   [2015] EWCA Civ 1214.
[77]   [1997] R.P.C. 737, 743.
[78]   [2002] R.P.C. 22, [80]. See also *Abbott Laboratories v Evysio* [2008] R.P.C. 23, at [114]–[130] ("substantially at").
[79]   [1996] F.S.R. 292, 302. See also *3M v Ati Atlas* [2001] F.S.R. 31, at [26]; *Unilin Beheer v Berry Floor NV* [2005] F.S.R. 6.

'The claim is for a device which "prevents air from contacting the surface of the ink" and the question is what is meant by "prevents". The claim must be read in the light of the object of the invention … It would be a very artificial construction of the claim to hold that, because an infringer's plug is not very efficient though sufficient for commercial purposes, therefore there is no infringement. That would simply be inviting infringers to take the invention but make it work inefficiently. This plug does prevent air from contacting the ink but it does not prevent all the air from doing so. I think that Lloyd-Jacob J was right in holding that a very substantial prevention was enough to constitute infringement.'

The same applies here. The closure is sufficient for commercial purposes. That the defendants' mats let through a little water is not enough to take them outside the scope of infringement."

Other illustrative examples include the following: **9-81**

- In *Taylor v Ishida*,[80] the claim included the word "fixed" but it was common ground that some movement was in fact required; the word was construed as covering devices where the extent of movement would not affect the working of the invention.
- In *Plastus*,[81] the relevant word was "opaque", in the context of a flap on an overhead projector document pocket. While its literal meaning was "impenetrable to light", it was held in context to mean sufficiently impenetrable to eliminate the disadvantages of the prior art.
- In *SEB v Societé De'longhi*[82] the words "closes" and "closed" did not imply a hermetic seal, but one "closed enough practically to prevent connection between the skirt and the vessel and the consequent escape of hot air, with the associated risk of burning". This was held as a practical matter to leave third parties with no uncertainty.
- The latter two cases were held in *Nikken Kosakusho Works v Pioneer Trading Co*[83] to demonstrate "that a word in the claim can take its colour from the specification and from the object that the patent was stated to be intended to realise, and that a word with absolute overtones can be made to bear relative ones".

Further examples involving words of degree ("large", "thin") are given below.[84]

The fact that the edge of the claim involves a question of fact and degree   **9-82**
therefore does not of itself render the scope of the claim impossible to determine, and the fact that it is possible to postulate difficult questions about a borderline does not make the claim so uncertain that there cannot be a reasonable degree of certainty for third parties.[85] Thus in *LG Philips v Tatung*,[86] Lord Neuberger considered that the word "behind" covered a component only partly behind another, as well as one wholly behind, having regard to the particular nature of the invention, but noted that "even if this were wrong, it may be that any uncertainty in this connection would be a 'puzzle at the edge of the claim' which did not invalidate it".

However, it was held in *Inhale Therapeutic Systems v Quadrant Healthcare*[87] that   **9-83**
where the claim requirement is a word importing a question of degree, the fact that

---

[80] [2001] I.P. & T. 1209; see [19] and [24].
[81] *Minnesota Mining & Manufacturing Co v Plastus Kreativ AB* [1997] R.P.C. 737, 752.
[82] [2003] EWCA (Civ) 952, [55].
[83] [2005] F.S.R. 15.
[84] See para.9–333, et seq.
[85] *Milliken Denmark v Walk off Mats Ltd* [1996] F.S.R. 292; *Unilin Beheer v Berry Floor BV* [2005] F.S.R. 6.
[86] [2007] R.P.C. 21, [26].
[87] [2002] R.P.C. 21, [28].

there is then a continuum is not a reason for assuming that it has been used so loosely as to have little or no effect, for otherwise "The same argument could be used where, say, a patentee refers to an ingredient being 'large'. Because there is no clear distinction between large, medium and small, a reference in a claim to 'large' could be read to include things which are small". There, the word in issue was "dissolved" and it was held impermissible to read it as covering any kind of dispersion, bringing in a molecular solution at one extreme, a colloidal suspension in the middle and a suspension at the other extreme.

Figurative meanings

9-84   Purposive construction may also operate to treat an expression in a claim as having a figurative meaning: standing as representative of a wider class. Cases where such an argument has succeeded are less common; thus in *Improver v Remington*, discussed further below, the patentee failed (in the UK, though not in Germany) to show that the expression "helical spring" would be understood also to cover a slitted rod. But as Hoffmann J made clear in the *Improver* case, purposive construction is the process of working out how the patentee has used the words in their claim: have they used them figuratively so as to encompass classes of meanings of which the particular word is an instance, or have they restricted themselves to that instance.[88]

9-85   The issues that arise are considered further below after the "Protocol" questions have been discussed,[89] although it is instructive here to note two contrasting illustrations, both involving chemical structures, where a meaning of the claim was urged which went beyond a simple question of degree.

9-86   In *Pharmacia v Merck*,[90] the claim was for a class of compounds including a hydroxy substituent which chemically was an enol form. In the presence of water, however, it would exist in equilibrium with its keto tautomer. The patent was however silent as to keto tautomers. The alleged infringement was the solid keto form. The Court of Appeal agreed with the judge below that there was no literal infringement, as "hydroxy" in the claim did not cover the keto form. However, differing from the decision at first instance, it held that on a purposive construction the claim nonetheless covered the keto tautomer (in the light of evidence as to what the skilled reader would appreciate about the tautomer forms). Arden LJ held on the facts that:

> "I do not agree with the judge's holding that 'the natural conclusion' to draw is that constituents not mentioned were expressly excluded. That cannot be a general rule. It would mean that the terms of a patent could never include an unspecified variant."[91]

9-87   This case is a relatively unusual one where the words of the claim were treated as having a figurative meaning and were found to cover something which did not vary merely in degree; the issue was not mere approximation, but a physically distinct product.

9-88   In *SmithKline Beecham Plc's (Paroxetine Anhydrate) Patent*,[92] however, the patentee sought to argue that a reference to "propan-2-ol" in the phrase "substan-

---

[88]   *Horne Engineering v Reliance Water Controls* [2000] F.S.R. 90, [11].
[89]   See para.9–134, et seq.
[90]   [2002] R.P.C. 41.
[91]   At [176].
[92]   [2003] R.P.C. 49 also known as *BASF A.G. v Smithkline Beecham Plc* [2003] EWCA Civ 872.

tially free of bound propan-2-ol" in the claims would be understood by the skilled reader as in context a synecdoche, standing for whatever organic solvent was used in the course of production. (A prior art process had used a different solvent, so that the product disclosed was indeed free of bound propan-2-ol, though not of the solvent actually used in preparation). Aldous J held:

> "I accept that the skilled addressee would interpret the specification taking into account the nature of the technical contribution. However he would also realise that the patentee claimed his monopoly in words of his own choosing. To disregard the apparent intention of the patentee could lead to an unfair result. In the present case, I regard the suggestion that the words 'propan-2-ol' should not be given their ordinary meaning, but should be read as 'organic solvent' as a deviation from ordinary rules of construction. It would do violence to the language: a result that should be avoided unless no other reasonable construction is possible."

Since another reasonable construction was possible, making sense of the techni-   **9-89** cal teaching of the patent without leading to any contradiction in the technical contribution taught, the claim was held to have its ordinary meaning.

Purposive construction does not permit rewriting the claim

Purposive construction is therefore a principle of *construction* of the claim   **9-90** language, and does not entitle the court to rewrite or amend the claim in the guise of construing it.[93] As it was put by Lord Sutherland in *Conoco v Merpro Montassa*[94]:

> "[w]hile a purposive construction is necessary, it must be borne in mind that this is intended to be a method of construction and not an excuse for not construing the claims at all". Such an unfettered approach would be at the expense of any degree of certainty to third parties. In the end, the question is whether the absence of a feature mentioned in the claim is "an immaterial variant which a person skilled in the trade would have regarded as being *within the ambit of the language*"."[95]

Not entitled to widen claim by ignoring express limitations

This was further confirmed in *STEP v Emson*,[96] where Hoffmann LJ said: **9-91**

> "The well known principle that patent claims are given a purposive construction does not mean that an integer can be treated as struck out if it does not appear to make any difference to the inventive concept. It may have some other purpose buried in the prior art and even if this is not discernible, the patentee may have had some reason of his own for introducing it."

This was applied in *Medtronic CoreValve v Edwards Life Sciences*[97] in which it   **9-92** was argued unsuccessfully that to confine the word "cylindrical" to that which is approximately geometrically cylindrical would be to give the claim a purposeless limitation. Jacob LJ held (at [25]):

> "I cannot accept these arguments. They put far too great a strain on the word 'cylindrical'—they indeed amount to striking it out altogether. Of course in some cases a patentee by the use of a particular geometric term may not have intended mathematical precision (the classic is '*vertical*' in *Catnic* [1982] R.P.C. 183). But it is quite another thing to strike a limitation out altogether which is the effect of Mr Carr's suggested meaning of cylindrical."

---

[93] Cf. *Norton & Gregory v Jacobs* (1937) 54 R.P.C. 271, 276, where the Court of Appeal rejected a similar approach.

[94] [1994] F.S.R. 99, 106.

[95] *Improver v Remington* [1990] F.S.R. 181, 189–190, citing *Anchor Building Products v Redland Roof Tiles* [1990] R.P.C. 283. The emphasis is that of Hoffmann J.

[96] [1993] R.P.C. 513, 522.

[97] [2010] EWCA Civ 704; [2010] F.S.R. 34.

9-93   Even if the integer of a claim appears to have no bearing on the inventive concept, it is not legitimate to construe the claim more broadly merely because it appears to have been drafted more narrowly than necessary in view of that inventive concept.[98] To give a claim a purposive construction is not to extract some general principle or inventive concept from a patent specification and discard those features of the claim which are inconsistent with, or unnecessary for the implementation of, that principle. It must always be assumed that claims are in the form they are for good reason.[99]

9-94   This principle was also emphasised by Pumfrey J in *Palmaz's Patents*,[100] where he said:

> "This is not just a departure from some descriptive word or phrase, or a matter of degree: it is the omission of whole features of the claim. There is no basis for such an approach to construction, above all where the specification does not describe the reason for the presence of the features in the claim, which have been added by amendment. The construction of the claim must give reasonable protection for the patentee and a reasonable degree of certainty for third parties—see the Protocol on the Interpretation of Article 69 of the European Patent Convention set out above, which forms part of our domestic law of construction and infringement by virtue of section 125 of the Patents Act 1977. No construction of the words of this claim which managed to cover the NIR stent could be said to satisfy the requirement of a reasonable degree of certainty for third parties."

9-95   Jacob J stressed the practical considerations in *Beloit v Valmet (No.2)*,[101] observing as follows:

> "In all this it must be remembered that it is the patentee who has set out the limits of his monopoly. Moreover, those reading his claim are entitled to see that it has a scope that goes thus far and no further and to design around the patent. There is no such thing as the tort of non-infringement. Finally, if claims are given the sort of loose construction contended for, the whole approach to examination of patents is rendered more uncertain."

9-96   In *PCME v Goyen Controls*,[102] a phrase in a claim commencing "in order to …" was construed as "mere surplusage", describing the alleged benefits of using other claimed features and not adding any further limitation. However, this was questioned in *Siemens Schweiz v Thorn*,[103] and in *Vector v Glatt*,[104] an argument that seven words within a claim were "mere surplusage" was rejected; they did add an extra requirement.

Unexplained limitations in the claim

9-97   Sometimes there is no adequate reason apparent from the face of the patent why a particular limitation was included at all. This of course presents an obstacle to the application of a purposive approach. As already noted above, Hoffmann LJ held in *STEP v Emson*[105] that it was wrong to ignore such limitation or to treat it as struck out simply because it appeared to make no difference to the inventive concept, for:

---

[98]   *Dyson v Hoover* [2001] R.P.C. 26, [48(c)] and [48(d)], citing *STEP v Emson* [1993] R.P.C. 513, and *Brugger v Medic-Aid* [1996] R.P.C. 635, 649.
[99]   *Horne Engineering v Reliance Water Controls* [2000] F.S.R. 90, [11].
[100] [1999] R.P.C. 47, 77.
[101] [1995] R.P.C. 705, 720.
[102] [1999] F.S.R. 801, 809.
[103] [2008] R.P.C. 4, [15]; reversed on other grounds in [2009] R.P.C. 3.
[104] [2008] R.P.C. 10, [34].
[105] [1993] R.P.C. 513, 522.

"It may have some other purpose buried in the prior art and even if this is not discernible, the patentee may have had some reason of his own for introducing it."

It was emphasised in *Uni-Continental Holdings v Eurobond Adhesives*[106] that this passage in *STEP* is not an invitation to try to identify the reasons why in point of fact the patentee wrote their claims in the way they did. Even if the patent office file is available, it is not generally admissible as an aid to construction in any event; see further para.9–229, et seq. Indeed, it is in general not possible to know with certainty what the patentee's intentions were, either from within the four corners of the document or from the file or at all, since a patentee is under no obligation to disclose to the Patent Office any prior art of which they are aware.[107]   **9-98**

Lord Hoffmann made the following observations regarding the inability to know the patentee's intentions in *Kirin-Amgen*[108]:   **9-99**

"One of the reasons why it will be unusual for the notional skilled man to conclude, after construing the claim purposively in the context of the specification and drawings, that the patentee must nevertheless have meant something different from what he appears to have meant, is that there are necessarily gaps in our knowledge of the background which led him to express himself in that particular way. ... It is however frequently impossible to know without access, not merely to the file but to the private thoughts of the patentee and his advisors as well, what the reason was for some apparently inexplicable limitation in the extent of the monopoly claimed. One possible explanation is that it does not represent what the patentee really meant to say. But another is that he did mean it, for reasons of his own; such as wanting to avoid arguments with the examiners over enablement or prior art and have his patent granted as soon as possible. This feature of the practical life of a patent agent reduces the scope for a conclusion that the patentee could not have meant what the words appear to be saying. It has been suggested that in the absence of any explanation for a restriction in the extent of protection claimed, it should be presumed that there was some good reason between the patentee and the patent office. I do not think that it is sensible to have presumptions about what people must be taken to have meant but a conclusion that they have departed from conventional usage obviously needs some rational basis."

In *Telsonic A.G.'s Patent*,[109] no technical reason could be discerned as to why the claim had been limited in the way that it was. As a result the first two Protocol questions were answered in the patentee's favour: the alleged variant worked in the same way and this would have been obvious. However, this circumstance also proved fatal in the case of the third question. Laddie J held that "The skilled reader would not know why the inventor limited his claim as he did. Therefore he would be unable to decide that the limitation could not have been intended by the patentee", and explained: **9-100**

"One is driven to ask, why the inventor put any limitations at the end of the claim. To that there is no stated or obvious answer. One can only speculate. Perhaps it was prior art. Perhaps it was a mistake. In the circumstances, to adopt the approach in *Catnic*, it would not be apparent to the skilled addressee that the limitations 'cannot have been intended by the patentee'. Both from the claims and the specification it is apparent that limitations were intended. Alternatively, to use the approach suggested in *Merck v Generics*, the addressee could not conclude with reasonable confidence that the Single Bent Rod design was one the patentee wanted to cover."

Not entitled to use specification to narrow or limit the claim

Just as purposive construction does not mean that an integer can be treated as ignored, it also does not permit an additional limitation to be implied into the claim,   **9-101**

---

[106] [1999] F.S.R. 263, 271.
[107] See *Chiron v Organon Teknika (No.7)* [1994] F.S.R. 458, 468.
[108] *Kirin-Amgen v Hoechst Marion Roussel* [2005] R.P.C. 9, [35].
[109] [2004] R.P.C. 38, [55] and [58].

even if connected with the way in which the invention works, if that does not arise from a proper construction of the language of the claim itself.

9-102 In *Hewlett Packard v Waters*, the judge at first instance had proceeded on the basis that the claim required continuous adjustment, and the alleged infringement which used step-wise adjustment was to be considered as a "variant". The Court of Appeal reversed this decision, holding[110] that:

> "No doubt the words of the claim have to be construed in the context of the whole specification having regard to what was the common general knowledge at the priority date; but it would not be right to imply a limitation into the words chosen by the patentee to define his monopoly. ... The claim does not state that every change in flow rate has to be accompanied by a change in stroke volume and it would be wrong to imply such a limitation into the claim by importing a word such as continuously."

9-103 Similarly, in *Auchincloss v Agricultural & Veterinary Supplies*[111] the claim was for a biocidal composition comprising a number of stated components, two of which were to react to generate hypohalite ions. The Court of Appeal criticised the construction held by the court below which was that the extent of this reaction must be such as to have a substantial biocidal effect. Aldous LJ held:

> "The reaction must be real in the sense that the skilled addressee would consider that what took place was a reaction generating hypohalite ions. There is nothing in the claim requiring that the generated hypohalite ions should be materially or substantially responsible for the biocidal action of the composition. To introduce such a requirement, as the judge did, is impermissible. In effect it is introducing, by way of construction, a requirement that the claim must be fairly based on the patent specification which was a requirement under the Patents Act 1949, but is not under the Patents Act 1977."

9-104 It follows that if the defendant's product or process does fall within the language of the claims, then even if it does not take all the stated advantages of the invention this does "not mean that he was not using the invention as he may have decided to use it badly".[112]

9-105 However, in *Mabuchi Motor K.K.'s Patent*[113] there was a dispute as to the meaning of the word "crimping" in the context of the specification. The text of the specification taught such a method of mechanically and electrically connecting two other integers by bending over and gripping, and stated that it was preferred over riveting which was undesirable as adding to manufacturing complexity. The defendants used a rivet as the primary means of connection but also had a bent-over flap. Jacob J rejected a submission that this amounted to infringement, holding:

> "It was argued that Johnson were adding 'riveting to robbery'. But it hardly seems to be robbery to use as a necessary step that which the patentee intended to say was unnecessary. Moreover it would hardly be consistent with 'reasonable degree of certainty for third parties' (see Protocol on Article 69 of the EPC) for a patent which teaches that riveting is unnecessary to cover a device which depends on rivets to work satisfactorily. Nor would a patent with that scope give 'fair protection' to the patentee. It would be unfairly wide."

Relationship between the claims and the description

9-106 It is the normal principle of construction of any document that it should be construed as a whole so as to give a sensible consistent meaning to every part of

---

[110] [2002] EWCA Civ 612; [2003] I.P. & T. 143, [34]–[35].
[111] [1999] R.P.C. 397, 402.
[112] *Union Carbide v B.P. Chemicals* [1999] R.P.C. 409, 419, CA.
[113] [1996] R.P.C. 387, 406.

it. In the context of patents, the specification and the claim are part of the same document and are to be construed as such. This is confirmed by the statutory principles of construction as laid down in the 1977 Act. As Jacob J said in *3M v Plastus Kreativ*[114]:

> "Based on Article 69 of the EPC and the Protocol thereto one is told that the monopoly is defined by the claim. To decide what that means one is to read its language in the context of the patent including the drawings. The exercise does not involve an arid study of the claim outside of its context. The words are to be construed having regard to the inventor's purpose as set out in the rest of his patent. That is why the words 'purposive construction' are apt."

Laddie J summarised the law concisely in *Brugger v Medic Aid*[115] in these terms: **9-107**

> "The claims and the specification are to be read together. It is to be expected that they will be consistent with each other (i.e. claims to specification and claims to each other). A construction which achieves such internal consistency has much to commend it but, as with all other guides, this is but one of the factors the court should take into consideration when construing the patent."

Description and claims have different functions

The claims and the description perform different functions, however, as **9-108**
respectively defined in PA 77 subss.14(3) and 14(5) and in EPC arts 83 and 84. This was explained by Laddie J in *Merck & Co Inc v Generics (UK) Ltd*[116]:

> "38. The purpose of the patent is to convey to the public what the patentee considers to be his invention and what monopoly he has chosen to obtain. These are not necessarily the same. The former is primarily to be found in the specification and the latter is primarily to be found in the claims. Although he is not deemed to be a patent lawyer, the patentee should be taken to be aware of the primary, and rather different, purposes of the specification and the claims when he is drafting his patent. So, the patentee must be taken to know the framework of the form and purpose when drafting his patent. It is his duty to communicate his invention and his assertion of monopoly to the public in language it will understand. He is warned by the Protocol that his exclusive rights will not necessarily extend to everything which, from a reading of the specification and claims, it can be seen that he contemplated. ... The patentee can be taken to be aware of the fact that there is always a balance to be achieved between width of protection and validity. It is up to the patentee to choose the level of risk he wishes to run."

In the light of the different functions of the description and claims, it is not to be **9-109**
assumed that the scope of the claim is necessarily co-extensive with the teaching of the description. As Lord Hoffmann stated in *Kirin-Amgen*[117]:

> "There is no presumption about the width of the claims. A patent may, for one reason or another, claim less than it teaches or enables."

This may be for a variety of possible reasons; one obvious one is that the claims **9-110**
were narrowed in the course of prosecution in order to distinguish prior art which came to the attention of the patentee after the application had been filed. A practical consideration that may be borne in mind here is that the specification itself is seldom substantially modified after filing (save for consistory clauses reciting the claims, and addition of references to prior art of which the patentee becomes aware), because of the risks of inadvertently adding matter (which can arise when material is removed: see para.3–16); although the claims are frequently amended dur-

---

[114] [1997] R.P.C. 737, 743.
[115] [1996] R.P.C. 635, 642.
[116] [2004] R.P.C. 31, [38].
[117] *Kirin-Amgen v Hoechst Marion Roussel* [2005] R.P.C. 9, [33].

ing prosecution in the light of prior art that emerges during examination. The description of the invention as originally conceived and the scope of the invention as ultimately claimed, may therefore diverge for good reason and this may not be apparent on the face of the document.

9-111   The converse is of course also true: a patent may claim more than it expressly teaches (but obviously at risk as to validity), for the description may focus on specific embodiments while the claim may cover a wider general class exemplified by those embodiments.

Not legitimate to import "gloss" from the description

9-112   Although the claims are to be read purposively, in the light of the inventor's purpose as set out in the description, it has never been legitimate either to cut down or to extend the clear meaning of the language of a claim by references to the body; for that would be not to construe but to amend the claims.

9-113   In *Glaverbel v British Coal (No.4)*, (a case involving a patent granted under the 1949 Act, but decided post-*Catnic*), Mummery J explained the principle thus[118]:

> "In reading the specification as a whole the different function of the claim and the rest of the specification should be observed. The claim, cast in precise language, marks out the legal limit of the monopoly granted by the patent; and 'what is not claimed is disclaimed'. The specification describes how to carry out the process claimed and the best method known to the patentee of doing that. Although the claims are construed in the context of the specification as a whole, it is not permissible to restrict, expand, or amend the clear language of a claim by reference to a limitation or gloss in the language used in the earlier part of the specification, but not repeated in the claim itself. It is legitimate, however, to refer to the rest of the specification to explain the background to the claims, to ascertain the meaning of the technical terms and resolve ambiguities in the construction of the claims."

9-114   In the same case in the Court of Appeal,[119] Staughton LJ said:

> "(4)   The whole document must be read together, the body of the specification with the claims. But if a claim is expressed in clear language, the monopoly sought by the patentee cannot be extended or cut down by reference to the rest of the specification."

9-115   In *Improver*,[120] Hoffmann J, as he then was, summarised the principle thus:

> "[T]he scope of the invention must be found in the language of the claims. Extrinsic material such as the description can be used to interpret those claims but cannot provide independent support for a cause of action which the language of the claim, literally or figuratively construed, simply cannot bear."

9-116   Floyd J explained the underlying reasoning in *Nokia v Ipcom*[121]:

> "Where a patentee has used general language in a claim, but has described the invention by reference to a specific embodiment, it is not normally legitimate to write limitations into the claim corresponding to details of the specific embodiment, if the patentee has chosen not to do so. The specific embodiments are merely examples of what is claimed as the invention, and are often expressly, although superfluously, stated not to be "limiting". There is no general principle which requires the court to assume that the patentee intended to claim the most sophisticated embodiment of the invention. The skilled person understands that, in the claim, the patentee is stating the limits of the

---

[118] [1994] R.P.C. 443, 486, [3].
[119] [1995] R.P.C. 255, 269. See also Peter Gibson LJ's judgment at 281, referring to *EMI v Lissen* quoted below.
[120] [1990] F.S.R. 181, 190.
[121] [2009] EWHC 3482 (Pat), [41].

monopoly which it claims, not seeking to describe every detail of the manifold ways in which the invention may be put into effect."

But nonetheless the colour taken from the specification can sometimes narrow **9-117** the acontextual meaning which the claim would bear when read alone: thus in *Kirin-Amgen* the words "host cell" were held in the context of the specification held to mean "cell which is host to an exogenous DNA sequence encoding for EPO", and this was proper because:

> "This is not reading words into the claim any more than when one says that in a particular context "the City" means 'the City of London."[122]

The principle that the description cannot be used to cut back or extend the claims **9-118** has long been emphasised, in authorities decided many years before *Catnic*, but the earlier authorities now have to be treated with caution as they may have leaned too far towards the over-literal principles of construction there criticised, and which the Protocol to EPC art.69 says is to be avoided. The principal pre-*Catnic* authorities are however summarised below, as the reasoning remains persuasive.

In *British Hartford-Fairmont v Jackson Bros*[123] Romer LJ stated: **9-119**

> "where the construction of a Claim when read by itself is plain, it is not in my opinion legitimate to diminish the ambit of the monopoly claimed merely because in the body of the Specification the Patentee has described his invention in more restricted terms than in the Claim itself. The difference may well have been intentional, and created with the object ... of holding in reserve a variety of constructions for use if the patent should be called in question, and in the meantime to frighten off those who might be disposed to challenge the patent."

In *Norton-Gregory v Jacobs*,[124] the Court of Appeal observed: **9-120**

> "Now if Claim 1 be read by itself and construed in accordance with the ordinary meaning of the language used, it is apparent that the use of any reducing agent falls within it. ... But it is said ... that the language of the Claim must be construed so as to exclude any reducing agent which a chemist of ordinary skill would know, with or without experiment, to be unsuitable in view of the result to be achieved. ... To adopt the latter proposition would not be to construe the Specification but to amend it, and it would, in our opinion, be mere self-deception to hold otherwise. ... It is illegitimate to whittle away clear words in a claim by reading into them glosses and limitations extracted from the body of the Specification whose function is in its essence different from that of the claim. ... This does not mean that regard is not to be paid to the fact that the claim as well as the body of the Specification is addressed to persons skilled in the art and must be construed accordingly, But the argument here goes far beyond this and, under the pretence of construing the claim, in reality seeks to reform it."

In the more recent case of *American Home Products v Novartis*[125] the Court of **9-121** Appeal similarly rejected a submission that the claim integer "rapamycin" should be understood as meaning rapamycin itself and derivatives which exhibit the same type of activity and were suitable for preparation as a medicament. It added that the patent would have been invalid for insufficiency on that construction.

In *Electric and Musical Industries Ltd v Lissen Ltd*[126] it was accepted that "if the **9-122** claims have a plain meaning in themselves, then advantage cannot be taken of the

---

[122] *Kirin-Amgen v Hoechst Marion Roussel* [2005] R.P.C. 9, [59].
[123] [1932] 49 R.P.C. 495 at 556, per Romer LJ: but his overall view of the patent and patentee in that case are also illustrated by his remark on the same page: "A man who could make that Claim is capable of claiming anything".
[124] [1937] 54 R.P.C. 271, 276.
[125] [2001] R.P.C. 8.
[126] [1939] 56 R.P.C. 23.

language used in the body of the specification to make them mean something different"[127] (per Lord Porter). Lord Russell said:

> "The function of the claims is to define clearly and with precision the monopoly claimed, so that others may know the exact boundaries of the area within which they will be trespassers. Their primary object is to limit and not to extend the monopoly. What is not claimed is disclaimed. The claims must undoubtedly be read as part of the entire document, and not as a separate document; but the forbidden field must be found in the language of the claims and not elsewhere. It is not permissible, in my opinion, by reference to some language used in the earlier part of the specification, to change a claim which by its own language is a claim for one subject-matter into a claim for another and a different subject-matter, which is what you do when you alter the boundaries of the forbidden territory. A patentee who describes an invention in the body of a specification obtains no monopoly unless it is claimed in the claims. As Lord Cairns said,[128] there is no such thing as infringement of the equity of a patent."

9-123   But, as Lord Evershed MR stated in *Rosedale Associated Manufacturers Ltd v Carlton Tyre Saving Co Ltd*[129]:

> "It is no doubt true and has been well established (see, for example, the speech of Lord Russell of Killowen in the *E.M.I. v Lissen* case) that you must construe the claims according to their terms upon ordinary principles, and that it is not legitimate to confine the scope of the claims by reference to some limitation which may be found in the body of the specification, but is not expressly or by proper inference reproduced in the claims themselves. On the other hand, it is clearly no less legitimate and appropriate in approaching the construction of the claims to read the specification as a whole. Thereby the necessary background is obtained and in some cases the meaning of the words used in the claims may be affected or defined by what is said in the body of the specification."

9-124   These authorities were considered and explained by Lord Sutherland in *Conoco v Merpro Montassa*,[130] who after quoting from Lord Russell's speech in *EMI v Lissen* said:

> "I do not take this passage to mean that if words in a claim can be construed by reference to their normal English meaning, this is necessarily conclusive and that reference to the body of the specification is prohibited. The words in a claim must be read in the light of the terms of the specification as a whole and given the appropriate meaning in that context. As was said in *Rosedale Association Manufacturers Ltd v Carlton Tyre Saving Co Ltd* [1960] R.P.C. 59, reading the specification as a whole provides the necessary background, and in some cases the meaning of the words used in the claims may be affected or defined by what is said in the body of the specification. Once so construed however, it is not permissible to go back to the body of the specification to put a gloss on the claim extending or restricting the ambit of the monopoly; see *Poseidon Industri A.B. v Cerosa Ltd* [1982] F.S.R. 209."

9-125   The quotations from *EMI* and *Rosedale* above were more recently considered by Robert Walker LJ in *Cartonneries De Thulin v CTP White Knight*[131]:

> "That passage [from *Rosedale*] was recently approved by this court in *Lubrizol Corporation v Esso Petroleum* [1998] R.P.C. 727, 738, a case which illustrates an inadmissible attempt to use other parts of the specification to put a gloss on the clear language of a claim".

In the same case Robert Walker LJ had earlier observed that:

> "The other complicating factor is the special importance of the claims made in a patent specifica-

---

[127] [1939] 56 R.P.C. 23, 57.
[128] In *Dudgeon v Thomson* (1877) 3 App. Cas. 34. The point was echoed by Jacob J in Beloit, quoted at para.9-95: "There is no such thing as the tort of non-infringement".
[129] [1960] R.P.C. 59, 69. See also *Insituform v Inliner* [1992] R.P.C. 83, 90; *Lubrizol v Esso Petroleum* [1998] R.P.C. 727, 738 and 742.
[130] [1994] F.S.R. 99, 106.
[131] [2001] R.P.C. 6, [21].

tion, and the degree to which the construction of the claims may be influenced by other parts of the specification. ... Although a patent specification must, like any other legal document, be read as a whole in its technical and commercial context, the claims set out in the specification have a special importance".

Relationship between the claim and the essence or principle of the invention

The correct approach is therefore to construe the language of the claims, albeit purposively, rather than merely to seek to extract a general principle from them. However, on a true purposive construction it may be that the language can be understood as referring to the function of the components rather than the specific described embodiments performing that function.   **9-126**

This can for example arise in a case where the true inventive concept lies in a general technique but the claim happens to be drafted by reference to a particular manner of application which would have been the appropriate one at that time. Such a situation arose in *Codex Corp v Racal-Milgo*,[132] where the patent in suit related to modems. It described the implementation of the invention in terms of analogue signal processing technology, in which a waveform was generated and processed in a number of sequential steps. The allegedly infringing product was implemented using very different digital technology in which waveforms were stored or computed in one overall operation rather than by separate stages. The Court of Appeal upheld the trial judge's finding that there had been infringement, in spite of the very different digital technology used in the infringing device, and declined to give the claims a narrow reading so as to limit them to embodiments using the older analogue technology as described in the specification itself and in relation to which the literal language of the claim was more readily suited. At first instance,[133] Whitford J said: **9-127**

"The advance of technology has led, so far as the alleged infringement is concerned, to a device which presents differences over the techniques described in the patent; techniques which were in themselves old at the date of the patent. These new techniques no doubt have their own advantages. No instructed reader considering the *Codex* patent would in my judgment have thought that strict compliance with the techniques of application, which in a field like this are forever rapidly changing, was an essential requirement of the invention."

On appeal, the Court of Appeal confirmed the finding of infringement and explained how they had reached this conclusion as follows[134]:   **9-128**

"[T]here is no suggestion in Lord Diplock's speech that one should look only to the essence or principle of a patent in suit and hold there to have been an infringement merely because that essence or principle has been made use of by the alleged infringer. There may have been, or there may not. The question to be asked is one of construction, but of purposive or realistic construction through the eyes and with the learning of a person skilled in the art, rather than with the meticulous verbal analysis of the lawyer alone."

Similarly, in *Societé Nouvelle des Bennes Saphem v Edbro*[135] the Court of Appeal, differing from the court below, considered that the claim of the patent there in suit was on its true purposive construction directed to three functional features. Although on its literal construction it was directed to specific apparatus, the language was directed to the function which it would perform when used.   **9-129**

---

[132] [1983] R.P.C. 369.
[133] Unreported, 1981.
[134] [1983] R.P.C. 369, 381.
[135] [1983] R.P.C. 345, 361.

9-130   The overall approach in such cases was considered by Lord Hoffmann in *Kirin-Amgen* in a section of his speech headed "New technology".[136] In response to an argument that if the claims could not be construed in terms sufficiently general to include methods unknown at the priority date, the value of a patent would be destroyed as soon as some new technology for achieving the same result was invented, he observed:

> "I do not dispute that a claim may, upon its proper construction, cover products or processes which involve the use of technology unknown at the time the claim was drafted. The question is whether the person skilled in the art would understand the description in a way which was sufficiently general to include the new technology. There is no difficulty in principle about construing general terms to include embodiments which were unknown at the time the document was written. One frequently does that in construing legislation, for example, by construing 'carriage' in a 19th century statute to include a motor car. In such cases it is particularly important not to be too literal. It may be clear from the language, context and background that the patentee intended to refer in general terms to, for example, every way of achieving a certain result, even though he has used language which is in some respects inappropriate in relation to a new way of achieving that result".

9-131   In contrast, an example of a case where the patentee sought to extend the principle of purposive construction too far was *Willemijn Houdstermaatschappij v Madge Networks*,[137] where the plaintiff's approach was criticised as involving an attempt to distil the essence or principle of the patent in suit (and to do so in the light of the alleged infringement), contrary to the dictum in *Codex* quoted above.

Scope of claim and disclosure

9-132   Merely because it is possible to envisage an embodiment which falls within the scope of a claim does not mean that such an embodiment (or any particular feature thereof) is disclosed by the specification and claim. Not everything which is merely encompassed by a patent is necessarily disclosed by it. Thus in *M-Systems v Trek 2000*,[138] Kitchin J stressed, in considering an allegation that an amendment to the claim would add matter, that:

> "Secondly, and more importantly, it was not disputed before me that devices which have no cable fall within the *scope of the claims* of the application. But this does not mean to say they were *disclosed* by it. As I reiterated in *European Central Bank*, not everything which falls within the scope of the claims is necessarily disclosed and, as a matter of UK law, it is important to maintain this distinction."

9-133   He therefore held to be inadmissible an amendment to introduce a new limitation which, while narrowing the scope of the claim, would introduce matter not previously disclosed: although the invention described in the application as filed included and would cover devices falling within the scope of the new claim, they were not clearly and unambiguously disclosed by it.

5. THE "IMPROVER" OR "PROTOCOL" QUESTIONS

9-134   The tests set out by Lord Diplock and quoted at para.9-46, et seq. were analysed and broken down by Hoffmann J in *Improver v Remington* as follows[139]:

> "If the issue was whether a feature embodied in an alleged infringement which fell outside the

---

[136] *Kirin-Amgen v Hoechst Marion Roussel* [2005] R.P.C. 9, [78].
[137] [1992] R.P.C. 386.
[138] [2008] R.P.C. 18, [65], [86].
[139] [1990] F.S.R. 181, 189.

primary, literal or acontextual meaning of a descriptive word or phrase in the claim ('a variant') was nevertheless within its language as properly interpreted, the court should ask itself the following three questions:

(1) Does the variant have a material effect upon the way the invention works? If yes, the variant is outside the claim. If no—

(2) Would this (i.e. that the variant had no material effect) have been obvious at the date of publication of the patent to a reader skilled in the art. If no, the variant is outside the claim. If yes—

(3) Would the reader skilled in the art nevertheless have understood from the language of the claim that the patentee intended that strict compliance with the primary meaning was an essential requirement of the invention. If yes, the variant is outside the claim.

On the other hand, a negative answer to the last question would lead to the conclusion that the patentee was intending the word or phrase to have not a literal but a figurative meaning (the figure being a form of synecdoche or metonymy)[140] denoting a class of things which included the variant and the literal meaning, the latter being perhaps the most perfect, best-known or striking example of the class."[141]

The issue in that case was whether the requirement in the claim for a "helical spring" would be satisfied by a flexible slitted rod, the slits performing the same function as the gaps between adjacent windings of the spring's helix. The slitted rod was not, literally speaking, a helical spring, but it had relevant qualities of "springiness" and "slittiness" enabling it to perform the relevant function in a similar way, and the issue was therefore whether it was a "variant" which still fell within the scope of the claim.   **9-135**

These "*Improver*" questions were subsequently referred to as "the Protocol questions" by the Court of Appeal in *Wheatley v Drillsafe*,[142] and that designation has continued to be used. The underlying reasoning for posing the questions in this way was there explained by Aldous LJ as follows: **9-136**

"It is reasonable to infer, absent express words to the contrary, that the patentee intended to include within his monopoly what can be termed immaterial variants, in the sense that they were not material to the way the invention worked. Also it is reasonable to infer that a patentee did not intend to include within the ambit of his monopoly a variant which had a material effect upon the way the invention worked, otherwise his claims could, to the detriment of the patentee, include variants which had little if anything to do with what he had invented. However, third parties have to be considered and therefore they should not be held to infringe if it was clear that such a variant was not intended to be within the ambit of the monopoly either because of the words chosen or because it would be seen to have materially affected the way the invention worked."

Prior to the speeches in *Kirin-Amgen*, this three-part "*Improver* test" was frequently applied as an aid to achieving the proper purposive construction and therefore as a "normally useful tool".[143] The House of Lords in *Kirin-Amgen* was however at pains to stress that these questions are mere guidelines for applying the principle of purposive construction in the context of equivalents.[144] They are not to   **9-137**

---

[140] Synecdoche: "a figure of speech in which a part is made to represent the whole or vice versa (e.g. new faces at the meeting)"; Metonymy: "the substitution of the name of an attribute or adjunct for that of the thing meant (e.g. Crown for the king)" (Concise Oxford Dictionary).

[141] See also the similar approaches by Aldous J in *Southco v Dzus* [1990] R.P.C. 587, at 606; and in *Lux Traffic Controls v Pike Signals* [1993] R.P.C. 107, at 126, in which he independently put forward a similar three-part formulation.

[142] [2001] R.P.C. 7, [23].

[143] Per Aldous LJ in *Pharmacia v Merck* [2002] R.P.C. 41, at [40], though he there held that their difficulties in application outweighed their advantages in that case.

[144] See *Kirin-Amgen v Hoechst Marion Roussel* [2005] R.P.C. 9, per Lord Hoffman, at [51]–[52], [69],

be treated as legal rules and they are not always even useful or helpful. See the section of this chapter "When are the Protocol questions useful" at para.9–164.

Falls outside the primary, literal or acontextual meaning?

9-138   This phrase echoes the strict pre-*Catnic* literal approach to construction, though now for the purpose of differentiating it. Lord Hoffmann in *Kirin-Amgen*[145] suggested that the meaning of this expression might itself give rise to difficulty, for every utterance has some context, but stated that here it must be taken to mean a construction which assumes that the author used words strictly in accordance with their conventional meanings. Thus "helical spring" (in the context of *Improver* itself) exemplified this.

The "variant"

9-139   In applying the Protocol questions, it is first necessary to identify what the relevant variant is. An example of a case where identifying the variant made a material difference to the answer obtained to this question is *Union Carbide v B.P. Chemicals*,[146] where the defendant's characterisation of the variant was rejected and therefore a number of its submissions as to materiality fell away. In *Wesley Jessen v CooperVision*,[147] HHJ Fysh stated:

> "First, I wish to consider whether *anything* may be a 'variant' merely on the *ipse dixit* of the patentee. There must I think be a threshold question that is, whether, applying commonsense to the language and facts, the skilled man would be likely to reject the description 'variant' outright as an abuse of language. Furthermore, the fact that the first two Protocol questions may be answered in the affirmative, does not in itself demonstrate that the word or phrase in question must therefore be a variant."

9-140   In *Ultraframe v Eurocell Building Plastics*,[148] Jacob LJ felt that the requirement to identify the variant—"from what?"—posed unnecessary difficulties and therefore declined to apply the three-stage Protocol questions.

9-141   From the way in which the *"Improver* test" is formulated, it might perhaps be thought that the claim construction using this approach can only be widened (enlarged so as to embrace additional "variants" outside its "literal" scope) and never narrowed. But, of course, where there are several possible acontextual meanings of a word, purposive construction involves selecting that which corresponds to the meaning as it would be understood in context, which may or may not be the narrower of the possible acontextual meanings.[149] In the former event, the narrower meaning is correct and the claim does not include the "variant" sought to be incorporated by the wider meaning.

9-142   **(1) Does the variant affect the way the invention works?** The first and second *"Improver"* questions require findings of fact but they cannot be considered without recourse to the patent. They are to be considered in the light of what the specification teaches as to what the invention is, for the variant may have a material effect

---

[81]–[84], and Lord Walker, at [138]–[139].
[145] *Kirin-Amgen v Hoechst Marion Roussel* [2005] R.P.C. 9, [63]–[64].
[146] [1999] R.P.C. 409, 421.
[147] [2003] R.P.C. 20, [84].
[148] [2005] EWCA (Civ) 761.
[149] See, e.g. the meaning given to "conduit" in *STEP v Emson* [1993] R.P.C. 513, 522.

on some other aspect of the machine but not upon the way that the invention itself works.[150] It is therefore necessary to determine how the invention works, and as Pumfrey J pointed out in *Horne Engineering v Reliance Water Controls*[151]:

> "This is a question of disclosure. It is not a process of substituting or adding explanations if the explanation is provided by the specification itself."

It does not necessarily follow that because the variant works in a different way **9-143** or has advantages of its own, the variant therefore has a material effect on the way in which the invention as such works.[152]

This first question has to be answered by describing the working of the inven- **9-144** tion at the level of generality with which it is described in the claim.[153] Lord Hoffmann stated in *Kirin-Amgen*[154]:

> "I agree with the Court of Appeal that the invention should normally be taken as having been claimed at the same level of generality as that at which it is defined in the claims. It would be unusual for the person skilled in the art to understand a specification to be claiming an invention at a higher level of generality than that chosen by the patentee."

It was however suggested in *Telsonic A.G.'s Patent*[155] that relying on the claim **9-145** alone for this purpose (in the context of an exercise to determine the scope of that very claim) could lead to circular reasoning, so that Laddie J there proceeded on the basis that "the level of generality is that indicated by the inventor". (As discussed below,[156] an alternative approach would have been to abandon the Protocol questions entirely). Although in that case, the claim included a limitation which appeared arbitrarily to exclude products which would work in the same way, and so the patentee's real problem was with the third Protocol question.

In *Kirin-Amgen*, Lord Hoffmann pointed out that the German courts approach **9-146** equivalents with similar guidelines, but which are not identical.[157] In relation to this first Protocol question, he explained:

> "For example, German judges do not ask whether a variant 'works in the same way' but whether it solves the problem underlying the invention by means which have the same technical effect. That may be a better way of putting the question because it avoids the ambiguity illustrated by *American Home Products Corporation v Novartis Pharmaceuticals UK Ltd* [2001] R.P.C. 159 over whether 'works in the same way' involves an assumption that it works at all. On the other hand, as is illustrated by the present case, everything will depend upon what you regard as "the problem underlying the invention.""

In the case referred to, *American Home Products v Novartis*[158] the patentee had **9-147** urged a construction of "rapamycin" that included derivatives that would work,

---

[150] *Kastner v Rizla* [1995] R.P.C. 585, 598; and see *Improver v Remington* itself at [1990] F.S.R. 181, 191.
[151] [2000] F.S.R. 90, [11].
[152] *Insituform v Inliner* [1992] R.P.C. 83, 92. Compare Bowen LJ's famous dictum in *Wenham Co v Champion Gas* (1892) 9 R.P.C. 49, at 56: "The superadding of ingenuity to a robbery does not make the operation justifiable", and *British Liquid Air v British Oxygen* (1909) 26 R.P.C. 509, at 528.
[153] *Improver v Remington* [1990] F.S.R. 181, 192; *Sundstrand v Safe Flight Instrument Corp* [1994] F.S.R. 599, 614, PCC; *Kastner v Rizla* [1995] R.P.C. 585, 598–599; *Union Carbide v B.P. Chemicals* [1999] R.P.C. 409, 421; *Wheatley v Drillsafe* [2001] R.P.C. 7, [26], [34], [88].
[154] *Kirin-Amgen v Hoechst Marion Roussel* [2005] R.P.C. 9, [70].
[155] [2004] R.P.C. 38, [45]–[46].
[156] See "When are the Protocol questions useful?", para.9–164.
[157] As noted by Floyd LJ in the Court of Appeal in *Actavis v Eli Lilly* [2015] EWCA Civ 555, at [48].
[158] [2001] R.P.C. 8

based on a functional limitation at the end of the claim. However, this formulation led to the conclusion that the first two questions would therefore inevitably be answered in the patentee's favour, an approach rejected by the Court of Appeal. The Court of Appeal took the view that this pointed away from the construction being advanced (which would also have led to the claim being insufficient). In *Kirin-Amgen*,[159] Lord Hoffman instead took this as an example of a case where the Protocol questions were not useful.

9-148   The claim is to be read as a whole and therefore it is artificial, when the claim has been divided into its individual integers for convenience, to look at each feature separately in considering the relevant variant.[160] Where several integers are to be read together, it is inappropriate to compare the variant with those integers one at a time.

9-149   **(2) Would this have been obvious to the skilled reader?** Hoffmann J explained in *Improver*[161] that the question supposes that the skilled person is told of both the invention and the variant, and asked whether the variant would obviously work in the same way. It is not correct to ask whether "the variant must be one which would have suggested itself to the skilled man as an obvious alternative", for the variant may itself have been inventive.

9-150   However, where the patent was a "pioneering" patent in its field, it was held that due to the lack of information available at the time as to the subject matter, even if the variant did not affect the way the invention worked, this would hardly have been obvious to the skilled reader.[162] Lord Hoffman similarly asked rhetorically in *Kirin-Amgen*[163]:

> "When one asks whether it would have been obvious to the person skilled in the art that the variant worked in the same way as the invention, does one assume that it works? Otherwise, in the case of a technology which was unknown at the priority date, the person skilled in the art would probably say that it was by no means obvious that it would work in the same way because it was not obvious that it would work at all."

9-151   He went on to suggest that such cases were instances where the Protocol questions were not useful.

9-152   This second question only arises if it has already been concluded that the answer to the first question is that the variant does not affect the way the invention works, and so the second question should be considered on that assumption.[164]

9-153   The correct test is therefore to assume that the skilled reader was told of the variant, and on the basis that it does not in fact make any difference to the way the invention works, consider what his reaction would have been. In *Union Carbide v B.P. Chemicals*[165] the Court of Appeal answered this question by stating "A skilled man, told of the variant, would immediately realise that it was immaterial whether [the variant was adopted or not]"; he would realise that the factor which was important in ensuring success was not affected by the variant.

---

[159] *Kirin-Amgen v Hoechst Marion Roussel* [2005] R.P.C. 9, [82].
[160] *Kastner v Rizla* [1995] R.P.C. 585, 596.
[161] *Improver v Remington* [1990] F.S.R. 181, 192.
[162] *Sundstrand v Safe Flight Instrument Corp* [1994] F.S.R. 599, 615, PCC.
[163] *Kirin-Amgen v Hoechst Marion Roussel* [2005] R.P.C. 9, [81].
[164] *Kastner v Rizla* [1995] R.P.C. 585, 599.
[165] [1999] R.P.C. 409, 421.

In *Actavis v Eli Lilly*[166] Floyd LJ considered the issue of what information it must **9-154** be assumed that the skilled reader has available to them for the purpose of asking whether it was obvious that the variant will in fact have no material effect on the way the invention works. He regarded it as axiomatic that "one is concerned with what would be obvious, in the sense of immediately apparent, to the skilled reader from a reading of the specification informed by common general knowledge". Thus the notional addressee is not presented with information which they cannot derive from the patent or their common general knowledge about whether the variant will in fact have no material effect on the way the invention works. A submission that there may be situations where the missing information is so easy for the skilled person to obtain that it should be taken to have been reasonably available to them when they read the patent was only not considered because it had not been advanced before the trial judge and there was no relevant evidence on the point.

It will be seen that in this question the skilled person is again pressed into the **9-155** service of patent jurisprudence. However, their role is not identical to their statutory role under s.3 of the Act. In *Merck & Co Inc v Generics (UK) Ltd*[167] Laddie J held that the test for obviousness in the second Protocol question cannot be the same test as used to invalidate a patent over published prior art; for whereas in considering obviousness it is enough to demonstrate that the reader of the prior art found the prospects of achieving the desired result sufficiently encouraging to warrant trying it out, in the case where one is attempting to broaden the patent monopoly to cover variants which are not within the acontextual meaning of the claims, a higher degree of confidence of success must be involved. The reader must have little or no doubt that the variant will, not may, work in the same way to produce the same results.

(3) Would strict compliance have been understood to be required? Hoff- **9-156** mann J stated in the *Improver* case itself[168]:

"It is worth noticing that Lord Diplock's first two questions, although they cannot sensibly be answered without reference to the patent, do not primarily involve questions of construction: whether the variant would make a material difference to the way the invention worked and whether this would have been obvious to the skilled reader are questions of fact. The answers are used to provide the factual background against which the specification must be construed. It is the third question which raises the question of construction and Lord Diplock's formulation makes it clear that on this question the answers to the first two questions are not conclusive. Even a purposive construction of the language of the patent may lead to the conclusion that although the variant made no material difference and this would have been obvious at the time, the patentee for some reason was confining his claim to the primary meaning and excluding the variant. If this were not the case, there would be no point in asking the third question at all."

In *Wheatley v Drillsafe*[169] Aldous LJ said of the third Protocol question: **9-157**

"... third parties have to be considered and, therefore, they should not be held to infringe if it was clear that such a variant was not intended to be within the ambit of the monopoly either because of the words chosen or it would be seen to have materially affected the invention worked."

---

[166] [2015] EWCA Civ 555, 48–49.
[167] [2004] R.P.C. 31, [78].
[168] *Improver v Remington* [1990] F.S.R. 181, 190.
[169] [2001] R.P.C. 7, [23].

9-158   The above-quoted passage from *Improver* itself emphasises that the answers to the first two questions cannot be conclusive. As Laddie J observed in *Merck & Co v Generics (UK) Ltd*[170]:

> "At the most the answer to these questions provide shortcuts to the only important question, namely question (3)."

9-159   In the same case, Laddie J also suggested that the third *Improver* question was the wrong way round, at least if itself applied rigidly and literally:

> "In formulating the questions, Hoffmann J said he was applying the guidance in *Catnic*. There is no doubt that the binding authority on construction in this jurisdiction is the latter case. That was confirmed by the Court of Appeal in *Kastner v Rizla* [1995] R.P.C. 585. Yet there appears to be a potential difference between the way the issue of construction was put in *Catnic* to the way it is explained in *Improver*. Imagine the case where the notional skilled reader does not understand why the patentee put a limitation in the claim. According to *Catnic*, in such a case the limitation is effective because it is not 'apparent' that the limitations 'cannot have been intended by the patentee'. The variants will be *excluded* from the monopoly. By contrast the same facts would be answered differently if *Improver* question (3) is applied rigidly. Where the reason for introducing the limitation is unclear, the skilled reader could not say that he understood 'that the patentee intended to con ne his claim'. Thus *Improver* question (3) would be answered in the negative and the claim will be construed to *include* the variants. I think that this difference is more imagined than real. At p.197 of *Improver* it appears to have been accepted that if the notional skilled addressee would speculate that the patentee had good reason for including the limitation in the claims, the limitation is effective. In other words the *Catnic* approach was adopted."

9-160   However, such arguments cannot be taken to extremes, for it is always possible to speculate that the patentee might for some unknown reason, not apparent on the face of the patent, have intended to be taken literally. (Such speculation is all too easy: perhaps in *Catnic* itself, the word "vertically" had deliberately not been qualified by the word "substantially" because the patentee had been aware of prior art at an angle of 5° and wanted to keep a literal construction in reserve.) It may also be noted that Lord Diplock answered his "nutshell" question by pointing out that no "plausible" reason had been given why the patentee would have wanted to limit his claims to a strict literal meaning.

9-161   An over-rigid approach to the third question is not appropriate, as this would itself contravene the Protocol as not being fair to the patentee.[171]

9-162   The claim is to be considered for this purpose in the light of the specification as a whole, as required by s.125 of the 1977 Act.[172] The analysis therefore involves consideration of the way in which the invention is described, but through the eyes of the skilled reader, so that in many of the authorities the resolution of this issue is promptly followed by the characterisation of the unsuccessful party's approach as involving the over-meticulous verbal analysis deprecated by Lord Diplock.

9-163   One practical reason why the patentee would want to exclude variants is that they would not work to solve the stated problem addressed by the patent.[173] Although where the specification recited a number of advantages to the invention, in particular that the use of certain additional equipment was not required, and the variant did

---

[170] [2004] R.P.C. 31, [56].
[171] *Kastner v Rizla* [1995] R.P.C. 585, 595.
[172] *Kastner v Rizla* [1995] R.P.C. 585, 599.
[173] *3M v Plastus Kreativ* [1997] R.P.C. 737, at 747, per Jacob J.

not achieve them all, this did not mean that the claim excluded it since there was no such limitation appearing in the claim.[174]

When are the Protocol questions useful?

As has already been noted above, the House of Lords in *Kirin-Amgen* was at pains to stress that the Protocol questions are not to be treated as legal rules, but are mere guidelines and not always useful.[175] Lord Hoffmann noted at [52] that they had been used by English courts for the past 15 years as a framework for deciding whether equivalents fall within the scope of the claims, and went on to say:

9-164

> "On the whole, the judges appear to have been comfortable with the results, although some of the cases have exposed the limitations of the method. When speaking of the '*Catnic* principle' it is important to distinguish between, on the one hand, the principle of purposive construction which I have said gives effect to the requirements of the Protocol, and on the other hand, the guidelines for applying that principle to equivalents, which are encapsulated in the Protocol questions. The former is the bedrock of patent construction, universally applicable. The latter are only guidelines, more useful in some cases than in others. I am bound to say that the cases show a tendency for counsel to treat the Protocol questions as legal rules rather than guides which will in appropriate cases help to decide what the skilled man would have understood the patentee to mean."

Lord Walker made similar observations in his speech at [138] and [139].

Similarly, in *Pharmacia v Merck*,[176] where the question was whether a claim to an enol tautomer also covered a keto tautomer, the Court of Appeal found that the difficulties in applying the Protocol questions outweighed the advantages. Arden LJ observed at [163]:

9-165

> "The courts use the '*Improver*' questions as a tool of analysis and the disciplined approach it offers promotes consistency and transparency in this important field. The habits of those who draft patents are no doubt conditioned by the law's requirements, and that is another reason for following a structured approach. ... However, it bears repetition that the *Improver* questions are no more than guidelines: the final conclusion on interpretation must be found by asking the Protocol questions [semble: the requirements of the Protocol to Art.69 itself]. But they make it clear that the touchstone for a variant to be within a patent is not that it is necessary so that the monopoly granted by the patent is effective. On the contrary the variant must be immaterial, obvious and consistent with the language of the patent."

An initial difficulty identified by Lord Hoffmann[177] was to decide what is meant by a "primary, literal or acontextual meaning". He stated that it must be taken to mean a construction which assumes that the author used words strictly in accordance with their conventional meanings. In *Ultraframe v Eurocell Building Plastics*[178] Jacob LJ simply dealt with the problem in this way:

9-166

> "Although the Protocol questions can be a guide, their application often produces unnecessary difficulties. They require, for instance, the court to consider a 'variant'—which begs the question 'from what?' I therefore propose to go straight to the compulsory question."

Lord Hoffmann went on in *Kirin-Amgen* to say[179]:

9-167

---

[174] *Union Carbide v B.P. Chemicals* [1999] R.P.C. 409, 422.
[175] See *Kirin-Amgen v Hoechst Marion Roussel* [2005] R.P.C. 9, per Lord Hoffman, at [51]–[52], [69], [81]–[84], and Lord Walker at [138]–[139].
[176] [2002] R.P.C. 41.
[177] *Kirin-Amgen v Hoechst Marion Roussel* [2005] R.P.C. 9, [63]–[65].
[178] [2005] EWCA (Civ) 761.
[179] [2005] R.P.C. 9, [65].

"The notion of strict compliance with the conventional meanings of words or phrases sits most comfortably with the use of figures, measurements, angles and the like, when the question is whether they allow for some degree of tolerance or approximation. That was the case in *Catnic* and it is significant that the 'quintet' of cases in which the German Bundesgerichtshof referred to *Catnic* and said that its approach accorded with that of the House of Lords were all concerned with figures and measurements. In such cases, the contrast with strict compliance is approximation and not the rather pretentious figures of speech mentioned in the Protocol questions."

9-168   However, he went on to acknowledge that the Protocol questions can also be usefully applied where the word in question was not said to be used as an approximation, but to have a figurative meaning. Thus in the *Improver* case itself, the question was whether a slitted rod satisfied the claim's requirement for a "helical spring", so that in that context, the contrast with strict compliance could not be said to involve merely a penumbra of tolerance.

9-169   Lord Hoffman went on to explain why the Protocol questions may in some circumstances be superfluous. He said[180]:

"No doubt there are other cases, not involving figures or measurements, in which the question is whether a word or phrase was used in a strictly conventional or some looser sense. But the present case illustrates the difficulty of applying the Protocol questions when no such question arises. No one suggests that 'an exogenous DNA sequence coding for EPO' can have some looser meaning which includes 'an endogenous DNA sequence coding for EPO'. The question is rather whether the person skilled in the art would understand the invention as operating at a level of generality which makes it irrelevant whether the DNA which codes for EPO is exogenous or not. That is a difficult question to put through the mangle of the Protocol questions because the answer depends entirely upon what you think the invention is. Once you have decided that question, the Protocol questions answer themselves."

Similarly, he stated (at [69]):

"The determination of the extent of protection conferred by a European patent is an examination in which there is only one compulsory question, namely that set by article 69 and its Protocol: what would a person skilled in the art have understood the patentee to have used the language of the claim to mean? Everything else, including the Protocol questions, is only guidance to a judge trying to answer that question. But there is no point in going through the motions of answering the Protocol questions when you cannot sensibly do so until you have construed the claim. In such a case—and the present is in my opinion such a case—they simply provide a formal justification for a conclusion which has already been reached on other grounds."

9-170   The risk is therefore that the Protocol questions may force circular reasoning. One cannot consider the first question—does the variant work in the same way—unless one has decided what the invention is, but to do that one first has to construe the claim. (As noted at para.9-100 a similar problem had been identified in *Telsonic A.G.'s Patent*.[181]) Once the claims have been construed, the question of infringement has been answered and it becomes unnecessary and indeed liable to cause confusion then to attempt to apply the Protocol questions as well.[182] Lord Hoffmann therefore concluded that[183]:

"The Protocol questions are useful in many cases, but they are not a substitute for trying to understand what the person skilled in the art would have understood the patentee to mean by the language of the claims."

---

[180] *Kirin-Amgen v Hoechst Marion Roussel* [2005] R.P.C. 9, [66].
[181] [2004] R.P.C. 38, [45]–[46].
[182] *Kirin-Amgen v Hoechst Marion Roussel* [2005] R.P.C. 9, [70].
[183] *Kirin-Amgen v Hoechst Marion Roussel* [2005] R.P.C. 9, [71].

This problem arises in particularly acute form in the case of new technology, where the claim was drafted in terms of techniques known at the date of the patent and could not have anticipated subsequent developments in the art. The court's approach in such cases has been discussed at the section headed "Equivalents and construction" at para.9–63, et seq. As there explained, Lord Hoffmann confirmed that in such cases, "The question is whether the person skilled in the art would understand the description in a way which was sufficiently general to include the new technology". Although after discussing the particular problems which arise in such cases with the second Protocol question—how does one ask whether it would have been obvious that the variant would work in the same way, when the new techniques were not available at the relevant time?—he went on to conclude that[184]: **9-171**

> "So perhaps a better answer to the dispute over the second Protocol question is that new technology is another situation in which the Protocol questions may be unhelpful. On the other hand, if the claim can properly be construed in a way which is sufficiently general to include the new technology, the Protocol questions tend to answer themselves."

In the light of Lord Hoffmann's comments in *Kirin-Amgen*, the Protocol questions went largely unasked until their revival in *Actavis v Lilly*.[185] This was probably in part due to the fact that a number of European jurisdictions whose law the court was applying in *Actavis* apply tests akin (albeit not identical) to the Protocol questions, as considered further below. **9-172**

In *Actavis*, claim 1 was in Swiss-form (i.e. the general form "use of substance X in the manufacture of a medicament for treating disease Y". Specifically, claim 1 referred to the use of pemetrexed disodium. The claimant intended to sell pemetrexed dipotassium (amongst other variants of pemetrexed disodium) and hence the task for the court was to determine what the skilled reader would have understood "pemetrexed disodium" to mean. **9-173**

In addressing this issue, the court reviewed the judge's application of the Protocol questions. **9-174**

It was common ground that the variants in issue had no material effect on the way the invention works. As to whether this would be obvious to the skilled team (as it was in that case) Floyd LJ explained that the judge had concluded that the view of the chemist on the skilled team would be that he would not be able to predict the effect on the overall solubility of the pemetrexed salt of the substitution of the sodium counter-ion with another. **9-175**

An argument that the judge had been wrong to include a chemist in the skilled team was rejected.[186] A second argument was that it is permissible to assume that the skilled chemist knows that the variants would be soluble, and that it was permissible to take into account that the claimant had committed sums of money to its development project (including the costs of litigation) in reliance on the fact that the variants would be satisfactory. This argument was also rejected on the basis that it was not a legitimate exercise to assume that the skilled reader could be fed information about the variants to deal with their technical concerns about their workability. The answer to such concerns must be found in the specification or in the common general knowledge. **9-176**

---

[184] *Kirin-Amgen v Hoechst Marion Roussel* [2005] R.P.C. 9, [84].
[185] [2015] EWCA Civ 555.
[186] The inclusion in the skilled team of a person whose skill is relevant to the manufacturing step of a Swiss-form claim is discussed at para.8–41.

9-177   A third argument was that the judge had focused on the wrong problem when considering whether it was obvious that the variant had a material effect on the way the invention worked. In the context of claim 1 being in Swiss-form, it was said that the problem underlying the invention was not a manufacturing one but a therapeutic one and that the oncologist would know that the source of pemetrexed anions would have no effect at all in this context. However, Floyd LJ agreed with the judge below, saying:

> "I agree with the judge's reasoning. Once the claim includes the step of manufacturing a medicament for treating a disease, it necessarily includes a requirement that the manufactured medicament is to some extent effective for treating the disease. If the skilled chemist is unable to predict that a variant will be sufficiently soluble to deliver an effective amount of pemetrexed anions in solution, then he is unable to say that the variant would have no material effect on the way the invention works."

9-178   When it came to the third Protocol question, upon consideration of the specification of the patent and the common general knowledge, Floyd LJ agreed with the judge that the skilled team would understand that the patent was clearly limited to the disodium salt and did not extend to any of the variants in issue. Floyd LJ attributed to the skilled reader an understanding that there are plausible reasons why the patentee might have wished to limit his claim to the disodium salt: in particular the skilled reader would have understood that the patentee might have been content with a claim limited to his commercial embodiment. The claimant's pemetrexed dipotassium was therefore held not to infringe on the basis of the third Protocol question.

The approach in other EPC jurisdictions

9-179   The objective of art.69 of the EPC and its Protocol is of course to secure uniformity of approach to claim construction throughout the member states of the EPC. While in the absence of any supra-national court there is no means of ultimate review to secure this, the line of authority cited above has striven to ensure that the approach in the UK remains in conformity with that in other jurisdictions.

9-180   The Court of Appeal in *PLG v Ardon*[187] reviewed some of the principal German authorities, although in *Assidoman*[188] Aldous J demonstrated that they had not done so accurately, and pointed out that it could not be concluded that the German approach was more in accordance with the Protocol unless one first performed a comparison of the approaches and a review of the extent to which each provided fair protection to the patentee and reasonable certainty to third parties. In *Kastner v Rizla*,[189] it was conceded that in *PLG* the Court of Appeal had not accurately expressed the approach taken by the German courts.

9-181   In *Kirin-Amgen*, Lord Hoffmann summarised the principles applied by the German and Dutch courts, in the light of suggestions that these jurisdictions were continuing to apply the pre-EPC approach of using claims merely as a guide or a point of departure. He concluded that both jurisdictions were giving the claims a central role, and that although the guidelines applied in Germany were in some respects different, the German courts were indeed "also approaching the question

---

[187] [1995] R.P.C. 287, 307–309.
[188] [1995] R.P.C. 321, 335–336.
[189] [1995] R.P.C. 585, 594.

of equivalents with a view to answering the same ultimate question as that which I have suggested is raised by Article 69, namely what a person skilled in the art would have thought the patentee was using the language of the claim to mean".[190]

Differences in result do from time to time arise when the courts of different jurisdictions consider the same patents, but this does not of itself illustrate a difference in approach; for even within the UK different results may be achieved in different courts.[191] The fact that validity is reserved to individual national courts means that differences in outcome are inevitable (just as differences between first instance and appeal courts within the same jurisdiction are inevitable from time to time, if the latter are to be useful).   **9-182**

The case of *Improver Corp v Remington Inc*[192] is instructive in illustrating how the UK and German courts can still come to different conclusions as to the protection to be afforded to a patentee in respect of the same patent, even though the courts of both countries were purporting to apply the Protocol. As Aldous J commented in *Assidoman*,[193] there are procedural differences in the two jurisdictions, the evidence before each would have been different, and the conclusion in one of the courts could have been wrong even if the principles of law applied were right. Jacob J's comments on the *Terfenadine* and *Improver* cases in *Beloit v Valmet (No.2)*[194] and in *3M v Plastus Kreativ*[195] are also instructive.   **9-183**

The court here will therefore not necessarily follow a decision on a parallel European patent, but will apply its own independent judgment based on the material before it. Indeed it has a duty to do so. Thus in *American Home Products v Novartis*[196] Aldous LJ noted that the District Court of the Hague had come to the same conclusion as he had done, but stated that he had not relied upon the reasons given as it was to be appealed and was decided upon different evidence.   **9-184**

The Court of Appeal in *Occlutech v AGA Medical*[197] was invited to examine the law in Germany in the light of an article in the *Yale Law Journal*[198] co-authored by the late Pumfrey LJ and other distinguished judges including Dr Peter Meier-Beck. Patten LJ noted that the first instance courts of The Netherlands and the UK on the one hand and the Düsseldorf Higher Regional Court on the other had arrived at different conclusions as to construction. He considered the summary of the German approach to the question of equivalents and commented: **9-185**

"38. Assuming (as I do) that this represents a comprehensive summary of the German position on equivalents, it is immediately apparent that it does not contain anything similar to the third of the questions posed by Hoffmann J (as he then was) in *Improver Corp v Remington Consumer Products Ltd* [1990] F.S.R. 181 as part of his re-statement of Lord Diplock's approach to construction in *Catnic*: i.e.

'(3) Would the reader skilled in the art nevertheless have understood from the language of the claim that the patentee intended that strict compliance with the primary

---

[190] *Kirin-Amgen v Hoechst Marion Roussel* [2005] R.P.C. 9, [72]–[75].
[191] Thus, e.g. in *ICI v Montedison* [1995] R.P.C. 449, each of the three members of the Court of Appeal reached a different conclusion on construction of the "whereby ..." clause—see para.9–329.
[192] Hoffmann J there discussed why he had come to a different conclusion from the German court—see [1990] F.S.R. 181, at 197–199.
[193] [1995] R.P.C. 321, 335.
[194] [1995] R.P.C. 705, 720–721.
[195] [1997] R.P.C. 737, 743.
[196] [2001] R.P.C. 8, [57].
[197] [2010] EWCA Civ 702.
[198] "The Doctrine of Equivalents in Various Patent Regimes—Does Anybody Have It Right?" (2009) 11 Yale J.L. & Tech 261.

meaning was an essential requirement of the invention? If yes, the variant is outside the claim.'

On one view this is likely to deprive the skilled addressee of one possible explanation of the words used: i.e. that they have been deliberately chosen so as to narrow the scope of the claims over the teaching in order to accommodate the considerations described by Lord Hoffmann in paragraph 35 of his speech quoted earlier. But it is not feasible in the context of this appeal to carry out an exhaustive comparison of the relevant principles of German and Dutch law so as to be able to express a confident view as to whether the underlying principles at play in the two European decisions on infringement do or do not equate to what the House of Lords has stated as the correct English approach to that question. I therefore propose to examine the rival contentions as to the proper construction of claims 1 and 16 in the light of the principles set out in Kirin-Amgen and to consider AGA's reliance on the decision of the Oberlandesgericht in those terms."

9-186   In an unusual case where the English Court was seised with jurisdiction over the issue of infringement in France, Italy and Spain, the first instance decision of Arnold J in *Actavis v Eli Lilly*[199] provided an unprecedented opportunity for the English Court to analyse the law of infringement in each of these jurisdictions.

9-187   At the time of the trial, the *Actavis* product had been held to infringe in Germany by the Düsseldorf Regional Court (although that finding was subsequently reversed shortly before the Court of Appeal hearing in England). In the case of French law, Arnold J held that the French doctrine of equivalence did not apply in circumstances where the claim is narrowly worded to cover specific means (as opposed to general means) and the function of those means is not novel. On the facts of the case, the means in issue—"pemetrexed disodium"—was a specific means whose function (being its efficacy in inhibiting tumour growth) was not novel.[200] He held that although the variants in question were equivalents to the claimed pemetrexed disodium, under Italian law they were nevertheless excluded from the scope of protection. This was for two reasons. First, because on its face the patent clearly demonstrated a conscious intention of the patentee to limit the claims to pemetrexed disodium. Secondly, because if there was any doubt about that, it was amply confirmed by the prosecution history, which he held could, under Italian law in an appropriate case, be relied upon as an aid to construction of the claims, particularly where it is clear the applicant has intentionally limited the scope of the claims during the course of prosecution. Lastly, concerning Spanish law, he held that in a pharmaceutical case a test that is particularly likely to be applied is an adapted *Improver* test which involves asking the following questions:

"1.   Does the variant alter the functioning of the invention? If the answer is yes, equivalence does not exist. If the answer is no, i.e. the functioning of the invention is not altered, it is necessary to ask the next question.

2.   Would the variant have been obvious to a skilled person who read the patent on the date when it was published? If the variant was not obvious i.e. it is inventive, there is no equivalence. If the answer is yes, it is still necessary to ask the third question.

3.   Would the person skilled in the art who read the patent have understood, given the terms used in the claim, that the patent holder intended that strict compliance with the literal wording was an essential requirement of the invention? If the answer is yes then there can be no equivalence. But if strict compliance is not essential then the variant may be equivalent."

9-188   Applying those adapted *Improver* questions, although the answer to the first question was not disputed to be yes, the answer to the second was no, for the reasons

---

[199] [2014] EWHC 1511 (Pat), [2015] R.P.C. 6.
[200] [2014] EWHC 1511 (Pat); [2015] R.P.C. 6, [164]. The judge also relied on the prosecution history which he also held to be available under French law.

given when answering the equivalent question under UK law—an answer which, as seen above, was upheld on appeal. Furthermore, even if the answer to question 2 was yes, the answer to question 3 was also yes, also for the reasons given when answering the equivalent question under UK law. Accordingly the judge held that the variants on pemetrexed disodium did not fall within the scope of the claims.

6. EVIDENCE RELATING TO CONSTRUCTION

The proposition that "Construction is for court alone"

It is often said that construction is a matter for the court alone, the explanation being that the claim's meaning is a question of law and therefore one left to the judge rather than to the jury when their functions were distinct. However, there are two important qualifications that need to be made to that bare proposition: **9-189**

(1) First, since the addressee of a patent specification is assumed to be a "person skilled in the art" (and similar principles will apply to prior art documents), evidence is admissible to assist the court in reading it through the eyes of such a person. This includes in particular evidence as to the common general knowledge in the relevant art, as to the meaning of technical terms, and as to the technical consequences of what is described or of any putative construction.

(2) Secondly, the teaching of the specification, once construed, is a question of fact, as is what the skilled reader would do with that teaching. A distinction is to be drawn between construction—the meaning of the words used—and disclosure—what they would teach the reader. As the latter is a question of fact, evidence is also admissible as to those matters.

While patent cases are now tried by a judge alone, so that issues as to the different functions of judge and jury do not directly arise, they may assume importance in the context of admissibility of evidence, and the extent to which decisions on construction by the Court of Appeal may be binding if the same patent is subsequently re-litigated against a different opponent. These considerations will be reviewed below. **9-190**

Admissibility of evidence as to the meaning of the claim

Many authorities have held that the construction of the specification is for the court alone when properly instructed as to the notional skilled addressee. The court construes the patent objectively, but adopting the mantle of the notional addressee to whom it is directed and in the light of the common general knowledge with which he is assumed to be imbued.[201] Once having understood the relevant background knowledge, the court reserves to itself the ultimate question of the meaning of the words used, in view of the fact that it is a notional reader to be considered. **9-191**

The consequence is that evidence of expert witnesses as to the meaning of the claim is inadmissible. Lindley LJ in *Brooks v Steele and Currie*[202] said: **9-192**

> "The judge may, and indeed generally must, be assisted by expert evidence to explain technical terms, to show the practical working of machinery described or drawn, and to point out what is old and what

---

[201] *Dyson v Hoover*, [2001] R.P.C. 26, [48(f)].
[202] (1896) 13 R.P.C. 46, 73.

is new in the specification. Expert evidence is also admissible, and is often required to show the particulars in which an alleged invention has been used by an alleged infringer, and the real importance of whatever differences there may be between the plaintiff's invention and whatever is done by the defendant. But, after all, the nature of the invention for which a patent is granted must be ascertained from the specification, and has to be determined by the judge and not by a jury, nor by any expert or other witness. This is familiar law, although apparently often disregarded when witnesses are being examined."[203]

9-193   Lord Tomlin in *British Celanese v Courtaulds*[204] emphasised the same point as follows:

"He [that is, an expert witness] is not entitled to say nor is Counsel entitled to ask him what the specification means, nor does the question become any more admissible if it takes the form of asking him what it means to him as an engineer or as a chemist."

9-194   This was confirmed and expressly applied both at first instance and in the Court of Appeal in *Glaverbel v British Coal*.[205] Similarly, in the context of a 1977 Act patent, Aldous LJ stated in *Dyson v Hoover*[206]:

"The parties agreed that the construction of the claims was for the Court, when properly instructed. As the Court is not required to construe the specification in a vacuum, evidence as to the factual matrix can be helpful as can evidence to explain technical terms. In this case, the parties went further and adduced evidence from two distinguished professors who gave their views as to the meaning that should be attributed to certain words and phrases in the claims. I have not found their evidence helpful as they did not seek to attribute to those words and phrases the meaning required by the Protocol, namely a meaning, between the extremes of literal and patentee's contemplated interpretation, and which provides fair protection and a reasonable degree of certainty. That of course is the task required by section 125 of the 1977 Act. It is not a skill which scientists have."

9-195   In *Qualcomm v Nokia*[207], Floyd J stated:

"It is for the court and not the witnesses to come to conclusions about what the claim means. Subject to the well known exception about technical terms with a special meaning, the construction of a patent is a question of law. So an expert report which seeks to parse the language of the claim, and opine that a particular ordinary English word can only in his opinion have a particular meaning is not admissible, or helpful."

9-196   It follows that disclosure will not generally be ordered relating to how a party has construed expressions in equivalent patents, at least where those expressions are not terms of art.[208] The court is also not obliged to accept the construction placed on the claim by either of the parties.[209]

9-197   In *Scanvaegt v Pelcombe*[210] it was held that a party is entitled to advance a submission on construction even if it is contrary to the evidence, where that

[203] And see *Neilson v Harford* (1841) 1 W.P.C. 331, at 370; *Seed v Higgins* (1860) 30 L.J.Q.B. 314, at 317; *Hill v Evans* (1860) 31 L.J.Ch. 457, at 460; *Kaye v Chubb & Sons Ltd* (1887) 4 R.P.C. 289, at 298; *Gadd & Mason v Mayor, etc., of Manchester* (1892) 9 R.P.C. 516, at 530; *British Dynamite Co v Krebs* (1896) 13 R.P.C. 190, at 192; *Nestlé & Co v Eugene* (1921) 38 R.P.C. 342, at 347; *Canadian General Electric Co v Fada Radio* (1930) 47 R.P.C. 69, at 90; *British Celanese v Courtaulds* (1935) 52 R.P.C. 171, at 196; *Glaverbel S.A. v British Coal Corp (No.2)* [1993] R.P.C. 90.
[204] (1935) 52 R.P.C. 171, 196.
[205] [1993] R.P.C. 90, at 95, per Mummery J; [1995] R.P.C. 255, 268, (CA).
[206] [2002] R.P.C. 22, [13]. See also per Aldous LJ in *American Home Products v Novartis* [2001] R.P.C. 8, [19]; *Hoechst Celanese v B.P. Chemicals* [1999] F.S.R. 319, 325–326.
[207] [2008] EWHC 329, [9].
[208] *Abbott v Medinol* [2010] EWHC 1731 (Pat), [9].
[209] *Consafe v Emtunga* [1999] R.P.C. 154, 163.
[210] [1998] F.S.R. 786, 796.

construction is not dependent on the words under consideration having any technical meaning. Aldous LJ there went on to emphasise Lord Tomlin's statement in the *British Celanese* case quoted above, and to say that inadmissible evidence should not be included in the evidence and might give rise to sanctions in costs.

The technical content of many claims which are litigated, and indeed the nature **9-198** of purposive construction with its emphasis on the skilled reader, has however meant that the boundary between admissible and inadmissible evidence has become unclear and indeed is frequently crossed. The court in more recent times has been less inclined to exclude evidence touching on the meaning of a claim, where supporting technical reasons for preferring a particular construction are given. Thus in *DSM NV's Patent*,[211] Neuberger J said:

> "Of course, the fact that a patent is to be construed through the eyes of a relevantly skilled person or persons does not alter the fact that, subject to one point, the construction of the specification is for the Court alone. However, expert evidence is admissible, indeed it is sometimes necessary, even on the issue of construction, for instance to explain technical terms."

As a purely practical matter, an expert's report may simply be more readable if, **9-199** in addition to setting out relevant admissible reasons, it provides context by identifying any construction which they are intended to support (or indeed rebut).

Admissible evidence relating to construction

While Lord Tomlin in *British Celanese v Courtaulds*[212] stressed that ultimately **9-200** the construction of the patent is a matter for the court alone, he did confirm that evidence was admissible on a number of aspects touching on the question of construction. He said:

> "The area of the territory in which in cases of this kind an expert witness may legitimately move is not doubtful. He is entitled to give evidence as to the state of the art at any given time. He is entitled to explain the meaning of any technical terms used in the art. He is entitled to say whether in his opinion that which is described in the specification on a given hypothesis as to its meaning is capable of being carried into effect by a skilled worker. He is entitled to say what at a given time to him as skilled in the art a given piece of apparatus or a given sentence on any given hypothesis as to its meaning would have taught or suggested to him. He is entitled to say whether in his opinion a particular operation in connexion with the art could be carried out and generally to give any explanation required as to facts of a scientific kind."

This has continued to be the position in relation to patents granted under the 1977 **9-201** Act.[213] In *Unilever v Schöller Lebensmittel*,[214] the defendants applied to strike out a patent action summarily, contending that on no construction could they be held to infringe. Aldous J declined to do so, saying:

> "I believe that there should be relevant evidence as to the background against which this specification should be construed. The claim must, in my view, be interpreted as part of the whole document; it must be given a purposive construction read through the eyes of the skilled man in the art and in the light of what has been done before.
>
> On that basis it is possible that any prima facie view that I have arrived at could in fact be changed by evidence as to what was on the market and what the skilled person would have in his mind when reading this patent."

It also follows from Lord Diplock's speech in *Catnic* and from the "*Improver*" **9-202**

---

[211] [2001] R.P.C. 35, [55].
[212] [1935] 52 R.P.C. 171, 196.
[213] *Scanvaegt v Pelcombe* [1998] F.S.R. 786, 796.
[214] [1988] F.S.R. 596.

questions that evidence of a skilled person can also be received as to the materiality of any variant.

9-203   However, there are still limits to the evidence which may be led. In *Glaverbel v British Coal (No.2)*,[215] Mummery J reviewed the extent to which evidence was admissible. While he confirmed that evidence of the surrounding circumstances, the meaning of technical terms, of what the specification would have taught and whether it could be put into effect were all admissible, he held as inadmissible: (a) direct evidence of the subjective intentions of the inventor, (b) evidence of subsequent conduct showing how the invention was acted upon and understood, and (c) opinions of expert witnesses on the construction of the specification. He did, however, in that case allow part of the disputed evidence to be taken *de bene esse* pending appeal. On appeal, these rulings were upheld.[216]

Evidence relating to technical expressions

9-204   The claims and specification may contain technical expressions which need to be explained by suitable evidence.[217] Evidence from a skilled person as to his or her understanding of the meaning to be given to various words or phrases appearing in the claim is therefore admissible,[218] if it be shown that they have a technical meaning. But once it is shown that any word or phrase in a specification is not a technical one having a special trade meaning, evidence from witnesses as to their meaning becomes inadmissible; their meaning within the context of the patent then becomes a matter for the court alone.[219]

9-205   There is no presumption that technical words used in technical documents should prima facie be given their technical meaning. The court is entitled to hear evidence as to the meaning of technical words and thereafter must decide the meaning from the context in which they are used.[220]

Dictionaries

9-206   Although the exercise of looking up a disputed word in a dictionary may be a useful starting point, it cannot be determinative as the dictionary will give only the acontextual meaning or meanings, and the dispute is always as to what the word means in the context of the patent as a whole. In *3M v Plastus Kreativ AB*[221] Aldous LJ said:

> "The documents to which [counsel] referred us cannot be of any help in construction of a patent. Dictionaries can provide a useful starting point, but cannot be determinative as the task laid down in the 1977 Act requires the court to seek the middle ground between 'literal' and 'liberal'

---

[215] [1993] R.P.C. 90, 93.

[216] [1995] R.P.C. 255, 268.

[217] *Brugger v Medic-Aid* [1996] R.P.C. 635, 642.

[218] Doubts that arose in the early cases are thus now resolved: contrast *British Celanese v Courtaulds* (1935) 52 R.P.C. 171 at 195; *Allmanna Svenska Electriska AB v The Burntisland Shipbuilding Co Ltd* (1951) 69 R.P.C. 63, 76; *American Cyanamid Co v Ethicon Ltd* [1979] R.P.C. 215, 249.

[219] See, e.g. *STEP v Emson* [1993] R.P.C. 513, at 522.

[220] *Hoechst Celanese v B.P. Chemicals* [1999] F.S.R. 319, 326–327, where the disputed word "dimension" had a strict scientific meaning, but a wider ordinary meaning given in the *Oxford English Dictionary*.

[221] [1997] R.P.C. 737, 752; see also per Jacob J at 744 and see *Wesley Jensen v Coopervision*, 2003 R.P.C. 20, at [39(b)], where there was no relevant dictionary meaning.

construction. Thus it is to the specification that the court must turn to ascertain the sense in which a word or phrase is used and the purpose of the use."

Thus in *Hoechst Celanese v B.P. Chemicals*,[222] the dispute was whether the word   **9-207**
"dimension" in its context in the patent meant linear dimension (length) or the property normally measured in the art (volume); the Oxford dictionaries gave both meanings and thus gave no assistance as to which was appropriate.

In *Visx v Nidek*[223] Neuberger J stressed that it was wrong to rely on what   **9-208**
individual words or expressions are capable of meaning, rather than considering what they mean, in light of their textual, technical and factual context. To similar effect, the Supreme Court of Canada has held in *Whirlpool v Camco*[224] that use of a simple dictionary approach is incompatible with the principles of purposive construction, and added that:

"A second difficulty with the appellants' dictionary approach is that it urges the Court to look at the words through the eyes of a grammarian or etymologist rather than through the eyes and with the common knowledge of a worker of ordinary skill in the field to which the patent relates".

Reference to how the relevant word or expression is used in materials forming   **9-209**
part of the relevant common general knowledge may assist in showing how the word or expression would be understood by the reader of the patent. However, care must be taken that these are using the term in the same way as in the specification itself, for as Neuberger J noted in *Rohm & Haas v Collag*[225]:

"The cases to which I have referred emphasise the danger of trying to construe a word or expression acontextually, that is outside the context of the patent in which it is found. There can be even greater danger, I think, if one is seeking to construe the meaning of a word in one context by reference to how it is used in another context."

Technical consequences of a particular construction

In *Qualcomm v Nokia*,[226] after pointing out that evidence seeking to parse the   **9-210**
language of the claim was inadmissible, Floyd J went on to say:

"What is both admissible and helpful expert evidence is something rather different: evidence about the technical inter-relationship between rival claim meanings and the teaching of the specification. The expert is well able to assist the Court about the impact of different assumptions about the correct legal construction of the claim. It may be that it is only on one construction of the claim that general technical statements made in the body of the patent about what the invention achieves will hold good. It is perfectly legitimate for an expert to point that out, and to give a technical explanation of why, if the rival construction is adopted, the claim would extend to embodiments which would not achieve the patent's technical objective."

He added that "None of the above requires the expert to go through the claim and   **9-211**
give his definition (wide or narrow) of every word or phrase in it".

---

[222] [1999] F.S.R. 319.
[223] [1999] F.S.R. 405, 426.
[224] [2001] F.S.R. 46, [52]–[52].
[225] [2001] F.S.R. 28, [88].
[226] [2008] EWHC 329, [10].

Experimental evidence and construction

9-212   In *Merck & Co Inc v Generics (UK) Ltd*,[227] the claimant carried out extensive and costly experiments directed to issues which it perceived to arise on the first two "Protocol" questions. This was strongly criticised by Laddie J, who held that "in the future, no experiments should be conducted going to *Catnic*-type questions of construction unless the court has given informed permission for them in advance". He observed that:

> "One can stand back and think how courts construe other documents, such as contracts, deeds and wills. It is doubtful that in any of them would it be appropriate to have expert evidence of the breadth and complexity of the evidence served here. A patent is a document written by the patentee for publication to the world at large and designed not only to set out clearly what the invention is but to describe the monopoly sought in unambiguous terms. It is supposed to be comprehensible to members of the relevant trade simply on reading. If our law has reached the stage where experiments and extensive expert evidence is admissible to aid in construing patents, then it suggests that something has gone wrong".

Construction contrasted with disclosure (teaching) of a document

9-213   The role of expert witnesses in patent actions was considered in *Technip France SA's Patent*,[228] where in the particular context of obviousness, in a passage quoted more fully at para.12–97. Jacob LJ there stated:

> "But it also is permissible for an expert witness to opine on an 'ultimate question' which is not one of law. I so held in *Routestone v Minories Finance* [1997] BCC 180 and see s.3 of the Civil Evidence Act 1972."

9-214   The qualification "which is not one of law" confirms the position that the expert's opinion on a pure question of construction is not relevant.

9-215   However, the teaching of the specification, once construed, is a pure question of fact, as is what the skilled man would do with that teaching without the exercise of inventive ingenuity.[229] It follows that evidence relating to a document's disclosure is admissible. Thus in *SmithKline Beecham Plc v Apotex Europe*,[230] Jacob LJ referred back to his previous judgment in the *Technip* case, and supplemented it thus:

> "To that I would add this: although it is inevitable that when an expert is asked what he would understand from a prior document's teaching he will give an answer as an individual, that answer is not as such all that helpful. What matters is what the notional skilled man would understand from the document. So it is not so much the expert's personal view but his reasons for that view—these the court can examine against the standard of the notional unimaginative skilled man." The expert may therefore give evidence of "what [the skilled reader] would understand".

Evidence relating to a document's disclosure is admissible

9-216   It also follows that fresh evidence may be adduced in a subsequent action for the purpose of showing that that which before was not regarded as an anticipation is

---

[227] [2004] R.P.C. 31, [34]; see also [40], [54]–[56], and [88].
[228] [2004] R.P.C. 46.
[229] *Inpro's Patent* (2006) R.P.C. 20, [112].
[230] [2005] F.S.R. 23, [52]–[53].

so in fact.[231] In *SmithKline Beecham Plc v Apotex Europe*,[232] there had been a previous unsuccessful action to revoke the patent by a third party, BASF. Apotex brought a subsequent action to revoke, with different evidence. Pumfrey J therefore had to consider the respective roles in a patent action of the judge (whose exclusive role was to determine the law) and a notional jury (whose role is to determine the facts). He said:

"... the construction of the documents themselves is a question of law, and cannot change from case to case. But it has to be remembered that the construction of the documents is not the end of the question. Their disclosure is still a question of fact, upon which evidence is admissible, and accordingly the parties to the present proceedings cannot be circumscribed in their contentions as to the disclosure of the documents except by the evidence—see Lord Westbury in the well-known case of *Hills v Evans* (1861) 31 L.J. Ch (NS) 457 at 460:

'and so the rule is given by Parke, B., in delivering the judgment of the Court of Exchequer in the case ... of *Neilson v Harford*. The language of the learned Judge, which I adopt, is in these words: "The construction of all written instruments belongs to the Court alone, whose duty it is to construe all such instruments as soon as the true meaning of the words in which they are couched, and the surrounding circumstances, if any, have been ascertained as facts by the jury; and it is the duty of the jury to take the construction from the Court either absolutely, if there be no words to be construed as words of art or phrases used in commerce, and so surround circumstances to be ascertained; or conditionally, when those words or circumstances are necessarily referred to in them."

Now, adopting that as the rule in the comparison of two specifications, each of which is filled with terms of art, and with the description of technical processes, the duty of the Court would be confined to this, to give the legal construction of such documents taken independently. But after that duty is discharged, there would remain a most important function to be still performed, which is the comparison of the two instruments when they have received their legal exposition and interpretation; and as it is always a matter of evidence what external thing is indicated and denoted by any description, when the jury have been informed of the meaning of the description contained in each specification, the work of comparing the two, and ascertaining whether the words, as interpreted by the Court, contained in specification A, do or do not denote the same external matter as the words as interpreted and explained by the Court contained in specification B is a matter of fact, and is, I conceive, a matter within the province of the jury, and not within the function of the Court. Granting, therefore, to the full extent, the propriety of the expression of the rule which is here contained, and taking either specification as so interpreted, whether the two specifications that are brought into comparison do or do not indicate the same external matter, must be determined by the jury, and not be determined as matter of law by the Court.'

In a modern context, I take this to indicate that the narrow question of the grammatical and legal meaning of the words aside, that which they actually describe is, as a thing, a question of fact. My conclusion is, therefore, that while I must follow the judgment of the Court of Appeal in the BASF case both as to the meaning of the patent in suit and as to the prior art, in particular '407, I must have regard to the evidence adduced in this case as to what the description actually conveys to the skilled man."

On appeal,[233] this passage was not criticised, and indeed was supported by Jacob **9-217** LJ's statement at [4] that:

---

[231] *Shaw v Day* (1894) 11 R.P.C. 185, 189; *Edison v Holland* (1889) 6 R.P.C. 243, 277; *Flour Oxidizing Co Ltd v Carr & Co Ltd* (1908) 25 R.P.C. 428, 448; *Higginson and Arundel v Pyman* (1926) 43 R.P.C. 291, 300.

[232] [2004] F.S.R. 26, [12].

[233] [2005] F.S.R. 23, [4] and [51]–[52]; see para.9–215.

"It is not suggested that Pumfrey J in this action was, or this court is, any way bound by the previous decision so far as it turned on evidence."

and by the passage from Jacob LJ's judgment at [53], already quoted above.

The effect of previous findings of construction of a patent

9-218   In *Novartis v Dexcel-Pharma*,[234] the Court again had to consider the question of the extent to which a previous decision on construction of a patent was binding on a lower court. In an interim decision, Floyd J reviewed the authorities including *SKB v Apotex* discussed in the previous paragraph above, and held:

> "The problem with treating questions of construction as pure questions of law is that they frequently are not. Although direct evidence as to the meaning of non-technical terms is inadmissible, the court does not reach its conclusion as to the meaning of the claim in a factual vacuum. Evidence as to the common general knowledge can frequently have an important bearing, as part of the factual matrix against which construction is decided, as can factual evidence about the consequences of the teaching of passages in the specification. ... Also, as *SKB v Apotex* shows, the meaning of a claim feature may be dependent on external evidence about what it conveys which may change from case to case.
>
>   Thus while a subsequent court is bound on questions of law, care is necessary to identify the precise point of law to be derived from the previous court's decision. ... if the evidence on which the legal conclusion is founded is different in a relevant way, one may ask legitimately, why should subsequent litigants be bound by the evidence adduced in a previous action? The point of law to be decided once the evidence is different is itself different. I think this comes within what Jacob LJ had in mind in *SKB v Apotex* when he said that the subsequent court is not bound by the previous court's decision 'so far as it turned on evidence'".

9-219   At the subsequent trial of the action,[235] the defendant did not contend that an earlier decision on construction of the patent was binding, but merely that the earlier reasoning was persuasive, and so the point of law was not further considered.

Scientific adviser

9-220   The Court has power to appoint a scientific adviser, given by s.70(3) of the Senior Courts Act 1981. Relevant provision is made in CPR 35.15 and under para.4.10 of the Practice Direction under CPR Pt 63. The role of such an adviser was considered by the Court of Appeal in *Halliburton v Smith (No.2)*,[236] in which it held that such role is not limited to understanding technical evidence, but also providing assistance where needed on matters of fact in dispute between the parties. This latter role was subject to an overriding requirement of fariness, which could be met by disclosure and a "right of response sufficient to comply with the requirements of natural justice". However, the scientific adviser is not the decision maker, and it is the task of the court and not the adviser to decide the case.[237]

7.   OTHER GENERAL PRINCIPLES OF CONSTRUCTION

9-221   Purposive construction is plainly an essential means for determining the true scope of the claims of a patent, but it is not the whole story, and has to be applied as one tool amongst many when a patent and its claims are being construed. All

---

234   [2008] F.S.R. 31, [15]–[23].

235   [2009] EWHC 336 (Pat), [54].

236   [2007] R.P.C. 17.

237   See also *Qualcomm v Nokia*, [2008] EWHC 329 (Pat), at [27].

canons of construction are in the end guides, and an over-rigid application of any of them is not appropriate.[238]

The extent to which approaches from other fields of jurisprudence are ap-   **9-222** plicable to the construction of patents has attracted a range of judicial comment. It has been said that the principles that the courts have developed for the interpretation of patents are, in many respects, similar to the principles that they have developed for the interpretation of contracts (although, of course, a patent is a unilateral expression of intention).[239] In *Pharmacia v Merck*[240] Arden LJ discussed the similarities and differences between patent construction and the interpretation of contracts and statutes. In *SmithKline Beecham Plc's (Paroxetine Anhydrate) patent*,[241] Sedley LJ took a more extreme position and stated that because the law has historically been suspicious of monopolies for well-known reasons of public policy, there is no useful analogy between a patent and a deed or a written contract—the latter two will have been drafted for a purpose which, assuming it not to be illegal or contrary to public policy, the law will do what it properly can to uphold. By contrast, he pointed out, there was no rule of benevolent construction by which courts should strive to uphold a patent.

A useful review of some of the more general applicable principles is to be found   **9-223** in the judgment of Staughton LJ in *Glaverbel S.A. v British Coal*,[242] where he set them forth in a series of propositions as follows:

> "(1)   The interpretation of a patent, as of any other written document, is a question of law. That does not mean that the answer to it will necessarily be found in our law books. It means that it is for the judge rather than a jury to decide, and that evidence of what the patent means is not admissible. In particular, evidence of the patentee as to what he intended it to mean should not beadmitted, nor indirect evidence which is said to point to his intention. Compare the rule that the parties to a deed or contract cannot give evidence of what they intend it to mean. A patent is construed objectively, through the eyes of a skilled addressee.
>
> (2)   The court may, and indeed should, have regard to the surrounding circumstances as they existed at the date of the publication of the specification (or perhaps the priority date). Those circumstances, sometimes described as 'the matrix' in a commercial context, would include common general knowledge. I imagine that they would not include circumstances known only to the patentee or a limited class of persons, since every skilled addressee should be able to know what the patent means and therefore have equal access to material available for interpretation.
>
> (3)   The court should admit evidence of the meaning of technical terms. It may be that expert evidence can go somewhat further than that in aid of interpretation; but I need not decide that in the present case.
>
> (4)   The whole document must be read together, the body of the specification with the claims. But if a claim is expressed in clear language, the monopoly sought by the patentee cannot be extended or cut down by reference to the rest of the specification.
>
> (5)   The court must adopt:
>
> 'a purposive construction rather than a purely literal one derived from applying to it the kind of meticulous verbal analysis in which lawyers are too often tempted by their training to indulge.'
>
> *Catnic Components Ltd v Hill & Smith Ltd* [1982] R.P.C. 183 by Lord Diplock at page 243. This has become a popular theme in recent times, for the interpretation of contracts and statutes. But what does it mean? There is a clear contrast with meticulous verbal analysis, or the 'narrowly semantic approach' (also described by Lord Diplock, in *Fothergill v Monarch Airlines*

---

[238] *Brugger v Medic-Aid* [1996] R.P.C. 635, 642.

[239] Per Lewison J in *Ultraframe (UK) Ltd v Eurocell Building Plastics Ltd* [2005] R.P.C. 7, [68].

[240] [2002] R.P.C. 41, [158]–[161].

[241] [2003] R.P.C. 49, [103]; also known as *BASF A.G. v SmithKline Beecham Plc* [2003] EWCA Civ 872.

[242] [1995] R.P.C. 255, 268–270.

Ltd [1981] A.C. 251 at 280). If possible, the meaning of the document must be moulded to conform with the purpose of its author or authors—the purpose being judged from the document as a whole and the surrounding circumstances. To put it another way, there is a conflict with the purpose if a judge is disposed to say to himself—'he cannot have meant that'. In the *Catnic* case itself, Lord Diplock said (at page 244):

'No plausible reason has been advanced why any rational patentee should want to place so narrow a limitation on his invention. On the contrary, to do so would render his monopoly for practical purposes worthless ...'

That is in my view an example of the purposive method of construction. It is at least allied to, and perhaps an example of, what Lord Reid said in *L. Schuler A.G. v Wickman Machine Tool Sales Ltd* [1974] A.C. 235 at 251:

'The fact that a particular construction leads to a very unreasonable result must be a relevant consideration. The more unreasonable the result the more unlikely it is that the parties can have intended it, and if they do intend it the more necessary it is that they should make their intention abundantly clear.'

(6) Subsequent conduct is not available as an aid to interpretation of a written document. That too was established by the *Schuler* case, reaffirming an earlier decision of the House of Lords.

(7) A claim must not be construed with an eye on prior material, in order to avoid its effect: *Molins v Industrial Machinery Co Ltd* (1938) 55 R.P.C. 31 at 39."

9-224   *Glaverbel* itself was a decision on a patent granted under the 1949 Act, although the relevant principles, and in particular the "purposive" approach to construction, have as discussed above not changed.

Subsequent conduct of the patentee

9-225   In interpreting the patent, the court is not concerned with what the patentee meant by the words he used, but what those to whom the specification is addressed would have understood him to mean.[243] Evidence of the subsequent conduct of the patentee, said to demonstrate how he understood his claim or intended it to be understood, is not admissible.[244] A contention that the patent must have been intended to cover the patentee's own product (subsequently introduced onto the market, and therefore not novelty destroying) is also irrelevant.[245] The rationale is that the meaning of a document cannot as a matter of construction have been altered or ascertained by evidence of how the parties subsequently acted upon it or interpreted it.[246] Such matters may in some circumstances be relevant to estoppel or other equitable remedies, but not to determining the meaning of the document as it stands.

9-226   It follows that no assistance is provided in construing the claim by the mere fact that the patentee has previously asserted a wide construction of his claim (but in subsequent proceedings contends for a narrow one in order to save its validity), nor (subject to the comments below relating to prosecution history) by the fact that he has subsequently asserted a narrow construction (but in subsequent proceedings asserts a wide one, in order to catch an alleged infringement). While the House of Lords understandably expressed astonishment in *BTH v Charlesworth*[247] that the patentee should have maintained an action on one patent up to the House of Lords,

---

[243] *Kirin-Amgen v Hoechst Marion Roussel* [2005] R.P.C. 9, [32]. See also *Osram v Pope* [1917] 34 R.P.C. 369, at 391.

[244] *Glaverbel v British Coal (No.2)* [1993] R.P.C. 90, per Mummery J.

[245] *M-Systems v Trek 2000*, [2008] R.P.C. 18, [85]–[87].

[246] *Glaverbel v British Coal (No.2)* [1993] R.P.C. 90, citing *Schuler A.G. v Wickman Machine Tool Sales* [1974] A.C. 235.

[247] (1925) 42 R.P.C. 180, see in particular 203–204.

and then in subsequent litigation on another patent maintained before them that the earlier patent was not workable, the Court of Appeal declined in *Glaverbel (No.4)*[248] to rely on that case as establishing any principle that a patentee was not permitted to "blow hot and cold".

For similar reasons, caution may be required when considering products of the patentee said to embody the invention of the patent in suit.[249]   **9-227**

Patentee's internal documentation relating to construction

The patentee's internal documentation showing how he interpreted his claim is similarly irrelevant. In *Qualcomm v Nokia*[250] Floyd J explained: **9-228**

"The addressee of the specification is the person skilled in the art, equipped with the common general knowledge, no more and no less. The addressee does not have access to documents which are not part of the common general knowledge. This may seem trite, but there was a sustained attempt by Nokia in cross examination to make use of Qualcomm's confidential internal documents (disclosed as relevant to other issues) on the issue of construction. This is wrong, and counterproductive. It is easy to explain why this is so. It is wrong because, if the effect of such an internal document were to force an interpretation different from that which would be arrived at without it, the patent would mean different things to different people. In particular, it would mean different things in the course of the grant procedure (where there is no disclosure) and in litigation (at least when there is chance disclosure on other issues). It is wrong because the process of construction is designed to elicit objectively what the patentee's intention is, not to inquire into his subjective intention. It is counterproductive because (like file wrappers) it leads to lengthy and irrelevant satellite arguments as to the meaning and effect of other documents, which not everybody has access to or can be bothered to read.

No doubt the purpose of deploying such documents is that it is thought that the court, once it has seen what the subjective intention of the patentee was, will be reluctant to hold that the skilled person would have understood that he meant something different. For my part I can say that there is no such reluctance. If anything, it alerts the tribunal to the fact that, without the document, there may be something to be said for the alternative construction. The same goes for file wrappers, which I noticed had been prepared into court bundles, but were not deployed."

Use of prosecution history as an aid to construction

The US doctrine of "file wrapper estoppel", under which statements made by or on behalf of the patentee during the course of prosecution may be taken as binding on issues of construction, does not exist as such under English law. However, in *Furr v Truline*[251] Falconer J accepted a submission that statements made by the patentee in the Patent Office amounted to an admission against interest, so that it was not open to them to contend for a wider construction thereafter. (It should also be noted that in that case it was the patentee itself which originally put the documents in evidence, a matter regarded by Falconer J as significant.)   **9-229**

In *Bristol Myers Squibb v Baker Norton*,[252] Jacob J made a number of observations on the use of the prosecution history as an aid to construction, as follows: **9-230**

"First, whether that history can, and if so how, be used as an aid to construction would not be governed by national rules of construction. Claim construction is no longer a matter for national law but is governed by Article 69 and the Protocol. Thus, by way of example, specific English law no-

---

[248] [1995] R.P.C. 255, 270.
[249] See *Ultraframe v Eurocell Building Plastics* [2005] R.P.C. 36, [76] (but note that Neuberger LJ's judgment was a dissenting one on the facts); *M-Systems v Trek* [2008] R.P.C. 18, [87].
[250] [2008] EWHC 329, [5]–[6].
[251] [1985] F.S.R. 553, 563–564.
[252] [1999] R.P.C. 253, 274.

tions of estoppel, cannot, as such, be used to construe the claim. Preventing him from asserting such a wide construction may be different—a specific English law defence. Second, there is an obvious important practical difference between merely referring to the specification as originally filed as an aid to construction and referring to detailed matter (e.g. contentions in correspondence or evidence) as contained in the EPO file. The specification as filed is a published document (the 'A' specification) and is referred to in the specification as granted. The intermediate processing correspondence with the examiner is different in volume and character, not least because it is not normally translated. Thirdly, there is another obvious difference between using the prosecution history to *widen* the claim and using that history to *narrow* it. It would be unfair on the public if material they would not normally look at could serve as a basis for supporting a wide construction of the claim. But there is not the same sort of unfairness if a patentee having contended for a narrow construction of his claim during prosecution is held to that construction later (cf. *Furr v Truline (Building Products) Ltd* [1985] F.S.R. 553, an English case). Fourthly, there is a difference between merely resolving a puzzle in the specification (though not the claim) by reference to the specification as filed and using the specification as filed as an aid to construction of the claim itself. I used the former in relation to an example in the patent in *Milliken Denmark AS v Walk Off Mats Ltd* [1996] F.S.R. 292 at 299. All these are matters to be considered, perhaps by the Enlarged Board of Appeal or, if current proposals were to proceed, by a European Patent Court. Fortunately I do not have to consider them here."

9-231   However, in a case in which the patent as granted posed a puzzle as to what its examples were describing and teaching—*Milliken Denmark A/S v Walk Off Mats*[253]—Jacob J considered that the skilled reader would go back to the specification as filed or the priority document, which were cross-referred in the granted patent.

9-232   Similarly, in *Rohm & Haas v Collag*, resolution of a dispute over the scope of the word "surfactant" was rendered difficult by the lack of explanation as to its purpose in the specification. The Court of Appeal observed[254]:

"A purposive construction is however possible only if the purpose of the patentee can be ascertained in an objective way, by studying the specification (and any other admissible material). The specification of the patent in suit is open to criticism not only for a lack of precision in the use of words. It also fails to make clear the main thrust of its inventive purpose."

9-233   There was however some explanation in a letter to the EPO from the patentee which contained statements material to the construction issue. The Court of Appeal considered that persuasive guidance could be derived from the following passage in the decision of the Dutch Supreme Court in *Ciba-Geigy v Oté Optics*[255]:

"Article 69, paragraph 1 of the EPC as interpreted in accordance with the Protocol relating thereto does indeed purport (among other things) to ensure reasonable certainty for third parties, but it does not follow that the information from the granting file that is available to third parties may never be used in support of the interpretation given by the patentee to his patent. The requirement of reasonable certainty for third parties does, however, call for restraint in using arguments derived from the granting file in favour of the patentee. Consequently, a court will only be justified in using clarifying information from the public part of the granting file, when it holds that even after the average person skilled in the art has considered the description and the drawings, it is still open to question how the contents of the claims must be interpreted."

The Court of Appeal itself then proceeded to hold[256]:

"The letter to the European Patent office did not have the same status as published prior art identified in a specification, which is readily admissible. But it did contain objective information about and commentary on experiments which were conducted in response to official observations, and it could

---

[253] [1996] F.S.R. 292, 299.
[254] [2002] F.S.R. 28, [25].
[255] Decision of 13 January 1995.
[256] [2002] F.S.R. 28, [42].

be of assistance in resolving some puzzling features of the specification. Although the prosecution process may sometimes superficially resemble a process of negotiation between the applicant and its advisers and the officials who scrutinise the file, it is not the sort of commercial negotiation which is still rigidly excluded in the construction of a written contract. ... Had it been necessary for the judge to take account of the letter in order to resolve the issue of construction, I consider that he would have been entitled to do so."

It is therefore the case that there is no absolute prohibition on the use of the prosecution file, though there are many reasons not to encourage such a reference. Lord Hoffmann noted in *Kirin-Amgen*[257] that: **9-234**

"The courts of the United Kingdom, the Netherlands and Germany certainly discourage, if they do not actually prohibit, use of the patent office file in aid of construction. There are good reasons: the meaning of the patent should not change according to whether or not the person skilled in the art has access to the file and in any case life is too short for the limited assistance which it can provide."

In *Monsanto v Cargill*[258] the patent had been previously considered, in earlier proceedings between the parties, by the EPO TBA, which had arrived at a construction of a phrase in the specification. Pumfrey J held that it was nonetheless open for the parties to argue for a different construction (because art.69 EPC and its Protocol gives claim construction "something of an autonomous aspect") but went on to hold that although reference to the EPO file is discouraged: **9-235**

"... here we are considering an interpretation arrived at in contested proceedings by a Board of Appeals of the EPO which should be treated with respect. I think one needs a good reason to depart from an interpretation placed on a claim by a TBA in contested proceedings and which forms part of one of the grounds of decision".

In *Wesley Jessen v Coopervision*,[259] the court having arrived at a construction of the relevant integer ("dots"), noted that its conclusion was "bolstered" by the unusual circumstance that the patentee had been required in prosecution to narrow the claim (from "patterns"), thus shedding light on the underlying purpose of the patentee's choice of words. Although in *Telsonic A.G.'s Patent*,[260] Laddie J took the opposite view, holding that: **9-236**

"In the absence of binding authority or legislation, I would be reluctant to accept that this doctrine has any part to play in construing a patent and its claims. Patents and their claims are meant to be statement made by the patentee to the relevant public. Their meaning and effect should be discernible from the face of the document. However, for reasons set out below, I do not think it necessary to resolve this issue in this case. The meaning of the claim appears to me to be clear enough without resort to this material. In the result I have not looked at any of the prosecution history of the patent. I will treat the claims as if they had always been in their current form. I have paid no attention to what Mr Howe says is the reason for the amendments made. I have not read any of the documents relating to this issue".

In *Actavis v Eli Lilly*[261] Arnold J reviewed the case law set out above, including the judgment in *Rohm & Haas*,[262] commenting in respect of it that: **9-237**

"In my judgment this reasoning is persuasive, and it is supported by the subsequent judgment of the Court of Appeal in *Virgin v Premium*. I accept that, for the reasons explained by Jacob J in *Bristol-Myers Squibb* and Lord Hoffmann in *Kirin-Amgen*, courts should be cautious before relying upon

[257] *Kirin-Amgen v Hoechst Marion Roussel* [2005] R.P.C. 9, [35].
[258] [2008] F.S.R. 7, [82].
[259] [2003] R.P.C. 20, [87]–[88].
[260] [2004] R.P.C. 38, [30].
[261] [2014] EWHC 1511 (Pat); [2015] R.P.C. 6, [108]–[110].
[262] [2002] F.S.R. 28.

prosecution history as an aid to construction. In the real world, however, anyone who is interested in ascertaining the scope of a patent and who is professionally advised will obtain a copy of the prosecution file (most, if not all, of which is generally open to public inspection) and will consider it to see if it sheds light on the matter. In some cases, perhaps not very many, the prosecution history is short, simple and shows clearly why the claims are expressed in the manner in which they are to be found in the granted patent and not in some broader manner. In such a situation, there is no good reason why the court should shut its eyes to the story told by the prosecution file. On the contrary, consideration of the prosecution file may assist in ensuring that patentees do not abuse the system by accepting narrow claims during prosecution and then arguing for a broad construction of those claims for the purpose of infringement. For the reasons discussed below, I consider that the present case provides a good illustration of this."

9-238   Arnold J went on[263] to reject an argument that if the prosecution history was useful as an aid to construction at all, this was only if the claims had been limited during prosecution to avoid objections of novelty or obviousness over prior art, and not where the claims had been limited to avoid objections of lack of support/ added matter or clarity—an argument advanced on the basis that an amendment made in the latter case could not shed light on the meaning which the patentee intended because of the distinction between the disclosure of a specification and the scope of a claim.

9-239   This decision was later considered in the Court of Appeal by Floyd LJ (with whom Kitchen LJ and Longmore LJ agreed). After noting at [60] that it was common ground between the parties that the prosecution history was "not inadmissible" as a guide to construction and that this was said to be consistent with what Lord Hoffmann had stated on the topic in *Kirin-Amgen* at [35] supra, Floyd LJ identified that in the *Rohm & Hass* case the material in question was expressly drawn to the attention of the reader by a note in the specification itself. He also noted the summary of problems associated with taking such material into account in *Bristol-Myers Squibb Co v Baker Norton Inc*[264] but commented that a rule which merely discourages reference to material, as opposed to treating it as inadmissible, has obvious practical disadvantages, in that in the absence of an exclusionary rule, the cost and expense associated with its deployment will almost invariably be incurred. In reviewing Arnold J's reasoning as set out above he said:

> "58.   The difficulty I feel with endorsing this reasoning is as follows. Firstly it assumes that the skilled reader will always read the prosecution history. I do not see why this should be so, given the limited value which, at least before the judgment in this case, it was generally recognised to have. Secondly, and more importantly, it suggests that the story told by the prosecution history of how the claims came to be drafted as they were will assist the court in preventing abuse of the system. To my mind this will be a very rare case indeed. Unless the acceptance of a restriction in a claim is to operate as some kind of estoppel against the patentee arguing for wider claims (a proposition for which neither side contended and which Jacob J rejected, at least on the basis of domestic estoppel, in *Bristol Myers*), there will always remain an issue as to whether the applicant needed to accept the restriction notwithstanding that he did so. In those circumstances, the light which the prosecution history sheds on the ultimate question of construction is likely to be extremely limited.
>
> 59.   I therefore do not regard it as useful to go to the prosecution history in order to discover that the patentee accepted a restriction to his claim against an objection of lack of support in the specification. It is always open to a party attacking the patent to argue that the claims as sought to be construed by the patentee lack support in the specification: see for example *American Home Products v Novartis* [2001] R.P.C. 8 at [31]. What purpose does it serve to illustrate this point by showing that the patentee was faced with an official objection to that effect and amended his claims in the light of it? It is still open to the patentee to say that he need not have

---

[263]   At [112].
[264]   [1999] R.P.C. 253, 274–275, addressed at para.9-230.

done so, and the apparent concession he made in prosecution was wrongly made. If it is not open to the patentee so to contend, then the prosecution history is indeed creating a form of estoppel.

60. In any event, patent offices are usually concerned with patentability, not scope of protection. If an applicant were to conclude every letter by saying that he did not accept that by accepting this or that limitation he was necessarily restricting the scope of protection, no inference could be drawn from his conduct in accepting it. I would be reluctant to put the patent attorneys' profession to this unnecessary trouble."

In *Idenix v Gilead*[265] Arnold J himself commented on his judgment in *Actavis v Lilly*, noting that in that case he had held that, in principle, a limitation made to a claim to avoid an objection of lack of clarity could be relied on as an aid to construction. He explained that although he adhered to that view, with the benefit of the arguments in the case now before him, he would add that such an amendment is less likely to be a useful aid to construction than a limitation to avoid an objection of lack of support. On the facts before him in *Idenix*, the amendment made by the patentee before the EPO was in order to meet the examiner's objection that a particular expression ("leaving group") lacked clarity. The fact of the deletion of the unclear term did not, in the absence of discussion of the meaning of the term now in issue which remained in the claim ("phosphate"), shed any light on the meaning which the skilled team would understand the patentees to be conveying by the use of that term.

9-240

The position has thus been reached in England and Wales that whilst reference to the prosecution history is "not inadmissible", it is discouraged and is likely to be considered of very limited assistance, if any.

9-241

In *Free World Trust v Électro Santé*,[266] the Supreme Court of Canada took a stricter view and rejected admissibility of prosecution history as an aid to construction, holding:

9-242

"References to the intention of the inventor in *Catnic* ... are said to leave the door ajar to the possibility of reconsideration. In my view, those references to the inventor's intention refer to an objective manifestation of that intent in the patent claims, as interpreted by the person skilled in the art, and do not contemplate extrinsic evidence such as statements or admissions made in the course of patent prosecution. To allow such extrinsic evidence for the purpose of defining the monopoly would undermine the public notice function of the claims, and increase uncertainty as well as fuelling the already overheated engines of patent litigation. The current emphasis on purposive construction, which keeps the focus on the language of the claims, seems also to be inconsistent with opening the pandora's box of file wrapper estoppel. If significant representations are made to the Patent Office touching the scope of the claims, the Patent Office should insist where necessary on an amendment to the claims to reflect the representation."

No rule of benevolent construction

Prior to the 1977 Act, the form of the patent provided "that these our letters patent shall be construed in the most beneficial sense for the advantage of the patentee", but these words applied to the patent grant itself and had no relation to the words of the specification.

9-243

The modern practice is that the court does not resolve doubt in favour of the patentee, as this is not part of the purposive approach to construction.[267] To apply

9-244

[265] *Idenix Pharmaceuticals, Inc v Gilead Sciences* [2014] EWHC 3916, [318].
[266] [2001] F.S.R. 45, [65]–[66].
[267] *Assidoman Multipack v Mead* [1995] R.P.C. 321, 332.

such a principle would be in conflict with the Protocol insofar as it requires there to be certainty for third parties.[268]

9-245   In *Merck & Co Inc v Generics (UK) Ltd*,[269] Laddie J rejected a submission that the requirement for fairness means that the court should give as much protection as it feels is justified having regard to the inventive contribution made by the patentee even if that includes embodiments which the patentee intended to exclude, for example because he misunderstood how their own invention works—"The courts are not a branch of the social services". There is no canon of construction which would justify the courts in granting a patentee more protection than that which, objectively assessed, they indicated they wanted, and to do so could prove to be unfair to the patentee, by broadening their monopoly so as cover the prior art, thus invalidating it and leaving them with no protection at all. The judge went on to hold as follows:

> "It seems to me that what the Protocol requires is that the monopoly should cover all embodiments, whether explicitly mentioned in the claims or not, which the notional skilled reader would conclude, with reasonable confidence, the inventor wanted to cover. Where it is clear that the patentee did not intend to obtain protection for particular variants, it is not open to the court to extend the monopoly to cover them. Similarly, if a notional skilled addressee cannot conclude with reasonable confidence that the inventor wanted to obtain protection for a particular embodiment, it must follow that the patent conveys the message that the patentee might well have intended to exclude that embodiment. To give protection in such circumstances would run the risk of going against the intention of the patentee, thereby being unfair to him, and would not be giving third parties a reasonable degree of certainty as required by the Protocol.
>
> Determining whether a skilled reader would conclude with reasonable confidence that a particular embodiment was one the patentee wanted to cover involves assessing all the facts of the case. The wording of the claims is the most important one, but is not necessarily determinative. Matters such as the way the inventor describes his inventive contribution and his explanation, if any, of how the invention achieves its claimed results are matters to be taken into account. The factors, and how they interrelate to each other, will vary from case to case."

9-246   In *SmithKline Beecham Plc's (Paroxetine Anhydrate) patent*,[270] a submission that any difficulty of construction should be resolved in favour of the patentee was firmly rejected as tending to reward opaque drafting. Sedley LJ reviewed the 19th century authorities (which need not be revisited here) and noted that with one exception they would have endorsed the modern practice. (He also noted that it was equally wrong to reward a defendant who sought out opacity where on a fair-minded reading there was none.)

9-247   In *Scanvaegt v Pelcombe*[271] the Court of Appeal also doubted a submission to the opposite effect, that a patent should be construed *contra proferentem*, strictly against the patentee. While it was not necessary to decide the point, it suggested that such an approach would also contravene the Protocol.

Legal consequences of the construction adopted

9-248   The issue sometimes arises as to whether the balance to be achieved as required by the Protocol to art.69 is to be answered by reference to purely technical issues arising out of the specification, or whether the legal consequence of strict compliance or otherwise may also be taken into account in achieving the balance required.

---

[268] See *Wesley Jessen v CooperVision* [2003] R.P.C. 20, at [39(c)].

[269] [2004] R.P.C. 31, [48]–[49].

[270] [2003] R.P.C. 49, [103]; also known as *BASF A.G. v SmithKline Beecham Plc* [2003] EWCA (Civ) 872.

[271] [1998] F.S.R. 786, 796.

In *Optical Coating Laboratory v Pilkington*[272] Balcombe LJ said: **9-249**

"It is in answering this third [Protocol] question that the matter of obviousness becomes relevant. If one asks the question: why should the patentee have intended that the variant of placing a stack of reflective layers on an absorbing substrate should not be within the ambit of the invention claimed? Then the answer may well be: because such a solution to the problem posed was then obvious to a person skilled in the art. Or as Lord Diplock said in Catnic (supra) at page 244:

'No plausible reason has been advanced why any rational patentee should want to place so narrow a limitation on his invention.'

A plausible reason in the present case is that to make the invention as wide as is now claimed would have been to risk rendering the whole patent void for obviousness ...

Thus in our judgment there was a perfectly good reason why OCLI should have chosen not to include this variant in claim 1 of the specification."

The difficulty in applying this consideration in every case, rather than in the   **9-250**
particular circumstances of *Optical Coatings*, is that frequently the court is not
informed as to all of the prior art of which the patentee was aware in framing his
claim. A patentee is under no obligation to disclose to the Patent Office any prior
art of which he is aware.[273] It must also be borne in mind, as stated by Staughton
LJ in *Glaverbel v British Coal*,[274] that "a claim must not be construed with an eye
on prior material, in order to avoid its effect".

It is therefore submitted that the correct general approach is that stated by Jacob   **9-251**
J. in *Beloit v Valmet (No.2)*,[275] where he said the following:

"I believe Article 69 of the EPC does not legitimately allow courts to construe claims using the prior art either to widen them or narrow them. There is normally no reason to suppose the patentee when he set the limits of his monopoly knew of a particular piece of prior art which is therefore irrelevant in deciding what those limits are. Of course the position is different if the prior art is specifically acknowledged in the patent. The purposive construction would lead to a construction of a claim which did not cover that acknowledged prior art: it can hardly have been the inventor's purpose to cover that which he expressly recognises was old."

In *Ultraframe v Eurocell Building Products*[276] Lewison J at first instance referred   **9-252**
to the above passage from *Beloit* and added:

"... much depends on the way in which the prior art is acknowledged. A mere reference to a prior patent does not necessarily require the addressee of the patent to dig it out and study it in detail. On the other hand if the specification identifies some particular feature of the prior patent as disclosing a problem which the inventor claims to have overcome, it may be of considerable relevance in interpreting the width of the claim. It is not that the prior patent is irrelevant in interpreting the patent; it is a question of what to do with it."

Thus it is a "valuable canon of construction", though not a rigid rule, to avoid if   **9-253**
possible a construction of the claim which reads on to prior art referred to in the
patent.[277]

The overall principle is therefore that a construction which leads to a foolish   **9-254**

---

272 [1995] R.P.C. 145, 158.
273 See *Chiron v Organon Teknika (No.7)* [1994] F.S.R. 458, 468.
274 [1995] R.P.C. 255, 270.
275 [1995] R.P.C. 705, 720.
276 [2005] R.P.C. 7, [73]. In the same case in the Court of Appeal, [2005] R.P.C. 36, at [47], it was held "improbable" that the claim would be intended to cover a feature differentiated in prior art specifically acknowledged in the patent.
277 *Actavis v Janssen* [2008] F.S.R. 35, [56].

result should if possible, be rejected as being without the intention of the patentee,[278] for a construction which does not lead to an absurd result is to be preferred. However, a finding of invalidity cannot of itself be regarded as an absurd result, unless the relevant piece of prior art is specifically acknowledged and sought to be distinguished in the patent, or unless the invention would to the knowledge of the ordinary reader then be obvious simply in the light of the common general knowledge.

9-255   In *Adaptive Spectrum v British Telecommunications Ltd*[279] Floyd LJ referred to the above passage (at [108]–[111], noting that it follows the discussion of the *Optical Coating* case and pointed out that that case was decided at a time when the courts decided construction by making a distinction between the strict, literal or acontextual meaning of the language and its purposive meaning, as opposed to adopting the unitary approach propounded in *Kirin-Amgen*. One aspect of the old approach, he said, was that it invited speculation as to whether there was a possible reason why the patentee might have wanted to restrict itself to the strict, literal meaning. Accordingly, the proposition arrived at in *Optical Coating*, namely that a good reason for confining the meaning of the claims to the literal construction was that, if the wider construction was adopted, the patent would be rendered obvious in the light of the prior art, is not, he pointed out, a universal one. Floyd LJ then referred to the passages set out above in *Beloit* and *Ultraframe* before concluding:

"As with any canon of construction, one must be wary of treating it as a rigid rule. Moreover as soon as one departs from documents specifically acknowledged in the specification, the skilled reader has no basis for assuming that the patentee was aware of the document in question. Still further, where the objection is one of obviousness rather than lack of novelty, a value judgment is involved on which widely differing views are possible. It is true that if the document is said to form part of the common general knowledge, it might be said to be more likely that the patentee is aware of it. But a patentee may have been isolated from the common general knowledge, or may, despite the later finding of obviousness, have genuinely believed that he had made an invention over it. As will be seen below, the argument of invalidity over Kerpez involved, amongst other things, resolving a dispute between experts as to the feasibility of identifying noise sources. I am not persuaded therefore that it would be right to give weight to this factor in the present case."[280]

9-256   Similarly, it is incorrect to have an eye on the issue of infringement when applying this test. As Jacob J warned in *3M v Plastus Kreativ*[281]:

"Taken out of its original context there is always a danger in the nutshell question: there never is a plausible reason why the patentee (assuming his claim is valid) would want to exclude a competitor's product. That does not mean his claim covers it."

Ambiguous patent

9-257   In the absence of ambiguity as a ground of revocation for new Act patents, questions of construction may sometimes prove difficult, as the court no longer has the option of revoking the claims concerned[282] but has to grapple with them for better or worse. It must seek to give them a construction in accordance with the require-

---

[278] See also, e.g. *3M v Rennicks (UK) Ltd* [1992] R.P.C. 331, at 342–343.
[279] [2014] EWHC Civ 1462, [108] –[111].
[280] [2014] EWHC Civ 1462, [111]. This question was re-considered by Henry Carr J in *Stretchline Intellectual Properties v H&M Hennes & Mauritz* [2015] EWHC 3298 (Pat), [21] after citing the passage from *Terrell on the Law of Patents* and the judgment of Floyd J in *Adaptive Spectrum*.
[281] [1997] R.P.C. 737, 747.
[282] So that the trenchant warning given by Lord Loreburn to draftsmen in *Natural Colour Kinematograph* [1915] R.P.C. 256, at 266 no longer applies.

ment of the Protocol to art.69, combining fair protection with reasonable certainty, and approaching the specification as a practical document.

Usually the purposive approach will assist in determining the meaning from the way in which the invention is described in the specification, but sometime this is not possible. Pumfrey J observed in *Halliburton v Smith*[283]: **9-258**

> "Second, there may be obscurities and difficulties in a claim that cannot be resolved by an appeal to context. It is very rare that some sensible meaning cannot be attributed to the words used in a patent claim, but where a claim permits alternative interpretations it is possible to be left with no alternative but to take the most straightforward."

In *Raychem's Patents*,[284] the claim was of exceptional complexity; it was objected that it was an exercise in "parameteritis" and that the obscurity was calculated to make the claim dificult to work through and to prove invalidity. Laddie J pointed out that it was open to a patentee to use what language they like to define their invention, but that the court has to guard against being impressed by the form and language of the claims rather than the substance of the patentee's alleged technical contribution, and where claims were prolix and opaque it should break free of the actual language and consider what they really meant. These dicta were not criticised in the Court of Appeal, where the dispute on construction did not need to be resolved. One possible approach where a phrase in a claim cannot be understood is simply to ignore it altogether, so that it has no limiting effect and therefore cannot serve to distinguish the prior art. This approach may well be a reasonable one where the patent then fails for validity, as the patentee has only himself to blame. However, it has the disadvantage that it provides a wider scope of claim when infringement is being considered, so that the patentee is effectively being given the benefit of the doubt and a claim of the widest possible scope. **9-259**

It is submitted that it is open to the court to hold that infringement was not proven in a case where the language of the claim is so obscure that its boundary could not be determined with any proper precision.[285] But as Jacob J observed in *Milliken Denmark A/S v Walk Off Mats*[286]: "[t]hat it is possible to postulate difficult cases about a borderline does not make the claim so uncertain that there cannot be a reasonable degree of certainty for third parties". There is a difference between a "fuzzy boundary" and a true ambiguity or insufficiency.[287] **9-260**

European patents (UK): Translations

The text of a European patent in the language of the proceedings relating to the patent before the EPO is the authentic text for the purposes of any domestic proceedings before the Comptroller or the court.[288] However, where the language of the proceedings is French or German, and a translation has been filed at the UK Patent Office, the translation becomes the authentic text for the purposes of any domestic proceedings, other than proceedings for revocation of the patent, if the pat- **9-261**

---

[283] *Halliburton Energy Services v Smith International (North Sea) Ltd* [2005] EWHC 1623 (Pat) (21 July 2005).

[284] [1999] R.P.C. 497, CA; [1998] R.P.C. 31, per Laddie J.

[285] See *Scanvaegt v Pelcombe* [1998] F.S.R. 786, at 797; *Smithkline Beecham Plc v Apotex Europe* [2005] F.S.R. 243, at [115]. See also the section "Proof in case of ambiguous claim" at para.14–36 in the chapter of this work dealing with infringement.

[286] [1996] F.S.R. 292, 302.

[287] *SmithKline Beecham Plc v Apotex Europe* [2005] F.S.R. 23, [115].

[288] PA 1977 s.80(1).

ent as translated into English confers protection which is narrower than that conferred by it in French or German.[289] Any dispute as to the correct translation is a question of fact to be decided by the court on evidence. In *Siemens Schweiz v Thorn*,[290] the Court gave guidance as to the approach to be adopted in a case where there was a dispute surrounding the correctness of the English translation of the German original text, for the separate purposes of considering validity and considering infringement.

Construction of amended specification

9-262   Where an amendment has been made after the date of publication of a complete specification, the amendment is for all purposes deemed to form part of the specification,[291] and therefore the specification is to be read in the form in which it appears after amendment. In construing an amended specification under the 1949 Act, reference could be made to the specification as originally published,[292] but this provision has not been re-enacted.

8.   PARTICULAR FORMS OF CLAIM

Product and process claims

9-263   The different nature of these two types of claim is recognised by EPC art.64(2) which provides that:

> "If the subject-matter of the European patent is a process, the protection conferred by the patent shall extend to the products directly obtained by such process."

That article is given effect by PA 77 s.60(1)(c).

9-264   So far as a product claim is concerned, it will normally be infringed (or anticipated) if the device (or prior art) in question is capable of being used in a way falling within the claim, regardless of whether it in fact was, or indeed was ever intended to be, so used.[293]

9-265   A product claim will cover the product wherever found.[294] But if the claim, properly construed, is to an isolated product (e.g. an enantiomer) then it will not extend to the product when found in unseparated form (e.g. a racemate).[295]

9-266   Process claims may require and refer to the presence of particular hardware in order to carry them out, as for example in *Technip France SA's Patent*,[296] where Jacob LJ noted that:

> "It is an unusual claim structure, a process claim followed by a product-for-carrying-out-the-process claim. Moreover the process claim requires various items of hardware and is thus not 'pure

---

[289] PA 1977 s.80(2).

[290] [2008] R.P.C. 4, [11]–[13]; reversed on other grounds in [2009] R.P.C. 3.

[291] PA 1949 s.31(2); and PA 1977 s.75(3).

[292] PA 1949 s.31(2), proviso. And see *Tecalemit Ltd v Ewarts* (1927) 44 R.P.C. 488, at 500; *Multiform Displays Ltd v Whitmarley Displays Ltd* [1957] R.P.C. 260.

[293] See, e.g. *Technip France SA's Patent* [2004] R.P.C. 46, at [68] (infringement) and [78] (anticipation).

[294] *Merrell Dow v HH Norton* [1996] R.P.C. 76, 82 ll.36–44.

[295] *Generics v Lundbeck* [2007] R.P.C. 32, [62]–[64] (Patents Court); [2008] R.P.C. 19, [11]–[13] (CA); [2009] R.P.C. 13, [7] (HL, though the point was no longer live).

[296] [2004] R.P.C. 46.

process.' Nonetheless I do not think that the skilled man, to whom it is addressed, would have much difficulty in following it, guided as he will be by the drawings."

It is submitted that such claims remain process claims, albeit not "pure". **9-267**

"Swiss-style" or "use" claims

These are claims of the form "use of substance X in the manufacture of a medica- **9-268** ment for treating disease Y". Such a form is permissible in order to provide protection for inventions relating to second medical use. The underlying reasoning is described in more detail in para.2-49, et seq.

The significance of Swiss claims will diminish over time as they are now no **9-269** longer granted following the 2000 revisions to the European Patent Convention ("EPC 2000"). However, much of the case law will remain pertinent as claims are granted under EPC 2000 with medical use limitations which are intended to match as closely as possible the scope of protection to the scope provided by a Swiss-type claim as discussed further below.

Such claims are not claims to a method of medical treatment as such (contrast **9-270** "use of substance X for treating disease Y", which would be) and so do not fall foul of the requirement for industrial applicability.

Novelty and inventive step may arise from the application to a new medical use **9-271** (or indeed a new dosage regimen).

Such claims are process claims, as was held by Whitford J and Falconer J sit- **9-272** ting *en banc* in *John Wyeth & Brother Ltd's Application.*[297] The court said at 563:

"Mr Laddie, for the Comptroller, submitted, and we agree, that a claim in the Swiss-form, such as those in the *Wyeth* and *Schering* claims now under consideration, although in the form 'The use of substance A in the manufacture of a medicament to treat disease B', is, in reality, a claim to the method of manufacture of such a medicament by using substance A in its manufacture."

Central to the construction of both Swiss claims and EPC 2000 medical use **9-273** claims is what does the word "for" mean? Does it mean just "suitable for" or does it mean "suitable for and intended for" the particular medical application? If the latter, a number of questions arise: Is the intention subjective or objective? Whose intention is relevant (the doctor, pharmacist or end user)? At what date must the intention be assessed? These questions have now each been addressed, as considered below.

The Court of Appeal first reviewed the relevant law as to the background to **9-274** Swiss-form claims in *Actavis v Merck.*[298] It subsequently re-reviewed both the EPO and domestic law in *Warner-Lambert v Actavis*[299] at [51]–[68]. The review considered first *EISAI/Second medical indication* (G05/83)[300] and (*ABBOTT RESPIRATORY/dosage regimen claims* (G2/08), discussed above at para.2–52, et seq. and then *University of Texas Board of Regents/Cancer treatment* (T 1780/

---

[297] [1985] R.P.C. 545.
[298] [2008] R.P.C. 26, disapproving the Court's earlier decision in *Bristol Myers Squibb v Baker Norton*, [1999] R.P.C. 253 (Pat.Ct.) and [2001] R.P.C. 1 (CA). See above generally at para 2-30-2-37. See also *EISAI*, Decision G05/83; *Monsanto v Merck* [2000] R.P.C. 77 at 84; *Kos Life Sciences*, EPO Enlarged Board decision G2/08.
[299] [2015] EWCA Civ 556; [2015] R.P.C 25.
[300] [1985] O.J. EPO 64; [1979 – 85] E.P.O.R B241, considered above at para.2-49, et seq.

12).[301] That case concerned double patenting. The Technical Board of Appeal of the EPO explained that claims in Swiss-form have a different scope from EPC 2000 claims. Floyd LJ explained, at [56], that:

"…The former are purpose limited process claims, the latter are purpose limited product claims. EPC 2000 claims do not include, as a technical feature, the manufacture of a medicament. Because a claim to a process using a product (a physical activity) inherently involves less protection than a claim to a product (a physical entity), the scope of purpose limited process claim was inherently less than that of a purpose limited product claim.

57.   The Board however noted an argument that EPC 2000 protection was intended to be equivalent to Swiss claims, on the basis of a preparatory document. At [23] the Board said:

'23.   As regards the last argument of the examining division, namely that the EPC legislator considered the two claim formats equivalent (see section VII above), the board notes that it was the *intention* of the legislator to provide a claim format which afforded an equivalent protection, as far as the further medical uses are concerned, to that offered by the Swiss-type claim, see decision G 02/08 of the Enlarged Board (O.J. EPO 2010, 456, point 5.10.4 of the reasons) where it refers to preparatory document MR/18/00, point 4 as indicating the intention of the legislator when introducing Article 54(5) EPC as follows: "The new Article 54(5) EPC eliminates any legal uncertainty on the patentability of further medical uses. It unambiguously permits purpose–related product protection for each further new medical use of a substance or composition already known as a medicine." This protection is equivalent, as far as the further uses are concerned, to that offered by the 'Swiss type claim'. In contrast to previous Article 54(5), now Article 54(4) EPC, providing broad (generic) protection for use in a medical method for the inventor of such use for the first time, new Article 54(5) is expressly limited to a specific use. *This limitation is intended to match as closely as possible the scope of protection to the scope provided by a 'Swiss type claim'.* (Emphasis added).'

58.   The Board was not persuaded by this argument that it was wrong to ascribe a different, narrower scope to Swiss claims, at least in the context of the objection of double patenting."

9-275   Floyd LJ then went on to consider *Mobil (Friction reducing additive* (G 02/88)[302] holding at 59 that in that case:

"…the Enlarged Board of Appeal applied a similar novelty principle in the non-medical field. An engine oil additive which had previously been used for preventing rust was discovered to have friction reducing properties, even though the old use of the additive for preventing rust would inherently have realised the new friction effect. Mobil claimed the use of the known compound for the new purpose. The Board recognised at [7.2.1] that a claim which has no technical feature which reflects the new use, and has wording referring to such new use "which is merely mental in nature and does not define a technical feature" is not novel. However the Board explained that the proper construction of such claims is normally that the compound, when used, in fact achieves the technical effect. On that basis the known use does not, it is argued, deprive the claimed use of novelty.

60.   At paragraphs 10.1 and 10.2 the Board addressed the question of what happens to the user of the prior art additive for the old purpose (with its inherent effect) who continues after the patent is granted. Does he risk infringement by continuing? The Board, being only concerned with the novelty of the claim, considered that any question of his right to continue was a matter for national law. The Board went on to point out that the same problem would arise in connection with Swiss form claims in the medical field."

9-276   Floyd LJ then considered the English authorities, starting with *Wyeth*[303] and *Merrell Dow*.[304] In respect of the latter he pointed out that Lord Hoffmann had referred to the difficulties in applying the conventional approach of English patent law to

[301] [2014] EPOR 28, [16]–[24].
[302] [1999] E.P.O.R. 73. Considered at para.11-48.
[303] [1985] R.P.C. 545. See paras 2-50 and 9-272.
[304] [1996] R.P.C. 76.

infringement of *Mobil*-type claims, namely that liability is strict and does not depend on any mental element. He then turned to *Bristol Myers Squibb* and *Actavis v Merck*.[305] He noted that in the former Aldous LJ had explained that a Swiss-type claim could not be interpreted as "a product when used because that would constitute a method of treatment which is prohibited under the EPC." In respect of *Actavis* he set out Jacob LJ's explanation (itself taken from *BMS*) that a Swiss-type claim "steers clear of two obstacles to patentability, namely the requirement of novelty and the ban on methods of treatment of the human body by therapy" as well as noting that the court in that case had noted that the policy reasons for allowing *Mobil*-type claims and Swiss-form claims are "closely akin".[306]

Floyd LJ then came on to consider how *Actavis v Merck* and other authorities had considered the construction of the word "for" in such claims. He noted that in *Actavis* (at [10]) Jacob LJ had commented that in many cases the difficulty as to the infringement of Swiss-form claims, namely how to tell whether someone has used a product for the manufacture of a medicament for the treatment of a particular disease, might be more theoretical than real because manufacturers will have to say that a product is for the treatment of given diseases on the patient information leaflet. However, Floyd LJ said: **9-277**

"66. This passage is not addressing, let alone laying down any construction of the word 'for'. Instead it is concerned with how evidential difficulties of discovering the purpose element of the claim might in some cases be addressed. Moreover it is not in practice the case that a manufacturer 'will have to say that his product is for the treatment of Y on his product information leaflet' in order to benefit from the patentee's market for the novel use. By the means of a 'skinny label' he can say nothing at all about the novel indication, and leave it to the market to ensure that it is in fact dispensed for pain. The court was not addressing the problem which confronts the court on this appeal, where the PIL is silent as to an indication for which there is a large market, in circumstances where doctors and pharmacists are encouraged and incentivised towards generic prescribing, dispensing and cross-dispensing."

Floyd LJ also highlighted the comment in *Actavis v Merck* (at [75]) that: **9-278**

"In its essence the claim here is to the use of finasteride for the preparation of a medicament of the specified dosages. It is not aimed at and it does not touch the doctor—it is directed at the manufacturer."

Finally he noted that in *Hospira UK Ltd v Genentech Inc*[307] Birss J had recorded that it was common ground between the parties in that case that the word "for" in such claims meant "suitable and intended for" without being required to explore any further what the second part of that phrase meant.   **9-279**

Floyd LJ's extensive consideration of the background informed the issue under consideration in *Warner-Lambert v Actavis*[308] as to the requisite intention for the infringement of a Swiss-type claim. In his view the issue of infringement was a question of construction of the claim and, like any such question, the task was for the court to determine what the skilled reader of the patent would understand the patentee to be using the language of the claim to mean. He rejected the submission that subjective intent was required and held that the skilled person: **9-280**

"... would understand that the manufacturer who knows (and for this purpose constructive knowledge is enough) or could reasonably foresee that some of his drug will intentionally be used for pain is

---

[305] [2008] R.P.C. 26.
[306] See *Actavis v Merck*, at [30].
[307] [2014] EWHC 1094 (Pat), [58].
[308] [2015] EWCA Civ 556; [2015] R.P.C 25.

making use of the patentee's inventive contribution, in the same way as a manufacturer who actively desires that result. In my judgment, therefore, the skilled person would understand that the patentee was using the word 'for' in the claim to require that the manufacturer knows (in the above sense) or can reasonably foresee the ultimate intentional use for pain, not that he have that specific intention or desire himself."[309]

9-281 Subsequently, the issue of infringement in *Warner-Lambert v Actavis* went back before Arnold J on the substantive trial of the action.[310],[311] Although Arnold J expressed doubts as to the correctness of the Court of Appeal's analysis, he stated that he was not "entirely convinced" that it was wrong and therefore proposed to follow it.[312]

9-282 At trial, an issue that had not been addressed by the Court of Appeal was the date at which the relevant intention was to be assessed. On this Arnold J considered that the relevant date was the date of manufacture of the medicament.[313]

9-283 On the issue of the identity of the person who must have the requisite knowledge in the case of a claim to the use of a product for the manufacture of a medicament "for treating pain", Arnold J did not consider that there was intentional administration of the product for the treatment of pain if the product was dispensed in circumstances where the doctor has prescribed a generic version of the product for pain and the pharmacist did not know the indication for which it has been prescribed. There could only be infringement if the pharmacist dispensed the product when they knew that the product had been prescribed for pain.[314]

9-284 Swiss-type and medical use claims also raise the question of what level of efficacy is required by the words "for the treatment of". A claim of the form "The use of ... for the curative or prophylactic ... treatment of ..." is only fulfilled by the use of a compound which is both for the purpose of trying to treat the target illness and which also is suitable for treating that illness, that is to say that in relation to at least some individuals the treatment works.[315]

9-285 Furthermore, following EPO case law, it is now established that "attaining the claimed therapeutic effect is a functional technical feature of the claim". Hence in *Regeneron Pharmaceuticals v Genentech Inc*[316] the claims were both in Swiss-form and EPC 2000 format. The Swiss-type claim was for the "Use of a hVEGF antagonist in the preparation of a medicament for the treatment of a non-neoplastic disease or disorder characterised by undesirable excessive neovascularisation, wherein the hVEGF antagonist was inter alia an anti-VEGF antibody". The first issue of construction concerned the meaning of the words "a medicament for the treatment of a non-neoplastic disease or disorder characterised by undesirable excessive neovascularisation". The finding of Floyd J at first instance was that:

"In my judgment the skilled person would understand that the diseases in question were those

---

[309] [2015] EWCA Civ 556; [2015] R.P.C 25, [127].

[310] The judgment of the Court of Appeal was in the context of: (a) an appeal from the refusal of Arnold J to grant interim relief to Warner Lambert; and (b) an appeal by Actavis whereby Arnold J had refused to strike the claim out. The Court of Appeal upheld the refusal of interim relief on the balance of justice and therefore the Court of Appeal's consideration of the law of Swiss claims was strictly obiter.

[311] [2015] EWHC 2548 (Pat).

[312] See [632].

[313] See [641]-[648].

[314] See [638] and [666].

[315] *Pfizer Ltd's Patent* [2001] F.S.R. 16, [40]-[42]; *Bristol-Myers Squibb v Baker Norton* [2001] R.P.C. 1, [21]; *Teva v Merck* [2010] F.S.R. 17, [54]-[58].

[316] [2013] EWCA Civ 93; [2013] R.P.C. 28.

characterized by excessive undesired angiogenesis. That is the question which has to be answered for the purposes of infringement. I see no reason to recast the definition either as sought by Genentech or by the claimants. There was no evidence that anyone skilled in the art would have any difficulty in identifying a disease which is characterized by undesirable, excessive angiogenesis and one which is not. Further, the skilled person would not understand that the patentee was saying that the treatment would necessarily successfully deal with anything other than undesired angiogenesis in that disease. Thus, for example, the skilled person would not understand that the treatment would necessarily deal with other aspects of the disease state which were independent of angiogenesis."[317]

In rejecting the appeal from this finding Kitchin LJ found that the following points were material:

9-286

"39. ...First, the claim is concerned with non-neoplastic diseases which have, as one of their characteristics, undesirable excessive neovascularisation, that is to say angiogenesis. The angiogenesis must therefore contribute to the pathology of the disease though it need not necessarily be the cause of it. Hence the specification explains in the section to which I have referred at [24] above, angiogenesis is an important component of a variety of diseases of which a number are then identified.

40. Second, the medicament must treat the disease. That is not to say that the medicament must cure the disease; plainly many diseases characterised by angiogenesis cannot be cured. But it must improve the patient's condition, and it must do so by treating the angiogenic component of the disease from which the patient is suffering.

41. Third, the medicament does not have to treat all, or indeed any other, aspects of the disease, of which, in the case of some diseases, such as RA, there may be many. It is only directed at the angiogenic aspect of the disease and its efficacy is derived from its activity as a VEGF antagonist.

42. Against this background, I do not believe the judge's analysis can be faulted. It was not suggested by any party at trial that the claim does not require any therapeutic effect. It clearly does, and the judge so held. But it does not require a medicament which will cure or even treat all aspects of a disease and, in particular, it does not require treatment of those aspects of a disease which are independent of angiogenesis."

Kitchin LJ also held[318] that, as the Technical Board of Appeal of the EPO explained in decision *The Salk Institute for Biological Studies* (T609/02), at [9], where a therapeutic application is claimed in Swiss-form, attaining the claimed therapeutic effect is a functional technical feature of the claim.

9-287

This aspect of construction is of importance in the context of novelty where the prior art makes suggestions to treat, but that treatment is not actually realised or attained. For this reason, in *Regeneron*, the suggestion in the prior art that "Further, VEGF neutralizing mAbs could be potential therapeutic agents in diseases involving excess endothelial cell proliferation" was held not to be anticipation when it was "no more than a prediction that these antibodies could have therapeutic potential".[319]

9-288

In *Merck v Ono*[320] the claims were both in Swiss-form and EPC 2000 form to, respectively, "use of an anti-PD-1 antibody which inhibits the immunosuppressive signal of PD-1 for the manufacture of a medicament for cancer treatment (claim 1) and "anti-PD-1 antibody which inhibits the immunosuppressive signal of PD-1 for the use in cancer treatment". The judge addressed the construction of these claims as follows:

9-289

"117. There was an issue as to whether unamended claims 1 and 3 relate to the treatment of any and all cancers in general. The answer is plainly that they do. The skilled reader would understand that the inventors had used the language of the unamended claims to mean that no cancers are excluded, or in other words the use of an anti-PD-1 inhibitory antibody to treat any cancer

---

[317] *Regeneron Pharmaceuticals v Genentech* [2010] EWHC 657 (Pat), [53].
[318] See [56].
[319] See [62].
[320] [2015] EWHC 2973.

would be within claim 1. The claim is not limited to particular kinds of cancer and is not, for example, limited to cancers already thought to be immunogenic either at the priority date or later.

118. This question is of most significance in the context of sufficiency of disclosure, priority and plausibility. With an eye on these arguments, it is worth noting that cancers can be divided up in numerous ways. There is no simple list of types of cancer. For example although in some contexts one can refer simply to lung cancer, in other contexts one distinguishes between non-small cell lung cancer and other kinds of lung cancer. The fact that the skilled reader knows and understands this does not alter the conclusion on construction. The claim is as wide as possible.

119. Very few drugs work in every single patient to whom they are administered, for a variety of reasons. The fact that no skilled reader of the patent would expect this drug to work in every patient does not alter the point on claim construction either".

9-290   The further question of whether such claims cover use of the relevant compound at any stage in production, or whether such compound must be present as such in the medicament itself, arose for decision in *American Home Products v Novartis*,[321] where the claim was for:

"1.   Use of rapamycin for the preparation of a medicament for inhibiting organ or tissue transplant rejection in a mammal in need thereof."

9-291   The defendant had used rapamycin as a starting material to prepare a derivative used in their product, but the derivative and not rapamycin itself was the effective ingredient. The Court of Appeal held that there was therefore no infringement, saying (at [52]):

"The claim has to be construed in context. It is a Swiss-type claim to an invention for the second medical use of rapamycin. As the specification makes clear, the medicament that provides the inhibition is rapamycin. There is no disclosure of any other medicament. It would be unfair to the patentee to construe the word 'medicament' as meaning any product whether or not it contained rapamycin as that would render the patent invalid. ... It follows that the word 'medicament' must be construed as referring to the product rapamycin which is the product described in the specification as having been discovered by the inventor to have the beneficial immunosuppressant properties"

9-292   An alternative argument that 0.8 per cent of rapamycin itself remained in the product as an impurity was also rejected thus:

"It is only necessary to contemplate answering the Protocol questions in respect to a variant where the medicament included only 0.8 per cent of rapamycin to see that the claim must be construed as meaning that the medicament has to be essentially rapamycin."

9-293   However, the case does not necessarily stand for the proposition that "medicament" must in general be construed as meaning that the relevant compound must be present as such within it, for the reasoning turned in part on the particular facts of that case, including the way in which the invention was described and the fact that the claim would have been invalid for insufficiency if construed more broadly. This point arose directly in *Ranbaxy UK v AstraZeneca*.[322]

9-294   In *Ranbaxy UK v AstraZeneca* claim 1 of the Patent was in Swiss-form and was directed to the use of magnesium esomeprazole with an optical purity of $\geq$ 99.8 per cent e.e. (enantiomeric excess, a level of optical purity) for the manufacture of a medicament for the inhibition of gastric acid secretion. The product which the claimant wished to import was made in India. The process of manufacture began with magnesium esomeprazole with an optical purity of $\geq$ 99.8 per cent e.e.

---

[321] [2001] R.P.C. 8; see also *Monsanto v Merck* [2000] R.P.C. 77.
[322] [2011] EWHC 1831 (Pat); [2011] F.S.R. 45.

Thereafter the process involved the addition of a quantity of omeprazole racemate such that the finished product no longer contained magnesium esomeprazole of that optical purity.

The question therefore was whether the product which the claimant wished to **9-295** import was the direct product of a process in which magnesium esomeprazole with an optical purity of $\geq$ 99.8 per cent e.e. was used to make a medicament for the inhibition of gastric acid secretion. The answer to this question turned upon the proper construction of the claim according to the principles set out in *Kirin-Amgen*.[323]

As noted at para.8-53, Kitchin J held that the skilled person must be taken to **9-296** know the basic drafting conventions used to frame a patent and its claims and therefore that they would recognise that claim 1 has been drafted in Swiss-form.

He also found that it was inherent in the reasoning of *EISAI/second medical* **9-297** *indication*[324] that the skilled person would generally understand a Swiss-form claim to mean that the medicament must contain the active ingredient for which the new and inventive use has been found. But for the exclusion contained in art.52(4) EPC 1973, the claim would have been directed to the new and non-obvious use of that ingredient. Kitchin J did not go so far as to suggest that a claim cast in Swiss-form must always be construed as being directed to the use of an active ingredient for the manufacture of a medicament which contains that ingredient. The proper meaning of the claim must, he held, must be determined having regard to the words of the claim when construed purposively in the light of the specification and the common general knowledge, as the Court of Appeal emphasised in *Monsanto v Merck*.[325] However, that is how it would normally be understood. One reason for this was that the skilled person would appreciate that to construe it otherwise would render the claim vulnerable to an attack of insufficiency as illustrated by *American Home Products Corporation v Novartis Pharmaceuticals*.[326]

On the specific facts of that case the judge found that the whole teaching of the **9-298** specification was about the production of optically pure magnesium esomeprazole and its use in particular therapies and, for that purpose, its formulation with a conventional carrier. Recognising that the teaching of the specification that magnesium esomeprazole with an optical purity of $\geq$ 99.8 per cent e.e. was new, the skilled person would nevertheless understand claim 1 to be directed to the use of such magnesium esomeprazole to manufacture a medicament which contains that active ingredient.

Product-by-process claims: "obtainable by"

Under its current practice, the EPO does not usually permit[327] claims of the form **9-299** "A [product] ... obtained by the process of ..." as such claims provide no protection over and above a process claim.[328] Moreover a new process is not enough in

---

[323] [2004] UKHL 46; [2005] R.P.C. 9.
[324] (G5/83) [1985] O.J. EPO 64.
[325] [2000] R.P.C. 77.
[326] [2001] R.P.C. 8.
[327] The EPO recognises an exception where the product is new in the sense of being different but the difference cannot otherwise be defined in physical or chemical terms; *International Flavors & Fragrances* [1984] O.J. EPO 309.
[328] See PA 1977 s.60(1)(c).

itself to make the product new, for "it is still the same product even if made in a different way".[329]

9-300   Prior to the decision in *Hospira UK v Genentech*[330] it was not clear whether this is merely a rule of novelty, or whether it is a rule of construction (namely, that the words "obtained by the process of" are to be disregarded as adding no further limitation).

9-301   The EPO does however in principle permit "A [product] ... obtainable by the process of ...", because looked at as a matter of language it is a product claim, and it takes the view that such claims are therefore to be assessed for the purpose of novelty, etc. as product claims, and the method actually used is irrelevant. The EPO Guidelines state[331]:

> "Claims for products defined in terms of a process of manufacture are admissible only if the products as such fulfil the requirements for patentability, i.e. inter alia that they are new and inventive. A product is not rendered novel merely by the fact that it is produced by means of a new process (see T150/82, O.J. 7/1984, 309). A claim defining a product in the process is to be construed as a claim to the product as such and the claim should preferably take the form 'Product X obtainable by process Y', or any wording equivalent thereto, rather than 'Product X obtained by process Y'."

9-302   In some circumstances, this may provide useful and fair protection for inventors. Where there is a clearly defined class of products and a clear test for "obtainable by", a patentee who has such a claim can bring an action without having to establish the method of manufacture which an infringer actually used.

9-303   However, such claims give rise to serious problems of construction. If such a claim only covers products actually made by the processes taught in the specification, then it adds nothing. But if the claim is wider and covers products made by other processes, then questions arise as to how much wider, what test is to be applied in determining whether or not a product falls within the claim, and how skilled persons are to determine whether or not they infringe. These questions were addressed and answered in *Hospira UK v Genentech*.[332]

9-304   Claim 1 of the Genentech patent was a claim to a product. The product was a lyophilised (i.e. freeze fried) formulation of the antibody trastuzumab comprising at least four ingredients: a lyoprotectant, buffer, surfactant and antibody. The product claimed in claim 1 of the patent had to be "obtainable by" lyophilising the solution of Table 5 of the patent. Birss J explained that although most inventions are either products or processes there is no rule that an invention must either be one or the other. He explained that in the case of Swiss-form claims infringement is "often argued only under s.60(2) (infringement by supplying means essential) which avoids the problem of deciding whether it is a product or a process". He continued:

> "128. Another kind of claim which straddles the boundary between products and processes is a product by process claim. As a matter of language there are two kinds: (1) a product 'obtained by' a process, and (2) a product 'obtainable by' a process. At least at first sight they are different.
>
> 129. At first sight the scope of a claim to a product 'obtained by' a process would be only to products which had actually been made by the process. There might be problems of proof in an infringement case or for novelty but conceptually there is no difficulty. If no products had ever been made that way in the past, then the claim would be novel. The fact that such products are physically entirely identical to products made in the past would not alter the fact that no product

[329] See *Kirin-Amgen v Hoechst Marion Roussel* [2005] R.P.C. 9, at [90].
[330] *Hospira UK Ltd v Genentech Inc* [2014] EWHC 3857.
[331] See EPO Guideline for Substantive Examination C-III, 4.7b (56/196).
[332] [2014] EWHC 3857 (Pat).

made by that process had been made available to the public before. They would only be infringed by products actually made by the relevant process. This was the view taken of product by process claims in the Court of Appeal in *Kirin Amgen* ([2002] EWCA Civ 1096, [2003] RPC 3)."

The judge pointed out that an issue not addressed in *Kirin-Amgen* was whether **9-305** the rule that the process feature is irrelevant for novelty is a rule of the law of novelty or a rule of mandatory claim interpretation. He explained[333] how in *Kirin-Amgen* the House of Lords had required, for the purposes of being novel, a claim to erythropoietin made by the expression of a gene in a host cell, to be different from known urinary erythropoietin. On the other hand, when the House of Lords decided that the defendant's rEPO did not infringe, it was because it was not the product of the expression of a gene in a host cell. Hence it was, as the judge put it, "applying the process feature as a relevant limitation which was not satisfied for the purposes of (non-)infringement but ignoring it for the purposes of novelty". As he explained, that can only be on the basis that the product by process rule is a rule of novelty law, not claim construction. The paradoxical result is that a product not made by the claimed process had been found not to infringe because it was not made by that process while another product not made by that process was found to render the claim lacking novelty. When it comes to infringement however, Birss J considered that:

"It is not obvious that an inventor who drafted his or her claim in the form of a product 'obtained by' a process ever intended to cover other things or would be understood to be using language to mean that. The test for novelty is one thing but to ignore the clear words of the claim may result in it covering things which owe nothing to the inventor's technical contribution and risk insufficiency. It is hard to see how one can apply one of the key principles of construction emphasised by *Kirin-Amgen* itself, that the reader considers what the draftsman was using language to mean, in any other way."[334]

The judge derived the following principles from his consideration of the EPO and **9-306** UK authorities:

"i)   A new process which produces a product identical to an old product cannot confer novelty on that product. To be novel a product obtained or obtainable by a process has to have some novel attribute conferred on it by the process as compared to the known product.

ii)   This rule is a rule of the law of novelty. It is not a principle of claim construction. Although in effect the rule treats 'obtained by' language as 'obtainable by' language, nevertheless as a matter of claim construction a claim to a product 'obtained by' a process means what it says. That will be the relevant scope of the claim as far as infringement and sufficiency are concerned.

iii)   Although normally a patent is drafted by the inventor 'in words of his own choosing', the EPO will not permit overt product by process language unless there is no other alternative available. By no other alternative, they mean no other way of defining a particular characteristic of the product in question."

Accordingly, in the context of infringement, where a product is said to be **9-307** "obtained by process X" it must have been actually obtained by that process in order to infringe. However, when it comes to validity (specifically novelty), the wording "obtained by" does not exclude prior art material which is physically the same, even though it has not been obtained by the process claimed. In this respect therefore, though stated as a rule of novelty, the rule construes the words "obtained by" differently in the context of validity and infringement.

---

[333] See [143], et seq.
[334] [2014] EWHC 3857 (Pat), [146].

9-308   In the former case, it is not required that the prior art material is actually *obtained by* the process in order to deprive the claim of novelty, although in the latter case the product must be *obtained by* the process in order to infringe. While this contradicts the general rule that the construction of words used should be the same for validity and infringement, it is the only way to rationalise the decision reached in the House of Lords in *Kirin-Amgen* in which prior art material which had not been obtained by the claimed process was held to anticipate the claim which, in turn, is based on the EPO's case law on product-by-process claims.

Relevance of drafting practice

9-309   As discussed at para.8-49, the skilled reader is taken to know some patent law (probably with the benefit of skilled advice), and to suppose that the patentee knew some patent law. The Court of Appeal in *Virgin v Premium Aircraft Interiors*[335] held that "Knowledge of that may well affect how the claim is read—for instance one would not expect the patentee to have used language which covered what he expressly acknowledged was old". Thus, for example, if the skilled reader encountered terms of art such as "divisional application" or *"parent application"* they would if necessary seek advice as to their meaning. The case confirmed that the skilled reader should be taken to be aware of the function of reference numerals and of the two-part claim structure. It went on to hold at [21]:

> "Even without a two-part claim structure, because the skilled reader knows that the patentee is trying to claim something which he, the patentee, considers to be new, he will be strongly averse to ascribe to the claim a meaning which covers that which the patentee acknowledges is old. And if the patentee not only acknowledges that a particular piece of prior art is old but then has a pre-characterising clause which is fairly obviously based on it, the skilled reader will be even more strongly inclined to read that clause as intended to describe that old art".

9-310   As also discussed at para.8-52, in *Virgin v Delta*[336] Arnold J concluded that it followed from the logic of *Virgin v Premium Aircraft Interiors* that the skilled reader is also deemed to know about, and take into account, that:

> "(i)   it is possible to frame claims in a variety of different ways. In particular, claims may be directed, subject to constraints on unity of invention, both to the whole of an inventive product and to its key components separately.
>
> (ii)   It is possible to infringe a patent both directly under s.60(1) of the Patents Act 1977 corresponding to Art.25 of the Community Patent Convention and indirectly under s.60(2) of the 1977 Act corresponding to Art.26 CPC. As discussed in more detail below, the latter type of infringement involves the supply or offer to supply of "any of the means, relating to an essential element of the invention" i.e. less than the whole of a claimed product.
>
> (iii)   Patents are territorial in nature. This has two aspects to it. The first is that a UK patent prevents persons other than those "entitled to work the invention" (to use the language of s.60(2)) from doing things in the UK. The second is that a patentee can in principle obtain, and may well have in fact obtained, parallel patent protection in other countries. In saying this, I am not going so far as to presume that the skilled person will actually carry out a search to locate any corresponding foreign patents, even though a well-advised person would do so and nowadays would be able to locate most such patents quickly and easily using electronic databases."

The two-part claim format: "characterised by"

9-311   The structure of the claim itself may provide indications as to which features are important and which might be replaced by variants. One way in this may be done

---

[335]   [2010] R.P.C. 8, [13].
[336]   [2010] EWHC 3094 (Pat); [2011] R.P.C. 8, [49].

is the use of the two-part claim format preferred by the European Patent Office. Thus Laddie J in *Merck & Co Inc v Generics (UK) Ltd* said[337]:

"Furthermore, the patentee may choose a form of language which emphasises which features of an invention are important and which are not. For example it is common to find claims which start with general description followed by 'characterised in' followed by a list of features. The addressee would appreciate that the latter features are particularly important but the features before the words 'characterised in' are less so. If there is a variant to the latter which obviously does not affect the way in which the invention works, the notional reader may be reasonably confident that the inventor wanted to cover this variant as well. In these types of cases, the monopoly is likely to extend to the new variant."

Thus it is more likely that the patent requires strict adherence to the integers that follow the word "wherein", than to the integers that precede it.[338] **9-312**

Reference numerals

Reference numerals appearing in a claim, while helpful, are irrelevant to construction. Rule 29 (7) of the Implementing Regulations to the EPC provides that if the application contains drawings: **9-313**

"... the technical features mentioned in the claim shall preferably, if the intelligibility of the claim can thereby be increased, be followed by reference signs relating to these features and placed between parentheses. These reference signs shall not be construed as limiting the claim."

In *Virgin v Premium Aircraft Interiors*,[339] the Court of Appeal held that: **9-314**

"...we do not think that numerals should influence the construction of the claim at all—they do not illustrate whether the inventor intended a wide or narrow meaning. The patentee is told by the rule that if he puts numerals into his claim they will not be used to limit it. If the court subsequently pays attention to the numbers to limit the claim that is simply not fair. And patentees would wisely refrain from inserting numbers in case they were used against them. That is not to say that numbers are pointless. They help a real reader orient himself at the stage when he is trying to get the general notion of what the patent is about. He can see where in the specific embodiment a particular claim element is, but no more. Once one comes to construe the claim, it must be construed as if the numbers were not part of it. To give an analogy, the numbers help you get the map the right way up, they do not help you to read it to find out exactly where you are."

In *Jarden v SEB*, a case about deep fat fryers, it was argued by the appellant in the Court of Appeal[340] (on appeal from Arnold J[341]) that the judge had misinterpreted the term "the main body" as including the lid of the fryer. One of its main contentions was that the judge wrongly made use of identifying numerals in the patent to construe its meaning. Vos LJ accepted these submissions: **9-315**

"32. I agree with the judge that these arguments are, at least in some respects, finely balanced. But I should start with the question of whether the judge was justified in making the use that he did of the reference numerals. In this regard, I have no doubt that the judge fell into legal error by allowing the reference numerals to influence his construction of the claim. The judge was not simply using the reference numerals to identify which parts in Figure 2 were being referred to in the claims or the specification, but was relying on the use of the particular identifiers '2', '2A', '2B' and '2C' (referring to the main body, the base, the side flank and the lid respectively) to conclude that the lid was to be regarded on a proper construction of the claims

---

[337] [2004] R.P.C. 31, [42].
[338] *Ultraframe v Eurocell* [2005] R.P.C. 7, [76] (Lewison J).
[339] [2010] R.P.C. 8, [17].
[340] [2014] EWCA Civ 1629.
[341] [2014] EWHC (Pat) 445.

as a part of the main body. This can be clearly seen from the fact that the judge said at paragraph 81 that he considered 'for the reasons given by counsel for SEB' that 'the skilled reader of the specification would conclude that the lid was part of the main body'. One of those reasons was recited by the judge at paragraph 72 namely 'the specification describes the main body 2 as having three parts: a base 2A, a side skirt 2B and a lid 2C' and that the 'specification uses the same numbering scheme to describe a number of other assemblies'.

33.   The judge was, therefore, in my judgment, allowing the numerals themselves to influence the construction of the claim in violation of Jacob LJ's primary injunction in paragraph 17 of *Virgin Atlantic*. This was not a use of numerals simply to identify the parts of the patented device, or, to use Jacob LJ's analogy, to enable the reader to get the map the right way up. It was the use of numerals to direct the skilled reader to which parts of the patented device were to be read in the claims as being included when a particular term was used. Whilst, as the judge said, the point was not used to 'limit' the claims in direct violation of Rule 43(7), it was used to construe the claims and, in particular, to give an extended meaning to the term 'main body' so as to include the lid, which increased the scope of the patentee's protection. That was in my judgment impermissible."

Subsidiary claims

9-316   Where the specification contains a number of claims, the subsidiary (dependent) claims will often be drafted so as to add one integer to the combinations claimed in previous claims. In these circumstances it is submitted that the added integer would be likely to be the only inventive idea of that subsidiary claim and that a purposive construction could not, therefore, be applied to that subsidiary claim so as to extend its scope to combinations not having that integer.[342] The *Catnic* decision does, however, leave scope for argument based on the facts of each case.

9-317   In *3M v Plastus Kreativ*,[343] the Court of Appeal firmly rejected as untenable a suggestion that the ambit of a word of limitation contained in claim 1 could change, depending upon whether that claim was read on its own or together with certain other sub-claims.

Relevance of subsidiary claims to construction of antecedent claims

9-318   The court will if possible construe the claims so as to give a different meaning to different claims. In *Parkinson v Simon*,[344] Lord Esher MR said:

"When you find a patent with several claims in it, you must, if you can, so construe those claims as to give an effective meaning to each of them. If there are several claims which are identical with each other, then some of them have no effect at all. It follows from the ordinary rules of construction that you must construe the different claims so as to make them effective if possible, to be different from each other in some respects, or else they are not effective."[345]

As Peter Gibson LJ stated in *Glaverbel v British Coal (No.4)*[346]:

"I would mention one other aid to construction arising from the practice of those who draft claims for a patent. As is common ground between the parties, the characterising feature of a subordinate claim is treated as also embraced by any antecedent claim to which it is appended, the subordinate claims being narrower in scope. Thus guidance may properly be obtained from a subordinate claim on the true construction of the antecedent claim to which it is appended."

---

[342] See *C. Van der Lely N.V. v Bamfords Ltd* [1963] R.P.C. 61, 78; *Submarine Signal Co v Henry Hughes & Son Ltd* (1932) 49 R.P.C. 149, 175.

[343] [1997] R.P.C. 737, 752.

[344] [1894] 11 R.P.C. 493, 502.

[345] See also *Mergenthaler Linotype Co v Intertype Ltd* (1926) 43 R.P.C. 239, at 289; *Samuel Parkes & Co Ltd v Cocker Bros Ltd* (1929) 46 R.P.C. 241, 247.

[346] [1995] R.P.C. 255, 281.

The conventional hierarchy of claims is to start with the widest, and progress **9-319** through subsidiary claims of ever narrowing scope, so that it is reasonable to infer that an earlier claim would be read as wider than a later subsidiary claim. However, if after properly construing the specification and claims, little or no difference can be found between two of the claims, "this circumstance affords no ground for departing from the reasonable and natural meaning of the language".[347] Jacob LJ commented on this approach in *Ultraframe v Eurocell Building Plastics*[348]:

"The argument is this: that the width of claim 1 must be wider than claim 3 and that it was only claim 3 which contained a limitation requiring some prior restraint. It is an example of the argument epitomised by the late Anthony Walton QC: 'Claim 1 "A car"; Claim 2 "A car wherein the wheels are round"'—forcing you to the conclusion that claim 1 covers cars with non-round wheels. That sort of argument, although it has its uses, can descend into overmeticulous verbal analysis."

An express limitation in a dependent claim may also carry with it further implied **9-320** limitations, and the same principles apply: the fact that a product does not have the implied limitation of the dependent claim is not of itself a reason to exclude it from falling within the antecedent claim.[349]

Other expressions commonly arising in patent claims

The following paragraphs address a number of specific phrases or issues which **9-321** arise from time to time in patent claims and which the court has considered in the past. Of course, each case will turn on its own special facts, and these expressions (like individual words) take their meaning from their context, so that no general rule can be laid down.[350] Indeed, the fact that such expressions have in the past been the subject of argument indicates that more than one acontextual meaning is capable of being postulated. Thus, these examples are intended to be illustrative of the court's general approach, rather than either definitive or exhaustive.

"Comprising"

A requirement that a claim "comprises" certain elements does not mean that other **9-322** elements may not be present: "comprising" does not mean "only consisting of".[351]

"For" and "suitable for"

We have addressed the construction of "for" in the context of Swiss-type and **9-323** medical use claims in paras 9-273 to 9-281. More generally, a claim to an article "suitable for" a particular purpose is a claim to such an article, whatever its intended purpose, so that the actual use which is intended need not be shown.[352] An argument that "a device for operating ..." meant the device "when used for" was

---

[347] Per Tomlin J. in *Brown v Sperry Gyroscope Co Ltd* [1925] 42 R.P.C. 111, at 136. Also see *Wenham Co Ltd v Champion Gas Lamp Co* (1892) 9 R.P.C. 49, at 55; *New Vacuum, etc., Ltd v Steel & Wilson* (1915) 32 R.P.C. 162, at 171; *Samuel Parkes & Co Ltd v Cocker Bros Ltd* (1929) 46 R.P.C. 241, at 247.

[348] [2005] EWCA (Civ) 761, [41].

[349] *Napp v Ratiopharm* [2009] R.P.C. 18, [42].

[350] See Laddie J's comments on previous constructions of particular words in *Electrolux Northern v Black & Decker* [1996] F.S.R. 595, at 604.

[351] *Napp v Ratiopharm* [2009] R.P.C. 18, [65].

[352] *Adhesive Dry Mounting Co Ltd v Trapp & Co* (1910) 27 R.P.C. 341; *Furr v Truline (C.D.) (Building Products)* [1985] F.S.R. 553.

rejected in *Coflexip v Stolt*,[353] on the basis that it would then be a method claim although from its context it was clearly a device claim; it was construed as meaning "a device suitable for operating…".

9-324 However, in such cases it is of course still necessary to show that the relevant article is in fact suitable for such purpose, without modification.[354] In the case of computer apparatus for a particular function, computer hardware would not be suitable for the claimed function unless programmed for that function.[355]

9-325 In *Bühler v Satake*[356] the claim was to a "roller mill for the milling of cereals or the like". It was common ground that this was a limitation so that a device was only covered if it was capable of milling cereals or the like. A dispute as to how capable it had to be was resolved on the basis that the claim covered a mill if it could be shown to be suitable for milling cereal without alteration to make it so. The cited prior art would have needed an extra hopper to make it a practical device, and so was held not to anticipate.

9-326 In *Qualcom Inc v Nokia Corp*[357] Floyd J considered the expression in the context of apparatus which might or might not require physical modification to make it "suitable for" the purposes of the patent. He said:

> "73. Nevertheless, one has to be very cautious of any principle of construction which is said to codify the meaning of particular words. Perhaps more importantly in this particular case, it is important not to take the meaning of 'suitable for' too far. Mr Antony Watson QC, who argued the case on the 324 Patent for Qualcomm with Mr Thomas Hinchliffe, started from the premise that an apparatus did not cease to infringe merely because it was switched off. So an apparatus for toasting bread infringes whether connected to the mains or not. He says this is just one example, and there is a general principle that an apparatus is still suitable for performing a particular function if it can be readily modified so as to perform that function. Mr Silverleaf accepts that a claim will be infringed if all that is required is to supply power. But he contends that modifications to the apparatus are not what is contemplated by 'suitable for'.
>
> 74. I think Mr Silverleaf is right. Supplying power to a toaster does not change the apparatus: it simply puts into use the apparatus which is there already. The question in each case is whether the apparatus, as it stands, is suitable for use in that way. If the apparatus has to undergo physical modification before it can be used, then prima facie it is not suitable for use and does not infringe."

9-327 This same reasoning was applied by Mann J in *Rovi Solutions Corporation v Virgin Media*[358] in which it was held that without appropriate programming the apparatus cannot be regarded as "suitable for" the processes of the patent.

9-328 The term "for the treatment of" (a particular medical condition) has acquired particular significance in the case of further medical use claims (whether in Swiss-form or under the 2000 Revisions to the EPC) and this is addressed in paras 9-273 to 9-288.

"Whereby" and "in order to": claims that require a consequence

9-329 Such expressions can give rise to difficulty, because of the different possible shades of meaning which they can bear; must an integer be the sole cause, the

---

[353] [2001] I.P. & T. 1332; and see also *Insituform Technical Services v Inliner UK* [1992] R.P.C. 83, 95-96 and *Virgin v Delta* [2011] EWCA Civ 162.

[354] *Visx v Nidek* [1999] F.S.R. 405, 426. See also the discussion in *Zeno v BSM-Bionic* [2009] EWHC 1829 (Pat), at [26]-[37]; *Qualcomm v Nokia* [2008] EWHC 329 (Pat), at [72]-[73].

[355] *Phillips v Nintendo* [2014] EWHC 1959 (Pat), [98]-[105].

[356] [1997] R.P.C. 232, 239.

[357] [2008] EWHC 329 (Pat). See also [78]-[86] of *Schenck Rotec v Universal Balancing* [2012] EWHC 1920 (Pat), a decision of HHJ Birss QC sitting as a judge of the High Court.

[358] [2014] EWHC 1559.

dominant cause, or merely a contributing cause of a given effect? In *ICI Plc v Montedison*[359] the claim was for a composition comprising a stated combination of ingredients A, B and C "whereby" a certain result was achieved. In the Court of Appeal, the three members of the court each arrived at a different construction: Stuart Smith LJ held that C must be a causa sine qua non, Morritt LJ held that the effect had to be obtained by the combination of all three ingredients, and Sir John May held that C should be the causa sine qua non or the dominant cause. Further, the complexity of the technical evidence as to how the effect had been achieved in the alleged infringing product meant that the trial judge had been unable to conclude that the patentee's evidence was correct on this issue and therefore the patentee had failed on the balance of probabilities to prove infringement.

In *Thorn v Siemens*[360] the claim required the presence of a wax and recited it as "facilitating" an operation. The Court of Appeal considered that for the claim to be satisfied, a practical benefit as a result of its inclusion had to be shown; the claim was talking about something that mattered. By contrast, in *PCME v Goyen Controls*[361] a phrase commencing "in order to ..." was construed as mere surplusage, describing the alleged benefits of using other claimed features and not further limiting the claim.

9-330

"Preferably"

The word "preferably" in a claim imposes no limitation, though it serves to indicate that whatever else the claim may cover, it certainly covers that which is indicated as preferred. Its use in a claim is a customary draftsman's device which serves to facilitate amendment, should that ever be required, by a simple deletion.[362]

9-331

"Predetermined"

This commonly used word gave rise to difficulty in *Nikken Kosakusha Works v Pioneer Trading Company*,[363] where the issue was the meaning of the expression "an annular groove of predetermined depth". Mann J concluded that it meant no more than "a groove whose depth the maker has decided in advance". He rejected the criticism that this could introduce subjective intention into the issue of infringement, and also rejected a submission that it meant a groove of sufficient depth to achieve the object of the invention since this amounted to rewriting rather than construing the claim. In the Court of Appeal,[364] Jacob LJ said that "it beggars belief that a patent agent could draft a claim in such words or that the Patent Office would accept them. 'Predetermined depth' cries out for the question, by whom? And what does it mean?" The criticism was of course directed to its use of the word "predetermined" in that particular context, for while it is difficult to conceive of a groove whose depth is not determined in advance, the distinction between

9-332

---

[359] [1995] R.P.C. 449.
[360] [2009] R.P.C. 3.
[361] [1999] F.S.R. 801, 809.
[362] *Corevalve v Edwards* [2009] F.S.R. 8, [45].
[363] [2005] F.S.R. 15.
[364] [2006] F.S.R. 4, [2].

parameters decided at "design time" and not left open or variable until "run time" may of course be useful in other circumstances.[365]

Words of degree

9-333   Words of degree such as "large" or "thin" are sometimes found in claims. In *British Thomson-Houston v Corona Lamp Works*,[366] the claim required a lament of "large diameter". It was held that the word "large" carried the notion of comparison and in the absence of any standard stated in the specification, the comparison would be that which would be well understood in the trade as being the average for a given vacuum lamp. Lord Finlay suggested that if the particular dimensions had been defined arithmetically, the only usefulness would be to those who wished to take the substance of the invention while avoiding liability for infringement.

9-334   In *Cleveland Graphite v Glacier Metal*,[367] where the claimed bearing liner was required to be of "thin and flexible" metal, the relevant test was held by Somervell LJ in the Court of Appeal to be whether the liner obtained its strength from its own rigidity or, being flexible, from the housing. In the House of Lords, Lord Normand pointed out that this test differed only in words and not in substance from the test of comparison with existing liners of which the skilled person would be aware. He also stressed the undesirability of cutting down the protection due to an inventor who had made as clear a definition of his monopoly as the subject admitted of. Or, as Lord Kinnear observed in *Watson Laidlaw & Co v Pott Cassells and Williamson*[368]:

> "A patentee must not use language so vague as to enable him to secure a monopoly for more than his real invention and so to invade the rights of his free rivals. But, on the other hand, it is permissible to state the real invention in language of such generality as is essential to preserve it and to prevent those rivals from invading the rights of the patentee."

9-335   In *Palmaz's Patents*[369] the claim required the presence of "thin bars having a uniform thin rectangular cross-section". It was held that this merely required that the metal was thin enough to perform its required function but not so thin as to be liable to collapse when in position. A submission that the two uses of the word "thin" had two separate meanings, for different reasons, was rejected as involving the "meticulous verbal analysis" deprecated by Lord Diplock in *Catnic*.

Tests for infringement

9-336   The patentee is entitled to specify a test for infringement in the claim, though this may give rise to difficulties if it is unclear. As Jacob J said in *Millikin Denmark AS v Walk O Mats Limited*[370]:

> "It is possible to imagine claims which simply have no meaning to the skilled man. A lie detector which had been calibrated in Pinnochio units, no one knowing what these were, would be an example."

---

[365] See, e.g. the discussion in *Folding Attic Stairs v Loft Stairs* [2009] F.S.R. 24, at [43]-[56].
[366] (1922) 39 R.P.C. 49.
[367] [1950] 67 R.P.C. 149.
[368] (1911) 28 R.P.C. 565; cited with approval in *Poseidon v Cerosa* [1982] F.S.R. 209.
[369] [1999] R.P.C. 47. See also *Abbott Laboratories v Evysio* [2008] R.P.C. 23, at [114]-[130] ("substantially at").
[370] [1996] F.S.R. 292, 301. See also *Procter & Gamble Co v Peaudouce* [1989] F.S.R. 180, at 198; *Scanvaegt v Pelcombe* [1998] F.S.R. 786; *Novartis v Johnson* v Johnson [2010] EWCA Civ 1039.

In *Ratiopharm v Napp*[371] the relevant test required an average to be taken over a   **9-337**
number of samples in a batch. However the claim was to a "dosage form", i.e. a
single tablet, and so infringement was established by showing that a modest but
significant portion of tablets would pass the test, even though the batch as a whole
would not.

Numerical values and ranges

Patent claims frequently contain limitations to quantities of constituent   **9-338**
components expressed as numerical ranges with lower and/or upper limits. The
question arises as to whether those limits are to be treated as absolute, or whether
some deviation outside the stated range may still amount to infringement.

The *Catnic* case itself was concerned with a descriptive word ("vertical") rather   **9-339**
than a numerical limit; and it might be argued that Lord Diplock's comments on
over-meticulous verbal analysis would have no application in relation to a clearly
stated numerical limit. However, the purposive approach to construction is a general
one. Like "vertical", which had different meanings to a geometer or an engineer, a
number may or may not impart absolute precision depending on all the circumstances in which it is used. It is submitted that the correct consideration in each case
is to determine whether on its true construction the stated limit has to be read as
"exactly (X)" or as "about (X)", determination of which possible meaning is correct being approached in the same way as for any other form of claim limitation.

Such an approach was applied by Aldous J in *PLG Research Ltd v Ardon*   **9-340**
International Ltd,[372] to a numerical limit in a claim. The claim, relating to a method
of producing plastic netting, contained a requirement that junctions have "a
minimum thickness not less than 75 per cent of the thickness of the mid-point of
any of the strands passing into the junction". Aldous J held at 213-214 that:

> "There is no evidence that the 75 per cent limitation, as opposed to say 76 per cent or 74 per cent,
> was crucial, nor that it would be seen to be crucial by the skilled addressee. Thus, variants close to
> 75 per cent limitation for a minor part of the junctions would not have a material effect upon the way
> the invention worked and that would have been obvious to the skilled addressee. Further the patentee
> would not be thought to have intended to exclude such variants from his monopoly. The skilled ad-
> dressee would realise that the manufacture of plastics net structures by biaxially stretching was a
> process in which variations of thickness were certain and that the edges of the junctions could not
> be vertical. Thus there would be some variation apparent when measuring the strands and the junc-
> tions, and also the measurements taken at the extreme edge would not be the place contemplated for
> the patentee."

Aldous J went on to hold the patent invalid and not infringed for other reasons,   **9-341**
so that the above passage was not strictly part of his reasoning. He did, however,
hold at 217 that although significant parts of the defendant's junctions had an average thickness of only between 60 per cent and 72 per cent of the strand thickness,
he would have found infringement if the product had differed from the claim only
in that respect. This part of his judgment was not challenged on appeal.[373]

In *Lubrizol Corp v Esso Petroleum*[374] the figure of "1.3" in the claim was   **9-342**
construed as "1.3 to two significant figures", in accordance with the scientific
convention that numbers are given to the number of figures that are significant, and

---

[371] [2008] EWHC 3070 (Pat), [86]-[96].
[372] [1993] F.S.R. 197.
[373] See [1995] R.P.C. 287.
[374] [1998] R.P.C. 727, 748.

therefore "at least 1.3" was construed as meaning anything above 1.25. While this is a straightforward approach to the number itself, such a construction of the words "at least" is difficult to reconcile with the requirement for reasonable certainty for third parties, for the patentee could have said "at least 1.25" if he had meant this. Similarly, in *Rhône-Poulenc v Dikloride*,[375] a value of 5 per cent was held to fall within "4.8 per cent or less". Evidence as to what the skilled reader would understand to be the expected precision of the measurement in question may be material here. In *Halliburton v Smith*,[376] Pumfrey J construed "between 31 per cent and 35 per cent" as meaning "the specified number to two significant figures, so including 30.5 per cent to 35.4 per cent, or 30.50 per cent to 35.49 per cent, or 30.500 per cent to 35.499 per cent", in the light of such evidence relating to the simulation methods used to determine the relevant parameter.

9-343   In all of the above cases, the construction issue arose in the context of infringement and the claim was broadened beyond its strict mathematical limits. Logically it should follow that the same approach will be applied when the question arises in the context of a novelty attack, and this issue was addressed by the Court of Appeal in *Smith & Nephew v Convatec* (see further below).

9-344   A stricter approach was taken by the deputy judge in *Auchincloss v Agricultural and Veterinary Supplies*,[377] where after stating that he did not regard the departure from the stated numerical range as a "variant" at all in the *Catnic* sense, he held (in a passage not in issue in the subsequent decision of the Court of Appeal):

> "Where the patentee has expressed himself in terms of a descriptive word or phrase there may be room for supposing that he was using language figuratively, and did not intend to restrict himself to the purely literal meaning. But where the patentee has defined an integer of his claim in terms of a range with specified numerical limits at each end, his purpose must be taken to have been to claim thus far and no further. His reason for doing so may not be apparent, but it may exist all the same, for instance it may lie 'buried in the prior art'. Further, in this case I believe that there are evidence reasons of convenience and certainty which would have led him to claim in this way, as I have observed."

9-345   In *Smith & Nephew v Convatec*[378] Birss J had to consider the meaning of the phrase "the agent being present in a concentration between 1 per cent and 25 per cent of the total volume of treatment". On the lower boundary there were three possibilities. The claimant's primary case was that the claim would be understood as requiring rounding to the nearest whole number and so anything more than 0.5 per cent was caught. The defendant's primary case was that the claim "means what it says" and anything less, for example 0.9999 per cent, is outside the claim. The defendant's fall back position was that 1 per cent is expressed to one significant figure and so anything greater than or equal to 0.95 per cent is covered.

9-346   As regards numerical ranges in particular, the judge was referred to a number of cases in the English courts and the Technical Board of Appeal in the EPO, most of which applied a significant figures approach.[379] Counsel pointed out that in *Kirin-Amgen* Lord Hoffmann referred to numerical ranges at [65], observing that the no-

---

[375] [1988] F.S.R. 282, 290, High Court of Malaya.
[376] [2006] R.P.C. 2, [91].
[377] [1997] R.P.C. 649, 689–690.
[378] [2013] EWHC 3955 (Pat); [2014] R.P.C. 22.
[379] The cases were: *Lubrizol v Esso* 13 November 1996 in a passage not reported in the report at [1997] R.P.C. 195, *Goldschmidt v EOC Belgium* [2000] EWHC Pat 175, *Halliburton v Smith* [2006] R.P.C. 6, *FNM Corp v Drammock* [2009] EWHC 1294, *Auchinloss v Agricultural & Veterinary Supplies* [1997] R.P.C. 649, *PLG v Ardon* [1993] F.S.R. 197, T 74/98 (19 October 2000) and T 1186/05 (6

tion of strict compliance with the conventional meanings of words or phrases sits most comfortably with the use of figures, measurements, angles and the like, when the question is whether they allow for some degree of tolerance or approximation.

In his judgment the judge pointed out that the fact that in many earlier cases the courts in England and the EPO Boards of Appeal have held that the question of whether a value should be held to fall within a numerical limit should be decided by rounding that value to the same number of significant figures as the range is expressed in the claim, does not mean that this must always be the conclusion to be reached.[380]He came to the conclusion that a lower limit of 0.95 per cent was the correct approach.

9-347

This decision was appealed by both parties, the leading judgment being delivered by Kitchin LJ.[381] The correct approach to the interpretation of numerical ranges is set out in his judgment at [16], et seq., under "The approach to interpretation of a numerical range" starting with the general approach to be adopted to the interpretation of a patent claim set out by Lord Hoffmann in *Kirin Amgen* and later summarised by Jacob LJ giving the judgment of the court of appeal in *Virgin*. Kitchin LJ stressed (at [17] and [18]) that the following principles were just as applicable to a claim containing a numerical range as they are to a claim containing descriptive words or phrases:

9-348

"17. I would add the following two principles which are also drawn from Lord Hoffmann's speech and which have a particular bearing on this appeal. First, the reader comes to the specification with the benefit of the common general knowledge and on the assumption that its purpose is to describe and demarcate an invention. Second, the patentee is likely to have chosen the words appearing in the claim with the benefit of skilled advice and, in so far as he has cast his claim in specific rather than general terms, is likely to have done so deliberately."

Kitchin LJ considered a wide range of authorities and concluded:

9-349

"38. As I have said, the approach to be adopted to the interpretation of claims containing a numerical range is no different from that to be adopted in relation to any other claim. But certain points of particular relevance to claims of this kind do emerge from the authorities to which I have referred and which are worth emphasising. First, the scope of any such claim must be exactly the same whether one is considering infringement or validity. Secondly, there can be no justification for using rounding or any other kind of approximation to change the disclosure of the prior art or to modify the alleged infringement. Thirdly, the meaning and scope of a numerical range in a patent claim must be ascertained in light of the common general knowledge and in the context of the specification as a whole. Fourthly, it may be the case that, in light of the common general knowledge and the teaching of the specification, the skilled person would understand that the patentee has chosen to express the numerals in the claim to a particular but limited degree of precision and so intends the claim to include all values which fall within the claimed range when stated with the same degree of precision. Fifthly, whether that is so or not will depend upon all the circumstances including the number of decimal places or significant figures to which the numerals in the claim appear to have been expressed."

After considering the disclosure of the patent in suit Kitchin LJ considered that Birss J was right to reject Smith & Nephew's primary case that the limits of the claim were exactly 1 per cent and 25 per cent. Kitchin LJ found that taken as a whole, in the light of the common general knowledge and the teaching of the specification, the skilled reader would believe that the patentee intended the limits to be understood in a less precise way. However, there was no logical basis for preferring the significant numbers approach over the whole number (or zero decimal

9-350

December 2007).

[380] See [49].

[381] [2015] EWCA Civ 607.

places) approach in construing the claim in issue and Kitchin LJ found that the skilled reader would understand that the patentee intended the claim to embrace all concentrations of agent ≥ 0.5 per cent and < 25.5 per cent.

9-351   Lord Justice Christopher Clarke added:

> "68. To a person not possessed of the relevant common general knowledge and not skilled in the art, in which category I would until now have placed myself, the proposition that 0.75 (or 0.5) falls between 1 and 25 appears obviously incorrect. To jump to that conclusion would, however, ignore the fact that figures, no less than words, may take their meaning from the context in which they are used. A linguist may regard the word 'one' as meaning 'one'-no more and no less. To those skilled in the art it may, however, in context, imply a range of values extending beyond the integer. For the cogent reasons contained in the judgment of Lord Justice Kitchin, I agree that in the patent in suit the words 'between 1 per cent and 25 per cent' extend to all values ≥ 0.5 per cent and < 25.5 per cent."

9-352   An extreme case on numerical limits was where the claim called for two or more instances of a given integer, and the infringer had only one. In *Mabuchi Motor K.K.'s Patents*[382] the claim called for a "plurality" of projections. The defendant's device, which was alleged to infringe, had a single projection, but bent over and with a relief hole at the bend. Jacob J held that although "plurality" had to be construed, applying the "*Improver*"[383] principles, as excluding a single projection, the skilled person would consider that the defendant's device amounted in substance to two flaps or an immaterial variant from two flaps which was not excluded from the claim. However, the German court reached the opposite conclusion,[384] regarding one projection as an arrangement which was specifically excluded and which could not be recouped by the doctrine of equivalence.

9-353   The interaction between the word "approximately" and a stated ratio was considered in *Generics UK Ltd v Yeda*[385] where the question arose as to the meaning of "approximately 6:2:5:1". Each of the claims required the presence or production of "copolymer-1" and the patent stated that "Copolymer-1 is a mixture of polypeptides composed of alanine, glutamic acid, lysine and tyrosine in a molar ratio of approximately 6:2:5:1." The claimant's primary contention at first instance was that the word "approximately" covered compositions in which the molar fraction of any single amino acid did not differ from 6:2:5:1 by more than ±10 per cent, with the result that its product did not infringe. The claimant's secondary contention was that, if this were not correct, the patent failed to provide any criterion by which to determine what is covered by the word "approximately", and thus was ambiguous. The patentee's contention was that the word "approximately" meant what it said and reflected the fact that copolymer-1 is a random copolymer whose composition is not precisely defined. Thus the skilled reader would understand that, in this respect, the claims had a fuzzy boundary. The skilled reader would also understand, however, that the claims embraced compositions in which the molar ratios of the amino acids (as distinct from the molecular weight distributions) correspond to those of the prior art copolymer-1 compositions referred to in the patent. These broad contentions generated a number of sub-issues and a considerable volume of evidence was considered by Arnold J. Ultimately he held that:

> "219. Drawing these threads together, my conclusions are as follows. The skilled team would consider that the word 'approximately' was intended to cater for variations in both amino acid

---

[382] [1996] R.P.C. 387, 407-408.

[383] [1990] F.S.R. 181. See para.9-134, et seq.

[384] [1990] R.P.C. 411.

[385] [2012] EWHC 1848 (Pat).

analysis and the synthesis of copolymer-1. They would proceed on the basis that the inventors might well be intending to allow for a level of error in analysis of greater than ±per cent. As for the variability in synthesis, they would not think it was appropriate to take twice the variance in the analysis as marking the limit of compositions that could properly be regarded as constituting copolymer-1. They would take into account the effect of changes in molar ratio in terms of numbers of amino acids as shown by Prof Sampson's illustrations, and as a result would be inclined to accept a greater deviation in the proportion of tyrosine than in the case of the other amino acids. Accordingly, the skilled team would conclude that the claim was one that had a fuzzy boundary. It is therefore not possible to say precisely where that boundary lies. What can be said is that in my judgment the skilled team would not regard a relative difference in tyrosine of 29.6 per cent, as in the case of batch GMA2, as taking the batch outside the claim. Furthermore, I do not consider that the claim is ambiguous."

On appeal, the Court of Appeal[386] held that: **9-354**

"104. I think that there is in fact very little difficulty over the question of construction. The parties are agreed that the skilled team would understand the patentee to be using the term 'approximately 6:2:5:1' to allow for variations in amino acid analysis and variability in copolymer-1 synthesis. I think that the only other evidence which was material to the question of what the skilled person would have understood that term to mean was that given by Dr Coles and Professor Kent, namely that the skilled person would be concerned that variations might affect the known efficacy and safety of co-polymer-1. Accordingly the question to be asked on infringement was whether the percentage difference from 6:2:5:1 expressed as a molar fraction in any given sample is within the variability which can arise from amino acid analysis and copolymer-1 synthesis. The skilled person would not consider a difference which exceeded such variability as being within the scope of the claim.

105. That, in my judgment, is where the question of construction ended and the question of infringement should have begun. It did not matter that the skilled person would not have known from their common general knowledge how to quantify the maximum degree of variability. That was a question for evidence. I differ with respect from the judge when he derived from Professor Sampson's illustrations the proposition that the skilled team would tolerate a greater variation in tyrosine, and that such variation could be as much as 29.6 per cent. The evidence did not support the conclusion that the skilled team would think that the patentee was using the term 'approximately 6:2:5:1' to convey this meaning."

---

[386] [2013] EWCA Civ 925.

CHAPTER 10

INVALIDITY AND THE GROUNDS OF REVOCATION

CONTENTS

1. INTRODUCTION

The grounds upon which a patent may be revoked are codified in s.72(1) of the **10-01**
1977 Act, set out in full below. Subsections 72(1)(a)–(e) provides five grounds upon
which a patent may be revoked, and the section expressly states that these are the
only available grounds.

Subsection 72(1)(a), the ground that "the invention is not a patentable inven- **10-02**
tion", refers back to the definition of patentable invention in s.1. It therefore
incorporates within it the objections of lack of novelty (anticipation) and lack of
inventive step (obviousness) which in view of their importance are discussed more
fully in separate chapters which follow, as is the objection of insufficiency under
s.72(1)(c).

These grounds for revocation also define the grounds on which the validity of a **10-03**
patent may otherwise be put in issue. An exhaustive list of other proceedings in
which validity may be challenged is set out in s.74(1). Invalidity may be relied upon
as a defence to an action for infringement of a granted patent, or for infringement
of rights conferred by a published application. Validity may also be put in issue in
proceedings for a declaration of non-infringement, proceedings for groundless
threats, or disputes relating to Crown use; this is further discussed in the respective chapters of this work dedicated to those types of proceedings.

Section 74(2) expressly provides that validity may not be put in issue in any other **10-04**
types of proceedings (including an application for a declaration as to validity or
invalidity), and s.74(3) confirms that the only grounds on which validity may be put
in issue are those set out in s.72. Nevertheless, the terms of a settlement agreement may preclude a party from putting validity in issue when it is sued for infringements committed after the agreement.[1]

History

Section 26(1) of the Patents Designs and Trade Marks Act 1883 abolished the **10-05**
proceeding by *scire facias* to repeal a patent and s.26(3) provided that:

> "Every ground on which a patent might, at the commencement of this act, be repealed by scire facias
> shall be available by way of defence to an action for infringement and shall also be a ground of
> revocation."

Those grounds were those that had been established by the common law. A **10-06**

---

[1] *Stretchline v H&M* [2015] EWCA Civ 516, see [40].

similar provision was contained in s.20(2) of the Patents and Designs Act 1907 as originally enacted. However, this section was amended by s.3 of the Patents and Designs Act 1932, which instead introduced a statutory list of grounds of invalidity, as a codification of those previously established by the common law.

10-07   The Patents Act 1949 followed to a large extent these statutory grounds, and s.32(1)(a)–(l) set out 14 separate grounds upon which a patent could be revoked for invalidity. By s.32(4) each of these grounds of invalidity could be relied upon as a defence to an action for infringement without the necessity of seeking revocation of the patent.

10-08   The grounds of invalidity in the 1949 Act were a complete code and whatever flexible powers the court had under the common law were absorbed into the Act.[2] However, in *Bristol Myers Co (Johnson's) Application*[3] Lord Diplock held that recourse to earlier decisions of scire facias was still permissible where the meaning of the Act was in doubt.

10-09   The grounds provided by s.32 of the 1949 Act were extensive and related both to what were known as external and internal grounds of validity. The external grounds were so called because they involved consideration of material (in particular prior art) outside the patent itself and covered matters such as prior claiming, lack of novelty (anticipation), lack of inventive step (obviousness), and prior secret use. The internal grounds covered insufficiency of the specification, inutility of the invention, ambiguity of the claims, lack of fair basis in the specification for the scope of claims granted and non-disclosure of the best method of carrying out the invention.

Relevance of authorities decided under the old law

10-10   The grounds of revocation set out in the 1977 Act are also a complete code. It was a new code with a marked change in language. Furthermore, the actual grounds of revocation, as shown below, are mostly based upon the corresponding grounds in the EPC.

10-11   Under the 1977 Act there are far fewer grounds for attacking the validity of a patent than existed under the previous law. Further, since the wording of the 1977 Act (and of the Convention) differs from that of previous Acts, care must be taken when considering the reasoning in cases decided under equivalent provisions of the previous law.[4]

10-12   In *Dr Reddy's Laboratories v Eli Lilly*,[5] the Court of Appeal had to consider the law relating to "selection patents" and the rules which had been developed under pre-1977 law. It declined to follow the old law and instead adopted the approach taken by the EPO Boards of Appeal in applying the EPC. The Master of the Rolls observed that:

> "In my opinion, in so far as there is a difference between them, the approach of the Board since the 1977 Act came into force, rather than the approach of the English courts proceeding under the earlier law, is to be preferred, unless the former approach can be shown to be one-off, impractical, illogical, inconsistent with principle, not open as a matter of domestic law, or (perhaps) not applied in domestic courts of other signatory states of the EPC. Of course, where the approach is not well-established, for instance, because it was taken only in one Board decision, or does not represent the

---

2   *Amerian Cyanamid Co (Dann's) Patent* [1971] R.P.C. 425.
3   [1975] R.P.C. 127, 156.
4   See, e.g. *Mentor Corp v Hollister Inc* [1991] F.S.R. 557, at 561.
5   [2010] R.P.C. 9, [102]–[103].

consistent approach of the Board, different considerations may well apply. So, too, at least where that approach has not been approved by the Enlarged Board of Appeal, it would often be different if the domestic court considered that the Board's approach was impractical illogical or inconsistent with principle. Obviously, there would be no question of following the Board's approach, if an English court were precluded from such a course as a matter of domestic law. It may also be easier to justify a refusal to follow the Board's approach if courts in, say, Germany or the Netherlands, had also declined to do so."

In that case the Court of Appeal chose to follow the EPO approach to selection patents, rather than the domestic decisions made under the old law. **10-13**

To the extent that general principles developed under the earlier law relating to the grounds of anticipation, obviousness, and insufficiency remain useful, they are incorporated into the discussion in the separate chapters addressing them below. The reader interested in any of the other grounds (which are now only of historical interest) may find them discussed in earlier editions of this work. **10-14**

2.   THE INDIVIDUAL GROUNDS OF REVOCATION UNDER THE 1977 ACT

Under the Patents Act 1977 the grounds upon which a patent may now be revoked are set out in s.72. Section 72(1) provides: **10-15**

"Subject to the following provisions of this Act, the court or the comptroller may by order revoke a patent for an invention on the application of any person (including the proprietor of the patent) on (but only on) any of the following grounds, that is to say—

(a)   the invention is not a patentable invention;
(b)   that the patent was granted to a person who was not entitled to be granted that patent;
(c)   the specification of the patent does not disclose the invention clearly enough and completely enough for it to be performed by a person skilled in the art;
(d)   the matter disclosed in the specification of the patent extends beyond that disclosed in the application for the patent, as filed, or, if the patent was granted on a new application filed under sections 8(3), 12, or 37(4) above or as mentioned in section 15(9) above, in the earlier application, as filed;
(e)   the protection conferred by the patent has been extended by an amendment which should not have been allowed."

Section 72(1) is one of the sections governed by s.130(7) of the Act and is therefore framed to have, as nearly as practicable, the same effect in the UK as the corresponding provisions of the European Patent Convention ("EPC"). **10-16**

Subsections 72(1)(a), (c), (d) and (e) have their origin in arts 100 and 123 of the EPC which identify the grounds for opposition to the grant of a European patent at the EPO and the restrictions subject to which a patent or application may be amended. **10-17**

Subsection 72(1)(b) relates to a wrongful claim to entitlement. The EPC does not provide a mechanism for determining a dispute over entitlement, expressly leaving such matters to be determined by the appropriate national court.[6] **10-18**

Not a patentable invention

Section 72(1)(a) provides that it is a ground of revocation if "the invention is not a patentable invention". This subsection refers back to s.1(1), where a "patentable invention" is defined as being an invention in respect of which the following four conditions are satisfied, that is to say— **10-19**

---

[6]   See EPC art.61; and the Protocol on Recognition thereto. And see para.4–35.

    (a) the invention is new;

    (b) it involves an inventive step;

    (c) it is capable of industrial application; and

    (d) the grant of a patent for it is not excluded by subss.1(2) and 1(3) or s.4A.

10-20   The first of these requirements (novelty, and its converse, anticipation) and the second (inventive step, and its converse, obviousness) will be considered in separate chapters below. The differences between them are described below at para.10–22, et seq. of this chapter.

10-21   The third and fourth of these conditions have been considered in Ch.2.[7] For a granted patent to be revoked on the ground of lack of industrial applicability has hitherto been unusual (perhaps because patents with no industrial application, even if granted, are not usually worth litigating), but it was the principal ground of objection addressed in *Eli Lilly v Human Genome Sciences*.[8] In that case the Patents Court revoked a patent concerned with a newly discovered protein and its gene, the decision was upheld in the Court of Appeal but the Supreme Court overturned the decisions of the lower courts. In doing so the court reviewed the underlying policy and the cases in the EPO under the corresponding art.57 EPC and sought to align UK law on industrial applicability closely with the law developed in the EPO.

The difference between novelty and obviousness

10-22   Lack of novelty is established if the claim, when properly construed, includes within its scope something which has previously been made available to the public. Any prior document relied upon has to be construed as at its date of publication.[9] If it in fact discloses something embodying each of the features of the claim then it will anticipate, even if the underlying or intended purpose of what is disclosed is quite different (a so-called "accidental anticipation").

10-23   In addressing the question of obviousness, it is assumed that the invention is novel and therefore differs in some identifiable respect from the prior art. The question then has to be asked whether it was obvious and hence did not involve any inventive step to devise a product or process falling within the scope of the claim in question.[10] (In considering whether the invention claimed is obvious, the relevant comparison is not between the preferred embodiment of the invention claimed and the prior art. If any embodiment within the scope of the claim is obvious, then the claim is invalid.[11])

10-24   As Lord Hoffmann explained in *Synthon*[12]:

"... it is this requirement that performance of an invention disclosed in the prior art must necessarily infringe the patent which distinguishes novelty from obviousness. If performance of an invention disclosed by the prior art would not infringe the patent but the prior art would make it obvious

---

[7] See respectively para.2–16, et seq., para.2–63, et seq. and para.2–127, et seq.

[8] [2011] UKSC 51, considering the following EPO cases in particular: T 0870/04, T 1329/04, T 0604/ 04, T 0898/05, T 1452/06 and T 1165/06.

[9] See para.11–57.

[10] See *Gadd and Mason v May of Manchester* [1892] 9 R.P.C. 516, at 525; *Molins v Industrial Machinery Co* (1938) 55 R.P.C. 31; *EMI Ltd v Lissen Ltd* [1937] 54 R.P.C. 307, at 324; and *3M v Bondina Ltd* [1973] R.P.C. 491.

[11] *Woodrow v Long Humphreys & Co Ltd* (1934) 51 R.P.C. 25; *Non-Drip Measure Co Ltd v Strangers Ltd* (1942) 59 R.P.C. 1, 23 (reversed in HL on other grounds).

[12] *Synthon BV v SmithKline Beecham Plc (Paroxetine)* [2006] R.P.C. 10, [25]: see also *General Tire v Firestone* [1972] R.P.C. 457, 485–6; *Inpro's Patent* [2006] R.P.C. 20, [111].

to a skilled person how he might make adaptations which resulted in an infringing invention, then the patent may be invalid for lack of an inventive step but not for lack of novelty."

Such a situation may arise for instance where the prior publication could be implemented in alternative ways, only one of which would fall within the claims of the patent: in such a case an attack of novelty would fail as the claimed invention would not be the inevitable result of the disclosure, but if the relevant alternative was one obvious implementation, then a finding of obviousness would follow.[13]   **10-25**

It is important, therefore, not to blur the distinction between novelty and obviousness. A near miss from the point of view of novelty may sometimes readily lead to a finding of obviousness instead. In such a case, where a prior art citation is so close that it will invalidate the patent for obviousness even if it is not strictly an anticipation, and the only issue is the disclosure of that citation, it may be convenient to treat the two issues together,[14] though care is needed to avoid confusion.[15]   **10-26**

However, a near miss does not necessarily mean that the claim is obvious, for if an "accidental anticipation" argument fails then it may be difficult to show that the necessary modification to bring the cited art within the claim would be obvious. Validity in some cases is a "question of anticipation or nothing".[16] Since obviousness involves different considerations from novelty, there can be cases where once the novelty test has failed, an invention will not be obvious even though the differences between the prior art and what is claimed are small and would involve only reasonable trial and experiment or workshop modification. Once the differences are identified, it remains to be shown that what is claimed is obvious. It is not always the case that small variants from the prior art would be so.[17]   **10-27**

Indeed the fact that the prior art missed the invention may instead be a significant pointer in favour of non-obviousness. And as Jacob J said in *Honeywell v ACL*[18]   **10-28**

"The only surviving attack is one of obviousness. When I say "one" of obviousness, I actually mean that there are several such attacks. One always has suspicions when several obviousness attacks are run. Mr Trevor Watson QC (a doyen of the Patent Bar of the 1930s) used to say, I was taught, that "too many shots at the target make for subject-matter". However when there are several attacks it is of course the court's duty to examine each in turn. That I proceed to do."

However, in *Discovision Associates v Disctronics (UK) Limited*[19] Pumfrey J held as follows: **10-29**

"There is a risk of taking this epigram too literally. While it may be a useful tool for the advocate, it proves too much. Too many shots at the target only make for subject matter when the target is the same, the others have missed it, the common general knowledge is the same for each and the inventors did not have idiosyncratic reasons for doing what they did. As Jacob J said, the court must look at each citation relied on individually. I think also that there is a suggestion in the epigram that the existence of a number of other solutions to a given problem may suggest that the next has subject matter. This is quite illogical, but it is a line of argument which is frequently encountered. The fact that there are a number of ways of approaching a problem does not mean that any one of them is obvious or not obvious."

---

13 See, e.g. *Gemstar v Virgin Media* [2010] R.P.C. 10, [64]-[70].
14 See, e.g. *Akzo's (tibolone) patent, Arrow v Norton Healthcare* (Scottish Court of Session), [2007] R.P.C. 11, [105]-[106].
15 *Hickman v Andrews* [1983] R.P.C. 147, 169–170.
16 *Hickman v Andrews* [1983] R.P.C. 147, 169–170.
17 *Ferag v Muller Martini* [2007] EWCA Civ 15, [12].
18 Unreported, 22 February 1996.
19 Unreported, 29 July 1998.

10-30   A near miss on novelty will be fatal to an attack on validity where the attack is based on a prior application pursuant to s.2(3), since such documents are only treated as prior art for the purpose of novelty and not for the purpose of obviousness.[20]

10-31   The appellate approach in cases involving novelty is different from that applied to obviousness cases; novelty is a question of law and an appellate court may consider afresh, while in a case of obviousness it is reluctant to interfere unless the court below has erred in principle.[21]

Grantee not entitled to be granted the patent

10-32   Section 72(1)(b) of the 1977 Act provides that a patent may be revoked if "the patent was granted to a person who was not entitled to be granted that patent." This ground of revocation is only open to a person who has established his right to be entitled to be granted the patent, or a patent for part of the matter comprised in the specification of the patent sought to be revoked,[22] and in any case cannot be made if the attempt to establish his right was started after the second anniversary of the date of grant of the patent sought to be revoked, unless it is proved that the registered proprietor at the time of grant or when the patent was transferred to him knew he was not entitled to the patent.[23]

10-33   The substantive law on entitlement to a patent is dealt with in Ch.4 of this work.

10-34   The section used to provide, prior to its amendment by the Copyright Designs and Patent Act 1988, that revocation could also be sought if a patent had been granted to someone who was not the *only* person entitled to it. The effect of the amendment is that, whereas a sole owner of the patent who is not named as a proprietor has the right to have the patent revoked, the same does not now apply to co-owners. They can only be registered as co-proprietors.[24]

Insufficiency

10-35   Section 72(1)(c) of the 1977 Act provides that a patent may be revoked if its specification "does not disclose the invention clearly enough and completely enough for it to be performed by a person skilled in the art", the objection known as insufficiency.

10-36   The substantive law on insufficiency is considered in its own dedicated Ch.13 of this work. As noted below, an allegation of insufficiency may form part of a "squeeze" argument as an alternative to obviousness.

10-37   Lack of clarity of a claim is not as such a separate ground of revocation. Lack of clarity (resulting in a claim failing to satisfy the requirement of s.14(5)(b) of the Act that the claim be clear and concise) is of course a reason for refusing grant, and may be a reason for refusing an amendment.[25] It may also result in a finding that it is not possible to tell that the claim has been infringed.[26] However, a claim that lacks

---

[20] *Hoechst Celanese Corp v B.P. Chemicals* [1997] F.S.R. 547; and see para.11–107. See also the various "paroxetine" cases *SmithKline Beecham's Patent (No.2)* [2003] R.P.C. 6, 33 and 43.

[21] *Biogen v Medeva* [1997] R.P.C. 1; and see further para.12–16.

[22] PA 1977 s.72(2)(a).

[23] PA 1977 s.72(2)(b), as amended by the Intellectual Property Act 2014.

[24] *Henry Bros v Ministry of Defence* [1999] R.P.C. 442, 451. And see para.16–158.

[25] See, e.g. the discussion in *LG Philips v Tatung* [2007] R.P.C. 21 (CA).

[26] Consider the example of the lie detector which had to be calibrated in Pinnochio units, no one know-

clarity may also be vulnerable to an insufficiency attack. See para.13–51, et seq. in the chapter dedicated to insufficiency.

Added matter and extension of scope

Two grounds of invalidity are provided which are available in the event of there **10-38** having been improper changes to the content or scope of a patent. In substance, each of the grounds renders invalid a patent which has been amended in circumstances where the amendments do not comply with the requirements of the Act as laid down in s.76 (which are in turn based on the restrictions on amendment set out in EPC art.123). These requirements are considered in Ch.15.

First, the objection generally referred to as "added matter". By subs.72(1)(d) of **10-39** the 1977 Act a patent may be revoked if:

> "the matter disclosed in the specification extends beyond that disclosed in the application for the patent, as filed, …".

The subsection goes on to state that the same applies where matter in a patent **10-40** granted on a new application filed under ss.8(3), 12, or 37(4) above, or as mentioned in s.15(9), extends beyond that in the earlier application as filed.

The leading case is now *Nokia v IPCom*.[27] The rule can be summarised in a single **10-41** sentence, as per Jacob J in *Richardson-Vicks' Patent*[28]:

> "I think the test of added matter is whether a skilled man would, upon looking at the amended specification, learn anything about the invention which he could not learn from the unamended specification"

Secondly, the objection of "extension of scope". By subs.72(1)(e), a patent may **10-42** be revoked if:

> "the protection conferred by the patent has been extended by an amendment which should not have been allowed".

Cases in which objections under these subsections succeed should be relatively **10-43** uncommon, as the amendments in question will already have been scrutinised before acceptance, although experience shows that subsequent litigation can throw up new issues on construction. These objections may be usefully deployed as "squeeze" or "shepherding" arguments,[29] preventing the patentee from asserting a wider reading of the material or claim integer in question. Furthermore, it is relatively common for patentees to seek to amend their patents at trial, usually in order to address novelty or obviousness concerns raised by the pleaded prior art, and the objection of added matter is frequently deployed in relation to such amendments.

3. COMBINING THE INDIVIDUAL GROUNDS OF REVOCATION

The individual grounds of revocation have been identified and described above. **10-44** The immediately following three chapters of this work will address separately and

---

ing what these were, given by Jacob J in *Milliken Denmark AS v Walk Off Mats Limited* [1996] F.S.R. 292.
[27] [2013] R.P.C .5, [46]–[60].
[28] [1995] R.P.C. 568, 576; cited in *Nokia v IPCom*, at [49]; and see also [60] thereof.
[29] See para.10–48.

in detail the most important of those grounds, and in respect of which the case law is the most developed, namely anticipation, obviousness and insufficiency. However, before doing so, it is convenient to comment more generally here on the relationships and interactions between some of them.

10-45   It is of course entirely possible for a patent to be invalid on more than one of the above grounds: for example it may be anticipated by citation X, rendered obvious by citation Y, and also contain objectionable amendments.

10-46   It would be less common for a claim to be simultaneously obvious and insufficient, though this could arise if the claim was over-broad and thus insufficient on the *"Biogen"* principle.[30] In *Horne Engineering v Reliance Water Controls*[31] it was held that it was obvious to make some articles within the claim for other reasons, but the specification was also insufficient in failing to teach that some lengths of baffle tube would not work or would lead to the device working in the same way as the prior art. In *Novartis v Johnson and Johnson*,[32] Jacob LJ pointed out that obviousness and insufficiency may both come into play when a claim is not clear and concise.

10-47   An attempt to run both arguments simultaneously (alleging that a claim is obvious but nonetheless the skilled reader would be unable to put the claimed invention into efffect) may however instead be glaringly inconsistent (as Lord Hoffmann noted in *Conor v Angiotech*,[33] "The specification did claim that a taxol coated stent would prevent restenosis and Conor did not suggest that this claim was not plausible. That would have been inconsistent with the evidence of its experts that taxol was just the thing to try").[34] However, as discussed below, squeezes between obviousness and insufficiency in the alternative can arise.

Validity and "squeeze" arguments

10-48   There can often be an interaction between the individual grounds of invalidity such that they may constitute true alternatives, so that it is also common in UK patent litigation for more than one such ground to be argued so as to raise to a so-called "squeeze" argument. "Squeeze" arguments are less common in jurisdictions where validity and infringement are bifurcated such as in Germany. Nevertheless, the German courts do recognise the concept, as can be seen from the *Formstein* decision[35] which is similar to the *"Gillette"* defence (see below).

10-49   A "squeeze" arises when a patentee is faced with two contentions which constrain them such that their attempt to answer the one may worsen his position as regards the other. A common case is the squeeze between infringement and validity, exemplified by the *"Gillette"* defence[36] if the claim is construed widely enough to cover the defendant's product then it is also wide enough to cover the prior art and must be invalid, whereas if it is construed narrowly enough to avoid the prior art then it does not cover the defendant's product and there is no infringement.

---

[30] See para.13–45.

[31] [2000] F.S.R. 90, [38].

[32] [2010] EWCA Civ 1039, [19].

[33] [2008] R.P.C. 28, [36].

[34] The concept of "plausibility" was considered in the context of industrial applicability in *Eli Lilly v Human Genome Sciences* [2001] UKSC 51, in the context of insufficiency by the Court of Appeal in *Regeneron Pharmaceuticals v Bayer Pharma* [2013] R.P.C. 28, at [95]–[103], and in relation to inventive step in *Generics (UK) Ltd v Yeda Research & Development Co* [2014] R.P.C. 4, at [49].

[35] [1986] GRUR 803, 805.

[36] See para.14-262, et seq.

Such squeeze arguments are highly sensitive to the facts of a particular case and the following paragraphs merely provide some illustrative examples of such situations which have arisen, without attempting to be comprehensive. **10-50**

Novelty and obviousness

The difference between these two grounds has been explained above. While novelty and obviousness are distinct and it is important to avoid confusing the two, they may sometimes be considered together on the basis that either the claim does not distinguish the prior art at all, or if it does then the only differences are obvious modifications of the prior art. **10-51**

Insufficiency and obviousness

It is not uncommon for the grounds of obviousness and insufficiency to be argued in the alternative, the contention in an appropriate case being that either the difference between the cited prior art and the claim is such that the invention would have been obvious to the skilled addressee given the state of his/her common general knowledge, or if not (because some necessary aspect was not part of the common general knowledge) then the specification insufficiently discloses how the invention is to be performed. **10-52**

Such an interrelationship was considered by the Court of Appeal in *Halliburton v Smith*,[37] where it was stated: **10-53**

> "We would add one further comment here: there is an interrelationship between obviousness and insufficiency. At first blush one might suppose that an idea which requires masses of work to implement would be more readily rejected by, or less likely to occur to, the notional unimaginative skilled person/team who is the addressee than one which can be readily put into practice. This produces an apparent paradox: the less sufficient the description, the less is an idea likely to be obvious. The answer to the paradox is this: that if the notional skilled person/team is one that is prepared to contemplate an immense amount of work, that attribute must also be considered part of the person/team's consideration of what is obvious. Obviousness and sufficiency of description must be considered by the same person/team."

However the last sentence must be qualified having regard to the subsequent decision in *Schlumberger v EMGS*.[38] **10-54**

Such a "squeeze" (also sometimes known as a "shepherding" argument) may constrain the patentee's case as to the constitution of the relevant skilled team and the matters comprising common general knowledge, as well as claim construction. Against that, obviousness must of course be considered on the assumption that the skilled addressee was not previously aware of the invention, whereas for the purpose of sufficiency the skilled reader is assumed to be provided with the patent specification. **10-55**

The "squeeze" may be based on classic insufficiency, or on "*Biogen*" insufficiency. Lord Hoffmann noted in *Kirin-Amgen*[39] **10-56**

> "The complaints of insufficiency are four. First, if (contrary to the view I have expressed on infringement) the claims cover EPO made by any form of recombinant DNA technology, it is said that they are insufficient because the specification does not enable TKT's technology. I shall call this the 'breadth of claim objection'. It is a classic patent law squeeze".

---

[37] [2006] EWCA Civ 1715, [22].
[38] [2010] EWCA Civ 819, [54]–[55].
[39] *Kirin-Amgen v Hoechst Marion Roussel* [2005] R.P.C. 9, [105].

10-57   In *Schering-Plough v Norbrook Laboratories*,[40] Floyd J warned that an initial issue may arise:

> "A habit of patent lawyers (which it is easy to fall into) is to talk about directions being sufficient to enable the invention to be 'worked' without specifying what working the invention really means. It is essential in a case such as this to identify what is meant. Moreover it is important to be even-handed with the issue of obviousness."

10-58   In that case, the claims for a combination product required the retention of long-acting effect of one of its components. This aspect, and therefore the claims, were held non-obvious because this effect would not have been expected. However, sufficiency required that the skilled reader should be capable of making a combination having that effect. So far as the broader claims were concerned, this was unpredictable and would require undue effort to determine: those claims failed for insufficiency.

Novelty and insufficiency

10-59   Such a squeeze may in principle arise, in the same way as for obviousness and insufficiency. In *SmithKline Beecham's (Paroxetine Methanesulfonate) patent*[41] the House of Lords held that the test of enablement of a prior disclosure for the purpose of anticipation is the same as the test of enablement of the patent itself for the purpose of sufficiency. The Technical Board of Appeal in the EPO has also held that the tests are the same.[42]

Added matter and novelty/obviousness

10-60   An allegation of added matter may support a powerful squeeze on construction, where there has been a previous amendment of the specification or claims. The patentee is constrained to say that the amendment has introduced no new matter of relevance, and this may limit his ability to contend that the amendment had the effect desired. Thus in *M-Systems v Trek 2000*,[43] the patentee relied upon a proposed amendment to distinguish the prior art, giving rise to this position:

> "M-Systems contended that neither the claim as granted nor as proposed to be amended is limited to such devices but, in the alternative, and if it was right in its submission as to the disclosure of the application, then the introduction of such a limitation by amendment, whether pre or post grant, must necessarily have added to the disclosure. Accordingly, it argued, Trek must either fall victim to the Scylla of the prior art or the Charybdis of the prohibition against adding matter by amendment."

10-61   In *European Central Bank v Document Security Systems*,[44] the patent was attacked on the grounds of obviousness and added matter. The added matter case succeeded at first instance, and on appeal the ECB raised obviousness only on a contingent, "squeeze", basis: that if the skilled person had sufficient common general knowledge and was clever enough to deduce what was claimed in the

---

[40]   [2006] F.S.R. 18, [99].
[41]   [2006] R.P.C. 10, [27].
[42]   *ICI/Pyridine Herbicides* (T206/83) [1987] O.J. EPO 5, [1986] 5 E.P.O.R. 232, [2]; *COLLABORATIVE/Preprorennin* (T81/87) [1990] O.J. EPO 250, [1990] E.P.O.R. 361, [15].
[43]   [2008] R.P.C. 18, [19].
[44]   [2008] EWCA Civ 192.

granted patent simply from the specification as filed, then the claimed invention would likewise be obvious to him over the cited prior art.

Infringement and insufficiency

In *Regeneron Pharmaceuticals v Bayer Pharma*,[45] the Court of Appeal had to consider a squeeze on insufficiency and infringement. The argument was that the development of the alleged infringing product had required a major research effort and a good deal of ingenuity, and if it infringed, then the patent must be bad for insufficiency. This argument was rejected: the claim was for an invention of broad application and the skilled team would have been able to work the invention across its breadth even if they would not have produced the actual infringing product.[46]

10-62

---

[45] [2013] R.P.C. 28.
[46] See also *Kirin-Amgen* [2005] R.P.C. 9, [117].

CHAPTER 11

INVALIDITY DUE TO LACK OF NOVELTY (ANTICIPATION)

CONTENTS

1. INTRODUCTION

Novelty under the 1977 Act

Section 1 of the Act defines a "patentable invention", and one of the require-   **11-01**
ments of that definition is that the invention is new. By s.2(1) of the 1977 Act, an
invention shall be taken to be new if it does not form part of the "state of the art".
A claim that is not new is said to be anticipated (although this term does not appear in the Act itself, other than in a reference in s.128 to the old law under the 1949
Act).

The ambit of the "state of the art" for this purpose is defined by the remainder   **11-02**
of s.2. Subsection 2(2) incorporates all matter (information) which has been made
available to the public before the priority date of the invention. Subsection 2(3)
further incorporates (but only for the purpose of assessing novelty) matter contained
in certain patent applications which matter has an earlier priority date. Subsection
(4) relates to exceptional circumstances where a prior disclosure is to be
disregarded. The issues arising under each of these subsections are considered in
turn below.

The current law was concisely summarised by Lord Hoffmann sitting in the Court   **11-03**
of Appeal in *H Lundbeck A/S v Generics (UK) Ltd*[1] as follows:

"In order to anticipate a patent, the prior art must disclose the claimed invention and (together with
common general knowledge) enable the ordinary skilled person to perform it".

To "disclose the claimed invention" as here required, the prior art must disclose   **11-04**
subject matter which, if performed, would necessarily result in an infringement of
the patent.[2]

The need for an "enabling disclosure" is equally important. A disclosure of, e.g.   **11-05**
the existence of a chemical substance is not enabling (and therefore not an anticipation) if the skilled reader would not know from the information given how to

---

[1]   [2008] R.P.C. 19, [9]; see also the (obiter) comments of Lord Scott in the House of Lords decision
in the same case at [2009] R.P.C. 13, [5]–[8].
[2]   *Synthon BV v SmithKline Beecham Plc (Paroxetine)* [2006] R.P.C. 10, [22]; see also *Inpro's Patent* [2006] R.P.C. 20, at [111]; *Ferag v Muller Martini* [2007] EWCA Civ 15, at [7].

produce or obtain it, or how to obtain or to make the required starting materials. Merely being told that it exists is not of itself enough.

History

11-06   The objection that the invention is not new has long been an objection to validity, but the relevant law has changed significantly with the coming into force of the 1977 Act. Successive earlier Acts codified the law, until s.32(1) of the 1949 Act contained 12 different ground of revocation, including three relevant to novelty. First, s.32(1)(a) set out the objection known as "prior claiming":

> "that the invention, so far as claimed in any claim of the complete specification, was claimed in a valid claim of earlier priority date contained in the complete specification of another patent granted in the United Kingdom".

11-07   Secondly, s.32(1)(e) contained the lack of novelty objection, relating to what was "known or used" in the United Kingdom:

> "that the invention, so far as claimed in any claim of the complete specification, is not new having regard to what was known or used, before the priority date of the claim, in the United Kingdom".

11-08   Thirdly, there was a separate objection of "prior secret use" under s.32(1)(l) of that Act, namely:

> "that the invention, so far as claimed in any claim of the complete specification, was secretly used in the United Kingdom, otherwise than as mentioned in subsection (2) of this section, before the priority date of that claim".

11-09   The former requirement for local novelty, i.e. having regard only to disclosure in the United Kingdom, has now gone, and availability of the relevant anticipatory material anywhere in the world will invalidate. This is implicit in art.54 of the EPC. The draftsman of the 1977 Act has not only provided in s.130(7) that s.2 is intended to have the same effect but has also expressly confirmed this by incorporating the additional words "whether in the United Kingdom or elsewhere" in s.2(2).

11-10   The objection of prior secret use no longer applies. On the contrary, a key requirement of the law is now that the relevant matter has been made available to the public. Use in secret will no longer invalidate, though persons who have been previously working a claimed invention may be able to benefit from the "right to continue" provisions of s.64. In *Lubrizol v Esso*[3] a prior use invalidated a patent granted under the 1949 Act because the *fact* of the prior use was not secret, even though the *details* of the product supplied were confidential and therefore neither public nor enabling: the result would have been different under the 1977 Act.

11-11   The old objection of prior claiming no longer exists. As explained below, the problem which it was intended to meet is now instead addressed by the provision of PA77 s.2(3) (derived from EPC art.54(3)), which treats applications of earlier priority date as part of the state of the art for the purposes of novelty but not obviousness.

2.   SECTION 2(2): THE STATE OF THE ART

11-12   Section 2(2) defines the main body of material which constitutes the state of the art. It provides:

---

[3]   See [1998] R.P.C. at 767 (lines 29–31) and 768 (lines 31–45).

> "(2)   The state of the art in the case of an invention shall be taken to comprise all matter (whether a product, a process, information about either, or anything else) which has at any time before the priority date of that invention been made available to the public (whether in the United Kingdom or elsewhere) by written or oral description, by use or in any other way."

A number of separate questions will have to be addressed in resolving any allegation of lack of novelty:

    (1)   What constitutes the relevant "matter"?
    (2)   To whom must the relevant "matter" be made available?
    (3)   How was the "matter" made available?
    (4)   What information is thereby made available?
    (5)   Does that "matter" make the invention available?

11-13

(1)   What constitutes the relevant "matter"?

Section 2(2) introduces the concept of "matter", a potentially confusing expression, particularly when taken in conjunction with the explanation in parenthesis, namely "(whether a product, process or any information relating to either)". The equivalent provision in the EPC, art.54(2), is in somewhat simpler terms and refers more economically to "everything":

11-14

> "(2)   The state of the art shall be held to comprise everything made available to the public by means of a written or oral description, by use, or in any other way, before the date of filing of the European patent application."

The relevant concept is the information that has already been made available to the public. As Lord Hoffmann stated in *Merrell Dow*[4]:

11-15

> "An invention is a piece of information. Making matter available to the public within the meaning of section 2(2) therefore requires the communication of information."

The general wording of these provisions means that there is, in theory, no limit to the way in which such information can be made available.

11-16

It was settled by the House of Lords in *Asahi's Application*[5] that the relevant "matter" should amount to an "enabling disclosure"; put shortly, sufficient information has to be provided for the recipient to be able to put the invention into practice himself. This expression was further analysed by the House of Lords in *Synthon*,[6] discussed further at para.11-92.

11-17

Asahi was a case involving a prior publication in a document. In *Merrell Dow*[7] the House of Lords had to consider what "matter" meant in the context of a prior use. The House confirmed that "matter" means information, so that one had to consider what information had been made available by the prior use. The House again there confirmed that information had to be an "enabling disclosure".

11-18

(2)   To whom must the matter be made available?

"One member of the public free in law and equity to use it"

The words "made available to the public" in s.2(2) are not new to UK patent law in that they formed part of the definition of "published" in s.101(1) of the 1949 Act

11-19

---

4   [1996] R.P.C. 76 at 86.
5   [1991] R.P.C. 485.
6   *Synthon BV v SmithKline Beecham Plc (Paroxetine)* [2006] R.P.C. 10, [2005] UKHL 59.
7   [1996] R.P.C. 76.

and the definition of "published" at s.130(1) of the 1977 Act equates it with being made available to the public. Although the Act does not use the word "published" in respect of the novelty provisions, Aldous J in *PLG Research Ltd v Ardon International Ltd*[8] stated that "made available to the public" should be given the same meaning as those words used in the definition of "published" in s.101 of the 1949 Act:

"Thus to form part of the state of the art, the information given by the use must have been made available to at least one member of the public who was free in law and equity to use it."[9]

(This part of his judgment involved a prior use, but the principle applies equally in the case of documents and other types of prior disclosure.)

11-20   Availability to just one member of the public suffices, for the law imposes no higher threshold for the extent of the availability. Lord Parker CJ said in *Bristol Myers Co's Appn*[10]:

"It seems to us that we are bound ... to reject the contention that publication depends in some way upon anything in the nature of a dedication to the public or upon the degree of dissemination of the information alleged to have been published. On the contrary, if the information, whether in documentary form or in the form of the invention itself, has been communicated to a single member of the public without inhibiting fetter that is enough to amount to a making available to the public ...."

11-21   **Obscurity of publication irrelevant**   The words "made available to the public" also impose no requirement that any person should actually have received the information. It is sufficient if it is available to be received, as, for example, being placed on the shelves of a library open to the public, no matter how obscure or remote the library is. Equally, it makes no difference, if the material is in fact available, whether the skilled person would have had a reason to look for it.[11] In *Lux Traffic Controls Ltd v Pike Signals*[12] Aldous J applied the EPO Board of Appeal decision in *Telemecanique*[13] confirming that a single sale without an obligation of secrecy was enough to invalidate a subsequent patent. He said:

"It is settled law that to invalidate a patent, a disclosure has to be what is called an enabling disclosure. ... Further it is settled law that there is no need to prove that anybody actually saw the disclosure provided the relevant disclosure was in public."

11-22   Thus, once the information is made available to one single person who is free to make such further use of the information as they please, including communicating it to others, then the information is part of the "state of the art"; it can no longer be held back. The underlying principle here is that since, in theory at least, it could then immediately be freely disseminated to and used by anybody, a subsequently granted patent should not validly prevent its use. Whether in practice the information actually was so disseminated is completely irrelevant. Thus the presence of a single document in a little-used foreign language on the shelves of an obscure library is enough to make its contents part of the state of the art, even if in fact it was never

---

8   [1993] F.S.R. 197.
9   [1993] F.S.R. 197, 226.
10   [1969] R.P.C. 146, 155.
11   See *Availability to the Public* (G01/92) [1993] O.J. EPO 277; [1993] E.P.O.R. 241.
12   [1993] R.P.C. 107, 133.
13   (T482/89) [1993] E.P.O.R. 259.

read, because its contents are thereby available to be further disseminated without restriction.[14]

Confidential disclosures have no invalidating effect

The test of "one member of the public free in law and equity" contrasts with the position where the recipient is under some legal or equitable obligation, express or implied, to keep the information confidential. It follows that if the communication is encumbered with an obligation of confidence, expressed or implied, the communication has no invalidating effect.   **11-23**

In *Qualcomm v Nokia*,[15] the defendant submitted that where a document is effectively circulated to every person having an interest in it, it should be treated as made available to the public, even if individual recipients were supplied the document in confidence. Floyd J rejected the submission, holding that it was contrary to the decision of the EPO TBA in Decision T 482/89[16] which relied upon German law to the same effect. However, this decision was doubted in *LG Electronics v Sony Europe*,[17] an application for summary judgment. Arnold J held that there was room for debate as to the correct legal test to be applied in such circumstances.   **11-24**

Cases have arisen where a document has initially been disclosed in confidence, but the confidentiality obligation has subsequently been released. The question is then whether the information is at the moment of release treated as "made available to the public" or whether some further act of dissemination is necessary. The EPO Board of Appeal has indicated that the critical issue is whether the recipient could be treated as representative of the public at the time of receiving the information, or whether he was in some special relationship with the donor.[18] The position where information is imparted under a time-limited embargo, but the recipient is then free to publish it, seems not to have been explored (though in most such cases a subsequent act of publication will take place and may be relied upon).   **11-25**

Nor do disclosures to a third party who keeps it to himself, or cannot understand it

The language of the section also serves to distinguish the case where a third party discovers something but keeps it to himself and discloses it to nobody. In such circumstances nothing has been made available to the public and his mere private knowledge cannot invalidate the patent (a well-settled principle going back to *Dollond's Case* in 1776; see the discussion of it in *Catnic v Evans*[19]). Thus where the information is embodied in a prior use which has remained secret, the information will not be made available to the public and cannot be relied upon in order to invalidate the patent, but s.64 of the 1977 Act provides a limited defence to a secret   **11-26**

---

[14] Jacob LJ said in *Unilin Beheer BV v Berry Floor NV* [2007] F.S.R. 25, at [46]: "… my favourite pretend example is an anticipation written in Sanskrit wrongly placed in the children's section of Alice Springs public library…". See also *Zipher v Markem* [2009] F.S.R. 1, at [248] and *Folding Attic Stairs v Loft Stairs* [2009] F.S.R. 24, at [31]–[32], [66] and [83].

[15] [2008] EWHC 329 (Pat), at [112].

[16] O.J. EPO 1992 646, [2.1]–[2.8].

[17] [2011] EWHC 2319 (Pat).

[18] *New Japan Chemicals/Acetals, Zipher v Markem* (T108/01) [2009] F.S.R. 1, [242]–[244].

[19] [1983] F.S.R. 401, 414.

user to continue that use.[20] (This may be contrasted with the previous law[21] where prior secret use could serve to invalidate a claim to an invention on the ground of lack of novelty.[22])

11-27   It may therefore be possible that there is no "making available" if the only relevant disclosure was to a person who simply could not understand it at all and was therefore not in a position either to use or to disseminate it. Such persons may be considered not to have received the information at all, or, while not under any fetter of confidentiality, as being under a disability in being incapable of taking any further action based on such information.

11-28   In *Folding Attic Stairs v Loft Stairs*,[23] a prototype of the claimed invention was located at the patentee's factory. There it was not ordinarily accessible to the public but it was on display during a visit by a minister and photographer upon who were imposed no terms of confidentiality (and indeed it was partially visible in a newspaper photograph of the visit). The defendants contended that this was therefore an anticipating prior disclosure. The deputy judge held that there is no irrebuttable presumption of law that information that is capable of being perceived by persons who are on private premises is in fact perceived by them, if the circumstances are such as to make it unlikely that those persons were interested in the subject-matter. Examples considered included an abstruse chemical formula disclosed to a child too young to understand it (though the key concept here would appear to be an incapacity to understand and further disseminate or use, not a mere lack of interest). It was pertinent that the premises were not open to the public at large, so that the only viewing had been by a small and defined class of persons who were unskilled and in the relevant sense uninterested; on the facts, the details could not have been further disseminated.

11-29   Such circumstances must be rare. Proof has never been required that the recipient was in fact actually motivated to analyse or further circulate the relevant information—its mere "availability" is enough. It is noteworthy that the section refers to availability to the "public" rather than to the "person skilled in the art". Thus in *Wesley Jessen v CooperVision*[24] it was held that a patent for a contact lens was anticipated by supply of prior art products to patients who were free to use or discuss them—there was no suggestion that any of these end-users had any special knowledge or interest or were other than ordinary members of the public in the widest sense.

11-30   **Whether a disclosure is in fact confidential**   A legal obligation of confidence might be, for example, a contractual non-disclosure agreement. However, aside from any contract, it is well established in English law that there can, in appropriate circumstances, be implied and enforced an equitable obligation of confidence.

11-31   A very frequently cited authority on the requirements for a confidential information action in modern times is *Coco v Clark*,[25] in which Megarry J stated:

"In my judgment, three elements are normally required if, apart from contract, a case of breach of confidence is to succeed. First, the information itself, in the words of Lord Greene MR in the *Salt-*

---

[20]   See para.14-199, et seq.
[21]   PA 1949 s.32(1)(b).
[22]   See per Lord Hoffmann in *Merrell Dow Phamaceuticals v H.N. Norton & Co Ltd* [1996] R.P.C. 76, at 86.
[23]   [2009] F.S.R. 24, [73]–[89].
[24]   [2003] R.P.C. 20, [109].
[25]   [1969] R.P.C. 41.

man case on page 215, must 'have the necessary quality of confidence about it'. Secondly, that information must have been imparted in circumstances importing an obligation of confidence. Thirdly, there must be an unauthorised use of that information to the detriment of the party".

In relation to the second of these requirements, he went on to say: **11-32**

"It seems to me that if the circumstances are such that any reasonable man standing in the shoes of the recipient of the information would have realised that upon reasonable grounds the information was being given to him in confidence, then this should suffice to impose upon him the equitable obligation of confidence. In particular, where information of commercial or industrial value is given on a business-like basis and with some avowed common object in mind, such as a joint venture or the manufacture of articles by one party for the other, I would regard the recipient as carrying a heavy burden if he seeks to repel a contention that he was bound by an obligation of confidence: see the *Saltman* case at page 216."

More recently, Lord Goff stated as follows in the *Spycatcher* case, *A-G v Guard-* **11-33**
ian Newspapers (No 2)[26]:

"I start with the broad general principle (which I do not intend in any way to be definitive) that a duty of confidence arises when confidential information comes to the knowledge of a person … in circumstances where he has notice, or is held to have agreed, that the information is confidential, with the effect that it would be just in all the circumstances that he should be precluded from disclosing the information to others."

This approach appears to accord with the UK's obligations under art.39 of the **11-34**
TRIPS Agreement (Agreement on Trade Related Aspects of Intellectual Property Rights), which provides:

"Natural and legal persons shall have the possibility of preventing information lawfully within their control from being disclosed to, acquired by, or used by others without their consent in a manner contrary to honest commercial practices so long as such information:

(a)   is secret in the sense that it is not, as a body or in the precise configuration and assembly of its components, generally known among or readily accessible to persons within the circles that normally deal with the kind of information in question;
(b)   has commercial value because it is secret; and
(c)   has been subject to reasonable steps under the circumstances, by the person lawfully in control of the information, to keep it secret".

Both the "contrary to honest commercial practices" test and subpara.(c) reflect **11-35**
the requirement that the recipient should have appreciated from the circumstances that the relevant information was secret.

Examples

The above principles relating to implied obligations of confidentiality have been **11-36**
consistently applied in the English authorities addressing the question of "made available to the public", where the question arises whether the recipient was "free in law and equity" to make use of information disclosed to him. Some examples are as follows:

(a)   In *Catnic v Evans*[27] (a case involving a patent granted under the 1949 Act), an architect had shown a model lintel to several parties whom he hoped to interest in making it commercially, in the expectation (to their knowledge) of some reward if they did so. While he had not expressly

---

[26]   [1990] 1 A.C. 109, 281. This approach was cited with approval by Lord Nicholls and Lord Hoffmann in *Campbell v Mirror Group Newspapers* [2004] 2 A.C. 457, at [14] and [48] respectively.
[27]   [1983] F.S.R. 401, 407.

bound them in confidence, it was held that they were under implied obligations of confidence. As a result, the lintel did not become "known" as a result of those disclosures.

(b) In *Pall v Commercial Hydraulics*,[28] a case involving a patent under the 1977 Act, Falconer J had to consider two alleged prior uses: (i) a supply to a potential customer of experimental samples for a comparison test, and (ii) a supply to five other companies of samples for purposes of testing. In relation to use (i), he held that the samples were experimental and secret and that no details of their construction could have been determined; in the circumstances he held that there was not an "enabling disclosure" and thus no anticipation. As for (ii), he held that as the primary purpose for sending the experimental samples was to obtain testing feedback for further development into a commercial product, they were sent under conditions of confidence.

(c) In *Strix v Otter*,[29] the defendants relied on prior disclosures between Strix and Philips. Ferris J held that those parties had been acting pursuant to a joint venture in which there was a mutual obligation of confidence within the tests set out in *Coco v Clark*, which he expressly applied. Thus neither party was free to disseminate information provided to it by the other, and so there was no invalidating prior disclosure.

(d) In *Kavanagh Balloons v Cameron Balloons*,[30] HHJ Fysh similarly applied *Coco* and *Strix*.

(e) By contrast, in *BAYER/Plasterboard*[31] the patentee had before the priority date of its patent carried out experimentation at the premises of its customer. There was no formal development agreement and no formal *secrecy* agreement. An argument that secrecy should be assumed as the parties had a common interest in maintaining it was rejected; the Board of Appeal rejected this, holding that there was no common interest and thus no obligation of secrecy so that the patent was invalid.

(f) In *Aga Medical Corporation v Occultech (UK)*[32] Roth J held that no obligations of confidence applied to medical devices used in clinical trials conducted in Bratislava. This was despite the fact that the Opposition Division of the EPO had held that the same disclosure was confidential.[33]

(g) In *Eugen Seitz v KHS Corpoplast*[34] Roth J held that a fax sent by one defendant to the other nine years prior to the patent was written and intended to be viewed in the context of a joint project which neither defendant was free to disclose to third parties: hence it was confidential. In the same case an issue arose as to whether the supply of a particular machine from one to company (Soplar) to an independent company (Alpla) was done under conditions of confidence. The evidence showed

---

28 [1990] F.S.R. 329.
29 [1995] R.P.C. 607.
30 [2004] R.P.C. 5, [45]–[46].
31 (T602/91) [1996] E.P.O.R. 388.
32 [2015] R.P.C. 12.
33 See [2015] R.P.C. 12, at [53]. However, that Opposition Division decision was itself under appeal: see [2015] R.P.C. 12, at [4].
34 [2015] R.P.C. 11.

that at the relevant time all of Soplar's machines were built for Alpla and that the companies' relationship was unusually close. Roth J nevertheless held that Alpla was under no obligation of confidence as regards the Soplar machines.

The approach which the English Court has taken is also in accordance with the **11-37** EPO Examination Guidelines (November 2015 edn) at Part G, Chapter IV, section 7.2.2, which now states:

> "The basic principle to be adopted is that subject-matter has not been made available to the public by use or in any other way if there is an express or tacit agreement on secrecy which has not been broken, or if the circumstances of the case are such that such secrecy derives from a relationship of good faith or trust. Good faith and trust are factors which may occur in contractual or commercial relationships. Reference should be made to the particular case of a non-prejudicial disclosure arising from an evident abuse in relation to the applicant, in accordance with art.55(1)(a)."

Both Falconer J in *Quantel* and Aldous J in *PLG* expressly referred to and **11-38** relied upon similar statements in previous versions of these Guidelines.

Burden of proof for establishing "free in law and equity" The question of **11-39** where the burden of proof lies was reviewed by the Court of Appeal in *Dunlop Holdings' Application*,[35] (a case under the Patents Act 1949). The position on onus may be summarised as being that the burden lies on the party seeking to invalidate to show that the prior use on which he relies is public (non-secret), but the burden can shift.[36] The *Dunlop* decision was followed and applied in the case of a 1977 Act patent in *Visx v Nidek*.[37]

The concept of a shifting burden is of course a familiar one generally. Where the **11-40** evidence is fragmentary (e.g. purely oral disclosures) the question of who bears the burden may be very significant. Thus in *Dunlop*, where the evidence was thin, the issue was important: there was a divergence of views and the Patent Office held non-secret, the High Court held secret, and the Court of Appeal held non-secret again. In *Visx*, Neuberger J considered that discussions between co-workers were on the facts of that case probably subject to an obligation of confidentiality, though it is clear from the judgment that these were borderline decisions on imperfect evidence. But in cases on prior use where the facts are clearer, e.g. from contemporaneous records, the court is usually able to reach an overall view as to the circumstances of disclosure on the usual "balance of probabilities" standard, without needing to worry about where the burden formally lies.

(3) How was the matter made available?

Section 2(2) requires absolute novelty. It makes no difference to the question of **11-41** novelty where the material forming the state of the art has been made available, whether in the United Kingdom or elsewhere in the world. Similarly, the language of the disclosure will make no difference (though as a practical matter it may give rise to disputes of fact as to the correct translation).

---

[35] [1979] R.P.C. 523, 541–544 (Buckley LJ) and 547 (Bridge LJ).
[36] See especially *Dunlop* at 542/20–543/2. See also *Qualcomm v Nokia* [2008] EWHC 329 (Pat), at [113].
[37] [1999] F.S.R. 405, 440, applied at 442–3, 445, 449; see also *Kavanagh Balloons v Cameron Balloons* [2004] R.P.C. 5, at [46].

11-42   The following paragraphs illustrate means by which information can be communicated and the way in which the nature of the information is to be ascertained.

Making available by documents

11-43   A claim is invalidated if the invention claimed in it was previously "made available to the public", and, accordingly, the nature of the document which made it available is immaterial. In the case of a book or other document containing a description of the invention, it is not necessary that it should have been sold in order to constitute disclosure. Mere exhibition in a bookseller's window for sale, or sending it to a bookseller to be sold, is sufficient disclosure.[38] Prior publication in a foreign journal and in a foreign language will suffice. Where a German specification, six weeks earlier in date, was placed on the shelves of the Patent Office library in a place where members of the public in search of information of the kind in question would normally go, this was sufficient publication.[39] Where a document had been obtained from South Africa by an employee of a company, it was held that it had been published as the document had been communicated to a single member of the public without any inhibiting fetter.[40] Whether or not the document is ordinarily accessible to the public still appears to be the crucial test.[41]

11-44   It is often the case that an author submits a work for publication some considerable time before it is duly published as intended. While it will be a question of fact turning on the circumstances of each case whether submission of the manuscript by the author to the publisher of itself amounts to making it available, it would seem more likely (particularly in the case of scientific papers to be subjected to peer review) that it is held in confidence until actual publication.[42]

Making available by prior use

11-45   Prior to the coming into force of the 1977 Act it had been the law that no patent could be validly granted to prevent the public in the United Kingdom doing either that which was done in public or in secret before the priority of the patent applied for.[43]

11-46   As indicated above, this is no longer the case under the 1977 Act. The whole question of prior use was considered by the House of Lords in the *Merrell Dow* case.[44] It was there contended that the expression "all matter" in s.2(1) must include products or processes which were publicly available in the sense of being available for inspection but which conveyed no information about themselves. Lord Hoffmann rejected this argument[45]:

---

[38]   *Lang v Gisborne* (1862) 31 Beav 133 at 136; 31 L.J.Ch. 769.
[39]   *Harris v Rothwell* (1887) 4 R.P.C. 225, 232; 35 Ch D. 416, at 431; and see *Humpherson v Syer* (1887) 4 R.P.C. 407, at 415.
[40]   *Bristol-Myers Co Application* [1969] R.P.C. 146.
[41]   See *Availability to the Public* (G01/92) (above); and *JAPAN STYRENE PAPER/Foam particles* (T 444/88) [1991] E.P.O.R. 94.
[42]   See *BILFINGER/Sealing Screen*; *Zipher v Markem* (T842/91) [2009] F.S.R. 1, at [240]–[241].
[43]   See PA 1949 s.32(1)(l).
[44]   *Merrell Dow Pharmaceuticals Inc v H.N. Norton & Co Ltd* [1996] R.P.C. 76.
[45]   *Merrell Dow Pharmaceuticals Inc v H.N. Norton & Co Ltd* [1996] R.P.C. 76, at 86. See also *PLG Research Ltd v Ardon International* [1993] F.S.R. 197; and *Evans Medical Ltd's Patent* [1998] R.P.C. 517.

"I think that this argument, which in any event depends upon a rather refined *inclusio unius* construction of the parenthetical expansion of the words 'all matter', dissolves completely when one looks, as one must, at Article 54. This provision makes it clear that to be part of the state of the art, *the invention* must have been made available to the public. An invention is a piece of information. Making matter available to the public within the meaning of section 2(2) therefore requires the communication of information. The use of a product makes the invention part of the state of the art only so far as that use makes available the necessary information.

The 1977 Act therefore introduced a substantial qualification into the old principle that a patent cannot be used to stop someone doing what he has done before. If the previous use was secret or uninformative, then, subject to section 64, it can. Likewise, a gap has opened between the tests for infringement and anticipation. Acts done secretly or without knowledge of the relevant facts, which would amount to infringements after the grant of the patent, will not count as anticipations before."

In all cases, therefore, it will be necessary to prove not only that the prior product or process was publicly available but also to adduce evidence as to what information was conveyed by the prior use to the notional skilled addressee.

11-47

In *MOBIL/Friction reducing additives*,[46] this principle was applied by the EPO to the case of a new use of an old material. Use of the known material for the known purpose would in fact also have achieved the purpose which was the subject of the later patent. However, the previous use would not have revealed the fact that the new purpose was being achieved. A patent was therefore granted. This case, and the problems to which it gives rise, is further considered under the heading "Use claims" at para.11-136, et seq.

11-48

A practical example of the question of ascertaining the information disclosed by a prior use is contained in *Lux Traffic Controls Ltd v Pike Signals Ltd*[47] where there was a prior public use of a prototype set of traffic lights. Aldous J stated[48]:

11-49

"There is a difference between circumstances where the public have an article in their possession to handle, measure and test and where they can only look at it. What is made available to the public will often differ in those circumstances. In the latter case it could be nothing material; whereas in the former the public would have had the opportunity of a complete examination"

and continued:

"In the case of a written description, what is made available to the public is the description and it is irrelevant whether it is read. In the case of a machine it is that machine which is made available and it is irrelevant whether it is operated in public. A machine like a book can be examined and the information gleaned can be written down. Thus what is made available to the public by a machine, such as a light control system, is that which the skilled man would, if asked to describe its construction and operation, write down having carried out an appropriate test or examination. To invalidate the patent, the description that such a man would write down must be a clear and unambiguous description of the invention claimed."

Similarly in *Wagner International v Earlex*[49] Floyd J held that a skilled person who examined the prior art sprayer device which was alleged to anticipate the patent at a trade show would not have been able to deduce two key features of the claims "clearly and unambiguously" from that disclosure. For that reason the novelty attack failed, even though the device itself actually fell within the claims of the patent.[50]

11-50

---

46 G02/88 [1990] O.J. EPO 93; [1990] E.P.O.R. 73.
47 [1993] R.P.C. 107, 132, et seq.
48 [1993] R.P.C. 107, 134.
49 [2012] EWHC 984 (Pat).
50 See [65]–[71].

Standard of proof of prior use

11-51   As to the standard of proof in relation to a prior use, patent litigation applies the ordinary standard in civil litigation generally, namely the overall "balance of probabilities", and this applies equally to proof of prior use. This was confirmed in *Kavanagh Balloons v Cameron Balloons*,[51] where HHJ Fysh declined to follow EPO and US decisions purporting to impose a higher standard in such cases, and concluded that the evidence relating to prior use should be assessed on a flexible and proportionate basis but within the overall requirement of proof on the balance of probabilities.

11-52   Where the facts of prior disclosure are within the knowledge of the patentee, the patentee will be expected to adduce proportionately cogent answers, positive and negative, to gainsay such factual evidence as the opponent is able to establish with the disadvantage of having been privy to none of it.[52]

11-53   Thus all the circumstances can be taken into account when deciding whether a party has discharged an onus upon him, but this can be and always is done within the context of the civil standard.

Making available by oral disclosure

11-54   Publication by oral description is explicitly included in s.2(2) of the 1977 Act[53] but it had long been accepted that an invention can become "known" by a prior oral disclosure equally as by a prior published document or by a prior use. As Bowen LJ said in *Humpherson v Syer*[54]:

> "I put aside questions of public use and treat this as a question of whether there has been a prior publication: that is, in other words, had this information been communicated to any member of the public who was free in law and equity to use it as he pleased. ... If so, the information had been given to a member of the public and there was nothing further to serve as consideration for any patent."

Plainly, evidential difficulties may arise in proving what was said.

(4)   What information was thereby made available?

11-55   Once a particular document or other prior disclosure has been identified, it is necessary to determine what information is conveyed. The prior document or disclosure is to be treated as read or understood through the eyes of the relevant skilled person, the notional addressee. In appropriate cases, the skilled person may have to be a team of people with different scientific backgrounds so that the import of the document may be fully understood.[55]

11-56   This may involve two separate steps: first, construing the prior disclosure as a matter of law, and secondly determining what the skilled reader would derive from it. Pumfrey J stated in *Inpro's Patent*[56] that "The teaching of the specification, once construed, is a pure question of fact, as is what the skilled man would do with that teaching without the exercise of inventive ingenuity". As noted below, he went on

---

[51]   [2004] R.P.C. 5, at [51]–[58].
[52]   *Memcor Australia Pty Ltd v Norit Membraan Technologie BV* [2003] F.S.R. 43, [30].
[53]   See also *IBM/lonetching* (T534/88) [1991] E.P.O.R. 18.
[54]   (1887) 4 R.P.C. 407, 413; and see *Dollond's Case* (1776) 1 W.P.C. 43.
[55]   *Tetra Molectric Ltd v Japan Imports* [1976] R.P.C. 547, 583.
[56]   *Research in Motion v Inpro* [2006] R.P.C. 20, [111].

to explain that the relevant teaching may involve both explicit and implicit disclosure.

The general rule for the construction of prior documents is the same as that for any other documents, namely "that the document should be construed as if the court had to construe it at the date of publication, to the exclusion of information subsequently discovered".[57] The meaning of the document does not change over time. As Jacob LJ said in *SmithKline Beecham Plc v Apotex Europe*[58]: **11-57**

> "A reader (and I suppose this is true of all documents) who wants to find out what the writer was actually saying, must try to read it with eyes of a contemporary to the publication. If an eighteenth-century recipe says 'use dephlogisticated X' one uses what the writer must have meant—the ash of X after burning. One does not say there is no such thing as phlogiston."

In determining the meaning of the document, regard may be had only to what is stated in the document itself, and parol evidence can be admitted merely "for the purpose of explaining words or symbols of art ... and ... of informing the court of relevant surrounding circumstances".[59] Its interpretation at that date is as always for the appropriately skilled addressee.[60] Care must be taken in approaching prior documents for the purposes of anticipation to ensure that the disclosure is not supplemented by the addition of knowledge which would not have been present in the mind of the skilled reader at the date of the publication of the document in question but which would have been known by the priority date of the patent in suit.[61] **11-58**

A prior document which is so obscure in meaning that does not clearly tell the reader what to do does not make anything truly old; a document which has no clear meaning is not "clear and unambiguous" and not novelty-destroying.[62] **11-59**

The target audience may be a relevant consideration: in *Gemstar v Virgin Media*,[63] an issue arose as to whether a feature was displayed to a user or was merely an internal aspect of a database; it was resolved having regard to the fact that the document was written for consumers who would be interested in what they could see and would have no interest in its underlying implementation. **11-60**

Mosaicing

Each document must be interpreted on its own in order to determine the information it contains. It is not legitimate to piece together a number of prior documents in order to produce an anticipation of the invention. In *Von Heyden v Neustadt*,[64] the defendants pleaded anticipation, and put in evidence a mass of paragraphs extracted from a large number of publications. James LJ, in his judgment, said: **11-61**

---

[57] *Ore Concentration Co (1905) Ltd v Sulphide Corp Ltd* (1914) 31 R.P.C. 206, 224; *Nobel's Explosives Co Ltd v Anderson* (1894) 11 R.P.C. 519, 523; see also *British Thomson-Houston Co Ltd v Metropolitan-Vickers, etc. Ltd* (1928) 45 R.P.C. 1, 20; see also *Teva v Astrazeneca* [2014] EWHC 2873, (2015) 142 B.M.L.R. 94, [75].

[58] [2005] F.S.R. 23, [89].

[59] *Canadian General Electric Co Ltd v Fada Radio Ltd* (1930) 47 R.P.C. 69, 90.

[60] *Dyson v Hoover* [2001] R.P.C. 26, [112].

[61] See the observations of Sir Lionel Heald QC in *Minnesota Mining & Manufacturing Co v Bondina Ltd* [1973] R.P.C. 491, at 520–521; cited with approval in *Mölnlycke A.B. v Procter and Gamble Ltd (No.5)* [1994] R.P.C. 49, at 114.

[62] *Schlumberger v EMGS*, [2010] EWCA Civ 819, [164]–[165].

[63] [2009] EWHC 3068, [154].

[64] (1880) 50 L.J. Ch.126.

"We are of opinion that if it requires this mosaic of extracts, from annuals and treaties spread over a series of years, to prove the defendants' contention, that contention stands thereby self-condemned ... And even if it could be shown that a patentee made his discovery of a consecutive process by studying, collating and applying a number of facts discriminated in the pages of such works, his diligent study of such works would as much entitle him to the character of an inventor as the diligent study of the works of nature would do."[65]

11-62   And in *Lowndes' Patent*[66] Tomlin J said:

"It is not open to you to take a packet of prior documents and ... by ... putting a puzzle together produce what you say is a disclosure in the nature of a combination of the various elements which have been contained in the prior documents. I think it is necessary to point to a clear and specific disclosure of something which is said to be like the patentee's invention."

11-63   However, a series of papers which form a series of disclosures and refer to each other, so that "anyone reading one is referred by cross-reference to the others", do not form an impermissible mosaic and can be relied upon together as an attack on novelty.[67]

11-64   Equally, it may be impermissible to "cherry-pick" different aspects of the disclosure of a single document and seek to combine them in such a way as to produce an end result falling with the later claim; this does not necessarily demonstrate that such a combination is itself disclosed to the skilled addressee. See the discussion of proving inevitable result at para.11-84, et seq.

Generic and optional disclosures

11-65   A generic disclosure will not normally take away the novelty of a subsequent claim to a member of the class. For example disclosure of "fixing means" is not a disclosure of a nail.[68] See also the discussion of selection patents at para.11-131.

11-66   Something may be disclosed even if it is described as optional or less preferred; to describe the thing as optional is to describe the thing.[69] In *Ranbaxy v Warner-Lambert*[70] it was held that the relevant enantiomer was indeed specifically disclosed, albeit as one of a number of alternatives that could be made following the teaching of the prior document, and did not require "adaptation" of that teaching. The claim was not novel: it would have covered one of the alternatives explicitly taught by the citation. The fact that the prior art discloses a number of alternative options does not mean that there is no clear and unambiguous disclosure.[71]

11-67   However, a direction not to do something, even though explicitly mentioned, would seem not to be a disclosure of that thing, as following such a direction would not result in doing it. The context, including the suggested reasons for not doing it, may however be material, in particular to an alternative case based on obviousness. A statement that "no epoxy group was found" in a prior document was

---

65   *Von Heyden v Neustadt* (1880) 50 L.J.Ch. 126, at 128; *Rondo Co Ltd v Gramophone Co Ltd* (1929) 46 R.P.C. 378, at 391; *Pope Appliance Corp v Spanish River, etc. Ltd* (1929) 46 R.P.C. 23, [1929] A.C. 269.
66   (1928) 45 R.P.C. 48, 57.
67   *Sharpe & Dohme Inc v Boots Pure Drug Co Ltd* (1927) 44 R.P.C. 367; (1928) 45 R.P.C. 153, 180
68   *Dr Reddy's Laboratories v Eli Lilly* (Floyd J at first instance) [2009] F.S.R. 5, [78].
69   *Ranbaxy v Warner-Lambert* (at first instance) [2006] F.S.R. 14, [52]; *Zipher v Markem* [2009] F.S.R. 1, [252].
70   [2007] R.P.C. 4, [32]–[41].
71   See also *Laboratorios Almirall v Boehringer Ingelheim* 2009 F.S.R. 12, [212].

held by the EPO in case T310/88 not to anticipate even though repetition of the example showed that it was there; the document taught away.

Implicit disclosure

11-68 The disclosure need not be explicit; it may be implicit. As Jacob J said in *Hoechst Celanese v BP Chemicals*[72]:

"...it must be right to read the prior document with the eyes of the skilled man. So if he would find a teaching implicit, it is indeed taught. The prior document is novelty-destroying if it explicitly teaches something within the claim, or as a practical matter, that is what the skilled man would see it is teaching him."

11-69 Pumfrey J stated in *Inpro's Patent*[73] that

"As ever, the question is what is explicitly disclosed and what also is necessarily implicit in the teaching. The skilled man must be taken to read documents in an intelligent way, seeking to find what is disclosed as a matter of substance."

11-70 The reference to what was "necessarily" implicit is important, in ensuring that the relevant disclosure will inevitably result in something falling within the claim. He there held that because the relevant citation taught a particular step, and the only purpose for which that would be taken would be to achieve a requirement of the claim in issue, the relevant requirement was implicitly disclosed and anticipation was established. Such cases where the relevant feature is not explicitly disclosed will clearly generate disputes of construction and of fact, but in that case he was in any event able to make a finding of obviousness in the alternative.

11-71 The approach of the EPO is the same. In the Guidelines for Examination in the EPO,[74] the test is stated as follows:

"A document takes away the novelty of any claimed subject-matter derivable directly and unambiguously from that document including any features implicit to a person skilled in the art in what is expressly mentioned in the document, e.g. a disclosure of the use of rubber in circumstances where clearly its elastic properties are used even if this is not explicitly stated takes away the novelty of the use of an elastic material. The limitation to subject-matter 'derivable directly and unambiguously' from the document is important. Thus, when considering novelty, it is not correct to interpret the teaching of a document as embracing well-known equivalents which are not disclosed in the documents; this is a matter of obviousness."

11-72 Disclosure by inevitable result is further discussed at para.11-84, et seq.

Photographs and drawings

11-73 Particular difficulties may be posed by photographs and drawings where the court will need to be instructed as to the information which any particular document will convey to the skilled addressee. In *C. Van der Lely N.V. v Bamfords Ltd* Lord Reid stated[75]:

"There is no doubt that, where the matter alleged to amount to anticipation consists of a written description, the interpretation of that description is, like the interpretation of any document, a ques-

---

[72] [1998] F.S.R. 586 at 601. See also *Research In Motion v Motorola*, [2010] EWHC 118 (Pat) at [181].
[73] *Research in Motion v Inpro* [2006] R.P.C. 20 at [128].
[74] Part G, Chapter VI—Novelty at Section 2 (November 2015 edn).
[75] [1963] R.P.C. 61, 71.

tion for the court assisted where necessary by evidence regarding the meaning of technical language. It was argued that the same applies to a photograph. I do not think so. Lawyers are expected to be experts in the use of the English language, but we are not experts in the reading or interpretation of photographs. The question is what the eye of the man with appropriate engineering skill would see in the photograph, and that appears to me to be a matter of evidence. Where the evidence is contradictory the judge must decide. But the judge ought not in my opinion to attempt to read or construe the photograph himself; he looks at the photograph in determining which of the explanations given by the witnesses appears to be most worthy of acceptance."

(5) Does that "matter" make the invention available? Disclosure and enablement

11-74   As noted above,[76] it is settled that for anticipation to be established, there must be an "enabling disclosure". This concept has now been further explained by the House of Lords in *Synthon*,[77] which has stressed the importance of separating the concepts of disclosure and of enablement. As Lord Hoffman explained:

"In order to make good their case, Synthon had to satisfy the judge on two points. The first was that their application disclosed the invention which had been patented as claim 1. I shall call this requirement 'disclosure'. The second was that an ordinary skilled man would be able to perform the disclosed invention if he attempted to do so by using the disclosed matter and common general knowledge. I shall call this requirement 'enablement'. If both these requirements are satisfied, the invention is not new."

Disclosure

11-75   As regards the requirement of disclosure, this has been set out in two statements of the law from judgments which were held in *Synthon*[78] to be of "unquestionable authority". The first such statement is from Lord Westbury's speech in *Hill v Evans*[79]:

"I apprehend the principle is correctly thus expressed: the antecedent statement must be such that a person of ordinary knowledge of the subject would at once perceive, understand and be able practically to apply the discovery without the necessity of making further experiments and gaining further information before the invention can be made useful. If something remains to be ascertained which is necessary for the useful application of the discovery, that affords sufficient room for another valid patent."

(Although, as noted at para.11-92 when considering the separate question of enablement, the person skilled in the art may be assumed to be willing to make trial and error experiments to get the matter disclosed to work—provided that the end result for which he is aiming is itself disclosed.)

11-76   The second such statement is from the very frequently cited judgment of Sachs LJ in *General Tire & Rubber Co v Firestone Tyre & Rubber Co Ltd*[80]:

"To determine whether a patentee's claim has been anticipated by an earlier publication it is necessary to compare the earlier publication with the patentee's claim. The earlier publication must, for this purpose, be interpreted as at the date of its publication, having regard to the surrounding circumstances which then existed, and without regard to subsequent events. ... If the earlier publica-

---

[76] See para.11-03.
[77] *Synthon BV v SmithKline Beecham Plc (Paroxetine)* [2006] R.P.C. 10, [14].
[78] *Synthon BV v SmithKline Beecham Plc (Paroxetine)* [2006] R.P.C. 10, [20].
[79] (1862) 31 L.J.(N.S.) 457, 463.
[80] [1972] R.P.C. 457, 485.

tion, so construed, discloses the same device as the device which the patentee by his claim, so construed, asserts that he has invented, the patentee's claim has been anticipated, but not otherwise.

The earlier publication and the patentee's claim must each be construed as they would be at the respective relevant dates by a reader skilled in the art to which they relate having regard to the state of knowledge in such at the relevant date. The construction of these documents is a function of the court, being a matter of law, but, since documents of this nature are almost certain to contain technical material, the court must, by evidence, be put in the position of a person of the kind to whom the document is addressed, that is to say, a person skilled in the relevant art at the relevant date. If the art is one having a highly developed technology, the notional skilled reader to whom the document is addressed may not be a single person but a team, whose combined skills would normally be employed in that art in interpreting and carrying into effect instructions such as those which are contained in the document to be construed. We have already described the composite entity deemed to constitute the notional skilled addressee.

When the prior inventor's publication and the patentee's claim have respectively been construed by the court in the light of all properly admissible evidence as to technical matters, the meaning of words and expressions used in the art and so forth, the question whether the patentee's claim is new for the purposes of section 32(1)(e) [of the 1949 Act] falls to be decided as a question of fact. If the prior inventor's publication contains a clear description of, or clear instructions to do or make, something that would infringe the patentee's claim if carried out after the grant of the patentee's patent, the patentee's claim will have been shown to lack the necessary novelty, that is to say, it will have been anticipated. The prior inventor, however, and the patentee will have approached the same device from different starting points and may for this reason, or it may be for other reasons, have so described their devices that it cannot be immediately discerned from a reading of the language which they have respectively used that they have discovered the same device; but if carrying out the directions contained in the prior inventor's publication will inevitably result in something being made or done which, if the patentee's patent were valid, would constitute an infringement of the patentee's claim, this circumstance demonstrates that the patentee's claim has in fact been anticipated.

If, on the other hand, the prior publication contains a direction which is capable of being carried out in a manner which would infringe the patentee's claim, but would be at least as likely to be carried out in a way which would not do so, the patentee's claim will not have been anticipated, although it may fail on the ground of obviousness. To anticipate the patentee's claim the prior publication must contain clear and unmistakable directions to do what the patentee claims to have invented: *Flour Oxidizing Co Ltd v Carr & Co Ltd* (1908) 25 R.P.C. 428 at 457, line 34, approved in *BTH Co Ltd v Metropolitan Vickers Electrical Co Ltd* (1928) 45 R.P.C. 1 at 24, line 1. A signpost, however clear, upon the road to the patentee's invention will not suffice. The prior inventor must be clearly shown to have planted his flag at the precise destination before the patentee."

Thus, where the directions are capable of being carried out in a variety of ways, some of which fall within the claim and others do not, then there is no clear and unambiguous direction but at best a signpost (though it may lead to an alternative finding of obviousness).[81] This is the qualitative difference being stressed in *General Tire* between "inevitable result" in the claimed way and "at least as likely" in some other way.   **11-77**

Lord Hoffman in *Synthon*[82] went on to explain: **11-78**

"If I may summarise the effect of these two well-known statements, the matter relied upon as prior art must disclose subject-matter which, if performed, would necessarily result in an infringement of the patent. That may be because the prior art discloses the same invention. In that case there will be no question that performance of the earlier invention would infringe and usually it will be apparent to someone who is aware of both the prior art and the patent that it will do so. But patent infringement does not require that one should be aware that one is infringing: 'whether or not a person is working [an]... invention is an objective fact independent of what he knows or thinks about what he is doing': *Merrell Dow Pharmaceuticals Inc v H N Norton & Co Ltd* [1996] R.P.C. 76, 90. It follows that, whether or not it would be apparent to anyone at the time, whenever subject-matter described in the prior disclosure is capable of being performed and is such that, if performed, it must

---

81   *Rocky Mountain Traders v Hewlett Packard* [2002] F.S.R. 1, [34].
82   *Synthon BV v SmithKline Beecham Plc (Paroxetine)* [2006] R.P.C. 10, [22].

result in the patent being infringed, the disclosure condition is satisfied. The flag has been planted, even though the author or maker of the prior art was not aware that he was doing so."

11-79   The need for clear and unmistakable directions therefore does not require equivalence of language—merely of teaching. The question arose for consideration by the House of Lords in *Merrell Dow*[83] where the prior disclosure related to the use of terfenadine in vivo as an anti-histamine. This use would inevitably have produced the compound of the invention although no one would have appreciated this. Lord Hoffmann there reasoned as follows:

> "There is an infinite variety of descriptions under which the same thing may be known. Things may be described according to what they look like, how they are made, what they do and in many other ways. Under what description must it be known in order to justify the statement that one knows that it exists? This depends entirely upon the purpose for which the question is being asked. Let me elaborate upon an example which was mentioned in argument. The Amazonian Indians have known for centuries that cinchona bark can be used to treat malarial and other fevers. They used it in the form of powdered bark. In 1820, French scientists discovered that the active ingredient, an alkaloid called quinine, could be extracted and used more effectively in the form of sulphate of quinine. In 1944, the structure of the alkaloid molecule (C20H24N2O2) was discovered. This meant that the substance could be synthesised"

and concluded:

> "My Lords, I think that on this point the Patents Act 1977 is perfectly clear. Section 2(2) does not purport to confine the state of the art about products to knowledge of their chemical composition. It is the *invention* which must be new and which must therefore not be part of the state of the art. It is therefore part of the state of the art if the information which has been disclosed enables the public to know the product under a description sufficient to work the invention."[84]

11-80   In consequence, in so far as the claim to the compound covered its production in vivo, the claim was invalid. A means of synthetic preparation was not, however, disclosed in the prior art and a claim to the compound when prepared synthetically was allowed.

11-81   It follows as a consequence from the *Merrell Dow* case that the question of whether a prior published document makes an invention available to the public cannot necessarily be confined to an analysis of the prior published document and the patent. The Court of Appeal held in *SmithKline Beecham Plc's Patent*[85] that:

> "As *General Tire* made clear, the prior published document may have approached the device or chemical from a different point of view. If however the prior document is enabling so that by carrying out the directions it inevitably leads to the flag being planted within the claim, the patent will lack novelty."

11-82   In particular, it does not matter whether the prior document discloses the invention itself, or merely discloses directions which would inevitably result in the invention being performed. Lord Hoffmann stated in *Synthon*[86]:

> "Although it is sometimes said that there are two forms of anticipatory disclosure: a disclosure of the patented invention itself and a disclosure of an invention which, if performed, would necessarily infringe the patented invention (see, for example, Laddie J in *Inhale Therapeutic Systems Inc v Quadrant Healthcare Plc* [2002] R.P.C. 21 at para.43) they are both aspects of a single principle,

---

[83] *Merrell Dow Pharmaceuticals v H.N. Norton & Co Ltd* [1996] R.P.C. 76, 88.
[84] See also *BAYER/Diastereomers* (T12/81) [1979–85] E.P.O.R. Vol.B. 308, at 312.
[85] [2003] R.P.C. 6, [18].
[86] *Synthon BV v SmithKline Beecham Plc (Paroxetine)* [2006] R.P.C. 10, [2005] UKHL 59, [24].

namely that anticipation requires prior disclosure of subject-matter which, when performed, must necessarily infringe the patented invention."

So another way of looking at the question is to ask whether what has been disclosed falls within the claim—if it were carried out, would it necessarily infringe?[87] As Lord Hoffmann went on to say[88]:

11-83

"it is this requirement that performance of an invention disclosed in the prior art must *necessarily* infringe the patent which distinguishes novelty from obviousness. If performance of an invention disclosed by the prior art would not infringe the patent but the prior art would make it obvious to a skilled person how he might make adaptations which resulted in an infringing invention, then the patent may be invalid for lack of an inventive step but not for lack of novelty."

"Inevitable results" must be strictly proved

The test for inevitability is strict: as was pointed out in *Ferag v Muller Martini*,[89] the phrases "necessarily result" and "must result" in Lord Hoffmann's speech are significant. An invention cannot be new if the prior art contains a teaching which, when followed, will inevitably produce something falling within the claims[90] provided the teaching is clear and unambiguous.[91]

11-84

Thus in *Inhale v Quadrant*[92] Laddie J held that even though it was "overwhelmingly likely" that the prior art had formed a composition within the claims of the patent in suit, this was not enough for the purposes of anticipation: see below. In *BASF v SKB*[93] Pumfrey J noted at [44] that the same test was also applied in the EPO, the examination guidelines stating that the inevitable result objection should only be raised where there "can be no reasonable doubt as to the practical effect of the prior teaching".[94] In *Swarovski-Optik v Leica Camera*[95] the prior art device was adjustable. In normal operation it did not anticipate the claim but it would do so if adjusted to suit a set of unusual conditions. The argument was whether the possibility that it might be so adjusted was enough to establish anticipation. The Court of Appeal doubted the legitimacy of this approach but did not find it necessary to decide the issue.

11-85

Nature of experiments necessary to prove "inevitable results"

In repeating any prior art proposal by experiment with a view to proving lack of novelty, the party seeking to do so must adhere faithfully to the teaching of the source document. Moreover, the interpretation of the cited document for the purpose of such experiment is deemed to be assessed as of the date of its publication, and that interpretation is also deemed to be the job of the skilled worker, whose

11-86

---

[87] *Technip France SA's Patent* [2004] R.P.C. 46, [77]; *Ferag v Muller Martini* [2007] EWCA Civ 15, [8].

[88] *Synthon BV v SmithKline Beecham Plc (Paroxetine)* [2006] R.P.C. 10, [25].

[89] [2007] EWCA Civ 15, [7].

[90] See *Evans Medical Ltd's Patent* [1998] R.P.C. 517, at 571 and 576; *Quantel Ltd v Spaceward Microsystems* [1990] R.P.C. 83, at 112.

[91] See *Hoechst Celanese Corp v B.P. Chemicals Ltd* [1998] F.S.R. 586.

[92] [2002] R.P.C. 21, [103]–[104].

[93] [2002] EWHC 1373, [44].

[94] See Part G, Chapter VI, at para.6 (November 2015 edn).

[95] [2014] EWCA Civ 637. See [103], [105] and [106].

knowledge must not be supplemented by later knowledge.[96] Thus as Sir Lionel Heald QC said in *Minnesota Mining & Manufacturing Co v Bondina*[97]:

"All the judgments ... are insistent on the limitation of the effect of the prior publication to what is clearly and unmistakably disclosed in the document itself, with no substantial addition, subtraction or alteration, and with no 'hindsight' of any kind, particularly excluding any reference to the specification of the patent being attacked. Just as Lord Moulton condemned 'ex post facto analysis of the invention', so these authorities condemn what one might call 'ex post facto synthesis of the invention', starting from a prior publication."

11-87 Likelihood, even overwhelming likelihood, does not suffice. In *Inhale v Quadrant*[98] Laddie J said:

"In the terminology of *General Tire*, van de Beek must be shown to have planted his flag at the precise destination before the patentee. That has not been proved. The teaching is a clear signpost, hence the finding of obviousness, but it does not anticipate. ... Once again, it is overwhelmingly likely that such a Tg would have been achieved, but that is not enough for the purpose of anticipation."

11-88 Lord Hoffmann in *Synthon* confirmed[99]:

"But the infringement must be not merely a possible or even likely consequence of performing the invention disclosed by the prior disclosure. It must be necessarily entailed. If there is more than one possible consequence, one cannot say that performing the disclosed invention will infringe. The flag has not been planted on the patented invention, although a person performing the invention disclosed by the prior art may carry it there by accident or (if he is aware of the patented invention) by design. Indeed, it may be obvious to do so. But the prior disclosure must be construed as it would have been understood by the skilled person at the date of the disclosure and not in the light of the subsequent patent."

11-89 He then cited with approval the decision of the European Patent Office in *Union Carbide*[100] which is as follows:

"4.4 It may be easy, given a knowledge of a later invention, to select from the general teachings of a prior art document certain conditions, and apply them to an example in that document, so as to produce an end result having all the features of the later claim. However, success in so doing does not prove that the result was inevitable. All that it demonstrates is that, given knowledge of the later invention, the earlier teaching is capable of being adapted to give the same result. Such an adaptation cannot be used to attack the novelty of a later patent.

4.5 An opponent relying on inevitable result as a ground of invalidity must do one of two things; either reproduce the earlier example so closely that there is no scope for serious challenge to the validity of the repetition, or, if some material deviation is unavoidable, show convincingly that the deviation is not material to the end result."

11-90 Similarly, in *Smithkline Beecham Plc v Apotex Europe Ltd*[101] Jacob LJ said:

"SKB invoke was what said by the EPO Board of Appeal in *Union Carbide* T396/89 [1992] E.P.O.R. 312:

'4.7 ... the Board observes that a party attacking the validity of a patent is free to choose his weapons of attack to suit his own convenience, taking into account relevant considerations of cost and effectiveness. If he seeks to establish that an example taken from a prior art document inevitably produces a given result, he thereby assumes the burden of perform-

---

[96] *Dyson v Hoover* [2001] R.P.C. 26.
[97] [1973] R.P.C. 491, 521.
[98] [2002] R.P.C. 21, [103]. See also *Fomento Industrial SA v Mentmore Manufacturing Co Ltd* [1956] R.P.C. 87, at 115, line 19.
[99] *Synthon BV v SmithKline Beecham Plc (Paroxetine)* [2006] R.P.C. 10; [2005] UKHL 59, [23].
[100] (T396/89) [1992] E.P.O.R. 312, [4.4] and [4.5].
[101] [2005] F.S.R. 23, [74] and [77]–[78].

ing his own repetition in such a way as to demonstrate that the repetition is valid. In the light of all the material before it, the Board is not satisfied that a valid repetition of Example 4 of document (1) would lead inevitably to a product falling within Claim 1, and the objection of lack of novelty based on this citation therefore fails.' ...

The plain fact is that the experiments look contrived—litigation chemistry. In the *SmithKline Beecham Plc's Patent (No.2)* [2003] R.P.C. 33 case I castigated what appeared to me to be a deliberate departures (by both sides) from the actual recipe of the prior art. I said ([61]):

'Again for the life of me, I cannot understand why the experimenters were not just given the unembellished disclosure.'

That was said in December 2002 when this action had just started. It is most improbable that those concerned with this case were unaware of it. But whether they were or not, it stands to reason that if you want to prove that a skilled man carrying out a recipe will, using his ordinary skills, be able to do so, the thing to do is to give it (without any hints) to a scientist of ordinary skills and ask him to try. Of course lawyers do not like that approach—they lose control and fear that he will fail. But if he does, then probably the attack on that ground is no good. It may be that for a similar situation in future this sort of experiment is better conducted by a court appointed single joint expert. This is a matter which should at least be considered when an application for leave to adduce experimental evidence is made."

In *Mayne Pharma v Debiopharm*[102] it was held that where an experiment had been done purporting to prove inevitable result, the service of the notice of experiments waived privilege otherwise attaching to documents relating to the work up or preliminary investigation of that experiment.

11-91

Enablement

Compliance with the "necessarily result" test is not in itself sufficient for a piece of prior art to be novelty destroying. The prior art must also be "enabling"—it must provide enough information to enable the skilled man to make or do that which is covered by the impugned claim.[103] This is the requirement of enablement. Lord Hoffmann explained in *Synthon*[104]:

11-92

"Enablement means that the ordinary skilled person would have been able to perform the invention which satisfies the requirement of disclosure. This requirement applies whether the disclosure is in matter which forms part of the state of the art by virtue of section 2(2) or, as in this case, section 2(3). The latter point was settled by the decision of this House in *Asahi Kasei Kogyo KK's Application* [1991] R.P.C. 485."

The necessary test for enablement was therefore equated to that required for sufficiency under ss.14(3) and 72(1)(c) of the Act,[105] with the caveat that when considering anticipation the skilled person could not have the subsequent patented invention in mind.

11-93

The words in the above-quoted passage from *General Tire* "If the prior inventor's publication contains a clear description of, or clear instructions to do or make..." therefore need to be qualified with the caveat that a mere description of something which the skilled reader would not be able to do or make, or otherwise obtain, is not sufficient to anticipate.

11-94

There is no pithy summary of the test for enablement, no doubt because it would

11-95

---

[102] [2006] F.S.R. 37.

[103] *Ferag v Muller Martini* [2007] EWCA Civ 15, [9].

[104] *Synthon BV v SmithKline Beecham Plc (Paroxetine)* [2006] R.P.C. 10; [2005] UKHL 59, [26].

[105] *Synthon BV v SmithKline Beecham Plc (Paroxetine)* [2006] R.P.C. 10, [2005] UKHL 59, [27], and [61]–[63].

be impossible to cater for the variety of factual situations which may arise.[106] The onus of proving enablement will depend on the nature of the case and the nature of the prior art.[107]

11-96   The question of whether or not there has been an enabling disclosure arises most frequently in cases involving chemical compounds or processes for making them. Thus, for example, while a prior art document may contain directions for making a product, a dispute may arise as to whether they are complete or what would actually be obtained as a result of following those directions. However, of course the principle is not limited to the chemical field. Evidence is admissible to determine whether the disclosure is enabling.[108]

Enablement, medical use claims and plausibility

11-97   Medical use claims owe their novelty to the discovery of the new therapeutic use of the medicament.[109] The actual achievement of the therapeutic effect is a functional technical feature of such a claim.[110] This is true for Swiss-style claims and EPC 2000 claims. Therefore, in order for prior art to deprive a medical use claim of novelty, there must be an enabling disclosure of the claimed therapeutic effect.[111] So if and to the extent that plausibility forms part of the requirements for enablement in the context of sufficiency (so held in *Regeneron*[112]), logically it must play the same role in the context of novelty.[113]

Reasonable experimentation

11-98   In the well-known passage from *Hills v Evans* quoted above,[114] Lord Westbury stated that a "person of ordinary knowledge of the subject would at once perceive and understand and be able practically to apply the discovery without the necessity of making further experiments". However, this passage was explained by Lord Reid in *C. Van der Lely N.V. v Bamfords Ltd*[115] as follows:

> "Lord Westbury must have meant experiments with a view to discovering something not disclosed. He cannot have meant to refer to the ordinary methods of trial and error which involve no inventive step and generally are necessary in applying any discovery to produce a practical result … The other requirement is that 'the information given by the prior publication must for the purpose of practical utility be equal to that given by the subsequent patent.' There may be cases where the skilled man has to have the language of the publication translated for him or where he must get from a scientist the meaning of technical terms or ideas with which he is not familiar, but once he has got this he must be able to make the machine from what is disclosed by the prior publication."

---

[106] *Mölnlycke Health Care AB v Brightwake Limited* [2011] EWHC 376 (Pat), [244], the decision was overturned on appeal, [2012] EWCA 602 (Civ), although not on this point.

[107] See *Mölnlycke Health Care AB v Brightwake Limited* [2011] EWHC 376 (Pat), at [245]–[247]. In that case, the prior art disclosure was held to assert that a particular result had been achieved and the evidential onus therefore shifted to the party challenging enablement. The decision was overturned on appeal, [2012] EWCA 602 (Civ), although not on this point.

[108] *SmithKline Beecham Plc's Patent* [2003] R.P.C. 6, [42].

[109] Per Floyd LJ in *Warner Lambert v Actavis* [2015] EWCA Civ 556, [120]–[121].

[110] *Regeneron v Genentech* [2013] EWCA 93 Civ, [56] and see para.9–285.

[111] Birss J in *Merck v Ono* [2015] EWHC 2973, at [173].

[112] *Regeneron v Genentech* [2013] EWCA 93 Civ, [100]–[101] and see para.13–59.

[113] Birss J in *Merck v Ono* [2015] EWHC 2973, at [175].

[114] See para.11–75.

[115] [1963] R.P.C. 61, 71.

Lord Hoffmann explained in *Synthon*[116] that these passages were to be understood in the context of enablement rather than disclosure. He there stated: **11-99**

> "For example, I have explained that for the purpose of disclosure, the prior art must disclose an invention which, if performed, would necessarily infringe the patent. It is not enough to say that, given the prior art, the person skilled in the art would without undue burden be able to come up with an invention which infringed the patent. But once the very subject-matter of the invention has been disclosed by the prior art and the question is whether it was enabled, the person skilled in the art is assumed to be willing to make trial and error experiments to get it to work. If, therefore, one asks whether some degree of experimentation is to be assumed, it is very important to know whether one is talking about disclosure or about enablement."

In the *Synthon* case itself, the prior art disclosed the existence of a crystalline material, PMS. However, the infrared spectrum provided was wrong, and the procedure for making it would not work as stated. Nonetheless, it was held to anticipate a later claim to crystalline PMS. The existence of a crystalline form PMS was disclosed and it was shown that PMS is monomorphic so that (notwithstanding the error in the spectrum), the relevant form was disclosed. Further, a skilled reader would have been able to produce it because, notwithstanding the problem with the stated procedure, some reasonable experimentation with solvents would have provided the crystalline form: that satisfied the requirement of enablement. **11-100**

Thus in a less straightforward case, the reason that it is necessary to draw the distinction between disclosure and enablement is that confusion may arise if the skilled addressee of the prior art may need to carry out trial and error experimentation to put it into practice. It is then necessary to consider whether or not such experimentation is merely part of the exercise of enabling him to apply what has already been disclosed, or whether it amounts to finding out something more. **11-101**

Pumfrey J explained the point in the following passage from *Inpro's Patent*[117]: **11-102**

> "In cases of anticipation by inevitable result, the prior art discloses those things which, if the skilled man does them, will fall within the claim. But enablement must be of something inevitably within the claim. If the skilled person is given a target, in the shape of a disclosure of the invention, the law of enablement permits reasonable experimentation, error correction and so on while yet holding that the prior disclosure is enabling. If the only target the skilled man is given is a course of action, then following that course of action must inevitably result in something within the claim, and there is no space for experimentation except in getting what is disclosed to work on the prior document's own terms".

In the following passage from *Monsanto v Cargill*[118] Pumfrey J noted the consequence: **11-103**

> "It should be noted that when the case is based on clear and unmistakeable directions contained in the prior document the skilled man may only use his knowledge of the result called for by the claim if that result is, itself, disclosed by the prior document. To this extent, the requirements of sufficiency of description, where the end is known, and of enabling disclosure may differ."

As the Court of Appeal pointed out in *Ferag v Muller Martini*,[119] to satisfy the "necessarily result" test, it is not good enough to show that a skilled reader, by making reasonable or sensible adjustments or additions to what is actually described in **11-104**

---

[116] *Synthon BV v SmithKline Beecham Plc (Paroxetine)* [2006] R.P.C. 10; [2005] UKHL 59, [31].
[117] *Research in Motion v Inpro* [2006] R.P.C. 20, [111].
[118] [2008] F.S.R. 7, [107].
[119] [2007] EWCA Civ 15, [11].

the prior art, would make or do something within the claim. That would be to move from the objection of anticipation to that of obviousness.

11-105   Of course the same disclosure may satisfy the requirements of both disclosure and enablement. As was held in *Synthon*[120]:

> "The prior art description may be sufficient in itself to enable the ordinary skilled man, armed with common general knowledge of the art, to perform the subject-matter of the invention. Indeed, when the prior art is a product, the product itself, though dumb, may be enabling if it is 'available to the public' and a person skilled in the art can discover its composition or internal structure and reproduce it without undue burden."

11-106   To similar effect, Lord Walker said[121]:

> "In the case of a low-tech invention (for instance a simple agricultural machine such as the hay rake with ground-driven wheels in *Van der Lely*) the simple disclosure of the invention will probably be enough to enable the skilled person to perform it. By contrast in the case of a high-tech invention in the field of pharmaceutical science the bald assertion of the existence of the invention may have to be accompanied by detailed disclosure enabling the skilled person to perform it. But in testing the adequacy of the enablement it may be assumed that the skilled person will have to use his skill, and may have to learn by his mistakes (see Lord Reid's reference to 'trial and error' in *Van der Lely* [1963] R.P.C. 61, 71)."

3. SECTION 2(3): UNPUBLISHED PATENT APPLICATIONS

11-107   A particular problem is posed in patent law in the case of co-pending patent applications. There is always a lapse of time between the application for a patent and the publication of that application. In that intervening period the contents of the application remain secret and are thus not part of the "state of the art" as defined by s.2(2) of the 1977 Act. Hence, the application cannot be relied upon by virtue of that subsection to seek to invalidate a later-filed application in respect of the same subject-matter and hence to prevent "double patenting". This could create anomalies in a "first-to-file" system.

11-108   Under the old law, this problem was dealt with by the law of prior claiming.[122] The law was that a patent would be invalidated if the invention claimed in the later application was shown to have been the subject of a valid prior grant. Prior publication was immaterial. Problems arose in deciding whether the ground of invalidity was limited to cases where the two claims were identical or whether it extended to the case where carrying out the invention claimed in one case would infringe the claims in the other.[123]

11-109   As an alternative solution to the problem of conflicting concurrent applications, art.4(3) of the Strasbourg Convention of 1963 proposed that contracting States should be permitted to deem the contents of all applications for patents to be comprised in the state of the art, to the extent to which the contents of those applications had an earlier priority date. By this mechanism an unpublished application, to the extent that it was entitled to an earlier priority date, could be deemed

---

[120] *Synthon BV v SmithKline Beecham Plc (Paroxetine)* [2006] R.P.C. 10; [2005] UKHL 59, [29].
[121] *Synthon BV v SmithKline Beecham Plc (Paroxetine)* [2006] R.P.C. 10, [2005] UKHL 59 at [64].
[122] PA 1949 s.32(i)(a).
[123] See *Kromschroders Patent* [1960] R.P.C. 75; *Syntex S.A.'s Application* [1966] R.P.C. 560; *Merck & Co (Macek's) Patent* [1967] R.P.C. 157; *Ethyl Corporation's Patent* [1970] R.P.C. 227; *Daikin Kogyo's Application* [1974] R.P.C. 559.

to have been published on that priority date or, perhaps, immediately prior to the priority date of the claim of the later patent.[124]

The EPC—in art.54(3)—and the Patents Act 1977—in s.2(3)—adopt this approach[125] subject to an important limitation contained in art.56 and the equivalent section of the Act (s.3) which provides that an unpublished application cannot be relied upon in relation to obviousness. Section 2(3) provides: **11-110**

> "(3) The state of the art in the case of an invention to which an application for a patent or a patent relates shall be taken also to compromise matter contained in an application for another patent[126] which was published on or after the priority date of that invention, if the following conditions are satisfied, that is to say—
>
> (a) that matter was contained in the application for that other patent both as filed and as published; and
>
> (b) the priority date of that matter is earlier than that of the invention."

It was confirmed in *Woolard's Application*[127] that the purpose of this provision is to prevent double patenting. **11-111**

In *Asahi Kasei Kogyo K.K.'s Application*[128] the interpretation of s.2(3) was considered. It was held that, just as an enabling disclosure was required to invalidate a later claim on the ground of lack of novelty under s.2(2), so also an enabling disclosure was required for s.2(3). Lord Oliver reviewed the existing authorities,[129] in the course of which he stated: **11-112**

> "It is the appellant's contention that, as indicated in the *Genentech* case, the test for whether 'matter' disclosed in an application unpublished at the priority date of the application in suit constitutes an anticipation under subsection (3) must, as a matter of construction of the two subsections, be the same as the test under subsection (2), so that here too an enabling disclosure is required. It would, it is argued, be absurd that an application which, if published on the day prior to the priority date of the application in suit, would not constitute an anticipation because, for want of an enabling disclosure, it did not make the invention available to the public, should nevertheless constitute an anticipation and thus deprive the application in suit of novelty if published on the day following such priority date."

Accordingly, in order to rely on an unpublished application for the purposes of an allegation of lack of novelty it is necessary to show: **11-113**

(a) that the matter contained in the unpublished application constitutes an anticipation in the same way as if the document were published, including the requirement that the matter constitutes an enabling disclosure[130];

(b) that the matter relied on for (a) above is—

   (i) included both in the application as filed and as published; and

   (ii) entitled to a priority date earlier than the priority date of the claim attacked.[131]

Subject therefore to proving the matters referred to in (b) above, so far as **11-114**

---

[124] See *Genentech Inc (Human Growth Hormone) Patent* [1989] R.P.C. 613, 644.

[125] s.2(3) is one of the sections governed by s.130(7).

[126] This includes an application for a European patent (UK) and an international application for a patent designating the UK. See PA 1977 ss.77 and 89.

[127] [2002] R.P.C. 39.

[128] [1991] R.P.C. 485.

[129] [1991] R.P.C. 485, 537–542.

[130] See Section 2 of this chapter (particularly paras 11–74 to 11–106 as to an enabling disclosure); and see *Minnesota Mining and Manufacturing Co's (Suspension Aerosol Formulation) Patent* [1999] R.P.C. 135.

[131] See Ch.7.

concerns novelty an unpublished application stands on all fours with a prior published application. There is no different test for novelty depending on whether a document is cited under s.2(2) or s.2(3).[132]

11-115   It makes no difference whether the application subsequently matures into a granted patent or, conversely, whether it is subsequently withdrawn before grant.[133] An application which is withdrawn before the date of publication, but which is nonetheless published because preparations for publication had been completed before withdrawal, is however not part of the state of the art under s.2(3).[134] Finally, it is important to note that s.2(3) has no application to questions of obviousness.[135] The distinction between the correct approach to novelty and that for obviousness is thus crucial in the case of an unpublished application.[136]

11-116   In some circumstances a patent can be anticipated by its own priority application (so-called "poisonous priority"). This happened in *Nestec v Dualit*,[137] where the claims had been broadened between the priority application and the patent application as filed. Meanwhile the priority application itself had been published and was taken to be part of the state of the art under s.2(3) of the Act. Hence the claims of the patent were not entitled to priority but were anticipated. *Nestec* was considered by the EPO Technical Board of Appeal in *Partial Priority/Infineum*,[138] which referred a number of issues relating to poisonous priority to the Enlarged Board.

4.   SECTION 2(4): EXCEPTIONS TO THE STATE OF THE ART

11-117   Disclosure of any matter constituting the invention made within six months prior to the date of filing the application is to be disregarded if:

    (a)   the matter was obtained unlawfully or in breach of confidence either from the inventor or from any third party who had obtained it in confidence from the inventor[139]; or

    (b)   the disclosure was due to or made in consequence of the inventor displaying the invention at an international exhibition.[140]

11-118   Section 2(4)—like its equivalent in the EPC, art.55—limits the six-month period of grace expressly to the date of filing of the application and not to the priority date of the application.

11-119   Article 89 of the EPC deems the date of priority to count as the date of filing for the purpose of arts 54(2) and (3) and 60(2) but does not do so for art.55. However, in *PASSONI/Stand Structure*,[141] the Opposition Division of the EPO held that, where the European application claimed priority from an earlier application, the six-month period should be deemed to run from the priority date. The reasoning for reaching this conclusion is somewhat tortured and may not commend itself to an

---

[132] *SmithKline Beecham Plc's Patent* [2003] R.P.C. 6.
[133] See PA 1977 s.78(5A), as amended by CDPA 1988 Sch.5 para.22, reversing *L'Oréal's Application* [1986] R.P.C. 19.
[134] *Woolard's Application* [2002] R.P.C. 39.
[135] See PA 1977 s.3.
[136] See *Beloit Technologies Inc v Valmet Paper Machinery Inc (No.2)* [1995] R.P.C. 705, at 738.
[137] [2013] R.P.C. 32.
[138] (T-0557/13), 17 July 2015.
[139] PA 1977 s.2(4)(a) and (b).
[140] PA 1977 s.2(4)(c).
[141] [1992] E.P.O.R. 79.

English court. It has, however, been accepted in Holland[142] but rejected in Germany.[143]

In the latter case, the Bundesgerichtshof justified a finding in accordance with the plain language of art.55 as follows: **11-120**

"Under Article 54(4) EPC earlier applications are only taken into consideration for the examination as to novelty if the territorial scope matches that of the earlier application. This confirms that the system is intended to help avoid double patenting ... This suggests that the purpose of the time limit prescribed in Section 3(4) PatG 1981 and Article 55(1) EPC is ... to give the entitled person sufficient opportunity—particularly in the case of misuses—to file an application himself and, hence, that it is correct to refer solely to the age of the first application ..."

Whilst this reasoning provides a justification for the language used, the decision is harsh for it will not, in many cases, serve to avoid the potentially important problem of misuse of confidential information prior to the priority date. The provision is in need of further judicial consideration.   **11-121**

5. PARTICULAR FORMS OF CLAIM

The general principles discussed above are of course applicable to claims of all kinds. Different forms of claim however give rise to particular considerations and some are reviewed further below.[144]   **11-122**

Product claims

A product claim will cover the product wherever found. As Lord Hoffmann stated in *Merrell Dow v H H Norton*:[145]   **11-123**

"The monopoly covers every aspect of manufacture and every form which comes within the description in the claim. So claim 24 includes the making of the acid metabolite in one's liver just as much as making it by synthetic process; in the body as well as in isolation."

A claim to a product as such is anticipated by any article falling within the words of the claim, irrespective of the purpose for which it was or is to be used. As noted in the chapter addressing construction,[146] words in a product claim such as "for" or "for use in" are ordinarily construed as meaning "suitable for use", so a prior disclosure of an article may fall within the claim even though never intended for such use.   **11-124**

However, the question of suitability will still have to be determined, for any article can be used for a purpose for which it was not intended and an overlap between the uses to which two articles can be put does not necessarily itself make one an anticipation of a claim to the other,. In *Hickman v Andrews*[147] the word "workbench" was construed in its context and held to exclude a prior art bookbinder's press. Graham J (whose judgment was upheld in the Court of Appeal) said: **11-125**

"I think one must be realistic about these things when construed in a patent specification and must

---

[142] *Organon International B.V. v Applied Systems ARS Holding B.V.* [1998] O.J. EPO 278, a decision of the Hoge Raad (Supreme Court).
[143] *Corioliskraft* [1998] O.J. EPO 263, a decision of the Bundesgerichtshof (Federal Court of Justice).
[144] See also Part 8 of Ch.9 which also deals with various types of claim.
[145] [1996] R.P.C. 76, 82, lines 36–44.
[146] See para.9–323.
[147] [1983] R.P.C. 147. See also *Dyson v Hoover* [2001] R.P.C. 26, [113].

avoid, if one can, falling into the trap of being astute after the event by ex post facto synthesis to build up an anticipation out of a prior document or prior user in order to make it fit the claim."

11-126   In *Akzo's (tibolone) patent*[148] it was noted that the context in which the prior product was found was irrelevant, as was the quantity present, the reason it was being studied or even whether the researcher knew what it was or what value it might have: so the prior disclosure of a single crystal anticipated a claim to a compound characterised in that it was "crystalline pure". The Court of Session there also followed EPO authority to the effect that the prior disclosure of a compound made available all grades of purity achievable by conventional methods using common general knowledge, though expressing some doubt as to whether this objection was one of anticipation or obviousness.

11-127   Although, if the claim on its proper construction is limited to an isolated product (e.g. an enantiomer) then it will not be anticipated by the product when found in unseparated form (e.g. a racemate).[149] Conversely, a claim to a chiral compound normally found as a racemate (but not so limited) was held broad enough to cover a pure enantiomer.[150]

11-128   A product may still be novel even if it could be described and was known to be desirable, if the prior art did not also enable it. In *Generics v Lundbeck*,[151] the claim was to one of the two enantiomers (asymmetrical left- and right-handed configurations of a molecule) of a racemate (50–50 mixture of the two), citalopram. The racemate was known, as was how to make it. The existence of the two enantiomers was also known, but a method of separating them or synthesising each individually was not known. The patentee found a way of isolating one of the enantiomers, which had a beneficial therapeutic effect. A claim to that one specific enantiomer was upheld as novel in the Court of Appeal: it was common ground that the isolated enantiomer was not enabled in the prior art. In the House of Lords, the only contested issue was insufficiency, but although novelty was not in issue, Lord Scott briefly reviewed the law and observed[152] that:

> "It is common ground that prior to the priority date claimed by the respondent for its 'product' invention the (+) enantiomer of citalopram had not been made available to the public otherwise than as an unseparated part of the racemate that constituted the citalopram molecule. In its *separated* form the (+) enantiomer had not at any time before the priority date been made available to the public. It follows, therefore, that the (+) enantiomer was 'new' for the purposes of section 1(1)(a) of the Act."

Product-by-process claims

11-129   A claim to a product when made by a new process is not enough in itself to make the product new, for "it is still the same product even if made in a different way".[153] However this is a rule of the law of novelty, not a rule of mandatory claim interpretation. Thus the process feature in question has to be ignored for the

---

[148] *Arrow v Norton Healthcare* [2007] R.P.C. 11 (Scottish Court of Session), [17] and [105].
[149] *Generics v Lundbeck* [2007] R.P.C. 32, [62] (Patents Court); [2008] R.P.C. 19 (CA); not in issue in the House of Lords [2009] R.P.C. 13.
[150] *Ranbaxy v Warner-Lambert* [2007] R.P.C. 4.
[151] [2008] R.P.C. 19 (CA); [2009] R.P.C. 13 (HL).
[152] [2009] R.P.C. 13, [6].
[153] See *Kirin-Amgen v Hoechst Marion Roussel* [2005] R.P.C. 9, at [90]; but note also see *International Flavors & Fragrances Inc* [1984] O.J. E.P.O. 309. See further para.9–263, et seq.

purposes of novelty but taken into account for the purposes of infringement and insufficiency.[154]

In any event a claim to a new process of making a known product may be valid, **11-130** and by virtue of s.60(1)(c) may be infringed by dealings in products obtained directly by that process.

Selection patents

Under the pre-1977 law, disclosure of a class (typically, a class of chemical **11-131** compounds) prima facie amounted to a disclosure of each and every member of that class. It was however possible to obtain a valid patent for a specific compound or subclass, as a so-called "selection patent", if it could be shown that the subclass possessed some special advantage which was enjoyed by the subclass as a whole but also peculiar to it. These requirements were formulated in the so-called "IG rules", named after the case in which they were formulated, *IG Farbenindustrie's Patents*.[155] Their subsequent application gave rise to problems in reconciling them with the statute and with other authorities on novelty, since there was nothing in the 1949 Act which recognised any special approach for selection patents as a special category. The pre-1977 law was considered by the House of Lords in *E.I. Du Pont De Nemours & Co (Witsiepe's) Application*.[156]

However the position has changed, and the Court of Appeal considered the law **11-132** now applicable to such cases in *Dr Reddy's Laboratories v Eli Lilly*,[157] there observing that the pre-1977 jurisprudence including the IG rules were now part of legal history rather than applicable law. (Indeed it held the patent in suit to be valid, even though noting that it would not have satisfied the IG rules had they still been applicable.)

So far as novelty was concerned, the Court rejected the broad proposition that **11-133** the disclosure of a generalised class necessarily amounted to a disclosure of each and every member of it. Such rejection applied whether the earlier class was described by way of a general formula or by an itemised listing out of all the members. What was required for anticipation was an "individualised description" of the later claimed compound or class. Absent that, it could not be said that performing any part of the earlier generalised disclosure would inevitably produce a result within the later claim. This approach mirrored that of the EPO and Germany.

Jacob LJ there noted that what an "individualised description" amounted to might **11-134** involve questions of degree. (Contrast, e.g. *Ranbaxy v Warner-Lambert*[158] where the claim was held anticipated because alighting on the claimed compound was merely picking one of the class of compounds disclosed in the prior art, so that "if the claim were valid it would cover one of the alternatives explicitly taught by the citation".)

So far as obviousness was concerned, the Court held, following the practice of **11-135** the EPO, that where there is what can fairly be regarded as a mere arbitrary selection from the wider class, there is no technical advance or technical contribution

---

154 *Hospira UK v Genentech Inc* [2014] EWHC 3857. At the time of writing an appeal is still outstanding.
155 (1930) 47 R.P.C. 289.
156 [1982] F.S.R. 303.
157 [2010] R.P.C. 9.
158 [2007] R.P.C. 4, [40].

and the later selection will be obvious.[159] However, a selection that makes a real technical advance in the art will be patentable. This aspect of the case is discussed further in the chapter on obviousness below.[160]

"Use" claims

11-136   If a product is known in the prior art, then a claim to the known product as such will not be novel, but a process claim may still be allowable for the use of the old product in a new way. (The position is more complicated in the case of known pharmaceutical products, however, because EPC art.53(c) prohibits patents for methods of medical treatment. This may be overcome by a claim in "Swiss" form, described in the next section below.)

11-137   In *MOBIL/Friction reducing additives* (G02/88)[161] the Enlarged Board of Appeal had to consider a claim to a new use of an old material. Use of the known material for the known purpose would in fact also have achieved the purpose which was the subject of the later patent. However, the previous use would not have revealed the fact that the new purpose was being achieved. The Board emphasised[162] that under art.54(2) of the EPC the question to be decided is what has been "made available" to the public: the question is not what may have been "inherent" in what was made available (by a prior written description, or in what has previously been used (prior use), for example). Under the EPC, a hidden or secret use, because it has not been made available to the public, is not a ground of objection to the validity of a European patent.

11-138   The Enlarged Board summarised their conclusions in this way at [10.3] of their decision:

> "... with respect to a claim to a new use of a known compound, such new use may reflect a newly discovered technical effect described in the patent. The attaining of such a technical effect should then be considered as a functional technical feature of the claim (e.g. the achievement in a particular context of that technical effect). If that technical feature has not been previously made available to the public by any of the means set out in article 54(2) EPC, then the claimed invention is novel, even though such technical effect may have inherently taken place in the course of carrying out what has previously been made available to the public."

11-139   The reasoning in the latter part of this passage is difficult to follow,[163] and is difficult to reconcile with other authorities on anticipation by inevitable result, in particular the decision of the House of Lords in *Merrell Dow*.[164] It was however referred to but not expressly disapproved in the latter case. As was also discussed in *Merrell Dow*, there may be difficulties in considering infringement; for example, the position of the party who had made the prior use, if he continued to do exactly the same thing after the date of the patent and therefore continued inherently to at-

---

[159]   In *Ranbaxy v Warner-Lambert at first instance* [2006] F.S.R. 14, at [64], Pumfrey J suggested that, absent a disclosure of the advantages of the class, a mere arbitrary selection among things already disclosed would lack novelty, though the relevance of advantages would seem to be related only to obviousness.

[160]   See para.12–43, et seq.

[161]   [1990] O.J. EPO 93; [1990] E.P.O.R. 73.

[162]   [1990] E.P.O.R. 73, 88.

[163]   The Court of Appeal considered it in *Bristol-Myers Squibb v Baker Norton* [2001] R.P.C. 1, at [39]–[41]; however, it did not shed any light on the infringement issue, and note also that the Court of Appeal in *Actavis v Merck* [2008] R.P.C. 26 has explained and declined to follow *Bristol-Myers Squibb*.

[164]   [1996] R.P.C. 76, 92.

tain the relevant technical effect. It is hard to see that infringement might turn on whether he then knew that the new technical effect was being obtained, or on whether he told his customers that it was. If the principle in *Mobil* were confined to true new uses, as opposed to mere discoveries about old uses,[165] then its application would be straightforward, but its reasoning appears to be wider.

In *Actavis v Merck*[166] the Court of Appeal noted that the allowability of the claim **11-140** in *Mobil* turned on similar policy considerations to those underlying Swiss-style claims. It also noted that the difficulties in considering infringement in the case of Swiss-style claims would in many cases be more theoretical and real, because of the way in which medical products are marked: but it did not address the question of infringement in the case of other "use for" claims. (In *Mobil* the EPO Enlarged Board stated at [10.1] that it considered that the infringement problems would be "analogous": but this seems to overlook the different practical considerations which apply when marketing medicines and when marketing motor oil).

The case was also unsuccessfully prayed in aid by the patentee in *Actavis v Jans-* **11-141** *sen*,[167] where Floyd J noted that, "if *Mobil* is correctly decided", unadvertised technical effects which underlie new uses of old materials are an exception to the rule about inevitable results, noting an analogy with second medical use cases (the first medical use might inherently have assisted patients who happened also to have the second condition). However, he was able to decide the case before him on the basis that merely explaining the mechanism underlying a use already described in the prior art cannot without more give rise to novelty, thus differentiating it from *Mobil* on the facts. This area of the law remains in need of clarification.

Swiss-style and second medical use claims

Swiss-style claims are claims of the form "use of substance X in the manufacture **11-142** of a medicament for treating disease Y". In this way, they avoid the problem that a claim to "use of substance X for treating disease Y" would be a method of medical treatment and therefore not patentable (EPC art.52(4), now EPC 2000 art.53(c)). These have now been superseded by EPC 2000 claims in the form "product X for treating disease Y" by virtue of EPC 2000 art.54(5). The two types of claim are not the same: in particular, Swiss-type claims are purpose-limited process claims whereas EPC 2000 claims are purpose-limited product claims.[168] The nature of and principles of construction applicable to such claims have been described in Ch.9 of this work,[169] hence this chapter will focus on the implications as regards novelty.

In particular, such claims may be novel even where the substance in question has **11-143** previously been known for treating a different medical condition (a "second medical use" claim). In *Actavis v Merck*[170] the relevant compound was already known for treating the relevant condition, and the only new aspect lay in a different dos-

---

165 As suggested by Jacob J at first instance in *Bristol-Myers Squibb v Baker Norton* [1999] R.P.C. 253, at [65].
166 [2008] R.P.C. 26, [10], [30].
167 [2008] F.S.R. 35, [88]–[100].
168 See *Warner-Lambert v Actavis* [2015] R.P.C. 25, at [56]. In *University of Texas Board of Regents/ Cancer treatment* (T 1780/12) [2014] E.P.O.R. 28, at [16]–[24], it was explained that EPC 2000 claims created greater legal certainty in relation to the patentability of further medical use claims and overcame doubts as to the validity of Swiss-type claims.
169 See para.9-268, et seq.
170 [2008] R.P.C. 26. See also *EISAI/Second medical indication* (G05/83) [1979–85] E.P.O.R B241, [1985] O.J. EPO 64 and *Monsanto v Merck* [2000] R.P.C. 77, 84.

age regime. The Court of Appeal, in considering whether or not such a claim could be regarded as novel, reviewed in detail the law relating to Swiss-style claims. The EPO Enlarged Board of Appeal has reached a similar conclusion in its decision *Kos Life Sciences* (G2/08).

11-144   As also explained in Ch.9 the word "for" in a claim to an article "for" a particular purpose will generally mean "suitable for": i.e. that the article is suitable for that purpose, whether or not so used. However, Swiss-type claims and EPC 2000 claims are an exception to this rule. For instance in *Hospira v Genentech*,[171] the relevant claim was to use of a particular antibody in the manufacture of a medicament "for use in a method for treating a human patient with a breast cancer" of a particular type. It was common ground that: (a) the claim was to something which was indeed an effective treatment of the disease[172]; (b) that in this context the word "for" meant "suitable and intended for", not merely "suitable for".

11-145   The first point confers novelty over a mere proposal to administer the drug in question to patients in the manner claimed, since a mere proposal does not disclose that the treatment is indeed efficacious.[173] However, Hospira did not need to consider what was meant by "intended for": in particular, whose intention was relevant and what the nature of such intention was.

11-146   In *Warner-Lambert v Actavis*[174] this question was answered. In particular the Court of Appeal held that "for" meant that the manufacturer of the product knew, or could reasonably foresee, the intentional use of the product for the relevant purpose. The effect of this point is that the claim is novel over the product itself, since there is no disclosure of any intentional use of that product for the relevant purpose.

Disclaimers

11-147   Where there is an "accidental anticipation", it may be possible for the patentee to insert a specific disclaimer of the prior material. The EPO Enlarged Board of Appeal held in *PPG/Disclaimer* (G1/03)[175] that a specific disclaimer is not considered to add matter if inserted into a claim to avoid an "accidental" anticipation, but it does add matter if it is inserted to avoid a "non-accidental" anticipation. An accidental anticipation involves a "disclosure…belong[ing] to a remote technological field or [one whose] subject-matter suggested it would not help to solve the problem [addressed by the patent in question]". It further stated that "the disclosure has to be completely irrelevant for assessing the inventive step" and "the disclosure in question must be so unrelated and remote that the person skilled in the art would never have taken it into consideration when working on the invention". The Enlarged Board concluded that:

> "When an anticipation is taken as accidental, this means that it appears from the outset that the anticipation has nothing to do with the invention. Only if that is established, can the disclaimer be allowed."

---

[171] [2014] EWHC 1094 (Pat).

[172] See also *Regeneron v Genentech* [2013] R.P.C. 28, at [56]. The same construction was common ground in a later dispute between the same parties: see *Hospira v Genentech* [2015] EWHC 1796 (Pat), at [52].

[173] However, the Court went on to observe that if it was obvious that the treatment would be efficacious or at least obvious to conduct a trial of the treatment which would involve treating patients, then the claim was likely to lack inventive step.

[174] [2015] R.P.C. 25.

[175] [2004] E.P.O.R. 331; applied by the Court of Appeal in *LG Philips v Tatung* [2007] R.P.C. 21.

CHAPTER 12

INVALIDITY DUE TO OBVIOUSNESS (LACK OF INVENTIVE STEP)

CONTENTS

1. INTRODUCTION

Obviousness under the 1977 Act

Section 1 of the Act defines a "patentable invention", and one of the require-   **12-01**
ments there set out is that the invention involves an inventive step. This is defined
in s.3, which provides:

> "An invention shall be taken to involve an inventive step if it is not obvious to a person skilled in
> the art, having regard to any matter which forms part of the state of the art by virtue only of section
> 2(2) above (and disregarding section 2(3) above)."

Section 130(7) of the Act provides that this is equivalent to art.56 of the EPC.   **12-02**
Thus even if a claim of a patent is novel having regard to the state of the art as
defined by s.2 of the 1977 Act, it may nevertheless be invalid as lacking in inventive step having regard to s.3. As Pumfrey J observed in *Conor v Angiotech*[1]:

> "... it is essential to remember that the objection of obviousness is available even when the inven-
> tion is not anticipated. This proposition may be trite, but it is important to guard against the sugges-
> tion that lack of anticipation is in itself an indication of non-obviousness in the technically objec-
> tive sense. It is not. The second is that inventions may be obvious even though the art missed them.
> That is a corollary of my first observation. It is absurd to suggest that everything objectively obvi-
> ous at the priority date should have been done or contemplated either then or at any time thereafter.
> Patents should not be granted for things that have been obvious for a long time."

History

Revocation on the ground of obviousness was first codified in the 1932 Act,   **12-03**
although prior to that a patent was always liable to be revoked under the common
law for "want of subject matter", a ground that did not always clearly differentiate
between anticipation and obviousness. The relevant provision in the Patents Act
1949 was s.32(1)(f), which provided that a patent was liable to be revoked on the
ground

> "that the invention, so far as claimed in any claim of the complete specification, is obvious and does

---

[1] [2006] R.P.C. 28, [37]: but note that his overall decision was reversed by the House of Lords.

not involve any inventive step having regard to what was known or used, before the priority date of the claim, in the United Kingdom".

12-04   As with novelty,[2] the restriction which limited the prior art to matter available in the United Kingdom is now no longer the law. However the general principles developed under the previous law continue to be useful, as the question of whether an invention is obvious remains "a kind of jury question".

2.   OBVIOUSNESS—GENERAL PRINCIPLES

Obvious in what way? The meaning of "obvious"

12-05   The word "obvious" is an ordinary English word and the court has repeatedly refused to attempt to define or paraphrase the statutory requirement. It is therefore a mistake to apply a particular methodology of assessing obviousness slavishly in substitution for that requirement.

12-06   As Jacob LJ said in *Generics v Daiichi*[3]:

"There is at bottom only one test, namely that posed by Art. 56 of the EPC transposed into UK law by s.3 of the Patents Act 1977. Was the invention obvious to a person skilled in the art having regard to any matter which forms part of the state of the art? Judicial or patent office attempts to formulate the test in other words, or to provide a formula, can be helpful, provided that one does not lose sight of the statutory question. One must not take any such other test or formula as if it were the statute—they are only tools for answering the statutory question. Adherence to any rigid formula can be a mistake."

12-07   However, whilst no alternative formulation can be a perfect substitute for the statutory test, a formula can sometimes be useful and they are frequently applied in practice.[4] It follows that a number of methods of considering obviousness have been developed, notably the "obvious to try" question and the "*Windsurfing/ Pozzoli*" test in the UK, and the "problem/solution" approach in the EPO. As these tests are to be regarded as merely an aid to answering the sole question "is it obvious" rather than a substitute for it, the court has from time to time noted that use of the "*Windsurfing /Pozzoli*" test is not essential[5] or identified circumstances where it is not appropriate or helpful.[6] It also follows that failure to apply it is not of itself an "error of principle" for purposes of an appeal.[7]

12-08   In *Mölnlycke v Procter & Gamble*[8] Sir Donald Nicholls drew attention to the following warning given by Lopes LJ in *Savage v Harris*[9]:

"Cases, so far as regards the law, are most useful, but when they are applied to particular facts, they, as a rule, are of little service. Each case depends upon its own particular facts and the facts of almost every case differ."

12-09   He went on to state that citing previous decisions on a question of fact is not a

---

2   See para.11-09.
3   [2009] R.P.C. 23, [17]. See also Lewison LJ at [178]–[185] of *MedImmune v Novartis* [2012] EWCA 1234; [2013] R.P.C. 27.
4   See also *Nichia v Argos* [2007] F.S.R. 38, at [21]–[22].
5   See, e.g. *Research in Motion v Inpro* [2007] EWCA Civ 51, at [7].
6   See, e.g. *SmithKline Beecham Plc v Apotex Europe Ltd* [2005] F.S.R. 23, at [35].
7   *Nampak Cartons v Rapid Action Packaging* [2010] EWHC 1458 (Pat), [40].
8   [1994] R.P.C. 49, 112.
9   (1896) 13 R.P.C. 364, 370.

useful, nor is it a proper, exercise.[10] However, authorities on the principles to be applied and the approach to be taken of course remain relevant and helpful.

If anything falling within the claim is obvious, then the claim is invalid for obviousness. The EPO TBA explained the rationale in *Triazoles/AgrEvo*[11]:

    12-10

> "The reason for this is, that it has for long been a generally accepted legal principle that the extent of the patent monopoly should correspond to and be justified by the technical contribution to the art …. Now, whereas in both the above decisions this general legal principle was applied in relation to the extent of the patent protection that was justified by reference to the requirements of Articles 83 and 84 EPC, the same legal principle also governs the decision that is required to be made under Article 56 EPC, for everything falling within a valid claim has to be inventive. If this is not the case, the claim must be amended so as to exclude obvious subject-matter in order to justify the monopoly."

The underlying policy

Hoffmann LJ stated in *STEP v Emson Europe Ltd*[12] that:

    12-11

> "The words 'obvious' and 'inventive step' involve questions of fact and degree which must be answered in accordance with the general policy of the Patents Act to reward and encourage inventors without inhibiting improvements of existing technology by others. The question is therefore whether in accordance with this policy the patent discloses something sufficiently inventive to deserve the grant of a monopoly."

Subsequently Sir Donald Nicholls VC, sitting in a differently constituted Court of Appeal, stated in *Mölnlycke v Procter & Gamble*[13] that the Court did not consider that it assisted to ask whether "the patent discloses something sufficiently inventive to deserve the grant of a monopoly". However, this principle was expressly applied by Laddie J in *Haberman v Jackel*[14] and appears to be consistent with patent law policy and difficult to fault as stated. Similarly, Pumfrey J observed in *Conor v Angiotech*[15] that:

    12-12

> "The point of the objection of obviousness is to prevent the too-ready grant of patents from hampering them in the ordinary technical development that must take place in an industry."

and expressly noted that while he was bound by *Mölnlycke*, he was also "obliged to remember" the observations in the above-quoted passage from *Step v Emson*.

Obviousness is ultimately "a kind of jury question"

As will appear from what follows, the question of whether an invention is or is not obvious is one that requires the court to take account of all relevant evidence and to reach an overall view on the totality of that evidence. In *Windsurfing International Inc v Tabur Marine (Great Britain) Ltd*[16] Oliver LJ pointed out:

    12-13

> "The question to be decided when an objection is made on the ground of obviousness is, as Jenkins L.J. … observed in [*Allmanna Svenska Elektriska A/B v The Burntisland Shipbuilding Co Ltd*]:
>
> > 'in the end of all … as it were a kind of jury question'."

---

[10] See also *Norton Healthcare v Beecham Group Plc*, Unreported, 19 June 1997, CA; cited in *Glaxo Group's Patent* [2004] R.P.C. 43, at [42].

[11] (T0939/92) at [2.4.2].

[12] [1993] R.P.C. 513, 519 (a decision under the 1949 Act).

[13] [1994] R.P.C. 49, 112.

[14] [1999] F.S.R. 683, [45].

[15] [2006] R.P.C. 28, [34]: but note that his final decision was reversed by the House of Lords.

[16] [1985] R.P.C. 59, 73–74.

12-14   In *Conor v Angiotech*[17] Lord Hoffmann approved the following statement of the law made by Kitchin J in *Generics v Lundbeck*[18]:

> "The question of obviousness must be considered on the facts of each case. The court must consider the weight to be attached to any particular factor in the light of all the relevant circumstances. These may include such matters as the motive to find a solution to the problem the patent addresses, the number and extent of the possible avenues of research, the effort involved in pursuing them and the expectation of success."

12-15   Obviousness has therefore also been described as a "multi-factorial question".[19] These considerations will be reviewed separately below, but such discussion remains subject to the overriding principle that none is of itself decisive and the Court is required to weigh all relevant factors in reaching an overall conclusion.

12-16   It follows that the Court of Appeal is unwilling to substitute its own view on the question of obviousness for that of the trial judge in the absence of any error of principle, and the following passage from Lord Hoffmann's speech in *Biogen v Medeva*[20] is frequently cited on appeal:

> "The need for appellate caution in reversing the judge's evaluation of the facts is based upon much more solid grounds than professional courtesy. It is because specific findings of fact, even by the most meticulous judge, are inherently an incomplete statement of the impression which was made upon him by the primary evidence. His expressed findings are always surrounded by a penumbra of imprecision as to emphasis, relative weight, minor qualification and nuance (as Renan said, *la vérité est dans une nuance*), of which time and language do not permit exact expression, but which may play an important part in the judge's overall evaluation. It would in my view be wrong to treat *Benmax* as authorising or requiring an appellate court to undertake a de novo evaluation of the facts in all cases in which no question of the credibility of witnesses is involved. Where the application of a legal standard such negligence or obviousness involves no question of principle but is simply a matter of degree, an appellate court should be very cautious in differing from the judge's evaluation."

12-17   The *Biogen* principle (which in short is that an appellate court must exercise caution in differing from the trial judge's evaluation of the facts unless he has erred in principle) applies to obviousness but not to novelty, save in special cases, for instance where there is a conflict of expert testimony on the meaning of a technical term or as to what exactly is disclosed by the prior art.[21] Also, where a judge has made an error in his starting point by wrongly construing the prior art so as to find anticipation, then rather less weight can be placed on any finding of obviousness.[22] It is also in general not correct for the Court of Appeal to apply the *Biogen* principle only to a part of the overall reasoning leading to the ultimate conclusion, but leave other parts.[23]

---

[17]   [2007] UKHL 49; [2008] R.P.C. 28, [42].

[18]   [2007] R.P.C. 32, [72].

[19]   *Actavis v Novartis* [2010] F.S.R. 18, [41]; *Nichia v Argos* [2007] EWCA Civ 741, [22].

[20]   [1997] R.P.C. 1, 45. See also *Designers Guild Ltd v Russell Williams (Textiles) Ltd* [2001] F.S.R. 11 and *Merck v Co Inc's Patents* [2004] F.S.R. 16.

[21]   *Technip France SA's Patent* [2004] R.P.C. 46, [74]; *Smithkline Beecham Plc v Apotex Europe Ltd* [2005] F.S.R. 23, [36].

[22]   *Ferag v Muller Martini* [2007] EWCA Civ 15, [14].

[23]   *Saint-Gobain PAM v Fusion Provida* [2005] EWCA Civ 177, [37].

Technical not commercial obviousness

Patents are granted for technical advances, not for appreciating that a techni- **12-18** cally obvious development can be exploited commercially. In *Hallen Company v Brabantia (UK) Ltd*,[24] Aldous J stated:

"The word 'obvious' in section 3 is, I believe, directed to whether or not an advance is technically or practically obvious and not to whether it is commercially obvious. Although the law is encapsulated in section 3 of the Patents Act 1977, the law on obviousness goes back many hundreds of years. The basis of the law is that the public are entitled to manufacture that which has been published, in the sense of made available to the public, with obvious modifications. By 'obvious modifications' are meant that which technically or practically would be obvious to the unimagina- tive skilled addressee in the art. Such a skilled man should be assured that his actions will not be covered by any monopoly granted to another if he does that which is part of the state of the art with modifications which are workshop modifications or otherwise technically or practically obvious alterations. He does not and should not have to look further and consider whether the step he is tak- ing is obvious or not for commercial reasons. The prize for a good commercial decision or idea is a head start on the competition and not a monopoly for twenty years."

Thus in contrast to perceived obstacles to manufacture (which may lead the **12-19** skilled person to consider a step not worth trying, and require invention to overcome), mere obstacles to lawful sale, e.g. regulatory approval, are not relevant obstacles[25]: if an invention is technically obvious, an allegation that a likely failure to obtain regulatory approval would make it not obvious to try has been rejected.[26]

However, the principle set out in the above-quoted passage from *Hallen* now has **12-20** to be understood in the light of subsequent decisions regarding the "mindset" of the skilled person.[27] As Aldous LJ subsequently explained in *Dyson v Hoover*[28]:

"Since at least the *Hallen* case, it has been recognised that the patent system is not available to protect mere commercial improvements. The observation of Slade LJ were directed at that issue which is step four of the *Windsurfing* steps. … The mantle of the skilled person is that of an actual skilled person. The purpose of assuming the mantle of the skilled person is to enable the decision as to what is obvious to be a decision based on actual facts. They include all the attitudes and perceptions of such a person."

The nature of the "mindset" with which the skilled person is deemed to be **12-21** imbued is discussed at para.12-54, et seq.

Obvious when?—The date for determining obviousness

Obviousness is to be judged as of the priority date of the relevant claim of the **12-22** patent, and the skilled reader is assumed to be considering each separate prior art citation as of that date. The relevant question is then how the reader would react to it, as of that date. (Contrast the position when considering novelty: for novelty purposes, a prior art citation is simply to be construed as of its own date of publica- tion, and the question of how it might be modified does not arise: see para.11-57.)

It is possible for an invention to be obvious over a citation at one date, but **12-23**

---

[24] [1989] R.P.C. 307, 327, upheld at [1991] R.P.C. 195.
[25] See further para.12-39.
[26] *Richardson-Vicks Inc's Patent* [1997] R.P.C. 888; *Ivax v Akzo* [2007] R.P.C. 3, [41]–[43].
[27] See Mance LJ's discussion in *Panduit Corp v Band-It Co* [2003] F.S.R. 8, [46]–[49].
[28] [2002] R.P.C. 22, [56]–[57]. See also the judgments of Sedley LJ at [87]–[88] and Arden LJ at [95]– [97].

subsequently cease to be obvious as at the priority date, because of other intervening contradictory knowledge.[29]

Obviousness of what?—The invention specified in the claim

12-24   The House of Lords in *Conor v Angiotech*[30] had to consider how one identifies the concept embodied in the invention which may constitute the "inventive step" for the purposes of art.56 of the EPC and s.1(1)(b) of the Patents Act 1977. There, the claim was essentially for a stent coated with taxol, which proved to be particularly effective in solving the problem of restenosis. However, the patent specification did not provide clear proof of this. Conor argued that the patent taught no more than that coating with taxol was worth trying (among other things), that this was obvious albeit without a prior expectation of success, and that the patent therefore added nothing to existing knowledge. This argument, accepted below, was rejected by the House of Lords. Lord Hoffmann said (at [17]):

> "I shall say at once that in my opinion this argument was an illegitimate amalgam of the requirements of inventiveness (article 56 of the EPC) and either sufficiency (article 83) or support (article 84) or both. It is the claimed invention which has to involve an inventive step. The invention means prima facie that specified in the claim: see section 125(1) of the 1977 Act. In the present case, the invention specified in claim 12 was a stent coated with taxol. There was no dispute that this was a new product. The question should therefore simply have been whether it involved an inventive step. As in the case of many product claims, there was nothing inventive in discovering how to make the product. The alleged inventiveness lay in the claim that the product would have a particular property, namely, to prevent or treat restenosis. (*Compare Pharmacia Corp v Merck & Co Inc* [2002] R.P.C. 41). So the question of obviousness was whether it was obvious to use a taxol-coated stent for this purpose. And this, as I have said, was the question to which the experts addressed themselves.
>   In my opinion, however, the invention is the product specified in a claim and the patentee is entitled to have the question of obviousness determined by reference to his claim and not to some vague paraphrase based upon the extent of his disclosure in the description. There is no requirement in the EPC or the statute that the specification must demonstrate by experiment that the invention will work or explain why it will work."[31]

12-25   The above passage states that "alleged inventiveness lay in the claim that the product would have a particular property, namely, to prevent or treat restenosis". It should however be noted that had the product been obvious for some other purpose (but would have still been suitable also for treating restenosis), then the claim would have been invalid for obviousness. Conversely, had the claimed products not had that property then the patent would have been invalid for insufficiency (as Lord Hoffmann then noted at [23]).

Obvious with respect to what?—The relevant "matter"

12-26   The "matter" which is said to form part of the state of the art can be any disclosure which would form part of the state of the art for the purposes of s.2(2), and can therefore be a prior written or oral disclosure or a prior use; all the considerations discussed in relation to novelty in the previous chapter apply. The exception is that an unpublished prior patent application, even if relevant to novelty under s.2(3), is irrelevant to the question of obviousness under s.3, as the section expressly states.

---

[29]   *Actavis v Merck* [2008] R.P.C. 26, [109]–[119].
[30]   [2008] R.P.C. 28.
[31]   But Lord Hoffmann subsequently referred to a "threshold test" of plausibility: see the further discussion of this requirement at para.12-35.

The prior art must have been "made available to the public" but (in contrast to   **12-27**
material relied upon as common general knowledge), there is no requirement that
it should have been widely disseminated or actually known to those skilled in the
art. Laddie J explained in *Pfizer Ltd's Patent*[32]:

> "A real worker in the field may never look at a piece of prior art—for example he may never look at
> the contents of a particular public library—or he may be put off because it is in a language he does
> not know. But the notional addressee is taken to have done so. This is a reflection of part of the policy
> underlying the law of obviousness. Anything which is obvious over what is available to the public
> cannot subsequently be the subject of valid patent protection even if, in practice, few would have
> bothered looking through the prior art or would have found the particular items relied on. Patents are
> not granted for the discovery and wider dissemination of public material and what is obvious over
> it, but only for making new inventions. A worker who finds, is given or stumbles upon any piece of
> public prior art must realise that that art and anything obvious over it cannot be monopolised by him
> and he is reassured that it cannot be monopolised by anyone else."

In the EPO, focus is placed on the citation determined to be the "closest prior art".   **12-28**
In the UK court, each pleaded citation is considered separately on its merits.
However, pleading a large number of citations may be counterproductive, tending
to generate an impression that a party "does not feel it has a real killer".[33] This
consideration was explained in *Alan Nuttall v Fri-Jado*[34]:

> "The Defendants for their part cited a considerable number of items of prior art in support of their
> case on obviousness. That is seldom sound policy because, if the alleged invention was indeed obvi-
> ous in the light of one particular item of prior art, it does not make the case any better that there were
> other items that were not quite as good. On the contrary, to cite numerous pieces of prior art in an
> obviousness case tends, if anything, to suggest that the invention was not so obvious after all. At the
> trial the Defendants dropped most of those and wanted to rely on four, including a prior user of their
> own. In the end they decided to rely on just the two best citations, plus common general knowledge".

Mosaicing: combining cited art with other material

The "mosaicing" together of individual cited documents or prior uses is not   **12-29**
permissible, unless it can be shown that the skilled person, confronted with a
particular citation, would turn to some other citation to supplement the information provided by the first.[35] Whether they would do so is a question of fact. Lord
Reid said in *Technograph v Mills & Rockley*[36]:

> "When dealing with obviousness, unlike novelty, it is permissible to make a 'mosaic' out of the
> relevant documents, but it must be a mosaic which can be put together by an unimaginative man with
> no inventive capacity."

In *Pfizer Ltd's Patent*[37] Laddie J referred to the passage in the 15th edn of this   **12-30**
work dealing with mosaicing in the context of novelty (see para.11-61), and
continued:

> "This passage is directed particularly at the issue of mosaicing when applied to the law of novelty.
> The same approach applies to obviousness. There may well be invention in patching together
> disclosures from unrelated sources (see *Von Heyden v Neustadt* (1880) 50 L.J.Ch. 126). But, at least

---

[32] [2001] F.S.R. 16, [62].
[33] *Generics v Daiichi* [2009] R.P.C. 23, [3]; see also *Corus v Qual-Chem* [2008] EWCA Civ 1177, [2];
Ratiopharm v Napp [2009] R.P.C. 11, [7], and see para.10-28.
[34] [2008] EWHC 1311 (Pat).
[35] *Glaxo Group Ltd's Patent* [2004] R.P.C. 43, [35].
[36] [1972] R.P.C. 346, 355.
[37] [2001] F.S.R. 16, [65]–[66].

in relation to obviousness, the second part of this statement [that reliance on express cross-referencing is permissible] does not represent a rigid but limited exception. When any piece of prior art is considered for the purposes of an obviousness attack, the question asked is "what would the skilled addressee think and do on the basis of this disclosure?" He will consider the disclosure in the light of the common general knowledge and it may be that in some cases he will also think it obvious to supplement the disclosure by consulting other readily accessible publicly available information. This will be particularly likely where the pleaded prior art encourages him to do so because it expressly cross-refers to other material. However, I do not think it is limited to cases where there is an express cross-reference. For example if a piece of prior art directs the skilled worker to use a member of a class of ingredients for a particular purpose and it would be obvious to him where and how to find details of members of that class, then he will do so and that act of pulling in other information is itself an obvious consequence of the disclosure in the prior art."

12-31   Account has therefore been taken of information which, although not part of the skilled person's common general knowledge, would have been acquired by him as a matter of routine before embarking on the problem to which the patented invention provides the solution.[38] However, in *Generics (UK) Ltd v Daiichi Pharmaceutical*[39] Kitchin J explained that:

"I can readily accept that, faced with a disclosure which forms part of the state of the art, it may be obvious for the skilled person to seek to acquire further information before he embarks on the problem to which the patent provides a solution. But that does not make all such information part of the common general knowledge. The distinction is a fine one but it may be important. If information is part of the common general knowledge then it forms part of the stock of knowledge which will inform and guide the skilled person's approach to the problem from the outset. It may, for example, affect the steps it will be obvious for him to take, including the nature and extent of any literature search."

12-32   In the Court of Appeal in the same case,[40] Jacob LJ referred to the above passage and stated:

"I agree with that although I personally do not find the point of principle 'subtle'. It would be wholly subversive of patents and quite unfair to inventors if one could simply say 'piece of information A is in the standard literature, so is B (albeit in a different place or context), so an invention consisting of putting A and B together cannot be inventive.' The skilled man reads each specific piece of prior art with his common general knowledge. If that makes the invention obvious, then it does. But he does not read a specific citation with another specific citation in mind, unless the first causes him to do so or both are part of the matter taken to be in his head."

12-33   In *KCI Licensing v Smith & Nephew*[41] Arnold J held in relation to the above decisions:

"It follows that, even if information is neither disclosed by a specific item of prior art nor common general knowledge, it may nevertheless be taken into account as part of a case of obviousness if it is proved that the skilled person faced with the problem to which the patent is addressed would acquire that information as a matter of routine. For example, if the problem is how to formulate a particular pharmaceutical substance for administration to patients, then it may be shown that the skilled formulator would as a matter of routine start by ascertaining certain physical and chemical properties of that substance (e.g. its aqueous solubility) from the literature or by routine testing. If so, it is legitimate to take that information into account when assessing the obviousness of a particular formulation. But that is because it is obvious for the skilled person to obtain the information, not because it is common general knowledge."

---

[38]   *KCI Licensing v Smith & Nephew* [2010] EWHC 1487 (Pat), [108]–[112]; and see the authorities there cited.
[39]   [2009] R.P.C. 4, [40].
[40]   [2009] R.P.C. 23, [27].
[41]   [2010] EWHC 1487 (Pat), [112].

Combining cited art with common general knowledge

Where a case of obviousness, as opposed to novelty, is being run, then there will **12-34** be some difference between what is described in the prior art and what is claimed in the claim under attack. The argument on obviousness is then typically whether the skilled person would have bridged the gap in the light of their common general knowledge.

The definition of common general knowledge, discussed at para.8-56, et seq. in **12-35** Ch.8, is potentially a very wide one (albeit the common general knowledge must be established in the UK[42]). But of course it does not follow that, merely because some piece of information falls within that definition, it is necessarily obvious to combine it with a cited piece of prior art. Whether such a combination would be made is a question of fact in each case. It may simply not have occurred to the skilled reader absent some spark of ingenuity; or in the more extreme case there may have been a "mindset" against applying such material to the problem in hand. The point is exemplified by *Dyson v Hoover*, in which cyclones were held to be part of the common general knowledge of vacuum cleaner designers (at first instance this was expressly qualified as "latent" common general knowledge), but making practical use of this knowledge was not obvious to them: see the further discussion of this case, and the topic of mindset, at para.12-54.

Obviousness over common general knowledge alone

In some cases, it may not be necessary to rely on any particular disclosure, for **12-36** the invention may be obvious merely in the light of the common general knowledge possessed by the skilled person.[43] However, such allegations must be approached with caution as they are unencumbered by any detail which might point to non-obviousness and are particularly prone to be tainted by hindsight.[44]

In *Ratiopharm v Napp*[45] Floyd J noted that it was not the general practice to plead **12-37** the relevant common general knowledge relied upon in support of such a case but considered that some formal exposition in advance of expert reports would be appropriate. He then made a number of observations regarding the approach to be taken to an allegation of obviousness over common general knowledge alone. The first was self-evident: it is that it is essential that the starting point for the plea is indeed established to be common general knowledge. Secondly, it is important to be precise about what it is that is asserted to be common general knowledge; for example it may be important to distinguish between knowledge of the existence of a product and knowledge of particular applications. Thirdly, it is vital to have in mind the requirements for matter to be part of the common general knowledge: see in particular the passage in *Beloit v Valmet*,[46] discussed at para.8-66 of this work. Fourthly, allegations of obviousness in the light of common general knowledge alone need to be treated with a certain amount of care. They can be favoured by parties attacking the patent because the starting point is not obviously encumbered with inconvenient details of the kind found in documentary disclosures, such as misleading directions or distracting context. It is vitally important to make sure that the

---

[42] See Arnold J in *Generics (UK) v Warner Lambert* [2015] EWHC 2548 (Pat), at [123]–[124].

[43] See, e.g. *Lucas (Joseph) (Batteries) Ltd v Gaedor Ltd* [1978] R.P.C. 297, 377.

[44] *3M v Ati Atlas* [2001] F.S.R. 31, [32]; *Abbott Laboratories v Evysio* [2008] R.P.C. 23, [180].

[45] [2009] R.P.C. 11, [154]–[159]. See also *Nokia v Ipcom* [2009] EWHC 3482 (Pat), [109].

[46] [1997] R.P.C. 489, 494–5.

whole picture presented by the common general knowledge is considered, and not a partial one.[47] Finally, the common general knowledge does not include knowledge which does not inform the skilled person's approach from the outset. The judge explained the final point thus:

"Whether knowledge is common and general depends on the considerations explained by Aldous LJ in *Beloit*. If information does not satisfy that criterion, it does not become common general knowledge by postulating a set of steps that the skilled team might take to find it if they had already embarked on an attempt to solve a particular problem. That is not to say that it is illegitimate, in assessing an obviousness attack, to take account of material which would inevitably be found and treated as reliable in consequence of a step or steps which it is obvious to take. If the material so found is such as would be accepted, then it may assist in showing obviousness of a further step. But what it cannot be used for is in support of an argument that the series of steps being undertaken were obvious from the start."

12-38   He found that the patent in suit was not obvious over common general knowledge on the facts of the case before him, and this aspect of his decision was not appealed.

Lack of "technical contribution"/"AgrEvo" obviousness/"Plausibility"

12-39   An allegation of obviousness may sometimes succeed where the patent has made no "technical contribution" to the art. This is a free-standing allegation in the sense that it may succeed even where a case of "conventional" obviousness over the cited prior art has failed (as was the case in *Eli Lilly v Human Genome Sciences*).[48]

12-40   Consideration of obviousness on this basis does not arise directly from either the Patents Act 1977 or the EPC. Its origin was explained by Floyd LJ in *Generics v Yeda*[49] as follows:

"Neither the European Patent Convention ("EPC") nor the Patents Act 1977 includes amongst the available grounds of invalidity of a granted patent an objection that the patent does not make a technical contribution to the art. However the "problem and solution" approach adopted by the EPO under the EPC to the ground of lack of inventive step necessarily involves isolating from the patent (in comparison with the prior art) some technical contribution or effect. The EPO adopt this approach in order to formulate a technical problem which is solved by the patent – achieving that technical effect – as a precursor to asking whether the patent solves that problem in an obvious or non-obvious way."

12-41   The policy behind the requirement for a technical contribution was explained by Kitchin J, in *Abbott Laboratories v Evysio* as follows[50]:

"There is no invention in stipulating a feature which is arbitrary and serves no useful purpose. It has long been established that a patent cannot be used to prevent a person from doing what is merely an obvious extension of what has been done or was known in the art before the priority date. The public are entitled to make obvious products using obvious and ordinary techniques. The selection of a number of these products by reference to an arbitrary parameter which has no technical significance does not involve an inventive step and does not create a patentable invention. It involves no technical ingenuity and solves no technical problem".

12-42   The EPO's jurisprudence on the issue of the technical contribution requirement for obviousness flows from the decision of the Technical Board of Appeal in

---

[47]   These difficulties are well illustrated in *Accord Healthcare v Medac* [2016] EWHC 24 (Pat), see [119]–[124].
[48]   [2009] R.P.C. 29, [317].
[49]   [2013] EWCA Civ 925, [37].
[50]   [2008] R.P.C. 23, [181].

AgrEvo (hence it is frequently referred to as "*AgrEvo* obviousness").[51] *AgrEvo* obviousness is a relatively new feature of UK jurisprudence. However, it has been considered in a comparatively large number of recent cases. It should also be noted that the central considerations relating to *AgrEvo* obviousness are hard to separate (if at all) from very similar considerations, in particular plausibility, that arise in the context of sufficiency, industrial applicability and priority. These are discussed in greater detail in paras 2-20, 7-37, 11-97 and 13-54.[52]

In *Generics v Yeda*[53] Floyd LJ considered *AgrEvo* and the cases that followed, **12-43** and summarised the position as follows:

"(i)   Article 56 of the EPC is in part based on the underlying principle that the scope of the patent monopoly must be justified by the patentee's contribution to the art.

(ii)   If the alleged contribution is a technical effect which is not common to substantially everything covered by a claim, it cannot be used to formulate the question for the purposes of judging obviousness.

(iii)   In such circumstances the claim must either be restricted to the subject matter which makes good the technical contribution, or a different technical solution common to the whole claim must be found.

(iv)   A selection from the prior art which is purely arbitrary and cannot be justified by some useful technical property is likely to be held to be obvious because it does not make a real technical advance.

(v)   A technical effect which is not rendered plausible by the patent specification may not be taken into account in assessing inventive step.

(vi)   Later evidence may be adduced to support a technical effect made plausible by the specification.

(vii)   Provided the technical effect is made plausible, no further proof of the existence of the effect is to be demanded *of the specification* before judging obviousness by reference to the technical effect propounded."

A central question is what standard of disclosure is required to render a techni- **12-44** cal effect plausible. This has been the subject of judicial consideration in a number of recent cases, although uncertainty remains as to the boundaries of the concept.

In *HGS v Lilly*[54] the Supreme Court considered the meaning of "plausible" in the **12-45** context of an objection for lack of industrial applicability. The Supreme Court drew a distinction between "speculation" and concepts such as "plausible" or "reasonably credible". Lord Hope expressed the position as follows:[55]

"I would not quarrel with Jacob LJ's comment, after consulting the *Shorter Oxford English Dictionary*, that the sense that word conveys is that there must be some real reason for supposing that the statement is true: para.111. The important point, however, is that the standard is not any higher than that."

The test for plausibility is therefore a threshold test, and it would appear that the **12-46** standard required in the circumstances in *HGS v Lilly* (a product claim) is comparatively low.

Later cases make clear, however, that there is no single standard for demonstrat- **12-47**

---

51   *Triazoles/AgrEvo* (T939/92), [2.4]–[2.6], especially [2.5.3].

52   And see *Actavis v Lilly* [2015 EWHC 3294 (Pat); *Regeneron v Genentech* [2013] R.P.C. 28; *Lilly v HGS* [2011] UKSC 51; and *Hospira v Genentech* [2014] EWCA 1094.

53   [2013] EWCA Civ 925, [2014] R.P.C. 4, [49]. A review of the underlying authorities is given by Arnold J in *Idenix v Gilead* [2014] EWHC 3916 (Pat). See also *Teva v Boehringer* [2015] EWHC 2963 (Pat).

54   *Idenix v Gilead* [2014] EWHC 3916 (Pat), [443]. And see *Merck v Ono* [2015] EWHC 2973(Pat), [133]–[134] and *Generics v Secretary of State for Health* [2015] EWHC 2548 (Pat).

55   *HGS v Lilly* [2011] UKSC 51, [149]. See also Lord Neuberger in the same case at [107(viii)] and [120]–[123].

ing plausibility. In *Merck v Ono*[56] Birss J stated that:

"Whenever one is considering plausibility it must be done in the context of the invention determined by properly construing the claim and one must keep in mind the particular legal objection which is under consideration. Moreover it is worth reminding oneself that "plausible" is not a term found in the relevant parts of either the EPC or the 1977 Patents Act. It has proved to be a useful concept in various factual situations but just because that has proved to be true in one case does not mean that everything said in that context applies in a very different context. There is no law of plausibility as such".

12-48   Birss J went on to explain that the material relied on must make the particular claimed use, whatever it is, plausible. Thus, a pure product claim and a Swiss claim would require material of different breadth to make them plausible. For a pure product claim, such as that in *HGS v Lilly*, there were no functional or technical features. It followed that it was enough if the product claimed would have a plausible therapeutic effect. In comparison, for an EPC2000 or Swiss claim, the material relied on to establish plausibility must be both sufficiently specific, and have a sufficient breadth of application, to fairly support the claim both in terms of the nature of the agent claimed to have an effect, and in terms of the effect claimed.

12-49   In *Actavis v Lilly*[57] Carr J considered the test for plausibility, finding that the standard required was lower than that for an expectation of success[58]:

"There is no requirement in the EPC that a patent should contain data or experimental proof to support its claims. The reference in *Salk* (T609/02) to the provision of experimental tests to support the claimed therapeutic use was by way of example. In respect of claims to therapeutic applications which are of wide scope, such experimental tests may well be required. In the case of narrow claims, they may not be

In my judgment, the policy considerations underlying plausibility for sufficiency are different from those underlying fair expectation of success for obviousness, which indicates that the standard for assessment of plausibility is not the same as assessment of obviousness. For obviousness, a fair expectation of success is required because, in an empirical art, many routes may be obvious to try, without any real idea of whether they will work. The denial of patent protection based upon the "obvious to try" criterion alone would provide insufficient incentive for research and development in, for example, pharmaceuticals and biotechnology, and would lead to the conclusion that a research program of uncertain outcome would deprive a patent of inventive step. The reason why the court requires that the invention of a patent should be plausible is different. It is to exclude speculative patents, based on mere assertion, where there is no real reason to suppose that the assertion is true.

The cases on which Lilly relies (to which I have referred above) establish that the test of plausibility is a threshold test which is satisfied by a disclosure which is 'credible', as opposed to speculative. That disclosure may subsequently be confirmed or refuted by further evidence obtained subsequent to the priority date. If it is subsequently shown that the invention does not work with substantially all of the products or methods falling within the scope of the claim then the scope of the monopoly will exceed the technical contribution and the patent will be invalid. This indicates why plausibility is only a threshold test. A plausible invention may nonetheless be shown to be insufficient. In my judgment the standard for assessment of plausibility is not the same the standard for assessment of expectation of success in the context of obviousness".

12-50   The question of "technical contribution" is particularly relevant where it is alleged that the patentee has done no more than make an arbitrary selection. The position was summarised by Arnold J in *Sandvik v Kennametal*[59] as follows:

"Where it is suggested that a claimed invention is obvious as being an arbitrary selection, the key question is whether the specification 'passes the threshold test of disclosing enough to make the inven-

56   [2015] EWHC 2973 (Pat), [133]–[139].
57   [2015] EWHC 3294 (Pat), [176]–[177].
58   Which would appear to be consistent with EPO jurisprudence in cases such as *Ipsen* (T578/06).
59   [2011] EWHC 3311 (Pat) [2012] R.P.C. 23, [185].

tion plausible' as Lord Hoffmann put it in Conor v Angiotech, that is to say, to make it plausible that the selection has the technical significance claimed for it."

It should also be noted that the old (pre-1977) law under which selection patents were treated as a special case is now to be regarded as part of legal history and is not relevant to current jurisprudence.[60]   **12-51**

Obvious to whom?—The "person skilled in the art"

Section 3 is one of those sections which gives express statutory recognition to   **12-52**
the "person skilled in the art". This may be a team with differing scientific knowledge, whose general characteristics and attributes have been considered in Ch.8. In the context of obviousness, such person is deemed to be normally skilled but unimaginative. Laddie J described such a person in *Pfizer Ltd's Patent*[61] in the following way:

"The question of obviousness has to be assessed through the eyes of the skilled but non-inventive man in the art. This is not a real person. He is a legal creation. He is supposed to offer an objective test of whether a particular development can be protected by a patent. He is deemed to have looked at and read publicly available documents and to know of public uses in the prior art. He understands all languages and dialects. He never misses the obvious nor stumbles on the inventive. He has no private idiosyncratic preferences or dislikes. He never thinks laterally. He differs from all real people in one or more of these characteristics."

Obviousness is to be judged by reference to such a person: in the well-worn   **12-53**
phrase, the court is required to "assume the mantle of the skilled person" when assessing obviousness. Pumfrey J noted in *Conor v Angiotech*[62] that:

"To an inappropriately defined skilled man, nothing may be obvious or everything may be obvious. The most difficult part of any obviousness case is the attribution of the relevant skill and knowledge to the notional addressee of the patent".

The common general knowledge and the "mindset" of the skilled person

The person skilled in the art will, by definition, be acquainted with the common   **12-54**
general knowledge in the art. This topic has been discussed in Ch.8 of this work. Whether they would apply it to the problem in hand, or combine it with the cited prior art, is a question of fact in each case.

Further, it may be pertinent to show that they will also have the "mindset" of   **12-55**
those skilled in the art at the priority date. This will include not only technical knowledge but also the technical prejudices that existed at the relevant date.

In *Dyson v Hoover*[63] the judge at first instance referred to one aspect of the   **12-56**
relevant skilled person's common general knowledge as "latent"—something of which they would be aware as a result of his graduate training in general mechanical engineering. However, that knowledge, namely aspects of cyclone technology, would not have been regarded as applicable to the design of vacuum cleaners. At first instance, the judge held that[64]:

"... Common general knowledge has both positive and negative aspects. I have so far considered

---

[60] *Dr Reddy's Laboratories v Eli Lilly* [2010] R.P.C. 9, [19].
[61] [2001] F.S.R. 16, [62].
[62] [2008] R.P.C. 28.
[63] [2001] R.P.C. 26, [34] and [41].
[64] [2001] R.P.C. 26, [156].

under this topic, as is customary, only positive aspects of the knowledge with which the skilled addressee is to be imbued. In my view in certain cases (and I believe this to be one of them), negative aspects of knowledge must in approximation to reality play their part. At the priority date of the patent, I believe that such was the 'mindset' within the vacuum cleaner industry, no notional, right-thinking addressee would ever have considered the viability of purifying dirt-laden air from a vacuum cleaning operation, other than by means of using a bag or bag and final filter. For present purposes, the addressee is nonetheless deemed to have been presented with (in effect) three items of prior art wherein it is proposed to clean dirt-laden air by means not of bags but by cyclonic action alone. He is also assumed to take some interest in them however inimical the proposals may be to his likely way of thinking at the time. In terms of its impact on the issue of obviousness, I believe that this negative thinking which as Mr Kitchin suggested amounted to prejudice, would at least have caused the addressee to regard modification to any of these prior art proposals with considerable reserve if not overt scepticism. This likelihood must, I consider, be given due weight. In my view of the matter, I cannot think that any of the cited prior art would ex facie be likely to have led the addressee at the relevant date with any enthusiasm to effect the often substantial changes which would bring these proposals within a claim of the patent. ... My view in this regard is bolstered (but not precipitated) by Mr Dyson's evidence of what actually happened when he tried to interest the industry in Dyson I".

12-57   In the same case in the Court of Appeal, Sedley LJ said the following[65]:

"The vacuum-cleaner industry was functionally deaf and blind to any technology which did not involve a replaceable bag. The fact that the handicap was entirely economically determined made it if anything more entrenched. The industrial perception of need was consequently, in the judge's happy coinage, bagridden. It is entirely in accordance with what we know about innovation that this commercial mindset will have played a part in setting the notional skilled addressee's mental horizon, making a true inventor of the individual who was able to lift his eyes above the horizon and see a bag-free machine."

12-58   The Court of Appeal did not itself take up the designation "latent" to characterise the pre-existing common general knowledge of cyclones. Such knowledge remained common general knowledge but absent some stimulus it was not appreciated that it could be applied. (One may contrast the position as regards sufficiency, when the skilled reader will have the patent before him and may then be sufficiently well equipped to apply it without further detailed teaching.) The case demonstrates that even if aspects of an invention may be available to the skilled person, whether it was obvious to apply them or to combine them with a specific citation is still a question that must be addressed.

12-59   Where there were commonly understood reasons why the trade had previous adopted a certain practice, those reasons are part of the mantle of the skilled person through whose eyes obviousness had to be judged.[66] Thus in an art (fluidised beds) where the behaviour was not well understood and developments were empirical, so that those involved were conservative in outlook, it was held that this mindset meant that the skilled person would be wary of modifying designs on paper in the prior art.[67]

12-60   A technical prejudice must be general: it is not enough that some persons actually engaged in the art at the material time labour under a particular prejudice if a substantial number of others do not. Thus a prejudice which is insufficiently widespread for it properly to be regarded as commonly shared will not be at-

---

[65] [2002] R.P.C. 22, [89].

[66] *Panduit Corp v Band-It Co* [2003] F.S.R. 8, [27].

[67] *Vector v Glatt* [2007] R.P.C. 12, [134]–[135]. But note that the final decision was reversed on other grounds (added matter) on appeal: [2008] R.P.C. 10.

tributed to the notional skilled person.[68] For example, a single statement in a patent specification recording the prejudice will not suffice.[69] The standard of proof in the UK court is mirrored by the strict approach taken by the Technical Boards of Appeal in the EPO.[70]

In *Ivax v Akzo*[71] it was held that commercial reasons may be relevant in considering whether a skilled person would follow a particular path (there, the cited prior art was a subsisting patent which prevented one possible route from being taken; it was held that this was relevant to and supportive of the obviousness of other routes, recognised but not claimed in that patent).

12-61

In *Dyson v Samsung*[72] it was held that it was not necessary for the patent to expressly identify or address any prejudice or to explain how or why contrary to the prejudice, the invention worked or was practical (the patent only needed to make it plausible that the invention would work or be practical). However, the failure to address the prejudice in the patent might well be of evidential significance.

12-62

The skilled person's level of interest in the prior art

All material forming part of the state of the art is deemed to be considered carefully and completely by the skilled person,[73] They are to be assumed to take an interest in the prior art cited, and thus the obscurity of a citation is not to be counted against it. To allow documents to be discounted on the ground of obscurity would run against the policy of the law that any person must be free to enter a library and exploit what they find there, provided that they exercise no invention in that exploitation.[74] Similarly they should not be discounted purely on grounds of age,[75] though the age of a piece of prior art may be relevant to the wider question of "why was it not done before".

12-63

In the *Windsurfing* case itself, Oliver LJ explained[76]:

12-64

"The hypothetical Skilled Man is, no doubt, (together with his cousins the Reasonable Man and the Officious Bystander) a useful concept as setting a standard and, in the instant case, as providing the touchstone by which the question of obviousness may be judged by the equally hypothetical Juror; but he must not be allowed to obscure the nature of the inquiry which the words of the statute require, and one cannot help feeling that his image may lead to confusion if one seeks to attribute to him human qualities either of constitutional idleness or of perception beyond the knowledge and skill in the field in which he is hypothetically supposed to operate. It is accepted by the appellants that the question of whether the alleged invention was obvious has to be answered objectively by reference to whether, at the material time (that is, immediately, prior to the priority date), the allegedly inventive step or concept would have been obvious to a skilled addressee, but Mr. Pumfrey submits that, whilst one has to assume that Darby was within the cognisance of the skilled man, one is not to assume that he has any interest in it. The burden, he suggests, lies upon the defendants to show some reason why such an interest should be aroused.

What Mr. Pumfrey's refinement on this seeks to suggest is not only that the skilled man, who is

---

68 *Glaxo Group Ltd's Patent* [2004] R.P.C. 43, [30].
69 *Farrow Holdings Group Inc v Secretary of State for Defence* [2014] EWHC 2047 (Pat).
70 See the *Case Law of the Boards of Appeal of the EPO*, 7th edn (Munich: EPO, 2013), para.10.2.
71 [2007] R.P.C. 3, [44]–[49], [71]. And see *Teva v Boehringer* [2015] EWHC 2963 (Pat), [114]–[117].
72 [2009] EWHC 55 (Pat); [2009] F.S.R. 15, [153]–[157].
73 *Technograph Printed Circuits Ltd v Mills & Rockley Electronics Ltd* [1972] R.P.C. 346; see also the *Windsurfing* case [1985] R.P.C. 59, 74.
74 *Glaxo Group Ltd's Patent* [2004] R.P.C. 43, [37]; see also *Gillette Safety Razor Co Ltd v Anglo-American Trading Co Ltd* (1913) 30 R.P.C. 465, 480.
75 *Brugger v Medic-Aid* [1996] R.P.C. 635, 653.
76 [1985] R.P.C. 59, 71.

to set the standard, is uninventive but that, in the absence of some evidence to the contrary, he is uninterested; and that is, in our judgment, a view which obscures the real question that has to be answered and which is not supported in authority. What has to be determined is whether what is now claimed as inventive would have been obvious, not whether it would have appeared commercially worthwhile to exploit it.

...

We agree, of course, that one must not assume that the skilled man, casting his experienced eye over Darby [the prior art], would at once be fired with knowledge that here was something which had a great commercial future which he must bend every effort to develop and improve, but he must at least be assumed to appreciate and understand the free-sail concept taught by Darby and to consider, in the light of his knowledge and experience, whether it would work and how it will work."

12-65   This principle was applied and explained by the Court of Appeal in *Asahi Medical Co Limited v Macopharma (UK) Limited*[77]:

"I will come later to analyse the judge's reasoning, but must first make it clear that a decision on obviousness does not require a conclusion as to whether or not the skilled person would be slightly, moderately or particularly interested in any document. The court has to adopt the mantle of the skilled person. That mantle will include the prejudices, preferences and attitudes that such persons had at the priority date. Thereafter the court has to decide whether the step or steps from the prior art to the invention were obvious. That decision has to be taken without the invention in mind and through the eyes of the skilled person. Of course any prior art document relied on must be deemed to be read properly and in that sense with interest. To conclude otherwise would deprive the public of their right to make anything which is an obvious modification of a published document."

12-66   The skilled reader must therefore be assumed to be sufficiently interested to consider the teaching of the prior citation: to read it properly. But whether, having given it such consideration, he would find it useful is a different matter. It may be that its potential significance can only be identified with the benefit of hindsight, without which he would have dismissed it as not relevant to him. This issue was considered by Laddie J in *Inhale v Quadrant*,[78] where he said:

"However, there is one issue which is of significance to one of the pieces of prior art relied on in this action. A fiction in patent law is that the notional uninventive skilled man in the art is deemed to have read and assimilated any piece of prior art pleaded by the party attacking the patent claim. If the invention is obvious to that person in the light of a particular piece of prior art, the claim in invalid. It is no answer to say that in real life the prior art would never have come to the attention of a worker in the field, for example because it was tucked away on the top shelf of a public library or because it was in a language which nobody in the art knew. The notional skilled person is assumed to have read and understood the contents of the prior art. However that does not mean that all prior art will be considered equally interesting. The notional skilled person is assumed to be interested in the field of technology covered by the patent in suit, but he is not assumed to know or suspect in advance of reading it that any particular piece of prior art has the answer to a problem he faces or is relevant to it. He comes to the prior art without any preconceptions and, in particular, without any expectation that it offers him a solution to any problem he has in mind. Some pieces of prior art will be much more interesting than others. A document directed at solving the particular problem at issue will be seized upon by the skilled addressee. Its very contents may suggest that it is a worthwhile starting point for further development. But the same may not be the case where a document comes, say, from a distant and unrelated field. For example, in theory a notional skilled person engaged in trying to improve the operation of an internal combustion engine is assumed to know, have read and assimilated the contents of all published material including those, say, in the baking field. It may be that a document in the latter field discloses something which, if applied to the internal combustion art, would produce a marked improvement in performance. However, the person skilled in the art is not deemed to read the baking document in the knowledge, or even with a suspicion, that it is of significance to the problems he has to deal with. It may be that it is written in such a way that, although he understands it, the skilled person will dismiss it as irrelevant to his work. The more distant a prior

[77]   [2002] EWCA Civ 466, [21].
[78]   [2002] R.P.C. 21, [47]. And see *Collingwood Lighting v Aurora* [2014] EWHC 228 (Pat).

art document is from the field of technology covered by the patent, the greater the chance that an intelligent but uninventive person skilled in the art will fail to make the jump to the solution found by the patentee."

It follows that in a more extreme case, if the court is satisfied that a particular **12-67** piece of prior art would be seen by a skilled person as being so flawed as to present no useful starting point for development, then it would be right to reject the document.[79] In *Schlumberger v EMGS*[80] one of the prior art citations was held to be "so obscure in meaning as not really to have one": an argument that it was obvious to cherry-pick parts of it was rejected and its obscurity was unsurprisingly held to be a very telling factor against obviousness. Ultimately, the question turns on the facts. HHJ Birss put it this way in *Vernacare v Environmental Pulp Products*[81]:

> "As a matter of principle, the skilled person reads any given piece of prior art with interest. However, as a matter of principle again, once they have done so there is nothing to say as a matter of law that the skilled person is not entitled to say having read it with interest, 'I have read it with interest, but I am not interested.' The context is vital".

3.   STRUCTURED APPROACHES TO OBVIOUSNESS

As Jacob LJ noted in *Nichia v Argos*[82]:   **12-68**

> "Because obviousness is a multi-factorial question, it is impossible to devise a more detailed sort of question, suitable for all cases. *Windsurfing* (4) cannot be further refined. The statutory question is the statutory question and none other. Attempts in the past to try to devise a question have all been built around the circumstances of the particular case, see e.g. Graham J's discussion of the 'Cripps question' in *Olin Mathieson v Biorex* [1970] R.P.C. 157 at 188–189. Similarly, attempts to force all questions of obviousness into a 'problem-solution' approach can lead to trouble, though often the test can be a helpful guide."

The *Windsurfing/Pozzoli* test is however still frequently applied in the UK courts, **12-69** and the problem/solution approach continues to be preferred in the European Patent Office. The following paragraphs therefore review these structured approaches, though neither is a universally applicable replacement for the sole statutory question "is it obvious".

The structured approach in the "Windsurfing" and "Pozzoli" cases

A structured approach to determining the issue of obviousness, which has **12-70** frequently been followed and applied in subsequent cases, is provided by the four questions posed by Oliver LJ in *Windsurfing International Inc v Tabur Marine (Great Britain) Ltd*.[83] After observing that the question of obviousness was in the end "a kind of jury question", he went on to explain:

> "But it is one which has to be answered, not by looking with the benefit of hindsight at what is known now and what was known at the priority date and asking whether the former flows naturally and obviously from the latter, but by hypothesizing what would have been obvious at the priority date to a person skilled in the art to which the patent in suit relates, who is assumed to have access to what was known of the art in the United Kingdom immediately before the priority date."

---

[79]   See, e.g. *Hoechst Celanese Corp v B.P. Chemicals* [1998] F.S.R. 586.
[80]   [2010] EWCA 819, [164], [181].
[81]   [2012] EWPCC 41.
[82]   [2007] EWCA Civ 741, [22]. And see *MedImmune v Novartis* [2012] EWCA Civ 1234, [85]–[95].
[83]   [1985] R.P.C. 59, 71 and 73–74.

He then set out a four-stage test. This was subsequently reviewed by the Court of Appeal in *Pozzoli v BDMO SA*[84] and restated as follows:

"(1)
    (a)   Identify the notional "person skilled in the art";
    (b)   Identify the relevant common general knowledge of that person;
(2)   Identify the inventive concept of the claim in question or if that cannot readily be done, construe it;
(3)   Identify what, if any, differences exist between the matter cited as forming part of the 'state of the art' and the inventive concept of the claim or the claim as construed;
(4)   Viewed without any knowledge of the alleged invention as claimed, do those differences constitute steps which would have been obvious to the person skilled in the art or do they require any degree of invention?"

12-71   The Court is of course not obliged to apply the *Windsurfing/Pozzoli* analysis (and a failure to do so, is therefore not necessarily a good ground of appeal); ultimately the sole issue is that posed by s.3.[85] However the Court of Appeal observed in *Wheatley v Drillsafe*[86] that failure to follow its structured approach had led the judge below into the error of applying hindsight reasoning and failing to distinguish what was known from what was common general knowledge.

12-72   It will be noted that in the final step, the statutory test for inventive step is restated. The first three steps are essentially for the purpose of putting the court in the right frame of mind (they "merely orientate the tribunal properly"[87]) as necessary preparation for the final question—which is the only question—which is, is it obvious?[88] Thus in *DSM NV's Patent*,[89] Neuberger J said:

"In a sense, I suppose that it can be said that this four stage approach really involves ending up back where one started, namely with the original issue, embodied in the fourth question. However, I believe that it is appropriate to apply this four stage approach, not merely because it has been approved and applied in a number of previous cases, including in the Court of Appeal. It is also because it ensures that one does not go straight to the question of obviousness by reference to a general impression as to the evidence as a whole. By adopting the structured approach, one ensures that there is a measure of discipline, reasoning and method in one's approach. Indeed, it helps to ensure that there is consistency of approach in different cases involving the issue of obviousness."

Windsurfing/Pozzoli step (1): Identify the skilled person and the common general knowledge

12-73   The first step requires the court to identify the skilled person (or team), and the common general knowledge. This is so that it may "adopt the mantle of the skilled person" for the purpose of the subsequent steps. These issues have already been discussed in Ch.8 of this work. In the context of obviousness, they also give rise to subsidiary questions as to the level of interest which such person is taken to show to the prior art, and the "mindset" to be assumed. These topics are discussed in more detail at para.12-94, et seq.

---

[84] [2007] F.S.R. 37, [14]–[23].
[85] *Instance v Denny* [2002] R.P.C. 14, [17]; *SmithKline Beecham Plc v Apotex Europe Ltd* [2005] F.S.R. 23, [34]–[35]; see also *Sabaf v MFI* [2005] R.P.C. 10, [20]–[24].
[86] [2001] R.P.C. 7, [45], [54], [72].
[87] *Virgin v Premium Aircraft Interiors* [2010] R.P.C. 8, [115]; *Actavis v Novartis* [2010] F.S.R. 18, [21].
[88] *Degussa-Huls SA v The Comptroller-General of Patents* [2005] R.P.C. 29, [24].
[89] [2001] R.P.C. 35, [55].

Windsurfing/Pozzoli step (2): Identify the inventive concept, or construe the claim

The ultimate question is whether or not the claim covers something which is obvious. In this step, the court is not seeking to alter the scope of the claim being considered, but merely to strip out unnecessary verbiage or make a précis.[90] As Pumfrey J stated in *Inpro's Patent*[91]:

12-74

> "The inventive concept of the patent in suit is on the face of it what is specified by the claims, freed from any prolixity, obscurity and meaningless characterisation of the kind described by Laddie J in *Raychem's Patents* [1998] R.P.C. 31."

Jacob LJ had earlier explained in *Unilever v Chefaro*[92]:

12-75

> "It is the inventive concept of the claim in question which must be considered, not some generalised concept to be derived from the specification as a whole. Different claims can, and generally will, have different inventive concepts. The first stage of identification of the concept is likely to be a question of construction: what does the claim mean? It might be thought there is no second stage—the concept is what the claim covers and that is that. But that is too wooden and not what courts, applying Windsurfing stage one, have done. It is too wooden because if one merely construes the claim one does not distinguish between portions which matter and portions which, although limitations on the ambit of the claim, do not. One is trying to identify the essence of the claim in this exercise."

Stripping out unnecessary verbiage which is irrelevant to the matters in dispute may be helpful, but in some cases the exercise may cause more trouble than it is worth. In *Pozzoli*[93] itself, Jacob LJ repeated the above-quoted passage from *Unilever v Chefaro* but went on to add:

12-76

> "In some cases the parties cannot agree on what the concept is. If one is not careful such a disagreement can develop into an unnecessary satellite debate. In the end what matters is/are the difference(s) between what is claimed and the prior art. It is those differences which form the 'step' to be considered at stage (4). So if a disagreement about the inventive concept of a claim starts getting too involved, the sensible way to proceed is to forget it and simply to work on the features of the claim."

Whichever approach is taken here, it is the claim itself that is paramount. As Lord Hoffmann said in *Conor v Angiotech*[94]:

12-77

> "The patentee is entitled to have the question of obviousness determined by reference to his claim and not to some vague paraphrase based upon the extent of his disclosure in the description".

Just as mis-paraphrasing the claim too widely would be unfair to inventors, considering it too narrowly may equally be unfair to the public. The importance of considering the inventive concept of the claim over its full width was stressed by Laddie J in *Brugger v Medic-Aid Ltd*,[95] for the following reasons:

12-78

> "The important issue as far as this case is concerned is to identify correctly the inventive concept which the patentee must be taken to have put forward as underpinning his monopoly. For this purpose it is necessary to bear in mind that the relevant inventive step must apply to all embodiments falling within the claims which are said to have independent validity. It is not legitimate to define the inventive step as something narrower than the scope of the relevant claims. In particular it is not legitimate to identify a narrow sub-group of embodiments falling within the claim and which have certain

---

90   *Pozzoli* [2007] F.S.R. 37, [18].
91   Research in *Motion v Inpro* [2006] R.P.C. 20, [132].
92   [1994] R.P.C. 567, 580.
93   [2007] F.S.R. 37, [19]; see also *Actavis v Novartis AG* [2010] EWCA Civ 82, [22]; and *Population Diagnostics v Comptroller General* [2012] EWHC 3541 (Ch), [26]–[30].
94   [2008] R.P.C. 716, [19].
95   [1996] R.P.C. 635, at 656.

technical advantages and then to define the inventive step in terms which apply to that sub-group but not the rest of the claim. …

The fact that the patentee was aiming to achieve certain functional advantages when designing his new nebulizer may well explain how he arrived at his preferred embodiments but what the court is concerned with is not the inventive concept, if any, in the preferred embodiments but the inventive concept put forward in the claims. If the patentee chooses to advance broad claims, the inventive concept will be broadened in an equivalent way. After all, *Windsurfing* was only putting forward a convenient way of approaching the statutory question; 'is anything falling within the scope of the claims obvious?'"

12-79   It is therefore only where technical advantages are possessed by everything falling within the claim, or at least all sensible embodiments of what is claimed, that it is legitimate to bear in mind the technical advantages of the invention.[96] A wide inventive concept which includes but is not limited to embodiments with technical merit may be more vulnerable to an attack on the ground of lack of inventive step than a narrow one which is limited to or traps the advantageous features.[97]

Windsurfing/Pozzoli step (3): Identify the differences between the cited art and the invention

12-80   The third question requires the court to have regard to the piece of prior art in question, to identify what that prior art is teaching the skilled person and then to identify the gap between that teaching and the inventive concept. As noted at para.12-36, it may also be necessary to identify the gap between the invention and the common general knowledge.

Windsurfing/Pozzoli step (4): Decide whether those differences represent obvious steps

12-81   It is, of course, the fourth question which requires the court to answer the question, formerly left to a jury: is the invention obvious? Pumfrey J sought to identify the balance to be achieved in *Glaxo Group Ltd's Patent*[98]:

"It is a question of fact in every case. Both the Scylla of considering nothing obvious except that to which the skilled man is driven and the Charybdis of considering every invention obvious that can be decomposed into a sequence of obvious steps must be avoided. The former is unfair to industry because it stifles natural development. The latter is unfair to inventors and not countenanced by English patent law."

12-82   In answering this question, the gap identified in step 3 must then be considered without assuming knowledge of the invention; the court must take care not to allow hindsight to colour its judgment. The *Windsurfing* case itself, in the passage already quoted above[99] stresses this, as have many subsequent cases. The first three steps involve knowledge of the invention, which must then be forgotten for the purposes of step 4. It has to be remembered that the skilled person, without possession of the patent, is not in a position to perform his own *Pozzoli* analysis.[100]

---

[96]   See further para.12-188.
[97]   *Schering-Plough v Norbrook Laboratories* [2006] F.S.R. 18, per Floyd J.
[98]   2004 R.P.C. 43, [41].
[99]   See para.12-70.
[100]   *Zipher v Markem* [2009] F.S.R. 1, 284; *Qualcomm v Nokia* [2008] EWHC 329 (Pat), [116].

The "problem-solution" approach in the EPO compared with Windsurfing/ Pozzoli

In considering obviousness, both the UK courts and the EPO are seeking to ap-   **12-83** ply the same overall test, that stipulated in EPC art.56. However, in seeking to develop structured approaches to the ultimate question, they have expressed them in somewhat different terms. This raises the question of whether, leaving aside differences in procedure, the two approaches would invariably reach the same result on the same facts, or whether either or both imposes inappropriate "glosses" on the correct test. It also raises the question of the extent to which the UK courts are bound by the jurisprudence of the EPO. The latter question was addressed by Lord Neuberger in *HGS v Lilly*[101] as follows:

"Further, while national courts should normally follow the established jurisprudence of the EPO, that does not mean that we should regard the reasoning in each decision of the Board as effectively binding on us. There will no doubt sometimes be a Board decision which a national court considers may take the law in an inappropriate direction, misapplies previous EPO jurisprudence, or fails to take a relevant argument into account. In such cases, the national court may well think it right not to apply the reasoning in the particular decision. While consistency of approach is important, there has to be room for dialogue between a national court and the EPO (as well as between national courts themselves). Nonetheless, where the Board has adopted a consistent approach to an issue in a number of decisions, it would require very unusual facts to justify a national court not following that approach."

As to the relationship between the problem-solution approach and *Windsurfing/*   **12-84** *Pozzoli*, the following should be noted.

In *Actavis v Novartis*[102] Jacob LJ responded to a suggestion that *Windsurfing/*   **12-85** *Pozzoli* is a peculiarly British approach. He explained that it is no more than a structure by which the question, obvious or not, is to be approached, and merely makes explicit that which is implicit in all other approaches. He went on to compare the *Windsurfing/Pozzoli* approach with the EPO's "problem-solution" approach. This is explained in the EPO's *Guidelines for Substantive Examination* as follows:

"In the problem-and-solution approach, there are three main stages

   (i)   determining the "closest prior art",
   (ii)   establishing the "objective technical problem" to be solved, and
   (iii) considering whether or not the claimed invention, starting from the closest prior art and the objective technical problem, would have been obvious to the skilled person."

In relation to the first step, identifying the closest prior art, Jacob LJ noted that   **12-86** this was a practical approach to keep oppositions manageable, though deciding which piece of prior art is the closest can lead to satellite disputes. He pointed out that this was not a requirement of *Windsurfing/Pozzoli*, but in practice litigants before the English courts have confined themselves to their best cases. (As noted in para.12-28, where an attacker cites too many "near misses" the court may instead be inclined to infer non-obviousness against him.)

In relation to the second step—establishing the "objective technical problem"—   **12-87** Jacob LJ noted that this may present difficulties, as it involves the court or tribunal artificially creating a problem supposed to be solved by the invention, and the final result may depend on how the problem is formulated. The approach does not cope

---

[101] [2011] UKSC 51; [2012] R.P.C. 6, [87].
[102] [2010] F.S.R. 18. See also *Generics v Daiachi* [2009] R.P.C. 23, [18]-[21].

well with cases where the invention involves perceiving that there is a problem, or in appreciating that a known problem, perhaps "put up with" for years, can be solved. Pumfrey J also expressed concerns about this aspect of the problem/solution approach in *Ranbaxy v Warner-Lambert*.[103]

12-88   As he also stressed, the problem/solution approach is not a compulsory approach, but merely one which should normally be applied.[104] It makes sense for an examining office which needs a structured approach. A national court making a full multifactorial assessment of all relevant factors may use it less often, particularly where there may be significant dispute as to, e.g. how to formulate the problem.

12-89   The *Windsurfing/Pozzoli* analysis was also compared with the problem/solution approach by Pumfrey J in *Glaxo Group's Patent*.[105] He stated that:

> "I am not persuaded that this is substantially different from the *Windsurfing* approach, subject to one qualification. The EPO will consider obviousness on the basis of the closest prior art only. Every pleaded starting point, however remote, needs to be considered in coming to a conclusion on obviousness in the domestic context, but I suspect that the need to concentrate on the 'best' citation has a result that is not much different. When one reaches the final step (the last *Windsurfing* step seems to be the same) the factors to be taken into account in assessing obviousness are not, so far as I can see, much different. The summaries of decisions contained in the 'Case Law of the Boards of Appeal', ss.6.1–6.2 clearly indicate the wide variety of factors that the EPO consider relevant to an assessment of obviousness. Interestingly, the question of the expectation of success seems to be considered particularly relevant where the course of action in question is long and consists of much labour, and understandably it is in the field of genetic engineering and biotechnology that the question becomes important (see s.6.2). Obviousness is a question of fact, a so-called 'jury question', and I see no basis for the suggestion that UK law is out of step with the principles applied in the EPO."

12-90   It may also be noted that the problem/solution approach does not expressly include anything corresponding to *Windsurfing/Pozzoli* step 1, namely identifying the person skilled in the art and the common general knowledge. However this must be implicit: the need to consider inventive step from the viewpoint of the skilled person is expressly required in EPC art.56 in any event.

12-91   In EPO jurisprudence the third step of the problem-solution approach gives rise to a subsidiary investigation—the so called "could-would" approach. This approach is explained in the EPO Guidelines for Substantive Examination[106] as follows:

> "*Could-would approach*
> In the third stage the question to be answered is whether there is any teaching in the prior art as a whole that *would* (not simply could, but would) have prompted the skilled person, faced with the objective technical problem, to modify or adapt the closest prior art while taking account of that teaching, thereby arriving at something falling within the terms of the claims, and thus achieving what the invention achieves (see G-VII, 4).
> In other words, the point is not whether the skilled person could have arrived at the invention by adapting or modifying the closest prior art, but whether he *would have done* so because the prior art incited him to do so in the hope of solving the objective technical problem or in expectation of some improvement or advantage (see T 2/83). Even an implicit prompting or implicitly recognizable incentive is sufficient to show that the skilled person would have combined the element from the prior art (see T257/98 and T/35/04). This must have been the case for the skilled person before the filing or priority date valid for the claim under examination."

---

[103] [2006] F.S.R. 14, [68]–[73].

[104] The EPO has itself held that the problem/solution approach is not always appropriate and is "no more than one possible route for the assessment of inventiveness. Accordingly, its use is not a sine qua non when deciding inventiveness": see *Aluminium alloys/Alcan* (T465/92).

[105] [2004] R.P.C. 43, [43]–[45].

[106] November 2015 edn, at G-VII, 5.3.

The scope of the "could-would" approach was discussed by Jacob LJ in *Actavis*   **12-92**
v Novartis[107]:

"I do not read [the EPO's could/would approach] as involving a requirement that the notional skilled person would actually physically implement the idea. What the passage is saying, sensibly enough, is that it is not enough the skilled man could have arrived at the invention from the prior art, it must be shown that he would have done. Whether he would actually press ahead and implement the idea depends on a host of other, commercial considerations."

The UK court has shown no enthusiasm for a mechanistic adoption of the could-   **12-93**
would approach. Thus, in *Hospira v Genentech*,[108] Birss J cautioned:

"Second, the law of obviousness cannot be accurately summarised simply by stating that the question is whether the skilled person *would* have arrived at the claimed invention, not whether they *could* have. The issue is multifactorial and based closely on the particular circumstances.
    Third, the word "would" is not always straightforward. Sometimes asking simply if a skilled person "would" do something risks placing too much weight on what are really minor or irrelevant factors like cost, instead of focusing on the technical issues. Moreover, the well known 9 ½ inch plate is not something a skilled person *would* make. It is more accurate to say that it is not patentable because the skilled person could make it without any inventive step".

4. EVIDENCE RELATING TO OBVIOUSNESS

"Primary" and "secondary" evidence

Since obviousness is a "jury-type question", to be decided on the facts of each   **12-94**
case, relevant evidence may take many different forms. The two types of evidence relating to obviousness were defined and distinguished by the Court of Appeal in *Mölnlycke v Procter & Gamble*,[109] in which Sir Donald Nicholls VC stated:

"The Act requires the court to make a finding of fact as to what was, at the priority date, included in the state of the art and then to find again as a fact whether, having regard to that state of the art, the alleged inventive step would be obvious to a person skilled in the art. In applying the statutory criterion and making these findings the court will almost invariably require the assistance of expert evidence. The primary evidence will be that of properly qualified expert witnesses who will say whether or not in their opinions the relevant step would have been obvious to a skilled man having regard to the state of the art. All other evidence is secondary to that primary evidence. ...In the nature of things, the expert witnesses and the court are considering the question of obviousness in the light of hindsight. It is this which may make the court's task difficult. What with hindsight seems plain and obvious often was not so seen at the time. It is for this reason that contemporary events can be of evidential assistance when testing the experts' primary evidence."

Primary evidence

The primary evidence is therefore that of the expert witnesses called by the par-   **12-95**
ties, who can give evidence as to the identity and attributes of the skilled person or team, the common general knowledge which they would possess and the way in which such persons would, as a matter of routine, approach problems in the relevant art. The expert evidence can also identify steps which would either be routine, or require a degree of lateral thinking and hence not be obvious to the skilled person.
    In practice, the experts called by the parties tend to be over-skilled. However, the   **12-96**

[107] [2010] EWCA 82; [2010] F.S.R. 18, [45]–[46].
[108] [2014] EWHC 1094 (Pat), [228]–[229].
[109] [1994] R.P.C. 49, 112.

courts have generally found it helpful to have the best possible guidance from persons steeped in the art, and have been able to make allowance where necessary.[110] It must be recalled that experts are not called as living embodiments of the unimaginative and uninventive skilled person: so it is not a contest to see whose expert most closely represents the skilled person.[111] As well as being over-qualified, the experts may come to the case with personal prejudices or preferences that must be discounted.[112]

12-97   The role of expert witnesses in giving evidence on obviousness in patent actions was considered by Jacob LJ in *Technip France SA's Patent*,[113] who said as follows:

> "... sometimes the requirement that the skilled man be uninventive is used by counsel for a patentee in an attempt to downgrade or dismiss the evidence of an expert called to say that a patent is obvious—'my witness is more nerdlike than his' is the general theme. I do not find this a helpful approach.
> ...
> I must explain why I think the attempt to approximate real people to the notional man is not helpful. It is to do with the function of expert witnesses in patent actions. Their primary function is to educate the court in the technology—they come as teachers, as makers of the mantle for the court to don. For that purpose it does not matter whether they do or do not approximate to the skilled man. What matters is how good they are at explaining things.
> But it also is permissible for an expert witness to opine on an 'ultimate question' which is not one of law. I so held in *Routestone v Minories Finance* [1997] B.C.C. 180 and see s.3 of the Civil Evidence Act 1972. As regards obviousness of a patent Sir Donald Nicholls V-C giving the judgment of the Court of Appeal in *Mölnlycke v Procter & Gamble* [1994] R.P.C. 49 at page 113 was explicit on the point:

> > 'In applying the statutory criterion [i.e. as to whether an alleged inventive step was obvious] and making these findings [i.e. as to obviousness] the court will almost invariably require the assistance of expert evidence. The primary evidence will be that of properly qualified expert witnesses who will say whether or not in their opinions the relevant step would have been obvious to a skilled man having regard to the state of the art.'

> But just because the opinion is admissible:

> > 'it by no means follows that the court must follow it. On its own (unless uncontested) it would be "a mere bit of empty rhetoric" ... What really matters in most cases is the reasons given for the opinion. As a practical matter a well-constructed expert's report containing opinion evidence sets out the opinion and the reasons for it. If the reasons stand up the opinion does, if not, not. A rule of evidence which excludes this opinion evidence serves no practical purpose. What happens if the evidence is regarded as inadmissible is that experts' reports simply try to creep up to the opinion without openly giving it. They insinuate rather than explicate'

> Because the expert's conclusion (e.g. obvious or not), as such, although admissible, is of little value it does not really matter what the actual attributes of the real expert witness are. What matters are the reasons for his or her opinion. And those reasons do not depend on how closely the expert approximates to the skilled man."

12-98   In *SmithKline Beecham Plc v Apotex Europe*[114] Jacob LJ referred back to his previous judgment as quoted above, and supplemented it thus:

> "To that I would add this: although it is inevitable that when an expert is asked what he would understand from a prior document's teaching he will give an answer as an individual, that answer is not as such all that helpful. What matters is what the notional skilled man would understand from the document. So it is not so much the expert's personal view but his reasons for that view—these

---

[110] See, e.g. HHJ Fysh's comments in *Wesley Jessen v CooperVision* [2003] R.P.C. 20, at [32].
[111] *Schering-Plough v Norbrook Laboratories* [2006] F.S.R. 18, [39].
[112] *Glaxo Group Ltd's Patent* [2004] R.P.C. 43, [32].
[113] [2004] R.P.C. 46.
[114] [2005] F.S.R. 23, [52]–[53].

the court can examine against the standard of the notional unimaginative skilled man. There is an analogy here with the well-known *Bolam* test for professional negligence—what matters is not what the individual expert witness says he personally would have done, but whether the conduct said to be negligent falls short of what a reasonable professional would have done.

Thus in weighing the views of rival experts as to what is taught or what is obvious from what is taught, a judge should be careful to distinguish his views on the experts as to whether they are good witnesses or good teachers—good at answering the questions asked and not others, not argumentative and so on, from the more fundamental reasons for their opinions. Ultimately it is the latter which matter—are they reasons which would be perceived by the skilled man?"

The greater difficulty with expert evidence is that it is prepared and given long **12-99** after the relevant date, and so runs the risk of being tainted by hindsight. Further, the expert evidence is almost invariably conflicting. In *Schlumberger v EMGS*[115] Jacob LJ gave further guidance as to how the court should deal with the conflicting opinions of the experts on obviousness:

"It is not a matter to be decided by choosing between one expert who says 'tis and one who says 'tisn't. A mere assertion of opinion is of no real value. … Reasons for the opinion are what really matter. It follows that it is generally not enough for the court to conclude that it accepts the opinion of one expert or the other. It too must descend into the reasons for the opinions."

There would seem to be no objection in principle to expert evidence explaining **12-100** technical issues arising in matters which would be categorised as secondary evidence.

Secondary evidence

Since obviousness is in the nature of a jury question, factual evidence is admis- **12-101** sible showing for example how the inventor in fact made the invention, how others were addressing the problem solved by the patent, the reaction of others, and the reaction of the marketplace. In *Mölnlycke v Procter & Gamble*[116] Sir Donald Nicholls VC stressed that the test for obviousness is an objective one and went on to note that a difficulty with secondary evidence (there defined broadly as "all other evidence" except the primary evidence of the experts) is that the court can quickly find itself caught up in an investigation of what was or was not obvious to certain identified individuals at certain dates, as to the true reasons for the events in question, as to the level of expertise of those involved, as to the material which they had considered, or as to the reasons for commercial success. He then stated:

"Secondary evidence of this type has its place and the importance, or weight, to be attached to it will vary from case to case. However, such evidence must be kept firmly in its place. It must not be permitted, by reason of its volume and complexity, to obscure the fact that it is no more than an aid in assessing the primary evidence".

However, secondary evidence may be, as Birss J said in *Accord v Medac*[117] **12-102** *"decisive in a proper case"* (although on the facts of that case it was not).

In *Schlumberger v EMGS*[118] Jacob LJ referred to the passage from *Mölnlycke v* **12-103** *Procter & Gamble* quoted above and stated:

---

[115] [2010] EWCA Civ 819, [86].
[116] [1994] R.P.C. 49, 112.
[117] [2016] EWHC 24 (Pat), [116].
[118] [2010] EWCA Civ 819, [84]–[85].

"It would be wrong to read this decision as saying that secondary evidence is always of minor importance. That would be to throw away a vast mass of jurisprudence, including many House of Lords cases, (e.g. *Siddell* and *Technograph*)."

He there described the relevance of secondary evidence as follows:

"It generally only comes into play when one is considering the question 'if it was obvious, why was it not done before?' That question itself can have many answers showing it was nothing to do with the invention, for instance that the prior art said to make the invention obvious was only published shortly before the date of the patent, or that the practical implementation of the patent required other technical developments. But once all other reasons have been discounted and the problem is shown to have been long-standing and solved by the invention, secondary evidence can and often does, play an important role. If a useful development was, in hindsight, seemingly obvious for years and the apparently straightforward technical step from the prior art simply was not taken, then there is likely to have been an invention. ...

Other types of secondary evidence can also point to inventiveness. One well-known type is the commercial success of the patented product, particularly if it met a long-standing need. Again one has to be able to strip out all other possible causes of that success, such as advertising, low production costs due to factors other than the invention, good design features and so on. But if one can do that (normally it works only in the case of simple inventions), and one is left with a successful product, which, if anyone had thought of it earlier, would have met a large market earlier, there may well be an invention. Also of clear common sense relevance (though of course not decisive) is a situation where another party has thought the development sufficiently important to apply to patent it itself".

12-104   Further, in *Conor v Angiotech*[119] Pumfrey J noted that "when assessing the attributes of the skilled person, it is essential to try to reflect, to the extent that the evidence permits, the actual ordinary skills of the real-life contemporaries of the skilled man at the priority date" and so identified another issue to which contemporary evidence could be relevant:

"It is perhaps a surprising feature of the passage that I have quoted from *Mölnlycke* that the Vice-Chancellor does not refer expressly to the common general knowledge and to the light that may be thrown on the level of skill and the common general knowledge by the contemporary history."

Contemporaneous events and contemporaneous reactions

12-105   Evidence of contemporaneous events, and in particular the contemporaneous reactions to the invention, unaffected by hindsight, of real skilled people may be of real value, for it will not have been tailored or selected for the trial, often many years later.[120] In some cases such evidence may suggest obviousness, in others it may point to an act of invention. Whitford J stated in *Lucas v Gaedor*[121]:

"... the question of obviousness is probably best tested, if this be possible, by the guidance given by contemporaneous events. ..."

12-106   In *Technograph Printed Circuits v Mills & Rockley*[122] Lord Reid said:

"Being wise after the event counsel for the appellants pointed out that this was really an easy problem to solve ... The whole history of this matter shows the falsity of that analysis. Dozens of inventors, and no doubt others as well, had tried and failed to find a satisfactory solution."

---

[119] [2006] R.P.C. 28, [34]–[35].
[120] *Schlumberger v EMGS* [2010] EWCA Civ 819, [115].
[121] [1978] R.P.C. 297, 358.
[122] [1972] R.P.C. 346, 353.

Aldous J put it this way in *Chiron v Organon Teknika (No.3)*[123]: **12-107**

"... it will be necessary to go back to November, 1987 [the priority date] and try to understand the attitudes and thinking of those in the art at the time. That can best be achieved by looking at what was happening and the attitudes of those concerned in the field in the 1980s. Such evidence does, I believe, enable me to decide whether the opinions of the witnesses are consistent with the facts or hindsight reconstructions of the type which are not persuasive."

In *Schlumberger v EMGS*[124] Jacob LJ noted that in *Mölnlycke*[125] itself Sir Donald **12-108**
Nicholls, while earlier stating that secondary evidence should be kept in its place, had then placed reliance on the defendant's own reaction to the invention. Jacob LJ went on to say:

"Also of clear common sense relevance (though of course not decisive) is a situation where another party has thought the development sufficiently important to apply to patent it itself. *Siddell v Vickers*[126] is an early example where this was given weight. One has to be a bit careful about this: even where an invention is obvious, someone has to be first to get there. And, these days, people apply for patents for all sorts of reasons, including as a precaution against attempts by others to preclude the field. But where another party has not only applied to patent the same invention but has given reasons for why it is inventive, greater weight can be given to the fact—the reasons can be compelling evidence of inventiveness."[127]

However, care has to be taken to see that any contemporaneous reaction is in fact **12-109**
material to the question of whether the invention was obvious over the cited art. The fact that others have been grappling with the problem solved by the patent for many years when they were aware of the disclosure relied upon as constituting the nearest prior art may carry weight.[128] But if those persons were unaware of the cited prior art, then of course this can scarcely provide assistance in relation to the question of whether the invention was obvious over that particular citation. They may also simply have missed the obvious.[129] Laddie J considered these issues in detail in *Pfizer Ltd's Patent*[130] (the "*Viagra*" case at first instance) as follows:

"Of particular importance in this case, in view of the way that the issue has been developed by the parties, is the difference between the plodding unerring perceptiveness of all things obvious to the notional skilled man and the personal characteristics of real workers in the field. As noted above, the notional skilled man never misses the obvious nor sees the inventive. In this respect he is quite unlike most real people. The difference has a direct impact on the assessment of the evidence put before the court. If a genius in a field misses a particular development over a piece of prior art, it could be because he missed the obvious, as clever people sometimes do, or because it was inventive. Similarly credible evidence from him that he saw or would have seen the development may be attributable to the fact that it is obvious or that it was inventive and he is clever enough to have seen it. So evidence from him does not prove that the development is obvious or not. It may be valuable in that it will help the court to understand the technology and how it could or might lead to the development. Similarly evidence from an uninspiring worker in the field that he did think of a particular development does not prove obviousness either. He may just have had a rare moment of perceptiveness. This

[123] [1994] F.S.R. 202, 223.
[124] [2010] EWCA Civ 819, [83] and [85].
[125] [1994] R.P.C. 49, 123.
[126] (1890) 7 R.P.C. 293: see Lord Halsbury, at 304: "the contention that they had themselves invented it, is the strongest possible proof of what they thought about it; and they certainly were persons likely to know and appreciate whether the apparatus was new".
[127] See also *Unilever v Chefaro* [1994] R.P.C. 567, at 586; cf. *Qualcomm v Nokia* [2008] EWHC 329, [422].
[128] See, e.g. Laddie J in *Haberman v Jackel International Limited* [1999] F.S.R. 683, at 697, et seq.
[129] *Panduit Corp v Band-It Co* [2003] F.S.R. 8, [33].
[130] [2001] F.S.R. 16, [63]–[64].

difference between the legal creation and the real worker in the field is particularly marked where there is more than one route to a desired goal. The hypothetical worker will see them all. A particular real individual at the time might not. Furthermore, a real worker in the field might, as a result of personal training, experience or taste, favour one route more than another. Furthermore, evidence from people in the art as to what they would or would not have done or thought if a particular piece of prior art had, contrary to the fact, been drawn to their attention at the priority date is, necessarily, more suspect. Caution must also be exercised where the evidence is being given by a worker who was not in the relevant field at the priority date but has tried to imagine what his reaction would have been had he been so.

This does not mean that evidence from those in the art at the relevant time is irrelevant. It is not. As I have said, it may help the court to assess the possible lines of analysis and deductions that the notional addressee might follow. Furthermore, sometimes it may be very persuasive. If it can be shown that a number of ordinary workers in the relevant field at the relevant time who were looking for the same goal and had the same prior art, missed what has been patented then that may be telling evidence of non-obviousness. This is particularly the case where the commercial benefits of the development would have been apparent and a long time had passed between the publication of the prior art and the priority date of the patent. Hence, the impact and interrelationship between the familiar concepts of long felt want and commercial success. Likewise evidence that ordinary men in the art and working from the same prior art at the relevant time independently came to the same development may be some evidence that the notional skilled man would have done likewise. However, the evidence is rarely that simple. In most substantial patent cases the technology at issue is sophisticated and the witnesses called are experts in their fields. In most cases, of which this is a good example, they are either renowned academics or researchers who have been immersed in the Research and Development departments of major companies. In either case they come to the issues not only with a profound understanding of the technology but also frequently with knowledge of additional private and relevant information which is not deemed to be known to the notional addressee. For example, a research worker in the field will almost always have knowledge of highly confidential prior work done in his department which cannot but affect his attitude to the prior art. This is all material of which the notional man skilled in the art will be ignorant."

12-110 The history of what those skilled in the art at the relevant time is therefore of little interest unless it can be shown that they were aware of the relevant art, and time and money spent investigating what particular groups were doing at a particular time may be disproportionate to the usefulness of the evidence obtained.[131] In *Halliburton Energy Services, Inc v Smith International*[132] Pumfrey J explained:

"In the final assessment of a finely balanced argument on obviousness, it is possible that the balance will be tilted in favour of the patent if it is established that many were trying and failing: but this sort of consideration is secondary, and will draw attention away from the main question, which is what is obvious to the skilled person in the light of each cited document, taken separately and interpreted through the eyes of the skilled person. In the usual case, I think, the fact that some investigators tried and failed to solve the problem allegedly solved by the patent is irrelevant to the question with which I am confronted, unless it can be shown that those who failed were aware of the publication under consideration, and the fact of failure will therefore have the strongest effect when the common general knowledge alone is relied on, although even then it must be shown that those who tried and failed were possessed of the common general knowledge and were not the victims of idiosyncratic prejudice or ignorance."

12-111 The contemporary history may also throw light on the level of skill and the common general knowledge in the relevant art.[133]

[131] *3M v Ati Atlas* [2001] F.S.R. 31, [32].
[132] [2006] R.P.C. 2, [172].
[133] Per Pumfrey J at first instance in *Conor v Angiotech* [2006] R.P.C. 28, at [34]–[35], cited at para.12-104.

The inventor's evidence

Similarly, it is possible that evidence from inventors or disclosure of docu- **12-112** ments relating to the making of the invention, may shed light on the particular thought processes which they went through in devising their inventions,[134] and therefore on the issue of obviousness. However, it needs to be treated with caution for a number of reasons.[135] The inventor may not have the same level of skill (either higher or lower) than that of the notional skilled person. What may have seemed ingenious to the inventor may therefore nonetheless have lacked inventive step in that it would have been obvious to a notional skilled person who was actually in possession of the cited art. Thus in *Hickman v Andrews*,[136] the Court of Appeal said:

"It is clear from his evidence, that Mr. Hickman arrived at the 'Workmate', even in its simplest form as specified in claim 1, without the refinements of collapsibility, and portability, by an independent and highly ingenious and skilled inventive process; but that is not conclusive, because he may have missed the obvious owing to his complete lack of knowledge of the prior art in the book binding craft."

Conversely, what may have seemed trivial to the actual inventor may nonethe- **12-113** less be inventive when assessed objectively. If he is an inventive man then he will no doubt see things more clearly than his notional non-inventive colleague.[137]

Further, the inventor may not have been familiar with the relevant prior art (or **12-114** indeed even the common general knowledge). Where the question is whether the invention was obvious over a particular citation but the inventor was at the time unaware of it, then the fact that the invention came as a surprise to them cannot assist. Thus in *Lilly ICOS Ltd v Pfizer*,[138] the *"Viagra"* case, the Court of Appeal held:

"Mr Young also relied on the way that Pfizer came to make the invention. He drew attention to the fact that they were testing sildenafil citrate to treat complaints such as hypertension. Erections were reported as a side effect. That led to the realisation that it could be used for the treatment of MED.
That history does show that the invention of claim 1 of the patent was a surprise to Pfizer and that could have indicated invention. However account must be taken of the Rajfer and Murray articles."

In the same case,[139] a third party had also filed a patent application stating that **12-115** "the patentees had unexpectedly found that the claimed compounds were useful in the treatment of MED" but (absent evidence that the statement was correct and its basis) this did not impugn the evidence that the invention was obvious in the light of the cited art.

Commercial success

Evidence of the commercial success of the invention may be a material factor in **12-116** determining whether the new result was obvious or not,[140] but it is always neces- sary to consider whether any commercial success is due to the patented invention

---

[134] *SKM v Wagner Spraytech* [1982] R.P.C. 497.
[135] See *Nichia v Argos* [2007] F.S.R. 38: Jacob LJ's dissenting judgment reviews the history and practice.
[136] [1983] R.P.C. 147, 188–189.
[137] *Hoechst Celanese Corp v BP Chemicals Ltd* [1997] F.S.R. 547, 565.
[138] [2002] EWCA Civ 1, [59]–[60].
[139] [2002] EWCA Civ 1, [61].
[140] See *Hinks & Son v Safety Lighting Co* (1876) 4 Ch D. 607.

or to extraneous causes. In the latter event, commercial success is quite irrelevant when deciding whether the invention is obvious.

12-117   In *Longbottom v Shaw*,[141] Lord Herschell said:

> "Great reliance is placed upon the fact that when this patent was taken out and frames were made in accordance with it, there was a larger demand for them…I do not dispute that that is a matter to be taken into consideration; but, again, it is obvious that it cannot be regarded in any sense as conclusive … If nothing be shown beyond the fact that the new arrangement results in an improvement, and that this improvement causes a demand for an apparatus made in accordance with the patent, I think that it is of very little importance."

12-118   More recently, Laddie J in *Pfizer Ltd's Patent*[142] made the same point in the following way:

> "Doing what is obvious can be commercially successful. Commercial success comes into its own as a secondary indication of inventiveness where both the relevant prior art has been available and the need for a solution to a known problem has been sought for a long time. Failure to make the step which is covered by the patent in those circumstances may be some indication that it is not as obvious as it might at first appear. That has no application here where the gap between the prior art and the priority date is so very short."

12-119   However, commercial success was an important consideration in *Haberman v Jackel*,[143] where the invention seemed very simple but had met with immediate demand even though the embodiment first marketed was very simple and did not benefit from appealing design or heavy marketing. Laddie J's non-exhaustive summary of the factors relevant when a patent is defended against a charge of obviousness by commercial success (which as Jacob LJ subsequently said "remains a masterpiece"[144]) was as follows:

> "The mere existence of large sales says nothing about what problems were being tackled by those in the art nor, without more, does it demonstrate that success in the market place has anything to do with the patented development nor whether it was or was not the obvious thing to do. After all, it is sometimes possible to make large profits by selling an obvious product well. But in some circumstances commercial success can throw light on the approach and thought processes which pervade the industry as a whole. The plaintiffs rely on commercial success here. To be of value in helping to determine whether a development is obvious or not it seems to me that the following matters are relevant:
>
> (a)   What was the problem which the patented development addressed? Although sometimes a development may be the obvious solution to another problem, that is not frequently the case.
>
> (b)   How long had that problem existed?
>
> (c)   How significant was the problem seen to be? A problem which was viewed in the trade as trivial might not have generated much in the way of efforts to find a solution. So an extended period during which no solution was proposed (or proposed as a commercial proposition) would throw little light on whether, technically, it was obvious. Such an extended period of inactivity may demonstrate no more than that those in the trade did not believe that finding a solution was commercially worth the effort. The fact, if it be one, that they had miscalculated the commercial benefits to be achieved by the solution says little about its technical obviousness and it is only the latter which counts. On the other hand evidence which suggests that those in the art were aware of the problem and had been trying to find a solution will assist the patentee.

---

[141]   (1891) 8 R.P.C. 333, 336.

[142]   [2001] F.S.R. 16, [63]–[64].

[143]   [1999] F.S.R. 683, [32]. See also Pumfrey J's discussion in *Conor v Angiotech* [2006] R.P.C. 28, at [32]–[37].

[144]   In *Schlumberger v EMGS* [2010] EWCA Civ 819, at [80], then citing it in full.

(d) How widely known was the problem and how many were likely to be seeking a solution? Where the problem was widely known to many in the relevant art, the greater the prospect of it being solved quickly.

(e) What prior art would have been likely to be known to all or most of those who would have been expected to be involved in finding a solution? A development may be obvious over a piece of esoteric prior art of which most in the trade would have been ignorant. If that is so, commercial success over other, less relevant, prior art will have much reduced significance.

(f) What other solutions were put forward in the period leading up to the publication of the patentee's development? This overlaps with other factors. For example, it illustrates that others in the art were aware of the problem and were seeking a solution. But it is also of relevance in that it may indicate that the patentee's development was not what would have occurred to the relevant workers. This factor must be treated with care. As has been said on more than one occasion, there may be more than one obvious route round a technical problem. The existence of alternatives does not prevent each or them from being obvious. On the other hand where the patentee's development would have been expected to be at the forefront of solutions to be found yet it was not and other, more expensive or complex or less satisfactory, solutions were employed instead, then this may suggest that the ex post facto assessment that the solution was at the forefront of possibilities is wrong.

(g) To what extent were there factors which would have held back the exploitation of the solution even if it was technically obvious? For example, it may be that the materials or equipment necessary to exploit the solution were only available belatedly or their cost was so high as to act as a commercial deterrent. On the other hand if the necessary materials and apparatus were readily available at reasonable cost, a lengthy period during which the solution was not proposed is a factor which is consistent with lack of obviousness.

(h) How well has the patentee's development been received? Once the product or process was put into commercial operation, to what extent was it a commercial success. In looking at this, it is legitimate to have regard not only to the success indicated by exploitation by the patentee and his licensees but also to the commercial success achieved by infringers. Furthermore, the number of infringers may reflect on some of the other factors set out above. For example, if there are a large number of infringers it may be some indication of the number of members of the trade who were likely to be looking for alternative or improved products (see (iv) above).

(i) To what extent can it be shown that the whole or much of the commercial success is due to the technical merits of the development, i.e. because it solves the problem? Success which is largely attributable to other factors, such as the commercial power of the patentee or his license, extensive advertising focusing on features which have nothing to do with the development, branding or other technical features of the product or process, says nothing about the value of the invention.

I do not suggest that this list is exhaustive. But it does represent factors which taken together may point towards or away from inventiveness."

If commercial success is to be relied upon as an answer to obviousness, it must be formally pleaded with supporting particulars.[145]   **12-120**

Copying

An allegation of copying by the defendant is of little weight, for "a trader is entitled to copy a competitor unless there is a valid legal restraint on doing so. The mere fact of copying does not prove that a patent is valid. At most copying is one very small factor which is relevant to the issue of commercial success".[146] Conversely, proving that there was independent design and not copying may not assist either; it does not prove obviousness. However, if the defendant or others have   **12-121**

---

[145] Practice Direction 63 —Intellectual Property Claims, para.4.6, 6.3; see further para.14-233. And see *Blue Gentian v Tristar* [2013] EWHC 4098 (Pat), [13].

[146] *Haberman v Jackel International Ltd* [1999] F.S.R. 683, [47].

also sought to patent the same invention, giving reasons why they considered it inventive, then this may be highly material.

12-122   Allegations of copying, if made, should not take the defendant by surprise. In *3M v Ati Atlas*[147] Pumfrey J said:

> "I should add that I consider that it is desirable that allegations of copying of this sort should in future be pleaded. In order to rebut the allegation of copying evidence may have to be given which could not be relevant to the principal issues in a patent action. It may be that a suggestion of copying can only be made after disclosure has taken place, but that is no reason not to plead it. It may also change the scope of standard disclosure. Copying is anyway equivocal on the issue of validity. If a defendant forms the view that what is in the patent is obvious, why should he not copy?"

Disclosure relating to secondary evidence

12-123   The law and practice of disclosure of inventor's records was reviewed by the Court of Appeal in *Nichia v Argos*.[148] In a dissenting judgment, Jacob LJ reviewed the authorities and noted that cases where such disclosure made any significant difference to the overall outcome were rare. However, the majority considered that it was wrong to impose a blanket rule of no disclosure, but that considerations of proportionality should guide any search.

12-124   Most authorities on disclosure relating to secondary evidence have involved documents relating to the making of the invention by the patentee but it is also possible that a challenger may have relevant documents also. Floyd J stated in an interim decision in *Schlumberger v EMGS*[149]:

> "The basis for this application is the usual one. Those who say a patent is obvious in litigation should be faced with their own contemporaneous reaction: for it is obviousness in ignorance of the invention which is important and not obviousness with the benefit of hindsight. If they said at the time, 'How on earth did they think of that?', it can cut across the opinions of experts all expressed with the benefit of hindsight."

12-125   The current practice relating to disclosure is further considered at para.19-248, et seq.

5.   RELEVANT CONSIDERATIONS IN ASSESSING OBVIOUSNESS

12-126   While Nicholls VC in the *Mölnlycke* case[150] cited Lopes LJ's salutary warning about each case turning on its own facts, he also noted that evidentiary considerations and forensic tools have been developed through the cases. The considerations that the Court has regarded as significant will obviously vary from case to case, but the following sections of this chapter discuss various issues of principle that have wider relevance. An attempt has been made to break them down into individual topics, but inevitably there is overlap both in the principles and in the way that they have been applied in individual cases. On any given issue it is usually possible to find cases going each way, depending on the particular facts, and ultimately the only question is that posed by the statute, namely is it obvious?

---

[147] [2001] F.S.R. 31, [41].
[148] [2007] F.S.R. 38.
[149] [2008] EWHC 56 (Pat), [35].
[150] See para.12-08.

Obvious to try

A question that has been considered in many cases is whether the inventive step   **12-127**
would have been "obvious to try" to a skilled person in possession of the cited prior
art. The classic formulation of this aspect of the law is by Diplock LJ in *Johns
Manville Corporation's Patent*[151]:

> "I have endeavoured to refrain from coining a definition of 'obviousness' which counsel may be
> tempted to cite in subsequent cases relating to different types of claims. Patent law can too easily be
> bedevilled by linguistics, and the citation of a plethora of cases about other inventions of different
> kinds. The correctness of a decision upon an issue of obviousness does not depend upon whether or
> not the decider has paraphrased the words of the Act in some particular verbal formula. I doubt
> whether there is any verbal formula which is appropriate to all classes of claims. The superintend-
> ing examiner used the expression 'alerted to the possibilities' of using polyacrylamides in improv-
> ing the filterability of asbestos cement slurries. I find no fault with this phrase in the context of the
> claim in the appellants' specification. The learned judge preferred the expression 'see without dif-
> ficulty that these newly-introduced polymers would be of advantage in his filtration step.' I think that
> 'would be' puts it too high if it postulates prior certainty of success before actually testing the
> polymers in the filtration process; it is enough that the person versed in the art would assess the likeli-
> hood of success as sufficient to warrant actual trial."

As Lord Diplock himself stressed at the start of the above passage, there is no   **12-128**
single verbal formula applicable to all classes of claims. The "obvious to try"
standard was not being advanced as a definitive and universal test, but merely as a
lower test in the circumstances of that case and in contradistinction to a test which
required certainty of success.

The expectation of success

At the heart of the "obvious to try" test is the question of how much of an   **12-129**
expectation of success is required. This must of course depend on the facts of each
case, and as shown below it has been suggested that it may give rise to irrational
results, particularly when one is considering inventions made in research-based
industries. The difficulties in applying the test were highlighted by Professor Sir
Hugh Laddie (extra judicially) as follows[152]:

> "The problem can be approached by considering first the concept of 'obvious to try'. The classic state-
> ment of this principle is set out in the judgment of the Court of Appeal in *Johns-Manville
> Corporation's Patent*. It was said that a development should be treated as obvious if 'the person
> versed in the art would assess the likelihood of success as sufficient to warrant actual trial'. State-
> ments to similar effect have been made by the EPO.
>   On its face, this produces an unworkable or irrational test. If the reward for finding a solution to
> a problem and securing a monopoly for that solution is very high, then it may well be worthwhile
> for large players to examine all potential avenues to see if one gives the right result, even though the
> prospects of any one of them succeeding are much less than 50/50. What makes something worth
> trying is the outcome of a simple risk to reward calculation. Yet, if the reward is very large, the
> avenues worth trying will be expanded accordingly. So, the more commercially attractive the solu-
> tion and the more pressing the public clamour for it, the harder it will be to avoid an obviousness
> attack. In those circumstances a solution which is quite low down a list of alternatives, all of which
> are more or less worth trying, will fail for obviousness; a consequence which is consistent with the
> decision in *Brugger v Medic-Aid*."

---

[151] [1967] R.P.C. 479, 493.
[152] In "Patents — what's invention got to do with it?", cited with approval by Carr J in *Actavis v Lilly*
[2015] EWHC 3294 (Pat), 102–107.

12-130   In *Brugger v Medic-Aid* Ltd[153] Laddie J stated:

"First a route may still be an obvious one to try even if it is not possible to be sure that taking it will produce success, or sufficient success to make it commercially worthwhile. The latter point is inherent in *Johns Manville Corporation's Patent* [1967] R.P.C. 479, a decision of the Court of Appeal under the Patents Act 1949 which is just as relevant to obviousness under the 1977 Act. Secondly, if a particular route is an obvious one to take or try, it is not rendered any less obvious from a technical point of view merely because there are a number, and perhaps a large number, of other obvious routes as well. If a number of obvious routes exist it is more or less inevitable that a skilled worker will try some before others. The order in which he chooses to try them may depend on factors such as the ease and speed with which they can be tried, the availability of testing equipment, the costs involved and the commercial interests of his employer. There is no rule of law or logic which says that only the option which is likely to be tried first or second is to be treated as obvious for the purpose of patent legislation."

12-131   This passage was expressly approved by the Court of Appeal in *Palmaz's European Patents*.[154] In *Glaxo Group's Patent*[155] it was held that if it is obvious to try something for other reasons, there need be no superadded requirement that there should also be some expectation of success.

12-132   However, in *Saint-Gobain PAM v Fusion Provida*[156] the Court of Appeal also considered the above passage from *Johns-Manville* but held on the facts that "there was simply no likelihood of success. One just did not know what would happen if one tried"; the prior art document was silent on the vital question. Jacob LJ held:

"None of this to my mind remotely makes the idea of using Zn/Al alloy for pipes *obvious*—as something which is simply self-evident to the unimaginative man skilled in the art. Mere possible inclusion of something within a research programme on the basis you will find out more and something might turn up is not enough. If it were otherwise there would be few inventions that were patentable. The only research which would be worthwhile (because of the prospect of protection) would be into areas totally devoid of prospect. The "obvious to try" test really only works where it is more-or-less self-evident that what is being tested ought to work."

12-133   The phrase "more-or-less self-evident that what is being tested ought to work" was explained by Lord Hoffmann in *Conor v Angiotech*[157] as a "fair expectation of success", with the degree of expectation depending on the facts of the case.[158] Thus, the fact that something is well worth investigating, or on the basis of a hope of success, is not enough in and of itself—there must also be a fair expectation of success.[159]

12-134   The application of the "obvious to try" test was considered by the House of Lords in *Conor v Angiotech*.[160] The relevant claim, claim 12, was to a stent coated with taxol "for treating or preventing recurrent stenosis". The lower courts had held the claim obvious because it would have been obvious to try to make such a stent to see whether it would work to treat restenosis, albeit without any expectation of success. The argument put by Conor (who were seeking revocation) was that taxol,

---

[153] [1996] R.P.C. 635, 661.
[154] [2000] R.P.C. 631, [48].
[155] [2004] R.P.C. 43, [42].
[156] [2005] EWCA Civ 177, [28].
[157] [2007] R.P.C. 20; and see the discussion in *Actavis v Novartis (first instance)* [2009] EWHC 41 (Ch), [149]–[163].
[158] And see *Regeneron v Genentech* [2013] EWCA Civ 93.
[159] *Teva v Leo* [2015] EWCA Civ 779, [21]. And see the quote from MedImmune at the end of this section.
[160] [2007] R.P.C. 20.

like many other anti-proliferative drugs, was worth a try: this was, they said, obvious, and it was not necessary to show that it was obvious actually to use taxol to treat restenosis because the patent did not teach that it would work. In the House of Lords, Lord Hoffmann rejected this argument (at [16]) and went on to say (at [17]):

> "There was no dispute that this was a new product. The question should therefore simply have been whether it involved an inventive step. As in the case of many product claims, there was nothing inventive in discovering how to make the product. The alleged inventiveness lay in the claim that the product would have a particular property, namely, to prevent or treat restenosis."

He noted that the patent specification did sufficiently disclose the fact that a taxol-coated stent would prevent or treat restenosis, and went on to hold (at [28]): **12-135**

> "The question was whether that was obvious and not whether it was obvious that taxol (among many other products) *might* have this effect. It is hard to see how the notion that something is worth trying or might have some effect can be described as an invention in respect of which anyone would be entitled to a monopoly. It is therefore perhaps not surprising that the test for obviousness which Pumfrey J devised for such an 'invention' was whether it was obvious to try it without any expectation of success. This oxymoronic concept has, so far as I know, no precedent in the law of patents."

The issue was whether what was claimed was obvious, and not merely whether it might have been worth trying. While, as has subsequently been noted, it is not entirely clear that the ultimate decision in *Conor* on the facts (the claim was held non-obvious) should inevitably have followed in that case,[161] Lord Hoffmann felt able to deduce what the trial judge would have held if he had approached the issue correctly. **12-136**

In *MedImmune* Kitchin LJ summarised the correct approach regarding whether it was obvious to try a particular route as follows (emphasising in so doing that different considerations might apply in different technical fields)[162]: **12-137**

> "One of the matters which it may be appropriate to take into account is whether it was obvious to try a particular route to an improved product or process. There may be no certainty of success but the skilled person might nevertheless assess the prospects of success as being sufficient to warrant a trial. In some circumstances this may be sufficient to render an invention obvious. On the other hand, there are areas of technology such as pharmaceuticals and biotechnology which are heavily dependent on research, and where workers are faced with many possible avenues to explore but have little idea if any one of them will prove fruitful. Nevertheless they do pursue them in the hope that they will find new and useful products. They plainly would not carry out this work if the prospects of success were so low as not to make them worthwhile. But denial of patent protection in all such cases would act as a significant deterrent to research.
>
> For these reasons, the judgments of the courts in England and Wales and of the Boards of Appeal of the EPO often reveal an enquiry by the tribunal into whether it was obvious to pursue a particular approach with a reasonable or fair expectation of success as opposed to a hope to succeed. Whether a route has a reasonable or fair prospect of success will depend upon all the circumstances including an ability rationally to predict a successful outcome, how long the project may take, the extent to which the field is unexplored, the complexity or otherwise of any necessary experiments, whether such experiments can be performed by routine means and whether the skilled person will have to make a series of correct decisions along the way.
>
> Ultimately the court has to evaluate all the relevant circumstances in order to answer a single and relatively simple question of fact: was it obvious to the skilled but unimaginative addressee to make a product or carry out a process falling within the claim... ."

---

161 See the discussion in *Actavis v Novartis* at first instance, [2009] EWHC 41 (Ch) at 149–163, and *Teva v Merck* [2010] F.S.R. 17, at [88]–[98].
162 *MedImmune Ltd v Novartis Pharmaceuticals Ltd* [2012] EWCA Civ 1234; [2012] R.P.C. 27, [90]–[93].

The expectation of success and research-based industries

12-138   The *Johns Manville* case itself involved a low-technology process in an industry that would not be characterised as research-based. Lord Walker's speech in *Conor*[163] reviewed the "obvious to try" test, and pointed out the difficulties to which its application may give rise in high-technology industries. In the course of so doing, he cited an extra-judicial article by Sir Hugh Laddie quoted above.

12-139   Lord Walker also referred to similar observations made in the same case in the Court of Appeal, with a "useful anthology of citations from different jurisdictions" which included this passage in Judge Rich's decision in the US Court of Appeal for the Federal Circuit in *Tomlinson's Appn*[164]:

> "Slight reflection suggests, we think, that there is usually an element of 'obviousness to try' in any research endeavour that is not undertaken with complete blindness but rather with some semblance of a chance of success, and that patentability determinations based on that as the test would not only be contrary to statute but result in a marked deterioration of the whole patent system as an incentive to invest in those efforts and attempts which go by the name of 'research'."

12-140   This problem has also been considered in *Teva v Merck*,[165] in which Floyd J concluded:

> "I think that [counsel] is right that one must proceed with caution when faced with an obviousness attack based on a suggestion that the skilled person would embark on a research program in the course of which he would discover that a product or compound was effective. This is particularly so where the technical effect is one which is newly discovered, or impossible or very hard to predict. That is because the expectation of success may be zero, or inadequate to drive the research forward. In the end it will all depend on weighing the various factors as they appear from the evidence in the case. That is what I have endeavoured to do in the present case."

12-141   In contrast, some aspects of pharmaceutical research are unlikely to be protectable as there is nearly always likely to be at least a fair expectation of success. This is particularly true of new dosage regimes, as Jacob LJ observed in *Actavis v Merck*[166]:

> "Only in an unusual case such as the present where, see below, treatment for the condition with the substance had ceased to be worth investigating with any dosage regime) could specifying a dosage regime as part of the therapeutic use confer validity on an otherwise invalid claim."

"Obvious to try" is only one of many considerations

12-142   Obviousness is in the end a "jury-type question", and no single test is universally applicable. In *Pfizer's Patent*[167] Aldous LJ stressed this point as follows:

> "Mr Young is correct that when considering what is obvious it cannot be assumed that the skilled person would try every possible permutation or carry out extensive research (see *Hallen Co v Brabantia (UK) Ltd* [1991] R.P.C. 195 at 212). What would have been obvious will depend on all the circumstances. As I said in *Norton Healthcare Ltd v Beecham Group Plc* CA (unreported) 19th June 1997:

---

[163]   [2008] R.P.C. 28, [45]–[51].

[164]   (1966) 363 F 2d 298, 931.

[165]   [2010] F.S.R. 17, [88]–[98]. And see *Teva v Leo* [2015] EWCA Civ 799, at [32]–[33] and the quotation from *MedImmune* at para.12-137.

[166]   [2008] EWCA Civ 444 and see also *Hospira v Genentech* [2015] EWCA Civ 57.

[167]   [2002] EWCA Civ 1, [57]. And see *MedImmune v Novartis* [2012] EWCA 1234, at [85]–[95].

'When deciding whether a claimed invention is obvious, it is often necessary to decide whether a particular avenue of research leading to the invention was obvious. In such circumstances the extent of the different avenues of research and the perceived chances of any one of them providing a successful result can be relevant to the decision whether the invention claimed was obvious. Whether the subject matter was obvious may depend upon whether it was obvious to try in the circumstances of that particular case and in those circumstances it will be necessary to take into account the expectation of achieving a good result. But that does not mean that in every case the decision whether a claimed invention was obvious can be determined by deciding whether there was a reasonable expectation that a person might get a good result from trying a particular avenue of research. Each case depends upon the invention and the surrounding facts. No formula should be substituted for the words of the statute. In every case the Court has to weigh up the evidence and decide whether the invention was obvious. This is the statutory task.'"

These considerations remain applicable. In *Conor*[168] itself, Lord Hoffmann specifically endorsed what Kitchin J had said in *Generics (UK) Ltd v H Lundbeck*[169]: **12-143**

"The question of obviousness must be considered on the facts of each case. The court must consider the weight to be attached to any particular factor in the light of all the relevant circumstances. These may include such matters as the motive to find a solution to the problem the patent addresses, the number and extent of the possible avenues of research, the effort involved in pursuing them and the expectation of success."

Thus expectation of success, and therefore the "obvious to try" question itself, is but one of many factors that the court will have to weigh.[170] **12-144**

Hindsight and Ex post facto analysis

Obviousness is to be tested (and, when the *Windsurfing/Pozzoli* test is used, the fourth step is to be applied) without assuming knowledge of the invention. The inventor did not have the advantage that hindsight brings. In *Non-Drip Measure Co Ltd v Strangers Ltd*[171] Lord Russell said: **12-145**

"Whether there has or has not been an inventive step in constructing a device for giving effect to an idea which when given effect to seems a simple idea which ought to or might have occurred to anyone, is often a matter of dispute. More especially is this the case when many integers of the new device are already known. Nothing is easier than to say, after the event, that the thing was obvious and involved no invention. The words of Moulton LJ in *British Westinghouse v Braulik*[172] may well be called to mind in this connection: 'I confess' (he said) 'that I view with suspicion arguments to the effect that a new combination, bringing with it new and important consequences in the shape of practical machines, is not an invention, because, when it has once been established, it is easy to show how it might be arrived at by starting from something known, and taking a series of apparently easy steps. This ex post facto analysis of invention is unfair to the inventors and, in my opinion, it is not countenanced by English patent law ..."

The quoted passage from the *British Westinghouse* case continues to be cited and was held in *Technip SA's Patent*[173] to be as true today as when it was first said. **12-146**

---

[168] [2008] R.P.C. 28, [42].

[169] [2007] R.P.C. 32, [72].

[170] For an example of such a balancing exercise see, e.g. *Generics v Daiichi* [2009] R.P.C. 23, at [43]–[44].

[171] (1943) 60 R.P.C. 135, 142.

[172] (1910) 27 R.P.C. 209, 230.

[173] [2004] R.P.C. 46, [112]; see also *Smithkline Beecham Plc v Apotex Europe* [2005] F.S.R. 23, at [65]; *Ferag v Muller Martini* [2007] EWCA Civ 15, at [13].

The "step-by-step" approach

12-147   In *Technograph Printed Circuits Ltd v Mills & Rockley (Electronics) Ltd*[174] Lord Reid said:

> "But the question is not whether it is now obvious to the court (or to the jury) but whether at the relevant date it would have been obvious to the unimaginative skilled technician."

12-148   In the same case, Lord Diplock said in a passage that has been often cited:

> "The cross-examination of the respondents' expert followed with customary skill the familiar 'step by step' course. I do not find it persuasive. Once an invention has been made it is generally possible to postulate a combination of steps by which the inventor might have arrived at the invention that he claims in his specification if he started from something that was already known. But it is only because the invention has been made and has proved successful that it is possible to postulate from what starting point and by what particular combination of steps the inventor could have arrived at his invention. It may be that taken in isolation none of the steps which it is now possible to postulate, if taken in isolation, appears to call for any inventive ingenuity. It is improbable that this reconstruction a posteriori represents the mental process by which the inventor in fact arrived at his invention, but, even if it were, inventive ingenuity lay in perceiving that the final result which it was the object of the inventor to achieve was attainable from the particular starting point and in his selection of the particular combination of steps which would lead to that result."

12-149   It has been held as a consequence that where a patentee's expert has conceded in cross-examination that the invention is obvious, his evidence has to be treated with caution as it may have been given a result of a step-by-step cross-examination[175]; but of course the concession may also be correct, and indeed an invention may look obvious with hindsight because it was in fact obvious. Situations in which this will be the case were highlighted by Birss J in *Hospira v Genentech*[176] as follows:

> "The particular point made in *Technograph* was that it was wrong to find an invention was obvious if it was only arrived at after a series of steps which involve the cumulative application of hindsight. In some circumstances success at each step in a chain is a necessary predicate for the next one and it is only the hindsight knowledge of the invention as the target which could motivate a skilled person to take each step without knowledge about the next one. In a situation like that, *Technograph* is important.
>
> But other cases, of which I believe this is an example, have other factors. Factors which characterise this case are:
>
> i)   Although a number of choices have to be made, the existence of these choices is not tainted with hindsight.
>
> ii)   Although the point cannot be taken too far since the ingredients interact and have to work in combination, nevertheless a number of the choices here fall to be made in parallel not in series.
>
> iii) This is a highly empirical field and is one in which the skilled team will, without hindsight, want to test a range of ingredients.
>
> iv)   The tests themselves are run in parallel. The skilled team does not test one combination at a time. It tests a number together."

---

[174] [1972] R.P.C. 346, 362.
[175] *Rocky Mountain Traders v Hewlett Packard* [2002] F.S.R. 1, [53].
[176] [2014] EWHC (Pat), [240]–[241].

Simplicity no objection

In *Siddell v Vickers & Sons Ltd*[177] Lord Herschell said: **12-150**

"If the apparatus be valuable by reason of its simplicity there is a danger of being misled by that very simplicity into the belief that no invention was needed to produce it. But experience has shown that not a few inventions … have been of so simple a character that once they have been made known it was difficult … not to believe that they must have been obvious to everybody."[178]

A similar issue arose more recently, in *Haberman v Jackel International Ltd*,[179]   **12-151**
which involved what appeared to be a very simple idea. Laddie J said:

"In all cases where obviousness is in issue the court is trying to look back to what paths would have been seriously considered by a notional skilled but uninventive person in the relevant art at the priority date. The task is made more difficult because the patentee's development is already known to the parties and the court. Therefore inevitably the court will know not only that a solution is possible but what it is. Many patented inventions operate in accordance with simple principles of physics, chemistry or other sciences. It is normally easy to understand why they work. From this it is but a short step to thinking that a competent technician in the art would have realised, starting from the same simple principles, why the solution proposed by the patentee should have worked. So, working from those principles, the solution must be obvious. In such cases it is also easy to take the relevant expert witnesses under cross-examination through a series of logical steps which lead to the solution. The simpler the solution, the easier it is to explain. The easier it is to explain, the more obvious it can appear. This is not always fair to inventors."

At [45] of the judgment he continued: **12-152**

"Mrs Haberman has taken a very small and simple step but it appears to me to be a step which any one of the many people in this trade could have taken at any time over at least the preceding ten years or more. In view of the obvious benefits which would flow from it, I have come to the conclusion that had it really been obvious to those in the art it would have been found by others earlier, and probably much earlier. It was there under their very noses. As it was it fell to a comparative outsider to see it. It is not obvious. This finding can be expressed in the language used by Hoffmann LJ as he was in *STEP v Emson* [1993] R.P.C. 513. Mrs Haberman's patent discloses something sufficiently inventive to deserve the grant of a monopoly."

There may be invention in what is merely simplification[180] or in recognising that   **12-153**
the entire industry was going in the wrong direction.[181] Nevertheless, matters of
ordinary skilled designing or mere workshop improvements cannot be considered
as requiring the exercise of invention.[182]

Age of the cited art and "why was it not done before"

The age of a piece of prior art may have a bearing on the issue of obviousness,   **12-154**
though the weight to be attached to such consideration will depend on the
circumstances. Where a piece of prior art was only available shortly before the

---

[177] (1890) 7 R.P.C. 292, 304.
[178] See also *Thierry v Riekman* (1897) 14 R.P.C. 105. This echoes Milton's description in book 6 of Paradise Lost of Satan's invention of the cannon: "The invention all admired, and each, how he To be the inventor missed, so easy it seemed Once found, which yet unfound most would have thought Impossible".
[179] [1999] F.S.R. 683, [29].
[180] *Pope Applicance Corp v Spanish River, etc. Mills Ltd* (1929) 46 R.P.C. 23, 55.
[181] *Beloit Technologies Inc v Valmet Paper Machinery Inc (No.2)* [1995] R.P.C. 705, 750.
[182] See *Safveans Aktie Bolag v Ford Motor Co (Eng.) Ltd* (1927) 44 R.P.C. 49, at 61; *Curtis & Son v Heward & Co* (1923) 40 R.P.C. 53, at 183; *Shaw v Burnet & Co* (1924) 41 R.P.C. 432.

priority date of the invention, then this may of itself explain why it had not already been taken up and modified by others; even obvious developments do not happen overnight. On the other hand, if sufficient opportunity to make a worthwhile invention had been available to others, then this raises the question: "why was it not done before?" In *Technip SA's Patent*, Jacob LJ said:

> "All the 'bits and pieces' of the invention were known separately for many years. The question 'why was it not done before' is always a powerful consideration when considering obviousness, particularly when all the components of a combination have been long and widely known. Sometimes there is a good answer (e.g., no demand, not worth the expense, prior art only recent)."

12-155   There, the invention was found not be obvious over the prior art, none of the answers to the "why was it not done before" question being satisfactory.[183] However, there may be other perfectly valid explanations, some of which were considered by Laddie J in *Brugger v Medic-Aid Ltd*,[184] as follows:

> "No doubt a manufacturer with existing tooling is likely to follow a line of modification which is least likely to result in him having to retool completely or significantly. This may act as a commercial constraint which will reduce his willingness to embark on certain lines of development. Indeed the cost of retooling may be such that he will not consider the rewards which would flow from the improved product would justify the change. These purely commercial considerations are likely to affect the direction, if any, in which the established manufacturer may go. However they give a distorted picture of what, from a technical and patent point of view, is obvious. As I have said, a new entrant into the trade may well have different commercial constraints. The court has to be alert to the difference between commercial attractiveness and technical obviousness. They are not always the same. Failure to modify a piece of prior art, even if that delay extends over a long period, may be due to commercial factors rather than perceived technical obstacles. It may also be because the pleaded prior art has rested obscurely on a library shelf for all that time—although that is something which cannot be said of the prior art here. The above considerations do not mean that the age of prior art is irrelevant. The fact that a piece of prior art has been available for a long time may indicate, contrary to first impressions, that it was not obvious to make the patented development from it. It is useful to bear in mind in this regard the concept of long felt want. This is a particularly efficient expression. An apparently minor development which meets a long felt want may be shown to be non-obvious because, although the prior art has long been available, the development was not hit upon by others notwithstanding that there was a need for improvement (the 'want') and an appreciation of that need (the 'felt'). In other words the age of prior art may be an indication that a development from it is not obvious if it can be shown that the circumstances in the relevant trade were such that a failure of the development to appear earlier is surprising. There may be numerous explanations for why a development was not made earlier such as complacency in relation to existing products or processes (which in turn may depend on the number of competitors in the trade and the extent to which they attempted to compete with each other in terms of new products as opposed to on price and marketing), the adequacy of the existing products, the comparative poverty of the trade, the commercial difficulties which would be expected to be faced if an attempt was made to introduce a new product, whether it was reasonable to expect that the commercial benefits of introducing a new product would be too small or too long term to justify the investment and so on. It is only when the answer to the question 'why was this not developed earlier' is 'a likely and reasonable explanation is that people looking for a way round an existing problem did not see this as the answer' that the age of the prior art should play a part in meeting an obviousness attack. If it is likely that in the real world no one was looking for an answer the fact that none was found says nothing about whether the answer proposed in the patent under attack was obvious."

12-156   In short, there may be many reasons why something was not done before, and one cannot simply conclude that everything that is not anticipated was not obvious.

---

[183] See also *Schlumberger v EMGS* [2010] EWCA Civ 819, at [77].
[184] [1996] R.P.C. 635, 654–5.

Alternative paths

It is sometimes contended that there would have been a number of routes open **12-157** to the skilled person faced with the problem solved by the patent, and that the particular claimed route was only obvious with hindsight. In *Olin Mathieson Chemical Corporation v Biorex Laboratories*,[185] a Dr Margaret Simkins produced a lengthy list of information which she as a researcher would have produced if asked for information on the relevant problem; such a list has come to be known as a "Simkins list". This may, depending on the surrounding facts, help to demonstrate that although there was a known problem, the route taken by the patentee was not perceived by others and that there was invention in finally overcoming it.

But it may carry little weight where the various routes are each obvious ones. In **12-158** *Brugger v Medic-Aid Ltd*,[186] following the passage cited in the preceding paragraph above, Laddie J went on to say:

> "For these reasons a Simpkins [sic] List of prior art proposals, as furnished in this case, will frequently be of little assistance in resolving the issue of obviousness. Such a list may demonstrate that the particular route followed by the patentee was studiously avoided by others in the art in which case it may be of some assistance in countering arguments of obviousness. But it may only show that a number of other designs are possible and have been proposed. This does not strengthen the patentee's case."

In particular, a Simkins list is no answer where the patented route was obvious **12-159** over the particular item of cited art anyway. In *Pfizer Ltd's Patent*[187] Laddie J stated:

> "The fact that there are alternative routes is no answer to a case of obviousness based on a particular piece of prior art. On the contrary, the notional skilled addressee is expected to have read the pleaded prior art carefully and to bring to it his interest in the field. If he does that and finds the patented step was an obvious one to make, it is no answer to say that if he had started with other prior art other solutions would have come to mind."

In *Ivax v Akzo*[188] the cited prior art was a subsisting patent which prevented one **12-160** possible route from being taken; it was held that this was relevant to and supportive of the obviousness of other routes (recognised but not claimed in that patent).

Motive

It may be relevant to consider whether there is any a priori motive to take the step **12-161** in question. In *Mölnlycke v Procter & Gamble*[189] Sir Donald Nicholls VC said that:

> "obviousness connotes something which would at once occur to a person skilled in the art who was desirous of accomplishing the end",

thus implicitly assuming that there was some "end" in contemplation.

Some of the authorities suggest that it is always necessary to show such a mo- **12-162** tive, although in others it has been considered not to be a requirement (though still

---

185 [1969] F.S.R. 361.
186 [1996] R.P.C. 635, 661.
187 [2001] F.S.R. 16, [78].
188 [2007] R.P.C. 3, [44]–[49], [71].
189 [1994] R.P.C. 49.

a relevant consideration). In *Hickman v Andrews*[190] the *"Workmate"* case, the Court of Appeal said:

> "There is another preliminary question and that is what the expert is supposed to be doing. It cannot be that he is to look to the whole store of his imaginary knowledge and see if it is obvious to turn something therein to better account. He must think I have some definite object in view, and in the instant case, for example, he would be seeking to make a workbench which would be an improvement on those already on the market."

12-163 Similarly, in *Hallen Co v Brabantia*,[191] Slade LJ said:

> "We ... accept the plaintiff's submission that, for the purpose of testing obviousness, one cannot assume that the skilled person simply makes technical trials for the sake of doing so."

12-164 In *Hoechst Celanese Corp v BP Chemicals*[192] Laddie J reviewed the authorities and concluded:

> "All of those passages are consistent with the Object/Solution approach to obviousness adopted by the Technical Board of Appeal of the EPO. Even if the step from the prior art is a small one, to prove obviousness it is necessary to demonstrate that there is some reason for taking it."

12-165 The EPO TBA made a very similar point in *Triazoles/AgrEvo*[193]:

> "Moreover, in the Board's judgment, it follows from this same legal principle that the answer to the question what a skilled person would have done in the light of the state of the art depends in large measure on the technical result he had set out to achieve. In other words, the notional 'person skilled in the art' is not to be assumed to seek to perform a particular act without some concrete technical reason: he must, rather, be assumed to act not out of idle curiosity but with some specific technical purpose in mind."

12-166 In *Napp v Ratiopharm*[194] it was contended that the necessary modification from the prior art to the claim would be apparent to the formulator: but the obviousness attack failed because of an absence of any prior but necessary motivation of the clinician.

12-167 Other authorities have expressed the position less rigidly and do not require motive as a necessary element. The true position appears to be that an absence of motive to take the step in question makes the argument of obviousness more difficult, but does not rule out obviousness entirely. Laddie J subsequently stated in *Brugger v Medic-Aid Ltd*[195]:

> "On the basis of this they say there is no reason why it should have been obvious to modify the prior art in any particular direction. That, it appears to me, is a non sequitur. The fact, if it be one, that existing commercial products are highly successful and satisfactory does not indicate that there are no obvious modifications to make to them. It merely demonstrates that there may be little incentive to those already making those products to change the design—a quite different matter."

12-168 Similarly, the Court of Appeal has nonetheless held that a step from the prior art, albeit made without reason, can still be obvious.[196] The statutory test is obvious-

---

[190] [1983] R.P.C. 147, 169–170.
[191] [1991] R.P.C. 195, 212.
[192] [1997] F.S.R. 547, 565.
[193] T0939/92, at [2.4.2].
[194] [2009] R.P.C. 18, [112]–[113].
[195] [1996] R.P.C. 635, 655.
[196] *Pharmacia v Merck* [2002] R.P.C. 41, [123]–[124]. See also *Asahi Medical v Macopharma* [2002] EWCA Civ 466, at [23]–[25], and Jacob LJ's further discussion of the "5 1/4 inch plate paradox"

ness and any modification which is obvious will not be patentable, whereas one which is not obvious will be. Whether or not there is a reason for taking the step from the prior art may well be an important consideration, although that does not mean that it is an essential requirement of a conclusion of obviousness.[197]

Invention may lie in the idea

In some cases, the desired end result may be known but elusive and the inventive step lies in finding a way of achieving it.[198] In others, there may be invention in perceiving the new result, even though no further act of invention is required to put it into practice.[199] In *Olin Mathieson Chemical Corporation v Biorex Ltd*[200] Graham J said:

> "... the invention may lie in the idea of taking the step in question. Why should anyone want to take this step unless he had first appreciated that such a step might give him a useful product? ... and it is in my judgment not obvious to take the step in question unless and until it has been conceived that the idea of doing so might lead to a useful result. Of course, once one has the idea of doing so it is perfectly obvious how to do it but that is not the material question."

Similarly, as Whitford J said in *Genentech*[201] in a passage subsequently referred to by Lord Hoffmann in *Kirin-Amgen*[202]:

> "It is trite law that you cannot patent a discovery, but if on the basis of that discovery you can tell people how it can be usefully employed, then a patentable invention may result. This in my view would be the case, even though once you have made the discovery, the way in which it can be usefully employed is obvious enough."

Lord Hoffmann distinguished different possible classes of invention in *Biogen v Medeva*[203]:

> "Whenever anything inventive is done for the first time it is the result of the addition of a new idea to the existing stock of knowledge. Sometimes, it is the idea of using established techniques to do something which no one had previously thought of doing. In that case, the inventive idea will be doing the new thing. Sometimes, it is finding a way of doing something which people had wanted to do but could not think how. The inventive idea would be the way of achieving the goal. In yet other cases, many people may have a general idea of how they might achieve a goal but not know how to solve a particular problem which stands in their way. If someone devises a way of solving the problem, his inventive step will be that solution, but not the goal itself or the general method of achieving it."

Floyd J further considered the "idea" type of invention in *Schering-Plough v*

12-169

12-170

12-171

12-172

---

in *Actavis v Novartis* [2010] EWCA Civ 82, at [36]–[37].

[197] *Pharmacia v Merck* [2002] R.P.C. 41, at [123]–[124]. See also *Asahi Medical v Macopharma* [2002] EWCA Civ 466, at [23]–[25], and Jacob LJ's further discussion of the "5 1/4 inch plate paradox" in *Actavis v Novartis* [2010] EWCA Civ 82, at [36]–[37].

[198] *Pharmacia v Merck* [2002] R.P.C. 41, [124]. See also *Dyson v Hoover* (at first instance) [2001] R.P.C. 26, at [153].

[199] For example, separating and characterising the enantiomers in *Generics v Lundbeck* [2009] R.P.C. 13.

[200] *Hickton's Patent Syndicate v Patents, etc. Ltd* (1909) 26 R.P.C. 339. See also, e.g. *Muntz v Foster* (1843) 2 W.P.C. 93; *Lane Fox v Kensington, etc. Co Ltd* (1892) 9 R.P.C. 413, at 416.

[201] [1970] R.P.C. 157, 192.

[202] [1987] R.P.C. 553, 566.

[203] *Kirin-Amgen v Hoechst Marion Roussel* [2005] R.P.C. 9, [76].

Norbrook Laboratories[204] as follows:

> "An invention may simply consist in an idea which, once it has been conceived, is one which will obviously work. For those cases a party attacking the patent only needs to show that the idea was an obvious one. But there are other cases where the invention involves something more than the bare idea, because it is not immediately apparent that the idea could be made to work. In these cases the attacking party needs to show something more: that it was obvious to have the idea and to try it to see whether it would work."

12-173 He went on to add that the "obvious to try" test had the further requirement of a reasonable expectation of success: see para.12-129. Likewise, invention may also lie in finding out the problem.[205]

Overcoming a prejudice

12-174 Invention may lie in overcoming the preconceptions of the skilled person in a particular field of technology. As Jacob J put it in *Union Carbide Corp v BP Chemicals*[206]:

> "Invention can lie in finding out that that which those in the art thought ought not be done, ought to be done. From the point of view of the purpose of patent law it would be odd if there were not patent incentive for those who investigate the prejudices of the prior art."

12-175 Subsequently, in *Pozzoli v BDMO*[207] he referred to this passage but observed that there was something odd about "technical prejudice" in that a prejudice can only come into play if you have had the idea first; and then the idea would seem to be old or obvious. He explained:

> "Patentability is justified because the prior idea which was thought not to work must, as a piece of prior art, be taken as it would be understood by the person skilled in the art. He will read it with the prejudice of such a person. So that which forms part of the state of the art really consists of two things in combination, the idea and the prejudice that it would not work or be impractical. A patentee who contributes something new by showing that, contrary to the mistaken prejudice, the idea will work or is practical has shown something new. He has shown that an apparent 'lion in the path' is merely a paper tiger. Then his contribution is novel and non-obvious and he deserves his patent. Where, however, the patentee merely patents an old idea thought not to work or to be practical and does not explain how or why, contrary to the prejudice, that it does work or is practical, things are different. Then his patent contributes nothing to human knowledge. The lion remains at least apparent (it may even be real) and the patent cannot be justified."

12-176 However, the prejudice may be a general one, and the invention may be a more specific answer to it. Thus in *Dyson Appliances v Hoover Ltd*,[208] both at first instance and on appeal, the "mindset" within the vacuum cleaner industry was treated as prejudice "making a true inventor of the individual who was able to lift his eyes above the horizon and see a bag-free machine" (see the passage from the judgment quoted at para.12-57). The claim there was narrower than merely a bag-free machine but was a specific combination which overcame a relevant defect. As

---

[204] [1997] R.P.C. 1, 34.
[205] [2006] F.S.R. 18, [35].
[206] See *Beecham Group Ltd's (Amoxycillin) Application* [1980] R.P.C. 261, Buckley LJ.
[207] [1998] R.P.C. 1, 13. See also *Ivax v Akzo* [2007] R.P.C. 3, [48].
[208] [2001] R.P.C. 26; [2002] R.P.C. 22.

to the standard of proof required in the UK Courts, see Birss J in *Farrow v Secretary of State for Defence*.[209]

It is necessary to distinguish technical from mere commercial prejudice. Pumfrey J explained in *Glaxo Group's Patent*[210]:   **12-177**

> "Such a prejudice may be a merely commercial one ("this device won't sell") or it may be a technical one ("this won't work and it is not worth bothering with"). A 20-year monopoly is conferred for overcoming a prejudice of the second kind, but not for overcoming a commercial prejudice (see *Hallen Co v Brabantia (UK) Ltd* [1989] R.P.C. 307 (Aldous J.)). A technical prejudice must be general: it is not enough that some persons actually engaged in the art at the material time labour under a particular prejudice if a substantial number of others do not. A prejudice which is insufficiently widespread for it properly to be regarded as commonly shared will not, in my view, be attributed to the notional skilled person."

It is not necessary for the patent to explain why the prejudice is wrong or provide a scientific explanation of how the invention works to overcome it.[211] Thus, in *Synthon v Teva*,[212] Birss J stated: **12-178**

> "I do not accept that much can be made of the fact that the patent does not expressly assert that this or that element in the disclosure was surprising or difficult. Such language appears sometimes in patents but it can be a hostage to fortune when it turns out that prior art, which perhaps was unknown to the inventors, shows that something was not so surprising after all. When that occurs it may or may not lead to the invalidity of a given claim but an approach which made invalidity more likely because one element disclosed in the specification in the section describing the invention was not flagged as unexpected would create unwelcome incentives to those drafting the documents. They will get even longer. The primary task of the specification is to explain the invention so that the claims are supported and can be understood and so that the skilled person can perform the invention to the standard required by the law. That is quite enough."

Merely doing something which scientific opinion considered pointless is not overcoming a prejudice.[213]   **12-179**

Unforeseeable advantages: bonus effects

Most inventions the subject of a patent, in particular those that are worth litigating, will have some advantage over the prior art. (If they do not then they may be inherently obvious, as in effect a mere arbitrary collection of features that fail to co-operate to solve any problem, or may be invalid as incapable of industrial application, or perhaps insufficient by claiming more than they enable.[214]) Patentees therefore almost invariably seek to show that the invention does possess advantages over the prior art, with a view to supporting a case that the invention is not obvious. This is of course a relevant consideration when judging obviousness: a surprising and unexpected technical effect may be regarded as an indication of inventive step. One may then ask why the prior art did not take or at least mention the course proposed. It may not have been obvious to try with any expectation of success; only once the inventor took the step in question did the advantage of doing so become apparent. As Floyd J stated in *Schering-Plough v Norbrook Laboratories*[215]:   **12-180**

---

[209] [2014] EWHC 2047 (Pat).
[210] [2007] F.S.R. 37, [25]–[28].
[211] *Buhler v FP Spomax* [2008] F.S.R. 27, [46]–[48].
[212] [2015] EWHC 1395, [115]. At the time of writing this decision was under appeal.
[213] *Ancare New Zealand Ltd's Patent* [2003] R.P.C. 8 (Privy Council).
[214] And see para.12-39, et seq., particularly at para.12-50.
[215] [2006] F.S.R. 18, [34].

"In answering the statutory question it may help to show that the benefits which the invention neces-sarily brings with it are unexpected. Again, by 'necessarily' I mean that everything falling within the claim will bring those benefits. That is because, where a seemingly simple step brings with it a valu-able and unexpected benefit, it may only be obvious with hindsight to show that the step was one which would have been taken by the skilled person."

12-181   Nevertheless, note if an invention as claimed is obvious for one reason, the fact that it brings with it another benefit (even an unexpected one) does not stop it be-ing obvious. The statutory purpose is to allow workers in the art to take obvious steps: if in doing so they hit on something useful, then that is a bonus that they are entitled to take without fear of being sued for infringement of a patent.[216] In *Hal-len v Brabantia*[217] Slade LJ said:

"True it is that, as the Judge found, it was not obvious that coating a self-puller with PTFE would have the dramatic effect that it did in extracting the cork, and indeed that probably without the intervention of the patent in suit such a corkscrew would not have been marketed for many years. However, as he rightly appreciated, these were in law irrelevant considerations. The dramatic improvement in extraction was for the Plaintiffs a golden bonus; but it is common ground that an added benefit, however great, will not found a valid patent if the claimed invention is obvious for another purpose."

12-182   In *Bristol-Myers Squibb v Baker Norton*[218] Jacob J at first instance addressed obviousness in this way:

"The true question is, do the directions given by Winograd make the discovery of the neutropenic effect obvious? It is wrong to ask whether you would have predicted that effect. The obvious course of action as a result of the talk would have revealed the result. Reduced neutropenia was truly *ob via*—in the way—to go back to the Latin root of the word 'obvious'. There is no inventive step."

12-183   This reasoning however requires that the invention would have been obvious for other reasons. In *Napp v Ratiopharm*[219] the Court of Appeal explained:

"An unexpected advantage only fails to defeat an obviousness attack where there is a real motive to use the idea apart from that advantage. For only then will the skilled man more or less inevitably bump into the unexpected advantage. And even that may not be enough to destroy a patent—for there may be room in some cases (we express no opinion) for an invention by selection."

Is there a need to identify the advantages in the patent specification?

12-184   Ultimately the relevant test is whether the claim is obvious, and claims themselves do not set out explanations. Although, as discussed at para.12-180, whether the claim is adjudged obvious or not may depend at least in part upon whether what is claimed has advantages over the prior art. Then the question arises whether those advantages need to be set out in the description of the patent or whether the patentee is entitled to lead evidence of unstated advantages. The authorities have taken different standpoints, depending on the particular facts, and the answer may be sensitive to the overall context. However, all such considera-tions are subject to the requirement that the invention be plausible (see para.12-35).

---

[216] *Schering-Plough v Norbrook Laboratories* [2006] F.S.R. 18, [34].
[217] [1991] R.P.C. 195, 216, lines 11–25. See also *Hoechst/Enantiomers* (T296/87), cited in *Laboratorios Almirall v Boehringer Ingelheim* [2009] F.S.R. 12, at [228].
[218] [1999] R.P.C. 253: upheld on appeal.
[219] [2009] R.P.C. 18, [115].

The patentee is not required to explain the reasons why the invention works. As   **12-185**
was said long ago in *British Ore v Minerals Separation*[220]:

"An inventor patents a process and not its scientific explanation."

Fletcher Moulton LJ, giving the judgment of the Court of Appeal, then said: **12-186**

"He may not, and in many cases does not, know the modus operandi of Nature in bringing about the
results he obtains, and I know of inventions in which, to this day, it is a matter of controversy as to
how they act to produce their results".

More recently, in *Conor v Angiotech*,[221] Lord Hoffman pointed out that: **12-187**

"There is no requirement in the EPC or the statute that the specification must demonstrate by experiment that the invention will work or explain why it will work"

(but note that (at [37]) Lord Hoffman referred to the need to satisfy the plausibility
threshold).

In *Glaxo Group Ltd's Patent*[222] Pumfrey J stated: **12-188**

"It is sometimes thought that a patent may be saved from a finding of obviousness if a combination
otherwise obvious has some unexpected advantage, and, in particular, an advantage caused by an
unpredictable co-operation between the elements of the combination. I do not consider that such an
approach is in general justified. There is a limited class of cases in which the patentee has identified
an advantageous feature possessed by some members only of a class otherwise old or obvious, has
described the advantageous effect in his specification and has limited his claim to the members of
the class possessing this advantageous feature. Such a claim may be justified on the basis of what is
called selection. Unexpected bonus effects not described in the specification cannot form the basis
for a valid claim of this kind. I think that the matter is described with complete correctness by Jacob
J in *Richardson-Vicks' Patent* [1995] R.P.C. 568 at 581:

'Whether or not there was a synergy demonstrated by experiments conducted after the date of the
patent cannot help show obviousness or non-obviousness. Nor can the amended claim be better
if only the components of the amended claim (as opposed to the unamended claim) can be shown
to demonstrate synergy. The patent does not draw any such distinction and it would be quite wrong
for later-acquired knowledge to be used to justify the amended claim.'

If a synergistic effect is to be relied on, it must be possessed by everything covered by the claim, and
it must be described in the specification."

In that case, there was no effect described in the specification that was not the   **12-189**
natural prediction from the properties of the two components of the combination;
that combination being obvious, the claim was held obvious. Kitchin J noted in
Generics v Lundbeck[223] that these cases were concerned with synergistic effects
(both involved combinations of two known drugs), but stated that he did not
consider the principle to be confined to those cases and held:

"A patentee cannot seek to bolster the inventive nature of his monopoly by relying on a discovery
which he had not made at the time of the patent. That is the position here. At the date of the Patent,
Lundbeck had not found that escitalopram was more efficacious or was effective in treating more
patients than citalopram. Those discoveries were not made until some time later. They are nowhere
hinted at in the specification and could not have been predicted from what is described. In these

---

[220] (1909) 26 R.P.C. 124, 144, line 32 (CA); see also *Buhler v FP Spomax*[2008] F.S.R. 27, at [47]–
[49].
[221] [2008] R.P.C. 28, [19].
[222] [2004] R.P.C. 43, 113–114. See also *Laboratorios Almirall v Boehringer Ingelheim* [2009] F.S.R.
12, at [174]–[182].
[223] [2007] R.P.C. 32, [237]; reversed on other grounds in higher courts.

circumstances I do not believe that it is legitimate for Lundbeck to rely upon them in support of the alleged invention."

12-190 This issue did not arise in the Court of Appeal nor in the House of Lords where the sole question was insufficiency.

12-191 It is submitted that the above statement is relevant where some fresh discovery has had to be made before any "technical contribution" was apparent (in which case an objection of lack of industrial applicability may also apply[224]). By contrast, where the advantages of an invention are either self-evident anyway or inherent and capable of being explained without introducing after-acquired discoveries, there can be no objection to the patentee identifying and relying upon them even though they were not expressly set out in the specification.

12-192 Any statements which the patentee does make regarding the advantages of the invention and any reasons that they provide, may of course also be relevant when considering the purposive construction of the claim,[225] and hence its obviousness. However, once construed, the fact that an alleged infringer did not obtain those advantages "did not mean that he was not using the invention as he may have decided to use it badly".[226] If this latter situation applies, then it would appear that the advantages are not available to all embodiments falling within the claim and so are not relevant to its validity.

Combinations contrasted with mere collocations

12-193 In *British Celanese Ltd v Courtaulds Ltd*[227] Lord Tomlin said:

> "It is accepted as sound law that a mere placing side by side of old integers so that each performs its own proper function independently of any of the others is not a patentable combination, but that where the old integers when placed together have some working interrelation producing a new or improved result then there is patentable subject-matter in the idea of the working interrelation brought about by the collocation of the integers."[228]

12-194 The principle is illustrated by the old and well-known case of *Williams v Nye*[229] (the "*Sausage Machine Case*"). The patent was for a machine for mincing meat and filling the minced meat into skins so as to make sausages. In fact, it consisted of combining in one apparatus two machines which had formerly been used separately. The mincing part performed no more than its already well-known functions, and the same was true of the filling part. The ultimate result was novel and useful, although there was no difficulty to be overcome and no invention.[230]

12-195 In *Sabaf SpA v MFI Furniture Centres*,[231] the claim had two separate characterising features. While each had been separately disclosed in the prior art, there was

---

[224] See, e.g. *Eli Lilly v Human Genome Sciences* [2010] R.P.C. 14, citing *ZymoGenetics* (T0898/05), at [5] and [6].

[225] See, e.g. *M-Systems v Trek 2000* [2008] R.P.C. 18, at [45], [53], where such statements were inconsistent with the case which the patentee wished to advance.

[226] *Union Carbide v B.P. Chemicals* [1998] R.P.C. 1, 16.

[227] (1935) 52 R.P.C. 171, 193.

[228] See also *Klaber's Patent* (1906) 23 R.P.C. 461, at 469; *British United Shoe Machinery Co Ltd v A. Fussell & Sons Ltd* (1908) 25 R.P.C. 631, 657; *Wood v Gowshall Ltd* (1937) 54 R.P.C. 37, at 40; *Sabaf v MFI Furntire Centres* [2005] R.P.C. 10—discussed below.

[229] (1890) 7 R.P.C. 62.

[230] See also *Wood v Raphael* (1897) 13 R.P.C. 730, (1898) 14 R.P.C. 496; *Layland v Boldy & Sons Ltd* (1913) 30 R.P.C. 547.

[231] [2005] R.P.C. 10. See also *Nokia v Ipcom* [2009] EWHC 3482 (Pat), at [108].

no item of prior art which taught both. However, neither made the other function any differently or produced any combined effect except that each contributed separately to produce a slim hob which was suitable for a work surface over a cupboard. The House of Lords considered that the principle stated in the *British Celanese* case, which had been applied by the judge at first instance to find the claim obvious, remained sound; while the Court of Appeal's approach which was to consider whether it was obvious to combine the two features was on these facts wrong in principle. Lord Hoffman explained:

"I quite agree that there is no law of collocation in the sense of a qualification of, or gloss upon, or exception to, the test for obviousness stated in section 3 of the Act. But before you can apply section 3 and ask whether the invention involves an inventive step, you first have to decide what the invention is. In particular, you have to decide whether you are dealing with one invention or two or more inventions. Two inventions do not become one invention because they are included in the same hardware. A compact motor car may contain many inventions, each operating independently of each other but all designed to contribute to the overall goal of having a compact car. That does not make the car a single invention."[232]

Lord Hoffman noted that s.14(5)(d) contemplated that a claim may "relate to one invention or to a group of inventions which are so linked as to form a single inventive concept", and stated that one must not try to consider as a whole what are in fact two separate inventions. He therefore considered the correct approach to be as follows: **12-196**

"If the two integers interact upon each other, if there is synergy between them, they constitute a single invention having a combined effect and one applies section 3 to the idea of combining them. If each integer 'performs its own proper function independently of any of the others', then each is for the purposes of section 3 a separate invention and it has to be applied to each one separately."[233]

This principle is limited to cases involving the analysis of known features merely juxtaposed and has no wider implications.[234] In *Abbott v Evysio*[235] it was contended that the claim requirements of "curved flexure means" and "flat apices" each performed their own ordinary and separate functions; however it was held on the evidence that while this was largely true, the features interacted to some degree to produce a satisfactory balance of properties, so that each element could not be regarded merely as an individual element for obviousness purposes. **12-197**

6. PARTICULAR FORMS OF CLAIM

Computer implemented inventions

The law relating to excluded inventions (including programs for computers) is considered in Ch.2 of this work. In relation specifically to inventive step, in G0003/08[236] the Enlarged Board held at [10.13] that: **12-198**

"The present position of the case law is thus that ... a claim in the area of computer programs can avoid exclusion under Articles 52(2)(c) and (3) EPC merely by explicitly mentioning the use of a computer or a computer-readable storage medium. But no exposition of this position would be

---

232 [2005] R.P.C. 10, [24].
233 [2005] R.P.C. 10, [26].
234 *Degussa-Huls SA v C-G* 2005 R.P.C. 29, [34].
235 [2008] R.P.C. 23, [182]–[185].
236 ss.7 (see 7.3.4 and 7.3.8), 10.8–10.12, 11.3, 12.4, 13.4. See also *Comvik/Two Identities*.

complete without the remark that it is also quite clear from the case law of the Boards of Appeal since T1173/97 that if a claim to program X falls under the exclusion of Articles 52(2) and (3) EPC, a claim which specifies no more than 'Program X on a computer-readable storage medium,' or 'A method of operating a computer according to program X,' will always still fail to be patentable for lack of an inventive step under Articles 52(1) and 56 EPC. Merely the EPC article applied is different. While the Enlarged Board is aware that this rejection for lack of an inventive step rather than exclusion under Article 52(2) EPC is in some way distasteful to many people, it is the approach which has been consistently developed since T1173/97 and since no divergences from that development have been identified in the referral we consider it not to be the function of the Enlarged Board in this Opinion to overturn it, for the reasons given above (see point 7.3.8)."

12-199   The approach to inventive step in such cases was summarised in *Estimating sales activity/Duns*.[237] The reasoning, whether or not "distasteful", is also not straightforward and indeed in *Aerotel*,[238] Jacob LJ proposed that one of the questions that might be put to an Enlarged Board was "How should those elements of a claim that relate to excluded subject matter be treated when assessing whether an invention is novel and inventive under Articles 54 and 56?" This question was however not contained in the referral leading to decision G0003/08, as there noted at [10.3.2].

12-200   The current approach also appears difficult to reconcile with the principle stated in *Conor v Angiotech*[239] that a patentee is entitled to have obviousness determined "by reference to his claim and not to some vague paraphrase" of it, and with the holding in case T388/04 that "The extent to which subject-matter or activities are excluded from patentability under art.52(2) and (3) EPC is notionally distinct from, and may be considered independently of, the question of inventive step." Be that as it may, the EPO has shown no sign yet that it will deviate from its current approach.[240]

---

[237] T154/04.
[238] [2007] R.P.C. 7, [76].
[239] [2008] R.P.C. 28. See para.12-24.
[240] See, e.g. *UNILOCK/Two Keys* (T1461/12) [2016] E.P.O.R. 5, and T1784/06 *COMPTEL/ Classification method* [2013] E.P.O.R. 9.

CHAPTER 13

INVALIDITY DUE TO INSUFFICIENCY

CONTENTS

1. INTRODUCTION

The relevant statutory provisions

Section 72(1)(c) of the 1977 Act provides that a patent may be revoked if: **13-01**

"the specification of the patent does not disclose the invention clearly enough and completely enough for it to be performed by a person skilled in the art".

This corresponds to the ground of opposition provided in EPC art.100(b) and also   **13-02**
reflects the requirement that art.83 EPC provides:

"The European patent application shall disclose the invention in a manner sufficiently clear and complete for it to be carried out by a person skilled in the art.[…]"

Section 14 of the 1977 Act sets out certain requirements that claims are required   **13-03**
to possess. These include that the specification be sufficiently described according
to s.14(3), mirroring the language of art.83 EPC. The following additional requirements are found in subs.14(5) (which corresponds to EPC arts 82 and 84):

"(5) The claim or claims shall—
  (a) define the matter for which the applicant seeks protection;
  (b) be clear and concise;
  (c) be supported by the description; and
  (d) relate to one invention or to a group of inventions which are so linked as to form a single
       inventive concept".

Failure to comply with requirements of subs.14(5) does not of itself give rise to   **13-04**
a finding of invalidity, the section being directed to examination. Nevertheless, the
case law relating to allegations of insufficiency under s.72 of the 1977 Act has
developed not only to embrace "classical insufficiency" but also to embrace
complaints of excessive claim breadth ("*Biogen* insufficiency") and ambiguity.[1]

---

[1] See Floyd J in *Regeneron v Bayer and Genentech* [2012] EWHC 657 and Arnold J in *Sandvik v Kennametal* [2011] EWHC 3311.

History

13-05   The Patents and Designs Act 1932, which codified the grounds of revocation, expressly introduced the ground of lack of sufficiency at s.25(2)(h). Prior to that, the patentee had long been required to disclose details of their invention (see, e.g. s.2(2) of the 1907 Act), and failure to do so rendered the patent liable to be revoked under the common law.

13-06   Section 32(1) of the 1949 Act contained, amongst others, the following grounds of revocation (sometimes referred to as "internal" invalidity objections, because in contrast to the "external" objections they did not depend on the consideration of prior art):

"(g)   that the invention, so far as claimed in any claim of the complete specification, is not useful;

(h)   that the complete specification does not sufficiently and fairly describe the invention and the method by which it is to be performed, or does not disclose the best method of performing it which was known to the applicant for the patent and for which he was entitled to claim protection;

(i)   that the scope of any claim of the complete specification is not sufficiently and clearly defined or that any claim of the complete specification is not fairly based on the matter disclosed in the specification;

(j)   that the patent was obtained on a false suggestion or representation;"

13-07   After joining the European Patent Convention, and the introduction of the 1977 Act, the law became unsettled regarding how the courts may intervene if patent claims are excessively broad: the removal of the objection of lack of fair basis (the second limb of (i)) as a ground of revocation, and the failure to comply with s.14(5) not giving rise to a ground of invalidity, was initially thought to limit the courts' entitlement to strike down excessively broad claims. It is this issue which laid the ground for the subsequent decision of the House of Lords in *Biogen v Medeva*.[2]

13-08   A second complication arose because of a misinterpretation of EPO jurisprudence regarding what was required to satisfy the obligation of sufficiency. Courts of first instance had interpreted *Genentech I/Polypeptide Expression* (T292/85) as evidencing a "one way" rule: that in order to make an invention sufficient, it was only necessary to enable a single embodiment. This led to the suggestion that excessive claim breadth from the perspective of insufficiency could only be addressed by identifying multiple inventions within the claim, each invention requiring the enablement of a single embodiment (see Aldous J in *Chiron Corporation v Organon Teknika LTD (No.3)*.[3] It was in *Biogen v Medeva* in the Court of Appeal[4] that the correct position was described; being that the disclosure in the specification must enable the invention to be performed across its breadth.

13-09   The decision of the House of Lords in *Biogen v Medeva* is particularly important because it resulted in English jurisprudence diverging from that of the EPO and other European jurisdictions. It is of course necessary that courts can render invalid claims which exceed the technical contribution but this can be done in different ways. The Patents Court has sought to achieve this goal by introducing concepts of fair basis through art.83 of the EPC. This is sometimes referred to as "*Biogen* insufficiency" and is contrasted with "classical insufficiency". Under English law it is said a patent can be insufficient even if it is possible to work the specification across the scope of the claim when the scope of the claims exceed the technical

---

[2]   [1997] R.P.C. 1.

[3]   [1994] F.S.R. 202, 241–242.

[4]   [1995] R.P.C. 25, 98.

contribution; whereas in the approach taken at the EPO, if it is possible to work the specification across the scope of the claim that is usually the end of the enquiry into sufficiency. Other objections of excessive claim breadth are dealt with under art.56.

Biogen v Medeva

Biogen v Medeva was an unusual case on its facts and consequently its applica- **13-10** tion in other circumstances needs to be approached with caution. This became particularly apparent in *Generics v Lundbeck*[5] which is considered below. The essential facts in *Biogen* were that the inventor took the non-obvious step of expressing HBV proteins in a recombinant system when it was not known whether introns were present in the viral sequence. It was however obvious to sequence HBV and had it been sequenced it would have been discovered that introns were not present. Lord Hoffmann held that the contribution in these circumstances did not justify a monopoly extending to the recombinant antigens per se.

The principal discussion of validity occurred in relation to the claim to priority. **13-11** Under s.5(2) of the 1977 Patents Act, in order for the claim to be entitled to priority it must be "supported" by matter disclosed in the earlier application. Support embraces the requirement that there must be an enabling disclosure. Lord Hoffmann placed reliance upon *Genentech I/Polypeptide Expression* (T292/85) to extend his reasoning to concepts beyond enablement (at 51):

> "This shows that there is more than one way in which the breadth of claim may exceed the technical contribution to the art embodied in the invention. The patent may claim results which it does not enable, such as making a wide class of products when it enables only one of those products and discloses no principle which would enable others to be made. Or it may claim every way of achieving a result when it enables only one way and it is possible to envisage other ways of achieving that result which make no use of the invention."

Lord Hoffmann having held that if a claim extends beyond the technical contribu- **13-12** tion (without non-enablement) it will not be supported by the priority document, went on to state that the same reasoning applied to insufficiency under s.72(1)(c). He did not explain how that aspect of "support" was reflected in the requirement that the invention be disclosed "clearly enough and completely enough". Although dealt with briefly in his speech, it is this reasoning which has given rise to the English concept of "*Biogen* insufficiency".

Relevance of earlier authorities

The Court of Appeal stated in *Halliburton v Smith International*,[6] after setting **13-13** out the provisions of EPC art.83, that:

> "This precise language is new. However, the basic requirement, that a patent should teach the practice of the invention sufficiently well for the notional addressee to perform the invention is fundamental to the patent system: the teaching is the price the patentee pays for his time-limited monopoly. No one suggests that the EPC changed anything in relation to this topic. Older English cases which contain useful discussions about the subject remain relevant in understanding the concept more fully."

---

5 [2009] R.P.C. 13.
6 [2006] EWCA Civ 1715, [12].

Different aspect of Insufficiency

13-14   General summaries of the law of insufficiency can be found from Floyd J in *Regeneron and Bayer v Genentech*[7] and Arnold J in *Sandvik v Kennametal*.[8] Floyd J described insufficiency as being a single objection to the validity of a patent which can arise in different ways. Those different ways include classical insufficiency, *Biogen* insufficiency and ambiguity.

2. CLASSICAL INSUFFICIENCY

13-15   A convenient summary of the general principles underlying the requirement of sufficiency was set out by Kitchin J in *Eli Lilly v Human Genome Sciences*[9]:

> "The specification must disclose the invention clearly and completely enough for it to be performed by a person skilled in the art. The key elements of this requirement which bear on the present case are these:
>
> (i)   the first step is to identify the invention and that is to be done by reading and construing the claims;
> (ii)   in the case of a product claim that means making or otherwise obtaining the product;
> (iii)   in the case of a process claim, it means working the process;
> (iv)   sufficiency of the disclosure must be assessed on the basis of the specification as a whole including the description and the claims;
> (v)   the disclosure is aimed at the skilled person who may use his common general knowledge to supplement the information contained in the specification;
> (vi)   the specification must be sufficient to allow the invention to be performed over the whole scope of the claim;
> (vii) the specification must be sufficient to allow the invention to be so performed without undue burden."

To whom is the specification to be sufficient?

13-16   The relevant addressee is the person skilled in the art. The nature and attributes of this person, or, in an appropriate case, team of persons, has been considered in Ch.8 of this work and see specifically paras 8-11 to 8-16. The person skilled in the art for the purpose of assessing inventive step is not necessarily the same person (or team) as the skilled person to whom the patent specification is addressed for the purpose of assessing sufficiency: the art in each circumstance may be different (*Schlumberger v EMGS*[10]) although practical examples of this are rare.

On what date is the sufficiency of a specification to be judged?

13-17   The House of Lords in *Biogen Inc v Medeva Plc*[11] held that the correct date for assessing sufficiency for the purposes of the 1977 Act was the date of application, because matter may not be added and an insufficient application should not become sufficient because of general developments in the state of the art after the filing date.

---

7   [2012] EWHC 657, [96].
8   [2011] EWHC 3311, [106].
9   [2008] R.P.C. 29, [239]. See also *Novartis v Johnson and Johnson* [2010] EWCA Civ 1039.
10   [2010] EWCA Civ 819, [30]–[70].
11   [1997] R.P.C. 1, 53. See also *Asahi Kasei Kogyo K.K.'s Application* [1991] R.P.C. 485, 536.

It had previously been considered that the relevant date was the date of publication of the complete specification (under the 1949 Act).[12]

What degree of enablement is required for the patent to be sufficient?

Classical insufficiency arises where the directions in the patent are inadequate to enable the addressee to perform the invention without undue effort. A frequently cited passage is the following by Aldous J in *Mentor Corp v Hollister Inc*[13]:

13-18

> "The section requires the skilled man to be able to perform the invention, but does not lay down the limits as to the time and energy that the skilled man must spend seeking to perform the invention before it is insufficient. Clearly there must be a limit. The sub-section, by using the words, clearly enough and completely enough, contemplates that patent specifications need not set out every detail necessary for performance, but can leave the skilled man to use his skill to perform the invention. In so doing he must seek success. He should not be required to carry out any prolonged research, enquiry or experiment. He may need to carry out the ordinary methods of trial and error, which involve no inventive step and generally are necessary in applying the particular discovery to produce a practical result. In each case, it is a question of fact, depending on the nature of the invention, as to whether the steps needed to perform the invention are ordinary steps of trial and error which a skilled man would realise would be necessary and normal to produce a practical result."

In *Mentor v Hollister* in the Court of Appeal,[14] Lloyd LJ stated:

13-19

> "When, a little later, Aldous J came to apply the law to the facts of this case, he refers to 'routine trials' and 'normal routine matters that the skilled man would seek to do and would be able to do'. Mr. Thorley criticises the use of the word 'routine'. To require the performance of routine trials is, he said, to ask too much of the addressee. I do not agree. 'Routine' is just the word I would have chosen myself to describe the sort of trial and error which has always been regarded as acceptable; and 'routine trials' has the further advantage that it is a positive concept, which is easily understood and applied. In practice, therefore, it may provide a surer test of what is meant by 'clearly enough and completely enough' in s.72(1) of the Act than the negative test proposed in *Valensi*, namely the absence of prolonged research, enquiry and experiment. If the trials are unusually arduous or prolonged, they would hardly be described as routine."

The test of "routine trials", although of assistance, must be considered in the light of the more recent judgments. Whether or not the teaching of a specification is sufficient to enable the invention to be performed across the full width of the claim is a question of fact, the answer to which is highly sensitive to the nature of the invention and also depends upon the attributes of the skilled person and the effort which they can reasonably be required to apply. In *Halliburton v Smith International*[15] the Court of Appeal approved the following statement of the law of insufficiency by Pumfrey J at first instance:

13-20

> "The sufficiency of a specification is a question of fact and necessarily depends upon the nature of the invention and the attributes of the skilled person. There is no general rule, and although statements like 'you may not set a man a problem and call it a specification' or 'the skilled person must be enabled to perform the invention without prolonged research, enquiry and experiment' give a flavour of the problem they do not really help." (See *Mentor v Hollister*.[16])

---

[12] *Standard Brands' Inc's Patent (No.2)* [1981] R.P.C. 499, 529–530.
[13] [1991] F.S.R. 557, 162.
[14] [1993] R.P.C. 7, 14.
[15] [2006] EWCA Civ 1715 (CA), from [11], Pumfrey J; [2006] R.P.C. 2, from [131]. See also *Kirin Amgen v TKT* [2004] UKHL 46; *Valensi v British Radio Corporation* [1973] R.P.C. 337; *Helitune v Stewart Hughes* [1991] F.S.R. 171, 201; *Edison and Swan Electric Light v Holland* [1892] R.P.C. 198, 201.
[16] [1993] R.P.C. 7, 10–14.

13-21   Pumfrey J went on to review the decision of the Court of Appeal *Mentor v Hollister*[17] and then continued:

> "All the same, one must be on one's guard against formulations that gloss the statutory requirement as there is always a risk that they will end up being substituted for it. This is a particular risk where the subject of the specification is very complex and its development would anyway be expected to be accompanied by a great amount of work. What is 'prolonged' in this context? It is always necessary to keep a balance between the interests of the public and the interests of the patentee in the sense that it is necessary to guard against imposing too high a standard of disclosure merely because the subject matter is inherently complex."

It follows that the standard for sufficiency is necessarily sensitive to the nature of the subject matter of the patent.[18]

13-22   The Court of Appeal in the *Halliburton* case[19] added:

> "Patents are meant to teach people how to do things. If what is 'taught' involves just too much to be reasonable allowing for all the circumstances including the nature of the art, then the patent cannot be regarded as an 'enabling disclosure'. That is the basic concept behind the requirement of sufficiency and one that lies at the heart of patent law ('central' as Lord Hoffmann put it in *Biogen v Medeva* [1997] R.P.C. 1 at p.47). The setting of a gigantic project, even if merely routine, will not do. ...
>
> The European Patent Office test of 'undue effort' is apposite for testing sufficiency. It was developed principally to deal with claims of undue width or those limited by function—see e.g. *GENENTECH/Human t-PA* T929/92. But it is also of general application. It is another way of applying the very words of the objection which emphasise the question is one of degree ('clearly enough and completely enough'). ...
>
> The answer is that the line is one to be drawn by an exercise of judgment, taking into account all of the relevant factors, one of which is of course the nature of the invention itself and its field of technology. But there are other factors too—for instance, the width of the patent claim or whether it has functional limitations which require too much work to explore."

13-23   In *UNILEVER/Stable bleaches* (T 226/85)[20] the Technical Board of Appeal of the EPO made a finding of insufficiency because the skilled person was in no position to carry out the invention without an undue burden of experimentation and search for the right conditions. The Board noted that:

> "Even though a reasonable amount of trial and error is permissible when it comes to the sufficiency of disclosure in an unexplored field or,—as it is in this case—, where there are many technical difficulties, there must then be available adequate instructions in the specification or on the basis of common general knowledge which would lead the skilled person necessarily and directly towards success through the evaluation of initial failures or through an acceptable statistical expectation rate in case of random experiments."[21]

13-24   Lawyers attacking the sufficiency of a patent are inclined to adduce evidence that in order to put an invention into effect it is necessary to engage in a "research project", inviting the court to imply that this is necessarily the point at which trial and error becomes excessive. But just as routine work may be of a scale such that a patent is insufficient, equally attaching the label "research" is not determinative either. The point at which the burden upon the skilled person becomes an undue burden is a judicial assessment dependent on the nature of the art.

13-25   A particular circumstance which may give rise to a finding of insufficiency is

---

[17]   [1993] R.P.C. 7.
[18]   *Merck Sharp & Dohme Ltd v Ono Pharmaceutical Co Ltd* [2015] EWHC 2973 (Pat), [130]–[132].
[19]   [2006] EWCA Civ 1715, [13] and [18]–[21].
[20]   [1988] O.J. EPO 336; [1989] E.P.O.R. 18.
[21]   Cited in *Eli Lilly v Human Genome Sciences* [2008] R.P.C. 29, [239].

when a claim contains a functional limitation and the specification gives a measure of guidance as to how to identify products which may possess that property. *American Home Products Corporation v Novartis Pharmaceuticals*[22] concerned a Swiss-form claim to rapamycin for use in the inhibition of transplant rejection. A competitor produced a derivative which gave rise to the issue of whether the derivative was in the scope of the claim. The Court of Appeal held that the claim did not extend to derivatives but considered the position of sufficiency on the assumption it did. Aldous LJ held that the patent would in these circumstances be insufficient because it required an undue burden to identify the compounds which had the required activity:

"42. The judge held that the number of possible derivatives was vast and whether any particular molecule derived from rapamycin would work at all was impossible to predict with certainty. Many derivatives would not exhibit immunosuppressant activity. Those which involved small changes to the side chain would be the most likely to work. Thus the skilled person could make up a list of possibles, with those believed to be the most likely at the top of the list. Even so, finding appropriate derivatives, if they existed, would involve a systematic and iterative process. Further, when a derivative which had appropriate activity had been identified, it would be impossible to be certain that it did not exhibit unpredictable defects. To discover whether it did would require further tests which would take a long time.

43. The very uncertainty and unpredictability found by the judge meant that the skilled person was being required to carry out research. The duty upon the patentee is to provide a description which enables the skilled person to perform the invention, in this case across the breadth of the claim; not to supply a starting point for a research programme. If the claim includes derivatives of rapamycin, an enabling description of such derivatives is needed so that the products of the claim can be ascertained."

In *Merck v Ono*[23] this part of the decision in *American Home Products* was taken to establish the proposition that when considering whether the task set for the skilled person produced an undue burden would depend on the quality of the work required as well as its quantity. Leaving the skilled person to find out what works is not sufficient.

13-26

In *Novartis v Johnson & Johnson*[24] the patent had claims to extended wear contact lenses. The claim was limited by reference to certain functional criteria including oxygen permeability, ion permeability, "ophthalmic compatibility" and being "suited to extended wear". Insofar as the claim contained limits regarding the material from which the lens could be made of, they were broad. Kitchin J relied referred to *American Home Products* in his judgment and concluded:

13-27

"It follows, in my judgment, that a claim to a class of products said to possess a useful activity must be based upon the identification of a common principle which permits a reasonable prediction to be made that substantially all the claimed products do indeed share that activity. Further, it is not permissible to by-pass that requirement simply by adding a functional limitation which restricts the scope of the claim to all the products which do have the relevant activity, that is to say all those which "work". In the case of a claim limited by function, it must still be possible to perform the invention across the scope of the scope of the claim without undue effort. That will involve a question of degree and depend upon all the circumstances including the nature of the invention and the art in which it is made. Such circumstances may include a consideration of whether the claims embrace products other than those specifically described for achieving the claimed purpose and, if they do, what those other products may be and how easily they may be found or made; whether it is possible to make a

22 [2001] R.P.C. 8.
23 *Merck Sharp & Dohme Ltd v Ono Pharmaceutical Co Ltd* [2015] EWHC 2973 (Pat), [130].
24 Kitchin J [2009] EWHC 1671, [244]; upheld by Court of Appeal [2010] EWCA Civ 1039. See also *Idenix v Gilead* for another example of leaving the person skilled in the art a research project to synthesise and test the compounds which may have the desired antiviral activity (at [595]–[598]).

reasonable prediction as to whether any particular product satisfies the requirements of the claims; and the nature and extent of any testing which must be carried out to confirm any such prediction."

13-28　In *Regeneron and Bayer v Genentech*[25] Floyd J explained there was nothing wrong with a functional limitation provided the patent specification, with or without the common general knowledge, provides the skilled person with the means of achieving that functional result across the breadth of the claim without undue effort. He went on to state that a claim cannot be rendered "insufficiency proof" by claiming only things which work.

13-29　In the case of claims relating to clinical applications of pharmaceutical products, there is no general requirement that clinical data must be provided. In *Regeneron Pharmaceuticals Inc v Genentech Inc*,[26] Kitchin LJ stated (at [103]):

> "... the Boards of Appeal of the EPO have recognised that in the case of a claim to the use of a product to make a medicine for a particular therapeutic purpose it would impose too great a burden on the patentee to require him to provide absolute proof that the compound has approval as a medicine. Further, it is not always necessary to report the results of clinical trials or even animal testing. Nevertheless, he must show, for example by appropriate experiments, that the product has an effect on a disease process so as to make the claimed therapeutic effect plausible."[27]

Enablement across the breadth of the claim

13-30　It is necessary not just to enable something falling within the scope of the claim but to enable the claim across its breadth. In the context of classical insufficiency, there is limited guidance in the case law as to how to determine whether a claim is enabled across its breadth. Although case law recognised that a distinction may be drawn between *Biogen* insufficiency and classical insufficiency, discussion of enablement across the breadth of a claim often blends both these species.

13-31　It is clear that it is not a requirement of patentability that everything falling within the scope of a claim must be enabled. If that were the case there would be no possibility of improvement patents falling within the scope of earlier patents. In the *Kirin-Amgen* case, Aldous LJ stated[28]:

> "The law contemplates that patents will not lack sufficiency even though the claims cover inventive improvements. If the law was otherwise there would be no room for patents which disclosed a principle of general application unless the specification described how to carry out later inventions using the principle."

13-32　Generally if a claim specifies a particular embodiment it will be necessary to enable that embodiment. If it covers an embodiment which it does not specify then depending on the nature of the technical contribution it may not be necessary to enable it. In *Genentech I/Polypeptide Expression* (T292/85)[29] the claim was essentially to a plasmid with certain features comprising inter alia heterologous DNA which was suitable for transforming a bacterial host resulting in an expression product. There was no limitation to a particular plasmid, a particular heterologous gene or a particular bacterial host. The Board stated:

> "3.1.2 ...The suggested features in the claims are essentially functional terns in this particular context, in spite of structural connotations, and may cover an unlimited number of possibili-

---

[25] [2012] EWHC 657, [157].
[26] [2013] EWCA Civ 93.
[27] See also *Salk Institute* (T609/02).
[28] [2002] EWCA 1096, [69].
[29] See also *Oncomouse* (T19/90).

ties, it follows that the features may generically embrace the use of unknown or not yet envisaged possibilities, including specific variants which might be provided or invented in the future....

In appropriate cases, such as the present, it is only possible to define the invention (the matter for which protection is sought – Article 84 EPC) in a way which gives a fair protection having regard to the nature of the invention which has been described, by using functional terminology in the claims...

3.1.4   The objection raised against the terms "plasmid" and "bacteria" that they are too broad since some of them rely on yet unavailable entities is untenable. The Board is of the opinion that this is quite normal practice in many technical fields where terms as "carriers", "resilient means", or "amplifying means" are common place and embrace new components, be they inventive or not....

3.1.5   The above examples show that the need for a fair protection governs both the considerations of the scope of claims and of the requirements for sufficient disclosure. Unless variants of components are also embraced in the claims, which are, now or later on, equally suitable to achieve the same effect in a manner which could not have been envisaged without the invention, the protection provided by the patent would be ineffectual...

3.1.6   The Examining Division's tentative suggestion that such terms should be restricted to those available in the art has no basis in existing law. Unless broad, yet proper terminology is allowable, subsequent investigations by third parties might be encouraged to concentrate on finding alternatives outside the claims instead of trying to pursue progress through dependent inventions. The lack of recognition of the full significance and the interdependency of technical contributions could adversely affect progress in the area of microbiology and biochemistry...."

In *Erythropoietin II/Kirin Amgen* (T0636/97) it was stated: **13-33**

"4.5   For the board it is a fundamental principle of patent law that a claim can validly cover broad subject matter, even though the description of the relevant patent does not enable every method of arriving at that subject matter to be carried out. Otherwise no dominant patent could exist, and each developer of a new method of arriving at that subject matter would be free of earlier patents. In many cases in the field of biotechnology, patent protection would then become illusory. This is not to say that some claims might not be too broad in scope and not be enabled over their whole scope for the purpose of Article 83 EPC ... The boards have considered this question of allowability of a broad claim versus the requirements of Article 83 EPC, strictly on a case by case basis, influenced by the extent to which the information in the patent could be used to develop further embodiments without a major conceptual leap."

In *Kirin-Amgen v Hoechst Marion Roussel*[30] Lord Hoffmann made obiter comments relating to breadth of claim objections. One objection which had been raised against the patent was that *if* the claims covered any form of recombinant DNA technology, the claim was insufficient because it did not enable TKT's technology. Another was whether the claim should be limited to expression in CHO cells given that was the expression system enabled by the specification. Lord Hoffmann held that it was necessary to ask whether the patent disclosed a principle of general application: **13-34**

"In my opinion there is nothing difficult or mysterious about it. It simply means an element of the claim which is stated in general terms. Such a claim is sufficiently enabled if one can reasonably expect the invention to work with anything which falls within the general term."

Without expressing a concluded view he indicated that the patent did not teach making EPO using recombinant technology using the TKT process. He then went on to observe that the patentee should be entitled to cover expression of EPO through improved cell expression systems which were not enabled by the specification.   **13-35**

---

[30]   [2004] UKHL 46, from [110].

13-36   In *Regeneron Pharmaceuticals v Kymab and Novo Nordisk*[31] Carr J considered a process claim to the in situ replacement of a murine immunoglobulin gene locus with human V, D and J segments. The judge held that because the process covered doing this with inserts of a certain size which were covered by the claim, the claim was not enabled across its breadth and was insufficient.

13-37   In some cases the question of enablement is intimately linked to the question of technical contribution. An example is *Novartis v Johnson & Johnson* where the claims were insufficient because the person skilled in the art could not without undue effort identify compound which would have the desirable properties required by the claim. In other cases insufficiency may arise for other reasons: it may, for example, properly be anticipated that certain compounds falling within the scope of a claim would have the promised properties with which the technical contribution is associated but those compounds cannot be made without undue effort. An example of such a case is *Gilead v Idenix*[32] where the technical contribution was said to be the identification of antiviral activity but one the defects of the patent was the inability of the skilled person to make the compounds (note the claims were also insufficient for additional reasons). One allegation in *Merck v Ono*[33] was that a claim to the use of an anti-PD-1 antibody for cancer treatment could not be sufficient (or plausible) because the evidence was that the agent did not work for all cancers. The judge held on the facts that although there were cancers for which the agent did not work, the generality of the principle disclosed in the patent was not undermined by the lack of success in these instances. The agents were found to work for substantially all cancers and the claim was sufficient.[34]

Markush claims

13-38   A Markush formula describe a class of chemical compounds by reference to a backbone chemical structure within which optional substitutions may be made at various positions. Such formulae are used commonly to describe class of organic compound in respect of which a new use is claimed, such as a use in therapy. For reasons which are not entirely clear, a practice has developed in these circumstances of granting claims to compounds per se notwithstanding that the technical contribution resides not in the mere drawing of the chemical structure, nor in a method of synthesis, but only in the novel use. This would seem in theory to raise questions concerning the scope of such claims for the purpose of infringement. It also raises issues in relation to sufficiency.

13-39   In *Pharmacia v Merck*[35] the court was concerned with broad compound claims in Markush form. The patent taught that such compounds were anti-inflammatory and in particular were gastric sparing by reason of their being COX II selective but the claims were drafted as compounds per se. Aldous LJ rejected the suggestion that functional limitations should not be read into the "invention", although it is not clear whether he read functional limitations into the claims. He held at [17]:

> "17. Mr Kitchin QC, who appeared for the patentees, drew attention to section 125 of the 1977 Act which provides that an invention 'shall, unless the context otherwise requires be that specified in a claim.' He then drew to our attention claims 1-12 which claim chemical compounds.

31 [2016] EWHC 87.
32 [2014] EWHC 3916, from [470].
33 [2015] EWHC 2973.
34 [2015] EWHC 2973, [157]–[172].
35 [2002] R.P.C. 41.

He submitted that they could be used for any purpose because they were claimed without limitation as to use.... It followed that the invention of claim 1 was the compounds themselves. [...]

18. Mr Kitchin is correct that claims 1 to 12 do not include any limitation as to use. Thus when construed without recourse to the rest of the specification, the invention claimed is to the chemical compounds set out. But that construction makes the invention inconsistent with, amongst other passages, the description of the invention in the specification. It states that 'A class of compounds useful in treating inflammation-related disorders is defined by Formula 1'. I will deal with this submission and the other submissions on construction later in this judgment in the context in which they arise. But I will first decide whether the judge was right to accept Merck's submission which is set out in paragraph 42 of his judgment as to what was the 'invention' or 'technical contribution' in the specification.....

20. I agree with the judge. Nobody reading the specification could believe that the 'invention' was the compounds claimed in claim 1. The specification makes clear that the patentees had found a class of compounds that could be made which at least had anti-inflammatory action. It was that contribution that merited a 20 year monopoly. In my view the only question capable of argument is whether the compounds in the class were chosen merely for their anti-inflammatory action or because in addition they had reduced side-effects due to them being Cox II selective."

In *Pharmacia* the validity of the claims was judged under the objection of insufficiency by reference to whether or not the property of selective COX II inhibition was present across the class. Irrespective of the apparently broad scope of the claims, the "invention" was the activity disclosed in the specification. In *HGS v Eli Lilly*[36] (at [31]) Jacob LJ observed:

  13-40

"...I am not clear that *Pharmacia* would be decided for the same reasons today. The objection is an *AgrEvo* type – that the claim included within it many compounds as to which there was no technical contribution today."

In *AgrEvo*[37] the patent claimed a class of triazole derivatives by reference to a Markush formula. The specification asserted that all the compounds had herbicidal activity but the credibility of that claim across the breadth of the class was questioned. In particular there was only data relating to *some* of the claimed compounds and there was not sufficient evidence to lead to an inference that substantially all the claimed compounds possessed this activity. There were two differences to the approach under *Pharmacia*. The first difference being that the objection was brought under lack of inventive step rather than insufficiency. The second is that the objection board considered whether the claims as to activity were credible (plausible) whereas in *Pharmacia* the court considered the actual activity of the compounds falling within the scope of the claims.

  13-41

In *Idenix v Gilead*[38] Arnold J considered a Markush claim to a class of nucleoside analogues which the patent disclosed were useful for treating Hepatitis C virus. He held that it was not plausible that the claimed compounds had such activity and this gave rise to a finding that the claims were obvious following the reasoning in *AgrEvo*, and insufficient.

  13-42

It is essential to have in the patent system a ground of objection which prevents speculative patents remaining on the register. Patents are granted because of a technical advance not speculation—anyone can speculate about anything at any time. The modern approach to the rejection of such patents is to determine whether the relevant promise of the claimed subject matter is "plausible" or "credible". If not the claims will be obvious and/or insufficient. When *Pharmacia* was decided

  13-43

---

[36] [2012] EWCA Civ 1185.
[37] T0939/92.
[38] [2014] EWHC 3916.

the approach of considering speculative patents through the requirement of "plausibility" was not developed in the case law and consequently experimental evidence was introduced to determine whether the claimed compounds in fact had the required properties. The requirement of "plausibility" is considered further below.

Quality of the product or process enabled

13-44   In *Mentor v Hollister*[39] the court accepted that the requirement was not to produce a successful commercial product but rather a workable prototype. While the claimed invention must be enabled across the full scope of the claim, it is not a further requirement that it should be as good as the patent promises. In *Zipher v Markem*[40] Floyd J held that:

> "If the skilled team would not be able to make something within the claim, insufficiency will be established. But what if the skilled team would be able to make something falling within the claim, but which is not as good as the patent promises? In my judgment that will not be insufficiency, although it may help in some cases (for the purposes of the separate objection of lack of inventive step) in showing that the technical advance made by the claim is less great than contended for by the description."

3.   BIOGEN INSUFFICIENCY

13-45   As explained above, in *Biogen v Medeva* Lord Hoffmann held that if a claim extends beyond the technical contribution it will not support the invention and will be insufficient. This objection is independent of classical insufficiency under English law.

13-46   Underpinning the jurisprudence of the EPO is the recognition that the claimed monopoly of a patent should not extend beyond its technical contribution. This does not however give rise to a free-standing objection nor does it follow that excessive claim breadth necessarily gives rise to a finding of insufficiency. In practice the EPO decides many cases of excessive claim breadth under art.56 of EPC.

13-47   In practice it may rarely matter whether an objection to excessive claim breadth is brought under art.56 or art.83 as the result will usually be the same. As observed above in the context of Markush claims, the courts have recently adopted *AgrEvo* obviousness in preference to *Biogen* insufficiency but there is no reason to suppose that this change in approach will lead to different conclusions as to validity. Insofar as inconsistencies have occurred between findings of UK courts and those of the EPO (or courts of other contracting states) these can more often be attributed to a different view of the technical contribution of a patent rather than a difference in law.

13-48   The reasoning in *Biogen v Medeva* was relied upon by Kitchin J in *Generics v Lundbeck*.[41] In this case the main claim was to one of two enantiomers of citalopram. The racemate was known, as was how to make it. The existence of the two enantiomers was also known, although a method of separating them or synthesising each individually was not known. The patentee found *one* way of isolating one of the enantiomers but claimed the product (the particular enantiomer) rather than the method it had found. At the priority date there was no other obvi-

---

[39] [1993] R.P.C. 7, 17, lines 4–14.
[40] [2009] F.S.R. 1, [365].
[41] [2007] R.P.C. 32; [2008] R.P.C. 19 (CA); [2009] R.P.C. 13 (HL).

ous way of making the product. Kitchin J reasoned that the inventive step resided in the particular process not in the known *desideratum* of the isolated enantiomer and that the first person who achieves an obviously desirable goal should not be entitled to monopolise the goal. There were factual analogies with *Biogen* in that Professor Murray had found one way of making HBV antigens but was not entitled to claim the antigen per se.

In the Court of Appeal,[42] unusually, Lord Hoffmann was a presiding judge. He **13-49** expressly sympathised with Kitchin J's application of *Biogen* and then distinguished it in an analysis which appeared to suggest the patent in *Biogen* might have been held obvious rather than insufficient. In any event he then held the technical contribution in *Lundbeck* was the enantiomer and this should not be confused with the inventive step which may have resided in the particular method (see [36]).

In the House of Lords[43] (following the judgment of Lord Hoffmann below) Lord **13-50** Neuberger held:

"it can be said that the respondent's technical contribution in this case was to make available, for the first time, a product which had previously been unavailable, namely the isolated (+)-enantiomer of citalopram. On that basis, it would appear to follow that the respondent was entitled to claim the enantiomer".

Lord Mance thought that "inventive concept" and "technical contribution" were synonymous, whereas Lord Walker considered that the "technical contribution" was concerned with the *evaluation* of the inventive concept (how far forward had it carried the state of the art) and so differed from it.[44]

4. LACK OF CLARITY/AMBIGUITY

Clarity of claims is an issue upon which a patent is examined under art.84 EPC **13-51** and s.14 of the Patents Act 1977. Objections under these provisions cannot be raised after grant. The courts have nevertheless indicated that ambiguities can give rise to findings of non-infringement and insufficiency.

In *Kirin-Amgen v Hoechst Marion Roussel*[45] Lord Hoffmann considered an **13-52** ambiguity arising from the use of the term "higher molecular weight" where the term was ambiguous. He held:

"125. The judge decided that the lack of clarity made the specification insufficient. It did not merely throw up the possibility of doubtful cases but made it impossible to determine in any case whether the product fell within the claim. The invention was not disclosed 'clearly enough and completely enough for it to be performed by a person skilled in the art': section 72(1)(c).

126. The Court of Appeal disagreed. They said that it was sufficient that some uEPO could be tested against rEPO by SDS-PAGE. The fact that it did not specify which uEPO and that choosing one uEPO would bring the product within the claim and another would not was "lack of clarity dressed up to look like insufficiency." For my part, I do not think that can be right. If the claim says that you must use an acid, and there is nothing in the specification or context to tell you which acid, and the invention will work with some acids but not with others but finding out which ones work will need extensive experiments, then that in my opinion is not merely lack of clarity; it is insufficiency. The lack of clarity does not merely create a fuzzy boundary between that which will work and that which will not. It makes it impossible to work the invention at all until one has found out what ingredient is needed."

It follows that there is a blurring between issues of clarity and impediments to **13-53**

---

42 [2008] R.P.C. 19.
43 [2009] R.P.C. 13.
44 [2009] R.P.C. 13, [30] and [45].
45 [2004] UKHL 46.

working the invention. A similar obiter observation was made by Jacob LJ in *SmithKline Beecham v Apotex*[46] (at [115]):

"It would seem to follow, if points (3)–(4) are accepted, that the meaning of the words 'solvate' and 'anhydrate' are truly ambiguous—are words which do not just have a 'fuzzy boundary' (per Lord Hoffmann in *Kirin-Amgen* (at [126]). One just does not know what the patentee meant at all. If this logic is right, then not only can there be no infringement (see, e.g. *Milliken v Walk-Off Mats* [1996] F.S.R. 292 (the 'Pinocchio units' case) and *Scanvaegt v Pelcome* [1998] F.S.R. 786) but the claims would be truly ambiguous and thus insufficient on the principles laid down by Lord Hoffmann in *Kirin-Amgen*."

5. PLAUSIBILITY

13-54   Chapter 13 of the last edition ("Invalidity Due to Insufficiency") contained no reference to the objection of want of plausibility. At the time of writing most cases of invalidity being argued before the Patents Court now contain an allegation that the teaching of the patent is not plausible. This represents a significant change in law and practice.

13-55   The need to distinguish patents that contain teaching which is plausible from those that are entirely speculative is well-established at the EPO in the context of inventive step. The problem of speculative claiming may arise in various contexts but is particularly notable where claims to classes of chemical compounds are filed as Markush formulae. In medicinal chemistry rival applicants may be tempted, at an early stage of research, to file broad claims to classes of novel chemical in the anticipation that within those classes there may be compounds with particularly useful properties but without, at that point, having shown which compounds will be useful. The approach of the EPO has been to refuse such patents as lacking an inventive contribution.

13-56   The problem-solution approach used by the EPO to analyse inventive step requires the formulation of a problem that has been solved by the claims. Where claims are speculative and where the patent does not plausibly solve any problem there is no inventive step: the drawing out of chemical formulae does not of itself represent a technical contribution. In *AgrEvo* (T0939/92) the Technical Board of Appeal observed that in order to be patentable a selection of chemical compounds should not be arbitrary but must be justified by a hitherto unknown technical effect which is caused by the structural features claimed such that the "technical effect which justifies the selection of the claimed compounds must be one which can be fairly assumed to be produced by substantially all the selected compounds". On the facts of that case it was held that it was not possible to predict the technical effect of herbicidal activity from the structural features described by the claims. It followed that the requirements of art.56 of EPC were not met.

13-57   The approach in *AgrEvo* was followed *in John Hopkins/Factor-9* (T1329/04). The question which arose, again in the context of art.56 of the EPC, was whether a claimed polynucleotide was plausibly a member of the TGF-beta superfamily. It was only in post-priority date publications that the evidence to support this contention, beyond speculation, could be found. It was held that this was not enough to support a finding under art.56 in the patentee's favour:

"12.   …The definition of an invention as being a contribution to the art, i.e. as solving a technical problem and not merely putting forward one, requires that it is at least made plausible by the

---

46   [2004] EWCA Civ 1568.

disclosure in the application that its teaching solves indeed the problem it purports to solve. Therefore, even if supplementary post-published evidence may in the proper circumstances also be taken into consideration, it may not serve as the sole basis to establish that the application solves indeed the problem it purports to solve."

This reasoning, again in the context of inventive step, was referred to in Lord **13-58** Hoffmann's speech in *Conor Medsystems Inc v Angiotech Pharmaceuticals Inc*.[47] The courts have subsequently applied this requirement of plausibility as part of the test of sufficiency. This is perhaps not surprising given that the approach taken in *Biogen v Medeva* has led the UK courts to use art.83 to invalidate patents in circumstances where the EPO would only apply art.56.

In *Regeneron Pharmaceuticals v Genentech*[48] Kitchin LJ explained (at [100]– **13-59** [101]):

"100. It must therefore be possible to make a reasonable prediction the invention will work with substantially everything falling within the scope of the claim or, put another way, the assertion that the invention will work across the scope of the claim must be plausible or credible. The products and methods within the claim are then tied together by a unifying characteristic or a common principle. If it is possible to make such a prediction then it cannot be said the claim is insufficient simply because the patentee has not demonstrated the invention works in every case.

101. On the other hand, if it is not possible to make such a prediction or it is shown the prediction is wrong and the invention does not work with substantially all the products or methods falling within the scope of the claim then the scope of the monopoly will exceed the technical contribution the patentee has made to the art and the claim will be insufficient. It may also be invalid for obviousness, there being no invention in simply providing a class of products or methods which have no technically useful properties or purpose."

This requirement of plausibility as a threshold test of sufficiency has been ap- **13-60** plied in a number of cases subsequently. In *Eli Lilly & Company v Janssen Alzheimer Immunotherapy* Arnold J stated:

"245. I do not accept this submission. In my judgment it is well established that it is permissible for a party attacking the validity of a patent to rely on post-dated evidence. If domestic authority is required for that proposition, it is not necessary to go further back than Kitchin LJ's statement in *Regeneron v Genentech* quoted above: 'if it is shown the prediction is wrong and the invention does not work with substantially all the products or methods falling within the scope of the claim then … the claim will be insufficient'.

255. For the reasons set out above, the court must undertake a two-stage enquiry. The first stage is to determine whether the disclosure of the Patent, read in the light of the common general knowledge of the skilled team, makes it plausible that the invention will work across the scope of the claim. If the disclosure does make it plausible, the second stage is to consider whether the later evidence establishes that in fact the invention cannot be performed across the scope of the claim without undue burden."

This new test of plausibility may not represent a substantive change in the law **13-61** if the threshold is low and the test used only to identify those patents which fail to disclose any technical contribution: the courts have always found ways of invalidating patents which are entirely speculative and whether this is done through arts 56 or 83 EPC may be a matter of detail. However, if it is to be the case that the test of plausibility represents more than this, and that a patent may fall for want of plausibility in circumstances where it is otherwise sufficient, this emerging area of jurisprudence may represent a significant change. It is of note that a practice is emerging in litigation of inviting experts to opine upon the quality of evidence

---

47   [2008] UKHL 49; [2008] R.P.C. 28.
48   [2013] EWCA Civ 93.

disclosed in a patent and whether it makes the claims plausible. This raises the question, "how stringent is the test of 'plausibility'"?

13-62   In the context of industrial applicability, in *Human Genome Sciences Inc v Eli Lilly & Co*[49] it was said that the word "plausible" conveys that there must be some real reason for supposing the statement is true, but the standard is not any higher than that. In *Hospira v Genentech*[50] Birss J left open the question of whether the test for plausibility was the same as the standard for obviousness: in other words if a technical effect is plausible in the light of the disclosure in the patent, does it follow that the same disclosure in the prior art would render the invention obvious? In the subsequent case of *Actavis v Eli Lilly and Company*[51] Carr J held that the two were not the same and that the test of plausibility was a threshold test which sought to distinguish the credible from the speculative:

> "173. …Susceptibility of industrial application, sufficiency and inventive step are all part of the requirements of the relevant treaties and legislation. Necessarily, it is the task of the courts and the Boards of Appeal of the EPO to interpret these requirements. In so doing, plausibility has been referred to at the highest level as one factor that should be taken into account. Nonetheless it is relevant to bear in mind that plausibility does not form a separate ground of objection to the validity of a patent. Therefore it falls to be considered within the context of the statutory objections to validity, and having regard to their respective purposes…
>
> 176. There is no requirement in the EPC that a patent should contain data or experimental proof to support its claims. The reference in *Salk* to the provision of experimental tests to support the claimed therapeutic use was by way of example. In respect of claims to therapeutic applications which are of wide scope, such experimental tests may well be required. In the case of narrow claims, they may not be…
>
> 178. The cases on which Lilly relies (to which I have referred above) establish that the test of plausibility is a threshold test which is satisfied by a disclosure which is "credible", as opposed to speculative. That disclosure may subsequently be confirmed or refuted by further evidence obtained subsequent to the priority date. If it is subsequently shown that the invention does not work with substantially all of the products or methods falling within the scope of the claim then the scope of the monopoly will exceed the technical contribution and the patent will be invalid. This indicates why plausibility is only a threshold test. A plausible invention may nonetheless be shown to be insufficient. In my judgment the standard for assessment of plausibility is not the same the standard for assessment of expectation of success in the context of obviousness."

13-63   In *Generics(UK) v Warner Lambert*[52] Arnold J held that a claim to pregabalin for the treatment of neuropathic pain was required to make plausible both the treatment of central neuropathic and peripheral neuropathic pain because the person skilled in the art understood that both types of pain were known. The learned judge held that because the experimental evidence disclosed in the patent related to central sensitisation, and this was not understood to be associated with central neuropathic pain, the claim of treating neuropathic pain was not plausible across its breadth.

13-64   In *Merck v Ono*[53] Birss J considered allegations of insufficiency on the ground of lack of plausibility and reviewed what was required to establish the plausibility of a claim to the therapeutic use of an agent, as compared to the claim in *Human Genome Sciences*. He stated at [139]:

> "In *HGS* it was found to be plausible that the product claimed would have some sort of therapeutic

---

[49] [2011] UKSC 51, [149], Lord Hope.
[50] [2014] EWHC 1094. In the same case Birss J held that the same test of plausibility was applicable to issues of priority, thereby disagreeing with the Technical Board of Appeal, see para.7-37.
[51] [2015] EWHC 3294.
[52] [2015] EWHC 2548.
[53] [2015] EWHC 2973.

utility. At the level of individual diseases one could not say which might be treated but that did not matter because the claim was not so limited. For a purpose limited medical use claim, more specificity is likely to be required than was necessary in *HGS* but on the other hand, material which is too narrowly focussed may not support a wide claim. The principle applicable to purpose limited medical use claims must be that the material relied on to establish plausibility must be both sufficiently specific, and have a sufficient breadth of application, to fairly support the claim both in terms of the nature of the agent claimed to have an effect, and in terms of the effect claimed."

6. OTHER ASPECTS OF INSUFFICIENCY

Biological material

Failure to make biological material available by its deposit in a deposit institution may give rise to a finding of insufficiency.[54]   **13-65**

Effect of errors

An error in a specification (whether in the description or a drawing) will not render the patent invalid provided that it is an error which the skilled addressee would at once observe and be in a position to correct.[55]   **13-66**

The following test was set out by Aldous J, in a passage warmly approved by the Court of Appeal in *Mentor Corporation v Hollister Incorporated*[56]:   **13-67**

"The test to be applied for the purpose of ascertaining whether a man skilled in the art can readily correct the mistakes or readily supply the omissions, has been stated to be this: Can he rectify the mistakes and supply the omissions [without] the exercise of any inventive faculty? If he can, then the description of the specification is sufficient. If he cannot, the patent will be void for insufficiency."

The reader will not necessarily be misled by incorrect nomenclature or other errors of description in the priority document.[57] However, while obvious errors may be corrected, the tests of enablement and obviousness differed. For a document to be enabling, it must lead the reader to the invention clearly. A disclosure which if embodied in a priority document would not give enabling support to a patent claim directed at a particular step might still render the step obvious if incorporated in a piece of prior art.[58]   **13-68**

Where the inventor states an erroneous theory as to the operation of the invention, this will not invalidate the patent[59] unless it amounts to a statement that would in practice be misleading.[60] The test is whether the specification is sufficient to enable the invention to be performed. Laddie J further observed in *Evans Medical Ltds' Patent*[61]:   **13-69**

"If an inventor through clever foresight or lucky guess work describes something which works and how to do it, his disclosure is enabling. It is *nihil ad rem* that he never carried out the experiments

---

54 See PA 1977 s.125A(4); and Patent Rules 2007 r.13(1) and Sch.1 para.3. See also paras 3–21 and 3–64.

55 *No-Fume Ltd v Frank Pitchford Co Ltd* (1935) 52 R.P.C. 231, 243; see also, *Valensi v British Radio Corp* [1973] R.P.C. 337; *Visx v Nidek* [1999] F.S.R. 405, 461.

56 [1993] R.P.C. 7, 14.

57 *Evans Medical Ltds Patent* [1998] R.P.C. 517, 535.

58 *Evans Medical Ltd's Patent* [1998] R.P.C. 517, 560.

59 See *"Z" Electric Lamp Co v Marples, Leach Co* (1910) 27 R.P.C. 737, at 746.

60 As in *Monnet v Beck* (1897) 14 R.P.C. 777, 847. See also, *"Z" Electric Lamp Co v Marples Leach Co* (1910) 27 R.P.C. 737.

61 [1998] R.P.C. 517, 550.

themselves or faked the results. The more complex the area of technology, the less likely it is that the inventor will be able to predict the results of experiments he never carried out or that he will strike lucky, but what is important is what the document teaches, not how the contents got there."

Appeals on insufficiency

13-70   A decision on insufficiency, like that on obviousness, involves an assessment and weighing of a number of factors. Therefore, as with obviousness, where a finding of classical insufficiency below involves no question of principle but is simply a matter of degree, an appellate court may be cautious in differing from the judge's evaluation.[62]

---

[62]   *SmithKline Beecham's Patent* [2006] R.P.C. 10 (HL), [38]; *Halliburton v Smith International* [2006] EWCA Civ 1715 (CA), [24].

CHAPTER 14

PATENT INFRINGEMENT

CONTENTS

1. INTRODUCTION

Patent infringement is and always has been a form of tort[1] actionable by the patentee or, if applicable, by their exclusive licensee.[2] Prior to the Patents Act 1977, there was no statutory definition of infringement. The infringement of a patent was instead the doing, after the date of publication of the complete specification,[3] of that which the Letters Patent had prohibited being done, and the substantive law on infringement involved construing the terms of the Royal Command, which were as follows:

14-01

"We do by these presents for Us, our heirs and successors, strictly command all our subjects whatsoever within our United Kingdom of Great Britain and Northern Ireland, and the Isle of Man, that they do not at any time during the continuance of the said term either directly or indirectly make use of or put in practice the said invention, nor in anywise imitate the same, without the written consent, licence or agreement of the patentee, on pain of incurring such penalties as may be justly inflicted on such offenders for their contempt of this our Royal Command, and of being answerable to the patentee according to the law for damages thereby occasioned."[4]

Patents granted under the 1977 Act no longer contain any Royal Command, and the law of infringement has instead now been codified by the definition in s.60. The 1977 Act contains transitional provisions which preserved the old law of infringement under limited circumstances,[5] but it is no longer practically possible for these to apply.

14-02

The definition of infringement contained in s.60 of the 1977 Act arises out of the CPC wherein it was resolved that the Member States should adjust their patent laws so as to bring them into conformity with the corresponding provisions of the EPC, the CPC and the PCT. As a result, there is a "striking and unusual"[6] provision in s.130(7) of the 1977 Act declaring that certain sections of the Act (including ss.60

14-03

---

[1] *Sevcon v Lucas CAV* [1986] R.P.C. 609.
[2] See PA 1977 s.67; and further at para.16-22.
[3] PA 1949 s.13.
[4] See Patents Rules 1968 Sch.4.
[5] Patents Rules 1968 Sch.4 para.3.
[6] Per Oliver J in *Smith, Kline & French Laboratories v R.D. Harbottle (Mercantile) Ltd* [1980] R.P.C.

and 69) are so framed as to have, as nearly as practicable, the same effects in this country as the corresponding provisions of the EPC, CPC, and PCT have in the territories to which those Conventions apply.

14-04   Article 25 of the CPC provides as follows:

"A Community patent shall confer on its proprietor the right to prevent all third parties not having his consent:

(a)   from making, offering, putting on the market or using a product which is the subject matter of the patent, or importing or stocking the product for these purposes;

(b)   from using a process which is the subject-matter of the patent or, when the third party knows, or it is obvious in the circumstances, that the use of the process is prohibited without the consent of the proprietor of the patent, from offering the process for use within the territories of the Contracting States;

(c)   from offering, putting on the market, using, or importing or stocking for these purposes the product obtained directly by a process which is the subject matter of the patent."

14-05   Section 60(1) of the 1977 Act is, however, in the following terms:

"**60.**—(1)   Subject to the provisions of this section, a person infringes a patent for an invention if, but only if, while the patent is in force, he does any of the following things in the United Kingdom in relation to the invention without the consent of the proprietor of the patent, that is to say—

(a)   where the invention is a product, he makes, disposes of, offers to dispose of, uses or imports the product or keeps it whether for disposal or otherwise;

(b)   where the invention is a process, he uses the process or he offers it for use in the United Kingdom when he knows, or it is obvious to a reasonable person in the circumstances, that its use there without the consent of the proprietor would be an infringement of the patent;

(c)   where the invention is a process, he disposes of, offers to dispose of, uses or imports any product obtained directly by means of that process or keeps any such product whether for disposal or otherwise."

(Notwithstanding the usage of the words "if but only if" in this subsection, a further form of infringement is then defined in s.60(2), modelled on art.26 of the CPC, which will be further considered below.)[7]

14-06   As may be noted by comparison of the texts above, the draftsman of s.60 has seen fit (notwithstanding the declaration contained in s.130(7)) to make significant changes to the language of art.25. The words "putting on the market" and "stocking" have been altered and it is difficult to understand the reason why they have been changed since the declared intention was to have "as nearly as practicable" the same effect. Nonetheless, in the light of that declaration regard has to be had to his intentions, and reference back to the text of the CPC itself may sometimes be necessary when construing the Act. (Jacob J has observed in a different context that such rewriting helps nobody[8] and suggested in *Bristol Myers Squibb v Baker Norton*[9] that it would be easier for those concerned with patent matters in the UK and elsewhere in Europe to work on the basis that the Conventions are of direct effect, thus avoiding argument based on detailed language differences and also resulting in use of a unified numbering system.)

14-07   Jacob J noted in *Union Carbide v B.P. Chemicals*[10] that the words "if but only

---

363, at 372.
[7]   See para.14-94, et seq.
[8]   In *Beloit Technologies Inc v Valmet Paper Machinery Inc (No.2)* [1995] R.P.C. 705, at 737.
[9]   [1999] R.P.C. 253, 258.
[10]   [1998] F.S.R. 1, 5.

if" in s.60(1) of the 1977 Act are not to be found in art.25 of the CPC. However, he did not regard them as adding anything. Although he expressed uncertainty in that case as to whether s.61 could be regarded as a complete code so far as remedies are concerned (once liability is established), it is submitted that s.60 must be regarded as exhaustive as to what constitutes infringement.

2. GENERAL PRINCIPLES APPLYING TO INFRINGEMENT

Ascertainment of whether there is infringement

In all cases, it is necessary to show that the "invention" has in some respect been taken. The invention is defined in s.125(1) as "that specified in a claim of the specification of the application or patent, as the case may be, as interpreted by the description and any drawings contained in that specification". This involves construing the specification and claims so as to determine whether the product or process in question falls within the claims. Construction of patent claims is fully considered in Ch.9 of this work. **14-08**

If the relevant product or process does not fall within the claims, properly construed, then there can be no infringement. As Jacob J said in *Beloit Technologies Inc v Valmet Paper Machinery Inc (No.2)*[11], there is no tort of non-infringement; a defendant is entitled to design around the patent. There is no further equity in a patent beyond its claims. **14-09**

Once it is shown that the relevant product or process falls within one or more claims, it is then necessary in order to determine whether there has been infringement: **14-10**

(a) to decide whether the acts alleged to have been done by the defendant were of such a nature that they fell within the statutory definition of infringement;

(b) to determine who is liable for those acts; and

(c) to decide whether such acts are excused by any statutory exceptions or rules of law, or whether the relief available to the patentee is restricted.

Each of these questions will be considered in turn in subsequent sections of this chapter, and thereafter the position under the various conventions applying to patents will be discussed.

"Infringement" of invalid patent

It has been said that there cannot in any event be an infringement of an invalid patent. Thus Jacob J said in *Organon Teknika v Hoffmann-La Roche*[12]: "in English law validity and infringement are part of the same questions. You cannot infringe an invalid claim, even if you fall within its language". However, the word "infringement" is used in the statutes and has been used in many judgments as meaning "within the scope of the monopoly claimed," and it will be used in this chapter in that sense. **14-11**

---

[11] [1995] R.P.C. 705, 720.

[12] [1996] F.S.R. 383, 386; and see also *Pittevil & Co v Brackelsberg Melting Processes Ltd* (1932) 49 R.P.C. 23.

Infringement of published application

14-12   By s.69 of the 1977 Act, once an application for a patent has been published, the applicant has the same rights to bring proceedings for damages for infringement as if the patent had been granted on the date of publication of the application, in respect of any act which would have infringed. However, they are only entitled to bring such proceedings once the patent has actually been granted, and only if the relevant act would have infringed both the patent as granted and the claims in the application immediately before the Patent Office completed preparations for its publication (s.69(2)). This therefore requires the scope of the claims both as published and as granted to be determined and infringement of both sets of claims to be established.[13] Other limitations contained in s.69 as to relief are discussed in Ch.21 at para.21-79, et seq.

Defendant's knowledge

14-13   A patent has been said to provide an "absolute" monopoly, in the sense that a patent may be infringed regardless of whether or not the defendant copied the invention, or indeed was even aware of the invention or of the patent. Its historic origin as "Letters Patent" (open letters, setting forth the Royal Command) meant that further notice was not required. The expression "absolute monopoly" is therefore used by way of contrast with other forms of intellectual property such as copyright, where copying is an essential element of infringement. The expression is substantially accurate, but contains an element of oversimplification in that the various forms of infringement defined in s.60 of the 1977 Act include some where knowledge is a requirement.

Knowledge or intention ordinarily irrelevant

14-14   With the important exceptions of:

(a)   an offer of a process for use[14];

(b)   claims which are limited by the use or purpose to which the product is to be put (so-called "purpose-limited claims"[15]); and

(c)   contributory or indirect infringement under s.60(2),

it is and always has been the law in relation to infringement that the knowledge or intention of the infringer is irrelevant.

14-15   Thus, there is no duty cast upon a patentee to inform persons that what they were doing amounted to an infringement of their patent. If they knew of the infringement and omitted to give a warning, they were not estopped from subsequently bringing an action. In *Proctor v Bennis*[16] Cotton LJ said:

> "The right of the patentee does not depend on the defendant having notice that what he is doing is an infringement. If what he is doing is in fact an infringement, even although the defendant acts in the way which … was bona fide or honest, he will not be protected from an injunction by that. It does not depend on notice."

---

[13]   See *Unilever v Chefaro* [1994] R.P.C. 567, at 590, et seq.

[14]   See para.14-90.

[15]   Examples are Swiss-type claims, MOBIL-type claims and medical use claims in the EPC 2000 format.

[16]   (1887) 4 R.P.C. 333, 356.

However, the patentee would be denied relief if their conduct amounted to acquiescence.[17]

Exceptions where knowledge is relevant

However, the defendant's knowledge is relevant in the case of infringements involving: (a) an offer of a process for use[18]; (b) purpose-limited claims[19]; and (c) indirect (contributory) infringement under s.60(2).[20]   **14-16**

Innocence may also prevent an award of damages or an order for an account of profits, even where lack of knowledge is irrelevant to a finding of infringement.[21]   **14-17**

Defendant's intention to infringe

Just as a defendant's knowledge of infringement is ordinarily irrelevant, so too is their intention. The situation commonly arises where the defendant had been aware of the existence of the patent when creating their own product and sought to "design around" it, so that their intention was to avoid infringement. The situation is no different in principle from that in which they were unaware of the patent; no presumption will be made either in their favour or against them. Infringement is judged objectively. Thus in *Stead v Anderson*,[22] Wilde CJ said: "We think it clear that the action is maintainable in respect of what the defendant does, not what he intends."[23] In *Palmaz's Patents*[24] Pumfrey J rejected a submission that the alleged infringing devices were in any reasonable sense a copy of the patentee's product, and observed that "whether or not it was designed with an eye to that stent is quite irrelevant to the question of infringement" and "this is not the correct approach to the question 'infringing or not?' which calls for an entirely objective investigation".   **14-18**

Equally, if a person who intended to infringe a patent did not in fact do so, they would not be taken to have infringed.[25] However, proof of an intention to infringe in the future, which did not amount to an actual act of infringement, may justify an injunction to restrain infringement.[26] In *Hoechst Celanese Corporation v B.P. Chemicals*,[27] the defendant contended that if its process had fallen within the parameters at all, these were only short-term unintended fluctuations which did not satisfy the claim's requirement that the parameters be "maintained", and were de minimis. Jacob J observed that this argument, if correct, could introduce the subjective question of the level at which an infringer intended to operate, which could not be a relevant matter.   **14-19**

Intention in the case of the infringement of "purpose-limited" claims

Purpose-limited claims arise in several contexts. First, in respect of claims which are for the use of old products for a new use—sometimes referred to as *MOBIL-*   **14-20**

---

17 (1887) 4 R.P.C. 333, 356.
18 PA 1977 s.60(1)(b); see para.14-90.
19 See para.14-20.
20 See para.14-94.
21 PA 1977 s.62(1) and see para.19-166, et seq.
22 (1847) 2 W.P.C. 151, 156.
23 See also *Wright v Hitchcock* (1870) L.R. 5 Ex. 37, at 47; *Young v Rosenthal* (1884) 1 R.P.C. 29, at 39.
24 [1999] R.P.C. 47, 78 and 92. See also *Haberman v Jackel* [1999] F.S.R. 683, at 706.
25 *Newall v Elliott* (1864) 10 Jur. (N.S.) 954, 958.
26 See paras 14-67, 19.86 and para.21-15, et seq.
27 [1998] F.S.R. 586, 597.

type claims following the decision of the EPO in *MOBIL/Friction reducing additive* (G02/88).[28] Secondly, in respect of Swiss-type claims where the claim is for the use of a product in the manufacture of a medicament *for* a particular therapeutic use. Thirdly, in respect of claims in EPC 2000 format (the successor to Swiss-type claims) where the claim is to a product *for* a particular therapeutic use (such as "substance X *for use in* the treatment of Y").

14-21 Each of these claim types is alike in that their novelty resides not in the product per se but in the new use or purpose for that product. The recognition that an old product can have a new and inventive application is the technical contribution of these claims and leads to the conclusion that it would exceed that technical contribution if the word *for* in such claims was read in the sense of merely *suitable for*. After all, the old substance was always "suitable" for the new use, it is just that no-one had recognised the benefits of the new use. For this reason, in determining infringement, regard has to be had to the purpose or intent with which the infringer is putting the old product onto the market.

14-22 Lord Hoffmann, with whom the other four members of the House of Lords agreed, pointed out in *Merrell Dow v H.N. Norton*[29] that since liability is absolute, and the alleged infringer's state of mind is irrelevant, there are difficulties in applying the law of infringement to claims of the kind allowed by the EPO's Enlarged Board of Appeal in *MOBIL/Friction reducing additive*,[30] i.e. those for the use of a known substance in a known way for a new purpose. He did not, however, need on the facts of that case to decide how the principle of absolute liability was to be applied in a case where the only novel aspect of a claim lay in the purpose for which the product was used.[31]

14-23 Given the length of time that *MOBIL*-type and Swiss-type claims have been granted, it is perhaps surprising that it was not until the decisions in *Warner-Lambert v Actavis*[32] that the issue of the requisite intent was subjected to close judicial scrutiny.[33]

14-24 In summary, for the reasons given in Section 9 above, purpose-limited claims are infringed where the defendant knows, or it is obvious to a reasonable person in the circumstances, that the product in question will intentionally be put to the claimed use. The subsidiary questions of the time when such intention must be held and the persons who must have such intent are addressed at paras 9-282 and 9-283.

---

[28] EPO Enlarged Board of Appeal decision G02/88 [1990] E.P.O.R. 73.
[29] [1996] R.P.C. 76, 92.
[30] EPO Enlarged Board of Appeal decision (G02/88) [1990] E.P.O.R. 73.
[31] See the discussion in Ch.9 above at para.9–275.
[32] See *Warner-Lambert v Actavis Warner-Lambert Company, LLC v Actavis Group Ptc EHF* [2015] EWHC 72 (Pat) (21 January 2015); *Warner-Lambert Company, LLC v Actavis Group PTC EHF* [2015] EWHC 223 (Pat) (6 February 2015); *Warner- Lambert Company LLC v Actavis Group PTC EHF* [2015] EWHC 249 (Pat) (6 February 2015); *Warner-Lambert Company, LLC v Actavis Group PTC EHF* [2015] EWHC 485 (Pat) (2 March 2015); *Warner-Lambert Company, LLC v Actavis Group Ptc EHF* [2015] EWCA Civ 556 (28 May 2015); *Generics (UK) Ltd (t/a Mylan) v Warner-Lambert Company LLC* [2015] EWHC 2548 (Pat) (10 September 2015).
[33] The problems of making intention a relevant issue on infringement had previously been considered obiter, by Jacob J in *Bristol Myers Squibb* [1999] R.P.C. 253, at 271–273 in the context of Swiss-type claims.

Damage

Damage is not, and has never been, an essential of the cause of action. In *SmithKline Corp v DDSA Pharmaceuticals*[34] Buckley LJ said: **14-25**

"So it seems to me ... that it is not incumbent to show that he has suffered commercial loss. It is an infringement if his monopoly has been infringed, and he is entitled to a remedy."

The existence of a cause of action irrespective of the right to claim damages is demonstrated by the case of *SmithKline Beecham v Apotex Europe Limited*[35] per Aldous LJ (at [18]) (emphasis added): **14-26**

"Care must be taken before extrapolating the views expressed in the *Polaroid* and *Peaudouce* cases into a rule of law or practice applicable to other cases. The facts in those cases were not typical and questions of recoverability of damages could have been crucial. However it must be remembered that the grant of an interlocutory injunction is a discretionary remedy that should be available to prevent injustice. It would be unusual to grant an interlocutory injunction to protect a property right if no damages for infringement could be recovered. But if the claimant has a cause of action to protect a property right recognised by the law, there is no reason in principle why the court should not grant an interlocutory injunction to protect that right, even if damages are not recoverable".

See also per Carnwarth LJ (at [43]): **14-27**

"Aldous LJ has also quoted from Lord Diplock's classic statement in *American Cyanamid Co v Ethicon Ltd* [1975] A.C. 396, 406, where he said:

'The object of the interlocutory injunction is to protect the plaintiff against injury by violation of his right for which he would not be adequately compensated in damages recoverable in the action if the uncertainty were resolved in his favour at the trial ...'

The purpose of an interlocutory injunction therefore is protection, not just against 'loss which would sound in damages', but against violation of any right where damages would not be adequate compensation. An obvious example of the need for that wider formulation is the case of trespass to land. A landowner whose title is not disputed is normally entitled to an injunction to restrain trespass on his land, even if the trespass does not harm him (see *Patel v W.H. Smith (Eziot) Ltd* [1987] 1 W.L.R. 853, 858F). With great respect to Robert Walker J, therefore, I think that the passage in *Peaudouce* may be too narrowly stated. I also think he would have been surprised by the use sought to be made of it by Mr Watson".

Of course, even once liability has been established, the nature of the remedy may depend upon the nature of the loss sustained; see generally Ch.19. **14-28**

Onus of proof

The onus of proving infringement lies in general on the claimant, as with any other cause of action. It is up to them to produce sufficient evidence to establish infringement on the balance of probabilities.[36] There is a statutory exception in the case of processes for producing new products, discussed further at para.14-33. While the onus initially lies on the patentee to prove infringement, if they are able to make out a prima facie case that there has been, the onus may thereafter shift to the defendant to answer such case. **14-29**

In general, the evidential onus of proving infringement lies on the patentee even where relevant manufacturing steps had taken place abroad; this is and always has **14-30**

---

34 [1978] F.S.R. 109, 114.
35 [2003] EWCA Civ 137.
36 *ICI plc v Montedison* [1995] R.P.C. 449.

been the law. In *Cartsburn Sugar Refining Co v Sharp*, Lord Kinnear said[37]:

> "No witness has been examined of sufficient skill as a mechanic to give a detailed description of the machine in question. All that is proved is that it does not correspond in all respects, though in some respects it does correspond, to the description in *Hersey's* Patent. It is said that as the manufacture complained of had taken place in America, it was incumbent on the respondents, upon the principle which received effect in the case of *Neilson v Betts*,[38] to prove by negative evidence that it was not manufactured according to the specified process. I think no such onus lies upon the respondents in the present case, because there can be no question on the evidence that such articles as were sold by the respondents may have been produced by machinery which involved no infringement of the complainers' patent. That being so, it lay upon the complainers to prove their case, and as they took a commission to America for the purpose of proving it, there could have been no difficulty in their obtaining a sufficient description of the machine to which it is alleged they have traced the cubes of sugar sold by the respondents to enable them to establish the infringement, if infringement there was."

14-31   But where the articles were made abroad and the plaintiffs in consequence could not be afforded full opportunity of inspecting the machinery by which they were made, it was held that it lay with the defendants to rebut a prima facie case made out by the plaintiffs.[39] In the various "Saccharin" cases,[40] the plaintiffs were the owners of patents which covered all known processes of making saccharin. They were able to produce evidence to the effect that although it was conceivable that saccharin might be made in some other way, no other processes were then known to the scientific world. The defendants, who imported saccharin, could not give any satisfactory account of the way in which the imported substance was actually made. It was held that infringement had been established.

14-32   The Act does not impose any duty on a defendant to keep records to establish non-infringement, although adverse inferences might be drawn if relevant material had actually been disposed of.[41]

Onus in case of process for obtaining new product

14-33   By s.100(1) of the 1977 Act, if the invention is a process for obtaining a new product, the same product produced by a person other than the proprietor of the patent, or a licensee of theirs, shall, unless the contrary is proved, be taken in any proceedings to have been obtained by that process. Thus, the onus is in this case shifted to the defendant. It is, however, provided that in considering whether a party has discharged the burden imposed on them, the court shall not require him to disclose any manufacturing or commercial secrets if it appears to the court that it would be unreasonable to do so.[42] It is anticipated that in most cases the court will order limited disclosure as has been done in the past.[43]

---

37   (1884) 1 R.P.C. 181, 186.

38   (1871) L.R. 5 H.L. 1.

39   *Saccharin Corp v Dawson* (1902) 19 R.P.C. 169; *Saccharin Corp v Jackson* (1903) 20 R.P.C. 611; *Saccharin Corp v Mank & Co* (1906) 23 R.P.C. 25; *Saccharin Corp Ltd v National Saccharin Co Ltd* (1909) 26 R.P.C. 654; and *see British Thomson-Houston Co v Charlesworth, Peebles & Co* (1923) 40 R.P.C. 426, at 456.

40   *Saccharin Corp v Dawson* (1902) 19 R.P.C. 169; *Saccharin Corp v Jackson* (1903) 20 R.P.C. 611; *Saccharin Corp v Mank & Co* (1906) 23 R.P.C. 25; *Saccharin Corp Ltd v National Saccharin Co Ltd* (1909) 26 R.P.C. 654.

41   *Hoechst Celanese v B.P. Chemicals* [1998] F.S.R. 586.

42   PA 1977 s.100(2).

43   See, e.g. *Warner-Lambert v Glaxo* [1975] R.P.C. 354; *Centri-spray Corp v Cera International Ltd* [1979] F.S.R. 175; *Roussel Uclaf v ICI* [1990] R.P.C. 45, CA, affirming [1989] R.P.C. 59.

In *Generics v Lundbeck*[44] the interpretation of s.100 was described as difficult (per   **14-34**
Jacob LJ at [8]). In *Crystal Fibres v Fianum*[45] it was described as difficult to
construe and apparently quite narrow (per Floyd J as he then was, at [24]).
However, neither case had to address the actual meaning of the section.

The "new product" in the context of s.100 was considered by Birss J in   **14-35**
Magnesium Elektron Limited v Molycorp Chemicals & Oxides (Europe) Limited.[46]
The issue was whether there was a sufficiently arguable case to give permission to
serve proceedings out of the jurisdiction in China. Birss J held that it is the product
made by the claimed process which must be novel, not that the product per se needs
be novel—for if a patent disclosed a novel product per se then a product claim
would have been available in addition to the process claim. In the case of a claim
to a process for making "zirconium-cerium-based mixed oxides" it was not required
that zirconium-cerium-based mixed oxides were novel per se. Hence Birss J held
that:

"... There is nothing in the section which requires that the product which must be a new product is
a thing defined in the same level of generality as the words used in the process claim. This case illustrates the difference. The claimant says the preliminary results establish that products made by the
patented process have a particular fingerprint which is unique to that process. The fact that products
with that fingerprint are produced by that process and no other process known to [*the witness*] is what
the claimant contends means that the patented process satisfies s.100. The products produced by that
process are novel. They have not been made available to the public before. The fact that the patent
does not assert that products made that way have a unique fingerprint does not matter. In my judgment that is the right way to approach the section ... The [*allegedly infringing product*] is the same
product as the new product produced by the process because (says the claimant) it has the same
characteristics which make the product new. It is not the same product because it consists of
zirconium-cerium-based mixed oxides, it is the same product because it has the same fingerprint. That
fingerprint is what makes the products obtained by the process new."[47]

Proof in the case of ambiguous claim

As already noted in the chapter dealing with construction,[48] it is possible that the   **14-36**
court may decline to find for a patentee on the basis that the claim is so ambiguous
that infringement has not been or cannot be proved, and the patentee has thus failed
to discharge the onus of proving it. In *Procter & Gamble v Peaudouce*,[49] a decision involving a patent granted under the Patents Act 1949, Fox LJ held that "A
claim must be sufficient and clear so as to define the monopoly upon which there
can be no intrusion. If there is no clarity, intrusion cannot arise. It is fundamental
to the law that a producer of a product must know where he cannot intrude." Jacob
J indicated obiter in *Milliken Denmark A/S v Walk Off Mats*[50] that this would also
appear to be correct when construing a claim under the 1977 Act and this comment was approved by Aldous LJ in *Scanvaegt v Pelcombe*,[51] where he said:

---

44 [2006] EWCA Civ 1261.
45 [2009] EWHC 2149 (Pat).
46 [2013] EWHC 3596 (Pat).
47 [2015] EWHC 3596, [31]–[32].
48 See para.9-257.
49 [1989] F.S.R. 180, 198.
50 [1996] F.S.R. 292.
51 [1998] F.S.R. 786, 797.

"I believe that Jacob J is right and that despite the fact that lack of clarity is no longer a matter that results in a patent being invalid, it can result in the patentee being unable to establish infringement. If you cannot define the invention claimed, you cannot conclude that it is being used."

Infringement de minimis

14-37   As with any other tort, the court may be prepared to disregard as de minimis an act which amounts to infringement only in a trifling respect. However, in *Hoechst Celanese v B.P. Chemicals*[52] (a case where the claim expressly required certain process conditions to be "maintained") Jacob J noted that while the patentee may not be interested in truly transient "spikes", there could be no reason why they should not be interested in catching significant commercial production; in that case a single day's production amounted to some 400 tonnes of product. *In Monsanto Technology LLC v Cargill International SA*[53] Pumfrey J said "There is, generally, no authority in favour of trace quantities of infringing material being held not to infringe, and some authority against it". It is submitted that the authority mentioned by Pumfrey J is likely to have been *Hoechst Celanese*.

14-38   In *Warner-Lambert v Actavis*[54] Arnold J held that since only a small proportion of pharmacists knew that the generic product was being dispensed for pain (the indication the subject of the claim) this was de mimimis and hence non-infringing.

14-39   In *Stretchline Intellectual Properties v H&M Hennes & Mauritz Limited*[55] levels of about 5–6.6 per cent of fusible yarn (figures found to be present in the alleged infringements despite the much lower figures given in the PPDs) were close to, or within, the preferred range specified in the description and this fact defeated any argument that the percentage of fusible yarn in the alleged infringements was de minimis.

14-40   For the issue of whether a contribution is de minimis in the context of joint tortfeasance, see para.14-156.

3. NATURE OF THE INFRINGING ACT

Jurisdiction

14-41   Section 60 of the 1977 Act makes it clear that infringement only occurs if a person does an act "within the United Kingdom" without the consent of the proprietor.[56]

14-42   Section 132(2)–(3) provides that references to the UK shall be construed as including references to the Isle of Man and that the territorial waters shall be treated as part of the UK. However, s.132(4) of the 1977 Act also applies to acts done in an area designated by order under s.1(7) of the Continental Shelf Act 1964 or specified by order under s.10(8) of the Petroleum Act 1998 in connection with any activity falling within s.11(2) of that Act, as it applies to acts done in the UK. The effect of s.132(4) is to bring the off-shore oil and gas industry within the compass of the 1977 Act, particularly in the UK sector of the North Sea.

---

52 [1998] F.S.R. 586, 598.
53 [2008] F.S.R. 7.
54 [2015] EWHC 2548 (Pat), [671], [673] and [676].
55 [2015] EWHC 3298, [82].
56 See also *Plastus Kreativ v Minnesota Mining and Manufacturing* [1995] R.P.C. 438, 442.

Direct and indirect infringement

The ambit of infringement is defined by s.60 of the 1977 Act and in so far as any **14-43** difficulties in construction arise reference is to be had to s.130(7).[57] Acts which (subject to the other provisions of s.60) constitute infringing acts are set out in ss.60(1) and (2). Subsection (1) applies to acts done in relation to patented products or processes; these are generally referred to as "direct" infringement. In contrast, subs.(2) applies to acts which do not directly involve patented products or processes but which nonetheless constitute infringement and are thus indirect infringing acts.

Product and process inventions

Section 60 distinguishes between two possible cases, namely where the inven- **14-44** tion is a product and where the invention is a process. The section thus draws a clear dividing line between product and process inventions. This distinction was not always recognised and under the old law products of a patented machine had been held to be infringements of a patent for that machine.[58] This is no longer the law.

The "invention" is defined in s.125(1) as that specified in a claim and so the **14-45** expression "where the invention is a product" means no more than where the allegedly infringed claim is a product claim. It is submitted that the expression "where the invention is a product" is not a reference to a patented product as defined in s.130(1) of the 1977 Act, namely "a product which is a patented invention or, in relation to a patented process, a product obtained directly by means of the process or to which the process has been applied". This would have the effect of making all products obtained directly by means of a patented process "products" within the meaning of s.60(1)(a) and hence s.60(1)(c) would become otiose.[59]

Direct infringement where the invention is a product

Where the invention is a product, s.60(1)(a) provides that the patent will be **14-46** infringed by any person who:

(a) makes,
(b) disposes of,
(c) offers to dispose of,
(d) uses,
(e) imports the product, or
(f) keeps it whether for disposal or otherwise.

(a) Makes

No difficulty should arise with the word "makes" as it is an ordinary English word **14-47** with wide meaning; it also formed part of the old Royal Command in the grant of Letters Patent and thus the law developed under the 1949 Act and earlier statutes will continue to give guidance.

Making and selling all of the constituent parts of a machine as a collection or kit **14-48** so that they may easily be put together might amount to direct infringement under

[57] See para.2-04.
[58] See, e.g. *Townsend v Haworth* 12 Ch D. 831; *United Horse Shoe v Stewart* (1885) 2 R.P.C. 122; *Wilderman v E.W. Berk & Co Ltd* (1925) 42 R.P.C. 79.
[59] See also "where the invention is a process", at para.14-73.

this head, such a kit amounting in substance to the complete article.[60] Laddie J expressed doubts in *Lacroix Duarib v Kwikform*,[61] a strike-out case, as to whether this was the correct approach under s.60 where the kit was to be exported in unassembled form so that there was no making of the claimed invention (a complete structure) within the UK but allowed the action to proceed.

14-49   Whether there can be infringement under s.60(1)(a) by selling a "kit of parts" was considered by Arnold J in *Virgin Atlantic Airways v Delta*.[62] This was a summary judgment application which turned, inter alia, on the questions of: (i) whether claim 1 of the patent was properly construed as being limited to a passenger seating system assembled and arranged "on an aircraft"; and (ii) even if claim 1 was so construed, whether it was arguable that it had been infringed by the making, offering to dispose of and disposing of a "kit of parts" in the UK.

14-50   Arnold J set out the preceding domestic case law on kits of parts (*Rotocrop* (see below) and *Lacroix* (see above))[63] as well as foreign case law from Australia, Canada, France, Germany and the Netherlands.[64] In his subsequent analysis of the law, he took as his starting point Laddie J's observation in *Lacroix* that s.60(1) and (2) are based on an international agreement as to what acts shall constitute infringement of a patent and that case law and commentaries based on or derived from earlier provisions, whether in England or in other countries, may be misleading. He first considered cases where there is no extra-territorial dimension, explaining that in such cases there is no need for a doctrine of infringement under s.60(1)(a) by dealings in a kit of parts since if a defendant supplies or offers to supply a complete kit of parts for assembly into a product falling within a product claim then there will almost inevitably be infringement pursuant to s.60(2). The same will be true if a defendant supplies or offers to supply an incomplete kit of parts which includes all the main elements of the claimed product, the customer obtaining or providing the missing part. The defendant may also be liable as a joint tortfeasor if they also provide instructions for assembly of the kit, as in the *Rotocrop* case. Despite this he accepted that it was arguable that there could be infringement under s.60(1)(a) in supplying a kit of parts for assembly in the UK.

14-51   When it came to cases with an extra-territorial dimension he divided his analysis into those in which the kit provided is complete and those in which it was not. In the case of the former, he regarded it as arguable that dealing in a complete kit of parts in the UK, for assembly outside the UK, constituted an infringement, despite the fact that infringement under s.60(2) requires it to be intended that the invention be put into effect in the UK. In contrast he held that it is not an infringement to deal in a kit of parts in the UK where the defendant's customer obtains or provides the missing part and where assembly takes place outside the jurisdiction. In such cases the defendant has not dealt in the claimed product in the UK even in disassembled form.

14-52   Accordingly, provided that the "kit of parts" is of a complete unit once assembled, it was at least arguable that such a kit infringes a claim to the assembled

---

[60]   See *United Telephone Co v Dale* (1884) 25 Ch D. 778, at 782; *Dunlop Pneumatic Tyre Co Ltd v David Moseley & Sons Ltd* (1904) 21 R.P.C. 274, at 280; and cf. *Cincinnati Grinders (Inc) v BSA Tools Ltd* (1931) 48 R.P.C. 33, at 46–48, 58 and 76; *Rotocrop International Ltd v Genbourne Ltd* [1982] F.S.R. 241, at 259.

[61]   [1998] F.S.R. 493.

[62]   [2010] EWHC 3094; [2011] R.P.C. 8.

[63]   See [88]–[109].

[64]   See [2010] EWHC 3094, at [110]–[126].

unit under s.60(1)(a). However, since the defendant's kit was capable of being arranged differently to the system claimed, a declaration of non-infringement was granted summarily.

On appeal[65] the proposition that, as a matter of law, it was arguable that **14-53** manufacture in the UK of a complete kit of parts for assembling into a patented device could infringe a patent was not challenged. Furthermore, Jacob LJ (with whom Patten LJ and Smith LJ agreed) held that the patentee was correct on the point of construction: the claim was not limited to a unit that was fitted into an aircraft. It covered a system capable of being so fitted (as the defendant's was). Accordingly the declaration of non-infringement was discharged. However, Jacob LJ did not go on to consider the challenge to the judge's conclusion that an incomplete kit of parts subsequently exported did not infringe, on the basis that the position across Europe is not well settled, there is room for development of the law and the question could be highly fact sensitive and was not suitable for determination on a summary judgment application.

(b) Disposes of

In its widest meaning the word "disposes" (which was not used in earlier statutes **14-54** or in the Royal Command) would prima facie cover any loss of physical possession including destruction. The CPC, however, does not use the word "dispose" but instead uses the more specific expression "putting on the market". "Dispose" therefore has a more limited meaning covering only loss of physical possession by transferring that possession to another in the course of trade (e.g. by way of sale). This will, it appears, extend also to lending[66] but delivery to or by a mere warehouseman or carrier will not amount to disposal in this sense.[67]

In the case of goods manufactured abroad, the goods themselves had to come into **14-55** this country to constitute infringement under the old law and the same is now required by s.60. In *Badische Anilin und Soda Fabrik v Johnson and the Basle Chemical Works*,[68] a trader in England ordered goods from the defendant in Switzerland to be sent by post to England. The defendant addressed the goods to the trader in England and delivered them to the Swiss Post Office, by whom they were forwarded to England. The goods were manufactured according to an invention protected by the plaintiff's patent. It was held by the House of Lords that, since the contract of sale was completed by the delivery to the Post Office in Switzerland, and since the Post Office was the agent of the buyer and not of the vendor, the vendor had not made, used, exercised or vended the invention within the ambit of the patent, and that the patentee had no right of action against the vendor for an infringement of the patent.[69] Similarly, in *Badische Anilin und Soda Fabrik v Hickson*,[70] it was argued on behalf of the plaintiff that, as the vendor had set aside the goods in the foreign country, the property in them had passed and there was a complete sale. Lord Loreburn said that although there was appropriation to the

---

[65] [2011] EWCA Civ 162. See in particular [10].
[66] Under the old law, lending was not an infringement—see *United Telephone Co Ltd v Henry & Co* (1885) 2 R.P.C. 11.
[67] See *Smith, Kline & French Laboratories Ltd v R.D. Harbottle (Mercantile) Ltd* [1980] R.P.C. 363; *Kalman v PCL Packaging (UK)* [1982] F.S.R. 406.
[68] (1897) 14 R.P.C. 919.
[69] See also *Morton Norwich Products Inc v Intercen Ltd* [1978] R.P.C. 501, at 516; *Saccharin Corp Ltd v Reitmeyer* (1900) 17 R.P.C. 606.
[70] (1906) 23 R.P.C. 433.

purchaser and a completed sale, the operation of completing the sale had not taken place in this country, and consequently there had been no infringement. More recently, in *Sabaf SpA v MFI Furniture Centres Ltd*[71] the Italian manufacturer who sold the goods in Italy to a British purchaser so that property passed in Italy was not liable as a primary infringer.

14-56 However, although in the circumstances of a given case the vendor may not be liable as a primary infringer they might instead be liable for the subsequent acts of infringement of the recipient of the goods as a joint tortfeasor, if they acted in concert with the recipient pursuant to a common intention that there be further dealing in the goods within the jurisdiction.[72]

14-57 While the word "disposes" would also seem appropriate to cover exporting the goods in question, it is not so clear whether an act of export would be "putting on the market" within the jurisdiction. But in any event, an act of export would ordinarily be preceded by other infringing acts including keeping "for disposal or otherwise".[73]

(c) Offers to dispose of

14-58 This expression is apt to cover in particular an offer for sale but is not so limited. In *Gerber v Lectra*,[74] the defendant contended that it excluded those activities such as pre-contractual negotiations or advertising which in contract law would be regarded as mere "invitations to treat" rather than offers capable of acceptance so as to create a binding contract. Jacob J rejected this submission as being unduly legalistic and not consistent with the provisions of art.25 of the CPC, which refers to "putting on the market". He preferred the plaintiff's contention that the matter should be viewed as one of commercial substance, and stated the law as follows:

> "I think the approach to construction of section 60 (and the CPC) should be purposive. A party who approaches potential customers individually or by advertisement saying he is willing to supply a machine, terms to be agreed, is offering it or putting it on the market. If that is to happen during the life of the patent he infringes.
>
> He is disturbing the patentee's monopoly which he ought not to do. So I think the early advertisements were infringements, not mere threats.
>
> The position is not the same in relation to the near-expiry negotiations. I see no reason to regard an 'offer' to supply purely post-expiry as an infringement in itself, even if made during subsistence. It is not a disturbance of the monopoly. I can, for instance, see no reason why a trader should not say 'X's product is coming off patent at the end of the year. I will take orders now for supply next year.' That is not 'offering a product which is the subject-matter of the patent.' The product offered is off patent. If such an activity causes X's customers not to buy but to wait until next year then X will not like it, but I can see no interference with his monopoly. Even if it causes him to reduce his prices he cannot complain—the cause has been an indication of a willingness to conduct a non-infringing activity, just like an offer of a competing non-infringing product during the life of the patent. So the position is quite different from an advertisement early in the life of the patent indicating a willingness to supply an infringing product in breach of the monopoly."

14-59 In any event an advertisement will also ordinarily amount to a threat to dispose of the products being advertised, and thus injunctive relief may be obtained on a

---

[71] [2005] R.P.C. 10, 209.

[72] See para.14-64, et seq.

[73] *Smith, Kline & French Laboratories Ltd's (Cimetidine) Patents* [1990] R.P.C. 203, 225–226 (Falconer J). See also *American Cyanamid Co's (Fenbufen) Patent* [1990] R.P.C. 309, 328; [1991] R.P.C. 409. *Research Corporation's (Carboplatin) Patent* [1990] R.P.C. 663, 702. Compare (under the old law) *SmithKline Corp v DDSA Pharmaceuticals Ltd* [1978] F.S.R. 109.

[74] [1995] R.P.C. 383, 411.

quia timet basis whether or not a completed act of infringement has taken place. The offer must be an offer within the jurisdiction to dispose of infringing products within the jurisdiction.[75]

(d) Uses

The word "use" takes its ordinary meaning, and no further limitation is required by reason of art.25 of the CPC. The word would, however, seem to indicate making practical use of the invention itself, rather than simply handling for commercial purposes (e.g. stocking and supplying), as the latter acts are separately covered in the subsection. Subject to that reservation, it may be noted that the word "use" was included in the old Royal Command and the law as developed thereunder will continue to provide guidance.

14-60

In the case of *Neilson v Betts*,[76] the facts were as follows: Betts (the plaintiff) was the patentee of an invention for the manufacture of capsules for the purpose of covering bottles of liquid and protecting the contents from the action of the atmosphere. The patent did not extend to Scotland. The defendants bottled beer in Glasgow for the Indian market and covered it with capsules, which were apparently made in Germany in accordance with Betts' specification. The beer was shipped in vessels which called at Liverpool to complete their cargoes; on some occasions the beer was transhipped in England, but no cases of beer were opened, nor was any of the beer sold in this country. It was held by the House of Lords (affirming the judgments in the courts below) that as the object of Betts' invention was to make a capsule that would preserve beer, whilst the beer was in England it was being preserved by the use of Betts' invention, and consequently that there was an infringement of the patent. Lord Chelmsford, in giving judgment in the court below, said[77]:

14-61

> "It is the employment of the machine or article for the purpose for which it was designed which constitutes its active use, and whether the capsules were intended for ornament, or for protection of the contents of the bottles upon which they were placed, the whole time they were in England they may be correctly said to be in active use for the very objects for which they were placed upon the bottles by the vendors. If the beer, after being purchased in Glasgow, had been sent to England, and had been afterwards sold here, there can be no doubt, I suppose, that this would have been an infringement, because it would have been a profitable user of the invention, and I cannot see how it can cease to be a user because England is not the final destination of the beer."[78]

In the case of *Adair v Young*,[79] certain pumps, which were an infringement of the plaintiff's patent, were fitted on board a British ship. There was no evidence of their having been used. It was held by the Court of Appeal that there had been no infringement, but as there was evidence of an intention to use the pumps, an injunction was granted against the use of the pumps.

14-62

---

[75] *Kalman v PCL Packaging (UK)* [1982] F.S.R. 406, 417–418.
[76] (1871) L.R. 5 H.L. 1.
[77] L.R. 3 Ch. App. 429, 439.
[78] See also *Nobel's Explosives Co v Jones, Scott & Co* (1881) 17 Ch.D. 721; *Universities of Oxford and Cambridge v Richardson* 6 Ves. 689; *Dunlop Pneumatic Tyre Co Ltd v British and Colonial Motor Car Co Ltd* (1901) 18 R.P.C. 313; *Hoffmann-La Roche & Co A.G. v Harris Pharmaceuticals Ltd* [1977] F.S.R. 200; *Morton Norwich Products Inc v Intercen Ltd* [1978] R.P.C. 501; *SmithKline Corp v DDSA Pharmaceuticals Ltd* [1978] F.S.R. 109.
[79] (1879) 12 Ch D. 13.

14-63   In *Research Corporation's Supplementary Protection Certificate (No.2)*,[80] it was (not surprisingly) held that "use" of a patented substance (there, the drug carboplatin) included its formulation into a medicinal product.

14-64   The section is directed to use of the patented product itself, so that an application to regulatory authorities to sell a product in the UK, even though accompanied by data relating to the patented product, is not "use" of the product in the UK.[81] (Although the position will of course be different if samples are supplied.[82]). Similarly, under the old law, taking out a patent for a process or machine that infringed a prior patent did not amount to infringement,[83] nor did the granting of a licence to manufacture under a subsequent patent constitute infringement.[84] Each of these cases involved merely use of information about the patented invention but not use of the invention itself.

(e) Imports

14-65   Section 60(1) of the 1977 Act on its face appears to prohibit importation for any purpose; but it is to be interpreted consistently with art.25 of the CPC which refers to "making, offering, putting on the market or using a product which is the subject-matter of the patent, or importing or stocking the product for these purposes". The purpose for which the importation takes place may therefore be material, although a commercial purpose can ordinarily be inferred.

14-66   Importation by way of trade of patented goods, or goods made abroad by a patented process was an act of infringement under the old law, and it is submitted that the authorities decided thereunder will continue to apply. It was decided in *Pfizer Corporation v Ministry of Health*, as stated by Lord Upjohn:

> "[T]hat where an importer imports into this country articles made abroad, but in accordance with a British patent, for the purpose of distributing and selling them in this country, he quite plainly is using and exercising the patent, and he thereby infringes the patent the moment he introduces them into this country."[85]

14-67   As noted at para.14-55, the goods themselves had to come into this country to constitute infringement. A contract of sale concluded abroad but providing for delivery in the UK would almost certainly be actionable on a quia timet basis as constituting a threat to import.

14-68   Questions will often arise as to who, on the facts of any given case, is the importer. In *Sabaf SpA v MFI Furniture Centres Ltd*.[86] Lord Hoffmann made it plain that the person who contracts with the carrier is not necessarily the importer: the importer is to be determined as a question of law, usually by reference to the possession of title to the goods. In *Fabio Perini v PCMC*[87] it was held (obiter) that despite title passing in England, as a matter of commercial reality the supply was

---

[80] [1996] R.P.C. 320, 327–328.

[81] *Upjohn v Kerfoot* [1988] F.S.R. 1, 7; compare *Smith, Kline & French Laboratories Ltd v Douglas* [1991] F.S.R. 522.

[82] See *Generics v Smith, Kline & French Laboratories Ltd* [1997] R.P.C. 801.

[83] *Tweedale v Ashworth* (1890) 7 R.P.C. 426, 431.

[84] *Montgomery v Paterson* (1894) 11 R.P.C. 221, 663.

[85] [1965] R.P.C. 261. And see *Beecham Group Ltd v Bristol Laboratories Ltd* [1978] R.P.C. 153, at 199 where Lord Diplock said that the doctrine was well established by the date of *Von Heyden v Neustadt* (1880) 14 Ch D. 230.

[86] [2005] R.P.C. 10, 209, [34]–[45].

[87] [2012] EWHC 911 (Ch); [2012] R.P.C. 30.

in Italy when the goods were delivered unconditionally ex works. The decision in *Sabaf* did not preclude that finding. *Sabaf* decided that the foreign vendor could not be the importer after title had passed: it did not hold that the foreign vendor must be the importer if title had not passed.

(f) Keeps ... whether for disposal or otherwise

While the term "keeping, whether for disposal or otherwise" prima facie extends to all forms of keeping including warehousemen and carriers, it is to be construed consistently with the terms of the CPC which in art.25 refers to "stocking" for the other commercial purposes there enumerated.

14-69

The question arose in *Smith, Kline & French Laboratories Ltd v R.D. Harbottle (Mercantile) Ltd*[88] where British Airways were alleged to have infringed the plaintiff's patent by keeping a product covered by that patent in their capacity as warehousemen. Oliver J held that having regard to s.130(7) of the 1977 Act and the words of the CPC, the word "keeping" did not extend to the activities of mere warehousemen and carriers such as British Airways.[89] He favoured construing the term in the sense of "keeping in stock", although as this was an interlocutory application he expressly declined to arrive at a definitive interpretation.

14-70

This approach was followed by the Court of Appeal in *McDonald v Graham*,[90] where Ralph Gibson LJ held the defendant was keeping the infringing products "in the sense of keeping them in stock for the purposes of his business in order to make use of them as and when it would be beneficial for him to do so".

14-71

Under the old law, once goods had been imported, mere purchase, ownership, possession, or transport did not amount to infringement although an injunction could be justified on the ground that it was strong evidence of a threat to use. On the other hand, where such purchase, ownership, possession or transport involved use of the invention, there was infringement.[91] In *SmithKline Corp v DDSA Pharmaceuticals Ltd*[92] the defendants imported infringing goods into this country for the purpose of re-exporting the same to Nigeria. Buckley LJ said[93]:

14-72

"It seems to me that in the light of these authorities, Whitford J was fully justified in saying, as he did in the course of his judgment in the *Hoffmann-La Roche* case[94] at page 207:

'I entirely agree with the views which have been expressed that possession with the intention of using the articles for trade purposes and for the securing of a profit amounts to an infringement: whether the dealing which you are proposing to carry on is a dealing with a customer in this country or with an export customer.'"

---

88 [1980] R.P.C. 363.
89 [1980] R.P.C. 363, 371–374; see also *Nobel's Explosives v Jones, Scott & Co* (1881) 17 Ch D. 721.
90 [1994] R.P.C. 407, 431.
91 *Moet v Pickering* [1878] 8 Ch D. 372; *Adair v Young* (1879) 12 Ch D. 13; *Pressers, etc., Ltd v Newell & Co* (1914) 31 R.P.C. 51 (disapproving *United Telephone Co v London Globe, etc., Co* (1909) 26 Ch D. 766); *British Motor Syndicate v John Taylor & Sons Ltd* (1900) 17 R.P.C. 723; *British United Shoe Machinery Co v Simon Collier Ltd* (1909) 26 R.P.C. 21, 534 and (1910) 27 R.P.C. 567; *Non-Drip Measure Co Ltd v Strangers Ltd* (1942) 59 R.P.C. 1; and see the passage from *Neilson v Betts* (1871) L.R. 5 H.L. 1 set out at para.14-161.
92 [1978] F.S.R. 109.
93 [1978] F.S.R. 109, 113.
94 [1977] F.S.R. 200.

Direct infringement where the invention is a process

Use of a process

14-73   By s.60(1)(b) of the 1977 Act, regardless of knowledge, a person who uses a patented process in the UK without the consent of the proprietor infringes that patent.

14-74   In *Union Carbide v B.P. Chemicals*[95] Jacob J refused to permit the patentees to add as a new cause of action an allegation that by reason of its acts of infringement the defendant had developed a process of its own which it had been able to license abroad and thereby unjustly enrich itself. The allegation that it was offering abroad a process that had been derived from infringement was not within s.60(1)(b) and was therefore not of itself actionable. As discussed above[96] in relation to using a patented product, the complaint was in reality about use of data or information about the process, rather than use of the process itself.

14-75   In *Fabio Perini v PCMC*[97] it was held that the claimant could recover damages for lost sales of a machine as a result of the infringing use (for which the defendant was liable as a joint tortfeasor) of a patented process employed by machines, which were sold by the defendant, on the basis that the infringing process was written into the contract for sale of the machine, even though the infringing use for which the defendant had been held jointly liable only started after the sales had been lost.

Dealing in the products of a process

14-76   Section 60(1)(c) of the 1977 Act further provides that it is an infringement where the invention is a process, if a person disposes of, offers to dispose of, uses or imports any product obtained directly by means of the process or keeps any such product whether for disposal or otherwise. Again, generally speaking, this is so regardless of the knowledge of the individual dealing in the product. However, as addressed above[98] in the case of Swiss-form claims, knowledge or reasonable foresight on the part of the manufacturer that their product will intentionally be used for the claimed therapeutic application is required for the claim to be infringed.

14-77   The section is limited to the situation where the invention is a process. Authorities under previous Acts, in which claims to machinery were held to be infringed by the products produced by the machine, are no longer good law.[99] A claim to a machine as such will be a product not a process claim, and such a claim can only be infringed by the machine itself. Thus it is submitted that dealings in products produced by a patented machine are not now covered by s.60(1)(c) if the patent contains only product claims for the machine itself. However, under modern drafting practice most patents for such a new machine will also include process claims.

14-78   The expressions "uses", "disposes", "imports", and "keeps" will be construed in the same manner as in s.60(1)(a).[100] Thus, the subsection assimilates dealings in the products of a process invention with dealings in product inventions.

---

[95] [1998] F.S.R. 1.
[96] See para.14-74.
[97] [2012] EWHC 911 (Ch); [2012] R.P.C. 30.
[98] See para.14-23.
[99] See the section "Product and process inventions" at paras 14-44 and 14-45.
[100] See para.14-24, et seq.

No distinction is drawn by the subsection between a process used in this country **14-79** and one used abroad; just as in the case of products which infringe product claims, if the products of the process are dealt with in an infringing manner in this country, then it is immaterial where they were originally made.

The scope of the words "obtained directly" was considered by the Court of Ap- **14-80** peal in *Pioneer v Warner*.[101] The Court noted that the qualifying word "directly" had its origin in German law, which used "*unmittelbar*" which has the sense of "without intermediary". The Court therefore held that the section applied to products which were the direct and immediate result at the end of applying the patented process. However, such a product did not cease to be so obtained if it was thereafter subjected to further processing which did not cause it to lose its identity, there being no such loss of identity if it retained its essential characteristics in spite of the further processing.

Whether or not any further processing applied after the patented process results **14-81** in a loss of identity, is of course a question of fact in any given case. In the course of its judgment, the Court reviewed the European authorities including nine German decisions in which the loss of identity test had been applied. Once the immediate output of the patented process has been transformed by further processing into an inseparable component of a composite object, the latter can no longer be regarded as directly obtained by the process. Conversely where the result of performing the claimed method was a CAD file, which was itself used to manufacture a drill bit, it was held that the manufactured product was the direct product of the claimed method since the bit so manufactured was "as much the direct product of the design process as it is the product of the manufacturing process of which the design is part".[102]

In *Monsanto Technology LLC v Cargill International SA*[103] the claim in ques- **14-82** tion was for "a method of producing genetically transformed plants ..." and the alleged infringement consisted of importing genetically modified soya bean meal into the UK. It was held that this claim only referred to the production of a parent strain, which had subsequently been grown and harvested over many generations to produce many thousands of tonnes of material. Although this "huge mountain" of material was the ultimate product of the original transformation of the parent plant, and contained the same informational content, it was not the direct product of that transformation nor did it even contain any of the original reproductive material.

The same claimant brought proceedings in the Netherlands in respect of a similar **14-83** type of infringement. However the substantive Dutch patent law had been amended to incorporate art.9 of Directive 98/44/EC ("the Biotech Directive)[104] which states:

"The protection conferred by a patent on a product containing or consisting of genetic information shall extend to all material ... in which the product is incorporated and in which the genetic information is contained and performs its function".

On a reference to the Court of Justice of the European Union,[105] it was held that **14-84** the protection provided for in art.9 was not available when the genetic information has ceased to perform the function it performed in the initial material from which the material in question was derived. The soy meal imported was a dead

---

[101] [1997] R.P.C. 757.
[102] *Halliburton Energy Services Inc v Smith International (North Sea) Ltd* [2006] R.P.C. 2.
[103] [2008] F.S.R. 7.
[104] See para.2–131 and para.2–132, et seq.
[105] *Monsanto Technology LLC v Cefetra BV* (C-428/08) (Judgment of the Grand Chamber, 6 July 2010).

material obtained after the soy had undergone several treatment processes, and the mere fact that genetic material could be extracted therefrom and transferred into the cell of a living organism was not sufficient.

14-85   Section 60(1)(c) has therefore altered the law as applied under previous legislation, in which infringement could be found whether an imported product had been directly or indirectly obtained from a patented process, provided always that there had been substantial use of the process.[106]

14-86   Section 130(1) of the 1977 Act defines a patented product as "a product which is a patented invention or, in relation to a patented process, a product obtained directly by means of the process or to which the process has been applied". It is not clear what is added by the words "or to which the process has been applied": it is submitted that they cannot be construed as extending the definition of infringement beyond s.60(1)(c) because of the words "if, but only if" at the beginning of s.60.

14-87   In *MedImmune v Novartis Pharmaceutical Research*[107] the claims in issue involved methods for producing and selecting bacteriophage particles that bound to target epitopes or antigens with "desired specificity" (also referred to as the "phage display" process). It was argued that claim 5 was to a method of identifying a desired molecule, while claim 8 was to method of manufacturing the molecule so identified and the antibody alleged to infringe is not a product obtained directly by the identification process. Hence it was said that it was only as a result of the inclusion of further, non-inventive, manufacturing steps in the claim, that MedImmune was able to allege that the defendant's antibody infringed the claims. It was said that, for these reasons, it could not be right to apply the loss of identity test without qualification. Furthermore, it was argued that the test cannot depend on the precise manner in which the claims of the patent in suit are drafted. Instead, the test which should be applied should focus upon the inventive claim or inventive part of the claim, in addition to asking whether the allegedly infringing product is obtained directly from that process.

14-88   Arnold J rejected this argument for the following three reasons:

(1)   First, the loss of identity test adopted by the Court of Appeal in that case was a general test stated without qualifications.

(2)   Secondly, both Aldous J and the Court of Appeal in *Pioneer* treated the opinion of Dr Bruchhausen's as authoritative, which was that the issue depended on the manner in which the claims were drafted and that it was legitimate for the patentee to obtain protection going beyond an inventive intermediate by framing claims to the whole process.

(3)   Thirdly, the argument is fundamentally one about territoriality and although the patent system is territorial, it is not rigidly so.[108] There was nothing inherently objectionable about affording MedImmune a remedy in the UK given that defendant's product was sold here. Nor did art.64(2) EPC and art.25(c) CPC compel the conclusion that this should be excluded.

14-89   For these reasons, Arnold J concluded that, if the defendant's antibody was

---

[106] *Saccharin Corp Ltd v Anglo-Continental Chemical Works* (1900) 17 R.P.C. 307; *Wilderman v E.W. Berk & Co Ltd* (1925) 42 R.P.C. 79; *Beecham Group Laboratories Ltd v Bristol Laboratories Ltd* [1978] R.P.C. 153.
[107] [2011] EWHC 1669 (Pat).
[108] Citing *Menashe Business Mercantile Ltd v William Hill Ltd* [2002] EWCA Civ 1702; [2003] 1 W.L.R. 1462 and *Virgin Atlantic Airways Ltd v Delta Air Lines Inc* [2011] EWCA Civ 162.

produced by a process falling within the claims in issue, it would have been a product obtained directly by means of that process. This issue was raised by the defendant in the Court of Appeal by their respondent's notice. However, since the judge's finding of invalidity was upheld, it did not fall for consideration.[109]

Offer of a process for use

The only form of direct infringement where knowledge is a prerequisite to liability is where the invention is a process and the infringing act consists of offering the process for use. In this case, s.60(1)(b) of the 1977 Act provides that the offer is only an infringement if the person offers it for use in the UK when they know, or it is obvious to a reasonable person in the circumstances, that its use there without the consent of the proprietor would be an infringement of the patent. There is thus a subjective and an objective test for knowledge, only one of which has to be satisfied for infringement to occur. This provides protection for an innocent infringer[110] provided that their innocence is reasonable.   **14-90**

The nature of the knowledge required may be contrasted with that required by s.60(2).[111] Section 60(1)(b) requires knowledge that use would be "an infringement of the patent", whereas s.60(2) only requires knowledge of suitability and intention to put "the invention into effect". The former appears to require knowledge not only that the use involves applying the inventive concept in question but also that that inventive concept is protected by the patent in suit.   **14-91**

In *Tamglass Ltd OY v Luoyang North Glass Technology Co Ltd*,[112] Mann J held that offers to sell the first defendant's machine which were faxed to UK companies amounted to offers of the claimed process in the UK although it is not clear from the report whether the machines (which also infringed product claims) were incapable of operating in any other way. As regards knowledge, the judge held that the first defendant (a Chinese manufacturer) probably knew its machine infringed; alternatively, a reasonable person with the attributes of the skilled man would have found it obvious that the machine infringed at the time of the offers for use in the UK. The first defendant was a significant company with over 20 engineers; it claimed to produce many machines each year; the machine in question cost over $900,000; it claimed to have development expertise; and it exhibited at international exhibitions.   **14-92**

In the same case, the second defendant was also held to infringe under this head in that it offered the relevant machine for the purpose of bending and tempering glass as per the process claims. The claimant gave evidence that the second defendant's managing director had visited the claimant's premises; had been told that the claimant's machines were protected by patents and that machines supplied by Chinese manufacturers were infringements; and had responded by saying he was not concerned about patents because infringement was difficult to prove and he would not allow anyone into his factory to see the machine. The second defendant's managing director served a witness statement claiming no recollection of this conversation but did not participate in the trial nor challenge the claimant's evidence.   **14-93**

---

[109] [2012] EWCA Civ 1234.
[110] See also PA 1977 s.62; and para.19-166.
[111] See para.14-119, et seq.
[112] [2006] F.S.R. 32.

Indirect infringement under s.60(2)

14-94   This type of infringement is covered by s.60(2) of the 1977 Act which provides that a person (other than the proprietor of the patent) infringes a patent for an invention if, while the patent is in force and without the consent of the proprietor, they supply or offer to supply in the UK a person other than a licensee or other person entitled to work the invention with any of the means, relating to an essential element of the invention, for putting the invention into effect when they know, or it is obvious to a reasonable person in the circumstances, that those means are suitable for putting, and are intended to put, the invention into effect in the UK.

14-95   It is therefore potentially an infringement to supply or offer to supply "means relating to an essential element of the invention" with the requisite knowledge. However, there are two territorial limitations. First, the supply or offer to supply must be "in the United Kingdom" and secondly, the invention must be "put into effect in the United Kingdom". Section 60(2) is based upon art.26 of the CPC and s.130(7) applies.

Supply or offer to supply

14-96   These words are not used in s.60(1), which instead refers to "disposal". "Supply" clearly contemplates a transfer to a third party, whereas "disposal" considered in isolation does not necessarily do so. However, since the latter word has to be understood in the same sense as the more specific expression "putting on the market" used in art.25 of the CPC,[113] it is submitted that the meaning is the same.

Means relating to an essential element

14-97   Whether or not any particular means is an essential element of a given invention will be a question of fact in each case. It will clearly cover the supply of a product in kit form to be assembled by the purchaser into an infringing item within the UK,[114] although where the dividing line is to be drawn between essential and inessential elements is not clear. In *Schutz v Werit*[115] Floyd J found it unnecessary to decide the question but recorded his "provisional view that not every feature in the claim is necessarily an essential element of the invention".

14-98   The issue fell for consideration by Arnold J in *Nestec SA v Dualit Limited*[116] in which the question arose as to whether a disposable capsule for a coffee machine related to an essential element of a coffee making system. Arnold J held that a disposable capsule did constitute "means relating to an essential element" of a claim for a coffee making apparatus. However, he went on to hold that such capsules did not "put the invention into effect".

14-99   Arnold J observed that the Supreme Court of the Netherlands and the Bundesgerichtshof (Federal Court of Justice) in Germany have adopted different approaches to the question of what constitutes means relating to an essential element of an invention. He preferred the German approach set out first in *Impeller Flow*

---

[113] See para.14–06.
[114] *Grimme Maschinenfabrik GmbH & Co KG v Scott* [2010] EWCA Civ 1110; [2011] F.S.R. 7, [99]–[104].
[115] [2010] F.S.R. 22.
[116] [2013] EWHC 923; [2013] R.P.C. 32, [168]–[176].

Meter,[117] a decision of the Federal Court of Justice in relation to s.10 of the German Patents Act, which implements art.26 CPC:

"The criterion of the suitability of the means to interact functionally with an essential element of the invention in the implementation of the protected inventive idea excludes such means that—such as the energy needed for the operation of a protected device—might be suitable for being used in the exploitation of the invention but which contribute nothing to the implementation of the technical teaching of the invention. If a means makes such a contribution, it will, on the other hand, generally not depend on the feature or features of the patent claim that interact with the means. For, what is an element of the patent claim is, as a rule for this reason alone, also an essential element of the invention. The patent claim defines the protected invention and limits the protection granted to the patent holder to forms of exploitation that implement all the features of the invention. As a mirror image of each individual feature's function to limit protection in this way, each individual feature is fundamentally also an appropriate point of reference for the prohibition on the supply of means within the meaning of Sec. 10 of the Patent Act. In particular, it is not possible to determine the essential element of an invention according to whether they distinguish the subject matter of the patent claim from the state of the art. It is not infrequently the case that all the features of a patent claim as such are known in the state of the art. For this reason, this does not provide a suitable criterion for differentiation."

Thus the German Court proceeded on the basis that the means in question must contribute to implementing the technical teaching of the invention. It rejected the contention that a feature could only be an essential element of the claim for this purpose if it served to distinguish the subject matter of the claim from the prior art, i.e. was novel in its own right.[118]   **14-100**

Arnold J. concluded[119]:   **14-101**

"175. In my judgment the German approach is more consonant with the apparent purpose of Article 26(1), which is that third parties should not be allowed to benefit from the invention by supplying means the market for which has been created by the invention, than the Dutch one. Furthermore, I consider that the Dutch approach is difficult to reconcile with Article 26(2), which makes it clear that a staple commercial product may constitute means relating to an essential element. Accordingly, I propose to follow the German approach.

176. Applying that approach, I consider that the capsule does constitute means relating to an essential element of claim 1 of the Patent. In my view the capsule does contribute to the implementation of the technical teaching of the invention, and is not of completely subordinate importance. Although the invention takes the capsule as a given, and claim 1 only requires the capsule to have a guide edge in the form of a flange, the flange of the capsule plays a significant role in the way in which the claimed invention works."

Means suitable for putting the invention into effect

In addition to the requirement that the means relate "to an essential element of the invention", s.60(2) requires also that they must be "suitable for putting the invention into effect". This depends on whether a person who obtains and uses the means in question thereby either makes a product falling within the claims of the patent or uses the means in a process falling within the claims of the patent.   **14-102**

In *Nestec* it was not suggested that a person who purchased a coffee capsule for use together with a Nespresso machine was repairing or re-conditioning either the machine itself or the system comprised by the combination of the machine and the capsule. Nevertheless, it was common ground that the guidance provided by the   **14-103**

---

[117] See Case X ZR 48/03.
[118] This reasoning was amplified by the court in the second of the German cases relied on by Arnold J: *Pipette System* (X ZR 38/06), at [18]–[21] set out at [171] of *Nestec*.
[119] At [175]–[176] of *Nestec*.

House of Lords in *United Wire* and the Supreme Court in *Schutz v Werit*[120] was relevant to the issue of what constitutes the "making" of a product.

14-104   The *United Wire* case involved two patents for a screen consisting of a frame to which two meshes of different mesh sizes were adhesively secured at the periphery so as to be at different tensions. The meshes quickly became torn in use. The defendants sold reconditioned screens made from the patentee's own frames. The House of Lords held that the defendants had made products in accordance with the patents. Lord Bingham and Lord Hoffmann gave reasoned speeches, with which the other Law Lords agreed. Lord Bingham thought the issue was simply whether the defendants "made" the patented article, to which the answer was a question of judgment, and that it was better not to ask whether the defendants' work involved "repair".

14-105   Lord Hoffmann also said that the real issue was whether the defendants had made the patented product. He quoted with approval a statement made by Lord Halsbury LC in *Sirdar Rubber Co Ltd v Wallington, Weston & Co*[121] that "you may prolong the life of a licensed article but you must not make a new one under the cover of repair" but then he also warned of the dangers of asking whether the work constituted repair. Having recorded the appellant's submission that the question was one of fact and degree and therefore the Court of Appeal ought not to have reversed the trial judge, he concluded (at [73]) by saying that:

> "... in this case the Court of Appeal was in my opinion entitled to substitute its own evaluation because I think, with great respect to the judge, that he did not correctly identify the patented product. He said that the frame was an important part of the assembly and that the defendants had prolonged 'the screen's useful life'. It is quite true that the defendants prolonged the useful life of the *frame*. It would otherwise presumably have been scrapped. But the *screen* was the combination of frame and meshes pre-tensioned by attachment with adhesive according to the invention. That product ceased to exist when the meshes were removed and the frame stripped down to the bare metal. What remained at that stage was merely an important component, a skeleton or chassis, from which a new screen could be made."

14-106   In *Schutz v Werit* the patent concerned large containers used for the transport of liquids (called intermediate bulk containers or "IBCs"). IBCs of a two-part construction resting on a flat pallet had been well known for many years. They consisted of a metal cage into which a large plastic container (or "bottle") is fitted. While the cage has a limited life-span, it has a significantly longer life expectancy than a bottle: on average, it is about five or six times as long. "Reconditioners" engage in "re-bottling" or "cross-bottling" used IBCs. In either case the old bottle is removed, any damage to the cage repaired, and a new bottle is fitted within the cage. Re-bottling involves replacing the bottle with a fresh bottle from the original manufacturer. Cross-bottling involves replacing the bottle with a bottle from a different source.

14-107   The patented invention concerned the use of the idea of flexible weld joints in the cage to increase its strength and durability. Claim 1 of the patent was to a complete IBC, i.e. a pallet, a bottle and a cage. The specification acknowledged that the bottle was "exchangeable", i.e. replaceable. The issue in the Supreme Court was whether a third party (who used the defendant's bottles to cross-bottle cages from the patentee's used IBCs) had made IBCs falling within claim 1 of the patent. The Supreme Court held that it had not.

---

[120] [2013] UKSC 16; [2013] 2 All E.R. 177; [2013] Bus. L.R. 565; [2013] 3 Costs L.O. 500; [2013] R.P.C. 16
[121] (1907) 24 R.P.C. 539, 543.

Lord Neuberger (along with the other members of the Supreme Court) set out in **14-108** his judgment a number of considerations in interpreting the word "makes" in s.60(1):

"26.   ... First, the word 'makes' must be given a meaning which, as a matter of ordinary language, it can reasonably bear. Secondly, it is not a term of art: like many English words, it does not have a precise meaning. Thirdly, it will inevitably be a matter of fact and degree in many cases whether an activity involves 'making' an article, or whether it falls short of that.

27.   Fourthly, the word 'makes' must be interpreted in a practical way, by reference to the facts of the particular case. Fifthly, however, there is a need for clarity and certainty for patentees and others, and for those advising them. Sixthly, it should be borne in mind that the word applies to patents for all sorts of products, from machinery to chemical compounds. Seventhly, one should bear in mind, at least as part of the background, the need to protect the patentee's monopoly while not stifling reasonable competition.

28.   Eighthly, the word 'makes' must be interpreted bearing in mind that the precise scope of a claim may be a matter almost of happenstance in the context of the question whether the alleged infringer 'makes' the claimed product. Lord Diplock described the specification of a patent as 'a unilateral statement by the patentee, in words of his own choosing' by which he states 'what he claims to be the essential features of the new product'—*Catnic Components Ltd v Hill & Smith Ltd* [1982] R.P.C. 183, 242. As Lord Hoffmann explained in *Kirin-Amgen Inc v Hoechst Marion Roussel Ltd* [2004] UKHL 46, [2005] 1 All E.R. 667, [2005] R.P.C. 169, para 21, a claim is, or at least should be drafted 'not only ... in the interest of others who need to know the area "within which they will trespassers" but also in the interests of the patentee, who needs to be able to make it clear that he lays no claim to prior art or insufficiently enabled products'. As Lord Hoffmann went on to explain in para 35, all sorts of factors, only some of which may appear to be rational, can influence the person drafting a claim.

29.   Ninthly, where, as here, there is a decision (*United Wire*) of the House of Lords or this court on the meaning of the word, it cannot be departed from save for very good reasons indeed. Finally, particularly given that section 60 (like section 125) is one of the sections mentioned in section 130(7) of the 1977 Act, the word should be interpreted bearing in mind that it is included in a provision which is intended to be part of a scheme which applies in many other jurisdictions."

Lord Neuberger then summarised the approach involved in deciding whether a **14-109** particular activity involves making the patented article:

"Deciding whether a particular activity involves 'making' the patented article involves, as Lord Bingham said, an exercise in judgment, or, in Lord Hoffmann's words, it is a matter of fact and degree. In some such cases, one can say that the answer is clear; in other cases, one can identify a single clinching factor. However, in this case, it appears to me that it is a classic example of identifying the various factors which apply on the particular facts, and, after weighing them all up, concluding, as a matter of judgment, whether the alleged infringer does or does not 'make' the patented article. In the present case, given that (a) the bottle (i) is a freestanding, replaceable component of the patented article, (ii) has no connection with the claimed inventive concept, (iii) has a much shorter life expectancy than the other, inventive, component, (iv) cannot be described as the main component of the article, and (b) apart from replacing it, Delta does no additional work to the article beyond routine repairs, I am of the view that, in carrying out this work, Delta does not 'make' the patented article".[122]

Arnold J applied the *United Wire* and *Schutz* cases in *Nestec*. He considered that **14-110** a number of matters were of significance in determining whether the owner of a Nespresso machine of a relevant kind "makes" the system claimed in claim 1 of the patent when they acquire a capsule.

First, he concluded that the capsule was an entirely subsidiary part of the **14-111** system.[123] Secondly, both the machines and the capsules had an independent commercial existence. Thirdly, given that the capsules were consumables, purchasers

---

[122] At [78].
[123] On the grounds of: (i) cost (the Nespresso machines sold for hundreds of pounds, whereas the

of machines would assume that they were entitled to obtain capsules to use with the machine from whatever source they pleased. Fourthly, the capsule did not embody the inventive concept of the patent. Fifthly, it was manifest that the owner of the machine was not even doing anything which would ordinarily be described as repairing a product, let alone making one.

14-112   In the light of all these matters, Arnold J concluded that owners of relevant Nespresso machines did not "make" the claimed system when they used Nespresso capsules.[124]

Knowledge

14-113   In *Grimme Maschinenfabrik GmbH & Co KG v Scott*[125] the finding at first instance was that the patentee's invention was "put into effect" when the patentee's machine was fitted with rubber rollers. The supply of a steel-rollered machine, which was designed and promoted to enable the steel rollers to be changed for rubber rollers, was the supply of means by which that could be achieved, and was the supply of a means essential for that purpose. This finding was upheld on appeal. The issue was therefore whether the supplier "knows … that those means … are intended to put the invention into effect".

Jacob LJ identified three particular questions[126]:

"i)   Whose intention is referred to? The possible candidates are the supplier himself, his direct customer or the ultimate user. Or perhaps no specific person at all—the inquiry being whether the 'means' and the circumstances surrounding it being offered or supplied are such that some ultimate users will intend to use or adapt the 'means' so as to infringe. We call this the 'inherently probable' view.

ii)   How specific must the intention be? Must it be a present settled intention at the time of alleged infringement? Or will a contingent future intention do? Here for instance a purchaser of Mr Scott's steel-rollered machine may say to himself: 'I know I can change to rubber rollers. That may be handy if in some conditions the metal roller is not aggressive enough'.

iii)   When must the intention be formed? Must it exist at the time of the supply (or offer to supply) or can it be formed later?"

14-114   In finding that the "inherently probable" view was the correct one, Jacob LJ answered these questions as follows:

"108. First then the person who must have the intention. One can rule out the supplier himself. The required intention is to put the invention into effect. That the supplier himself does not intend to do. The question is what the supplier knows or ought to know about the intention of the person who is in a position to put the invention into effect—the person at the end of the supply chain. Arnold J put it pithily in *KCI Licensing v Smith & Nephew* [2010] EWHC 1487 (Pat), [2010] F.S.R. 740 at [200]:

It is implicit in this reasoning [i.e. that of Lewison J in *Cranway v Playtech* [2009] EWHC 1588 (Pat) [2010] F.S.R. 3] that the relevant intention is not that of the supplier. In my judg-

---

capsules sold for 20–30p each); (ii) comparative durability (the machines were intended to last for many years and make thousands of cups of coffee, whereas the capsule was intended to be used once and then discarded); (iii) the short life-span of the capsules (the capsules contained ground coffee which was perishable); (iv) the independence of function of the machine (the functioning of the machine was not altered by the presence or absence of the capsule); and (v) the economic value of the machine (presence or absence of a capsule did not affect the economic value of the machine, although the machine would be useless without a supply of capsules).

[124] See [200]–[204].

[125] [2010] EWCA Civ 1110; [2011] F.S.R. 7, [107]–[132], overruling *Cranway v Playtech* [2010] F.S.R. 3 on this point.

[126] At [107].

ment this is correct. S.60(2) makes it clear that there can be infringement not merely if the supplier knows that the means are intended to put the invention into effect, but also if that would be obvious to a reasonable person in the circumstances. That is inconsistent with a requirement of intention on the part of the supplier. Thus the relevant intention must be that of the person supplied.

109. Next, must the required intention be that of the person directly supplied by the alleged infringer? Lewison J took that view in *Cranway*, saying at [156]:

> Whether means are *suitable for* putting an invention into effect must be a purely objective test. But whether they are intended to put an invention into effect cannot be wholly objective. Only human beings can have intentions, although their intentions may be attributed to other legal persons, according to rules of attribution. Thus this limb of the test must depend on the subjective intention of someone. A supplier of essential means might reasonably be supposed to know what the intention of his immediate counter-party is. But it would be a far stronger thing to expect him to discern the intention of a person far down the supply chain. Moreover, at the time of the supplier's supply of the essential means the person who ultimately forms the intention to use the means to put the invention into effect may not be ascertainable and he may not have formed that intention. It thus seems to me to be more likely that s.60(2) was directed to a supply of essential means to a direct infringer rather than to another secondary infringer ….

110. We do not agree for two reasons. First, if that view were right, a party who only supplied essential means to middlemen could never fall within the provision. It cannot have been intended that the legislation would not catch a primary supplier to the ultimate market even if he very well knew that the ultimate users would adapt the means so as to infringe.

111. Secondly, the reasoning presupposes an actual, already formed, intention in the user. We do not think that is necessary (see below).

112. What then of the 'inherently probable' view? This was essentially that for which Mr Chacksfield argued. He submitted that it was enough if the supplier knew (or it was obvious in the circumstances) at the time of his offer to supply or supply that *some* (disregarding freak use) ultimate users would intend to use, adapt or alter the 'means essential' so as to infringe.

113. Against this view it can be said that Article 26 requires that the alleged infringer must know (or it must be obvious etc) that the means *are* intended to put the invention into affect. The present tense is used. So it can be said that a future intention—even a probable future intention—is not enough.

114. Notwithstanding the force of that linguistic point, we conclude that the 'inherently probable' view is indeed the correct construction of the provision. We do so for a number of reasons."

The reasons given by Jacob LJ included the French and German translations of art 26.1 CPC ("moyens sont … destinés à cette mise en oeuvre" in the French version and also "bestimmt" in the German version). Both versions convey the notion of what will happen ultimately rather than a need to look for the intention of a presently identifiable user. Also persuasive were a number of German cases.[127]   **14-115**

After consideration of these, Jacob LJ summarised the position as follows[128]:   **14-116**

"In short, the knowledge and intention requirements of Art. 26 and section 60(2) are satisfied if, at the time of supply or offer of supply, the supplier knows, or it is obvious in the circumstances, that ultimate users will intend to put the invention into effect. That is to be proved on the usual standard of balance of probabilities. It is not enough merely that the means are suitable for putting the intention into effect (for that is a separate requirement), but it is likely to be the case where the supplier proposes or recommends or even indicates the possibility of such use in his promotional material."

---

[127] *Deckenheizung* [BGH X ZR 153/03] 13 June 2006; *Haubenstretchautomat* [BGH X ZR 173/02] 9 January 2007; and *Pipettensystem* [BGH X ZR 38/06] 27 February 2007 and three earlier cases: *Luftheizgerät*, [BGH X ZR 176/98] 10 October 2000; *DI B.V.*[2004] ENPR 194 of 25 March 1999 (Oberlandsgericht, Düsseldorf); and *Antriebsscheibenaufzug* [BGH X ZR 247/02] 7 June 2005.
[128] At [131].

14-117   Subsequently, in *KCI Licensing Inc v Smith & Nephew plc*[129] Jacob LJ summarised the law in this way, giving cross-references to his judgment in *Grimme*:

"i)   The required intention is to put the invention into effect. The question is what the supplier knows or ought to know about the intention of the person who is in a position to put the invention into effect—the person at the end of the supply chain, [108].

ii)   It is enough if the supplier knows (or it is obvious to a reasonable person in the circumstances) that some ultimate users will intend to use or adapt the 'means' so as to infringe, [107(i)] and [114].

iii)   There is no requirement that the intention of the individual ultimate user must be known to the defendant at the moment of the alleged infringement, [124].

iv)   Whilst it is the intention of the ultimate user which matters, a future intention of a future ultimate user is enough if that is what one would expect in all the circumstances, [125].

v)   The knowledge and intention requirements are satisfied if, at the time of supply or offer to supply, the supplier knows, or it obvious to a reasonable person in the circumstances, that ultimate users will intend to put the invention into effect. This has to be proved on the usual standard of the balance of probabilities. It is not enough merely that the means are suitable for putting the invention into effect (for that is a separate requirement), but it is likely to be the case where the supplier proposes or recommends or even indicates the possibility of such use in his promotional material, [131]."

14-118   The Court of Appeal in *KCI*[130] reversed the decision of Arnold J on the basis that there is no requirement that the ultimate users must have decided to use the means to put the invention into effect at the time they first take possession of the means. The relevant intention may be formed at a later time. However, the supplier must know (or it must be obvious to them in all the circumstances) that some ultimate users will indeed form that intention.

Section 60(2) and Swiss-type claims

14-119   As discussed at para.9-269, Swiss-type claims are drafted as process claims which are directed at the manufacturer. It is relatively straightforward to envisage a situation where a supplier supplies a formulator with material for manufacturing a product knowing that it is suitable and intended for a given indication. Nevertheless, what of the act of supplying that product into the market? Can this amount to contributory infringement?

14-120   Arnold J held not at an interim stage in *Warner-Lambert v Actavis*[131] where he thought it right that counsel for Warner-Lambert did not press this claim. He held that under s.60(2) there can only be infringement by the person supplied or by a user further down the chain of supply (although it is not necessary for there actually to be an infringing act). That was not the case in *Warner-Lambert* since no wholesaler or pharmacist used the product in issue for any process of manufacture or preparation.

14-121   On appeal from a successful application by Actavis to strike out the claim under s.60(2)[132] Floyd LJ gave three reasons, each of which was in his judgment sufficient to allow the indirect infringement case to go to trial.

"136. The first reason is that which I have already given, namely that the courts of two EPC member states considering this same question have held that, at face value, indirect infringement can arise in these circumstances.

137. The second reason is that, if, as I have held, there is a case of threatened or actual infringe-

---

[129] [2010] EWCA Civ 1260; [2011] F.S.R. 8, [53].
[130] See [55].
[131] [2015] EWHC 72 (Pat), [113].
[132] *Warner-Lambert v Actavis* [2015] EWCA Civ 556, [136].

ment of the process claim under section 60(1)(b), then it follows that dealings downstream in the direct product of the process are also infringements under section 60(1)(c). Although this may not add anything to the direct infringement case, it is wrong to strike it out as a viable additional cause of action.

138. The third reason is that I consider it is arguable to say that when section 60(2) speaks of 'putting the invention into effect', it may be legitimate to look not just at whether any one person is carrying out the invention in a sense which would give rise to liability of that person for an act of infringement. It may be that the invention is put into effect if pregabalin is manufactured by one person and supplied to another who intentionally uses it for the treatment of pain. In those circumstances, a person who supplies pregabalin with the requisite knowledge (i.e. that prescribed in section 60(2) itself) does provide means suitable and intended to put the invention into effect, albeit by the combination of manufacturer and user, rather than by any one person alone. It may be that this is the reasoning which underlies the decisions in the Dutch and German cases which I have referred to.

139. An analogous problem arises where one step of a two step process is carried out by A and the second step is carried out by B. Absent a claim of joint tortfeasance, could it not be said that by supplying the result of the first step to B, A is contributing to putting the invention into effect (by A and B together)?"

At trial, the claim under s.60(2) was dismissed by Arnold J for the reasons given in *Warner-Lambert v Actavis*.[133] Arnold J rejected each of the three reasons Floyd LJ. had given for restoring the claim at [679]–[684] and held at [684]: **14-122**

"The fundamental difficulty with Pfizer's claim under section 60(2) remains, as it has always done, that claims 1 and 3 of the Patent are claims to processes of manufacture, but there is no act of manufacture by any party downstream from Actavis, nor even the prospect of such an act. This is so even if manufacturing (or 'preparation', to use the word in the claims) for this purpose includes packaging with appropriate instructions. In particular, there is no act of manufacture by pharmacists, nor any prospect of such an act. It follows that, although there is no difficulty in concluding that Lecaent's active ingredient is 'means, relating to an essential element of the invention, for putting the invention into effect', Lecaent is not suitable for putting, or intended to put, the invention into effect: either the invention has already been put into effect by the time that Lecaent leaves Actavis' hands or it is not put into effect at all. Accordingly, I conclude that Actavis have not infringed claims 1 and 3 of the Patent pursuant to section 60(2)."

At the time of writing this later judgment is itself under appeal. **14-123**

Contributory infringement and EPC 2000 claims

It should be noted that, as the number of claims in EPC 2000 format increases and the number of Swiss-type claims diminishes, the issue of contributory infringement of EPC 2000 format claims becomes relatively straightforward. EPC 2000 claims are not to the process of manufacture (as Swiss-type claims are) but to the particular product *for use in* the particular therapy. **14-124**

Accordingly as regards such EPC 2000 format claims, where a person who supplies or offers to supply a particular product has the requisite knowledge (following *Grimme* and *KCI* (mentioned above)) that at least some of the product in question will be used for the claimed treatment, then contributory infringement will arise from the supply of such a product. The same applies where the EPC 2000 format claims cover a particular dosage regime or method of application. **14-125**

---

[133] [2015] EWHC 2548 (Pat), [678]–[684].

The territorial limitations

14-126   The territorial limitations were considered by the Court of Appeal in *Menashe Business Mercantile v William Hill Ltd*.[134] The claim in question was to a gaming system for playing an interactive computer game which required the presence of both a host computer and a terminal computer on which the game was played. The host computer was remote from the player's computer and was located in Antigua (or Curacao). To play the game, the player had to purchase a CD which when loaded onto his computer allowed it to interact with the host computer so as to create an "infringing" system. The defendant accepted that the CD was a means relating to an essential element of the invention and that this had been supplied to the player in the UK. However, it was contended that although the player would be located in the UK, the invention was not being put into effect in the UK since the host computer, itself an essential element of the invention, was not located within the UK.

14-127   The Court of Appeal accepted that the nature of the invention had to be determined by reference to the claim and held that the means had to be such as to put the claimed apparatus into an infringing state in the UK.[135] In doing so the Court of Appeal rejected Jacob J's conclusion at first instance that regard should be had as to whether the infringement merely had an effect within the UK.[136] Aldous LJ concluded (at [29]):

> "29. I do not consider it appropriate to introduce through section 60(2) the concept of infringement by supplying means which merely have an effect in the United Kingdom. As Mr Arnold pointed out the effect could be economic, physical or perhaps in some cases emotional. The Judge's recourse to the Brussels Convention was not helpful as that is concerned with where the effect of an event is felt, whereas the judge's construction is concerned with the effect of an invention. Mr Prescott pressed into use the phrase a 'technical effect', whatever in this context that may be. There is in my view no basis for introducing into the definition of infringement that the supply of a s.60(2) means must have an effect. It must put something, namely the invention, into effect."

14-128   However, the court went on to hold that there was infringement under s.60(2) because it did not matter on the facts of the case where the host computer was situated. The gaming system was being used in the UK and, to that extent, the host computer was being used in the UK by the punter in question.[137]

14-129   *Menashe* was considered and applied by Arnold J in *Research in Motion v Motorola*.[138] So far as s.60(1)(b) was concerned, the method of operating the messaging gateway system alleged to infringe was offered for use by RIM in Canada, not in the UK. So far as s.60(2) was concerned, Arnold J considered the facts of *Menashe*:

> "155. The alleged infringing act was the supply of software by the defendant to a punter for running on his computer. The software effectively turned the punter's computer into the terminal of the claim. The punter was able to connect his computer to the host computer, which was located outside the UK. Thus, the punter was able to use the claimed system in the UK by reason of the supply of the software and it did not matter that the host computer was not in the UK. The use of the system in the UK by the punter was sufficient for the invention to be put into effect in the UK for the purposes of section 60(2). As Aldous LJ said at [33]:

---

[134] [2003] R.P.C. 31, 575.
[135] [2003] R.P.C. 31, [24]–[29].
[136] [2002] R.P.C. 47, 950.
[137] [2003] R.P.C. 31, [33].
[138] [2010] EWHC 118 (Pat), [153]–[157].

'If the host computer is situated in Antigua and the terminal computer is in the United Kingdom, it is pertinent to ask who uses the claimed gaming system. The answer must be the punter. Where does he use it? There can be no doubt that he uses his terminal in the United Kingdom and it is not a misuse of language to say that he uses the host computer in the United Kingdom. It is the input to and output of the host computer that is important to the punter and in a real sense the punter uses the host computer in the United Kingdom even though it is situated in Antigua and operates in Antigua. In those circumstances it is not straining the word "use" to conclude that the United Kingdom punter will use the claimed gaming system in the United Kingdom, even if the host computer is situated in, say, Antigua. Thus the supply of the CD in the United Kingdom to the United Kingdom punter will be intended to put the invention into effect in the United Kingdom.'

156. I agree with RIM that asking and answering Aldous LJ's questions in this case leads to a different answer. Who uses the method of operating a messaging gateway system that has the claimed features? The answer is RIM. Where do they operate it? The answer is in Canada."

Hence there was no infringement under s.60(2) either. **14-130**

The double territorial limitation of s.60(2) also precluded a finding of infringe- **14-131** ment in respect of the seat units in *Virgin v Delta*[139] (considered above at para.14-49, et seq.) in that, although the supplier had supplied or offered to supply seat units, which would plainly constitute means relating to an essential element of the invention of claim 1, to Delta in the UK, the seat units were assembled and arranged into the seating system on aircraft only in the USA.

Accordingly the double territorial limitation is fundamental to the operation of **14-132** s.60(2). The requisite offer for sale or sale must be in the UK and the invention must be put into effect in the UK. However, care must be taken properly to identify what the invention is and where it is being put into effect.

Persons entitled to work the invention

This expression does not extend to persons protected from infringement by virtue **14-133** of s.60(5)(a), (b) or (c).[140] It does, however, extend to a Crown user[141] and, under s.60(6)(b), to uses authorised by s.20B(4) (use, or preparation for use, commenced during a period prior to re-instatement of an application which had been refused or treated as having been refused or withdrawn), s.28A(4) or (5) (use, or preparation for use, commenced during a period when the patent had lapsed), s.64 (use, or preparation for use, commenced before the priority date), s.78(5) (use, or preparation for use, commenced during a period when the European patent application or UK designation has been refused or withdrawn or deemed so), s.80(4) (use, or preparation for use, commenced during a period before a corrected English translation of a French or German European patent has been filed) or s.117A(4) or (5) (use, or preparation for use, commenced during a period before correction of an error or mistake in a withdrawal of an application for a patent).[142]

Staple commercial products

Special protection against infringement under s.60(2) of the 1977 Act is however **14-134** given to suppliers of staple commercial products. Section 60(2) does not apply to the supply or offer of such a product unless the supply or the offer is made for the purpose of inducing the person supplied to do an act which constitutes infringe-

---

[139] [2010] EWHC 3094; [2011] R.P.C. 8.
[140] PA 1977 s.60(6); and see para.14–219, et seq.
[141] PA 1977 s.60(6)(a).
[142] See para.14-219.

ment by virtue of s.60(1).[143] There is no definition of a staple commercial product in the 1977 Act and the expression does not appear in the instruments referred to in s.130(7). The use of the word "staple" is presumably a reference to raw materials or other basic products commonly available and with a multitude of possible applications, and the purpose of the subsection is to protect the supplier of such products even if he has knowledge that they are to be put to an infringing purpose. The scope of the words is far from clear and the dividing line between protecting the supplier of raw materials on the one hand and giving a fair monopoly to the patentee must be a question of fact in each case.

14-135   In *Nestec v Dualit*[144] Arnold J held that the disposable coffee capsules for use in Nespresso machines were not staple commercial products.[145] He referred to the single European authority cited to him[146] and noted that, following from that authority, it was accepted before him that "products that are of a kind which is needed every day and can be generally obtained" was a useful working definition "staple commercial product". The product in question is the actual product supplied by the defendant, not the feature of the claim which the product satisfies, and the date at which the test is to be applied is the date of the alleged infringement not the date of the patent. The consequence is that a product can be a staple commercial product at the date of the alleged infringement even if it was not at the date of the patent. However, a product which has become a staple commercial product as a result of the invention will not qualify. On the facts of the case before him he held:

> "184. Turning to the facts of the present case, I do not consider that NX capsules are staple commercial products. I agree with the view expressed by Justice Crennan of the High Court of Australia in *Northern Territory of Australia v Collins* [2008] H.C.A. 49 at [145], albeit in a slightly different statutory context, that in order to qualify as a staple commercial product, a product must ordinarily be one which is supplied commercially for a variety of uses. NX capsules were specifically designed for use with Nespresso machines. When they were first introduced, they had no other use. Subsequently, Dualit have introduced the NX Adapter, which enables NX capsules to be used in some other types of coffee machines. More recently, Dualit have also launched their own design of coffee machine, which accepts NX capsules among other options. Thus even now NX capsules have no other use other than with a limited range of portionised coffee machines."

14-136   As to the inducement given by the supplier of a staple commercial product which renders them subject to the provisions of s.60(2), no limitation is placed on the wording so that any inducement whether oral or written, express or implied will suffice. The test is, however, a subjective one.

4. WHO IS LIABLE FOR THE INFRINGING ACTS?

14-137   As a basic principle, the person or persons who actually performed the infringing acts are liable to the patentee. However, the rights of the patentee are not restricted merely to an action against the actual infringer.

14-138   Section 60(1) of the 1977 Act provides that a person infringes if, but only if, they perform the acts there set out. However, s.60, which relates essentially to the types of act which constitute infringement, does not limit the liability of persons for the commission of those acts. Accordingly, liability may arise where a person com-

---

[143] PA 1977 s.60(3).
[144] [2013] EWHC 923; [2013] R.P.C. 32.
[145] At [178]–[182].
[146] *Pavel v Sony Corporation*, Unreported, 13 January 1993.

mits an infringing act through the agency of another; or where the relationship between two people is such as to make them liable as joint tortfeasors so that when one infringes a patent, both will be liable.[147] In this respect the pre-1977 decisions on joint tortfeasorship and agency will continue to apply. But the suggestion that there might have been a quite separate tort of procuring infringement by others[148] is no longer good law, except where s.60(2) applies.[149]

Infringement by agents and servants

A person can infringe a patent by making the article themselves, or by their agent, **14-139** or by their servants. The agent and servants themselves could infringe the patent, and actions could be brought against them individually, but that did not absolve the person who employed them for that purpose. Where an infringing act is committed by an employee of a company, then they personally will have infringed, and their employer will be vicariously liable in the ordinary way. However, actions against mere workmen who innocently helped in an infringement and were not the really guilty persons, were not encouraged.[150]

In *Sykes v Howarth*[151] the invention consisted in the application of cards or strips **14-140** of leather covered with wire to rollers at "wide distances". A person who contracted to clothe rollers, and supplied to a "nailer" cards of such width that when applied to the rollers they must of necessity leave wide spaces, and who himself paid the nailer, was held to have infringed the patent, though he alleged that his business was that of a card-maker only, and did not include the nailer's work. Fry J said:

> "I have come to the conclusion that the nailer must be deemed to have been the agent, for the purpose of nailing on, of the defendant ... there is a contract to clothe in the manner prescribed by the particulars given to the defendant, and that contract was carried into effect by a person paid by the defendant ... the defendant himself receiving the total amount for which he contracted. The consequence is that in my judgment all the defences fail."

In *Gibson and Campbell v Brand*[152] it was held that an order given by the defend- **14-141** ant for the making of silk by a process which infringed the plaintiff's patent, which order was executed in England, was sufficient to satisfy the allegation that the defendant made, used, and put in practice the plaintiff's invention, although the silk was in fact made through the agency of others. Sir N.C. Tindal CJ said: "This is quite sufficient to satisfy an allegation that he made those articles, for he that causes or procures to be made, may well be said to have made them himself."

---

[147] See *Sabaf SpA v MFI Furniture Centres Ltd* [2005] R.P.C. 10, at 209; see also *CBS Songs Ltd v Amstrad Consumer Electronics* [1988] R.P.C. 567, at 606–609, HL.

[148] Which was sometimes put forward under the old law; see, e.g. *Belegging v Witten Industrial Diamonds Ltd* [1979] F.S.R. 59, at 66; citing *Lumley v Gye* (1853) 2 E. & B. 216; *Rotocrop Inc Ltd v Genbourne Ltd* [1982] F.S.R. 241, at 260; *Dow v Spence Bryson* [1982] F.S.R. 598, at 626–630.

[149] See para.14–94, et seq.

[150] See *Savage v Brindle* (1896) 13 R.P.C. 266.

[151] (1879) 12 Ch D. 826, 832.

[152] (1841) 1 W.P.C. 631.

Joint tortfeasorship

14-142   Persons may be liable for infringement if their acts are such as would make them joint tortfeasors under the general law.[153] The general law is as stated by Scrutton LJ in *The Koursk*[154] when he said:

"Certain classes of persons seem clearly to be joint tortfeasors: the agent who commits a tort in the course of his employment for his principal, and the principal; the servant who commits a tort in the course of his employment and his master; two persons who agree on common action, in the course of, and to further which, one of them commits a tort. These seem clearly joint tortfeasors; there is one tort committed by one of them on behalf of, or in concert with, another."

14-143   But before a person can be said to be a joint tortfeasor, they must have acted in concert with another person in the commission of the tort.[155] In *Morton-Norwich Products Inc v Intercen Ltd*, Graham J referred to "a concerted design".[156] The mere sale in the ordinary way of business of goods, which the vendor is entitled to sell, is not tortious, even though the purchaser may subsequently use the goods wrongly. Thus, the mere sale of articles which are not themselves protected by a patent but which can be used for the purposes of infringement, will not amount to an infringement,[157] even if the seller knows the articles will be used for this purpose.[158] While they may be facilitating the tort, they are neither procuring nor involved in it.[159] This distinction was emphasised by Buckley LJ in the *Belegging* case when he said[160]: "Facilitating the doing of an act is obviously different from procuring the doing of the act."[161] Dillon LJ explained this latter dictum in *Mölnlycke v Procter & Gamble (No.4)*,[162] in which he said:

"A person who merely facilitated but did not procure the infringement, was not a joint tortfeasor with the infringer and so was not liable if, for instance, he sold articles which could be used for infringing or non-infringing purposes even though he knew that they would probably be used and were intended to be used for the infringing purposes. More recently however a new concept has been developed. Parties will be regarded as joint tortfeasors if on the facts they had a common design to market in the United Kingdom articles which in truth infringe a United Kingdom patent."

14-144   Although as noted above,[163] sale of a kit of parts intended to be assembled into a patented product may make the seller a joint tortfeasor with the purchaser. The distinction between conduct which does or does not create liability as a joint tortfea-

---

[153] *Morton-Norwich Products Inc v Intercen Ltd* [1978] R.P.C. 501.
[154] [1924] P. 140, 155. See also *CBS Songs Ltd v Amstrad Consumer Electronics* [1988] R.P.C. 567, at 606–609, HL.
[155] *Innes v Short* (1898) 15 R.P.C. 449; *Morton-Norwich Products Inc v Intercen Ltd* [1978] R.P.C. 501; *Belegging v Witten Industrial Diamonds Ltd* [1979] F.S.R. 59, 66. *Rotocrop International Ltd v Genbourne Ltd* [1982] F.S.R. 241; *Lancashire Fires v S.A. Lyons* [1996] F.S.R. 629.
[156] [1978] R.P.C. 501, 513.
[157] *Sykes v Howarth* (1879) 12 Ch. 826; *Townsend v Haworth* (1875) 48 L.J. Ch D. 770; *Dunlop Pneumatic Tyre Co Ltd v David Moseley & Sons Ltd* (1904) 21 R.P.C. 274, 278; *Adhesive Dry Mounting Co v Trapp & Co* (1910) 27 R.P.C. 341, 353; *White v Todd Oil Burners Ltd* (1929) 46 R.P.C. 275, 293; *Belegging v Witten Industrial Diamonds Ltd* [1979] F.S.R. 59, 64.
[158] *Townsend v Haworth* (1875) 48 L.J. Ch. 770; *Kalman v PCL Packaging (UK)* [1982] F.S.R. 406.
[159] Compare also *CBS Songs Ltd v Amstrad Consumer Electronics* [1988] R.P.C. 567, HL.
[160] [1979] F.S.R. 59.
[161] See *Dow Chemical A.G. v Spence Bryson & Co (No.2)* [1982] F.S.R. 397 and 598, at 626–630; *Kalman v Packaging (UK)* [1982] F.S.R. 406; *Rotocrop International v Genbourne* [1982] F.S.R. 241, at 260.
[162] [1992] R.P.C. 21, 29.
[163] See para.14–50; see also *Incandescent Gas Light Co v New Incandescent Mantle Co* (1898) 15 R.P.C. 81.

sor will depend on the facts of each case. The authorities were reviewed by the Court of Appeal in *Unilever v Gillette*[164] in which the plaintiff applied to amend its pleadings to allege joint tortfeasorship by the US parent company of the defendant and for leave to serve out of the jurisdiction. Mustill LJ said[165]:

> "As to the authorities on this subject, if I am right in the view just expressed that they are really cases on the facts, I suggest that little is to be gained by matching the circumstances of each case against each of the allegations in the draft amended statement of claim. For my part, I prefer to take the relevant part of the amendment as a whole, and to ask whether, if the allegations therein are proved to be true (and there seems no dispute that they will be), and if they are set in the context of the relationship between the companies in the Gillette Group, when that has emerged at the trial, a judge directing himself correctly could reasonably come to the conclusion that:
>
> (a) there was a common design between Boston and G.U.K. to do acts which, if the patent is upheld, amounted to infringements, and
>
> (b) Boston has acted in furtherance of that design.
>
> I use the words 'common design' because they are readily to hand, but there are other expressions in the cases, such as 'concerted action' or 'agreed on common action' which will serve just as well. The words are not to be construed as if they formed part of a statute. They all convey the same idea. This idea does not, as it seems to me, call for any finding that the secondary party has explicitly mapped out a plan with the primary offender. Their tacit agreement will be sufficient. Nor, as it seems to me, is there any need for a common design to infringe. It is enough if the parties combine to secure the doing of acts which in the event prove to be infringements."

A good arguable case was held established on the facts of that particular decision, and amendment of the pleading was allowed together with leave to serve the US parent company out of the jurisdiction. **14-145**

In *Unilever v Chefaro*,[166] the Court of Appeal returned again to this issue, this time setting aside service on the second defendant on the basis that it had not been shown to be arguably liable. In order to show infringement by common design it was necessary to show some act in furtherance of the common design and not merely an agreement. The mere fact that the party had overall control of the company which actually committed the allegedly infringing act in the sense that it could override the latter's decisions by financial and voting control was not sufficient to establish joint liability, or even to give rise to an inference that there was a common design and that the party sought to be joined had acted in furtherance of it. **14-146**

This decision was subsequently considered and further explained in *The Mead Corporation v Riverwood International*[167] and in *Sandman v Panasonic*.[168] In the former case, a similar result on the facts was achieved; it was not enough to show that the defendants were closely related by shareholding or otherwise, and it was necessary to produce some evidence that the foreign party was actually involved in furthering the common design to infringe. Mere looking on was not enough. By contrast, in the latter case (for infringement of copyright) the court declined to strike out a case of joint tortfeasorship at the interlocutory stage, because of the particular circumstance that the foreign parent company manufactured equipment abroad which was specifically adapted for use in the UK. It was held that there was an argu- **14-147**

---

[164] [1989] R.P.C. 583.

[165] [1989] R.P.C. 583, 608.

[166] [1994] F.S.R. 135.

[167] [1997] F.S.R. 484; see also *Coin Controls Ltd v Suzo International (UK) Ltd* [1997] F.S.R. 660.

[168] [1998] F.S.R. 651.

able case fit for trial that the parent and its UK subsidiary were jointly engaged in a common design to sell in this country.

14-148 The authorities, many of which concern intellectual property, were also reviewed by the Court of Appeal in a fraud case, *Crédit Lyonnais v EGCD*,[169] where Hobhouse LJ confirmed that:

"Mere assistance, even knowing assistance, does not suffice to make the secondary party jointly liable as a joint tortfeasor with the primary party. What he does must go further. He must have conspired with the primary party or procured or induced his commission of the tort (my first category) or he must have joined in the common design pursuant to which the tort was committed (my third category)."

14-149 It is not necessary to show a common design deliberately to infringe; it is sufficient that the common design related to acts which in the event constituted infringement.[170]

14-150 In *Generics (UK) Ltd v H. Lundbeck A/S*[171] Jacob LJ summed up the position as follows:

"There is no real dispute as to the principles by which a party is made liable as a joint tortfeasor with another for patent infringement. There is no need to go to any authority other than the last in point, *Sabaf v Meneghetti*.[172] Peter Gibson LJ, giving the judge of the court said this at paragraph 59:

'The *underlying* concept for joint tortfeasance must be that the joint tortfeasor has been so involved in the commission of the tort as to make himself liable for the tort. Unless he has made the infringing act his own, he has not himself committed the tort. That notional seems to us what underlies all the decisions to which we were referred. If there is a common design or concerted action or otherwise a combination to secure the doing of the infringing acts, then each of the combiners has made the act his own and will be liable. Like the judge, we do not think that what was done by Meneghetti was sufficient. It was merely acting as a supplier of goods to a purchaser which was free to do what it wanted with the goods. Meneghetti did not thereby make MFI's infringing acts its own.'"

14-151 Jacob LJ went on to conclude that merely supplying outside the jurisdiction goods to a party who later sells them within the jurisdiction is not enough for joint tortfeasorship, even if the supplier knows his customer intends so to sell; nor was it enough that the supplier in question also supplied information to the regulatory authorities.

14-152 In *Twentieth Century Fox Film Corp v Newzbin*[173] Kitchin J, after considering the leading authorities on the issue[174] summarised the principles:

"I derive from these passages that mere (or even knowing) assistance or facilitation of the primary infringement is not enough. The joint tortfeasor must have so involved himself in the tort as to make it his own. This will be the case if he has induced, incited or persuaded the primary infringer to engage in the infringing act or if there is a common design or concerted action or agreement on a common action to secure the doing of the infringing act".

14-153 Arnold J further reviewed the law as to joint tortfeasance (to which he refers also

---

[169] [1998] 1 Lloyd's Rep. 19; an appeal to the House of Lords was subsequently dismissed—see [1999] 1 Lloyd's Rep. 563. See also *Napp v Asta* [1999] F.S.R. 370; and *Sepracor v Hoechst Marrion Roussel* [1999] F.S.R. 746.

[170] *Unilever v Gillette* [1989] R.P.C. 583, 609; *Unilever v Chefaro* [1994] F.S.R. 135, 138.

[171] [2006] EWCA Civ 1261, [24].

[172] [2003] R.P.C. 264.

[173] *Twentieth Century Fox Film Corpn v Newzbin Ltd* [2010] EWHC 608 (Ch); [2010] F.S.R. 21, [108].

[174] *CBS v Amstrad* [1988] A.C. 1013, *Unilever v Gillette* [1989] R.P.C. 583; *Crédit Lyonnais v Exports Credits Guarantee Dept* [1988] 1 Lloyd's Rep. 19; and *Sabaf v Meneghetti* [2002] EWCA Civ 976.

as "accessory liability") in *L'Oréal SA v eBay International AG*.[175] It follows from that analysis[176] that A will be jointly liable for patent infringements committed by B in either of two (closely-related) situations: (i) where A procures B to commit the infringing act by inducement, incitement or persuasion, and (ii) where A and B act in concert with one another pursuant to a common design.

In *Fabio Perini SpA v LPC Group plc*[177] the Court of Appeal upheld the trial judge's decisions that PCMC Italia, but not PCMC UK, was jointly liable for infringements committed by LPC. The infringed claims were process claims and the judge had held PCMC Italia and LPC had acted in concert pursuant to a common design because it was clear from the contract between PCMC Italia and LPC that the machine supplied by PCMC Italia to LPC was to operate in accordance with the patented process and PCMC Italia had constructed the machine on LPC's premises and caused it work in that way. Lord Neuberger of Abbotsbury MR, with whom Hughes and Jackson LJJ agreed, said: **14-154**

> "104. So far as joint liability is concerned, both Perini and PCMC refer to a decision of this court (which went to the House of Lords, but not on the point at issue here), *Sabaf v Meneghetti and MFI* [2003] R.P.C. 14, where, at paragraphs 58–59, the Court of Appeal rejected the contention that the supply of infringing goods from abroad into this country was sufficient to fix the supplier with liability even where the supplier 'knew that [the goods] were going to be imported into the UK'. The supplier in that case had 'merely been acting as a supplier of goods to a purchaser, which was free to do what it wanted with the goods'. Peter Gibson LJ said that, in order to be liable, the alleged joint tortfeasor must have 'been so involved in the commission of the tort as to make himself liable for the tort', and that he must have 'made the infringing act his own'. While I agree with the decision, I must confess to finding the reasoning rather circular, which is not surprising as the circumstances in which joint liability arises are difficult, probably impossible, to define fully satisfactorily in abstract.
>
> 105. At least to my mind, the test propounded by Mustill LJ in an earlier patent case, *Unilever v Gillette* [1989] R.P.C. 583, 608–609, is rather more helpful in the present case. At the end of a brief analysis of the principles (quoted by the Judge at [2009] EWHC 1929 (Pat), paragraph 177), Mustill LJ said that it was 'enough if the parties combined to secure the doing of acts which in the event prove to be infringements'. Merely exporting a machine from another country to a third party in the UK, even helping to install the machine in the third party's premises in the UK, would not, at least in ordinary circumstances, amount to such an act, as it is the use of the machine (which, in that case at least, was a matter entirely for the third party) which constitutes the tort."

Subsequently, in *Football Dataco Ltd v Sportradar GmbH*[178] Sir Robin Jacob, with whom Lewison and Lloyd LJJ agreed, held that the earlier authorities establish that the seller of physical goods for infringements carried out by his purchaser with those goods is not a joint tortfeasor where: (a) the goods he sells themselves are not infringing but can be used by the ultimate consumer to make infringing goods, even if the seller knows that many ultimate consumers will do just that[179]; and (b) the seller of infringing goods is abroad and is not responsible for their importation.   **14-155**

Most recently in *Fish & Fish Limited v Sea Shepherd UK*[180] the Supreme Court reviewed the law on common design in the context of the argument that the   **14-156**

---

[175] [2009] EWHC 1094 (Ch); [2009] R.P.C. 21, [346]–[382].

[176] As summarised and applied by Arnold J. in *Resolution Chemicals Ltd v H. Lundbeck A/S* [2013] EWHC 739.

[177] [2010] EWCA Civ 525.

[178] [2013] EWCA Civ 27.

[179] On the basis that in such a case the choice as to whether to infringe is made by the consumer alone and there is no common design to infringe—see the speech of Lord Templeman in *CBS v Amstrad* [1988] A.C. 1013.

[180] [2011] EWCA Civ 162; [2015] A.C. 1229; [2015] 2 W.L.R. 694.

contribution of the alleged joint tortfeasor to the tort was such as to be de minimis. The claim was for loss and damage allegedly suffered by the claimant in an incident in the Mediterranean Sea on 17 June 2010 when conservationists mounted an operation designed to disrupt the bluefin tuna fishing activities of the claimant. The appeal arose from the determination of a preliminary issue as to whether the incident was directed and/or authorised and/or carried out by the appellant, Sea Shepherd UK (a conservation group), its servants or agents, and whether it was liable, directly or vicariously, for any damage sustained by the claimant.

14-157 Lord Toulson, Lord Neuberger and Lord Kerr held that the trial judge had been entitled to find that the contribution of the appellant had been de minimis and that accordingly there was no joint liability. Lord Sumption and Lord Mance, dissenting, took the view that the contribution was above the de minimis threshold. Their Lordships however stressed that there was no difference between them as a matter of legal principle.

14-158 Lord Toulson stated the law in relation to common design to be as follows:

"To establish accessory liability in tort it is not enough to show that D did acts which facilitated P's commission of the tort. D will be jointly liable with P if they combined to do or secure the doing of acts which constituted a tort. This requires proof of two elements. D must have acted in a way which furthered the commission of the tort by P; and D must have done so in pursuance of a common design to do or secure the doing of the acts which constituted the tort. I do not consider it necessary or desirable to gloss the principle further."[181]

14-159 Lord Sumption's summary was that:

"...the defendant will be liable as a joint tortfeasor if (i) he has assisted the commission of the tort by another person, (ii) pursuant to a common design with that person, (iii) to do an act which is, or turns out to be, tortious."[182]"

Although none of their Lordships expressly considered the relationship between procurement and common design in exactly those terms, Lord Sumption made the following observation[183]:

"Inducing or procuring a tort necessarily involves common intent if the tort is then committed."

14-160 Lord Sumption identified two limiting features relevant to the scope of joint liability. The first was the alleged joint tortfeasor's intent:

"Intent in the law of tort is commonly relevant as a control mechanism limiting the ambit of a person's obligation to safeguard the rights of others, where this would constrict his freedom to engage in activities which are otherwise lawful. The economic torts are a classic illustration of this. The cases on joint torts have had to grapple with the same problem, and intent performs the same role. What the authorities, taken as a whole, demonstrate is that the additional element which is required to establish liability, over and above mere knowledge that an otherwise lawful act will assist the tort, is a shared intention that it should do so."[184]

14-161 Thus for the alleged joint tortfeasor to be liable they must have intended that their own act would assist the tort (although they need not have been aware that the act of the primary tortfeasor was, in law, a tort). By implication it is necessary that they knew of the intended act of the primary tortfeasor at the time of their own act.

14-162 The second limiting feature is the requirement that the alleged joint tortfeasor has

181 See [21].
182 See [37]. See also Lord Neuberger's summary in very similar language at [55].
183 See [41].
184 See [44].

actively co-operated with the primary tortfeasor. The two features are to be taken together:

"The required limitation on the scope of liability is achieved by the combination of active co-operation and commonality of intention. It is encapsulated in Scrutton LJ's distinction between concerted action to a common end and independent action to a similar end, and between either of these things and mere knowledge of the consequences of one's acts."[185]

In *Vertical Leisure v Poleplus*[186] HHJ Hacon interpreted this to mean that in order **14-163** to fix an alleged joint tortfeasor with liability, it must be shown both that they actively co-operated to bring about the act of the primary tortfeasor and also that they intended that their co-operation would help to bring about that act (the act found to be tortious). Liability will always be subject to the threshold requirement that the alleged joint tortfeasor's contribution to the act was more than de minimis (see [66]).

Joining parties in order to obtain disclosure

As is apparent from the authorities cited above, a common circumstance in which **14-164** joint tortfeasance is alleged is so that the claimant can bring in not only the company which is actually carrying out the infringing acts in the UK, but also its foreign parent company, usually the head of a multinational group. This may be done for a number of reasons concerned with the final remedy: there may be doubt as to whether the local subsidiary could meet an award of damages, an injunction may be needed against the parent to prevent it from continuing the infringing acts through another subsidiary, or there may be a desire to obtain a final decision on the merits which could be relied upon for purposes of issue estoppel elsewhere. One reason for joining a foreign parent which frequently arises in the cases, however, is a desire to obtain disclosure from the parent; often because it is the parent that has researched and developed the product which is the subject of the action, and the local subsidiary may have few if any documents relating to the design or the design history.

In *Mölnlycke v Procter & Gamble (No.4)*,[187] the Court of Appeal declined to **14-165** strike out an action against the third defendant, a member of the same group as the other defendants, against all of whom a good arguable case of joint tortfeasorship had been pleaded. The plaintiff conceded that its only purpose for seeking joinder of the third defendant was in order to obtain discovery. The Court of Appeal held that common design may be pleaded in such circumstances without being an abuse of the process of the court, even though the effect of the concept of common design was that discovery in cases involving multinational companies could become burdensome. Dillon LJ referred to the power of the court to control discovery so as to prevent oppression, and said:

"It is a long-established rule that a plaintiff who has been injured by a number of joint tortfeasors can choose which he will sue. But the defendants have no right whatsoever to dictate which the plaintiff shall sue or make the choice for him."[188]

---

185 At [44].
186 [2015] EWHC 841 (IPEC).
187 [1992] R.P.C. 21.
188 [1992] R.P.C. 21, 35. See also *Lubrizol Corp v Esso Petroleum Co Ltd* [1992] R.P.C. 281, 296; affirmed on appeal on other grounds—see [1992] R.P.C. 467.

14-166   As the pleading supported an arguable case of joint tortfeasorship in that case, on the principles of *Unilever v Gillette*,[189] the action was allowed to proceed.

14-167   In *Sandvik v Kennamental*[190] Arnold J considered an application to set aside service out of the jurisdiction on a foreign defendant in a patent case in which the claim against the foreign defendant was based on joint tortfeasance. In considering this question, the judge considered that the correct test to apply with regard to jurisdictional issues was that of a good arguable case. This test itself derives from the judgment of Waller LJ in *Canada Trust v Stolzenberg (No 2)*.[191] He also noted the observations made by Laddie J in *Napp v Astra*[192] about the particular considerations raised by reliance on a claim of joint tortfeasance as the basis for bringing a foreign defendant into a claim for infringement of a UK intellectual property right. The observations were:

> "... but the earlier cases illustrate that the court is careful to ensure that foreign defendants are not brought unnecessarily into English proceedings, and that the courts therefore look carefully at allegations of joint tortfeasance to see whether there is anything of substance in them. In case after case it has been said that the mere fact that a company is a parent company of a subsidiary which is a primary infringer does not make the parent itself an infringer. The fact that one company owns a trade mark which another infringing company uses on infringing goods does not make the trade mark owner an infringer. At all times the courts are looking to see whether there is a credible case made out that the joint tortfeasor has really become involved in some way with the tort in the jurisdiction which is the subject of the action."[193]

14-168   Laddie J's approach was recently endorsed by Birss J in *Magnesium Elektron Limited v Molycorp Chemicals & Oxides (Europe) Limited*.[194]

14-169   The Court of Appeal in *Unilever v Chefaro*[195] observed that it was a "heresy" that a party could be joined simply in order to obtain discovery from them; it was necessary first to show that they were arguably liable. However, Hoffmann LJ questioned whether a change in the law might be desirable in order to make such discovery available and under CPR Pt 31.17 disclosure can now be made against non-parties, although this is the exception rather than the rule.[196]

14-170   In *Teva v Amgen*[197] in circumstances where the former registered proprietor of the patent in suit had assigned it, but not other members of the same patent family, to a manufacturing subsidiary Arnold J accepted a submission in principle, on an application to remove the parent company from proceedings, that although it was not legitimate to bring proceedings against a party purely in order to obtain disclosure, it was a factor which could be taken into account in deciding whether a party should remain or cease to be a party to proceedings. Arnold J decided it was not desirable for the parent company to cease to be a party on the basis that in the context of applications for declarations of invalidity and non-infringement, it was arguable that it would be affected by the court's determination of the issues before

---

[189] See also *Puschner v Palmer* [1989] R.P.C. 430, another case where the court declined to strike out an allegation of common design.
[190] [2010] EWHC 3417 (Pat).
[191] [1998] 1 W.L.R. 547 (CA).
[192] [1999] F.S.R. 370.
[193] At 375.
[194] [2015] EWHC 3596 (Pat).
[195] [1994] F.S.R. 135.
[196] *Frankson v Home Office* [2003] 1 W.L.R. 1952, CA.
[197] [2013] EWHC 3711 (Pat).

it. In so doing he applied the criteria set out by Aikens LJ in *Rolls-Royce plc v Unite the Union*[198] as to the principles concerning the grant of declaratory relief.

Company directors

The courts have been understandably reluctant to undermine the principle of limited liability by holding that each time a director gave instructions for a company to do an act which turned out to be tortious, they incurred joint liability. Something more has to be shown, so that it can properly be said that the director has in some sense made the act his own and not merely that of the company. Directors of a limited liability company would only be liable for infringements committed by the company if it is proved that the company acted as their agent, or that they expressly authorised the infringement.[199] Once again, as with the closely related law concerning joint tortfeasors, each case will turn on its particular facts as to whether the director in question has so acted as to incur joint liability. **14-171**

In *PLG Research v Ardon International*,[200] Aldous J held that a director is not liable for tortious acts of a company unless their involvement had been such as to render them liable as a joint tortfeasor if the company had not existed. Ferris J interpreted this in *Springsteen v Flute International*,[201] a copyright case, to mean that it is necessary to look carefully at the conduct of the individual director and to see whether, if it had not been done as agent in the name and on behalf of the company, it would have made the director a joint tortfeasor. In the latter case, the company and the individual were in substance "one and the same", their identity being so complete that everything the company did was determined and directed by him without reference to anyone else: he was found to be personally liable. By contrast, in *PLG v Ardon*, Aldous J relied upon the distinction drawn in the law between merely facilitating and actually procuring a tort; a person who only facilitates a tort is not liable whereas a person who procures a tort is liable.[202] He held that the fourth defendant, the sole administrator of the third defendant who had been involved in a number of ordinary business decisions but who had a general role and did not deal with details, had at the most facilitated the alleged acts of infringement, and he was therefore held not to be personally liable for them. **14-172**

In *MCA v Charly Records*,[203] a copyright case, the Court of Appeal reviewed the authorities and concluded as follows: **14-173**

"49. First, a director will not be treated as liable with the company as a joint tortfeasor if he does

---

[198] [2009] EWCA Civ 387; [2010] 1 W.L.R. 318.

[199] *British Thomson-Houston Co Ltd v Sterling Associates Ltd* [1924] 2 Ch. 33, (1924) 41 R.P.C. 311; see also *Cropper Minerva Machines Co Ltd v Cropper, Charlton & Co Ltd* (1906) 23 R.P.C. 388, at 392; *Pritchard and Constance (Wholesale) Ltd v Amata Ltd* (1925) 42 R.P.C. 63; *Reitzmann v Grahame-Chapman and Derustit Ltd* (1950) 67 R.P.C. 178, at 185; *T. Oertli A.G. v E.J. Bowman Ltd* [1956] R.P.C. 282; *PLG v Ardon* [1992] F.S.R. 59. Compare also decisions on infringement of other intellectual property rights: *PRS v Ciryl* [1924] 1 K.B. 1; *Walker (John) & Sons v Ost (Henry) & Co* [1970] R.P.C. 489; *Hoover v Hulme (STO)* [1982] F.S.R. 565; *White Horse Distillers v Gregson Associates* [1984] R.P.C. 61; *Evans (C.) & Son v Spritebrand* [1985] F.S.R. 267; *Besson (A.P.) v Fulleon* [1986] F.S.R. 319; *BBC Worldwide v Pally Screen Printing* [1998] F.S.R. 665; *British Sky Broadcasting Group Plc v Sky Home Services Ltd* [2007] F.S.R. 14, [278]–[279].

[200] [1993] F.S.R. 197, 238.

[201] [1999] E.M.L.R. 180, 227.

[202] *CBS Songs v Amstrad Consumer Electronics* [1988] R.P.C. 567, HL; *Belegging v Witten Industrial Diamonds* [1979] F.S.R. 59; *PLG v Ardon* [1993] F.S.R. 197. See generally the discussion of joint tortfeasorship above.

[203] [2002] F.S.R. 26.

no more than carry out his constitutional role in the governance of the company—that is to say, by voting at board meetings. That, I think, is what policy requires if a proper recognition is to be given to the identity of the company as a separate legal person. Nor, as it seems to me, will it be right to hold a controlling shareholder liable as a joint tortfeasor if he does no more than exercise his power of control through the constitutional organs of the company—for example by voting at general meetings and by exercising the powers to appoint directors. Aldous LJ suggested, in *Standard Chartered Bank v Pakistan National Shipping Corporation (No.2)*[204],—in a passage to which I have referred—that there are good reasons to conclude that the carrying out of the duties of a director would never be sufficient to make a director liable. For my part, I would hesitate to use the word "never" in this field; but I would accept that, if all that a director is doing is carrying out the duties entrusted to him as such by the company under its constitution, the circumstances in which it would be right to hold him liable as a joint tortfeasor with the company would be rare indeed. That is not to say, of course, that he might not be liable for his own separate tort, as Aldous LJ recognised at paragraphs 16 and 17 of his judgment in the *Pakistan National Shipping* case.

50. Second, there is no reason why a person who happens to be a director or controlling shareholder of a company should not be liable with the company as a joint tortfeasor if he is not exercising control though the constitutional organs of the company and the circumstances are such that he would be so liable if he were not a director or controlling shareholder. In other words, if, in relation to the wrongful acts which are the subject of complaint, the liability of the individual as a joint tortfeasor with the company arises from his participation or involvement in ways which go beyond the exercise of constitutional control, then there is no reason why the individual should escape liability because he could have procured those same acts through the exercise of constitutional control. As I have said, it seems to me that this is the point made by Aldous J (as he then was) in *PLG Research Ltd v Ardon International Ltd*.[205]

51. Third, the question whether the individual is liable with the company as a joint tortfeasor—at least in the field of intellectual property—is to be determined under principles identified in *C.B.S. Songs Ltd v Amstrad Consumer Electronics Plc*[206] and *Unilever Plc v Gillette (U.K.) Limited*.[207] In particular, liability as a joint tortfeasor may arise where, in the words of Lord Templeman in *C.B.S. Songs v Amstrad* at page 1058E to which I have already referred, the individual 'intends and procures and shares a common design that the infringement takes place'.

52. Fourth, whether or not there is a separate tort of procuring an infringement of a statutory right, actionable at common law, an individual who does 'intend, procure and share a common design' that the infringement should take place may be liable as a joint tortfeasor. As Mustill LJ pointed out in *Unilever v Gillette*, procurement may lead to a common design and so give rise to liability under both heads.

53. In the light of the authorities which I have reviewed I am satisfied that no criticism can be made of the test which the judge applied.[208] But, in my view, the test can, perhaps, be expressed more accurately in these terms: in order to hold Mr Young liable as a joint tortfeasor for acts of copying, and of issuing to the public, in respect of which CRL was the primary infringer and in circumstances in which he was not himself a person who committed or participated directly in those acts, it was necessary and sufficient to find that he procured or induced those acts to be done by CRL or that, in some other way, he and CRL joined together in concerted action to secure that those acts were done."

14-174   In *Societa Explosivi Industrial SpA v Ordnance Technologies (UK) Ltd*,[209] it was submitted that the first proposition (the so-called "constitutional exception") was not supported by previous case law but it was not necessary to decide the point. It was also pointed out that the test ultimately applied was essentially a circular one, but that this area of the law involved elusive and difficult questions, hence framing a precise definition which was suitable for all cases was likewise difficult.

---

204 [2000] 1 Lloyd's Rep. 218, 235.
205 [1993] F.S.R. 197.
206 [1988] A.C. 1013.
207 [1989] R.P.C. 583.
208 See the judgment at [37], which cites the test applied at first instance.
209 [2006] R.P.C. 12

Since 2002 *MCA v Charly Records* has been consistently applied in consider- **14-175**
ing the issue of director's liability[210]; see most recently for example *Twentieth*
Century Fox v Harris[211] in which the earlier decision of Kitchin J in *Twentieth*
Century Fox v Newzbin[212] was considered and applied to find the director of
Newzbin personally liable as joint tortfeasor with his company.

5. STATUTORY EXCEPTIONS TO INFRINGEMENT

The 1977 Act enacts a number of exceptions to the rights conferred by a patent. **14-176**
The exceptions stem from art.27 of the Community Patent Convention.[213] In the
case of some of the exceptions, it is possible to trace their origin even further
back.[214] More recently, further exceptions have been introduced into the 1977 Act
by the Patents Regulations 2000 (implementing arts 1–11 of the Biotech Directive)[215] and by the Medicines Marketing Authorisations Etc) Amendment Regulations 2005 (implementing art.10(6) of Directive 2001/83/EC and art.13(6) of Directive 2001/82/EC).[216]

At least in the case of those exceptions which stem from EU law, they must be **14-177**
read and construed in the light of the wording and purpose of the TRIPS Agreement[217] and, in particular, art.30 of TRIPS which states:

"Members may provide limited exceptions to the exclusive rights conferred by a patent, provided that
such exceptions do not unreasonably conflict with a normal exploitation of the patent and do not
unreasonably prejudice the legitimate interests of the patent owner, taking account of the legitimate
interests of third parties."

Private use

Under s.60(5)(a) of the 1977 Act, an act which would otherwise infringe a pat- **14-178**
ent will not do so if it is done privately and for purposes which are not commercial.
However, if there is a dual purpose and one of those purposes is commercial, then
this exception will not apply.[218]

Experimental use

Similarly, under s.60(5)(b), an act done for experimental purposes relating to the **14-179**
subject-matter of the action will not be an infringement.

The subsection was considered by the Court of Appeal in *Monsanto Co v Stauffer* **14-180**
Chemical Co,[219] where Dillon LJ held that the word "experiment" was to be given
its ordinary meaning, and that, in view of the statutory history of the section, deci-

---

[210] For example, *Boeglis-Gravures SA v Darsail-ASP Ltd* [2009] EWHC 2690 (Pat) in which one of
the defendant's directors was held personally liable having been found to have exceeded his
constitutional role in the company.

[211] [2014] EWHC 1568 (Ch), at [135]–[139].

[212] *Twentieth Century Fox Corpn v Newzbin Ltd* [2011] EWHC 608 (Ch).

[213] See para.1-70, et seq.

[214] See, e.g. s.60(5)(d) is derived from art.5 of the Paris Convention (see para.1-60). See also art.27 of
the Convention on International Civil Aviation of 7 December 1944.

[215] See para.1-46, et seq.

[216] See para.1-51, et seq.

[217] See para.1-72, et seq.

[218] *Smith, Kline & French Laboratories Ltd v Evans Medical Ltd* [1989] F.S.R. 513; *McDonald v
Graham* [1994] R.P.C. 407, 431.

[219] [1985] R.P.C. 515; compare also *Monsanto v Stauffer (New Zealand)* [1984] F.S.R. 559; *Smith, Kline*

sions under the old law as to what constituted "experimental purposes" were not of assistance.

14-181   He went on to hold that, although experimental purposes could have an ultimate commercial end in view (hence the difference in wording between subparas 60(5)(a) and (b)):

> "Trials carried out in order to discover something unknown or to test a hypothesis or even in order to find out whether something which is known to work in specific conditions, e.g. of soil or weather, will work in different conditions can fairly, in my judgment, be regarded as experiments. But trials carried out in order to demonstrate to a third party that a product works or, in order to amass information to satisfy a third party, whether a customer or a body such as the PSPS or ACAS [regulatory bodies], that the product works as its maker claims are not, in my judgment, to be regarded as acts done 'for experimental purposes'. The purposes for which tests or trials are carried out may in some cases be mixed and may in some cases be difficult to discern; indeed, in the present case, if fuller evidence is given at the trial, a different result may then be reached. On the affidavit evidence before this court, it is not clear to me what the defendants are still wanting to find out about TOUCHDOWN. On that evidence, if I ask, in relation to the defendants' proposed field trials of category (2) to be carried out by the second defendant's personnel on land rented on other farms, the broad question whether those trials would be carried out, or done, for experimental purposes, my answer is that they would not; they would be carried out in order to obtain the approval of the PSPS and ACAS."[220]

14-182   The approach in *Monsanto* has been followed in a number of subsequent cases.[221] The German Federal Supreme Court has taken a similar view, holding in *Klinische Versuche II*[222] that:

> "The ground for granting a patent to the inventor is therefore ultimately the public interest in scientific and technological progress.
>
> Therefore the unlimited protection of the patent is not justified in a case where the further development of technology is hindered ... However, with this purpose of the patent right it is impossible to stipulate that research activities which are concerned with the research and further development of technology would be impermissible if they are at the same time undertaken with the additional, or even overwhelming, motivation of using the results of the tests to prepare for commercial exploitation."[223]

14-183   It was submitted in *Monsanto* that the words "relating to the subject-matter of the invention" ought to be narrowly construed so as to exclude any experiments directed to commercial exploitation, but the Court of Appeal rejected this submission, since the difference in wording between subparas (a) and (b) of s.60(5) indicated that the experimental purposes may yet have a commercial end in view. In *Smith Kline & French Laboratories Ltd v Evans Medical Ltd*,[224] Aldous J considered that the words nonetheless had a limiting effect, and held that for the protection to apply the act must be done for purposes relating to the subject-matter of the invention found in the claims of the patent alleged to be infringed, in the sense of having a real and direct connection with that subject-matter. Hence a company seeking to investigate a chemical patent using a reagent which is itself patented would have a defence under the chemical patent but not under the reagent

---

& *French Laboratories Ltd v Evans Medical Ltd* [1989] F.S.R. 513.
[220] [1985] R.P.C. 515, 542.
[221] *Smith Kline & French Laboratories Ltd v Evans Medical Ltd* [1989] F.S.R. 513; *Auchincloss v Agricultural and Veterinary Supplies* [1999] R.P.C. 397.
[222] Case X ZR 68/94, reported at [1998] R.P.C. 423.
[223] In *Corevalve Inc v Edwards Lifesciences AG* [2009] F.S.R. 8 it was suggested that where the defendant's acts are done for mixed purposes, it may be necessary to consider their preponderant purpose.
[224] [1989] F.S.R. 513.

patent, since the investigations only relate to the chemical patent. The German Federal Supreme Court has taken a similar approach.[225]

On the basis of these authorities, it is submitted that, in the case of pharmaceutical products, carrying out clinical trials, including Phase III clinical trials, will be entitled to a defence under s.60(5)(b) to an infringement action. This submission is supported by the fact that in Directive 2004/27/EC, it is expressly provided that clinical trials necessary to obtain regulatory approval for a generic medical product shall not be regarded as contrary to patent rights.[226] No equivalent provision is made in respect of medicinal products intended for research and development which would have been required if no defence was available under s.60(5)(b) (and equivalent provisions in other member states). **14-184**

Where an infringing product was sold for experimental use by another, the vendor was liable for infringement[227]; it is submitted that the same result would follow under the 1977 Act as it is has been held that seeking to exploit and sell technology cannot be experimental use.[228] To purchase and use infringing articles for the purpose of instructing pupils and to enable them to pull them to pieces and put them together again was not mere experimental use, and amounted to an infringement.[229] **14-185**

Extemporaneous preparation on prescription

The extemporaneous preparation in a pharmacy of a medicine for an individual in accordance with a prescription given by a registered medical or dental practitioner is excluded by s.60(5)(c) from infringement, as are all dealings with medicines so prepared. The provision was new in the 1977 Act; it is consistent with the policy of s.4(2). **14-186**

Vessels, vehicles and aircraft

Ships

Under s.60(5)(d), an act which consists of the use, exclusively for the needs of a relevant ship, of a product or process in the body of such a ship or in its machinery, tackle or apparatus or other accessories, in a case where the ship has temporarily or accidentally entered the internal or territorial waters of the UK does not constitute infringement.[230] **14-187**

"Relevant ship" is defined in s.60(7); the definition expressly excludes ships registered in the UK. **14-188**

The protection extends only to uses "exclusively for the needs of a relevant ship" so that a distinction is to be drawn between a use which is exclusively for such needs and one which is not. Thus where a ship is used for laying marine cable, that operation is not protected by s.60(5)(d) because it is not "exclusively for the needs of a relevant ship". The cable laying is for the needs of the party which has asked **14-189**

---

225 *Klinische Versuche I* (X ZR 99/92) [1997] R.P.C. 623, 639.
226 See art.10(6) of Directive 2001/83/EC as amended by art.1(8) of Directive 2004/27/EC. The same applies to veterinary products, see Directive 2004/28/EC. But note the amendment to PA 1977 s.60 referred to at para.14-196 which came into force on 30 October 2005.
227 *Hoffmann-La Roche & Co A.G. v Harris Pharmaceuticals Ltd* [1977] F.S.R. 200.
228 *Inhale Therapeutics v Quadrant* [2002] R.P.C. 21, 419.
229 *United Telephone Co v Sharples* (1885) 2 R.P.C. 28.
230 PA 1977 s.60(5)(d).

the cable to be laid and the vessel is being used for that purpose.[231] Section 60(5)(d) comes into play to protect the vessel in so far as it is engaged in inter-state passage.[232]

14-190　　The protection is also limited to the case where the ship has "temporarily or accidentally" entered the internal or territorial waters of the United Kingdom. The meaning of the word "temporarily" was considered in *Stena Rederi AB v Irish Ferries Ltd*[233] where a ferry registered in Eire which sailed regularly between Dublin and Holyhead was alleged to infringe a UK patent by virtue of its frequent presence within UK territorial waters. This allegation was rejected by the Court of Appeal which held that the shipowner was entitled to the defence provided by s.60(5)(d) and held that "temporarily" meant transient or for a limited period of time and did not depend on frequency.

14-191　　Accidental entry may occur when a ship gets lost or when bad weather blows it off course. In the case of accidental entry, the entry may be permanent (e.g. shipwreck).

Aircraft, hovercraft and vehicles

14-192　　Use of a product or process in the body or operation of a relevant[234] aircraft, hovercraft or vehicle which has temporarily or accidentally entered or is crossing the UK (including the airspace above it and its territorial waters) or the use of accessories for such aircraft, hovercraft or vehicle is also protected.[235] In this subsection, there is no requirement of "exclusive use" but otherwise the protection is complementary to that for ships. Further protection is given in respect of the use of exempted[236] aircraft which are lawfully entering or crossing the UK (as defined above) and of the importation into the UK or the use or storage there of any part or accessory for such an aircraft.[237]

Agricultural exceptions

14-193　　Two new agricultural exceptions have been introduced by an amendment to subs.(5).[238] Section 60(5)(g) relates to the use by a farmer of the product of their harvest for propagation or multiplication by them on their own holding, where the farmer has been sold patented propagatory material by the patentee or with their consent. The farmer is however required to pay equitable remuneration in respect of their use[239] and complex provisions are provided in Sch.1A of the Act to regulate the relationship between the farmer and the patentee.[240]

14-194　　Section 60(5)(h) permits a farmer who has been sold by the patentee or with their consent breeding stock or other animal reproductive material which constitutes or contains the patented invention to use the animal or animal reproductive material

---

[231] Per Laddie J in *Stena Rederi AB v Irish Ferries Ltd* [2002] R.P.C. 50, 990, [74]–[75].

[232] *Stena Rederi AB v Irish Ferries Ltd* [2002] R.P.C. 50, 990, [74]–[75].

[233] [2002] R.P.C. 50, 990 and [2003] R.P.C. 36, 668.

[234] Defined in PA 1977 s.60(7), as amended.

[235] PA 1977 s.60(5)(e).

[236] Defined in PA 1977 s.60(7), as amended.

[237] PA 1977 s.60(5)(f).

[238] PA 1977 s.60(5)(g) and (h) as amended by reg.4 of the Patents Regulations 2000 (SI 2000/2037). The amendments apply to applications for patents made on or after 28 July 2000 (see reg.9).

[239] PA 1977 Sch.1A para.3.

[240] See PA 1977 s.60(6A).

for agricultural purposes. Use "for an agricultural purpose" includes making an animal or animal reproductive material available for the purposes of pursuing the farmer's agricultural activity, but does not include sale within the framework, or for the purposes, of commercial reproduction activity.[241]

In the case of s.60(5)(g) and (h), "sale" includes any other form of commercialisation.[242] **14-195**

Studies, tests or trials

Further exceptions to infringement in respect of studies, tests or trials have been introduced by amendment to subs.(5).[243] The amendment is to implement art.10(6)[244] of Directive 2001/83/EC of the European Parliament and of the Council on the Community Code relating to medicinal products for human use, and art.13(6)[245] of Directive 2001/82/EC on the Community Code relating to veterinary medicinal products. As amended, s.60(5)(i) provides that an act done in conducting a study, test or trial which is necessary for and is conducted with a view to the application of art.10(1)–(4) of Directive 2001/83/EC (applications for generic medicinal products) or art.13(1)–(5) of Directive 2001/82/EC, and any other act which is required for the purpose of the application of those paragraphs, shall not constitute an infringement of a patent. **14-196**

It should be noted that the Directive provides that such acts do not infringe any patent rights *for medicinal products* (see art.10(6)) whereas s.60(5)(i) of the 1977 Act, as amended in order to implement the Directive, could be read as providing that such acts do not infringe any patent rights at all.[246] However, under EU law, the court is required to construe s.60(5)(i) in the light of the wording and the purpose of the Directive in order to achieve the result envisaged by the Directive. Consequently, when properly construed, there may be no difference between the scope of s.10(5)(i) and that of the Directive. **14-197**

Other potential differences between the scope of the UK implementing legislation and the directive can be seen by comparison of the UK implementing legislation with the corresponding implementing legislation of other Member States. For example the UK implementation of the directive is at least limited to permitting acts done for purposes of the abridged procedure for European marketing authorisation, whereas the French implementing legislation allows acts done for purposes of any marketing authorisation in the EU, and the German implementation allows any acts done for purposes of any marketing authorisation in any country. **14-198**

Right to continue use begun before priority date

Under the 1949 Act, no protection was given to an infringer who commenced his infringing activity before the priority date of the patent. However, secret use was a ground for revocation of a patent and thus secret use was protected. Under the 1977 Act, secret use no longer invalidates a patent, although rights are given under **14-199**

---

[241] PA 1977 s.60(6B).

[242] PA 1977 s.60(6C).

[243] PA 1977 s.60(5)(i), as amended by the Medicines (Marketing Authorisations Etc.) Amendment Regulations 2005 (SI 2005/2759) reg.3. The Regulations come into effect on 30 October 2005.

[244] Substituted by art.1(8) of Directive 2004/27/EC.

[245] Substituted by art.1(6) of Directive 2004/28/EC.

[246] Note the absence of any reference to art.10(6).

s.64 to any person who in the UK before the priority date of the invention does in good faith an act which would constitute an infringement of the patent if it were in force, or makes in good faith effective and serious preparations to do such an act.

14-200   In *Schenck v Universal Balancing*[247] it was submitted that s.64 was contrary to Directive 2004/48/EC on the Enforcement of Intellectual Property Rights ("the Enforcement Directive") and had been impliedly repealed by the secondary legislation[248] which was passed in the light of the Enforcement Directive. HHJ Birss QC sitting as a judge of the High Court rejected the submission, noting that although doubts had been raised to whether the section is compliant with European Union law, those doubts relate to the territorial limitations in the section. Section 64 is not concerned with remedies for patent infringement, it is concerned with whether certain acts constitute infringement. The Enforcement Directive on the other hand, is concerned with harmonising remedies, not infringement itself.

In the UK

14-201   Although the 1977 Act specifies that the act in question must be in the UK, it is submitted that this will extend to all forms of potentially infringing acts including importation.

In good faith

14-202   The act or preparations must be in good faith and, thus, use of an invention in contravention of the inventor's rights, for example in breach of confidence or possibly in infringement of an earlier patent, will be excluded.

Which would constitute an infringement

14-203   It is necessary that the act in question would, if the patent had been granted, have constituted infringement. Thus, if the act in question was one for which protection was given by the 1977 Act (e.g. private or experimental use) the user will not be able to benefit from the rights granted by s.64. However, experimental use may constitute effective and serious preparations to do an "infringing" act.

Effective and serious preparations

14-204   This concept was new in the 1977 Act and occurs in both s.64 and s.28. Whether preparations have become effective and serious will be a question of fact in any given case, and in view of the wide range of possible circumstances that could arise, it is difficult to predict what extent of protection the section will afford. In *Helitune v Stewart Hughes*,[249] the defendant had produced prototypes of the products in issue but at the priority date had not sold any and instead was concentrating on producing a different "non-infringing" product. It was held that the stage of making effective and serious preparations had not been reached. In *Lubrizol v Esso Petroleum*,[250] it was also held that the necessary stage of effective and serious preparations to manufacture in the UK had not been reached (although the court ap-

---

[247] [2012] EWHC 1920 (Pat), [194].
[248] i.e. SI 2006/1028.
[249] [1991] F.S.R. 171.
[250] [1998] R.P.C. 727, 770.

pears to have overlooked that importation and disposal had actually taken place before the priority date). Aldous LJ held that:

> "The word 'effective' qualifies the word 'preparations'. It follows that there must be something more than preparations to do an infringing act. What more will depend upon the nature of the product and all the surrounding circumstances, but in all cases the preparations must be so advanced as to be about to result in the infringing act being done."

In many factual circumstances it may be difficult to identify the moment when **14-205** activities move to a stage of being effective and serious preparations; for example, as a product moves from a paper proposal to a commercial trial, or where negotiations, e.g. to import an article, move from mere preparatory discussions to contractual negotiations. Once the contract is concluded, it is submitted that the preparations will have been completed, although before then the position is less clear. The court will have to decide the question on the basis of the user's evidence and the onus will be on them to plead[251] and show the necessary preparations.

The rights given

The section provides "what can be called a statutory licence".[252] The rights given **14-206** are set out in ss.64(1) and (2) of the 1977 Act (as amended by CDPA 1988), which provide that any person who has in good faith done the necessary act, or made preparations to do it, shall have the right:

(1) to continue to do or, as the case may be, to do that act (but their right does not extend to granting a licence to another person to do the act); and

(2) if the act was done, or the preparations were made, in the course of a business, to

    (a) authorise the doing of that act by any partners of theirs for the time being in that business, and

    (b) assign that right, or transmit it on death (or in the case of a body corporate on its dissolution), to any person who acquires that part of the business in the course of which the act was done or the preparations were made.

Continue to do that act

The meaning to be given to the word "act" has given rise to difficulties. Clearly, **14-207** the word covers a single infringing act which extends over a period of time (for example, the building of a ship), although it is submitted that it is also intended to cover a situation in which infringing acts are repeated, for example, by the use of a machine which repeatedly produces infringing products day after day, even though the making of each individual article will be a separate act of infringement for the purposes of damages and of the Limitation Acts. It is further submitted that the right to continue is therefore not limited merely to completing one infringing act which appears to span the moment of grant.[253]

The Act imposes no quantitative restrictions. If a person has manufactured one **14-208** potentially infringing product they should be at liberty to repeat that act as and when they please even if this involves the purchase of new plant since any quantitative

---

[251] *Instance v Denny* [1994] F.S.R. 396.

[252] Per Aldous J in *Helitune v Stewart Hughes* [1991] F.S.R. 171, at 206.

[253] See *Rotocrop International v Genbourne* [1982] F.S.R. 241, at 262.

restriction would be inconsistent with one of the objects of patent law which is to contribute to the increase of knowledge without fettering the right of others to use their pre-existing knowledge. The right is restricted to continuing to do that act and not any infringing act. Thus, if the potentially infringing act was making (which no doubt would also be effective and serious preparations for disposal), this would not entitle the person in question to import instead of make. Such a conclusion is consistent with the provisions of s.64(3).

14-209 A further question which can give rise to difficulty is that of the extent to which the section permits any qualitative change in the act to be repeated. In *Lubrizol v Esso Petroleum*,[254] Aldous LJ clarified the position and laid to rest some of the doubts which had arisen in earlier authorities. He set out the law thus:

> "It seems that the words used by me in *Helitune* have been read in a way not intended. Clearly, the right given by section 64 cannot be a right to manufacture any product nor a right to expand into other products. However, I do not believe that identicality is required. I believe that the judge was right in this case when he said:
>
> > 'If the protected act has to be *exactly* the same (whatever that may mean) as the prior art then the protection given by the section would be illusory. The section is intended to give practical protection to enable a man to continue doing what in substance he was doing before.'"

14-210 It is submitted that some measure of freedom to incorporate qualitative changes must properly be given to the prior user, and that they will be permitted to modify their prior use in ways that do not affect the essential nature of their product or process, but not in ways that materially alter and improve its nature; for the prior user should generally be able to show that the placing of a product on the market in itself involved an intention to make modifications of the former kind during the lifetime of the product. However, where the claimed invention was to a process, the prior act which would have been an infringement was the importation of the product made by the claimed process. Accordingly the defence applied to the importation of the product made by that process, not to the importation of the product however made.[255] Of course, the question of whether or not they are in substance doing what they did before may give rise to difficult questions of fact.

Right to assign to successors

14-211 Section 64(2) provides a right to assign the right to continue to do the prior use to successors and to authorise business partners to do the prior use. The right is limited to cases where the prior use or preparation was done in the course of a business and the assignment is to a person acquiring that part of the business.

No right to grant licences

14-212 A prior user obtaining rights under s.64 cannot licence another to exercise those rights.[256]

---

[254] [1998] R.P.C. 727, 770.
[255] *H. Lundbeck A/S v Norpharma SpA* [2011] EWHC 907 (Pat); [2011] R.P.C. 23, [163]–[173]. Note also that the importation of a racemic mixture was held not to be substantially the same act as the importation of one of the enantiomers.
[256] PA 1977 s.64(4).

Protection on disposal

Where a patented product is disposed of by any person to another in exercise of **14-213** a right conferred by s.64(2), that other and any person claiming through them shall be entitled to deal with the product in the same way as if it has been disposed of by a sole registered proprietor.[257]

Right to continue use commenced in other circumstances

There are also a number of instances where the Act makes provision for the **14-214** protection of those who in good faith begin to do an act, or in good faith make effective and serious to do an act, during a period in which the patent is for one reason or another not in force but subsequently comes back into effect. As with s.64, there may well be difficulties in all these cases in determining the date by which effective and serious preparations can be said to have been made.

Restoration following failure to pay renewal fees

A patent, which has lapsed by reason of failure to pay renewal fees,[258] may be **14-215** restored in certain circumstances.[259] In these circumstances, s.28A of the 1977 Act contains provision for the protection of persons who may have begun to use the invention in the meantime. Provided such acts are begun, or serious and effective preparations to do such acts are made, in good faith after the period when it was no longer possible for the patent to be renewed under s.25(4) but before publication of notice of the application for restoration, then similar protection is provided as under s.64.[260] However, if such acts were begun before the end of the period of six months after lapse (i.e. were either begun before lapse, or begun less than six months after lapse), then they are treated as infringements.[261]

Reinstatement following failure to comply with a time period

An application for a patent may also be reinstated after it has been refused, or **14-216** treated as having been refused or withdrawn, because of the applicant's failure to comply with a time period set out in the Act or rules or specified by the Comptroller.[262] In these circumstances, protection of persons who may have begun to use the invention prior to its reinstatement is provided by s.20B of the 1977 Act. Provided that the application has been published before its termination and that such acts are begun, or serious and effective preparations to do such acts are made, in good faith after the termination of the application but before publication of notice of the request for reinstatement, then similar protection is provided as under s.64.[263] However, if such acts were begun before the expiry of the time when it was pos-

---

[257] PA 1977 s.64(4).
[258] PA 1977 s.25(3).
[259] PA 1977 s.28.
[260] PA 1977 s.28A(4)–(6).
[261] PA 1977 s.28A(3).
[262] PA 1977 s.20A and see para.3-49.
[263] PA 1977 s.20B(4)–(6).

sible to extend the period which the applicant has failed to comply with, then they are treated as infringements.[264]

Re-establishment under the European Patent Convention following loss of rights

14-217 Similar provisions to the above apply in relation to those who have begun in good faith to do (or made in good faith effective and serious preparations to do) an act which would constitute infringement of the rights conferred by publication of a European patent application after such application is refused, withdrawn or deemed withdrawn, or after the designation of the UK in the application is withdrawn or deemed withdrawn, and before the rights of the applicant are subsequently re-established under the European Patent Convention.[265] Such persons have the right to do, or continue to do, the act notwithstanding such re-establishment and any subsequent grant of the patent.

Correction of inaccurate translation

14-218 Where the authentic text of a European patent or application is French or German a translation into English of the specification or claims shall be treated as the authentic text for the purpose of domestic proceedings (other than proceedings for revocation of the patent) if the translation confers narrower protection than the original.[266] In such circumstances the proprietor or application may file a corrected translation with the Patent Office, and if they do so:

(a) payments made for use of the invention are not recoverable, and the proprietor cannot bring proceedings, in respect of acts which infringe the correct translation but not the original translation—except where the corrected translation has been published or communicated to the alleged user of the invention before the relevant acts were committed; and

(b) a person who begins in good faith to do (or makes in good faith effective and serious preparations to do) an act which would not constitute infringement of the originally translated version, but would do so under the amended translation, shall have the right to do, or continue to do, such act notwithstanding such corrected translation and any subsequent grant of the patent.[267]

Resuscitation of patent following withdrawal

14-219 Similarly an application for a patent which has been withdrawn may be resuscitated where there has been an error or mistake in the withdrawal.[268] In these circumstances, s.117A of the 1977 Act contains provision for the protection of persons who may have begun to use the invention prior to its resuscitation. Provided that the application (and details of its withdrawal) have been published and that such acts are begun, or serious and effective preparations to do such acts are made, in

[264] PA 1977 s.20B(3).
[265] PA 1977 ss.77(5) and 78(6) and (6C), as substituted by Patents Act 2004 s.5 Sch.1 para.3(3) with effect from 13 December 2007 (SI 2007/3396).
[266] PA 1977 s.80(2).
[267] PA 1977 s.80(3) and s.80(4)–(7), as substituted by Patents Act 2004 s.5 and Sch.1 para.4 with effect from 13 December 2007 (SI 2007/3396).
[268] PA 1977 s.117 and see para.3-50.

good faith after withdrawal but before publication of the notice of the request to correct the error or mistake in the withdrawal, then similar protection is provided as under s.64.[269] However, if such acts were begun before withdrawal, there is no protection.[270]

6. OTHER DEFENCES TO INFRINGEMENT

Consent of the proprietor of the patent

It is a prerequisite of infringement under ss.60(1) and (2) of the 1977 Act that **14-220** the act complained of should be done without the consent of the proprietor of the patent. There is no requirement that this consent should be express and the normal rules of law will apply to determine whether consent is to be implied.

Express instructions by patentee

Express instructions given by the patentee, or on their behalf, negative infringe- **14-221** ment if they were specific directions to do that which was claimed in the patent, such directions amounting in effect to a licence.

This can cause embarrassment in cases where the patentee, seeking to obtain **14-222** evidence of a prospective defendant's infringing acts, has placed trap orders which turn out to be too specific as to what was required. In *Kelly v Batchelar*,[271] the plaintiff's patent was for a telescopic ladder, being two ladders joined together, the inner being raised or lowered by means of an endless cord. The plaintiff, for the purpose of adducing evidence of infringement, instructed an agent to order from the defendant an adjustable ladder with the endless cord. The defendant made a ladder to this order but without a cord. The agent of the plaintiff said that it would not do, but must have a cord with pulleys, whereupon the defendant added the cord as instructed. In the action for infringement brought against the defendant, North J held that the defendant acted upon the express instructions of the plaintiff's agent, who had power and authority to give such instructions, and consequently that making this ladder did not amount to an infringement of the plaintiff's patent.[272]

By contrast, in *Dunlop Pneumatic Tyre Co v Neal*,[273] the agent of the plaintiffs **14-223** was sent to the defendant to ask him to repair an old tyre, the subject of the plaintiff's patent, with a view to ascertaining whether the defendant was infringing the patent by purporting merely to repair tyres. The agent gave no express instructions as to what was to be done to the worn tyres beyond saying that they were to be repaired. It was held that what was done by the defendant amounted to infringement, and that in such a case he could not shelter himself behind the instructions of the plaintiff's agent.

Effect of sale by patentee

Where a patentee alone or along with their agent, sold the patented article without **14-224** limitation, they sold the right of free disposition as to that article, and if they sold

---

[269] PA 1977 s.117A(4)–(6).
[270] PA 1977 s.117A(3).
[271] (1893) 10 R.P.C. 289.
[272] See also *Henser & Guignard v Hardie* (1894) 11 R.P.C. 471.
[273] (1899) 16 R.P.C. 247.

the article abroad, the purchaser could import and sell it in England. Lord Hatherley, in *Betts v Willmott*,[274] said:

"Unless it can be shown, not that there is some clear injunction to his agents, but that there is some clear communication to the party to whom the article is sold, I apprehend that inasmuch as he had the right of vending the goods in France, or Belgium or England, or in any other quarter of the globe, he transfers with the goods necessarily the licence to use them wherever the purchaser pleases. When a man has purchased an article he expects to have control of it, and there must be some clear and explicit agreement to the contrary to justify the vendor in saying that he has not given the purchaser his licence to sell the article, or to use it wherever he pleases as against himself."

14-225 This reasoning amounts to saying that the patentee has impliedly licensed the acts complained of, and as a result the patentee may exclude such an implied licence, by expressly limiting the rights granted to the purchaser. As noted below[275] to be effective, however, this limitation must be notified to subsequent purchasers of the goods. An alternative explanation adopted by some other legal systems is that of exhaustion of rights which leaves no patent rights to be enforced.[276]

14-226 Where, however, goods are made under licence abroad, it is a question of fact in each case whether the licence implies permission to sell the licensed product in this country in violation of the patent.[277] Similarly, if the patentee has assigned their patent rights in this country, prima facie, they cannot then manufacture infringing articles abroad and seek to sell them in this country.[278] However, any sale in this country under such circumstances may not be a violation of the patent either under the doctrine of exhaustion of rights[279] or by reason of an implied licence or consent.[280] In *HTC v Nokia*[281] Arnold J held he was bound by the principle that there was a fundamental distinction between a sale of a product and a licence under a patent, in that in the case of the former, the purchaser acquired all rights that were not expressly reserved, although in the case of the latter, the licensee acquired only those rights which were expressly or necessarily granted. However, he noted that on the alternative analysis of the sale exhausting the patentee's rights, no contractual restriction could revive those rights.

Limited licence

14-227 If a person acquired goods covered by a patent and at the time when he acquired those goods they had knowledge that a restrictive condition had been imposed in relation to them, any dealing with the goods in breach of such restrictive condition constituted an infringement.[282] The restrictive condition was not effective if such

---

[274] (1871) L.R. 6 Ch.App. 239, 245.

[275] At para.14–227.

[276] See Lord Hoffmann in *United Wire Ltd v Screen Repair Services (Scotland) Ltd* [2001] R.P.C. 24, at [68]–[69].

[277] See *Société Anonyme des Manufactures de Glaces v Tilghman's Patent Sand Blast Co* (1883) 25 Ch D. 1; *Beecham Group Ltd v International Products Ltd* [1968] R.P.C. 129; *Beecham Group Ltd v Shewan Tomes (Traders) Ltd* [1968] R.P.C. 268, at 284; *Minnesota Mining & Manufacturing Co v Geerpres Europe Ltd* [1974] R.P.C. 35; *Wellcome Foundation Lrd v Discpharm Ltd* [1993] F.S.R. 433; *Football Association Premier League Ltd v QC Leisure (No. 2)* [2008] WEHC 1411 (Ch), [2008] F.S.R. 32, [171]–[173].

[278] *Betts v Willmott* (1871) L.R. 6 Ch.App. 239.

[279] See para.14–240, et seq.

[280] See *Revlon Inc v Cripps & Lee Ltd* [1980] F.S.R. 85.

[281] [2013] EWHC 3247 (Pat); [2014] R.P.C. 19.

[282] *National Phonographic Co of Australia Ltd v Menck* (1911) 28 R.P.C. 229; *Columbia Gramophone*

person gained knowledge of it only after they had acquired the goods, even though they might receive such knowledge before reselling the goods.[283]

In *Roussel Uclaf v Hockley International*,[284] Jacob J stated the law as follows: **14-228**

> "It is the law that where the patentee supplies his product and at the time of the supply informs the person supplied (normally via the contract) that there are limitations as to what may be done with the product supplied then, provided those terms are brought home first to the person originally supplied and, second, to subsequent dealers in the product, no licence to carry out or do any act outside the terms of the licence runs with the goods. If no limited licence is imposed on them at the time of the first supply no amount of notice thereafter either to the original supplyee (if that is the appropriate word) or persons who derive title from him can turn the general licence into a limited licence."

Repairing

Difficult questions of fact may arise where it is alleged that the patent has been **14-229**
infringed by what amounts to the manufacture of a new article under the guise of repairing an old article which had been made under the patent. In *Sirdar Rubber Co Ltd v Wallington, Weston & Co*,[285] Lord Halsbury said: "The principle is quite clear, although its application is sometimes difficult; you may prolong the life of a licensed article, but you must not make a new one under cover of repair."[286]

In *British Leyland Motor Corp v Armstrong Patents Co*,[287] Lord Bridge cited the **14-230**
above passage with approval, and said:

> "Letters patent, on their face, always granted to the patentee the exclusive right 'to make, use, exercise and vend' the invention. A literal application of this language would lead to the absurdity that a person who acquired the patented goods would infringe the patent if he used or resold them. To avoid this absurdity the courts had recourse to the doctrine of implied licence. In the field of repair it is clear that a person who acquires a patented article has an implied licence to keep it in repair, but must stop short of renewal."

This decision was however considered by the Privy Council in *Canon K.K. v* **14-231**
Green Cartridge,[288] where it was held that replacement of toner cartridges (the subject of a patent) could not be regarded as "repair" of the copier or printer in which they were used.

In *Solar Thompson Engineering Co Ltd v Barton*[289] Buckley LJ expressed the law **14-232**
as follows:

> "The cardinal question must be whether what has been done can fairly be termed a repair, having regard to the nature of the patented article. If it is, any purchaser of such an article, whether from the patentee or from a licensee of the patentee or from a purchaser from the patentee or such a licensee or purchaser, is impliedly licensed to carry it out or to contract with someone else to carry it out for him; for clearly the implied licence must be as transferable as the patented article and must include permission to authorise an agent or contractor to carry out whatever the owner of the article could himself do under the licence, had he the required skill and equipment."

The law on this topic was most recently reviewed by the House of Lords in **14-233**

Co Ltd v Murray (1922) 39 R.P.C. 239; *Columbia Gramophone Co Ltd v Thoms* (1924) 41 R.P.C. 294; *Sterling Drug Inc v C.H. Beck Ltd* [1973] R.P.C. 915.

[283] *Gillette Industries Ltd v Bernstein* (1941) 58 R.P.C. 271, 282.

[284] [1996] R.P.C. 441, 443.

[285] (1907) 24 R.P.C. 539, 543.

[286] See also *Dunlop Pneumatic Tyre Co v Neal* (1899) 16 R.P.C. 247.

[287] [1986] R.P.C. 279, 358.

[288] [1997] F.S.R. 817.

[289] [1977] R.P.C. 537, 555. See also *Dellareed v Delkim Developments* [1988] F.S.R. 329.

United Wire v Screen Repair Services[290] and by the Supreme Court in *Schutz v Werit*.[291] These cases have been considered above in the context of what is meant by "means, relating to an essential element of the invention" for the purposes of s.60(2) PA 1977.[292]

14-234   In *United Wire* the House of Lords upheld the reasoning of Aldous LJ in the Court of Appeal[293] who considered that the concept of implied licence was not an apt analysis, since such a licence could be excluded by the patentee, and consideration of whether an act was "repair" involved a subjective element. He held that the correct starting point was the definition of infringement in the 1977 Act and the Conventions, and to ask on the facts of the case whether what the defendant had done would fall within the definition of infringing acts as amounting to making the product of the invention. The mere patching of a tyre would not amount to making a tyre, but more extensive operations could amount to making the product even if an original article supplied by the patentee was used as a starting point.[294]

14-235   In the House of Lords, Lord Bingham expressly approved the reasoning of Aldous LJ[295] and Lord Hoffman explained the matter as follows:[296]

> "Repair is one of the concepts (like modifying or adapting) which shares a boundary with 'making' but does not trespass upon its territory. I therefore agree with the Court of Appeal that in an action for infringement by making, the notion of an implied licence to repair is superfluous and possibly even confusing. It distracts attention from the question raised by section 60(1)(a), which is whether the defendant has made the patented product. As a matter of ordinary language, the notions of making and repair may well overlap. But for the purpose of the statute, they are mutually exclusive. The owner's right to repair is not an independent right conferred upon him by licence, express or implied. It is a residual right, forming part of the right to do whatever does not amount to making the product."

14-236   In *Schutz v Werit*[297] Floyd J distinguished *United Wire* on the basis that that was not a case in which the invention resides in the part retained. He regarded the correct approach as being to ask "whether, when the part in question is removed, what is left embodies the whole of the inventive concept of the claim". He was reversed on appeal,[298] Jacob LJ holding that it was inappropriate to determine the issue by reference to the inventive concept.

14-237   In the Supreme Court the judgment of Floyd J was upheld "albeit for somewhat more nuanced reasons". Lord Neuberger started by interpreting the word "makes" in s.60(1)(a) PA 1977 and the considerations he applied to that interpretation have been set out at para.14-108. Ultimately however, the question of whether replacing a part of a patented article constitutes "making" it is a matter of fact and degree.

14-238   In answering that question Lord Neuberger considered it helpful to consider the question of whether the bottle part of the Intermediate Bulk Container was such a subsidiary part of the patented article that its replacement, when required, did not involve "making" a new article. On the facts before him he held that the bottle was such a subsidiary part—it had a much lower life expectancy than the cage and was

---

[290] [2001] R.P.C. 24, 439.
[291] [2013] UKSC 16; [2013] 2 All E.R. 177; [2013] Bus. L.R. 565; [2013] 3 Costs L.O. 500; [2013] R.P.C. 16.
[292] See para.14-102.
[293] [2001] R.P.C. 24, [25].
[294] See also Lord Hoffmann in *Canon K.K. v Green Cartridge* [1997] F.S.R. 817, at 735, PC; and *Hazel Grove v Euro-League Leisure* [1995] R.P.C. 529, PCC.
[295] [2001] R.P.C. 13, [55].
[296] [2001] R.P.C. 13, 459, [71].
[297] [2010] F.S.R. 22, [196]–[197].
[298] [2011] EWCA Civ 303; [2011] Bus. L.R. 1510; [2011] F.S.R. 19.

easily physically replaceable. Moreover it was legitimate, in the context of addressing the question whether a person "makes" the patented article by replacing a worn
out part, to consider whether that part includes the inventive concept, or has a function which is closely connected with that concept. The bottle did not include any
aspect of the inventive concept of the patents in issue. Lord Neuberger noted that
the case before Floyd J was indeed different to *United Wire* in that in that case the
part replaced, the wire mesh system, had no independent identity from the retained
part, the frame, such that it was much easier to say that the original product ceased
to exist when the mesh was removed. He also contrasted the defendant's operations in *United Wire*, which involved a much more complex operation than the
replacement of the bottle involved in *Schutz*. Merely replacing a damaged plastic
bottle (albeit one of considerable size) with a new plastic bottle (even allowing for
the fact that the replacement had to be made) appeared to him to be an exercise of
a very different order. Finally, he held that the fact that an end-user is paid for a used
IBC could be relevant. He explained that "if an article has no value when it has been
used and before it is worked on, and has substantial value after it has been worked
on, that could fairly be said to be a factor in favour of the work resulting in the
'making' of a new article, or, to put the point another way, in favour of the work
involved amounting to more than repair". However, this is a factor that needs to be
approached with caution.

Lord Neuberger weighed up the various factors on the facts and concluded at [78]   **14-239**
with the passage set out above at para.14–109.

Exhaustion of rights under European Law

It was established by the European Court of Justice in *Parke Davis v Probel*[299]   **14-240**
that the mere existence and exercise of patent rights does not of itself infringe arts
101 and 102 of the Treaty on the Functioning of the European Union[300] (ex-arts 81
and 82 of the EC Treaty). Further, although the exercise of patent rights to prevent
importation is prima facie contrary to art.34 of the TFEU (ex-art.28 of the EC
Treaty), as amounting to a quantitative restriction on trade between Member States,
the "normal" exercise of such rights will ordinarily be within the "specific subject
matter" of the patent right and thus fall within the exception provided for industrial
property rights in art.36 of the TFEU (ex–art.30).[301]

However, the doctrine of exhaustion of rights developed under EC law serves to   **14-241**
restrict the right of a patentee to bring proceedings for infringement in this country
where the patentee has already consented to the marketing of the goods in question in another Member State. The principle of the free movement of goods must
then prevail.

Section 60(4) of the 1977 Act, which was never brought into force and has now   **14-242**
been repealed,[302] contained an express reference to the doctrine of exhaustion of
rights as set out in art.81(1) of the CPC. However, the doctrine is well established
by decisions of the European Court of Justice under arts 34 and 36 of the TFEU (ex-

---

[299] [1968] C.M.L.R. 47; [1968] F.S.R. 393, ECJ. See also *Thetford Corp v Fiamma SpA* [1987] 3 C.M.L.R. 266.
[300] See paras 1-82 and 1-84.
[301] See the passage in *Centrafarm v Sterling* quoted below, and see also *Generics v Smith, Kline & French Laboratories Ltd* [1997] R.P.C. 801 (post-expiry injunction).
[302] PA 2004 Sch.2 para.13.

arts 28 and 30 of the EC Treaty),[303] which is part of UK domestic law by virtue of the European Communities Act 1972.

14-243 The doctrine takes its name from the concept that once a patentee has dealt in or consented to dealings in the goods within the EC, their patent rights are said to be "exhausted" and they cannot then revive them to prevent further circulation. Its application can be seen from two landmark decisions of the European Court.

14-244 In *Centrafarm v Sterling*[304] the ECJ held that it was incompatible with the rules of the EC Treaty concerning free movement of goods for a patentee to seek to exercise their rights to prevent sale in a Member State of products originally marketed in another Member State by the patentee or with their consent. The fact that the defendants, parallel importers, were able to profit from price differences between the states concerned as a result of different national legislation was irrelevant. The court held:

> "As a result of the provisions in the Treaty relating to the free movement of goods and in particular of Article 30 [now Article 34 of the TFEU], quantitative restrictions on imports and all measures having equivalent effect are prohibited between Member States."

14-245 By art.36 of the TFEU (ex-art.30) these provisions shall nevertheless not include prohibitions or restrictions on imports justified on grounds of the protection of industrial or commercial property.

14-246 Nevertheless, it is clear from this same Article, in particular its second sentence, as well as from the context, that whilst the Treaty does not affect the existence of rights recognised by the legislation of a Member State in matters of industrial and commercial property, yet the exercise of these rights may nevertheless, depending on the circumstances, be affected by the prohibitions in the Treaty.

14-247 Inasmuch as it provides an exception to one of the fundamental principles of the Common Market, art.36 of the TFEU (ex-art.30) in fact only admits of derogations from the free movement of goods where such derogations are justified for the purpose of safeguarding rights which constitute the specific subject matter of this property.

14-248 In relation to patents, the specific subject matter of the industrial property is the guarantee that the patentee, to reward the creative effort of the inventor, has the exclusive right to use an invention with a view to manufacturing industrial products and putting them into circulation for the first time, either directly or by the grant of licences to third parties, as well as the right to oppose infringements.

14-249 An obstacle to the free movement of goods may arise out of the existence, within a national legislation concerning industrial and commercial property, of provisions laying down that a patentee's right is not exhausted when the product protected by the patent is marketed in another Member State, with the result that the patentee can prevent importation of the product into their own Member State when it has been marketed in another state.

14-250 Whereas an obstacle to the free movement of goods of this kind may be justified on the ground of protection of industrial property where such protection is invoked against a product coming from a Member State where it is not patentable and has been manufactured by third parties without the consent of the patentee and in cases where there exist patents, the original proprietors of which are legally and economically independent, a derogation from the principle of the free movement

---

[303] And prior to the Treaty of Amsterdam arts 30 and 36.
[304] (15/74) [1974] E.C.R. 1147; [1974] 2 C.M.L.R. 480; [1975] F.S.R. 161.

of goods is not, however, justified where the product has been put onto the market in a legal manner, by the patentee themselves or with their consent, in the Member State from which it has been imported, in particular in the case of a proprietor of parallel patents.

In fact, if a patentee could prevent the import of protected products marketed by themselves or with their consent in another Member State, they would be able to partition off national markets and thereby restrict trade between Member States, in a situation where no such restriction was necessary to guarantee the essence of the exclusive rights flowing from the parallel patents. **14-251**

In *Merck v Stephar*[305] a similar result was reached in a case in which it had been impossible for the patentee to obtain a patent in the other Member State; he had nevertheless placed the relevant goods on the market there themselves. The court held: **14-252**

> "It is for the proprietor of the patent to decide, in the light of all the circumstances, under what conditions he will market his product, including the possibility of marketing it in a Member State where the law does not provide patent protection for the product in question. If he decides to do so he must then accept the consequences of his choice as regards the free movement of the product within the Common Market, which is a fundamental principle forming part of the legal and economic circumstances which must be taken into account by the proprietor of the patent in determining the manner in which his exclusive right will be exercised."

The decision in *Merck v Stephar* was reviewed by the ECJ in *Merck v Primecrown*,[306] and its reasoning upheld and followed so as to permit parallel imports. **14-253**

In all the cases, it has been emphasised that consent is the cornerstone of the doctrine.[307] Thus, the doctrine does not apply to goods placed on the market by a third party pursuant to a compulsory licence,[308] for in view of the compulsory nature of the licence, such goods cannot be considered to have been marketed with the true consent of the proprietor. It does not apply to goods modified to such an extent as no longer to be in substance the patentee's goods.[309] The doctrine does not apply to goods placed on the market outside the EC.[310] **14-254**

Abuse of dominant position as a defence

Article 102 of the Treaty on the Functioning of the European Union[311] (ex– art.82 of the EC Treaty) prohibits the abuse of a dominant position within the EU. However, even though a patent may enable its proprietor to establish a dominant position in some relevant market, the mere exercise of his patent rights to prevent competitors from making the protected products cannot amount to an "abuse"; it is after all what patents are for.[312] A patentee is therefore not obliged to licence at **14-255**

---

[305] (187/80) [1981] E.C.R. 2063; [1981] 3 C.M.L.R. 463; [1982] F.S.R. 57.
[306] [1995] F.S.R. 909, per Jacob J; [1997] F.S.R. 237, ECJ.
[307] See the Advocate-General's summary of the case law in *Cnl-sucal N.V. S.A. v Hag G.F. A.G.* (C-10/89) [1990] E.C.R. I–3711, at 3729.
[308] *Pharmon v Hoechst* (19/84) [1985] E.C.R. 2281; [1985] 3 C.M.L.R. 775; [1986] F.S.R. 108.
[309] *Dellareed v Delkim Developments* [1988] F.S.R. 329, 347.
[310] *EMI v CBS* (51/75) [1976] E.C.R. 811; [1976] 2 C.M.L.R. 235.
[311] See paras 1–82 and 1–84.
[312] See *CICRA v Renault* (53/87) [1988] E.C.R. 6039; [1990] 4 C.M.L.R. 265. See also *Huawei Technologies Co Ltd v ZTE Corp* (C-170/13) [2015] Bus. L.R. 1261; [2015] 5 C. M.L.R. 14, at [45]–[46].

all, and a fortiori cannot be compelled to grant licences on reasonable terms.[313] The Treaty does not impose compulsory licences through the back door.

14-256   It has, however, also been held that exercise of the patent right may give rise to abusive conduct contrary to art.102, for example by the arbitrary refusal to supply spare parts to independent repairers, fixing of prices for spare parts at an unfair level, or the withdrawal of spare parts for certain models altogether.[314] It has also been held arguable that where the patentee's attempt to enforce his monopoly would assist them in conduct which does constitute such an abuse, this may constitute a defence to an infringer sued under the patent. In *Pitney-Bowes v Francotyp-Postalia GmbH*,[315] Hoffmann J reviewed the authorities and said:

> "It is sufficient that the existence of the intellectual property right creates or buttresses the dominant position which the plaintiff is abusing. The remedy contemplated by the court is that the plaintiff may have to be deprived of the means of maintaining his dominant position."

14-257   However, in that case he struck out a number of the pleaded allegations of abuse; and as for the rest, the decision merely determined that they were arguable.

14-258   Furthermore, in the context of the giving of undertakings to licence standard essential patents on FRAND (fair, reasonable and non-discriminatory) terms, a refusal to licence may in principle constitute an abuse of art.102.[316]

14-259   In *Chiron v Murex*,[317] the Court of Appeal upheld the decision of Aldous J that a number of alleged abuses should be struck out; but an allegation of abuse by charging excessive prices for patented products was held arguably to constitute an abuse which might give rise to a defence to the action, in that the grant of an injunction in the action could buttress the ability of the plaintiff to continue their abusive conduct by continuing to charge high prices. However, the allegation was struck out on the ground that no effect on inter-state trade was shown.

14-260   In *Philips Electronics v Ingman*[318] the patentees owned a number of patents relating to compact discs; they licensed these to CD manufacturers on standard terms. The defendants declined to take a licence and alleged in their defence that the proceedings were being used in furtherance of an abuse contrary to art.82 of the EC Treaty (now art.102 of the TFEU). Laddie J held that it was wrong to define the relevant market by reference to the patent right alone, as the market for licences under the patent; the correct market was the market in the goods concerned. On the facts pleaded, there was no discernible abuse in this market and he therefore struck out all the pleaded breaches of art.82 (now art.102). He did, however, allow pleaded allegations of breach of art.81 (now art.101 of the TFEU), based on the licence terms, to remain in the case, but ordered them to be tried separately and to be stayed pending the outcome of a complaint to the EC Commission.

---

[313] *Volvo v Erik Veng(UK)* (238/87) [1988] E.C.R. 6211, [1989] 4 C.M.L.R. 122; cf. *Radio Telefis Eireann v Commission* (T-69/89) [1991] 4 C.M.L.R. 586, CFI; and *RTE and ITP v Commission* (C-241 and 242/91P) [1995] E.C.R. I-743, [1995] 4 C.M.L.R. 718, [1995] All E.R. 416, ECJ ("the *Magill* case"); and see *Intel Corp v Via Technologies Inc* [2003] F.S.R. 12 (Laurence Collins J) and [2003] F.S.R. 33, CA. But see *Huawei Technologies Co Ltd v ZTE Corp* (C-170/13) in the context of the giving of an undertaking to licence under FRAND terms.

[314] *CICRA v Renault* (53/87) [1988] E.C.R. 6039, [1990] 4 C.M.L.R. 265.

[315] [1991] F.S.R. 72.

[316] *Huawei Technologies Co Ltd v ZTE Corp* (C-170/13) [2015] Bus. L.R. 1261; [2015] 5 C. M.L.R. 14, [52]–[54]. See Ch.18, "FRAND".

[317] [1994] F.S.R. 187; see also *Digital Equipment Corp v LCE Computer Maintenance* (Mervyn Davies J, 22 May 1992, unreported, a copyright case); and *IBM v Phoenix* [1994] R.P.C. 251.

[318] [1999] F.S.R. 112.

In *Sandvik AB v K.R. Pfiffner (UK) Ltd*,[319] a large number of Euro defences were   **14-261**
struck out but the defendants were given permission to amend to raise defences
under the then numbered arts 85 and 86 of the EC Treaty (now arts 101 and 102 of
the TFEU) relating to allegations of charging excessive prices, price fixing and
licence and supply discriminations. Neuberger J. emphasised that, in principle, a
patentee is entitled to seek to enforce his monopoly and that proceedings to enforce
it cannot lightly be impugned.[320] In *Intel Corp v Via Technologies Inc*[321] the Court
of Appeal reinstated certain defences under arts 81 and 82 (now arts 101 and 102
of the TFEU) accepting that there were exceptional cases in which the exercise of
an exclusive right might involve abusive conduct.[322] The case was however settled before trial.

"Infringement not novel" (Gillette defence)

Since no relief could be obtained in respect of an invalid patent, if the defend-   **14-262**
ant could prove that the act complained of was merely what was disclosed in a
publication which could be relied on against the validity of the patent, without any
substantial or patentable variation having been made, they had a good defence. This
is the so-called "*Gillette* defence" arising out of the words of Lord Moulton in *Gillette Safety Razor Co v Anglo-American Trading Co*[323] where he said:

> "I am of opinion that in this case the defendant's right to succeed can be established without an
> examination of the terms of the specification of the plaintiff's letters patent. I am aware that such a
> mode of deciding a patent case is unusual, but from the point of view of the public it is important
> that this method of viewing their rights should not be overlooked. In practical life it is often the only
> safeguard to the manufacturer. It is impossible for an ordinary member of the public to keep watch
> on all the numerous patents which are taken out and to ascertain the validity and scope of their claims.
> But he is entitled to feel secure if he knows that that which he is doing differs from that which has
> been done of old only in non-patentable variations such as the substitution of mechanical equivalents
> or changes of material, shape or size. The defence that 'the alleged infringement was not novel at
> the date of the plaintiff's letters patent,' is a good defence in law, and it would sometimes obviate
> the great length and expense of patent cases if the defendant could and would put forth his case in
> this form, and thus spare himself the trouble of demonstration on which horn of the well-known
> dilemma the plaintiff had impaled himself, invalidity or non-infringement."[324]

Lord Moulton's dicta in the *Gillette* case were, however, considered and   **14-263**
explained in *Page v Brent Toy Products Ltd*,[325] where the prior document in question was more than 50 years old and, therefore, could not be relied on as destroying novelty.[326] Evershed MR said[327]:

> "Lord Moulton was not stating that this plea, that the infringement was not novel, was a separate
> defence against a claim of infringement, but was confining himself to the case where the alterna-
> tives of invalidity or non-infringement were open to the defendant. He was stating: 'This is a conveni-

---

[319] [2000] F.S.R. 17.
[320] Applying *ITT Promedia NV v Commission* [1998] 5 C.M.L.R. 491.
[321] [2003] F.S.R. 33, 574.
[322] *Applying RTE v Commission* [1995] F.S.R. 530 and *ITT Promedia NV v Commission* [1998] 5
C.M.L.R. 491.
[323] (1913) 30 R.P.C. 465, 480.
[324] See also *Proctor v Bennis* (1887) 4 R.P.C. 333 at 351; *Cincinnati Grinders (Inc) v BSA Tools Ltd*
(1931) 48 R.P.C. 33, at 58; *Merrell Dow v H.N. Norton* [1994] R.P.C. 1, at 13, [1995] R.P.C. 233,
CA, [1996] R.P.C. 76, HL.
[325] (1950) 67 R.P.C. 4.
[326] Under PA 1949 s.50(1)(a).
[327] (1950) 67 R.P.C. 13.

ent brief form of raising, by way of pleading, the whole case. If the allegation is made good, then where the dilemma is present, the result must be that the plaintiff fails by being impaled on one horn or the other.' It follows therefore in my judgment … that since … in this case … there is no dilemma for the plaintiff: the plea of invalidity is not open to the defendants on this particular matter. And, in my judgment, the language of Lord Moulton does not entitle the defendants here to raise as a separate defence this form of words."

14-264 Such a defence was argued in *Hickman v Andrews*,[328] and although it failed on the facts of the case, Graham J said of it: "It is a good defence if it is strictly proved."[329] The principle was again considered by the Court of Appeal in *Windsurfing v Tabur Marine*,[330] in which Lord Oliver explained that the policy behind the invalidity ground of obviousness was that it would be "wrong to prevent a man from doing something which is merely an obvious extension of what he has been doing or what was known in the art before the priority date of the patent granted." The defendant's obviousness attack succeeded (so that the other horn of the dilemma, non-infringement, apparently did not need to be considered).

14-265 The principle was again invoked, and the *Gillette* case was held still to be correct in law, by Aldous J in the *Merrell Dow*[331] case. In the House of Lords, Lord Hoffmann said[332]:

"Ever since the power of the Crown to grant monopolies was curbed by parliament and the courts at the beginning of the seventeenth century, it has been a fundamental principle of UK patent law that the Crown could not grant a patent which would enable the patentee to stop another trader from doing what he had done before."

14-266 It is submitted that although Lord Moulton's test may be helpful in assisting a manufacturer to decide whether or not to proceed with some art which may appear to fall within the claim of a patent, it does not provide any additional defence to an infringement action. It is in reality an attack on validity which invokes the policy underlying the grounds of anticipation and obviousness.

Comity

14-267 In the rather unusual circumstances of *A Ltd v B Bank and Bank of X*,[333] the patent in suit claimed a type of security paper which was said to be used in banknotes issued by the state of X, and the patentee alleged that B Bank had infringed the patent by issuing such banknotes in the UK. The defendants asserted that the issues were not justiciable here in that the English court should not interfere with the prerogative right of a state to issue paper money and that the relief sought would be a breach of international comity. The Court of Appeal rejected these arguments: the banknotes were to be regarded as commodities here rather than as legal tender, and their issue here was a private act rather than a sovereign one.

---

[328] [1983] R.P.C. 147.
[329] [1983] R.P.C. 147, 172.
[330] [1985] R.P.C. 59.
[331] *Merrell Dow Pharmaceuticals v H.N. Norton Pharmaceuticals* [1994] R.P.C. 1, 13.
[332] [1996] R.P.C. 76, 83. See also the parallel German and US decisions reported at [1998] F.S.R. 145 and 158. respectively.
[333] [1997] F.S.R. 165.

7. INFRINGEMENT UNDER THE EPC, CPC AND PCT

The European Patent Convention

Any infringement of a European patent is to be dealt with by national law.[334] The **14-268** 1977 Act[335] provides that as from publication[336] of the mention of its grant in the *European Patent Bulletin* a European patent UK shall be treated as if it were a patent granted under the 1977 Act. Accordingly, infringement will be considered under the law applicable to patents granted under the 1977 Act and, in particular, express provision is made to cover cases where the European Patent is found partially valid after commencement of infringement proceedings.[337] Provisions are also made to deal with amendment and revocation generally.[338] The law relating to actions for infringement of European patent applications before grant but after publication will be the same as national law.[339]

The question has arisen as to whether the court of one country to which a **14-269** European patent extends is entitled to consider infringements alleged to occur in other territories, or to grant an injunction restraining infringements in such territories, as a result of jurisdiction conferred initially by the Brussels Convention and now by Council Regulation (EC) 44/2001.[340] By art.22(4) of the Regulation (art.16(4) of the Convention), exclusive jurisdiction over proceedings concerned with the registration or validity of patents (and other IP rights) is given to the national court where the patent has effect. Equivalent exclusive jurisdiction has not been given in respect of infringement proceedings[341] and the question therefore arises as to the circumstances in which infringement proceedings are in fact "concerned with the validity" of a patent. This matter is considered further at para.19-61, et seq.

The Community Patent Convention

The CPC did not enter into force and it is clear that it will not now enter into **14-270** force.[342]

The provisions relating to infringement of Community patents were set out in arts **14-271** 29–32 of the CPC (1975) and arts 25 to 28 of the CPC (1989). Whilst there were differences in wording between these Articles and the corresponding provisions of the 1977 Act,[343] the differences in wording would not have given rise to any differences in practice because of the provisions of s.130(7) of the 1977 Act.[344] It was originally envisaged that the CPC would be given legal effect in the United

---

[334] EPC art.64(3).
[335] PA 1977 s.77(1).
[336] Formerly special provisions applied where a European patent (UK) was in French or German, see PA 1977 ss.77(6) and (9). But s.77(6) ceased to have effect from the date when the London Agreement came into force (see para.1-51, et seq. and see also Patents Rules 2007 r.56(9) and 56(10)). Section 78(7) still requires the filing of a translation into English of the claims of a European patent application in French or German in the circumstances set out in that subsection.
[337] PA 1977 s.77(3).
[338] PA 1977 ss.77(4) and (5).
[339] PA 1977 s.78.
[340] In effect from 1 March 2002 except in Denmark.
[341] See the Jenard Report (OJC59 5.3.79, p.36).
[342] See para.1–70, et seq.
[343] PA 1977 ss.60 and 64.
[344] See para.14–03, et seq.

Kingdom by ss.86 and 87 of the 1977 Act. However, these sections were never brought into force and they have now been repealed.[345] It is to be noted, however, that the references to the Community Patent Convention in s.130(7) of the 1977 Act remain.

The Patent Co-operation Treaty

14-272   In essence, the PCT provides a convenient method of applying for national patents in a multitude of countries.[346] National patents are thereby obtained, and the question of infringement will be decided in respect of a patent granted pursuant to a PCT application in the same way as a patent granted pursuant to any other kind of application.

---

[345] PA 2004 s.5 and Sch.1 para.6 Sch.3.
[346] See para.1-61, et seq. and para.3-80, et seq.

CHAPTER 15

AMENDMENT OF SPECIFICATIONS

CONTENTS

1. INTRODUCTION

The ability to amend the specification or claims of a patent application during   **15-01**
prosecution as relevant prior art is disclosed as a result of searches carried out by
patent offices around the world or of a granted patent, particularly during revocation proceedings, has been recognised for many years. There must however be
restrictions on the right of an applicant or patentee to alter the scope of the
disclosure or the ambit of the claims.

As is set out below, the 1977 Act introduced statutory limitations on the right to   **15-02**
amend, but as originally enacted many of the discretionary restrictions on amendment developed under earlier legislation were maintained. In particular, for post-
grant amendments, the statutory limitations were equivalent to those imposed upon
the right of a patentee to amend a European patent during the course of post-grant
opposition proceedings in the European Patent Office under the EPC, but the
discretionary restrictions contained in the 1977 Act, as originally enacted, had no
equivalent in the EPC.

Section 2 of the Patents Act 2004 implemented a provision of the EPC 2000   **15-03**
designed to harmonise the approach to amendment of national courts and patent offices of the contracting states of the EPC. Sections 27 and 75 of the 1977 Act
(general power to amend specification after grant and amendment of patent in
infringement or revocation proceedings respectively) have been amended to provide
that in considering whether or not to allow an application to amend, the Comptroller or the court (as the case may be) shall have regard to any relevant principles applicable under the EPC. The effect of the amendments is to limit the discretion

hitherto exercised by the Comptroller and the court in the amendment proceedings in the UK.[1] The amendments came into force on 13 December 2007.[2]

15-04   Separately, the Intellectual Property (Enforcement, etc) Regulations 2006[3] amended ss.62 and 63 of the 1977 Act (restrictions on recovery of damages for infringement, and relief for infringement of partially valid patent respectively) with effect from 29 April 2006,[4] thereby overtaking more limited amendments to those sections contained in ss.2(3) and (4) of the 2004 Act which were never brought into force.

2.   HISTORY OF THE LAW

Amendment at common law

15-05   During the period when specifications were filed or enrolled in the Court of Chancery, the Master of the Rolls, as Keeper of the Records, had power at common law to correct errors in a specification, but this power was strictly limited to the correction of verbal or clerical errors arising from mistake or inadvertence.[5]

Statutory powers of amendment

15-06   The common law power of amendment was too restricted to be of use in such cases and by the Acts of 1835 and 1844[6] the patentee was given power to file a "disclaimer of any part of either the title of the invention or of the specification, stating the reason for such disclaimer, or … a memorandum of any alteration in the said title or specification (not being such disclaimer or such alteration as shall extend the exclusive right granted by the said letters patent)." Any such disclaimer or amendment, however, was made at the patentee's own peril, and, in a subsequent action involving the validity of the patent, objection might be taken on the ground that it in fact extended the monopoly.

15-07   Section 18 of the Patents, Designs and Trade Marks Act 1883 permitted, in cases where there were no legal proceedings relating to the patent pending, amendments by disclaimer, correction or explanation to be effected by the Comptroller. Where there were such legal proceedings pending, the patentee had by s.19 to petition the court for permission to apply to the Comptroller, only amendments by disclaimer being allowed in this case. Section 18(9) also provided that the granting of leave to amend should be conclusive as to the permissibility of the amendment, save in cases of fraud, though this provision was not given its full effect until the decision of the House of Lords in *Moser v Marsden*.[7]

15-08   The Patents and Designs Act 1907, by s.21, substantially re-enacted s.18 of the Act of 1883, and by s.22 (corresponding in other respects to s.19 of the Act of 1883) conferred upon the court itself power to allow amendments by way of disclaimer

---

[1]   See para.15–109, et seq.
[2]   See the Patents Act 2004 (Commencement No.4 and Transitional Provisions) Order 2007 (SI 2007/ 3396). There were no relevant transitional provisions.
[3]   SI 2006/1028 regs 2 and 3. The UK Regulations implement Directive 2004/48/EC of the European Parliament and of the Council of 29 April 2004 on the enforcement of intellectual property rights ("the IP Enforcement Directive").
[4]   See paras 19–165, 21–63 to 21-65 and para.21-155, et seq.
[5]   *Sharp's Patent* (1840) 1 W.P.C. 641, 649; *Gare's Patent* (1884) 26 Ch D. 105.
[6]   Patents Act 1835 (5 & 6 Will. 4, c.83) and Administration of Justice Act 1884 (7 & 8 Vict., c.69).
[7]   (1892) 9 R.P.C. 214.

in any action for infringement or proceeding for revocation. This power was extended to cases of amendments by way of correction or explanation, by the alteration effected in s.22 of the 1907 Act by the Patents and Designs Act 1919.

Under the Acts prior to the Patents Act 1949 it was a requirement that the amended specification should not claim an invention "substantially larger than or substantially different from" the invention previously claimed. This led to many reported cases on the topic of "substantially different", which was interpreted in a manner which in many cases rendered the ostensible right of a patentee to amend largely illusory.

15-09

The 1949 Act generally contained the same provisions as to amendment as its predecessor, the 1907 Act, save that the omission of the requirement that the invention should not be "substantially different" was a great advantage to patentees. The patentee could at any time after acceptance of the complete specification apply to amend by way of disclaimer, correction or explanation. Unless the amendment was for the purpose of correcting an obvious mistake, it was necessary that the amended specification should not claim or describe matter not in substance disclosed in the specification before the amendment; and everything covered by an amended claim must have fallen within the scope of at least one claim prior to the amendment.[8] Amendments once made were conclusive and could not be questioned save on the grounds of fraud.

15-10

3. THE 1977 ACT AND THE EPC 2000

Amendment under the 1977 Act

The Patents Act 1977 adopted a different manner of prescribing what amendments are permissible. The requirement that the amendment must be by way of disclaimer, correction or explanation was dropped, and replaced with a requirement (which must be satisfied in the case of amendments both before and after grant) that the amendment must not result in the disclosure of additional matter ("added matter").[9] In addition, no amendment of the specification of a patent shall be allowed if it extends the protection conferred by the patent.[10] The correctness of a decision allowing amendment either before or after grant can be challenged at a later date and if, in revocation proceedings, the court is satisfied that matter has been added by amendment or that the protection conferred by a patent has been extended by an amendment which should not have been allowed, the patent will be revoked.[11] These provisions stem from corresponding provisions in the EPC.

15-11

Discretion

As originally enacted, the 1977 Act retained many of the discretionary restrictions on amendment developed under earlier legislation and relating to the patentee's past conduct, see *Kimberley Clark v Procter & Gamble*.[12] In general these discretionary restrictions had no corresponding provisions in the EPC. As mentioned at para.15–03, the EPC 2000 has brought about changes to the discre-

15-12

---

[8]   PA 1949 s.31(1).
[9]   See para.15–29, et seq.
[10] See paras 15–63 to 15-65.
[11] See paras 15-27 to 15-28.
[12] [2000] R.P.C. 422.

tion exercised by the court and the Comptroller in amendment proceedings in the United Kingdom. These changes were implemented in the UK by the Patents Act 2004 which amended the 1977 Act. The changes are discussed further below.[13]

Errors and mistakes

15-13   The 1977 Act also gave the comptroller wider powers to correct "mistakes"— including obvious mistakes, see s.117[14] and, in relation to errors in translations of European patents and applications for European patents, s.80(3).[15] Neither section is referred to in s.130(7) as being so framed as to have, as nearly as practicable, the same effects in the United Kingdom as corresponding provisions of the EPC or another Convention.

The EPC 2000

15-14   Prior to the EPC 2000, the national legal systems of a number of contracting states did not permit amendment post-grant in an equivalent manner. Furthermore, in the EPO, no post-grant amendment could be effected otherwise than in the course of opposition proceedings. Once the opposition proceedings (if any) were terminated, there was no mechanism by which a patentee could effect amendments by a single application to all the individual national patents stemming from the grant of a European patent, with the result that amendments could be made in some contracting states but not in others with resultant disconformity.

15-15   Various amendments were therefore adopted in the EPC 2000 with a view: (a) to enabling the patentee to effect post-grant amendment to all the national patents by a single application to the EPO, and (b) to requiring all contracting states to make provision in their national laws to permit amendments of the kind which would be permitted by the EPO.

(a) Amendment in the EPO

15-16   Post-grant amendments in the EPO, otherwise than in the course of opposition proceedings, have been achieved by art.105(a) to the EPC which provides:

> "(1)   At the request of the proprietor, the European patent may be revoked or be limited by an amendment of the claims. The request shall be filed with the European Patent Office in accordance with the Implementing Regulations. It shall not be deemed to have been filed until after the limitation or revocation fee has been paid.
>
> (2)   The request may not be filed while opposition proceedings in respect of the European patent are pending."

15-17   This procedure, which is known as "the limitation procedure", allows a patentee at any time after grant (except where opposition proceedings are pending) to seek an amendment. The procedure is ex parte. There is no provision for opposition. The requirements of art.84 (clarity of claims and support by the description) and art.123 (no added matter or extension of protection) must be met[16] and if they are met, the

---

[13]   See para.15–109.
[14]   See para.15–91, et seq.
[15]   See para.15-107.
[16]   EPC Rules r.95(2).

amendment must be allowed.[17] If the amendment is allowed, it has effect in all the contracting states in which the European patent has been granted.[18] Once granted, the amended specification must be published[19] and the amendments are deemed to have had effect from the outset.[20] There is provision for an appeal against refusal.[21] This central limitation procedure under art.105(a) is intended to be simple and relatively quick.

A request to limit or revoke may not be filed while opposition proceedings in respect of the European patent are pending.[22] If a request is filed while opposition proceeding are pending, then the request is "deemed not to have been filed".[23] Opposition proceedings have precedence. However, where opposition proceedings are pending, the patentee may amend the patent in the course of those proceedings provided that the amendments are occasioned by a ground for opposition under art.100, even if that ground has not been invoked by the opponent.[24] **15-18**

There is no such prohibition of the limitation procedure with respect to proceedings in the national courts of the contracting states in which the European patent has been granted, although it might be said that opposition proceedings and national proceedings should be treated equally, especially where there was a risk that the claims were limited differently in national proceedings. In *Samsung Electronics Co Ltd v Apple Retail UK Ltd*[25] the Court of Appeal was faced with an appellant patentee who commenced a central limitation application before the EPO after trial. The Court held that the mere making of application for central limitation before the EPO could not be an abuse of the English Court's process (and indeed justified an adjournment of the appeal for the limitation procedure so that the Court could consider the amended claims on appeal).[26] The Court found support for that approach in the decision of the Supreme Court in *Virgin v Zodiac* in which reliance on retrospective amendment of a patent was permitted.[27] However, crucially the Court in *Samsung* left open the question of whether or not a patentee's attempted later reliance before the appeal court upon a patent which has been amended pursuant to a central amendment application made after trial was an abuse of process.[28] That must depend upon all the circumstances, including whether it would be necessary to remit the case for retrial and, if so, what the consequences of that would be.[29] Those questions could only be addressed once the amendment had been determined **15-19**

---

[17] EPC Rules r.95(3).

[18] EPC art.105b(3). See also PA 77 s.77(4).

[19] EPC art.105c.

[20] EPC art.68. Since PA 77 s.77(4) deems that the amendment shall have effect as if the specification of the patent had been amended under the PA 77, this would presumably be under s.27 or s.75 and both these provisions deem that the amendment shall be regarded always to have had effect from the grant of the patent.

[21] EPC art.106.

[22] EPC art.105a(2).

[23] EPC Rules r.93(1).

[24] EPC Rules r.80.

[25] [2015] EWCA 250 (Civ), [2015] R.P.C. 3. See also *Rovi Solutions Corp v Virgin Media Ltd* [2015] R.P.C. 5, in which an adjournment of trial was reluctantly ordered by Mann J, who made it clear that an adjournment would not be automatically granted in such circumstances.

[26] *Samsung Electronics Co Ltd v Apple Retail UK Ltd* [2015] EWCA 250 (Civ), [2015] R.P.C. 3, [30] and [52].

[27] *Virgin Atlantic Airways Ltd v Zodiac Seats UK Ltd* [2013] UKSC 46, [27].

[28] *Samsung Electronics Co Ltd v Apple Retail UK Ltd* [2015] EWCA 250 (Civ), [2015] R.P.C. 3, [51]–[57].

[29] *Samsung Electronics Co Ltd v Apple Retail UK Ltd* [2015] EWCA 250 (Civ), [2015] R.P.C. 3, [51]–[57].

and the matter returned to court, although before this could happen in *Samsung* the case had settled.

(b)   Amendment in the national courts

15-20   Article 138 of the EPC, which provides for revocation proceedings to be brought in the national courts of contracting states, has been amended so as to provide that, in addition to revocation (with effect to that contracting state only[30]) limitation by way of amendment can also be effected under art.138(2) and (3) which, as amended, provide:

> "(2)   If the grounds for revocation affect the European patent only in part, the patent shall be limited by a corresponding amendment of the claims and revoked in part.
>
> (3)   In proceedings before the competent court or authority relating to the validity of the European patent, the proprietor of the patent shall have the right to limit the patent by amending the claims. The patent as thus limited shall form the basis for the proceedings."

15-21   Thus the contracting states of the EPC have been required to make provision for amendment proceedings in their national law and this has been done in the United Kingdom by amendments to ss.27 and 75.

15-22   In particular s.2(1) of the 2004 Act has amended s.27 of the 1977 Act so as to insert an additional subs.(6) which reads:

> "(6)   In considering whether or not to allow an application under this section, the Comptroller shall have regard to any relevant principles applicable under the European Patent Convention."

15-23   Similarly s.2(5) of the 2004 Act has amended s.75 of the 1977 Act by the introduction of a new s.75(5) which states:

> "(5)   In considering whether or not to allow an amendment proposed under this section, the court or the comptroller shall have regard to any relevant principles under the European Patent Convention."

15-24   After some initial doubts as to the proper construction of the phrase "shall have regard to", it is now apparent that the UK court should apply the same approach when considering amendment during the course of proceedings in the UK as the EPO applies in prosecution and in opposition proceedings before it.[31] And, by analogy, the Comptroller should apply the same approach when considering an application to amend under s.27. Accordingly it now appears settled that the pre-existing domestic law in the UK relating to the court's discretion in amendment proceedings has been changed and the discretion is now more limited. These developments are discussed further below.[32]

15-25   **Court may require amendment in other designated states**   In addition, s.63 of the 1977 Act has been amended[33] so that it may be made a condition of granting relief in respect of a partially valid patent that an application be made to limit the claims in all the designated states of the European patent by an application to the EPO under the Limitation Procedure of art.105a. Similarly s.72(4A) has been

---

[30]   EPC art.138(1), as amended.

[31]   *Zipher Ltd v Markem Systems Ltd* [2009] F.S.R. 1, *Hospira v Genentech* [2014] EWHC 3857, [141].

[32]   See para.15–109, et seq.

[33]   See PA 1977 s.63(4) as introduced by PA 2004 s.3(1). A similar provision applies in relation to PA 1977 s.58(9A) (reference of disputes as to Crown use) by virtue of PA 2004 s.3(2).

inserted[34] so that where a patent is found invalid to a limited extent, the court may order its revocation unless amended to its satisfaction under s.75 or by application to the EPO.

4. PERMISSIBLE AMENDMENTS UNDER THE 1977 ACT

The amendment of patents granted under the 1977 Act is covered by ss.27, 62, 63, 72, 75, 76 and 117 of the 1977 Act. Section 27 provides the general power to amend after grant before the comptroller. Sections 62 and 63 deal with the inter-relationship between amendments and infringement proceedings, and s.72 similarly concerns revocation. Section 75 provides the general power to amend in the course of infringement or revocation proceedings, and s.76 sets out the conditions which an amendment must satisfy. Section 117 permits the comptroller to correct errors. In addition, ss.17–19 provide for amendment of applications before grant.

15-26

Pre-and post-grant

By virtue of s.19, with one significant exception, amendment prior to grant is placed on a similar footing to amendment after grant, in that any amendment can be made whether before or after grant provided that it complies with the require-ments of s.76. The important exception to this general statement is that the prohibi-tion in s.76(3)(b) against an amendment which "extends the protection conferred by the patent" only applies to granted patents, and there is no corresponding provi-sion applying to amendment pre-grant.[35]

15-27

It follows, therefore, that while the prohibition against added matter applies equally to amendment before and after grant, the facility still remains for the patentee to submit wider claims during pre-grant proceedings. Thus, there is no objection to a patentee seeking to delete narrow claims and substitute broader ones provided this is carried out before grant and provided that new matter is not introduced, bearing in mind that amendment of a claim in this way could itself amount to disclosure of added matter.[36]

15-28

A. Sections 76(2) and 76(3)(a): Added Matter

The application as filed

In the case of amendments to applications, the prohibition in s.76(2) is against the disclosure of "matter extending beyond that disclosed in the application as filed", whereas in the case of granted patents s.76(3)(a) simply states that no amend-ment shall be allowed if it results in the specification "disclosing additional matter". The effect is the same in each case: the comparison is to be with the application as filed. This is stated expressly in s.76(2) but by implication in s.76(3)(a).[37] Confirma-tion may be obtained from the language of s.72(1)(d), which provides that the pat-ent may be revoked if "the matter disclosed in the specification of the patent extends

15-29

---

34 PA 2004 s.4.
35 Compare s.76(3) with s.76(2), and see the following paragraph.
36 *Southco Inc v Dzus Fastener Europe Ltd* [1992] R.P.C. 299 and see para.15–62, et seq.
37 This statement was approved by Pumfrey J in *Triumph Actuation Systems LLC v Aeroquip-Vickers Ltd* [2007] EWHC 1367 (Pat), at [36]–[41]; see also *Monsanto Technology LLC v Cargill International SA* [2008] F.S.R. 7, at 155–156.

beyond that disclosed in the application for the patent, as filed"; no distinction is made between matter added during the application stage and the post-grant stage. It follows that when a patentee is considering amendment (or when a defendant who believes that they can invalidate the patent as it stands is considering what amendments they might have to face), it is always necessary to look at the application as filed. The content of the granted specification alone could be misleading: matter present in the application as filed can be deleted during the course of prosecution, but then re-introduced after grant.[38]

Divisionals

15-30   However, it is not permitted to delete subject matter from a member of a sequence of divisional applications (i.e. parent—divisional—2nd generation divisional—etc.) and reintroduce that matter to a succeeding application in the sequence. Content of a member of a sequence of divisional applications must be disclosed in each of the preceding applications in the sequence as filed, albeit that the claims of such a member need not be "nested", i.e. within the scope of, the claims of the preceding applications in such sequence.[39]

Meaning of "matter"

15-31   There is no definition of "matter" in the 1977 Act, and Aldous J suggested in *Southco v Dzus*[40] that the word was broad enough to cover both structural features of the mechanism (the case involved a mechanical product) and inventive concepts. He went on to say that the Act was seeking to prevent a patentee altering his claims in such a way as to claim a different invention from that which was disclosed in the invention, so that the section would not be contravened if the invention in the amended claim was disclosed in the application when read as a whole.

Test for extension of disclosure adopted by the court

15-32   In *Bonzel v Intervention Ltd*, Aldous J stated[41]:

"The decision as to whether there was an extension of disclosure must be made on a comparison of the two documents read through the eyes of a skilled addressee. The task of the Court is threefold:

(a)   To ascertain through the eyes of the skilled addressee what is disclosed, both explicitly and implicitly in the application.
(b)   To do the same in respect of the patent as granted.
(c)   To compare the two disclosures and decide whether any subject matter relevant to the invention has been added whether by deletion or addition.

The comparison is strict in the sense that subject matter will be added unless such matter is clearly and unambiguously disclosed in the application either explicitly or implicitly."

15-33   In *Vector Corporation v Glatt Air Techniques*,[42] Jacob LJ pointed out that Aldous J used the expression *"subject matter"* (as did art.123(2) of the EPC) whereas s.76

---

38   *Triumph Actuation Systems LLC v Aeroquip-Vickers Ltd* [2007] EWHC 1367 (Pat), [39].
39   *SEIKO/Sequences of divisionals* (G1/06) [2008] O.J. EPO 307, a decision of the Enlarged Board of Appeal.
40   [1990] R.P.C. 587, at 616.
41   *Bonzel v Intervention (No.3)* [1991] R.P.C. 553, 574; cited in *AP Racing v Alcon Components* [2014] EWCA Civ 40.
42   [2008] R.P.C. 10

merely used the expression *"matter"*. He concluded that there was no difference and that the formulation provided by Aldous J was both helpful and had stood the test of time. In a nutshell, the test is whether the skilled person would, upon looking at the amended specification, learn anything about the invention which he could not learn from the application as filed.[43]

Jacob LJ also went on to approve the elaboration upon the *Bonzel* formulation in *European Central Bank v Document Security Systems Inc*,[44] where Kitchin J said: **15-34**

> "97.   A number of points emerge from this formulation which have a particular bearing on the present case and merit a little elaboration. First, it requires the court to construe both the original application and specification to determine what they disclose. For this purpose the claims form part of the disclosure (s.130(3) of the Act), though clearly not everything which falls within the scope of the claims is necessarily disclosed.
>
> 98.   Second, it is the court which must carry out the exercise and it must do so through the eyes of the skilled addressee. Such a person will approach the documents with the benefit of the common general knowledge.
>
> 99.   Third, the two disclosures must be compared to see whether any subject matter relevant to the invention has been added. This comparison is a strict one. Subject matter will be added unless it is clearly and unambiguously disclosed in the application as filed.
>
> 100. Fourth, it is appropriate to consider what has been disclosed both expressly and implicitly. Thus the addition of a reference to that which the skilled person would take for granted does not matter: *DSM NV's Patent* [2001] R.P.C. 25 at [195]–[202]. On the other hand, it is to be emphasised that this is not an obviousness test. A patentee is not permitted to add matter by amendment which would have been obvious to the skilled person from the application.
>
> 101. Fifth, the issue is whether subject matter relevant to the invention has been added. In case G1/93, Advanced Semiconductor Products, the Enlarged Board of Appeal of the EPO stated (at paragraph [9] of its reasons) that the idea underlying Art.123(2) is that that an applicant should not be allowed to improve his position by adding subject matter not disclosed in the application as filed, which would give him an unwarranted advantage and could be damaging to the legal security of third parties relying on the content of the original application. At paragraph [16] it explained that whether an added feature which limits the scope of protection is contrary to Art.123(2) must be determined from all the circumstances. If it provides a technical contribution to the subject matter of the claimed invention then it would give an unwarranted advantage to the patentee. If, on the other hand, the feature merely excludes protection for part of the subject matter of the claimed invention as covered by the application as filed, the adding of such a feature cannot reasonably be considered to give any unwarranted advantage to the applicant. Nor does it adversely affect the interests of third parties.
>
> 102. Sixth, it is important to avoid hindsight. Care must be taken to consider the disclosure of the application through the eyes of a skilled person who has not seen the amended specification and consequently does not know what he is looking for. This is particularly important where the subject matter is said to be implicitly disclosed in the original specification."

The Courts' approach to the test of added matter was encapsulated by Floyd LJ   **15-35**
in *AP Racing v Alcon Components*[45]:

> "In the end the question is the simple one posed by Jacob J (as he then was) in *Richardson-Vick Inc's Patent* [1995] R.P.C. 568 at p.576 (approved by him as Jacob LJ in *Vector Corp v Glatt Air Techniques Ltd* [2007] EWCA Civ 805, [2008] R.P.C. 10 at [4]):
>
>> 'I think the test of added matter is whether a skilled man would, upon looking at the amended specification, learn anything about the invention which he could not learn from the unamended specification.'
>
> The policy behind the rule against adding matter was also examined in *Vector v Glatt* at [5] to [6].

---

[43]   *Vector Corporation v Glatt Air Techniques* [2008] R.P.C. 10, [4], citing *Richardson-Vicks Inc's Patent* [1995] R.P.C. 568, 576; see also *M-Systems Flash Disk Pioneers v Trek 2000 International* [2008] R.P.C. 18, at [33].

[44]   [2007] EWHC 600 (Pat).

[45]   [2014] EWCA Civ 40.

> One of the reasons for the rule which was identified is that third parties should be able to look at the application and draw a conclusion as to the subject matter which is available for supporting a claimed monopoly. If subject matter is added subsequently the patentee could obtain a different monopoly to that which the application originally justified."

15-36   As pointed out by Kitchin J in *European Central Bank*, the claims are part of the relevant disclosures and the status of information in the claims is no different from that in the body of the specification.[46] The claims of an application or specification themselves constitute a separate disclosure, but they are not disclosures of the detail of how a product may be constructed to achieve the aims of the invention, which is why not all products within the ambit of a claim are disclosed.[47]

The distinction between disclosing a feature and covering a feature

15-37   A number of authorities have explained that the fact that a claim in the patent as granted would cover embodiments not disclosed in the application does not mean that there is added matter,[48] since a patentee need not limit their claim to all the details of their disclosure.[49] Indeed a claim may include within its scope far more than a specification expressly discloses.[50] The Court of Appeal in *Nokia v IPCom*[51] re-emphasised this point citing Jacob LJ:

> "In *Napp Pharmaceutical Holdings Ltd v Ratiopharm* [2009] EWCA Civ 252, [2009] R.P.C. 18, Jacob LJ re-emphasised at [98]–[99] that not everything falling within the scope of a claim is necessarily disclosed:
>
>> '98.   We can deal with this quite shortly. The added subject-matter is said to be contained in claim 6. Mr Silverleaf put it this way:
>>
>>> "We say that if that claim covers water soluble spheronising agents, it must also disclose the possibility of using them or it does not actually read on to them at all; because otherwise the teaching of the document is to use water insoluble ones. We say if in fact the claim is wide enough to cover water soluble spheronising agents, there must be added matter."
>>
>> 99.   The trouble with that submission is that claim 6 does not mention – so cannot possibly teach – water soluble spheronising agents. It just specifies "a spheronising agent." The fallacy in the argument is to equate disclosure of subject matter with scope of claim, a fallacy struck down as long ago as 1991 in *A.C. Edwards v Acme Signs & Displays* [1992] R.P.C. 131 (see e.g. per Fox LJ at p.143).'"

15-38   In *Hospira v Genentech*[52] Birss J observed that although there is a clear line of authority to this effect in the UK, it is not always easy to see which cases fall on the *A.C. Edwards* side of the line[53]and moreover this is not a distinction which is drawn as sharply by the EPO. He stated:

---

[46]   See PA 1977 s.130(3); and *Asahi Kasei Kogyo K.K.'s Applications* [1991] R.P.C. 485; but see also *A.C. Edwards Ltd v Acme Signs & Displays Ltd* [1992] R.P.C. 131, at 143 and *Texas Iron Works Inc's Patent* [2000] R.P.C. 207, at 244.

[47]   *Bonzel v Intervention Ltd* [1991] R.P.C. 553, 578; *Beloit v Valmet (No. 2)* [1995] R.P.C. 705, 740; *Spring Form Inc v Playhut Ltd* [2000] F.S.R. 327, [26]; *Dyson Technology Ltd v Samsung Gwangju Electronics Co* [2009] F.S.R. 15, [228].

[48]   *Siegfried Demel v Jefferson* [1999] F.S.R. 204, 216.

[49]   *Assidoman Multipack v Mead* [1995] R.P.C. 321.

[50]   *Virgin Atlantic Airways Ltd v Premium Aircraft Interiors UK Ltd* [2010] R.P.C. 8, [71].

[51]   [2012] EWCA Civ 567, [50].

[52]   [2014] EWHC 3857.

[53]   See [168]–[171]. The line of cases referred to was *A.C. Edwards v Acme* [1992] R.P.C. 131, *Texas Iron Works* [2000] R.P.C. 207, and *AP Racing v Alcon* [2014] EWCA Civ 40. Another in the same

"The task of applying the law in this area is made more difficult by the fact that the EPO does not approach added matter this way at all. It is notable that neither side has cited an EPO decision supporting the *A.C. Edwards* principle. In *AP Racing* Floyd LJ referred in paragraph 32 to a decision in the EPO (T065/03) in which a broader term used in a claim was found to add matter. That was because the Board held that the effect of the broader language (combustion engine when only a diesel engine was disclosed) was to teach that the invention was suitable for any type of engine, a teaching absent from the application and therefore new matter."[54]

The judge continued:

A.C. Edwards v Acme, Texas Iron Works and *AP Racing* are each concerned with mechanical inventions in which a word or phrase has been used to identify or describe a structure in the application ('spring means' for a coil spring and cotter arrangement in *A.C. Edwards*, 'liner hanger unit' for an arrangement of slips and cones in *Texas Iron Works*, and 'asymmetric peripheral stiffening band' for a hockey stick shaped peripheral stiffening band in *AP Racing*). In each of those cases the inevitable effect of using this new descriptive language is that the claim will not be limited to the particular arrangement described in the application. The claim will have a broader scope. But in each case the court found that no other construction or thing was disclosed by the patent in which this language appeared in the claim.

I can see that this result follows in cases about descriptive language like this. Plainly the law cannot be that any change in descriptive language will never add matter but these cases show that some kinds of change in descriptions do not. Of course there is no reason to limit this principle to mechanical inventions, it just comes up naturally in those cases. I have more difficulty applying that principle to a case in which the skilled reader knows that the art is empirical, that the disclosure is a form of recipe, and that the point of the exercise is to produce a material which has certain properties, determined by carrying out tests on the material produced (e.g. stability)."[55]

Added matter is for the court

Furthermore, because the court carries out the exercise (through the eyes of the skilled addressee) it follows that construction of both the application as filed and the patent as granted are matters for the judge; the views of skilled men may be helpful but are not determinative.[56] The court is concerned with what is disclosed and not what might have been disclosed.[57] The principle of there being an implicit disclosure has been recognised by the EPO[58] and has been followed by the Court of Appeal.[59]

15-39

The test is applied strictly

The prohibition against the amended application or specification disclosing matter which extends beyond that previously disclosed has been enforced by the court and the Patent Office in a number of decisions.[60] These decisions show that the sec-

15-40

---

line is *Gedeon Richter v Bayer Pharma* [2012] EWCA Civ 235.
54 At [172].
55 See [173]–[174].
56 *Siegfried Demel v Jefferson* [1999] F.S.R. 204, 214.
57 *Flexible Direction Indicators' Application* [1994] R.P.C. 207.
58 *THOMSON-CSF/Collector for high-frequency tube* (T151/84) [1988] 1 E.P.O.R. 29; and *THOMSON-CSF/Spooling process* (T467/90) [1991] O.J. EPO 115.
59 *A.C. Edwards Ltd v Acme Signs & Displays Ltd* [1992] R.P.C. 131.
60 *Protoned's Application* [1983] F.S.R. 110; *B & R Relays Ltd's Application* [1985] R.P.C. 1; *RTL Contactor Holding's Application*, unreported, 1983, Patents Court; *Raychem Ltd's Application* [1986] R.P.C. 547; *Van der Lely's Application* [1987] R.P.C. 61; *Southco v Dzus Fasteners Ltd* [1992] R.P.C. 299; *Bonzel v Intervention Ltd (No.3)* [1991] R.P.C. 553. See also *Glatt's Application* [1983] R.P.C. 122; *Chinoin's Application* [1986] R.P.C. 39 and *Ward's Application* [1986]

tion is to be interpreted strictly, and as noted above the crucial question is "whether any subject matter relevant to the invention has been added whether by deletion or addition".[61] In *Raychem's Application*,[62] an amendment to omit the necessity of a final process step was disallowed since there was no disclosure in the overall process described that the last step could be omitted. In *Van der Lely's Application*,[63] an amendment to claim as a separate invention a part of a hay-baling machine was refused since the specification did not disclose the existence of the particular feature independently of the total machine disclosed in the specification. Compare also *Windsurfing International Inc v Tabur Marine (GB) Ltd*,[64] where the Court of Appeal refused to allow an amendment limiting the monopoly claimed in the broadest claim to a feature claimed in a subsidiary claim, on the grounds that the particular feature was disclosed as being non-essential and the proposed amendment would not simply "amend the specification but turn it on its head".[65] In *Merck & Co Inc's Patents*[66] the Court of Appeal refused an amendment seeking to delete passages in the specification so as to make it plain that the invention resided in a single unit dosage form. This was not disclosed as being any part of the invention in the patent as filed.

15-41 These decisions illustrate that great care is necessary when formulating and seeking amendments, in view of the danger that the patent may be invalidated by adding matter or by a widening amendment—see para.15–63, et seq.

Where two or more inventions are disclosed

15-42 Where an application discloses two or more different inventions it is not added matter later to claim them separately. Indeed that is precisely what the divisional application system is designed to permit.[67] For instance in *Buhler AG v FP Spomax SA*[68] a deletion of various cereals formerly mentioned in the claim, leaving only a reference to wheat, was allowable as not adding matter: the claim as so amended did not say anything about the other cereals. Similarly in *Teva v Merck*[69] an amendment limiting the claim to only one of two disclosed options was allowed.

Adding references to the prior art

15-43 It is, however, a well-established practice in the EPO that it is permissible to add references to prior art, and indeed to allow limitation of the claim by reference to the prior art so acknowledged,[70] although even here there are dangers that new matter may be added, for example, by pointing out additional advantages of the invention when comparing it with the prior art. It would clearly be wrong that such a limitation, originally introduced merely to distinguish a piece of art, should

---

R.P.C. 50.

[61] *Bonzel v Intervention (No.3)* [1991] R.P.C. 553, 574.

[62] [1986] R.P.C. 547.

[63] [1987] R.P.C. 61.

[64] [1985] R.P.C. 59.

[65] *Windsurfing International Inc v Tabur Marine (GB) Ltd* [1985] R.P.C. 59, 82.

[66] [2004] F.S.R. 16, 330 at [45]–[49].

[67] *Virgin Atlantic Airways Ltd v Premium Aircraft Interiors UK Ltd* [2010] R.P.C. 8, [68].

[68] [2008] F.S.R. 27.

[69] [2010] F.S.R. 17.

[70] *ADVANCED SEMICONDUCTOR PRODUCTS/Limiting feature* (G01/93) [1995] E.P.O.R. 97, [7]; *Palmaz* [1999] R.P.C. 47, 70.

subsequently be turned into a virtue and relied upon positively as a part of the inventive concept. But an amendment deleting references to advantages of an embodiment no longer claimed, and extolling the virtues of the embodiment still claimed, was held to be permissible as merely confining the ambit of the specification.[71]

Hindsight

At [102] of his judgment approved by the Court of Appeal in *European Central Bank* (above), Kitchin J referred to the danger of hindsight. An example of a case in which hindsight could play a part was *Liversidge v Owen Mumford*[72] in which extensive amendments had been made via a sequence of divisionals so that the features claimed in the granted patent were presented as related to one aspect (sequencing) and as distinct from another optional second aspect (safety). Reading the application with hindsight, knowledge of the granted patent could have led to the wrong result. The application only disclosed the second aspect and not the first. Read without hindsight the claimed features were disclosed in the application only as part of the safety mechanism. They were not optional.

15-44

Features derived from drawings

The law on added matter does not prohibit the derivation of features from the drawings of an application for a patent and they are to be treated on an equal footing with other parts of the document. However, it is the practice of the EPO only to allow amendments to introduce such features into the claims where the structure and function of such features is clearly and unambiguously derivable from the drawings and it is possible to isolate them from the other features shown.[73]

15-45

Intermediate generalisations

Difficulty can arise out of amendments of the kind known as "intermediate generalisations", where the specification provides a number of examples and the patentee seeks to generalise from these examples to claim a range or class which they are said to illustrate and exemplify. Several EPO cases have considered the matter, including the Enlarged Board decisions in *Advanced Semiconductor Products/Limiting feature* (G1/93)[74] and *PPG Industries/Disclaimer* (G1/03).[75] In *LG Philips LCD v Tatung*[76] the Court of Appeal specifically rejected the argument that because the concept of intermediate generalisation was not to be found in the Act or in the EPC, it was an unhelpful and illegitimate concept. It held that the Enlarged Board had merely developed the law on added matter in ways which involved superimposing a degree of policy over what had been perceived by the English courts as a relatively pure issue of principle. In recent years a large number of added matter objections have been pleaded as intermediate generalisations.

15-46

---

[71] *Mölnlycke AB v Procter & Gamble (No.5)* [1994] R.P.C. 49.
[72] [2012] EWPCC 33, see [85]–[116], especially [107]–[116].
[73] *Abbott Laboratories Ltd v Evysio Medical Devices Ulc* [2008] R.P.C. 23. See also *Strix v Otter* [1995] R.P.C. 607.
[74] [1994] O.J. EPO 541, [1995] E.P.O.R. 97.
[75] [2004] O.J. EPO 413, [2004] E.P.O.R. 33.
[76] [2007] R.P.C. 21.

15-47   This type of amendment was considered under the old law in *Ethyl Corporation's Patent*.[77]

15-48   At first instance in *Palmaz's European Patents*,[78] an attempt to amend in such a manner was refused on the facts. Pumfrey J identified the issue as follows:

> "If the specification discloses distinct sub-classes of the overall inventive concept, then it should be possible to amend down to one or other of those sub-classes, whether or not they are presented as inventively distinct in the specification before amendment. The difficulty comes when it is sought to take features which are only disclosed in a particular context and which are not disclosed as having any inventive significance and introduce them into the claim deprived of that context. This is a process sometimes called 'intermediate generalisation.'"

15-49   This passage was subsequently cited with approval by the Court of Appeal in both *LG Philips v Tatung*[79] and *Vector v Glatt*.[80] In *Palmaz* itself Pumfrey J refused to permit an amendment which sought to incorporate into the claim a feature selected from a description given in only one form of construction of the product in question, whose significance was nowhere disclosed and which was for the first time suggested to have technical significance. The suggestion for the first time that it had technical significance, whether in its original context or in other embodiments, was held to amount to addition of matter to the specification. The facts of *Palmaz* may be contrasted with the facts of *Generics (UK) v Daiichi Pharmaceutical*[81] where it was held that the skilled person would immediately recognise the claimed method to be of general application, even though it was not presented in the application as being inventively distinct.[82] Similarly in *Smith & Nephew v Convatec*[83] the judge said:

> "Although the words of Pumfrey J in *Palmaz* and approved in *Vector v Glatt* refer to features not being disclosed 'as having any inventive significance', I do not understand that to mean that only features expressly asserted as being inventive in the specification may be added to a claim by amendment. A patentee does not have to repeatedly assert, with every line of the disclosure, that he thinks each point is or may be inventive. On the other hand of course, the context is crucial and a patentee cannot extract features disclosed in one context and introduce them into a claim stripped of their context. That is what I understand the principle to be."

15-50   In *A.C. Edwards v Acme Sign & Displays Ltd*[84] the defendants unsuccessfully argued that amendments made to claim 1 of the patent in suit, which were generalisations on what was specifically described, constituted an extension of the disclosure in the application as filed. The decision can be explained by reference to one of the factual issues. The specification only disclosed an embodiment where there were two studs retaining a particular component. Originally, the claim had no limitation to the presence of such studs but by amendment a limitation was introduced that the component was attached by "a stud". It was argued that since a requirement for "a stud" included within its scope a device having only one stud, the amendment to the claim had extended the disclosure of the patent by the ad-

[77] [1972] R.P.C. 169.
[78] [1999] R.P.C. 47, 71. The point was not considered in the Court of Appeal in *Palmaz* itself (see [2000] R.P.C. 631, at [61]).
[79] [2007] R.P.C. 21.
[80] [2008] R.P.C. 10.
[81] [2009] R.P.C. 4, [191]–[196].
[82] See also *Teva v Merck* [2010] F.S.R. 17.
[83] [2012] EWHC 1602 (Pat), [88].
[84] [1992] R.P.C. 131.

ditional information that there should be one stud per component. The Court of Appeal held that the mere fact that the amended claim covered such an arrangement within its monopoly did not mean that there was an extension of the disclosure.[85]

In *Nokia Corporation v IPCom*[86] Kitchin LJ explained that it was permissible to generalise a feature if it is apparent to the skilled addressee that the feature is generalisable:

> "56. Turning to intermediate generalisation, this occurs when a feature is taken from a specific embodiment, stripped of its context and then introduced into the claim in circumstances where it would not be apparent to the skilled person that it has any general applicability to the invention... .
>
> 59. It follows that it is not permissible to introduce into a claim a feature taken from a specific embodiment unless the skilled person would understand that the other features of the embodiment are not necessary to carry out the claimed invention. Put another way, it must be apparent to the skilled person that the selected feature is generally applicable to the claimed invention absent the other features of that embodiment.
>
> 60. Ultimately the key question is once again whether the amendment presents the skilled person with new information about the invention which is not directly and unambiguously apparent from the original disclosure. If it does then the amendment is not permissible."

Specific disclaimer

It not infrequently occurs that a claim is anticipated by the disclosure of an earlier patent or other publication in circumstances where the prior publication can fairly be regarded as accidental or fortuitous in the sense that the publication merely discloses something which falls within the claims of the later patent rather than disclosing the basic invention contained in the patent. It is often impossible to amend the claims to avoid anticipation by such prior art without unduly narrowing the scope of the claims and it is a convenient way to avoid anticipation merely to disclaim what is specifically disclosed in the prior publication. Such an amendment, known as a specific disclaimer, is normally inserted in the body of the specification just before the claims.

The Enlarged Board of Appeal in *PPG Industries/Disclaimer* (G1/03)[87] established that a disclaimer which is not disclosed in the application as filed may nevertheless be allowable in order to:

(a) restore novelty by delimiting a claim against co-pending applications which form part of state of the art under art.54(3) and (4) EPC;

(b) restore novelty by delimiting a claim against an accidental anticipation under art.54(2) EPC; and

(c) disclaim subject-matter which, under arts 52–57 EPC, is excluded from patentability for non-technical reasons.

A disclaimer should not remove more than is necessary either to restore novelty or to disclaim subject matter excluded from patentability for technical reasons. A disclaimer which is or becomes relevant for the assessment of inventive step or sufficiency of disclosure adds subject matter, contrary to art.123(2) EPC.

In G2/10 the Enlarged Board drew a distinction between the position in G1/03, where the disclaimer had no basis in the specification and those cases where the

15-51

15-52

15-53

15-54

15-55

---

85 See also *Assidoman Multipack v Mead* [1995] R.P.C. 321, at 354.
86 [2012] EWCA Civ 567.
87 [2004] O.J. EPO 413, [2004] E.P.O.R. 33. Cited and followed by the Court of Appeal in both *Napp Pharmaceutical Holdings Ltd v Ratiopharm GmbH* [2009] R.P.C. 18 and *LG Philips LCD Co v Tatung (UK)* [2007] R.P.C. 21.

disclaimer related to an area or subgroup of the disclosure. Reference was made to the judgment of Jacob LJ in *Napp v Ratiopharm*[88] in reaching the conclusion that such a disclaimer may be permissible provided it does not prevent the skilled addressee with technical information which would not be derivable directly and unambiguously from the application as filed.

15-56   In *Idenix v Gilead*[89] Arnold J considered a case in which the application as filed comprised 23 classes of compounds which could be screened for antiviral activity. The patent claimed only one of these classes. It was argued that the task which the person skilled in the art was set – fishing in a pond of one class as opposed to 23 classes - was materially different and consequently there was added matter. Arnold J rejected this submission holding there was nothing additional taught about the subclass by the amendment.

Delimiting a claim against co-pending applications

15-57   In the Court of Appeal in *Napp Pharmaceutical Holdings Ltd v Ratiopharm GmbH*,[90] Jacob LJ gave an example where the original description claimed a process to be carried out at a range of 0–100° C. If patentee later discovers that it only works at between 75° and 80° C, an amendment to the narrow range (never before mentioned) would be adding later acquired matter in order to make the patent sufficient. Conversely such an amendment would not be adding anything new where the disclaimed range was simply that disclosed in a co-pending application.

15-58   In *Napp* itself, the disclaimer in question appeared in the claim of a divisional application so as to delimit the scope of the divisional from that of its parent. It was held that the disclaimer did not distinguish any matter which formed part of the state of the art, and that no matter relating to the invention had been added.

Delimiting a claim against accidental anticipation

15-59   A disclaimer does not add matter if it is inserted into a claim to avoid an "accidental" anticipation, but it does add matter if it is inserted to avoid a "non-accidental" anticipation.[91] An "accidental" anticipation involves a disclosure belonging to a remote technological field or one whose subject-matter suggested it would not help to solve the problem addressed by the patent in question. In other words, "the disclosure has to be completely irrelevant for assessing the inventive step" and: "When an anticipation is taken as accidental, this means that it appears from the outset that the anticipation has nothing to do with the invention. Only if that is established, can the disclaimer be allowed".[92]

Relationship with obviousness

15-60   As such an amendment merely disclaims what is specifically disclosed, it will not prevent the patent being found invalid for obviousness unless the nature of the prior disclosure is such that it would not be obvious to modify what is disclosed in any

---

88   [2009] EWCA Civ 252.
89   [2014] EWHC 3916.
90   [2009] R.P.C. 18, [74].
91   *LG Philips LCD Co v Tatung (UK)* [2007] R.P.C. 21, CA. See also *Abbott Laboratories Ltd v Evysio Medical Devices* [2008] R.P.C. 23.
92   *LG Philips LCD Co v Tatung (UK)* [2007] R.P.C. 21, CA, quoting with approval *PPG Industries/ Disclaimer* (G1/03) [2004] O.J. EPO 413, [2004] E.P.O.R. 33, at [37] and [46].

material way, and so a disclaimer of this type is rarely appropriate to distinguish prior publications which are not so old or obscure as to be of no practical relevance. The court will not allow an amendment of this type if it is clear that the amended specification is still invalid for obviousness.[93]

Disclaimer must be clear, etc.

As with any other form of amendment, the disclaimer must be clear and otherwise allowable under the Act. An example of such a disclaimer is provided by the *Merrell Dow* case; after the patent was held invalid by the House of Lords,[94] the patentee was permitted to amend by adding to the end of claim 1 the words "other than formed by metabolism of terfenadine *in vivo*".   **15-61**

Widening claims pre-grant

The application of s.76(2) of the 1977 Act to pre-grant amendments of claims, where the amendment widened the monopoly was considered in *Southco Inc v Dzus Fasteners Ltd*.[95] The Court of Appeal held that amendments to claims which deleted integers do not offend against s.76(2) where, from the terms of the original disclosure, it is quite apparent to the skilled reader that the matter sought to be omitted was not meant to be an essential feature of the inventions. In the same case in the Patents Court,[96] Aldous J held that: **15-62**

"it was not material whether pre-grant amendment had the effect of widening or narrowing the monopoly claimed, provided the invention in the amended claim was disclosed in the application when read as a whole. What the Act sought to prevent was a patentee altering his claim in such a way as to claim a different invention from that which was disclosed in the application. Section 76 did not prevent the granted patent claiming a different combination from that in the application if the amended claim had in it the essential elements required by both the application and the specification of the patent to achieve the objects of the invention. The section prevented the patentee disclosing either by deletion or addition any inventive concept which was not disclosed before, but did not prevent him claiming the same invention in a different way."

B. Section 76(3)(b): Extending the Protection

Meaning of "extending the protection"

In *Hospira v Genentech*[97] Birss J said the following about this objection: **15-63**

"106. This rarely comes up at trial in the UK, no doubt because the law is clear and usually easy to apply. The correct approach is to compare the scope of the claims as granted with the scope of the claims as proposed to be amended. In both cases the scope is that of the claims properly construed in accordance with the Protocol. If the proposed amended claim covers something that would not have been covered by the granted claims then the prohibition is engaged.

107. Usually to make the argument good the person challenging the amendment needs to identify a concrete thing which did not fall within the scope as granted but which would fall within the scope after amendment if the amendment was allowed. If such a thing cannot be identified in concrete terms, that is usually an indication that there is no extension. Because the prohibition is absolute, the thing need not be commercially realistic.

---

[93] See *Esso Research and Engineering Co's Application for Revocation of Shell's Patent* [1960] R.P.C. 35; and *Holliday & Company Ltd's Application* [1978] R.P.C. 27.

[94] [1996] R.P.C. 76.

[95] [1992] R.P.C. 299.

[96] [1990] R.P.C. 587.

[97] [2014] EWHC 3857, [106]–[108].

108. The purpose of the prohibition is the protection of the public. Once a patent has been granted, the public can rely on its scope and know that it will not get any wider by amendment. There is no corresponding prohibition pre-grant. The law of added matter is different. It applies both pre-and post-grant."

15-64   Extension of the scope of an individual claim is not objectionable provided that it does not extend the protection of the patent overall.[98] The fact that limitations have been added to a claim does not justify removal of some other limitation in the claim.[99]

Amending the body of the specification may extend the protection

15-65   It should also be borne in mind that because, by reason of s.125, the disclosure in the body of the specification may affect the construction of the claims, amendment to the body of the specification even without any change in the words of the claims themselves could nonetheless result in a widening of the scope of the claims. While in most cases an amendment to the body of the specification which could affect the construction of the claims in a widening manner would be contrary to the requirement that the disclosure should not extend beyond that disclosed in the unamended specification, there could be cases where deletion of matter would also widen the claims.[100]

C.   Clarity, Support and Other Matters

Clarity and support

15-66   In addition to complying with s.76, the amended specification must continue to comply with the requirements of s.14(5) of the 1977 Act, and in particular that the claims should be clear and concise and supported by the description.[101] This is also a requirement of post-grant amendments at the EPO (both in Opposition proceedings[102] and under the Limitation Procedure[103]) and it is submitted that the changes to UK law brought about by the 2004 Act have not altered the position.

15-67   The court will only consider objections under s.14(5) that arise out of the amendments themselves. The court will consider the amendments to ensure that they are in a form which would have been accepted by the Patent Office, although where a deletion was sought which did not affect the ambit of the valid claims which had already been granted, it was not open to an opponent to reopen these issues, unless perhaps the claims were obtained through deliberate dishonesty.[104]

15-68   An amendment by way of explanation may be permissible if it turns what might

---

98 *Siegfried Demel v Jefferson* [1999] F.S.R. 204, 213.

99 Cf. *Sinkler's Application* [1967] R.P.C. 155.

100 *Merck & Co Inc's Patent* [2004] R.P.C. 31, [45]–[49].

101 *Genentech Inc's Patent* [1989] R.P.C. 147; *Schering Biotech Corp's Application* [1993] R.P.C. 249; *Chiron v Organon (No.5)* [1994] F.S.R. 258 (approved by the Court of Appeal in [1995] F.S.R. 589); *Strix v Otter* [1995] R.P.C. 607, 651; *Horne Engineering v Reliance Water Controls* [2000] F.S.R. 90, 111.

102 EPC art.101(3)(a). And see *SIEMENS/Unity* (G1/91) [1992] O.J. EPO 253, [1992] E.P.O.R. 356, [5.2].

103 EPC Rules r.95(2).

104 *Chiron v Organon (No.5)* [1994] F.S.R. 258.

be regarded as a vague or ambiguous specification into a clear specification, and does not extend the disclosure of the specification.[105]

Where an amendment is of a vague nature and would create uncertainty as to **15-69** what the new claim really means, it will be refused.[106] If the original claim is ambiguous and susceptibleof two interpretations, it has been held that, in the exercise of the court's discretion, no amendment will be permitted which gives the patentee the benefit of the wider interpretation,[107] as this may result in enlarging the scope of the monopoly. It is submitted, however, that under the modern law, the court would not refuse the amendment on the ground that it *may* have that effect; rather the court would, if possible, construe the claims and decide the position definitively one way or the other.

An amendment to delete a subsidiary claim will be refused if the deletion of the **15-70** subsidiary would obscure the scope of the main claim.[108]

Amendment fails to cure invalidity

It is not the normal procedure to attack the validity of a patent as it is proposed **15-71** to be amended (other than in the course of other proceedings in which validity is in issue), and it has been held that it is not permissible when deleting claims to allege that the remaining unamended claims should never have been granted.[109]

However, the court or Comptroller will not allow an amendment which is sought **15-72** to strengthen the validity of the patent if the amendment still clearly leaves the patent invalid or if what remains is so small as not to warrant the grant of a patent.[110]

Where validity is in issue in the same proceedings, and the proposed amended **15-73** claims are held to be still invalid, the court may either formally allow the amendment but then find the amended patent invalid and order its revocation,[111] or it may refuse leave to amend on the basis that the amendment is pointless and simply revoke the patent in its existing form.[112] Given that the court has a wide discretion as to costs in either event, the difference appears to be one of form only.

Amendments which succeed in curing invalidity

If the amendment is sought in response to an attack on the validity of the patent **15-74** so as to avoid anticipation or obviousness, it is not an objection that the amendment will validate the patent, and indeed that it is the whole purpose of the amendment in these circumstances.

Similarly, an amendment to remove added matter, i.e. material improperly added **15-75** by a previous amendment, is also in principle permissible provided that it does not thereby widen the scope of the protection granted by the patent.

---

[105] *Polymer Corp's Patent* [1972] R.P.C. 39.
[106] *Parkinson's Patent* (1896) 13 R.P.C. 509, 514. See also *J. Lucas (Batteries) Ltd v Gaedor Ltd* [1978] R.P.C. 297, 350; *ICI Ltd (Whyte's) Patent* [1978] R.P.C. 11; *Beloit Corporation's Application (No.2)* [1974] R.P.C. 478; and see *Hauni-Werke Korber & Co K.G.'s Application* [1982] R.P.C. 327.
[107] See *Chain Bar Mill Co Ltd's Application* (1941) 58 R.P.C. 200, at 205 and *Union Carbide Corp's Application* [1969] R.P.C. 530, at 543.
[108] *Plastic S.A.'s Patent* [1970] R.P.C. 22.
[109] *Chiron v Organon (Amendment)* [1994] F.S.R. 458.
[110] See *Comptroller's Ruling A* (1911) 28 R.P.C.; *Great Lakes Carbon Corp's Patent* [1971] R.P.C. 117, at 123; *VEB Pentagon Application* [1971] R.P.C. 368, at 373; *Bristol Myers Co's Application* [1979] R.P.C. 450; and *Minister of Agriculture's Patent* [1990] R.P.C. 61.
[111] As in *Richardson Vicks' Patents* [1995] R.P.C. 568.
[112] As in *Texas Instruments v Hyundai* (1999) 22(12) I.P.D. 22116.

15-76   Amendments to cure insufficiency will ordinarily offend against the prohibition on adding matter, if an attempt is made to make good a previous omission in the teaching, but there may be sufficient directions given in relation to some of the claimed embodiments and in such a case amendment by deletion of the other insufficient claims would again appear to be permissible.

Amendment to subsidiary claims

15-77   Where the broadest claim is amended by disclaimer it is permissible to add further limitations not added to the broadest claim into dependent subsidiary claims.[113]

15-78   Similarly it is permissible to introduce completely new subsidiary claims, not in existence at the date of grant, in order to provide fall-back positions in the event of an invalidity attack on the patent in the future.[114]

Amendment after expiry

15-79   A patent can be amended after it has expired.[115]

Double grant

15-80   An amendment can be made to overcome an objection of double grant under s.73 of the 1977 Act.[116]

Further amendments

15-81   The fact that an amendment has already been made is not of itself an objection to a subsequent application for a further amendment.[117]

Further amendment to cure internal invalidity

15-82   In some cases, however, it may be impossible to re-amend the specification to remove matter which has created invalidity under s.72(1)(d) or (e) without further contravening s.76. Thus, if a limitation to the claim had been added which was found to be objectionable as adding matter, it may be impossible to save the patent either by leaving it in (because the patent would remain invalid under s.72(1)(d)) or by taking it out (because removing such a limitation would widen the protection conferred by the patent, contrary to s.76(3)(b) and s.72(1)(e)).

15-83   This "added matter trap" or "inescapable trap" was discussed by the EPO Enlarged Board of Appeal in *ADVANCED SEMICONDUCTOR PRODUCTS/ Limiting feature* (G01/93).[118] Particular care should be taken with regard to narrowing amendments to claims or disclaimers introduced during examination or opposition proceedings and relating to subject matter not disclosed in the application as filed under art.123(2) EPC. A later attempt to remove this amendment or disclaimer would result in an extension of protection under art.123(3) EPC. To avoid such a

---

[113] *ICI's Patent* [1978] R.P.C. 11.
[114] *Norling v Eez-away (UK) Ltd* [1997] R.P.C. 160, [37]-[39].
[115] *Bristol Myers Co v Manon Freres Ltd* [1973] R.P.C. 836.
[116] *Turner & Newall Ltd's Patent* [1984] R.P.C. 49.
[117] *Chatwood's Patent Safe and Lock Co v Mercantile Bank of Lancashire Ltd* (1900) 17 R.P.C. 23.
[118] [1994] O.J. EPO 541, [1995] E.P.O.R. 97.

trap, it may often be safer to amend claims by the addition of features rather than by disclaimer.

There may, however, be situations where the wrong amendment (for example, a claim which had widened the monopoly) could be removed by amendment. Section 72(4) of the 1977 Act provides that rather than revoking a patent where it has been established that it is invalid "to a limited extent" the Comptroller may order that the patent be revoked unless within a specified time an application to amend under s.75 be made. In *Harding's Patent*,[119] the Comptroller found a patent invalid under s.72(1)(d) but allowed the patentee to attempt to cure the invalidity by amendment. The Patents Court, whilst not dealing with the point, apparently upheld the decision by remitting the case back to the Comptroller to consider an application to amend. The Comptroller indicated that amendment would normally be allowed unless bad faith was established. It is submitted that this is the correct approach and that where the added matter was only the result of accident, incompetence or error of judgment then the court would ordinarily accede to such an application.

15-84

Adequacy of original drafting

There is no burden on an applicant in an amendment proceeding affirmatively to establish either good faith or reasonable skill and knowledge in the original drafting of the complete specification as an essential pre-requisite for the grant of leave to amend,[120] although as a matter of discretion leave might be refused where the original drafting involved a deliberate intention to mislead the Patent Office.[121] The question of the good faith, reasonable skill and knowledge of the original drafting may, however, be relevant to the question of whether damages or an account of profits or costs will be awarded in respect of any infringement occurring prior to the decision allowing amendment or where the patent is found to be partially valid.[122]

15-85

In *Unilin Beheer v Berry Floor NV (No. 2)*[123] the patentee had in the course of amending its patent failed to remove two passages which were irrelevant to the invention as eventually claimed. It was not suggested that the two passages rendered the claims non-compliant with the EPC, nor that there was any nexus between these passages and the amendment itself. The first instance judge held that the failure to do so amounted to lack of reasonable skill, but that the patent as a whole was drafted with reasonable skill. The Court of Appeal dismissed the appeal, holding that reasonable skill and knowledge only extended to that which was relevant, and not to irrelevant matter. There would only be a lack of reasonable skill and knowledge where the irrelevant matter led to difficulties in interpreting the claim and had been left in through negligence.

15-86

---

[119] [1988] R.P.C. 515.

[120] *Schwark's Patent* [1958] R.P.C. 53.

[121] This was suggested as being a proper ground for the EPO refusing an amendment in *Richardson Vicks Inc's Patent* [1995] R.P.C. 568, at 577. See also *Kimberly-Clark Worldwide Inc v Procter & Gamble Ltd (No.2)* [2001] F.S.R. 22, 339 at [56]-[62], where the allegation was one of covetousness. But see also paras 15-119 to 15-120.

[122] PA 1977 s.62(3) and s.63(2) as amended by the Intellectual Property (Enforcement, etc) Regulations 2006 (2006/1028) so as to secure compliance with art.13 of the Enforcement Directive 2004/48/EC; and see para.15-169.

[123] [2006] F.S.R. 26.

15-87   In *Nokia v IPCom*[124] Floyd J noted that s.63(2), after amendment, only required the court to take account of three factors, and the former requirement of "good faith and with reasonable skill and knowledge" was no longer a pre-condition to obtaining relief. The amended s.63(2) (and presumably s.62(3) as well) was not intended to act as a sanction against careless drafting or lack of good faith when they had no bearing on the remedy sought by the patentee. Further, the burden was on the party asserting s.63(2) to prove that the factors set out were present and relevant.

Obvious mistake

15-88   For the reasons set out above, s.76 of the 1977 Act prohibits any amendment which has the effect of widening the claims. It follows that an application to amend a mistake in the claims under ss.27 or 75 cannot be permitted if its correction would result in a widening of the claims. However, if the mistake and its correction was obvious in the sense that the skilled person would always have appreciated from the document itself that there was a mistake and what was really meant, then on a proper construction of the claim,[125] it would have always had the corrected meaning anyway; and thus there would be no obstacle to amendment under s.76(3)(b).

15-89   Similarly an amendment to correct an obvious mistake in the body of the specification will not add matter contrary to s.76(3)(a) where the mistake and the correction are obvious to the skilled person from the document itself. In *Norling v Eez-away (UK) Ltd*[126] the specification of the patent was in "pidgin English" as a result of a poor translation of the application from Swedish into English. The patentee sought to clarify the specification by a large number of amendments intended to correct the translational errors. The amendments were opposed as being added matter. Commencing at [35], Laddie J said:

> "The defendant's objection to the first category of amendments centred on an assertion that any amendment which truly clarifies or explains the specification must be adding matter to the specification and were therefore is not allowable. ... The proposition that all amendments made to clarify text must be adding matter, in the s.76 sense, is false. Where the meaning of the text is not altered by the amendment, then it adds nothing. That is the position here. The effect of the amendments is to remove some of the pidgin English and replace it with text which reads more easily but means the same thing ... I will allow those amendments."

15-90   In addition the 1977 Act also provides some facility for the correction of obvious mistakes under s.117, discussed in the next paragraph.

D.   Section 117: Correction of Errors

The legislation

15-91   Section 117(1) of the 1977 Act provides that:

> "The Comptroller may, subject to any provision of rules, correct any error of translation or transcription, clerical error or mistake in any specification of a patent or application for a patent or any document filed in connection with a patent or such an application."

15-92   The general procedure before the Comptroller under this section is set out in

---

[124] [2012] R.P.C. 21.
[125] i.e. in accordance with *Kirin-Amgen v Hoechst Marion Roussel* [2005] R.P.C. 9 (HL). See also *Chartbrook v Persimmon Homes* [2009] 4 All E.R. 677 (HL).
[126] [1997] EWHC 369 (Pat).

r.105 of the Patents Rules 2007. The application must be advertised (except when the Comptroller determines that no party could reasonably object)[127] and, if a party wishes to oppose, the subsequent procedure is governed by Pt 7 of the Patent Rules 2007.[128]

Rule 105(3) and (4) provide that: **15-93**

"(3)   Where the request is to correct a specification of a patent or application, the request shall not be granted unless the correction is obvious (meaning that it is immediately evident that nothing else could have been intended in the original specification).

(4)   But paragraph (3) does not apply where the error in the specification of the patent or application is connected to the delivery of the application in electronic form or using electronic communications."

Despite the similar wording of r.105 of the UK Rules and r.139 of the Implement-   **15-94**
ing Regulations of the EPC, s.117 is not one of those sections listed in s.130(7) of the 1977 Act as being so framed as to have, as nearly as practicable, the same effects in the United Kingdom as the corresponding provisions in the EPC or another Convention.

Meaning of "immediately evident"

While r.105(3) requires that the correction is "immediately evident", it does not   **15-95**
state in terms to whom it must be immediately evident. However, it is submitted that, as with questions of obviousness, the person to whom the question should be directed is the notional addressee, namely a person skilled in the relevant art. Further, the subrule does not make it clear as to what material can be considered in deciding whether the correction is obvious in the sense that it is immediately evident that nothing else could have been intended. For example, if the question must be answered on the face of the specification alone, a given mistake may well not be self-evident, let alone its correction. However, the same mistake and its correction would be self-evident if the mistake was due to an error of transcription[129] and the notional skilled addressee was allowed to consider the original document which had been wrongly transcribed.

This question was considered in *Dukhovskoi's Applications*,[130] a case involving   **15-96**
a mistranslation of a word in the claim. It was held that the fact that there was an error was apparent on the face of the document. Whitford J held that, taking a common-sense view, once that was established then the only way to determine what correction was required was to go back to the original mistranslated document, and on doing so then the correct translation was immediately apparent. At least in the case of mistranslations, therefore, one is not confined to considering the specification alone. There would seem to be no reason in principle why the same approach should not apply, for example, in the case of mistranscriptions producing nonsense chemical formulae or mathematical equations.

In *CELTRIX/Correction of errors* (G11/91)[131] the Enlarged Board held that the   **15-97**
error must be so obvious that a skilled person would be in no doubt that the informa-

---

127   Patents Rule 2007 r.75 and Sch.3 Pt 2 and r.105(5).
128   See, generally, para.15-138.
129   Other than an error connected to the delivery of the application in electronic form or using electronic communications, in which case sub-rule (3) does not apply in any event.
130   [1985] R.P.C. 8. See also *Antiphon A.B.'s Application* [1984] R.P.C. 1 where the Patent Office held that the question must be answered on the face of the specification alone.
131   *CELTRIX/Correction of errors* (G11/91) [1993] O.J. EPO 125; [1993] E.P.O.R. 245.

tion in question was not correct and, considered objectively, could not be meant to be read as such. This test was applied by Arnold J in *CompactGTL v Velocys*.[132]

Meaning of "mistake"

15-98   In so far as the section allows for correction of errors of translation or transcription or clerical errors the jurisdiction seems clear in that the types of mistakes are identified. However, the reference to the word "mistake" is not qualified in any way and problems are likely to arise as to what other types of "mistake" can be corrected under this section. In so far as the mistake can be corrected under ss.27 or 75 and is allowable under s.76, no difficulty will probably arise in practice. It is possible, however, that an attempt could be made under s.117 to obtain an amendment which would otherwise be prohibited as extending the disclosure or extending the protection. In such circumstances, the question will arise as to whether it is the type of mistake that can be corrected, and in particular whether matters such as errors of judgment can fairly be regarded as mistakes.

Drawings

15-99   Section 15(8) of the 1977 Act[133] allows an application under s.117(1) to correct errors or mistakes with respect to the filing of drawings, thereby reversing the decision in *Antiphon A.B.'s Application*.[134]

Added matter and extending the scope of protection

15-100   Subsections (2) and (3) of s.76 do not extend the effect of that section to s.117 and it would seem to follow, therefore, that provided the correction sought is obvious in the sense set out by sub-rule (3), or sub-rule (3) does not apply by virtue of sub-rule (4), provision is made in the 1977 Act for the correction of mistakes which would widen the claim.

15-101   Similarly, there is no power to revoke a patent under s.72(1)(e) (extension of protection) if the amendment was lawfully allowed under s.117. However, the position with regard to s.72(1)(d) (added matter) is less clear unless it can be said that an amendment under s.117 takes effect for all purposes from the date of the original document, so that an application for a patent which has been amended under s.117 becomes, in law, the application as filed for the purposes of s.72(1)(d).

15-102   Alternatively, where both the error and its correction are obvious from the face of the document itself, then it is submitted that, on a proper construction of the document, the unamended and amended versions will have the same meaning[135] because the amendment simply brings the wording of the claims into line with the meaning which the skilled person would understand them to bear anyway.[136] Consequently there can be no question of added matter or widening of the scope of the claims in these circumstances.

---

[132] *CompactGTL Limited v Velocys plc* [2014] EWHC 2951 (Pat).
[133] Formerly s.15(3A) inserted by CDPA 1988 Sch.5 para.2.
[134] [1984] R.P.C. 1.
[135] See the discussion on obvious mistakes at paras 15-88 to 15-89.
[136] *CompactGTL Limited v Velocys plc* [2014] EWHC 2951 (Pat), at [76].

Discretion

It is to be noted that s.117 contains the word "may" and accordingly amend- **15-103** ment under s.117 is discretionary.

Where the patentee sought to correct an error in the translation of a European pat- **15-104** ent (UK) filed at the Patent Office, the Comptroller refused the correction under s.117 by allowed it under s.80(3) on the basis that s.117 does not contain any safeguards for third parties whereas s.80(3) does.[137]

Section 117 is not one of those sections listed in s.130(7) as being so framed as **15-105** to have, as nearly as practicable, the same effects in the United Kingdom as the corresponding provisions in the EPC or another Convention and it was not amended by the 2004 Act so as to provide that the Comptroller must have regard to any relevant principles applicable under the EPC. However, it does not follow that the discretion under s.117 is subject to the wide-ranging discretionary considerations relating to the patentee's conduct which applied (pre-2004 Act) to applications to amend under ss.27 and 75.

E.   Section 80(3): Translation of European Patent Applications

European patents applications not in English

Apart from the general power under s.117 to correct errors of translation, the **15-106** 1977 Act contains special provisions for correcting errors of translation of European patents (UK) which are not processed in English. Formerly, s.77(6) provided that a European patent (UK) published in French or German did not have effect in this country unless a translation of the specification into English was filed at the Patent Office but s.77(6) ceased to have effect on 1 May 2008 when the London Agreement came into force.[138] However, s.78(7) still requires filing of a translation into English of the claims of a European patent application in French or German in the circumstances set out in that subsection.

Correction of errors

If errors in such translations occur, by s.80(3) of the 1977 Act provision is made **15-107** for the filing of corrected translations. Section 80(4) contains provisions protecting persons whose action only became an infringement as a result of correction of a translation provided such acts were commenced prior to the publication of the corrected translation.

Interrelationship of ss.80 and 117

The interrelationship between correcting a translation under s.117 and filing a **15-108** corrected translation under s.80(3) was considered in *Rhône-Poulenc*,[139] in which the hearing officer held that there was no distinction in result, but there was a significant difference in the safeguards available to third parties in that s.117

---

[137] *Rhône-Poulenc-Santé's European Patent (UK)* [1996] R.P.C. 125.
[138] Patent Rules 2007 r.56(10) and see paras 1-69, 3-72, 5-12 and 14-268. The translation requirements are not invalid under EC law, see *BASF A.G. v Präsident des Deutschen Patentamts* (C-44/98) [2001] 2 C.M.L.R. 21, 435.
[139] [1996] R.P.C. 125.

provides none whereas s.80(3) is subject to s.80(4). In his discretion, he therefore refused amendment under s.117 and required a corrected translation (which widened the claim) to be filed under s.80(3).

5. DISCRETION AND CONDITIONS UNDER SS.27 AND 75

Introduction

15-109   Both s.27 (amendment before the Comptroller) and s.75 (amendment before the court) contain the word "may" and therefore, prima facie, they provide a discretion to the tribunal whether to allow or refuse an amendment, even if the amendment is not otherwise precluded by express provisions of the 1977 Act.

15-110   This discretion also existed under the old law (i.e. pre-1977 Act) by virtue of the word "may" in ss.29 and 30 of the 1949 Act. One of the factors which was taken into account was the conduct of the patentee and a considerable body of case law developed under the old law as to the principles under which this discretion should be exercised.

15-111   The old law principles were initially also applied by the court in the case of amendments sought to patents granted under the 1977 Act, although the court then had to consider in a number of cases how the discretion should be exercised where there were concurrent proceedings in the UK and in the Opposition Division of the EPO and the patentee had sought the same amendments in both forums. In such cases, an apparent inconsistency arose by the UK Court applying a more rigorous test than that applied by the EPO. In *Kimberley Clark v Procter & Gamble*,[140] the Court of Appeal resolved the doubts which had begun to emerge in a line of first instance decisions by holding that the approach to exercising discretion under the 1977 Act as originally enacted continued to be that formerly applied to 1949 Act patents.

15-112   However ss.27 and 75 of the 1977 Act were amended by subs.(1) and (5) of s.2 of the 2004 Act, which came into effect on 13 December 2007. In *Markem v Zipher*[141] Floyd J held that, following these amendments, the approach to the exercise of discretion had changed and that the old law approach is no longer correct.

The principles on which discretion is exercised

15-113   Section 75(5) of the Patents Act 1977 as introduced by s.2(5) of the 2004 Act,[142] is as follows:

> "(5) In considering whether or not to allow an amendment proposed under this section, the court or the comptroller shall have regard to any relevant principles applicable under the European Patent Convention."

15-114   In *Markem v Zipher*[143] Floyd J noted that there was "very little by way of express guidance in the European Patent Convention" as to the principles to be applied when considering whether or not to allow amendments. In that context he observed as follows:

---

[140] [2000] R.P.C. 422.
[141] [2009] F.S.R. 1.
[142] See also new s.27(6) of the 1977 Act introduced by s.2(1) of the 2004 Act.
[143] [2009] F.S.R. 1, [206].

"209. Article 102(3) of the Convention refers in passing to "amendments made by the proprietor in the course of the opposition proceedings". The relevant rules are rr.57 and 57A [now Rule 80]:

> 57—(1)   The Opposition Division shall communicate the opposition to the proprietor of the patent and shall invite him to file his observations and to file amendments, where appropriate, to the description, claims and drawings within a period to be fixed by the Opposition Division.

> 57A   Without prejudice to Rule 87, the description, claims and drawings may be amended, provided that the amendments are occasioned by grounds for opposition specified in Article 100, even if the respective ground has not been invoked by the opponent.

210. It will be seen that r.57A restricts the discretion to amend to those amendments which are occasioned by grounds for opposition (including unpleaded ones). Until the introduction of that rule, the EPO only permitted amendments under Arts 102(3) and 123 which were responsive to a validity attack actually raised by an opponent.

211. The case law of the Boards of Appeal shows that appropriateness of the amendments to the proceedings, their necessity and procedural fairness are the main, perhaps only, factors considered relevant to the discretion to allow amendment in opposition proceedings. The EPO's publication, Case Law of the Boards of Appeal states at 570:

> As already mentioned, the boards of appeal have derived in particular from R. 57(1) EPC the principle that the proprietor has no right to have amendments admitted at any stage of the proceedings. At the discretion of the opposition division or the board of appeal, amendments can be refused if they are neither appropriate nor necessary."

Separately (at [212]–[216]), Floyd J considered the new procedure for central limitation introduced by EPC 2000 itself and held that neither art.105b nor the Implementing Regulations appear to give the EPO a discretion to reject a limitation request which complies with the prescribed formalities.   **15-115**

Having regard to the above matters Floyd J concluded as follows: **15-116**

"217. The position under the EPC would therefore appear to be that:
  (i)   in opposition proceedings, appropriateness of the amendments to the proceedings, their necessity and procedural fairness are the main, perhaps only, factors considered relevant to the discretion to allow amendment;
  (ii)   in central amendment proceedings, compliance with the procedural requirements gives rise to a right to have the patent limited in accordance with the request.

218. If a proper amendment is now brought forward in opposition proceedings in good time and which is necessary and appropriate to meeting the opposition, it seems inescapable that it will be allowed. It would, it seems to me, be an odd result if an amendment which would be available as of right under the central amendment procedure was refused simply because the patent was under opposition. Such a result would only be justified if either (a) the amendments would have no effect on the opposition and could accordingly be made after its conclusion if the patent survives or (b) procedural fairness to the opponents meant that it could not be considered. I appreciate that (b) might result in a patent being revoked before it could be amended: but if it were not so, the patentee could derail the proceedings by claiming the right to amend at the last moment.

219. I think what I have derived so far can fairly be described as the principles on which in future, if not in the past, the power to allow amendment will be exercised in the EPO under the EPC. It follows that if I am to have regard to the principles applicable under the EPC, the discretion which I have to refuse amendments which comply with the Act has been limited. Considerations such as those formerly considered relevant to the discretion, such as the conduct of the patentee, are no longer relevant."

Although in this passage Floyd J refers to the "appropriateness of the amendments" to the opposition proceedings, this needs to be seen in the light of r.57A (now r.80) which allows that patentee to bring forward an amendment in opposition proceedings provided that it is occasioned by grounds for opposition specified in art.100, even if the respective ground has not been invoked by the opponent.   **15-117**

The restrictions on what is appropriate or necessary may be more extensive before the Board of Appeal than before the Opposition Division.[144]

15-118   Consequently under the current law discretion does remain relevant, but only to a limited degree.[145] Where the application is made in response to revocation proceedings or a counterclaim for revocation, it may be refused if the proposed amendments are not appropriate to the proceedings or are unnecessary or are procedurally unfair. For example, in *Akzo NV and Akzo Nobel's Patents*,[146] a Scottish case, an application to amend made three months before trial was refused as being too late and hence procedurally unfair. In *Hospira v Genentech*[147] Birss J refused an application to amend to introduce product by process language on the ground that applying the relevant principles which the EPO would apply, it would be refused.

Covetous claiming

15-119   Under the old law, covetous claiming (that is, deliberately obtaining or maintaining a claim which the patentee knows to be invalid) was considered to be grounds for refusing an application to amend in the exercise of the court's discretion. Since the EPO does not concern itself with this question, the right view must be that today the court will not do so either when considering whether to allow an amendment.

15-120   It is also to be noted that both ss.62 and 63 of the 1977 Act have been amended by the 2004 Act so as to provide that the court may take into account whether the proceedings were brought in good faith when deciding whether to award damages or an account of profits or costs for an infringement committed prior to the decision to allow the amendment or where the patent is found only partially valid. It is submitted that proceedings brought to enforce a covetous claim would not be proceedings brought in good faith and thus, in most cases, the court will have other means within its disposal for dealing with patentees found guilty of covetous claiming apart from refusing the amendments sought.

Reasons for the amendment

15-121   Under the old law (pre-2004 Act), the patentee was required to put before the court the whole story of how it was that amendment had come to be sought, so that the necessary material was present for the court to consider when exercising its discretion.[148] There was a "heavy onus" on those seeking to amend, see Graham J in *Chevron Research Company's Patent*.[149]

15-122   Under the new law, the proprietor is still required to state the grounds upon which

---

[144] *Motorola* (G4/93) [1994] O.J. EPO 875.

[145] See *Datacard Corporation v Eagle Technologies* [2011] R.P.C. 17, at [232]-[233] where discretion to refuse amendment was exercised since the proposed amendment expanded the scope for contributory infringement.

[146] [2007] R.P.C. 11, [57]-[58]. The application was renewed at the end of trial and again refused, on the same and additional grounds.

[147] [2014] EWHC 3857, [148]-[160], especially [156]-[159].

[148] See, e.g. *Mabuchi Motor K.K.'s Patents* [1996] R.P.C. 387, at 398.

[149] [1970] R.P.C. 580, at 586, approved by the Court of Appeal in *SCM Corp Application* [1979] R.P.C. 341; see also *du Pont de Nemour's Application* [1972] R.P.C. 545; *Smith, Kline & French Laboratories Ltd v Evans Medical Ltd* [1989] F.S.R. 561; and *Hsiung's Patents* [1992] R.P.C. 497.

amendment is sought.[150] However, it is submitted that the heavy onus of the old law no longer applies.

Privilege

Under the old law, there was no obligation upon a patentee seeking to amend their patent to waive privilege[151] and the same approach to privilege will continue to apply under the new law.

15-123

The two categories of amendment

Under the pre-1977 Act law a distinction was drawn between two essentially different types of amendment. These may conveniently and aptly be styled the "deletion" type of amendment, where (wider) claims are to be deleted and the patent is thereafter to be maintained with its remaining (narrower) claims; and the "rewriting" type of amendment, where a new claim is to be created which does not correspond exactly in scope to any existing claim. The distinction mattered most in the context of discretion. Deletion amendments were only refused in an extreme case when the patentee should be "driven from the judgment seat"[152] whereas the position on rewriting amendments shifted over time from a strict position in which any lack of diligence would be grounds for refusal to a more liberal approach whereby, as a general rule, the discretion would not be adversely applied unless the patentee had deliberately elected to maintain invalid claims which they knew or should have known required amendment: "covetous claiming".[153] For a more detailed exposition of this, the reader is referred to earlier editions of this work.

15-124

Deletion amendments: amendment of partially valid patent

Section 63 of the 1977 Act provides that relief can be granted in an action in respect of a patent which is "only partially valid" and infringed.[154] There was a similar provision in s.62 of the 1949 Act. This is addressed at paras 15-169 to 15-179.

15-125

Leave to amend by deleting invalid claims may be granted subject to conditions—see paras 15-180 to 15-192.

15-126

Removal of embarrassing matter

Under the old law (pre-2004 Act), an amendment was refused in the exercise of the court's discretion in a case where the patentee sought to delete matter which was embarrassing and might have assisted an attack on the validity of the patent[155] but

15-127

---

[150] CPR r.63.10. And see Patents Rules 2007 r.35(1)(c) for applications to amend under s.27.

[151] *Oxford Gene Technology Ltd v Affymetrix Inc (No.2)* [2001] R.P.C. 18.

[152] See *Chiron v Organon* [1994] F.S.R. 258; [1994] F.S.R. 458, at 463; upheld in the Court of Appeal, sub nom. *Chiron v Organon (No.11)* [1995] F.S.R. 589. See also *Van der Lely (C) N.V. v Bamfords Ltd* [1964] R.P.C. 54, at 76, *Mabuchi Motor K.K.'s Patents* [1996] R.P.C. 387.

[153] *Smith, Kline & French Laboratories Ltd v Evans Medical Ltd* [1989] F.S.R. 561; see also *Bentley Engineering Co Ltd's Patent* [1981] R.P.C. 361; *Donaldson Co Inc's Patent* [1986] R.P.C. 1; and *Autoliv Developments A.B.'s Patent* [1988] R.P.C. 425.

[154] As to a "partially valid patent", see *Hallen v Brabantia* [1990] F.S.R. 134.

[155] *Union Carbide Corporation's Application* [1972] R.P.C. 854.

the patentee remained free to lead evidence to contradict it.[156] Similarly, where a patent was revocable on the grounds of fraud, amendment was not allowed to disclaim the parts fraudulently claimed[157] and in another case leave was refused to remove a false suggestion.[158] However, these cases must now be considered against the background of the new principles for the exercise of the court's discretion in amendment proceedings introduced by the 2004 Act.

Double patenting

15-128   In the EPO one ground for refusing amendments is double patenting. In *Koninklijke Philips v Nintendo*[159] the defendant argued that an amendment sought at trial in the Patents Court should be refused in the exercise of the court's discretion under s.75(5) on the basis of applying the principles applied by the EPO on double patenting. The court reviewed the authorities in the UK and the EPO on the topic[160] and held as follows:[161]

> "[…] as a matter of UK law a double patenting objection taken as a ground for refusing a post-grant amendment to a claim can be taken but should only be taken in the following circumstances:
>
> i)   The two patents must have the same priority dates and be held by the same applicant (or its successor in title);
>
> ii)   The two claims must be for the same invention, that is to say they must be for the same subject matter and by this I mean they must have the same scope. The scope is considered as a matter of substance. Trivial differences in wording will not avoid the objection but if one claim covers embodiments which the other claim does not, then the objection does not arise.
>
> iii)   The two claims must be independent claims. This necessarily follows from the rejection of the point on overlapping scope. If two independent claims have different scope then there is no reason to object even if the patents contain dependent claims with the same scope. The point might arise later if an amendment is needed e.g. to deal with a validity attack but in the case the point can be taken then.
>
> iv)   If the objection arises in the Patents Court in which both patents are before the court then it can be cured by an amendment or amendments to either patent.
>
> v)   Even if the objection properly arises in the sense that two relevant claims have the same scope, if the patentee has a legitimate interest in maintaining both claims then the amendment should not be refused."

Impositions of conditions

15-129   Both the Comptroller and the court have a general discretionary power to impose conditions when granting leave to amend. Section 27 expressly makes provision for the Comptroller to allow amendment "subject to such conditions, if any, as he thinks fit", and it would also appear to be covered by the words "subject to such terms as

---

[156] *Gerber v Lectra* [1995] F.S.R. 492.

[157] *Ralston's Patent* (1908) 25 R.P.C. 13.

[158] *Parry Husband's Application* [1965] R.P.C. 382.

[159] *Koninklijke Philips Electronics N.V. v Nintendo of Europe GmbH* [2014] EWHC 1959 (Pat), see [290]-[311] and [440]-[449].

[160] s.18(5) of the 1977 Act, *IBM (Barclay and Biggar's) Application* [1983] R.P.C. 283, *Marley's Roof Tile* [1994] R.P.C. 231, *Divisional/ASTROPOWER* (G1/05) and *Sequences of Divisionals/SEIKO* (G1/06), *ARCO/Double Patenting* (T307/07), *BOEHRINGER INGELHEIM/Cyclic Amine Derivative* (T 1423/07); *HITACHI/Thermal-type air flow measuring instrument*.

[161] *Koninklijke Philips Electronics N.V. v Nintendo of Europe GmbH* [2014] EWHC 1959 (Pat), see [310].

to advertising the proposed amendment and as to costs, expenses or otherwise" in s.75.

However, although conditions were imposed many years ago[162] (e.g. preventing suing for infringements committed prior to the application to amend) this is rarely done today.   **15-130**

In *Hallen v Brabantia*[163] Aldous J stated: **15-131**

"In my view it is for a defendant to establish that special conditions exist before terms will be imposed or a patentee will be deprived of part of his damages. A patentee who has made an invention, disclosed it to the public in his specification and established that his specification was framed in good faith and with reasonable skill and knowledge is entitled to the full rewards provided by the law unless some special circumstances exist. For instance, it would be right to safeguard a person who has been led by a defect in a patent specification to act to his detriment. Where an amendment is to be made and a defendant establishes no more than he received reasonable advice that a patent was not infringed or was invalid, no limitation on damages or conditions should be imposed. It seems to me that a defendant must also establish that he acted on the advice to his detriment and that the advice given was based in some way upon the defect to be cured by the amendment."

Given that the exercise of discretion is now to be exercised with regard to the relevant principles applicable under the EPC, it is submitted that, in future, it will require an exceptional case before the court will impose conditions when granting leave to amend.[164]   **15-132**

6. PRACTICE

Amendment of UK patent applications before grant

The procedure is governed by r.31 of the Patents Rules 2007. Amendment cannot be made prior to receipt of the examiner's report under s.17(5) of the 1977 Act unless the Comptroller requires or consents.[165] After receipt of the report under s.17(5) and before receipt of the examiner's first report under s.18, the applicant may amend the specification without formality. If such report states that the application complies with requirements under the Act the applicant can amend within two months of receipt thereof. If not, and the applicant receives such report before preparations for the application are complete, then they can amend if in any event. If not, but the application does not receive the report until after such preparations are complete, they can still amend it once at the same time as responding to such report.[166] Any further amendment may only be made with the consent of the Comptroller and the application must be made in writing giving reasons for seeking the amendments sought.[167]   **15-133**

---

[162] See, e.g. *Dorr Co Inc's Application* (1942) 59 R.P.C. 113, at 118; *Bray v Gardiner* (1887) 4 R.P.C. 40; *Deeley v Perkes* (1896) 13 R.P.C. 581; *Ludington Cigarette Machine Co v Baron Cigarette Machine Co* [1900] 17 R.P.C. 214, at 745; *Geipel's Patent* (1903) 20 R.P.C. 545; (1904) 21 R.P.C. 379; *Gillette Safety Razor Co v Luna Safety Razor Co Ltd* (1910) 27 R.P.C. 527; *White's Patent* [1958] R.P.C. 287.

[163] [1990] F.S.R. 134, 149.

[164] For an unusual case in which conditions were imposed under s.63 for *not* amending the patent, see *Koninklijke Philips v Nintendo* Patents Court, Birss J (17 July 2014).

[165] See Patents Rules 2007 rr.31(3) and 31(5).

[166] See Patents Rules 2007 r.31(4).

[167] See Patents Rules 2007 rr.31(5) and 31(6).

Amendment of UK patents after grant

15-134 Following grant there are two national routes for making amendments. The first route is to apply to the Comptroller under s.27 of the 1977 Act. The jurisdiction under s.27 is limited in that, by reason of s.27(2), the Comptroller cannot allow amendments under that section if there are "pending before the court or the Comptroller proceedings in which the validity of the patent may be put in issue".

15-135 On the other hand s.75, as amended by the Patents Act 2004,[168] allows an application to the court or Comptroller, as the case may be, to amend in proceedings in which validity *may be* put in issue. This will cover the case where proceedings are in being, such as infringement proceedings, in which validity may be put in issue, even if, at the date of the application to amend, a counterclaim for revocation has not been served.

15-136 Prior to the amendment of s.75, an application could only be made under that section in proceedings in which validity *is* put in issue. Thus the 1977 Act, as originally enacted, apparently left a lacuna in that, as Jacob J observed in *Lars Eric Norling v Eez-Away*,[169] the unavoidable effect was that if there was an infringement action pending with no plea of invalidity, the Comptroller had no jurisdiction (under s.27) because validity may be put in issue in the infringement action, and the court has no jurisdiction (under s.75) because validity had not in fact been put in issue.

Proceedings "pending before the court or the Comptroller"

15-137 As to when proceedings are "pending before the court or the Comptroller", doubt formerly arose as to the position where an action was settled between the parties but this has now been clarified. Once the court is seised of an amendment application properly made in existing proceedings by virtue of s.75, it continues to have jurisdiction to deal with amendment even if the proceedings subsequently come to an end, for example by settlement. It was so held in *Lars Eric Norling v Eez-Away*,[170] pointing out that there was a significant change in the language of the 1977 Act so that earlier authorities to the contrary[171] could be distinguished. This avoids the obviously inconvenient alternative that the court loses jurisdiction, no matter how far the amendment application has advanced, and the application to amend has to be restarted in the Patent Office, resulting in an obvious waste of time and costs. In *ICI Plc v RAM Bathrooms Plc*,[172] a case under the 1949 Act, Aldous J gave guidance as to the types of amendment that the Patents Court would hear where there has been a settlement (i.e. in the probable absence of effective opposition).

Amendment before Comptroller after grant under s.27

15-138 The procedure is governed by r.35 and, if an opposition is filed, by Pt 7 of the Patents Rules 2007. The application to amend is made in writing and must identify

---

[168] PA 2004 s.16 Sch.16 para.19.
[169] [1997] R.P.C. 160.
[170] [1997] R.P.C. 160.
[171] See *Lever Bros Patent* (1955) 72 R.P.C. 198; *Critchley Bros Ltd v Engleman & Buckham Ltd* [1971] R.P.C. 346; *Congoleum Industries Inc v Armstrong Cork Co Ltd* [1977] R.P.C. 77; *ICI Plc v RAM Bathrooms Plc* [1994] F.S.R. 181.
[172] [1994] F.S.R. 181.

the proposed amendment and state the reason for making it.[173] The application is
then advertised by the Comptroller and any person may oppose within four weeks
from the date of the advertisement in the journal by filing in duplicate Patents Form
15 and a statement of grounds.[174] In the case of an application to amend under s.27,
it is the opposition under s.27(5) which starts the proceedings for the purposes of
Pt 7.[175] Where an error in the advertisement was corrected in a subsequent advertisement, the time for entering opposition was held to run from the date of the second
advertisement.[176] Neither the 1977 Act nor the Rules appear to make any provision requiring an opponent to show that they have a locus standi.[177]

The Rules provide that reasons for seeking the amendment must be given,[178] and **15-139**
an application may be refused unless the patentee discloses his reasons.[179] It is not
the practice to require the reasons for amendment to be inserted in the statutory
advertisements.

Rule 76(4) provides that the opponent's statement of grounds must include a **15-140**
concise statement of the facts and grounds in which he relies. The Comptroller is
required to notify the proprietor of the commencement of the proceedings and to
send them the Opponent's Patents Form 15 and statement of grounds and at the
same time to specify a period within which the proprietor must file a
counterstatement.[180] If the proprietor fails to file a counterstatement within the
period specified, then the Comptroller will treat the proprietor as supporting the opponent's case.[181] On the other hand, if a counterstatement is filed, then the
Comptroller must as soon as practicable send it to the opponent and specify a period
within which the opponent must file Patents Form 4 and the periods within which
evidence may be filed by the parties.[182] The opponent must file Patents Form 4
within the specified period if they wish to continue the proceedings; if they fail to
file the form, then they will be deemed to have filed a request to withdraw from the
proceedings.[183] Evidence is generally given by signed witness statement but, if they
think fit, the Comptroller may direct evidence to be given by affidavit or statutory
declaration instead of, or in addition to, a witness statement; where necessary they
may also take evidence *viva voce*.[184] The Comptroller also has power to order
disclosure and the attendance of witnesses where appropriate.[185]

An appeal from the Comptroller lies to the Patents Court and thereafter, with **15-141**
leave of the Patents Court or the Court of Appeal, a further appeal lies from the
Patents Court to the Court of Appeal.[186]

---

[173] Patent Rules 2007 r.35(1).
[174] PA 1977 s.27(5); Patent Rules 2007 rr.73(1)(b), 75, 76(2)(b), 76(3) and Sch.3 Pt 2. The period for
opposing may not be extended except where there are pending before the court or the comptroller
proceedings in which the validity of the patent is put in issue, see r.108 and Sch.4 Pt 1.
[175] Patent Rules 2007 r.73(1)(b) and Sch.3 Pt 2.
[176] *Hughes & Co's Application* (1931) 48 R.P.C. 125.
[177] *Braun AG's Appln* [1981] R.P.C. 355.
[178] Patent Rules 2007 r.35(1)(c).
[179] See *Waddington Ltd's Patent* [1986] R.P.C. 158 where particulars of the prior art in question were
required from the patentee. See also *Clevite Corp's Patent* [1966] R.P.C. 199.
[180] Patent Rules 2007 r.77(1), (4) and (5).
[181] Patent Rules 2007 r.77(6) and (9), and applied in *Norsk Hydro A/S's Patent* [1997] R.P.C. 89.
[182] Patents Rules 2007 r.80(1).
[183] Patents Rules 2007, rr.80(1A) and 81A.
[184] Patents Rules 2007 r.87.
[185] Patents Rules 2007 r.86.
[186] PA 1977 s.97.

Amendment under s.75 during proceedings before Comptroller

15-142   Amendment before the Comptroller under s.75 is governed by the same principles as amendment under s.27, namely those set out in r.35 and Pt 7 of the Patents Rules 2007 discussed in the preceding paragraph. However, in the case of an opposition under s.75(2), notice of opposition must be given before the end of the period of two weeks beginning with the date of the advertisement.[187]

15-143   In *Osterman's Patent*[188] it was held by the Comptroller that there was a presumption that amendment was offered with a view to meeting the grounds of revocation, thus differing from the position under s.27 of the 1977 Act, where grounds had to be stated. However, this decision would appear to have been superseded by the requirement of r.35(1)(c) that reasons be given.

15-144   In *Coal Industry (Patents) Ltd's Patent*,[189] it was held on appeal to the Patent Court that when in Patent Office proceedings, the patentee first sought to delete apparatus claims, then reinstated and defended them, and finally sought to delete them again by amendment, some sort of explanation ought to have been given for this sequence of blowing cold, hot, and cold again; this was a matter calling for explanation and evidence. Patentees and opponents are not entitled to exclude the public interest question of whether an application to amend should be allowed.

15-145   The Comptroller has a discretion whether or not to hear an amendment application under s.75 separately from the main proceedings before him, although the usual course is to hear them together.[190]

Amendment under s.75 during proceedings before the Patents Court

15-146   The procedure is now governed by CPR Pt 63.10.[191] The procedure as laid down by the rule is summarised below.

15-147   The application must be by application notice giving particulars of the amendment sought and the grounds therefor. It must state whether the applicant contends that the claims prior to amendment are valid. Amendment may be sought on a conditional basis (i.e. if the patent as granted is held to be invalid) or an unconditional basis (i.e. where the validity of the patent as granted is not defended).[192] The application notice must be served on the Comptroller as well as the other parties to the litigation within seven days. Unless the court otherwise orders, the application must be advertised in the *Official Journal (Patents)*.

15-148   Any person desiring to oppose the amendment must give notice within 14 days of the publication of the advertisement, and such notice must include the grounds of opposition relied upon.[193]

15-149   Within 28 days of the first appearance of the advertisement the applicant must apply to the court for directions. At that first hearing the court will determine whether the application should be heard forthwith or at the hearing of the main proceedings or separately, what evidence is necessary and in what form, and

---

[187] Patents Rules 2007 r.76(2)(a). This period may not be extended, see r.108 and Sch.4 Pt 1.

[188] [1985] R.P.C. 579.

[189] [1994] R.P.C. 661.

[190] *Norsk Hydro A/S's Patent* [1997] R.P.C. 89.

[191] See also the Pt 63 Practice Direction—Intellectual Property Claims at paras 10.1-10.2.

[192] The propriety of conditional (contingent) requests was expressly considered and upheld by the Court of Session (Outer House) in *Akzo NV and Akzo Nobel's Patents* [2007] R.P.C. 11.

[193] CPR r.62.10(6).

whether disclosure is necessary (as to which, see the following section). By this stage statements of reasons and of opposition will have been exchanged so that the issues will have been identified.

The usual procedure is for the court to order the application to amend and the trial **15-150** of the action to be heard together since this avoids duplication of evidence and the necessity to "educate" the court twice in the art. If there are a large number of opponents it may, exceptionally, be more convenient to hear the application separately from the action but even in such cases it is usually more convenient to hear the trial immediately after the application. Which course is to be adopted is entirely in the discretion of the judge, and the Court of Appeal will not review it.[194]

If the court orders the application to be heard at the trial, the first hearing is **15-151** merely used to set directions and frequently the only direction necessary in relation to the application itself is an order that all evidence, disclosure (if any), and documents served in relation to the trial shall be admissible in relation to the application, and vice versa. On this basis, any evidence served should address both the patent as granted (if the amendment is sought on a conditional basis) and the patent as proposed to be amended.

Provision is normally made for witnesses to be cross-examined on their written **15-152** evidence at the full hearing of the application to amend.[195] Provision may also be made for disclosure, although the patentee ordinarily provides voluntary disclosure by annexing relevant documents to witness statements.[196]

The court will also consider whether to include in the order conditions that the **15-153** patentee will not (pending the full hearing of the application) proceed with any other pending actions for infringement, or threaten other actions and will abide by any terms subsequently imposed as to costs, etc.[197] Where an injunction had been granted in an action for infringement and the defendants subsequently petitioned for revocation and the patentees applied in the revocation proceedings for leave to amend, the injunction was dissolved as one of the terms of leave being given,[198] in as much as it would be highly inconvenient to try what might be a new issue on an application to commit for breach of an injunction obtained before amendment.[199] An interim injunction will not be granted if the patentee indicates that they intend to amend the patent in suit.[200] The court has an inherent discretion as to any terms that should be imposed.[201] But in exercising that discretion a court must act judicially and, if it errs in principle or comes to a conclusion unsupported by the

---

[194] See *British Celanese Ltd v Courtaulds Ltd* (1932) 49 R.P.C. 345.

[195] As to scope of cross-examination on affidavits filed in amendments proceedings at the trial of the action see *E.I. du Pont de Nemours v Enka A.G.* [1986] R.P.C. 417.

[196] In *M-Systems Flash Disk Products v Trek 2000 International* [2008] R.P.C. 18 an application to amend was refused on the grounds of lack of disclosure, but although the appeal itself was heard after the entry into force of the Patents Act 2004 the decision under appeal was not, and the appeal was a review rather than a rehearing, see [99]-[100].

[197] *Rheinische Gummi und Celluloid Fabrik v British Xylonite Co* (1912) 29 R.P.C. 672, 673; see also *Hollandsche (N.V.) Glas-en Metaalbank v Rockware Glass Syndicate Ltd* (1931) 48 R.P.C. 181.

[198] *Kennick and Jefferson's Patent* (1912) 29 R.P.C. 25.

[199] See *Dudgeon v Thomson* (1877) 3 App. Cas. 34; and *PLG Research Ltd v Ardon International Ltd* [1993] F.S.R. 698.

[200] *Mölnlycke AB v Procter & Gamble Ltd (No.2)* [1990] R.P.C. 487.

[201] See *Strachan and Henshaw Ltd v Pakcel Ltd* (1949) 66 R.P.C. 49, at 58; as to costs, see *Leopold Rado v John Tye & Sons* (1955) 72 R.P.C. 64.

evidence or fails to give due weight to all relevant considerations, then an appellate court will exercise its own discretion.[202]

15-154　Following the full hearing of the application the applicant must within seven days serve the order on the Comptroller.[203] If the amendment is made before the trial of the main proceedings, leave is usually granted to proceed on the specification as amended, and to make the amendments necessary in the pleadings for that purpose.[204]

15-155　If a successful challenge is made, the amendments are disallowed and the specification remains in its unamended form (with possibly fatal consequences to its validity).

Costs

15-156　Costs are in the discretion of the court and it now ordinarily exercises its discretion in the same way as in any other kind of proceeding. The old practice that the amending patentee had to pay the costs of the defendants/opponents whether the amendments are allowed or refused does not apply.

Multiple amendments

15-157　In general the attitude of the court has been to discourage the seeking of multiple amendments in the alternative; cf. the practice of the EPO where multiple auxiliary requests are common.[205] The practice is that a patentee should formulate his amendments at an early stage and indicate whether he maintains that the unamended claims are invalid. Evidence will then be addressed to the claims in issue.[206] However, in *Inpro Licensing Sarl's Patent*[207] the court considered three sets of claims, consisting of amendments to the claims as granted and two additional sets which were referred to as the A claims and B claims respectively.

Altering amendment

15-158　The court or Comptroller may allow amendment in a different form to that sought and advertised. If the alteration is substantial, it should be re-advertised.[208] Where the amendments proposed (and allowed) on appeal differed from those proposed before the Comptroller, the matter was referred back to the Comptroller to

---

[202] *Raleigh Cycle Co Ltd v H. Miller & Co Ltd* (1950) 67 R.P.C. 226; *Van der Lely (C) N.V. v Bamfords Ltd* [1964] R.P.C. 54.

[203] CPR r.63.10(8).

[204] *Lilley v Artistic Novelties* (1913) 30 R.P.C. 18, 20; see also *Hollandsche (N.V.) Glas-en Metaalbank v Rockware Glass Syndicate Ltd* (1931) 48 R.P.C. 425; *Haslam Foundry and Engineering Co v Goodfellow* (1887) 37 Ch D. 118, at 123; and *Gillette Safety Razor Co v Luna Safety Razor Co Ltd* (1910) 27 R.P.C. 527.

[205] See the judgment of Aldous LJ in *Lubrizol v Esso Petroleum* [1998] R.P.C. 727 cited at para.15-185.

[206] See also *Beloit Technologies Inc v Valmet Paper Machinery Inc* [1997] R.P.C. 489 at 501 and *Sara Lee Household v Body Care UK Ltd* v Johnson Wax Ltd [2001] F.S.R. 17, 261.

[207] [2006] R.P.C. 20.

[208] See, e.g. *Lucas (Joseph) (Batteries) Ltd v Gaedor Ltd* [1978] R.P.C. 297, at 351. But cf. *Pavel v Sony Corp (No.3), The Times,*22 March 1996, CA, where the need to re-advertise and permit additional opponents and perhaps new evidence meant that alteration to the amendments would cause prejudice and was therefore refused.

determine whether re-advertisement was necessary, in which case any opponent would have been "at liberty to argue the matter afresh."[209] Having advertised the deletion of certain claims a patentee may not be allowed to withdraw such deletion.[210]

Effect of amendment being allowed

By ss.27(3) and 75(3) of the 1977 Act, amendments made under ss.27 and 75 respectively are deemed always to have had effect as from the grant of the patent. The reasons for an amendment form no part of the amendment itself.[211] **15-159**

Subsequent challenge to allowability of amendments

By s.72(1)(d) of the 1977 Act it is a ground of invalidity that the matter disclosed in the specification of a patent extends beyond that disclosed in the application for that patent. By s.72(1)(e) of the 1977 Act it is also a ground of invalidity that the protection conferred by the patent has been extended by an amendment which should not have been allowed. Clearly, the latter subsection expressly permits the question of the allowability of an amendment to be reopened, and the same must be true of the former subsection also. This is in contrast with the position under the 1949 Act, under which an amendment once made was conclusive except in the case of fraud.[212] **15-160**

Amendment of European patent (UK) before the Comptroller or the court

After grant, European patents (UK) are treated as if they had been granted pursuant to an application made under the 1977 Act.[213] It follows that after grant European patents, in so far as they relate to the UK, may be amended in exactly the same way and with the same consequences as amendments of patents granted under the 1977 Act, and the practice described above applies without any distinction being drawn. **15-161**

Amendments of European patents and applications before EPO

Prior to grant, European patent applications can be amended in the EPO, in accordance with essentially the same principles as amendment under the 1977 Act.[214] **15-162**

Amendment in the course of opposition proceedings

During the course of any opposition before the EPO after grant, a European patent can also be amended.[215] If a European patent is so amended, the amendment takes effect in the UK as if it had been made under the 1977 Act, and in particular **15-163**

---

[209] *Union Switch and Signal Co's Application* (1914) 31 R.P.C. 289, 293.

[210] *Quantel Ltd v Spaceward Microsystems Ltd* [1990] R.P.C. 83.

[211] *Cannington v Nuttall* (1867) L.R. 5 H.L. 205, 227-228; and *Dow Chemicals A.G. v Spence Bryson* [1984] R.P.C. 359.

[212] PA 1949, s.31(2). See *Trubenising Ltd v Steel & Glover Ltd* (1945) 62 R.P.C. 1, at 13.

[213] PA 1977 s.77(1).

[214] See EPC art.123, and EPC Rules r.137; and *Appeal Practice Decision No.4* [1981] R.P.C. 80.

[215] EPC art.101; and EPC Rules rr.80–82.

the provisions of ss.62(3), 63(1) and 63(2) will apply.[216] After amendment in an opposition the European patent is republished.[217] This has the effect that if an amendment is effected in the EPO subsequent to a trial in the English Courts but prior to an appeal to the Court of Appeal, the Court of Appeal can only consider the validity of the amended claim, no other claim being in existence.[218]

Amendment after grant under the limitation procedure

15-164   Provided that opposition proceedings are not pending, a European patent may be amended by the EPO after grant by an application for limitation under EPC art.105a. If the amendment ld is allowed, then it takes effect in the UK in the same way as an amendment made in the course of opposition proceedings.[219]

Procedure where there are proceedings before the court

15-165   Where there are proceedings before the court in which the validity of a European patent (UK) may be put in issue, the proprietor of the patent must serve on all parties to the proceedings a copy of their intended request for limitation of the patent at least 28 days prior to filing of the request with the EPO.[220] Thereafter any party may apply to the court for directions or such other order as may be appropriate.

Amendment in EPO while appeal pending in UK

15-166   The opportunities for amendment in the EPO mean that it is possible for an amendment to be effected in the EPO subsequent to a trial in the English Courts but prior to an appeal to the Court of Appeal. Where this situation arises, the Court of Appeal can only consider the validity of the amended claim, no other claim being in existence.[221]

15-167   In *Eli Lilly v Human Genome Services*[222] there were parallel proceedings in the UK and in the EPO. Both the Opposition Division and the first instance judge in the UK found that the patent was invalid, but the orders for revocation were stayed pending appeal. By the time the UK appeal came to be heard the EPO had maintained the patent with more restricted claims. The UK appeal was conducted on the basis of the claims allowed by the EPO.[223]

15-168   An application to amend centrally while an appeal is pending in the UK is not an abuse of process but reliance on such amended claims on appeal may be.[224]

---

[216] PA 1977 s.77(4).

[217] EPC art.103.

[218] *Palmaz's European Patents* [2000] R.P.C. 631.

[219] PA 77 s.77(4).

[220] Pt 63 Practice Direction—Intellectual Property Claims paras 11.1–11.4.

[221] *Palmaz's European Patents* [2000] R.P.C. 631.

[222] [2010] R.P.C. 14.

[223] Note that the only issue was whether the claims were excluded for lack of industrial application, and the amendment made no difference for this purpose.

[224] *Samsung Electronics Co Ltd v Apple Retail UK Ltd* [2015] EWCA 250 (Civ), [2015] R.P.C. 3, see para.15–19.

7. AMENDMENT AFTER JUDGMENT

Where patent is found partially valid

By s.63(1) of the 1977 Act, where in infringement proceedings a patent has been **15-169** found to be only partially valid, relief may be granted in respect of that part of it which has been found to be valid and infringed. This is, however, subject to s.63(2), which provides that when awarding damages, costs, or making an order for an account of profits the court shall take into account the following[225]:

(a) whether at the date of the infringement the defendant knew, or had reasonable grounds to know, that he was infringing the patent;

(b) whether the specification of the patent was framed in good faith and with reasonable skill and knowledge; and

(c) whether the proceedings are brought in good faith.

Subsection (a) stems from the Intellectual Property Enforcement Directive and **15-170** in particular art.13 of the Directive which requires Member States to ensure that the court orders the infringer who knowingly or with reasonable grounds to know engaged in an infringing activity to pay the right holder damages. Although directed to Member States, the duty to take all appropriate measures to ensure the fulfilment of a Member State's obligation to achieve the result envisaged by the directive is binding on all authorities of the Member State including the court.[226]

Subsection (b) was part of the old law, see paras 21–172 to 21–183. **15-171**

Subsection (c) is directed to proceedings which are not brought in good faith, for **15-172** example proceedings to enforce a covetous claim, that is a claim which the patentee knows to be invalid, see paras 15–119 to 15-120, 21-161 and 21-188.

Meaning of "partially valid" in s.63(1) and the effect of s.63(2)

The meaning of "partially valid" in s.63(1) and the effect of s.63(2) are **15-173** considered in more detail at para.21–155, et seq. of this work.

Directing amendment under s.63(3) and/or limitation under s.63(4)

As a condition of granting relief under s.63 the court may direct that the **15-174** specification be amended upon an application made under s.75 and such an application may be made whether or not all other issues in the proceedings have been determined.[227]

In the case of a European patent (UK), the court may also grant relief under s.63 **15-175** on condition of relief that the claims of the patent are limited to its satisfaction by the EPO at the request of the proprietor.[228]

The court has a discretion whether or not to direct amendment. The court has **15-176** power to grant relief without requiring amendment.[229] Ordinarily, it would seem appropriate to require amendment to be made to excise those parts found to be invalid,

---

[225] See para.19–168, et seq.
[226] See paras 1–86 and 1-87. See also para.21–54, et seq.
[227] PA 77 s.63(3).
[228] PA 77 s.63(4).
[229] *Gerber v Lectra* [1994] F.S.R. 471, 483.

but in *Gerber v Lectra*,[230] one of the patents ("Gerber I") had expired prior to judgment, and although claim 1 was held to be invalid Aldous J held that there was no need for amendment provided that appropriate undertakings were given.

15-177   In *Koninklijke Philips v Nintendo*[231] relief was granted under s.63 without requiring the deletion of an invalid claim because the invalid claim had been held to have a bearing on the construction of a valid claim and deleting the invalid claim could alter that construction. The court reviewed the authorities and held that a jurisdiction to do this did still exist.[232] Whereas the terms of art.138(2) EPC in its post-EPC 2000 form could be read as requiring deletion in every case of invalidity, s.63 is not a section referred to in s.130(7) as being framed to follow the EPC and was not amended when the 1977 Act was amended to implement EPC 2000. The patentee was required to give undertakings in order to protect the public.

Procedure where s.63 applies

15-178   Where s.63 applies, the patentee will usually also wish an opportunity to prove that the specification of the patent as published was framed in good faith and with reasonable skill and knowledge, as this is a precondition for recovering damages, costs, or an order for an account of profits.[233] Following its judgment finding the patent partially valid, the court will give any necessary directions for this to be considered at a subsequent hearing, and for the application to amend to be heard at the same time.[234]

Procedure in Court of Appeal

15-179   There have been cases where the Court of Appeal has itself ordered the amendment to be made, but where there is any difficulty an appellate court would presumably order the application to be made in the High Court, possibly accompanied by an indication of the general kind of amendment that the appellate court would regard as satisfactory.[235]

Where patent is found wholly invalid

15-180   Section 63(1) only applies to partially valid patents, in which there is at least one patentable invention validly claimed, and the normal form of amendment will therefore be a deletion-type amendment to excise invalid claims (or parts of claims). The question arises as to whether the court may permit a rewriting-type amendment in a case where a patent has been found wholly invalid.

15-181   There is no express limitation in s.75 as to the stage at which an application to amend may be made, and indeed s.63(3), relating to partially valid patents, contemplates an amendment being made after a judgment on validity has been delivered. There are, however, no cases in recent times where amendment has been allowed following a judgment in which all claims of the patent in suit have been

---

230 [1994] F.S.R. 471, 474.
231 Patents Court, Birss J (17 July 2014) and later Patents Court, Birss J (25 July 2014).
232 The authorities were *Gerber v Lectra*, Patents Court, Aldous J (5 May 1993), *Kirin-Amgen's Patent*, Neuberger J [2002] EWHC 471 and *Zipher v Markem*, Lewison J [2007] EWHC 154.
233 See para.15–169 and see paras 19–168 to 19–169.
234 See, e.g. *David Kahn Inc v Conway Stewart & Co Ltd* [1974] R.P.C. 279, at 327; *Hallen v Brabantia* [1990] F.S.R. 134.
235 See *Van Der Lely v Ruston's Engineering Co Ltd* [1993] R.P.C. 45.

held invalid. The prevailing attitude has been that a patentee who has had their chance should not be permitted a second attempt to reformulate a valid claim which they could have placed before the court earlier, and that where a defendant has come before the court and proved a patent to be invalid it would be wrong to put them into jeopardy a second time.

In *Windsurfing International Inc v Tabur Marine (GB) Ltd*,[236] the patentee ap-   **15-182** plied to amend immediately after the judgment at first instance had been delivered, but Whitford J held that he could see no scope for any amendment and leave to amend was refused. On appeal, the Court of Appeal refused to allow the patentee an opportunity to attempt to amend the patent to produce a valid claim. The court held that the amendment sought would not be allowable but also indicated that since considering a newly formulated monopoly would require effectively a new trial, the court "would require considerable persuasion that the imposition upon a successful defendant of such a manifestly inconvenient and oppressive course would be a proper exercise of discretion in an otherwise strong case".

Similarly, in *Procter & Gamble v Peaudouce*,[237] the Court of Appeal, which had   **15-183** held the patent in suit invalid, refused an application to allow the patentees to formulate amendments which might validate the patent. The court indicated that a question concerning amendment should have been raised earlier than after judgment in the Court of Appeal. (This notwithstanding the fact that the patent had been found valid at first instance and therefore not in need of amendment.)

In *Pavel v Sony*[238] an application that the Court of Appeal should consider   **15-184** substantially different amendments from those originally before the trial judge was refused, and the appeal was heard on the basis of the claims as granted because it was "not in the public interest, nor in the interest of justice, that proposed amendments should be altered at trial nor after trial".

In *Lubrizol v Esso Petroleum*,[239] the patent (granted under the 1949 Act) was held   **15-185** invalid at first instance and on appeal; the patentee then sought, but was refused, leave to amend after judgment in the Court of Appeal to meet the court's findings.

In *Nikken v Pioneer*[240] the patentee had fought and lost the first instance trial on   **15-186** the basis of a claim containing the key words "an annular groove of predetermined depth". The patentee then applied to amend these words by replacing "predetermined depth" with "approximately 3 to 5mm in depth". Mann J refused permission for a second trial and his decision was upheld by the Court of Appeal.

In *Nokia v IPCom*[241] Jacob LJ elaborated upon the reasoning in *Nikken v Pioneer*.   **15-187** He started by observing that while the substantive limits as to permissible amendments are harmonised throughout all Convention countries, the EPC leaves procedural matters concerning infringement and revocation of patents granted by the EPO to national courts. Next he summarised the amendment procedure for UK patents and commented on it as follows:

"The procedure for amendment of a UK patent, whether granted by the EPO or the UK Patent Office in legal proceedings is governed by the procedural rules of the Court, CPR Pt 63.10. I summarised it in *Nikken* [2006] F.S.R. 4:

'[9] … The procedure is by way of an application notice, service on the Comptroller, subsequent

---

[236] [1985] R.P.C. 59.
[237] [1989] F.S.R. 614; and see also *British Thomson-Houston Co's Patent* [1919] 36 R.P.C. 251.
[238] *The Times*, 22 March 1996, CA.
[239] [1998] R.P.C. 727.
[240] [2006] F.S.R. 4.
[241] [2011] EWCA Civ 6.

advertisement and so on. The procedures can, in appropriate circumstances, be gone through quickly or gone through provisionally on the basis that probably no third party will ever come in to oppose. It may be noted that the rules specifically require by Part 63.10 that the patentee must state whether he will contend that the claims prior to amendment are valid. That means that in advance of trial everyone knows where they stand. The patentee is either saying that the original claims are all right or not, and he is plainly also saying that the proposed amendment claims are all right.'

This is important. It means that once the patentee knows the attacks being made on his patent (and in particular the cited prior art) he is fully entitled to formulate what is called in the EPO a 'fallback' position by way of seeking an amendment—indeed he can formulate several. And he can make it clear that he is only seeking amendment if his patent as it stands is found invalid, or is seeking the amendment anyway: conditional or unconditional. Rule 63.10 specifically requires that the patentee must state whether he 'will contend that claims prior to the amendment are valid….

All three members of the Court gave judgments. I said at [8] after having pointed out that s.75(1) of the Patents Act 1977 says the Court 'may allow the proprietor of the patent to amend':

> 'There are different situations in which the exercise of the discretion to allow amendment of a patent may be sought: (a) before a trial; (b) after trial, at which certain claims have been held valid but other claims held invalid, the patentee simply wishing to delete the invalid claims (I would include here also the case where the patentee wishes to re-write the claims so as to exclude various dependencies as in *Hallen Co v Brabantia (UK) Ltd* [1990] F.S.R. 134. There the patentee is in effect continuing to claim which he had claimed before but in a much smaller way); and (c) after a trial in which all claims have been held invalid but the patentee wishes to insert what he hopes are validating amendments.'"

15-188   Jacob LJ held that the application before the Court of Appeal was of a class (c) type and referred to *Nikken* this way:

> "100. I described the position for such a type in *Nikken* [2006] F.S.R. 4:
>
> > '[11]   Class (c) involves something different, a proposed claim which was not under attack and *could not have been* under attack prior to trial. If the court is to allow such a claim to be propounded after trial, there is almost bound to be a further battle which would arise in the proposed amendment proceedings. That battle will be over whether or not the proposed amended claim is valid. I say "almost bound" because I can just conceive a case where the point was covered by the main litigation in some way or other.'
>
> I should have added that a further battle may also arise about the allowability of the amendments. In this case if IPCom were allowed to apply for the amendments, there would indeed be battles both about allowability (and clarity) and validity.
>
> 101. In *Nikken* [2006] F.S.R. 4, I then went on to say that an exercise of discretion to allow two trials would be improper for three reasons which I can summarise here:
>
> (a)   It would breach the general procedural rule laid down as long ago as1843 in *Henderson v Henderson* (1843) 3 Hare 100, that a party should normally not be allowed to advance in a second proceeding matter he could have advanced in the first.
>
> (b)   That rule had been applied in patent cases by this Court in *Windsurfing International Inc v Tabur Marine (Great Britain) Ltd* [1985] R.P.C. 59, CA and Aldous J in *Lubrizol Corp v Esso Petroleum Co Ltd (No.5)* [1998] R.P.C. 727, CA. I said Aldous J had epitomised the position when he said, at p.790: 'I believe it is a fundamental principle of patent litigation that a party must bring before the court the issues that he seeks to have resolved, so as to enable the court to conclude the litigation between the parties.'
>
> (c)   The general court rules were 'dead against' allowing amendment proceedings requiring a second trial after a first trial had determined the patent was invalid. […]"

15-189   Jacob LJ then turned to consider whether this approach was inconsistent between *Nikken* and the speeches in the *Johnson v Gore Wood*,[242] holding as follows:

> "108. …I do not think there is anything inconsistent between these speeches and *Nikken*. I accept entirely that the true test is one of abuse of process—procedural fairness—and that the burden

---

[242] [2002] 2 A.C. 1.

lies on the party objecting to the second action to show this. However where a party fails to advance a case he could have advanced much earlier and does so without any real justification, he is abusing the process and the other party is therefore entitled to object. It is not normally procedurally fair to subject the other side to successive cases when you could readily have put them all in one go.

109. There are exceptions, depending on the facts (such as the facts of *Gore-Wood* [2002] 2 A.C. 1). But there is nothing exceptional about the facts here. IPCom had every opportunity of proposing the amendments in time so that there could be a trial about them, it did not do so (whether deliberately or not we do not know), it only proposed amendments too late for them to be dealt with fairly at the trial, it elected to go to trial on the patent as it stood, and only when it lost did it seek to prolong matters thereby to vex Nokia again with the same patent. The judge was fully entitled to regard that as procedurally unfair and to refuse to allow that to happen."

Similarly, in *Vector v Glatt*[243] the trial judge had allowed an amendment and held the patent valid on that basis. An appeal made against a single amended claim was successful, and the patentee then applied for a further amendment which involved deletion of certain wording appearing in that claim. The appellant alleged that the further amendment required a new trial for three reasons. Jacob LJ held that he would not have ordered a new trial for the first two reasons, but that the third would require a fresh trial, and that in the interests of finality the patentee should be refused permission to apply for the further amendment. **15-190**

In *Generics v Warner Lambert*[244] Arnold J refused an application to amend the specification after judgment holding that art.138 of the EPC did not affect the principles stated by Jacob LJ in *Nokia v IPCom* nor did the fact that it was possible to make a central amendment affect those principles either (referring to Kitchin LJ in *Samsung Electronics v Apple Retail*). **15-191**

It would seem therefore that, except perhaps in a case where there is an obvious amendment which clearly would validate the patent without requiring a new trial, the Court of Appeal will not entertain an application to amend, and the same considerations would appear to apply equally in the case of a patentee applying after an adverse judgment in the Patents Court. It follows that patentees who feel that their existing claims might be found invalid should raise the possibility of amendment before the trial. **15-192**

[243] [2008] R.P.C. 10.
[244] [2015] EWHC 3370 (Pat).

CHAPTER 16

DEVOLUTION, ASSIGNMENTS AND LICENCES, CO-OWNERSHIP AND REGISTRATION

CONTENTS

1. DEVOLUTION

The applicant and the proprietor

Upon publication of the application for a UK national patent the Comptroller causes the name, etc. of the applicant or applicants to be entered in the Register of Patents, which is kept at the Patent Office,[1] and upon grant of the patent the Comptroller also causes the name, etc. of the grantee or grantees to be entered if different to that of the applicant.[2]   **16-01**

In the case of an application for a European patent, upon publication of the application by the EPO the name of the applicant is entered upon the Register of European Patents maintained at the EPO in Munich and entries concerning applications for European patents (UK) are copied through to the UK Register.[3] Upon grant, a European patent (UK) is treated as if it were a UK national patent[4] and the Comptroller makes entries upon the UK Register in respect of it.   **16-02**

The UK Register is only prima facie evidence of anything required to be registered under the Patents Act 1977.[5] Accordingly, registration as applicant or as proprietor is not conclusive proof that the person registered is entitled to be granted a patent or is in fact the proprietor of the patent.[6] The rights conferred by a patent, and in particular the right to sue for infringement of the patent, are vested in the proprietor as opposed to the person registered as the proprietor.[7] Unlike the Patents Act 1949,[8] the 1977 Act does not contain any provision to the effect that, subject to the equities, the person registered as proprietor of the patent has title to assign the same or grant rights under the patent. Protection of persons taking an assignment from the proprietor of a patent or from an applicant is provided for by the   **16-03**

---

1   Patents Rules 2007 r.44(1).
2   Patents Rules 2007 r.44(4).
3   See paras 16-172 to 16-176.
4   PA 1977 s.77(1); EPC art.64.
5   PA 1977 s.32(9), as amended by Patents, Designs and Marks Act 1986 (hereafter "PDMA 1986") s.1 and Sch.1 para.4.
6   See also PA 1977 s.7(4).
7   PA 1977 s.61.
8   PA 1949 s.74(4).

provisions relating to conflicting transactions set out below.[9] It is to be noted that the 1977 Act contains no definition as to who is the proprietor of the patent and, in particular, the Act does not provide that the proprietor is the registered proprietor. In the normal way, the proprietor of the patent is the original grantee or a person who obtains title to the patent by an assignment which meets the requirements of the 1977 Act.[10] However, where the original grantee's entitlement to the patent is challenged, the true proprietor is the person who can trace their title from one or other of the persons specified in ss.7(2)(a) and 7(2)(b) of the Act.[11]

Nature of property in patents and applications

16-04   Any patent or application for a patent is personal property (without being a thing in action)[12] and may be transferred by assignment[13] or vested by operation of law (as on death, bankruptcy or dissolution of a company) in the same way as any other personal property.[14] The 1977 Act also proceeds on the basis that a patentable invention is personal property.[15] Assignments of patentable inventions are discussed above in the context of the right to be granted a patent[16] and the right to claim priority from an earlier application.[17]

European patents (UK) and applications, PCT applications

16-05   As well as applying to UK national patents and applications, these provisions also apply to European patents (UK)[18] and to applications for European patents (UK)[19] and to applications made via the PCT whether for a UK national patent[20] or for a European patent (UK).[21]

Devolution on death

16-06   The property in a patent or application passes, by operation of law, when the proprietor or applicant dies. Upon the death of a proprietor or applicant their interest in the property passes to their executors or administrators, as the case may be, in a like manner to the rest of their personal estate, that is to say, upon trust to fulfil the provisions of the will, or, in the case of intestacy, upon trust for sale with power to postpone such sale.[22] If, however, the proprietor or applicant dies intestate and

---

9   PA 1977 s.33; see also para.16-39.
10 See para.16-29.
11 *Hartington Conway Ltd's Patent Application* [2004] R.P.C. 7. And see Ch.4.
12 PA 1977 s.30(1).
13 PA 1977 s.30(2). See para.16-29, et seq.
14 PA 1977 s.30(3).
15 *KCI Licensing v Smith & Nephew* [2010] EWHC 1487 (Pat), [66]. Decision reversed in part on appeal on other grounds ([2010] EWCA Civ 1260; [2011] F.S.R. 8).
16 See para.4-20.
17 See para.7-11.
18 PA 1977 s.77.
19 PA 1977 s.78.
20 PA 1977 s.89(1).
21 PA 1977 s.79.
22 See Administration of Estates Act 1925 s.33(1).

without any next of kin the patent or application, as the case may be, vests in the Crown as bona vacantia.[23]

Any step which, by the 1977 Act, is required to be taken by the proprietor of a patent or application may be taken by his executor or administrator; and an application for a patent may also be made by (and the patent granted to) the successor of any deceased person who, immediately before dying, was entitled to make such an application.[24] A patent or an application may be vested by an assent of personal representatives.[25] The assent will be void unless in writing.[26] The death of the proprietor of a patent or application and the vesting by an assent of personal representatives are events to which s.33 of the 1977 Act applies,[27] and should be registered without delay to prevent loss of rights in an infringement action.[28]

16-07

Devolution on dissolution of a company

If a company is the proprietor of a patent or application (or a patent or application is held in trust for it) and is dissolved without having assigned such property, it vests in the Crown as bona vacantia.[29] It has been held that in the case of a patent there is no merger in the Crown in these circumstances because the monopoly right given by the patent "is not a right against the Crown only; but is a right to prevent others from using the invention".[30] Where, however, the company at the time of its dissolution holds the patent or application as a trustee for some other person, the property does not vest in the Crown as bona vacantia,[31] and the court may make a vesting order vesting the rights in such person as the court may appoint.[32]

16-08

Charges on patents, etc. by a company

A charge on a patent, or on a licence under a patent, created by a company will be void against the liquidator/administrator and the creditors of the company unless a statement of particulars of the charge is delivered to the Registrar of Companies within 21 days of the creation of the charge.[33] For charges already in existence when the patent or licence is acquired by the company, see s.859C of the Companies Act 2006. As to the registration of mortgages, etc. in the Register of Patents, see para.16-39, et seq. and para.16-177, et seq.

16-09

---

[23] See Administration of Estates Act 1925 s.46(1)(vi); and Inheritance (Provision for Family and Dependants) Act 1975 s.24.
[24] PA 1977 ss.7(2)(c), 8(8) and 30(3).
[25] PA 1977 s.30(3).
[26] PA 1977 s.30(6).
[27] PA 1977 s.33(3)(d).
[28] PA 1977 ss.68 and 69(1). And see para.16-47, et seq.
[29] See Companies Act 2006 s.1012.
[30] *Dutton's Patent* (1923) 40 R.P.C. 84, 86 (dissenting from *Re Taylor's Agreement Trusts* (1904) 21 R.P.C. 713); see also *Bates' Patent* (1921) 38 R.P.C. 385; and Law of Property Act 1925 s.185.
[31] See Companies Act 2006 s.1012.
[32] See Trustee Act 1925 s.41; see also s.51(1)(ii); and Law of Property Act 1925 ss.9 and 181. For vesting orders made under Trustee Act 1893 (when a patentee's right was a chose in action) see, e.g. *Heath's Patent* (1912) 29 R.P.C. 389; *Dutton's Patent* (1923) 40 R.P.C. 84.
[33] Companies Act 2006 ss.859A, 859D and 859H. As to the court's power to extend the period allowed for delivery see s.859F.

Devolution on bankruptcy

16-10   Patents and applications which are the property of a bankrupt pass on their bankruptcy to the trustee in bankruptcy.[34] A secret process also has to be disclosed where it is part of the assets and goodwill of a business.[35] The trustee in bankruptcy is also entitled to call for after-acquired patents[36] and royalties,[37] however a bona fide sale for value without notice of the bankruptcy will be valid against them.[38] A patent held by a bankrupt patentee in trust for others does not pass upon bankruptcy, even though the circumstances be such that they are the reputed owner.[39]

16-11   The so-called anti-deprivation rule renders void and unenforceable a contract which provides that a patent or application will remain a person's property until their bankruptcy and, on the happening of that event, go over to someone else (and thus be taken away from his creditors).[40] The same rule also applies in the case of insolvency of a business.[41]

Writ of fieri facias

16-12   Under the old law a patentee's right, being merely that of preventing others from working their invention, was a chose in action, and was incapable of seizure under a writ of fieri facias.[42] Now that it is specifically provided[43] that a patent is not a chose in action it must be doubtful whether this proposition is still correct. So also in respect of an application for a patent.[44] A receiver will not be appointed in execution of a judgment, at any rate where it is not shown that the patentee is in receipt of profits by way of royalties or otherwise.[45] The extent to which a patentee's right can be said to have "no locality" is, however, doubtful.[46]

16-13   Articles manufactured in accordance with a patent can be seized and sold under a writ of fieri facias, but such seizure and sale do not give to the purchaser any rights beyond those which they would have acquired in the ordinary way; thus, if a person in possession of a patented chattel has only a limited and personal licence to use it, a purchaser, with notice of such licence, from a sheriff who has seized the article, does not acquire any licence to use it.[47]

---

[34] Insolvency Act 1986 s.306.

[35] See *Re Keene* [1922] 2 Ch. 475; *Cotton v Gillard* (1874) 44 L.J. Ch. 90.

[36] Insolvency Act 1986 s.307(1); *Hesse v Stevenson* (1803) 3 Bos. & Pul. 565, 577; approved in *Re Roberts* [1900] 1 Q.B. 122.

[37] See *Re Graydon, ex p. Official Receiver* [1896] 1 Q.B. 417, at 419.

[38] Insolvency Act 1986 s.307(4).

[39] Insolvency Act 1986 s.283(3).

[40] *Belmont Park Investments v BNY Corporate Trustee Services* [2011] UKSC 38; [2012] 1 A.C. 383. See also *Fraser v Oystertec Plc* [2004] F.S.R. 22.

[41] *Belmont Park Investments v BNY Corporate Trustee Services* [2011] UKSC 38; [2012] 1 A.C. 383. See also *Fraser v Oystertec Plc* [2004] F.S.R. 22.

[42] *British Mutoscope and Biograph Co v Homer* (1901) 18 R.P.C. 177; and see *Edwards & Co v Picard* [1909] 2 K.B. 903, 905.

[43] PA 1977 s.30(1).

[44] PA 1977 s.30(1).

[45] *Edwards & Co v Picard* [1909] 2 K.B. 903 (Moulton LJ dissenting).

[46] See *English Scottish and Australian Bank Ltd v Inland Revenue Commissioners* [1932] A.C. 238; overruling *Smelting Co of Australia Ltd v Commissioners of Inland Revenue* [1897] 1 Q.B. 175; and see also *British Mutoscope and Biograph Co v Homer* (1901) 18 R.P.C. 177 and *Edwards & Co v Picard* [1909] 2 K.B. 903.

[47] *British Mutoscope and Biograph Co v Homer* (1901) 18 R.P.C. 177.

Devolution of licences and sub-licences

Any licence or sub-licence under a patent or application vests by operation of law **16-14** in the same way as any other personal property and may be vested by an assent of personal representatives.[48]

The death of a licensee or sub-licensee under a patent or application and the vest- **16-15** ing of any such licence or sub-licence by an assent of personal representatives are events to which s.33(3) applies.[49] It is particularly important to ensure that these events are registered in the case of an exclusive licence for otherwise the ability to recover costs in a subsequent infringement action may be prejudiced.[50]

In order to prevent licences from vesting in the manner referred to, it is com- **16-16** mon to include express provisions in licence agreements providing for the automatic determination of the licence upon the death of the licensee or in the event that the licensee should be adjudicated bankrupt or, in the case of a company, go into receivership or liquidation (otherwise than for the purposes of amalgamation or reconstruction).

2. ASSIGNMENTS AND LICENCES

Under the 1977 Act

By s.30(2) of the 1977 Act, any patent or application or any right in a patent or **16-17** application may be assigned or mortgaged, and by s.30(4) licences may be granted under any patent or any application. To the extent that the licence so provides, a sub-licence may be granted thereunder, and any such licence or sub-licence may be assigned or mortgaged.[51]

An assignment of a patent or an application and an exclusive licence granted **16-18** under any patent or application may confer on the assignee or licensee, as the case may be, the right of the assignor or licensor to bring proceedings for a previous infringement.[52]

Under the old law[53] an assignment for a part only of the UK could be made. The **16-19** present Act contains no specific provisions but presumably such a limited assignment would be covered by the words "any right in it" in s.30(2). In any event the same practical effect could be achieved by granting an exclusive licence.[54]

The rights of co-owners to assign and grant licences are dealt with at para.16- **16-20** 160, et seq.

Difference between assignment and licence

There is a fundamental distinction between an assignment of a patent (or an ap- **16-21** plication for a patent) and a licence. By the former the assignee stands in the shoes of the assignor, and is fully entitled to deal with the patent or application as they please, subject to the provisions of the 1977 Act as to the grant of compulsory

[48] PA 1977 s.30(4)(b).
[49] PA 1977 s.33(3)(d).
[50] PA 1977 s.68. And see para.16-47, et seq.
[51] PA 1977 s.30(4)(a).
[52] PA 1977 s.30(7).
[53] PA 1949 s.21(1).
[54] See para.16-22.

licences.[55] A non-exclusive licensee, on the contrary, is merely permitted to do acts which would, but for the licence, be prohibited.[56] Other contractual rights as between the parties may be created by the licence, as in the case of an exclusive licence where the patentee or applicant contracts not to grant other licences or to exercise the licensed rights themselves.

Exclusive licence

16-22   An exclusive licensee has the same right as the proprietor of the patent to bring proceedings in respect of any infringement of the patent committed after the date of the licence.[57] Thus, an exclusive licensee has a right in relation to the patent or application which is more than contractual; nevertheless, an exclusive licence is a right under, not in, the patent or application.[58] An exclusive licensee under an application may also bring proceedings in their own name in respect of any infringement of the rights arising upon publication of the application.[59] An exclusive licence may also confer on the licensee the right to bring proceedings for a previous infringement.[60] The proprietor or applicant, as the case may be, must be made a party to the proceedings. However, if made a defendant, the proprietor/applicant will not be liable for any costs or expenses unless they enter an appearance and take part in the proceedings.[61] Where both the proprietor and the exclusive licensee sue as co-claimants, each is entitled, if successful, to damages assessed on normal principles.[62]

16-23   As in the case of proprietorship, there is no requirement in the 1977 Act to the effect that the exclusive licence must be registered before proceedings are commenced. However, non-registration may affect the licensee's ability to recover their costs of the proceedings.[63]

16-24   An exclusive licence is defined as being[64]:

"a licence from the proprietor of or applicant for a patent conferring on the licensee, or on him and persons authorised by him, to the exclusion of all other persons (including the proprietor or applicant), any right in respect of the invention to which the patent or application relates, and 'exclusive licensee' and 'non-exclusive licence' shall be construed accordingly."

16-25   There may, therefore, be several exclusive licensees, each having an exclusive licence in their own field and each may sue in respect of an infringement committed in contravention of their particular right.[65] The definition of an exclusive licence

---

[55] See Ch.17.
[56] This has been well settled since the eighteenth century, see per Lord Diplock in *Allen & Hanburys v Generics (UK) Ltd* [1986] R.P.C. 203, at 246.
[57] PA 1977 s.67(1).
[58] *Insituform Technical Services v Inliner UK* [1992] R.P.C. 83, 105; *Dendron GmbH v University of California (No.3)* [2004] F.S.R. 43, [23].
[59] PA 1977 ss.67(1) and 69, subject to the restrictions of s.69(2).
[60] PA 1977 s.30(7).
[61] PA 1977 s.67(3).
[62] *Optical Coating Laboratory Inc v Pilkington PE Ltd* [1993] F.S.R. 310, PCC, reversed on other grounds on appeal, see [1995] R.P.C. 145.
[63] PA 1977 s.68; and see para.16-47, et seq.
[64] PA 1977 s.130.
[65] *Spring Form Inc v Toy Brokers Ltd* [2002] F.S.R. 17, [20]; *Dendron GmbH v University of California (No.3)* [2004] F.S.R. 43, [25].

may not prevent the proprietor retaining some measure of control of sub-licences, perhaps through an agency relationship.[66]

An exclusive licensee who has the right to grant sub-licences may grant an **16-26** exclusive licence to another and such a licence will fall within the definition of s.130(1) if it deprives the first exclusive licensee of rights in respect of the invention to which the patent relates.[67] However, a person who merely has the exclusive right to manufacture to an exclusive licensee's specification is not an exclusive licensee within the definition of s.130(1) because an exclusive right to manufacture to another's specification does not constitute an exclusive licence of a right "in respect of the invention to which the patent... relates."[68]

In the absence of evidence establishing that the claimant is an exclusive licensee **16-27** their claim will be struck out but there should be no additional finding to the effect that they are *not* in fact an exclusive licensee unless there is evidence to justify that finding.[69]

Where the exclusive licensee sues in respect of goods supplied by the proprie- **16-28** tor of the patent, the defendant will not be liable unless he acquired the goods with notice of the exclusive licence.[70]

Form of assignment

Under the old law an assignment had to be by deed to convey the legal estate and **16-29** thereby alter the proprietorship in a patent, as that which is created by deed can only be assigned by deed.[71] Under the present law however there is no need for an assignment to be under seal. By s.30(6) of the 1977 Act, as originally enacted, it was provided that any assignment or mortgage of a patent or any application, or any right in a patent or any application or any assent relating to any patent or any such application shall be void unless it is in writing and is signed by or on behalf of the parties to the transaction. It is to be noted that as originally enacted all the parties to the transaction (normally two) were required to sign the document. However, s.30(6) was amended by art.10 of the Regulatory Reform (Patents) Order 2004[72] with effect from 1 January 2005 so as to dispense with the requirement that all parties must sign. Thus for an assignment or mortgage made on or after 1 January 2005 it is sufficient if the document is signed by the assignor or mortgagor only. Likewise an assent may be signed by or on behalf of the personal representative only. Yet for transactions taking place before 1 January 2005, the requirement remains that all parties must have signed. In *Wright Hassall v Horton*[73] HHJ Cooke held that an instrument in writing which satisfied s.30(6) is effective as a legal assignment without any additional requirement for consideration.

Article 72 EPC provides that an assignment of a European patent application **16-30** shall be made in writing and shall require the signature of the parties to the contract.

---

[66] *Peaudouce S.A. v Kimberley Clark Ltd* [1996] F.S.R. 680, 690.
[67] *Dendron GmbH v University of California (No.3)* [2004] F.S.R. 43.
[68] *Bondax Carpets v Advance Carpet Tiles* [1993] F.S.R. 162.
[69] *Procter & Gamble v Peaudouce (UK) Ltd* [1989] F.S.R. 180, CA.
[70] *Heap v Hartley* (1889) 6 R.P.C. 499; *Cochrane & Co v Martins* (1911) 28 R.P.C. 284; *Scottish Vacuum Cleaner Co Ltd v Provincial Cinematograph Theatres Ltd* (1915) 32 R.P.C. 353; *Christian Salvesen v Odfjell Drilling* [1985] R.P.C. 569 see also para.16-108.
[71] *Stewart v Casey* (1892) 9 R.P.C. 9, 11 and 13.
[72] SI 2004/2537.
[73] [2015] EWHC 3716 (QB).

Assignment of the right to file an application

16-31   The right to file an application for a patent is a right in an application for a patent and, consequently, s.30(6)(a) of the Act applies to an assignment of such a right, i.e. it must be in writing and signed by or on behalf of the appropriate parties.[74] The right to file an application for a patent in respect of an invention may be validly assigned before the invention has been made.[75]

Defective assignment

16-32   A purported assignment which does not comply with the requirements of the 1977 Act will normally amount to an agreement to assign in equity and, accordingly, the assignee will be regarded in equity as the owner of the patent or application. An equitable owner of a patent is entitled to commence proceedings for infringement without joining the assignor, provided that before judgment the assignor is made a party to the proceedings or the legal title is perfected.[76]

Lost assignment

16-33   Where an assignment has been lost or there are good reasons why the original document cannot be adduced in evidence, the court will admit secondary evidence of the assignment and will attach such weight to it as it considers appropriate in all the circumstances.[77] The "best evidence" rule does not prevent the admission of such evidence.[78]

Assignment or licence?

16-34   Disputes can sometimes arise as to whether a particular agreement is an assignment or a licence. The outcome of such disputes turns on the proper construction of the agreement in question.[79]

Form of licence

16-35   The 1977 Act does not require that a licence, whether exclusive, or non-exclusive be in any particular form and, therefore, subject to proof of the existence of the same, an oral licence will be enforceable.[80] In view, however, of the problems of uncertainty with regard to an oral contract and the advisability of registering any licence, dealt with in para.16-47, it is sensible that any licence be in writing.

---

[74]   *Hartington Conway Ltd's Patent Application* [2004] R.P.C. 6 (the Comptroller), [65]–[66]; [2004] R.P.C. 7 (Pumfrey J), [25].

[75]   PA 1977 s.7(2)(b). And see *KCI Licensing Inc v Smith & Nephew PLC* [2010] EWHC 1487 (Pat); [2010] F.S.R. 31, reversed on other grounds on appeal.

[76]   *Baxter International Inc v Nederlands Produktielaboratorium voor Bloedtransfusiapparatuur B.V.* [1998] R.P.C. 250. See also para.16-36.

[77]   *Springstein v Masquerade Music Ltd* [2001] E.M.L.R. 25 (a decision in respect of an assignment of copyright).

[78]   *Springstein v Masquerade Music Ltd* [2001] E.M.L.R. 25.

[79]   See, e.g. *Messenger v British Broadcasting Co Ltd* [1929] A.C. 151; *JHP Ltd v BBC Worldwide Ltd* [2008] F.S.R. 29.

[80]   See *Morton-Norwich Products Inc v Intercen* [1981] F.S.R. 337.

Agreements to assign or grant licences

Agreements to assign or to grant licences are specifically enforceable in equity, **16-36** and are governed by the ordinary rules relating to contract as to specific performance, consideration, etc. Such agreements must, however, be of the degree of definiteness required by law to constitute an enforceable contract; thus, an agreement to grant a licence for a definite period and on stated terms would be enforceable.[81] So, too, an agreement to assign which fails as an assignment for non-compliance with s.30(6).[82] An agreement to assign does not alter the proprietorship of a patent, but gives right in equity to have the proprietorship altered in law.[83]

Agreements to assign or to grant licences may be made prior to the filing of the **16-37** application for the patent concerned. Thus, an agreement relating to a subsisting patent may, subject to EU law,[84] contain provisions for the assignment of, or the grant of licences under, patents in respect of future improvements.

Section 7(2)(b) of the 1977 Act provides that a patent for an invention may be **16-38** granted to any person who was, at the time of the making of the invention, entitled to the whole of the property in it by virtue of any enforceable term of any agreement entered into with the inventor before the making of that invention. Consequently, where such an agreement has been entered into, it is not necessary to execute an assignment of the right to apply for the patent after the invention has actually been made.[85]

Effect of registration on rights in patents

Section 33 of the 1977 Act makes provision for the situation where a transac- **16-39** tion, instrument or event in relation to a patent or application is incompatible with an earlier transaction, instrument or event relating to that patent or application. The section provides that a person claiming under the later transaction shall be entitled to the property in the patent or application as against the person claiming under the earlier transaction, if the earlier transaction was not registered or, in the case of an application which has not been published, notice of the earlier transaction had not been given to the Comptroller and in both cases the person claiming under the later transaction did not know of the earlier transaction. The provisions apply equally to the case where any person claims to have acquired any right in or under a patent or application by virtue of a transaction, instrument or event to which the section applies, and that right is incompatible with any such right acquired by virtue of an earlier transaction, instrument or event to which the section applies.[86]

Early registration of a licence, assignment or other agreement conferring rights **16-40** with regard to a patent or application is therefore of great importance, the existence of such registration preventing the patentee from granting licences under or otherwise dealing with the patent in an incompatible manner.

---

[81] See, e.g. *Brake v Radermacher* (1903) 20 R.P.C. 631.
[82] *Baxter International Inc v Nederlands Produktielaboratorium voor Bloedtransfusiapparatuur B.V.* [1998] R.P.C. 250, a decision prior to the amendment of PA 1977 s.30(6).
[83] *Stewart v Casey* (1892) 9 R.P.C. 9, 14, CA.
[84] See para.16-123, et seq., particularly paras 16-143 to 16-144.
[85] *KCI Licensing Inc v Smith & Nephew PLC* [2010] EWHC 1487 (Pat); [2010] F.S.R. 31, reversed on other grounds on appeal.
[86] PA 1977 s.33(2).

Transactions, instruments and events to which s.33 applies

16-41   The transactions, instruments and events to which s.33 applies are set out in subs.(3) of that section and cover assignments of a patent or application for a patent or a right in a patent or application, the mortgage of a patent or application, the grant or assignment of a licence or sub-licence, mortgage of a licence or sub-licence, the death of a proprietor of a patent or application or any person having a right in or under a patent or application, the vesting of a patent or application by an assent of personal representatives, and any order of the court transferring a patent or application to any person or that an application should proceed in the name of any person. But the section does not apply to all transactions affecting the proprietorship in patents and, in particular, it does not apply to an agreement to assign a patent.[87]

16-42   The word "assignment" in s.33(3)(a) is to be given a wide meaning and may be an instrument in some circumstances or an event in other circumstances or a combination of the two.[88] Thus an assignment of a UK patent by operation of law of the kind involved in a universal succession following the merger of two companies under Swiss law is within s.33(3)(a).[89]

16-43   It is unclear whether the wide meaning of "assignment" in s.33(3)(a) has the effect of catching the transfer by operation of law of a patent or application (or any right in or under a patent or application) which occurs when, for example, a person becomes bankrupt or a company is dissolved.[90] In *Siemens Schweiz AG v Thorn Security Ltd*[91] the Court of Appeal declined to decide the question but suggested that in these circumstances there may no assignment for the purpose of s.33(3)(a) until the trustee in bankruptcy or the Crown (as the case may be) assigns the asset to a third party.

16-44   Section 33(3)(d) relates to the death of the proprietor of a patent or application (or any person having a right in or under a patent or application) and the vesting by an assent of personal representative of a patent, application or any such right. Although the property in a patent or application, etc. passes by operation of law to personal representatives on death, it would seem that death per se may not be an event falling within section 33(3)(d) but rather the subsection is directed to the vesting by an assent of personal representatives following death.[92]

16-45   Section 33(3)(e) is intended to cover the case where the order or directions are dispositive and involve the exercise of some discretion conferred by law.[93]

---

[87] *Coflexip Stena Offshore Ltd's Patent* [1997] R.P.C. 179, 188; *Siemens Schweiz AG v Thorn Security Ltd* [2009] R.P.C. 3, CA, [97].

[88] *Siemens Schweiz AG v Thorn Security Ltd* [2009] R.P.C. 3, CA, [91].

[89] *Siemens Schweiz AG v Thorn Security Ltd* [2009] R.P.C. 3, CA, 94], overruling *Tamglass Ltd OY v Luoyang North Glass Technology Co Ltd (No.3)* [2006] F.S.R. 34.

[90] See paras 16-06 to 16-11.

[91] *Siemens Schweiz AG v Thorn Security Ltd* [2009] R.P.C. 3, CA, [95].

[92] *Siemens Schweiz AG v Thorn Security Ltd* [2009] R.P.C. 3, CA, [95].

[93] *Siemens Schweiz AG v Thorn Security Ltd* [2008] R.P.C. 4 (Mann J), [106]; [2009] R.P.C. 3, CA, [97].

European patents (UK) and applications

Section 33 applies equally to UK national patents and European patents (UK) and **16-46** applications therefore.[94] In the case of applications for European patents (UK), registration is made at the EPO and the entry is copied through to the UK Register.[95]

Effect of non-registration on infringement proceedings

Non-registration of title to a patent does not prevent a proprietor or exclusive **16-47** licensee commencing proceedings or from seeking interlocutory relief.[96] However, the ability of an unregistered proprietor or exclusive licensee to recover their costs of infringement proceedings may be affected.

Section 68 (as amended[97] with effect from 29 April 2006) provides that where a **16-48** person becomes the proprietor or exclusive license of a patent by virtue of a transaction, instrument or event to which s.33 applies, the court shall not award them costs in proceedings for a subsequent infringement unless the transaction, instrument or event is registered within six months of its date or the court is satisfied that it was not practicable to register within that period but it was registered as soon as practicable thereafter.

It has been held that s.68 as originally enacted, which placed a bar on damages **16-49** or an account of profits rather than on recovery of costs, applies to acts of infringements committed prior to 29 April 2006 even if the date of issue of the Claim Form or the date of judgment are later.[98]

In the context of s.68, "practicable" means that the applicant for registration must **16-50** take all the steps which the reasonable applicant acting on competent advice would take in the circumstances to secure registration.[99]

The section is not directed to punishing the applicant for delay but to protecting **16-51** the infringer from a claim to costs or expenses of someone whose interest they could not have ascertained from an inspection of the register.[100] The primary purpose of s.68 is to inform the public who is the owner (or exclusive licensee) of the patent monopoly.[101] Section 68 (and s.33) are intended to coerce patentees and others entering into relevant transactions concerning patents to register their interests.[102]

The effect of s.68 in circumstances where a licence was registered late, but before **16-52** judgment in the proceedings, was considered in *Schütz v Werit*. In the Court of Appeal,[103] Jacob LJ[104] held that the section operates to preclude recovery of costs incurred whilst the licence remains unregistered. However, on appeal to the

---

94 PA 1977 ss.77 and 78.
95 See para.16-176.
96 *Baxter International Inc v Nederlands Produktielaboratorium voor Bloedtransfusiapparatuur B.V.* [1998] R.P.C. 250; *Christian Salvesen v Odfjell Drilling* [1985] R.P.C. 569.
97 Intellectual Property (Enforcement, etc) Regulations 2006 (SI 2006/1028).
98 *Siemens Schweiz AG v Thorn Security Ltd* [2008] R.P.C. 4 (Mann J); as to the effect of s.68 as originally enacted, see para.16-26 of the 17th edn of this work.
99 *Mölnlycke A.B. v Procter & Gamble Ltd (No.5)* [1994] R.P.C. 49, 139, CA.
100 *Mölnlycke A.B. v Procter & Gamble Ltd (No.5)* [1994] R.P.C. 49, 109, per Morritt J.
101 *LG Electronics Inc v NCR Financial Solutions Group Ltd* [2003] F.S.R. 24, [18] and cited with approval by Lord Neuberger in *Schütz v Werit* [2013] UKSC 16; [2013] R.P.C. 16.
102 *Spring Form Inc v Toy Brokers Ltd* [2002] F.S.R. 17, 287.
103 *Schütz v Werit* [2011] EWCA Civ 927.
104 With whom Ward and Patten LLJ agreed.

Supreme Court,[105] Lord Neuberger[106] noted that this interpretation left the section with "very little bite" as the consequences of the section could be avoided by registering immediately before issuing proceedings. He concluded, albeit obiter, that the correction interpretation was that the licensee could not recover its costs in so far as they are attributable to a claim for relief in respect of pre-registration infringements but could recover costs attributable to a claim for relief in respect of post-registration infringements. Where both categories of infringement were alleged an apportionment would have to be made.[107]

16-53   Where an existing agreement granting an exclusive licence under a patent is replaced by a second agreement which also grants an exclusive licence under the patent, it is unclear whether the second licence must be registered to avoid the consequences of s.68. It has been held that it is the second agreement which should be recorded on the register, as the licensee "becomes" an exclusive licensee by virtue of the second agreement notwithstanding that they were previously an exclusive licensee by virtue of the first agreement.[108] However, the Court of Appeal held in *Schütz v Werit*[109] that re-registration was not required in such circumstances. This conclusion was itself doubted upon appeal to the Supreme Court but the point was left undecided.[110] Pending clarification of this point it would seem sensible to register such second licences as a precaution.

16-54   Where a patent is assigned together with the right of the assignor to sue for previous infringements, the assignee takes the assignor's right to sue subject to any defect in that right under s.68.[111] The practical consequences of this will of course depend upon the resolution of the question discussed above as to how much "bite" s.68 has.

16-55   Section 68 also applies where relief is claimed in respect of infringement of the rights conferred by publication of the application and the assignment of the application was made (or the exclusive licence was granted) after the application was published.[112]

16-56   However, s.68 does not apply to an agreement to assign a patent because s.33 does not apply to such an agreement.[113]

16-57   If a party wishes to rely upon the provisions of s.68 to limit its liability in costs, it must specifically raise such reliance in its pleadings.[114]

Notice of equitable interests

16-58   Section 33 of the 1977 Act only applies to some of the potential transactions relating to a patent. It does not apply to, for example, an agreement to assign[115] or a purported assignment which acts merely as an agreement to assign because it is

---

[105] *Schütz v Werit* [2013] UKSC 16; [2013] R.P.C. 16.
[106] With whom Lord Walker, Lady Hale, Lord Mance and Lord Kerr agreed.
[107] *Schütz v Werit* [2013] UKSC 16; [2013] R.P.C. 16, [97]–[100].
[108] *Spring Form Inc v Toy Brokers Ltd* [2002] F.S.R. 17, 287. See also *Minnesota Mining & Manufacturing v Rennicks* [1992] R.P.C. 331; [1992] F.S.R. 118.
[109] [2011] EWCA Civ 1337.
[110] *Schütz v Werit* [2013] UKSC 16; [2013] R.P.C. 16, [101]–[106].
[111] *LG Electronics Inc v NCR Financial Solutions Group Ltd* [2003] F.S.R. 24.
[112] PA 1977 s.69. See also *Spring Form Inc v Toy Brokers Ltd* [2002] F.S.R. 17.
[113] *Cofiexip Stena Offshore Ltd's Patent* [1997] R.P.C. 179, 188; *Siemens Schweiz AG v Thorn Security Ltd* [2009] R.P.C. 3, CA, [97].
[114] *Schütz v Werit* [2013] UKSC 16; [2013] R.P.C. 16, [88]–[91].
[115] *Cofiexip Stena Offshore Ltd's Patent* [1997] R.P.C. 179, 188; *Siemens Schweiz AG v Thorn Security Ltd* [2009] R.P.C. 3, CA, [97].

invalid for failure to comply with the requirements of s.30(6).[116] Such agreements to assign, and any other equitable right arising in relation to a patent not covered by s.33(3), are subject to the usual conditions of equitable assignments, and a person obtaining a legal assignment without notice of the equitable one can claim priority,[117] and can convey a good title, even though the subsequent purchaser from them may in fact have had notice.[118] Similarly, a licensee who before entering into a licence agreement has notice of a prior agreement to assign may be restrained from infringing by the new proprietor, as soon as the latter's title has been perfected by a legal assignment.[119] Thus, under the 1977 Act, if a person taking an assignment of a patent had notice that the assignor was holding the patent on trust for a third party, the assignment would not give the assignee priority as against the interest of the third party. The misdescription of the nature of a previous agreement as where an assignment was described to a party as a licence, may not prevent such party's knowledge of its existence constituting constructive notice.[120]

Covenants attaching to patents

Where an assignee of a patent covenants with the assignor for themselves and they assign that they will work the patent and pay certain royalties thereon to the assignor, a subsequent assignee with notice takes the patent subject to those covenants.[121] In such a case there is no privity of contract between the assignor and the second assignee. However, the rights of the assignor are analogous to a vendor's lien, and the second assignee cannot hold the rights which they have acquired without also fulfilling the obligations which may be said to attach to those rights, and consequently the terms of the original assignment become a matter of great importance.   **16-59**

In *Dansk Rekylriffel Syndikat Aktieselskab v Snell*,[122] Neville J said: **16-60**

"The obligation to fulfil the terms of the agreement, being with regard to the assignees not personal, but attached to the property which they acquired with notice on the terms upon which it was held by their assignor, disables them from holding the property without fulfilling the terms. It appears to me that such an interest of the vendor, if not properly described as a vendor's lien, is closely analogous to it.[123] The question involved is whether, upon the true construction of the original assignment, it was intended that the vendor should retain a charge upon the property, or that he should part with the property completely, looking solely to the personal liability of the purchaser to pay the consideration."[124]

In that case the existence of clauses in the original contract to the effect that the purchaser thereunder should keep the patent in force and should pay royalties, was held to indicate a reservation of interest in the vendor sufficient to bring the case within the above principle.   **16-61**

---

116 See para.16-29, et seq.
117 e.g. as in *Wapshare Tube Co Ltd v Hyde Imperial Rubber Co* (1901) 18 R.P.C. 374.
118 *Actiengesellschaft für Cartonnagen Industrie v Temler and Seeman* (1901) 18 R.P.C. 6.
119 See, e.g. *New Ixion Tyre and Cycle Co v Spilsbury* (1898) 15 R.P.C. 380, 567.
120 *Morey's Patent* (1858) 25 Beav. 581.
121 *Werderman v Société Générale d'Electricité* (1881) 19 Ch D. 246, 251 and 252.
122 [1908] 2 Ch. 127, 136.
123 See also *British Association of Glass Bottle Manufacturers v Foster & Sons Ltd* (1917) 34 R.P.C. 217, at 224.
124 See also *Bagot Pneumatic Tyre Co v Clipper Pneumatic Tyre Co* (1902) 19 R.P.C. 69, at 75; *Barker v Stickney* [1919] 1 K.B. 121.

Assignor estopped from impeaching validity

16-62   The circumstances in which an assignor may be prevented from denying the validity of the patent purely as a matter of the national law of estoppel are set out in this section. However, in some cases an assignment may constitute an agreement within the scope of art.101 of the Treaty on the Functioning of the EU (or the corresponding provisions of the Competition Act 1998) and therefore its effects must be also considered as a matter of competition law. See para.16-123, et seq.

16-63   When a patent has been assigned the new proprietor is entitled, in the absence of any provision in the assignment to the contrary, to prevent the assignor from manufacturing the patented article;[125] and in any action brought for that purpose by the assignee (or by any person deriving title through them) the assignor is estopped by his deed of assignment from impeaching the validity of the patent.[126] Similarly, the assignor of a licence is estopped from alleging as against their assignees that the patent is invalid.[127] The estoppel in such cases is of a personal nature and does not extend to the partner of an assignor even in an action in which both are joined as co-defendants.[128] Estoppel can "only operate in the same transaction as that in which it arises"[129]; it is limited to such implication of validity as may be contained in the deed to which the assignor has put their hand and seal, and does not exist, for example, where there is an assignment by operation of law, as upon bankruptcy of the patentee.[130] The former patentee is not estopped as against the new owner of the patent either by matter of record contained in the letters patent itself, or by statements contained in a specification (which professes only fully to declare the nature of the invention and how it is to be carried into effect), or by representations contained in the application for letters patent unless it be shown that the other party relied upon such representations.

16-64   It is probable that there would be such estoppel against the patentee as between themselves and the Crown.[131]

16-65   An assignor, where they are estopped from denying the validity of the patent, may, of course, contend for a construction of the specification which will exclude what they are in fact doing. So long as it does not impugn the validity of the patent, they may call evidence as to the state of the art in the light of which the specification must be construed.[132]

16-66   A person estopped from disputing the validity of a patent is, nevertheless, entitled to give evidence and assist in attacking its validity in proceedings to which they are not a party.[133]

Estoppel against licensee

16-67   The circumstances in which a patent licensee may be prevented from denying the validity of the patent purely as a matter of the national law of estoppel are set out

---

[125] See, e.g. *Franklin Hocking & Co Ltd v Franklin Hocking* (1887) 4 R.P.C. 255.
[126] *Chambers v Crichley* (1864) 33 Beav. 374.
[127] *Gonville v Hay* (1904) 21 R.P.C. 49.
[128] *Heugh v Chamberlain* (1877) 25 W.R. 742.
[129] *Fuel Economy Co Ltd v Murray* (1930) 47 R.P.C. 346, 353; *V.D. Ltd v Boston Deep Sea Fishing, etc., Ltd* (1935) 52 R.P.C. 303, 331; see also *Compania Naviera Vasconzada v Churchill & Sim* [1906] 1 K.B. 237, 251.
[130] *Cropper v Smith and Hancock* (1884) 1 R.P.C. 81.
[131] *Cropper v Smith and Hancock* (1884) 1 R.P.C. 81, 96.
[132] *Franklin Hocking & Co Ltd v Franklin Hocking* (1887) 4 R.P.C. 255, 434; (1889) 6 R.P.C. 69.
[133] *London and Leicester Hosiery Co v Griswold* (1886) 3 R.P.C. 251.

in this section. However, the propositions stated should be treated with caution as the effect of EU and national competition law in relation to the validity of no-challenge clauses, discussed at para.16-145, et seq., must also be considered.

A licensee may be estopped from denying the validity of the patent but there is not "an absolute estoppel in all cases and in all circumstances … but only an estoppel which is involved in and necessary to the exercise of the licence which the licensee has accepted."[134]

16-68

If the licence is limited in its scope, e.g. in area, and the patentee brings an action against the licensee, not under the licence, but for infringement of the patent in respect of acts done outside the licensed area, then the licensee would not be estopped in the action for infringement from disputing the validity of the patent.[135] It appears that a licensee would never be estopped from alleging that the patent is invalid, if the action brought against them is for infringement of patent, but only when an action is brought against him under the licence to enforce its provisions. As Luxmore J said in *Fuel Economy Co Ltd v Murray*[136]:

16-69

"A licensee cannot challenge the validity of a patent in an action under the licence, the licence being admitted by the licensee, because the title is not in issue. But in an action for infringement a different set of circumstances arises altogether. It is not an action under the licence at all, and in such a case, so far as my judgment goes, no estoppel arises."

Further, where there is in an agreement for sale, or for a licence, a covenant that the patent is valid, the question of validity is open to the assignee or licensee, and may go to the root of the consideration.[137] The real question to be decided in such cases is: "Did the defendant buy a good and indefeasible patent right, or was the contract merely to place the defendant in the same situation as the plaintiff was with reference to the alleged patent?"[138] Where a patentee contracted to give to the defendant the *exclusive right to sell* certain things for which patents had been obtained, it was held that if one of the patents was invalid the consideration failed as the patentee could not confer the privileges which he agreed to confer.[139] The decision upon this point might have been otherwise if he had refrained from inquiring into the validity and had worked the patent for a long time and subsequently, when called upon to pay royalty, refused upon the ground of invalidity.[140] In a case, however, where there was a covenant that payments should cease if the patent became void for lack of novelty, it was held that this referred to the patent being held void in proceedings between the patentee and other parties, and that the licensee was not entitled to put the validity of the patent in issue in an action upon

16-70

---

[134] *Fuel Economy Co Ltd v Murray* (1930) 47 R.P.C. 346, 358; see also *V.D. Ltd v Boston Deep Sea Fishing, etc., Ltd* (1935) 52 R.P.C. 303, 331; and *Kerbing Consolidated Ltd v Dick* [1973] R.P.C. 68.

[135] *Fuel Economy Co Ltd v Murray* (1930) 47 R.P.C. 346.

[136] *Fuel Economy Co Ltd v Murray* (1930) 47 R.P.C. 346, 353.

[137] *Nadel v Martin* (1906) 23 R.P.C. 41; *Henderson v Shiels* (1907) 24 R.P.C. 108.

[138] See *Hall v Conder* (1857) 26 L.J.C.P. 138, 143. See also *Suhr v Crofts (Engineers) Ltd* (1932) 49 R.P.C. 359.

[139] *Chanter v Leese* (1839) 5 Mee. & W. 698, as explained in *Hall v Conder* (1857) 26 L.J.C.P. 138, 143.

[140] *Chanter v Leese* (1839) 5 Mee. & W. 698, as explained in *Hall v Conder* (1857) 26 L.J.C.P. 138, 143.; see also *Suhr v Crofts (Engineers) Ltd* (1932) 49 R.P.C. 359.

the licence.[141] The above principles apply equally where there is a licence not under seal[142] and where the licence is a verbal one.[143]

16-71   A licensee is entitled to contend that what they are doing is not within the terms of their licence, and where (as is ordinarily the case) such terms are defined by the claims of the specification, they are at liberty to adduce evidence of common knowledge in the light of which the claims will be construed. They are not, however, entitled, in an action brought under the licence, to prove facts which would be inconsistent with the validity of the patent,[144] though obviously they may plead that the patent has expired,[145] and also may dispute that the patent should be extended and the length of its extension.[146]

Fraud

16-72   A licensee is, of course, entitled to repudiate their licence on the ground of fraud or common mistake, and the invalidity of the patent, if known to the licensor at the time of granting the licence, may be an element constituting fraud[147]; if the licensee proposes to take this course they must plead fraud in distinct terms.[148]

Circumstances in which there is no estoppel against licensee

16-73   Where the licence has been determined prior to the expiration of the patent and the patentee consequently sues the former licensee for infringement instead of for royalties under the licence, the former licensee may contest the validity of the patent, and, it appears, is not under any estoppel merely because they once were a licensee.[149]

16-74   If the agreement to assign or grant a licence is purely executory, there is no estoppel.[150]

16-75   It would appear that the mere purchase of a patented article from the patentee or a licensee does not compel the purchaser to assume the position of a licensee in respect of the article and in consequence to be estopped from attacking the validity of the patent.[151]

Construction and implied terms

16-76   The ordinary rules of construction apply to assignments and licences, and their meaning may be determined by the court in the same way as in the case of other

---

[141] *Mills v Carson* (1892) 9 R.P.C. 9.

[142] *Lawes v Purser* (1856) 6 El. & Bl. 930.

[143] *Crossley v Dixon* [1863] 10 H.L.C. 293.

[144] See *Clark v Adie* (1877) 2 App.Cas. 423, 426 and 436; *Young and Beilby v Hermand Oil Co Ltd* (1892) 9 R.P.C. 373; *Jandus Arc Lamp, etc., Co Ltd v Johnson* (1900) 17 R.P.C. 361, at 376; *Hay v Gonville* (1907) 24 R.P.C. 213, at 218.

[145] *Muirhead v Commercial Cable Co* (1895) 12 R.P.C. 317, 325; (1895) 12 R.P.C. 39, CA.

[146] *Bristol Repetition Ltd v Fomento* [1960] R.P.C. 163.

[147] See *Lawes v Purser* (1856) 6 El. & Bl. 930, 936.

[148] *McDougall Bros v Partington* (1890) 7 R.P.C. 216; *Ashworth v Law* (1890) 7 R.P.C. 231, 234.

[149] *Crossley v Dixon* [1863] 10 H.L.C. 293; *Axmann v Lund* (1874) L.R. 18 Eq. 330, 337 and 338. See also *Neilson v Fothergill* (1841) 1 W.P.C. 287; *Noton v Brooks* (1861) 7 H. & N. 499; *Ashworth v Law* (1890) 7 R.P.C. 231.

[150] See *Basset v Graydon* (1897) 14 R.P.C. 701, at 709; *Henderson v Shiels* (1907) 24 R.P.C. 108, at 113 and 115; *Suhr v Crofts (Engineers) Ltd* (1932) 49 R.P.C. 359, at 365.

[151] See *Gillette Safety Razor Co v A.W. Gamage Ltd* (1908) 25 R.P.C. 492, at 500, per Warrington J; (1909) 26 R.P.C. 745, per Parker J.

documents.[152] The limited circumstances in which terms will be implied were recently summarised by Lord Neuberger in *Marks and Spencer v BNP Paribas Securities Services Trust*.[153]

Caveat emptor

In the absence of express warranty the maxim caveat emptor ordinarily applies   **16-77**
to the assignments of patents and the grant of licences and there is no implied warranty that the patent is valid; the invalidity of the patent is no defence to an action brought by the assignor or patentee for the purchase price or for royalties.[154] This proposition must, however, be doubted in light of developments in competition law, discussed below.[155]

There is not ordinarily any implied warranty in an assignment of a patent or a   **16-78**
licence under a patent that the manufacture or sale of articles made under the patent will not infringe any other patents. Knowledge of and concealment of such a fact by the patentee might, however, amount to fraud on their part, and entitle the assignee or licensee to rescission of the contract.

No implied covenant to work the invention

There is not ordinarily any implied covenant that the licensee shall work the   **16-79**
invention[156]; express provisions are, therefore, commonly inserted in licence agreements whereby the licensee undertakes to pay a minimum royalty whether he manufactures or not; and in the case of an exclusive licence, where there may be danger of what was formerly called "Abuse of Monopoly", it is often thought desirable that the licensee should be bound actually to manufacture a certain number of articles each year.

"Best endeavours"

Some clauses of a commonly occurring kind have been interpreted, e.g. an audit   **16-80**
clause[157] and an obligation by licensees to use "all diligence" and their "best endeavours" to promote the sale of the patented articles.[158] The last mentioned obligation is a particularly onerous one for a licensee.

---

[152] See, for example, *Oxford Gene Technology Ltd v Affymetrix Inc* [2000] F.S.R. 741 (Jacob J); [2001] F.S.R. 12, CA, applying the approach to construction set out by Lord Hoffmann in *Investors Compensation Scheme Ltd v West Bromwich Building Society* (1998) 1 W.L.R. 896, at 912, HL. See also *Cambridge Display Technology Ltd v E.I. du Pont de Nemours & Co* [2005] F.S.R. 14; *Cambridge Antibody Technology Ltd v Abbott Biotechnology* [2005] F.S.R. 27; *JR French Ltd v Redbus LMDS Ltd* [2006] F.S.R. 13.

[153] [2015] UKSC 72; [2015] 3 W.L.R. 1843, [15]–[21].

[154] *Hall v Conder* (1857) 26 L.J.C.P. 138; *Smith v Buckingham* (1870) 21 L.T. 819; *Liardet v Hammond Electric Light & Power Co* (1883) 31 W.R. 710; *Bessimer v Wright* (1858) 31 L.T. (O.S.) 213; *Chanter v Hopkins* 4 M & W 399; cf. *Chanter v Leese* (1839) 4 M. & W. 295; 5 M. & W. 698 where it was held that the contract was for the sale of an exclusive right.

[155] See para.16-123, et seq.

[156] See, e.g. *Re Railway and Electrical Appliances Co* (1888) 38 Ch D. 597 at 608; *Cheetham v Nuthall* (1893) 10 R.P.C. 321, at 333.

[157] *Fomento (Sterling Area) Ltd v Selsdon Fountain Pen Co Ltd* [1958] R.P.C. 8.

[158] *Terrell v Mabie Todd & Co Ltd* (1952) 69 R.P.C. 234. See also *IBM (UK) Ltd v Rockware Glass Ltd* [1980] F.S.R. 335; *Transfield Pty v Arlo International* [1981] R.P.C. 141, Aust. High Ct.

"Beneficial owner"

16-81   Where the assignor conveys as "beneficial owner" on a disposition made before 1 July 1995, the covenants set out in Pt I of Sch.2 to the Law of Property Act 1925 will be implied.[159] The same covenants will also be implied in certain cases where a disposition is made after 1 July 1995 in pursuance of a contract entered into before that date.[160]

"Full" or "limited title guarantee"

16-82   Since 1 July 1995, a disposition may be expressed to be made with "full title guarantee" or with "limited title guarantee" and, if so, the covenants specified at s.1(2) and set out in ss.2–5 of the Law of Property (Miscellaneous Provisions) Act 1994 will be applicable to the disposition. The provisions replace the old provisions contained in the Law of Property Act 1925.

Rectification

16-83   In an appropriate case the court may order rectification of a patent licence agreement.[161]

Breach of licence

16-84   The general law relating to breach of contract is applicable to breaches of the terms contained in a licence.[162] It is, of course, open to a licensee to contend that no royalties are payable on the articles they are producing as they do not fall within the scope of the claims of the patent,[163] unless they are estopped from so contending by their previous conduct.[164]

Conflict of laws

16-85   Where there is an agreement between British nationals for the grant of a licence under British patents and an order of a foreign court purports to make such grant illegal, the matter must be resolved in accordance with the law relating to the comity of nations.[165]

16-86   On the other hand, it was held to be no answer to a defence raised under the now repealed s.44(3) of the 1977 Act (namely, that at the time of the infringement there was in force a contract containing a condition or term void under s.44(1) thereof) to say that the contract in question is governed by a foreign law which does not give effect to s.44(1).[166] For these purposes, the foreign law was held to be irrelevant.[167]

16-87   Where an agreement grants a licence under certain foreign patents but is

---

[159] Law of Property Act 1925 s.76; Law of Property (Miscellaneous Provisions) Act 1994 s.10.

[160] Law of Property (Miscellaneous Provisions) Act 1994 s.11.

[161] *QR Sciences Ltd v BTG International Ltd* [2005] F.S.R. 43, *JR French Ltd v Redbus LMDS Ltd* [2006] F.S.R. 13.

[162] See *National Carbonising Co Ltd v British Coal Distillation Ltd* (1937) 54 R.P.C. 41.

[163] *Dobson v Adie Bros Ltd* (1935) 52 R.P.C. 358; *Pytchley Autocar Co Ltd v Vauxhall Motors Ltd* (1941) 58 R.P.C. 287.

[164] *Lyle-Meller v A. Lewis & Co (Westminster) Ltd* [1956] R.P.C. 14.

[165] *British Nylon Spinners Ltd v Imperial Chemical Industries Ltd* (1952) 69 R.P.C. 288; [1954] 71 R.P.C. 327.

[166] *Chiron Corp v Organon Teknika Ltd (No.2)* [1993] F.S.R. 324; [1992] 3 C.M.L.R. 813; [1993] F.S.R.

governed by English law and confers exclusive jurisdiction on the English court, the English court will determine such issues of foreign patent law as may be necessary in order to resolve any dispute which may arise between the parties.[168] Where the agreement provides that the scope of the claims of the foreign patent is to be decided by the English court but the validity of the claims is to be decided by the court of the country where the patent is registered, the English court will not necessarily stay the English proceedings pending the outcome of the invalidity proceedings in the foreign court.[169]

Termination of licences

The question of the rights of one or other party to terminate a licence has, where there has been no express provision in the agreement dealing with the matter, given rise to considerable difficulty. It would seem that a certain amount of confusion has existed between equitable rights as arising from contract between licensor and licensee, and such purely legal rights as a licensor may in general possess to withdraw at their pleasure such permission as they may have given. The case of *Wood v Leadbitter*,[170] which was heard at common law before the Judicature Act 1873, turned upon a technical point not of contract but of trespass upon land, and decided that a mere permission to go upon a person's land, unless accompanied by some transfer of interest or property, as where a right was conferred, for example, to cut and remove the hay upon the land, was revocable at the pleasure of the owner of the land. An attempt was made in *Ward v Livesey*[171] to apply this doctrine to a case of a licence under a patent, and it was held that the revocability of a licence depended on whether it was or was not "coupled with an interest". It appears, however, not to have been realised that, since the fusion of law and equity by the Judicature Act, the real point at issue is not any purely legal right that an owner may have of revoking their licence, but whether, upon the true construction of the *contract* between the parties, one or the other is debarred in equity from the exercise of such legal right.[172]

16-88

It may be that one or the other party is entitled to terminate at pleasure or upon the happening of certain events, and inferences have been drawn as to this from the nature of the obligations imposed upon one or other of the parties by the contract.[173] For example, where a patentee by granting an exclusive licence debarred themselves from working the invention and received a lump sum as part consideration for the grant of the licence, they were held not entitled to revoke it at their pleasure.[174] In an ordinary verbal licence, however, where nothing is said as to any precise dura-

16-89

567, CA.
[167] *Chiron Corp v Organon Teknika Ltd (No.2)* [1993] F.S.R. 324; [1992] 3 C.M.L.R. 813; [1993] F.S.R. 567, CA.
[168] See, for example, *Celltech (Adair's) US Patent* [2003] F.S.R. 25; [2004] F.S.R. 3.
[169] *Celltech R&D Ltd v MedImmune Inc* [2005] F.S.R. 21.
[170] (1845) 13 Mee. & W. 838.
[171] (1888) 5 R.P.C. 102.
[172] *Guyot v Thomson* (1894) 11 R.P.C. 541, 552; and see *Kerrison v Smith* [1897] 2 Q.B. 445; *Hurst v Picture Theatres Ltd* [1915]1K.B.1; *British Actors Film Co Ltd v Glover* [1918] 1 K.B. 299.
[173] *Guyot v Thomson* (1894) 11 R.P.C. 541.
[174] *Guyot v Thomson* (1894) 11 R.P.C. 541.

tion of the term, the presumption is that the licence is terminable at the pleasure of either party.[175]

16-90   Where there are express provisions for termination upon certain specified events or by one of the parties to the contract, it will be inferred that there is no right of termination upon other events not so specified or by the other of the parties.[176] Thus, a breach of an independent covenant by the licensor to pay the renewal fees will not go to the root of the contract[177]; nor will the breach of a covenant to sue infringers,[178] or to give instruction as to the working of the invention.[179]

Termination if patent held invalid

16-91   Provisions are frequently inserted providing for the termination of the licence in the event of the patent being held to be invalid by a court of competent jurisdiction. In such a case, where the decision of the court of first instance is against the patent but is reversed upon appeal and the patent is eventually upheld, the licence is still in force and the licensee liable for royalties thereunder.[180] The simplest course is to provide that the licence shall continue so long as the patent remains subsisting.

Continued payment of royalties after patent expiry

16-92   A term which requires the licensee to continue to pay royalties after all the patents have expired (or otherwise ceased to have effect) could infringe art.101 TFEU or the corresponding prohibition under the Competition Act 1998 but will not necessarily do so.[181]

Where no express power to determine

16-93   In a case where the licence contained no provision as to the period for which it was to remain in force, it was held that the licence was determinable on reasonable notice.[182] The assessment of what length of time amounts to reasonable notice should be made with regard to the facts as existing at the time when the notice is given, not at the time when the contract is made.[183]

Licences under several patents

16-94   Where licences are granted under several patents or a group of patents, care is necessary to define the state of affairs which is to prevail when some but not all of the patents have expired. Such licences are often drafted in such a way that the licensee remains liable to pay royalties until the expiry of the last patent, even

---

[175] *Crossley v Dixon* [1863] 10 H.L.C. 293; 32 L.J.Ch. 617; *Coppin v Lloyd* (1898) 15 R.P.C. 373.
[176] *Guyot v Thomson* (1894) 11 R.P.C. 541; *Cutlan v Dawson* (1896) 13 R.P.C. 710; (1897) 14 R.P.C. 249; *Patchett v Sterling Engineering Co Ltd* (1953) 70 R.P.C. 269.
[177] *Mills v Carson* (1893) 10 R.P.C. 9.
[178] *Huntoon Co v Kolynos (Inc)* (1930) 47 R.P.C. 403, 416–429.
[179] *Campbell v Jones* (1796) 6 Term Rep. 570.
[180] *Cheetham v Nuthall* (1893) 10 R.P.C. 321.
[181] Guidelines on the Application of Article 101 of the Treaty on the Functioning of the European Union to technology transfer agreements, O.J. C 89, 28 March 2014, pp.3–50, point 187.
[182] *Martin Baker Aircraft Co Ltd v Canadian Flight Equipment Ltd* (1955) 72 R.P.C. 236.
[183] *Martin Baker Aircraft Co Ltd v Canadian Flight Equipment Ltd* (1955) 72 R.P.C. 236.

though they may be working only under the patents which have expired and not under the surviving ones at all.[184]

Notices

All notices required to be served under an assignment or licence must be in writing, and will be deemed to have been sufficiently served if they are left at, or sent by registered letter or by recorded delivery to, the last-known address of the party to be served.[185] In all such assignments and licences, the word "month" is to be deemed to mean "a calendar month" unless the context requires otherwise.[186]   **16-95**

Ambit of licences

There are a number of acts specified in s.60 which constitute an infringement of the rights conferred by a patent and care should be taken in drafting licence arrangements to ensure that the licence granted is clearly defined. A licence to "use and exercise" conveys the fullest rights, including that of importation.[187] A licence to "make" does not imply a licence to use or vend.[188] But a purchaser from a person who is licensed to "make and vend" has been held to be entitled to use and vend the article so purchased.[189] If it is intended to give all rights under the patent it is better to use general wording rather than attempting to set out seriatim the various permitted acts.   **16-96**

Purchase of articles abroad from patentee

The owner of a UK patent who, by themselves or with their agent, sells the patented article abroad without reservation or condition, cannot restrain the importation of the article so sold into this country,[190] as the unconditional sale of an article implies the grant of authority to use and sell it co-extensive with the right of the vendor at the date of the sale.[191] And a subsequent assignee of the patent is not entitled to restrain the further use or sale of goods sold under conditions such as to confer an absolute authority to use and sell so far as patent rights are concerned.[192] However, if a patentee assigned their patent and subsequently continued to make the goods abroad, the assignee could, no doubt, restrain their importation or sale,[193]   **16-97**

---

[184] See, e.g. *Siemens v Taylor* (1892) 9 R.P.C. 393.

[185] Law of Property Act 1925 s.196(1), (3), (4), (5); Recorded Delivery Service Act 1962 ss.1 and 2.

[186] Law of Property Act 1925 s.61.

[187] *Dunlop Pneumatic Tyre Co v North British Rubber Co* (1904) 21 R.P.C. 161, 181 and 183.

[188] *Basset v Graydon* (1897) 14 R.P.C. 701 at 708 and 713; and see *Huntoon Co v Kolynos (Inc)* (1930) 47 R.P.C. 403, 422.

[189] *Thomas v Hunt* (1864) 17 C.B.(N.S.) 183. See also *National Phonograph Co of Australia v Menck* (1911) 28 R.P.C. 229.

[190] *Betts v Willmott* (1871) L.R. 6 Ch.App. 239.

[191] *Betts v Willmott* (1871) L.R. 6 Ch.App. 239; see also *Incandescent Gas Light Co Ltd v Cantelo* (1895) 12 R.P.C. 262, at 264; *National Phonograph Co of Australia Ltd v Menck* (1911) 28 R.P.C. 229; *Roussel-Uclaf S.A. v Hockley International* [1996] R.P.C. 441.

[192] *Betts v Willmott* (1871) L.R. 6 Ch.App. 239; see also *Incandescent Gas Light Co Ltd v Cantelo* (1895) 12 R.P.C. 262, at 264; *National Phonograph Co of Australia Ltd v Menck* (1911) 28 R.P.C. 229; *Roussel-Uclaf S.A. v Hockley International* [1996] R.P.C. 441.; see also *Gillette Safety Razor Co Ltd v Gamage (A.W.) Ltd* (1907) 24 R.P.C. 1.

[193] See *Betts v Willmott* (1871) L.R. 6 Ch.App. 239, at 244.

unless in the case of imports from another Member State of the EU the doctrine of exhaustion of rights applies.[194]

Purchase of articles abroad from licensee under foreign patent

16-98   Subject to EU law,[195] a licence in respect of a foreign patent to manufacture and sell thereunder granted by a patentee who also owns a British patent does not imply any licence to the purchase of articles so manufactured or sold by the licensee to import the same into this country.[196]

Exhaustion of rights within the European Union

16-99   As discussed in detail at para.14-240, et seq. under EU law,[197] the proprietor of a patent may not exercise their patent rights to prevent the importation into the UK of a product put into circulation for the first time by them or with their consent in another Member State of the EU.[198]

16-100   On the other hand, the proprietor of a patent is entitled to exercise their patent rights against a product first put into circulation in another Member State by a third party *without* their consent.[199] Furthermore, the consent must be voluntary and thus the doctrine does not apply where the product in question was first put into circulation in a Member State under a compulsory licence from the proprietor.[200] Nor will the patentee be deemed to have given their consent where they were legally obliged to market the product in a Member State.[201]

Specific mechanism

16-101   For a limited period, a specific mechanism applied in respect of the importation of certain products from Spain or Portugal.[202] Under these provisions, the proprietor of a patent for a chemical or pharmaceutical product or a product relating to plant health filed at a time when a product patent could not be obtained for that product in Spain or Portugal was entitled to rely on their patent rights to prevent the importation into the UK of that product, even if that product was first put on the

---

[194] See para.14-240, et seq. *Cnl-Sucal N.V.S.A. v Hag G.F.A.G.* (C-10/89) [1990] E.C.R. I-3711; [1990] 3 C.M.L.R. 571; [1991] F.S.R. 99; *IHT Internationale Heiztechnik GmbH v Ideal-Standard GmbH* (C-9/93) [1994] 3 C.M.L.R. 857.

[195] See para.14-240, et seq.

[196] *Société Anonyme des Manufactures de Glaces v Tilghman's Patent Sand Blast Co* (1930) 25 Ch D. 1, 9; and see *Beecham Group Ltd v International Products Ltd* [1968] R.P.C. 129; *Minnesota Mining and Manufacturing Co v Geerpres Europe* [1974] R.P.C. 35; *Smith, Kline & French Laboratories Ltd v Global Pharmaceuticals* [1986] R.P.C. 394; *Wellcome Foundation v Discpharm Ltd* [1993] F.S.R. 433.

[197] arts 34, 35 and 36 of the Treaty on the Functioning of the European Union.

[198] *Centrafarm B.V. v Sterling Drug* (15/74) [1974] E.C.R. 1147; [1974] 2 C.M.L.R. 480; [1975] F.S.R. 161.

[199] *Parke Davis v Probel* (24/67) [1968] C.M.L.R. 47; *Thetford v Fiamma SpA* (C-35/87) [1989] F.S.R. 57; *EMI Electrola GmbH v Patricia Im-und Export Verwaltungsgessellschaft mbH* (C-341/87) [1989] E.C.R. 79, [1989] 2 C.M.L.R. 413, [1989] F.S.R. 544.

[200] *Pharmon B.V. v Hoechst A.G.* (19/84) [1985] 3 C.M.L.R. 775; [1985] E.C.R. 2281; [1986] F.S.R. 108.

[201] *Merck v Primecrown* (C-267/95 and C-268/95) [1997] F.S.R. 237, [50].

[202] arts 47 and 209 of the Treaty of Accession of the Kingdom of Spain and the Portuguese Republic; European Communities (Spanish and Portuguese Accession) Act 1985.

market in Spain (or Portugal) for the first time by them or with their consent.[203] Where these provisions applied, their effect was to put Spain and Portugal in the same position as non-EC countries so far as concerns importation from either of them.[204] The provisions expired on 6 October 1995 and 31 December 1994 in respect of Spain and Portugal respectively.[205]

Likewise a specific mechanism applies in relation to the import and marketing **16-102** of pharmaceutical products from the Czech Republic, Estonia, Latvia, Hungary, Poland, Slovenia and Slovakia.[206] The mechanism is similar but not identical to that which applied in relation to the import and marketing of products from Spain and Portugal. The main differences are that: (1) the mechanism applies to both patents and SPCs, (2) it applies to pharmaceutical products only, (3) the mechanism lasts for the life of the patent or SPC rather than for a fixed period, and (4) the person intending to import or market a pharmaceutical product covered by the mechanism must give at least one month's prior notice to the proprietor of the patent or SPC and demonstrate to the competent authorities in the application regarding that import that such notice has been given. The person intending to import or market the pharmaceutical product in question need not give notification themselves, provided that it is possible from the notice to ascertain their identity clearly.[207]

A holder of a patent or SPC who receives a notice from a person intending to **16-103** import is not obliged to respond with notification of their intention to oppose the proposed importation before invoking their rights to prevent importation. However, if they do not indicate such an intention during the one-month waiting period, the person proposing to import the pharmaceutical product in question may legitimately apply to the competent authorities for authorisation to import the product and, where appropriate, import and market it.[208] The holder forfeits their right to compensation for importation and marketing occurring prior to the date on which they indicate their intention to oppose the same, but does not forfeit the right to prevent future importation and marketing.[209]

The specific mechanism has also been included in the subsequent Acts of Acces- **16-104** sion of Bulgaria and Romania[210] and Croatia.[211]

Limited licences

Licences frequently contain clauses limiting the licensee's right so that they are **16-105** not entitled to work the patent in any way they choose. Care is necessary that such

---

[203] *Wellcome Foundation Ltd v Discpharm Ltd* [1993] F.S.R. 433, PCC.

[204] *Generics (UK) Ltd v Smith, Kline & French Laboratories Ltd* (C-191/90) [1993] R.P.C. 333, [1993] F.S.R. 592, [1992] E.C.R. I-5335, [1993] 1 C.M.L.R. 89, ECJ; *Smith, Kline & French Laboratories Ltd's (Cimetidine) Patents* [1990] R.P.C. 203, 261 and 262, CA.

[205] *Merck v Primecrown* (C-267/95 and C-268/95) [1997] F.S.R. 237.

[206] art.22 and Annex IV, Ch.2, of the Act concerning the conditions of accession of the Czech Republic, the Republic of Estonia, the Republic of Cyprus, the Republic of Latvia, the Republic of Lithuania, the Republic of Hungary, the Republic of Malta, the Republic of Poland, the Republic of Slovenia and the Slovak Republic.

[207] *Merck Canada v Sigma* (C-539/13).

[208] *Merck Canada v Sigma* (C-539/13).

[209] *Merck Canada v Sigma* (C-539/13).

[210] art.21 and Annex V, Ch.1, of the Act concerning the conditions of accession of the Republic of Bulgaria and Romania.

[211] art.16 and Annex IV, Ch.1 of the Act concerning the conditions of accession of the Republic of Croatia and the adjustments to the Treaty on European Union, the Treaty on the Functioning of the European Union and the Treaty establishing the European Atomic Energy Community.

licences do not contravene arts 101 or 102 of the Treaty on the Functioning of the European Union[212] or the corresponding national provisions of the Competition Act 1998. However, subject to those exceptions which will be referred to subsequently in this chapter[213]:

> "a patentee has a right, not merely by sale without reserve to give an unlimited right to the purchaser to use, and thereby to make in effect a grant from which he cannot derogate, but may attach to it conditions, and if these conditions are broken, then there is no licence, because the licence is bound up with the observance of the conditions."[214]

16-106   The previous restrictions contained in s.44 of the Patents Act 1977, the Resale Prices Act 1976 and the Restrictive Trade Practices Act 1976 have all been repealed by the Competition Act 1998 with effect from 1 March 2000 although transitional provisions provide that s.44 continues to apply in respect of any agreement made before that date.[215]

Purchaser without notice of limited licence

16-107   A purchaser of patented goods without notice of restrictions affecting such goods is free to use and sell them in any way they choose.[216] However, if at the time of purchase they have notice of any restrictions affecting the patented goods (other than restrictions that are void) and contravenes such restrictions they are liable to be sued for infringement by the patentee, as the restrictions are "not contractual but are incident to and a limitation of the grant of the licence to use, so that, if the conditions are broken, there is no grant at all."[217]

16-108   The question of the knowledge of the defendant is one of fact in each case, as to which the passing of some leaflet or label with the goods at the time of sale may or may not be sufficient evidence according to the nature of the goods and the general circumstances. It is not essential that the purchaser should have knowledge of the precise restrictions concerned so long as they have knowledge of their nature and existence and means of knowledge of their exact extent.[218] Registration of the limited licence at the Patent Office (now the UKIPO) is not in itself equivalent to notice of the limitations to a purchaser of an article.[219]

---

[212] ex-arts 81 and 82 of the EC Treaty and, prior to the Treaty of Amsterdam arts 85 and 86.

[213] See para.16-123, et seq.

[214] Per Kennedy J in *Incandescent Gas Light Co Ltd v Brogden* (1899) 16 R.P.C. 179, at 183; and see *Incandescent Gas Light Co Ltd v Cantelo* (1895) 12 R.P.C. 262, at 264. See also *Sterling Drug Inc v C.H. Beck Ltd* [1973] R.P.C. 915.

[215] Competition Act 1998 ss.1, 70 and 74(3) and Sch.14. Article 3 of The Competition Act 1998 (Transitional, Consequential and Supplemental Provisions) Order 2000 (SI 2000/311).

[216] See *Betts v Willmott* (1871) L.R. 6 Ch.App. 239, at 245; *Incandescent Gas Light Co Ltd v Cantelo* (1895) 12 R.P.C. 262; *Incandescent Gas Light Co Ltd v Brogden* (1899) 16 R.P.C. 179; *Scottish Vacuum Cleaner Co Ltd v Provincial Cinematograph Theatres Ltd* (1915) 32 R.P.C. 353; *Hazeltine Corp v Lissen Ltd* (1939) 56 R.P.C. 62.

[217] Per Farwell J in *British Mutoscope and Biograph Co Ltd v Homer* (1901) 18 R.P.C. 177, at 179; see also *National Phonograph Co of Australia Ltd v Menck* (1911) 28 R.P.C. 229, at 248; see also *Columbia Graphophone Co v Vanner* (1916) 33 R.P.C. 104; *Columbia Graphophone Co Ltd v Murray* (1922) 39 R.P.C. 239; *Columbia Graphophone Co Ltd v Thoms* (1924) 41 R.P.C. 294; *Dunlop Rubber Co Ltd v Longlife Battery Depot* [1958] R.P.C. 473; all cases decided prior to Resale Prices Act 1964 and 1976 and relating to breaches of restrictions as to the resale prices of articles.

[218] See *Columbia Graphophone Co Ltd v Murray* (1922) 39 R.P.C. 239; cf. *Badische Anilin und Soda Fabrik v Isler* (1906) 23 R.P.C. 633.

[219] *Heap v Hartley* (1889) 42 Ch D. 461, (1888) 5 R.P.C. 603, 608, (1889) 6 R.P.C. 495, CA; *Scottish*

Limited licence imposed by licensee

It is submitted that just as a patentee may impose restrictions on the otherwise **16-109** unlimited licence implied by the sale of a patented article, so a licensee may similarly impose restrictions upon articles made and sold by them pursuant to their licence. Provided these restrictions are not void and have been sufficiently brought to the notice of the purchaser, any contravention of them constitutes an infringement in respect of which a patentee or an exclusive licensee[220] may take action. The contrary is suggested in one reported case,[221] but there the order of the court of first instance was discharged by the Court of Appeal[222] and in the subsequent proceedings the contention that the limitation of the licence was invalid appears to have been dropped.[223]

Assignment of licence and sub-licensing

By s.30(4)(a) of the 1977 Act, to the extent that the licence so provides, a sub- **16-110** licence may be granted under the licence and any such licence or sub-licence may be assigned. It is submitted, that the licence may so provide either expressly or impliedly and that the extent to which sub-licences may be granted or the licence (or sub-licences) assigned is, therefore, essentially a matter of construction. In drafting a patent licence care should be taken to make it clear by express language whether the licence is to be personal to the licensee or is to be assignable.

If a licensee is not entitled to assign, and the licensor knowingly accepts royal- **16-111** ties from a purported assignee, the licensor is thereby estopped from disputing the assignment.[224]

Although a licensee under a personal licence is entitled to exercise their rights **16-112** by their servants or agents, they are not entitled to exercise their rights in such a way that their "agents" are in substance "independent contractors".[225]

Where the benefit of a licence, in which the consideration is payable by way of **16-113** a share of profits is assigned by the licensor, the assignee is entitled to an account from the licensee, provided that they put themselves into the position of the licensor by agreeing to pay any moneys due from the licensor to the licensee.[226] However, if the assignment be of a share only of the benefit of the licence, they must join the other persons entitled, as the licensee is not bound to account separately to several parties.[227]

If the licensee has power to grant sub-licences, such sub-licences will determine **16-114** upon the determination of their own licence unless it appears from the terms of their own licence that the contrary is intended.[228]

Vacuum Cleaner Co v Provincial Cinematograph Theatres Ltd (1915) 32 R.P.C. 353, OH.
[220] See para.16-22, et seq.
[221] *Gillette Safety Razor Co Ltd v A.W. Gamage Ltd* (1908) 25 R.P.C. 492. For a modern case see *Sterling Drug Inc v C.H. Beck Ltd* [1973] R.P.C. 915.
[222] (1908) 25 R.P.C. 782; see also *Liverpool v Irwin* [1977] A.C. 239.
[223] (1909) 26 R.P.C. 745.
[224] *Lawson v Donald Macpherson & Co* (1897) 14 R.P.C. 696.
[225] *Howard and Bullough Ltd v Tweedales and Smalley* (1895) 12 R.P.C. 519.
[226] *Bergmann v Macmillan* (1881) 17 Ch D. 423.
[227] *Bergmann v Macmillan* (1881) 17 Ch D. 423.
[228] See *Austin Baldwin & Co Ltd v Greenwood & Batley Ltd* (1925) 42 R.P.C. 454 and *VLM Holdings Ltd v Ravensworth Digital Services* [2013] EWHC 228 (Ch) (a copyright case).

16-115   Sub-licences or an assignment of a licence should be registered, see para.16-39, et seq.

Covenants for improvements

16-116   Covenants are frequently inserted in assignments and licences whereby the assignor or licensor undertakes to communicate to the other party any new discovery or invention which they may make or acquire connected with his invention and, if they obtain a patent for such new invention, to assign it to or to grant a licence to the other party. In other cases the covenants are mutual, each party communicating improvements to the other.

16-117   Such covenants require care in wording in order to ensure that there is no danger of their being in restraint of trade, and in order to avoid unnecessary difficulties in deciding what is and what is not an "improvement".

16-118   Certain types of improvement clause may no longer be permissible, in certain circumstances, as contravening art.101 of the Treaty on the Functioning of the European Union. See para.16-123, et seq.

Ambit of covenants for improvements

16-119   It is difficult to foretell at the time of making a contract the precise nature of the "improvement" which it will be desired to cover. The ambit of the rights conferred depends entirely upon the construction of the contract.[229] The word "improvement" is not a term of art and can have wider or narrower meanings according to context.[230] Sometimes "improvements" are defined as being confined to articles or processes which would be an infringement of the patent in question; in other cases it may be desired to secure any further inventions relating to the particular art. The words "improvement upon", unless otherwise qualified, are ambiguous in that, for instance, in the case of a machine, they may relate to some alteration in its design which will enable it to perform its duty better or more cheaply, or they may relate to a different machine which performs the same duty in a different and better way; the former meaning is that usually adopted, and a separate and distinct invention, although relating to the same general subject-matter, cannot usually be described as an improvement.[231] Notwithstanding this ambiguity, it is usually best, when drafting a licence, merely to use the word "improvements", without attempting any more precise definition, as the parties are usually reluctant to agree to anything more detailed and even an elaborate and complicated clause often gives rise to disputes as to its true construction.

16-120   In *Linotype and Machinery Ltd v Hopkins*,[232] where the licensor covenanted to communicate "every improvement in or addition to the Hopkins machine or mode of applying the same or any discovery useful to the manufacture thereof", the Court of Appeal, having regard to those words, would not agree that any improvement of which the company was to have the benefit should necessarily be limited to

---

[229]   See *Valveless Gas Engine Syndicate Ltd v Day* (1899) 16 R.P.C. 97; *Osram-Robertson Lamp Works Ltd v Public Trustee* (1920) 37 R.P.C. 189; *Vislok Ltd v Peters* (1927) 44 R.P.C. 235.

[230]   Per Lord Hoffman in *Buchanan v Alba Diagnostics Ltd* [2004] R.P.C. 34, HL.

[231]   *Davies v Davies Patent Boiler Ltd* (1908) 25 R.P.C. 823; *Sadgrove v Godfrey* (1920) 37 R.P.C. 7, at 20 and 21; *Vislok Ltd v Peters* (1927) 44 R.P.C. 235. See also *Davies v Curtis & Harvey Ltd* (1903) 20 R.P.C. 561.

[232]   (1908) 25 R.P.C. 349 at 665; affirmed by (1910) 27 R.P.C. 109.

something that was an infringement of the original patent assigned, and in the same case Lord Loreburn[233] said:

"I think that any part does constitute an improvement, if it can be adapted to this machine, and it would make it cheaper and more effective or in any way easier or more useful or valuable, or in any other way make it a preferable article in commerce."

In *National Broach, etc., Co v Churchill Gear Machines Ltd*[234] the licensee **16-121** covenanted to "communicate to [the licensor] all details of any improvements which may be developed during the subsistence" of the licence agreement and to apply for patents if so requested by the licensor. A question in the case was when the duty to communicate something which had been developed arose. The House of Lords held it was impossible to lay down any criterion and the court, looking at the matter through technical eyes, must answer the question in any particular case in all the circumstances of that case, but, if an idea has arisen which may lead to some patentable improvement, the obligation to communicate will arise at a very early stage as the licensor must have time to consider whether he wanted patents applied for.

Patents subsequently acquired

Agreements by the vendors of a patent to assign to the purchasers all patent rights **16-122** that they may subsequently acquire of a like nature to the patent sold are not contrary to public policy at common law.[235] The danger to the purchasers of the destruction of the value of the rights which they have bought would otherwise be great, as inventors frequently continue to make inventions relating to the same art, and without such protection the purchasers would be exposed to competition from the vendors with the benefit of their previous experience.[236] The validity of such contracts at common law, as always where the question is one of restraint of trade, depends upon whether the restrictions extend further than is reasonably necessary to protect the legitimate interests of the parties in the circumstances of the case. The period over which the disability imposed is to last, and the area over which it is to extend are material factors to be considered in each case. Although covenants by a vendor not to make or sell the invention at all, or the product obtained by the patented or any similar process which would be in competition with it, may be perfectly valid under national law,[237] such covenants might well contravene art.101 of the Treaty on the Functioning of the European Union and/or the Chapter I prohibition of the Competition Act 1998.[238]

Technology Transfer Agreements

A comprehensive study of arts 101 and 102 of the Treaty on the Functioning of **16-123** the European Union and the corresponding provisions of the Competition Act 1998 on patent assignments, and licences and agreements relating to patented products is outside the scope of this work. However, Commission Regulation (EU) No 316/

---

[233] (1910) 27 R.P.C. 109 at 113. See also *Buchanan v Alba Diagnostics Ltd* [2004] R.P.C. 34, 690, HL.
[234] [1967] R.P.C. 99, 110 and 111. See also *Beecham v Bristol Laboratories* [1978] R.P.C. 521; and *Regina Glass v Schuller* [1972] R.P.C. 229.
[235] *Printing and Numerical Registering Co v Sampson* (1875) L.R. 19 Eq. 462.
[236] *Printing and Numerical Registering Co v Sampson* (1875) L.R. 19 Eq. 462.
[237] See *Nordenfelt v Maxim Nordenfelt, etc., Co Ltd* [1894] A.C. 535; *Mouchel v Cubitt & Co* (1907) 24 R.P.C. 194; cf. *Dranez Anstalt v Hayek* [2003] F.S.R. 32.
[238] See para.16-123, et seq.

2014 of 21 March 2014 on the application of art.101(3) of the Treaty on the Functioning of the European Union to categories of technology transfer agreements is of particular relevance to patent licensing and is considered in detail here. The Regulation provides a block exemption to art.101 TFEU which prohibits all agreements between undertakings which may affect trade between Member States which have as their object or effect the prevention, restriction or distortion of competition within the internal market.

16-124 Further Regulations deal with Vertical Agreements,[239] Specialisation Agreements[240] and Research and Development Agreements.[241] Each of these regulations may exempt agreements containing provisions relating to patents although, in the case of Vertical Agreements and Specialisation Agreements, those provisions must not constitute the primary object of such agreements.[242]

16-125 The effect of non-compliance with art.101 TFEU is also considered.[243]

Regulation 316/2014—the Technology Transfer Block Exemption Regulation (TTBER)

16-126 The TTBER came into force on 1 May 2014, replacing Regulation 772/2004 and will expire on 30 April 2026.[244] Transitional provisions provided that agreements in force on 30 April 2014 which did not satisfy the requirements of Regulation 316/2014 but did satisfy the requirements of Regulation 772/2004 continued to enjoy exemption from art.101(1) until 30 April 2015.[245]

16-127 The TTBER applies to agreements between two undertakings only[246] but for these purposes connected undertakings are treated as a single undertaking.[247] As to subject-matter, the block exemption applies to "technology transfer agreements" where that term is defined as meaning either:[248]

"(i) a technology rights licensing agreement entered into between two undertakings for the purpose of the production of contract products by the licensee and/or its sub-contractor(s),

(ii) an assignment of technology rights between two undertakings for the purpose of the production of contract products where part of the risk associated with the exploitation of the technology remains with the assignor;"

---

239 Commission Regulation 330/2010, [2010] O.J. L102/1, replacing Regulation 2790/1999, [1999] O.J. L336/21 which itself replaced, inter alia, Regulation 1983/83 [1983] O.J. L173/1, as amended by [1983] O.J. L281/24. See also the Commission Notice on Guidelines on vertical restraints [2010] O.J. C130/1.
240 Commission Regulation No 1218/2010 of 14 December 2010 on the application of art.101(3) of the Treaty to categories of specialisation agreements.
241 Commission Regulation No 1217/2010 of 14 December 2010 on the application of art.101(3) of the Treaty on the functioning of the European Union to categories of research and development agreements, replacing Regulation 2658/2000 [2000] O.J. L304/3 and Regulation 2659/2000 [2000] O.J. L304/7; replacing Regulation 417/85 [1985] O.J. L53/1 and Regulation 418/85 [1985] O.J. L53/5 (both as amended by Regulation 151/93 [1993] O.J. L21/8). See also the Commission Notice on Guidelines on the applicability of Article 101 of the Treaty on the Functioning of the European Union to horizontal co-operation agreements [2011] O.J. C11/1.
242 For vertical agreements, see Commission Regulation No. 330/2010 art.2(3); for specialisation agreements, see Commission Regulation No 1218/2010 art.2(2).
243 See para.16-154.
244 art.11 and Recital (2).
245 art.10.
246 Recital (2) and art.1(1)(c).
247 art.1(2).
248 art.1(1)(c).

The expression "contract product" means a product produced, directly or **16-128** indirectly, on the basis of the licensed technology rights.

An agreement may be exempted by the TTBER even if conditions are stipulated **16-129** for more than one level of trade, by, for instance, requiring the licensee to set up a particular distribution system and specifying the obligations the licensee must or may impose on resellers of the products produced under the licence.[249] However, such conditions and obligations should nevertheless comply with the rules applicable to supply and distribution agreements.[250] A number of agreements are expressly excluded from the TTBER, namely: (1) supply and distribution agreements concluded between a licensee and buyers of its contract products,[251] (2) agreements in the context of research and development and specialisation which are covered by other block exemption regulations,[252] (3) agreements relating to the mere reproduction and distribution of software copyright protected products (such agreements being more akin to distribution agreements),[253] and (4) agreements for the pooling of technologies with the purpose of licensing them to third parties, or to agreements whereby the pooled technology is licensed out to those third parties.[254]

The Commission has published a detailed Notice entitled Guidelines on the ap- **16-130** plication of Article 101 of the Treaty on the Functioning of the European Union to technology transfer agreements.[255] The Guidelines deal with both the application of the TTBER and the application of art.101 to technology transfer agreements that fall outside the scope of the TTBER. The Guidelines (and the TTBER itself) do not address the potential parallel application of art.102 to technology transfer agreements.[256]

The exemption

Article 2(1) TTBER provides that art.101(1) of the TFEU shall not apply to **16-131** technology transfer agreements (the definition of which is discussed above). The exemption also applies to "provisions, in technology transfer agreements, which relate to the purchase of products by the licensee or which relate to the licensing or assignment of other intellectual property rights or know-how to the licensee, if, and to the extent that, those provisions are directly related to the production or sale of the contract products".[257]

The exemption lasts unless the licensed technology rights expire, lapse, are are **16-132** declared invalid or, in the case of know-how, become publicly known (unless it becomes so as a result of action by the licensee).[258]

---

[249] Recital (6).
[250] See Commission Regulation (EU) No. 330/2010.
[251] Recital (6).
[252] Recital (7) and art.9. In relation to such agreements see Commission Regulation (EU) No 1217/2010 (research and development agreements) and Commission Regulation (EU) No 1218/2010 (specialisation agreements).
[253] Recital (7).
[254] Recital (7).
[255] O.J. C 89, 28 March 2014, pp.3–50.
[256] Guidelines, point 2.
[257] art.2(3) TTBER.
[258] art.2(2).

Relevant market

16-133   Article 1(1)(m) defines the relevant market for the purposes of the TTBER as the combination of the relevant product or technology market with the relevant geographic market. The relevant product market is the market for the contract products and all products which are regarded as interchangeable or substitutable for the contract products by the buyer, by reason of the products' characteristics, their prices and their intended use.[259] The relevant technology market is the market for the licensed technology rights and all technology rights which are regarded as interchangeable or substitutable for the licensed technology rights by the licensee, by reason of the technology rights' characteristics, the royalties payable in respect of those rights and their intended use.[260] The relevant geographic market is the area in which the undertakings concerned are involved in the supply of and demand for products or the licensing of technology rights, in which the conditions of competition are sufficiently homogeneous and which can be distinguished from neighbouring areas because the conditions of competition are appreciably different in those areas.[261]

Market shares

16-134   Article 3 sets different market share thresholds depending on whether the parties to the agreement are "competing undertakings" (as defined by art.1(1)(n)) or not.

16-135   Article 3(1) provides that where the parties are competing undertakings, the exemption of art.2 applies on condition that the combined market share of the parties does not exceed 20 per cent on the relevant market(s). Where the parties are not competing undertakings, art.3(2) the threshold is 30 per cent. Article 8 sets out rules to be applied in determining the market share for the purposes of art.3.

16-136   Where the market share is initially below the appropriate threshold level set by art.3(1) or 3(2) but subsequently rises above that level, the exemption continues to apply for a period of two consecutive calendar years following the year in which the relevant threshold level was first exceeded.[262]

16-137   If the market share thresholds of the parties to a particular agreement are above the levels set out in art.3, it does not follow that the agreement will fall within the scope of art.101(1). There is no presumption that such an agreement infringes art.101(1).[263]

Hardcore restrictions

16-138   Article 4 sets out what are termed the "hardcore restrictions". If an agreement contains any of these restrictions, then the whole agreement is excluded from the benefit of the block exemption.[264] The hardcore restrictions differ depending on whether the parties to the agreement are, or are not, competing undertakings (as defined in art.1(1)(n)).

---

[259] art.1(1)(j).
[260] art.1(1)k).
[261] art.1(1)(l).
[262] art.8(e).
[263] Recital (13).
[264] art.4 and Recital (14).

In the case of competing undertakings, art.4(1) provides that the exemption of **16-139** art.2 does not apply to agreements which, directly or indirectly, in isolation or in combination with other factors under the control of the parties, have as their object any of the following:

"(a) the restriction of a party's ability to determine its prices when selling products to third parties;

(b) the limitation of output, except limitations on the output of contract products imposed on the licensee in a non-reciprocal agreement or imposed on only one of the licensees in a reciprocal agreement;

(c) the allocation of markets or customers except:

  (i) the obligation on the licensor and/or the licensee, in a non-reciprocal agreement, not to produce with the licensed technology rights within the exclusive territory reserved for the other party and/or not to sell actively and/or passively into the exclusive territory or to the exclusive customer group reserved for the other party,

  (ii) the restriction, in a non-reciprocal agreement, of active sales by the licensee into the exclusive territory or to the exclusive customer group allocated by the licensor to another licensee provided the latter was not a competing undertaking of the licensor at the time of the conclusion of its own licence,

  (iii) the obligation on the licensee to produce the contract products only for its own use provided that the licensee is not restricted in selling the contract products actively and passively as spare parts for its own products,

  (iv) the obligation on the licensee, in a non-reciprocal agreement, to produce the contract products only for a particular customer, where the licence was granted in order to create an alternative source of supply for that customer;

(d) the restriction of the licensee's ability to exploit its own technology rights or the restriction of the ability of any of the parties to the agreement to carry out research and development, unless such latter restriction is indispensable to prevent the disclosure of the licensed knowhow to third parties."

In the case of non-competing undertakings, art.4(2) provides that the exemp- **16-140** tion of art.2 does not apply to agreements which, directly or indirectly, in isolation or in combination with other factors under the control of the parties, have as their object any of the following:

"(a) the restriction of a party's ability to determine its prices when selling products to third parties, without prejudice to the possibility of imposing a maximum sale price or recommending a sale price, provided that it does not amount to a fixed or minimum sale price as a result of pressure from, or incentives offered by, any of the parties;

(b) the restriction of the territory into which, or of the customers to whom, the licensee may passively sell the contract products, except:

  (i) the restriction of passive sales into an exclusive territory or to an exclusive customer group reserved for the licensor,

  (ii) the obligation to produce the contract products only for its own use provided that the licensee is not restricted in selling the contract products actively and passively as spare parts for its own products,

  (iii) the obligation to produce the contract products only for a particular customer, where the licence was granted in order to create an alternative source of supply for that customer,

  (iv) the restriction of sales to end-users by a licensee operating at the wholesale level of trade,

  (v) the restriction of sales to unauthorised distributors by the members of a selective distribution system;

(c) the restriction of active or passive sales to end-users by a licensee which is a member of a selective distribution system and which operates at the retail level, without prejudice to the possibility of prohibiting a member of the system from operating out of an unauthorised place of establishment."

Where the parties are not competing undertakings when the agreement is **16-141** concluded but subsequently become competing undertakings, then they will be treated as non-competing undertakings for the full life of the agreement, unless the agreement is subsequently amended in any material respect (including by the conclusion of a new technology transfer agreement between the parties concerning competing technology rights).[265]

Excluded restrictions

16-142   Article 5 sets out "excluded restrictions". In contrast to hardcore restrictions, if an agreement contains an excluded restriction, it is only that restriction that is excluded from the benefit of the block exemption, not the whole agreement.

16-143   Article 5(1) provides that the art.2 exemption shall not apply to two categories of obligation. Article 5(1)(a) relates to exclusive grant-back obligations, namely:

> "any direct or indirect obligation on the licensee to grant an exclusive licence or to assign rights, in whole or in part, to the licensor or to a third party designated by the licensor in respect of its own improvements to, or its own new applications of, the licensed technology;"

16-144   In this context "exclusive" means the right of the licensee to exploit the improvement is excluded.[266] Non-exclusive grant-back obligations do fall within the TTBER block exemption, even if non-reciprocal (i.e. imposed on the licensee only).[267]

16-145   Article 5(1)(b) relates to non-challenge clauses, namely:

> "any direct or indirect obligation on a party not to challenge the validity of intellectual property rights which the other party holds in the Union, without prejudice to the possibility, in the case of an exclusive licence, of providing for termination of the technology transfer agreement in the event that the licensee challenges the validity of any of the licensed technology rights."

16-146   Non-challenge clauses are excluded from the TTBER because licensees are normally well-placed to determine the validity of an intellectual property right and it is in the interest of undistorted competition that invalid intellectual property rights are eliminated.[268]

16-147   Non-challenge clauses relating to the ownership of the right in question (as opposed to its validity) are not excluded from the block exemption and are generally not regarded as contrary to art.101(1).[269]

16-148   Non-challenge clauses in the context of settlement agreements (whether within the TTBER or otherwise) are addressed below.[270]

16-149   In the case of non-competing undertakings, art.5(2) further provides that the block exemption does not apply "to any direct or indirect obligation limiting the licensee's ability to exploit its own technology rights or limiting the ability of any of the parties to the agreement to carry out research and development, unless such latter restriction is indispensable to prevent the disclosure of the licensed know-how to third parties".

---

[265]   art.4(3).

[266]   Guidelines on the application of Article 101 of the Treaty on the Functioning of the European Union to technology transfer agreements O.J. C 89, 28 March 2014, pp.3–50, point 129.

[267]   Guidelines on the application of Article 101 of the Treaty on the Functioning of the European Union to technology transfer agreements O.J. C 89, 28 March 2014, pp.3–50, point 131.

[268]   Guidelines on the application of Article 101 of the Treaty on the Functioning of the European Union to technology transfer agreements O.J. C 89, 28 March 2014, pp.3–50, point 134.

[269]   Guidelines on the application of Article 101 of the Treaty on the Functioning of the European Union to technology transfer agreements O.J. C 89, 28 March 2014, pp.3–50, point 135.

[270]   See para.16-151.

Withdrawal of exemption

Under art.6 the Commission may withdraw the benefit of the block exemption **16-150** pursuant to art.29(1) of Regulation (EC) 1/2003 where it finds in a particular case that a technology transfer agreement to which the block exemption applies nevertheless has certain effects which are incompatible with the conditions laid down in art.101(3) TFEU.

Non-challenge clauses in settlement agreements

The Commission takes the view that non-challenge clauses in settlement agree- **16-151** ments generally fall outside art.101(1) of the Treaty.[271] The purpose of the agreement is to settle an existing dispute and/or to avoid future disputes and it is therefore inherent that the parties agree not to challenge the rights to which the dispute related.

Non-challenge clauses in settlement agreements may, however, be objection- **16-152** able in certain circumstances. Examples of such circumstances include: where a patent was granted on the basis of incorrect or misleading information; and where the licensor, besides licensing the technology rights, induces, financially or otherwise, the licensee to agree not to challenge the validity of the technology rights.[272]

Effect of non-compliance with art.101(1)

Any agreement prohibited by art.101(1) (and not saved by the de minimis rule **16-153** or art.101(3)) is automatically void.[273] However, the nullity applies only to those elements of the agreement which are subject to the prohibition unless those elements are not severable in which case the nullity will apply to the agreement as a whole.[274] The consequences of the nullity are determined by the national law.[275] The Commission and the competition authorities of the Member States[276] also have power to impose fines on the parties infringing art.101.[277] Further, the ECJ has held that any individual may claim damages for the loss caused to them by the offending agreement.[278] Non-compliance with art.101(1) may also give rise to a defence to an action for infringement of a patent.[279]

---

[271] Guidelines on the application of Article 101 of the Treaty on the Functioning of the European Union to technology transfer agreements O.J. C 89, 28 March 2014, pp.3–50, point 242.

[272] Guidelines on the application of Article 101 of the Treaty on the Functioning of the European Union to technology transfer agreements O.J. C 89, 28 March 2014, pp.3–50, point 243.

[273] TFEU art.101(2).

[274] *Technique Minière v Maschinenbau Ulm GmbH* (56/65) [1966] E.C.R. 235; [1966] C.M.L.R. 357.

[275] *VAG France S.A. v Etablissements Magne S.A.* (10/86) [1986] E.C.R. 4071, [1988] 4 C.M.L.R. 98, ECJ; *Chemidus Wavin v TERI* [1977] 3 C.M.L.R. 514, [1977] F.S.R. 181, CA; *Inntrepreneur Estates v Mason* [1993] 2 C.M.L.R. 293.

[276] The Competition and Markets Authority in the case of the United Kingdom.

[277] Council Regulation (EC) 1/2003 arts 4, 5 and 23(2). Fines may be up to 10% of the undertaking's turnover in the preceding business year. See also Commission Regulation (EC) 773/2004 relating to the conduct of proceedings by the Commission pursuant to arts 81 and 82 of the EC Treaty, [2004] O.J. L123/18.

[278] *Courage v Crehan* (C-453/99) [2001] E.C.R. I-6297; [2001] 5 C.M.L.R. 28, 1058.

[279] *Intel Corp v Via Technologies Inc* [2003] F.S.R. 33; and see para.14-261, et seq.

Refusal to license under EU law

16-154   It has been argued that it may be unlawful to refuse to grant a licence under a patent in certain circumstances, particularly where such refusal is an abuse of a dominant position and therefore contrary to art.102 of the TFEU.[280] However, in *Volvo v Veng*[281] the CJEU ruled that the refusal by the proprietor of a registered design to grant a licence, even in return for a reasonable royalty, cannot in itself constitute an abuse of a dominant position.[282]

16-155   Where a party intends to rely on a refusal to licence as a defence to a patent infringement action, it is incumbent on him to plead explicitly the exceptional features which take the case outside *Volvo v Veng*.[283]

Refusal to license/cancellation of conditions under national law

16-156   Under UK national law, a refusal by the proprietor of a patent to grant licences on reasonable terms may result in the patent being endorsed "licences of right". The endorsement may be made by the Comptroller on the application of any person under the provisions relating to compulsory licences.[284]

16-157   Under UK national law, a patent may also be endorsed "licences of right" by the Comptroller on the application of the Competition and Markets Authority or the Secretary of State following a merger and market investigation or on the application of the appropriate Minister following a report of the Competition and Markets Authority.[285] In both cases, as an additional or alternative remedy, the Comptroller may by order cancel or modify any condition in licences granted under a patent by the proprietor restricting the use of the invention by the licensee or the right of the proprietor to grant other licences.[286]

3.   CO-OWNERSHIP

Co-ownership

16-158   Co-ownership of a patent or an application for a patent may arise by the patent being applied for by or granted to joint applicants or by assignment. The title of a co-owner should be entered in the register. Apart from an agreement to the contrary, each co-owner is entitled to an equal undivided share in the patent[287] and is entitled, "by himself or his agents", to do for his own benefit and without the consent of or need to account to the other co-owner(s) any act which would otherwise amount

---

[280] *Pitney Bowes Inc v Francotyp-postalia GmbH* [1991] F.S.R. 72, [1990] 3 C.M.L.R. 466; see also *Chiron Corp v Organon Teknika Ltd (No.2)* [1993] F.S.R. 324, [1992] 3 C.M.L.R. 813; *Chiron Corp v Murex Diagnostics Ltd (No.2)* [1994] F.S.R. 187, CA; *Sandvik AB v K R Pfiffner (UK) Ltd* [2000] F.S.R. 17, and see paras 14-256 to 14-261.

[281] *Volvo v Erik Veng (UK) Ltd* (238/87) [1988] E.C.R. 6211; [1989] 4 C.M.L.R. 122, [8].

[282] Cf. *Radio Telefis Eireann v Commission* (T-69/89) [1991] 4 C.M.L.R. 586, CFI; *RTE and ITP v Commission* (C-241 and 242/91P) [1995] E.C.R. I-743, [1995] 4 C.M.L.R. 718, [1995] All E.R. (EC) 416, ECJ ("the *Magill* case"); and see *Intel Corp v Via Technologies Inc* [2003] F.S.R. 12 (Lawrence Collins J) and [2003] F.S.R. 33, CA.

[283] *Philips Electronics N.V. v Ingman* [1999] F.S.R. 112, 134.

[284] PA 1977 ss.48(1)(b), 48A(1)(c) and 48B(1)(d) and (e).

[285] PA 1977 ss.50A and 51.

[286] PA 1977 ss.50A(4) and 51(3).

[287] PA 1977 s.36(1).

to an infringement of the patent concerned.[288] However, one co-owner may not without the consent of the other co-owner(s) grant a licence under the patent or assign or mortgage a share in it or amend the specification of the patent or apply for such an amendment to be allowed or for the patent to be revoked.[289] These provisions also have effect in relation to an application for a patent.[290]

Ownership of patent for limited area

Assuming it is still possible to assign a patent for a limited part of the UK or to **16-159** achieve the same result by granting an exclusive licence,[291] in such circumstances the "assignee" would be owner of their share of the patent in severality and could sue or grant licences in respect of acts done or to be done in the area to which their portion of the patent extended and would not, apart from contract, be liable to account in any way to the owner of the rest of the patent.

Right of one co-owner to work the invention and to grant licences

As noted above, subject to any agreement to the contrary, a co-owner of a pat- **16-160** ent may do "by himself or his agents" and "for his own benefit" (and without the consent of or need to account to the other co-owner(s)) any act which would otherwise amount to an infringement of the patent concerned[292]; but they may not grant a licence under the patent without the consent of the other co-owner(s).[293] A person may supply a co-owner of a patent for an invention with the means relating to an essential element of the invention, for putting the invention into effect, and such supply will not amount to an infringement of the patent.[294] If a co-owner disposes of a patented product to any person, then that person (and any other person claiming through them) is entitled to deal with the product in the same way as if it had been disposed of by a sole registered proprietor.[295]

In *Henry Bros v Ministry of Defence*,[296] the Court of Appeal said, obiter, that the **16-161** general purpose of s.36(2) of the 1977 Act is to permit what might be called domestic enjoyment or "home use" while not permitting larger scale exploitation through the grant of licences. Exactly where the dividing-line should be drawn in every case will depend on the facts. For example, "home use" for the Crown has an extraordinarily wide scope, far wider than it has for an ordinary individual.[297] The court also expressed the view (at 450) that the word "agents" in s.36(2) does not draw any sharp distinction between employees and independent contractors—although in some situations that distinction might correspond to the important distinction between "home use" and commercial exploitation.

---

[288] PA 1977 s.36(2) and (4).
[289] PA 1977 s.36(3), as amended by PA 2004 s.9.
[290] PA 1977 s.36(7).
[291] See para.16-19.
[292] PA 1977, s.36(2).
[293] PA 1977 s.36(3).
[294] PA 1977 s.36(4).
[295] PA 1977 s.36(5).
[296] [1997] R.P.C. 693; [1999] R.P.C. 442, CA.
[297] [1997] R.P.C. 693; [1999] R.P.C. 442, CA.

The right to sue

16-162   One co-owner can sue for infringement of the patent[298] or of the rights arising on publication of the application[299] but must join their fellow co-owners, either as co-claimant(s) or as defendant(s). If a co-owner joined as a defendant takes no part in the proceeding they shall not be liable for costs.[300]

Counterclaim for revocation

16-163   Where a co-owner is joined as a co-defendant and a counterclaim for revocation of the patent is made by other defendants, the court will not enter judgement in default against the defendant co-owner if they fail to serve a defence to the counterclaim.[301] However, if the defendant co-owner does not serve a defence to the counterclaim, they will not be permitted to adduce evidence at trial relating to the validity of the patent although they may be ordered to give disclosure relating to the issue of validity.[302]

Assignment, mortgage, amendment and revocation

16-164   Apart from an agreement to the contrary, a co-owner cannot amend or apply to amend the patent, apply for revocation of the patent, or assign or mortgage a share in the patent without the consent of all persons who are co-owners of the patent or application, as the case may be.[303]

Devolution of title

16-165   The rules of law applicable to the devolution of personal property generally apply in relation to co-owned patents and applications.[304] Accordingly, the undivided share of a co-owner of a patent or an application devolves upon death to their personal representatives.

Powers of the Comptroller

16-166   Under the 1977 Act any co-owner of a patent may apply to the Comptroller for directions regarding whether any right in or under the patent should be transferred or granted to any other person.[305] This provision is to prevent the proper exploitation of a patent being unreasonably prevented by one or more co-owners.[306]

---

[298] PA 1977 s.66.
[299] PA 1977 s.69.
[300] PA 1977 s.66(2).
[301] *MMI Research Ltd v Cellxion Ltd* [2008] F.S.R. 23.
[302] *MMI Research Ltd v Cellxion Ltd* [2008] F.S.R. 23.
[303] PA 1977 s.36(3) and (7).
[304] PA 1977, s.36(6) and (7).
[305] PA 1977 s.37(1)(c), *Hughes v Paxman* [2007] R.P.C. 2.
[306] *Hughes v Paxman* [2007] R.P.C. 2.

Procedure

The procedure on an application to the Comptroller under s.37 is governed by **16-167** Pt 7 of the Patents Rules 2007.[307] If a person ordered to execute any instrument or do any other acts fails to do so within 14 days of being requested to do so, the Comptroller may, on an application made to them, give directions empowering some other person to perform such act.[308]

Applications for patents

There is a similar provision enabling the Comptroller to determine whether any **16-168** right in or under an application for a patent should be transferred or granted to any other person.[309] The jurisdiction also extends to foreign and convention patent applications.[310] For UK patent applications, the Comptroller is also empowered to resolve disputes between joint applicants for a patent as to whether, or in what manner, the application should be proceeded with.[311] The procedure on an application to the Comptroller under ss.8, 10 or 12 is also governed by Pt 7 of the Patents Rule 2007.[312]

Appeal

An appeal lies to the Patents Court from a decision of the Comptroller under ss.8, **16-169** 10, 12 or 37 and, with leave, from the Patents Court to the Court of Appeal.[313]

Trustees and personal representatives

The provisions of the Act as to co-ownership do not affect the mutual rights or **16-170** obligations of trustees or personal representatives or their rights and obligations as such.[314]

Revocation by co-owner

The co-owner of a patent who is registered as sole proprietor is liable to have **16-171** their co-owner included as registered proprietor under s.37(2)(a) of the 1977 Act. However, the patent can no longer be revoked on the application of the unregistered co-owner under s.72(1)(b).

4. REGISTRATION

Register of Patents

There is kept at the UK Patent Office (now the UKIPO) a Register of Patents in **16-172**

---

[307] Patents Rules 2007 r.73(1)(a) and Sch.3 Pt 1.
[308] PA 1977 s.37(3). *Florey's Patent* [1962] R.P.C. 186. See also *Cannings US Application* [1992] R.P.C. 459.
[309] PA 1977 s.8(1)(b).
[310] PA 1977 s.12(1)(b).
[311] PA 1977 s.10.
[312] Patents Rules 2007 r.73(1)(a) and Sch.3 Pt 1.
[313] PA 1977 s.97(1) and (3).
[314] PA 1977 s.37(6).

which are entered particulars of published applications, patents, assignments, licences and other matters in compliance with the Patents Rules 2007.[315] Subject to rules, the public have a right to inspect the Register at all convenient times.[316]

16-173 A Register of European Patents is also maintained at the EPO.[317] The Register is open to public inspection and extracts from the Register are available on request on payment of an administrative fee.[318] Registration of an application for a European patent (UK) in the European Register is treated as registration under the 1977 Act.[319]

16-174 No entry can be made in the UK Register or in the European Register in respect of any application for a patent before the application has been published.[320]

Relationship between the two Registers

16-175 The Register of European Patents relates only to European patents and applications. Rules made under the EPC provide for the contents of the Register and, in the main, it records matters relating to applications up to and including the date of publication of the mention of the grant of the European patent in the *European Patent Bulletin*.[321] If an opposition is filed after grant or a request is filed by the proprietor to revoke or limit the claims, then matters relating to the opposition or the request, as the case may be, are also registered.[322] A transfer of a European patent application will be recorded on the European Register on request.[323] If a European patent is opposed, then where a person provides evidence that in a contracting state, following a final decision, they have been entered in the patent register of such state instead of the previous proprietor, they shall at his request replace the previous proprietor in respect of such state.[324] Provision is also made for the registration of licences and other rights in respect of European patent applications.[325]

16-176 The UK Register of Patents relates to UK national patents and European Patents (UK). However, the 1977 Act prohibits any requirements as to the registration of applications for European patents (UK) although registration of such an application in the European Register is treated as registration under the Act.[326] Thus assignments, licences, etc. relating to applications for European Patents (UK) are registered at the EPO. Once a European Patent (UK) is granted, it takes effect as a national patent granted under the 1977 Act[327] and thereafter assignments, licences, etc. are registered at the UKIPO.

Registration, etc. of certain transactions

16-177 Where a person acquires the property in a patent, the application for a patent or any right in or under a patent or application, by virtue of a transaction, instrument

---

[315] PA 1977 s.32, as amended by Patents, Designs and Marks Act 1986 s.1 and Sch.1 para.4; Patents Rules 2007 r.44.
[316] PA 1977 ss.32(1) and 32(5).
[317] EPC art.127.
[318] EPC arts 127 and 128; EPC Rules r.145.
[319] PA 1977 s.78(3)(f).
[320] Patents Rules 2007 r.44(1); EPC art.127.
[321] EPC Rules r.143.
[322] EPC Rules r.143(1)(q)–(x).
[323] EPC Rules r.22.
[324] EPC art.99(4).
[325] EPC Rules r.23.
[326] PA 1977 s.78(4) and s.78(3)(f).
[327] PA 1977 s.77(1); EPC art.64(1).

or event to which s.33(3) of the 1977 Act applies, there is no requirement to apply to have the title registered but registration is strongly advisable. Failure to register may result in the title being defeated by a subsequent conflicting transaction[328] and/or in the loss of the ability to recover costs in an action for infringement of the patent.[329]

Registrable documents, etc. in the UK Register

The 1977 Act provides the statutory framework for registration in the UK **16-178** Register of all transactions, instruments or events affecting rights in or under national patents or applications,[330] The procedure for registration of any transaction, instrument or event mentioned in ss.32(2)(b) or 33(3) is set out in r.47 of the Patents Rules 2007. The Comptroller also retains a discretion to register such other particulars as he may think fit.[331] Nevertheless, no notice of any trust whether express, implied or constructive may be entered in the Register and the Comptroller is not affected by any such notice.[332] It has been held that a document which affects the proprietorship of a patent, whether by creating trusts or otherwise, is not excluded from the Register by this provision.[333] However, to be registrable, documents containing an agreement must be complete and of such a nature that the agreement could be enforced by specific performance as otherwise no legal or equitable interest in the patent or proprietorship thereof would pass.[334]

The Comptroller may refuse to register documents if he is not satisfied that they **16-179** are properly stamped.[335] Nevertheless, Stamp Duty has been abolished for instruments executed on or after 28 March 2000 for the sale, transfer or other disposition of intellectual property and, accordingly, in future it is likely that such a refusal will become increasingly rare but it could arise, for example, where it is sought to register an assignment or other instrument made prior to 28 March 2000,[336] or an instrument which deals in part with a patent and in part with property on which stamp duty is payable.[337]

The application to register a transaction, instrument or event

The requirements for an application to register a transaction, instrument or event **16-180** are set out in guidance issued by the UKIPO.[338] The application should be made on Patents Form 21 and should include evidence establishing the transaction, instrument or event.[339] If the Form is signed by or on behalf of at least the assignor, mortgagor or grantor of a licence or security, to confirm the rights affected the requirement for evidence will normally be taken to be satisfied. In other cases ad-

---

[328] PA 1977 s.33(1) and (2). See also para.16-39, et seq.
[329] PA 1977 s.68. See also para.16-47, et seq.
[330] PA 1977 s.32(2)(b), as amended by PDMA 1986 s.1 and Sch.1 para.4. See also Patents Rules 2007 r.44(6).
[331] Patents Rules 2007 r.44(7).
[332] PA 1977 s.32(3), as amended by PDMA 1986 s.1 and Sch.1 para.4.
[333] *Kakkar v Szelke* [1989] 1 F.S.R. 225, 237.
[334] *Haslett v Hutchinson* (1891) 8 R.P.C. 457; *Fletcher's Patent* (1893) 10 R.P.C. 252; *Morey's Patent* (1858) 25 Beav.581; *Parnell's Patent* (1888) 5 R.P.C. 126.
[335] See Stamp Act 1891 s.17; cf. *Maynard v Consolidated Kent Collieries* [1903] 19 T.L.R. 448.
[336] See further paras 17-18 to 17-26 of the 16th edn of this work.
[337] *UKIPO Manual of Patents Practice* (published 1 July 2015, updated 31 December 2015), para.32.09.
[338] *UKIPO Manual of Patents Practice* (published 1 July 2015, updated 31 December 2015), para.32.09.
[339] Patents Rules 2007 r.47.

ditional evidence may be required. A translation must be supplied for any documentary evidence not in English.

Certificate of the Comptroller

16-181   A certificate by the Comptroller as to any entry which he is authorised to make or as to any other thing which he is authorised to do is prima facie evidence of the matters so certified.[340] Certified copies of any entry will be furnished by the Comptroller on payment of the prescribed fee, and will be admitted in proceedings in all courts without further proof or production of the originals.[341]

Information request

16-182   Any person interested in a particular national patent or application for a patent may, after publication of the application, leave a request at the UKIPO to be informed of certain matters, for example, of any attempt to register an assignment or other document in connection with the patent or application in question.[342] Notice will then be given to the person who has left the request and registration will be suspended for a few days so as to enable the person interested to apply to the courts to prevent registration if he so desires. The matters in respect of which information may be obtained are set out in r.54 of the Patents Rules 2007 and include when a request for substantive examination has been filed, when the specification of a patent or application for a patent has been published, when an application for a patent has been withdrawn or taken to be withdrawn or treated as withdrawn or refused or treated as refused, when a renewal fee has been paid within the period of six months referred to in s.25(4) of the 1977 Act, when a patent has ceased to have effect, and when an entry has been made in the register or an application has been made for making such an entry. Nevertheless, s.118 (and thus the Rules made thereunder) do not require the Comptroller to provide any information save that which is available from official UKIPO records.[343] Further, s.118 does not entitle persons to demand the dates of withdrawal of *unpublished* applications.[344]

Inspection of documents

16-183   In addition to inspection of the UK Register,[345] it is also possible after the date of publication of an application for a patent to inspect all documents filed or kept at the UKIPO in relation to the application or any patent granted in pursuance of it.[346] There are special provisions in respect of certain documents, including documents which the applicant or proprietor has requested to be treated as confidential and the Comptroller has so directed.[347] Similarly, after publication of an applica-

---

[340] PA 1977 s.32(10), as amended by PDMA 1986 s.1 and Sch.1 para.3.
[341] PA 1977 ss.32(6) and 32(11); Patents Rules 2007 r.46.
[342] PA 1977 s.118.
[343] *Haberman v Comptroller-General* [2004] R.P.C. 21.
[344] *Haberman v Comptroller-General* [2004] R.P.C. 21.
[345] See para.16-172, et seq.
[346] PA 1977 s.118.
[347] Patents Rules 2007 rr.51 and 53.

tion for a European patent, the files relating to the application may be inspected on request made to the EPO.[348]

Where prior to the publication of a national application for a patent the applicant threatens a person with proceedings after publication of the application, a request may be made by that person to the Comptroller for information and inspection of documents notwithstanding that the application has not been published.[349] There are similar provisions in respect of an application for a European patent, although the request must of course be made to the EPO.[350] **16-184**

Rectification of the UK Register by the court

The court may, on the application of any person aggrieved, rectify the UK register.[351] **16-185**

The application for rectification is a claim under the Patents Act 1977 and consequently, it is a claim which must be dealt with in the Patents Court or the Intellectual Property Enterprise Court.[352] The claim must also be served together with the accompanying documents on the Comptroller, who is entitled to take part in the proceedings.[353] **16-186**

Clerical errors in the register may be corrected by the Comptroller on application made to him in the prescribed manner. **16-187**

Falsifying entries

It is an offence to make a false entry in the UK register or a writing falsely purporting to be a copy of any entry, or to produce or tender in evidence any such writing knowing it to be false.[354] **16-188**

False use of "Patent Office"

If any person uses the words "Patent Office" (or any other words suggesting that their place of business is, or is officially connected with, the Patent Office) within their place of business or on any document issued by them, they are liable on summary conviction to a fine not exceeding level 4 on the standard scale.[355] **16-189**

---

[348] EPC art.128(4).
[349] PA 1977 s.118(4); Patents Rules 2007 r.52. See also, *Buralls of Wisbech Ltd's Application* [2004] R.P.C. 14, 285.
[350] EPC art.128(2).
[351] PA 1977 s.34.
[352] CPR r.63.2.
[353] CPR rr.63.14(3) and 63.15.
[354] PA 1977 s.109.
[355] PA 1977 s.112; "… not exceeding level 4 on the standard scale" means not exceeding £2,500; see the Criminal Justice Act 1982 s.37(2) as substituted by the Criminal Justice Act 1991 s.17. This section of the Act continues to refer to the Patent Ofiice, not the UKIPO.

CHAPTER 17

COMPULSORY LICENCES AND LICENCES OF RIGHT

CONTENTS

1. COMPULSORY LICENCES UNDER UK NATIONAL LAW

A. Legislative Bases for the Grant of a Compulsory Licence

The 1977 Act

Section 48(1) of the 1977 Act (as amended) provides that at any time after the **17-01**
expiration of three years[1] from the date of the grant of a patent, any person may apply to the comptroller for a licence under the patent, for an entry to be made in the
register to the effect that licences under the patent are to be available as of right,
or, where the applicant is a government department, for the grant to any person
specified in the application of a licence under the patent.

The applicant must establish at least one relevant ground upon which such relief **17-02**
can be granted under one of two regimes: the first applies where the patent proprietor is a "WTO proprietor"[2] and the second in other cases. This distinction was
introduced by the Patents and Trade Marks (World Trade Organisation) Regula-

---

[1] This period may be varied by a rule laid before, and approved by resolution of, each House of Parliament (s.48(6) PA 1977) but has not, to date, been varied.
[2] i.e. a World Trade Organisation proprietor. This term is defined by PA 1977 s.48(5), see para.17–
   17.

tions 1999[3] which, with effect from 29 July 1999, modified the 1977 Act so as to make the compulsory licence regime compliant with the UK's obligations under the TRIPS Agreement.

17-03   Where the proprietor of the patent in issue is a WTO proprietor, the relevant grounds are those set out in s.48A(1):

"(a)   where the patented invention is a product, that a demand in the United Kingdom for that product is not being met on reasonable terms;

(b)   that by reason of the refusal of the proprietor of the patent concerned to grant a licence or licences on reasonable terms–

(i)   the exploitation in the United Kingdom of any other patented invention which involves an important technical advance of considerable economic significance in relation to the invention for which the patent concerned was granted is prevented of hindered, or

(ii)   the establishment or development of commercial or industrial activities in the United Kingdom is unfairly prejudiced;

(c)   that by reason of conditions imposed by the proprietor of the patent concerned on the grant of licences under the patent, or on the disposal or use of the patented product or on the use of the patented process, the manufacture, use or disposal of materials not protected by the patent, or the establishment or development of commercial or industrial activities in the United Kingdom, is unfairly prejudiced."

17-04   In cases where the patent proprietor is not a WTO proprietor, the relevant grounds are set out in s.48B(1):

"(a)   where the patented invention is capable of being commercially worked in the United Kingdom, that it is not being so worked or is not being so worked to the fullest extent that is reasonably practicable;

(b)   where the patented invention is a product, that a demand for the product in the United Kingdom–

(i)   is not being met on reasonable terms, or

(ii)   is being met to a substantial extent by importation from a country which is not a member State;

(c)   where the patented invention is capable of being commercially worked in the United Kingdom, that it is being prevented or hindered from being so worked–

(i)   where the invention is a product, by the importation of the product from a country which is not a member State;

(ii)   where the invention is a process, by the importation from such a country of a product obtained directly by means of the process or to which the process has been applied;

(d)   that by reason of the refusal of the proprietor of the patent to grant a licence of licences on reasonable terms–

(i)   a market for the export of any patented product made in the United Kingdom is not being supplied, or

(ii)   the working or efficient working in the United Kingdom of any other patented invention which makes a substantial contribution to the art is prevented or hindered, or

(iii) the establishment or development of commercial or industrial activities in the United Kingdom is unfairly prejudiced;

(e)   that by reason of conditions imposed by the proprietor of the patent on the grant of licences under the patent, or on the disposal or use of the patented product or on the use of the patented process, the manufacture, use or disposal of materials not protected by the patent, or the establishment or development of commercial or industrial activities in the United Kingdom, is unfairly prejudiced."

17-05   These provisions must be read in light of CJEU decisions regarding free movement of goods arising from of art.34 of the Treaty on the Functioning of the European Union (TFEU). In particular the CJEU has held that by treating a case where demand for a patented product is satisfied on the domestic market by imports from other Member States of the EU as a case where a compulsory licence may be

---

[3]   SI 1999/1899.

granted for insufficiency of exploitation of the patent, the UK had failed to fulfil its obligations under art.30 of the EEC Treaty (now art.34 TFEU).[4] Moreover, in a subsequent case the European Court held that, where a patent is endorsed "licences of right", it is also contrary to the Treaty for the Comptroller to exercise his discretion in granting licences of right so as to permit a licensee to import products from outside the EC if the patentee works the invention in another Member State but not if the patentee works it within the UK.[5] Such an exercise of discretion discriminates against the patentee who decides to manufacture in another Member State of the EU.[6]

The Patents and Plant Variety Rights (Compulsory Licensing) Regulations 2002

The Patents and Plant Variety Rights (Compulsory Licensing) Regulations 2002[7] implement art.12 of Directive 98/44/EC of the European Parliament and of the Council on the legal protection of biotechnological inventions (the Biotech Directive).[8] The Regulations[9] enable the Comptroller General of Patents and the Controller of Plant Variety Rights, acting jointly, to grant non-exclusive compulsory licences and cross-licences where the exploitation of a plant variety right would infringe a patent and vice versa. The conditions and the procedure for the grant of a compulsory licence under the Regulations will be discussed in more detail below.[10]

17-06

The Patents (Compulsory Licensing and Supplementary Protection Certificates) Regulations 2007

The Patents (Compulsory Licensing and Supplementary Protection Certificates) Regulations 2007[11] assist in the implementation of Regulation (EC) 816/2006 of the European Parliament and of the Council of 17 May 2006 on compulsory licensing of patents relating to the manufacture of pharmaceutical products for export to countries with public health problems. The EC Regulation stems from the TRIPS Agreement and, in particular, the Decision of 30 August 2003 of the General Council of the World Trade Organisation on the implementation of para.6 of the Doha Declaration of 14 November 2001.[12] The UK Regulations, which came into effect on 17 December 2007, amend the Patents Act 1977 by inserting a new

17-07

---

4   *Re Compulsory Patent Licences: EC Commission v United Kingdom* (C-30/90)[1992] 1 E.C.R. 777; [1992] 2 C.M.L.R. 709; [1993] R.P.C. 283; [1993] F.S.R. 1.
5   *Generics (UK) Ltd v Smith Kline & French Laboratories Ltd* (C-191/90) [1992] E.C.R. I-5335; [1993] 1 C.M.L.R. 89; [1993] R.P.C. 333; [1993] F.S.R. 592.
6   See also *Allen & Hanburys Ltd v Generics (UK) Ltd* (434/85) [1988] E.C.R. 1245; [1988] C.M.L.R. 701; [1988] F.S.R. 312, where the ECJ held that it was also contrary to the EC Treaty for the Comptroller to exercise his discretion in granting a licence of right so as to permit a licensee to manufacture product in the UK but to prohibit him from importing product manufactured in another Member State of the EC. Subsequently s.46(3)(c) of the 1977 Act was amended by the CDPA 1988 to take account of this decision.
7   SI 2002/247, as amended by Reg.3 of the Patents (Compulsory Licensing and Supplementary Protection Certificates) Regulations 2007 (SI 2007/3293).
8   [1998] O.J. L213.
9   which came into force on 1 March 2002.
10 See para.17–132, et seq.
11 SI 2007/3293.
12 See para.1–75, et seq.

s.128A, thereby assisting in giving effect under national law to a compulsory licence granted under Regulation (EC) No.816/2006. The conditions and procedure for the grant of a compulsory licence under the EC Regulation will be discussed in more detail below.[13]

Community patents

17-08   The special provisions in the 1977 Act[14] relating to the grant of a compulsory licence in respect of a Community patent were never brought into force and were repealed by the Patents Act 2004.[15]

B.   Application for a Compulsory Licence or other Relief

Who may apply and when

17-09   The Act states[16] that "any person" may apply for a compulsory licence, however the Act also requires the Comptroller to take account of the ability of the applicant to work the invention[17] so that in effect the applicant has to show a proper interest. An application for a compulsory licence under UK national law or to have the patent endorsed "licences of right" cannot be made until three years have elapsed from the date of the grant of the patent.[18]

Infringement or revocation action pending

17-10   An application for a compulsory licence may be made to the Comptroller even though in parallel proceedings before the court the applicant denies infringement (and therefore denies he needs a compulsory licence) or asserts that the patent is invalid.[19] However, if a compulsory licence is applied for by a defendant, an interlocutory injunction may still be granted against them: they may fail to establish any of the grounds for such a licence or they may fail in the exercise of the Comptroller's discretion. Alternatively, they may be unable to pay the damages which may be awarded against them—even though such damages may be quantifiable.[20] An action for infringement will not, in general, be stayed pending the outcome of an application for a compulsory licence.[21] Nevertheless, an application for a compulsory licence may be stayed pending the final outcome of an infringement action.[22]

---

[13] See para.17–142, et seq.
[14] PA 1977 ss.53(1) and 86.
[15] PA 2004 s.16, Sch.2, para.12 and s.5, Sch.1, para.6.
[16] PA 1977 s.48(1).
[17] PA 1977 s.50(2)(b); see *J.R. Geigy S.A.'s Patent* [1964] R.P.C. 391; *Enviro-spray Systems Inc's Patents* [1986] R.P.C. 147; *Therma-Tru Corp's Patent* [1997] R.P.C. 777.
[18] PA 1977 s.48(1). This period may be varied by a rule laid before, and approved by resolution of, each House of Parliament (s.48(6) PA 1977) but has not, to date, been varied.
[19] *Halcon S.D. Group Inc's Patents* [1989] R.P.C. 1.
[20] *Dyrlund Smith A/S v Turberville Smith Ltd* [1998] F.S.R. 774, CA (a design right case).
[21] *Pfizer Corp v DDSA Pharmaceuticals Ltd* [1966] R.P.C. 44.
[22] *Halcon S.D. Group Inc's Patents* [1989] R.P.C. 1.

What the applicant must establish

The applicant must establish one of the relevant grounds for relief and thereafter the Comptroller has a discretion as to whether to grant relief and, if a licence is to be granted, upon what terms.[23]

17-11

The 1977 Act (as amended) provides for different grounds for relief depending on whether the proprietor is, or is not, a WTO proprietor.[24] For WTO proprietors there are now three grounds for relief[25] which are based on three of the five grounds for relief prior to amendment of the 1977 Act by the 1999 Regulations.[26] For non-WTO proprietors there continue to be five grounds for relief[27] which are the same as the five grounds prior to amendment, except that modifications have been made to take account of certain CJEU decisions referred to above.[28]

17-12

Similarly, the nature of the Comptroller's discretion differs in that the more limited grounds for relief in the case of a WTO proprietor are indicative of a less onerous policy to be achieved by the Comptroller by the exercise of his discretion where the proprietor is a WTO proprietor.[29] Further, s.50(1) of the Act (as amended) does not apply in the case of a WTO proprietor and instead s.48A(6) does.

17-13

Reasons for the differences

The reason for most of the differences in the case of the WTO proprietor stem from art.27(1) of TRIPS which provides that "… patents shall be available and patent rights enjoyable without discrimination as to place of invention, the field of technology and whether products are imported or locally produced". In consequence of the final part of this provision, the compulsory licensing rules of WTO members may not treat the WTO proprietor who chooses to import in a different manner to the WTO proprietor who chooses to manufacture locally. Thus, referring to the 1977 Act in its original form, ss.48(3)(a) and 48(3)(c) could not stand in the case of a WTO proprietor because they provided grounds for a compulsory licence where the invention was "capable of being commercially worked in the United Kingdom" but, for one reason or another, it was not being so worked. Thus, it was inherent in these provisions that they might discriminate against the proprietor who has chosen not to work their invention in the UK but rather to supply the UK market by importation. Similarly, s.48(3)(b)(ii), in its original form, could not stand as a ground for relief in the case of the WTO proprietor because it also sought to discriminate against the patentee who chooses to import.

17-14

Article 31(f) of TRIPs also provides that any use under a compulsory licence "shall be predominantly for the supply of the domestic market of the Member authorising such use". Consequently in the case of the WTO proprietor, the compulsory licensing rules may no longer be concerned with licensing manufacture solely for export. Thus, referring again to the 1977 Act in its original form, s.48(3)(d)(i) could not stand in the case of the WTO proprietor. Indeed the wording of s.48A(6)(c), as amended, substantially reproduces that of art.31(f) of TRIPs.

17-15

---

[23] PA 1977 s.48(2).

[24] PA 1977 s.48(4), and ss.48A and 48B.

[25] PA 1977 s.48A(1).

[26] The Patents and Trade Marks (World Trade Organisation Regulations) 1999 (SI 1999/1899).

[27] PA 1977 s.48B(1).

[28] See para.17–05.

[29] The grounds for relief may properly be taken into account in determining the policy to be achieved by exercise of the Comptroller's discretion, see *Allen & Hanburys Ltd v Generics (UK) Ltd* [1986] R.P.C. 203, at 249, HL.

17-16 As to the Comptroller's discretion, s.50(1)(a) requires the Comptroller to exercise his discretion so as to ensure that inventions which can be worked on a commercial scale in the UK shall be worked there without delay and to the fullest extent possible. Also, s.50(1)(c) directs the Comptroller to protect those developing or working an invention in the UK under the protection of a patent. It will be appreciated from what has been said above that the approach which underlies these requirements is at odds with TRIPS, under which the WTO proprietor may, if they so choose, supply the UK market by importation and is not to be penalised for so doing. Moreover, these requirements necessarily mean that the Comptroller is to encourage working of the invention in the UK in order to supply export markets but, again, such a requirement is not compatible with TRIPS. Thus, s.50(1), as amended, no longer applies in the case of a WTO proprietor. This means, of course, that s.50(1)(b) also does not apply in the case of a WTO proprietor but that provision is replaced by s.48A(6)(d) which enacts art.31(h) of TRIPS.[30]

Who is a WTO proprietor?

17-17 A WTO proprietor is defined by s.48(5) of the 1977 Act. A proprietor is a WTO proprietor if:

(a) they are a national of, or is domiciled in, a country which is a member of the World Trade Organisation; or

(b) they have a real and effective industrial or commercial establishment in such a country.

17-18 A list of current members of the WTO is maintained on the WTO website.[31]

Other special provisions applicable to WTO proprietors only

17-19 Quite apart from the differences in the grounds for relief and the nature of the Comptroller's discretion, there are a number of special provisions which apply in the case of a WTO proprietor but not in the case of a non-WTO proprietor.

Efforts to agree are mandatory

17-20 Section 48A(2), as amended, provides that no order or entry shall be made under s.48 in respect of a patent whose proprietor is a WTO proprietor unless:

(a) the applicant has made efforts to obtain a licence from the proprietor on reasonable commercial terms and conditions; and

(b) their efforts have not been successful within a reasonable time.

17-21 This provision gives effect to art.31(b) of TRIPs. It is to be noted that the efforts must be made before the order or entry is made, not before the application is made. Accordingly, there would seem to be no reason why the application should not be initiated with a view to agreement being reached thereafter. The analogous licence of right provisions provide that the Comptroller is to settle terms for a licence of right "in default of agreement" (see s.46(3)(a)) and it has been held that this does not make unsuccessful negotiations a pre-requisite to the application. As Whitford

---

[30] See para.17–26.

[31] *https://www.wto.org/english/thewto_e/whatis_e/tif_e/org6_e.htm* [Accessed 10 March 2016].

J said in *R. v Comptroller-General, ex parte Bayer A.G.*:[32]

"… an attempt to reach an agreement is not a pre-condition to the making of an application. If it were a great many rather difficult questions might arise. At what point in time must the attempt to agree terms be made? Over what period of time must the attempt to agree terms continue? How much of the four year [statutory] extension can be occupied by a patentee anxious to avoid the grant of a licence in countering proposals for agreed terms? I regard this as a bad point. A potential licensee makes his application and suggests appropriate terms. If these are acceptable to the patentee that is an end of the matter; if not the Comptroller has to adjudicate."

The compulsory licence provisions go a stage further than the licence of right **17-22** provisions in that the applicant must make efforts to obtain a licence from the proprietor "on reasonable commercial terms and conditions". Clearly, this provision will have to be applied with some flexibility. It is submitted that provided the applicant's proposals are made bona fide, the Comptroller should be slow to refuse relief on the ground that the applicant has not made efforts to obtain a licence from the proprietor on reasonable commercial terms and conditions.

Semi-conductor technology

Section 48A(3) prevents any order or entry under s.48 if the patented invention **17-23** is in the field of semi-conductor technology. The provision gives effect to art.31(c) of TRIPs. It does not prevent a patent being endorsed licences of right under s.51 of the 1977 Act following a report by the Competition Commission (see para.17-168).

The Comptroller's discretion: objects to be attained

As mentioned above,[33] the nature of the Comptroller's discretion differs depend- **17-24** ing on whether the proprietor is, or is not, a WTO proprietor.

WTO proprietor

The more limited grounds for relief in the case of a WTO proprietor, and the **17-25** reasons for those more limited grounds (discussed at paras 17–14 to 17–16), may be taken into account in determining the policy to be achieved by the Comptroller in the exercise of his discretion where the proprietor is a WTO proprietor.[34] In the light of those grounds, it is clear that the Comptroller may not exercise his discretion so as to discriminate against the WTO proprietor who chooses to import patented products, rather than manufacture them locally.

Furthermore s.50(1) of the 1977 Act does not apply in the case of a patent whose **17-26** proprietor is a WTO proprietor. However, the Act does place certain limits on the scope of the Comptroller's powers and in particular s.48A(6) provides that a licence granted in pursuance of an order or entry under s.48 in respect of a patent whose proprietor is a WTO proprietor:

(a) shall not be exclusive;
(b) shall not be assigned except to a person to whom there is also assigned the

---

[32] Unreported, 9 May 1985. The passage cited above was quoted and followed by Falconer J in *Roussel-Uclaf (Clemence & le Martret's) Patent* [1987] R.P.C. 109, at 117. See also *Rhône-Poulenc S.A.'s (Ketoprofen) Patent* [1989] R.P.C. 570.
[33] See para.17–16.
[34] *Allen & Hanburys Ltd v Generics (UK) Ltd* [1986] R.P.C. 203, 249, HL.

part of the enterprise that enjoys the use of the patented invention, or the part of the goodwill that belongs to that part;

(c)   shall be predominantly for the supply of the market in the United Kingdom;

(d)   shall include conditions entitling the proprietor of the patent concerned to remuneration adequate in the circumstances of the case, taking into account the economic value of the licence; and

(e)   shall be limited in scope and in duration to the purpose for which the licence was granted.

17-27   All of the above provisions originate from TRIPS, particularly art.31(c)–(f) and (h). Subsections (c) and (d) in particular throw some light on the objects to be attained by the Comptroller when exercising his discretion.

Non-WTO proprietor

17-28   Section 50(1) continues to apply in the case of a non-WTO proprietor. Thus in such a case, the Comptroller is to exercise his powers with a view to securing the following purposes:

(a)   that inventions which can be worked on a commercial scale in the UK shall be worked there without undue delay and to the fullest practicable extent;

(b)   that the inventor or other person entitled shall receive reasonable remuneration having regard to the invention; and

(c)   that the interests of any person working or developing an invention in the UK shall not be unfairly prejudiced.

17-29   The Patents and Designs Act 1919 contained a special definition of "working on a commercial scale",[35] but neither the 1949 Act nor the 1977 Act provides any definition of "commercial scale" and these words must, therefore, be given their natural and ordinary meaning, i.e. "in contradistinction to research work or work in the laboratory".[36]

17-30   These powers of the Comptroller must be applied in the light of the TFEU which has the effect of prohibiting the grant of a compulsory licence which does not permit importation from another Member State of the EU.[37] Nor may the Comptroller exercise his powers so as to discriminate against the patentee who decides to manufacture in another Member State.[38] However, so far as concerns the latter restriction on the Comptroller's powers, the grounds for relief in the case of a non-WTO proprietor have been amended by the 1999 Regulations[39] so as to give effect to the rulings of the CJEU.[40]

---

35   Patents and Designs Act 1919 s.93.

36   *McKechnie Bros Ltd's Application* (1934) 51 R.P.C. 461, 468.

37   *Allen & Hanburys Ltd v Generics (UK) Ltd* (434/85) [1988] E.C.R. 1245; [1988] 1 C.M.L.R. 701; [1988] F.S.R. 312.

38   *Generics (UK) Ltd v Smith, Kline & French Laboratories Ltd* (C-191/90) [1992] E.C.R. I-5335; [1993] 1 C.M.L.R. 89; [1993] R.P.C. 333; F.S.R. 592. See also *Re Compulsory Patent Licences: EC Commission v United Kingdom* (C-30/90) [1992] E.C.R. I-777; [1992] 2 C.M.L.R. 709; [1993] R.P.C. 283; [1993] F.S.R. 1.

39   The Patents and Trade Marks (World Trade Organisation) Regulations 1999 (SI 1999/1899).

40   See ss.48B(1)(b)(ii) and 48B(1)(c)(i) and (ii). See also s.48B(3) which qualifies s.48B(1)(a) in cases where the patented invention is being worked in a country which is a Member State and demand in the UK is being met by importation from that state.

WTO and Non-WTO proprietors

Under s.50(2) (which applies to both WTO and non-WTO proprietors), the **17-31**
Comptroller is also to take into account:

(a) the nature of the invention, how long the patent has been granted and the
    measures taken by the patentees or any licensee to make full use of the
    invention;
(b) the ability of a prospective licensee to work the invention; and
(c) the risks the latter must undertake;

but the Comptroller need not take into account matters arising subsequent to the application for a compulsory licence.[41]

Where the prospective licensee cannot show a sufficient ability to work the inven- **17-32**
tion, the application for a compulsory licence will be refused in the exercise of the
Comptroller's discretion.[42] In such circumstances, the Comptroller will not grant
a licence conditional upon the licensee returning to the Comptroller in due course
with satisfactory evidence of ability to exploit.[43]

Similarly, the Comptroller will not grant a compulsory licence if it would be **17-33**
futile to do so, e.g. if manufacture under that licence would necessarily infringe
another patent in respect of which no compulsory licence could be obtained.[44]

C.   Grounds for Relief: WTO Proprietors

In the case of an application in respect of a patent whose proprietor is a WTO **17-34**
proprietor, there are three classes of cases in which the act or default of the patentee
can give rise to an application for a compulsory licence which are set out in
s.48A(1) of the 1977 Act, as amended by the 1999 Regulations.[45] These classes are
not mutually exclusive; but unless the circumstances relied upon fall within one or
other of the classes, no relief can be granted under the section.[46] The classes are:

(a)   Unreasonable terms—s.48A(1)(a)

"Where the patented invention is a product, that demand in the United Kingdom for that product is **17-35**
not being met on reasonable terms."

Demand must be existing

The demand must be an actual one and not merely one which the applicant for a **17-36**
licence hopes and expects to create if and when they obtain a licence.[47]

Reasonable terms

The matters which have to be taken into consideration in determining what **17-37**
constitutes "reasonable terms" are similar to those which have to be considered

---

[41]   PA 1977 s.50(2).
[42]   *J.R. Geigy S.A.'s Patent* [1964] R.P.C. 391; *Enviro-spray Systems Inc's Patents* [1986] R.P.C. 147;
       Therma-Tru Corp's Patent [1997] R.P.C. 777.
[43]   *Enviro-spray Systems Inc's Patents* [1986] R.P.C. 147, 156–157.
[44]   *Cathro's Application* (1934) 51 R.P.C. 75, 88.
[45]   The Patents and Trade Marks (World Trade Organisation Regulations) 1999 (SI 1999/1899).
[46]   See *Brownie Wireless Co Ltd's Application* (1928) 45 R.P.C. 457, at 471.
[47]   *Cathro's Application* (1934) 51 R.P.C. 75, 82.

under para.(b) in the context of a patentees refusal to license on reasonable terms. These are dealt with at para.17–40.

17-38   In *Robin Electric Lamp Co Ltd's Petition*[48] the patentees required an undertaking from their licensees not to sell articles (in which the patented invention was used) below a specified price. This resulted in the price of such articles being considerably higher in this country than abroad. The supply was adequate to meet the demands of the public, and there was no evidence that the price was "so high as to be a serious burden to the consumer or to be unreasonable"; and it was held that there had not been a default by the patentees. This case should, however, be treated with caution in light of developments in competition law and the law relating to free movement of goods within the EU.

17-39   In a licence of right case—*Research Corporation's (Carboplatin) Patent*[49]— Hoffmann J stated that if the price charged by a patentee was reasonable and demand at that price was being met then it was irrelevant to say that demand would have been greater at a lower price. The question was whether or not a given price was reasonable bearing in mind that patentees are entitled to recoup research costs, fund further research in the public interest, and make a profit from their monopoly.

(b)   Refusal to grant licences on reasonable terms—s.48A(1)(b)

17-40   *"That by reason of the refusal of the proprietor of the patent to grant a licence or licences on reasonable terms—*

   (i)   *the exploitation in the United Kingdom of any other patented invention which involves an important technical advance of considerable economic significance in relation to the invention for which the patent concerned was granted is prevented or hindered; or*

   (ii)   *the establishment or development of commercial or industrial activities in the United Kingdom is unfairly prejudiced."*

Reciprocal licences

17-41   No order is to be made on ground (i) unless the proprietor of the patent for the other invention is willing to grant a reciprocal licence on reasonable terms.[50]

"Refusal of the proprietor"

17-42   It was held that before any application could be made (under the provisions of the 1907 Act corresponding to this paragraph) there must have been either a complete refusal to grant a licence or the terms upon which it was offered must have been unreasonable.[51] It is submitted that this general principle will continue to be followed but the applicant is now in no way prejudiced by the fact that he has already accepted a licence or made any admission in relation thereto.[52]

---

48   (1915) 32 R.P.C. 202.
49   [1990] R.P.C. 663.
50   PA 1977 s.48(7).
51   *Loewe Radio Co Ltd's Applications* (1929) 46 R.P.C. 479, 489 and 490.
52   PA 1977 s.48(8).

"Reasonable terms"

As to what constitutes "reasonable terms", Luxmoore J in *Brownie Wireless Co* **17-43**
Ltd's Applications[53] said:

> "The answer to the question must in each case depend on a careful consideration of all the surround-
> ing circumstances. The nature of the invention ... the terms of the licences (if any) already granted,
> the expenditure and liabilities of the patentee in respect of the patent, the requirements of the purchas-
> ing public, and so on".

It was argued that the royalty was out of proportion to the cost and selling price, **17-44**
and that a reduction would result in a greatly increased public demand. The learned
judge held there was no evidence to support the later contention, and said[54]:

> "There is in fact no necessary relationship between cost price or selling price ... and the royalty which
> a patentee is entitled to ask ... The best test of whether a royalty is reasonable in amount or the reverse
> is: How much are manufacturers who are anxious to make and deal with the patented article on com-
> mercial lines ready and willing to pay? ..."

He held on the evidence that the royalty was reasonable, that terms prohibiting **17-45**
export and providing for payment of royalty on non-patented articles were reasonable in the circumstances, and that in view of the nature of the invention it was
reasonable to require licensees to take a licence under all patents belonging to a
given group and to refuse to grant licences under individual patents.

"Commercial or industrial activities"

Under the corresponding provisions of the Patents and Designs Act 1919 it was **17-46**
held that the words "trade or industry of the United Kingdom" should be construed
in a wide sense.[55] It is submitted that the words "commercial or industrial activities in the United Kingdom" are even wider than the former words. The requirement under the Patents and Designs Act 1907 under this ground that "it is in the
public interest that a licence or licences should be granted"[56] has been abolished and
this must be borne in mind when considering cases decided under the earlier Acts.

(c)   Unreasonable conditions—s.48A(1)(c)

> *"That by reason of conditions imposed by the proprietor of the patent concerned on the grant of* **17-47**
> *licences under the patent, or on the disposal or use of the patented product or on use of the patented*
> *process, the manufacture, use or disposal of materials not protected by the patent, or the establish-*
> *ment or development of commercial or industrial activities in the United Kingdom is unfairly*
> *prejudiced."*

The "patented product" and "patented process"

These terms are defined in s.130(1). A "patented process" is a process for which **17-48**
a patent is granted. A "patented product" means a product which is a patented

---

[53]   (1929) 46 R.P.C. 457, 473.
[54]   (1929) 46 R.P.C. 457, 475; see also *Research Corp's Patent* [1991] R.P.C. 663.
[55]   *Brownie Wireless Co Ltd's Applications* (1929) 46 R.P.C. 457, 478; and see *Robin Electric Lamp
       Co Ltd's Petition* (1915) 32 R.P.C. 202, at 213.
[56]   Patents and Designs Act 1907 s.27(2)(d).

invention or, in relation to a patented process, a product obtained directly by means of the process or to which the process has been applied.[57]

"Commercial or industrial activities"

17-49   The meaning of these words has already been considered in the context of s.48A(1)(b)—see para.17-46.

"Unfairly prejudiced"

17-50   An activity may be prejudiced by the patentee's conduct but the subsection also requires that it be unfairly prejudiced. In deciding whether an activity is unfairly prejudiced, it is proper to view the matter from the patentee's perspective and in particular to take into account any investment made by the patentee which they wish to recoup.[58]

17-51   Where the patentee inserted in a limited licence conditions which prohibited the sale of the patented article to a specified class of retailers, it was held that such retailers were not "unfairly prejudiced" within the meaning of the provisions of the 1907 Act.[59] This case should, however, be treated with caution in light of developments in competition law.

D.   Grounds for Relief: non-WTO Proprietors

17-52   In substance, the grounds for relief in the case of an application in respect of a patent whose proprietor is not a WTO proprietor are the same as under the old law prior to amendment by the 1999 Regulations.[60] There are five classes of cases in which the act or default of the patentee can give rise to an application for a compulsory licence. As with WTO proprietors, these classes are not mutually exclusive; but unless the circumstances relied upon fall within one or other of the classes, no relief can be granted under the section.[61] The classes must continue to be applied in the light of the rulings of the CJEU that it is not legitimate under EU law to discriminate against commercial working of the invention by importation from another Member State and in favour of production in the UK.[62] However, as amended by the 1999 Regulations, the grounds for relief themselves give effect to those rulings.[63] The classes are:

(a)   Non-working in the UK—s.48B(1)(a)

17-53   *"Where the patented invention is capable of being commercially worked in the United Kingdom, that it is not being so worked or is not being worked to the fullest extent that is reasonably practicable"*

---

[57]   See also para.14–43, et seq.

[58]   *Colbourne Engineering Co Ltd's Application* (1955) 72 R.P.C. 169.

[59]   *Co-operative Union Ltd's Application* (1933) 50 R.P.C. 161, 164 and 165.

[60]   Patents and Trade Marks (World Trade Organisation) Regulations 1999 (SI 1999/1899).

[61]   See *Brownie Wireless Co Ltd's Application* (1928) 45 R.P.C. 457, at 471.

[62]   *EC Commission v United Kingdom* (C-30/90) [1992] E.C.R. I-777, [1992] 2 C.M.L.R. 709, [1993] R.P.C. 283, [1993] F.S.R. 1; and *Generics (UK) Ltd v Smith, Kline & French Laboratories Ltd* (C-191/90) [1992] E.C.R. I-5335, [1993] R.P.C. 333, [1993] F.S.R. 592. Also see PA 1977 s.53(5).

[63]   See PA 1977 ss.48B(1)(b)(ii) and 48B(1)(c)(ii). See also s.48B(3) which qualifies s.48B(1)(a) in cases where the patented invention is being worked in a country which is a Member State and demand in the UK is being met by importation from that state.

What must be shown

The onus is upon the applicant to establish that the patented invention is not be- **17-54** ing worked to the fullest extent that is reasonably possible, i.e. at the rate of production which is practicable and necessary to meet the demand of the patented invention. In order to establish a case under this subsection it will normally be necessary for an applicant to bring evidence to show what the demand for the invention might reasonably be expected to be and how far short production in the UK or importation from another Member State of the EU fails to supply that demand.[64] Where the invention is not being worked to the fullest extent that is reasonably practicable whether by manufacture in the UK or by importation from another Member State of the EU, a compulsory licence may be granted.[65] Thus once it is shown that manufacture in the UK is possible and demand is being met by importation from outside the EC, ground (a) is established.[66]

"Patented invention"

The meaning of the words "patented invention" requires some discussion in **17-55** considering the obligation on the patentee to establish working on a commercial scale.[67] In the case of an invention involving a small improvement in a complicated machine, a question arises as to the obligation on the patentee to manufacture. Again, if the patent is for the combination of old parts, there is the question whether the mere assembling in this country of parts made abroad is sufficient to comply with the section. In *Lakes' Patent*,[68] the Comptroller said:

"As a general rule a patentee ought not to be called upon to manufacture any mechanism or machine which he has not specifically described and claimed in his specification ... There may be, of course, cases in which it is impossible to sever the various elements claimed in combination, and in such cases different considerations may arise. If, however, the general principle stated is correct, the following general results would seem to follow, viz. if the patentee has claimed a wholly new machine or mechanism, he must manufacture that in this country or run the risk of coming within the provisions of the section ... If he claims a new improvement in a well-known machine, he must manufacture the improvement, and not necessarily the whole machine; but if he claims the improvement in combination with a machine consisting of well-known parts it may be that he must besides manufacturing the improvement put together the whole machine in this country, or at any rate the combination he claims. If his invention merely consists in a new combination of old and well-known elements, it would seem sufficient for him prima facie to put together the whole machine in this country, and it is not necessary for him to manufacture the old and well-known parts which are also possibly the subject-matter of prior patents; but different considerations may again arise where important alterations in the known parts are necessary for the new combination. Each case must, of course, be decided on its merits, and in each case it will have to be determined on a proper construction of the patentee's specification, what the patentee's invention really is, and what are its essential features."[69]

---

[64] *Kamborian's Patent* [1961] R.P.C. 403, 405.
[65] *Gebhardt's Patent* [1992] R.P.C. 1, 18. See also *Extrude Hone Corp's Patent* [1982] R.P.C. 361, at 383; that part of the judgment concerned with the EC Treaty cannot be sustained in the light of the subsequent rulings of the European Court, particularly *EC Commission v United Kingdom* (C-30/90) [1992] E.C.R. I-777; [1992] 2 C.M.L.R. 709; [1993] R.P.C. 283; [1993] F.S.R. 1.
[66] *Therma-Tru Corp's Patent* [1997] R.P.C. 777, applying *Fette's Patent* [1961] R.P.C. 396.
[67] The words "patented invention" are defined in s.130(1) as meaning "... an invention for which a patent is granted."
[68] (1909) 26 R.P.C. 443, 447.
[69] And see *Hill's Patent* (1915) 32 R.P.C. 475; *Wardwell's Patent* (1913) 30 R.P.C. 408; and cf. *Co-operative Union Ltd's Application* (1933) 50 R.P.C. 161.

17-56   In *Smith, Kline & French Laboratories Ltd's (Cimetidine) Patents*,[70] Falconer J said:

> "… it seems to me that the mere formulation in the United Kingdom of cimetidine manufactured in Ireland and imported therefrom does not, as a matter of substance, amount to a commercial working of the patented invention of each of the patents to the fullest extent reasonably practicable in the United Kingdom. The patents contain product and process claims and it seems to me that, even for the formulation claim in each patent commercial working in the United Kingdom to the fullest extent reasonably practicable of the invention so claimed is not obtained with the manufacture of the basic active ingredient in a foreign country."

Manufacture by infringers

17-57   The words "patented invention"[71] are comparable with the words "patented article or process" in s.27 of the 1907 Act. It was held under that section that the words were descriptive of the manufacture itself, and that manufacture by infringers might be relied upon by the patentee.[72] This would appear to be the case under the present law also. However, it is submitted that it would be wrong to refuse a compulsory licence merely because the market was being met by infringers.

Commercial working discontinued

17-58   A patentee cannot resist an application for a compulsory licence merely on the ground that there has at one time been commercial working in this country if such working has been discontinued.[73]

Fullest extent that is reasonably practicable

17-59   Under s.27 of the Patents and Designs Act 1907 an applicant had to show that the patented invention was worked exclusively or mainly abroad, and the patentee had to furnish satisfactory reasons why manufacture to an adequate extent was not carried on in the UK. The cases decided under that section may be of some assistance in construing the words "fullest extent that is reasonably practicable" of the present section.

17-60   In *Hatschek's Patent*,[74] Parker J said:

> "I do not think that any reasons can be satisfactory which do not account for the inadequacy of the extent to which the patented article is manufactured or the patented process is carried on in this country by causes operating irrespective of any abuse of the monopoly granted by the patent. The first thing, therefore, for the patentee to do is, by full disclosure of the manner in which he has exercised his patent rights, to free himself from all suspicion of having done anything to hamper the industry of the United Kingdom."

17-61   The learned judge then dealt with the case of a patentee who had favoured foreign manufacturers to the disadvantage of British ones. Under the present section, although the British and foreign manufacturers may have been treated equally by the patentee, they are, nevertheless, under the obligation to furnish an explanation of the circumstances which have prevented the establishment of commercial

---

[70]   [1990] R.P.C. 203, 224.
[71]   See also the definition of those words in PA 1977 s.130(1).
[72]   See Parker J in *Mercedes Daimler Co's Patents* (1910) 27 R.P.C. 762, at 768.
[73]   *Cathro's Application* (1934) 51 R.P.C. 75, 79.
[74]   [1909] 2 Ch. 68; 26 R.P.C. 228, 241.

manufacture in this country. On this point the further observations of the learned judge[75] are applicable.

"Certainly the fact that persons who were carrying on the industry in this country would make smaller profits than persons carrying it on abroad would, in my opinion, be no satisfactory reason at all. I can conceive cases in which a patentee … may find it impossible to work … in the United Kingdom because of the nature of the invention, or because of local conditions which prevail here but not in other countries, although these cases must, I think, be rare … But it can never, in my opinion, be sufficient for a patentee, defending himself under the section, to prove that he cannot now start an industry with any chance of profit."

The last sentence of the learned judge needs further explanation: he went on to say that the reason for there being no chance of profit might be that the foreign manufacturers had become firmly established in consequence of the patentee having favoured foreign trade at the expense of home trade. It is suggested that, in the absence of circumstances of that kind, the fact that there was no hope of profit, or that a loss was to be expected, would constitute a defence to an application under the present section.[76]   **17-62**

Absence of demand

The proof of absence of any demand for the invention in this country is not itself a sufficient defence. In *Boult's Patent*,[77] the Comptroller said: **17-63**

"The consideration of the adequacy of manufacture in this country does, no doubt, depend to some extent upon the demand existing for the article here or in neutral markets, but it does not follow that, if there is no demand existing, there is no obligation on a patentee to start an industry here. If he does in fact manufacture in foreign countries, and if there is in fact a demand for the article or process abroad, the absence of any demand here does not seem to be a valid excuse. The patentee must, in such cases, make an effort to create a demand here, and the establishment of an industry will in itself help to create in many cases a demand for the article or process in question."

Where, however, the type of engine to which the invention was applicable had been almost superseded, so that it would not have been commercially advisable to establish a manufacture of the patented mechanism in this country, and the patentee had merely charged royalties on imported French machines of a special kind, containing the patented mechanism, it was held that he had furnished a sufficiently satisfactory reason to comply with the requirements of the former law.[78] However, it is not: **17-64**

"open to a patentee, who has already filled the bulk of a largely non-recurrent demand for a patented article in this country by importation from abroad and who then, under the stimulus of an application for a compulsory licence, has arranged for a manufacture to be started here, to say that such a manufacture must be considered to be 'adequate and reasonable under all the circumstances' for the purpose in question merely because it is sufficient, or he considers it sufficient, to meet so much of the demand as has remained unsupplied from abroad."[79]

The Comptroller will not usually consider whether the demand would be increased if a lower price were charged; but if the price asked for articles made in   **17-65**

---

75 [1909] 26 R.P.C. 228, 243.
76 See also *Boult's Patent* (1909) 26 R.P.C. 383, at 387; *Kent's Patent* (1909) 26 R.P.C. 666, at 670.
77 (1909) 26 R.P.C. 383, 387.
78 *Osborn's Patent* (1909) 26 R.P.C. 819.
79 *Fabricmeter Co Ltd's Application* (1936) 53 R.P.C. 307, 312.

this country is higher than that charged for the imported article, it becomes necessary to inquire whether the price is a bona fide one, or one merely adopted for the
purpose of checking and diminishing the demand for the home-manufactured
article.[80]

Fear of infringement action

17-66   In *Taylor's Patent*[81] the patentee showed that he dared not establish manufacture
in this country for fear of an infringement action under a master patent owned by
the applicants for revocation, who had in fact refused the offer of a licence under
the patent in question. Parker J refused to revoke the patent and held that the
patentee was not bound, as the applicants contended, to apply for a voluntary or a
compulsory licence under the applicants' patent. Had the applicants been able to
show, however, that they had been ready and willing to grant the patentee a licence
on reasonable terms the decision might have been otherwise.

Requisite skill exclusively foreign

17-67   It will not avail the patentee to allege that the special skill and experience necessary to enable the invention to be carried into effect can only be found abroad,[82]
although it may well be that an invention requiring special skill and the establishment of a factory with special tools may need a longer time to develop than one in
which these features are not present. It is incumbent on the patentee to take steps
to import the necessary tools and skilled labour to effect manufacture in this country.
17-68   In *Kent's Patent*[83] the Comptroller said:

> "I shall always decline to accept, as a rule, any argument based on the impossibility of securing an
> efficient manufacture of special machinery in this country,[84] but I think it is natural for a patentee who
> desires to put the best possible machine upon the market to be somewhat over-scrupulous at first in
> obtaining his materials, and supervising the construction of his machine."

Circumstances beyond patentee's control

17-69   Under the Patents and Designs Act 1907, if the patentee could be shown to have
done their best to establish a manufacture in the UK and to have failed for reasons
beyond their control, they were not held to have abused their monopoly. In
Bremer's Patent,[85] Parker J said:

> "In my opinion, the company have throughout used, and still are using, their best endeavours to fulfil
> the obligation arising under the Act of 1907 by establishing in this country an industry in the article,
> the subject of their patent, and they have further proved, to my satisfaction, that their want of suc-
> cess up to the present time has been due to circumstances beyond their own control, and not to the
> manner in which they have exercised the rights conferred upon them by the patent in question. The
> Act of 1907 was never meant to penalise want of success when the patentee has done his best, and I
> cannot, therefore, come to the conclusion that the patent ought to be revoked."

---

[80]   *Kent's Patent* (1909) 26 R.P.C. 666, 670.
[81]   (1912) 29 R.P.C. 296.
[82]   *Johnson's Patent* (1909) 26 R.P.C. 52.
[83]   (1909) 26 R.P.C. 666 at 670.
[84]   See also *Wardwell's Patent* (1913) 30 R.P.C. 408; *A. Hamson & Son (London) Ltd's Application*
       [1958] R.P.C. 88.
[85]   (1909) 26 R.P.C. 449, 465.

But having regard to the changed language of the present section[86] it is doubtful whether this decision would now be followed.   **17-70**

Power to adjourn the application

If the circumstances are such as to justify the Comptroller in affording the   **17-71**
patentee more time to establish manufacture in this country, he may adjourn the
application.[87] Further, having regard to EU case law,[88] it is submitted that the
Comptroller should take the same approach in the case of a patentee who intends
to work the patented invention in a country which is a Member State of the EU and
to meet the demand in the United Kingdom by importation from that country.

(b)   Unreasonable terms and importation—s.48B(1)(b)

"Where the patented invention is a product, that a demand for the product in the United Kingdom—   **17-72**
(i) is not being met on reasonable terms, or (ii) is being met to a substantial extent by importation
from a country which is not a member State."

"A demand" and "reasonable terms"

The meaning of these terms has already been discussed in the context of   **17-73**
s.48A(1)(a)—see para.17-36, et seq.

Importation

With the rapid growth of international trade and the tendency of large companies   **17-74**
to centralise manufacture in a particular country, it is likely that there will be an
increasing tendency for the demand for many patented products to be met solely
by importation.

Where the importation is from outside the EU it is submitted that, subject to ques-   **17-75**
tions of discretion,[89] a compulsory licence should be granted to anybody willing to
set up manufacture in this country.[90] There may be cases where there is some good
reason (other than economics) for manufacture abroad but this will be rare and
generally speaking if it can be shown the patentee is meeting the demand by
importation from outside the EU a compulsory licence should be ordered. Such an
approach would be consistent with s.50(1)(a). See also the older cases set out at
paras 17–59 to 17–62. If the invention is actually being adequately worked in this
country, it is not necessarily a ground for granting a compulsory licence under this
head that certain specialised applications of the invention are not being met by
manufacture here.[91]

---

[86] PA 1977 s.48B(1)(a).
[87] PA 1977 s.48B(2). See also *Therma-Tru Corp's Patent* [1997] R.P.C. 777, at 797–798.
[88] See para.17–05.
[89] In *Therma-Tru Corp's Patent* [1997] R.P.C. 777, the licence was refused on grounds of discretion
      notwithstanding that the demand was being met by importation from outside the EC although
      manufacture in the UK was possible.
[90] The licence would also permit importation from the EC. See *Allen & Hanburys Ltd v Generics (UK)
      Ltd* [1988] E.C.R. 1245; [1988] 1 C.M.L.R. 701; [1988] F.S.R. 312.
[91] *Cathro's Application* (1934) 51 R.P.C. 75, 81.

(c)   Working prevented by importation—s.48B(1)(c)

17-76   *"Where the patented invention is capable of being commercially worked in the United Kingdom, that it is being prevented or hindered from being so worked—*

> (i)   *where the invention is a product, by the importation of the product from a country which is not a member State,*
> (ii)   *where the invention is a process, by the importation from such a country of a product obtained directly by means of the process or to which the process has been applied."*

Scope of s.48B(1)(c)(ii)

17-77   Apart from the fact that s.48B(1)(c)(ii) clearly extends to importation of a product made by a patented process, it is not easy to envisage a likely commercial situation to which this subsection would apply but s.48B(1)(b)(ii) would not.

(d)   Refusal to grant licences on reasonable terms—s.48B(1)(d)

17-78   *"That by reason of the refusal of the proprietor of the patent to grant a licence or licences on reasonable terms—*

> (i)   *a market for the export of any patented product made in the United Kingdom is not being supplied; or*
> (ii)   *the working or efficient working in the United Kingdom of any other patented invention which makes a substantial contribution to the art is prevented or hindered; or*
> (iii) *the establishment or development of commercial or industrial activities in the United Kingdom is unfairly prejudiced."*

Relief available under s.48B(1)(d)(i)

17-79   No order for endorsement of the patent "licences of right" is to be made on ground (i) (above) and any licence granted on that ground may restrict the countries in which the patented article may be sold or used by the licensee.[92]

Reciprocal licences

17-80   No order is to be made on ground (ii) (above) unless the proprietor of the patent for the other invention is willing to grant a reciprocal licence on reasonable terms.[93]

"Refusal of the proprietor"

17-81   The nature of refusal has already been considered in the context of refusal by a WTO proprietor under s.48A(1)(b)—see para.17-42.

"Reasonable terms"

17-82   The meaning of "reasonable terms" has already been discussed in the context of s.48A(1)(a) and (b)—see paras 17-37 to 17-39 and 17-43 to 17-49.

---

[92]   PA 1977 s.48B(4).
[93]   PA 1977 s.48B(5).

Export market

In *Penn Engineering & Manufacturing Corporation's Patent*,[94] Graham J stated: **17-83**

"In my judgment, particularly at the present time, public interest does demand that exports from this country should be on as large a scale as possible. At the same time it would not be right to deprive the inventor of such reasonable remuneration as he may be able himself to get from his own exploitation of his patent.

If the patentee is already manufacturing in this country and exporting to foreign countries it might well be reasonable for him to ask that the grant of a compulsory licence should be restricted so as to prevent export by the licensee to those countries to which he (the patentee) is already exporting. If however, the patentee is not manufacturing here and does not possess foreign patents in countries in which there is likely to be a market for export from this country, there seems very little, if any, reason to put restrictions on export in a compulsory licence to be granted. Any such restriction will prevent working 'to the fullest extent that is reasonably practicable', and it is, in my judgment, incumbent upon the patentee to ask for and justify such a restriction if he wishes to get it inserted in a compulsory licence order made against him."

"Commercial or industrial activities"

The meaning of "commercial or industrial activities" has already been discussed **17-84**
in the context of s.48A(1)(b)—see para.17-46.

(e) Unreasonable conditions—s.48B(1)(e)

"That by reason of conditions imposed by the proprietor of the patent on the grant of licences under **17-85**
the patent, or on the disposal or use of the patented product or on use of the patented process, the
manufacture, use or disposal of materials not protected by the patent, or the establishment or
development of commercial or industrial activities in the United Kingdom is unfairly prejudiced."

Effect of the section

The section has already been discussed in the context of the grounds for relief **17-86**
against the WTO proprietor—see s.48A(1)(c) and para.17-47, et seq.

Prohibiting compulsory licence by Order in Council

Section 54 of the 1977 Act provides that by Order in Council, the Comptroller **17-87**
may be prevented from granting a compulsory licence under s.48 on the grounds
of the demand being met by importation from non-Member States specified in the
Order. To date no such Order has been made.

E. Relief

The Comptroller's powers

Where the Comptroller is satisfied that one or more of the grounds set out above **17-88**
is satisfied, he may: (a) order the grant of a licence to the applicant, (b) order the
patent to be endorsed "licences of right" (thus enabling any person interested
thereafter to obtain a licence on reasonable terms as of right),[95] or (c) where the ap-

---

[94] [1973] R.P.C. 233, 242.
[95] See para.17-168, et seq.

plicant is a government department, he may order the grant of a licence to the person specified in the application.[96]

17-89   The 1977 Act[97] does not appear to enable the Comptroller to give relief other than in respect of the specific relief requested and it may therefore be advisable in appropriate cases to seek relief in the alternative.

Exceptions

17-90   If the only ground made out is that under s.48A(1)(b)(i) or, in the case of a non-WTO proprietor, s.48B(1)(d)(ii), then relief is conditional on the Comptroller being satisfied that the proprietor of the patent for the other invention is able and willing to grant the proprietor of the patent concerned, and their licensees, a licence under the patent for the other invention on reasonable terms.[98]

17-91   Further, in the case of the non-WTO proprietor, the Comptroller cannot order a patent to be endorsed "licence of right" where the only ground established is that set out in s.48B(1)(d)(i) (export market not being supplied) and any licence granted on that ground may restrict the countries in which the patented article may be sold or used by the licensee.[99]

17-92   In the case of a WTO proprietor, s.48A(3) also prohibits any order or entry under s.48 if the patented invention is in the field of semi-conductor technology.[100]

Licence to applicants' customer

17-93   If the Comptroller is satisfied that conditions imposed by the patentee on the grant of licences or on the disposal or use of the patented product or process unfairly prejudice the manufacture, use or disposal of materials not protected by the patent, he may also order the grant of licences to customers of the applicant.[101]

Amendment of existing licence

17-94   If the applicant is already a licensee, the Comptroller may amend the existing licence or order it to be cancelled and grant a new licence.[102]

Depriving the patentee of their patent rights

17-95   The power to deprive the patentee of any right to work the invention or grant licences and to revoke existing licences has been repealed.[103]

---

[96] PA 1977 s.48(2). For an example of compulsory licences, see *McKechnie Bros Ltd's Application* (1934) 51 R.P.C. 441, 461 and 472; *Cathro's Application* (1934) 51 R.P.C. 75, at 83; and *Zanetti-Streccia's Patent* [1973] R.P.C. 227.
[97] PA 1977 s.48(1) and (2).
[98] PA 1977 ss.48A(4) and 48B(5).
[99] PA 1977 s.48B(4).
[100] See para.17-23.
[101] PA 1977 s.49(1).
[102] PA 1977 s.49(2).
[103] PA 1977 s.49(3) deleted by CDPA 1988 Sch.5 para.13. See also PA 1977 s.48A(6)(a).

Terms of licence

In each case the terms upon which a compulsory licence will be granted will   **17-96**
depend on the particular facts of the case. The nature of the Comptroller's discretion and the manner in which it is to be exercised is discussed above[104] and in the
section dealing with licences of right.[105]

Imports

In *Farmers Marketing & Supply Ltd's Patent*,[106] a licence to manufacture abroad   **17-97**
and import was refused. However, a licence to import has been granted,[107] although
in that case a bar was placed on the licensee to prevent export. The principles applied in these cases are now subject to the TFEU and to the amendments to the 1977
Act made by the 1999 Regulations,[108] and if the country of manufacture from which
importation is to take place is a Member State of the EU, refusal of a licence to
import would today be contrary to the law.[109]

Exports

The export of a patented product or of the product of a patented process is not   **17-98**
specifically stated to be an infringing act in s.60(1)(a) or (c) of the 1977 Act but,
as a practical matter, export would necessarily involve the "keeping" for export of
the products in question and "keeping" does amount to an infringement.[110]
Consequently, a licensee cannot lawfully export patented products or the products
of a patented process without a licence to keep such products for export. Further,
in an appropriate case, the Comptroller may impose an export ban as a term of the
licence.[111]

In the case of a WTO proprietor, the licence must be predominantly for the sup-   **17-99**
ply of the market in the United Kingdom and limited in scope and in duration to
the purpose for which it was granted.[112] Accordingly, any licence to export must be
restricted to that extent.

On the other hand, in the case of a non-WTO proprietor, the Comptroller may   **17-100**
order a licence to include the right to export, and may do so even though the
grounds for granting the licence are not based on an export market not being
supplied.[113] Alternatively, the Comptroller may restrict the scope of that licence, e.g.
the Comptroller may restrict the countries to which the patented products may be
exported.[114]

---

[104] See para.17-24, et seq.
[105] See para.17-182, et seq.
[106] [1966] R.P.C. 546.
[107] *Hoffman-La Roche & Co A.G.'s Patent* [1969] R.P.C. 504 and also [1970] F.S.R. 225.
[108] The Patents and Trade Marks (World Trade Organisation Regulations) 1999 (SI 1999/1899).
[109] *Allen & Hanbury's Ltd v Generics (UK) Ltd* (434/85) [1988] E.C.R. 1245; [1988] 1 C.M.L.R. 701;
[1988] F.S.R. 312.
[110] *Smith, Kline & French Laboratories Ltd's (Cimetidine) Patents* [1990] R.P.C. 203, 225–226
(Falconer J).
[111] *American Cyanamid Co's (Fenbufen) Patent* [1990] R.P.C. 309, 328; [1991] R.P.C. 409. *Research
Corporation's (Carboplatin) Patent* [1990] R.P.C. 663, 702.
[112] See PA 1977 s.48A(6)(c).
[113] *Penn Engineering Patent* [1973] R.P.C. 233.
[114] *Smith, Kline & French Laboratories Ltd's (Cimetidine) Patents* (above); see also PA 1977 s.48B(4).

Financial terms

17-101   Guidance as to the financial terms can be obtained from the many licence of right decisions discussed at paras 17-188 to 17-198. In respect of mechanical inventions, royalty rates for compulsory licences are often in the range 5–7 per cent,[115] though there can be no hard and fast rules as each case will depend on its own facts.

Sub-licensing

17-102   Although a compulsory licence can permit sub-licensing, such cases are exceptions.[116] In any event the person who it is intended should be responsible for manufacture and sale should be a party to the application.[117]

Assignment

17-103   In the case of a WTO proprietor, s.48A(6)(b) of the 1977 Act imposes a specific prohibition on the assignment of a licence granted under s.48, except to a person to whom there is also assigned the part of the enterprise that enjoys the use of the patented invention, or the part of the goodwill that belongs to that part. It is submitted that, even in the case of a non-WTO proprietor, the Comptroller would not normally permit assignment of a compulsory licence.

Exclusivity

17-104   The Comptroller may not grant an exclusive licence in exercise of his powers under s.48 of the 1977 Act.[118]

Effective date of licence

17-105   The Comptroller has no power to antedate the grant of a licence,[119] and the licence will run from the decision or order of the Comptroller which settles all the terms of the licence.[120]

Revocation of order or cancellation of entry

17-106   The 1977 Act and the 1999 Regulations contain provisions whereby an order or entry made under s.48 may in certain circumstances be cancelled. Thus, unlike the non-WTO proprietor, the WTO proprietor may recover his full monopoly in certain circumstances.

[115] *Kalle & Co A.G.'s Patent* [1966] F.S.R. 112; *Penn Engineering Corp's Patent* [1973] R.P.C. 233; *Extrude Hone Corp's Patent* [1982] R.P.C. 361.
[116] *Therma-Tru Corp's Patent* [1997] R.P.C. 777, applying *Allen & Hanbury Ltd's (Salbutamol) Patent* [1987] R.P.C. 327. See also *Hilti A.G.'s Patent* [1987] F.S.R. 594 and *Research Corporation's (Carboplatin) Patent* [1990] R.P.C. 663, 702.
[117] *Therma-Tru Corp's Patent* [1997] R.P.C. 777.
[118] *Allen & Hanburys Ltd v Generics (UK) Ltd* [1986] R.P.C. 203, HL. See also s.48A(6)(a) in the case of a WTO proprietor.
[119] *Hoffman-La Roche & Co A.G. v Inter-Continental Pharmaceuticals Ltd* [1965] R.P.C. 226.
[120] *Geigy S.A.'s Patent* [1966] R.P.C. 250; *Allen & Hanburys Ltd v Generics (UK) Ltd* [1986] R.P.C. 203, HL.

Change of circumstances

Under s.52(2)(a) of the 1977 Act, where an order or entry has been made under **17-107**
s.48 in respect of a patent whose proprietor is a WTO proprietor, the proprietor or
any other person may apply to the Comptroller to have the order revoked or entry
cancelled on the grounds that the circumstances which led to the making of the
order or entry have ceased to exist and are unlikely to recur. Section 52(2)(b)
provides that any person wishing to oppose such an application may do so by notice
to the Comptroller.

If the Comptroller is satisfied that the circumstances have changed, he is not **17-108**
obliged to revoke the order or cancel the entry but he may do so.[121] He may also
terminate any licence granted to a person in pursuance of the order or entry subject
to such terms and conditions as he thinks necessary for the protection of the
legitimate interests of that person.[122]

The procedure upon an application under s.52(2)(a) to cancel an order or entry **17-109**
made under s.48 is governed by Pt 7 of the Patents Rules 2007[123] and, in general
terms, is similar to that described below.[124]

Orders or entries made or licences granted prior to the 1999 Regulations

Under Reg.8(1) of the 1999 Regulations, a WTO proprietor of a patent in respect **17-110**
of which an order or entry has been made under s.48 before the relevant date[125] may
apply to the Comptroller: (a) to have the order revoked or entry cancelled on the
grounds that the grounds on which the order or entry was made are not those set
out in s.48A(1),[126] or (b) to have the conditions subject to which any licence was
granted before that date in pursuance of the order or entry modified on the grounds
that the licence does not satisfy the requirement set out in s.48A(6).[127] Regulation
8(4) provides for opposition by any person.

If the application is made out, the Comptroller may revoke the order or cancel **17-111**
the entry.[128] He may also terminate any licence granted to a person in pursuance of
the order or entry subject to such terms and conditions as he thinks necessary for
the protection of the legitimate interests of that person.[129] On an application to
modify the conditions of a licence, he may modify those conditions but in so doing he must have regard to the need to protect the legitimate interests of the
licensee.[130]

---

[121] PA 1977 s.52(3)(a).
[122] PA 1977 s.52(3)(b).
[123] Patents Rules 2007 r.73(1)(a) and Sch.3 Pt 1.
[124] See para.17-112, et seq.
[125] The relevant date is the commencement date (29 July 1999) or, if later, the date on which the proprietor of the patent became a WTO proprietor—see Reg.8(8).
[126] See paras 17-34 to 17-51.
[127] See para.17-26.
[128] Reg.8(2)(a).
[129] Reg.8(2)(b).
[130] Reg.8(3).

F. Practice

The application

17-112   The procedure to be followed in respect of an application under s.48 is laid down in rules contained in Pt 7 of the Patents Rules 2007. The application is started by filing in duplicate Patents Form 2 and a statement of grounds which must include a concise statement of the facts on which the claimant relies and specify the relief that they seek.[131] Where appropriate, the statement must also include the period or terms of the licence which the claimant believes are reasonable.[132] The statement must be verified by a statement of truth but otherwise it is not necessary to file evidence verifying the statement with the application.[133]

17-113   The Comptroller must then notify the proprietor of the patent that proceedings have been commenced and, in addition, he may notify any persons who appear to him to be likely to have an interest in the case.[134] The notification must include the relevant form and the statement of grounds.[135] The application is also advertised in the *Official Journal*.[136]

Opposition

17-114   The patent proprietor, or any other person desiring to oppose the application, must file a counter-statement in duplicate before the end of the period of four weeks beginning immediately after the date of the advertisement.[137] If a person who was notified of the application by the Comptroller fails to file a counter-statement, the Comptroller will treat him as supporting the claimant's case.[138] Accordingly the patent proprietor should file a counterstatement even if they only wish to dispute the terms of the licence.[139] The counter-statement must state which of the allegations in the statement of grounds the defendant (that is, the opponent) admits, which they deny (in which case they must also state their reasons for doing so and any positive case of their own) and which they are unable to admit or deny but require to be proved.[140] Failure to deal with an allegation will be taken as an admission.[141] The counter-statement must also be verified by a statement of truth and be accompanied by a copy of any document to which it refers.[142]

17-115   When a counter-statement is filed, the Comptroller must as soon as practicable send it to the claimant and specify the period within which they must file Patents Form 4 and the periods within which evidence may be filed by the claimant and the

---

[131] Patents Rules 2007 rr.76(1) and 76(4)(a)–(d).

[132] Patents Rules 2007 r.76(4)(c).

[133] Patents Rules 2007 r.76(4)(f). See also r.87(5). Cf. Patent Rules 1995 r.68.

[134] Patents Rules 2007 rr.77(1) and (2).

[135] Patents Rules 2007 r.77(5).

[136] Patents Rules 2007 r.75 and Sch.3 Pt 3. The application may be opposed under s.52(1).

[137] PA 1977 s.52(1); Patents Rules 2007 r.77(8) and Sch.3 Pt 3. This period cannot be extended, see r.108(1) and Sch.4 Pt 1.

[138] Patents Rules 2007 r.77(9).

[139] They may, however, be permitted to make written submissions for consideration by the Comptroller, see *Ultimatte Corp's Patent* (BL O/1/84).

[140] Patents Rules 2007 rr.78(1)(a)–(c) and 78(2).

[141] Patents Rules 2007 r.78(3).

[142] Patents Rules 2007 rr.78(1)(d) and 79(1).

defendant.[143] If the claimant wishes to continue the proceedings following the receipt of the counter-statement, they must file Patents Form 4 within the specified period; if they fail to file the form within that period, they will be deemed to have filed a request to withdraw the proceedings.[144] The Comptroller may direct evidence to be filed simultaneously or sequentially depending on the circumstances of the case; usually six weeks is allowed for each round of evidence.[145] Evidence is by witness statement unless the Comptroller or any enactment requires otherwise.[146]

The hearing and the decision

Following completion of the evidence stage, the Comptroller must give the parties an opportunity to be heard[147] and, if a party requests to be heard, the Comptroller must send to the parties notice of a date for the hearing.[148] A hearing will be in public unless a party applies for it to be in private.[149] The Comptroller will order the hearing to be in private where he considers there is good reason for it to be held in private and all the parties to the proceedings have had an opportunity to be heard on the matter.[150] When the Comptroller has decided the matter, he must notify all the parties of his decision, including his reasons for making the decision.[151]   **17-116**

Costs

The Comptroller may also award costs. The Comptroller's Practice with regard to costs is set out at para.5.35, et seq. of the Patent Hearings Manual.[152] Costs are normally awarded by reference to a scale.   **17-117**

The Comptroller's case management powers

The Comptroller has wide case management powers to control the proceedings before him.[153] Thus, for example, he may limit the issues on which he requires evidence or the nature of the evidence.[154] He may also stay the proceedings where appropriate[155] or strike out a case unless supported by sufficient evidence to make out a prima facie case.[156] However, if an applicant puts in sufficient evidence to make their case, it is immaterial that the evidence in question is not the best   **17-118**

---

143 Patents Rules 2007 rr.80(1).
144 Patents Rules 2007 rr.80(1A) and 81A.
145 *UKIPO Litigation Manual* (January 2015 edn), para.1.41, et seq.
146 Patents Rules 2007 r.87(3).
147 Patents Rules 2007 r.80(4).
148 Patents Rules 2007 r.80(5).
149 Patents Rules 2007 r.84(1)(2).
150 Patents Rules 2007 r.84(3).
151 Patents Rules 2007 r.80(6).
152 Published 20 June 2014.
153 Patents Rules 2007 rr.82 and 83.
154 Patents Rules 2007 r.82(2).
155 Patents Rules 2007 r.82(1)(f). See also, *Halcon S.D. Group Inc's Patents* [1989] R.P.C. 1.
156 Patents Rules 2007 r.83. See also, *Richco Plastic Co's Patent* [1989] R.P.C. 722; *Rhône-Poulenc S.A.'s (Ketoprofen) Patent* [1989] R.P.C. 570; and *Co-operative Union Ltd's Applications* (1933) 50 R.P.C. 161.

evidence.[157] The Comptroller may also order security for costs or expenses in an appropriate case[158] or order the discovery and production of documents.[159]

17-119   Rule 74 sets out "the overriding objective" applicable in proceedings before the Comptroller which is similar to that applicable under the Civil Procedure Rules. The Comptroller is required to give effect to the overriding objective when he exercises any power given to him by Pt 7 of the 2007 Rules or interprets any rule in that Part.[160] The parties are also required to help the Comptroller to further the overriding objective.[161]

Reference to arbitrator

17-120   If the parties consent, or the proceedings require a "prolonged examination of documents or any scientific or local investigation", the Comptroller may refer the whole proceedings, or any issue of fact, to an arbitrator.[162] Where the whole proceedings are so referred, unless the parties otherwise agree before the award of the arbitrator or arbiter is made, an appeal lies from the award to the court.[163]

Appeal

17-121   An appeal from any order of the Comptroller under the compulsory licence provisions of the 1977 Act lies to the Patents Court.[164] The provisions relating to appeal, and any further appeal to the Court of Appeal, are the same as those applicable in the case of licences of right and are discussed in paras 17-206 to 17-207.

17-122   Where a patentee did not oppose an application, they were allowed to appeal against the decision granting a compulsory licence.[165] However, it is submitted that this decision may now be of doubtful authority in view of the terms of r.77(9) of the Patents Rules 2007 (whereby a patent proprietor who fails to file a counter-statement is to be treated as supporting the claimant's case) and of the increasing importance attached by the courts to the need for a party to put forward their entire case at the proper time or not at all.

17-123   Where an appeal is brought, the Attorney General has the right to appear and be heard.[166]

Further evidence on appeal

17-124   If more recent financial accounts become available between the dates of the hearing in the Patent Office and the hearing of the appeal, such accounts will be admit-

---

[157] *Monsanto's CCP Patent* [1990] F.S.R. 93, following *Fette's Patent* [1961] R.P.C. 396.
[158] Patents Rules 2007 r.85.
[159] Patent Rule 2007 r.86(b).
[160] Patents Rules 2007 r.74(3).
[161] Patents Rules 2007 r.74(4).
[162] PA 1977 s.52(5).
[163] PA 1977 s.52(6).
[164] PA 1977 s.97.
[165] *Zanetti Streccia's Patent* [1973] R.P.C. 227.
[166] PA 1977 s.52(4).

ted on appeal together with evidence to explain the financial position apparently revealed by them.[167]

G. The Competition and Markets Authority

Powers following merger or market investigations

Following a merger or market investigation under any of the provisions of the **17-125** Enterprise Act 2002 listed in s.50A(1)(a) of the 1977 Act,[168] the Competition and Markets Authority[169] or, as the case may be, the Secretary of State may apply to the Comptroller to take action under s.50A of the 1977 Act for the purpose of remedying, mitigating or preventing a matter which cannot be dealt with under the enactment concerned where that matter involves conditions in licences granted under a patent restricting the use of the invention by the licensee or the right of the proprietor to grant other licences or a refusal by the proprietor of a patent to grant licences on reasonable terms.[170]

Before making such an application, the Competition and Markets Authority or, **17-126** as the case may be, the Secretary of State, must publish a notice describing the nature of the proposed application and must consider any representations which may be made within 30 days of such publication by persons who appear to be affected.[171]

On an application under s.50A of the 1977 Act, the Comptroller may by order **17-127** cancel or modify any condition in a licence of the kind referred to above and/or may make an entry in the register to the effect that licences under the patent are to be available as of right.[172]

Powers following a report of the Competition and Markets Authority

Where a report of the Competition and Markets Authority has been laid before **17-128** Parliament containing conclusions to the effect that a person was engaged in an anticompetitive practice which operated or may be expected to operate against the public interest or is pursuing a course of conduct which operates against the public interest,[173] the Minister to whom the report has been made[174] may apply to the Comptroller to take action under s.51 of the 1977 Act.

As under s.50A, before making such an application the Minister must publish a **17-129** notice describing the nature of the proposed application and must consider any representations which may be made within 30 days of such publication by persons who appear to be affected.[175]

If, on an application made under s.51, it appears to the Comptroller that the mat- **17-130**

---

[167] *Therma-Tru Corp's Patent* [1997] R.P.C. 777.
[168] As amended by the Enterprise Act 2002 s.278 and Sch.25 para.8(2).
[169] Since 1 April 12015 the Competition and Markets Authority has taken over the functions of the Competition Commission.
[170] PA 1977 s.50A(1)–(2).
[171] PA 1977 s.50A(3).
[172] PA 1977 s.50A(4).
[173] See PA 1977 s.51(1), as amended by CDPA 1988 Sch.5 para.14 and by Enterprise Act 2002 s.278, Sch.25 para.8(3), and Sch.26.
[174] PA 1977 s.51(1) and (4).
[175] PA 1977 s.51(2).

ters specified in the Commission's report as being against the public interest include:

(a) conditions in licences granted under a patent by its proprietor restricting the use of the invention by the licensee or the right of the proprietor to grant other licences; or

(b) a refusal by the proprietor of a patent to grant licences on reasonable terms;

then the Comptroller may by order cancel or modify any such condition or may instead or in addition, make an entry in the Register to the effect that licences under the patent are to be available as of right.[176]

2. COMPULSORY LICENCES UNDER EU LAW

A. Introduction

17-131   It is not possible to draw a clear line between compulsory licences under national law and compulsory licences under EU law because the reality of EU law is that it impacts upon the national system of compulsory licences as explained, for example, at para.17-05. Indeed all of the amendments made to the UK national system of compulsory licences by the Patents and Trade Marks (World Trade Organisation) Regulations 1999 (see para.17-06) could fairly be said to be required by EU law.[177] Nevertheless, there are two instances where the EU has legislated to create its own distinct grounds for the grant of compulsory licences, namely:

(1) art.12 of Directive 98/44/EC of the European Parliament and of the Council on the legal protection of biotechnological inventions (the Biotech Directive),[178] and

(2) Reg.(EC) 816/2006 of the European Parliament and of the Council of 17 May 2006 on compulsory licensing of patents relating to the manufacture of pharmaceutical products for export to countries with public health problems.[179]

B. Article 12 of Directive 98/44/EC (the "Biotech Directive")

The object of the Directive

17-132   In broad terms the object of art.12 of Directive 98/44/EC (the "Biotech Directive") is to enable the grant of non-exclusive compulsory licences and cross-licences where the exploitation of a plant variety right would infringe a patent and vice versa. In that respect art.12(1) and (2) of the Directive provide:

"1.   Where a breeder cannot acquire or exploit a plant variety right without infringing a prior patent, he may apply for a compulsory licence for non-exclusive use of the invention protected by the patent inasmuch as the licence is necessary for the exploitation of the plant variety to be protected, subject to payment of an appropriate royalty. Member States shall provide that, where such a licence is granted, the holder of the patent will be entitled to a cross-licence on reasonable terms to use the protected variety.

---

176 PA 1977 s.51(3).
177 The TRIPS Agreement was signed by the UK and by the Council of the EU. It has also been ratified by the Council and, under UK national law, it is to be regarded as a Community Treaty as defined in s.1(2) of the European Communities Act 1972. See para.1–72, et seq.
178 [1998] O.J. L213.
179 [2006] O.J. L157.

2. Where the holder of a patent concerning a biotechnological invention cannot exploit it without infringing a prior plant variety right, he may apply for a compulsory licence for non-exclusive use of the plant variety protected by that right, subject to payment of an appropriate royalty. Member States shall provide that, where such a licence is granted, the holder of the variety right will be entitled to a cross-licence on reasonable terms to use the protected invention."

The Patents and Plant Variety Rights (Compulsory Licensing) Regulations 2002

The Patents and Plant Variety Rights (Compulsory Licensing) Regulations 2002[180] implement art.12 of the Biotech Directive in the United Kingdom. The UK Regulations came into force on 1 March 2002.   **17-133**

What the applicant must show

In order to secure a compulsory licence in respect of a patent under the Regulations, the applicant must show[181]:   **17-134**

(a) that they cannot acquire or exploit plant breeders' rights or a Community plant variety right without infringing a prior patent;

(b) that they have applied unsuccessfully to the proprietor of the prior patent for a licence to use that patent to acquire or exploit plant breeders' rights or a Community plant variety right; and

(c) the new plant variety, in which the applicant wishes to acquire or exploit the plant breeders' rights or Community plant variety right, constitutes significant technical progress of considerable economic interest in relation to the invention protected by the patent.

Opposition to grant and terms of licence

The proprietor (or any other person wishing to oppose) may give notice of opposition.[182] However, if the Comptroller General of Patents and the Controller of Plant Variety Rights are satisfied of the above three matters, they must order the grant to the applicant of a licence to use the invention protected by the patent insofar as the licence is necessary for the exploitation of the new plant variety on the conditions set out in Reg.7 and on such other terms as they think fit.[183]   **17-135**

Regulation 7(1)(a) provides that the compulsory patent licence must not be exclusive. Further, Reg.7(1)(b) provides that the proprietor of the patent is entitled to an appropriate royalty. Under Reg.7(1)(c), the proprietor may also request a cross-licence on reasonable terms in respect of plant breeders' rights or a Community plant variety right where the applicant has been granted, or has yet to acquire, such rights or right in the new variety.[184]   **17-136**

---

[180] SI 2002/247, as amended by Reg.3 of the Patents (Compulsory Licensing and Supplementary Protection Certificates) Regulations 2007 (SI 2007/3293).

[181] The Patents and Plant Variety Rights (Compulsory Licensing) Regulations 2002 Regs 3 and 6. See also the Biotech Directive art.12(1) (3) and paras (52) and (53) of the pre-amble.

[182] The Patents and Plant Variety Rights (Compulsory Licensing) Regulations 2002 Reg.5(1).

[183] The Patents and Plant Variety Rights (Compulsory Licensing) Regulations 2002 Reg.6.

[184] See also the Patents and Plant Variety Rights (Compulsory Licensing) Regulations 2002 Reg.7(2)–(4).

Variation and revocation

17-137   The Regulations also provide for variation of any order for grant of a compulsory licence or cross licence[185] and for revocation of such an order if the circumstances which led to it have ceased to exist or are unlikely to recur.[186]

Compulsory cross licences in respect of patents

17-138   A compulsory cross licence in respect of a patent may be ordered on reasonable terms where a compulsory licence has been granted by the Controller of Plant Variety Rights in respect of plant breeders' rights[187] or by the Community Plant Variety Office in respect of a Plant Variety Right.[188] Regulation 16 makes provision for the variation or revocation of any such compulsory licence.

Application of the 1977 Act

17-139   The provisions of the 1977 Act in respect of proceedings before the Comptroller, decisions of the Comptroller (including orders for grant of compulsory licences), appeals and other matters, as and to the extent that they relate to compulsory licences under s.48(1) of the Act, extend and apply to, and are to be taken as making corresponding provision in the UK in respect of matters related to compulsory patent licences and cross licences ordered to be granted under the Regulations[189] with the exception of the provisions of ss.48, 48A, 48B, 49, 50 and 52.[190]

Practice: Application of the Patent Rules

17-140   The Patent Rules 2007 in respect of applications for the grant and revocation of compulsory licences under s.48(1) of the 1977 Act and proceedings before the Comptroller and other matters in relation to such applications[191] extend and apply to and are to be taken as making corresponding provision in respect of applications for the grant of licences under Reg.3(1) and the variation or revocation of or revocation of compulsory patent licences and cross licences under Regs 7(2), 7(3) and 15(3) and other matters related to or arising under the Regulations.[192]

Appeals

17-141   An appeal lies from a decision of the controllers or Comptroller under the Regulations.[193] Where a decision of the controllers relates to a compulsory patent licence or cross licence under Reg.7(2) or (3) or where a decision of the Comptrol-

---

[185] The Patents and Plant Variety Rights (Compulsory Licensing) Regulations 2002 Reg.8.
[186] The Patents and Plant Variety Rights (Compulsory Licensing) Regulations 2002 Reg.9.
[187] The Patents and Plant Variety Rights (Compulsory Licensing) Regulations 2002 Reg.14(2).
[188] The Patents and Plant Variety Rights (Compulsory Licensing) Regulations 2002 Reg.15(3).
[189] The Patents and Plant Variety Rights (Compulsory Licensing) Regulations 2002 Reg.26(1).
[190] The Patents and Plant Variety Rights (Compulsory Licensing) Regulations 2002 Reg.26(2).
[191] See para.17-112, et seq.
[192] The Patents and Plant Variety Rights (Compulsory Licensing) Regulations 2002 Reg.22. The definition of "Patent Rules" in Reg.2(1) was amended by the Patents (Compulsory Licensing and Supplementary Protection Certificates) Regulations 2007 (2007/3293) Reg.3(2)(b).
[193] The Patents and Plant Variety Rights (Compulsory Licensing) Regulations 2002 Reg.17(1).

ler relates to a cross licence under Reg.15(3), an appeal may be brought to the Patents Court.[194]

C. Regulation (EC) 816/2006 (the "Compulsory Licensing Regulation")

The object of the Compulsory Licensing Regulation

The Compulsory Licensing Regulation stems from the TRIPS Agreement and, **17-142** in particular, the Decision of 30 August 2003 of the General Council of the World Trade Organisation on the implementation of para.6 of the Doha Declaration of 14 November 2001.[195] It is intended to be part of wider European and international action to address public health problems faced by least developed countries and other developing countries, and in particular to improve access to affordable medicines which are safe and effective.[196] The Regulation emphasises that, as the compulsory licensing system which it sets up is intended to address public health problems, it should be used in good faith and should not be used by countries to pursue industrial or commercial policy objectives.[197] Thus the Regulation states that it is imperative that products manufactured pursuant to the Regulation reach only those who need them and are not diverted from those for whom they were intended and that consequently any licence should impose clear conditions upon the licensee for that purpose.[198] Likewise the Regulation states that provisions should be made at external borders for customs action to deal with products made and sold for export which a person subsequently attempts to re-import.[199]

The Patents (Compulsory Licensing and Supplementary Protection Certificates) Regulations 2007

The Patents (Compulsory Licensing and Supplementary Protection Certificates) **17-143** Regulations 2007[200] assist in the implementation the Compulsory Licensing Regulation in the United Kingdom by amending the Patents Act 1977 by introducing a new s.128A. However, as the Compulsory Licensing Regulation is directly applicable in all Member States, the UK Regulations do not purport to implement those provisions of the Compulsory Licensing Regulation which are already enforceable in relation to UK patents. Thus the substantive provisions relating to the application and conditions for the grant of an EU compulsory licence are to be found in the Compulsory Licensing Regulation itself, not the UK Regulations.

Scope of the Compulsory Licensing Regulation

Article 1 of the Compulsory Licensing Regulation sets out the scope of the **17-144** Regulation in the following terms:

"This Regulation establishes a procedure for the grant of compulsory licences in relation to patents

---

[194] The Patents and Plant Variety Rights (Compulsory Licensing) Regulations 2002 Reg.17(2).
[195] See para.1–75, et seq. See also, the preamble to the Regulation, paras (1) and (2).
[196] Preamble para.(5).
[197] Preamble para.(6).
[198] Preamble para.(8).
[199] Preamble para.(9). See also arts 13 and 14.
[200] SI 2007/3293.

and supplementary protection certificates concerning the manufacture and sale of pharmaceutical products, when such products are intended for export to eligible importing countries in need of such products in order to address public health problems.

Member States shall grant a compulsory licence to any person making an application in accordance with Article 6 and subject to the conditions set out in Articles 6 to 10."

17-145   The expression "eligible importing countries" is defined by art.4 and it includes: (a) any least developed country appearing as such in the United Nations list, (b) any member of the WTO that has given the requisite notice to the Council of TRIPS of its intention to use the system as an importer in whole or in a limited way, and (c) any non-member of the WTO that satisfies the low-income criteria set out in art.4(b)(c) and has given the requisite notice to the Commission of its intention to use the system as an importer in whole or in a limited way.[201]

17-146   However, any WTO member that has made a declaration to the WTO that it will not use the system as an importing WTO member is not an eligible importing country.

Who may grant a compulsory licence under the Compulsory Licensing Regulation

17-147   Under arts 2(4) and 3 of the Compulsory Licensing Regulation, the "competent authority" for granting compulsory licences under the Regulation is the national authority which has competence for the granting of compulsory licences under national patent law, unless the Member State determines otherwise. Consequently, in the United Kingdom, the competent authority is the Comptroller.

Who may apply?

17-148   Article 6(1) provides that "any person" may submit an application for a compulsory licence under the Regulation to a competent authority in the Member State or states where patents or supplementary protection certificates have effect and cover their intended activities of manufacture and sale for export.

17-149   However, art.6(2) requires that if the person applying is submitting applications to authorities in more than one country for the same product, they must indicate that fact in each application together with the quantities and importing countries concerned.

17-150   Further, art.6(3) provides that the application must set out: (a) the name and contact details of the applicant, (b) the non-proprietary name of the pharmaceutical product or products which the applicant intends to manufacture and sell for export, (c) the amount of product that the applicant seeks to produce, (d) the importing country or countries, (e) where applicable, evidence of prior negotiations with the right holder, and (f) evidence of a specific request from authorised representatives of the importing country or a non-governmental organisation or a UN body or other international health organisation acting with the formal authorisation of the importing country and indicating the quantity of product required.

Notification to the rights holder

17-151   Article 7 provides that the competent authority must notify the rights holder "without delay" of the application and, before the grant of the compulsory licence,

---

[201] And see the additional requirements applicable to non-members of the WTO in art.5.

give them an opportunity to comment on the application and to provide the competent authority with any relevant information regarding the application.

Verification

Article 8 provides that it is the responsibility of the competent authority to verify **17-152** that each importing country cited in the application has given the requisite notice to the WTO or to the Commission, as the case may be, and that the quantity of product cited in the application does not exceed that notified by the importing country to the WTO or to the Commission and that, taking into account other compulsory licences granted elsewhere, the total amount of product authorised to be produced for any importing country does not "significantly" exceed the amount notified by that country to the WTO or to the Commission, as the case may be.

Prior negotiation

Article 9(1) provides that the applicant shall provide evidence to satisfy the **17-153** competent authority that they have made efforts to obtain authorisation from the rights holder and that such efforts have not been successful within a period of 30 days before submitting the application. This requirement is consistent with para.(6) of the pre-amble which states that the Regulation is designed to create a secure legal framework and to discourage litigation.

However, art.9(2) provides that the requirement will not apply in situations of **17-154** national emergency or other circumstances of extreme urgency or in cases of public non-commercial use under art.31(b) of the TRIPS Agreement.

Licence conditions

Article 10 sets out the conditions upon which a compulsory licence will be **17-155** granted. The licence must be non-assignable (except with that part of the enterprise or goodwill which enjoys the licence) and non-exclusive. The amount of product to be manufactured under the licence must not exceed what is necessary to meet the needs of the importing country cited in the application taking into account the amount of product manufactured under other compulsory licences granted elsewhere. The duration of the licence is to be indicated. The licence must be strictly limited to all acts necessary for the purpose of manufacturing the product in question for export and distribution in the country cited in the application. Products made under the licence must be clearly identified through specific labelling or marking as being produced pursuant to the Regulation and, where feasible, the products must be distinguished from those made by the rights holder. The packaging and associated literature must specify clearly that the that the product is exclusively for export to and distribution in the importing country concerned and, before shipment, the licensee must post on a website the quantities supplied and the counties to which they are supplied and the distinguishing features of the product or products concerned. If there is patent protection for the products in the importing country, they shall only be exported if that country has issued a compulsory licence for their import, sale and/or distribution. The competent authority may, at the request of the rights holder, request access to the license's books and records for the sole purpose of checking whether the terms of the licence have been met.

Royalty

17-156   The provisions in respect of the payment of royalty are contained in art.10(9) of the Regulation. The licensee must pay "adequate remuneration" to the rights holder as determined by the competent authority as follows:

    (a) in cases of national emergency or other circumstances of extreme urgency or in cases of public non-commercial use under art.31(b) of the TRIPS Agreement, the remuneration shall be a maximum of 4 per cent of the total price to be paid by the importing country or on its behalf; and

    (b) in all other cases, the remuneration shall be determined taking into account the economic value of the use authorised under the licence to the importing country or countries concerned, as well as humanitarian or non-commercial circumstances relating to the issue of the licence.

17-157   According to para.(15) of the pre-amble, "the simple formula" for setting remuneration is intended to accelerate the process of granting a compulsory licence in cases of national emergency, etc. However, the figure of 4 per cent "could be used as a reference point for deliberations on adequate remuneration in circumstances other than those listed above".

Refusal of application

17-158   Article 11 provides that an application must be refused if any of the conditions set out in arts 6–9 are not met or if the application does not contain the elements necessary to allow the competent authority to grant the licence in accordance with art.10 (see licence conditions above).

17-159   Before refusing an application, the competent authority shall give the applicant an opportunity to rectify the situation and to be heard.

Modification of licence

17-160   Under art.16(4), when notified by the importing country that the amount of pharmaceutical product has become insufficient to meet its needs, the competent authority may, following an application by the licensee, modify the conditions of the licence permitting the manufacture and export of additional quantities of the product to the extent necessary to meet the needs of the importing country concerned.

17-161   In such cases the licensee's application is to be processed in accordance with a simplified and accelerated procedure as described in art.16(4). For example, no further evidence of negotiation with the rights holder will be required, provided that the additional amount requested does not exceed 25 per cent of the amount granted under the original licence.

Termination of licence

17-162   Under art.16(1) a compulsory licence may be terminated by the competent authority in the event of breach by the licensee. In the event of termination, the competent authority must set a reasonable period of time within which the licensee must re-direct any remaining product to eligible importing countries or otherwise dispose of such product as prescribed by the competent authority.

Practice

The procedure for application for an EU compulsory licence and for other ap- **17-163**
plications under the Compulsory Licensing Regulation is governed by Pt 7 of the
Patents Rules 2007.[202]

Appeals

Article 17 provides that appeals against any decision of the competent authority **17-164**
shall be heard by the appropriate body under national law. Section 128A(4) of the
1977 Act applies the provisions contained in the Act relating to legal proceedings
(including appeals) to the Compulsory Licensing Regulation. Accordingly the
provisions for appeals in respect of decisions under the Compulsory Licensing
Regulation, and the practice and procedure on appeal are governed by the UK Act
and are the same as those applicable to decisions in respect of compulsory licences
under national law.

3.   LICENCES OF RIGHT

A.   The Endorsement

Voluntary endorsement

By the provisions of s.46 of the 1977 Act a patentee may voluntarily throw their **17-165**
invention open to anyone who cares to ask for a licence on terms to be agreed with
them or, in default of agreement, on terms to be settled by the Comptroller. In each
case the terms will depend on the relevant facts of that case.[203] The patentee gains
some advantages: they reduce the risk that they may be held at any time to have
abused their monopoly; to some small extent they advertise their invention and give
manufacturers or financiers the knowledge that the invention may be used on
reasonable terms; and by subs.(3)(d) their renewal fees are reduced to a half of what
they would otherwise have been. The application is made on Patents Form 28.[204]
The patentee must satisfy the Comptroller that they are not precluded by contract
from granting licences under the patent.[205] The Comptroller must give notice of the
application to any person registered as having a right or interest in or under the patent[206] but, unlike the 1949 Act,[207] the Comptroller is not required to give any such
person an opportunity to be heard. Doubtless the Comptroller will consider any
observations which any such person may make. After an entry is made in the
register to the effect that licences under the patent are to be available as of right,
the Comptroller must advertise the entry in the *Official Journal*.[208]

Cancellation of endorsement by persons other than the patent proprietor

Any person who claims that the patent proprietor is precluded by a contract from **17-166**
granting licences, in which contract the claimant is interested, may apply under

---

202 See Patents Rules 2007 r.73(1)(a) and Sch.3 Pt 1.
203 See *Cassou's Patent* [1970] F.S.R. 433.
204 Patents Rules 2007 r.43(1).
205 PA 1977 s.46(2).
206 PA 1977 s.46(2).
207 PA 1949 s.35(1).
208 Patents Rules 2007 r.43(2).

s.47(3) for cancellation of the endorsement within a period of two months begin-ning immediately after the date on which the entry was made.[209] The application and the subsequent procedure is governed by Pt 7 of the Patent Rules 2007.[210] The Comptroller must advertise the application[211] and give notice of it to the patentee.[212] Only the patentee may oppose.[213] The patentee's notice of opposition and counter-statement must be filed before the end of the period of four weeks beginning im-mediately after the date of the advertisement.[214] If the Comptroller is satisfied that the patentee is and was so precluded, he must cancel the endorsement and the patentee must then pay within a period specified by the Comptroller a sum equal to the balance of all renewal fees which would have been payable if the endorse-ment had not been made. If that sum is not paid, then the patent ceases to have ef-fect at the expiration of that period.[215]

Cancellation of endorsement by the patent proprietor

17-167   The patentee may apply at any time under s.47(1) for cancellation of the endorse-ment "licences of right" where the endorsement is voluntary and if the balance of renewal fees is paid as though there had been no endorsement. If the Comptroller is satisfied that there is no existing licence or that all licensees agree, the endorse-ment will be cancelled.[216] In that case the rights and liabilities of the patentee after cancellation will be the same as if the endorsement had not been made.[217] However, where a patentee sought to cancel an endorsement after an application for a licence had been made, the cancellation was allowed subject to the grant of the licence for which application had been made.[218] The application under s.47(1) for cancella-tion of the endorsement is made by the proprietor on Patents Form 30[219] and must be advertised.[220] Any person may give notice of opposition before the end of the period of four weeks beginning immediately after the date of the advertisement.[221] The opposition proceedings are started by filing in duplicate Patents Form 15 and a statement of grounds.[222] The Comptroller shall, in considering the application, determine whether the opposition is justified.[223] The 1977 Act does not require that the opponent be a "person interested"[224] but, it is submitted, that the interest of the opponent may be a factor in determining whether his opposition is justified.

---

[209] Patents Rules 2007,r.43(4). This period cannot be extended, see r.108(1) and Sch.4 Pt 1.
[210] Patents Rules 2007 r.73(1)(a) and Sch.3 Pt 1.
[211] Patents Rules 2007 r.75 and Sch.3 Pt 3.
[212] Patents Rules 2007 r.77(1). See also r.73(1)(a) and Sch.3 Pt 1.
[213] PA 1977 s.47(6).
[214] Patents Rules 2007 rr.77(7), (8) and (10). This period cannot be extended, see r.108(1) and Sch.4 Pt 1.
[215] PA 1977 s.47(4).
[216] PA 1977 s.47(2).
[217] PA 1977 s.47(5).
[218] *Cassou's Patent* [1970] F.S.R. 433.
[219] Patents Rules 2007, r.43(3).
[220] Patents Rules 2007 r.75 and Sch.3 Pt 2.
[221] Patents Rules 2007 r.76(2)(b). This period cannot be extended, see r.108(1) and Sch.4 Pt 1.
[222] Patents Rules 2007 rr.76(1) and 76(3)(c). And see r.76(4) for the contents of the statement.
[223] PA 1977 s.47(6).
[224] PA 1977 s.47(6)(a). Cf. PA 1949 s.36(5)(a); *Serengi's Patent* (1938) 55 R.P.C. 228; *Glaverbel's Pat-ent* [1987] R.P.C. 73, [1987] F.S.R. 153.

Endorsement by order of Comptroller

If a case of abuse of monopoly is made out against a patentee under s.48 of the **17-168**
1977 Act, the Comptroller may, as one of the remedies applicable, make an order
throwing the invention open to licences of right.[225] Also, under ss.50A(4) and 51(3)
of the 1977 Act (as amended), the Comptroller has power to make an entry in the
Register to the effect that licences under a patent are to be available as of right in
consequence of a merger and market investigation or a report of the Competition
and Markets Authority.[226]

Statutory endorsement

The 1977 Act extended the term of all 1949 Act patents having at least five years **17-169**
to run as at the appointed day (1 June 1978) to 20 instead of 16 years but all such
patents were to be treated as endorsed "licences of right" for the period of the
extension.[227] All the patents so endorsed have now expired and consequently the
provision is of historical interest only. Most of the cases decided from 1983 onwards
are a consequence of statutory endorsement.

B.   Consequences of Endorsement

Licences of right

Where an entry is made in the Register to the effect that licences are available **17-170**
as of right, any person shall, at any time after the entry is made, be entitled as of
right to a licence under the patent on such terms as may be settled by agreement
or, in default of agreement, by the Comptroller on the application of the proprietor
or the person requiring the licence.[228]

Exchange of licence

After the endorsement "licences of right" has been made, any existing licensee **17-171**
may apply to the Comptroller to exchange their licence for one granted pursuant
to the endorsement.[229]

Remedies for infringement after endorsement

An infringer of a patent endorsed "licences of right" may undertake to accept a **17-172**
licence to be settled by the Comptroller, in which case no injunction will be granted
against them and the damages will be limited to double what the royalties would
have been if the licence had been granted before the earliest infringement.[230] This

---

[225] PA 1977 ss.48(1)(b) and 48(2)(b), as amended.
[226] See para.17–125, et seq.
[227] See PA 1977 s.127 and Sch.1 para.4. Note also the excepted uses in Sch.1 para.4A, as introduced
by CDPA 1988 s.293. Further details of the scheme are set out in the 14th edn of this work at paras
9–45 and 9–46.
[228] PA 1977 s.46(3)(a).
[229] PA 1977 s.46(3)(b).
[230] PA 1977 s.46(3)(c).

restriction on the remedies against an infringer does not apply to infringement by importation from a country which is not a Member State of the EU.[231]

17-173   The undertaking may be given at any time before final order in the proceedings, without any admission of liability,[232] and may be given even if the patent has expired.[233]

Interim injunction

17-174   In resisting an interim injunction, it is not sufficient for a defendant to state that they will apply for a licence of right if they lose at trial; an undertaking to apply is required, although the application need not be made until after judgment.[234] Further, the defendant must show that the undertaking is one which they could reasonably expect to honour, i.e. that they have the money to pay should they lose.[235]

17-175   An interim injunction may be granted in the case of imports from outside the EU notwithstanding that the defendant offers an undertaking to apply for a licence of right and the undertaking is one that the defendant could reasonably be expected to honour.[236]

Renewal fees

17-176   The renewal fee payable in respect of a patent endorsed licences of right is half the fee which would be payable if the entry had not been made.[237]

C.   Settlement of Terms by Comptroller

Date when application can be made

17-177   In the case of a patent endorsed "licences of right" by statute,[238] it was held that an application for a licence of right could be made before the date when the patent was so endorsed but that the licence could not be granted until after that date.[239] Applications in anticipation of a voluntary endorsement or endorsement by order of the Comptroller present practical difficulties because, until such endorsements are actually made, the potential applicants for licences of right will be unaware that they have any right to apply.[240] However, where such practical obstacles can be overcome (e.g. because the proprietor has stated their intention that the patent will be endorsed licences of right from a certain date and there are no existing licensees) it is submitted that the jurisdiction exists for the application to be made prior to the date when the patent is so endorsed. However, the licence may not be granted until

---

[231] See the amendments made to s.46(3)(c) of the 1977 Act by CDPA 1988 s.295 and Sch.5 para.12(2) in consequence of the decision of the *European Court in Allen & Hanburys v Generics (UK) Ltd* (434/85) [1988] E.C.R. 1245; [1988] 1 C.M.L.R. 701; [1988] F.S.R. 312.

[232] PA 1977 s.46(3A), inserted by CDPA 1988 s.295 and Sch.5 para.12(3).

[233] *Ultraframe (UK) Ltd v Eurocell Building Plastics* [2005] R.P.C. 36, CA, at [109] onwards (a design right case).

[234] *Dyrlund Smith A/S v Turberville Smith Ltd* [1998] F.S.R. 403 and 774, CA (a design right case).

[235] *Dyrlund Smith A/S v Turberville Smith Ltd* [1998] F.S.R. 403 and 774, CA (a design right case).

[236] Note the difference in wording with regard to imports from outside the EU between CDPA 1988 s.239(1)(a) (design rights) and PA 1977 s.46(3)(c) (patents).

[237] PA 1977 s.46(3)(d).

[238] See para.17-169.

[239] *Allen & Hanburys Ltd v Generics (UK) Ltd* [1986] R.P.C. 203, 251 and 253, HL.

[240] *Allen & Hanburys Ltd v Generics (UK) Ltd* [1986] R.P.C. 203, 251.

after that date. There is no pre-requisite that the applicant must attempt to reach agreement with the patentee before applying for a licence of right.[241]

Date when licence takes effect

A licence granted by the Comptroller pursuant to the licence of right provisions **17-178** takes effect from the date when terms are settled by the Comptroller, not from the date of application.[242] Terms are settled when the Comptroller gives his final decision or makes his order irrespective of any appeal[243] and the licensee may accept those terms without prejudice to any appeal.[244] Where the royalty is increased on appeal, it will be backdated to the date of the original grant by the Comptroller by requiring a further royalty payment in respect of the increase.[245]

If a licence is granted by the Comptroller pursuant to the licence of right provi- **17-179** sions, the licensee will be entitled to the retrospective benefit of the cap on damages as from the date of the earliest infringement.[246]

Applicant attacking validity

There is jurisdiction to entertain an application for a licence of right under a pat- **17-180** ent, notwithstanding that the applicant is attacking the validity of the patent by way of defence to infringement proceedings.[247] The two courses of action are not inconsistent courses requiring an election.[248] An application for a licence of right does not amount to an admission of validity.[249] The application for a licence may, however, be stayed in an appropriate case but it will not be stayed where the applicant wishes to operate the licence pending the outcome of their invalidity attack.[250]

Non-trading applicant

There is also jurisdiction to entertain an application for a licence of right from a **17-181** non-trading company and application from such a company will not be summarily struck out or stayed.[251] But if as a practical matter the applicant would not be able

---

[241] *Roussel-Uclaf (Clemence & Le Martret's) Patent* [1987] R.P.C. 109; *Rhône-Poulenc S.A.'s (Ketoprofen) Patent* [1989] R.P.C. 570. See also *Stafford Enginering Services Ltd's Licence of Right (Copyright) Appln* [2000] R.P.C. 21, 806.

[242] *Allen & Hanburys Ltd v Generics (UK) Ltd* [1986] R.P.C. 203, 252, HL, overruling *R. v Comptroller-General of Patents, Designs and Trade Marks, ex p. Gist Brocades N.V.* [1985] F.S.R. 379.

[243] *Allen & Hanburys Ltd (Salbutamol) Patent* [1987] R.P.C. 327, CA.

[244] *Allen & Hanburys Ltd (Salbutamol) Patent* [1987] R.P.C. 327, CA.

[245] See Falconer J in *Smith, Kline & French Laboratories Ltd's (Cimetidine) Patents* [1990] R.P.C. 203, 230–234.

[246] See the closing words of s.46(3)(c). See also, *Ultraframe (UK) Ltd v Eurocell Building Plastics* [2005] R.P.C. 36, CA, at [110] (a design right case); *Halcon S.D. Group Inc's Patent* [1989] R.P.C. 1.

[247] *Du Pont (E.I.) (Blades) Patent* [1988] R.P.C. 479.

[248] *Halcom SD Group Inc's Patent* [1989] R.P.C. 1.

[249] *Du Pont (E.I.) (Blades) Patent* [1988] R.P.C. 479; *Halcom SD Group Inc's Patent* [1989] R.P.C. 1

[250] *Du Pont (E.I.) (Blades) Patent* [1988] R.P.C. 479; *Halcon S.D. Group Inc's Patent* [1989] R.P.C. 1.

[251] *Roussel-Uclaf (Clemence & Le Martret's) Patent (No.2)* [1989] R.P.C. 405.

to use the licence of right which they sought, the Comptroller may reject the application as an abuse of the process.[252]

Terms of licence

17-182   The Comptroller's discretion to impose limitations and conditions upon what the licence of right authorises the licensee to do is a wide one and his jurisdiction is not limited to terms as to the amount of royalties and security for their payment.[253] The Comptroller cannot impose upon the licensee any positive obligation to do any of the acts so licensed. Nor can he settle terms which would have the effect of debarring future applications for a similar licence. At least in the case of a non-WTO proprietor these are the only fetters on his jurisdiction to settle terms of licences of right.[254] In the case of a WTO proprietor, the Comptroller's powers are also limited by the provisions of s.48A(6) (see para.17–26).

17-183   Since by s.53(4) of the Act a compulsory endorsement of a patent with the words "licenses of right" has for all purposes the same effect as a voluntary endorsement under s.46, recourse may be had to the grounds on which the Comptroller is empowered to make a compulsory endorsement in order to identify the policy to the achievement of which Parliament intended the Comptroller's exercise of his discretion to be directed.[255] As discussed above,[256] those grounds differ depending on whether the proprietor of the patent is, or is not, a WTO proprietor.

17-184   The previous cases provide guidance as to the limitations and conditions which may be imposed by the Comptroller in the exercise of his discretion. These include: a prohibition on imports[257] (but, under EU law, there can be no prohibition on imports from other Member States of the EU)[258]; quality controls[259]; a clause allowing termination of the licence if the licensee comes under the control of any other company in the field[260] or if the licensee attacks the validity of the patent[261]; and a prohibition on assigning or sub-licensing.[262] All of these cases were decided under the old law, i.e. pre the amendments to the 1977 Act by the 1999 Regulations.

17-185   Under EU law, the Comptroller may not, in settling the terms, discriminate against the patentee who manufactures in another Member State of the EU and imports into the UK.[263] Moreover, in the case of a WTO proprietor, it is clear from the grounds for a compulsory licence set out in s.48A(1) of the 1977 Act,

---

252 *Rhône-Poulenc S.A.'s (Ketoprofen) Patent* [1989] R.P.C. 570.
253 Per Lord Diplock in *Allen & Hanburys Ltd v Generics (UK) Ltd* [1986] R.P.C. 203, at 248, HL.
254 Per Lord Diplock in *Allen & Hanburys Ltd v Generics (UK) Ltd* [1986] R.P.C. 203, at 248, HL.
255 Per Lord Diplock in *Allen & Hanburys Ltd v Generics (UK) Ltd* [1986] R.P.C. 203, at 249, HL.
256 See para.17–24, et seq.
257 *Allen & Hanburys Ltd v Generics (UK) Ltd* [1986] R.P.C. 203, HL.
258 *Allen & Hanburys Ltd v Generics (UK) Ltd* (434/85) [1988] E.C.R. 1245, [1988] 1 C.M.L.R. 701, [1988] F.S.R. 312, ECJ; *Allen & Hanburys Ltd (Salbutamol) Patent* [1987] R.P.C. 327; *Ciba Geigy A.G.'s Patent* [1986] R.P.C. 403; *American Cyanamid Co's (Fenbufen) Patent* [1990] R.P.C. 309, [1991] R.P.C. 409; *Research Corp's (Carboplatin) Patent* [1990] R.P.C. 663; *Smith, Kline & French Laboratories Ltd (Cimetidine) Patents* [1990] R.P.C. 203.
259 Per Lord Diplock in *Allen & Hanburys Ltd v Generics (UK) Ltd* [1986] R.P.C. 203, at 249–250, HL; Cf. *Cabot Safety Corp's Patent* [1992] R.P.C. 39, at 64.
260 *Syntex Corp's Patent* [1986] R.P.C. 585; See also *Smith, Kline & French v Harris* [1992] F.S.R. 110.
261 *Du Pont (E.I.) (Blades) Patent* [1988] R.P.C. 479; *Cabot Safety Corp's Patent* [1992] R.P.C. 39.
262 *Allen & Hanbury Ltd's (Salbutamol) Patent* [1987] R.P.C. 327, CA; Cf. *Cathro's Application* (1934) 51 R.P.C. 75; *Hilti A.G.'s Patent* [1988] R.P.C. 51.
263 *Generics (UK) Ltd v Smith, Kline & French Laboratories Ltd* (C-191/90) [1992] E.C.R. 5335; [1993] 1 C.M.L.R. 89; [1993] R.P.C. 333; [1993] F.S.R. 592, ECJ.

particularly when read against the background of art.27(1) of TRIPs, that the Comptroller may not discriminate against the proprietor who chooses to supply the UK market by importation, rather than by manufacture in the UK.[264] Accordingly, in such cases, the licence should contain the same terms (particularly as to importation from non-EU countries) as it would have done if the patentee had been manufacturing in the UK.

The following clauses have been refused: clauses aimed at preventing passing off **17-186** by the licensee, the proprietor being left to their remedies in tort[265]; a most favoured nation clause[266]; an export ban, other than to countries where parallel patents are in force[267] or where such exports would significantly affect manufacture in the UK[268]; a clause allowing immediate termination of the licence without prior warning for even trivial or accidental breaches[269]; and a clause requiring a patent attribution.[270]

In an appropriate case the Comptroller may order a grant by way of sub-licence **17-187** from an existing licensee with provision for it to become a licence from the patentee if the head licence is terminated.[271] However, generally sub-licensing is not permitted.[272]

Financial terms

Royalties are commonly expressed as a fixed price per unit of product rather than **17-188** as a percentage of the sales price.[273] Royalties based on sales price may be unjust to the patentee because it enables the licensee to reduce the royalty payable by price cuts. Royalties based on a fixed price per unit enables both sides to know where they stand.[274] The price per unit may also be subject to indexing.[275] A bank guarantee may be required to secure payment.[276]

In the case of a non-WTO proprietor, s.50(1)(b) of the 1977 Act provides that **17-189** the person beneficially entitled to the patent "shall receive reasonable remuneration having regard to the nature of the invention". On the other hand, in the case of the WTO proprietor, s.50(1)(b) of the 1977 Act does not apply and instead s.48A(6)(d) provides that the licence shall include conditions "entitling the proprietor … to remuneration adequate in the circumstances of the case, taking into ac-

---

[264] See para.17–05.
[265] *Syntex Corp's Patent* [1986] R.P.C. 585; *Hilti A.G.'s Patent* [1988] R.P.C. 51; *Cabot Safety Corp's Patent* [1992] R.P.C. 39; Cf. *Shiley Inc's Patent* [1988] R.P.C. 97; *Farbwerke Hoechst A.G. (Sturm's) Patent* [1973] R.P.C. 253.
[266] *Allen & Hanbury's Ltd's (Salbutamol) Patent* [1987] R.P.C. 327, per Whitford J.
[267] *Allen & Hanbury's Ltd's (Salbutamol) Patent* [1987] R.P.C. 327, per Whitford J; see also *Smith Kline & French Laboratories Ltd (Cimetidine) Patent* [1990] R.P.C. 203.
[268] *American Cyanamid Co's (Fenbufen) Patent* [1990] R.P.C. 309; [1991] R.P.C. 409.
[269] *American Cyanamid Co's (Fenbufen) Patent* [1990] R.P.C. 309; [1991] R.P.C. 409.
[270] *Cabot Safety Corp's Patent* [1992] R.P.C. 39.
[271] *Research Corp's (Carboplatin) Patents* [1990] R.P.C. 663.
[272] *Allen & Hanbury's Ltd's (Salbutamol) Patent* [1987] R.P.C. 327; *Hilti A.G.'s Patent* [1988] R.P.C. 51; *Therma-Tru Corp's Patent* [1997] R.P.C. 777.
[273] *Syntex Corp's Patent* [1986] R.P.C. 585; *Allen & Hanburys Ltd's (Salbutamol) Patent* [1987] R.P.C. 327, CA; *Smith, Kline & French Laboratories Ltd's (Cimetidine) Patents* [1990] R.P.C. 203, 245 and 259, CA; *Research Corp's (Carboplatin) Patent* [1990] R.P.C. 663; *American Cyanamid Co's (Fenbufen) Patent* [1990] R.P.C. 309, [1991] R.P.C. 409; *Cabots Safety Corp's Patent* [1992] R.P.C. 39.
[274] Per Whitford J in *Allen & Hanbury's Ltd (Salbutamol) Patent* [1987] R.P.C. 327.
[275] *Shiley Inc's Patent* [1988] R.P.C. 97.
[276] *Shiley Inc's Patent* [1988] R.P.C. 97.

count the economic value of the licence". The wording of s.48A(6)(d) reproduces that of art.31(h) of TRIPs. Consequently, although such wording is different to that of s.50(1)(b), it does not necessarily indicate a different approach.

17-190   The effect of s.50(1)(b) is that, in assessing the level of royalty, the Comptroller must consider what a willing licensor and a willing licensee would have agreed upon as a reasonable royalty to be paid for the rights granted to the licensee under the licence of right.[277] The following approaches have been considered in the decided cases:

The "s.41" approach

17-191   Under the s.41 approach,[278] the royalty should cover three elements, namely allowances for the recovery by the patentee of the cost of discovering the product (usually a drug in the decided cases) and establishing its efficiency, for the recoupment to the patentee of the promotional expenses incurred in creating and maintaining the market for it, and a reward for the patentee for their contribution to the art secured by an appropriate measure of profit upon the capital investment they have been constrained to make in the project.[279] On the other hand, the patentee's position as manufacturer is not to be taken into account: the patentee is only entitled to remuneration qua patentee or inventor, not to remuneration qua manufacturer.[280]

17-192   For the purposes of the assessment of the research and development costs, it may be appropriate to treat the patentee and exclusive licensee as one.[281] Research and development do not include formulation work.[282] It is not necessary to reduce the promotion element in the s.41 calculation if part of the market created by the patentee is not available to the licensee because the licensee only pays royalties on the share of the market that they actually obtain.[283] Regardless, the patentee is not entitled to recoup their promotional expenditure, however large.[284] The appropriate measure of profit upon the capital investment may be the profit obtained by the patentee on their actual costs rather than the return on capital normally obtained in the industry.[285]

The "comparables" approach

17-193   Where there are comparable licences negotiated at arm's length, the rate of royalty may provide an appropriate measure of remuneration. However, it is more usual that the "comparables" are not entirely comparable and, although it may still

---

[277] *Allen & Hanburys Ltd's (Salbutamol) Patent* [1987] R.P.C. 327; *Smith, Kline & French Laboratories Ltd's (Cimetidine) Patent* [1990] R.P.C. 203, 236; *American Cyanamid Co's (Fenbufen) Patent* [1991] R.P.C. 409.

[278] So-called because this was the approach adopted in proceedings under the Patents Act 1949 s.41.

[279] *J.R. Geigy SA's Patents* [1964] R.P.C. 391, 411; *Allen & Hanburys Ltd's (Salbutamol) Patent* [1987] R.P.C. 327, 376, CA.

[280] *Allen & Hanburys Ltd's (Salbutamol) Patent* [1987] R.P.C. 327, 378, CA; following *Patchett's Patent* [1967] R.P.C. 237, CA, a case in respect of compensation for Crown user. See also *Shiley Inc's Patent* [1988] R.P.C. 97.

[281] *Research Corporation's (Carboplatin) Patent* [1990] R.P.C. 663.

[282] *Smith, Kline & French Laboratories Ltd's (Cimetidine) Patent* [1990] R.P.C. 203; following *Farbwerke Hoechst (Sturm's) Patent* [1973] R.P.C. 253.

[283] *Smith, Kline & French Laboratories Ltd's (Cimetidine) Patent* [1990] R.P.C. 203, CA; *American Cyanamid Co's (Fenbufen) Patent* [1990] R.P.C. 309; [1991] R.P.C. 409, CA.

[284] *American Cyanamid Co's (Fenbufen) Patent* [1990] R.P.C. 309; [1991] R.P.C. 409.

[285] *Smith, Kline & French Laboratories Ltd's (Cimetidine) Patent* [1990] R.P.C. 203, CA.

be appropriate to take such "comparables" into account, it may be necessary to make adjustments to the rate of royalty because of the differences.[286] What is or is not a comparable and how far it is a comparable is a question of fact.[287] Where the alleged comparability is not demonstrated in evidence, it will not be taken into account.[288] Either party may be required to give discovery of other patent licences.[289]

In cases of conflict between the s.41 approach and the "comparables" approach, **17-194** the latter may be preferred.[290]

The "profits available" approach

The "profits available" approach looks at the profits available to the licensee **17-195** under the licence, and then seeks to apportion those profits as between the patentee and licensee. Thus, using this approach, it is possible to work out an equivalent royalty rate expressed in terms of a fixed price per unit product.

In calculating the profits available to the licensee, issues may arise as to the level **17-196** of the licensee's anticipated profits. Similarly issues may also arise as to how the profits should be apportioned. These are essentially issues of fact to be determined on the evidence.[291] Where price-cutting is likely[292] or where there is no clear evidence to show how the profits should be split,[293] then the profits available approach may cease to be useful. However, if the profits which a licensee can expect to receive are high, then that is a factor which can properly be taken into account when fixing the amount of the patentee's remuneration.[294]

The apportionment of the profits on the basis that the licensee receives a reason- **17-197** able remuneration and the patentee receives the rest has been criticised as contrary to s.50(1)(b) of the 1977 Act in that it makes the licensee's reasonable remuneration the measure of what is an appropriate royalty, instead of the patentee's reasonable remuneration as required by the section.[295] Although, as the cases show, there are other ways of apportioning the profits.[296]

It has been said that the "profits available" approach should be used as a last **17-198** resort.[297] However, where there are no directly comparable licences, it is frequently the case that the Comptroller is faced with little else by way of satisfactory evidence

---

[286] *Allen & Hanbury's Ltd's (Salbutamol) Patent* [1987] R.P.C. 327, 377; *Syntex Corp's Patent* [1986] R.P.C. 585; *American Cyanamid (Fenbufen) Patent* [1990] R.P.C. 309; [1991] R.P.C. 409.

[287] *American Cyanamid (Febufen) Patent* [1990] R.P.C. 309, [1991] R.P.C. 409, 413; see also *Cabot Safety Corp's Patent* [1992] R.P.C. 39.

[288] *Research Corp's (Carboplatin) Patent* [1990] R.P.C. 663.

[289] *Smith, Kline & French Laboratories Ltd's (Cimetidine) Patents* [1988] R.P.C. 148; *Merrell Dow Pharmaceuticals Inc's (Terfenadine) Patent* [1991] R.P.C. 221.

[290] *American Cyanamid Co's (Fenbufen) Patent* [1990] R.P.C. 309, [1991] R.P.C. 409; *Smith, Kline & French Laboratories Ltd's (Cimetidine) Patents* [1990] R.P.C. 203.

[291] *Cabot Safety Corp's Patent* [1992] R.P.C. 39; see also the licence of right cases in other fields, e.g. *E-UK Controls Ltd's Licence of Right (Copyright) Application* [1998] R.P.C. 833, *Sterling Fluid Systems Ltd's Licence of Right (Copyright) Application* [1999] R.P.C. 775, *NIC Instruments Ltd's Licence of Right (Design Right) Application* [2005] R.P.C. 1.

[292] *Research Corp's (Carboplatin) Patent* [1990] R.P.C. 663.

[293] *American Cyanamid Co's (Fenbufen) Patent* [1990] R.P.C. 309; [1991] R.P.C. 409. See also Lloyd LJ in *Smith, Kline & French Laboratories Ltd (Cimetidine) Patent* [1990] R.P.C. 203, at 244.

[294] *Smith,Kline & French Laboratories Ltd's (Cimetidine) Patent* [1990] R.P.C. 203, per Nicholls LJ at 257.

[295] [1990] R.P.C. 203, at 244 per Lloyd LJ. Note that s.50(1)(b) no longer applies in the case of a WTO proprietor. But a similar argument may be made in relation to s.48A(6)(d).

[296] See, for example, *Cabot Safety Corp's Patent* [1992] R.P.C. 39.

[297] *Smith, Kline & French Laboratories Ltd's (Cimetidine) Patent* [1990] R.P.C. 203, per Lloyd LJ, at

upon which to base a decision and, consequently, the profits available approach continues to be widely used.[298]

Prevarication by patentee

17-199   It has been recognised that the value of the endorsement "licence of right" can be significantly reduced if there is disagreement between the parties, and the proceedings for settlement of the licence are lengthy.[299] However, the patentee's delay in licence of right proceedings, even if culpable, is not relevant in settling the royalty rate.[300] Nevertheless, where the delay increases the costs of the proceedings and is such as to amount to an abuse of the process, then costs may be awarded on a compensatory basis and may be ordered to be set against the royalty due from the licensee.[301]

17-200   The General Court has also held that delay in licence of right proceedings may amount to an abuse of a dominant position under art.102 of the Treaty on the Functioning of the European Union (formerly art.86 of the EEC Treaty).[302]

Licensee's right to sue for infringement

17-201   A licensee under a patentee endorsed "licences of right" may, apart from agreement to the contrary, call upon the patentee to take proceedings for infringement and if the patentee does not do so within two months the licensee may institute proceedings in their own name, joining the patentee as a defendant.[303] The patentee is not liable for costs unless they enter an appearance and take part in the proceedings.[304]

D.   Practice

The application

17-202   The procedure for application to the Comptroller under s.46(3) of the 1977 Act for settlement of the terms of a licence of right is governed by Pt 7 of the Patents Rules 2007.[305]

17-203   Where the application is made by a person other than the proprietor of the patent, it is started by filing in duplicate Patents Form 2 and two copies of the draft licence which the applicant seeks.[306] The Comptroller then notifies the proprietor of the application and sends them copies of these documents and, at the same time,

---

244.
[298] *Cabot Safety Corp's Patent* [1992] R.P.C. 39; *Gerber Garment Technology Inc v Lectra Systems Ltd* [1995] R.P.C. 383, 413 (a damages inquiry case where it was necessary to assess a reasonable royalty on the same footing as in the licence of right case, see 412–413).
[299] *Allen & Hanburys Ltd v Generic (UK) Ltd* [1986] R.P.C. 203, 252, HL.
[300] *Cabot Safety Corp's Patent* [1992] R.P.C. 39.
[301] *Stafford Engineering Services Ltd's Licence of Right (Copyright) Appln* [2000] R.P.C. 797.
[302] *Hilti A.G. v EC Commission* (C-53/92P) [1991] E.C.R. II-1439; [1992] 4 C.M.L.R. 16; [1992] F.S.R. 210. Affirmed on appeal [1994] E.C.R. I-667; [1994] 4 C.M.L.R. 614; [1994] F.S.R. 760.
[303] PA 1977 s.46(4).
[304] PA 1977 s.46(5).
[305] Patents Rules 2007 r.73(1)(a) and see Sch.3 Pt 1.
[306] Patents Rules 2007 r.89(1).

specifies a period within which the proprietor may file a statement of grounds.[307] The proprietor must file a statement within the period specified otherwise they will be treated as supporting the applicant's case.[308] Thereafter the proceedings continue as if they had been started under r.76(1) with the proprietor as the claimant and the applicant as the defendant.[309] Thus the applicant is given an opportunity to file a counter statement in response to the proprietor's statement.

Where the application is made by the proprietor of the patent, alternative provisions apply. The application is started by filing in duplicate Patents Form 2 and a statement of grounds.[310] The statement should include, where appropriate, the period or terms of the licence which the proprietor believes are reasonable.[311] The pleadings should provide a clear statement of the facts which are to be relied on and which will be proved by evidence.[312] After the pleadings are filed, the Comptroller may specify the period within which evidence may be filed.[313] The Comptroller has wide case management powers to control the proceedings before him.[314] Discovery may be, and often is, ordered.[315] Frequently licence of right applications will involve the disclosure of confidential information and, as in the case of litigation before the court, the parties should first endeavour to agree the terms for such disclosure but in default of agreement the Comptroller will set the terms.[316] In the public interest, all evidence should be in the public domain and the person seeking confidentiality has the burden of justifying a departure from this principle.[317] No distinction is normally made between employee patent agents and those in private practice.[318]   **17-204**

It is customary in licence of right cases for the Comptroller not to make an award of costs unless one side pursues unreasonable terms or the circumstances of the particular case are sufficiently unusual to warrant a departure from that practice.[319]   **17-205**

Appeal

An appeal from the Comptroller in all matters relating to licences of right lies to the Patents Court.[320] The appeal is governed by CPR Pt 52[321] and, unless the court orders otherwise, it will be limited to a review of the Comptroller's decision.[322] Permission to appeal is not required, but it must be made within 28 days.[323] If an extension of time for appeal is desired, permission must be sought from the Patents   **17-206**

---

[307] Patents Rules 2007 r.89(2),(3) (4).
[308] Patents Rules 2007 r.89(5).
[309] Patents Rules 2007 r.89(6).
[310] Patents Rules 2007 rr.76(1) and 76(3)(b). See also r.76(4) for the contents of the statement.
[311] Patents Rules 2007 r.76(4)(c).
[312] *Roussel-Uclaf (Clemence & Le Martret's) Patent* [1987] R.P.C. 109. See also *Rhône-Poulenc S.A.'s Patent* [1989] R.P.C. 570.
[313] Patents Rules 2007 r.80.
[314] Patent Rules 2007 rr.82 and 83.
[315] *Smith, Kline & French Laboratories (Cimetidine) Patents* [1988] R.P.C. 148. *Merrell Dow Pharmaceuticals Inc's (Terfenadine) Patent* [1991] R.P.C. 221. See also, Patent Rules 2007 r.86(b).
[316] *Schering A.G.'s Patent* [1986] R.P.C. 30.
[317] *Diamond Shamrock Technologies S.A.'s Patent* [1987] R.P.C. 91; *Knutsson's and Björk's Patent* [1996] R.P.C. 461.
[318] *Schering A.G.'s Patent* [1986] R.P.C. 30.
[319] UKIPO Patents Hearings Manual (published 20 June 2014), para 5.39.
[320] PA 1977 s.97(1).
[321] CPR r.63.16.
[322] CPR r.52.11(1).
[323] UKIPO Patents Hearings Manual (published 20 June 2014), para.7.08.

Court as the Comptroller has no such discretion nor can this be agreed between the parties.[324]

17-207   With leave of the Patents Court or of the Court of Appeal, an appeal lies from the Patents Court to the Court of Appeal under s.97(3) of the 1977 Act where the ground of appeal is that the decision of the Patents Court is wrong in law.[325] Although CPR r.52.13 generally requires the permission of the Court of Appeal in the case of a second tier appeal (which permission will not be given unless the criteria set out in r.52.13(2) are met), it was held by the Court of Appeal in *Smith International Inc v Specialised Petroleum Services*[326] that s.55 of the Access to Justice Act 1999—and thus CPR r.52.13—do not apply to appeals under s.97(3) of the Patents Act 1977.

---

[324] UKIPO Patents Hearings Manual (published 20 June 2014), para.7.08.
[325] PA 1977 s.97(3). See also *Smith, Kline & French Laboratories (Cimetidine) Patents* [1990] R.P.C. 203, CA; *American Cyanamid Co's (Fenbufen) Patent* [1990] R.P.C. 309, [1991] R.P.C. 409, CA.
[326] [2005] EWCA Civ 1357; [2006] F.S.R. 25, following *Henry Boot Construction (UK) Ltd v Malmaison Hotel* [2001] QB 388, CA.

CHAPTER 18

FRAND

CONTENTS

1. INTRODUCTION

Many patent holders today have given an undertaking to license some or all or **18-01**
their patents on fair, reasonable and non-discriminatory ("FRAND") terms. Those
patents are usually ones which are or have been declared to be essential to a
standard (so-called standards essential patents or SEPs). The nature and extent of
an obligation to license on FRAND terms, and the consequences of it, can be
important questions relating to patents in certain areas of technology. A FRAND
undertaking can affect the remedies available to a patentee for infringement, such
as the availability of injunctive relief and the measure of damages. Questions about
FRAND can also arise in the context of allegations of breach of contract and of anti-
competitive behaviour contrary to arts 101 and 102 TFEU.

The law and practice relating to FRAND is still very much under development. **18-02**
Although there have been some decisions dealing with some of the questions which
arise, other aspects are yet to be decided by the courts either fully or at all. This
chapter will address the issues raised by focussing on the following topics:

(a) What are FRAND undertakings and how does an obligation to grant them
    arise?
(b) What is the nature and scope of a FRAND obligation?
(c) Settlement of FRAND terms by the court.
(d) What does essential mean?
(e) Competition law.
(f) Consequences of FRAND issues for the management of a trial.
(g) Availability of injunctive relief.
(h) Measure of damages when a patentee has given a FRAND undertaking.

2. WHAT ARE FRAND UNDERTAKINGS AND HOW DOES AN OBLIGATION TO GRANT THEM ARISE?

Before dealing the consequences of a FRAND undertaking, it is helpful to **18-03**
understand why FRAND undertakings are given. Because the majority of the patent litigation relating to FRAND issues has occurred in the cases concerned with

mobile telephony, the focus of this section will be on that technology. Other fields in which these issues have arisen are MP3 players and DVD players/recorders. The principles are applicable to any field in which patentees are required to offer FRAND licences.

18-04   A mobile telephone network is extraordinary complex and is comprised of many pieces of equipment interacting with each other. In order for the different elements in the network to interact, there need to be agreed protocols which govern the network and the communication between those elements. Therefore, networks require a degree of standardisation in order to function at all. A distinct consideration is that, in order to promote competition, it is desirable that the equipment that makes up such a network can be made by multiple manufacturers. Handsets made by manufacturer A must be able to be guaranteed to work with base stations made by manufacturers B and C and with core network equipment from manufacturer D. That way there can be competition between handset manufacturers in the consumer market and also competition between base station manufacturers in the network operator market. There can also be competition between network operators since the rival networks operate in the same way as each other at a technical level. In order for this to be possible, the functionality required of all elements of the overall network has to be standardised. The standards mandate a minimum level of technical functionality for all the equipment. In practice the standards are sometimes called "recommendations" or "technical specifications".

18-05   Technical standards are set by entities called Standards Setting Organisations ("SSOs"). One of the most important SSOs in the context of patent litigation is the European Telecommunications Standard Institute ("ETSI"). ETSI was created in 1988, initially in order to take over the work of standardising the then embryonic Europe-wide digital radio communication system (which became the GSM system) from the "Groupe Spécial Mobile" which had initiated its development. GSM was the first successful digital mobile phone system.

18-06   GSM was referred to as 2G, because it represented the second generation of mobile phone systems, the first generation being analogue systems such as TACS. ETSI has remained a key player in the development of mobile telephony standards after the deployment of GSM. It is a partner in the Third Generation Partnership Project (3GPP), which developed the standards for 3G (UMTS) and 4G (LTE) systems amongst others.

18-07   The major industry players were (and continue to be) represented within the SSOs. Standards are developed within the SSOs by consensus. Generally proposals are made by representatives from one or more companies. These are often in the form of papers known as technical documents or "TDocs". The competing proposals are discussed in working groups which focus on different aspects of the overall system and the final standard agreed upon. The working groups operate in public and the papers making technical proposals are published on the internet. TDocs are often a source of pertinent prior art to SEPs.[1]

18-08   There is an inevitable interaction between standardisation and patent rights. It can arise during the standard setting process itself. A company proposing a solution to a particular issue may well have filed a patent application on that development. However, the adoption of a technical solution that has been protected by a patent could potentially lead to a situation where the industry is held to ransom by the patentee. Conversely, given that one wants the system under development to be able

---

[1]   See, e.g. *Unwired Planet v Huawei* [2015] EWHC 3366 (Pat).

to take advantage of the best technical solutions available, it would be unrealistic and undesirable to try and avoid using patented solutions altogether. In that way the standard setting process benefits from the availability of patents and the economic incentive underpinning the patent system applies just as much in the context of standardisation as it does in other fields. Indeed, it is probable that some patentable inventions will be made during the standardisation process itself. After all, that process consists of some of the most highly skilled engineers in the field focussing on the technical problems which have to be solved in order to make a new system operate successfully. A balance between the aims of standardisation and the aims of the patent system has to be struck.

In order to deal with this situation, SSOs have developed policies for dealing with **18-09** patents and other intellectual property rights (often compendiously referred to as IPRs). ETSI has a policy of requiring its members to reveal the existence of such intellectual property rights or IPRs. The ETSI IRP policy is Annex 6 to the 19 November 2014 edn of the ETSI Rules of Procedure. Paragraph 6 of that policy explains its objectives, which broadly is to balance the needs of standardisation in the field of telecommunications for public use with the rights of the owners of IPRs.

These objectives are achieved by a scheme that involves two essential **18-10** components. First, there is an obligation on ETSI members to inform ETSI of any patent that they believe is or might be essential to a standard. Secondly, there is an obligation on a party declaring a patent to be essential to a standard to offer licences under the patent on FRAND terms. The obligation to declare is set out in para.4 of the ETSI IPR policy (capitalised words being terms defined in the IPR policy):

"4.1 Subject to Clause 4.2 below, each MEMBER shall use its reasonable endeavours, in particular during the development of a STANDARD or TECHNICAL SPECIFICATION where it participates, to inform ETSI of ESSENTIAL IPRs in a timely fashion. In particular, a MEMBER submitting a technical proposal for a STANDARD or TECHNICAL SPECIFICATION shall, on a bona fide basis, draw the attention of ETSI to any of that MEMBER's IPR which might be ESSENTIAL if that proposal is adopted."

The key word in para.4.1 is "essential". This is defined in para.15(6) of the IPR policy as:

"'ESSENTIAL' as applied to IPR means that it is not possible on technical (but not commercial) grounds, taking into account normal technical practice and the state of the art generally available at the time of standardization, to make, sell, lease, otherwise dispose of, repair, use or operate EQUIPMENT or METHODS which comply with a STANDARD without infringing that IPR. For the avoidance of doubt in exceptional cases where a STANDARD can only be implemented by technical solutions, all of which are infringements of IPRs, all such IPRs shall be considered ESSENTIAL."

Thus a patent is "essential" to a standard if it is not possible on technical grounds to comply with the standard without infringing the patent. The meaning of the term "essential" is addressed below.

The requirement for an undertaking to offer licences is contained in para.6.1 of **18-11** the ETSI IPR policy:

"6.1 When an ESSENTIAL IPR relating to a particular STANDARD or TECHNICAL SPECIFICATION is brought to the attention of ETSI, the Director— General of ETSI shall immediately request the owner to give within three months an irrevocable undertaking in writing that it is prepared to grant irrevocable licences on fair, reasonable and non-discriminatory ('FRAND') terms and conditions under such IPR to at least the following extent:
— MANUFACTURE, including the right to make or have made customized components and sub-systems to the licensee's own design for use in MANUFACTURE;
— sell, lease, or otherwise dispose of EQUIPMENT so MANUFACTURED;
— repair, use, or operate EQUIPMENT; and

— use METHODS.

The above undertaking may be made subject to the condition that those who seek licences agree to reciprocate."

18-12 Article 6.1bis of the ETSI IPR Policy makes it clear that the obligation to grant FRAND licences binds the successor in title to the patent. Thus the overall effect of these provisions is that any patentee who declares a patent essential to a technical standard developed by ETSI is required to undertake to offer licences on FRAND terms.

3. WHAT IS THE NATURE AND SCOPE OF A FRAND OBLIGATION?

18-13 An issue that has yet to be judicially determined is the legal status of an ETSI FRAND undertaking. In *Unwired Planet v Huawei*[2] the court referred to an article by Sir Robin Jacob entitled: *"FRAND: A legal analysis"* published in October 2014.[3] In that article, Sir Robin Jacob expressed the view that a party declaring a patent as essential to a particular standard was making a contractual commitment, governed by French law, that could be enforced by third parties. The reason French law is relevant is that the ETSI rules are governed by French law. Although he did not analyse the reasoning that led to this conclusion, in *Unwired Planet v Huawei*, the judge proceeded on the basis that this was correct.

18-14 In the same decision, the court noted that there were three legally relevant contexts in which a patentee's compliance with a FRAND undertaking could be considered. These were:

    (a) compliance with the contractually enforceable obligation to ETSI in the terms of the ETSI declaration and the ETSI IPR policy;

    (b) compliance with competition law; and

    (c) in the context of granting and refusing of injunctions. The judge referred to the concept of whether an offer of a licence was "equitably refusable": that is whether the offer has the necessary characteristics and complied with the patentee's FRAND undertaking such that if a defendant refused it, an injunction would be granted.

18-15 The scope of a patentee's FRAND obligations are generally undecided. To date no determination of FRAND related issues has proceeded to trial in the United Kingdom. However, there have been various interim decisions (mostly strike out applications) where certain relevant issues have been identified and discussed to a greater or lesser extent. The issues that have been identified to date include the following:

---

[2] [2015] EWHC 1029 (Pat), [21].

[3] "FRAND: A legal analysis", October 2014 published as Ch.21 of *IP and Other Things* (London: Bloomsbury, 2015). The paper is available at:
http://is.jrc.ec.europa.eu/pages/ISG/EURIPIDIS/documents/RobinJacob.pdf [Accessed 10 March 2016].

Whether a patentee who has made a FRAND commitment is required to offer individual single patent FRAND licences (i.e. licences limited to a particular patent in a particular territory), or whether they can comply with their FRAND obligations by offering a portfolio licence

Sir Robin Jacob has taken the view that offers of portfolio licences to the patentee's SEPs is acceptable and that the court should not embark on an evaluation of the royalty of just the patents sued upon. In *Unwired Planet v Huawei*,[4] it was argued on a strike out application by the defendant[5] that the wording of the ETSI IPR Policy indicated that there was an obligation to offer single patent licences because the Policy deals with patents individually. The court refused to decide summarily that a patentee must offer individual licences because it found that it was arguable that the key part of the factual matrix against which these terms have to be construed was competition law and policy, which could only be determined at trial.[6] However, in *Vringo v ZTE*,[7] the successful patentee sought to use its success in the English court in relation to one SEP in its portfolio in order to pressure the losing defendant to sign up to its offered licence. The offered licence had been for a worldwide licence of all of the patentee's SEPs. The patentee sought an order that unless the defendant accepted its offered licence, the court ought to grant an injunction. The court refused to make such an order on the basis that it was wrong to force a defendant to take a licence under a global portfolio merely because they have been found to infringe a single patent in the UK, indicating that a patentee who wishes to be able to obtain injunctive relief may need to make a single patent offer. **18-16**

Whether a patentee is permitted to bundle a licence to their SEPs with a licence to their other, non-essential patents

In *Unwired Planet v Huawei*[8] the patentee's offer bundled SEPs and non-SEPs together. The court refused to decide summarily that this did not comply with the patentee's FRAND obligation for this reason and sent the issue for trial. However the judge, agreeing with Sir Robin Jacob, commented that it thought that the answer might well be that an offer that bundles SEPs and non-SEPs together would not comply with a FRAND obligation. The judge went on to say: **18-17**

> "I cannot imagine that the April proposal has the necessary characteristics to mean that if the defendants refused to accept it, an injunction to restrain infringement of any or all five SEPs would be granted. That is because the April proposal bundles SEPs and non-SEPs together. As a result it seems to be very likely to be equitably refusable."[9]

---

4   [2015] EWHC 1029 (Pat), [21].
5   The defendant was seeking to strike out those paragraphs of the patentee's Particulars of Claim asserting that he had made offers of FRAND licences.
6   [2015] EWHC 1029 (Pat), 34]–[45].
7   [2015] EWHC 214 (Pat); [2015] R.P.C. 23, [107]–[109].
8   [2015] EWHC 1029 (Pat), [57]–[59].
9   [2015] EWHC 1029 (Pat), [75].

Whether a patentee is required to offer a licence under SEPs relating to a particular territory

18-18   In *Unwired Planet v Huawei*,[10] a strike out based upon the submission that a licence that was not limited to a particular territory (there the UK) could never be FRAND failed. The court held that that would have to be determined at trial.

Whether a patentee is obliged to offer a licence under all SEPs essential to a particular standard (e.g. 2G, 3G, etc.)

18-19   The strike out application in *Unwired Planet v Huawei*[11] based on this ground failed for the same reason as that in relation to territories.

Whether any FRAND offer made needs to be capable of acceptance (i.e. be a complete licence) or whether a term-sheet of the key terms suffices

18-20   In *Unwired Planet v Huawei*[12] the court refused to decide this summarily and again sent the issue for trial. However, it commented that if a patentee makes proposals which cover the vital terms which a licensor and licensee would wish to know—territorial scope, standards scope and royalty rates—and the putative licensee makes it clear that it was not interested, then it did not see why a patentee should be obliged nevertheless to produce a draft contractual document, capable of being accepted, as there was no point in doing so.

18-21   Importantly, no English Court has yet decided how the payment for a FRAND royalty is to be calculated. Doubtless, as when the court is considering the issue of a reasonable royalty in the context of a damages inquiry, an important factor would be comparable licences.[13] However, other factors such as the importance of the technology to the standard in question, the importance of the standard in question to the products covered by the licence and the availability of alternative technologies will all likely be relevant. The court would also likely hear evidence from licensing experts and those with experience of negotiating FRAND licences as to how royalties are arrived at in practice. In contrast to the UK, courts in other jurisdictions have conducted such assessments. For example, in the US a FRAND royalty was assessed in *Microsoft v Motorola*.[14]

18-22   Another issue that has yet to be determined is whether the patentee merely has to make an offer of one licence that is FRAND in order to comply with their FRAND obligation. For any given patent or portfolio there are likely to be a range of licences that would comply with the FRAND undertaking. Does a patentee merely have to offer one such licence on FRAND terms or can a defendant require a patentee to enter into a licence on any set of terms that are FRAND? In *Unwired Planet v Huawei*, Birss J canvassed the issue without deciding it.[15]

18-23   A further question is whether a defendant who fights a case through trial and loses is entitled to demand a FRAND licence on the same terms as was offered to them

---

[10]   [2015] EWHC 1029 (Pat), [48]–[49].

[11]   [2015] EWHC 1029 (Pat), [46]–[47].

[12]   [2015] EWHC 1029 (Pat), [61].

[13]   And indeed, in many of the cases in which these issues have arisen, disclosure of comparable licences has been ordered. See, for example, *Vringo v ZTE* [2015] EWHC 1704 (Pat).

[14]   United States District Court for Western District of Washington at Seattle, 25 April 2013, 10-CV-01823-ORD, referred to in *Vringo v ZTE* [2013] EWHC 1591 (Pat).

[15]   [2015] EWHC 1029 (Pat), [44].

at the outset of the action. This too has not been decided, although it is possible that they will not. At the outset of an action, it was unknown if the patent was valid or not. The royalty rate would take into account that uncertainty. After the action, the uncertainty has been removed. Additionally, it would arguably be discriminatory to treat parties who take a licence without litigation in the same way as ones who challenged validity through the courts.

As the discussion above demonstrates, the case law in this area is undeveloped. **18-24** Many questions have arisen in the cases that have come before the courts. However, to date there have been very few final answers. Nevertheless, it is submitted that the following propositions are correct:

(1) Whether a licence offered by a party is FRAND is a question which the court can determine. That includes determining whether a licence offered by a patentee is FRAND but also includes determining whether licence terms proposed by a putative licensee are FRAND.

(2) A patentee subject to an undertaking to ETSI to offer a FRAND licence for a given SEP who fails to offer any licence terms at all, or who is only prepared to accept terms which are not FRAND, will be in breach of that undertaking.

(3) At the suit of a third party wishing to enter into a FRAND licence, the English court will enforce against the patentee a FRAND undertaking given by that patentee to ETSI. The reasoning set out by Sir Robin Jacob in his October 2014 paper[16] is compelling.

(4) That enforcement will include settling disputed terms of an offered licence in the sense that "settling" means declaring a given term or terms to be FRAND but query how far that settlement process can go without the consent of the parties (see below at paras 18-25 and 18-26).

(5) The court does not have jurisdiction to compel a third party to enter into a licence being offered by a patentee, even if that licence is FRAND. The court's powers are limited to granting or refusing relief such as an injunction (see below) and awarding damages.

(6) While competition considerations provide relevant background which explains why FRAND obligations relating to SEPs may arise, competition law itself is not necessarily engaged every time a FRAND dispute arises. The fact that a patentee holds a SEP does not necessarily mean that that patentee is in a dominant position and subject to art.102 TFEU. Nor does every dispute about licensing a SEP necessarily engage art.101 TFEU. Thus while competition law may have the effect of imposing a FRAND obligation on a patentee in certain circumstances, it cannot be the only source of that obligation.

(7) The terms of the current form of ETSI FRAND undertaking refer to its being irrevocable and to its binding successors in title. In policy terms it is obvious why such a FRAND undertaking ought to have those characteristics but, at least in theory, there may be difficulties. The fact that an assignor was in breach of their obligation to bind the successor with an obligation to third parties does not automatically mean that the successor is actually bound by

---

[16] "FRAND: A legal analysis"; October 2014 published as Ch.21 of *IP and Other Things* (London: Bloomsbury, 2015). The paper is available at: *http://is.jrc.ec.europa.eu/pages/ISG/EURIPIDIS/documents/RobinJacob.pdf* [Accessed 11 March 2016].

that obligation. The legal basis on which such an undertaking could always be imposed directly on a successor is not clear.

4. SETTLEMENT OF FRAND TERMS BY THE COURT

18-25   In two interim hearings[17] the question has arisen about the extent to which the court would be prepared to settle the terms of a FRAND licence. The court held that, unless both parties agree, it could only consider specific offers and decide whether they were FRAND. The court could not conduct an open ended consideration of what would be a FRAND licence (akin to a Copyright Tribunal-style exercise) without the consent of the parties. These decisions do not mean that the court cannot settle the terms of a FRAND licence, they relate to the extent to which that exercise can be conducted.

18-26   It is submitted that if a patentee is obliged to offer FRAND licences and if the only term in dispute is a FRAND royalty rate in a set of licence terms which are otherwise not disputed, then there can be little doubt that the court can settle that rate. In settling such a rate the court would not be bound simply to pick one of the proposed rates advanced by one side or another. It could arrive at whatever rate it thought was FRAND. Equally, it is no doubt true that a court asked to declare that a set of proposed terms does or does not amount to a FRAND licence could do so and, in addition, in the exercise of its discretion could declare that, but for a given term or terms, the licence would be FRAND. However, in neither of these examples is the court going as far as fashioning the terms of an entire licence from scratch. That was the problem with the second declaration sought in *Unwired Planet v Huawei*, which was refused.[18] If the parties agreed that the court should do so then no doubt a court could craft an entire licence agreement but it must be doubted whether its jurisdiction can extend that far absent agreement. Nevertheless, in practice, like some of the other questions in this field, the problem may be more apparent than real given that the parties are likely to advance full sets of terms alleged to be FRAND.

What does essential mean?

18-27   The concept of essentiality is an important one in the context of FRAND because it is the fact that a patent is essential in the first place which gives rise to the need to prevent a patent holder holding to ransom undertakings wishing to make, sell and use equipment in accordance with that standard. The definition of the term ESSENTIAL in the currently applicable ETSI IPR Policy (para.15(6)) is set out above. In summary the definition means that a patent is essential to a standard if it is not possible on technical grounds to comply with the standard without infringing the patent. This simple definition is adequate in many circumstances but not all. Although this discussion will focus on the ETSI definition, the issues are likely to be inherent in any attempt to define what a patent essential to a standard is.

18-28   The courts have held that essentiality is a sufficiently clear concept for it to be possible to grant declarations of essentiality. This question came before the Court of Appeal in two cases both between Nokia Corporation and Interdigital Technol-

---

17   *Vringo v ZTE* [2013] EWHC 1591 (Pat) and *Unwired Planet v Huawei* [2015] EWHC 1029 (Pat), [69]–[71].
18   [2015] EWHC 1029 (Pat), [71].

ogy Corporation. In the first case[19] the declaration sought related to GSM and was in the following terms:

> "A declaration that the importation, manufacture, sale, supply, offer for sale or supply or use of—
>
> (i) GSM mobile telephones, and
> (ii) GSM system infrastructure equipment
>
> and each of them compliant with [the ETSI standard] without the licence of the defendant does not require infringement of the three patents in suit or any of them such that [the said patents] are not essential IPR for GSM release four."

In relation to this declaration, Jacob LJ (with whom Rix and Mummery LJJ agreed) held as follows: **18-29**

> "21. The definition of 'essential' is clear. It is contained in the relevant standard and the standard is clear. No one suggests otherwise. It is entirely possible, and has been done, to set out why Interdigital claim that the claims are essential. We were shown the document which was produced before Mr Justice Pumfrey, or shortly thereafter. I can see nothing in the document whatever which suggests that the issue of essential or not is not well and clearly defined. You take the standard, you take the patents, you take the definition of 'essential' and you see whether there is any way around or not. This is not an application for a declaration of non-infringement of a specific article of the sort which is covered by section 71 of the Patents Act 1977 but equally it seems to me that the issue, one way or another, is clearly enough defined to be the subject of the court's inherent jurisdiction.
>
> 22. In this connection it was said that in some cases the standard provides for options and that only some of the options are covered by the patents. That, to my mind, makes no difference though it might qualify the ultimate declaration which would indicate which options are covered and which are not. That is also suggested to make the proposed declaration theoretical. I do not think so. It tells everybody exactly where they stand, which options are covered and which are not covered by the patents.
>
> 23. It is also said that there is no real extant dispute between the parties and so this is not an appropriate matter for a declaration. Nokia have a licence. No claim of infringement is asserted against them is the way the argument works. But to my mind, clearly, the essentiality or its degree affects the value of a patent. If they dominate then what one has to pay is quite different than if they cover nothing essential; and can be easily circumnavigated …"

The second *Nokia v Interdigital* case about essentiality declarations concerned 3G.[20] This time InterDigital raised further objections to declarations of this type which had not been taken before[21] but the court rejected them. Jacob LJ then went on to say: **18-30**

> "20. I do not say that anyone could apply for declarations of the kind sought by Nokia. There would have to be a real commercial reason for the person seeking the declaration to have standing to do so. An interest in making 3G telephones which must therefore comply with the standard is clearly sufficient."

It is now accepted that the court has, as part of its inherent jurisdiction, a discretion to grant a binding declaration as to whether the claims of a patent are essential or inessential to a particular standard. See, for example, *Nokia v IPCom*,[22] in which such jurisdiction was not in dispute between the parties, though Floyd J   **18-31**

---

[19] [2005] EWCA Civ 614.

[20] *Nokia Corp v Interdigital Technology Corp* [2006] EWCA Civ 1618; [2007] F.S.R. 23.

[21] First was an argument that *Unilever v Procter & Gamble* [2000] F.S.R. 344 had not been cited in the previous case, noting that the observations of Robert Walker LJ that the existence of the statutory remedy under s.71 of the 1977 Act meant there was less room for the court's inherent jurisdiction. Secondly, InterDigital argued that the court's previous decision had opened the floodgates to a flood of similar applications.

[22] *Nokia GmbH v IPCom GmbH & Co KG* [2012] EWHC 225 (Pat).

noted[23] that the grant of the declaration remained discretionary and may not be granted if it served no useful purpose.

18-32   As stated above, the simple definition of essential (not possible to comply with the standard without infringement) is often adequate for all purposes but the scope of the concept of essentiality is not limited to that simple definition. Many standards contain optional features. A patent may relate to that option. From a standard setting point of view, the SSO will want any patents on optional features to be subject to FRAND licences. However, by definition it will be possible to comply with the standard without implementing such options and so, by definition, a patent covering that option cannot be one which has to be infringed in order to comply with the standard. It is submitted that the better view is that a patent which covers an option expressly provided for in a standard is to be regarded as a standard essential patent. The fact it is essential to an optional feature may well affect what a FRAND royalty rate would be for that patent (and other terms) but that is a different question from whether it is subject to a FRAND obligation.

18-33   One difficulty caused by optional features in a standard is a practical one. The only basis a patentee is likely to have for a claim for infringement of a patent is that a piece of equipment has been sold as being compliant with a standard. For patents which are essential to options, an assertion that the equipment complies with the standard in general is not an assertion that the equipment complies with an option.[24] In order to commence proceedings on the basis of the assertion that the equipment is standards compliant, the patentee will need to identify some arguable basis for the assertion that the option is being employed.

18-34   The current ETSI definition seeks to address a problem related to options in the last sentence of para.15(6) which starts with the words "for the avoidance of doubt" and "in exceptional cases". This sentence provides that "where a STANDARD can only be implemented by technical solutions, all of which are infringements of IPRs, all such IPRs shall be considered ESSENTIAL." In *InterDigital v Nokia*[25] Pumfrey J explained that:

"The purpose of this deeming provision is clear enough. Where there are a number of ways of implementing a standard all of which are patented, the relevant patents must be considered essential as a group because, whichever solution is chosen, one of them will have to be used and so licensed on FRAND terms. The purpose of this limb of the definition of the word 'essential' is thus to ensure that a licence is available in respect of any patent which is chosen."[26]

18-35   Considerations of this kind were part of the early objections to making a declaration of essentiality at all but they can be resolved with appropriate case management. It is now clear that the court can grant declarations of essentiality including dealing with options.[27]

18-36   If both patents are held by the same undertaking then little difficulty arises but the last sentence of the definition is wider than that. How it would work in a case in which the patents are held by different parties is unclear. If, as the definition suggests, the circumstances in which this provision will apply will be exceptional, then this may not matter.

18-37   A different problem relating to the concept of essentiality arises from the nature

[23] *Nokia GmbH v IPCom GmbH & Co KG* [2012] EWHC 225 (Pat), [180].
[24] See, e.g. Pumfrey J in *Nokia v InterDigital* [2004] EWHC 2920, [46].
[25] [2007] EWHC 445.
[26] *Nokia v InterDigital* [2007] EWHC 445, [7].
[27] *Nokia v InterDigital* [2005] EWCA 614, [21].

of standards themselves. Some aspects of a standard are inherently technically necessary for different products to function in the system. An example will be a communications protocol. However, other aspects of standards may not have to be complied with technically in order for a product to work in the system. The standard may state that a product should behave in a particular way but nevertheless it may be that the equipment can still be entirely interoperable with the standardised system without doing so. Accordingly, for example, just because a patent is essential to the 3G standard and just because a product is said to be a 3G handset, it may not necessarily be the case that the product in fact infringes that patent. This is not a theoretical concern, since an example of the phenomenon arose in *Nokia v IPCom*.[28] At the time of writing this dispute is still continuing but whatever the final outcome, the case stands as an example of the point. The standard and the patent required a mobile phone to perform an internal calculation in a particular way. Technically the phone could still interact with the 3G network whether it performed that calculation in the manner required by the standard or in other ways. So while phones compliant with the letter of the standard would infringe, phones did not actually have to infringe in order to work as 3G phones.

One reason why the precise scope of the definition of essential may be important **18-38** is if a patent is not essential within the meaning of that term in an SSO's IPR policy then there may be no obligation under that policy to undertake to grant FRAND licences. To illustrate this point, note that the ETSI definition distinguishes between technical and commercial grounds. In other words, a patent which covers the only commercially realistic way of making a piece of equipment compliant with the standard is not an essential patent within the ETSI definition. So there is no requirement under the ETSI IPR policy to give an undertaking to offer FRAND licences. While this makes sense from a standard setting point of view, it is possible that competition law considerations would work in a different way. From the point of view of an analysis of competition between undertakings, the distinction between what is commercially realistic and what is technically possible is not so significant.

5. COMPETITION LAW

Allegations of breach of competition law arising out of the existing of a FRAND **18-39** undertaking are raised from time to time. There has been no full determination of such an issue in the UK courts. However, in *Huawei v ZTE*,[29] a German case referred to the CJEU, the issue of breach of art.102 TFEU by reason of asserting patents that have been declared essential. The court set out the following principles:

(a)   The exercise of patent rights, even by an undertaking in a dominant position, cannot by itself amount to an abuse of that dominant position.[30] However, in principle a refusal by the proprietor of a SEP to grant a licence on FRAND terms could constitute an abuse within the meaning of art.102 TFEU and can be raised as a defence by the defendant to actions for patent infringement seeking prohibitory injunctions or recall of products.[31] An ac-

---

[28]   [2011] EWHC 1470 (Pat) and [2011] EWHC 1871 (Pat); and on appeal [2012] EWCA Civ 567.
[29]   C-170/13.
[30]   C-170/13, [46], referring to *Volvo* (238/87), EU:C:1988:477, [8]; *RTE and ITP v Commission* (C-241/91 P and C-242/91 P), EU:C:1995:98, [49]; and *IMS Health* (C-418/01), EU:C:2004:257, [34].
[31]   In English terminology, an injunction and an Order for delivery up. See C-170/13, at [53]–[54].

tion seeking damages for past infringement of a SEP is not prohibited by art.102 TFEU.[32]

(b) In order for an action seeking an injunction and delivery up for infringement of a SEP not to constitute an abuse, the patentee must comply with various conditions:

   (i) First, prior to commencing the action the patentee must alert the alleged infringer of the infringement complained about by designating that SEP and specifying the way in which it has been infringed.[33]

   (ii) Secondly, after the defendant has expressed its willingness to enter into a licence on FRAND terms, the patentee must put a precise, written offer for a licence on FRAND terms, specifying, in particular, the amount of the royalty and the way in which that royalty is to be calculated.[34]

(c) There are also obligations on the defendant. The CJEU made it clear that the defendant must respond diligently to the offer and without delaying tactics. Should the defendant not accept the offer, they can only allege that the action is an abuse of a dominant position contrary to art.102 TFEU if they have submitted promptly and in writing a counter offer that they contend corresponds to FRAND terms.[35] Furthermore, if the defendant is already infringing the SEP, if their counter-offer is rejected they must provide appropriate security. The CJEU stated that the calculation of that security must include, inter alia, the number of the past acts of use of the SEP, and the alleged infringer must be able to render an account in respect of those acts of use.[36] Finally, the CJEU made it clear that a defendant is entitled, in parallel to negotiations/disputes over the terms of a licence, to challenge both the validity of any asserted SEP and whether they infringe it.[37]

(d) If the parties cannot agree on the details of FRAND terms, they must, by agreement, request that the royalty be determined by an independent third party without delay.[38] This would presumably include a court determination and arbitration.

(e) In contrast to an action for an injunction, an action for an award of damages does not have a direct impact on whether competitor standard-compliant products will appear or remain on the market, such that such an action cannot be regarded as an abuse under art.102.[39]

18-40   To date there has been no decision of the English court considering these provisions.

18-41   Although allegations of abuse of a dominant position contrary to art.102 TFEU have been more common in this context than allegations of breach of art.101 TFEU (agreements that have as their object or effect the prevention, restriction or distortion of competition within the internal market), the latter may arise when patents

---

[32] C-170/13, [72]–[76].
[33] C-170/13, [60]–[61].
[34] C-170/13, [63].
[35] C-170/13, [65]–[66].
[36] C-170/13, [67].
[37] C-170/13, [69].
[38] C-170/13, [68].
[39] C-170/13, [72]–[76].

(or some of the patents) in a portfolio are assigned.[40] In *Unwired Planet v Huawei*,[41] the patentee had been the assignee of a number of patents originally filed by Ericsson. It was alleged by the defendants that the assignment breached art.101 TFEU in three ways. The third allegation was a specific one in relation to certain of the terms in the transfer agreement. However, the first and second allegations were more general.

First, it was alleged that there was a failure to ensure a complete and proper effective transfer of an enforceable FRAND obligation. The court struck this allegation out as hopeless in the light of the assignment in question. In addition, it also struck out an allegation of breach of art.101 TFEU because the assignment did not transfer the *assignor's* FRAND obligation to the assignee but merely required to assignee to commit to FRAND afresh. The basis of this allegation was that the non-discriminatory part of FRAND would now be considered without reference to the other patents in the transferor's portfolio. However, it was held to have no prospects of success because: **18-42**

> "It would be unreal and commercially unworkable for competition law to require that the transferor's own FRAND obligation should somehow be transferred in the manner alleged by Samsung. That would mean looking back at the position of the transferor in order to decide what FRAND terms were today. So many questions arise. Some are the following: What happens if the patents are assigned more than once? When considering these patents now in the hands of Unwired Planet does one look at Ericsson's portfolio today or as it was at the date of transfer? Neither makes much sense when you start thinking about it. How does the transferee or putative licensee get access to information about the predecessor's portfolio? What happens when patents are acquired by someone with their own existing portfolio?"[42]

Secondly, it was alleged that by dividing the original patentee's portfolio into two parts (the original patentee retained some patents for itself) art.101 was breached because unfair higher royalties would be earned and competition would be restricted or distorted. Although the court was sceptical about this allegation because it appeared to lead to the conclusion that a subset of patents could never be assigned from a portfolio, it allowed the allegation to go forward to trial, primarily because the original patentee retained a share in the royalties from the transferred patents and because this is a developing area of the law.[43]   **18-43**

6. CONSEQUENCES OF FRAND ISSUES FOR THE MANAGEMENT OF A TRIAL

Because owners of patents in technologies where FRAND issues come into play tend to have large portfolios of patents, litigating such patents tends to give rise to specific issues. These are addressed below.   **18-44**

First, the action for infringement (or revocation if initiated by the person seeking to avoid paying a royalty under the patents) will often contain multiple patents.   **18-45**

---

[40] A practice that has become more common in recent years because of "privateering", where a patentee assigns parts of their portfolio to companies set up to enforce them. In these arrangements, the original patentee usually have an entitlement to a share of the damages recovered by the assignee. The patentees in the *Vringo v ZTE* and *Unwired Planet v Huawei* disputes are examples of "privateers".

[41] [2015] EWHC 2097 (Pat).

[42] [2015] EWHC 2097 (Pat), [35].

[43] [2015] EWHC 2097 (Pat), [37]–[49].

The approach the court tends to take is to break the action down into a number of trials and schedule these in a sequence two to four months apart.[44]

18-46   Secondly, the UK litigation will usually be part of a wider global dispute. The parties may have been negotiating for months or years in advance of the litigation commencing. Further, there will often be parallel actions in at least Germany and the United States and possibly many other jurisdictions. Disputes are generally resolved by a global settlement after a number of rounds of litigation and not by litigation of each and every patent in the patentee's portfolio.

18-47   Thirdly, claims for infringement or revocation are often coupled with claims for declarations that particular patents are, or are not, in fact "essential" (as defined in the ETSI IPR policy above) to the standards against which they have been declared. The issues raised by this type of action are dealt with at para.18.27, et seq.

18-48   Fourthly, where the patents in suit have been declared as essential to one or more technical standards, the defendant almost inevitably raises FRAND issues. These include: (i) a denial of an entitlement to an injunction because of the FRAND declaration, (ii) an offer to take a licence on FRAND terms under such of the patents in suit as are found to be valid and infringed, together with a denial that any offer of a licence made by the patentee was on FRAND terms, and (iii) allegations of abuse of a dominant position by reason of the patentee's licensing position.

18-49   At an early stage in any action (usually at the case management conference, or CMC) the court has to decide how to manage the trial. Usually the course adopted is to hear the "technical trials" first, i.e. trials of the issue of infringement, essentiality and/or validity of the patents in suit, with the trial of the FRAND issues to be tried later if needed.[45] This is first and foremost a pragmatic decision as the number of standards essential patents found to be valid and infringed is frequently much less than the number originally asserted. To date many asserted patents have been found to be invalid or not infringed or both.[46] Most scheduled FRAND trials have not occurred either for this reason or because the parties had settled before the FRAND trial occurred.

18-50   The court has on occasions considered whether there might be benefits in hearing the FRAND issues first.[47] In *Vringo v ZTE*[48] the patentee sought at the CMC to persuade the court to determine the FRAND issues first. In particular, it had sought declaratory relief as to whether the terms of the offer the patentee had made to the defendant to license its entire global portfolio complied with its obligations to license its patents (including the UK patents in suit in the action) on FRAND terms and wanted this heard first. The patentee's reasons for taking the FRAND issue first, was that doing so would likely resolve the global dispute between the parties and result in a global licence being entered into under the patentee's portfolio. However, the defendant opposed the course proposed because its position was that all the patents asserted were invalid. The court refused to schedule the FRAND issues first

---

[44]   As happened in *Interdigital v Nokia* [2008] EWHC 969 (Pat), at [2]; *Unwired Planet v Huawei* [2015] EWHC 2097 (Pat), at [9].

[45]   This happened in at least *Vringo v ZTE, Unwired Planet v Huawei, Nokia v IPCom* and *Samsung v Apple*. See also *Seiko Epson v DCI* [2012] EWHC 316 (Pat).

[46]   At the date of writing there have been three full trials in which an asserted SEP has been found valid and essential: *Nokia v IPCom* (but the claim was then amended in the EPO and the amended claim was found not to be essential), the first *Vringo v ZTE* trial and the first of the *Unwired Planet v Huawei* trials. Both *Nokia v IPCom* and *Unwired Planet v Huawei* are subject to pending appeals.

[47]   Floyd J in *Nokia v IPCom* [2009] EWHC 1017 (Pat), at [11]; Kitchin J in *Philips v Alba*, 24 October 2008.

[48]   [2013] EWHC 1591 (Pat).

because it held that the defendant was entitled to adopt a contingent position that it would take a FRAND licence on any patent found to be valid and infringed. Where such a contingent position is taken, Birss J held that there is no basis on which the court could compel the defendants to accept a licence arrived at by approaching the matter as if he was a licensee willing to take a licence without having a judicial determination of validity and/or infringement.[49]

A further procedural issue that arises in patents action in which FRAND issues **18-51** arise is disclosure of comparable licences (possibly from third parties) and the protection of those licences by confidentiality clubs. However, the principles are the same as for the protection of any confidential information.

As to the scope of such disclosure, in *Unwired Planet v Huawei*[50] the disclosure **18-52** of the parties' various licence agreements was ordered. A further application was then made for disclosure of the underlying documents relating to the negotiations for the licences. This further disclosure was sought for two reasons: (1) in order to understand the financial terms, and in particular, to understand the extent to which they were comparable; and (2) to test the reality of how the negotiations arrived at the figures in actual licences as against the assertions by the parties as to how they should be done. The further disclosure was refused. The judge held that although the documents were relevant, disclosure: (i) was premature and may not be necessary, and (ii) was disproportionate.

Availability of injunctive relief

Although an injunction is a discretionary remedy, in the normal course of events **18-53** a patentee who demonstrates that their patent is valid and has been infringed by a defendant is entitled to an injunction to restrain further infringement.

However, where a FRAND undertaking has been made, prima facie an injunc- **18-54** tion may not be appropriate. The offer to grant a licence on FRAND terms is not affected by the finding that the patent is valid and infringed and if the defendant takes a licence, an injunction will not required. However, it is too simplistic to say that a patentee who has given a FRAND undertaking can never obtain an injunction for infringement of their patent. If a losing defendant refused to take a licence but carried on their infringement, there is no reason in principle why an injunction should not be ordered, notwithstanding the FRAND undertaking. A more realistic scenario to an outright refusal by a defendant to take any licence is that the defendant would agree to take a licence under any patent found to be valid and infringed but would dispute that the terms proposed by the patentee were FRAND. It is submitted that in those situations, the parties could ask the court to determine whether the terms offered were FRAND once the patent had been found valid and infringed. An injunction would only be appropriate if the defendant refused to enter into a licence on the terms determined to be FRAND by the court and continued to infringe the patent. If the terms offers were found not to be FRAND, the offer would be "equitably refusable"[51] (to adopt Birss J's expression) and the losing defendant could refuse to accept them without being injuncted.

Another issue that has arisen in the context of injunctions relates to the nature **18-55** of the offer of a licence made by a patentee. Most patentees own not just one pat-

---

49 [2013] EWHC 1591 (Pat), [44]–[46] and [52]–[60].
50 [2015] EWHC 2901 (Pat).
51 *Unwired Planet v Huawei* [2015] EWHC 1029 (Pat), [29].

ent in the UK but a portfolio of patents worldwide. A common situation is for the patentee to make an offer to license their entire worldwide portfolio. The question arises as to whether a losing defendant ought to be compelled to accept this offer or face being injuncted. In *Vringo v ZTE*,[52] Birss J doubted this:

> "107. … I suspect the fallacy in the reasoning of Vringo at this stage may be that just because it may be so that the global portfolio offer is a FRAND offer, it does not follow that the global portfolio licence on offer is the only set of terms which could be FRAND. It seems to me that there is likely to be a FRAND rate for [the patent in suit]. I can see that the aggregate of individual FRAND rates for patents taken alone and on a territorial basis may well be far more than global portfolio rates and so a rational defendant may well prefer to take a global portfolio licence rather than a series of individual ones. Moreover I accept, as Vringo urges on me, that global portfolio licences are the kinds of licences industry normally enters into.
>
> 108. However this is very different from saying that somehow the fact that a global licence on a portfolio of patents is FRAND necessarily means that a defendant in one jurisdiction faced with one patent is forced to take a global portfolio licence in order to stave off a national injunction on that one patent.
>
> 109. I could see a very different circumstance if Vringo had made a FRAND offer for [the patent in suit] and that offer had not been accepted. Then an injunction might well follow. In that sort of case, unlike the one based on the global portfolio licence, the threat of the injunction, which is after all a territorial remedy, would not be being used to create some sort of international coercion or coercion about other patent rights."

18-56   However, in *Vringo v ZTE* the point was ultimately not decided because shortly after the above judgment, the patentee changed its position and made an offer of an individual FRAND licence under the patent in suit alone.

Measure of damages when a patentee has given a FRAND undertaking

18-57   This issue is relatively straightforward. Where a patentee has given a FRAND undertaking then their damages will likely be limited to the royalties that would be payable under a FRAND licence. The damages inquiry in such a situation would serve a dual purpose: in addition to quantifying the damages due for past infringements, it would also establish the key terms of a FRAND licence that the defendant could chose to enter into if it wants to continue to practice the invention and avoid an injunction going forward.

18-58   The English courts have yet to conduct a determination of a FRAND royalty rate. As such the criteria that would be taken into account have not been judicially considered. However, it is submitted that these would most likely include consideration of comparable licences, the importance of the technology to the standard in question, the importance of the standard in question to the products covered by the licence, and the availability of alternative technologies.

---

[52]   [2015] EWHC 214 (Pat); [2015] R.P.C. 23.

CHAPTER 19

ACTION FOR INFRINGEMENT

CONTENTS

1. THE TRIBUNAL

The Patents 1977 Act established the Patents Court which is composed of the **19-01** patents judges who are puisne judges of the High Court.[1] The Patents County Court, which had been created by ss.287–292 of the Copyright, Designs and Patents Act 1988, was abolished from 1 October 2013 by the repeal of ss.287–289 and 291 of the 1988 Act and the Intellectual Property Enterprise Court established in its place, as a specialist list of the Chancery Division of the High Court.[2] The Comptroller also has a limited jurisdiction to decide disputes as to infringement.

The regulation of practice

Practice in patent cases in England and Wales, whether in the High Court or **19-02** IPEC, is regulated by the Civil Procedure Rules. As specialist proceedings, the CPR is modified in respect of patent cases by the Practice Direction in respect of Patents and Other Intellectual Property Claims issued under Pt 63. These rules do not apply to the Scottish courts. Practice before the Comptroller is regulated by the Patents Rules 2007 and by Patent Office Practice Notes.[3]

The Patents Court

The patents judges are nominated by the Lord Chief Justice in consultation with **19-03** the Lord Chancellor and are attached to the Chancery Division of the High Court.

---

[1] PA 1977 s.96. Now repealed and replaced by Senior Courts Act 1981 ss.6 and 62.
[2] Civil Procedure (Amendment No.7) Rules 2013 r.26, CPR r,63.1(2)(g).
[3] e.g. TPN 1/2000 [2000] R.P.C. 587; TPN 2/2000 [2000] R.P.C. 598 (costs); TPN 1/2003 [2003] R.P.C. 46 (appeals); TPN 4/2007 [2008] R.P.C. 7; TPN 6/2007 [2008] R.P.C. 8; TPN 4/2008; TPN 1/2009; TPN 3/2009. All are available on the UK IPO website.

All patent proceedings in the High Court are assigned to the Chancery Division and taken by the Patents Court. The Patents Court may appoint scientific advisers or assessors to assist it.[4]

IPEC

19-04   The Enterprise Judge is a judge authorised by the Chancellor of the High Court to sit in the Intellectual Property Enterprise Court ("IPEC").[5] They are a judge appointed at the level of a circuit judge but are a "Judge of the High Court" for the purpose of jurisdiction to grant certain civil restraint orders.[6]

Choice of Patents Court or IPEC

19-05   The claimant has a choice of the tribunal in which to bring an action by issuing a claim form in either the Patents Court or IPEC.

19-06   IPEC was established to deal with smaller, shorter, less complex and lower value actions. Generally, the longer, heavier, more complex, more important and more valuable actions continue to belong in the High Court.[7] These factors will usually determine the choice of court. Other relevant factors are: (a) the cap of £500,000 on recoverable damages in IPEC,[8] (b) the cap of a maximum of £50,000 on recoverable costs in IPEC,[9] and (c) the differences in the procedure in IPEC. These are dealt with in more detail in the IPEC chapter of this work.

Transfer between the High Court and IPEC

19-07   The Patents Court has power to transfer any proceedings before it over which IPEC would have jurisdiction to that court. Likewise IPEC has power to transfer actions to the High Court of its own motion or on application.

19-08   The court has a discretion as regards such transfers. There is a body of case law on the relevant considerations, which is dealt with in the IPEC chapter of this work.

The Comptroller

19-09   Under the 1977 Act, the Comptroller's jurisdiction has been extended from the limited jurisdiction under the 1949 Act[10] and the parties may by agreement refer infringement to the Comptroller.[11] The Comptroller may decline to deal with it, if the matters involved would more properly be determined by the court.[12] The Comptroller may decide whether damages and a declaration are appropriate.[13]

---

[4]   Senior Courts Act 1981 s.70; CPR r.35.15 and Pt 63, Practice Direction—Intellectual Property Claims para.5.10(1).

[5]   CPR r.63.1(2)(h).

[6]   *Perry v FH Brundle* [2015] EWHC 2737 (IPEC).

[7]   Per Sir Thomas Bingham MR in *Chaplin Patents Holdings Co Inc v Group Lotus Plc and Lotus Car Ltd* (17 December 1993) *The Times,* 12 January 1994, CA.

[8]   See CPR r.61.17A(1).

[9]   £25,000 on a damages inquiry or an account. See CPR r.45.30–45.32, especially r.45.31(1)(a) and (b).

[10]   PA 1949 s.67.

[11]   PA 1977 s.61(3).

[12]   PA 1977 s.61(5). For the principles applicable see *Luxim v Ceravision* [2007] R.P.C. 33.

[13]   PA 1977 s.61(3).

However, the Comptroller can consider all matters of validity.[14] An appeal lies from any decision of the Comptroller on infringement or validity to the Patents Court and thereafter, with permission of the Patents Court or the Court of Appeal, to the Court of Appeal.[15]

Because of the Comptroller's inability to grant injunctive relief, questions of infringement are rarely referred to the Comptroller. Further, in many cases, the costs will be increased by adding a further tribunal in the normal chain of possible appeals. If discovery or cross-examination is necessary, then this is best done before the court which has the machinery and experience to deal with disputes relating thereto. The conduct of proceedings before the Comptroller was reformed in 2007 such that the new rules are more closely aligned to the CPR system of case management.[16] In proceedings before the Comptroller, costs are dealt with on a scale system but the Comptroller has freedom to deal with costs off the scale to deal with unreasonable behaviour.[17]

19-10

Stay of court proceedings in favour of Comptroller

An application may be made to stay the High Court proceedings pending the outcome of an application to the Comptroller either to revoke the patent or for a declaration of non-infringement. The grant or refusal of the stay will depend upon the circumstances of each case. In *Ferro Corporation v Escol Products*[18] a stay was refused. In *Hawker Siddeley Dynamics Engineering Ltd v Real Time Developments Ltd*[19] a stay was granted, although that case has since been described as very unusual.[20] In particular, the Patent Office proceedings had been commenced and the defendants could not afford High Court proceedings and had agreed to be bound by the decision of the Patent Office.

19-11

Stay of court proceedings in favour of EPO opposition proceedings

A similar situation also arises in the case of a European patent (UK) which is the subject of opposition proceedings in the EPO. The issue has arisen many times.[21] In 2008 the Court of Appeal reviewed the position authoritatively in *Glaxo Group v Genentech*[22] and gave general guidance on the Patents Court's discretion to stay legal proceedings on the ground that there are parallel proceedings pending in the

19-12

---

[14] PA 1977 s.72.

[15] PA 1977 s.97(3).

[16] *Tribunal Practice Note* (TPN 6/2007) [2008] R.P.C. 8.

[17] *Tribunal Practice Note* (TPN 4/2007) [2008] R.P.C. 7. Note paras 11 and 12 thereof provides that in the case of a Conditional Fee Arrangement, any success fee element will not be taken into account in assessing costs.

[18] [1990] R.P.C. 651; and see *Gen Set SpA v Mosarc Ltd* [1985] F.S.R. 302.

[19] [1983] R.P.C. 395.

[20] *Ferro Corporation v Escol Products* [1990] R.P.C. 651.

[21] Cases prior to *Glaxo Group v Genentech* (see below) include *Amersham International Plc v Corning Ltd* [1987] R.P.C. 53; and *Pall Corp v Commercial Hydraulics (Bedford) Ltd* [1989] R.P.C. 703, CA. *Kimberly-Clark Worldwide v Procter & Gamble* [2000] F.S.R. 633. *General Hospital Corp's European Patent* [2000] F.S.R. 633; *Unilever v Frisa* [2000] F.S.R. 708; *3M v Rennicks* [2000] F.S.R. 727; *GD Searle & Co's and Monsanto Co's Patent* [2002] F.S.R. 24, 381 (an Irish case which also considered by analogy the ECJ decision in *Master Foods v HB Ice Cream* (C-344/98) 14 December 2000; *GSK Biologicals v Sanofi Pasteur* [2006] EWHC 2333 (Pat), *Unilin Beheer v Berry Floor* [2007] EWCA Civ 364, [2007] F.S.R. 25. See also *Beloit Technologies Inc v Valmet Paper Machinery Inc (No.3)* [1996] F.S.R. 718, CA.

[22] [2008] EWCA Civ 23, [2008] F.S.R. 18, followed in *GlaxoSmithKline Biologicals SA v Novartis*

EPO concerning the validity of the patent in suit. This guidance was re-considered and slightly modified in *IPCom GmbH v HTC Co Europe Ltd*[23] in the light of the decision of the Supreme Court in *Virgin Atlantic Airways Ltd v Zodiac Seats UK Ltd*.[24] The guidance is as follows:

"1.   The discretion, which is very wide indeed, should be exercised to achieve the balance of justice between the parties having regard to all the relevant circumstances of the particular case.

2.   The discretion is of the Patents Court, not of the Court of Appeal. The Court of Appeal would not be justified in interfering with a first instance decision that accords with legal principle and has been reached by taking into account all the relevant, and only the relevant, circumstances.

3.   Although neither the EPC nor the 1977 Act contains express provisions relating to automatic or discretionary stay of proceedings in national courts, they provide the context and condition the exercise of the discretion.

4.   It should thus be remembered that the possibility of concurrent proceedings contesting the validity of a patent granted by the EPO is inherent in the system established by the EPC. It should also be remembered that national courts exercise exclusive jurisdiction on infringement issues.

5.   If there are no other factors, a stay of the national proceedings is the default option. There is no purpose in pursuing two sets of proceedings simply because the Convention allows for it.

6.   It is for the party resisting the grant of the stay to show why it should not be granted. Ultimately it is a question of where the balance of justice lies.

7.   One important factor affecting the exercise of the discretion is the extent to which refusal of a stay will irrevocably deprive a party of any part of the benefit which the concurrent jurisdiction of the EPO and the national court is *419 intended to confer. Thus, if allowing the national court to proceed might allow the patentee to obtain monetary compensation which is not repayable if the patent is subsequently revoked, this would be a weighty factor in favour of the grant of a stay. It may, however, be possible to mitigate the effect of this factor by the offer of suitable undertakings to repay.

8.   The Patents Court judge is entitled to refuse a stay of the national proceedings where the evidence is that some commercial certainty would be achieved at a considerably earlier date in the case of the UK proceedings than in the EPO. It is true that it will not be possible to attain certainty everywhere until the EPO proceedings are finally resolved, but some certainty, sooner rather than later, and somewhere, such as in the UK, rather than nowhere, is, in general, preferable to continuing uncertainty everywhere.

9.   It is permissible to take account of the fact that resolution of the national proceedings, whilst not finally resolving everything, may, by deciding some important issues, promote settlement.

10.   An important factor affecting the discretion will be the length of time that it will take for the respective proceedings in the national court and in the EPO to reach a conclusion. This is not an independent factor, but needs to be considered in conjunction with the prejudice which any party will suffer from the delay, and lack of certainty, and what the national proceedings can achieve in terms of certainty.

11.   The public interest in dispelling the uncertainty surrounding the validity of monopoly rights conferred by the grant of a patent is also a factor to be considered.

12.   In weighing the balance it is material to take into account the risk of wasted costs, but this factor will normally be outweighed by commercial factors concerned with early resolution.

13.   The hearing of an application for a stay is not to become a mini-trial of the various factors affecting its grant or refusal. The parties' assertions need to be examined critically, but at a relatively high level of generality."

19-13   The revised guidelines were applied in *Actavis v Pharmacia*,[25] a case where the stay was sought by the patentee. At the hearing, as is often the case, the patentee offered undertakings in order to mitigate the prejudice that would be caused to the other party by a stay. These were:

     AG [2009] EWHC 931 (Pat); *TNS Group Holdings v Nielsen Media Research* [2009] EWHC 1160 (Pat); *Smith & Nephew PLC v Convatec Technologies Inc* [2011] EWHC 1103; *Danisco A/S v Novozymes A/S* [2012] F.S.R. 21.

23   [2013] EWCA Civ 1496; [2014] R.P.C 12.

24   [2013] UKSC 46; [2013] R.P.C. 29.

25   [2014] EWHC 2265 (Pat).

(a) to seek expedition of the EPO proceedings;

(b) not to seek an injunction against the defendant or its customers until the determination of the EPO proceedings; and

(c) only to seek damages of 1 per cent of the defendant's net sales during the period from launch until the determination of the EPO proceedings if the patent was held valid both by the EPO and by the English courts.

The court refused the stay, primarily because the EPO proceedings had only just commenced and the English proceedings would be resolved sooner. Whilst the undertakings offered went a considerable way to reducing the commercial uncertainty to the defendant, the court held they did not address the uncertainty caused by the prospect that the defendant might be removed from the market by an injunction at a later date and that the defendant might have to pay ordinary damages or account for its profits for the last two of those years. In the light of a draft judgment indicating this, the patentee made a renewed application for a stay in which it additionally undertook: **19-14**

(a) not to seek an injunction in the UK against the defendant or its customers in relation to the product in question during the life of the patent; and

(b) only to seek damages of 1 per cent of the defendant's net sales in the UK during the life of the patent if the patent was ultimately held valid by the EPO and valid and infringed by the English courts.

In the light of these additional undertakings, the court granted the stay.[26]   **19-15**

Spin-off value of judgment

A further relevant factor, which militates against a stay of national proceedings, is the so called "spin-off" value of judgments. The Patents Court has held that it is perfectly legitimate for the claimant to seek to obtain an English judgment on the validity of the patent in the hope that it will lead to a settlement throughout Europe and that it is also legitimate to seek to rely on that judgment in the courts of other contracting states or the EPO if no settlement can be reached.[27] Equally, the existence of parallel proceedings in other contracting states of the EPC is a factor (albeit not a strong one) that the court will take into account when considering whether to expedite proceedings.[28]   **19-16**

Acceleration of parallel EPO proceedings

The EPO will accelerate proceedings before them in certain circumstances and the English courts have asked the EPO to accelerate parallel proceedings when appropriate to do so.[29]   **19-17**

---

[26] [2014] EWHC 2611 (Pat).

[27] *TNS Group Holdings v Nielsen Media Research* [2009] EWHC 1160 (Pat); [2009] F.S.R 23, see [22]–[26], especially [25].

[28] *Research in Motion UK Limited v Visto Corporation* [2008] EWHC 3025 (Pat), see [15].

[29] See para.5–43; See EPO Decision *Human Genome Sciences* (T18/09), [1]–[4]; *Eli Lilly v Human Genome Sciences* Court of Appeal, 23 February 2009; [2009] EWCA Civ 168 and full judgment on 9 February 2010; [2010] EWCA Civ 33, especially [6]–[10]; *Eli Lilly & Co v Biogen IDEC MA Inc* [2012] EWHC 184 (Pat); [2012] F.S.R. 25; see also *Novartis* (T25/09), paras III–VII. The co-operation of the EPO was also sought in expediting the opposition proceedings in *Biogen Inc v Medeva Plc* [1993] R.P.C. 475.

Stay of proceedings in favour of another jurisdiction

19-18   In *Affymetrix Inc v Multilyte Ltd*[30] the court refused to stay a patent infringement action in England in favour of a parallel German case. The position with a stay
pending EPO proceedings was distinguished on the ground that the outcome of
proceedings in the EPO has a direct bearing on the issues pending before the
national court whereas the determination of the German court does not have the
same effect.[31]

19-19   In *Ivax Pharmaceuticals v Akzo Nobel*[32] the court was asked to decline jurisdiction and stay a patent revocation action in England in favour of a parallel Scottish
case concerning different patents relating to the same drug. The court had to
consider whether some other forum was prima facie more appropriate.[33] Scotland
was not a more appropriate forum and therefore the only basis for the stay was the
existence of the pending Scottish proceedings and the risk of inconsistent findings
of fact. The Scottish case concerned different aspects of the manufacturing process
and there was no significant risk of inconsistency. No stay was ordered.

Scotland, Northern Ireland, etc.

19-20   The 1977 Act applies to the United Kingdom. Actions in respect of infringements committed in Scotland are heard in the Court of Session which has power
to hear proceedings for revocation of a patent.[34] The rules of procedure applicable
to patent cases in Scotland are found in Chapter 55 of the Rules of the Court of Session 1994.

19-21   Actions in respect of infringements committed in Northern Ireland are heard in
the Chancery Division of the High Court in Northern Ireland.[35] The rules of
procedure specific to patent cases in Northern Ireland are found in Order 104 of the
Rules of the Court of Judicature (NI) 1980.

19-22   The rules of procedure applicable to patent cases in Scotland and Northern
Ireland are essentially similar to the rules applicable in the Patents Court but there
are differences and parties should not assume that the practice will necessarily be
identical in all three jurisdictions. This chapter is concerned with the practice before
the English courts.

19-23   The application of the 1977 Act to the Isle of Man is provided for by s.132.

2. PARTIES

The claimant

19-24   The claimant will normally be the registered proprietor, i.e. the person or persons
for the time being entered on the register as grantee or proprietor of the patent.
However, the right to bring proceedings is vested in "the proprietor",[36] not the
registered proprietor; consequently, registration as proprietor is not a pre-

---

[30]   [2004] EWHC 291 (Pat); [2005] F.S.R. 1.
[31]   Similar comments were made in *Baxter Healthcare SA v Bayer Corp* [2006] EWHC 1890, see [21].
[32]   [2006] F.S.R. 46.
[33]   Based on *Spiliada Maratime Corp v Cansulex Ltd* [1987] A.C. 460.
[34]   See the definition of "court" in PA 1977 s.130(1) and see also s.98 and s.131A.
[35]   See the definition of "court" in PA 1977 s.130(1) and see also s.131. Order 104 r.2 of the Rules of
the Court of Judicature (NI) 1980 assigns the proceedings to the Chancery Division.
[36]   PA 1977 s.61(1).

condition to the bringing of proceedings. An equitable owner of a patent is also entitled to initiate proceedings for infringement. Although, in accordance with the general law, the equitable owner must perfect their legal title before final judgment.[37]

Section 67 of the 1977 Act also enables an exclusive licensee to sue for infringement in their own name. The patentee must, unless they consent to join as a claimant, be joined as a defendant, but they are not liable for any costs unless they acknowledge service and take part in the proceedings.[38] **19-25**

The register is prima facie evidence of anything required or authorised by the Act or the Patents Rules 2007 to be registered.[39] Accordingly, registration as proprietor or as exclusive licence is prima facie evidence that the person so registered is in fact the proprietor or exclusive licensee as the case may be. **19-26**

An assignee of a patent or an exclusive licensee may bring proceedings in respect of infringements occurring prior to the date of such assignment or licence provided that such right is included within the relevant grant of title.[40] However, an assignee of accrued rights of action can only acquire such rights as the assignor had to assign. Thus, the assignee can only recover damages to compensate for the assignor's loss caused by infringement, not their own loss.[41] **19-27**

After grant, a patentee may sue in respect of acts occurring prior to grant, but after publication of the application.[42] **19-28**

Licensees under s.46 of the Patent Act 1977

In the case of a licence granted under a patent endorsed "licences of right"[43] or granted compulsorily,[44] the licence may[45] call upon the proprietor to take proceedings for infringement, and if the proprietor refuses or neglects to do so within two months may institute such proceedings in their own name, making the patentee a defendant.[46] As in the case of an action by an exclusive licensee, the patentee is not liable for any costs unless they acknowledge service and take part in the proceedings.[47] **19-29**

Assignee

An assignment of a patent does not per se include an accrued right of action for infringements committed prior to the assignment.[48] Where the patent has been as- **19-30**

[37] *Baxter International Inc v Nederlands Produktielaboratorium voor Bloedtransfusiapparatuur B.V.* [1998] R.P.C. 250.
[38] PA 1977 s.67(3). See *British and International Proprietaries Ltd v Selcol Products Ltd* [1957] R.P.C. 3, Ch D.
[39] PA 1977 s.32(9) as amended by Patents, Designs and Marks Act 1986 and Criminal Justice Act 2003.
[40] PA 1977 s.30(7).
[41] *LG Electronics Inc v NCR Financial Solutions Group Ltd* [2003] F.S.R. 24.
[42] PA 1977 s.69.
[43] PA 1977 s.46(4).
[44] PA 1977 s.49(4).
[45] Unless, in the case of a licence the terms of which are settled by agreement, the licence otherwise expressly provides—see PA 1977 s.46(4).
[46] PA 1977 s.46(4).
[47] PA 1977 s.46(5).
[48] PA 1977 s.30(7); and see *Wilderman v E.W. Berk & Co Ltd* (1925) 42 R.P.C. 79, at 90; *United Horse*

signed after the commencement of the action the assignee may be added as a necessary party.[49]

Co-owners

19-31   Where two or more persons are co-owners of a patent, one may sue for infringement without the consent of the others, but the others must be parties to the proceedings.[50] If the others are joined as defendants, they are not liable for costs or expenses unless they acknowledge service and take part in the proceedings.[51] A co-owner joined as a defendant is not obliged to serve a defence in the proceedings nor to serve a defence to a counterclaim for revocation but in such a case the court may make an order debarring them from adducing evidence or calling witnesses contesting allegations in the counterclaim for revocation.[52]

The defendant

19-32   Any person infringing a patent by themselves or by their servants or agents, is liable and may be made a defendant and sued for damages or an account of the profits derived by them from the infringement, and, if there be shown by act or word any threat or intent to continue to infringe, for an injunction and, where appropriate, for an order for delivery-up or destruction.[53] Any person who is a joint tortfeasor with such a person is similarly liable,[54] but no other person is liable for the acts of infringement. Mere carriers, warehousemen and others who become mixed up in the infringing acts of another come under a duty in equity to assist the patentee[55] but they do not thereby become liable for the acts of infringement.

Assignee of infringer's business

19-33   It has been held that an assignee of the business of a defendant—the assignment being subsequent to the issue of the claim form—cannot be joined by the defendant as a co-defendant where the claimant objected.[56] However, if the claimant applies to join an assignee as co-defendant, it is no answer to say that there was not a cause of action at the date the action began, for such an amendment takes effect from the date when it is made.[57]

Manufacturers

19-34   It has been held that the manufacturer and patentee of a machine, the use of which is claimed to be an infringement of another patent, cannot compel the claimant to join them as a co-defendant with the person by whom the machine is used and

Shoe and Nail Co Ltd v Stewart & Co (1888) 5 R.P.C. 260.
[49] See *Bates Valve Bag Co v B. Kershaw & Co (1920) Ltd* (1933) 50 R.P.C. 43; and see also CPR, r.19.
[50] PA 1977 s.66(2).
[51] PA 1977 s.66(2).
[52] *MMI Research v Cellxion* [2008] F.S.R. 23.
[53] PA 1977 s.61(1).
[54] See para.14–137, et seq. and para.19-37.
[55] See paras 14–69 and 19-40.
[56] *Briggs v Lardeur* (1885) 2 R.P.C. 13.
[57] *Liff v Peasley* [1980] 1 W.L.R. 781, 803; *Ketteman v Hansel Properties* [1987] A.C. 189, 210; *Vax Appliances v Hoover* [1990] R.P.C. 656; *Beecham Group v Norton Healthcare* [1997] F.S.R. 81.

against whom the action for infringement is brought.[58] However, this decision has probably been overruled by the Court of Appeal which allowed a manufacturer to be joined on appeal in circumstances where the original defendant, a customer of the manufacturer, had fallen out with the manufacturer and evinced an intention not to contest the appeal.[59] The manufacturer would probably also be so entitled if the action were brought against their agent in respect of goods which were their property.[60]

Directors of company

Directors of a limited company may be liable in respect of the acts of infringe- **19-35**
ment committed by the company if it be proved that the company committed the infringements as their agent, or that they expressly authorised or directed the acts of infringement or that their involvement was otherwise such as to render them liable as joint tortfeasors with the company.[61] The circumstances in which a director may be liable are considered further at para.14–171, et seq. Where liability is alleged, particulars should be given of any facts on which the claimant intends to rely.[62]

The existence of the relationship of principal and agent and the necessary degree **19-36**
of control or direction of the acts complained of is not to be inferred from the mere fact that the directors in question may be sole directors and sole shareholders of the company.[63] If, however, a company is formed for the express purpose of doing a wrongful act, or if, when formed, those in control expressly direct that a wrongful act be done, such individuals as well as the company are responsible.[64] In each case it is necessary to examine with care what part the director played personally in regard to the act or acts complained of.[65]

Joint tortfeasors

The circumstances in which a person may be found liable as a joint tortfeasor are **19-37**
considered at para.14–142, et seq. Where an allegation of joint tortfeasorship is made, particulars of the facts and matters relied upon in support of the allegation must be given. Where the adequacy of the particulars is challenged, the court may

---

58 *Moser v Marsden* (1892) 1 Ch. 487; (1892) 9 R.P.C. 214.
59 *Tetra Molectric Ltd v Japan Imports Ltd* [1976] R.P.C. 541.
60 *Vavasseur v Krupp* (1878) 9 Ch D. 351.
61 *British Thomson-Houston Co Ltd v Sterling Accessories Ltd* (1924) 2 Ch. 33, (1924) 41 R.P.C. 311; see also *Cropper Minerva Machines Co Ltd v Cropper, Charlton & Co Ltd* (1906) 23 R.P.C. 388, at 392; *Pritchard and Constance (Wholesale) Ltd v Amata Ltd* (1925) 42 R.P.C. 63 (trade name); *Leggatt v Hood* (1950) 67 R.P.C. 134; *Oertli A.G. v E.J. Bowman Ltd* [1956] R.P.C. 282, [1957] R.P.C. 388; *White Horse Distillers Ltd v Gregson Associates Ltd* [1984] R.P.C. 61; *C. Evans & Sons Ltd v Spritebrand Ltd* [1985] F.S.R. 267 (copyright); *PLG Research Ltd v Ardon International Ltd* [1993] F.S.R. 197; *MCA Records Inc v Charly Records Ltd* [2002] F.S.R. 401 (copyrght) referring inter alia to *Unilever v Gillette* [1989] R.P.C. 583; *C.B.S. Songs Ltd v Amstrad Consumer Electronics Plc* [1988] A.C. 1013; *Boegli-Gravures SA v Darsail-ASP Ltd* [2009] EWHC 2690 (Pat).
62 *British Thomson-Houston Co Ltd v Irradiant Lamp Works Ltd* (1924) 41 R.P.C. 338.
63 *Rainham Chemical Works v Belvedere Fish Guano Co* [1921] 2 A.C. 465.
64 *Rainham Chemical Works v Belvedere Fish Guano Co* [1921] 2 A.C. 465. See also *Middlemas and Wood v Moliver & Co Ltd* (1921) 38 R.P.C. 97; *Performing Right Society Ltd v Ciryl Theatrical Syndicate Ltd* [1924] 1 K.B. 1.
65 *C. Evans & Sons Ltd v Spritebrand Ltd* [1985] F.S.R. 267; *PLG Research Ltd v Ardon International Ltd* [1993] F.S.R. 197.

look beyond the pleading to see whether any arguable case can be made.[66] The court will not tolerate speculative pleas of joint tortfeasorship.

Proper course where infringers numerous

19-38   In the case of *Bovill v Crate*,[67] it was stated by Sir W. Page-Wood VC that in cases where there were numerous infringers a patentee might well:

> "select that which he thought the best in order to try the question fairly, and proceed in that case to obtain his interlocutory injunction. He might write at the same time to all the others who were *in simili casu*, and say to them: 'Are you willing to take this as a notice to you that the present case is to determine yours? Otherwise I shall proceed against you by way of interlocutory injunction; and if you will not object on the ground of delay, I do not mean to file bills against all of you at once. Am I to understand that you make no objection of that kind? If you do not object I shall file a bill against only one of you.' I do not think any court could complain of a patentee for taking the course I am suggesting"

and stated further that such conduct would not in itself debar the patentee (owing to the delay) from obtaining interlocutory injunctions.[68] Such a letter would, however, have to be carefully drawn in the light of the law on unjustified threats of proceedings under s.70 of the 1977 Act.

19-39   The usual course is for the patentee to select the main sources of supply of infringing articles and to obtain a decision in an action against those main sources as representative infringers, and, if the decision on such action is in his favour, to proceed against the others. Where there were two actions on the same patent in which the issues and defences were substantially the same, the second action was stayed pending the trial of the first action, the defendant in the second action undertaking to submit to an order similar to any order which the claimant might obtain in the first action.[69]

Carriers, warehousemen, etc.

19-40   Whilst a mere carrier, warehouseman or agent for transhipment was not liable for infringement,[70] an action could properly be brought against them for an injunction to restrain them from dealing with or disposing of infringing articles in any way.[71] Further, an action for discovery lies against a non-infringer in order to identify infringers or infringing goods.[72]

---

[66] See, e.g. *Mead Corp v Riverwood* [1997] F.S.R. 484; *Coin Controls v Suzo International* [1997] F.S.R. 660; *Napp Pharmaceutical Group Ltd v Asta Medica Ltd* [1999] F.S.R. 370.

[67] (1865) L.R. 1 Eq. 388.

[68] See also *Foxwell v Webster* (1863) 3 New Rep. 103; *North British Rubber Co Ltd v Gormully and Jeffery Manufacturing Co* (1894) 11 R.P.C. 17.

[69] *Multiple Utilities Co Ltd v Souch* (1929) 46 R.P.C. 402; *McCreath v Mayor, etc, of South Shields and Baker* (1932) 49 R.P.C. 349; *Gillette Industries Ltd v Albert* (1940) 57 R.P.C. 85; *White v Glove (Industrial) Manufacturing Co Ltd* [1958] R.P.C. 142; *Reymes-Cole v West Riding Hosiery Ltd* [1961] R.P.C. 273.

[70] See para.14–69 and *Nobel's Explosives Co v Jones, Scott & Co* (1894) 17 Ch D. 721.

[71] *Washburn and Moen Manufacturing Co v Cunard Steamship Co* (1889) 6 R.P.C. 398, 403. See also *Upmann v Elkan* (1871) L.R. 7 Ch. App. 130.

[72] *Norwich Pharmacal Co v Commissioners of Customs & Excise* [1974] R.P.C. 101.

Nothing in the 1977 Act is inconsistent with the continuation under the protective jurisdiction of equity of these rights and, as is implicit in *Smith, Kline & French Laboratories v R.D. Harbottle (Mercantile) Ltd*,[73] they remain good law. **19-41**

Other interested parties

CPR Pt 19.2(2) permits a person to be joined as a party if: (a) it is it is desirable to add the new party so that the court can resolve all the matters in dispute in the proceedings; or (b) if there is an issue involving the new party and an existing party which is connected to the matters in dispute in the proceedings, and it is desirable to add the new party so that the court can resolve that issue. However, in *Daiichi v Comptroller General of Patents* it was held that this rule does not permit the court to join a party merely because it had an interest in the same point of law (in that case as to interpretation of the SPC Regulation) that arose in the case it sought to join.[74] Joinder was refused because it was not desirable to add the new party to decide the issues in the existing proceedings. Submissions on the law would be made by the existing parties and the addition of the additional party would not have any beneficial effect on the court's ability to resolve the maters in dispute. **19-42**

Third party procedure

Where an indemnity was given to the defendants, after the commencement of the action, by a third party who had manufactured the infringing articles, it was held that the person giving such an indemnity should be joined as party.[75] Such third party will only be bound by the decision of the court in so far as the court may direct, and if the claimants neglect to amend by joining them as a defendant they will not be able to obtain an injunction against them as well as against the actual defendant.[76] **19-43**

However, it has been held that a defendant is not entitled to compel the claimant to join as co-defendant a person who supplied the defendant with the machine, the use of which is alleged to be an infringement, and who, the defendant alleges, is a licensee of the claimant; the question of infringement can be properly and conveniently tried without such joinder.[77] Unless, therefore, the defendant can join such person as a third party under CPR r.20.6, their only course is to commence a separate action against them. **19-44**

3. CLAIM FORM

Issue of the claim form

Actions in either the High Court or IPEC are commenced by the issue of a claim form from the relevant Production Centre.[78] Every claim in the Patents Court will be allocated to the Multi-track and the CPR provisions relating to allocation **19-45**

---

[73] [1980] R.P.C. 363.
[74] [2010] EWHC 2898 (Pat).
[75] *Edison and Swan Electric Light Co v Holland* (1886) 33 Ch D. 497; (1886) 3 R.P.C. 395 (under RSC Ord.16 rr.1 and 2). See now CPR r.20.6.
[76] *Edison and Swan Electric Light Co v Holland* (1889) 41 Ch D. 28; 6 R.P.C. 243, 286.
[77] *Evans v Central Electric Supply Co Ltd* (1923) 40 R.P.C. 357.
[78] CPR rr.7.2(1) and 7.10.

questionnaires and track allocation will not apply.[79] Where a claim has been allocated to the Patents Court, an application for directions (including an application for a fixed date of hearing) shall be made by the claimant within 14 days of the date when all defendants who intend to file and serve a defence have done so. If the claimant does not make such an application, any other party may do so.[80]

Contents of claim form

19-46   The claim form must[81]:

(a)   contain a concise statement of the nature of the claim (e.g. "infringement of patent");
(b)   specify the remedy which the claimant seeks;
(c)   where the claimant is making a claim for money, contain a statement of value in accordance with r.16.3; and
(d)   contain such matters as are required by the PD 63—Intellectual Property Claims.[82]

19-47   The remedies sought are normally injunction; damages or, at the claimant's option, an account of profits; delivery up or destruction of all infringing articles; and costs.

The statement of value

19-48   The statement of value required under CPR r.16.3 is a statement of how much the claimant expects to recover by way of damages or profits. If the money claim is the only claim made by the claimant, then normally the claim form cannot be issued in the High Court unless the statement of value exceeds £100,000.[83] However, there is an exception where the claim form states that the claim is to be in one of the specialist High Court lists and states which list.[84] If the claim form contains a statement that the value of the claim is more than £10m, the action will be exempted from the costs management provisions of CPR.[85]

Service of the claim form

19-49   After a claim form has been issued, it must be served on the defendant.[86] The general rule is that a claim form must be served within four months of issue,[87] though that is extended to six months where the claim form is to be served out of this jurisdiction.[88] Service generally is regulated by CPR Pt 6. If no address for

---

[79]   CPR r.63.1(3).
[80]   PD63—Intellectual Property Claims, paras 5.3–5.6.
[81]   CPR, r.16.2.
[82]   See CPR r.16.2(1)(d) and PD 63—Intellectual Property Claims.
[83]   See CPR r.16.3(5)(a).
[84]   CPR r.16.3(5)(d).
[85]   CPR r.3.12(1) and (2).
[86]   CPR r.7.5(1).
[87]   CPR r.7.5(1).
[88]   CPR r.7.5(2).

direct service upon the defendant is available, service may be made at the address for service given in the Register under the 1977 Act.[89]

Service out of the jurisdiction

Service without permission

The Civil Jurisdiction and Judgments Act 1982 came into force on 1 January **19-50** 1987, giving effect to the 1968 Brussels Convention on Civil Jurisdiction and the Enforcement of Judgments. The Act has been amended by the Civil Jurisdiction and Judgments Act 1991 which gives effect to the 1988 Lugano Convention[90] and by the Civil Jurisdiction and Judgment Order 2001[91] which gives effect to the Judgments Regulation.[92] As from 1 March 2002 the Brussels Convention was largely superseded by the Judgments Regulation, save in relation to Denmark.[93] On 1 January 2010, the 2007 Lugano Convention came into force replacing the 1988 Lugano Convention. It governs the whole of the European Union (including Denmark) as well as Norway, Iceland and Switzerland. Under the Act, the Regulation and the Conventions, permission to serve out of the jurisdiction is not required in many cases.[94]

The Judgments Regulation was recast in Council Regulation (EC) 1215/2012. **19-51** The recast Judgments Regulation applies to all cases commenced on or after 10 January 2015. References to the Regulation in the rest of this section are to the recast Judgments Regulation.

The basic rule under the Regulation[95] is that a person domiciled in a contracting **19-52** state shall be sued in the courts of that state.[96] A person domiciled in a contracting state may be sued in the courts of another contracting state only by virtue of the rules set out in ss.2–7 of Chapter II of the Judgments Regulation.[97] In actions for infringement of a patent, the most important exceptions to the basic rule are art.7(2) and art.8(1).[98]

Article 7(2) provides that in matters relating to tort,[99] a person may be sued in **19-53** the courts for the place where the harmful event occurred or may occur.[100] Thus, a company which is domiciled in another contracting state but which has committed an act of infringement in England may be sued in the courts of this country in reliance of art.7(2). However, where art.7(2) is so invoked, the court's jurisdiction

---

89 CPR r.63.14(2). This address maybe in the UK (see r.63.14(2)(a)) or not (see r.63.14(2)(b)).
90 The principal difference between the two Conventions is the countries to which they apply.
91 SI 2001/3929.
92 Council Regulation (EC) 44/2001.
93 Council Regulation (EC) 44/2001 art.1 para.3.
94 See CPR r.6.33, which gives effect to the Act, the Regulation and the Conventions.
95 The text of the Judgments Regulation is set out in the White Book, Vol.2.
96 art.4.
97 art.5.
98 arts 7 and 8 appear in s.2 of Ch.II.
99 This includes patent infringement, see *Mölnlycke A.B. v Procter & Gamble (No.4)* [1992] R.P.C. 21, CA. See also *Athanasios Kalfelis v Bankhaus Schröder* (C-189/97) [1988] E.C.R. 5565, ECJ.
100 *Shevil v Presse Alliance* [1995] E.C.R. I–415; *Kitechnology B.v v Unicor GmbH* [1995] F.S.R. 765, CA; *Modus Vivendi v British Products Sanmex Co Ltd* [1996] F.S.R. 790; *Mecklermedia Corp v D.C. Congress GmbH* [1997] F.S.R. 627.

in respect of that company will be limited to those acts of infringement which it has committed in this country only.[101]

19-54   Article 8(1) provides that where a person is one of a number of defendants, they may be sued in the country for the place where any of them is domiciled. However, for art.8(1) to apply, the connection between the defendants must be of a kind that makes it expedient to determine the actions together in order to avoid the risk of irreconcilable judgments.[102] Thus, where proceedings are commenced against a UK company for infringement of a patent in England and it is also alleged that a company domiciled abroad in a contracting state is liable with the UK company as a joint tortfeasor, the foreign company may be sued in this country in reliance of art.8(1).[103]

19-55   Schedule 4 of the 1982 Act deals with the allocation of jurisdiction within the United Kingdom. Under the Act, permission to serve in Scotland and Northern Ireland is also not required in many circumstances.[104] Schedule 4 is a modified form of Title II to the Brussels Convention.

19-56   Where, in reliance upon the Judgments Regulation, a person is served out of the jurisdiction without permission, they may wish to dispute the court's jurisdiction and particularly the factual basis for the court's jurisdiction upon which the claimant relies.[105] In those circumstances, the proper course is for the defendant to file an acknowledgement of service in accordance with CPR Pt 10 and then make an application in accordance with CPR Pt 11. Upon the hearing of the application, the claimant must show that they have "a good arguable case" in respect of the allegations upon which they rely.[106]

19-57   The court may have to decide whether it was "first seised" of proceedings as compared with a foreign court.[107] This may involve the application of the Hague Convention[108] on service of documents abroad.

Service with permission

19-58   Where CPR Pts 6.32 and 63.33 do not apply, an application for permission to serve out of the jurisdiction must be made. There is no special rule for patent cases.[109] The witness statement should be full and frank in its disclosure.[110] A mere assertion of infringement is insufficient,[111] the evidence must be sufficiently full to

---

[101] See the comments of Jacob J in *Mecklermedia Corp. v D.C. Congress GmbH* [1997] F.S.R. 627, at 636–637.
[102] *Anthanasios Kalfelis v Bankhaus Schröder* (C-189/97) [1988] E.C.R. 5565, ECJ. *Roche Nederland BV v Primus Goldenberg* (C-539/03) [2007] F.S.R. 5.
[103] *Mölnlycke A.B. v Procter & Gamble (No.4)* [1992] R.P.C. 21, CA.
[104] See CPR r.6.32.
[105] For example, a defendant may wish to contend that they have in fact done nothing at all causing harm within the jurisdiction or that in fact they are not a joint tortfeasor with another person domiciled within the jurisdiction.
[106] *Mölnlycke A.B. v Procter & Gamble (No.4)* [1992] R.P.C. 21, CA. See also para.19-58 and paras 14–143 to 14–163 (and the cases cited therein).
[107] arts 29–34 of the Judgments Regulation.
[108] Hague Convention on Service Abroad of Judicial and Extra Judicial Documents in Civil and Commercial Matters; see *Molins Plc v G.D SpA* [2000] F.S.R. 893.
[109] *Cranway v Playtech* [2007] R.P.C. 22.
[110] *The Hai Hing* [2000] 1 Lloyd's Rep. 300.
[111] *Cranway v Playtech* [2007] R.P.C. 22 and see *Raychem Corp v Thermon (UK)* [1989] R.P.C. 423; *Puschner v Tom Palmer (Scotland) Ltd* [1989] R.P.C. 430.

show that there is a good arguable case for the relief claimed.[112] In *Magnesium Elektron Limited v Molycorp*[113] one of the ways in which the claimant satisfied this requirement was by reliance of s.100 PA 1977, which provides that where the invention for which a patent is granted is a process for obtaining a new product, the same product produced by a person other than the proprietor of the patent or a licensee of theirs shall, unless the contrary is proved, be taken in any proceedings to have been obtained by that process. The court held that the patented process satisfied the requirements of s.100 because products with a particular unique fingerprint were produced by the patented process and no other process known to the claimant's expert. There is nothing in the section that requires the "new product" to be a thing defined at the same level of generality as the words used in the process claim.

Where permission to serve out is required, the usual grounds in patent actions are that: **19-59**

(a) an injunction is sought to restrain a person from doing an act within the jurisdiction[114];

(b) a person is a necessary and proper party to an action properly brought against some other person duly served within the jurisdiction,[115] as, for instance, upon the consignees of infringing goods in respect of which an action had been brought against the carriers thereof[116]; and

(c) the claim is founded upon tort and the damage was sustained, or resulted from an act committed, within the jurisdiction.[117]

A person served out of the jurisdiction with permission may dispute the court's jurisdiction by filing an acknowledgment of service in accordance with CPR Pt 10 and then making an application in accordance with CPR Pt 11. **19-60**

European cross-border suits

Article 2 of the Brussels Convention (now art.4 of the recast Judgments Regulation) opened the way to actions in the English courts for infringement of foreign intellectual property rights. This is because where an English domiciled company has infringed a foreign intellectual property right, art.4 allows the proprietor of that right to sue the company in this country for those acts of infringement notwithstanding that they were committed abroad and infringed a foreign right.[118] **19-61**

Moreover, a European patent granted under the European Patent Convention **19-62**

---

112 *Seaconstar Far East Ltd v Bank Markazi Jomhouri Islam Iran* [1994] 1 A.C. 438, and see also *Cranway v Playtech* [2007] R.P.C. 22; *Vitkovice Horni a Hutni Tezirstvo v Korner* [1951] A.C. 869; *The Electric Furnace Co v Selas Corp of America* [1987] R.P.C. 23; *Unilever v Gillette UK* [1989] R.P.C. 583; and *Lubrizol Corp v Esso Petroleum Co Ltd* [1992] R.P.C. 281, High Court and 467, CA. See also paras 14–142 to 14–163.
113 [2015] EWHC 3596 (Pat).
114 CPR Pt 6, PD 6B r.3.1(2); and see *Magnesium Elektron Limited v Molycorp* [2015] EWHC 3596 (Pat), at [37]–[38] citing *Rosler v Hilbery* [1925] Ch 250 and *Watson v Daily Record* [1907] 1 KB 853.
115 CPR Pt 6, PD 6B r.3.1(3); and see *Massey v Haynes & Co* (1888) 21 Q.B.D. 330.
116 *Washburn and Moen Manufacturing Co v Cunard Steamship Co* (1889) 6 R.P.C. 398; see also *Magnesium Elektron Limited v Molycorp* [2015] EWHC 3596 (Pat), at [39]–[41].
117 CPR Pt 6, PD 6B r.3.1(9), see *Magnesium Elektron Limited v Molycorp* [2015] EWHC 3596 (Pat), at [42]–[48].
118 *Pearce (Gareth) v Ove Arup* [1999] F.S.R. 525, CA; [1997] F.S.R. 641; *Coin Controls v Suzo International* [1997] F.S.R. 660, per Laddie J; *Fort Dodge Ltd v Akzo Nobel N.V.* [1998] F.S.R. 222,

normally applies in identical form in each of the European States for which it is granted.[119] Consequently, some proprietors of European patents have seen it as but a short step to seek to have all the acts of infringement committed in Europe by a single defendant or group of defendants[120] in relation to a particular product tried before the courts of one state.

19-63   However, art.24(4) of the Judgments Regulation (formerly art.16(4) of the Brussels Convention) provides that in proceedings concerned with the registration or validity of patents, the courts of the contracting state in which the registration has taken place shall have exclusive jurisdiction regardless of the defendant's domicile. In *GAT v Luk*[121] the Court of Justice held that these rules were mandatory and could not be derogated from either by agreement (under art.25, formerly art.17) or by submitting to the jurisdiction (under art.26, formerly art.18). The Court of Justice also held that under art.27 (formerly art.25)[122] where a court is seized of a claim which is principally concerned with a matter over which the courts of another contracting state have exclusive jurisdiction by virtue of art.24, it shall declare of its own motion that it has no jurisdiction. Consequently, where an action is commenced in this country for infringement of foreign patent rights in reliance of the Convention, the court is required to decline jurisdiction if the defendant attacks the validity of the patent rights in question.[123] However, until the attack on validity is made, the English court will have jurisdiction over the claim and if the defendant does not attack the validity of the foreign patent rights, then the court will continue to have jurisdiction.[124] The CJEU has also ruled that art.24(4) does not preclude the granting of cross-border interim relief under art.35 (previously art.31), even when the defendants contend that the patent is invalid at that interim stage.[125]

19-64   *GAT v Luk*[126] was applied in the Patents Court in *Knorr-Bremse v Haldex*,[127] which concerned an application to stay English proceedings on the basis that the Dusseldorf court was said to have exclusive jurisdiction as a result of the terms of a settlement agreement. The stay was refused on two grounds, first that agreement did not have the effect contended for because it was not binding on the claimant (who was neither a party to it nor a successor to a party) and secondly because the claimant had indicated it would be challenging the validity of the patent in issue and that once that was clear, the English court had exclusive jurisdiction.

19-65   A further development in this area occurred in *Roche v Primus*.[128] In that case a patentee began patent infringement proceedings in the Netherlands against a Dutch company and included as co-defendants other members of the same group based

---

CA.

[119] It is to be noted, however, that the rights conferred by a European patent are not necessarily the same in each contracting state. This is because a European patent is essentially a bundle of national patents, that is to say for each state for which it is granted, it confers on the proprietor the same rights as would be conferred by a national patent granted in that state; see EPC art.64(1).

[120] As in *Coin Controls v Suzo International* [1997] F.S.R. 660 where the foreign companies in Germany and Spain were joined as co-defendants in reliance of art.6(1). See also *Expandable Grafts v Boston Scientific* [1999] F.S.R. 352, Court of Appeal in The Hague.

[121] (C-4/03) [2006] F.S.R. 45.

[122] Formerly art.19 of the Brussels Convention (the numbering used in the judgment).

[123] *Coin Controls v Suzo International* [1997] F.S.R. 660; *Fort Dodge v Akzo Nobel N.V.* [1998] F.S.R. 222, CA.

[124] *Coin Controls v Suzo International* [1997] F.S.R. 660.

[125] *Solvay v Honeywell* (C-616/10).

[126] (C-4/03) [2006] F.S.R. 45.

[127] [2008] EWHC 156 (Pat), [2008] F.S.R. 30.

[128] (C-539/03) [2007] F.S.R. 5.

in other European states and selling the same product on the basis that they were infringing in their own countries. The Court of Justice held that art.6 of the Brussels Convention (as it then was) did not apply to permit such a course. Divergent decisions by the courts of different states in such a case were not contradictory or irreconcilable even if the parties had acted in an identical or similar manner. Although procedural economy might militate in favour of the proceedings being constituted as they were, to permit it would undermine the principle of legal certainty which is the basis for the Convention.[129]

Cross-border non-infringement proceedings

As well as a patentee bringing cross-border proceedings for infringement of various designations of their European Patent in a single jurisdiction, defendants sometimes bring cross-border non-infringement proceedings seeking declarations that their product would not infringe a number of national designations of a European patent. A recent example of such a case in the English Courts was *Actavis v Eli Lilly & Co*.[130] In that case, the claimant sought declarations that its proposed product would not infringe any claim of either the UK, French or Spanish designations of Lilly's patent.[131]   **19-66**

Such cross-border cases can give rise disputes as to the identity of the court first seised and whether later proceedings for infringement ought to be stayed pursuant to arts 29 and 30 (previously arts 27 and 28) of the Judgments Regulation. In *Molnlyke v BSN*[132] proceedings for declarations for non-infringement over a number of national designations of a European patent, including the UK designation, had been commenced in Sweden. In order for a stay under art.29, there must be identity of parties and identity of cause of action.[133] Floyd J refused to stay later English infringement proceedings pursuant to art.29 on the basis that there was not identity of parties to the two pieces of litigation. In the Swedish proceedings the only party was the patentee whereas in the English proceedings, the UK exclusive licensee was also a party. The appeal was dismissed for the additional reason that the Swedish Court was not seised of the same issue because the non-infringement issue was not being conducted on the basis of actual samples as was the case in the UK (as was thought before the Patents Court), but on the basis of a written description. This was determined by the Court of Appeal by asking the Swedish Judge to identify the issues of which her court was seised.[134]   **19-67**

In some cases a litigant will commence proceedings for declarations of non-infringement in a single European country with a notoriously slow legal process. Italy has traditionally been the jurisdiction of choice for this tactic. It is alleged that this "torpedo" is intended to be a stifling device to hinder a patentee's attempt to enforce his patent rights in other European states. As the Court of Appeal said in *RIM v Visto*[135] "much ingenuity is expended on all this elaborate game playing",   **19-68**

---

[129] (C-539/03) [2007] F.S.R. 5, see [34]–[38].
[130] [2015] R.P.C 6 (Pat); [2015] EWCA Civ 555 (CA).
[131] Non-infringement of the German designation had also been in issue until shortly before the trial, when the German court decided the issue itself. See [2015] EWCA civ 555, [95]–[99] for a chronology of the various proceedings in relation to the German designation.
[132] [2009] EWHC 3370.
[133] *"The Tatry"* (C-406/92) [1999] QB 515.
[134] [2010] EWCA 988.
[135] *Research in Motion v Visto* [2008] F.S.R. 20, CA, see [15]–[16].

but nevertheless the court also held that merely "firing" such an Italian torpedo as took place in that case, was not abusing the system.

Anti-suit injunctions

19-69   The ECJ has held that an anti-suit injunction is tantamount to interference with the jurisdiction of the foreign court and, hence, so far as concerns the Brussels Convention, such an injunction is incompatible with the principle that the jurisdiction of a court cannot be reviewed by a court in another contracting state, other than in the exceptional cases listed in art.28. Accordingly the Convention precludes the grant by a court in one contracting state of an injunction prohibiting a party to proceedings pending before it from commencing or continuing proceedings before a court in another contracting state, even where that party was acting in bad faith.[136]

Jurisdiction in case of objectionable patenting activity

19-70   In *Scandisk v Koninklijke Philips*[137] the Patents Court considered whether it had jurisdiction over a case concerning an allegation of breach of the Competition Act 1998 and/or arts 81 or 82 of the EC treaty (now arts 101 and 102 of the TFEU) relating to the patenting and patent licensing activities of one of the parties. Pumfrey J held that the court had no jurisdiction under the Brussels Regulation. The only arguable basis was art.5(3) concerning the place of damage but that failed. One allegation related to divisional patents (including patents covering the UK) but even assuming the divisional portfolio was wider than it ought to be and that this had an effect in England and Wales, nevertheless art.5(3) was not satisfied because there was no immediate loss suffered in the jurisdiction.

Non-Convention countries

19-71   In *Lucasfilm v Ainsworth*[138] the Court of Appeal held that actions for infringement of foreign (i.e. non-EU, non-Lugano) intellectual property rights cannot be brought in this country because they were barred by the *Mocambique* rule.[139] However, on appeal the House of Lords overturned this decision in relation to actions for infringement of copyright. Their Lordships left open whether the *Mocambique* rule applied to patents, stating that it was possible to see how the rationale of that rule can be applied to patents, particularly where questions of validity are involved.[140] The point therefore remains one to be decided in a future case.

Acknowledgement of service

19-72   A defendant may file an acknowledgement of service if they are unable to file a defence within the period specified by r.15.4[141] or if they wish to dispute the court's jurisdiction.[142] In effect this means that either an acknowledgement of service or a defence should normally be filed within 14 days after service of the particulars of

---

[136] *Turner v Grovit* (C-159/02) [2005] 1 A.C. 101.
[137] [2007] EWHC 332 (Ch); [2007] F.S.R. 22.
[138] [2009] EWCA 1328 (civ); [2010] F.S.R. 10.
[139] *British South Africa Company v Companhia de Moçambique* [1893] A.C. 602.
[140] See [2011] F.S.R. 41, at [101] and [106].
[141] CPR r.10.1(3)(a).
[142] CPR r.10.1(3)(b).

claim[143] because the longer period for filing a defence provided by r.15.4(1)(b) (and extended to 42 days in the case of patent infringement cases)[144] does not apply unless the acknowledgement of service has been filed. However, a longer period for filing a defence may apply in any of the special cases set out in r.15.4(2).[145]

Failure to file an acknowledgement of service or a defence

It is not essential for a defendant who wishes to contest the claimant's claim to file an acknowledgment of service as they can file a defence instead.   **19-73**

However, where a defendant fails to file either an acknowledgment of service or a defence, the procedure is regulated by CPR Pt 12. Where, as is usually the case, there is a claim for an injunction, the claimant must apply to the court under CPR Pt 23. The court must be satisfied that the particulars of claim have been served on the defendant and that the relevant times for acknowledgment or defence have expired. The claim form and the particulars of claim must show prima facie entitlement to the relief sought and the order for delivery-up must identify the goods to be delivered-up.[146]   **19-74**

Where one defendant only appears

A question has arisen as to what should be done if, in an action against two defendants for the same infringement, one of them fails to appear. If the cause of action was severable the claimant might apply, under CPR Pt 12, for judgment against the defendant who failed to give notice of an intention to file either acknowledgment of service or a defence.[147] The defendant who is defending might, however, succeed in establishing the invalidity of the patent, and the difficulty arises as to the position of the other defendant.   **19-75**

On the whole it may be said that an injunction is an equitable remedy and that it would be contrary to principle for the same tribunal which had pronounced a patent to be invalid to restrain a member of the public from doing what could not be an infringement. Some old cases in which issues if this kind arose are collected together in this footnote.[148]   **19-76**

4.   INTERIM INJUNCTIONS

Where it appears to the court "just or convenient" the claimant can obtain an injunction to restrain the defendant from infringing pending judgment in the action. Such application is made to the Patents Court by application notice under CPR Pt 23 which must be served on the defendant at least three clear days before the   **19-77**

---

143 CPR r.15.4(1)(a).
144 CPR r.63.7(a).
145 See also CPR r.63.7(b).
146 *Paton Culvery & Co Ltd v Rosedale Associated Manufacturers Ltd* [1966] R.P.C. 61.
147 See *Weinberg v Balkan Sobranie Cigarettes Ltd* (1923) 40 R.P.C. 399 (trade mark).
148 See *Cropper v Smith and Hancock* (1885) 10 App. Cas. 249; (1885) 2 R.P.C. 17; *Actiengesellschaft für Cartonnagen Industrie v Remus and Burgon* (1896) 13 R.P.C. 94; *Savage Brothers Ltd v Brindle* (1900) 17 R.P.C. 228, 233.

hearing.[149] In cases of exceptional urgency, an application may be made without serving an application notice.[150]

Principles governing interim injunctions

19-78   The House of Lords in *American Cyanamid Co v Ethicon Ltd*[151] laid down the principles upon which interim injunctions should be granted. Lord Diplock stated that:

> "The object of the interlocutory injunction is to protect the plaintiff against injury by violation of his right for which he could not be adequately compensated in damages recoverable in the action if the uncertainty were resolved in his favour at the trial; but the plaintiff's need for protection must be weighed against the corresponding need of the defendant to be protected against injury resulting from his having been prevented from exercising his own legal rights for which he could not be adequately compensated under the plaintiff's undertaking in damages if the uncertainty were resolved in the defendant's favour at the trial. The court must weigh one need against another and determine where 'the balance of convenience' lies."[152]

19-79   Lord Diplock, in a speech which was agreed with by the rest of the House, laid down the following guidelines:

(i)   There is no rule that a claimant must make out a prima facie case. "The court no doubt must be satisfied that the claim is not frivolous or vexatious; in other words, that there is a serious issue to be tried.[153] ... So unless the material available to the court at the hearing of the application for an interlocutory injunction fails to disclose that the plaintiff has any real prospect of succeeding in his claim for a permanent injunction at the trial, the court should go on to consider whether the balance of convenience lies in favour of granting or refusing the interlocutory relief that is sought."[154]

(ii)   "It is no part of the court's function at this stage of the litigation to try to resolve conflicts of evidence on affidavit as to facts on which the claims of either party may ultimately depend nor to decide difficult questions of law which call for detailed agreement and mature considerations."[155]

(iii)   "If damages in the measure recoverable at common law would be an adequate remedy and the defendant would be in a financial position to pay them, no interlocutory injunction should normally be granted, however strong the plaintiff's claim appeared to be at that stage."[156]

(iv)   "If, on the other hand, damages would not provide an adequate remedy for the plaintiff ..., the court should then consider whether, on the contrary hypothesis that the defendant were to succeed at the trial ... he would be adequately compensated under the plaintiff's undertaking as to damages for the loss he would have sustained by being prevented from doing so between the time of the application and the time of the trial. If damages in the measure recoverable under such an undertaking would be an adequate remedy and the plaintiff would be in a financial position to pay

---

[149]   CPR r.23.7(1)(b).
[150]   CPR Pt 23, Practice Direction—Applications para.3.
[151]   [1975] R.P.C. 513.
[152]   [1975] R.P.C. 513, 540, 1.6.
[153]   [1975] R.P.C. 513, 541, 1.13.
[154]   [1975] R.P.C. 513, 541, 1.23.
[155]   [1975] R.P.C. 513, 541, 1.15. But see CPR Pt 24.
[156]   [1975] R.P.C. 513, 541, 1.32.

them, there would be no reason upon this ground to refuse an interlocutory injunction."[157]

(v)   "It is where there is doubt as to the adequacy of the respective remedies in damages available to either party or to both, that the question of balance of convenience arises. It would be unwise to attempt even to list all the various matters which may need to be taken into consideration in deciding where the balance lies, let alone to suggest the relative weight to be attached to them. These will vary from case to case."[158]

(vi)   "Where other factors appear to be evenly balanced it is a counsel of prudence to take such measures as are calculated to preserve the status quo."[159]

(vii)   "If the extent of the uncompensatable disadvantage to each party would not differ widely, it may not be improper to take into account in tipping the balance the relative strength of each party's case as revealed by the affidavit evidence adduced on the hearing of the application. This however should be done only where it is apparent upon the facts disclosed by evidence as to which there is no credible dispute that the strength of one party's case is disproportionate to that of the other party."[160]

As Lord Hoffmann explained when giving the advice of the Privy Council in **19-80** *National Commercial Bank Jamaica Ltd v Olint Corp Ltd*,[161] in practice it is often hard to tell whether either damages or the cross-undertaking will be an adequate remedy and the court has to engage in an exercise in trying to predict whether granting or withholding an injunction is more or less likely to cause irremediable prejudice (and to what extent). Ultimately, the basic principle is therefore that the court should take whichever course seems likely to cause the least irremediable prejudice to one party or the other.

An interim injunction may be granted if the defendant has applied for a **19-81** compulsory licence but they infringe the patent during a period when their application is still pending.[162] Further, an interim injunction may be granted in respect of a valid claim even though other claims in the specification are not prima facie valid.[163] It is also possible for an injunction to be granted pending an appeal on claims found to be invalid at trial, provided the court is satisfied that the appeal has real prospects of success.[164]

Types of interim injunction order

Generally, the orders sought by way of interim injunction are negative in **19-82** character, i.e. they seek to restrain a defendant, pending trial, from doing or continuing to do, a specific act. However, the court is able to grant any order that it concludes is just and convenient. Thus, if appropriate, the court will grant manda-

---

[157] [1975] R.P.C. 513, 541, 1.36.
[158] [1975] R.P.C. 513, 541, 1.46.
[159] [1975] R.P.C. 513, 542, 1.3.
[160] [1975] R.P.C. 513, 542, 1.19. See also *NWL v Woods* [1979] 3 All E.R. 614.
[161] [2009] UKPC 16, applied in the various injunction application in *Warner-Lambert v Actavis* [2015] EWHC 72 (Pat), at [90]; *Warner-Lambert v Sandoz* [2015] EWHC 3152 (Pat), at [82].
[162] *Hoffman-La Roche & Co A.G. v Inter-Continental Pharmaceuticals Ltd* [1965] R.P.C. 226.
[163] *Hoffman-La Roche & Co A.G. v DDSA Pharmaceuticals Ltd* [1965] R.P.C. 504. See also para.19-98 where an application to amend the patent is made
[164] *Novartis AG v Hospira UK Ltd* [2013] EWCA Civ 583; [2014] R.P.C. 3.

tory orders. However, the court is generally more reluctant to do so because such an order is more likely to cause irredeemable prejudice that a prohibitory order.[165]

19-83   In the pregabalin litigation, which concerned a Swiss form claim to the use of the drug to treat a particular disorder (pain) in circumstances where the drug was also used to treat other, non-patented disorders, the court granted an interim order against the Department of Health. The order required the Department of Health to issue guidance to medical practitioners and pharmacists advising them not to prescribe or dispense generic pregabalin for the patented pain indication but only to prescribe the patentee's product.[166]

Serious issue to be tried

19-84   Usually the first part of the *American Cyanamid* test is not particularly onerous of the patentee to surpass. They merely need to establish that there is an arguable case that the defendant is infringing. It is not uncommon for it to be accepted by the defendant that there is a serious issue to be tried. However, if the existence of a serious issue is not conceded, this can give rise to two issues: (i) whether the defendant's product or process falls within the scope of any claim of the patent, and (ii) whether the defendant has done any act capable of being an infringement.

19-85   The first type of issue can be resolved either by evidence from an expert witness or, in appropriate cases, by the performance of experiments.[167]

19-86   The second type of issue arose in *Merck v Teva*.[168] There the action and the application for an interim injunction were brought on a quia timet basis because the defendant had obtained a marketing authorisation before the expiry of the SPC protecting the drug in question and had refused to answer any questions about its launch plans. The judge held that whilst obtaining a marketing authorisation did lead to an inference that the defendant intended to use it, it did not lead to an inference it intended to do so before expiry of the SPC in infringement of the patentee's rights. However, the fact that the defendant had obtained its marketing authorisation nearly two years before expiry of the SPC did lead to the conclusion that it intended to use it before the SPC had expired. Thus a cause of action based upon a threat to infringe was found. In considering whether there was an imminent threat to use the marketing authorisation such that an interim injunction was necessary, the court relied upon the timing of the marketing authorisation, the absence of a statement as to the defendant's intentions and the defendant's conduct in a previous case, which showed that it was prepared to launch a generic product without notice in the face of a patent and in large quantities. In all these circumstances the court was prepared to draw the inference that the defendant was not prepared to wait for the conclusion of the proceedings before launching its product and accordingly found the requirement for an arguable case satisfied.

19-87   From time to time, defendants have sought to avoid an injunction on the basis of a submission that the patent is invalid. However, because issues such as claim

---

[165] *National Commercial Bank Jamaica Ltd v Olint Corp Ltd* [2009] UKPC 16, [19].
[166] *Warner-Lambert v Actavis* [2015] EWHC 485 (Pat); [2015] R.P.C. 24, relying upon the judgment in *Cartier International AG v British Sky Broadcasting Ltd* [2014] EWHC 3354 (Ch), [2015] E.T.M.R. 1, at [96]–[110].
[167] As happened in *Leo v Sandoz* [2008] EWHC 541 (Pat).
[168] [2012] EWHC 627 (Pat); [2012] F.S.R. 24.

construction, novelty and particularly obviousness can rarely be dealt with summarily, these attempts are rarely successful.

Adequacy of damages

Many patent cases are not appropriate ones for the grant of an interim injunc-   **19-88**
tion because damages would be an adequate remedy for the patentee. Where the
infringement causes the patentee to lose sales, provided the defendant keeps proper
records of the sales they have made, the court can award damages based upon its
assessment of the proportion of the defendant's sales that the patentee would have
made and the patentee's usual profit margin.

However, there is a well-established line of patent cases in which interim injunc-   **19-89**
tions are commonly granted. These all concern the launch of a generic pharmaceutical product. Although each case turns on its own facts, the court has shown itself
to be ready to accept an argument that the launch of a generic pharmaceutical
product will cause substantial and unquantifiable loss to the patentee because it will
permanently depress the patentee's price. The argument goes that entry of the
generic product(s) will result in a downwards spiral in the price of the product and
that even if the patentee were to be successful at trial and remove the generic
products from the market, they will not be able to put the price back to previous
levels. Examples of cases where this argument has been accepted are listed in the
footnote.[169] An exception to this general principle was *Cephalon v Orchid*.[170]
However, that was a case where the infringement claim only just passed the serious issue hurdle, the invalidity arguments looked strong and, most importantly,
there was evidence that the patentee had been able to raise the price of the product
after temporarily lowering it to compete with competition from parallel imports.

Injunction when no damages recoverable

It would be unusual to grant an interim injunction to protect a property right if   **19-90**
no damages for infringement could be recovered. Regardless, if the claimant has a
cause of action to protect a property right recognised by the law, there is no reason
in principle why the court should not grant an interim injunction to protect that right
even if damages are not recoverable.[171] Thus the fact that a claimant sought to
restrain infringement of one patent in order to protect its market in a product made
under a different patent was no bar to an interim injunction.[172]

---

[169] *SmithKline Beecham v Generics (UK)* Unreported, 23 October 2001; *SmithKline Beecham plc v
Apotex Europe Ltd* [2003] EWCA Civ 137, [2003] F.S.R. 31; *Novartis AG v Hospira UK Ltd* [2013]
EWCA Civ 583, [2014] 1 W.L.R. 1264.

[170] [2010] EWHC 2945 (Pat).

[171] Per Aldous LJ in *SmithKline Beecham v Apotex Europe Ltd* [2003] EWCA Civ 137; [2003] F.S.R.
31, reconciling the apparent conflict between *Polaroid Corp v Eastman Kodak* [1977] R.P.C. 379
and *Peaudouce SA v Kimberly-Clark* [1996] F.S.R. 680 with *Corruplast Ltd v George Harrison
(Agencies) Ltd* [1978] R.P.C. 761 and *Gerber Garment Technology v Lectra Systems Ltd* [1995]
R.P.C. 383.

[172] *SmithKline Beecham v Apotex Europe Ltd* [2003] EWCA Civ 137; [2003] F.S.R. 31.

Defendant with other business interests

19-91   The fact that a defendant may have other viable business interests to which it can turn its attention is not a strong ground for urging the grant of interlocutory relief.[173]

Clearing the way

19-92   When a basic patent for a pharmaceutical agent expires (or the relevant Supplementary Protection Certificate expires), the innovator company will often possess a number of further patents which may be infringed by a generic product otherwise due to be launched at expiry of the basic patent/SPC. While there is no obligation on a potential defendant to start proceedings, if a party who wishes to launch a generic product in such circumstances chooses to wait until there is insufficient time between notifying the innovator company of its intentions and the launch date, that fact can be taken into account by a court deciding whether or not to grant an interim injunction.[174] In other words:

> "Where litigation is bound to ensue if the defendant introduces his product, he can avoid all the problems of an interlocutory injunction if he clears the way first. That is what the procedures for revocation and declaration of non-infringement are for."[175]

19-93   Accordingly, on evidence before the court that an interim injunction would cause uncompensatable loss to both sides; because on the claimant's side there would be formidable difficulties in the way of trying to get back to its present market position after a major collapse in prices caused by generic competition and because on the defendant's side one could not determine what the defendant would have sold if it entered the market at the moment it wishes to, the failure to clear the way has led to interim injunctions being granted in a number of patent cases in recent years.[176]

Cross-undertakings in favour of the NHS/Department of Health

19-94   In *Abbott Laboratories and Abbott Laboratories Ltd v Approved Prescription Services, Ranbaxy Europe Ltd and Generics (UK) Limited*[177] which concerned a pharmaceutical product sold to the National Health Service, the Secretary of State for Health applied to be named in the cross-undertaking in damages which would have been required had the claimant succeeded in its application for an interim

---

173   *Conder International Ltd v Hibbing* [1984] F.S.R. 312.
174   *SmithKline Beecham v Apotex Europe Ltd* [2003] EWCA Civ 137; [2003] F.S.R. 31.
175   Per Jacob J in *SmithKline Beecham v Apotex Europe Ltd* [2003] EWHC 2556 (Pat), [2003] F.S.R. 30, [68], upheld on appeal in *SmithKline Beecham v Apotex Europe Ltd* [2003] EWCA Civ 137, [2003] F.S.R. 31. See also *Improver Corp v Remington Consumer Products Ltd* [1989] R.P.C. 69.
176   *SmithKline Beecham v Generics*, Unreported, 23 October 2001, Patents Court; *SmithKline Beecham v Apotex Europe Ltd* [2003] EWCA Civ 137, [2003] F.S.R. 31; *Abbott Laboratories and Abbott Laboratories Ltd v Approved Prescription Services, Ranbaxy Europe Ltd and Generics (UK) Limited* [2004] EWHC 2723 (Pat) in which Pumfrey J held that he would have granted an interim injunction on this basis but for the fact that he found the relevant claim to be invalid on an application for summary judgment; *Warner-Lambert v Actavis* [2015] EWHC 72 (Pat), at [13]–[136], where although no injunction was granted, the court held that the failure to clear the way would favour the grant of interim relief. *Warner-Lambert v Sandoz* [2015] EWHC3152 (Pat), at [99]–[102], where the failure to clear the path relied upon was the failure to seek a declaration of non-infringement.
177   [2004] EWHC 2723 (Pat) and see also *SmithKline Beecham Plc v Apotex Europe Ltd* [2005] EWCA 658 (Civ); [2007] F.S.R. 6, see [77].

injunction. Since the court decided the patent was invalid the issue was not determined. A similar cross-undertaking was given in the *Warner-Lambert* litigation concerning the drug pregabalin.[178] However, the effect of such a cross-undertaking and its extent are not wholly clear and as to date no inquiry on such a cross-undertaking has taken place. These issues therefore remain to be decided in a future case.

The "snowball" effect

It is often argued that unless a claimant is seen quickly to prevent infringements **19-95** of their patent, other persons will be encouraged to infringe. This may in a suitable case be a proper matter to be taken into account[179] but it must be supported by cogent evidence.

The "springboard" argument

In cases where a patent is reaching the end of its term, no lesser protection should **19-96** be afforded to a claimant.

> "A patent monopoly not only entitles the holder to exploit the invention without competition during the period of patent protection, it also enables him to approach or enter on the period after the monopoly ceases in a strong position in the market place."[180]

A defendant should not, therefore, pre-empt the expiry of a patent and thereby **19-97** acquire a valuable commercial bridgehead.[181] Nor will a defendant if subject to an injunction be permitted to carry out those tests and trials necessary to secure the regulatory approvals needed to commence marketing once the patent has expired.[182] However, an offer to supply post-expiry of the patent is not an infringement even if the offer itself is made pre-expiry.[183]

Amendment pending

The court will not grant an injunction to restrain infringement of a patent, the **19-98** scope of the monopoly of which could not be defined,[184] and if an interim injunction had been granted before an application was made to amend, the court would discharge that injunction.[185] On the other hand the court can enforce a partially valid patent by way of interim injunction where the enforcement was of a claim which was valid[186] and can even enforce a claim found invalid at trial pending appeal, provided it is satisfied that that appeal has a real prospect of success.[187]

---

[178] *Warner-Lambert v Actavis* [2015] EWHC 72 (Pat); *Warner-Lambert v Sandoz* [2015] EWHC 3152 (Pat).
[179] *Conder International Ltd v Hibbing* [1984] F.S.R. 312, 315.
[180] Per Eichelbaum J in *Monsanto Co v Stauffer Co (N.Z.)* [1984] F.S.R. 559, HC (N.Z.); and *Monsanto Co v Stauffer Chemical Co* [1984] F.S.R. 574, CA.
[181] See *Dyson Appliances v Hoover (No.2)* [2001] R.P.C. 27 in which a post expiry injunction (in final form) was granted in these circumstances.
[182] *Monsanto Co v Stauffer Chemical Co* [1985] R.P.C. 515.
[183] *Gerber Garment Technology Inc v Lectra Systems Ltd* [1995] R.P.C. 383, 412.
[184] *Mölnlycke A.B. v Procter & Gamble* [1990] R.P.C. 487.
[185] *Mölnlycke A.B. v Procter & Gamble* [1990] R.P.C. 487.
[186] *SmithKline Beecham v Apotex Europe Ltd* [2002] EWHC 2556 (Pat); [2003] F.S.R. 30 and the cases cited therein. The case went to the Court of Appeal—*SmithKline Beecham v Apotex Europe Ltd*

Impecunious defendant

19-99   Where damages are an adequate remedy to the claimant but doubt exists as to the financial standing of the defendant, the court may decline to grant an interlocutory injunction upon the undertaking of the defendant to pay a reasonable sum into a suitable bank account, usually in the names of the parties' solicitors.[188]

Impecunious claimant

19-100   The fact that a claimant may not be able to meet his liability on the cross-undertaking[189] is not conclusive. The course to be taken is that which would involve the least risk of ultimate injustice.[190]

Delay will bar right

19-101   An interim injunction will not be granted in cases where the claimant is guilty of delay after learning of the infringement.

19-102   In *North British Rubber Co v Gormully and Jeffery Co*,[191] Chitty J said:

> "Now I am not aware, having regard to patents, that there is any substantial ground of distinction between an interlocutory injunction upon a patent right and upon any other. The principles appear to me to be substantially the same; and the general rule of the court is that a person who comes to ask for that remedy, which is granted with despatch and for the purposes of protecting rights until the trial, should come promptly."[192]

19-103   Whether or not such delay will deprive a claimant of an interim injunction will be judged also by reference to any prejudice occasioned to the defendant.[193]

19-104   The amount of delay which will prevent the granting of an interlocutory injunction will, of course, vary with the nature of the patent and the circumstances of the trade.

19-105   The delay may, in some cases, be satisfactorily explained, as in a case where the claimants' solicitors advised the claimants not to commence an action until the defendants appeared to be in a condition of sufficient financial soundness to undertake manufacture of the infringing articles,[194] or when the defendant embarked on a deliberate course of action seeking to obstruct the patentee from preventing

---

[2002] EWCA Civ 137; [2003] F.S.R. 31 where this point was not taken. See also *Hoffman-La Roche & Co A.G. v D.D.S.A. Pharmaceuticals Ltd* [1965] R.P.C. 503. See also *Zipher Ltd v Markem Systems Ltd* [2007] F.S.R. 18, at [18]–[19] and [23] where an application to strike out a claim brought on a patent the subject of amendment proceedings was refused.

[187]   *Novartis AG v Hospira UK Ltd* [2013] EWCA Civ 583; [2014] R.P.C. 3.

[188]   *Vernon & Co (Pulp Products) Ltd v Universal Containers Ltd* [1980] F.S.R. 179; and *Brupat Ltd v Sandford Marine Products Ltd* [1983] R.P.C. 61.

[189]   See para.19-107.

[190]   *Fleming Fabrications Ltd v Albion Cylinders Ltd* [1989] R.P.C. 47; applying *Allen v Jambo Holdings Ltd* [1980] 1 W.L.R. 1252; and *Cayne v Global Natural Resources* [1984] 1 All E.R. 225.

[191]   (1894) 11 R.P.C. 17, 20.

[192]   See also *Bovill v Crate* (1865) L.R. 1 Eq. 388; *Aluminium Co v Domeiere* (1898) 15 R.P.C. 32; *Gillette Safety Razor Co v A.W. Gamage Ltd* (1907) 24 R.P.C. 1; *Versil Ltd v Cork Insulation and Asbestos Co Ltd* [1966] R.P.C. 76.

[193]   *Monsanto Co v Stauffer Chemical Co (N.Z.)* [1984] F.S.R. 559, 572; considering *Legg v ILEA* [1972] 1 W.L.R. 1245.

[194]   *United Telephone Co v Equitable Telephone Association* (1888) 5 R.P.C. 233.

the launch of the its product by refusing to provide samples, thereby forcing the patentee to wait until after it had launched.[195]

Delay in proceeding against persons who are not parties to the application in question is no ground for refusing an injunction, if there has been no delay in proceeding against the defendant.[196]   **19-106**

Cross-undertaking

A cross-undertaking in damages will be required from the claimant. The undertaking is primarily to compensate the defendant in damages for any loss caused by the order if it subsequently transpires that the order should not have been made, for example because the patent is not infringed and/or invalid. However, a cross-undertaking will not necessarily only be for the benefit of the defendant. Paragraph 5.A of CPR PD25A requires the court, when making an order for an injunction, to consider whether to require an undertaking from the applicant to pay any damages sustained by a person other than the respondent, including another party to the proceedings or any other person who may suffer loss as a consequence of the order. However, such other persons need to be identified in some suitable way and the court and the applicant for the injunction need to know the nature of the potential loss or harm which is said may arise.[197] In one case, a cross-undertaking in favour of "customers and potential customers" of the defendant was not required because that class of persons was too vague and the nature of the loss they might suffer was not clear. The cross-undertaking was however required to extend to all other companies in the same group as the defendant, because the court held that patentee did not need to know precisely which companies in that group were undertaking the allegedly infringing acts and it would be burdensome and ultimately pointless to require the defendant to return to court in the event of a corporate restructuring.[198] Care therefore should be taken by a defendant to ensure that the parties who may be affected by the injunction are identified as being entitled to recover on the cross-undertaking at the time the injunction is ordered, for example by being named as defendants or expressly included in the cross-undertaking (see Inquiry on a cross-undertaking below at para.19-111, et seq.).   **19-107**

As noted above, in cases concerning medicines purchased by the National Health Service, cross-undertakings in favour of the NHS (or the Department of Health) are sometimes required from patentees.   **19-108**

An undertaking in damages will normally be required from the Crown or anyone suing on the Crown's behalf.[199]   **19-109**

Giving an undertaking is not the same as offering one; so that although every party who applied for an interim injunction offered a cross-undertaking, he did not give it if the court declined the injunction.[200]   **19-110**

---

[195] *Leo Pharma A/S v Sandoz Ltd* [2008] EWHC 541 (Pat).
[196] *Pneumatic Tyre Co v Warrilow* (1896) 13 R.P.C. 284.
[197] *Actavis v Boehringer Ingelheim* [2013] EWHC 2927 (Pat).
[198] *Actavis v Boehringer Ingelheim* [2013] EWHC 2927 (Pat), [19]–[42].
[199] *Hoffman-La Roche & Co A.G. v Secretary of State for Trade and Industry* [1975] A.C. 295, covering the practice in *Secretary of State for War v Cope* (1919) 36 R.P.C. 273 (registered design).
[200] *Zipher v Markem* [2009] F.S.R 1, [161]; however, note that on the facts of the case the Court of Appeal overturned the decision that an undertaking had actually been given in this case *Zipher v Markem* [2009] F.S.R 14.

Inquiry on a cross-undertaking

19-111　The court will normally order an inquiry as to damages on a cross-undertaking if the claimant loses at trial. Nevertheless, the party who was granted an interim injunction but lost at trial was not a wrongdoer and the expression "wrongful injunction" was inaccurate.[201] There remains a question as to whether the basis for the damages is equitable compensation or common law damages. The better view is in favour of equitable damages.[202]

19-112　The Court of Appeal set out the principles applicable on the assessment of damages on a cross-undertaking in *AstraZeneca v KrKa*.[203] They are:

(a)　The undertaking is to be enforced according to its terms. The question is therefore: what loss did the making of the Order and its continuation until discharge cause the defendant?

(b)　The approach is essentially compensatory and not punitive.

(c)　The assessment is made upon the same basis as that upon which damages for breach of contract would be assessed if the undertaking had been a contract between the parties that the claimant would *not* prevent the defendant from doing that which they were restrained from doing by the terms of the injunction.

(d)　Whilst "the presence of all the contingencies on which the gaining of the prize might depend makes the calculation not only difficult but incapable of being carried out with certainty or precision" damages for the lost opportunity are assessable.

(e)　The fact that certainty or precision is not possible does not mean that a principled approach cannot be attempted. A principled approach in such circumstances requires the defendant first to establish on the balance of probabilities that the chance of making a profit was real and not fanciful: if that threshold is crossed then the second stage of the inquiry is to evaluate that substantial chance. As Lord Diplock explained in *Mallett v McMonagle*[204]:

> "... in assessing damages which depend on its view as to what.... would have happened in the future if something had not happened in the past, the Court must make an estimate as to what are the chances that a particular thing... would have happened and reflect those chances, whether they are more or less than even, in the amount of damages it awards...".

(f)　The conventional method of undertaking this exercise is to assess damages on a particular hypothesis and then to adjust the award by reference to the percentage chance of the hypothesis occurring. In many cases it is sufficient to postulate one hypothesis and make one discount: but there is no reason in principle why one should not say that either Scenario 1 or Scenario 2 would have occurred and to discount them by different percentages. This is a fact-sensitive evaluative exercise of the kind with which an appeal court is reluctant to interfere, unless the judge has erred in principle or is plainly wrong for some other reason.

---

[201]　*SmithKline Beecham Plc v Apotex Europe Ltd* [2005] EWCA 658 (Civ); [2007] F.S.R. 6, see [25].

[202]　See *Lilly ICOS LLC v 8pm Chemists Ltd* [2009] EWHC 1905 (Pat); [2010] F.S.R 4 but see also *SmithKline Beecham Plc v Apotex Europe Ltd* [2005] EWCA 658 (Civ); [2007] F.S.R. 6, see [83]–[84].

[203]　[2015] EWCA Civ 484, [12]–[16].

[204]　[1970] A.C. 166, 176E–G.

A person subject to an interim injunction cannot recover more damage than they **19-113** suffered.[205] An application after trial to allow parties who were not defendants to the action (and therefore not covered by the express terms of the cross-undertaking) but were affected by an interim injunction to be joined in the proceedings so as to be able to recover on a cross-undertaking was rejected.[206] It was brought on two bases (slip rule and an application to join the action as defendants) but both failed. In the same case an attempt was made to base a claim by those parties on restitution and on third party losses in contract. These also failed; the Court of Appeal reviewed the position in detail and held that neither claim was soundly based.[207] An attempt to draft a cross-undertaking in such a way as to allow a claim so that the patentee disgorged profits they made from the injunction was rejected however the undertaking was framed so as to allow customers who had paid for the patentee's products or services covered by the injunction to claim the benefit of the cross-undertaking.[208]

In *Les Laboratoires Serviers v Apotex*[209] an issue of illegality arose. The activ- **19-114** ity for which compensation was sought (manufacture of the products whose lost sales in the UK were the basis for the damages claimed on the inquiry) were said to be unlawful because they amounted to infringement of a foreign patent. In the Patents Court Arnold J had held that the defendant was not entitled to recover on the cross-undertaking by action of the ex turpi causa rule. The Supreme Court held that acts which constituted "turpitude" for the purposes of the ex turpi causa rule included criminal acts and acts which were quasi-criminal in that they were contrary to the public law of the state and engaged the public interest, that being the foundation of the illegality defence. However, it held that the public interest was not engaged in torts (other than those of which dishonesty was an essential element), in breaches of contract and in statutory and other civil wrongs which offended against interests which were essentially private. In patent infringement actions the only relevant interest affected was that of the patentee, and that was sufficiently vindicated by the availability of damages for the infringements in Canada, which were deducted from the recovery under the cross-undertaking in England.

Procedure on application

Applications for interim injunction follow the same procedure as is used for all **19-115** other court applications and the following is of general application save where express reference is made to interim injunction. The full procedure is set out in CPR Pt 23, modified where necessary by CPR Pt 63, and the Practice Directions associated with each Part.

---

[205] *R. v The Medicines Control Agency* [1999] R.P.C. 705 and see also *SmithKline Beecham Plc v Apotex Europe Ltd* [2005] EWCA 658 (Civ); [2007] F.S.R. 6.
[206] *SmithKline Beecham Plc v Apotex Europe Ltd* [2005] EWHC 1655 (Ch); [2005] F.S.R. 44, the case went on appeal to the Court of Appeal but neither the slip rule point nor the joinder point was taken— see *SmithKline Beecham Plc v Apotex Europe Ltd* [2005] EWCA 658 (Civ); [2007] F.S.R. 6, see [20].
[207] *SmithKline Beecham Plc v Apotex Europe Ltd* [2005] EWCA 658 (Civ); [2007] F.S.R. 6.
[208] *Wake Forest University Health Sciences v Smith & Nephew* [2009] EWHC 45 (Pat); [2009] F.S.R. 11.
[209] [2015] A.C 430; [2015] R.P.C 10.

Evidence required

19-116   The need to show a serious issue to be tried should not be taken to indicate that the court will proceed on hypotheses of fact; the burden is on the party seeking the relief to adduce evidence of a sufficiently precise nature to satisfy the court that is has a real prospect of succeeding in obtaining a permanent injunction at trial.[210] In a patent case the evidence must be sufficiently precise to enable the court to come to a view that there is a serious prospect that the patentee will be able to show that each of the features of the claim is present in the alleged infringement.[211]

The hearing

19-117   If the parties have reached agreement by the date of the hearing, an order may be made without a hearing.[212] This may be either an agreement which disposes of the application entirely, or (as is more usual) an agreement as to appropriate directions. For instance, a defendant will often ask for time to adduce evidence in opposition to the application.[213] If the defendant offers interim undertakings acceptable to the claimant pending the substantive hearing for interim injunction, the hearing is likely to be adjourned. If no satisfactory undertakings are forthcoming, the claimant may elect to make its application anyway, but even if successful relief is likely to be limited to a few days pending the preparation of the defendant's evidence. The substantive hearing may be conducted by telephone,[214] and any failure to do so where appropriate may be the subject of a penalty in costs.[215] However, it is more likely that the application will be held in open court. On the hearing the applicant opens the case by reference to their evidence and the skeleton argument; thereafter the respondent is heard in answer; finally, the applicant is heard in reply.

19-118   The court is prepared to move quickly in granting interim relief, particularly in circumstances where it appears that the defendant is seeking to benefit from a surreptitious launch. In *Warner-Lambert v Teva*,[216] the defendant commenced sales of its product on a Monday morning and was injuncted at an oral hearing that afternoon. In *Warner-Lambert v Sandoz*[217] the defendant gave notice that it had commenced selling its product on a Friday (at around lunchtime) and was injuncted after a weekend telephone application the next day. The judgment made it clear that the Patents Court expects litigants in patent disputes before it to behave responsibly to enable disputes to be resolved in an orderly manner and that that generally entails the giving of prior notice. The Patents Court will not hesitate to use its powers, and in particular its powers to grant urgent interim relief, to attempt to ensure that parties who try to steal a march on other parties and thereby present the court with a fait accompli do not benefit from such conduct.

---

[210]   *Re Lord Cable* [1976] 3 All E.R. 417, 430.
[211]   Per Floyd J in *Novartis v Dexcel* [2008] EWHC 1266 (Pat); [2008] F.S.R. 31, at [25], citing Slade J in *Re Lord Cable* [1976] 3 All E.R. 417, at 430.
[212]   CPR r.23.8(a).
[213]   Following which the claimant will often serve further evidence in reply.
[214]   CPR Pt 23, Practice Direction—Applications para.6.
[215]   *Robert Hewitt v P. McCann* [1998] F.S.R. 688.
[216]   [2011] EWHC 1691 (Pat).
[217]   [2015] EWHC 3151 (Pat).

Form of order

With any injunction or undertaking pending trial, it is desirable that the defend- **19-119** ant should know, with as much certainty as possible, what they may, or may not do. This is also in the claimant's interest as any breach is easier to identify and enforce. Accordingly the injunction should be directed towards restraining a specific act in relation to a particular product or process rather than infringing the claimant's patent generally.[218]

Costs

Historically, the usual order for costs at the conclusion of an application for an **19-120** interim injunction was for the successful party's costs in the cause. However, more recently, the court has stated that where an injunction has been granted on the balance of convenience, because it is "holding the ring" pending trial, the more appropriate order is "costs reserved".[219] However, ultimately the court has a wide discretion over costs and there are many possible interim costs' orders open to the court to do justice in the circumstances of the case.[220]

The court may also make use of its summary powers of assessment. Accord- **19-121** ingly, each party who intends to claim costs must, not less than 24 hours before the hearing, serve on the other party and file with the court a statement of costs.[221] The court will generally make a summary assessment of costs if the hearing lasts less than one day, though it is to be noted that many possible costs orders do not require summary assessment in any event.

Under the old practice, where a party prolonged an interim hearing by argu- **19-122** ment on the merits of the case in circumstances where such argument was unnecessary, an order for immediate payment of costs was made.[222] Under the new practice, it is likely that the court will more readily make such an order.

Claimant entitled to order in public

Where the defendants offered to consent to judgment, the order to be made on a **19-123** summons in Chambers (i.e. in private), it was held that the claimants were entitled to an order made in open court (i.e. in public), and to the costs of the motion for judgment.[223]

Appeal from grant or refusal of interim injunction

The decision to grant or refuse an interim injunction is an exercise of discretion **19-124** by the judge. Accordingly, an appeal against that decision is a review of the exercise

---

[218] *The Staver Co Inc v Digitext Display Ltd* [1985] F.S.R. 512; and *Video Arts Ltd v Paget Industries Ltd* [1986] F.S.R. 623 and cf. *Spectravest Inc v Aperknit Ltd* [1988] F.S.R. 161. See also at trial *Coflexip S.A. v Stolt Comex Seaway Ltd* [1999] F.S.R. 911; and *Microsoft Corp v Plato Technology Ltd*, [1999] I.P. & T. 1, CA; affirming [1999] F.S.R. 834.

[219] *Desquenne et Giral U.K. Ltd v Richardson* [2001] F.S.R. 1.

[220] e.g. "costs in the case", "costs reserved", "claimant's costs in the cause", etc. see CPR Pt 44, Practice Direction—General Rules about Costs para.4.2 for a full list.

[221] CPR Pt 44, Practice Direction, paras 4.1–4.11.

[222] *Apple Corps Ltd v Apple Computer Inc* [1992] R.P.C. 70.

[223] *Smith and Jones Ltd v Service, Reeve & Co* (1914) 31 R.P.C. 319.

of that discretion. In *Elan Digital Systems Ltd v Elan Computers Ltd*[224] (a case decided before permission to appeal was required) the Master of the Rolls stated that:

"I think it should be said, and said with great volume and clarity, that this court does not exist to provide a second bite at each interim cherry in the sense that it is open to parties, having failed in front of the learned judge, simply to start again and have a de novo hearing in the hope that they will succeed in front of the Court of Appeal. We are a court of appeal, and particularly in the field of interim injunctions it is primarily the trial judge who is appointed to decide whether or not an injunction should be granted. This is not of course to say that there is no right of appeal, but there is a heavy burden on the appellant to show that the learned judge has erred in principle, and that in exercising his discretion there is either an error of principle or—which is the same thing in a different form—he exercised his discretion in a way which no reasonable judge properly directing himself as to the relevant considerations could have exercised it."

5. STATEMENTS OF CASE

Particulars of claim

19-125 Particulars of claim must be included on the claim form, or (as is usual) on a separate document served with the claim form, or be on a separate document served within 14 days after service of the claim form.[225] It is intended that in most cases the particulars of claim will be served with the claim form. The content of the particulars of claim in patent matters is closely defined by CPR r.16.4 as modified by CPR Pt 63 and the Practice Direction—Intellectual Property Claims. Much of the case law and practice prior to 26 April 1999 has, however, remained of assistance.

19-126 The particulars of claim must include a concise statement of the facts on which the claimant relies[226] and must be verified by a statement of truth.[227] It is not necessary to plead that the patent is valid, because "a patent is prima facie good as long as it stands",[228] nor need any facts material to the validity be pleaded.[229]

19-127 The particulars of claim should allege that the claimant is the registered proprietor of the patent; if the claimant is not yet so registered they should give details of their title to proprietorship and any plans to register that title forthwith.[230]

19-128 If the specification has been amended, or an application is afoot, such facts should be pleaded. As originally drafted, s.63(2) of the 1977 Act placed the burden of proving that the specification and claims as originally published were framed in good faith and with reasonable skill and knowledge on the patentee. However, as from

---

[224] [1984] F.S.R. 373, 384; see also Browne-Wilkinson LJ, at 386.

[225] CPR r.7.4(1). The particulars of claim must in any event be served no later than the latest time for serving a claim form—normally four months but six months if the claim form is to be served out of the jurisdiction; see CPR r.7.5.

[226] CPR r.16.4. A claim to interest must also be pleaded: rr.16.4(1)b and 16.4(2).

[227] CPR Pt 22. Note that failure to verify a statement of case is a ground for striking out; see CPR r.22.2(2).

[228] *Halsey v Brotherhood* (1880) 15 Ch D. 514 at 521; see also *Amory v Brown* (1869) L.R. 8 Eq. 663, at 664.

[229] See *Amory v Brown* (1869) L.R. 8 Eq. 663; *Ward Bros v J. Hill & Son* (1901) 18 R.P.C. 481, at 491, per Wills J; following *Young v White* (1853) 23 L.J. Ch. 190; and *Harris v Rothwell* (1887) 4 R.P.C. 225.

[230] Note that a claimant with only equitable rather than full legal title can bring proceedings, provided either the legal owner is joined or (as is usually more convenient) an assignment of legal title is taken before final order in the proceedings; see *Baxter International v Nederlands* [1998] R.P.C. 250; and para.19-24.

April 2006 it has been amended and it has been held that the burden of establishing a deficiency in the criteria under that section as amended lies with the person alleging it. As such, it would seem that there is no long any need for the particulars of claim to make any averment in relation to such matters.[231]

If a certificate of contested validity has been granted in a previous action so as **19-129** to entitle the claimant to solicitor and client costs,[232] the certificate and the claim to such costs should be pleaded.[233]

If the claimant alleges infringement of the rights arising on publication of the ap- **19-130** plication for the patent,[234] that allegation should also be pleaded.

In IPEC the Particulars of Claim must plead concisely all the facts and argu- **19-131** ments relied on.[235] The requirements for pleadings in IPEC are considerably different and dealt with in the IPEC chapter.

When particulars of claim are served on a defendant, whether or not they are **19-132** contained in the claim form, they must be accompanied by[236]:

(a) a form for admitting the claim;
(b) a form for defending the claim; and
(c) a form for acknowledging service.

Particulars of infringements

Particulars of the alleged infringements must be provided and, by convention, the **19-133** claimant often serves "particulars of infringements" as a separate document. While this was provided for by the rules hitherto, it is no longer mandatory but remains common practice. The "particulars of infringements" should show which of the claims in the specification of the patent are alleged to be infringed and give at least one instance of each type of infringement alleged. Additionally, a copy of each document referred to in the statement of case, and where necessary a translation of the document, must be served with the particulars of infringements.[237]

Actionable infringement must be alleged

The particulars of infringements must allege an actionable infringement, i.e. an **19-134** act committed subsequent to the date of publication of the application for the patent,[238] or else the particulars of claim may be struck out.[239] However, a mere threat to infringe, if made after that date, is sufficient.[240] An allegation of infringement which is speculative, although disclosing a cause of action, may be struck out under the inherent jurisdiction of the court.[241]

---

[231] See *Nokia Oyj v IPCom GmbH* [2012] R.P.C. 21; PA 1977 s.63(2).
[232] Under PA 1977 s.65.
[233] *Pneumatic Tyre Co Ltd v Chisholm* (1896) 13 R.P.C. 488.
[234] PA 1977 s.69.
[235] CPR r.63.20(1).
[236] CPR r.7.8.
[237] See CPR Pt 63; Practice Direction—Intellectual Property Claims para.4.1.
[238] PA 1977 s.69.
[239] See *Schuster v Hine, Parker & Co Ltd* (1935) 52 R.P.C. 345.
[240] *Bloom v Shuylman* (1934) 51 R.P.C. 308.
[241] *Upjohn Co v Kerfoot & Co Ltd* [1988] 4 F.S.R. 1; considered in *Smith, Kline & French Laboratories Ltd v Evans Medical Ltd* [1989] F.S.R. 513, at 524.

Which claims infringed

19-135   The Patents Court practice does not require the claimant to place a construction upon their patent in their particulars of infringements.[242] All they need do is indicate which claims of the patent they relies upon and by what act they consider the defendant to have infringed. If these two points can be made clear without adducing specific instances, that will be sufficient.[243] There is no objection to a claimant stating that they rely on *all* the claims of their specification, and it is a matter of costs at the trial if this course has been taken unreasonably.[244] However, the opposite does not apply. A claimant who does not specify a particular claim in their particulars of infringements will not be able to rely at trial upon that claim.[245]

Independent validity

19-136   A claimant will be required to identify those claims which are alleged to have independent validity as early as possible. The purpose of this is to narrow the issues to be decided at trial and to save costs. Parties who assert too many claims as independently valid may be penalised in costs or, in more extreme cases, where no realistic attempt to identify independently valid claims has been made, the court may proceed on the basis that if the independent claims are invalid, the dependent ones are as well.[246] Nevertheless, care should be taken when deciding which claims to support as independently valid, especially at an early stage since the court may not permit a claimant to withdraw a concession once made.[247] "Independent validity" refers to any ground of invalidity and so a patentee who intended only to concede all other claims if claim 1 was obvious but not if claim 1 merely lacked novelty, was only permitted to withdraw the concession made in error on the footing that the issue of the validity of the other claims, in the event of anticipation but not obviousness succeeding against claim 1 was stayed and reserved for consideration at a separate hearing.[248]

Each type of infringement is a separate cause of action

19-137   Each type of infringement represents a separate cause of action and a claimant will not be allowed to amend to introduce a different type of infringement if such acts have become statute barred under the Limitation Act.[249]

Infringements after action brought

19-138   When an action is brought in respect of a particular type of infringement and to restrain the threatened infringement by continued manufacture of that type (the usual way in which an action is framed), the claimant will not be allowed to give

---

[242] *Wenham Co Ltd v Champion Gas Co Ltd* (1890) 7 R.P.C. 49.
[243] *Aktiengesellschaft für Anilin Fabrikation v Levinstein Ltd* (1912) 29 R.P.C. 677; but cf. *Marsden v Albrecht* (1910) 27 R.P.C. 785, CA; *Aktiengesellschaft für Autogene Aluminium Schweissung v London Aluminium Co Ltd* (1919) 36 R.P.C. 199.
[244] *Haslam & Co v Hall* (1887) 4 R.P.C. 203, 206.
[245] *Kirin-Amgen Inc v Transkaryotic Therapies Inc (No. 2)* [2003] R.P.C. 3, [20]–[41].
[246] Patents Court Guide, para.6.4. See also *Samsung Electronics Co Limited v Apple Retail UK Limited* [2013] EWHC 467 (Pat), at [60]–[63].
[247] See, e.g. *Cairnstores v Aktiebolaget Hässle* [2002] EWHC 309 (Ch), Laddie J, at [15].
[248] See, e.g. *Cairnstores v Aktiebolaget Hässle* [2002] EWHC 309 (Ch), Laddie J, at [15].
[249] *Sorata Ltd v Gardex Ltd* [1984] R.P.C. 317.

evidence of infringements of a different type, committed after action brought to justify the allegation of intention to infringe; the proper course is to apply to amend the particulars of infringements.[250]

Further information

If the particulars served are too general, the defendant should consider applying for further information under CPR Pt 18; but: "It lies on the party who alleges that for the honest purpose of his litigation he wants further information, to satisfy the court that he is really placed in a difficulty by the particulars as they stand."[251] The request should be made as early as possible, and before either the case management conference or the application for further directions. Further particulars of infringements have sometimes been postponed until after disclosure on the ground that the defendant knew the breaches which he had committed better than the claimant.[252] When a party consents to an order for the giving of particulars that party waives the right to object to any of the particulars sought and must comply so far as is possible with the request.[253] **19-139**

An order for further and better particulars of infringements before defence was refused on the ground that they were unnecessary where the plaintiff had given the best particulars that they could and the relevant facts were in the knowledge of the defendant.[254] **19-140**

Defendants have from time to time sought further information of the patentee's construction of their claim. This is often not ordered, because lengthy expositions on construction at an early stage can be unhelpful. Questions of construction are context dependent and the context may not be apparent at an early stage of the action.[255] However, recent experience from IPEC has shown that requiring a patentee to break down their claim into features and identify where the alleged infringing features are to be found in the alleged infringement can be helpful, does not prejudice patentees and does not significantly increase costs.[256] The court may therefore be more willing to order such further information in appropriate cases. **19-141**

Evidence admitted if within particulars

Hitherto, evidence of matters not particularised was not admissible except with leave of the court.[257] The purpose of the rule was to prevent a defendant from being taken by surprise. Today the court's case management powers include the power to control evidence[258] and as such are sufficient to guard against this. **19-142**

Particulars of infringements were also ordered in actions which, though not **19-143**

---

[250] *Shoe Machinery Co Ltd v Cutlan* (1895) 12 R.P.C. 342, 358; *Welsbach Incandescent Gas Light Co Ltd v Dowle* (1899) 16 R.P.C. 391. See also *Kirin-Amgen Inc v Transkaryotic Therapies Inc (No. 2)* [2002] R.P.C. 3, at [20]–[41].

[251] Per Wills J in *Haslam & Co v Hall* (1887) 4 R.P.C. 203, at 207.

[252] *Russell v Hatfield* (1885) Griff.P.C. 204; 2 R.P.C. 144. See also *Mullard Radio Valve Co Ltd v Tungsram Electric Lamp Works (Great Britain) Ltd* (1932) 49 R.P.C. 299.

[253] *Fearis v Davies* [1989] F.S.R. 555.

[254] *Intel Corp v General Instrument Corp* [1989] F.S.R. 640.

[255] See Mann J in *Electromagnetic Geoservices ASA v Petroleum Geo-Services ASA* [2015] EWHC 2391 (Pat), at [22]–[26].

[256] Per Birss J in *CompactGTL v Oxford Catalysts Group* [2013] 3935 (Pat), at [11].

[257] For the old practice see, e.g. *Sykes v Howarth* (1879) 12 Ch D. 826.

[258] CPR r.3.1.

strictly actions for infringement, involved the question of infringement as an issue.[259]

19-144   If it is alleged that the defendant only arrived at the alleged infringement by copying the patent,[260] that must be pleaded.[261]

Amendment of particulars of claim or particulars of infringement

19-145   The particulars may be amended either with the written consent of all the parties or with the permission of the court.[262]

19-146   Permission to amend a claim form to add a cause of action not in existence at the date of issue can be granted provided that: (i) the original cause of action was valid at the date of issue of the claim form; and (ii) the new cause of action was valid at the date of the application to amend.[263]

19-147   Permission to amend so as to add a cause of action against a person originally served out of the jurisdiction will only be granted, however, if the court would independently of the original claim have given permission to serve out of the jurisdiction a claim form solely concerned with the additional cause of action.[264]

19-148   An amendment which would have amounted to the abandonment of the existing claim and its replacement by a new claim was refused, the patentee being required to commence fresh proceedings in that case.[265]

Striking out/summary determination

19-149   In *Anchor Building Products Ltd v Redland Roof Tiles Ltd*,[266] the Court of Appeal upheld the striking out by Whitford J of a counterclaim alleging infringement of a patent on the ground that the patentee had been unable to put before the court any evidence of an arguable case of infringement. However, in *Strix Ltd v Otter Controls Ltd*,[267] the Court of Appeal distinguished *Anchor v Redland* and pointed out that it was not and never had been permissible, on a strike out application where the issues in an action included issues of fact, to conduct a mini-trial on affidavits. *Strix v Otter* was followed in *Monsanto v Merck*[268] when the Court of Appeal allowed an appeal on a summary determination of claim construction, sending the matter on to trial. Accordingly, the Patents Court will only determine claims for patent infringement in a summary fashion (whether as a strike out or summary hearing) in a straightforward case. In *Virgin Atlantic Airways Ltd v Delta Airways Inc*[269] Jacob LJ said:

> "Whilst the general rules as to summary judgment apply equally to patent cases as to other types of case, there can be difficulties, particularly in cases where the technology is complex. If it is, the court

---

[259]   See, e.g. *Wren v Weild* (1869) L.R. 4 Q.B. 213.
[260]   An allegation which may have a bearing on validity.
[261]   *Minnesota Mining and Manufacturing v Ati Atlas* [2001] F.S.R. 31.
[262]   CPR r.17.1.
[263]   *Liff v Peasley* [1980] 1 W.L.R. 781, at 803; *Ketteman v Hansel Properties* [1987] A.C. 189, at 210; *Vax Appliances v Hoover* [1990] R.P.C. 656; *Beecham Group v Norton Healthcare* [1997] F.S.R. 81.
[264]   *Beecham Group v Norton Healthcare* [1997] F.S.R. 81.
[265]   *Texas Electronics v Hyundai Electronics* [2000] F.S.R. 86.
[266]   [1990] R.P.C. 283.
[267]   [1991] F.S.R. 354.
[268]   [2000] R.P.C. 77.
[269]   [2011] EWCA Civ 162; [2011] R.P.C. 18.

may not be able, on a summary application, to form a confident view about the claim or its construction, particularly about the understanding of the skilled man. On the other hand in a case such as the present, where the technology is relatively simple to understand, there is really no good reason why summary procedure cannot be invoked. No one should assume that summary judgment is not for patent disputes. It all depends on the nature of the dispute.

That can cut both ways, of course. If the court is able to grasp the case well enough to resolve the point, then it can and should do so — whether in favour of the patentee or the alleged infringer."

In *Nampak v Alpla*[270] the Court of Appeal upheld a summary judgment on a claim **19-150** for a declaration of non-infringement. Whilst it was necessary for the court to proceed with caution when construing a patent for the purposes of a summary determination, it remained the law that expert evidence is not admitted as to the meaning of ordinary English words which have no special or technical meaning in the art. Therefore, the refusal of an application for summary determination which involves claim construction is not inevitable and a party who claims that the court is inadequately equipped to decide an issue of construction summarily must identify, perhaps in only quite general terms, the nature of the evidence of the common general knowledge which they propose to adduce, and explain why that evidence might reasonably be expected to have an impact on the issue of construction.

In *Abbott Laboratories v Advanced Prescription Services*[271] a patentee applied **19-151** for an interim injunction. The defendants retaliated with an application for summary judgment of invalidity. The court determined a lack of entitlement to priority (leading to anticipation) and the presence of added matter and ordered revocation.[272]

Defence

The defence must be served within 42 days from the service of the particulars **19-152** of claim.[273]

The defendant must state in their defence[274]: **19-153**

(a) which of the allegations in the particulars of claim they deny;
(b) which allegations they are unable to admit or deny, but which they require the claimant to prove; and
(c) which allegations they admit to.

Where the defendant denies an allegation they must state their reasons for do- **19-154** ing so.[275] The defence must be verified by a statement of truth under CPR Pt 22.

In IPEC the defence must plead concisely all the facts and arguments relied on.[276] **19-155**

The following defences are available in an action for infringement: **19-156**

(1) Denial that the claimant is the proprietor of the patient, or an exclusive licensee, as the case may be.
(2) Permission of the proprietor.
(3) Denial of infringement or, as a defence to a claim for an injunction, of any threat or intent to infringe.

---

[270] [2014] EWCA 1293.
[271] [2004] EWHC 2723 (Pat).
[272] The matter was appealed but the proceedings were compromised.
[273] CPR r.63.7 (a).
[274] CPR r.16.5(1).
[275] CPR, r.16.5(2).
[276] CPR, r.63.20(1).

(4) Allegation that all claims alleged to be infringed are invalid.

(5) As a defence to a claim for damages or an account of profits, an allegation of innocent infringement (s.62(1)), late payment of renewal fees (s.62(2)), or where the patent has been amended an allegation that any or all of the following matters apply (all arising under s.62(3)): (i) the patent, as published, was not framed in good faith and with reasonable skill and knowledge; (ii) the defendant did not know or have reasonable grounds to know that they were infringing; and (iii) the proceedings are not brought in good faith.

(6) Right to continue prior use under s.64 of the 1977 Act.

(7) Laches, acquiescence or estoppel.

(8) Statute bar under Limitation Act.

(9) Right to repair or exhaustion of rights.[277]

(10) That the defendant is a person entitled to the grant of the patent.[278]

(11) That the relief sought by the claimant is contrary to European law or the Competition Act 1998.

(1) Title to sue

19-157   The title which the claimant must show is dealt with at para.19–24.

19-158   Where a claimant is registered as proprietor of, or as an exclusive licensee under, the patent, they may prove their title by adducing evidence of their registration.[279] However, the register is only prima facie evidence of title[280] and it may be rebutted by further evidence showing that the claimant is not in fact the proprietor or an exclusive licensee as the case may be.

19-159   Where a claimant has not registered their title, they must adduce evidence of the assignment or licence whereby they claim to be entitled to sue. Further, they must establish that the assignor or licensor had the necessary title to make the grant. If the documents predate 28 March 2000 then they must be properly stamped, where appropriate, in order for them to be admitted in evidence.[281] The defence of want of title will be made out where a claimant fails to show any title at all at the date of issue of the claim form.[282]

(2) Permission of the proprietor

19-160   Where a defendant pleads that he has the patentee's permission or consent to do the acts complained of[283] they should particularise the circumstances, stating, if the licence be alleged to have been verbal, the time and place at which it was given and by whom, or if alleged to have been in writing, identifying the document by date and otherwise. The onus of proof is upon the defendant,[284] and subject to EU law a

---

[277] See para.14-114.

[278] See *Dolphin Showers Ltd v Farmiloe* [1989] F.S.R. 1.

[279] PA 1977 s.32(9) and (10), as substituted by PDMA 1986 s.1 and Sch.1.

[280] PA 1977 s.32(9) and (10), as substituted by PDMA 1986 s.1 and Sch.1.

[281] See Finance Act 2000 s.129(1). And see para.17-18, et seq. of the 16th edn of this work.

[282] *Procter & Gamble Co v Peaudouce (UK) Ltd* [1989] 1 F.S.R. 180.

[283] Often known as "leave or licence" in the past.

[284] *British Thomson-Houston Co Ltd v British Insulated and Helsby Cables Ltd* (1924) 41 R.P.C. 345, 375; see also *Whitehead and Poole v Farmer & Sons Ltd* (1918) 35 R.P.C. 241.

defendant relying on the existence of a licence cannot normally attack the validity of the patent.[285]

The substantive law is considered at para.14–220, et seq.   **19-161**

(3) Denial of infringement

A denial of infringement puts the claimant to the proof: **19-162**

(a) that the defendant has committed the acts complained of in the particulars; and

(b) that such acts are in infringement of the patent, and in proving infringement with regard to goods purchased by the defendant it is incumbent upon the patentee to give evidence that such goods were not produced by the defendant or their agents.[286]

Where a defendant admitted importing the substance alleged to infringe, but   **19-163** denied knowledge of the process by which it was made and denied infringement, particulars of the method by which the substance was made were not ordered.[287] However, by contrast in a case in which the importer denied knowledge of the process employed by its supplier in China, it emerged that the product (a food supplement) was certified as kosher under Jewish dietary law by a rabbinical organisation based in New York. The Patents Court issued Letters of Request to the New York court for the production of documents held in New York relating to inspections carried out by the rabbinical organisation. The New York court ordered production of the documents and they were admitted at trial where they were held to show conclusively that the process infringed.[288] In a further case on the same patent against different importers and a different factory, the foreign manufacturer agreed to a plant inspection but the circumstances of the inspection and various serious breaches of the court's directions relating to it were such that the court struck out the defendant's defence and gave default judgment for the claimant.[289]

(4) Invalidity

If the defendant disputes the validity of the patent, the allegation must be specifi-   **19-164** cally pleaded. Further, the defendant must deliver, with their defence, grounds of invalidity which state every ground on which validity is challenged and must include such particulars as will clearly define every issue (including any challenge to any claimed priority date) which it is intended to raise.[290]

(5) Defence to a claim for damages or an account of profits

There are several defences which prevent an otherwise successful claimant from   **19-165** being able to recover damages from an infringer and, in some instances (but not all), the defences are also good against a claim to an account of profits. Since 29 April

---

[285] See para.16–67, et seq.
[286] *Betts v Willmott* (1871) L.R. 6 Ch. App. 239.
[287] *Parke, Davis & Co v Allen and Hanburys Ltd* (1953) 70 R.P.C. 123.
[288] *Nutrinova Nutrition v Scanchem UK* [2001] F.S.R. 797.
[289] *Nutrinova Nutrititon v Arnold Suhr Netherlands BV* [2002] EWHC 1729.
[290] CPR Pt 63, Practice Direction—Intellectual Property Claims para.4.2; and see para.19–199, et seq.

2006, the IP Enforcement Directive[291] has become relevant. For example, it led to an amendment to s.62(3) and s.68, both provisions of the 1977 Act which placed limits on the recovery of damages in certain cases. The change to s.62(3) is addressed below. The amendment to s.68 (failure to register an assignment) removed the bar to damages but still applies to costs.[292]

19-166 **Innocent infringement**   Section 62(1) of the 1977 Act provides that a patentee shall not be entitled to recover damages or an account of profits from a defendant who proves that they were not aware of the patent, and had no reasonable grounds for supposing it existed.[293] The defendant has the onus of proof and the defence should be specifically pleaded in the defence.

19-167 **Failure to pay renewal fee**   Section 62(2) of the 1977 Act provides that the court or the Comptroller may refuse to award damages or make an order for an account of profits in respect of any infringement committed during any period in respect of which a renewal fee remained unpaid.[294] The failure to pay the fee and, if appropriate, the defendant's reliance on that failure should be pleaded in the defence.

19-168 **Amendment of specification**   Section 62(3) of the 1977 Act (as amended as a result of the Enforcement Directive[295]) provides that when awarding damages or making an order for an account of profits in proceedings for an infringement of the patent committed before the decision to allow the amendment, the court shall "take into account" a number of matters. They are:

    (a)   whether at the date of infringement the defendant or defender knew, or had reasonable grounds to know, that he was infringing the patent;

    (b)   whether the specification of the patent as published was framed in good faith and with reasonable skill and knowledge; and

    (c)   whether the proceedings are brought in good faith.

19-169 Prior to amendment the section simply provided that no damages would be awarded before the date of amendment unless the court is satisfied that the specification as originally published was framed in good faith and with reasonable skill and knowledge. Also, prior to amendment the restriction did not apply if the claimant elected to take an account of profits.[296] The substantive effect of the section as amended is considered elsewhere.[297]

19-170 **Failure to register title**   Prior to 29 April 2006, s.68 of the 1977 Act provided a defence to damages in a case in which there had been a failure to register the proprietor's title (or licensee's licence). This provision was amended and the version now in force relates only to costs. Its effect is dealt with below.[298] The defence should be specifically pleaded in the defence.

---

[291] See SI 2006/1028.
[292] See para.19.24, et seq. and para.21.58.
[293] See paras 21–58 to 21-61.
[294] See para.21-62.
[295] See SI 2006/1028.
[296] *Codex Corp v Racal-Milgo Ltd* [1983] R.P.C. 369.
[297] See para.21–63, et seq.
[298] See para.16–47 and para.21-69, et seq.

(6) Right to continue prior or other use

By s.64 of the 1977 Act a person who, in the UK before the priority date of the **19-171** invention, does in good faith an act which would constitute an infringement of the patent if it were in force or makes in good faith effective and serious preparations to do such an act has the right to continue to do that act. Analogous provisions applicable in other circumstances are contained in ss.20B, 28A and 117A of the 1977 Act.

The effect of these sections is dealt with in Ch.14, particularly para.14–199, et **19-172** seq. Such a defence is always specifically pleaded.[299]

(7) Laches, acquiescence or estoppel

All facts relied upon as supporting these defences must be pleaded timeously.[300] **19-173** For the principles to be considered generally see the judgment of Lord Neuberger in *Fisher v Brooker*[301] in the section marked "Laches, estoppel and acquiescence" and see also Oliver LJ in *Habib Bank Ltd v Habib Bank A.G. Zurich*.[302]

Estoppel by conduct   It is not every defendant who is entitled to attack the valid- **19-174** ity of a patent. The position in this respect of an assignor of, or a licensee under, a patent is dealt with in Ch.16.[303]

Cause of action estoppel   Where judgment is given for a claimant in an action **19-175** for infringement, the patent being held to be valid and to have been infringed, the defendant if sued again by the patentee will be estopped from denying that the acts previously complained of were an infringement or that the patent is valid.[304] Thus a party attacking the validity of a patent should put their full case. The estoppel applies even if the party sought to raise different grounds of invalidity second time round, unless those new grounds could not have discovered with reasonable diligence before.[305] See also the rule in *Henderson v Henderson* at para.19–177 and *Cinpres v Melea*,[306] a case concerning cause of action estoppel in relation to entitlement when the evidence at the first trial involved perjury. Cause of action estoppel was held to bar damages being sought in a damages inquiry in relation to certain acts of supply in the UK because they had already been decided at the liability part of the proceedings.[307] The court held that because the point was squarely raised on the pleadings, all of the material relevant to its determination was before the court and the court did not grant the relief sought, the issue had been determined. Alternatively, even if the point had not been substantively determined, the court held that it would be an abuse of process to advance it in the inquiry.

---

[299] See, e.g. *Helitune v Stewart Hughes* [1991] F.S.R. 171, at 205; *Instance v Denny Brothers Printing* [1994] F.S.R. 396; *Lubrizol Corp v Esso* [1996] R.P.C. 195, [1998] R.P.C. 727.

[300] See *M Systems Flash Disk Pioneers v Trek 2000 International* [2008] EWHC 102 (Pat), [2008] R.P.C. 18.

[301] [2009] UKHL 41; [2009] 1 W.L.R. 1764.

[302] [1982] R.P.C. 1, 36.

[303] See paras 16–62 to 16–75.

[304] *Thomson v Moore* (1889) 6 R.P.C. 426; (1890) 7 R.P.C. 325.

[305] *Hormel Foods v Antilles Landscape Investments* [2005] EWHC 13, [2005] R.P.C. 28 (a trade mark case but the court addressed itself to patents as well). See also *Special Effects v L'Oréal* [2007] EWCA Civ 1, [2007] R.P.C. 15 (another trade mark case) in which the Court of Appeal distinguished *Hormel*. *Virgin Atlantic Airways Ltd v Zodiac Seats UK Ltd* [2013] R.P.C. 29, at [22].

[306] [2008] EWCA Civ 9, [2008] R.P.C. 17.

[307] *Fabio Perini v LPC Group & PCMC* [2012] EWHC 911 (Ch), [2012] R.P.C. 30, [20]–[32].

19-176 In principle a cause of action estoppel may arise from a foreign judgment but given the territorial nature of patents worldwide and the exclusive jurisdiction rules under EU law (see para.19–61) it is no surprise that the Patents Court has not been faced with an attempt to rely on a cause of action estoppel in a patent case. However, attempts have been made to rely on issue estoppel (see below para.19–185).

19-177 **The rule in Henderson v Henderson** The court requires the parties to litigation to bring forward their whole case and:

> "will not (except under special circumstances) permit the same parties to open the same subject of litigation in respect of matter which might have been brought forward as part of the subject in contest, but which was not brought forward, only because they have, from negligence, inadvertence, or even accident omitted part of their case. The plea of res judicata applies, except in special cases, not only to point upon which the court was actually required by the parties to form an opinion and pronounce a judgment, but to every point which properly belongs to the subject of litigation, and which the parties, exercising reasonable diligence, might have brought forward at that time."[308]

19-178 Thus, where a party seeks to raise in subsequent litigation matter which could and should have been litigated in earlier proceedings, the action is liable to be struck out as an abuse of the process.[309]

19-179 The parties' desire for a speedy trial on one issue was held to be "special circumstances" justifying re-opening another issue on an inquiry as to damages on a cross-undertaking which could have been raised in the main action.[310]

19-180 Although in *Chiron v Organon Teknika (No.14)*,[311] it was held that a defence abandoned at an earlier trial could not be raised in subsequent proceedings.[312]

19-181 Thus, it is submitted that where a patentee has both a UK national patent and a European patent (UK) for the same invention which is under opposition in the European Patent Office[313] and they are not prepared to wait until the opposition has been finally disposed of before commencing proceedings against an infringer, they should sue on both patents in case either: (i) the European patent (UK) survives opposition and the UK patent is revoked by the Comptroller under s.73(2); or (ii) the European patent (UK) is revoked by the EPO leaving only the UK national patent in existence.

19-182 **Estoppel personal only** Estoppel is personal and exists only against those whose conduct gave rise to it and persons claiming through them or, in the case of estoppel by record, only in proceedings between the same parties. Thus, it does not run against the partner of a person estopped[314] nor against a person who was not actu-

---

[308] *Henderson v Henderson* (1843) 3 Hare 100.
[309] *Johnson v Gore Wood* [2002] 2 A.C. 1 and see *Markem v Zipher* [2005] EWCA Civ 267, [2005] R.P.C. 31.
[310] *Hodgkinson & Corby v Wards Mobility* [1998] F.S.R. 530, CA.
[311] [1996] F.S.R. 701.
[312] See also *Christopher French v Paul J. Mason* [1999] F.S.R. 597 where the claim was struck out in reliance of the rule.
[313] Under PA 1977 s.73(3), as amended by CDPA 1988 Sch.5 para.19, the UK national patent and the European patent (UK) may co-exist until: (a) the end of the period for filing an opposition to the European patent (UK) under the EPC, or (b) if later, the date on which the opposition proceedings are finally disposed of.
[314] *Heugh v Chamberlain* (1877) 25 W.R. 742; *Goucher v Clayton* (1865) 11 Jur. (N.S.) 107.

ally a party to the previous action[315] even though they may have supported one of such parties by financing their defence under a contract of indemnity.[316] It also does not run against a company that had been part of the same group of companies as the person estopped.[317] Where a question of infringement was submitted to an arbitrator who found that the letters patent were not illegal or void, it was held in a subsequent action for infringement between the parties that such an award did not estop the defendant from several pleas in which he alleged facts inconsistent with validity of the patent, it only being possible to gather by inference that the arbitrator must have considered such allegations in making his award.[318]

Discontinuance   The discontinuance of an action by a claimant does not create **19-183** any estoppel against them by record. Under the old rules, unless there was a term of the order allowing discontinuance that no fresh action shall be brought on the same patent against the defendant, the claimant was entitled to commence a fresh action in respect of the same infringement.[319] Under the CPR, the permission of the court is required before a new action can be commenced against the same defendant if the claimant discontinues after the defendant has filed a defence.[320]

Discontinuance without leave is permitted under CPR Pt 38 (save where an **19-184** interim injunction has been granted or an undertaking given). A defendant who opposes discontinuance or insists on terms must apply under CPR r.38.4 within 28 days. For instance, the defendant may seek an undertaking that no fresh action will be brought in respect of the same product[321] or may seek a final judgment in their favour.[322]

Issue estoppel   Issue estoppel has a place in patent actions in appropriate cases— **19-185** even where the decision relied upon as the basis of the estoppel is a decision of a foreign court.[323] For example, the same issue may arise in litigation in different countries as to whether a particular scientific effect occurs when a particular invention or manufacturing process is carried out, or how an allegedly infringing product is made, or the properties of such a product or its composition. However, there will be no issue estoppel unless:

   (i)   the facts as found by the foreign court were so fundamental to its decision that without them the decision could not stand;
   (ii) the party to the UK action shared privity of "blood, title or interest"[324] with a party to the foreign action; and

---

[315] *Heugh v Chamberlain* (1877) 25 W.R. 742; *Goucher v Clayton* (1865) 11 Jur. (N.S.) 107; see also *Otto v Steel* (1886) 3 R.P.C. 109.
[316] *Gammons v Singer Manufacturing Co* (1904) 21 R.P.C. 452, 459, CA.
[317] *Resolution Chemicals Ltd v H. Lundbeck A/S* [2014] R.P.C 5.
[318] *Newall v Elliot* (1863) 1 H. & C. 797; 32 L.J.Ex. 120.
[319] See, e.g. *Haskell Golf Ball Co Ltd v Hutchinson* (1904) 21 R.P.C. 205; *Murex Welding Processes Ltd v Weldrics* (1922) Ltd (1933) 50 R.P.C. 178, 183.
[320] CPR r.38.7.
[321] *Albright & Wilson v S.B. Chemicals* [1994] R.P.C. 608.
[322] *Discovision v Disctronics* [1999] F.S.R. 196.
[323] *Kirin-Amgen Inc v Boehringer Mannheim GmbH* [1997] F.S.R. 289 and see *M Systems Flash Disk Pioneers v Trek 2000 International* [2008] EWHC 102 (Pat), [2008] R.P.C. 18.
[324] Per Lord Reid in *Carl Zeiss (Ltd) Stiftung v Rayner & Keeler Ltd (No.2)* [1967] 1 A.C. 853. See also *Gleeson v J. Wippell & Co* [1977] 1 W.L.R. 510; *House of Spring Gardens Ltd v Waite* [1991] 1 Q.B. 241.

(iii)   the issue could not be re-litigated in the foreign jurisdiction.[325]

19-186   Whether or not there is privity is a question of fact to be determined for each individual case. It is, however, clear that mere curiosity or even a commercial interest in the result of the foreign action is insufficient. In *Resolution Chemicals Ltd v H. Lundbeck A/S*,[326] the Court of Appeal held that in assessing whether there is privity of interest between a new party and a party to previous proceedings, the court needs to examine:

(a)   the extent to which the new party had an interest in the subject matter of the previous action;

(b)   the extent to which the new party can be said to be, in reality, the party to the original proceedings by reason of their relationship with that party; and

(c)   against this background to ask whether it is just that the new party should be bound by the outcome of the previous litigation.

19-187   The effect of the construction of claims in a previous action is addressed in Ch.9.

19-188   Decision of EPO in opposition proceedings   An opponent who unsuccessfully opposes the grant of a European patent in the EPO is not estopped from alleging invalidity by way of a defence to a subsequent allegation of infringement in proceedings on the European patent (UK) in this country.[327] There is no cause of action estoppel because the causes of action are not identical and, more fundamentally, the decision of the Opposition Division is not a final and conclusive judicial decision to the validity of the patent, validity being finally decided in revocation proceedings by the courts of the contracting states.[328] Similarly, there can be no issue estoppel in the absence of a final decision.[329]

19-189   Effect of decision between different parties   Where there has been a previous decision upon the validity of a patent by a court of co-ordinate or superior jurisdiction, which by reason of having been given in proceedings between different parties does not operate as an estoppel, strong additional evidence will be required in order to reverse the previous finding, and the court will usually hold itself bound by previous decisions on the question of the construction of the specification.[330]

19-190   In *Coflexip SA v Stolt Offshore MS Ltd (No.2)*[331] a defendant the subject of an inquiry as to damages sought to stay the inquiry pending the outcome of an appeal in subsequent litigation between the patentee and a different party in which the pat-

---

[325]   *Kirin-Amgen Inc v Boehringer Mannheim GmbH* [1997] F.S.R. 289. See also Lewison J in *Barrett v Universal-Island Records* [2006] EWHC 1009 (Ch); [2006] E.M.L.R. 21, at [175]–[190] (on cause of action estoppel but the point is the same).

[326]   [2014] R.P.C 5.

[327]   *Buehler A.G. v Chronos Richardson Ltd* [1998] R.P.C. 609, CA, followed in *Special Effects v L'Oréal* [2007] EWCA Civ 1 [2007] R.P.C. 15 (a trade mark case). See also *Unilin Beheer v Berry Floor* [2007] EWCA Civ 364, [2007] F.S.R. 25.

[328]   *Buehler A.G. v Chronos Richardson Ltd* [1998] R.P.C. 609, 616, CA, followed in *Special Effects v L'Oréal* [2007] EWCA Civ 1, [2007] R.P.C. 15 (a trade mark case).

[329]   *Buehler A.G. v Chronos Richardson Ltd* [1998] R.P.C. 609, 616, CA, followed in *Special Effects v L'Oréal* [2007] EWCA Civ 1, [2007] R.P.C. 15 (a trade mark case).

[330]   *Otto v Steel* (1886) 3 R.P.C. 109, 114; *Automatic Weighing Machine Co v Combined Weighing Machine Co* (1889) 6 R.P.C. 367; *Edison v Holland* (1889) 6 R.P.C. 243; *Flour Oxidising Co Ltd v Carr & Co Ltd* (1908) 25 R.P.C. 428, 448; *Higginson and Arundel v Pyman* (1926) 43 R.P.C. 291, 300; *SmithKline Beecham v Apotex* [2003] EWHC 2939 (Ch), [2004] F.S.R. 26, [12].

[331]   [2004] F.S.R. 34.

ent had been found invalid at first instance.[332] The Court of Appeal refused the stay because, even if the patent was finally held invalid and revoked, the doctrines of cause of action estoppel and issue estoppel prevented the defendant from relying on such revocation on the inquiry. This decision was followed in *Unilin Beheer v Berry Floor*.[333] However, in *Virgin v Zodiac*[334] the Supreme Court overturned these decisions and held that where a judgment is given in an English court that a patent (be it a UK or European patent) is valid and infringed, and the patent is subsequently retrospectively revoked or amended (whether in the UK or at the EPO), the defendant is entitled to rely on the revocation or amendment on the inquiry as to damages in order to contend that they should pay no damages. The Supreme Court went on to say that once the inquiry is concluded, different considerations would arise because there would then be a final judgment for a liquidated sum and thereafter payment of that sum. Whether at that stage the defendant could recover any sums paid, for example by a restitutionary claim, will have to await a case in which it arises.

Where a party produces evidence at the trial of an action to prove a certain fact **19-191** and at the trial of a subsequent action against a different party produces other witnesses whose evidence is inconsistent with such fact, although the original evidence does not create any estoppel and is not admissible as evidence in the subsequent action,[335] the court will scrutinise the new evidence with great care, the more especially if the witnesses called in the first action do not give evidence in the second action to explain that the previous evidence was the result of some mistake.[336]

Delay and acquiescence In *Fisher v Brooker*[337] the House of Lords reviewed the **19-192** position regarding a delay in asserting an intellectual property right (copyright) for 38 years. Given the length of the patent term under the Act and including five years for a supplementary protection certificate and one year for a priority filing, a comparable delay of over two decades is at least possible in principle in a patent case. Their Lordships held that mere passage of time cannot of itself undermine a claim to an intellectual property right; there is no English law statutory equivalent in the field of intellectual property to the doctrine of adverse possession in relation to real property. Note that delay in asserting a right may give rise to difficulties in Scotland.[338] A case of "laches" may be available in such circumstances but as Lord Neuberger pointed out, as an equitable doctrine it could only be used to defeat a claim to equitable relief and was no bar to a declaration of rights (which was intended to affect the future).

---

[332] In the end the subsequent finding of invalidity was reversed by the Court of Appeal and the patent was held valid, see *Technip France SA's Patent* [2004] R.P.C. 46.
[333] [2007] EWCA Civ 364, [2007] F.S.R. 25.
[334] [2013] R.P.C 29, [22].
[335] *British Thomson-Houston Co Ltd v British Insulated and Helsby Cables Ltd* (1924) 41 R.P.C. 345, 353–357 and 376–390.
[336] *British Thomson-Houston Co Ltd v British Insulated and Helsby Cables Ltd* (1924) 41 R.P.C. 345, 408; (1925) 42 R.P.C. 180, 199 and 200.
[337] [2009] UKHL 41.
[338] See *Fisher v Brooker* [2009] UKHL 41, at [78].

(8) Limitation Act

19-193   Reliance upon the Limitation Act 1980 as a defence in respect of any acts committed more than six years prior to the issue of the claim form must be expressly pleaded.[339]

If not pleaded, the claimant is entitled to assume that the defendant does not intend to rely on the defence.[340] If the claimant wishes to rely on concealment or put forward any other case for extending the normal limitation period, then they should set out the facts upon which they rely in their reply.

(9) Right to repair

19-194   A defence based on a right to repair patented articles ought to be specifically pleaded. The substantive law is considered at para.14–229, et seq.

(10) Defendant entitled to grant of patent

19-195   Such a defence should be specifically pleaded.[341] The substantive law is considered in Ch.4.

(11) Relief contrary to European Union law or the Competition Act 1998

19-196   In principle, arts 34-36, 101 and 102 of the Treaty on the Functioning of the European Union (formerly arts 28–30, 81 and 82 of the EC Treaty)[342] and the corresponding provisions of the Competition Act 1998[343] provide defences which can be used in patent infringement actions. For example, in *Parke Davis v Probel*,[344] the European Court held, in the context of a Dutch action, that art.36 could restrict the right of a proprietor of a patent to restrain infringements if that action degenerated into an abuse of the proprietor's dominant position (assuming the proprietor was in such a position). See also para.14–255, et seq. and para.16–154.

19-197   Apart from those cases concerned with the doctrine of exhaustion of rights (see para.14–240, et seq. and para.16–99, et seq.) in practice, at the time of writing, no such defence has been ultimately successful in a patent action[345] although "Euro-defences" have been used in related cases to establish an arguable defence for the purposes of avoiding summary judgment.[346]

"Gillette" defence

19-198   In *Gillette Safety Razor Co v Anglo-American Trading Co*,[347] Lord Moulton set out what has been called the "*Gillette* defence" namely that the alleged infringe-

---

[339] CPR Pt 16, Practice Direction—Statement of Case para.13.1.
[340] *Ketteman v Hansel Properties Ltd* [1987] A.C. 189.
[341] See *Dolphin Showers v Farmiloe* [1989] F.S.R. 1.
[342] And prior to the Treaty of Amsterdam, arts 30, 85 and 86. See also para.1–81, et seq.
[343] See para.16–123, et seq.
[344] (24/67) [1968] E.C.R. 55; [1958] C.M.L.R. 47.
[345] See *Quantel v Electronic Graphics* [1990] R.P.C. 272. See also *Volvo v Erik Veng* (238/87) [1988] E.C.R. 6211, [1989] 4 C.M.L.R. 122; *Ransburg Gema v Electrostatic Plant Systems* [1989] 2 C.M.L.R. 712; *Pitney Bowes v Francotyp-postalia* [1991] F.S.R. 72.
[346] e.g. *Dymond v Britton* [1976] 1 C.M.L.R. 133 (a contract case). And see the cases cited at para.14–255, et seq. and para.16–156.
[347] (1913) 30 R.P.C. 465, 480 and see para.14–262, et seq.

ment was not novel at the relevant date. It is not a free standing defence.[348] In practice Grounds of Invalidity are not drafted in this way (it is submitted rightly) notwithstanding that it remains a useful test by which to judge the chances of success in the action and a basis for argument on behalf of the defendant.

Grounds of invalidity

If the defendant disputes the validity of the patent they must deliver with their defence Grounds of Invalidity (formerly known as "Particulars of Objections") which state every ground on which validity is challenged and must include such particulars as will clearly define every issue (including any challenge to any claimed priority date) which it is intended to raise.[349] Grounds of Invalidity in theory ought to give to the claimant such information as will inform them as to the case they have to meet, and enable them to prepare for trial by investigation or research without danger of surprise. However, in practice patent pleadings are sparse and provide limited information about the defendant's case, a situation that has led to increasing use by the court of subsequent, issues based, statements of case (for example on priority date or anticipation). In contrast, in IPEC the Grounds of Invalidity are not to be in a separate document and must set out concisely all the facts and arguments upon which the party relies.[350] This is dealt with in more detail in the IPEC chapter of this work. **19-199**

The grounds of invalidity which may be relied on as a defence to an action for infringement and also in a counterclaim for revocation, are set out in detail in s.72 of the 1977 Act. So far as concerns s.72(1)(a) (namely the invention is not a patentable invention), this refers back to s.1(1) of the Act which provides that a patent may be granted only for an invention if: **19-200**

    (a)   the invention is new;
    (b)   it involves an inventive step;
    (c)   it is capable of industrial application; and
    (d)   the grant is not excluded by s.1(2) and (3).

Each ground relied upon must be separately specified. **19-201**

Lack of novelty (ss.72(1)(a) and 1(1)(a) of the 1977 Act)

CPR Pt 63, Practice Direction—Intellectual Property Claims section I Patents paras 4.3 and 4.4 provide that if the grounds of invalidity include an allegation of want of novelty or want of inventive step, the particulars must state the date(s) and means by which it was made available to the public (unless it is clear from the fact of the matter) and, if prior use is alleged, must also: **19-202**

    (1)   specify the names of all persons making such use;
    (2)   specify the place of such use
    (3)   identify any written material which identifies such use;
    (4)   specify the existence and location of any apparatus employed in such use; and
    (5)   specify all facts and matters relied on to establish that such matter was made available to the public.

---

[348] See Evershed MR in *Page v Brent Toy Products* (1950) 67 R.P.C. 4, at 33 and see para.14–262, et seq.
[349] CPR Pt 63.6 and Practice Direction 63—Intellectual Property Claims para.4.2 (2).
[350] CPR Pt 63.20.

19-203   Although the Practice Direction is in mandatory form, the court nevertheless retains a discretion. In *Visx Inc v Nidex Co*,[351] Aldous LJ said of the corresponding provision in force in 1998[352]:

> "[Counsel] for the plaintiff also submitted that the word 'must' in RSC, Ord.104, r.6 made it obligatory for a defendant who challenged the validity of a patent to set out the particulars required by the rule. That being so, no amendment should be allowed unless it contained the required particulars. That in my view is too simplistic.
>
> A judge has a discretion whether to allow amendments before they have been properly particularised. He should exercise that discretion to prevent amendments being made with a view to obtaining documents to discover a cause of action or defence. But such amendments need to be contrasted with those which plead a genuine case which is suitable for determination and are in sufficient detail so as to limit the area of discovery to an appropriate extent. It is a question of degree in each case as to whether the amendments are of the fishing type or plead a genuine cause of action or defence. If it be the latter and the omitted particulars are likely to be within the knowledge of the other party, then it would in general be appropriate to allow the amendment and to delay further particularisation until after discovery. Each case will differ and will need to be decided upon its own facts."

19-204   In *Avery v Ashworth, Son & Co*,[353] the defendants in their particulars of objections stated that they would rely "either by way of anticipation or as showing the scope of the claims ... upon matters known to the plaintiffs, in consequence of which the plaintiffs" at an earlier date had applied to amend their specification by disclaimer. The defendants were directed to deliver full particulars of the "matters" alleged. The further particulars delivered consisted of a statement that the defendants would rely upon all the matters contained in the particulars of objections which had been delivered in an action by the plaintiffs against other defendants upon another patent several years before. This, and the original paragraph, were ordered to be struck out. The decision was considered and explained by Aldous LJ in *Visx Inc v Nidex Co*[354]:

> "*Avery* decided that discovery in patent actions should be confined to the issues of invalidity pleaded. The allegation which formed the basis of the claim for discovery did not raise an issue of invalidity. Therefore it had to be struck out as embarrassing unless appropriate particulars were given. It did not decide that where bona fide allegations of invalidity are pleaded all relevant particulars have to be given before discovery."

19-205   The *Visx* decision applies to the regime under the CPR.[355]

Written description

19-206   Prior documents must be pleaded specifically, together with the date and means by which it was made available. The usual course with regard to patent specifications or scientific papers being simply to refer to their date of publication, and with regard to books or newspapers to do the same and further to specify the pages or chapters relied upon.

19-207   Whether or not a defendant will be required to give particulars of the exact passages of the prior documents relied upon, or to point out specifically what part or parts of the claimant's specification they allege to be affected thereby, will depend

---

[351] [1999] F.S.R. 91.

[352] At 100. Roch LJ agreed that the court retains a discretion, see 109.

[353] (1915) 32 R.P.C. 463 and 560; (1916) 33 R.P.C. 235. See also *Intel v GI* [1989] F.S.R. 640.

[354] [1999] F.S.R. 91, 99.

[355] Applied by the Patents Court in *Dendron v University of California* [2004] F.S.R.23 and *MMI Research v Cellxion* [2008] F.S.R. 23.

upon the circumstances of the case and the nature of the documents.[356] Where it appeared that the defendant had, figuratively speaking, "thrown at the head" of the claimant a large number of complicated specifications without any attempt at discrimination, further particulars were required.[357] If, however, the defendant bona fide relies upon the whole of one or more documents, and the subject-matter is simple, their particulars of objections will not be interfered with.[358]

In the IPEC exact passages relied on ought to be identified up front.[359]   **19-208**

Prior use

In the case of prior use the defendant is required to provide details of the exist-   **19-209**
ence and location of any apparatus employed in the use. There was an old distinction between the pleading requirements when the case was about a process claim rather than a product claim but the modern formulation of the rule removes any such distinction.[360]

Where the defendants pleaded a public use and sale of articles manufactured by   **19-210**
certain specified machines, particulars were ordered of the names and addresses of persons to whom the articles were alleged to have been sold and of the dates of such sales.[361]

Oral disclosure

Under the 1977 Act, oral disclosure is relevant. Similar particulars will be   **19-211**
required as to disclosure by documents including the names of the parties, the place, time, circumstances and what was said.

Obviousness (ss.72(1)(a) and 1(1)(b) of the 1977 Act)

This ground of objection must be specifically pleaded and the same rules   **19-212**
concerning particulars of prior publication and user that apply to novelty (see para.19–202, et seq.) apply to obviousness.[362]

Common general knowledge

If the defendant proposes to rely on common general knowledge as an addition   **19-213**
to their pleaded prior art publications, they should at least state that they intend to do so, but detailed particulars are not generally required in the Patents Court.[363] However, if a case of obviousness over common general knowledge alone is go-

---

[356] *Heathfield v Greenway* (1893) 10 R.P.C. 17; *Marchant v J.A. Prestwich & Co Ltd* (1949) 66 R.P.C. 117.
[357] *Holliday v Heppenstall Bros* (1889) 6 R.P.C. 320; *Sidebottom v Fielden* (1891) 8 R.P.C. 266, 270; *Heathfield v Greenway* (1893) 10 R.P.C. 17.
[358] *Siemens v Karo, Barnett & Co* (1891) 8 R.P.C. 376; *Nettlefolds Ltd v Reynolds* (1892) 9 R.P.C. 410; *Edison-Bell Consolidated Phonograph Co v Columbia Phonograph Co* (1901) 18 R.P.C. 4.
[359] CPR r.63.20(1).
[360] See para.12–122 of the 16th edn of this work for the cases which drew this rather unreal distinction.
[361] See *British United Shoe Machinery Co Ltd v Albert Pemberton & Co* (1930) 47 R.P.C. 134, at 141.
[362] CPR Pt 63, Practice Direction—Intellectual Property Claims para.4.3.
[363] *Holliday v Heppenstall* (1889) 6 R.P.C. 320; *McCreath v Mayor, etc., of South Shields and Baker* (1932) 49 R.P.C. 349; *American Chain and Cable Co Inc v Hall's Barton Ropery Co Ltd* (1938) 55 R.P.C. 287, 293; *Walton v Hawtins Ltd* (1948) 65 R.P.C. 69.

ing to be advanced then it should be pleaded in detail to avoid surprise.[364] By the same token whether or not a document is said to represent common general knowledge, publications which will be relied on as starting points for an argument of obviousness must be pleaded.[365] In any event, parties may be required to give disclosure of those documents relied upon as part of common general knowledge.[366]

19-214   The meaning of common general knowledge is considered at para.8–56, et seq. The manner of proof of common general knowledge is dealt with at para.8–70.

Not capable of industrial application (ss.72(1)(a) and 1(1)(c) of the 1977 Act)

19-215   Although under the 1949 Act it was not necessary to particularise a plea that the subject matter of the claim was "not an invention within the meaning of the Act ",[367] the modern approach to pleadings will mean that particulars will be necessary.[368]

Excluded by s.1(2) or 1(3) (ss.72(1)(a) and 1(1)(d) of the 1977 Act)

19-216   These subsections exclude from patenting certain matter including, for example, a discovery or scientific theory, anything which consists of literary or artistic work and any invention the publication or exploitation of which would generally be expected to encourage offensive, immoral or anti-social behaviour.

19-217   The objection must be specifically pleaded and it must be made clear as to why the alleged invention of the patent in suit falls within the subsections of the Act.

Patentee not entitled to be granted the patent (s.72(1)(b) of the 1977 Act)

19-218   This attack on the validity of a patent may only be made by a person found by the court in an action for a declaration, or by the court or the comptroller on a reference under s.37, to be entitled to be granted the patent or to be granted a patent for part of the matter comprised in the specification of the patent sought to be revoked.[369] Further, a two-year time limit applies beginning with the date of grant of the patent unless the person registered as proprietor knew at the time of grant or transfer that they were not entitled to the patent.[370]

19-219   It is submitted, that the previous practice under the 1949 Act (where it was necessary to give particulars as to whom the defendant alleged to be the true and first inventor[371] but, if fraud was not alleged, no further particulars needed to be given[372]) would not be adopted under the CPR. A defendant ought to provide particulars of

---

[364] *Ratiopharm v Napp Pharmaceutical Holdings* [2009] R.P.C. 11. See also *Dyson Technology Ltd v Samsung Gwangju Electronics Co* [2009] F.S.R. 608 in which a change of tack at trial to advance a case based on common general knowledge alone was permitted in the particular circumstances of that case. See especially [210]–[211].

[365] *Nutrinova v Scanchem* [2001] F.S.R. 797, [81].

[366] *Aluma Systems Inc v Hunnebeck GmbH* [1982] F.S.R. 239.

[367] *Hardaker v Boucher & Co Ltd* (1934) 51 R.P.C. 278.

[368] This ground of invalidity was advanced in *Lilly v HGS* [2010] R.P.C. 14 and particulars were provided of the point.

[369] PA 1977 s.72(2)(a).

[370] PA 1977 s.72(2)(b).

[371] See *Stroud v Humber Ltd* (1907) 24 R.P.C. 141, at 151; *Smith's Patent* (1912) 29 R.P.C. 339.

[372] See *Sylow-Hansen v June Hair, etc., Ltd* (1948) 65 R.P.C. 421.

not only who it contends to be the true inventor but also why it contends that to be the case. Where fraud is alleged, particulars of the fraud will still be required.[373]

Insufficiency (s.72(1)(c) of the 1977 Act)

"The specification of the patent does not disclose the invention clearly enough and completely enough for it to be performed by a person skilled in the art."   **19-220**

The objection of insufficiency will require proper particulars.[374] In a particular   **19-221** case, where the objection was not that the directions given could not be carried out, but that if one does carry them out the result described is not attained, further particulars were not required.[375]

If it is intended to rely on the fact that an example of the invention cannot be   **19-222** made to work particulars are required. These particulars must specify the respects in which the example does not work or does not work as described.[376]

Added matter (s.72(1)(d) of the 1977 Act)

"The matter disclosed in the specification of the patent extends beyond that disclosed in the applica-   **19-223** tion for the patent, as filed, or, if the patent was granted on a new application filed under section 8(3), 12, or 37(4) above or as mentioned in section 15(4) above, in the earlier application, as filed."

Particulars will be necessary to identify the relevant application and the matter   **19-224** disclosed in the specification of the patent which is alleged to extend beyond that disclosed in the application.

Extension of protection (s.72(1)(e) of the 1977 Act)

"The protection conferred by the patent has been extended by an amendment which should not have   **19-225** been allowed."

Particulars will be necessary as to the date of amendment, the nature of the exten-   **19-226** sion of the protection and the reason why the amendment should not have been allowed.[377]

Amendment of Grounds of Invalidity

Amendment of a Grounds of Invalidity is, like any other statement of case,   **19-227** governed by the general rule of CPR Pt 17.

Amendment of grounds of invalidity before or at trial

The longstanding practice of allowing amendments to a grounds of invalidity by   **19-228** way of a specific order known as an "*Earth Closet*" or a *See v Scott Paine* order (by which the amendment would be allowed on terms that the patentee could elect to consent to the revocation of their patent and, if they did, have a substantial proportion of their costs paid by the successful defendant) was disapproved of by the Court

---

[373] CPR Pt 16, Practice Direction—Statements of Case para.8.2(1).
[374] *Crompton v Anglo-American Brush Corporation Ltd (No.2)* (1887) 4 R.P.C. 197; *Heathfield v Greenway* (1893) 10 R.P.C. 17. See also *Instance v Denny* [1994] F.S.R. 396.
[375] See, e.g. "*Z" Electric Lamp Manufacturing Co Ltd v Marples, Leach & Co Ltd* (1909) 26 R.P.C. 762, CA.
[376] CPR Pt 63, Practice Direction—Intellectual Property Claims para.4.3(2).
[377] See, e.g. *Liversidge v British Telecom* [1991] R.P.C. 229.

of Appeal in *Fresenius Kabi Deutschland GmbH v Carefusion 303, Inc.*[378] The Court of Appeal took the view that such an order was anomalous with modern practice and commented that: "The Earth Closet order should be consigned to the place that bears its name."

19-229   Accordingly, amendments to a grounds of invalidity are now dealt with under the CPR in the same way as any other pleading amendment.

19-230   Further, if an amendment is allowed which leads the patentee to discontinue their claim for infringement and consent to revocation of their patent in the light of the newly pleaded ground of invalidity, the costs of the discontinuance will be dealt with under CPR Pt 38 in the same way as any other type of case. The usual rule will be that the patentee will pay the costs of their discontinued claim unless they can persuade the court to make some other order as to costs.[379]

Amendment in after trial and in Court of Appeal

19-231   In *Shoe Machinery Co Ltd v Cutlan*,[380] the Court of Appeal decided that they had jurisdiction to permit amendment of the particulars of objections although in that particular case they declined to do so, and the same rule has been held to apply to the Scottish Inner House.[381] The Court of Appeal is, however, very reluctant to permit such amendments.[382]

Where after trial but before the final order has been drawn up a defendant seeks to amend their grounds of invalidity to introduce new prior art (and necessarily call further evidence at a further trial), the position is similar to when seeking to amend and lead fresh evidence in the Court of Appeal. However, the court is entitled to be somewhat more flexible, and will not proceed on the strict basis that each of these three *Ladd v Marshall* conditions always has to be fully satisfied before fresh evidence can be admitted.[383]

Reply

19-232   The claimant may deliver a reply setting out facts which may tend to negative some of the pleas raised by the particulars of objections, e.g. that the invention was obvious. Although evidence of such facts could be called at the trial without these being pleaded, to set them out in a reply may be advantageous from the point of view of obtaining wider disclosure.[384]

19-233   Where a party wishes to rely upon commercial success in reply to an allegation of obviousness, CPR Pt 63, Practice Direction—Intellectual Property Claims para.4.6 requires the party to state the grounds upon which they rely. This has been interpreted under the old Rules as requiring the party to identify any defect in the prior art, how it was overcome, whether long felt want was being sought to be

---

[378] [2012] R.P.C 8.

[379] CPR r.38.6. See *Fresenius Kabi Deutschland GMBH v Carefusion 303* [2012] R.P.C 8, at [10]–[15].

[380] [1896] 1 Ch. 108; (1895) 12 R.P.C. 530.

[381] *Watson, Laidlaw & Co Ltd v Pott, Cassels and Williamson* (1909) 26 R.P.C. 349, 360.

[382] *Coflexip S.A. v Stolt Comex Seaway MS Ltd* [2001] R.P.C. 9. See also, e.g. *Alsop Flour Process Ltd v Flour Oxidising Co Ltd* (1907) 24 R.P.C. 349, CA; (1908) 25 R.P.C. 477, HL.

[383] *Charlesworth v Relay Roads Ltd* [2000] R.P.C. 300; *Vringo Infrastructure Inc v ZTE (UK) Ltd* [2015] EWHC 214 (Pat), [2015] R.P.C. 23.

[384] See *Laurence Scott and Electronics Ltd v General Electric Co Ltd* (1938) 55 R.P.C. 233.

established and, if so, how it was going to be established.[385] Further, the patentee must, within such time as the court may direct (typically the same time as disclosure), serve a schedule containing the following details[386]:

(1) where the commercial success relates to an article or product:
    (a) an identification of the article or product (for example by product code number) which the patentee asserts has been made in accordance with the claims of the patent;
    (b) a summary by convenient periods of sales of any such article or product;
    (c) a summary for the equivalent periods of sales, if any, of any equivalent prior article or product marketed before the article or product mentioned in sub-para.(a);
    (d) a summary by convenient periods of any expenditure on advertising and promotion which supported the marketing of the articles or products mentioned in sub-paras (a) and (c);
(2) where the commercial success relates to the use of a process:
    (a) an identification of the process the patentee asserts has been used in accordance with the claims of the patent;
    (b) a summary by convenient periods of the revenues received from the use of such process;
    (c) a summary for the equivalent periods of the revenues, if any, received from the use of any equivalent prior art process; and
    (d) a summary by convenient periods of any expenditure which supported the use of the process mentioned in sub-paras (a) and (c).

Counterclaim for revocation

Where invalidity is alleged as a defence to the allegation of infringement, a **19-234** defendant may, and usually does, counterclaim for revocation of the patent; where they do so, the claimant should serve a defence to such counterclaim.

Admissions

Under CPR r.32.18 a party may serve on another party a notice to admit facts no **19-235** less than 21 days before trial. Typically the Patents Court will set a timetable for notices to admit facts and responses to those notices at the CMC. However, a party can serve notices to admit facts at any stage of the action.

The importance of the notice to admit is two-fold. First, it enables the real is- **19-236** sues in the action to be more closely defined. Secondly, it enables the court to order that the costs of issues needlessly contested shall be borne by the party refusing to make the admissions sought. In particular, a refusal to admit will be relevant both to the court's discretion as to costs under CPR r.44.3 and in deciding the precise amount of costs (whether on a detailed or summary assessment) under CPR r.44.6.

The statement of truth

Statements of case (such as particulars of claim or a defence, or responses to **19-237** requests for further information under CPR Pt 18) must be verified by a statement

---

[385] *John Deks Ltd v Aztec Washer Co* [1989] R.P.C. 413.
[386] CPR Pt 63, Practice Direction—Intellectual Property Claims para.6.3.

of truth—see CPR Pt 22. This requirement also applies to witness statements. Proceedings for contempt of court may be brought if a person makes or causes to be made a false statement in a document verified by a statement of truth without an honest belief in its truth.[387] However, if a parallel committal application would obstruct the sensible disposal of the proceedings, leave to bring such proceedings would not be given.[388]

19-238   In IPEC the requirements for a statement of truth are modified so that the statement must be signed by a person with knowledge of the facts alleged; and if no one person has such knowledge, then it must be signed by persons who between them have knowledge of all the facts alleged.[389] The purpose of this rule is to allow statements of case to stand as evidence.

6.   CASE MANAGEMENT DIRECTIONS

Case management conference

19-239   The case management conference is central to the case management by the court required under CPR Pt 3, although the court can and will use its powers of case management at any hearing. At the Case Management Conference the court will usual give directions to bring the case to trial. These may include:

(1)   the service of further pleadings or of further information pursuant to Pt 18 of the CPR;

(2)   disclosure and inspection of documents;

(3)   requests for or the making of admissions;

(4)   the preparation of a technical primer setting out the basic undisputed technology relevant to the dispute;

(5)   the obtaining and filing of witness statements of evidence of fact and the service of copies thereof on the other parties;

(6)   the holding of a meeting of such experts as the judge may specify, for the purpose of producing a joint report on the state of the relevant art;

(7)   the exchanging of experts' reports, in respect of those matters on which they are not agreed;

(8)   the making of experiments, tests, inspections or reports;

(9)   the determination, as a preliminary issue, of any question that may arise (including any questions as to construction of the specification or other documents);

(10)   whether to conduct the proceedings as a streamlined trial; and

(11)   whether to strike out the whole or part of a party's case;

and otherwise, as the judge thinks necessary or expedient for the purpose of giving effect to the overriding objective set out in CPR Pt 1.

19-240   At such hearing the judge shall also consider, if necessary of their own initiative, whether:

(a)   the parties' advisers should be required to meet for the purpose of agree-

---

[387] CPR r.31.14 as happened in the Patents County Court in *Utopia Tableware Ltd v BPP Marketing Ltd* [2013] EWPCC 28. The judgment on the committal hearing is reported at *Her Majesty's Solicitor General v Dodd* [2014] EWHC 240 (QB); [2014] F.S.R. 27. Sentences of six months and two months were imposed.

[388] *Malgar Ltd v R.E. Leach (Engineering) Ltd* [2000] F.S.R. 393.

[389] CPR r.63.21.

ing which documents will be required at the trial and of paginating such documents; and

(b) an independent scientific adviser should be appointed to assist the court, whether as an assessor under CPR r.35.15, or otherwise.

First case management conference in IPEC

In IPEC the first case management conference is a significant occasion. The parties Statements of Case are supposed to have already set out all facts and arguments and need for any further material at all in order to place the case in a position to be decided is to be controlled by the court. Thus at the first case management conference, the court will identify the issues and decide whether to make an order for any of the following: specific disclosure, a product or process description (or a description supplementary to an existing one), experiments, witness statements, experts reports, cross-examination at trial, written submissions or skeleton arguments.[390] Such an order will relate to specific issues and a cost benefit test must be satisfied before any such order is made.[391] Save in exceptional circumstances, the court will not consider an application by a party to submit material in addition to that ordered in this fashion.[392] This is dealt with in the IPEC chapter.

19-241

Striking out pointless and wasteful litigation

The court has power under CPR r.3.4(2)(b) to strike out a properly constituted claim on the ground that it is an abuse of process in circumstances where it is plain that the litigation is pointless and wasteful.[393] However, given that any person can apply to revoke a patent and that the applicant's motive is irrelevant, it follows that it is not an abuse of process to apply to revoke a patent even if the claimant has no sufficient commercial interest in bringing the claim.[394]

19-242

The streamlined procedure

The Patents Court Guide sets out a streamlined procedure for determining appropriate cases. These would be causes in which (save to the extent it is otherwise ordered):

19-243

(i) all factual and expert evidence is in writing,
(ii) there is no requirement for disclosure,
(iii) there are no experiments,
(iv) cross-examination is only permitted on topics where it is necessary and is confined to those topics,
(v) the total duration of the trial is fixed and will normally be less than one day, and

---

[390] CPR r.63.23(1) and CPR Pt 63, Practice Direction—Intellectual Property Claims, Section V—provisions about proceedings in the Intellectual Property Enterprise Court para.29.1.

[391] CPR Pt 63, Practice Direction—Intellectual Property Claims, Section V—provisions about proceedings in the Intellectual Property Enterprise Court para.29.2.

[392] CPR r.63.23(2).

[393] See *Jameel v Dow Jones and Co* [2005] EWCA Civ 75; [2005] 2 W.L.R. 1614, at [69]–[70]. See also *Lilley v DMG Events* [2014] EWHC 610, an IPEC case where a case valued by the court at £83 was struck out as being disproportionate to the time that would have been spent by the court to hear the matter (two days plus one day of case management).

[394] *TNS Group Holdings Ltd v Nielsen Media Research Inc* [2009] F.S.R. 23.

(vi)   the date for trial will be fixed when the order is made and will normally be in about six months thereafter.

19-244   The streamlined procedure includes minor variants of the above.[395] The decision to use the streamlined procedure is an objective one and there are no presumptions. In one case, although the subject matter was apparently simple, it was not appropriate for the streamlined procedure, one relevant factor being the commercial importance of the patent.[396] Another case was "rightly" conducted as a streamlined procedure[397] although it lasted just over one day and involved cross-examination of two witnesses. In another the issues of validity and infringement were split and infringement was ordered to be heard by the streamlined procedure.[398]

Directions at the court's own initiative

19-245   It should be noted that the court has very wide case management powers which it can exercise at any time in furtherance of the overriding objective.[399] It is not therefore restricted in any way by the orders sought by a party but may make further orders of its own initiative, even without a hearing or giving the parties an opportunity to make representations.[400] It must, however, give the parties at least three days notice of any hearing it decides to have[401] and in practice the court is most unlikely to refuse to have representations from the parties.

Decisions on paper

19-246   The Patents Court will often decide minor matters on paper without a hearing if all parties consent. The rules applicable to IPEC provide that the court will deal with an application without a hearing unless the court considers it necessary to hold one.[402]

Handlings cases concerning numerous patents

19-247   Cases often involve more than one patent but there are practical limits on the number of patents which can sensibly be dealt with on a single occasion (the current practice tends to be for the court only rarely to deal with more than two patents per trial). The rule is that a claimant may use a single claim form to start all claims which can be conveniently disposed of in the same proceedings.[403] However, over a century ago, where the claimants sued on 23 patents (all of which related to the process of making saccharin), the action was ordered to be limited to three patents to be selected by the claimants.[404] In modern times a similar problem is generally dealt with by breaking down the list of patents into groups and scheduling multiple

---

[395] See paras 7.6–7.8 of the Patents Court Guide.
[396] *Inpro Licensing Sarl's Patent* [2006] R.P.C. 20.
[397] *Mayne Pharma v Pharmacia Italia*, per Jacob LJ on appeal at [2005] EWCA Civ 137.
[398] *Canady v Erbe Electromedizin GmbH* [2006] F.S.R. 10.
[399] See CPR Pts 1 and 3, especially rr.3.2 and 3.4.
[400] CPR r.3.3(4).
[401] CPR r.3.3(3).
[402] CPR r.63.25(3).
[403] CPR r.7.3.
[404] *Saccharin Corp Ltd v Wild & Co* (1903) 20 R.P.C. 243; see also *Saccharin Corp Ltd v R. White & Sons Ltd* (1903) 20 R.P.C. 454, CA; cf. *Saccharin Corp Ltd v Alliance Chemical Co Ltd* (1905) 22 R.P.C. 175.

trials spaced apart in order to resolve all the issues.[405] In a case which involved numerous patents said to be essential to a working of a standard, in addition to scheduling multiple trials on the patents themselves a preliminary issue was ordered to decide first whether the court should exercise its discretion to grant declarations concerning essentiality at all.[406]

7. DISCLOSURE

Disclosure (formerly discovery) and inspection of documents is dealt with gener- **19-248** ally by CPR Pt 31. This Part applies in modified form to a claim for infringement of a patent, a declaration of non-infringement of a patent, or any proceedings where the validity of a patent is in issue.[407]

Standard disclosure

Standard disclosure is the disclosure order most commonly made. It requires a **19-249** party to disclose only[408]:

(a) the documents on which they rely; and
(b) the documents which:
    (i)   adversely affect their own case;
    (ii) adversely affect another party's case; or
    (iii) support another party's case; and
(c) the documents which they are required to disclose by a relevant Practice Direction.

When giving standard disclosure, a party is required to make a reasonable search **19-250** for documents falling within (b) and (c) above that are or have been in its control.[409] The factors relevant in deciding the reasonableness of a search include the number of documents involved, the nature and complexity of the proceedings, the ease and expense of retrieval of any particular document and the significance of any document which is likely to be located during the search. Where a party has not searched for a category or class of document on the grounds that to do so would be unreasonable, they must state this in their disclosure statement and identify the category or class of document.[410]

---

405 The judgment giving that direction is not available but see *Nokia v IPcom* [2009] EWHC 3482 (Pat), at [2].
406 The judgment giving that direction is not available but see *InterDigital v Nokia* [2008] EWHC 969 (Pat), at [1]–[2].
407 CPR r. 63.8.
408 CPR r.31.6.
409 CPR rr.31.5 and 31.8. This may not include documents in the control of an associated company; see *Sommer Allibert (UK) Ltd v Flair Plastics Ltd* [1987] R.P.C. 599, at 627; *Unilever Plc v Gillette UK Ltd* [1988] R.P.C. 416. In *Schlumberger v EMGS* [2008] EWHC 56 (Pat), [8]–[21] specific disclosure of documents in the possession of an associated company of the claimant was ordered because the claimant had indicated in its disclosure statement when giving standard disclosure that it had searched the records of associated companies, thereby demonstrating that those records were in its control.
410 CPR r.31.7.

Standard disclosure in patent actions

19-251   Standard disclosure in patent actions does not require the disclosure of documents in the following exempt classes[411]:

(1)   documents relating to the infringement of a patent by a product or process if, before or at the same time serving a list of documents, the defendant has served on the claimant full particulars of the product or process alleged to infringe, including if necessary drawings or other illustrations (commonly referred to as a "product description" or "process description", as the case may be);

(2)   documents relating to any ground on which the validity of a patent is put in issue, except documents which came into existence with the period beginning two years before the earliest claimed priority date and ending two years after the date (commonly referred to as the "four-year window"); and

(3)   documents relating to the issue of commercial success.[412]

Product and process descriptions

19-252   A product or process description ("PPD") must provide full particulars of the product or process alleged to infringe, including if necessary drawings or other illustrations (full particulars means particulars sufficient to enable all issues of infringement to be resolved).[413] The description must be complete in all relevant areas; a description of the product either in general terms of including tendencious assertions was not acceptable.[414] Equally, conclusory statements are not acceptable. Whenever a PPD asserts that something relevant is absent, it is incumbent on the party preparing a product description to explain why.[415] It is good practice in an appropriate case to provide a sample along with the description where appropriate.

19-253   The function of the description is in all respects equivalent to disclosure and the duties of all parties are the same as they would be in relation to disclosure.[416] A product or process description must contain information of at least the level of specificity of the claims. It is often the case that the product or process description needs to contain rather more detailed information than the claims. This is because, even if the claims are expressed in general terms, the issues on infringement often involve understanding precisely how the allegedly infringing product or process is constructed or functions. The parties have an obligation to co-operate in relation to the PPD. The claimant has the primary responsibility to articulate its infringement case as clearly as it can. The defendant has the primary responsibility to provide full particulars of its product or process. It is not legitimate for a defendant to seek to use a lack of clarity of the claimant's case on infringement as an excuse for not providing proper particulars of its product or process. If the defendant is genuinely

---

[411]   CPR Pt 63, Practice Direction—Intellectual Property Claims para.6.1.
[412]   But see Schedule required under CPR Pt 63, Practice Direction—Intellectual Property Claims para.6.3.
[413]   *Consafe v Emtunga* [1999] R.P.C. 154, [23]. See also Arnold J in *Starsight Telecast Inc, v Virgin Media Limited* [2014] EWHC 828 (Pat), at [6]–[10].
[414]   *Consafe v Emtunga* [1999] R.P.C. 154, [23].
[415]   *Vringo Infrastructure Inc v ZTE (UK) Ltd* [2015] EWHC 818 (Pat).
[416]   *Alfred Taylor v Ishida (Europe) Ltd* [2000] F.S.R. 224.

unsure about what particulars it needs to provide, it should apply to the court for directions.[417]

Sometimes a defendant may not be in a position to provide a product descrip- **19-254** tion in relation to the (or a relevant part of) the product alleged to infringe. This issue has arisen in a number of cases concerning mobile telephones where the alleged infringing functionality resides in a microchip which the defendant has bought and incorporated into his phones without knowing the details of how it functions (other than in operation it complies with the relevant technical standards). In such cases, the correct course is for the party to verify such parts as they are able, and to serve a disclosure list (which may or may not contain any documents) in relation to the remainder.[418]

The court will prevent the use of process descriptions served under para.(1) for **19-255** purposes collateral to the litigation.[419]

A PPD ought to be accompanied by a signed written statement which: (i) states **19-256** that the person making the statement is personally acquainted with the facts to which the description relates; (ii) verifies that the description is a true and complete description of the product or process; and (iii) contains an acknowledgement by the person making the statement that they may be required to attend court in order to be cross-examined on the contents of the description.[420] Therefore, unless a description is accepted by the claimant, the defendant ought formally prove it by calling as a witness at trial the person(s) who signed it.[421]

Procedure for disclosure

Two weeks prior to the CMC, each party is required to serve a disclosure report **19-257** verified by a statement of truth, which describes briefly what documents exist or may exist that are or may be relevant to the matters in issue in the case; describes where and with whom those documents are or may be located; and in the case of electronic documents, describes how those documents are stored.[422] Not less than seven days before the first case management conference or on any other occasion as the court may direct, the parties must, at a meeting or by telephone, discuss and seek to agree a proposal in relation to disclosure that meets the overriding objective.[423]

The court will use the disclosure reports in deciding the appropriate order for **19-258** disclosure. The court is not constrained to make any particular order for disclosure. However, options include[424]:

(a) an order dispensing with disclosure;
(b) an order that a party disclose the documents on which it relies, and at the same time request any specific disclosure it requires from any other party;
(c) an order that directs, where practicable, the disclosure to be given by each party on an issue-by-issue basis;
(d) an order that each party disclose any documents which it is reasonable to

---

[417] See *Starsight Telecast Inc v Virgin Media Limited* [2014] EWHC 828 (Pat), at [6]–[10].
[418] Patents Court Guide, para.10.5.
[419] *Chiron v Evans Medical (No.2)* [1997] F.S.R. 268. See also CPR r.31.22.
[420] Patents Court Guide, para.10.4.
[421] Per Jacob LJ in *Technip France SA's Patent* [2004] R.P.C. 46, at [43].
[422] CPR r.31.5(3).
[423] CPR r.31.5(5).
[424] CPR r.31.5(7).

suppose may contain information which enables that party to advance its own case or to damage that of any other party, or which leads to an enquiry which has either of those consequences;

(e) an order that a party give standard disclosure; and

(f) any other order in relation to disclosure that the court considers appropriate.

19-259 If disclosure is ordered, each party must make and serve on every other party a list of documents in the relevant practice form. The list must indicate the documents in respect of which the party claims a right or duty to withhold inspection (e.g. because legally privileged) and those documents no longer in the party's control (further stating what has happened to those documents) as well as those in respect of which inspection will be given. The list must include a disclosure statement setting out the extent of the search made and certifying that they understand and have carried out their duty to disclose documents.[425]

19-260 At any stage in the proceedings, the court may make an order for specific disclosure or specific inspection.[426] When an application is made for such an order, the procedure is as set out in CPR Pt 23; see also the procedure on application for an interim injunction at para.19-77, et seq.

Disclosure before commencement of proceedings

19-261 The court may order disclosure before proceedings start where: (1) both the applicant and respondent are likely to be a party to subsequent proceedings, (2) the respondent's duty by way of standard disclosure in such subsequent proceedings would extend to the documents or classes of documents of which the applicant seeks disclosure, and (3) disclosure before proceedings is desirable in order to dispose fairly of the anticipated proceedings, or assist the dispute to be resolved without proceedings, or save costs.[427] Pre-action disclosure was refused in a case which was speculative in nature; there being nothing to support the suggestion that the invention may have been incorporated in the defendant's product.[428] Pre-action disclosure of licenses granted by the patentee under the patent it has asserted against the applicant for disclosure was ordered in *The Big Bus Company v Ticketogo Ltd*.[429] In that case the court held that it was desirable for parties to be able to make a realistic assessment of the value of the claim at the earliest possible stage. Where the key information concerning the value of the claim was held by one party, then it was desirable for that party to be required to disclose that information by way of pre-action disclosure. That would place the parties on an equal footing, would enable both parties to make an informed assessment of whether the claim was worth litigating at all and would promote settlement of the dispute without having to resort to proceedings.

Disclosure by non-party

19-262 The court may also order disclosure by a person not a party to proceedings where the documents of which disclosure are sought are likely to support the case of the

---

[425] See CPR r.31.10.
[426] CPR r.31.12.
[427] CPR r.31.16.
[428] *BSW Ltd v Balltec Ltd* [2007] F.S.R. 1.
[429] [2015] EWHC 1094 (Pat); see also *Adaptive Signal and Spectrum v British Telecom* [2014] EWHC 4447 (Pat).

applicant or adversely affect the case of one of the other parties to the proceedings, and disclosure is necessary in order to dispose fairly of the claim or to save costs.[430] In *American Home Products v Novartis*[431] the Court of Appeal upheld an order requiring third parties to provide disclosure which bore on the issue of obviousness.

The normal rule is that the party against whom the order is sought will be **19-263** awarded their costs to be paid by the party seeking such order, although the court will have regard to the extent to which it was reasonable to oppose such order.[432]

Disclosure by US court (under 28 USC 1782) for use in UK proceedings

The United States of America has a domestic rule (28 USC 1782) by which a US **19-264** court can compel a person in its jurisdiction to produce depositions and discovery for use in proceedings elsewhere.[433] In *Nokia Corporation v InterDigital Technology Corporation*[434] the claimant in an action for revocation of three UK patents, sought to employ USC 1782 to obtain documents from a third party in the USA (who had been involved in litigation on corresponding US patents with the same patentee) for use in the UK proceedings. The documents it sought were prior art, claim construction and invalidity contentions, negotiations of a licence between the patentee and the third party and documents relating to performance or modification of the licence. The latter three categories were said to be sought in order to deploy the documents in opposition to the exercise of discretion on patent amendment in the UK action. Although observing that it was unlikely that the material sought would be of utility in the action, Pumfrey J refused to order an injunction restraining the USC 1782 proceedings in the USA.[435]

Implied undertaking and confidentiality clubs

The CPR expressly provide[436] and, it is submitted, there is an implied undertak- **19-265** ing given in corresponding terms, that the disclosed documents may only be used for the purpose of the action in which they are disclosed. Consequently, the documents may not be used for any collateral or ulterior motive and a breach of that undertaking is a contempt of court.[437]

[430] CPR r.31.17.
[431] [2001] F.S.R. 41. Approved of in *Three Rivers DC v Governor and Company of the Bank of England (No 4)* [2002] EWCA Civ 1182; [2003] 1 W.L.R. 210, where the Court of Appeal comprehensively reviewed the power to order disclosure from a non-party under CPR r.31.17.
[432] CPR r.48.1.
[433] See *South Carolina Insurance Co v Assurantie Maatschappij "De Zeven Provincien NV"* [1987] A.C. 24.
[434] [2004] EWHC 2920 (Pat). The case went to the Court of Appeal ([2005] EWCA Civ 614) but this issue had fallen away by then.
[435] Citing *South Carolina Insurance Co v Assurantie Maatschappij "De Zeven Provincien NV"* [1987] A.C. 24 and the US Supreme Court case of *Intel v AMD*.
[436] CPR r.31.22.
[437] *Home Office v Harman* [1983] A.C. 280; *Alterskye v Scott* [1948] 1 All E.R. 469; *Halcon International Inc v Shell Transport and Trading Co* [1979] R.P.C. 97; *Distillers Co (Biochemicals) Ltd v Times Newspapers Ltd* [1975] Q.B. 613; *Riddick v Thames Board Mills* [1977] Q.B. 881; *Sybron Corp v Barclays Bank* [1984] 3 W.L.R. 1055; *Wilden Pumps v Fusfeld* [1985] F.S.R. 583; *Bayer v Winter (No.2)* [1986] 1 W.L.R. 540; *CBS Songs Ltd v Amstrad*.

Confidentiality clubs

19-266   In cases where disclosable documents include trade secrets or other confidential information it is usual to limit the persons who may inspect such documents. These schemes are often called confidentiality clubs. There is no universal form of order as to who should be included and each case will turn on its own facts. The principles to be considered are set out in *Warner-Lambert Co v Glaxo Laboratories Ltd*[438] and the cases therein referred to. In *Lilly ICOS Limited v Pfizer Ltd*[439] when the Court of Appeal considered the principles governing the exercise of the power in CPR r.31.22,[440] one of the factors the court took into consideration was this aspect of practice in patent cases.

19-267   Although a party has the right to a fair trial under art.6 of the European Convention on Human Rights that does not mean that they have an absolute or unqualified right to see every document.[441]

Documents read or referred to in court

19-268   The undertaking not to use a document ceases to apply after it has been read to, or by the court, or referred to at a hearing which has been held in public unless the court orders otherwise.[442] Documents pre-read by the judge and referred to in the skeleton argument qualify as having been read or referred to in open court.[443] In *Chan U Seek v Alvis*[444] Park J made an order under the then CPR Pt 5.4(5) (now Pt 5.4C (4)) in favour of a non-party newspaper for the disclosure of certain pleadings, witness statements and exhibits from the court file. The judgment includes a helpful review of the law and practice in this area including the issue of inherent jurisdiction.

Preservation of undertaking not to use

19-269   Pursuant to CPR r.31.22, the court may on the application of a party or of the person to whom the document belongs, make an order restricting or prohibiting further use despite the fact that it has been read or referred to in open court.[445] In *Lilly ICOS Limited v Pfizer Ltd*[446] the Court of Appeal considered the principles governing the exercise of the power in CPR r.31.22, finding that the starting point was the principle that very good reasons were required before departing from the normal rule of publicity; that the role the document played at trial was a factor to place in the balance; that any chilling effect of an order on third parties had to be kept in mind; that simple assertions of confidentiality and damage that would be done by publication, even if supported by both parties, should not prevail; that it was highly desirable to avoid holding trials in private; that patent cases were subject to the same general rules as these but were subject to some special problems, and that the parties should not feel constrained to hold back from relevant issues because

---

[438] [1975] R.P.C. 354; see also *Roussel Uclaf v ICI* [1990] R.P.C. 45, CA.
[439] [2002] F.S.R. 54.
[440] See para.19-265.
[441] Per Cranston J in *Roberts v Nottinghamshire Healthcare NHS Trust* [2009] F.S.R. 4, [25].
[442] CPR r.31.22(1)(a). See also para.19-209.
[443] *SmithKline Beecham Biologicals v Connaught Laboratories* [2000] F.S.R. 1.
[444] [2005] E.M.L.R. 19.
[445] CPR r.31.22(2) and (3).
[446] [2002] F.S.R. 54.

of legitimate fears of publicity. The need for proper evidence addressing why documents sought to be protected by a permanent order under CPR r.31.22(2) are confidential was emphasised in *Smith & Nephew plc v Convatec Technologies Inc.*[447] In that case, the court also summarised the law and explained the Patents Court's practice in relation to handling confidential documents.

Permission or agreement to use documents covered by undertaking

The undertaking also ceases to apply if the court gives permission[448] or if the **19-270** party who disclosed the document and the person to whom the document belongs agree.[449] Only in exceptional circumstances will the court give its permission and release a party from the implied undertaking.[450] The existence of a co-pending EPO opposition involving the same parties, subject matter and issues is not such a circumstance.[451] However, in *SmithKline Beecham v Generics*[452] the Court of Appeal gave permission for documents to be used in a second action on the same patent before the same judge against a different defendant (on terms preserving their confidentiality in the second action). Permission was given because the documents had been seen by the judge in the first action, they were potentially discoverable under r.31.17 and not to do so could reflect badly on the administration of justice.

Translation of documents in a foreign language

There is no obligation upon a party giving disclosure of a document in a foreign **19-271** language to provide a translation.[453]

Time for disclosure

Since it is not possible to say precisely what the issues between the parties are **19-272** before the defence is delivered, as a general matter neither party will be allowed disclosure of documents until that stage of the action has been reached.[454] But thereafter disclosure will not be delayed merely because it is inconvenient to a party to give it immediately.[455]

Nor will disclosure be ordered as a matter of course before trial as to facts which **19-273** will only become relevant after trial as, for instance, with regard to the extent of the defendant's infringements—a fact which is not material until the inquiry as to damages.[456] The practice as to discovery upon such inquiry as to damages is dealt

---

[447] [2014] EWHC 146 (Pat).
[448] CPR r.31.22(1)(b).
[449] CPR r.31.22(1)(c).
[450] See, e.g. *Crest Homes Plc v Marks* [1988] R.P.C. 21; *Dory v Wolf GmbH* [1990] F.S.R. 266; *Cobra Golf v Rata* [1996] F.S.R. 819; and *Bourns v Raychem* [2000] F.S.R. 841.
[451] *Bonzel v Intervention (No.2)* [1991] R.P.C. 43. See also *Danisco A/S v Novozymes A/S* [2012] F.S.R 21.
[452] [2004] F.S.R. 8.
[453] *Bayer A.G. v Harris Pharmaceuticals* [1991] F.S.R. 170.
[454] *Woolfe v Automatic Picture Gallery Ltd* (1902) 19 R.P.C. 161; *RHM Foods Ltd v Bovril Ltd* [1983] R.P.C. 275; *Intel Corp v General Instrument Corp* [1989] F.S.R. 640.
[455] *British United Shoe Machinery Co Ltd v Holdfast Boots Ltd* (1934) 51 R.P.C. 489.
[456] *De La Rue v Dickenson* (1857) 3 K. & J. 388; *Lea v Saxby* (1875) 32 L.T.(N.S.) 731; *Fennessy v Clark* (1887) 37 Ch D. 184.

with below.[457] However, the court has a discretion to order such disclosure at an earlier stage if there is a good reason to do so.[458] Reasons to make such an order are if disclosure would aid settlement or so that the claimant can determine if it was proportionate to continue with the action given the likely amounts at stake. The court can even make such an order before commencement of the action.[459]

Continuing duty of disclosure

19-274   Any duty of disclosure continues until the proceedings are concluded.[460] A party may not rely on any document which he fails to disclose or in respect of which they fail to permit inspection unless the court gives permission.[461]

The issues relevant to disclosure in patent cases

19-275   The issues in patent cases to which disclosure of documents must be relevant are not the broad issues of validity and infringement, although those issues as narrowed down by the particulars of objections or infringements.

19-276   Thus, under the old Rules, where the particulars of infringements alleged infringement of a process in general terms and also specified a particular instance of infringement, it was held that the plaintiff was only entitled to interrogate as to the particular act complained of.[462]

19-277   Similarly, where the defendant alleged invalidity by reason of certain facts within the knowledge of the plaintiff, it was held that the issue was not the validity of the patent generally, but only as limited by the particulars of objections and that a plaintiff should not be ordered to disclose every document which might suggest invalidity irrespective of whether it related to the particular grounds relied upon by the defendant.[463]

Interrogatories

19-278   Interrogatories were formerly a means whereby parties could interrogate each other with a view to advancing their own case or undermining that of their opponent. Under the CPR, interrogatories have been replaced by requests for further information under CPR Pt 18 and written questions to experts under CPR r.35.6.

19-279   It is submitted, however, that much of the case law decided in relation to interrogatories will be applicable in determining the limits of requests for further information and written questions to experts.

---

457 See para.21-131.
458 *Hazeltine Corp v British Broadcasting Corp* [1979] F.S.R. 523; *Adaptive Signal and Spectrum v British Telecom* [2014] EWHC 4447 (Pat); *The Big Bus Company v Ticketogo Ltd* [2015] EWHC 1094 (Pat).
459 *The Big Bus Company v Ticketogo Ltd* [2015] EWHC 1094 (Pat).
460 CPR r.31.11.
461 CPR r.31.21.
462 *Aktiengesellschaft, etc., Aluminium Schweissung v London Aluminium Co Ltd* (1919) 36 R.P.C. 199; but see *Alliance Flooring Co Ltd v Winsorfior Ltd* [1961] R.P.C. 375.
463 *Avery Ltd v Ashworth, Son & Co Ltd* (1915) 32 R.P.C. 463 and 560; cf. *Edison and Swan United Electric Light Co v Holland* (1888) 5 R.P.C. 213; *Belegging v Witten Industrial Diamonds* [1979] F.S.R. 59; *Intalite International N.V. v Cellular Ceilings Ltd (No.1)* [1987] R.P.C. 532; *Intel Corp v General Instrument Corp* [1989] 1 F.S.R. 640.

Thus, for example, the questions must relate to the issues in the proceeding as **19-280** narrowed by the particulars of objections or infringement.[464]

Similarly, the implied undertaking may apply to any responses given to such **19-281** requests or questions.[465]

In the Patents Court, requests or questions which go to construction were refused **19-282** in the past.[466] However, in IPEC construction is inevitably addressed before trial as a result of the requirement to plead all facts and arguments in the Statement of Case.[467] It maybe that experience in IPEC will lead to a greater ordering of requests going to construction the Patent Court.[468]

Disclosure, requests or questions relating to particular issues

Infringement

As stated above,[469] special provision is made in the Practice Direction[470] as to the **19-283** disclosure of documents relating to the infringement of a patent by a product or process if the party against whom the allegation of infringement is made has served full particulars of the product or process alleged to infringe. Consequently any further disclosure, request for information or question is likely to be dependent on the court first being satisfied that the particulars served are inadequate.

Subject thereto, the claimant may question the defendant or obtain disclosure as **19-284** to facts relevant to points in issue[471] with respect to the particular act instanced as an alleged infringement in the particulars of infringements, both as to whether the act was performed and as to the details which tend to show whether or not it was an infringement.

In the past a claimant was required to give disclosure of documents generated in **19-285** other jurisdictions which disclose the approach which may be taken on the issue of infringement,[472] however given the modern approach to the preparation of cases it is doubtful that this would be necessary today.

Names of defendant's customers

A defendant cannot conceal the name of their customer in the case of the specific **19-286** article complained of, and as regards that article may be questioned as to whether they have supplied it to anybody and to whom, unless, of course, they have already admitted the sale thereof in their defence.[473] A claimant is not, however, entitled to discover before trial the names of the defendant's customers generally, as this only

---

[464] See para.19-275.

[465] As in, e.g. *Chiron v Evans Medical* [1997] F.S.R. 268 where the process description was held to be covered by the implied undertaking. See also *Grapha Holding A.G. v Quebecor Printing (UK) Plc* [1996] F.S.R. 711 where information obtained on an inspection was held to be covered by the implied undertaking.

[466] *Wenham Co Ltd v Champion Gas Lamp Co Ltd* (1890) 7 R.P.C. 22; *Delta Metal Co Ltd v Maxim Nordenfelt Guns and Ammunition Co Ltd* (1891) 8 R.P.C. 169; *Bibby & Baron Ltd v Duerden* (1910) 27 R.P.C. 283, CA; *Lux Traffic Controls v Staffordshire Public Works Co* [1991] R.P.C. 73.

[467] CPR r.63.20.

[468] See *CompactGTL v Oxford Catalysts Group* [2013] 3935 (Pat), at [11].

[469] See para.19-251.

[470] See CPR Pt 63, Practice Direction—Intellectual Property Claims para.6.1(1).

[471] See *Marriott v Chamberlain* (1886) 17 Q.B.D. 154, at 163; *Nash v Layton* [1911] 2 Ch. 71.

[472] *Vickers v Horsell Graphic Industries Ltd* [1988] R.P.C. 421.

[473] See *Lister v Norton Bros & Co Ltd* (1886) 3 R.P.C. 68; see also *Stahlwerk Becker A.G.'s Patent*

becomes relevant if they establish their case and obtain an inquiry into damages.[474] Even upon an inquiry the matter is discretionary and the defendant may not be required to identify the names of their customers.[475] However at the interim stage disclosure of the names of customers may be ordered in order to give the patentee the opportunity of preventing the further sale into the market of the product complained of, the matter being approached on the same basis as an interim injunction.[476] The names of the defendant's customers was ordered in *Wobben v Siemens*[477] using the principles of *Norwich Pharmacal v Customs and Excise Commissioners*,[478] having been refused under CPR Pt 18.

Names of defendant's suppliers

19-287   The names of the persons who supplied the defendant with goods alleged to infringe are not normally relevant to any issue between the parties, although the names of such suppliers may be disclosable under the principles of *Norwich Pharmacal v Customs and Excise Commissioners*,[479] even when the supplier is outside the jurisdiction[480] or under an application brought under CPR rr.31.16 or 31.17.

19-288   Where the defendants dealt in a chemical product, all known processes for the manufacture of which were alleged to be covered by patents owned by the plaintiffs, interrogatories under the old Rules as to the sources of the defendants' supply were permitted by the Court of Appeal on the ground that the answers would probably enable the plaintiffs to ascertain whether the substance had been manufactured by an infringing process or not.[481]

19-289   Such a probability has also been held to exist where the plaintiffs alleged that they had knowledge of the processes employed at certain works and that, if informed as to the source of the defendants' goods, they would be enabled, utilising such knowledge, to prove infringement.[482]

Validity

19-290   Disclosure of documents, requests for information and questions to experts relating to the issue of validity may be obtained or made by either party although the Practice Direction provides[483] that standard disclosure is limited to documents which came into existence within the period beginning two years before the earliest claimed priority date and ending two years after that date.[484]

(1917) 34 R.P.C 344.

[474] *Sega Enterprises Ltd v Alca Electronics* [1982] F.S.R. 516.

[475] *Murray v Clayton* (1872) L.R. 15 Eq.Cas. 115; and *Smith, Kline & French Laboratories Ltd v Doncaster Pharmaceuticals Ltd* [1989] F.S.R. 401, 405 and 406.

[476] *Eli Lilly & Co v Neolab Ltd* [2008] F.S.R 25.

[477] [2015] F.S.R. 18.

[478] See para.19-301, et seq.

[479] See para.19-301, et seq.

[480] *Smith, Kline & French Laboratories Ltd v Global Pharmaceutics Ltd* [1986] R.P.C. 394.

[481] *Saccharin Corporation v Haines* (1898) 15 R.P.C. 344; and see *Stahlwerk Becker A.G.'s Patent* (1917) 34 R.P.C. 344.

[482] *Osram Lamp Works Ltd v Gabriel Lamp Co* (1914) 31 R.P.C. 230, CA.

[483] CPR Pt 63, Practice Direction—Intellectual Property Claims para.6.1(2).

[484] See also para.19-251.

Prior use

As regards prior use, although the requirements with regard to particulars and **19-291** inspection are stringent, nevertheless as long as the pleading is sufficient to enable the patentee to understand the case he has to meet, disclosure can be ordered on the issue even though every detail has not been pleaded.[485]

Obviousness

The question of discovery in relation to obviousness was reviewed in detail in **19-292** *Nichia Corp v Argos Ltd*[486] where the Court of Appeal allowed an appeal from a judge's blanket refusal to order disclosure of documents concerning the making of the invention. The judge had held that such disclosure was disproportionate having regard to the secondary nature of such evidence. The Court of Appeal held that such a blanket approach was wrong and a more nuanced approach taking into account the particular facts of the case was appropriate. Notably in that decision Jacob LJ dissented on the basis that in his view the time had now come such the normally such disclosure should not be ordered in a straightforward case. Although this dissent needs to be seen in the subsequent light of the renewed status accorded to so-called secondary evidence in relation to obviousness following the Court of Appeal in *Schlumberger Holdings Limited v Electromagnetic Geoservices AS*,[487] it remains the case that disclosure of documents concerning the making of the invention rarely play any significant role in the outcome of a trial.

When commercial success is relied upon to rebut an allegation of obviousness, **19-293** standard disclosure is limited by the Practice Direction, although disclosure of licences granted by the patentee in respect of the patent may be ordered by way of specific disclosure.[488]

Interrogatories under the old Rules, as to the state of mind of particular research- **19-294** ers in the field at the relevant time were found to be unnecessary in the context of obviousness and the court ordered their withdrawal.[489]

Insufficiency

In contrast to the position on obviousness, disclosure going to pleaded insuf- **19-295** ficiency allegations is generally more readily ordered. It can be powerful evidence in support of an insufficiency if the patentee's own documents show that despite serious efforts to do so, they were unable to work the claimed invention, either at all or in some material respect. Similarly, attempts of the party alleging insufficiency will be equally relevant.

---

485 *MMI Research v Cellxion* [2008] F.S.R. 23 applying *Visx v Nidek* [1999] F.S.R. 91.
486 [2007] F.S.R. 38. See also *Halcon International Inc v Shell Transport and Trading Co Ltd* [1979] R.P.C. 459; considered in *The Wellcome Foundation v V.R. Laboratories (Australia) Pty. Ltd* [1982] R.P.C. 343; and followed in *SKM S.A. v Wagner Spraytech (UK) Ltd* [1982] R.P.C. 497.
487 [2010] EWCA Civ 819; see para.12-101, et seq.
488 *Mentor Corp v Hollister Inc* [1990] F.S.R. 577.
489 *Mentor Corp v Hollister Inc* [1990] F.S.R. 577.

Disclosure of litigation experiments

19-296   The question of disclosure in relation to experiments is addressed at para.19-321.

Claim of privilege

19-297   Communications between a litigant and their professional legal adviser for the purpose of getting legal advice are privileged, whether at the time they are made litigation be pending or anticipated or not. Similarly, communications from some other person to such adviser are also privileged but only if made when litigation is pending or contemplated and when they are made with a view to the litigation for advice or collecting evidence. US depositions taken in the presence of both parties to litigation are not privileged, nor are answers to interrogatories served in US actions. Neither is the type of document which it is necessary in the public interest to exclude from disclosure on the grounds of privilege.[490]

19-298   The meaning of "contemplated proceedings" in the context of inter partes litigation has been explained as requiring that the person who was in the position to bring the proceedings has indicated in some way or other that proceedings might be brought.[491]

19-299   Documents prepared by a party's solicitors for the purpose of obtaining the fiat of the Attorney General to enable the party to counterclaim for revocation (as was then necessary) were held to be privileged documents.[492]

Patent attorneys

19-300   Formerly, patent agents when performing their ordinary work were not considered as professional legal advisers and communications with them were not privileged.[493] However, the position of patent agents in this regard was altered by s.15 of the Civil Evidence Act 1968 and is now covered by s.280 of the 1988 Act. The section now applies only to patent attorneys (rather than to patent agents).[494] The privilege attaching to such communications under UK law may or may not be recognised abroad. In *Eli Lilly v Pfizer (No.2)*[495] the Federal Court of Australia held that the privilege to a communication between a UK patent agent (in house) and his employer did not fall within the equivalent Australian provisions. The fact the communication was privileged in the UK did not mean it was necessarily privileged in Australia.

Action for disclosure

19-301   A person may be made a defendant in an action brought specifically to obtain discovery of the identity of infringers where that person (whether knowingly or not) "has got mixed up in tortious acts of others so as to facilitate their wrong-

---

[490] *Visx Inc v Nidex Co* [1999] F.S.R. 91, CA; *Minnesota Mining & Manufacturing Co v Rennicks (UK) Ltd* [1991] F.S.R. 97, disapproved.
[491] *Rockwell International Corp v Serck Industries Ltd* [1987] R.P.C. 89.
[492] *Vigneron-Dahl Ltd v Pettitt Ltd* (1925) 42 R.P.C. 431.
[493] *Moseley v Victoria Rubber Co* (1886) 3 R.P.C. 35.
[494] The distinction is an important one. Any person may act as a patent agent but only qualified persons can be patent attorneys (see ss.274–278 of the 1988 Act, as amended).
[495] [2004] F.C.A. 850.

doing".[496] The costs of an innocent defendant in providing such information will be borne by the claimant as will the costs of proceedings if the defendant properly doubts whether they should have to provide such information and submit the matter for determination by the court. The claimant may, however, be able to recover such costs from the infringer in subsequent proceedings.[497]

The court has jurisdiction to order the disclosure of the name of a wrong-doer **19-302** outside the jurisdiction even though such wrong-doing is under the laws of another country, provided it is shown that the transaction in which the defendant and the wrongdoer here involved related to the same subject-matter.[498]

The CPR also gives wide powers to the court to order disclosure before proceed- **19-303** ings have started[499] and against a person not a party to the proceedings.[500]

8. INSPECTION

Inspection of machinery or process

The court may give directions for the inspection, detention, custody or preserva- **19-304** tion of relevant property under CPR r.25.1(c) and, in an appropriate case, may make an order to inspect property before commencement or against a non-party under CPR r.25.5. CPR Pt 63, Practice Direction—Intellectual Property Claims para.4.5 provides that an order for inspection of machinery or apparatus allegedly used before the priority date may be made.

A classic statement of the purpose of inspection is to ensure that "the true facts **19-305** of the case shall be carefully sifted",[501] but at the same time care will be taken that the process of the law is not abused and that an action for infringement shall not be made a means and lever for the discovery of other persons' secrets. Thus the court will in a proper case prevent the use of information obtained on an inspection for purposes collateral to the litigation, such as use in parallel proceedings overseas.[502]

Under the CPR applications of this kind are dealt with on a two-stage basis, first **19-306** the jurisdictional threshold to make the order must be satisfied and secondly, the court had to decide whether to exercise its discretion to make the order.[503]

Prima facie case of infringement necessary

If the property to be inspected relates to alleged infringement then an order will **19-307** be made if the court is satisfied that there is a genuine and substantial issue to be tried.[504]

---

[496] *Norwich Pharmacal Co v Customs & Excise Commissioners* [1974] A.C. 133; but note Pt 9 of the Enterprise Act 2002 which restricts the release of certain information by public authorities in some circumstances.

[497] *Morton-Norwich Products Inc v Intercen (No.2)* [1981] F.S.R. 337.

[498] *Smith, Kline & French Laboratories Ltd v Global Pharmaceutics Ltd* [1986] R.P.C. 394.

[499] CPR r.31.16.

[500] CPR r.31.17.

[501] See, e.g. *Osram Lamp Works Ltd v British Union Lamp Works Ltd* (1914) 31 R.P.C. 309.

[502] *Grapha Holding A.G. v Quebecor Printing* [1996] F.S.R. 711.

[503] See *Black v Sumitomo Corp* [2001] EWCA Civ 1819; [2002] 1 W. L. R. 1562; [2003] 3 All E.R. 643 and *Red Spider Technology v Omega* [2010] F.S.R. 6.

[504] See *British Xylonite Co Ltd v Fibrenyle Ltd* [1959] R.P.C. 252; followed in *Unilever Plc v Pearce* [1985] F.S.R. 475.

19-308   In *Red Spider Technology v Omega*[505] the patentee applied for inspection of a valve pursuant to CPR r.31.16 (the rule permitting pre-action disclosure). It may be questioned whether the application should more properly have been made under CPR r.25.5 but the point was not taken and no doubt the outcome would have been the same. The application was refused on the ground that the respondent had provided a written description which, if true meant the valve did not infringe and it was difficult to see what the claimant had to go on to make out a case for infringement. A mere assertion that it did not accept the explanation was not sufficient. Even if the jurisdiction threshold was reached, which was doubtful, the court's discretion would be exercised to refuse the order; no time limit was placed on the time Omega would have to keep the valve, the inspection order was to widely drawn and amounted to fishing and there was a concern about confidentiality.

Inspection may be limited

19-309   When the interests of justice require, the inspection will be limited to solicitors, counsel, patent agents, and independent experts who will be required to keep any secrets which they may have discovered and which do not affect the question of infringement.[506]

19-310   In *British Thomson-Houston Co Ltd v Duram Ltd (No.2)*,[507] the plaintiffs filed an affidavit of an expert who deposed that he had examined the defendant's products and believed that they could only have been produced by the aid of the plaintiffs' patented process. Inspection of defendants' process was asked for and the defendants swore that their process was a valuable secret. Astbury J gave leave to the plaintiffs to administer interrogatories and to ask for samples,[508] and refused to entertain the application for inspection until it should be shown that the answers by the defendants would be insufficient to enable the plaintiffs to present their case.

19-311   In a case where the plaintiff's right to inspection depended upon a contract, the construction of which was disputed and he was unable to show that inspection was necessary to prepare his case, it was held that no inspection should be granted, on the ground that the right depended upon the question to be determined at the trial.[509]

19-312   Also, where the defendant delivered to the plaintiff specimens of the alleged infringing articles, the latter was not allowed to see those articles in actual use on the defendant's premises.[510]

Mutual inspection

19-313   Where it is necessary, the court will order the defendant and the claimant to give mutual inspection and to show both the patented machine and the alleged infringe-

---

[505] [2010] F.S.R. 6.
[506] See, e.g. *Flower v Lloyd* [1876] W.N. 169, at 230; *Swain v Edlin-Sinclair Tyre Co* (1903) 20 R.P.C. 435; *British Celanese Ltd v Courtaulds Ltd* (1933) 52 R.P.C. 63, at 80; *Coloured Asphalt Co Ltd v British Asphalt and Bitumen Ltd* (1936) 53 R.P.C. 89. See also *British Syphon Co Ltd v Homewood* [1956] R.P.C. 225; *British Xylonite Co Ltd v Fibrenyle Ltd* [1959] R.P.C. 252.
[507] (1920) 37 R.P.C. 121.
[508] See also *Patent Type Founding Co v Walter* (1860) 8 W.R. 353.
[509] *McDougall Bros v Partington (No.2)* (1890) 7 R.P.C. 351, 472.
[510] *Sidebottom v Fielden* (1891) 8 R.P.C. 266.

ment at work, and also tos permit either party to take away any of the work or samples of the work which has been done in their presence.[511]

Costs of inspection and retaining samples for future use

In *Niche Generics Ltd v Lundbeck A/S*[512] a declaration of non-infringement was **19-314** sought relating to a process for making a pharmaceutical product in India. An inspection took place after the start of proceedings. After some time the patentee accepted that the declarations of non-infringement should be made, accepted it should pay the general costs but objected to paying the costs of the inspection. Pumfrey J held that the inspection was of substantial evidential importance and that the patentee was liable to pay the costs. The patentee also sought an order that samples from the process be provided in order to police the declaration of non-infringement. This was refused on the basis that the patentee had not demonstrated a future probative use for the samples and even if the jurisdiction existed to order them, there was no reason to do so.

9. EXPERIMENTS

Experiments

Under CPR Pt 63, Practice Direction—Intellectual Property Claims paras 7.1– **19-315** 7.3, where a party desires to establish any fact by experimental proof conducted for the purpose of litigation, they must serve upon the other party a notice which states the facts which they desire to establish and giving full particulars of the experiments proposed to establish them. Such a notice must be served at least 21 days before service of the application notice for directions.[513] Within 21 days of service of the notice, the party upon whom it is served must state in respect of each fact whether or not they admit it.[514] Where any fact is not admitted, directions must be sought on the directions hearing in respect of such experiments.[515]

It is the invariable practice to limit the evidence relating to experiments unless **19-316** the procedure of notice and subsequent directions has been followed. It is usual to provide that each party shall demonstrate their experiments to the other party and permit the other party with an opportunity of securing drawings, photographs, samples and such other data as the party may reasonably require. It is also desirable to order that reports of the experiments be prepared and, where possible, agreed.[516]

In IPEC experiments are considered at the case management conference.[517] **19-317**

---

[511] *Davenport v Jepson* (1862) 1 New Rep. 307; *Amies v Kelsey* (1852) 22 L.J.Q.B. 84; see also *Germ Milling Co v Robinson* (1884) 1 R.P.C. 11.
[512] [2004] F.S.R. 20.
[513] CPR Pt 63, Practice Direction—Intellectual Property Claims para.7.3.
[514] CPR Pt 63, Practice Direction—Intellectual Property Claims para.7.2.
[515] CPR Pt 63, Practice Direction—Intellectual Property Claims para.7.3.
[516] *Oak Manufacturing Co Ltd v The Plessey Co Ltd* (1950) 67 R.P.C. 71.
[517] CPR Pt 63, Practice Direction—Intellectual Property Claims, Section V Intellectual Property Enterprise Court para.29.1(3).

Scope of the rule and disclosure of work ups

19-318   It had previously been considered that an analysis to establish infringement was not an "experiment".[518] However, the wording of CPR Pt 63, Practice Direction— Intellectual Property Claims para.7 is such as to require any fact which requires experimental proof by means of an experiment conducted for the purposes of litigation to be subject to the notice procedure.

19-319   There is no obligation on a party to serve a notice of experiment in respect of an experiment conducted in the normal course of research.[519]

19-320   What constitutes an experiment for the purposes of the rule will be usually be apparent in most cases. A chemical reaction clearly is. It is submitted that merely measuring the length of an object is not. However, occasionally there are borderline cases. In *Consafe v Emtunga*[520] Pumfrey J held that finite element analysis did constitute an experiment because it did not always produce the same result and was an exercise in judgment on the part of the person conducting it. In *Mölnlyke v Brightwake* electron micrographs were held to be experiments for the same reasons—the preparation of the sample and the creation of the images required an exercise of judgment on the part of the experimenter.[521] In *Mylan v Yeda*[522] Arnold J held that a statistical analysis of pre-existing data using standard statistical software package was not an experiment. In the same case, the claimant served a notice of experiments in respect of an exercise calculating the area under a graph by tracing the curve onto graph paper and counting the squares under the graph. Whilst the service of a notice may have been a pragmatic approach, given the lack of real any skill or judgment in the exercise, it is submitted that it was probably not necessary.

19-321   There is an obligation to disclose "work up experiments" in addition to the experiment actually relied on, because giving notice of experiments waived any privilege which otherwise might attach to them.[523] Similarly, the court could order the production of samples of materials used in experiments where a party performed the experiments in the EPO and the UK.[524] Samples so produced would be subject to an undertaking not to use save for the purposes of the proceedings in which they were produced. That restriction would only be lifted in special circumstances and where the release or modification would not occasion injustice to the person providing them.[525]

19-322   An issue that sometimes arises when an experiment has been repeated is the relative status of the results obtained on the repeat as compared to those in the Notice of Experiments itself. Usually more weight is placed on the results of the repeat, although there is no reason why reliance cannot also be placed on the results in the

---

518   *International de Lavand Ltd v Stanton Ironworks Co Ltd* (1941) 58 R.P.C. 177, 198.
519   This is the case today because the relevant part of the practice direction refers only to experiments conducted for the purpose of litigation. For the position in the past, see *Richardson-Vicks Inc's Patent* [1995] R.P.C. 568; and *Practice Direction (Pat Ct: Practice Explanation)* [1997] R.P.C. 166.
520   [1999] R.P.C. 154.
521   [2011] F.S.R. 26.
522   [2012] EWHC 1288.
523   *Mayne Pharma v Debiopharm* [2006] EWHC 164.
524   *Shire v Mount Sinai School of Medicine* [2012] F.S.R. 18, [14]–[15].
525   *Shire v Mount Sinai School of Medicine* [2012] F.S.R. 18, [24]–[30].

Notice itself. However, the weight to be given to such results will depend on the evidence before the court as to how those original experiments were conducted.[526]

Admission of a third party's experiments

In *Monsanto v Cargill*[527] the court considered an application to admit experiments in order to support a case of invalidity which had been conducted by a third party and used in the EPO. Admission was refused in the exercise of the court's discretion, the decisive factor being the impossibility of organising a witnessed repeat. **19-323**

Amending Notice of Experiments

Although CPR Pt 63, Practice Direction—Patents, etc. para.9 requires notice to be served of the facts proposed to be established by experimental proof, if it comes to the attention of the party serving the notice that the experiments they have done establish some other facts they will be at liberty to amend the notice and, provided there is no prejudice or detriment to the other party, such an application to amend will be sympathetically received.[528] Experiments as to matters which arise in the course of a hearing of an action have also been allowed.[529] **19-324**

Costs of experiments

The costs of experiments can be considerable and these may be disallowed from a successful party unless the court considers that they were of assistance in resolving the issues before the court.[530] **19-325**

Contrived experiments

Before embarking on carrying out extensive and expensive experiments in a patent action, the observations of Jacob LJ about contrived experiments and "litigation chemistry" in two recent cases are worth bearing in mind.[531] In *Generics v Daiichi*[532] the Patents Court considered experiments designed to support a case of obviousness over the prior art. The court held that the experimental evidence did not support the obviousness case because the choice of an important reagent appeared to have been made by the solicitors reading a list of reagents to the independent expert under whose guidance the experiments were being designed and conducted, the list including the single agents known to work.[533] **19-326**

---

[526] Per Kitchin J in *Novartis v Johnson & Johnson* [2009] EWHC 1671 (Pat), [336]; and per HHJ Birss QC in *Convatec v Smith & Nephew* [2012] R.P.C. 9, at [109]–[110].

[527] [2008] F.S.R. 7.

[528] *Van der Lely N.V. v Watveare Overseas Ltd* [1982] F.S.R. 122, 123.

[529] *British Celanese Ltd v Courtaulds Ltd* (1933) 50 R.P.C. 63, 84.

[530] *Pall v Commercial Hydraulics* [1990] F.S.R. 329, 358.

[531] *SmithKline Beecham v Apotex Europe Ltd* [2005] F.S.R. 23, [77]–[81] and *SmithKline Beecham's Patent (No.2)* [2003] R.P.C. 33. But see the also the observations of Kitchin J in *Generics v Daiichi* [2008] EWHC 2413 (Pat), at [152].

[532] [2008] EWHC 2413 (Pat).

[533] [2008] EWHC 2413 (Pat), [154]–[158].

10. MISCELLANEOUS MATTERS

Security for costs

19-327   Where one or more of the conditions set out in CPR r.25.13 are satisfied then if, having regard to all the circumstances, the court thinks it just to do so, it may order the claimant to give such security for the defendant's costs of the proceedings as it thinks just.[534] The conditions are[535] the claimant is: (i) resident outside the jurisdiction (and not resident in a Brussels Convention, Lugano Convention or Judgments Regulation state), (ii) is a company and there is reason to believe that it will be unable to pay the defendant's costs if ordered to do so, (iii) has changed their address with a view to evading the consequences of the litigation, (iv) failed to give their address in the claim for or gave an incorrect address in that form, (v) is acting as a nominal claimant and there is reason to believe that they will be unable to pay the defendant's costs if ordered to do so, or (vi) has taken steps in relation to their assets that would make it difficult to enforce an order for costs against them.

19-328   For the circumstances which the court might take into account in deciding whether to order security, see *Sir Lindsay Parkinson & Co Ltd v Triplan Ltd*.[536] Security will not normally be ordered where the claimant has the benefit of a legal protection insurance policy which will be sufficient for the defendant's costs.[537] Nor will it be ordered if the claimant is impecunious at the time of the application but can show that they will be in funds at trial.[538] However, where a claimant seeks to rely on their own impecuniosity, the onus is on them to bring proper evidence of it to court.[539] Similarly, where a claimant asserts that it would be able to pay the defendant's costs but has no visible means demonstrating it could do so (because, for example, it does not have published accounts), the onus will be on it to demonstrate its ability to pay. Further, where a claimant with no visible means of support chooses to provide no or inadequate information as to its financial position, it is not a big step for the court to conclude that there is in fact a reason to believe that it would not be able to pay.[540]

19-329   Costs estimates should be realistic and estimates based on an excessive number of hours or an excessive hourly charging rate will be disregarded.[541] In a case where costs budgets are in place, security will be ordered by reference to the approved budgeted amounts.

19-330   Where security is ordered, the court may stay the proceedings until the security is given. Where the claimant fails to provide the security, the court may dismiss the proceedings.

Scientific advisers

19-331   On the hearing of an application for further directions under CPR Pt 63, Practice Direction—Intellectual Property Claims, section I Patents para.5.10(1), the judge may direct that a scientific adviser should be appointed under s.70(3) of the Senior

---

[534] CPR r.25.13 (1).
[535] CPR r.25.13 (2).
[536] [1973] Q.B. 609, 626 and 627.
[537] *Airmuscle v Spitting Image Productions* [1994] R.P.C. 604.
[538] *Uni-continental v Eurobond* [1996] F.S.R. 834.
[539] *M.V. Yorke Motors v Edwards* [1982] 1 W.L.R. 444.
[540] *Mbasogo v Logo* [2006] EWCA Civ 608.
[541] *Thomas (Arthur Edward) v Barcrest* [1995] R.P.C. 138.

Courts Act 1981 or s.63(1) of the County Courts Act 1984.[542] The rules and the legislation also refer to the possibility of appointing an "assessor" (see CPR r.35.15 and s.70(1) of the Senior Courts Act 1981). In practice in patent cases in recent years, scientific advisers have been appointed in order simply to assist the court on the technology in issue and not to perform any judicial function as an assessor might. The role of a scientific adviser was considered in some depth in *Halliburton Energy Services v Smith International (North Sea) Ltd (No. 2)*,[543] in which the Court of Appeal held that the assistance which assessors could give the court was not limited to understanding the technical evidence, assistance might be needed on matters of fact in dispute, subject to the overriding requirement of fairness. When a scientific adviser's acquaintance with one party's expert was nothing more than would be expected between two distinguished academics in the same field, that was no bar to the scientific adviser performing their function.[544]

19-332 Examples of cases in which scientific advisers have played a role include the following. In *Kirin-Amgen v TKT*,[545] a case about genetic engineering, the House of Lords heard a series of seminars on undisputed matters of biochemistry from an independent professor in advance of the hearing, while in *Nokia v InterDigital*,[546] a case about 3G mobile telephone technology, the Patents judge was given a tutorial over two days by an independent expert selected by the parties to educate the court on the relevant technical aspects of the European 3G system generally. In *Biogen v Medeva*[547] the House of Lords sat with two expert advisers who assisted their lordships both before and during the hearing. Presumably two were appointed because the parties could not agree on one. In *Eli Lilly v Human Genome Sciences*[548] the Court of Appeal had the benefit of a scientific adviser (Dr Murphy) and Jacob LJ said:

"Prior to the hearing Dr Murphy gave us some 'teach-ins' about the background technology. At the hearing he sat with us and provided valuable further explanation of the technology. At all times he meticulously refrained (as he had been asked) from commenting on the parties' respective cases and he played no part in our decision making process. I would like to go on record to express the court's thanks to him."

19-333 In the past experts have been called where there is a conflict of evidence to make experiments and to report to the court.[549] The duty of an expert so appointed "is, instead of determining issues of fact, or of law, to find the materials upon which the court is to act".[550] Such an approach could be adopted under the CPR by the parties instructing a joint expert pursuant to CPR r.35.7 and 35.8. However, as a practical matter it would be an unusual case where the parties would adopt such a course, as opposed to instructing their own expert to conduct an experiment.

---

[542] See also CPR r.35.15.
[543] [2006] EWCA Civ 1599; [2007] R.P.C. 17.
[544] *Halliburton Energy Services v Smith International (North Sea) Ltd (No. 2)* [2006] EWCA Civ 1599; [2007] R.P.C. 17.
[545] [2004] UKHL 46; [2005] R.P.C. 9, [135].
[546] [2007] EWHC 3077 (Pat).
[547] [1997] R.P.C. 1.
[548] [2010] EWCA Civ 33.
[549] See *Badische Anilin und Soda Fabrik v Levinstein* (1883) 24 Ch D. 156; *Moore v Bennett* (1884) 1 R.P.C. 129; *North British Rubber Co Ltd v Macintosh & Co Ltd* (1894) 11 R.P.C. 477.
[550] Per Bramwell LJ in *Mellin v Monico* (1877) 3 C.P.D. 142, at 149.

Primer

19-334   At the case management conference the court may direct that a document setting out basic undisputed technology ("primer") be produced.[551] Although undoubtedly useful in some cases, in the past primers often became a battleground for unnecessary disputes. However, recently there has been judicial encouragement for the parties to prepare a primer, well in advance of expert evidence, that sets out the agreed basic undisputed technology relevant to the case. This is so as to avoid substantially the same material being described by each expert in their reports.[552] Ideally primers should be agreed documents. Generally, where the parties are unable to agree whether a particular issue ought to be included in the primer, rather than having a "marked-up" primer showing the areas of dispute, the issue should be omitted and dealt with by the experts in their reports. Where a technical primer has been produced, the parties should identify those parts which are agreed to form part of the common general knowledge. Usually, this should be done either in, or shortly after exchange of, the expert reports but in any event a reasonable time prior to trial.[553]

Undertakings

19-335   In proceedings for infringement the patentee applied to amend the patent and the point arose whether an undertaking not to do so had been given in earlier entitlement proceedings on the same patent. The court held no such undertaking had been given but in doing so laid down general guidelines in relation to undertakings in general (one of the issues was that the putative undertaking was not recorded in a court order and therefore the transcripts of proceedings had to be considered).[554]

Chancery masters' jurisdiction

19-336   The jurisdiction of chancery masters (and deputy masters) in patent cases is a limited one. Practice Direction—Intellectual Property Claims, Section I Patents para.5.2(2) provides that a Master may only deal with:

    (1)   orders by way of settlement, except settlement of procedural disputes;
    (2)   applications for extensions of time;
    (3)   applications for permission to serve out of the jurisdiction;
    (4)   applications for security for costs;
    (5)   other matters as directed by a judge of the court; and
    (6)   enforcement of money judgments.

19-337   A master may also deal with applications under CPR r.5.4C by a non-party for a copy of the Grounds of Invalidity on the court file.[555]

---

[551] CPR Pt 63, Practice Direction—Intellectual Property Claims para.5.10(2).
[552] See, for example, *Warner-Lambert v Actavis* [2015] EWHC 2548 (Pat), at [36]; *Merck & Co Inc v Ono* [2015] EWHC 2973, at [10]–[11].
[553] Patents Court Guide, para.13.6.
[554] *Zipher v Markem* [2009] F.S.R. 14.
[555] Direction of Kitchin J, dated 16 July 2008.

11. THE TRIAL

Multiple parties but single trial

If there are multiple parties all engaged in suits about the same patent, it may be **19-338** convenient to arrange the cases to come to trial together and in an appropriate case to require the parties alleging invalidity to serve a consolidated grounds of invalidity.[556] It will not always be convenient to hear trials concerning the same patent together, particularly where there are infringement allegations made in each action and each defendant contends that aspects of their product are confidential and ought to be kept from the other.[557] However, where multiple cases are tried together, it is common for multiple parties attacking the same patent to agree to share experts and/or counsel and this can be made an express condition of the trials being heard together. However, there is no reason why multiple parties attacking the same patent ought to be limited to one set of costs, although the Costs Judge will only allow costs that have been reasonably incurred.[558]

Expedited trials

Absent an order for expedition, a trial will be fixed (generally shortly after the **19-339** CMC) in accordance with the current trial window being offered by the Chancery judges listing office. In his practice statement of 7 December 2015, Arnold J set out a number of measures to bring patent actions on more quickly, and where possible within 12 months. The most important of these are: (i) that the trial length for patent actions is to be determined excluding time for pre-reading and writing closing submissions, (ii) that where it will enable a case to be tried within 12 months or shortly thereafter, the court may list a trial up to one month earlier than the applicable Trial Window without the need for any application for expedition, and (iii) the court will use its case management powers to bring cases on more promptly. Thus a trial estimated for six days may be directed to be heard in five days so that it can fit into a small listing window.

Where a party feels that it is important that its trial is heard more quickly they **19-340** may apply for expedition. Expedition is not a binary issue and the court can and will order greater or lesser degrees of expedition depending on the circumstances. The criteria that the court will take into account when considering a request for expedition are those set out by Lord Neuberger MR in *W.L .Gore & Associates GmbH v Geox SPA*[559]:

> "To my mind, when considering such an application there are four factors to take into account. The first is whether the applicants (in this case, Gore) have shown good reason for expedition; the second is whether expedition would interfere with the good administration of justice; the third is whether expedition would cause prejudice to the other party; and the fourth is whether there are any other special factors."

Thus a party seeking an expedited trial must be able to provide good reason why **19-341** their trial ought to jump the queue. Often the reason for seeking an expedition is

---

[556] As was done in *Glaxo Group Ltd's Patent* [2004] R.P.C. 43, at [1] and [2].
[557] *Samsung v Apple* [2011] EWHC 2711.
[558] *Bristol-Myers Squibb Co v Baker Norton Pharmaceuticals Inc* [2001] R.P.C. 1, [72].
[559] [2008] EWCA Civ 622, [25].

to resolve the patent issues in advance of the launch of a product.[560] However, dispelling commercial uncertainty more generally has sometimes been used to justify expedition.[561] It has been held that the existence of parallel proceedings abroad (and in particular in Germany) is a factor, although not a strong factor, in favour of a degree of expedition.[562] However, no case has been expedited on this ground alone.[563] The effect on the good administration of justice involves consideration of other litigants. Whether the other party would be prejudiced by expedition usually revolves around whether it can be ready for an expedited trial. Other special factors can include the conduct of the parties, and in particular whether there has been any delay by the party seeking expedition.

Trial of preliminary issue

19-342   Where more than one issue is raised, directions may be given for the trial of one of the issues as a preliminary point.[564] In general, however, this will only be done where it appears probable that the trial of such issue will decide the action.[565]

19-343   Where a plea of joint tortfeasance is made against a foreign company, it may be appropriate to hold two trials: one on validity and infringement and the other on the joint tortfeasance issue.[566]

19-344   In *Sarason v Frenay*[567] the defendant pleaded, inter alia, that the plaintiff had inserted into a contract a condition contravening the then statutory provisions in s.44 of the 1977 Act. This point was ordered to be tried as a preliminary issue, and, being decided in favour of the defendant, the action was dismissed.

19-345   In *Hanks v Coombes*[568] where the trial of the issue of infringement would have involved heavy expense and related to apparatus of a secret character, the issue of validity was ordered to be heard first.[569]

19-346   In *Nokia v InterDigital*[570] the question of whether certain patents were essential to the relevant telecommunications standard was tried first, with a view to ensuring that a subsequent validity case (if any) only had to address patents found to be essential.

19-347   In *Canady v Erbe Electromedizin GmbH*[571] the issues of validity and infringement were split and infringement was ordered to be tried first under the streamlined procedure.

---

[560] For example, *Warner-Lambert v Teva* [2011] EWHC 2018, [2011] F.S.R. 44; *HTC v Apple* [2011] EWHC 2396 (Pat), 14–19; *Generics (UK) Limited (trading as Mylan) v Warner-Lambert Company LLC* [2014] EWHC 3115 (Pat); *Idenix Pharmaceuticals, Inc v Gilead Sciences, Inc* [2014] EWHC 1346.

[561] *Eli Lilly & Co v Sanofi -Aventis Deutschland GmbH* [2014] EWHC 3410 (Pat), [23].

[562] *Research in Motion UK Limited v Visto Corporation* [2008] EWHC 3025 (Pat), [15]; *HTC v Apple* [2011] EWHC 2396 (Pat), 14–19.

[563] *ZTE v Ericsson* [2011] EWHC 2709 (Pat), [13]–[14].

[564] See Chancery Guide, para.3.14; *Toogood & Jones Ltd v Soccerette Ltd* [1959] R.P.C. 265.

[565] See Jessel MR in *Emma Silver Mining Co v Grant* (1877) 11 Ch D. 918, at 927; *Piercy v Young* (1879) 15 Ch D. 475; see also *United Telephone Co v Mattishead* (1886) 3 R.P.C. 213; *Kurtz v Spence* (1887) 4 R.P.C. 161; *Bescol (Electrics) Ltd v Merlin Mouldings Ltd* (1952) 69 R.P.C. 159; *A/B Astra v Pharmaceutical Manufacturing Co* (1952) 69 R.P.C. 312, [1956] R.P.C. 265.

[566] *Napp v Asta* [1999] F.S.R. 370.

[567] (1914) 31 R.P.C. 252, 330.

[568] (1927) 44 R.P.C. 305; 45 R.P.C. 237.

[569] And see, e.g. *Woolfe v Automatic Picture Gallery Ltd* (1902) 19 R.P.C. 425; *Stephenson, Blake & Co v Grant, Legros & Co Ltd* (1917) 34 R.P.C. 192 (registered design); *Murex Welding Processes Ltd v Weldrics (1922) Ltd* (1933) 50 R.P.C. 178.

[570] [2007] EWHC 3077 (Pat), see [1]–[6].

[571] [2006] F.S.R. 10.

Preliminary issues appear to be more readily ordered in IPEC. A number of such trials have taken place in the past few years.[572]   **19-348**

Estimates of length

Not less than one week before the date set for commencement of the trial, the parties must inform the court in writing of the estimate of length of their oral submissions, examination in chief and cross examination.[573] For trials in IPEC see para.20-36.   **19-349**

Court bundles and reading guide

The documents in the form to be used at trial must be lodged by the claimant's solicitors at least four working days before the date for trial together with a "reading guide" for the judge.[574] The reading guide should be short, non-contentious and agreed if possible. It should not contain argument. It should shortly set out the issues, the parts of the documents to be read on each issue and the most convenient order that they should be read. If thought appropriate the relevant passages in text books and cases should be referred to.   **19-350**

Skeleton arguments

Skeleton arguments are filed and exchanged before trial, usually at or close to the same time as the reading guide. They do not become public documents unless and until referred to in open court.[575]   **19-351**

Right to begin

The normal rule applies that, unless the court directs to the contrary, the person bearing the onus of proof should begin. Accordingly in patent infringement actions, the patentee will normally begin. Where infringement is admitted and there is a counterclaim for revocation, the applicant for revocation should begin.[576]   **19-352**

Trial in private

Where the defendant alleges that their process is a secret, part of the hearing may be conducted in private[577] and the transcript for those aspects kept separate.[578] In an appropriate case the court's judgment can be produced in two forms, the public form having been edited to remove confidential information, see *SmithKline*   **19-353**

---

[572] e.g. *Environmental Defence Systems Ltd v Synergy Health Plc* [2015] F.S.R. 6 (obviousness); *Mastermailer Stationery Ltd v Everseal Stationery Products Ltd* [2013] EWPCC 6 (infringement); *Destra Software Ltd v Comada (UK) LLP* [2012] EWPCC 39 (a copyright case, ownership and licensing issues); *Horler v Everseal Stationery Products Ltd* [2011] EWPCC 029 (ownership of the patent); and *Musion Systems Ltd v Activ8-3D Ltd* [2011] EWPCC 12 (whether the defendant carried out the acts alleged to infringe).

[573] CPR Pt 63, Practice Direction—Intellectual Property Claims para.9.1.

[574] CPR Pt 63, Practice Direction—Intellectual Property Claims, paras 9.2–9.3.

[575] *SmithKline Beecham Biologicals S.A. v Connaught Laboratories Inc* [2000] F.S.R. 1, CA.

[576] As in *Genentech Inc's Patent* [1987] R.P.C. 553, at 558.

[577] Previously called "in camera".

[578] See *Badische Anilin und Soda Fabrik v Levinstein* (1885) 2 R.P.C. 73; 24 Ch D. 156 and the ruling of Aldous J in *Bonzel v Intervention (No.3)* [1991] R.P.C. 553.

Beecham v Apotex Europe.[579] The court will however need to be persuaded that there is genuine confidential information meriting protection before it will sit in private and will in any event seek to minimise the time not in open court.[580]

Burden of proof of infringement

19-354   The burden of proving infringement (where it is denied) is on the claimant, and, if they are unable to prove it, there is no necessity for entering upon the question of validity, unless there is a counterclaim for revocation. It may, however, not be possible for the claimant to ascertain precisely what the defendant has done, especially where the defendant's manufacture is carried on abroad; and in such circumstances, if the claimant makes out a prima facie case which the defendant does not answer, it will probably be sufficient.[581] Evidence of experiments a defendant had adduced for the purposes of amendment proceedings in the Patent Office is not subject to absolute privilege and can be used by a claimant to prove infringement.[582] Where the infringement complained of is the sale or use merely of a patented article and the claimant manufactures such articles themselves, they must, in order to throw the onus on to the defendant, prove that the article was not made by them or their agent.[583]

19-355   Where the defendant does not appear at the trial but has disputed the validity of the patent in their defence, it is usual for the claimant to give prima facie proof of validity. However, it has been doubted whether such proof is strictly necessary.[584]

Sequence of issues

19-356   In determining the issues raised in a patent action the court must first construe the specification and claims of the patent. Next it must be determined whether the claims, or some of them, are valid, having regard to the matters set out in the particulars of objections. The court must then consider the evidence relating to and the admissions concerning the alleged infringing act and come to a conclusion whether it falls within the ambit of one or more valid claims. Finally, the court must decide what relief shall be given.

Proof of title

19-357   The claimant must prove that they are the proprietor or exclusive licensee of the patent in suit. This, where not admitted, may be proved by the production of a certified copy of or extract from the register, which is admissible as evidence by virtue of s.32 of the 1977 Act. If the claimant's title is not registered, then they must establish their title by proof of the assignment or licence, as the case may be.

19-358   The claimant is never in practice required to prove the actual grant of the patent itself or the specification, though this can, if required, be done by the production of a certified copy of the certificate of grant or of the specification, as the case may be.

---

[579] [2004] F.S.R. 26, similarly see *Roberts v Nottinghamshire Healthcare NHS Trust* [2009] F.S.R. 4.
[580] See *Smith & Nephew plc v Convatec Technologies Inc* [2014] EWHC 146 (Pat) where the relevant law and the Patents Court's practice for dealing with confidential documents was explained.
[581] *British Thomson-Houston Co Ltd v Charlesworth Peebles & Co* (1923) 40 R.P.C. 426, 456.
[582] *Smith, Kline & French Laboratories Ltd v Evans Medical Ltd* [1989] 1 F.S.R. 513.
[583] *Betts v Willmott* (1871) L.R. 6 Ch. App. 239.
[584] See *Weber v Xetal Products Ltd* (1933) 50 R.P.C. 211.

If a defendant desires to prove the absence of an entry from the register they may **19-359**
do so by producing a certificate from the Comptroller.[585]

Issue of validity

The question whether a subsisting patent is to be regarded as prima facie valid **19-360**
has often been asked but rarely answered.

In *AstraZeneca AB v The Commission*[586] the General Court of Justice expressed **19-361**
themselves as follows:

> "When granted by a public authority, an intellectual property right is normally assumed to be valid
> and an undertaking's ownership of that right is assumed to be lawful."

The claimant invariably gives evidence in support of their patent in respect of the **19-362**
objections taken because it is forensically advantageous for them to do so.
Nevertheless, it is submitted that strictly there is no need for them to do more than
to establish their title to a subsisting patent, for the patent is, prima facie, valid.[587]
Having proved this much, the onus is thereby shifted on to the defendant.

The issue of validity is subdivided into the various objections pleaded in the **19-363**
particulars of objections. Where the objection is lack of novelty by reason of
publication in a written document, the actual publication of the document must, of
course, be proved by the defendant, unless, as is usual, publication is admitted by
the claimant. Similarly, the onus of proof of an alleged prior use is on the defendant and must be fully discharged.[588] Where publication was admitted by inadvertence, leave to withdraw the admission was granted on special terms as to costs.[589]

The decision as to the identity or otherwise of the process or apparatus disclosed **19-364**
by a prior document with that of the patent in suit is a question of fact, and where
the identity is not obvious upon the face of the documents expert evidence is admissible to resolve the issue.[590] The disclosure which a document (whether it be an alleged anticipation or a specification the sufficiency of which is in dispute) would
make to a competent technician is sometimes tested by handing it to a suitable
person who is ignorant of the points in issue in the case, and seeing what they do
in endeavouring to follow its instructions and what results they arrive at.[591]

---

[585] PA 1977 s.32(10).
[586] (T-321/05), at [362].
[587] When granted by a public authority, an intellectual property right is normally assumed to be valid
and an undertaking's ownership of that right is assumed to be lawful.
[588] See *Dick v Tallis & Sons* (1896) 13 R.P.C. 149. at 162; *British United Shoe Machinery Co Ltd v
Albert Permberton & Co* (1930) 47 R.P.C. 134, at 158; *Vax v Hoover* [1991] F.S.R. 307, at 317; cf.
the EPO which may require proof of prior use "to the hilt", e.g. decision T472/92.
[589] *Van der Lely N.V. v Bamfords Ltd* [1959] R.P.C. 99.
[590] *Betts v Menzies* (1957) 10 H.L.Cas. 117, 153 and 154; *British Thomson-Houston Co Ltd v British
Insulated and Helsby Cables Ltd* (1925) 41 R.P.C. 345, 399 and 400; *British Celanese v Courtaulds*
(1935) 52 R.P.C. 171, 196.
[591] For old cases on this see, e.g. *Aktiengesellschaft für Autogene Schweissung v London Aluminium Co
(No.2)* (1920) 37 R.P.C. 153, at 164; 39 R.P.C. 296, at 309; *British Thomson-Houston Co Ltd v British Insulated and Helsby Cables Ltd* (1924) 41 R.P.C. 345, at 407. For modern authorities on the
same point see *SmithKline Beecham v Apotex Europe Ltd* [2005] F.S.R. 23, [77]–[81] and *SmithKline
Beecham's Patent (No.2)* [2003] R.P.C. 33 but per contra see the observations of Kitchin J in *Generics v Daiichi* [2009] R.P.C. 4, at [152].

Photographs and drawings

19-365   Although the construction of a document is for the court, following the ordinary rules of construction relating to written documents, guided by appropriate evidence, this does not apply to photographs or presumably to drawings of any kind; as Lord Reid said in *Van der Lely (C.) N.V. v Bamfords Ltd.*[592]

> "There is no doubt that, where the matter alleged to amount to anticipation consists of a written description, the interpretation of that description is, like the interpretation of any document, a question for the court assisted where necessary by evidence regarding the meaning of technical language. It was argued that the same applies to a photograph. I do not think so. Lawyers are expected to be experts in the use of the English language, but we are not experts in the reading or interpretation of photographs. The question is what the eye of the man with appropriate engineering skill and experience would see in the photograph, and that appears to me to be a matter for evidence. Where the evidence is contradictory the judge must decide. But the judge ought not, in my opinion, to attempt to read or construe the photograph himself; he looks at the photograph in determining which of the explanations given by the witnesses appears to be most worthy of acceptance."

Interference with witnesses (fact or expert)

19-366   In *Glaxo Group Ltd's Patents*[593] it emerged at trial that a Senior Vice-President of the defendant (patentee) had telephoned one of the claimant's expert witnesses and told him he could no longer expect the patentee to be friends with him and that it would no longer fund his research activities. Pumfrey J took the opportunity to emphasise that any pressure and any act which may have effect of placing pressure on a witness may be contempt of court.[594] The judge decided not to refer the matter to the Attorney-General because the individual concerned had acted on his own initiative and his reasons for acting were silly.

19-367   In *Cinpres Gas Injection v Melea*[595] the court granted an interim remedy preventing contact by or on behalf of a person connected with one party with an important witness whose evidence now was that he admitted lying on oath in a previous case. The injunction was granted because of the court's need to protect its own proceedings and to prevent pressure being put on witnesses.

Expert evidence

19-368   The evidence usually given as to validity apart from that as to specific facts, such as prior users or commercial success, is that of witnesses who have expert scientific knowledge and are well acquainted with the art to which the invention relates. Such evidence is admissible as to the sufficiency of the specification to a competent technician, as to the novelty and inventive step of the invention, as to the state of common knowledge in the art at material dates, and as to the meaning of technical terms. The principles as to the degrees of sufficiency required, and to novelty and inventive step, of course, matters of law for the court, as also is the question of whether the alleged invention is inherently excluded from patentability under s.1(2) and (3) of the Patents Act 1977.

---

[592] [1963] R.P.C. 61, 71; followed in relation to video recordings in *Vax v Hoover* (1991) F.S.R. 307.
[593] [2004] R.P.C. 43.
[594] [2004] R.P.C. 43, [118]–[121].
[595] [2006] F.S.R. 36.

The expert's function

Historically experts were generally not asked to give their opinions directly upon **19-369** the questions which are before the court for its decision, whether they be of law or fact but the absolute bar to such evidence was removed by the Civil Evidence Act 1972.[596] Although strictly not necessary, in practice expert witnesses almost invariably do give evidence concerning issues such as whether there has been infringement or whether the invention comprises an inventive step, as well as the reason for those views. However, in *Technip France SA's Patent*[597] Jacob LJ said this of expert witnesses:

"Their primary function is to educate the court in the technology—they come as teachers, as makers of the mantle for the court to don. For that purpose it does not matter whether they do or do not approximate to the skilled man. What matters is how good they are at explaining things."

And in *SmithKline Beecham v Apotex*[598] Jacob LJ referred to this observation and **19-370** added:

"To that I would add this: although it is inevitable that when an expert is asked what he would understand from a prior document's teaching he will give an answer as an individual, that answer is not as such all that helpful. What matters is what the notional skilled man would understand from the document. So it is not so much the expert's personal view but his reasons for that view—these the court can examine against the standard of the notional unimaginative skilled man."

Jacob LJ's observations on the role of experts resonate with the explanation of **19-371** the function of an expert explained by Lindley LJ in 1896 in *Brooks v Steele and Currie*[599]:

"It is necessary to examine the patent, and to ascertain first what the patented invention really is; and, secondly, whether the defendants have used that invention. In this, as in all cases, the nature of the invention must be ascertained from the specification, the interpretation of which is for the judge, and not for any expert. The judge may, and, indeed, generally must, be assisted by expert evidence to explain technical terms, to show the practical working of machinery described or drawn, and to point out what is old and what is new in the specification. Expert evidence is also admissible and is often required to show the particulars in which an alleged invention has been used by an alleged infringer, and the real importance of whatever differences there may be between the plaintiff's invention and whatever is done by the defendant. But, after all, the nature of the invention for which a patent is granted must be ascertained from the specification, and has to be determined by the judge and not by a jury, nor by any expert or other witness. This is familiar law, although apparently often disregarded when witnesses are being examined."[600]

As to the function of an expert in proving "common knowledge", see para.8– **19-372** 70. As to the function of an expert in proving what a photograph or drawing discloses, see para.19–365.

The expert's expertise

Plainly an expert witness ought to be an expert in the field in question since one **19-373** of the main functions of an expert in a patent case is to educate the court in the

---

[596] Civil Evidence Act 1972 s.3; see *Glaverbel S.A. v British Coal (No.4)* [1995] R.P.C. 255, CA.
[597] [2004] R.P.C. 46, [12].
[598] [2005] F.S.R. 23, [51]–[52].
[599] (1896) 13 R.P.C. 46, [73].
[600] See also *Graphic Arts Co v Hunters Ltd* (1910) 27 R.P.C. 677, at 687; *Joseph Crosfield Ltd v Techno-Chemical Laboratories Ltd* (1913) 30 R.P.C. 297, at 309; *British Celenase v Courtaulds* (1935) 52 R.P.C. 171, at 196; *Glaverbel S.A. v British Coal Corp (No.2)* [1993] R.P.C. 90.

technology[601] and to put the judge in possession of the common general knowledge.[602] Sometimes an expert in a related field may read in to the field in question, so as be better able to apply their general knowledge to the field in question[603] and it has been said that a witness who lacks expertise in a particular area with which the patent is concerned can read in to the state of the art and can be of great assistance.[604] However, if the expert is not in possession of the common general knowledge, then their expert views on what steps might or might not be obvious are likely to be of little value.[605]

Expert evidence given in other proceedings not binding

19-374   A party is not bound in proceedings against one party by evidence given on its behalf by experts or others in previous proceedings against some other party, nor is such evidence admissible against it in the subsequent proceedings as an admission.[606] If, however, it be proved that such evidence was given, this fact may be very material as showing the previous conduct of the party or of the witnesses where such conduct throws light on any question in issue in the subsequent action.[607] Evidence given in previous proceedings may be admitted in the subsequent proceedings under the hearsay rules.[608] Witnesses may, of course, always be cross-examined as to statements which they themselves have made in previous proceedings.[609] The claimant's witnesses can be cross-examined on documents contained in the Patent Office file of the application for the patent in suit (see para.16–172). Where an expert has previously given evidence in parallel proceedings in another jurisdiction, parties sometimes seek to obtain disclosure of that evidence. Such an application was refused in *Abbott v Medinol*, primarily because the evidence was sought in relation to an issue of claim construction, which is ultimately a matter of law for the court.[610]

Expert's duty to the court

19-375   It is the duty of experts to help the court on matters within their expertise. This duty overrides any obligation to the person from whom experts have received instructions or by whom they are paid.[611] An expert's report must comply with the requirements set out in Practice Direction 35. At the end of an expert's report there must be a statement that the expert understands and has complied with their duty to the court. The expert's report must state the substance of all material instruc-

---

[601] See para.19–369.
[602] Per Floyd J in *Fabio Perini v PCMC* [2009] EWHC 1929 (Pat), [11].
[603] Per Floyd J in *Fabio Perini v PCMC* [2009] EWHC 1929 (Pat), [11].
[604] Per Pumfrey J in *Inpro Licensing SARL's Patent* [2006] R.P.C. 20, [6].
[605] Per Floyd J in *Fabio Perini v PCMC* [2009] EWHC 1929 (Pat), [11].
[606] *British Thomson-Houston Co Ltd v British Insulated and Helsby Cables Ltd* (1924) 41 R.P.C. 345; (1925) 42 R.P.C. 180.
[607] *British Thomson-Houston Co Ltd v British Insulated and Helsby Cables Ltd* (1924) 41 R.P.C. 345; (1925) 42 R.P.C. 180.
[608] Civil Evidence Act 1995; CPR Pt 33.
[609] See *British Hartford-Fairmont Syndicate Ltd v Jackson Bros (Knottingly) Ltd* (1932) 49 R.P.C. 495, at 532.
[610] [2010] EWHC 1731.
[611] CPR r.35.3(1)–(2).

tions, whether written or oral, on the basis of which the report was written.[612] There is further guidance for expert witnesses in the practice direction to CPR Pt 36 and in the Protocol for the Instruction of Experts to Give Evidence in Civil Claims[613] referred to in para.1 of the practice direction.

Arnold J reviewed the duties on an expert in detail in *MedImmune v Novartis*[614] **19-376** and gave this guidance about the importance of properly instructing and expert.

"109. Expert witnesses in patent litigation stand in a rather unusual position. They are generally leading scientists or engineers in the field in question. Frequently they are academics. Sometimes they are consultants. In most cases, they will not have given expert evidence in patent litigation before, although there are exceptions to this. Not only that, but also they will generally have little experience of the patent system. Where do they have experience, it will generally be as inventors named on patents. As such, they may have had scientific input, but generally they will have learnt little about patent law in the process. In some fields, they may also be accustomed to using patents and patent applications as sources of technical information, but again without necessarily understanding much about patents themselves. When asked to prepare an expert report in a patent case, they will have to consider such questions as the identity and attributes of the person skilled in the art to whom the patent is addressed, the common general knowledge of the skilled person and whether something would or would not be obvious to that person in the light of particular prior art given the constraints imposed by the law of obviousness. Usually, this is not a task of which they will have any previous experience.

110. For these reasons expert witnesses in patent actions require a high level of instruction by the lawyers. Furthermore, even if they are experienced authors, they need considerable assistance from the lawyers in drafting their report. In practice, most expert reports in patent cases are drafted by the lawyers on the basis of what the expert has told them and the draft is then amended by the expert. This, of course, requires the lawyers to understand what the expert is saying. It follows that the drafting of an expert's report in a patent action involves a steep learning curve for both the expert and the lawyers. The lawyers are learning the technology and the expert is learning enough of the law to understand the questions he must address. It follows that a high degree of consultation between the expert and the lawyers is required. Frequently, the preparation of the report will involve an iterative process through a number of drafts.

111. It is obvious that this process entails a risk of loss of objectivity on the part of the expert even if the expert is striving to remain independent and impartial. It is therefore crucial that the lawyers involved should keep the expert's need to remain objective at the forefront of their minds at all times. If they cause or allow the expert to lose his objectivity, they are doing both the expert and their client a disservice. They are doing the expert a disservice because he may be subject to criticism during cross-examination and in the court's judgment as a result. They are doing the client a disservice because partisan expert evidence is almost always exposed as such in cross-examination, which is likely to reduce, if not eliminate, the value of the evidence to the client's case."

A case illustrating the dangers of a party seeking to control an expert's evidence **19-377** by the instructions given was *Synthon v Teva*.[615] In that case, the report of the expert (who had not given evidence before) was criticised for omitting important matters in her written reports. However, it transpired that the expert had that drafted various paragraphs in response to the other party's expert's report, but had been advised that there was no need to serve a reply report and the points were better raised in cross-examination. Birss J said this:

"19. [The expert's] personal position is mitigated very considerably by the advice she was given by the legal team. That sort of advice puts an expert in an impossible position. Despite the fact that clients may not like it, experts need to be advised fully about their personal responsibilities and role. They need to be advised that they must exercise their own judgment in matters of this kind. Whether an expert serves a reply report is first and foremost a matter for the expert

---

[612] CPR r.35.10(1)–(3).
[613] Available at: *www.judiciary.gov.uk* [Accessed 15 March 2016].
[614] [2011] EWHC 1669 (Pat), [99]–[114].
[615] [2015] EWHC 1395 (Pat).

not a matter for the lawyers. [The expert] should have been advised accordingly but she was not. The real cause of the problem in this case was not [the expert]."

The sequence in which an expert is instructed

19-378 Sometimes, in an attempt to insulate an expert from suggestions of hindsight, parties instruct an expert to look at the prior art first, then the priority document and the application as filed and finally the patent itself. In *Medimmune v Novartis*[616] the expert was instructed in this way and Arnold J indicated that this had been useful in the context of that case. However, in *HTC v Gemalto*, Birss J stated that, whilst experts need to be aware of the risk of hindsight reasoning and of allowing ideas in the patent to influence their views, Arnold J's judgment should not be seen as seeking to lay down a rule that this is how experts must be instructed in all patent cases.[617] In particular, he said this of the exercise undertaken in that case:

"...I believe it is important to emphasise that approaches like this are servants and should not become elevated into masters. The approach can risk creating a number of potential difficulties. First the expert naturally may think there is a legal requirement that this be done and that somehow a breach of this protocol is wrong or is his or her fault. There is no legal requirement that expert evidence in patent cases must be given this way. It will not always be fair on the expert to place this burden on them. Second, many patent lawyers are highly skilled at presenting information to the expert which, consciously or subconsciously, has the effect of leading the expert to the conclusion sought. Neither the expert nor the legal team may be aware of it at all. The expert may genuinely think they have formed views without knowledge of the contents of the patent when in fact they may have been led there. Thus the approach may not in fact eliminate hindsight and is capable of giving a false impression.

The exercise in this case caused much more trouble than it could ever have been worth."[618]

Duplicative expert evidence

19-379 As a general matter it is highly undesirable for a party to adduce evidence from two different experts on the same issue. Such a course is likely to lead to an increase in the cost and complexity of the case and to provide no corresponding benefit to the court in dealing with the case justly and in accordance with the overriding objective. Moreover, it is likely to create practical difficulties for the party faced with such evidence. A party faced with duplicative evidence should raise the issue with the judge, preferably before or, at the latest, during the trial, and seek appropriate directions as to whether the party seeking to rely upon the evidence should be permitted to do so and, if they are, the appropriate course to be adopted in relation to it. The point should not be left to be taken on appeal.[619]

Putting case to opponent's witnesses

19-380 If a party is going to submit that a witness is to be disbelieved then they must give the witness a fair opportunity to deal with the allegation.[620]

---

[616] [2011] EWHC 1669 (Pat).
[617] [2014] R.P.C. 9, [273].
[618] [2014] R.P.C. 9, [274]–[275].
[619] *Regeneron Pharmaceuticals Inc, Bayer Pharma AG v Genentech Inc* [2013] EWCA Civ 93; [2013] R.P.C. 28, [125].
[620] See *Markem v Zipher* [2005] R.P.C. 31, [56]–[61] and the cases cited there.

Trial in IPEC

Although the parties give estimates of the timetable required as usual, trials in **19-381**
IPEC run to a timetable set by the court.[621] Equal time will be allocated to the parties as far as appropriate. Cross examination will be strictly controlled. The court
will endeavour to ensure that the trial lasts no more than two days.

Where all parties consent, IPEC may determine the whole claim on the papers **19-382**
without an oral hearing.[622]

Reconsideration of judgment

In a number of cases in recent years attempts have been made after a judgment **19-383**
has been handed down or an order entered, to alter the judgment or order. In *Kirin-
Amgen v Transkaryotic Therapies Inc*[623] the defendant who had lost at trial applied to the court to reconsider its judgment which had just been handed down on
the ground that a vital part of the reasoning was said to be inconsistent with binding Court of Appeal authority. The court acceded to the application to reconsider,[624]
although on reconsideration affirmed its original judgment. The mere fact a judge
had missed a point or overlooked something did not of itself justify review. Before
the court could review on this ground it was necessary that the oversight could well
have led to a wrong conclusion and that changing the conclusion would lead to at
least one of the issues between the parties being determined differently. In
Charlesworth v Relay Roads[625] the court acceded to an application to amend the
pleadings after judgment had been handed down but before the order was drawn
up. It had jurisdiction to do so because the order had not yet been drawn up.[626] In
Navitaire v EasyJet[627] the court refused to admit further evidence after the judgment had been given but before the order was perfected. The court applied the same
test as is applicable to admitting fresh evidence on appeal.[628]

In *Bristol Myers v Baker Norton*[629] the terms of an order of the court of appeal **19-384**
setting aside a costs order in a patent case had an unintended legal effect. Although
the slip rule could not be used in order to allow for second thoughts on an issue not
raised, it could be used if the terms of the order did not meet the intention of the
court, which was the case.

In *Apotex Europe Ltd v SmithKline Beecham*,[630] on receipt of a draft costs judg- **19-385**
ment, the paying party raised two matters before the judgment was handed down.

---

[621] CPR Pt 63, Practice Direction—Intellectual Property Claims, Section V, Patents County Court
para.31.2.
[622] CPR Pt 63.23(3) and CPR Pt 63, Practice Direction—Intellectual Property Claims, Section V, Patents
County Court para.29.1
[623] [2002] R.P.C. 2.
[624] Following *Stewart v Engel* [2000] 1 W.L.R. 2268, the power to review being in CPR, Pt 3.1.7. See
also *In re Barrell Enterprises* [1973] 1 W.L.R. 19. But see below, both these cases have now been
disapproved of by the Supreme Court to the extent they require "exceptional circumstances" before
the court can reconsider or reverse its decision before the order is drawn up. *In re L (Children)
(Preliminary Finding: Power to reverse)* [2013] UKSC 8.
[625] [2000] R.P.C. 300.
[626] [2000] R.P.C. 300, 304–305. See also *Stanelco Fibre Optic Ltd's Application (No.2)* [2005] R.P.C.
16 and *Navitaire Inc v EasyJet* [2005] EWHC 282 (Ch), [2006] R.P.C. 4.
[627] [2006] R.P.C. 4
[628] See para.19–406, et seq.
[629] [2001] R.P.C. 45.
[630] [2004] EWHC 2052 (Ch); the perfected judgment to which this refers is [2004] EWHC 964 (Ch).

The first point was a correction of a percentage which was not opposed. The second point, although suggested to be a correction, was in fact a fresh argument which had not been argued before but could have been. The court was satisfied as to the correctness of its draft judgment and did not accept the second point.

19-386   In *Kooltrade v XTS*[631] the court refused an application to join new defendants after judgment.

19-387   In *Vringo v ZTE*[632] after judgment but before the order was drawn up, the Patents Court refused an application by the losing defendant to amend its Grounds of Invalidity to raise a new item of prior art, to call further evidence and to reopen the trial. The application was made after the decision of the *Supreme Court in In re L (Children) (Preliminary Finding: Power to reverse)*.[633] In that case, the Supreme Court considered the power of the judge to reverse their decision before the order was drawn up and sealed. The Supreme Court held that the jurisdiction to do this does exist and, importantly, they disapproved of statements in *In re Barrell Enterprises*[634] and *Stewart v Engel*,[635] to the effect that exceptional circumstances were required before such a jurisdiction should be exercised. The Supreme Court explained that every case must depend on its circumstances and that the starting point was the overriding objective in CPR Pt 1 to deal with cases justly. Applying the test *In Re L* the Patents Court refused the application, primarily because the new prior art (a well-known mobile telephone standard) was an item of prior art which could readily have been found earlier.

19-388   In *Teva UK Ltd v AstraZeneca AB*[636] a reconsideration request of a different type was made. In the confidential draft judgment provided to the parties, the judge found the patent invalid on the basis of a ground (obviousness over the common general knowledge) not argued for by the claimant, and dismissed the argument made on the basis of the prior art relied upon. Following the guidance in the Court of Appeal in *Re M (A Child) (Non-accidental injury: burden of proof)*,[637] the error was pointed out to the judge before the judgment was handed down. As explained in the judgment as handed down (at [121]–[132]), in the light of this he reconsidered his decision. The judge considered that he had made an error in his approach to the case of obviousness over the pleaded prior art and held the patent invalid in the light of that document when read together with the common general knowledge.

12.   APPEALS TO THE COURT OF APPEAL

The governing rule

19-389   Appeals, including appeals from the Comptroller, are governed by CPR Pt 52.

---

[631] [2002] F.S.R. 49.
[632] [2015] EWHC 214 (Pat); [2015] R.P.C. 23.
[633] [2013] UKSC 8.
[634] [1973] 1 W.L.R. 19.
[635] [2000] 1 W.L.R. 2268.
[636] [2014] EWHC 2873 (Pat).
[637] [2008] EWCA Civ 1261, [36]–[40].

Permission

With certain limited exceptions which do not generally apply to patent litiga- **19-390**
tion,[638] permission is required for every appeal and cross-appeal to the Court of Appeal from a decision of a judge in a county court or the High Court. Permission may
be given by the court below or the Court of Appeal. Permission to appeal in patent
cases in not automatic and refused from time to time, particularly where the appeal involves a challenge to a decision in relation to inventive step (for example,
in *Glaxo Group Ltd's Patent*[639]). In *Pozzoli v BDMO*[640] the Court of Appeal held
that a decision by a Court of Appeal judge or judges whether nor not to grant
permission to appeal from an order for revocation (whether that decision was taken
on the papers or following an oral hearing) was a judicial decision and was "judicial
review" as called for by art.32 of TRIPs.

In *Pozzoli*[641] the Court of Appeal stated on the question of granting permission **19-391**
that:

> "Unless the case is very clear and can be understood sufficiently readily in an hour or so, the better
> course if normally for permission to be granted by the trial judge. For unlike the trial judge, the Court
> of Appeal judge(s) who have to decide whether permission should be granted (where the trial judge
> refused it) will not be immersed in the technology and evidence in the same way as the trial judge
> Faced with but an incomplete understanding and a plausible skeleton argument seeking permission,
> the Court of Appeal will generally be likely to grant permission even if it later discerns that the case
> is indeed clear."

Whilst this statement has never been formally disapproved of, it is unclear the **19-392**
extent to which the "hour or so" rule set out by Jacob LJ is actually applied in
practice. Normally, decisions on permission to appeal are based upon the criteria
in the CPR, namely whether the appeal has a real prospect of success. So for
example, in *Les Laboratoires Servier v Apotex*,[642] in a case about x-ray crystal-
lography and crystalline forms, the Patents Court had given permission to appeal
applying the *Pozzoli* test while at the same time refusing to extend an interim
injunction pending the appeal against the order for revocation on the ground the appeal had no real prospect of success. The Lord Chief Justice observed that in his
judgment that permission to appeal should not have been given.

Permission is not required in the case of an appeal from the Comptroller to the **19-393**
Patents Court.[643] However, permission is required for any further appeal from the
Patents Court to the Court of Appeal.[644] CPR r.52.13 generally requires the permission of the Court of Appeal in the case of a second tier appeal (which permission
will not be given unless the criteria set out in r.52.13(2) are met), but the Court of
Appeal held in *Smith International Inc v Specialised Petroleum Services*[645] that s.55
of the Access to Justice Act 1999—and thus CPR r.52.13—do not apply to appeals under s.97(3) of the Patents Act 1977.

---

[638] CPR r.52.3(1)(a)(i)–(iii).
[639] In this case the Court of Appeal refused leave. Such decisions are not reported.
[640] [2007] F.S.R. 37.
[641] [2007] F.S.R. 37.
[642] [2008] EWCA Civ 445.
[643] TPN 1/2003 [2003] R.P.C. 46.
[644] PA 1977 s.97(3).
[645] [2005] EWCA (Civ) 1357, [2006] F.S.R. 25 following *Henry Boot Construction (UK) Ltd v
Malmaison Hotel* [2001] Q.B. 388, CA.

Time for appealing

19-394   Every appellant's notice (including one seeking permission to appeal) must be filed not later than 21 days after the date of the decision of the lower court.[646]

19-395   Unlike the old practice, under the CPR the date on which the court hands down its reasons for its decision is the date of the decision (or judgment) within the meaning of the rule and the time for appealing starts to run from that date. However, where there is likely to be a delay before the court's order consequent upon its judgment is finalised, the court may adjourn the hearing to determine whether permission to appeal ought to be granted.[647]

Service of notice of appeal on the Comptroller

19-396   An appeal against revocation of a patent[648] or any appeal originating from a decision of the Comptroller[649] must also be served on the Comptroller who may appear on the appeal.

Nature of appeal

19-397   An appeal is by way of review, not rehearing, and the appeal court will not re-open particular factual issues previously decided by the judge without good reason (particularly where to do so would substantially prolong the appeal).

19-398   The approach of an appellate court to the exercise of a discretion or an evaluation of judgment analogous to the exercise of a discretion (such as reasonable care or obviousness[650]) was a "steeper appellate hurdle" than the approach to deciding the correctness of a judge's judgment on a question of fact.[651] The role of the appellate court was to determine whether that finding was wrong, giving full weight to the advantages enjoyed by any judge of first instance who heard oral evidence. Owing to the nature of appeals, parties are seldom permitted to argue points not run below. In *Apimed Medical Honey Ltd v Brightwake Ltd*[652] the Comptroller, acting when the parties' had settled, served a respondent's notice seeking to raise a point not taken at trial. As it raised technical issues which were not possible to resolve on the appeal, he was not permitted to advance it.

Appeal on question of obviousness

19-399   In *Biogen Inc v Medeva Plc*[653] Lord Hoffmann said:

> "The question of whether an invention was obvious had been called 'a kind of jury question' (see Jenkins L.J. in *Allmanna Svenska Elektriska A/B v The Burntisland Shipbuilding Co Ltd* (1952) 69 R.P.C. 63 at 70) and should be treated with appropriate respect by an appellate court. It is true that in *Benmax v Austin Motor Co Ltd* [1955] A.C. 370[654] this House decided that, while the judge's findings of primary fact, particularly if founded upon an assessment of the credibility of witnesses, were

---

[646] CPR r.52.4(2)(b).
[647] CPR Pt 52, Practice Direction 52A para.4.1(a).
[648] CPR Pt 52, Practice Direction 52D para.14.1(2).
[649] CPR Pt 52, Practice Direction 52D para.13.1.
[650] See para.19–399.
[651] *Thorn Securty v Siemens Schweiz* [2009] R.P.C. 3, CA.
[652] [2012] EWCA Civ 5; [2012] R.P.C. 17, [56]–[57].
[653] [1997] R.P.C. 1, 45, HC.
[654] (1955) 72 R.P.C. 39, 42.

virtually unassailable, an appellate court would be more ready to differ from the judge's evaluation of those facts by reference to some legal standard such as negligence or obviousness. In drawing this distinction, however, Viscount Simmonds went on to observe, at page 374, that it was 'subject only to the weight which should, as a matter of course, be given to the opinion of the learned judge'. The need for appellate caution in reversing the judge's evaluation of the facts is based upon much more solid grounds than professional courtesy. It is because specific findings of fact, even by the most meticulous judge, are inherently an incomplete statement of the impression which was made upon him by the primary evidence. His expressed findings are always surrounded by a penumbra of imprecision as to emphasis, relative weight, minor qualification and nuance (as Renan said, '*la vérité est dans une nuance*'), of which time and language do not permit exact expression, but which may play an important part in the judge's overall evaluation. It would in my view be wrong to treat *Benmax* as authorising or requiring an appellate court to undertake a de novo evaluation of the facts in all cases in which no question of the credibility of witnesses is involved. Where the application of a legal standard such as negligence or obviousness involves no question of principle but is simply a matter of degree, an appellate court should be very cautious in differing from the judge's evaluation."

And in dealing with the issue of lack of support for the claims, Lord Hoffmann went on to say[655]: **19-400**

"I am bound to say that I regret the decision of the Court of Appeal to revisit the evidence upon which the judge made his finding of fact. For the reasons given earlier in relation to the issue of obviousness, I think that this was a question on which greater respect should have been paid to the judge's findings. The Court of Appeal's reversal of the judge on this issue greatly lengthened the hearing before your Lordships' House, as no doubt it had done in the Court of Appeal. The House was invited to undertake a minute examination of the facts with a view to restoring the findings of the judge. It was even offered inspection of the autoradiographs claimed to show the positive results upon which Professor Murray had based his claim to success-an offer which your Lordships felt able to decline. But I think that your Lordships learned enough of the detailed facts to form the view that the judge's decision was one which was open to him upon the evidence and should not have been disturbed."

Biogen v Medeva has been considered and applied in a number of cases subsequently.[656] **19-401**

More recently, in *Datec Electronic Holdings v United Parcels Service Limited*[657] the House of Lords (per Lord Mance at [46]) approved the statement of Clarke LJ in *Assicurazioni Generali SpA v Arab Insurance Group*[658] as giving proper guidance as to the role of the Court of Appeal when faced with appeals on fact: **19-402**

"16. Some conclusions of fact are, however, not conclusions of primary fact of the kind to which I have just referred. They involve an assessment of a number of different factors which have to be weighed against each other. This is sometimes called an evaluation of the facts and is often a matter of degree upon which different judges can legitimately differ. Such cases may be closely analogous to the exercise of a discretion and, in my opinion, appellate courts should approach them in a similar way."

Appeal on questions of enablement or insufficiency

On appeal, the proper approach in relation to a decision on enablement or insufficiency is similar to the approach in relation to a decision on obviousness: where **19-403**

---

[655] [1997] R.P.C. 1, 50.
[656] *Cartonneries de Thulin SA v CTP White Knight Ltd* [2001] R.P.C. 6, CA; *United Wire Ltd v Screen Repair Servces (Scotland) Ltd* [2001] R.P.C. 24 HL; *Dyson v Hoover* [2002] R.P.C. 22, CA; *Pharmacia v Merck* [2002] R.P.C. 41, CA; see also *Designers Guild v Russell Williams* [2001] F.S.R. 11 (a copyright case); *Instance v Denny* [2002] R.P.C. 14, CA (a patent case citing *Designers Guild*); and *Buchanan v Alba* [2004] R.P.C. 34, HL citing both *Biogen v Medeva* and *Designers Guild; Merck & Co Inc's Patents* [2004] F.S.R. 16 in particular the comments of Buxton LJ on appeals at [63]–[72].
[657] [2007] UKHL 23, [2007] 1 W.L.R. 1325.
[658] [2003] 1 W.L.R. 577.

there is no point of principle involved, an appellate court should be very cautious in differing from the judge's evaluation, see the decision of the House of Lords in *SmithKline Beecham's Patent*[659]; and the decision of the Court of Appeal in *Halliburton v Smith International*[660], particularly [24]–[25].

Stare decisis and the EPO

19-404   Since the English courts aim to follow the EPO on matters of law[661] and since the EPO does not regard itself as bound by its own previous decisions, the English doctrine of precedent cannot stand unmodified in patent matters.[662] For example the special circumstances arising from the creation of the European patent system and the central importance given to decisions of the EPO Board of Appeal mean that there is a specialist and limited exception to the rule on *Young v Bristol Aeroplane* by which the Court of Appeal is bound by the ratio of previous Court of Appeal decisions.[663]

19-405   However, there is a fundamental difference between following the EPO Boards of Appeal on matters of law and on matters of fact. Questions of fact are determined by the evidence and there is nothing wrong in principle in the English courts reaching a different conclusion from the EPO on an issue involving matters of fact when the evidence and evidence testing mechanisms before the two tribunals was not the same.[664]

Admitting further evidence on appeal

19-406   Although the Court of Appeal has power to receive further evidence in general it will not do so unless the following circumstances are satisfied, namely:

> "first, it must be shown that the evidence could not have been obtained with reasonable diligence for use at the trial; secondly, the evidence must be such that, if given, it would probably have an important influence on the result of the case, though it need not be decisive; thirdly, the evidence must be such as is presumably to be believed, or in other words, it must be apparently credible though it need not be incontrovertible."[665]

19-407   In *Coflexip SA v Stolt Comex Seaway MS Ltd*[666] the defendants (who had failed at first instance in their attack on the patent) applied on appeal to amend their particulars of objections to rely on a new item of prior art and to adduce fresh evidence for the purpose of establishing that the patent was invalid in the light of

---

[659] [2006] R.P.C. 323, [38].

[660] [2006] EWCA Civ 1715.

[661] See *Merrell Dow Pharmaceuticals Inc v H.N. Norton & Co Ltd* [1996] R.P.C. 76, 82; *Conor Medsystems Inc v Angiotech Pharmaceuticals Inc* [2008] UKHL 49, [2008] R.P.C. 28, [2008] 4 All E.R. 621, at [3], per Lord Hoffmann; *Generics (UK) Ltd v H Lundbeck A/S* [2009] UKHL 12, [2009] R.P.C. 13, [46] and [86]. In addition, as was explained in *Grimme Landmaschinenfabrik GmbH & Co KG v Scott* [2010] EWCA Civ 1110; [2011] F.S.R. 7, at [80], the English court also tries to follow the reasoning of the courts of other EPC Member States, only departing if convinced that the reasoning of that other court is erroneous.

[662] Consider *Aerotel v Telco and Macrossan* [2007] R.P.C. 7 and *Symbian v the Comptroller* [2009] R.P.C. 1.

[663] *Actavis v Merck* [2008] R.P.C. 26.

[664] *Eli Lilly v Human Genome Sciences* [2010] R.P.C. 14. See also *Synthon v Teva* [2015] EWHC 1395 (Pat) where the Court explained its reasons for differing from the EPO.

[665] *Ladd v Marshall* [1954] 1 W.L.R. 1489, CA. See also *ICI v Montedison* [1995] R.P.C. 449; cases decided on the burden of proof are not an exception to these principles.

[666] [2001] R.P.C. 9,

that prior art. Although the defendants were unaware of the prior art at the time of the trial at first instance, the patentee's evidence established that if a fuller search had been made by the defendants at the outset of the action, the new prior art would have been found. In its decision the Court of Appeal concentrated on the application to amend the particulars of objections which it refused in the exercise of its discretion as the proposed amendment did not satisfy the overriding objective laid down in CPR r.1.1. Aldous LJ said:

"To ensure expeditious and fair resolution retrials must be avoided. Thus a defendant in a patent action must decide the extent of any search he wishes to make and, except in very unusual circumstances, will be held by this Court to the decision he takes. To conclude to the contrary would encourage applications to introduce fresh prior art to meet conclusions reached by the trial judge with consequent delay and increased cost. Further a retrial cannot be an acceptable allotment of an appropriate share of the court's resources except in very unusual circumstances. None arise in this case.

It is not for the court to decide whether a search for prior art carried out by a defendant was reasonable. What is reasonable depends on a variety of factors, such as cost, importance of the result to the defendant, and its resources. To ensure that litigation is carried out efficiently and fairly parties must bring before the court the case that they wish to rely on. That Stolt did in this case. They carried out searches which they believed were appropriate and which they believed and still believe were reasonable. It was their decision not to search more widely and it is not right to allow them to reopen their case in this Court. There are no exceptional circumstances which would make this an appropriate case for amendment requiring a new trial."

And Chadwick LJ, agreeing with Aldous LJ, said: **19-408**

"Where the court's resources have already been allotted to one trial of the issues between the parties, a party seeking a second trial to raise new issues has a heavy burden to discharge if he is to persuade the court that further resources should be allotted for that purpose. The court is entitled to expect that parties will bring before it for trial, at one and the same time, all the issues upon which they wish to have a decision. Two bites at the cherry is wasteful of resources.

I agree with Lord Justice Aldous that it is not enough for a party in a patent action to say that he acted reasonably in deciding what limit to place upon his searches for prior art when preparing for a trial. It is accepted by the appellants, as I understand it, that more extensive searches than those actually carried out would have revealed the additional prior art upon which they now seek to rely. Such an acceptance is inevitable, as it seems to me, where it cannot be disputed that the additional material was there to be found. In such a case the test is not whether a party did what was reasonable; it is whether he did what was necessary."

As noted above, the court will apply the same principles to an application to **19-409** amend a Grounds of Invalidity, call more evidence and/or reopen a trial after judgment but before the final order is drawn up, albeit that it will be somewhat more flexible.[667] However, in *Vringo Infrastructure v ZTE UK Ltd*,[668] Birss J explained that where such an application is made, in most cases it will not be allowed if the applicant does not meet the *Ladd v Marshall* test.

An appeal with no respondent

The appeal court will not normally make an order allowing an appeal unless satis- **19-410** fied that the decision of the lower court is wrong.[669] However, a patentee whose patent was found invalid at first instance may pursue an appeal in order to overturn the

---

[667] *Charlesworth v Relay Roads* [2000] R.P.C 300.
[668] [2015] EWHC 214 (Pat); [2015] R.P.C. 23.
[669] CPR Pt 52 PD para.13.1. For some old patent cases on this see *Martin v Selsdon Fountain Pen Co Ltd* (1949) 66 R.P.C. 294; *Sun Life Assurance Co of Canada v Jervis* [1944] A.C. 111. See also *Norton and Gregory v Jacobs* (1937) 54 R.P.C. 271; *Manbre and Garton v Albion Sugar Co* (1937) 54 R.P.C. 243.

finding of invalidity notwithstanding that they may have settled with their opponent and in these circumstances, the Court of Appeal have given the Comptroller the option to attend if he felt able to assist,[670] the Comptroller's costs would be paid by the patentee. The same procedure has been adopted in the House of Lords.[671] The Comptroller's stance on such a case is not win for the sake of winning but to defend the judgment below objectively and in a non-partisan manner.[672]

Procedure on appeal

19-411 The normal timetable for the filing of bundles and skeleton arguments do not apply in the case of an appeal from the Patents Court to the Court of Appeal. On 16 January 2015, Deputy Master Meacher issued the following directions for all Intellectual Property Appeals in the Court of Appeal, substantially replicating the directions that had been given by Aldous LJ in January 2002:

> "*Applications for Permission to Appeal*
> The appellant's notice, skeleton argument and bundle should be lodged as required by CPR PD 52C, sections 2, 4 and 7.
>
> *Appeals*
>   Where permission to appeal has been given by the lower court or granted by the Court of Appeal:
>
> - The Civil Appeals Office will ask the parties to provide an agreed time estimate where possible or, where agreement cannot be reached, separate time estimates for the hearing of the appeal together with an agreed time estimate for any necessary pre-reading.
> - The case will then be referred to the Supervising Lord Justice for listing directions.
> - Once the appeal is listed, the parties will be asked to lodge an agreed timetable for the filing of skeleton arguments, appeal bundles and bundles of authorities for approval by the Supervising Lord Justice.
> - Any subsequent request by the parties to amend the approved timetable will be referred to the Supervising Lord Justice for determination."

Costs

19-412 The costs of employing an expert to assist counsel in the Court of Appeal will not be allowed save under the most special circumstances.[673]

---

[670] *Halliburton Energy Services Patent* [2006] R.P.C. 26.
[671] *Conor v Angiotech* [2008] R.P.C. 28 (HL).
[672] *Aerotel v Telco and Macrossan* [2007] R.P.C. 7, [4].
[673] *Consolidated Pneumatic Tool Co v Ingersoll Sergeant Drill Co* (1908) 25 R.P.C 574; *Société Anonyme Servo-Frein Dewandre v Citroen Cars Ltd* (1930) 47 R.P.C 221, 282.

CHAPTER 20

THE INTELLECTUAL PROPERTY ENTERPRISE COURT

CONTENTS

1. INTRODUCTION

The Intellectual Property Enterprise Court (IPEC) is the successor to the Patents **20-01**
County Court (PCC). The rules of procedure in IPEC are virtually identical to the
rules introduced in the PCC on 1 October 2010, with the main exception being the
updating of the costs caps applicable to various stages of the proceedings.[1] Cases
decided in the PCC post-1 October 2010 but prior to its reorganisation into the
IPEC, therefore remain generally applicable as precedents in the IPEC post-1
October 2013.[2] The history of both courts is summarised in Ch.1, at 1-34 to 1-41.
Lessons learned from the process of reforming the court and from its early years
in operation afterwards were summarised in the 2015 Francis Gurry Lecture.[3]

Jurisdiction and enforcement

As part of the Chancery Division of the High Court, the IPEC has jurisdiction **20-02**
over any case which can be heard before that Division. This means that the IPEC
may hear proceedings which are mainly concerned with intellectual property but
which also include claims for defamation, malicious falsehood, and/or breach of
fiduciary duty.

Similarly all of the remedies available in the High Court[4] are available in the **20-03**
IPEC including preliminary and final injunctions, damages, accounts of profits,
delivery up and disclosure. This includes search and seizure (Anton Piller) and asset freezing (Mareva) orders. The IPEC has the power to commit for contempt of

---

[1]   The transitional provisions governing the reconstitution of the PCC into the IPEC are likely to be
       of limited practical interest since they only apply to proceedings which were already in the PCC as
       at 1 October 2013. See the Civil Procedure (Amendment No. 7) Rules 2013 (SI 2014/1974) r.30.
[2]   *Phonographic Performance Ltd v Hamilton (No.1)* [2013] EWHC 3467.
[3]   2015 Francis Gurry Lecture on Intellectual Property given by Birss J in September 2015, to be
       published in the *Australian Intellectual Property Journal*.
[4]   Which in practice means the Patents Court for any claim under the 1977 Act. See CPR Pt 63.1, 63.2.

court, including the power to issue a bench warrant to secure court attendance.[5] IPEC judges who are nominated under s.9(1) of the Senior Courts Act 1981[6] are judges of the High Court for the purposes of CPR PD3C, such that they have jurisdiction to grant both extended and general civil restraint orders.[7]

20-04   However, in addition to the procedural differences between High Court and IPEC which are discussed in more detail below, the IPEC cannot award more than £500,000 by way of either damages or profits.[8] This figure is calculated exclusive of interest (other than interest payable under an agreement) and costs[9] and can be waived by agreement.[10] Furthermore, the IPEC has no jurisdiction to hear appeals from the UK Intellectual Property Office, which have to be made to the High Court.[11]

20-05   The IPEC small claims track is primarily intended to deal with lower value claims relating to copyright but it can also deal with claims involving trade marks, passing off, and unregistered designs (UK or Community) and breach of confidence. It cannot deal with claims relating to patents, registered designs (UK or Community) and plant varieties.[12] For these reasons it will be of limited interest to readers of this work. The IPEC small claims track has the power to order final injunctions and to award damages and other final remedies, although it cannot grant any interim remedies such as preliminary injunctions, search and seizure (Anton Piller) and asset freezing (Mareva) orders.[13] Claims allocated to this track will be dealt with by a District Judge.[14]

20-06   Orders of the IPEC may be enforced in the same way as any other orders of the High Court.[15] All applications for the enforcement of any financial element of an IPEC judgment will be dealt with by a District Judge.[16] All such applications made for enforcement of an IPEC multi-track judgment must be made in accordance with the Court's Practice Note.[17]

---

[5] *Westwood v Knight* [2012] EWPCC 14, where the then PCC relied on CCR r.29. The difficulties with Pt 81.18 (committal application in relation to a false statement of truth or disclosure statement) which were identified in the PCC case of *Utopia v BBP Marketing* [2013] EWPCC 28 would appear to have been resolved following the court's reorganisation into IPEC.

[6] In practice all IPEC judges, including deputies, are so nominated.

[7] *Perry v F.H. Brundle* [2015] EWHC 2737 (IPEC). This was a case about an extended civil restraint orders but the relevant words are the same in both PD 3C paras 3.1(2) and 4.1(2).

[8] See Pt 63.17A(1). In *Comptroller-General v Intellectual Property Agency* [2015] EWHC 3256 (IPEC) the losing defendant had made a gross profit of £1,106,510, but the court could only award the maximum permitted under the IPEC cap, i.e. £500,000.

[9] See Pt 63.17A(2).

[10] See Pt 63.17A(3). The limit was waived in *AP Racing v Alcon Components*, Unreported on this point, but the final sum awarded turned out to be close to £500,000 in any event: see [2016] EWHC 116 (IPEC).

[11] Patents Act 1977 s.97(1), 97(2), but see s.97(4), and s.109(4), Sch.14 of the Constitutional Reform Act 2005. The appeal has to be made to the Patents Court, but the Lord Chief Justice may nominate a judicial office holder (who may apparently be a Recorder) to exercise his functions under s.97(2).

[12] See Pts 63.27(1), 63.2, and 63.13.

[13] See Pt 63.27(4)).

[14] Pt 63.19(2)(b).

[15] See, e.g. Pts 71 (order to obtain information from judgment debtors, commonly known as oral examination) and 73 (charging orders, etc.).

[16] Pt 63.19(2)(c).

[17] Intellectual Property Enterprise Court (Multi Track) Practice Note, 17 December 2015: *https://www.judiciary.gov.uk/publications/intellectual-property-enterprise-court-multi-track-practice-note/* [Accessed 15 March 2016]. The note does not apply to orders made in the IPEC small claims track.

2. ALLOCATION AND TRANSFER BETWEEN THE PATENTS COURT AND IPEC[18]

Where litigants seek to recover more than £500,000, they should commence proceedings in the Patents Court given that IPEC is unable to award more than that sum. In other cases litigants should consider which forum is more appropriate.

20-07

The IPEC has been established to handle the smaller, shorter, less complex, less important, lower value actions and the procedures applicable in the court are designed particularly for cases of that kind. The court aims to provide cheaper, speedier and more informal procedures to ensure that small- and medium-sized enterprises and private individuals are not deterred from innovation by the potential cost of litigation to safeguard their rights. Longer, heavier, more complex, more important and more valuable actions belong in the Patents Court or (in the case of other IP rights) the general Chancery list of the High Court.[19]

20-08

If a party to litigation in either the IPEC or a different court believes that the other court is a more appropriate forum for the case, they should apply to transfer it. In the IPEC itself an application to transfer to a different court must be made at or before the case management conference.[20] If the application is made in the Patents Court there is no such restriction, although it is submitted that it should be done as early as possible with a view to the case management conference being heard in the IPEC. The application is made under CPR Pt 30.5 as modified by Pt 63.18: see also PD30 paras 9.1 and 9.2. In addition, the following guidelines have been provided by the IPEC to assist users in determining which court is suitable:[21]

20-09

"Size of the parties. If both sides are small or medium sized enterprises then the case may well be suitable for the IPEC. If one party is a small or medium sized enterprise but the other is a larger undertaking then again the case may be suitable for the IPEC but other factors ought to be considered such as the value of the claim and its likely complexity.

The complexity of the claim. The procedure in the IPEC is streamlined and trials will seldom last more than 2 days. A trial which would appear to require more time than that even with the streamlined procedure of the IPEC is likely to be unsuitable.

The nature of the evidence. Experiments in a patent case may be admitted in the IPEC but a case which will involve substantial complex experimental evidence will be unsuitable for the IPEC.

Conflicting factual evidence. Cross-examination of witnesses will be strictly controlled in the IPEC. The court is well able to handle cases involving disputed factual matters such as allegations of prior use in patents and independent design as a defence to copying; but if a large number of witnesses are required the case may be unsuitable for the IPEC.

Value of the claim. Subject to the agreement of the parties, there is a limit on the damages available in the IPEC of £500,000. However, assessing the value of a claim is not only concerned with damages. Putting a value on a claim is a notoriously difficult exercise, taking into account factors such as possible damages, the value of an injunction and the possible effect on competition in a market if a patent was revoked. As a general rule of thumb, disputes where the value of sales, in the UK, of products protected by the intellectual property in issue (by the owner, licensees and alleged infringer) exceeds £1 million per year are unlikely to be suitable for the IPEC in the absence of agreement."

---

[18] The relevant transfer provisions have now been considered and applied in a number of cases. Among those not considered separately below are: *Caljan Rite-Hite v Solvex* [2011] EWHC 669 (Ch); *Environmental Recycling v Stillwell* [2012] EWHC 2097 (Pat); *Destra v Comada* [2012] EWPCC 39; *Crocuer Enterprises v Giordano Poultry-Plast SPA* [2013] F.S.R. 44; *Canon KK v Badger Office Supplies* [2015] EWHC 259 (Pat).

[19] See the comments of Sir Thomas Bingham MR in *Chaplin Patent Holdings v Group Lotus plc*, 17 December 1993, CA, in relation to an application to transfer from the PCC to the High Court.

[20] CPR r.63.25(4). The court will consider an application to transfer the claim later in the proceedings only where there are exceptional circumstances: r.63.25(5).

[21] *IPEC Guide*, para.1.3.

20-10   An important qualification is that the "complexity" of the claim is really a measure of the necessary trial time; it is not a measure of how difficult the issues are to consider, and does not relate to the numerical technical difficulty rating assigned in a patents case.[22] The IPEC has a specialist judge and so the real limitation on complexity is the two-day trial length. Conversely, the fact that a hearing in the IPEC will almost always have an intellectual property specialist sitting is not a factor militating against transfer to the Chancery Division.[23]

20-11   It is important to remember that the court may impose conditions or other terms upon the parties when ordering a transfer.[24] The court or the parties may propose such terms, either as conditions to be attached to transfer or conditions of remaining in the original forum. Examples considered by the court have included submitting to capped damages so as to remain in the IPEC[25] and the defendant agreeing to limit any application for security for costs to the IPEC costs cap of £50,000.[26] In *Liversidge v Owen Mumford*[27] the patentee agreed to forego his right to an injunction and restricted himself to a royalty claim.

3. STATEMENTS OF CASE

20-12   The IPEC rules applicable to statements of case (i.e. pleadings) so far as content and timing are concerned are generally the same as those applicable in the Patents Court, with the following exceptions.

Facts and arguments must be pleaded

20-13   Part 16 applies with the modification that a statement of case must set out concisely all the facts and arguments upon which the party serving it relies.[28] One of the key purposes behind this modification is to facilitate the particular type of case management conference used in the IPEC, discussed in more detail below.[29] Since all of the IPEC judges are specialists, it is unlikely that legal arguments will need to be set out in any detail: all that is likely to be required is a brief statement of the nature of the argument to be relied on.[30]

20-14   In *Glass v Freyssinet*[31] HHJ Hacon noted that arguments on construction of a patent claim fall into a special category, since the question of construction is liable to remain open up to and throughout the trial; and the court is in no way limited in its conclusions on construction by submissions made by the parties, but must do its best to arrive at the correct construction. He held:

"21. It would not be helpful for argument on construction as it develops during a trial to be interrupted by periodic challenges as to whether this or that proposed construction falls squarely within a pleaded case. I agree that it is possible for a party to be disadvantaged by a new argument on construction to the extent that they can claim to have been taken unawares and deprived of the op-

[22] *ALK Abello v Meridian* [2010] EWPCC 014.
[23] *A.S. Watson v The Boots Company* [2011] EWPCC 26.
[24] PD30 para.9.2(1).
[25] This was proposed in *Watson v Boots* but transfer was ordered nonetheless.
[26] *Comic Enterprises Ltd v Twentieth Century Fox Film Corp* [2012] EWPCC 13, [38]–[42].
[27] [2011] EWPCC 34, [5]–[6]. There was still provision for an injunction in the event that the defendant failed to pay sums due.
[28] Pt 63.20(1).
[29] *Westwood v Knight* [2010] EWPCC 16, [59].
[30] *IPEC guide*, para.2.5(c).
[31] [2015] EWHC 2972 (IPEC).

portunity to file evidence that would have been relevant to the opponent's case now being advanced on a new construction of the claim. Parties in the IPEC would be very well advised to include all arguments in their pleading, including those on construction, to avoid any risk of having part of their case disregarded. Moreover, deliberately concealing an argument for tactical advantage is liable to be met with a severe sanction. But so far as construction is concerned, provided there is no deliberate concealment and the opposing party is unable to prove significant prejudice caused by a failure to plead the argument, parties are unlikely to meet with any resistance from the court as to the arguments they wish to advance. I emphasise the proviso."

The IPEC has issued additional guidelines, including the following:[32] **20-15**

"In all proceedings copies of important documents referred to in a statement of case (e.g. an advertisement relied on or documents cited in Grounds of Invalidity) should be served with the statement of case. Where any such document requires translation, a translation should be served at the same time.

It is likely to be necessary to break down a patent claim into suitable integers (i.e. separate parts) in order to explain a case on infringement with reference to specific elements of the alleged infringing product or process. This may be most conveniently done in the form of a table or chart annexed to the statement of case. Points on construction should emerge from this exercise and may need to be identified but lengthy argument on them is not required.

A submission of lack of novelty of a patent is likely to require a similar approach to infringement (i.e. a claim break down, perhaps in the form of a table, with the claim integers compared with the relevant parts of the prior art disclosure(s) relied upon).

A case of obviousness of a patent is likely to require a statement addressing the allegedly obvious step(s).

Where a party raises the issue of validity of a patent, the patentee (or other relevant party) should identify which of the claims of the patent are alleged to have independent validity in his reply (or defence) to the allegation of invalidity.

A specific statement of what facts are said to be relevant and common general knowledge is likely to be necessary. A short summary of the relevant technical background may be helpful."

If a case is commenced in the Patents Court but subsequently transferred, it may **20-16**
be necessary to re-plead but this will not always be the case. The normal Patents
Court pleading requirements that apply in all patents cases also continue to apply.[33]

Statement of truth

Part 22 applies with the modification that the statement of truth verifying a state- **20-17**
ment of case must be signed by a person with knowledge of the facts alleged or, if
no one person has knowledge of all the facts, by persons who between them have
knowledge of all the facts alleged.[34] Where more than one person signs the statement of case, it is good practice to identify the particular passages in relation to
which each person is signing.

This rule, in combination with the requirement to plead facts and arguments, is **20-18**
designed to reduce or even remove any need for witness statements (see Pt 32.6 and
below).

Time limits

The particulars of claim must also state whether the claimant has complied with **20-19**
para.7.1(1) and Annex A (para.2) of the Practice Direction (Pre-Action Conduct).
If the particulars of claim contain such a confirmation, the period for filing a defence
where the defendant files an acknowledgment of service under Pt 10 is generally

---

[32] *IPEC guide*, para.2.5(c).
[33] See CPR Pt 63.6 and PD 63 paras 4.1–4.6.
[34] Pt 63.21.

42 days after service of the particulars of claim.[35] If they do not, the period for filing a defence where the defendant files an acknowledgment of service under Pt 10 is 70 days after service of the particulars of claim.[36] There appears to be no other sanction for failure to make the statement of compliance. Moreover, it would appear that the court will not of its own motion investigate the truth of such a declaration to determine the time-limit for filing a defence.[37] If the r.63.22 declaration is made, then the shorter, 42-day period will apply.[38]

20-20   Where the claimant files a reply to a defence it must be filed and served on all other parties within 28 days of service of the defence. Where the defendant files a reply to a defence to a counterclaim it must be filed and served on all other parties within 14 days of service of the defence to the counterclaim.[39]

20-21   The periods permitted for the defence and all subsequent pleadings can only be extended by order of the court and for "good reason".[40] The requirement for "good reason" is not found in the normal Patents Court rules and is specific to IPEC. It is submitted that consent of the parties will not necessarily be sufficient: if it were, the rules would say so.

4. INTERIM APPLICATIONS

Generally

20-22   Part 23 applies with the modifications set out in Pt 63.25. The two most important modifications for present purposes are as follows:

20-23   **(a) Only five days to respond to any application** Except at the case management conference provided for in r.63.23(1), a respondent to an application must file and serve on all relevant parties a response within five days of the service of the application notice.[41] When an application is to be resolved on paper, it is imperative that the applicant tells the court the date on which the application notice was served. This is necessary so that the court can know when the five-day period provided for by r.63.25(2) has expired. Unless the matter is urgent or for some other good reason, the court will generally not deal with a paper application until it can be seen that the five-day period provided for by r.63.25(2) has expired.[42]

20-24   **(b) Applications will generally be dealt with on paper, by telephone, or video conference** The court will deal with an application without a hearing unless the court considers it necessary to hold a hearing.[43] Even where the court considers that a hearing is necessary, the court will conduct a hearing by telephone or video

---

[35] See Pt 63.22(2) and 15.4(2).

[36] See Pt 63.22(3).

[37] The court is unlikely to have the resources to investigate such an issue unless it is specifically raised by either party. If the issue is so raised, the court can decide it on evidence in the same way as any other issue.

[38] Reasoned order of HHJ Hacon in *Guardian IP Ltd v Global Vessel Security Ltd*, Unreported.

[39] Pts 63.22(4) and 63.22(5) respectively.

[40] Pt 63.22(6).

[41] Pt 63.25(2).

[42] *IPEC Guide*, para.2.9.

[43] Pt 63.25(3).

conference unless it considers that a hearing in person would be more cost effective for the parties or is otherwise necessary in the interests of justice.[44]

Amendment of pleadings

There is an important distinction between applications to amend made at or before the case management conference and those made thereafter. The former are subject to the cost-benefit test set out in para.29.2 of the Pt 63PD.[45] Regarding the latter, CPR Pt 63.23(2) is engaged and "exceptional circumstances" are required: see below.   **20-25**

Security for costs

Applications for security for costs can be made in the IPEC as in the Patents Court[46] but the IPEC cost limits mean that the relevant sums are much lower. Thus where the claimant is a company, it may be more difficult to establish that "it will be unable" to pay the defendant's costs if ordered to do so;[47] and even where this requirement is met, the sum actually ordered by way of security will be reduced accordingly.   **20-26**

Costs of interim applications

Save where a party has behaved unreasonably, the court will reserve the costs of an application to the conclusion of the trial when they will be subject to summary assessment.[48] Where a party has behaved unreasonably, the court may make an order for costs at the conclusion of the hearing,[49] and any costs so awarded are in addition to the *total* costs that may be awarded to that party under r.45.31 (see below).[50] However, costs awarded against an unreasonable party are still subject to the *stage* caps on costs set out in Tables A and B.[51] Where the court makes a summary assessment of costs, it will do so in accordance with Section IV of Pt 45.[52]   **20-27**

Preliminary non-binding opinion on the merits

If both parties wish the court to do so, e.g. if it is likely to assist the parties in reaching a settlement, the IPEC is willing to express a preliminary and non-binding opinion on the merits of the case.[53] This does not prevent the matter going to trial if the action does not settle in the meantime.[54]   **20-28**

---

[44] Pt 63PD para.30.1.
[45] *Temple Island v New English Teas* [2012] EWPCC 1.
[46] Pt 25.12.
[47] Pt 25.13(2)(c).
[48] Pt 63.26(1).
[49] Pt 63.26(2).
[50] Pt 45.32.
[51] *Kemel Akhtar v Bhopal Productions (UK) Limited* [2015] EWHC 154 (IPEC), [32].
[52] Pt 63.26(3).
[53] See *Weight Watchers v Love Bites* [2012] EWPCC 12 and *Fayus v Flying Trade* [2012] EWPCC 43. Since those cases were decided the CPR has been amended to make clear that Early Neutral Evaluation can be conducted in all courts in which the CPR applies (r.3.1(2)(m)).
[54] As happened in *Bocacina Ltd v Boca Cafes*. HHJ Birss QC (as he then was) gave a preliminary non-binding opinion in favour of the claimant (not reported). The defendant did change its name but the

Case Management Conference

20-29   The case management conference ("CMC") in the IPEC is conducted by a judge (who may be a deputy judge). The purpose of the CMC is to manage the conduct of the case in order to bring the proceedings to a trial in a manner proportionate to the nature of the dispute, the financial position of the parties, the degree of complexity of the case, the importance of the case and the amount of money at stake.[55] Its timing is determined by Pt 63PD paras 5.3–5.7: in essence, the claimant should apply for a CMC within the 14 days following service of the defence. If the claimant fails to apply in that time, then another party may do so or the court will act of its own accord to appoint a CMC.

20-30   At the first CMC, the court will identify the issues and decide whether to make orders under para.29.1 of PD 63. These include orders permitting the filing of further material in the case such as witness statements, experts' reports, disclosure and orders permitting cross-examination at trial and skeleton arguments. The court will only do so in relation to specific and identified issues;[56] and if the court is satisfied that the benefit of the further material in terms of its value in resolving those issues appears likely to justify the cost of producing and dealing with it.[57] The fact that there is no automatic right in the IPEC to, e.g. witness statements, disclosure, and even skeleton arguments often comes as a surprise to first-time users of the court.

20-31   Certain specific issues come up regularly in patent cases and the IPEC has issued guidance accordingly.[58] In particular, the patentee may be required to rely on no more than three independently valid claims; and a party challenging validity may be required to rely on no more than three items of prior art. The reference to prior art includes all starting points for the obviousness analysis. In other words it does not encompass a party's general reliance on common general knowledge as part of its case on obviousness but it does include an argument of obviousness over common general knowledge alone. Evidence over and above the material in the statement of case may well only be required in relation to common general knowledge and obviousness. In general, if expert evidence is required, it may be possible for that evidence to be given by "in house" experts.

20-32   The trial date will be fixed at the CMC. In order to fix a date the parties and/or their legal representatives will be expected to attend the CMC with dates of all relevant persons' availability including their own and that of any witnesses. Although the CMC, like any other IPEC application, may be dealt with without a hearing[59] the need to fix a trial date means that in practice many CMCs are most efficiently dealt with in open court. Moreover as part of the IPEC's active approach to case management, it is not uncommon for the court to review the proposed directions even where the parties consent and this is often conveniently done at an oral hearing.

20-33   The IPEC does not operate a docketing system but the judge hearing the CMC

---

parties were unable to settle. The trial was then heard by a different judge, Daniel Alexander QC, and is reported at [2013] EWHC 3090 (IPEC). The claimant won but only recovered about 50% of its costs having regard to the defendant's settlement offer: see [2014] EWHC 26 (IPEC).

[55]   IPEC Guide, para.2.6.
[56]   PD63 para.29.2(1).
[57]   PD63 para.29.2(2).
[58]   *IPC Guide*, para.2.6(e).
[59]   Pt 63.25(3).

is much more likely to hear the trial than the equivalent Patents Court judge. This is because whilst both courts can call on deputies, there is at present only one permanent IPEC judge (HHJ Hacon) whilst there are 10 permanent Patents Court judges.[60]

It is important to note that save in exceptional circumstances the court will not permit a party to submit material in addition to that ordered at the first case management conference.[61] As the wording suggests, the test of "exceptional circumstances" is intended to operate as a substantial hurdle.[62]   **20-34**

However, r.63.23(2) is not engaged where the order made at the case management conference expressly permits subsequent applications. For instance, the court may refuse permission for reply evidence at the case management conference but allow the parties to make a subsequent application for the same. The advantage of this course is that it encourages the parties to consider whether they really need reply evidence, and if so on what topics, and the court retains control over the admission of such evidence.   **20-35**

5. TRIAL

The timetable for trial will already have been set at the CMC (e.g. by allocating one day or two days overall) but the parties are usually required to submit a more detailed estimate (i.e. proposing times for opening speeches, cross-examination, and closing submissions) shortly in advance of the hearing. The court will consider the parties' estimates and allocate time accordingly. So far as appropriate, the court will allocate equal time to the parties.   **20-36**

In an appropriate case and if the parties consent, the IPEC is able and willing to conduct a trial entirely on paper.[63]   **20-37**

6. COSTS

Applicable rules

Costs are always assessed summarily.[64] They are always awarded on the scale set out in Pt 45, Section IV[65] save where: (a) the court considers that a party has behaved in a manner which amounts to an abuse of the court's process, or (b) the claim concerns the infringement or revocation of a patent or registered design or registered trade mark the validity of which has been certified by a court or by the   **20-38**

---

[60] Currently Arnold J, Birss J, Carr J, Mann J, Warren J, Morgan J, Norris J, Roth J, Rose J, Nugee J.
[61] Pt 63.23(2).
[62] *Redd Solicitors LLP v Red Legal Ltd* [2012] EWPCC 50, [16]. The test was satisfied in *BODO Sperlein v Sabichi* [2015] EWHC 1242, IPEC, a copyright case; in *Gama Healthcare v Pal International*, 24 July 2015, Unreported, a passing off case; and in *T&A Textiles & Hosiery v Hala Textile UK Ltd* [2015] EWHC 2888 (IPEC), a copyright case.
[63] As was done in *Hoffmann v Drug Abuse Resistance Education (UK) Ltd* [2012] EWPCC 2.
[64] Pt 63.26(1).
[65] Pt 45.30(1). See also Pt 45.30(3).

Comptroller-General of Patents, Designs and Trade Marks in earlier proceedings.[66]
There are no costs budgets in IPEC.[67]

20-39   The rules state that save in the two specific cases mentioned above, the court will not order a party to pay total costs of more than £50,000 on the final determination of a claim in relation to liability and £25,000 on an inquiry as to damages or account of profits.[68] These figures apply after any set off has been applied.[69]

20-40   The maximum amount of scale costs that the court will award for each stage of the claim is set out in PD 45.[70] Table A sets out the scale costs for each stage of a claim up to determination of liability. Table B sets out the scale costs for each stage of an inquiry as to damages or account of profits. Court fees, costs relating to the enforcement of any court order and wasted costs may be recovered in addition to the amount of these scale costs,[71] as may VAT.[72]

20-41   Case law has made only very limited inroads into these prima facie clear provisions. In *Henderson v All Around the World Recordings*, HHJ Birss QC (as he then was) accepted that the overall discretion given to the court in relation to costs by CPR Pt 44.3 also applied in the PCC, but said that "to exercise it to depart from the cap in anything other than a truly exceptional case would undermine the point of the costs capping system".[73] The hurdle of "truly exceptional" is a high one since in *Brundle v Perry*[74] it was held that forging a letter from the trial judge, which purported to reverse the court's decision and make a large financial award to the losing party, did not satisfy this criterion.

20-42   For cases which have been transferred to the IPEC from elsewhere, either the County Court or another part of the High Court, the IPEC will deal with costs incurred in proceedings before transfer on a case by case basis. Costs incurred in the High Court before transfer are usually dealt with by being summarily assessed as High Court costs.[75]

Assessment procedure

20-43   The starting point is the same as adopted in Patents Court cases: i.e. identify the overall winner;[76] consider whether there are issues on which the winner should be deprived of its costs; finally (and exceptionally) consider whether there are issues

---

[66] Pt 45.30(2). The latter exception has the prima facie surprising result that the caps are disapplied in a second action on the same patent, assuming its validity has been certified in the first action, even where the second action involves completely different infringements and no challenge to validity is made.
[67] Pt 3.12(1)(c).
[68] Pt 45.31(1)(a), (b).
[69] Pt 44.31(2), 44.12(a).
[70] Pt 45.31(3) and 45PD paras 3.1–3.3 as revised by CPR Update 66, para.24, with effect from 1 October 2013. The caps prior to CPR Update 66 were slightly lower (see *White Book* 2013, Vol 1, para.45PD.11) and still apply to cases which were commenced in the PCC prior to 1 October 2013 and are continued in the IPEC (see CPR Update 66 at para.25). See *Phonographic Performance Limited v Hamilton Entertainment Limited & Hamilton (No.2)* [2013] EWHC 3801 (IPEC).
[71] Pt 45.31(4A), introduced by SI 2013/1974.
[72] Pt 45.31(5).
[73] [2013] EWPCC 19. See also *Brundle v Perry* [2014] EWHC 979 (IPEC), *Akhtar v Bhopal Productions (UK) Ltd* [2015] EWHC 154 (IPEC).
[74] [2014] EWHC 979 (IPEC). The court held that the letter in question was an example of "intemperate and eccentric behaviour", not a deliberate attempt to influence others: see ibid at [14]. Hence it was "strikingly unusual" but not "truly exceptional": see [17].
[75] *Westwood v Knight* [2011] EWPCC 11.
[76] Which is not always clear. See *Roache v New Group Newspapers* [1998] E.M.L.R. 161, 168 as cited

where the winner should actually pay the loser's costs of these issues.[77] However, as noted in *BOS GmbH v Cobra UK Automotive Products*[78] this requires modification given the existence of scale costs. In particular the IPEC will:

(a) start with a party's actual costs for each stage[79];
(b) perform a summary assessment on the normal IPEC basis;
(c) apply any issue-based discount to the summarily assessed figure; and
(d) compare the resultant figure to the scale figure, and take the lower of the two.

In *Westwood*[80] the court had to consider whether a party could recover (i) pre-action costs, and (ii) costs of considering the other party's statements of case. The court held in relation to both points that there was no need to take too narrow a view of the stages in Table A. For instance, if work done pre-action could properly be regarded as part of the defence and counterclaim (or, it is submitted by analogy, the Particulars of Claim) then such costs were potentially recoverable under that stage. Similarly, it was legitimate in principle to include the costs of considering the statement of case of the other side, although it did not follow that such costs would in fact be recoverable in every case.[81] For instance, the court doubted that it would normally be appropriate for a defendant to claim costs for dealing with the Particulars of Claim and then costs for preparing a defence: see *Westwood v Knight*. Similarly it is submitted that it would not normally be appropriate for a defendant to claim its own pre-action costs under the stage dealing with the Particulars of Claim. **20-44**

Multiple parties

The court will not order a party to pay total costs of more than the capped sum (i.e. £50, 000 for liability), even where multiple separately represented parties are involved.[82] As pointed out in *Gimex*, one can envisage difficult situations: e.g. where two sets of defendants run very different defences, and/or one set of defendants wins but the other set loses. It was recommended that such matters should be raised at the case management conference. **20-45**

Combined trial on liability and quantum

Where a case is conducted as a single proceeding, with one set of statements of case, one case management conference, one set of witness statements and one trial then only one cap should apply. Where liability and quantum were heard together, **20-46**

---

in *Wilkinson v London Strategic Health Authority* [2012] EWPCC 55, at [5].

[77] *MMI Research v Cellxion* [2012] EWCA Civ 139.

[78] [2012] EWPCC 44, [28]–[34].

[79] i.e. as per Table A (for liability) or Table B (for damages/profits), as the case may be. Costs schedules which are not prepared strictly in accordance with these tables are of little assistance to the court and may be ignored.

[80] *Westwood v Knight* [2011] EWPCC 11.

[81] Thus a claimant can in principle claim for the costs of both the Particulars of Claim and defence, provided costs were genuinely incurred on both issues, and so can a defendant.

[82] *Gimex v The Chill bag Company Ltd* [2012] EW PCC 34 and *Liversidge v Owen Mumford (costs)* [2012] EWPCC 40. In *Gimex* the claimant won against different sets of defendants, whereas in *Liversidge* the different sets of defendants won. The *Liversidge* defendants agreed between themselves how the £50 000 should apportioned: see *Gimex v The Chill bag Company Ltd* [2012] EW PCC 34, at [18].

the liability cap was applied.[83] Again it was recommended that any party wishing to object to such a course should raise the matter at the case management conference.

7. APPEAL

20-47   If a party wishes to appeal, permission is generally required. Permission may be sought from the judge making the order or from the court to which the appeal is addressed. Depending on the nature of the order being appealed, the destination of an appeal from the multi-track in the IPEC is either the Court of Appeal or the High Court.[84] It is not always appreciated that final orders are appealed to the Court of Appeal whereas interim orders are appealed to the High Court (Chancery Division). This arises by virtue of r.63.19(1A) which provides that for the purposes of PD 52A, a decision of the enterprise judge shall be treated as a decision by a circuit judge hearing a specialist claim in the County Court.[85]

20-48   Paragraphs 3.6 to 3.8 of PD 52A explain the difference between a final order and an interim order. This is not always obvious: e.g. summary judgment and striking out are both treated as interim decisions.[86]

20-49   When permission is sought from the judge making the order at the hearing at which it was made, the order must expressly identify four things:[87]

(1)   whether or not the judgment or order is final;
(2)   whether an appeal lies, and if so the route of appeal;
(3)   whether permission is given to appeal; and
(4)   if permission is refused, the court to which the applicant should address any further application for permission.

---

[83]   *Azzurri Communications v International Telecommunications Equipment t/a SOS Communications* [2013] EWPCC 22.
[84]   See *IPEC Guide*, para.1.8. Appeals from the IPEC small claims track are to the Enterprise Judge in the IPEC: see *Azzurri Communications v International Telecommunications Equipment t/a SOS Communications* [2013] EWPCC 22 and Pt 63.19(3).
[85]   See also Table I to PD 52A.
[86]   52A PD para.3.8(2).
[87]   r.40.2(4) CPR.

CHAPTER 21

REMEDIES FOR INFRINGEMENT

CONTENTS

1. INTRODUCTION

The remedies sought or granted in an action for infringement may consist of: an **21-01** injunction; a damages inquiry or (at the option of the claimant) an account of profits; delivery up or destruction of all infringing articles in the possession or power of the defendant; and/or an order that the unsuccessful party disseminate the result of the action at its own expense.[1] There is no discrete cause of action for unjust enrichment outside the scope of the Patents Act 1977.[2] That Act sets out the heads of relief available but regard must also be had to the corresponding European Directive: Directive 2004/48/EC of the European Parliament and of the Council of 29 April 2004 on the enforcement of intellectual property rights ("the IP Enforcement Directive") was transposed in the United Kingdom by the Intellectual Property (Enforcement, etc.) Regulations 2006, which came into force on 29 April 2006.

2. INJUNCTION

Injunction based on threat to infringe

The justification for an injunction arises from the threat, actual or implied, that **21-02** a party is about to act to violate the claimant's rights. Before granting an injunction, therefore, it must be clear that the claimant actually has such rights, and that the defendant has done something which induces the court to believe that they are about to infringe those rights.

The fact that he has been guilty of an infringement of the patent rights will, in **21-03** most circumstances, be sufficient evidence that they intend to continue their infringement. Whether they have actually infringed the patent or not, though, it will suffice if they have threatened to infringe it. Actual past infringement is merely evidence upon which the court infers an intention to continue to infringe.

This has been the law since the nineteenth century and for example in *Frearson* **21-04**

---

[1] PA 1977 s.61. See also TRIPs arts 41–49.
[2] *Union Carbide v B.P. Chemicals* [1998] F.S.R. 1.

v Loe,[3] Sir George Jessel MR said:

"I am not aware of any suit or action in the Court of Chancery which has been successful on the part of a patentee, without infringement having been proved; but in my opinion, on principle there is no reason why a patentee should not succeed in obtaining an injunction without proving actual infringement. I think, for this reason, where the defendant alleges an intention to infringe, and claims the right to infringe, the mischief done by the threatened infringement of the patent is very great, and I see no reason why a patentee should not be entitled to the same protection as every other person is entitled to claim from the court from threatened injury, where that threatened injury will be very serious. No part of the jurisdiction of the old Court of Chancery was considered more valuable than that exercise of jurisdiction which prevented material injury being inflicted, and no subject was more frequently the cause of bills for injunction than the class of cases which were brought to restrain threatened injury, as distinguished from injury which was already accomplished. It seems to me, when you consider the nature of a patent right, that where there is a deliberate intention expressed, and about to be carried into execution, to infringe certain letters patent under the claim of a right to use the invention patented, the plaintiff is entitled to come to this court to restrain that threatened injury. Of course, it must be plain that what is threatened to be done is an infringement."

21-05   In July 2000 in *Cofiexip S.A. v Stolt Comex Seaway MS Ltd*[4] Aldous LJ said:

"Section 61 of the Patents Act 1977 provides for "a claim for an injunction restraining the defendant … from any apprehended acts of infringement". In doing so the section accords with the general law prior to the passing of the Act. An injunction is a remedy against further injury and the court will not make the order if satisfied that no such injury is likely to occur. It is not because the defendant has done a wrong that an injunction will be granted against him. Where a patentee has conclusively established the validity of his patent and that it had been infringed, as a general rule an injunction will be granted. However that will not happen as a matter of course as an injunction is a discretionary remedy. It is for that reason that there have been cases where injunctions have been refused, for example, where the defendant satisfied the court that further infringement was not likely."[5]

Actual infringement is evidence of intention to continue

21-06   The actual infringement of the patent is taken by the court to imply an intention to continue the infringement, notwithstanding any promises not to do so. An injunction will be granted unless it is very clear that there is in fact no intention to continue infringing. For example, Shadwell VC in *Losh v Hague*[6] said:

"If a threat had been issued, and the defendant revokes the threat, that I can understand as making the plaintiff satisfied; but if once the thing complained of has been done, I apprehend this court interferes, notwithstanding any promise the defendant may make not to do the same thing again."[7]

Evidence of acts after action brought

21-07   Evidence of acts committed after an action has been brought may be deployed in order to show that the claimant was right in their allegation that, at the date the action was brought, the defendant was threatening and intending to infringe—see Romer J in *Shoe Machinery Co Ltd v Cutlan*.[8]

Mere possession is not necessarily a threat to use

21-08   Possession of an infringing machine may give rise to a presumption of a threat to use a machine. However, the presumption may be rebutted by evidence and if

---

3   (1878) 9 Ch D. 48, 65. See also *Dowling v Billington* (1890) 7 R.P.C. 191.
4   [2001] R.P.C. 9, [13].
5   As to this last point, see para.21–10.
6   (1838) 1 W.P.C. 200.
7   See also *Geary v Norton* (1846) 1 De G. & Sm. 9.
8   (1895) 12 R.P.C. 342, 358.

the court accepts that there is in fact no threat to infringe then no injunction will be granted.[9]

In the case of *Adair v Young*[10] the defendant was the captain of a ship which was fitted with certain pumps which were an infringement of the claimant's patent. No act of using the pumps was proved; but it was shown that the ship was not supplied with other pumps. It was held that the possession of the pumps under such circumstances, although not of itself amounting to an infringement, was evidence upon which the court would infer that the defendant intended to use the pumps should occasion require. And the court—Brett and Cotton LJJ (James LJ dissenting)—granted an injunction.

21-09

Situation where the defendant no longer intends to infringe

As pointed out by Aldous LJ in *Cofiexip S.A. v Stolt Comex Seaway MS Ltd*,[11] injunctions have been refused where the defendant has satisfied the court that further infringements were not likely.

21-10

For example, in *Proctor v Bayley & Son*,[12] the infringement complained of took place six years before the trial of the action. It was proved that the machines were used only for a few months, after which they were abandoned as unsatisfactory. It was held by the Court of Appeal, reversing the decision of Bristowe VC that it was clear that the defendants had no intention whatever of continuing the wrongful act, and consequently that it was not a proper case in which an injunction should be granted. Cotton LJ in his judgment said[13]:

21-11

> "There is no doubt that it was a good patent, and we must also take it that the defendants have infringed; but the point is this: Is there any ground here which would justify the court in exercising the extraordinary jurisdiction of the Court of Chancery in granting an injunction? That, I think, has been a good deal lost sight of in the argument. It is not because a man has done a wrong that an injunction will be granted against him. If a man has done a wrong which will not be continued, at common law damages may be obtained for the wrong done, which the common law says is sufficient indemnity for that wrong; but then the Court of Chancery says this, in the exercise of its extraordinary jurisdiction: We will not be satisfied with that; we will grant an injunction, because a wrongful act has been done, in order to prevent that wrongful act; and they grant an injunction where a wrongful act has been done, and the court is satisfied of the probability of the continuance of the wrongful act ... But here, although the defendants did infringe the plaintiff's patent, we must consider all the circumstances of the case in order to guide us in the consideration of this: Ought the court to draw the inference that there will be a continuance of the wrongful act so as to justify the court in granting the extraordinary interference and the protection which is exercised by the court of equity?"[14]

Similarly in the more recent case of *Landor v Hawa International v Azure Designs*,[15] Neuberger LJ said:

21-12

> "It seems to me plainly inappropriate in principle to grant an injunction in favour of a claimant against a defendant who clearly and unequivocally agreed, before the action for the injunction was even started, to refrain from taking that very action which the injunction would have forbidden him from taking."

---

[9] *British United Shoe Machinery Co Ltd v Simon Collier Ltd* (1908) 25 R.P.C. 567.
[10] (1879) 12 Ch D. 13.
[11] [2001] R.P.C. 9, [13]. See also para.21–41.
[12] (1889) 42 Ch D. 390; (1889) 6 R.P.C. 538.
[13] At 541.
[14] See also *Hudson v Chatteris Engineering Co* (1898) 15 R.P.C. 438; *Wilderman v E.W. Berk & Co Ltd* (1925) 42 R.P.C. 79, at 90; (1925) 1 Ch. 116.
[15] [2007] F.S.R. 9, [46]. See also the review of the law in this area in *Cantor Gaming Ltd v Gameaccount Global Ltd* [2008] F.S.R. 4, a copyright case.

21-13   In that case, the defendant had initially offered an unequivocal undertaking before the action was commenced but the undertaking was withdrawn in terms which made it clear that the defendant was again threatening to infringe the claimant's rights. An injunction was held by a unanimous Court of Appeal to have been rightly granted at trial.

21-14   There are more complex cases in which, although the defendant may have clearly and unequivocally agreed before the trial not to do the acts which the injunction would forbid them from doing, it may nonetheless be appropriate to grant an injunction so that the assurances given by the defendant are backed by court sanction. In *British Telecommunications Plc v Nextcall Telecom Plc*[16] the defendant gave contractual undertakings which it did not fully honour. The claimant sought an injunction in unqualified form to enforce the undertaking but the defendant sought to resist the injunction on the basis that it was impossible to guarantee compliance with the injunction because of rogue employees. Jacob J granted the injunction in unqualified form observing that the court was "only enforcing by injunction precisely what the defendants undertook not to do by contract." Jacob J also pointed out that it did not follow from the absence of qualification of the injunction that the claimant would sensibly bring proceedings for contempt of court for the slightest breach. He said:

> "If [they] were nonetheless so to proceed, then if the defendants had truly taken all reasonable precautions to prevent a breach, it is most unlikely that they would be punished. There may well be no order as to costs ... or even an order for costs against [the claimant] if the court thought the application pointless. All would depend on the circumstances."

Infringer refuses to confirm its intentions

21-15   In *Merck Sharp & Dohme Corp & Bristol-Myers Squibb Pharmaceuticals Ltd v Teva Pharma BV & Teva UK Ltd*,[17] Merck was the proprietor of an SPC covering the anti-HIV drug, efavirenz. BMS was the exclusive licensee of the SPC. Teva obtained regulatory approval for a generic efavirenz product before the expiry of the SPC. Accordingly, the claimants wrote to Teva seeking confirmation that they would not market such a product before the SPC's expiry. Teva refused to give such confirmation, saying that its plans were confidential. BMS sought and was granted an interim injunction against Teva on the basis that its refusal to provide that confirmation amounted to a threat to infringe.[18]

21-16   Following a trial, Teva was enjoined permanently (throughout the life of the SPC), quia timet. Having assessed the law in relation to final injunctions made on a quia timet basis, the judge said (at [56]) that:

> "The principle I derive from these authorities is that the question the court is asking in every case is whether, viewed in all the relevant circumstances, there was a sufficiently strong probability that an injunction would be required to prevent the harm to the claimant to justify bringing the proceedings. In adding the word sufficiently to the word strong I do not mean to put a gloss on the words of Chadwick LJ, rather I am seeking to encapsulate the idea that the degree of probability required will vary from case to case depending on all the circumstances but that mere possibilities are never enough. To justify coming to court requires there to be a concrete, strong and tangible risk that an injunction is required in order to do justice in all the circumstances."

21-17   Teva's prior conduct in another recent case was a further factor taken into ac-

---

[16] [2000] F.S.R. 679.
[17] [2013] EWHC 1958 (Pat), [2014] F.S.R. 3.
[18] [2012] EWHC 627 (Pat).

count by the court. The judge held that on the evidence Teva was "demonstrably prepared to launch products without notice and at risk of infringing an originator's patent if it chooses to do so." Assessing all the relevant factors he had identified in the judgment, the judge awarded the injunction sought by Merck/BMS.

Differences in the nature of the infringements

Over the course of proceedings there are often changes in the nature of the **21-18** product or process which a defendant uses or intends to use. The proper course for a claimant who is aware of the change and who maintains that the defendant still infringes is to amend promptly to allege infringement by the new subject matter. In *Shoe Machinery Co Ltd v Cutlan*[19] such a change emerged during the trial in a situation in which the originally pleaded machines were admitted not to infringe but the patentee wished to contend that the defendant's new machine did infringe. Romer J ultimately refused to grant an injunction against the new machine in the action as constituted, finding that the patentee ought to have applied to amend to bring the matter before the court. He said:

"... if an action, as originally brought by a plaintiff patentee, [concerns past infringements], but he finds that the defendant has, since action brought, infringed in a way substantially different from his former infringements, leave would be given by the court to the plaintiff in a proper case, and on proper terms, to amend his action, and to bring these subsequent infringements before the court to be dealt with once and for all with the prior infringements."

Considered from the perspective of the defendant, if they wish to contend that **21-19** the new product or process does not infringe, they would be well advised to raise the matter during the proceedings. That is because the normal form of injunction is wide enough to restrain any infringement, not only the particular product or process in issue—see *Cofiexip S.A. v Stolt Comex Seaway MS Ltd*[20] below. In the same vein in *3M v Rennicks*,[21] Aldous J said:

"As to whether there should be an injunction, the defendants have not pleaded a positive case that their process has changed. In those circumstances, there being continued marketing of this similar material, an injunction will follow unless the defendants plead and prove some material difference. The injunction would be to restrain infringement and therefore the defendants will incur difficulty whether their new product does infringe the patent."

Springboard injunctions

In *Smith & Nephew v Convatec (No. 2)*, S&N's commercial process was found **21-20** not to infringe Convatec's patent. However, the court also considered a series of work-up experiments that had been carried out in order to achieve regulatory approval; a number of these did infringe. So working the S&N commercial process was not an infringement, although it was said by Convatec to have relied upon one. Convatec sought a "springboard" injunction to stop S&N from working its process.

The Patents Court reviewed the law in relation to springboard relief. The judge **21-21** held that in a proper case the court can make an order for springboard relief and that such relief would then fall within art.3 of the IP Enforcement Directive. The judge identified the following factors to be considered when considering an award of

---

[19] (1895) 12 R.P.C. 342, 358.
[20] [2001] R.P.C. 9.
[21] Unreported, 1 October 1990.

springboard relief:

(i)   Caution is required before a final injunction is granted restraining an otherwise lawful activity. Nevertheless in a proper case it will be.

(ii)   The nature of any unwarranted advantage relied on should be identified. The precise relationship between the unlawful activity in the past and the later acts which are said to exploit that unwarranted advantage needs to be considered.

(iii)   If an injunction is to be granted it must be in an appropriate form and for a duration which is commensurate with the unwarranted advantage relied on.

(iv)   The court must be particularly careful not to put the claimant in a better position than it would be if there had been no infringement at all, especially if otherwise lawful competitive activity will be restrained.

(v)   In considering what relief to grant, the availability of other remedies apart from an injunction needs to be taken into account, not only damages but, as in *Vestergaard*, the availability of an account of profits should be considered too.

21-22   The Court of Appeal reversed the judge's judgment on infringement, so that the prospect of springboard relief did not remain in issue. Accordingly, the judgment of the Patents Court in relation to the principles governing springboard relief is not of binding effect, although it is submitted that the principles collected by the judge and quoted above, remain an informative guide to the relevant law.

Importation

21-23   In *Thetford v Fiamma*[22] the European Court of Justice, observing that the right of a proprietor to prevent importation of products manufactured under a compulsory licence abroad is part of the substance of patent law,[23] held that a proprietor of a patent was entitled to an injunction to prevent importation of products manufactured by a third party in a country where a corresponding patent had never subsisted.

Acquiescence and delay

21-24   Positive acquiescence will bar the right of the patentee to an injunction if it amounts to a representation to the defendant that they are free to do what would otherwise be an infringement.[24] Thus, if a defendant constructed machinery, for instance, in ignorance of the existence of the claimant's patent, and the claimant, aware of such ignorance, lay by in silence and later attempted to obtain an injunction, such relief would probably be refused.[25] Otherwise, however, laches, while a bar to the obtaining of an interlocutory order, would not bar the right to a perpetual injunction as "there must be more than mere delay to disentitle a man to his legal rights".[26]

---

[22]   [1989] F.S.R. 57. See also *Parke Davis v Probel* (24/67) [1968] C.M.L.R. 47.

[23]   *Pharmon v Hoechst* (19/84) [1985] E.C.R. 2281, [1985] 3 C.M.L.R. 775.

[24]   *Proctor v Bennis* (1887) 4 R.P.C. 333 at 356; (1887) 36 Ch D. 740.

[25]   *Proctor v Bennis* (1887) 4 R.P.C. 333 at 356; (1887) 36 Ch D. 740. See *Electrolux Ltd v Electrix Ltd* (1954) 71 R.P.C. 23.

[26]   *Van der Lely (C.) N.V. v Bamfords* [1964] R.P.C. 54, 81, per Harman LJ, citing *Fullwood v Fullwood* (1878) 9 Ch D. 176.

Stay of injunction

Where the immediate operation of an injunction would cause great public **21-25** inconvenience, such operation may be suspended for a time to minimise such inconvenience. Thus in *Hopkinson v St James and Pall Mall Electric Light Co Ltd*,[27] the injunction was suspended for six months on account of the exceptional public inconvenience which would be caused by suddenly stopping the use of the three-wire electric lighting system, the defendants undertaking to keep an account in the meantime. A stay has also been granted to avoid extensive unemployment.[28]

Stay of injunction pending appeal

In the past, it has been said that the operation of an injunction will not usually **21-26** be suspended pending an appeal.[29] However, the question of whether or not a stay should be ordered is a matter for the discretion of the court. The correct approach to exercising that discretion is to be found in the judgment of Buckley LJ in *Minnesota Mining and Manufacturing Co v Johnson & Johnson & Ltd*.[30] In recent years, it has become the practice to give to the patentee the chance of either giving a cross-undertaking as to damages to obtain an injunction or, if not given, granting a stay pending appeal. The usual order where a stay is granted is that the injunction[31] should be stayed for such time as to enable the defendants to give notice of appeal, the stay to continue thereafter so long as the defendant prosecuted their appeal with due diligence, provided that they undertook to keep an account or in some cases paid money into a joint account.[32] It may be appropriate to stay an injunction in so far as it may affect a new product introduced pending appeal.[33]

In *Virgin Atlantic Airways Ltd v Premium Aircraft Interiors Ltd*[34] Jacob LJ **21-27** explained that in general, when an appeal to a higher court is pending, the balance of convenience approach is the correct one. But this does not apply where the national court procedure is at an end and the only outstanding issue is an EPO opposition. When there is no possibility of an appeal in the UK a permanent injunction will only be withheld if its effect is "grossly disproportionate" to the right protected.[35]

---

27 (1893) 10 R.P.C. 46, 62.
28 See, e.g. *Leeds Forge Co Ltd v Deighton's Patent Flue and Tube Co Ltd* (1901) 18 R.P.C. 233, at 240; *British Thomson-Houston Co Ltd v British Insulated and Helsby Cables Ltd* (1924) 42 R.P.C. 345, at 375; and see *Bonnard v London General Omnibus Co Ltd* (1919) 36 R.P.C. 307.
29 See, e.g. *Samuel Parkes & Co Ltd v Cocker Bros Ltd* (1929) 46 R.P.C. 241.
30 [1976] R.P.C. 671, 676; see also *Minnesota Mining and Manufacturing Co v Rennicks (UK) Ltd* [1992] R.P.C. 331, at 368.
31 *Letraset Ltd v Dymo Ltd* [1976] R.P.C. 65; *Minnesota Mining & Manufacturing Co v Johnson & Johnson Ltd* [1976] R.P.C. 671; *E. Warnink B.V. v J. Townsend & Sons Ltd* [1980] R.P.C. 31.
32 *Martin v Selsdon Fountain Pen Co Ltd* (1949) 66 R.P.C. 193, 216; *Martin v H. Millwood Ltd* (1954) 71 R.P.C. 458, 472; *Rosedale Associated Manufacturers Ltd v Carlton Tyre Saving Co Ltd* [1959] R.P.C. 189, 219 and 220; *Bugges Insecticide Ltd v Herbon Ltd* [1972] R.P.C. 197; *Illinois Tool Works Inc v Autobars Co (Services) Ltd* [1974] R.P.C. 337; *Quantel v Spaceward Microsystems* [1990] R.P.C. 147.
33 *Unilever v Chefaro Proprietaries* [1994] R.P.C. 567, 593.
34 [2010] F.S.R. 15.
35 *Virgin Atlantic Airways Ltd v Premium Aircraft Interiors Ltd* [2010] F.S.R. 15. See also para.21-39.

21-28   A striking example of the application of the balance of convenience approach arose in the *Kirin-Amgen Inc v Transkaryotic Therapies Inc* litigation.[36] At trial Neuberger J found the patent valid and infringed and the patentee sought an injunction in the normal form. The defendant sought a stay pending appeal and although the parties were agreed in principle that a stay was appropriate, they did not agree on its terms. The defendant wished to continue clinical trials of its infringing product pending appeal and to use the data generated from the trials in order to obtain clinical marketing approval for its product. The patentee contended that, since the injunction if granted then and there would prevent the clinical trials altogether,[37] the proper price for the stay pending appeal was that the defendant should be placed in the position it would have been in if there was no appeal, that is to say it should be not be able to use any marketing authorisation (whether British or European) obtained relying on work done in infringement of the patent after the stay was granted. The defendant resisted the absolute prohibition and contended that the stay should be subject to further order after the appeal. In settling the terms and finding for the patentee Neuberger J applied the principle set out by Buckley LJ in *Minnesota Mining and Manufacturing* case (above) and said:

> "In other words, if possible I should arrange matters so that if the appeal is dismissed, Amgen will be in the same position as if there had been no appeal, and so that, if the appeal succeeds, TKT will be in the same position as if they had succeeded at first instance. That must be right. If the appeal fails, it would be unjust if TKT were better off or Amgen worse off, by TKT having pursued an unmeritorious appeal than if they had not appealed. Similarly, if the appeal succeeds, it would be undesirable that TKT should be worse off or Amgen better as a result of a first instance decision on invalidity and/or infringement which turned out to be wrong."

21-29   Accordingly he made an order preventing the defendant for taking advantage of any marketing authorisation obtained using data generated from infringements committed after the stay was granted.

21-30   A further issue which arose before Neuberger J was the scope of the cross-undertaking from the patentee. He held that a cross-undertaking was required in principle but it should only apply to the parts of the order which are operative during the period of the stay. In so far as any part of the order is stayed, there was no need for a cross-undertaking.

21-31   In *HTC Corp v Nokia Corp*,[38] the Patents Court had previously held that the defendant's patent was valid and infringed by various models of the claimant's mobile telephones. The judge awarded final injunctive relief in general terms, finding that a successful claimant for infringement was prima facie entitled to an injunction to restrain infringements, save in special circumstances. The criteria to be applied when deciding whether or not to grant a final injunction were, the judge found, those provided by art.3(2) of the IP Enforcement Directive, namely efficacy, proportionality, dissuasiveness, the avoidance of creating barriers to legitimate trade and the provision of safeguards against abuse.

21-32   The judge stayed the injunction in relation to the claimant's principal mobile telephone handset product, finding that the potential harm to HTC outweighed that to the patentee since (among other factors) that product had been on the market for a considerable time. However, he refused to stay the injunction in relation to HTC's

---

[36] [2005] F.S.R. 44.

[37] It was common ground that the issue of the experimental use exception under s.60(5) (b) would be decided at a later date.

[38] [2013] EWHC 3778 (Pat), [2014] R.P.C. 30.

other model of handset, in light of the relatively recent launch of that handset, and the fact that HTC was aware of the commencement of infringement proceedings when it was designed and launched.

A little over a week later, the Court of Appeal reversed the judge's refusal of the **21-33** stay, finding that the injunctive relief in its entirety ought to be stayed pending appeal. It found that the judge's treatment of the two models of handset had been inconsistent and that the proper focus of the assessment should have been the economic consequences to each party of injunctive relief or its refusal. The injunctive relief was therefore stayed pending appeal.

In *Adaptive Spectrum and Signal Alignment Inc v British Telecommunications* **21-34** *plc*,[39] the Court of Appeal heard a dispute about the correct form of final order following its finding that the claimant's patent was infringed. BT, the defendant, sought a short stay (of approximately two weeks) to render its systems non-infringing; ASSIA, the successful claimant, was prepared to agree to such a stay only in return for a weekly payment of damages, to take the place of the injunction to which they would otherwise be entitled. The Court of Appeal was "narrowly persuaded" to order a stay of the injunction, on terms. The fact that ASSIA's principal interest was in financial relief, since its business lay in licensing its invention, appears to have weighed heavily in this assessment.[40]

BT was ordered to pay a 10 per cent effective royalty rate but subject to its be- **21-35** ing made clear that such payments amounted to a periodic interim payment on account of damages, and that ASSIA would be liable to repay such damages in the event they became overcompensated.[41]

In *ASSIA*, BT sought a cross-undertaking in damages relating to the final **21-36** injunction. It was sought to account for the possibility of the patent in suit being revoked by the European Patent Office. The Court of Appeal refused the cross-undertaking, holding that the purpose of such a cross-undertaking was to protect against a judgment later shown to be wrong, which an EPO revocation could not establish.

Lifting of injunction

An injunction will not normally be lifted nor will a defendant be relieved from **21-37** an enquiry as to damages where a patent is revoked at the subsequent application of some other person.[42] However, the defendants' acts cease to be infringing by reason of the revocation of the patent in respect of which the injunction is granted.[43] It is likely that this would apply also to European patents found valid and infringed in the UK, but subsequently revoked in the EPO on a successful opposition.

---

[39] [2014] EWCA Civ 1513.
[40] [2014] EWCA Civ 1513, [4].
[41] [2014] EWCA Civ 1513. [7].
[42] *Poulton v Adjustable Cover & Boiler Block Co* (1908) 25 R.P.C. 529; *Cofiexip SA v Stolt Offshore MS Ltd (No.2)* [2004] F.S.R. 7 (Jacob J), [18]–[19], [2004] F.S.R. 34, CA. *Unilin Beheer BV v Berry Floor NV* [2007] F.S.R. 25; An attempt to challenge this rule by appeal to the Supreme Court was refused in *Virgin Atlantic v Premium Aircraft Interiors* [2010] F.S.R. 15.
[43] *Poulton v Adjustable Cover & Boiler Block Co* (1908) 25 R.P.C. 529; *Cofiexip SA v Stolt Offshore MS Ltd (No.2)* [2004] F.S.R. 7 (Jacob J), [2004] F.S.R. 34, CA; *Virgin Atlantic v Premium Aircraft Interiors* [2010] F.S.R. 15, [8].

21-38   An injunction was lifted where a change in the law meant that an injunction was no longer available.[44]

Refusal of injunction as a matter of discretion

21-39   Even if the patent is held valid and infringed and there is a clear threat to infringe, the court retains a discretion to refuse an injunction and award damages in lieu.[45] Prior to the IP Enforcement Directive[46] it was thought that the existence of the compulsory licence provisions under the 1977 Act itself left little scope for the court to create its own doctrine of compulsory licences.[47] However, in *Virgin Atlantic Airways Ltd v Premium Aircraft Interiors Ltd*[48] the Court of Appeal observed that under art.3 of the IP Enforcement Directive an injunction was now not merely a discretionary remedy in the traditional sense but that it also had to be proportionate.[49] The Court approved Pumfrey J's view as expressed in *Navitaire Inc v EasyJet Airline Co Ltd (No. 4)*[50] that a permanent injunction would only be withheld if its effect is "grossly disproportionate" to the right protected.[51] However, on the facts of *Virgin Atlantic* the Court of Appeal was satisfied, just, that an imposition of the injunction in question would indeed be grossly disproportionate to the right protected.

Form of injunction

21-40   The ordinary form in which injunctions are now granted is "that the defendants, by themselves, their servants or agents be restrained from infringing Patent No. [ ]." However it is worded though, an injunction not to infringe a patent cannot be effective after the patent has ceased to be in force.[52]

21-41   In *Cofiexip v Stolt Comex Seaway*,[53] Laddie J granted an injunction in "narrow" form (i.e. worded according to the precise infringement found) rather than "wide" form (i.e. to prevent infringement generally) on the basis that the injunction in wide form, and the threat of contempt proceedings, would cause the defendant to steer well clear of the patent thus giving to the patentee a wider monopoly than the patent entitled him to. The Court of Appeal overturned this order, and granted the injunction in wide form. Aldous LJ said:

> "When deciding what is the appropriate form of injunction in a patent action, it must be borne in mind that the injunction is being granted to prevent apprehended use of the patentees' statutory monopoly, as defined in his claim. The decision as to form is taken against the background of the claim having been construed by the court as between the parties."[54]

21-42   Likewise an injunction in wide form is normally appropriate in a case where the

---

44   *Du Pont (E.I.) de Nemours & Co v Enka B.V.* [1988] R.P.C. 497.
45   *Chiron Corporation and Others v Organon Teknika Ltd (No.10)* [1995] R.P.C. 325.
46   See paras 1–39 and 1–76.
47   *Biogen Inc v Medeva Plc* [1993] R.P.C. 475.
48   [2010] F.S.R. 15.
49   See para.1–86, et seq.
50   [2006] R.P.C. 4, [104].
51   See also *Shelfer v City of London Electric Lighting Co* (1895) 1 Ch 287; *Jaggard v Sawyer* [1995] 1 W.L.R. 269. And see *Vestergaard Frandsen A/S v Bestnet European Ltd* [2010] F.S.R. 2 (a breach of confidence case).
52   *DawvEley* (1867) L.R. 3 Eq. 496, 508.
53   [1999] F.S.R. 473 (Laddie J); [2001] R.P.C. 9, CA.
54   [2001] R.P.C. 9, [18].

defendant has been found liable for contributory infringement (see *Grimme Maschinenfabrik GmbH & Co KG v Scott*[55]).

In *Saccharin Corporation v Dawson*[56] and *Saccharin Corporation v Jackson*,[57] actions were brought upon several patents. It was impossible to say which patent had been infringed but it was clear that one of them must have been. An injunction was granted in respect of all the patents for the life of the patent which would earliest expire.   **21-43**

In *Dunlop Pneumatic Tyre Co Ltd v Clifton Rubber Co Ltd*,[58] where there was another action pending on the same patent against the defendants in which another type of infringement was alleged, the injunction was in general form but the claimants undertook not to move to commit in respect of such other alleged infringement but to raise the issue in the other action.   **21-44**

Where an infringer was also a Crown contractor within the meaning of s.29 of the Patents and Designs Act 1907 (now replaced by s.55 of the 1977 Act) the injunction was granted "without prejudice to the rights of the Crown under section 29."[59]   **21-45**

Post-expiry injunction

Before the introduction of the practice of ordering delivery up to the claimant or destruction of all infringing articles in the defendant's power or possession, it was customary, where necessary, to grant an injunction to restrain the defendant from using or selling, after expiry of the patent, infringing goods manufactured during the term of the patent,[60] but such an order would not now be necessary.   **21-46**

In *Dyson Appliance Ltd v Hoover Limited (No.2)*[61] an injunction was granted for a fixed period after expiry of the patent on the ground that the defendant's wrongful activity prior to expiry meant that it would otherwise be able to secure accelerated re-entry into the market for its infringing product.[62]   **21-47**

Enforcement of injunction

A person against whom an injunction has been granted or who has given an undertaking in court is liable to be committed, should they be guilty of a breach of such injunction or undertaking, and a person aiding and abetting such a person and with knowledge of the injunction is also guilty of contempt,[63] but an application for committal, involving as it does the liberty of the subject, will require the strictest proof in its support.[64] However, there is a distinction between proof of law and proof of fact: disputed facts must be proved beyond reasonable doubt (i.e. to the criminal standard) but where the dispute is of law (e.g. construction of the patent) the civil standard of the balance of probabilities will apply.   **21-48**

---

55 [2010] EWCA Civ 1110, [134].
56 (1902) 19 R.P.C. 169.
57 (1903) 20 R.P.C. 611.
58 (1903) 20 R.P.C. 393.
59 *Commercial Solvents Corp v Synthetic Products Co Ltd* (1926) 43 R.P.C. 185, 238.
60 See *Crossley v Beverley* (1829) 1 W.P.C. 112.
61 [2001] R.P.C. 544.
62 [2001] R.P.C. 544, [44]–[51] and see also *Chappell & Co Limited v Columbia Graphophone Company* [1914] 2. Ch. 745, especially Kennedy LJ, at 754 and *Generics BV v Smith Kline & French Laboratories* [1997] R.P.C. 801, ECJ.
63 *Incandescent Gas Light Co v Sluce* (1900) 17 R.P.C. 173.
64 *Dick v Haslam* (1891) 8 R.P.C. 196.

21-49   Where an injunction was granted against a limited liability company restraining it, its servants, agents and workmen from infringing a patent, and such injunction was broken by infringement, the injunction was enforced both against the company and its directors, though the enforcement was not pushed to the extent of an order for sequestration or committal.[65] It does not appear from the report precisely how the directors were concerned in the breach, though somewhat different considerations may be applicable in such a motion for contempt from those ordinarily in the case of an action for infringement in which directors are made parties.[66]

Subsequent amendment of specification

21-50   In *Dudgeon v Thomson,*[67] the claimant had obtained an injunction. The specification was subsequently amended, and after this had been done he took proceedings to enforce the injunction. The House of Lords held that he should have brought a new action, since the new specification might be open to objection, and was not the same as the old specification.

Enforcement of undertaking

21-51   Where, in settlement of an action, a defendant offers undertakings to the court these are of identical effect to an injunction in the same terms save that the order containing the undertakings need not be served (endorsed with a penal notice) as a prerequisite to enforcement, because a party giving an undertaking is presumed to know of it. Where an undertaking is contractual in form a separate action is required to secure compliance in the event of any breach. When the undertaking is in the form not to infringe a particular patent, a defendant in an action for breach of the undertaking was held not to be entitled to raise the validity of the patent in his defence. The defendant may, however, argue that the acts complained of are different and do not fall within the claims of the patent.[68]

3. DAMAGES AND PROFITS

Damages or account of profits

21-52   Under English national law, a successful patentee is entitled to damages in respect of actual infringement of their patent, or, at their option, an account of profits. This latter remedy was abolished by the Patents and Designs Act 1919, reintroduced by Patents Act 1949 and is kept in s.61 of the 1977 Act. The two remedies are alternatives and the successful patentee cannot have both in respect of the same infringement.[69] It is also to be noted that under national law the profits,

---

[65] *Spencer v Ancoats Vale Rubber Co Ltd* (1888) 5 R.P.C. 46; see also *Lancashire Explosives Co Ltd v Roburite Explosives Co Ltd* (1896) 13 R.P.C. 429, at 441; *Hattersley & Sons Ltd v Hodgson Ltd* (1905) 22 R.P.C. 229, 239.

[66] See paras 14–171 and 19–35. See also *Multiform Displays v Whitmarley Displays Ltd (No.2)* [1956] R.P.C. 143 (reversed in the House of Lords on other grounds [1957] R.P.C. 260 and [1957] R.P.C. 401); and *Re Galvanised Tank Manufacturers Association's Agreement* [1965] 1 W.L.R. 1074.

[67] (1877) 3 App. Cas. 34. See also *PLG Research v Ardon International (No.2)* [1993] F.S.R. 698.

[68] *Heginbotham Bros Ltd v Burne* (1939) 56 R.P.C. 399; and *Van der Lely N.V. v Maulden Engineering Co (Beds) Ltd* [1984] F.S.R. 157.

[69] PA 1977 s.61(2).

or, as the case may be, losses, made by the infringer are not of any relevance in computing the damage caused to the patentee by their infringements.[70]

A patentee is entitled to disclosure from the defendant to enable them where necessary to choose between damages or profits.[71] In these circumstances it may be sufficient in the case of a patented product if the defendant supplies an affidavit setting forth the numbers of infringing devices made and/or sold, the sums received or receivable and an approximate estimate of the costs incurred, that approximate estimate to include a statement as to how the estimate was made.[72] **21-53**

The IP Enforcement Directive

Under EU law, art.13 of the IP Enforcement Directive (which has been specifi- **21-54** cally implemented in the UK by art.3 of the Intellectual Property (Enforcement, etc.) Regulations 2006)[73] provides as follows:

"1.　Member States shall ensure that the competent judicial authorities, on application of the injured party, order the infringer who knowingly, or with reasonable grounds to know, engaged in an infringing activity, to pay the rightholder damages appropriate to the actual prejudice suffered by him/her as a result of the infringement.
　　　When the judicial authorities set the damages:
　　(a)　they shall take into account all appropriate aspects, such as the negative economic consequences, including lost profits, which the injured party has suffered, any unfair profits made by the infringer and, in appropriate cases, elements other than economic factors, such as the moral prejudice caused to the rightholder by the infringement; or
　　(b)　as an alternative to (a), they may, in appropriate cases, set the damages as a lump sum on the basis of elements such as at least the amount of royalties or fees which would have been due if the infringer had requested authorisation to use the intellectual property right in question.
2.　Where the infringer did not knowingly, or with reasonable grounds know, engage in infringing activity, Member States may lay down that the judicial authorities may order the recovery of profits or the payment of damages, which may be pre-established."

Thus, at least in the case of the infringer who knowingly, or with reasonable **21-55** grounds to know, engaged in an infringing activity, "damages" under the Directive (and the UK Regulations implementing the Directive) may not be purely compensatory in that, when assessing those damages, the court must also take into account inter alia any unfair profits made by the infringer.

Terms on which an enquiry or account may be ordered

The prosecution of the enquiry or account will not normally be stayed pending **21-56** an appeal although provision may be made to secure any sums which may be found due, for example, by an undertaking by the claimants' solicitors to repay such sums, or by payment into an account in the parties' solicitors names.[74] The enquiry proceeds at the successful claimant's risk as to costs if the appeal succeeds, and/or

---

70　*United Horse Shoe and Nail Co Ltd v Stewart & Co* (1888) 5 R.P.C. 260, 267.
71　*Island Records v Tring* [1995] F.S.R. 560.
72　*Brugger v Medicaid* [1996] F.S.R. 362, 364.
73　See paras 1–39 and 1–76.
74　See *Lucas (Joseph) (Batteries) Ltd v Gaedor Ltd* [1978] R.P.C. 389; *Minnesota Mining & Manufacturing Co v Rennicks (UK) Ltd* [1992] R.P.C. 331, at 371; and *Strix v Otter Controls* [1995] R.P.C. 675.

if the EPO revokes the patent in suit during parallel opposition proceedings.[75] Since the Supreme Court's decision in *Virgin v Zodiac*,[76] if there are parallel proceedings in the EPO, an undertaking to repay may be required, possibly together with a liberty to apply.[77]

Restrictions on damages or an account

21-57   The 1977 Act contains various provisions which restrict the successful patentee's right to damages or an account of profits.

Innocent infringers

21-58   Under s.62(1) of the 1977 Act, neither damages nor an account of profits shall be awarded against a defendant who proves that at the date of the infringement they were not aware and had no reasonable ground for supposing, that the patent existed.[78] However, the marking of an article with the word "patent" or "patented" is not sufficient notice to make an infringer liable in damages unless the number of the patent accompanies such words. This special defence is not available to an infringer who has been informed of the existence of a patent application in respect of the article in question.[79]

21-59   In *Lancer Boss Ltd v Henley Forklift Co Ltd*,[80] Graham J said:

> "Clearly the onus is on the defendant to prove that he is innocent at the date of the infringement. This must mean innocent at the date of each separate infringement of which he is accused. He must prove not only that he was not aware that the relevant patent existed, but also that 'he had no reasonable ground for supposing' that such patent existed. Furthermore, the concluding words of the section make it clear that marking goods with the word 'patent' or 'patented' without the actual number of the patent is not enough to justify the court in holding against him."

21-60   It is submitted that the test which should be applied as regards "reasonable grounds for supposing" is an objective one in the sense that it involves knowledge of facts from which a reasonable man would arrive at the relevant belief. This is the test applied by Morritt J in *L.A. Gear v Hi-Tech Sportswear*[81] in the context of secondary infringement of copyright where the question is whether an infringer had "reason to believe" that an item was an infringing copy. On this basis, some of the statements of Graham J in the *Lancer Boss* case may not be applicable.

21-61   Further, it is submitted that the words of s.62(1) call for an inquiry of the defendant's state of knowledge at the date of each act of infringement so that there may be a period of time during which the defendant can establish the defence for

---

[75]   *Virgin Atlantic Airways v Premium Aircraft Interiors* [2010] F.S.R. 15.
[76]   *Virgin Atlantic Airways Ltd v Zodiac Seats UK Ltd* [2013] UKSC 46.
[77]   *IPCom GmbH v HTC Europe Co Ltd* [2013] EWCA Civ 1496 and *Koninklijke Philips v Nintendo* [2014] EWHC 3172 (Pat), Birss J (17 July 2014).
[78]   The provision has a long legislative history. Its predecessor in the 1949 Act was s.59(1). For a case on the corresponding provision in the Patents and Designs Act 1907, see *Wilderman v F.W. Berk & Co Ltd* (1925) 42 R.P.C. 79, at 90. For a more recent case regarding s.62, see *Schenck Rotec GmbH v Universal Balancing Ltd* [2012] EWHC 1920 (Pat).
[79]   *Wilbec Plastics Ltd v Wilson Dawes Ltd* [1966] R.P.C. 513. See also *First Currency Choice v Main-Line Corporate Holdings Ltd* [2008] F.S.R. 13, [92]–[94].
[80]   [1975] R.P.C. 307, 314 and 317.
[81]   [1992] F.S.R. 121. Morritt J's test was approved by the Court of Appeal in that case. See also *Linpac Mouldings Ltd v Eagleton Direct Export Ltd* [1994] F.S.R. 545; *ZYX Music GmbH v King* [1997] 2 All E.R. 129; *Pensher Security Door Co Ltd v Sunderland City Council* [2000] R.P.C. 249.

acts of infringement committed during that period and a later period (e.g. after they have been fixed with notice of the patent) during which they cannot. It was so decided by Judge Ford in *Texas Iron Work's Patent* and the decision was subsequently upheld by the Court of Appeal.[82] There are, however, statements to the contrary although it is submitted that these are no longer good law.[83]

Infringement after failure to pay renewal fee

Under s.62(2), the court or Comptroller has a discretion to refuse to award any damages in respect of infringements committed during the further period specified in s.25(4) of the 1977 Act but prior to the date on which the renewal fee and additional fee are paid.[84] As well as an award of damages, the discretion also extends to refusing to make "any such order" which, it is submitted, is a reference back to the order for an account of profits mentioned in s.62(1).

21-62

Infringement before amendment of patent

As originally enacted, s.62(3) of the 1977 Act provided that no damages were to be awarded in respect of infringements occurring before the date of a decision allowing an amendment of the specification of a patent unless the court was satisfied that the specification as published was framed in good faith and with reasonable skill and knowledge.

21-63

As originally enacted, the section did not distinguish between a case involving a knowing infringer and a case involving an innocent infringer and consequently it had the potential to operate in a manner that was inconsistent with art.13 of the IP Enforcement Directive because damages must be awarded to the right holder in the case of an infringer who knowingly, or with reasonable grounds to know, engages in an infringing activity.[85] Thus s.62(3) was amended by the Intellectual Property (Enforcement, etc.) Regulations 2006[86] so as to provide:

21-64

"Where an amendment of the specification of a patent has been allowed under any of the provisions of this Act, the court of the comptroller shall, when awarding damages or making an order for an account of profits in proceedings for infringement of the patent committed before the decision to allow the amendment, take into account the following:

(a)   whether at the date of the infringement the defendant or defender knew, or had reasonable grounds to know, that he was infringing the patent;
(b)   whether the specification for the patent was framed in good faith and with reasonable skill and knowledge,
(c)   whether the proceedings are brought in good faith."

The former wording of s.62(3), unlike s.62(1) and (2), made no reference to an account of profits and in *Codex Corp v Racal-Milgo*,[87] the patentee was held entitled to an account without having to establish good faith or reasonable skill and knowledge. This distinction was criticised by the Court of Appeal in *Unilin Beheer*

21-65

---

[82]   [2000] R.P.C. 207. But as the patent was also found invalid in both courts, the decisions were, strictly speaking, obiter dicta.
[83]   See Lloyd Jacob J in *Benmax v Austin Motor Co Ltd* (1953) 70 R.P.C. 143, at 156.
[84]   See also "Restoration of Lapsed Patents" at para.5–04, et seq.
[85]   See para.21–54.
[86]   art.2(2) Sch.2 para.2. The UK Regulations came into force on 29 April 2006.
[87]   [1983] R.P.C. 369.

BV v Berry Floor NV (No.2)[88] and under the law as amended the distinction has been abolished. Of course, since an account of profits is an equitable remedy the court will always have a discretion whether to award it or not.[89]An amendment of a patent or its specification includes a decision of the EPO allowing the amendment under the limitation procedure introduced by the EPC 2000.[90]

21-66   The meaning and effect of subss.(a) to (c), including the genesis of subs.(c), is considered further at para.21–157, et seq.

Partially valid patent

21-67   Section 63(2) of the 1977 Act contains provisions limiting relief where a patent is found at trial to be only partially valid. As originally enacted, s.63(2) provided that no damages could be awarded in the case of a partially valid patent unless the plaintiff proved that the specification for the patent was framed in good faith and with reasonable skill and knowledge. However, as with s.62(3) discussed above,[91] s.63(2) did not distinguish between a case involving a knowing infringer and a case involving an innocent infringer and consequently it had the potential to operate in a manner that was inconsistent with art.13 of the IP Enforcement Directive. Thus s.63(2) was also amended by the Intellectual Property (Enforcement, etc.) Regulations 2006.[92]

21-68   Section 63(2) is discussed further below.[93]

Non-registration of a change in proprietorship or of an exclusive licence

21-69   Section 33 of the 1977 Act applies to a number of transactions, instruments or events,[94] in particular to assignments of patents or applications and to the grant or assignment of any licence under the patent. Provision is made in the Act for the entry on the Register of Patents of details of these transactions, instruments and events.[95] Infringement proceedings can be brought by a subsequent proprietor and also, if the assignment to them conferred on them the right, for infringements committed before that date.[96] An exclusive licensee is, subject to the provision of s.67 of the Act, given like rights to bring proceedings for infringement as a patentee.[97] The position of an exclusive licensee was reviewed in detail by Pumfrey J in *Spring Form Inc v Toy Brokers Ltd.*[98]

21-70   As originally enacted, s.68 of the 1977 Act provided that where by virtue of a transaction, instrument or event to which s.33 applies a person has become the proprietor or exclusive licensee of a patent and the patent is subsequently infringed, they shall be awarded neither damages nor an account of profits in respect of such

88   [2006] F.S.R. 26, [35].
89   See, for example, Pumfrey J in *Spring Form Inc v Toy Brokers Ltd* [2002] F.S.R. 17, [16].
90   PA 1977 s.130(5A). See also para.15–14, et seq.
91   See para.21–63.
92   art.2(2) Sch.2 para.3. The UK Regulations came into force on 29 April 2006.
93   See para.21–156, et seq.
94   See PA 1977 s.33(3). See also para.16–39, et seq.
95   See PA 1977 ss.32 and 33.
96   See PA 1977 ss.30(7) and 31(7).
97   PA 1977 s.67(1).
98   [2002] F.S.R. 17.

a subsequent infringement occurring before the transaction, instrument or event is registered unless:

(a) it was registered within the period of six months beginning with its date; or

(b) the court or the Comptroller is satisfied that it was not practicable to register it before the end of that period and that it was registered as soon as possible after that date.[99]

As with ss.62(3) and 63(2) discussed above,[100] s.68 as originally enacted did not distinguish between the knowing and innocent infringer and had the potential to operate in a manner which was inconsistent with art.13 of the IP Enforcement Directive by denying the right holder damages in the case of a knowing infringer. Thus s.68 was amended by the Intellectual Property (Enforcement, etc.) Regulations 2006[101] so that in place of restricting the award of damages or an account of profits, the restriction is imposed up the award of costs and expenses.[102] **21-71**

It was held at first instance in *Thorn Security Ltd v Siemens Schweiz AG*[103] that the amendment to s.68 does not have retrospective effect. Thus the old law applies to acts of infringement committed when the old law was in force even if the date of the Claim Form or the date of judgment are later. **21-72**

Under s.68 as originally enacted, the restriction on the right to claim damages or an account applies only to damages or an account in respect of a subsequent infringement and thus any right to recover damages in respect of earlier infringements which may have been transferred by virtue of s.30(7) or s.31(7) is unaffected. However, an assignee of a patent can only acquire such right to damages as the assignor has and thus if the assignor's right to damages is barred by s.68 for a particular period, then the assignee will also be barred from claiming damages for the same period.[104] Section 68 was interpreted by the Supreme Court in *Schütz v Werit*.[105] The Court of Appeal[106] had found that Werit did infringe the patent of which Schütz was the exclusive licensee; it had also dismissed Werit's argument based on Schütz's non-registration of its exclusive licence. **21-73**

The Supreme Court reversed the Court of Appeal on the substantive issue of infringement, and so its comments in relation to s.68 are strictly obiter. However, having been expressed relatively fully by Lord Neuberger PSC and agreed with unanimously by the other Justices,[107] those sections of the Supreme Court's judgment in *Schütz* concerned with s.68 will have considerable persuasive force. **21-74**

Lord Neuberger PSC explained that s.68 should be understood to mean that where a licensee successfully sued for infringement and sought damages or an account of profits, it could not recover its costs relating to infringements before the date of registration but could recover costs relating to infringements from the date of registration of the licence. He also made clear that if s.68 is to be relied upon in this regard, then it must be pleaded; the Supreme Court found that in the case before it, s.68 had been so pleaded. **21-75**

---

[99] PA 1977 s.68. See also para.16–47.
[100] See paras 21–63 and 21–67.
[101] art.2(2) Sch.2 para.4. The UK Regulations came into force on 29 April 2006.
[102] art.2(2) Sch.2 para.3.
[103] [2008] R.P.C. 4. The point was not challenged on appeal.
[104] *LG Electronics Inc v NCR Financial Solutions Group Ltd* [2003] F.S.R. 24.
[105] [2013] UKSC 16, [2013] 2 All E.R. 177, [2013] R.P.C. 16.
[106] [2011] EWCA Civ 303, [2011] F.S.R. 19.
[107] Lord Walker, Lady Hale, Lord Mance and Lord Kerr JJSC.

More than one exclusive licence

21-76   Where a first licence is unregistered, but a second one is granted to the same licensee which constitutes a fresh agreement, damages may be awarded from the date of the second licence.[108]

21-77   In *Spring Form Inc v Toy Brokers Ltd*[109] Pumfrey J held that where an agreement replaced an existing agreement, it was the later agreement which should be recorded on the register. The exclusive licensee in that case was able to claim relief only for the period between registration of the first agreement and its supersession by the second agreement and for the period after registration of the second agreement. However, in a claim for an account of profits, while there would have to be apportionment of the profits between claimants in respect of the period during which they could both claim the account, the patentee was entitled to the whole of the profits for the periods when the exclusive licensee was under a disability (due to non-registration of the licence).

Infringement before grant

21-78   The right to bring proceedings in respect of infringements of a patent occurring subsequent to the date of publication but prior to grant is provided for in s.69 of the 1977 Act.[110] As with s.60,[111] s.69 is to be construed as to have as nearly as practicable the same effect in the UK as the corresponding provision of the EPC, CPC and PCT have in the territories to which those conventions apply.[112] It is provided that subsequent to publication and prior to grant, subject to two restrictions, an applicant for a patent shall have the same right to bring proceedings before the court or the Comptroller in respect of acts which would have infringed the patent if granted as they would have had if the patent had been granted on the date of publication.[113]

21-79   The restrictions are first that no proceedings can be brought until the patent is granted.[114] Secondly, the onus is on the applicant to show that the alleged infringing act would, if the patent had been granted on the date of publication of the application, have infringed not only the patent, but also the claims (as interpreted by the description and any drawings referred to in the description or claims) in the form in which they were contained in the application immediately before the preparations for its publication were completed by the Patent Office. This latter requirement takes account of the fact that the claims as granted may be wider than the claims of the application, provided that the claims as granted do not extend the scope of the disclosure of the application.[115] Thus, the second restriction requires the ambit of the claims[116] both of the application and as granted to be ascertained, and no infringement prior to the grant will occur unless the infringing act would infringe both sets of claims.

21-80   Even if the two requirements above are satisfied, the court or Comptroller is given

---

[108] *Minnesota Mining & Manufacturing Co v Rennicks (UK) Ltd* [1992] F.S.R. 118.
[109] [2002] F.S.R. 17.
[110] See *Unilever v Chefaro Proprietaries* [1994] R.P.C. 567, at 590–593.
[111] See paras 14–02 to 14–07.
[112] PA 1977 s.130(7).
[113] PA 1977 s.69(1).
[114] PA 1977 s.69(1)(a).
[115] PA 1977 s.76(2).
[116] See Ch.9.

a discretion as to whether to reduce any award of damages for infringements occurring before grant.[117] The court or Comptroller is directed to consider whether it would have been reasonable to expect from a consideration of the application as published that a patent would be granted conferring on the proprietor of the patent protection against the infringing act.[118] The question is an objective one and does not depend on the knowledge of a particular defendant.[119]

In *Spring Form Inc v Toy Brokers Ltd*,[120] Pumfrey J rejected the submission that the remedy for pre-grant infringement was restricted to damages and held that an account of profits was also available.[121] **21-81**

Section 62(2) and (3) of the 1977 Act[122] does not apply to infringements before grant.[123] **21-82**

The cause of action accrues for the purposes of the Limitation Acts when the infringement takes place, in spite of the statutory bar on commencement of proceedings until after grant.[124] **21-83**

Principle on which damages assessed

The principle to be applied in assessing damages is that the claimant should be restored by monetary compensation to the position which they would have occupied but for the wrongful acts of the defendant, provided always that such loss as they prove are: (i) foreseeable, (ii) caused by the wrong, and (iii) not excluded from recovery by public or social policy.[125] Lord Wilberforce in *General Tire*[126] stated the principle thus: **21-84**

"As in the case of any other tort (leaving aside cases where exemplary damages can be given) the object of damages is to compensate for loss or injury. The general rule at any rate in relation to 'economic' torts is that the measure of damages is to be, so far as possible, that sum of money which will put the injured party in the same position as he would have been in if he had not sustained the wrong. (*Livingstone v Rawyards Coal Co* (1880) 5 App.Cas. 25 at 39, per Lord Blackburn.)

In the case of infringement of a patent, an alternative remedy at the option of the plaintiff exists by way of an account of profits made by the infringer—see Patents Act 1949, section 60. The respondents did not elect to claim an account of profits: their claim was only for damages. There are two essential principles in valuing that claim: first, that the plaintiffs have the burden of proving their loss: second, that the defendants being wrongdoers, damages should be liberally assessed but that the object is to compensate the plaintiffs and not punish the defendants. (*Pneumatic Tyre Co Ltd v Puncture Proof Pneumatic Tyre Co Ltd* (1899) 16 R.P.C. 209 at 215.)"

Fabio Perini v LPC

In *Fabio Perini SpA v LPC Group plc*,[127] a damages inquiry was heard in the Patents Court following an earlier liability trial. At that first trial,[128] the claimant's patent was found to be valid and infringed. The patent was directed to a method for **21-85**

---

[117] PA 1977 s.69(3).
[118] PA 1977 s.69(3).
[119] *Unilever v Chefaro Proprietaries* [1994] R.P.C. 567.
[120] [2002] F.S.R. 17.
[121] [2002] F.S.R. 17, [14]–[17].
[122] See paras 21-62 and 21-63.
[123] PA 1977 s.69(3).
[124] *Sevcon v Lucas CAV* [1986] R.P.C. 609.
[125] *Gerber v Lectra* [1997] R.P.C. 443, 452.
[126] *General Tire & Rubber Co v Firestone Tyre & Rubber Co Ltd* [1976] R.P.C. 197, 212.
[127] [2012] EWHC 911 (Ch), [2012] R.P.C. 30.
[128] [2009] EWHC 1929 (Pat), upheld on appeal: [2010] EWCA Civ 525.

sealing rolls of paper (particularly kitchen/bathroom tissue) by adhesion of the end of the paper to the roll. PCMC's machine—a "tail-sealer"—was held to infringe. PCMC manufactured its tail-sealer in Italy for LPC, who then imported it in the UK and used it to manufacture rolls of kitchen/bathroom tissue.

21-86 At the damages inquiry, the Patents Court considered the principles on which such an inquiry is to be carried out. It held that the starting point was the order made in consequence of the liability trial. That order had declared infringement by use on the part of LPC and that PCMC was jointly and severally liable for such infringement.

21-87 The judge noted (at [75]) that the exercise is not a scientific one:

> "The next step is assessment of the damage. The position to which Perini is entitled to be restored is that which would have obtained if PCMC's infringing tail sealer had not been on the market when LPC and Georgia-Pacific were looking for converting lines. The assessment of such damages requires the Court to to construct and value hypotheses. As Jacob J. put it *Gerber v Lectra Systems* [1995] R.P.C. 383 at 395, the Court is "asked to re-write history" and to form a view about "what would have been" (rather than its ordinary function in civil actions of determining "what was"). In that context one cannot expect much in the way of accuracy."

21-88 The judge reviewed the relevant principles of causation and identified the relevant loss in the case before him to have been the loss of the patentee's chance to have won the contract for the supply that was in fact carried out in infringement of the patent. He said:

> "Causation questions (like assessment questions) have to be approached in a commercially realistic and common sense way and with the ultimate object of yielding compensation that is fair (but no more than fair) for the wrong suffered. That is true whether one is considering causation in fact or causation in law. Looking at what (if any) loss was caused by the infringement, I hold that in this case the loss caused to Perini was the loss of the chance of securing the LPC contract. The loss of the chance of deploying the monopoly of profit and advantage that it was the object of the 929 Patent to grant is in these circumstances in itself compensatable loss. In the world of (what would have been) Perini was not the sole company offering converting lines to LPC, and LPC would not have been compelled to accept what Perini offered. 'What would have been' depends on the hypothetical actions of LPC, or Perini and of Gambini. I will follow the approach taken in *Gerber Garment Technology Inc v Lectra Systems Ltd* [1997] R.P.C. 443, CA."

Where the patentee grants licences

21-89 Patentees derive their remuneration in respect of their inventions either by utilising their monopoly rights to enable them to obtain increased profits as manufacturers, or by permitting others to use their inventions under licence in consideration of royalty payments. In the latter case, the determination of the damages accruing from infringements is usually a relatively simple matter, it being generally assumed that the damage is equal to the amount which the infringer would have had to pay had they had a licence upon the terms normally granted by the patentee.[129]

---

[129] See, e.g. *Penn v Jack* (1866) L.R. 5 Eq. 81; *English and American Machinery Co v Union Boot and Shoe Machine Co* (1896) 13 R.P.C. 64; *Pneumatic Tyre Co Ltd v Puncture Proof Pneumatic TyreCoLtd* (1899) 16 R.P.C. 209; *British Motor Syndicate v John Taylor & Sons Ltd* [1901] 17 R.P.C. 723; *Meters Ltd v Metropolitan Gas Meters* (1911) 28 R.P.C. 157; *British Thomson-Houston Co Ltd v Naamlooze Vennootschap Pope's Metaaldraadlampenfabriek* (1923) 40 R.P.C. 119,127, CS; *Catnic Components v Hill & Smith Ltd* [1983] F.S.R. 512.

Reasonable royalty

Where the patentee does not grant licences and cannot prove any loss as **21-90** manufacturer, the court may assess the damages upon a reasonable royalty basis. As Fletcher Moulton LJ said in the *Meters* case[130]:

"I am inclined to think that the court might in some cases, where there did not exist a quoted figure for a licence, estimate the damages in a way closely analogous to this. It is the duty of the defendant to respect the monopoly rights of the plaintiff. The reward to a patentee for his invention is that he shall have the exclusive right to use the invention, and if you want to use it your duty is to obtain his permission. I am inclined to think that it would be right for the court to consider what would have been the price which—although no price was actually quoted—could have reasonably been charged for that permission, and estimate the damage in that way. Indeed, I think that in many cases that would be the safest and best way to arrive at a sound conclusion as to the proper figure. But I am not going to say a word which will tie down future judges and prevent them from exercising their judgment, as best they can in all the circumstances of the case, so as to arrive at that which the plaintiff has lost by reason of the defendant doing certain acts wrongfully instead of either abstaining from doing them, or getting permission to do them rightfully."

And in *Watson, Laidlaw & Co Ltd v Pott, Cassels and Williamson*,[131] Lord Shaw **21-91** said:

"If with regard to the general trade which was done, or would have been done by the Respondents [the patentees] within their ordinary range of trade, damages be assessed, these ought, of course, to enter the account and to stand. But in addition there remains that class of business which the Respondents would not have done; and in such case it appears to me that the correct and full measure is only reached by adding that a patentee is also entitled, on the principle of price or hire, to a royalty for the unauthorised sale or use of every one of the infringing machines in a market which the infringer, if left to himself, might not have reached. Otherwise, that property which consists in the monopoly of the patented articles granted to the patentee has been invaded, and indeed abstracted, and the law when appealed to would be standing by and allowing the invader or abstractor to go free. In such cases a royalty is an excellent key to unlock the difficulty, and I am in entire accord with the principle laid down by Lord Moulton in *Meters Ltd v Metropolitan Gas Meters Ltd*.[132] Each of the infringements was an actionable wrong, and although it may have been committed in a range of business or of territory which the patentee may not have reached, he is entitled to hire or royalty in respect of each unauthorised use of his property. Otherwise, the remedy might fall unjustly short of the wrong."[133]

In such an event the royalty is restitutionary (for invasions of the monopoly) **21-92** rather than directly compensatory (in the sense of being due to actual damage).

In *Catnic Components v Hill & Smith Ltd*[134] Falconer J held that a proper notional **21-93** rate was that which a potential licensee not yet in the market would pay, disregarding the possibility that he could make and sell non-infringing lintels.

Where the patentee manufactures

Where the patentee makes their profits as manufacturer (whether or not they grant **21-94** licences in addition) rather more difficult questions arise, such as whether the infringement has deprived them of manufacturer's profits equivalent to those which

---

[130] (1911) 28 R.P.C. 157,164–165. Approved in the *General Tire* case [1976] R.P.C. 197, at 214.
[131] (1914) 31 R.P.C. 104, 120.
[132] (1911) 28 R.P.C. 157, 163.
[133] And see *British United Shoe Machinery Co Ltd v A. Fussell & Sons Ltd* (1910) 27 R.P.C. 205; *British Thomson-Houston Co Ltd v Naamlooze Vennootsschap Pope's Metaaldraadlampenfabriek* (1923) 40 R.P.C. 119, at 127 and 128, CS.
[134] [1983] F.S.R. 512.

they would have made had they had the sale of the infringing goods, and what, if any, other damage may have been occasioned to them by their unauthorised sale. In *Smith, Kline & French Laboratories v Doncaster Pharmaceuticals*[135] damages were assessed on the basis of the difference between the price a parallel importer of infringing products actually paid for the products and the price he would have had to pay in order lawfully, to import the products.

21-95 Other classes of damage which a manufacturer may well sustain by such illegal competition are loss of goodwill and business connection or losses due to the necessity to reduce the prices of their wares to meet such competition. The claimant must in each case show a personal cause of action and personal loss caused by the defendant, such as diminution in the value of the shareholding in a subsidiary company. In the case of a claim based on loss via a subsidiary company, it is not self-evident that every dollar lost to a subsidiary company reduces the value of the parent's shareholding by a like amount.[136]

21-96 The onus of proving damage is, of course, upon the claimant in each case, but the burden is greatly lightened by the readiness of the court to infer that the wrongful invasion of a patentee's monopoly will in the ordinary course of events cause damage to them, and, further, the court will not be deterred from awarding substantial sums in damages by reason of the difficulty or impossibility of proof of precise figures by means of which the amount of damage can be mathematically calculated.[137]

21-97 In *Ungar v Sugg*,[138] an action in respect of "threats", Wright J said: "No one can doubt that in this case there was substantial damage, and the difficulty and impossibility of stating the precise ground for assessing it at any particular figure does not seem to be a sufficient reason for giving only a nominal sum", and Lord Esher MR in the Court of Appeal said[139]: "They were problematical damages, and had to be what is called guessed at: that is, not a mere guess, as if you were tossing up for the thing, but it must come to a mere question of what, in the mind of the person who has to estimate them, was a fair sum."

21-98 The assessment of damages is especially difficult with regard to infringements which do not actually compete directly with the goods manufactured by the patentee; for instance, where they are of a totally different quality or price or where it is established that, for some other reason, the order in any case would not have gone to them. In such cases, the defendant is not excused from the payment of substantial damages but is compelled to pay what would, upon a reasonable estimate, be the royalty which the patentee could have fairly obtained under the circumstances.[140]

Convoyed goods

21-99 Damages in respect of infringement do not distinguish between profits on the sale of patented articles and profit on the sale of other goods commonly sold together

---

[135] [1989] F.S.R. 401.
[136] *Gerber Garment Technology v Lectra Systems* [1997] R.P.C. 443, 453 and 455, CA. See also *Johnson v Gore Woods* [2002] 2 A.C. 1.
[137] See *Gerber Garment Technology v Lectra Systems* [1997] R.P.C. 443, CA; [1995] R.P.C. 383, (Pat).
[138] (1891) 8 R.P.C. 385, 388.
[139] (1892) 9 R.P.C. 114, 117.
[140] See para.21-90.

with them, with the result that the latter are also recoverable.[141] However, it does not follow that if a customer was in the habit of purchasing a patented item at the patentee's supermarket, then the patentee is entitled to recover their lost profits in respect of that item and all the other items which the customer normally bought at the patentee's supermarket, but no longer buys.[142]

Extending an inquiry to new causes of action

As noted above,[143] in *Fabio Perini* it was determined that the proper scope of a damages inquiry was determined by construing the order arising out of the liability trial. The Patents Court rejected the defendants' contention that *Building Product Design Ltd v Sandtoft Roof Tiles Ltd*[144] identified a principle that the court on an inquiry will only look into further examples of the same types of infringement established at trial.   **21-100**

Norris J found that there are occasions in which a new cause of action can be raised and adjudicated upon in the inquiry. The question is one of fairness and of convenience, the judge held, that should always be raised and considered at the outset of the inquiry.   **21-101**

That had not been done in the case before the court. The claimant sought in the inquiry to broaden out its claim for relief. The inquiry in *Fabio Perini* was limited to the damage caused by those acts of infringement that had been established at trial; it was not a full investigation into the extent of all infringements. It was held to be just and convenient to extend the inquiry to other cases of infringement by use for which the defendant PCMC was jointly liable, since they involved the same types of infringements decided at trial. However, it was neither just nor convenient to extend the inquiry to deal with alleged sales to a further customer who was not a party.   **21-102**

Price reduction

Where a manufacturer seeks to recover damages on account of reduction of their prices they must establish that the reduction was necessitated by the defendant's wrongful competition and was not the result of the ordinary exigencies of trade.[145]   **21-103**

In *American Braided Wire Co v Thomson*,[146] the patent infringed was one for the manufacturer of a particular form of bustle; no one else being able to put a similar bustle on the market without infringing that patent, the plaintiffs did not reduce their prices until compelled to do so by the defendants, and then only reduced them to the level quoted by the defendants. The official referee came to the conclusion that the plaintiffs would have made, but for the infringement, all the sales that they did make and also the sales made by the defendants, in each case at the plaintiffs'   **21-104**

---

[141] *Gerber Garment Technology v Lectra Systems* [1997] R.P.C. 443, 453 and 455, CA. See also *Rite-Hite v Kelley* [1996] F.S.R. 496, U.S. CAFC.

[142] Staughton LJ in *Gerber Garment Technology v Lectra Systems* [1997] R.P.C. 443, at 456.

[143] See para.21–85.

[144] [2004] F.S.R. 40 (PCC).

[145] *Alexander & Co v Henry & Co* (1895) 12 R.P.C. 360, 367; *United Horse Shoe and Nail Co Ltd v Stewart & Co* (1888) 13 App. Cas. 401.

[146] (1890) 7 R.P.C. 152.

original prices, and awarded damages accordingly. This assessment of damages was upheld by the Court of Appeal.[147]

21-105   Price reductions may, to some extent, counterbalance the loss of profit which they cause to the patentee on each article by the increased demand for such articles which they create among the public and this may be taken into consideration.[148]

Incremental profits

21-106   In *Leeds Forge Co Ltd v Deighton's Patent Flue Co*,[149] it was held, that in arriving at the damages due to competition, regard should be had to the fact that, had the plaintiffs received the orders which in fact went to the defendants, they would have been able to make a profit larger than the profit actually made by themselves on similar articles, or by the defendants on the articles actually made in infringement, since the proportion borne on account of establishment charges by each article made would have been materially reduced.[150]

Importance of invention irrelevant

21-107   In *United Horse Shoe and Nail Co Ltd v Stewart & Co*[151] the House of Lords held that the importance of the invention or of the portion of that invention which the defendant has taken, or the ease with which the defendant could have manufactured his goods without infringing the patent, are not in themselves material upon the assessment of the damages suffered. The principle is that if the defendant's acts are wrongful, the degree of their wrongfulness does not matter, and the defendant must pay such damage as is, in fact, occasioned to the claimant by their acts.[152]

21-108   In *Cofiexip·SA v Stolt Offshore Ltd*[153] the patentee claimed his lost profits in respect of a number of pipelaying contracts performed by the defendant by use of an infringing process. The question arose as to whether it was necessary in these circumstances for the patentee to plead and prove that the defendants had secured the contracts in question by reason of their use, or proposed use, of the infringing process or whether it was sufficient that they had in fact performed the contracts using the infringing process and by such performance they had prevented the patentee from performing the contracts himself. The Court of Appeal considered the submission that the reasoning in the *United Horse Shoe* case was no longer good law in the light of the House of Lords decision in *Kuwait Airways Corp v Iraqi Airways Co*[154] but held that it was at least arguable that the damages claimed were recoverable having regard to the patentee's proposed amended pleading and refused to strike out the claim to loss of profits.

21-109   Where the infringement is a mere accessory of the article manufactured and sold by the defendant, the claimant is only entitled to recover damages in respect of that

---

[147] See also *Wellman v Burstinghaus* (1911) 28 R.P.C. 326.
[148] See, e.g. *American Braided Wire Co v Thomson* (1890) 44 Ch D. 274.
[149] (1908) 25 R.P.C. 209.
[150] See also *Gerber Garment Technology v Lectra Systems* [1995] R.P.C. 383 (Jacob J); [1997] R.P.C. 443, CA.
[151] (1888) 13 App. Cas. 401; (1888) 5 R.P.C. 260.
[152] See *United Horse Shoe and Nail Co Ltd v Stewart & Co* (1888) 13 App. Cas. 401; (1888) 5 R.P.C. 260, at 267.
[153] [2003] F.S.R. 41.
[154] [2002] UKHL 19; [2002] 2 A.C. 833; [2002] 2 W.L.R. 1353.

accessory alone.[155] However, where it is an integral part of a machine as a whole, damages may be based on the fact that the claimant has lost an order for the whole machine, and the profits on the whole machine must be taken into account.[156]

"Franked" articles

Where the patentee's custom was to hire out articles on an annual royalty basis **21-110** and they recovered an agreed sum by way of damages from the manufacturer of infringing articles, it was held that the articles were not "franked" thereby and that users were liable in respect of any use subsequent thereto.[157] Likewise, when an account of profits is taken, the articles which are the subject of such an account do not become franked in the sense that further use and disposal of such items are no longer infringing acts.[158] Yet, where a patentee accepts a payment of damages on terms that they will not sue any other person in respect of the articles made or sold by the defendant, they will not be entitled thereafter to sue the defendant's customers or any other person into whose hands such articles may pass.[159]

Types of infringement not fully determined

Where certain of the types of alleged infringement were not exemplified in the **21-111** particulars of infringements and so were not the subject of any express findings it was ordered that this question should be determined as a preliminary issue in the inquiry.[160]

Damages for infringement of the rights conferred by publication of an application

Damages for infringement of the rights conferred by publication of an applica- **21-112** tion are awarded under s.69 of the 1977 Act. The damages are assessed on the same principles as any other damages for infringement, subject to the exception provided under s.69(3), which it is for the defendant to prove they are within, that it would not have been reasonable to expect that the patentee would get a valid claim covering what they do.[161]

Exemplary damages

In the absence of any authority that exemplary damages had been awarded for **21-113** infringement of patent prior to the decision of the House of Lords in *Rookes v Barnard*,[162] it has been held that a claim for exemplary damages is not available to

---

[155] *Clement Talbot Ltd v Wilson* (1909) 26 R.P.C. 467; see also *United Telephone Co v Walker* (1886) 3 R.P.C. 63.
[156] *Meters Ltd v Metropolitan Gas Meters Ltd* (1911) 28 R.P.C. 157.
[157] *United Telephone Co v Walker* (1887) 4 R.P.C. 63; see also *Penn v Bibby* (1866) L.R. 3 Eq. 308, at 311; and *Catnic Components v C. Evans & Co* [1983] F.S.R. 401, at 419–423.
[158] *Codex Corp v Racal-Milgo Ltd* [1984] F.S.R. 87; considering *Neilson v Betts* (1871) L.R. 5 H.L. 1; and *Watson v Holiday* (1882) 20 Ch D. 480.
[159] See, for example, *Rose Records v Motown Record Corp* [1983] F.S.R. 361 (a copyright case).
[160] *Cleveland Graphite Bronze Co Ltd v Glacier Metal Co Ltd* (1951) 68 R.P.C. 181.
[161] See para.21-78.
[162] [1964] A.C. 1129.

a claimant.[163] However, this decision may no longer be good law having regard to the subsequent decision of the House of Lords in *Kuddas v Chief Constable of Leicestershire*[164] (overruling *AB v South West Water Services*[165]). Thus exemplary damages may be available in a patent infringement action where the case falls within one of the three categories referred to by Lord Devlin in *Rookes v Barnard*, namely: (1) oppressive, arbitrary or unconstitutional actions by the servants of government, (2) where the defendant's conduct has been calculated by them to make a profit for themselves which may well exceed the compensation payable to the plaintiff, or (3) where a statute expressly authorises the same.

21-114   The claimant cannot recover exemplary damages unless they are the victim of the punishable behaviour. However, the means of the parties, irrelevant in the assessment of compensation, are material in the assessment of exemplary damages. Likewise everything which aggravates or mitigates the defendant's conduct is relevant. Punitive damages have been awarded by the High Court of Delhi in the trade mark case of *Time Inc v Lokesh Srivastava*[166] and the trade mark/copyright case of *Microsoft Corp v Deepak Raval*,[167] in each instance on the second of Lord Devlin's three bases.

The IP Enforcement Directive and the knowing infringer

21-115   It should be noted, however, that under art.13 of the IP Enforcement Directive (and particularly art.3 of the UK Regulations implementing the Directive) the court is already required, in the case of the knowing infringer, to take into account the profit made by the infringer from their infringing activities when assessing the right holder's damages.[168]

21-116   The question of damages for "moral prejudice" in the case of a wilful, knowing infringer was addressed by the Patents County Court in *Xena v Cantideck*.[169] In that case, the judge declined to award damages for such moral prejudice. The more appropriate course was found to be to reflect the infringer's conduct when making an award of costs.[170]

Damages where exclusive licensee is claimant

21-117   In awarding damages or granting any other relief to an exclusive licensee who sues as claimant, the court must take into consideration only the loss suffered or likely to be suffered by the actual exclusive licensee. If the latter claims an account of profits in lieu of damages, the profits to be considered are those earned by means of the infringement so far as it constitutes an infringement of the rights of the exclusive licensee as such.[171] When both the patentee and exclusive licensee are

---

[163] *Catnic Components v Hill & Smith Ltd* [1983] F.S.R. 512, 539–541; following *Morton-Norwich Products Inc v United Chemicals (London) Ltd* [1981] F.S.R. 337.
[164] [2002] 2 A.C. 122.
[165] [1993] Q.B. 507.
[166] [2005] F.S.R. 33.
[167] [2007] F.S.R. 11.
[168] See para.21-54.
[169] [2013] EWPCC 1.
[170] See *Xena*, at [114].
[171] PA 1977 s.67.

claimants in a claim for an account of profits, an apportionment between them will be made.[172]

Date from which damages are recoverable

Under s.69(1) of the 1977 Act, damages are recoverable (subject to the Statute of Limitations) from the date of publication of the application, but no action can be brought until the patent is granted.[173] Further conditions for recovery of damages from that date are discussed above.[174] The date from which damage should be reckoned in cases where a patent has been amended or where some of the claims are held to be invalid is dealt with at para.21-193. The court may, if it thinks fit, refuse to award damages in respect of infringements committed during any period in which the patentee is in default of payment of renewal fees.[175] **21-118**

Warranty under Sale of Goods Act

On the sale of an article there is an implied warranty[176] that the purchaser will enjoy quiet possession of the goods and this possession is disturbed when the goods infringe a patent, whether or not that patent was in force at the date of sale.[177] Accordingly, where an infringer has obtained items under a contract to which the Sale of Goods Act applies, although they will have no defence to the infringement action—such that damages will be due to the patentee—they will be entitled to be indemnified by the vendor. **21-119**

Interest

A successful claimant may recover simple interest on all sums payable.[178] Such interest may be awarded from the date of each infringement complained of at a rate which reflects the rate which the claimant would have had to have paid had it borrowed the amount payable by way of damages.[179] This should be objectively determined by reference to what it would cost claimants in general to borrow money rather than the particular claimant of any one case. In *Catnic Components Ltd v Hill & Smith Ltd*,[180] this was taken to be 2 per cent above the clearing bank base rate. **21-120**

---

[172] *Spring Form Inc v Toy Brokers Ltd* [2002] F.S.R 17.
[173] PA 1977 s.69(2)(a); see also the conditions contained in s.69(2)(b).
[174] See para.21-78.
[175] PA 1977 s.62(2).
[176] Sale of Goods Act 1979 s.12(2)(b).
[177] *Niblett v Confectioner's Materials Co* [1921] 3 K.B. 387; *Microbeads A.G. v Vinhurst Road Markings* [1976] R.P.C. 19.
[178] Senior Courts Act 1981 s.35A.
[179] *Tate & Lyle Food & Distribution Ltd v GLC* [1981] 3 All E.R. 716; applied in *Catnic Components Ltd v Hill & Smith Ltd* [1983] F.S.R. 512, 542–544.
[180] [1983] F.S.R. 512.

Position of assignee

21-121   An assignment of a patent does not, per se, transfer an accrued right of action for infringement[181] but such a right can be expressly assigned in the same manner as any other chose in action.[182]

Patents indorsed "licences of right"

21-122   If a patent is indorsed "licences of right",[183] in proceedings for infringement (otherwise than by the importation of any article from a country which is not a Member State of the EU) and if (but only if)[184] the defendant undertakes to take a licence to be settled by the Comptroller no injunction will be made and the damages will not exceed double the amount payable by them as licensee if the licence had been granted before the earliest infringement.[185] There is no such limitation in relation to an account of profits.

Form of order

21-123   Where damages are given, the usual form of order is to direct an inquiry as to damages, the costs thereof being reserved, with liberty to apply[186]; and where the action is in respect of certain claims of the patent only, the inquiry is limited as to infringement of the claims sued upon.[187] A person may not on the inquiry seek to re-open questions of infringement determined by the trial judge.[188] In a case where the evidence was available and the parties consented, a liquidated sum was assessed at the end of a successful application for summary judgment rather than waiting for an enquiry.[189]

Interim award

21-124   Where it is clear that a certain irreducible minimum will be awarded at the enquiry (regardless of any particularly complex areas of law or fact) the defendant may be ordered to pay such minimum or at least a substantial portion thereof.[190]

Where patent afterwards revoked

21-125   The position previously had been that, where an injunction was obtained in an action and an inquiry as to damages ordered, and after judgment (but before the inquiry) the patent was revoked on the petition of another person who adduced further reasons for attacking its validity, it was held in *Poulton v Adjustable Cover*

---

[181] *Wilderman v E.W. Berk & Co Ltd* (1925) 42 R.P.C. 79, 90.
[182] *Wilderman v E.W. Berk & Co Ltd* (1925) 42 R.P.C. 79. See also paras 16–177 and 19-170 on the consequences of failing to register an assignment.
[183] See para.17–165, et seq.
[184] *Gerber v Lectra* [1995] R.P.C. 383.
[185] PA 1977 s.46.
[186] *British Thomson-Houston Co Ltd v G. and R. Agency* (1925) 42 R.P.C. 305.
[187] e.g. *Benjamin Electric Ltd and Igranic Co Ltd v Garnett Whiteley & Co Ltd* (1930) 47 R.P.C. 44.
[188] *Harrison v Project & Design Co (Redcar) Ltd* [1987] R.P.C. 151.
[189] *Smith, Kline & French Laboratories Ltd v Doncaster Pharmaceuticals Ltd* [1989] F.S.R. 401.
[190] *Chiron v Murex (No.13)* [1996] F.S.R. 578.

and Boiler Block Co,[191] this fact did not preclude the inquiry from being prosecuted and the damages recovered. Parker J decided the case on the basis of an estoppel operating against the defendant. The Court of Appeal, in confirming the judgment, decided the case on the basis of res judicata.

The submission that subsequent developments in the law of estoppel[192] meant that **21-126** the decision in *Poulton* was no longer good law was rejected in *Cofiexip SA v Stolt Offshore MS Ltd (No.2).*[193] At first instance, Jacob J held that the defendants were estopped from raising the issue of validity on the inquiry by cause of action estoppel. In the Court of Appeal it was held by a majority that the defendants were estopped by cause of action estoppel in relation to the particular instance of infringement pleaded in the Particulars of Infringement and proved at trial, and by issue estoppel in relation to all other instances of infringement, there being no special circumstances entitling the defendants to re-open the issue of validity upon the inquiry.[194]

Poulton, Cofiexip and *Unilin* were all overturned by the Supreme Court's judg- **21-127** ment in *Virgin Atlantic Airways Ltd v Zodiac Seat UK Limited.*[195] Lord Sumption JSC and Lord Neuberger PSC each gave reasoned judgments to similar effect; Lady Hale, Lord Clarke and Lord Carnwath JJSC each agreed with both judgments. Lord Sumption JSC summarised the conclusion their Lordships had all reached on the law, as follows[196]:

"35. In my opinion *Poulton* is no longer good law, and *Cofiexip* was wrongly decided. It follows that *Unilin* was also wrongly decided because it proceeded on the premise of the law stated in *Cofiexip*. The point with which *Unilin* was actually concerned, namely whether there is a different rule for European patents arising from the scheme of the relevant legislation, has been argued before us but it does not arise, because the anomaly in English law to which that point is directed does not exist. Accordingly, where judgment is given in an English court that a patent (whether English or European) is valid and infringed, and the patent is subsequently retrospectively revoked or amended (whether in England or at the EPO), the defendant is entitled to rely on the revocation or amendment on the inquiry as to damages.

36. Once the inquiry is concluded, different considerations will arise. There will then be a final judgment for a liquidated sum. At common law, that judgment could be challenged on the ground that the patent had later been revoked or amended only by way of appeal, and then only if an appeal is still open. I doubt whether an implied statutory right to reopen it could be derived from the scheme of the Patents Act 1977 , but that is a question which will have to await a case in which it arises."

Servier v Apotex—ex turpi causa

Apotex had been enjoined before Servier's patent was revoked and Apotex had **21-128** collected damages under the cross-undertaking that Servier had given when obtaining the injunction. Norris J had heard that inquiry[197] and made a damages award of £17.5m. Servier later claimed that the damages should be refunded, because the

---

191 (1908) 25 R.P.C. 529 (Parker J) and 661 (CA).
192 See, in particular, *Arnold v National Westminster Bank* [1991] 2 A.C. 93 and *Johnson v Gore Woods and Co* [2002] 2 A.C. 1.
193 [2004] F.S.R. 7 (Jacob J) and 34 (CA).
194 Cf. *Arnold v National Westminster Bank* [1991] 2 A.C. 93 where special circumstances were held to exist.
195 [2013] UKSC 46; [2014] A.C. 160; [2013] 3 W.L.R. 299; [2013] 4 All E.R. 715; [2013] R.P.C. 29.
196 [2013] UKSC 46; [2014] A.C. 160; [2013] 3 W.L.R. 299; [2013] 4 All E.R. 715; [2013] R.P.C. 29, [35]–[36]
197 *Les Laboratoires Servier, Servier Laboratories Ltd v Apotex Inc, Apotex Pharmachem Inc, Apotex Europe Ltd, Apotex UK Ltd* [2008] EWHC 2347 (Ch), [2009] F.S.R. 3.

sales to which they related arose out of acts of manufacture which infringed Servier's Canadian patent.[198] They argued that the legal principle ex turpi causa non oritur actio ("no action can arise out of an illegal/immoral act") was engaged so that the damages should not have been recovered by Apotex. Arnold J acceded to Servier's request and ordered that the damages be refunded.

21-129   The Court of Appeal reversed the decision of Arnold J. It found consideration of the ex turpi causa defence to be relevant but that in the present case the defence did not act to deprive Apotex of its right to the damages collected under the cross-undertaking. Apotex's acts had been "low on the scale of culpability" as relevant to the defence, and sale in the UK of goods whose manufacture had infringed a Canadian patent was not unlawful in Canada or the UK.

21-130   The Supreme Court heard an appeal by Servier,[199] with the leading judgment being given by Lord Sumption JSC. The Supreme Court judgment focussed on the scope of "turpitude" for the purposes of the defence. It found that the term only extended to criminal and quasi-criminal acts, since they engaged the relevant public interest. The ex turpi defence was therefore not engaged in the present case, and so the appeal from the Court of Appeal's judgment was dismissed.

Disclosure on inquiry as to damages

21-131   Where an inquiry as to damages is directed, the same principles as to disclosure of documents apply as in the case of any other issue which has to be tried between the parties.[200] Under the modern practice, disclosure is carefully controlled by the court in an inquiry as to damages but, in principle, the defendant may be required to give full disclosure. Where machines have been made in infringement of the patent the defendant will be required to set out the names and addresses of the persons to whom such machines have been sold[201] but not ordinarily the names of the agents concerned in the transaction.[202] A form of "confidentiality club" may be put in place in an appropriate case but, as in any other case, the burden was on the party seeking to restrict disclosure to show that the case was sufficiently exceptional to justify the restrictions sought.[203]

21-132   The deliberate destruction of records or, in particular circumstances a failure to keep records, will raise an inference of infringement in favour of the claimant.[204]

21-133   The claimant may also be ordered to disclose his business books if they allege a falling-off of profits[205]; and of documents relating to prime cost of machinery.[206]

---

[198] [2011] EWHC 730 (Pat), [2011] R.P.C. 20; Norris J had refused an amendment to introduce the same argument into the inquiry before him: see *Harrison v Project & Design Co (Redcar) Ltd* [1987] R.P.C. 151, at [61], et seq.
[199] [2014] UKSC 55, [2015] A.C. 430, [2014] 3 W.L.R. 1257, [2015] R.P.C. 10.
[200] *British United Shoe Machinery Co Ltd v Lambert Howarth & Sons Ltd* (1929) 46 R.P.C. 315, 317.
[201] *Murray v Clayton* (1872) L.R. 15 Eq. 115; *American Braided Wire Co v Thompson & Co (No.2)* (1888) 5 R.P.C. 375; *Saccharin Corp v Chemicals & Drugs Co Ltd* (1900) 17 R.P.C. 612.
[202] *Murray v Clayton* (1872) L.R. 15 Eq. 115.
[203] *Dyson Limited v Hoover Limited (No.3)* [2002] R.P.C. 42.
[204] *Seager v Copydex Ltd* [1969] R.P.C. 250, 258; applied in *General Tire and Rubber Co v Firestone Tyre and Rubber Co Ltd* [1975] R.P.C. 203, 228, per Graham J, and 267, per Russell LJ.
[205] *Hamilton & Co v Neilson* (1909) 26 R.P.C. 671.
[206] *British United Shoe Machinery Co Ltd v Lambert Howarth & Sons Ltd* (1929) 46 R.P.C. 315, 320.

Costs of inquiry

Under the old practice, if the defendant, before the inquiry, offered a sum in **21-134** satisfaction, that fact was to be recited in the order so that it may be considered upon the question of costs when that question comes to be decided.[207] Under the modern practice,[208] such an offer is "without prejudice save as to costs" and thus would not be communicated to the judge hearing the matter until its conclusion.[209] The costs of the inquiry will usually be given to the claimant if the damages found due exceed the sum offered by the defendant; but they will usually be given to the defendant if the damages did not exceed the sum offered.[210] The modern practice allows for claimants to make similar offers with sanctions in terms of interest and costs assessed on an indemnity basis if the claimant does better than their offer.[211]

Principles applicable to an account of profits

The principles applicable to an account of profits in a patent action are examined **21-135** in two first instance decisions, *Celanese International v B.P. Chemicals*,[212] and *Spring Form Inc v Toy Brokers Ltd*.[213]

An account of profits is a restitutionary remedy whose purpose is to deprive the **21-136** defendant of the profits which they have improperly made by wrongful acts committed in breach of the claimant's rights and transfer those profits to the claimant.[214]

The general principle in quantifying the account is that the infringer is required **21-137** to disgorge the profits made by reason of the infringement, and not just on the occasion of the infringement.[215] The proper approach to quantification of such profits is thus not the "incremental" one advocated by the defendants in *Celanese*, i.e. based on the difference between: (i) the profits made by use of the patented method and products obtained thereby, and (ii) the profits which would have been achieved without using the patented method; what matters in each case is the profits made in fact by the defendant by reason of the infringement.

The maximum payment is the total profit made by the defendant and they only **21-138** have to account for those processes (or products) which infringe. Where only part of a product or process infringes, profits are to be apportioned between those which were caused by or attributable to the use of the invention (and which the patentee may thus recover) and those which were not. However, where the invention is the essential ingredient in the creation of the defendant's whole product or process it may be appropriate not to apportion.[216]

Before apportionment, the defendant may deduct from revenues all allowable **21-139** costs such as research and development costs, and costs of financing the plant as well as more direct costs such as manufacturing and distribution costs. The patentee

---

207 *Fettes v Williams* (1908) 25 R.P.C. 511; *British Vacuum Co v Exton Hotels Co Ltd* (1908) 25 R.P.C. 617.
208 CPR Pt 36 generally.
209 CPR r.36.16(1) and (2).
210 *Clement Talbot Ltd v Wilson* (1909) 26 R.P.C. 467 and now see CPR r.36.17.
211 CPR r.36.17.
212 [1999] R.P.C. 203. In fact, the case settled immediately prior to judgment being handed down.
213 [2002] F.S.R. 17, [6]–[11].
214 Pumfrey J in *Spring Form Inc v Toy Brokers Ltd* [2002] F.S.R. 17, [7], citing Slade J in *My Kinda Town Ltd v Soll* [1983] R.P.C. 15, at 49.
215 *Imperial Oil v Lubrizol* [1996] 71 C.P.R. (3d.) 26, CA (Can. Fed.).
216 *Hoechst Celanese International v B.P. Chemicals* [1999] R.P.C. 203, 222.

has to take the defendant as they find them and may not complain if the defendant operates their process inefficiently, or unprofitably.[217]

21-140 Some logical basis for an apportionment has to be found, bearing in mind the importance of the patented process in the relevant business activities carried out by the defendant. A useful guide may be provided by ordinary accounting principles whereby, in the absence of some special reason to the contrary, the profits of a single project are attributed to different parts or aspects of the project in the same proportion as the costs and expenses are attributed to them.[218] In *Celanese*, the relative capital expenditure of the plant used for the infringing process as a proportion of that of the entire plant was adopted as a reasonable yardstick for apportionment.[219]

Collecting damages on cross-undertaking after interim injunction discharged

21-141 In *Astrazeneca AB v Krka dd Novo Mesto*,[220] an interim injunction had previously been granted, with Astrazeneca having at that time given to Krka an undertaking in damages. A little over a year later, Astrazeneca brought an unsuccessful infringement action against a different party, based on the same patent. In light of that decision, Astrazeneca did not appeal and informed Krka that it intended to discharge the interim injunction. The High Court therefore had to assess the damages payable to Krka on the cross-undertaking that Astrazeneca had given when it obtained the interim injunction. Sales J approved the principles set out by Norris J in *Servier*:[221]

> "The principles of law sufficient to enable me to quantify compensation in this case may be shortly stated:-
>
> (a) The undertaking is to be enforced according to its terms. In the instant case (as in many others) it is that Servier will comply with any order the court may make "if the court...finds that this Order has caused loss to the defendants." The question for me is therefore: what loss did the making of the Order and its continuation until discharge cause to Apotex?
>
> (b) The approach is therefore essentially compensatory and not punitive;
>
> (c) The approach to assessment is generally regarded as that set out in the obiter observation of Lord Diplock in *Hoffmann-La Roche v Secretary of State for Trade* [1975] A.C. 295 at 361E namely: "The assessment is made upon the same basis as that upon which damages for breach of contract would be assessed if the undertaking had been a contract between the plaintiff and the defendant that the plaintiff would not prevent the defendant from doing that which he was restrained from doing by the terms of the injunction: see *Smith v Day* (1882) 21 Ch D. 421 per Brett LJ at p. 427."
>
> (d) What Apotex was trying to do (and what the Order restrained it from doing) was to enter a new market for the sale of generic perindopril. It was denied exploitation of this opportunity. The outcome of such exploitation is attended by many contingencies but *Chaplin v Hicks* [1911] 2 KB 786 establishes (per Vaughan Williams LJ at p.791) that whilst "the presence of all the contingencies on which the gaining of the prize might depend makes the calculation not only difficult but incapable of being carried out with certainty or precision" damages for the lost opportunity are assessable.
>
> (e) The fact that certainty or precision is not possible does not mean that a principled approach cannot be attempted. The profits that Apotex would have made from its exploitation of the opportunity to sell generic perindopril depend in part upon the hypothetical actions of third parties (other potential market participants) and in part upon Servier's response

---

[217] See *Dart Industries v Décor Corp* [1994] F.S.R. 567, HC (Aus.).

[218] See Millett J (as he then was) in *Potton v Yorkclose* [1990] F.S.R. 11, at 18.

[219] It is submitted that each case will turn very much on its own facts, and relative capital expenditure will not always provide a reasonable yardstick.

[220] [2014] EWHC 84 (Pat)

[221] [2014] UKSC 55, [5].

to them. A principled approach in such circumstances requires Apotex first to establish on the balance of probabilities that the chance of making a profit was real and not fanciful: if that threshold is crossed then the second stage of the inquiry is to evaluate that substantial chance (see *Allied Maples v Simmons & Simmons* [1995] 1 W.L.R. 1602). As Lord Diplock explained in *Mallett v McMonagle* [1970] A.C. 166 at 176E-G "… in assessing damages which depend on its view as to what… would have happened in the future if something had not happened in the past, the Court must make an estimate as to what are the chances that a particular thing… would have happened and reflect those chances, whether they are more all less than even, in the amount of damages it awards…"

(f)   The conventional method of undertaking this exercise is to assess damages on a particular hypothesis and then to adjust the award by reference to the percentage chance of the hypothesis occurring. In many cases it is sufficient to postulate one hypothesis and make one discount: but there is no reason in principle why one should not say that either Scenario 1 or Scenario 2 would have occurred and to discount them by different percentages. That is the course which Mr Watson QC urged in the present case: and I note that it has some support in *Earl of Malmesbury v Strutt & Parker* [2007] P.N.L.R. 570."

Applying those principles to the facts as he had found them, the judge accepted **21-142** Krka's case that it was due damages for lost profits during the lifetime of the interim injunction, with an uplift to compensate it for loss of the advantage it would have had as the first generic entrant into the relevant market. The result was an award of damages under the cross-undertaking largely in line with what Krka had sought.

4. ORDER FOR DELIVERY UP OR DESTRUCTION

Under the modern practice, a successful claimant can obtain an order for the **21-143** destruction or delivery up of infringing goods in the possession of the defendant,[222] so as to ensure that such goods are not retained in order to be placed upon the market after the expiry of the patent. The terms of s.61(1)(b) provide for delivery up or destruction of "any patented product in relation to which the patent is infringed or any article in which that product is inextricably comprised."

History of order

In the early case of *Crossley v Beverley*,[223] the possibility above referred to was **21-144** dealt with by the grant of an injunction perpetually restraining the defendant from selling infringing goods made during the continuance of the patent.[224] In *Betts v De Vitre*[225] an inquiry was ordered as to what infringing goods the defendants had, and it was ordered that such goods should be destroyed in the plaintiff's presence.[226] In *Plimpton v Malcolmson*[227] the defendant was ordered to deliver up or to destroy or render unfit for use infringing articles.

---

[222] PA 1977 s.61(1)(b).
[223] (1829) 1 W.P.C. 112.
[224] See also *Crossley v The Derby Gas Light Co* (1834) 4 L.T.Ch. 25; but see *Monsanto Co v Stauffer Chemicals* [1988] F.S.R. 57, at 62.
[225] (1865) 34 L.J.Ch. 289.
[226] See also *Frearson v Loe* (1878) 9 Ch D. 48, at 67.
[227] A.R. Ingpen, F. Turner Bloxam and H.G. Garrett, *Seton on Judgments*, 7th edn (London: Stevens and Sons, 1912), p.630.

Form of order

21-145   One principle underlying the above cases (from which the practice of making the present form of order originated) has been said[228] to be that the court should protect the patentee from any use after the expiry of their patent of infringing articles made during its currency, and also that such destruction or delivery up would render still more effective the injunction ordinarily granted by the court prohibiting their use during the term of the patent.

21-146   In *Merck Canada Inc v Sigma Pharmaceuticals plc (No. 2)*,[229] HHJ Birss QC doubted the first of these justifications for the order for delivery up, noting that such a purpose had been considered and dismissed by the Supreme Court of South Africa.[230] The judge went on to find at [21]:

> "In my judgment orders for delivery up/destruction are ancillary to the injunction and their purpose is to act as an aid to the injunction (Jacob LJ in *Mayne*[231] *[...]*). Such an order, when made, will obviously have the effect of protecting the patentee from any use after expiry of articles made during the currency of the patent but I do not believe it is accurate to say that that in itself is a or the purpose of orders for delivery up/destruction. That is not to say that questions of springboards and the like do not have a role to play in the exercise of the discretion, I am sure they do and springboard relief generally is a different point. However I am not satisfied that the passages in *[the previous edition of] Terrell* on this first point are correct."

21-147   The normal form of the order is for actual destruction or delivery up of infringing articles, but may be modified in suitable cases, as, for instance, where an infringing article can be rendered non-infringing by some alteration or by the removal of some part.[232] Machinery and equipment specially adapted for using an infringing process may be the subject of an order for delivery up or destruction but only where it cannot be used for non-infringing purposes. Equally, no order may be made for the delivery up of an article which is not itself an infringement but which is capable of being used as part of an infringing apparatus if it is also capable of being used without infringement.[233]

21-148   In some cases a patentee may expressly seek an order for delivery up of articles which may not themselves be infringing products on the basis that the only use to which they can be put would be a breach of the injunction restraining infringement. Although outside the terms of s.61(1)(b) it is submitted that there is no reason why, in an appropriate case, such an order may not be made.[234] Careful attention should therefore be given to the exact form of the wording of any order for delivery up or destruction upon oath.[235]

---

[228]   Including previously in this work.

[229]   [2012] EWPCC 21, [2013] R.P.C. 2. The order for delivery up was upheld on appeal [2013] EWCA 326 (Civ), [88]–[95].

[230]   *Monsanto Co v Stauffer Chemical Co* [1988] F.S.R. 57.

[231]   *Mayne v Pharmacia* [2005] EWCA Civ 294.

[232]   *Mergenthaler Linotype Co v Intertype Ltd* (1926) 43 R.P.C. 381; see also *Siddell v Vickers, Sons & Co Ltd* (1890) 7 R.P.C. 81, at 101; *Howes and Burley v Webber* (1895) 12 R.P.C. 465; *Aktiengesellschaft für Autogene Aluminium Schweissung v London Aluminium Co Ltd (No. 2)* (1920) 37 R.P.C. 153, 170; *British United Shoe Machinery Co Ltd v Gimson Shoe Machinery Co Ltd* (1927) 44 R.P.C. 85.

[233]   *Electric and Musical Industries Ltd v Lissen Ltd* (1937) 54 R.P.C. 5, 35.

[234]   These two sentences were approved in principle in *KCI Licensing Inc v Smith & Nephew Plc* [2010] EWHC 2067 (Pat) but on the facts the possibility of alternative use was held not to be "wholly unrealistic".

[235]   *Codex Corp v Racal-Milgo Ltd* [1984] F.S.R. 87.

In *Kirin-Amgen Inc v Transkaryotic Therapies Inc (No.3)*[236] Neuberger J **21-149** considered whether to include within an order for delivery up certain recombinant cells which were intended to be used to make an infringing product (a recombinant protein). He held that the cells should be delivered up. Although they contained only a very small quantity of infringing protein, Neuberger J held that once it is accepted that infringing material exists, it would only be in exceptional circumstances that the court should refuse an order that the infringing material should be delivered up or destroyed. The cells fell within the language "inextricably comprised" in s.61(1)(b) of the 1977 Act. The fact that the cells were "priceless" was as much a reason why they should be delivered up from the patentee's point of view as it was a reason not to from the defendant's point of view.

Effective date of order

The normal order requires the delivery up of those goods which are both in the **21-150** United Kingdom and in the defendant's possession custody power or control on the day that the order for delivery up is made. In *Mayne Pharma v Pharmacia Italia*,[237] the Court of Appeal refused to back-date the effective date of the order to the date of judgment so as to require the defendant to re-import and deliver up to the patentee infringing goods which had been in the defendant's possession in this country on that date but which had subsequently been exported prior to finalisation of the form of order. Jacob LJ said:

"Furthermore, it is important to remember what the jurisdiction to grant an order for delivery up is for. It is not anything more than a way of making sure that the injunction is obeyed. Einfeld J in *Roussel Uclaf and Another v Pan Laboratories Pty Limited* in the Federal Court of Australia on 17th May 1994, in dealing with a very similar case, said this:

'In this case the products cannot, while they remain outside the jurisdiction, infringe the Australian patents of the applicants. Nor is there any evidence that, unless ordered to do so by the Court, the respondents intend to re-import them. All that can be said in support of such an order is that while in Australia the products infringed the patents and that the respondents should not be allowed to 'gain a benefit' by 'sneaking' them out of the jurisdiction. But an order for delivery up is not for punishment of the infringer or compensation to the patentee. It is to protect the patentee's rights. As I see it, the presence of the products in Papua New Guinea [the place of export] does not place the rights of the applicant at risk and in need of protection.'"

However, the court may restrain a defendant from exporting infringing goods **21-151** pending appeal even if the order for delivery up is to be stayed, so that they will be available to be delivered up after the appeal.[238] Additionally, in an appropriate case, the court may—as an alternative to delivery-up/destruction—order that an infringing party take immediate steps to render its acts non-infringing. It will ordinarily have to confirm (by witness statement or similar) that it has done so, and precisely what steps it has taken.[239]

---

[236] [2005] F.S.R. 41.
[237] [2005] EWCA Civ 294.
[238] *Kirin-Amgen Inc v Transkaryotic Therapies Inc (No.3)* [2005] F.S.R. 41.
[239] *ASSIA v BT* [2014] EWCA Civ 1513.

Compensation

21-152   The defendant is not entitled to any compensation for loss caused to them by such destruction or delivery up, and cannot set off the value of goods delivered up against a claim for damages.[240] The loss caused by the destruction of an infringing article may cause a loss to the infringer considerably greater than the costs of the infringing article. However, that loss is part of the risk an infringer incurs when they infringe.[241] But there is no question of confiscation of infringing articles, in the sense that the defendant is deprived of their property in them, the only purpose of the order being the rendering of the goods non-infringing to the satisfaction of the patentee.[242] The ordinary order, therefore, gives the infringer the choice between destruction or delivery up, although in a case where the order was made only for delivery up without any objection being made at the time by the defendant, it was held, upon a subsequent motion to vary the minutes so as to give the defendant the option, that the original order, not having been objected to, must stand.[243]

Disclosure

21-153   In aid of the order for delivery up, the defendant will be ordered to give disclosure as to any infringing goods in his possession or power.[244]

Stay of order

21-154   The order for delivery up or destruction may be stayed pending an appeal.[245] For terms on which it may be stayed see *Kirin-Amgen Inc v Transkaryotic Therapies Inc (No.3)*.[246]

5.   RELIEF FOR INFRINGEMENT OF PARTIALLY VALID PATENT

21-155   By s.63(1) of the 1977 Act, where in infringement proceedings a patent has been found to be only partially valid, relief may be granted in respect of that part of it which has been found to be valid and infringed. This is subject to two provisos, financial remedies are subject to s.63(2) and any relief under s.63 may be subject to amendments (s.63(3) and (4)).

21-156   Section 63(2) provides:

> "(2)   Where in any such proceedings it is found that a patent is only partially valid, the court or the comptroller shall, when awarding damages, costs or expenses or making an order for an account of profits, take into account the following—
>
> (a)   whether at the date of the infringement the defendant or defender knew, or had reasonable grounds to know, that he was infringing the patent;

---

[240] *United Telephone Co v Walker* (1886)3 R.P.C.63, 67.

[241] *Kirin-Amgen Inc v Transkaryotic Therapies Inc (No.3)* [2005] F.S.R. 41

[242] *Vavasseur v Krupp* (1878) 9 Ch D. 351, 360; and see *Codex Corp v Racal-Milgo Ltd* [1984] F.S.R. 87.

[243] *British Westinghouse Electric and Manufacturing Co Ltd v Electrical Co Ltd* (1911) 28 R.P.C. 517, 531.

[244] See, e.g. *British Thomson-Houston Co Ltd v Irradiant Lamp Works Ltd* (1923) 40 R.P.C. 243.

[245] See, e.g. *British United Shoe Machinery Co Ltd v Lambert Howarth & Sons Ltd* (1927) 44 R.P.C. 511; *Samuel Parkes & Co Ltd v Cocker Bros Ltd* (1929) 46 R.P.C. 241.

[246] [2005] F.S.R. 41.

(b)   whether the specification for the patent was framed in good faith and with reasonable skill and knowledge;

(c)   whether the proceedings are brought in good faith; and any relief granted shall be subject to the discretion of the court or the comptroller as to costs or expenses and as to the date from which damages or an account should be reckoned."

Section 63(2) its current form came into force as a result of amendments effec-   **21-157** tive from 29 April 2006.[247] In order to understand the purpose and true meaning of these amendments, it is necessary to consider their background.

In its current form the section includes an account of profits as well as damages,   **21-158** that change appears to stem from the comments of the Court of Appeal in *Unilin Beheer BV v Berry Floor NV (No.2)*.[248]

Section 63(2)(a) stems from art.13 of the IP Enforcement Directive.[249] As   **21-159** originally enacted, the section did not distinguish between a case involving a knowing infringer and a case involving an innocent infringer and consequently it had the potential to operate in a manner that was inconsistent with art.13. Section 63(2)(a) removes that potential for inconsistency by allowing the court to take into account the defendant's state of knowledge and to make an award which is consistent with the Directive.

Section 63(2)(b) is part of the old law and will be discussed further below.[250]   **21-160**

Section 63(2)(c) stems from changes made to UK law which were necessitated   **21-161** by the EPC 2000. In particular the EPC 2000 necessitated changes to the wide discretionary power which the court and the Comptroller previously exercised upon an application to amend a patent.[251] Under the law as amended in accordance with the EPC 2000, the previous discretionary power is now more limited.[252] In particular, whereas under the old law the court could refuse an application to amend a patent in a case of covetous claiming, it is now doubtful whether the court can continue to take that approach.[253] Nevertheless it would appear that Parliament has decided that the court and the Comptroller should retain at least some power to deal with a case where a patentee has brought proceedings upon one or more claims which he knows to be invalid. It is submitted that proceedings brought on a covetous claim would not be proceedings brought in good faith.

Although s.63(2)(c) was introduced by the Intellectual Property (Enforcement,   **21-162** etc) Regulations 2006, it should be noted that an earlier form of amendment of the section (which at that time included subs.(c), but not subs.(a)) was enacted by s.2(4) of the Patents Act 2004.[254] However s.2(4) was never brought into force and the amendment was superseded by the fuller amendment contained in the 2006 Regulations.

A number of issues arise under the section as follows. First, what is the mean-   **21-163** ing of "partially valid"? Secondly, what state of mind of the infringer must be proved in order to bring point (a) into play? Thirdly, how are good faith and reasonable skill and knowledge to be proved? Fourthly, when are proceedings not brought

---

[247] The amendments were made by the Intellectual Property (Enforcement, etc) Regulations 2006 art.2(2) Sch.2 para.3.
[248] [2006] F.S.R. 26, [35]. And see para.21-65.
[249] See para.21-54. And see also the discussion in relation to s.62(3) at para.21-63.
[250] See para.21-172, et seq.
[251] See para.15-14, et seq.
[252] See para.15-109, et seq.
[253] See para.15-119.
[254] See also s.2(3) of the 2004 Act for the corresponding amendment to s.62 of the 1977 Act.

in good faith? Fifthly, what are the principles which the court should follow when exercising the discretion provided to it under s.63(1)?

Meaning of "partially valid"

21-164   Section 63(1) (and its predecessors under previous Acts) swept away the old rule that the presence of one invalid claim rendered the entire patent invalid; the interesting history of the law relating to that rule and the way in which it was applied was reviewed by Aldous J at first instance, and subsequently Millett LJ in the Court of Appeal, in *Gerber v Lectra*.[255]

21-165   In *Hallen Co v Brabantia (UK) Ltd*[256] claim 10, when dependent on claims 1, 8 and 9, was found to be valid. However, the claim was not wholly valid as there was, within claim 10, a patentable invention and other non-patentable matter. However, Aldous J held that the patent was partially valid. He stated (at 140):

> "The 1977 Act substantially departed from the position under the 1949 Act. Under that act it was thought that a claim could only have one priority date and the practice arose of splitting up claims so that each claim could attract its own priority date: *Farbenfabriken Bayer A.G.'s Patent*, [1966] R.P.C. 278. Under the 1977 Act the need to split claims was removed by s.125(2) so that in cases where more than one invention is contained within a claim, multiple priority dates are possible. Thus, a claim may now include matter within it which is not a patentable invention, but it does not mean that the claim does not include within it an invention. If there is an invention in a claim the patent is partially valid."

21-166   And continuing (at 141), he said:

> "That a claim can contain within it a number of discrete claims was made clear by the Court of Appeal in *Daikin Kogyo Co Ltd (Shingu's Application* [1974] R.P.C. 559 ... In the same way, I am of the view that claim 9 of the patent in suit is in effect a number of discrete claims. This can be tested by applying the old law of prior claiming. If a claim in an earlier patent was of the same scope as claims 1, 8, 9 and 10, would it have been prior claimed? The answer would depend on whether claim 9 contained within it a discrete claim for the combination of claims 1, 8, 9 and 10. To my mind the answer would be yes, and that this is spelled out by the words 'according to any preceding claim'."

21-167   In *Lubrizol v Esso Petroleum*,[257] the patent (granted under the 1949 Act) was held invalid at first instance and in the Court of Appeal. The patentee submitted amendments and argued that since these would overcome the findings against them in the judgment, the patent was partially valid. This argument was rejected. Aldous LJ said:

> "However, it must be remembered that s.63 only applies when a court has held that a patent is partially invalid and partially valid. In such a case it can grant relief without requiring amendment or may direct that it be amended to its satisfaction. Thus, if a claim specifies more than one invention, it may grant relief in respect of one of those inventions even though the other invention is invalid. That is not this case. None of the claims specifies more than one invention."

21-168   Section 63(2) only applies where a court has made a finding that the patent was

---

[255] [1994] F.S.R. 471; [1995] F.S.R. 492. See also *Kirin-Amgen Inc's Patent* [2002] R.P.C. 43 (Pat) and [2003] R.P.C. 3, CA.

[256] [1990] F.S.R. 134. See also *Koninklijke Philips Electronics NV v Nintendo of Europe GmbH* [2014] EWHC 3177 (Pat).

[257] [1998] R.P.C. 727. And see also para. 9-163, et seq.

partially invalid, it does not apply when the patentee conceded a claim was invalid and the patent was duly amended.[258]

State of mind of the infringer

The state of mind of the infringer also arises under s.62(1) of the Act,[259] but that section poses the relatively straightforward question of whether at the date of the infringement the defendant was aware, or had reasonable grounds for supposing, that the patent existed. The issue of whether at the date of the infringement the defendant knew, or had reasonable grounds to know, that they were infringing the patent involves a much more sophisticated question. For instance, the defendant presumably needs to know, or have reasonable grounds to know: (a) that the patent exists, and (b) that their acts fall within the scope of the monopoly thereof as properly construed. In addition, since invalidity of the patent is a defence to infringement,[260] it would appear to follow that the defendant who knows that their acts fall within the scope of such monopoly but who does not know or have reasonable grounds to know that the patent is valid, will not have the relevant state of mind. However, since a granted patent is prima facie valid, it is submitted that a defendant would need to be able to adduce evidence in order to explain why the prima facie position did not, of itself, amount to reasonable grounds for knowing that the patent was valid. **21-169**

So far as concerns the test to be applied in determining whether the defendant had "reasonable grounds to know", it is submitted that the test which should be applied is the objective one suggested by Morritt J in *L.A. Gear v Hi-Tech Sportswear* and discussed above in relation to s.62(1) of the 1977 Act and supplied in *Schenck Rotec*.[261] Thus the defendant must have knowledge of facts from which a reasonable man would arrive at the relevant belief. However, the issue of whether an item is an infringing copy under copyright or trade mark law tends to be a much simpler question than whether a given act infringes a patent, particularly given that many of the copyright and trade mark cases where the issue arises involve obviously counterfeit goods. **21-170**

Further, it is submitted that the words of s.63(2)(a) also call for an inquiry of the defendant's state of knowledge at the date of each infringement. **21-171**

Good faith and reasonable skill and knowledge

The requirement to prove that the specification for the patent was framed with good faith and reasonable skill and knowledge arose under the old law and accordingly there already exists a body of case law in which the issue of "good faith and reasonable skill and knowledge" has been considered. Further the requirement arose (and still does arise) both under s.63(2), in the case where a patent is held partially valid, and also under s.62(3), in the case where the patent has previously been **21-172**

---

[258] *SmithKline Beecham Plc v Apotex Europe Ltd (No.2)* [2005] F.S.R. 24. See also *Zipher Ltd v Markem Systems* [2007] F.S.R. 18.

[259] See para.21-58, et seq. See also *Schenck Rotec GmbH v Universal Balancing Ltd* [2012] EWHC 1920 (Pat).

[260] PA 1977 s.74(1)(a).

[261] [1992] F.S.R. 121. Morritt J's test was approved by the Court of Appeal in that case. See also *ZYX Music GmbH v King* [1997] 2 All E.R. 129; *Pensher Security Door Co Ltd v Sunderland City Council* [2000] R.P.C. 249.

amended and damages are sought in respect of infringements committed prior to the decision to allow the amendment.[262]

21-173   The question is to be decided by considering any mistake in the patent in the context of the whole specification, making due allowance for any difficulty that the draughtsman has and of course the importance of the passage said to be mistaken.[263]

21-174   There are two separate tests in these subsections. That directed to good faith is essentially a test of honesty, based on what the patentee or their agent actually knew; ignorance of a fact which they ought to have known may have other consequences but do not indicate a lack of good faith.[264] Reasonable skill and knowledge is a separate consideration. Carelessness is in itself not enough.[265] In *Chiron Corp v Organon Teknika (No.7)*,[266] Aldous J held that a specification was framed with reasonable skill and knowledge if it was in a form which a person with reasonable skill in drafting patent applications and knowledge of the law and practice could produce with the patentee's knowledge of the invention. It follows that it is possible that this test will not be satisfied if the draftsman has not been properly instructed by the patentee. In *Kirin-Amgen Inc v Transkaryotic Therapies Inc*[267] the Court of Appeal held that the relevant knowledge must encompass the knowledge of the person which formed the basis of the information in the specification. The question had to be answered objectively and a patentee who used a contractor was not in any better or worse position than a patentee who did not. Thus where a specification contained an obvious mistake due to work done by a contractor, however skilled, the patentee had to shoulder the burden of establishing that the specification was framed with reasonable skill and knowledge.

21-175   It would seem that, where a party wishes to advance an allegation that an act of drafting or amendment was not carried out with "reasonable skill and knowledge", since no reasonable draftsman (patent attorney) could have done so, such an allegation will ordinarily need expert evidence in support. In *Nokia Corporation v IPCom GmbH & Co KG*,[268] IPCom's patent was attacked for obviousness, insufficiency and added matter. All of the attacks failed bar one of the nine added matter allegations. IPCom had put forward a conditional amendment before trial which cured the successful added matter attack and the amendment was accepted by the court.

21-176   Nokia contended that the patent had been found partially valid and that s.63(2)(b) applied to bar (or at least to limit) the relief available to IPCom. A further hearing was ordered after trial, directed to this matter and following relevant pleadings and evidence. Nokia's case was that the earlier amendment to the patent that led to the successful added matter attack was one framed without good faith, reasonable skill and knowledge ("GFRSK"). They asserted that no reasonable patent attorney could have believed that the amendment could be made without impermissible addition of matter.

21-177   Floyd J noted (at [19]) that the amended s.63(2) differed from its predecessor in several respects:

(i)   There is now a list of three factors to be taken into account.

---

[262] See para.21-63.
[263] *Kirin-Amgen Inc v Transkaryotic Therapies Inc* [2003] R.P.C. 3, [151], CA.
[264] *Hallen v Brabantia* [1990] F.S.R. 134; *Hoechst Celanese v B.P. Chemicals (No.1)* [1997] F.S.R. 547.
[265] *General Tire & Rubber Co v Firestone Tyre & Rubber Co Ltd* [1975] R.P.C. 203, 270.
[266] [1994] F.S.R. 458.
[267] [2003] R.P.C. 3, [152].
[268] [2011] EWHC 2719 (Pat), [2012] R.P.C. 21.

(ii) Neither GFRSK nor any of the other factors is an absolute pre-condition to obtaining relief: they are now merely factors to be taken account of in awarding relief.

(iii) It follows that relief may properly be awarded despite a finding of lack of GFRSK. The section enables a graduated approach, taking account of the factors referred to and their seriousness.

(iv) The section no longer explicitly allocates the burden of proving GFRSK on the patentee.

He went on to hold that the burden lay on the party making the allegation of draft- **21-178**
ing without GFRSK: here, that was Nokia. Since Nokia had not supported its allegation with evidence from an expert patent attorney, and since the EPO had accepted the amendment in question notwithstanding submissions on this point from
Nokia, the court found that it was not in a position to make a determination in relation to s.63(2)(b).

It was held by Lloyd-Jacob J in *Ronson Products Ltd v Lewis & Co* that: **21-179**

"where the drafting of the specification departs in a material respect from the intention of the applicant for protection, and this despite the transmission by the applicant to his patent agent of all
relevant information, an acknowledgement of such agent, that the way he expressed himself in the
passage in question was wrong in view of the information he had received, must establish the absence
of reasonable skill and knowledge."[269]

In the *General Tire & Rubber Co v Firestone Tyre & Rubber Co Ltd*, the Court **21-180**
of Appeal stated[270]:

"Section 59(3) [of the 1949 Act] does not speak of 'reasonable care' but of 'reasonable skill and
knowledge'. This we take to be limited to the field of expertise peculiar to those concerned with framing specifications, and in no way to refer to mere commonplace slips which are from time to time
the fate of those in many fields remote from patent expertise. A particular lack of reasonable care
may in any given case exhibit a lack of reasonable relevant skill, but not in every case by any means,
and certainly not in the case suggested."

In the same case, the court also stated: **21-181**

"On this question of good faith in framing a specification one is, we apprehend, basically in a field
of inquiry whether the patentee or his agent knew something detrimental to the patent, as applied for
in the form in which the specification was framed, which escaped the eagle eye of the examining officer in the Patent Office. If a patent agent puts forward something of which he had no knowledge,
which suffers from some fatal imperfection in the patent field we do not consider that, when the Patent Office accepts it without demur, it can be said that it was framed otherwise than in good faith. It
is, after all, the function of a patent agent to argue in honesty for the width of the application."[271]

However, more recently, in *Unilin Beheer BV v Berry Floor NV (No.2)*,[272] the **21-182**
Court of Appeal drew a distinction between relevant and irrelevant matter in the
specification of a patent and held that the requirement of "reasonable skill and
knowledge" did not extend to matter which was irrelevant. Thus the Court of Appeal held that if a specific passage in the specification of the patent has no

[269] [1963] R.P.C. 103, 138; see also *Lucas (Joseph) (Batteries) Ltd v Gaedor Ltd* [1978] R.P.C. 289.
[270] [1975] R.P.C. 203, 270.
[271] [1975] R.P.C. 203, 269. See also *Lucas (Joseph) (Batteries) Ltd v Gaedor Ltd* [1978] R.P.C. 389;
   Rediffusion Simulation v Link Miles [1993] F.S.R. 369; *Hallen v Brabantia* [1990] F.S.R. 134; and
   Chiron v Organon (No.7) [1994] F.S.R. 458.
[272] [2006] F.S.R. 26.

importance whatsoever, then, even if it is negligently wrong, s.63(2) of the 1977 Act is not engaged.[273]

21-183   The fact that the original claim was not "framed in good faith and with reasonable skill and knowledge" does not, however, affect the validity of the patent, after it has been amended.[274]

Meaning of "whether the proceedings are brought in good faith"

21-184   It is submitted that the meaning of "proceedings brought in good faith" is best understood against the background whereby the amendments to s.63(2) came to be made. This is discussed at para.21-157. It is submitted that proceedings brought to enforce a claim which the patentee knew to be invalid would not be proceedings "brought in good faith".

Practice

21-185   Under the old law it was held that questions under ss.62(3) and 63(2) are best decided by the trial judge.[275] They were sometimes left to the hearing of any enquiry as to damages, however, at least in cases where amendment was sought in an infringement action it was better practice to hear this question as part of the amendment proceedings since usually the court has most of the relevant facts before it for determining the allowability of the amendment.[276] Further, as the question went to the liability to pay damages, it was preferable that the question be determined before the costs of the inquiry are incurred, for otherwise such costs could be wasted.

21-186   Under the old law, the questions under ss.62(3) and 63(2) were "good faith and reasonable skill and knowledge" whereas under the law as amended there are or may be further issues. Nevertheless, it is submitted that the further issues only reinforce the view that they are best decided by the trial judge.

Onus of proof

21-187   Under the old law, the onus of proof that the original specification was framed in good faith and with reasonable skill and knowledge lay with the patentee.[277] However, it has been said by Greene MR that: "good faith and reasonable skill and knowledge would be assumed in the patentee's favour in the absence of internal or external evidence to the contrary."[278]

21-188   In *Johnson Electric v Mabuchi Motor K.K.*,[279] claims were obtained which were deliberately wide, but not deliberately invalid; this came about due to misunder-

---

[273] *Unilin Beheer BV v Berry Floor NV (No.2)* [2006] F.S.R. 26, [24] and [25].
[274] See *British United Shoe Machinery Co Ltd v A. Fussel & Sons Ltd* (1908) 25 R.P.C. 631, at 660.
[275] *Kirin-Amgen Inc v Transkaryotic Therapies Inc* [2003] R.P.C. 3, [148], CA.
[276] See, e.g. *Lucas (Joseph) (Batteries) Ltd v Gaedor Ltd* [1978] R.P.C. 389; and see *David Kahn Inc v Conway Stewart & Co Ltd* [1976] R.P.C. 279.
[277] See *British United Shoe Machinery Co Ltd v A. Fussell & Sons Ltd* (1908) 25 R.P.C. 368; *British United Shoe Machinery Co Ltd v Gimson Shoe Machinery Co Ltd (No.2)* (1929) 46 R.P.C. 137, at 164. Relief was granted in the following cases: *Hopkinson v St James and Pall Mall Electric Light Co Ltd* (1893) 10 R.P.C. 46; *J.B. Brooks & Co Ltd v E. Lycett Ltd* (1903) 20 R.P.C. 390; *J.B. Brooks & Co Ltd v Rendall, Underwood & Co Ltd* (1907) 24 R.P.C. 17; *Kirin-Amgen Inc v Transkaryotic Therapies Inc* [2003] R.P.C. 3, CA.
[278] *Molins & Molins Machine Co Ltd v Industrial Machinery Co Ltd* (1938) 55 R.P.C. 31, 33. See also *General Tire case* [1975] R.P.C. 203, at 269.
[279] [1996] R.P.C. 387.

standing and mistranslation between the UK and Japanese patent agents. It was held that there was no covetousness, although there was a lack of reasonable skill and knowledge.

Under the new law (i.e. as amended), there is no clear statement in s.63(2) as to **21-189** who has the onus of proof for any of the issues raised by subs.(a)–(c). It is submitted, however, that the onus will be upon the patentee for each of the issues although, as in all civil litigation, it will be a shifting onus and thus once the patentee has established a prima facie case for any of the issues raised by subs.(a)–(c) the onus will shift to the defendant to show otherwise.

Discretionary principles when considering relief

Section 63(2) of the 1977 Act, as amended, provides that the defendant's state **21-190** of knowledge, whether the specification was framed in good faith and with reasonable skill and knowledge, and whether the proceedings are brought in good faith, are all factors to be taken into account when awarding "damages, costs or expenses or making an order for an account of profits". In this respect it is similar to s.62(3) where the same factors are relevant to a claim awarding damages or making an order for an account of profits if a patent has been amended and where the infringement was committed before the decision to allow the amendment. No mention is made in s.63(2) of relief by way of injunction or delivery up and the reason for this, it is submitted, is because they are both equitable remedies and subject to the court's discretion in any event.[280] Once infringement of a valid claim is proved, the patentee is prima facie entitled under s.63 of the 1977 Act to an injunction. As Pearson LJ said in *Van der Lely (C.) N.V. v Bamfords Ltd*[281] in respect of s.62 of the 1949 Act:

> "Under these provisions ... it is clear that the claims can be considered separately, and the invalidity of some only of the claims does not invalidate the whole patent, and does not prevent the giving of relief in respect of the claims which are valid. Indeed, I think that the section gives to the patentee a prima facie right to relief subject to the qualifications provided. Under subsection (1) he can apply for an injunction and the court has the usual discretion with regard to the granting of an injunction. If a breach of a legal right is established and there is no equitable bar to the granting of an injunction, and no bar has arisen under subsection (3) of the section, the court will (or at any rate normally would) grant an injunction. It is to be noted that an injunction can be granted without any amendment of the patent."

This approach has been followed by Aldous J in *Hallen Co v Brabantia (UK)* **21-191** *Ltd*[282] in relation to s.63 of the 1977 Act.

Where a valid claim has been infringed, the mere fact that there has been delay **21-192** in seeking to amend is no ground for refusing an injunction. As Harman LJ stated in *Van der Lely (C.) N.V. v Bamfords Ltd*[283]:

> "If the relief asked be by way of injunction, on the ordinary principles well known in the Court of Chancery, where a man's legal rights have been invaded, mere delay will not deprive him of relief; that is stated by Fry J in the well-known decision *Fullwood v Fullwood*[284] where he said that there must be more than mere delay to disentitle a man to his legal rights."

---

280 See para.21-63 concerning the ability to seek an account of profits after amendment; and see *Codex Corp v Racal-Milgo Ltd* [1983] R.P.C. 369 as well as *Spring Form Inc v Toy Brokers Ltd* [2002] F.S.R 17.
281 [1964] R.P.C. 54, 73.
282 [1990] F.S.R. 134. See also *Chiron v Organon (No.7)* [1994] F.S.R. 458.
283 [1964] R.P.C. 54, 81.
284 (1878) 9 Ch D. 176.

Date from which damages should be reckoned

21-193   In a case to which the section applies, the court has an unfettered discretion to decide from what date any award of damages should run, and must take all relevant circumstances into account including not only the conduct of the parties but also the position of the general public; but it will remain the fact that the defendant has infringed a valid claim and the claimant ought not to be deprived of the right to damages without good reason. The Court of Appeal so held in *Gerber v Lectra*,[285] and it expressly approved the statement of Aldous J at first instance to the following effect:

> "The defendants accept that: (i) the specification was framed in good faith and with reasonable skill and knowledge; (ii) the claims which were held valid do not need alteration by amendment because the only appropriate amendment would be the deletion of Claim 1; (iii) they have infringed those claims; and (iv) they have not been prejudiced by the inclusion in the patent of the claim held invalid. They submit that the court should make an order that they should not pay anything for the infringements. In effect, the order that they seek would grant to the defendants a free licence because the patent contained an invalid claim. When so stated, the submission appears devoid of merit."

21-194   However, the effect of the presence of the invalid claims on the defendant will be taken into account, so that if the presence of the invalid claims has induced them to act as they did then it would be unjust to require them to pay damages. Although if they had no effect upon the defendant then ordinarily it would not be just to deprive the claimant of damages.[286]

Directing amendment as a condition of relief under s.63

21-195   Where a patent has been found partially valid, the court has a discretion under s.63(3) whether or not to direct amendment. The considerations raised by this subsection are considered at para.15-125 of this work.

Under s.63(4), as amended, the court may also make it a condition of relief in the case of the European patent (UK) that the claims of the patent are limited to its satisfaction by the European Patent Office at the request of the proprietor.[287]

6.   CERTIFICATE OF CONTESTED VALIDITY

21-196   At the close of an action for infringement where the issue of validity has been raised and the patent has been upheld, the patentee should obtain a certificate of contested validity entitling them to a special privilege in subsequent actions. In order to prevent a patentee from being put repeatedly to the expense of defending successive attacks on the validity of their patent, it is enacted that a court may in any proceedings certify that the validity of any claim[288] was contested in those proceedings and in that case, if in any subsequent proceedings for infringement or for revocation of the patent the patentee is successful, they are entitled, unless the court or the comptroller otherwise directs, to have their costs or expenses as

---

[285] [1995] F.S.R. 492, 499, CA.
[286] [1995] F.S.R. 492, 499, CA. See also *Hallen v Brabantia* [1990] F.S.R. 134.
[287] See also PA 1977 s.72(4A) as amended. See also para.15-16.
[288] See *Ludlow Jute Co Ltd v James Low & Co Ltd* (1953) 70 R.P.C. 69.

between solicitor and own client (other than the costs or expenses of any appeal in any such proceedings).[289]

Both as regards the grant of a certificate of contested validity and as regards any **21-197** subsequent direction depriving a claimant of solicitor and client costs, the power conferred upon the court is purely discretionary, and is exercised upon the facts of the particular case before the court. It is difficult, therefore, to extract from the many reported decisions any guiding principles upon which such certificates or directions should be granted.[290]

In general, however, a certificate will not be granted unless there has been a real **21-198** contest as to validity,[291] although in exceptional circumstances the court may depart from this rule.[292] Where the question of validity was disputed upon a certain construction of a specification only, and not generally, a certificate has been refused.[293] When a certificate of validity has once been granted there is no need for another in a subsequent action upon the same patent[294]; in one case, however, a fresh certificate was granted where validity was attacked on new grounds.[295] If the specification is amended after the granting of the certificate, so as to affect the claim or claims certified, the certificate will no longer hold good, and a new one must be applied for in any subsequent action.[296] Certificates are granted in respect of any individual claims of a patent which come into question.[297]

In *SmithKline Beecham Plc v Apotex Europe Ltd (No.2)*[298] the Court of Appeal **21-199** held that although s.65(2) did not apply to the costs on an appeal,[299] the same result could and would in an appropriate case be achieved by applying the general powers of the court to award indemnity costs.

Certificate of validity on appeal

A certificate of validity can also be granted by the Court of Appeal when a deci- **21-200** sion by the court of first instance is reversed.[300] However, where a patent which has been held to be invalid in the lower courts is held valid by the House of Lords, the practice is for the House of Lords to remit the matter to the Chancery Division with

---

[289] PA 1977 s.65.
[290] See *Letraset International Ltd v Mecanorma Ltd* [1975] F.S.R. 125.
[291] *Gillette Industries Ltd v Bernstein* (1941) 58 R.P.C. 271, 285; *Martin v C.B. Projection (Engineering) Ltd* (1948) 65 R.P.C. 361. See also *British Thomson-Houston Co Ltd v Corona Lamp Works Ltd* (1922) 39 R.P.C. 49, at 93; *Auster Ltd v Perfect Motor Equipments Ltd* (1924) 41 R.P.C. 482, 498; *Brupat v Smith* [1985] R.P.C. 156.
[292] *Gillette Industries Ltd v Bernstein* [1942] 58 R.P.C. 271, 285. See also *Brupat v Smith* [1985] F.S.R. 156, in which a challenge to validity was made but dropped in closing speeches as a result of cross-examination.
[293] *New Inverted Incandescent Gas Lamp Co Ltd v Globe Light Ltd* (1906) 23 R.P.C. 157; and see *Morris and Bastert v Young* (1895) 12 R.P.C. 455, at 464 and 465.
[294] *Edison and Swan Electric Light Co v Holland* (1889) 6 R.P.C. 243, 287.
[295] See *Flour Oxidising Co Ltd v J. and R. Hutchinson* (1909) 26 R.P.C. 597, at 638.
[296] *Brooks & Co Ltd v Rendall, Underwood & Co Ltd* (1907) 23 R.P.C. 17, 27.
[297] PA 1977 s.65; and see, e.g. *Marconi's Wireless Telegraph Co Ltd v Mullard Radio Valve Co Ltd* (1923) 40 R.P.C. 1, at 27; *British United Shoe Machinery Co Ltd v Gimson Shoe Machinery Co Ltd (No.2)* (1929) 46 R.P.C. 137.
[298] [2005] F.S.R. 24.
[299] Jacob LJ commented that this was "completely irrational". His views were shared by Ward LJ but not by Arden LJ.
[300] See *Cole v Saqui* (1889) 6 R.P.C. 41, at 45.

a direction to grant a certificate of validity and, where necessary such other certificates to which the patentee may be entitled.[301]

Appeal as to grant or refusal of certificate

21-201   It has been held that a certificate that the validity of a claim was contested is not a judgment or order within s.19 of the Judicature Act 1873 (now s.16(1) of the Senior Courts Act 1981[302]); and no appeal, therefore, lay from the decision of the judge granting or withholding the certificate.[303]

The subsequent action

21-202   Under the 1949 Act, it was the law that a certificate of contested validity granted in one action will not affect the costs in another, although decided at a later date, provided that the latter proceedings were instituted before the grant of the certificate in the earlier action.[304] Under s.65(2) of the 1977 Act, however, it has been held that a party to existing proceedings who has challenged the validity of a patent may elect either to proceed with the challenge or accept the certificate. If they adopt the former course and go on to lose, they will be liable to pay the higher scale costs.[305]

Effect of certificate on costs of subsequent action

21-203   The court in the subsequent action has an unlimited discretion, which it exercises in view of the facts of the particular case; thus, a direction depriving the claimants of solicitor and client costs was made where the second action was vexatious[306] or where the issue of validity was not raised therein, and the defendants were innocent infringers[307] or had a plausible argument with respect to non-infringement.[308] The mere fact that validity is not disputed in the subsequent action is not, however, sufficient to cause such a direction to be made,[309] some special reason being required.[310]

21-204   Solicitor and client costs are refused in respect of the issue of validity where the claimant is successful upon that issue but fails owing to non-infringement, as the party relying on the validity of the patent must obtain a final order or judgment in their favour.[311]

21-205   The court has on occasion refused to go behind the certificate of validity and

---

[301]   *British Thomson-Houston Co Ltd v Corona Lamp Works Ltd* (1922) 39 R.P.C. 49, 95; *Van der Lely v Ruston's* [1993] R.P.C. 45.

[302]   Formerly the Supreme Court Act 1981. See the Constitutional Reform Act 2005 Sch.11 Pt 1 para.19(1).

[303]   *Haslam & Co v Hall (No.2)* (1888) 5 R.P.C. 144.

[304]   *Automatic Weighing Machine Co v International Hygienic Society* (1889) 6 R.P.C. 475, 480; *Saccharin Corp Ltd v Anglo-Continental Chemical Works Ltd* [1901] 1 Ch. 414. See *Letraset International Ltd v Mecanorma Ltd* [1975] F.S.R. 125.

[305]   See *Mölnlycke A.B. v Procter & Gamble Ltd (No.5)* [1994] R.P.C. 49, at 140 and 141.

[306]   *Proctor v Sutton Lodge Chemical Co* (1888) 5 R.P.C. 184.

[307]   *Boyd v Tootal Broadhurst Lee Co Ltd* (1894) 11 R.P.C. 174, 185.

[308]   *Saccharin Corp Ltd v Dawson* (1902) 19 R.P.C. 169, 173.

[309]   *United Telephone Co Ltd v Patterson* (1889) 6 R.P.C. 140; *British Vacuum Cleaner Co v Exton Hotels Ltd* (1908) 25 R.P.C. 617, 629.

[310]   *Welsbach Incandescent Gas Light Co Ltd v Daylight Incandescent Mantle Co Ltd* (1899) 16 R.P.C. 344, 353.

[311]   PA 1977 s.65(2); and see *Higginson and Arundel v Pyman* (1926) 43 R.P.C. 113, at 136.

inquire as to the circumstances in which it was granted.[312] However, in later cases the court has ordered only party and party costs where the real substantial trial of validity has taken place in the subsequent action.[313]

In *Otto v Steel*,[314] solicitor and client costs were refused on the ground that the **21-206** validity of the patent was attacked on new grounds,[315] although it is unlikely that that case will be followed at the present time, save in exceptional circumstances.

Solicitor and client costs have also been refused where the patent has been **21-207** amended since the certificate of validity was granted.[316]

7. Costs

Practice under the Civil Procedure Rules

Prior to the entry into force of the CPR, quantification of costs had become an **21-208** unnecessarily complex, time-consuming and expensive process. This was true both of UK litigation generally and patent actions in particular. The CPR has introduced a new, and considerably simpler, code which applies to both the Patents Court and (with some important modifications, discussed in Ch.20) to the Intellectual Property Enterprise Court. The provisions of the CPR in relation to costs were revised and re-ordered with effect from 1 April 2013.

The court has a discretion as to whether costs are payable by one party to another, **21-209** the amount of these costs, and when they are paid but the general presumption is that the loser pays the winner's costs to an extent which reflects the extent to which the winner has been successful.[317] The court will, however, bear in mind all the circumstances, including the conduct of the parties and any payment into court or offer to settle (whether or not made in accordance with CPR Pt 36).[318] The conduct of the parties includes whether it was reasonable for a party to raise, pursue or contest a particular allegation or issue and the manner in which the party did in fact do so.[319]

The CPR provides that the conduct of the parties before, as well as during, the **21-210** proceedings is to be taken into account and in particular the extent to which the parties followed any relevant pre-action protocol.[320] However, not only is there no pre-action protocol for patents actions but it is unlikely that there will be, due to the possibility of threats actions and/or the encouragement of "torpedo" actions in other jurisdictions.

There are many costs orders which can be made.[321] In each case the court must **21-211** state whether the assessment is to be made on the standard or indemnity basis. Assessed on either basis only costs which are proportionate will be allowed.

---

[312] *Fabriques de Produits Chimique, etc. v Lafitte* (1899) 16 R.P.C. 61, 68; *Peter Pilkington Ltd v B. and S. Massey* (1904) 21 R.P.C. 421, 438; *Badische Anilin und Soda Fabrik v W.G. Thompson & Co Ltd* (1904) 21 R.P.C. 473, 480.

[313] *British Thomson-Houston Co Ltd v Corona Lamp Works Ltd* (1922) 39 R.P.C. 49, 93; *Auster Ltd v Perfecta Motor Equipments Ltd* (1924) 41 R.P.C. 482, 498.

[314] (1886) 3 R.P.C. 109, 120.

[315] See also *Flour Oxidising Co Ltd v J. and R. Hutchinson* (1909) 26 R.P.C. 597, at 638.

[316] *J.B. Brooks & Co Ltd v Rendall, Underwood & Co Ltd* (1907) 24 R.P.C. 17, 27.

[317] CPR r.44.2(1), (2), (4)(b).

[318] CPR r.44.2(4)(a), (c).

[319] CPR r.44.2(5)(b), (c).

[320] CPR r.44.2(5)(a).

[321] CPR r.44.2(6).

Disproportionate costs will be disallowed even if they were reasonably or necessarily incurred. Assessment on the standard basis resolves doubts in favour of the paying party while assessment on the indemnity basis resolves doubts in favour of the receiving party.[322]

21-212   Where the court orders a party to pay costs to another party[323] it may either make a summary assessment of the costs, or order detailed assessment of the costs by a costs officer.[324] The court also has power to order a party's legal representatives to pay wasted costs personally,[325] where the conduct of such legal representative has been unreasonable or improper.[326]

Apportionment of costs

21-213   Lord Woolf MR was anxious to move away from the position that any success is sufficient to obtain an order for costs and this concern was reflected in the CPR provisions about costs when they were brought in.[327] Apportionment had long been a concern of the Patents Court which developed its own jurisprudence on the subject. Today it can be seen that the policy applied in patent cases is no different from that applicable to other cases. The fact that patent costs are generally approached in the same way in the majority of cases is a reflection of the application of that policy to the particular circumstances.

21-214   An example of the problems which can arise occurs when the patentee lost the action as a whole but succeeded either on the issue of infringement (the patent being invalid) or validity (but no infringement). In making orders apportioning the costs of an action and counterclaim, in the exercise of its discretion, the court had to reconcile two competing principles, on the one hand, prima facie, the costs of litigation should follow the event,[328] but on the other hand the costs order ought to reflect the extent to which costs have been thrown away by one party raising and pursuing unsuccessful points.[329]

21-215   The modern approach to the costs of patent cases is that explained in *SmithKline Beecham Plc v Apotex Europe Ltd (No.2)*.[330] After referring to cases in other fields and to the earlier patent cases of *Stena v Irish Ferries*[331] and *Rediffusion Simulation Ltd v Link Miles Ltd*,[332] Jacob LJ said[333]:

"An issue-by-issue approach is therefore one which should be applied so far as it reasonably can. On

---

[322] CPR rr.44.3 and 44.4. For example of costs being ordered on the indemnity basis, see *Connaught Laboratories Inc's Patent* [1999] F.S.R. 284 and *Marshalltown Trowel Co v CeKa Works Ltd* [2001] F.S.R. 36.

[323] Other than fixed costs. Fixed costs ordinarily apply only to claims for a specified sum of money or the delivery of goods (CPR r.45.1(2)(a),(b)) and are therefore not relevant to claims in the Patents Court. There is a fixed costs regime in the Small Claims Track of the IPEC, however; see para.20-05.

[324] CPR r.44.6(1).

[325] CPR r.44.11.

[326] *Bell Fruit Manufacturing Co v Twinfalcon* [1995] F.S.R. 144, in which a patent agent who acted without authority and caused the claimant to incur substantial costs was ordered to pay such costs.

[327] *Phonographic Performance Ltd v AEI Redifussion Music Ltd* [1999] EWCA Civ 834.

[328] See now CPR, r.44.3 (2)(a).

[329] The provision of certificates is an application of this principle.

[330] [2005] F.S.R. 24, [24]–[41]. See also *Kavanagh Balloons Pty Ltd v Cameron Balloons Ltd* [2003] EWCA Civ 1952; [2004] F.S.R. 33.

[331] [2003] EWCA Civ 214; [2003] R.P.C. 37.

[332] [1993] F.S.R. 369, 410.

[333] [2005] F.S.R. 24, [26] and [27].

the other hand such an approach is not the be-all and end-all. Whether or not 'it was reasonable for a party to raise, pursue or contest a particular allegation' remains a relevant factor to be taken into account as part of the conduct of the parties (see CPR 44 r.(4)(a) and (5)(b)).

The impossibility of great precision

Before turning to this particular case I should say something about this. Although an issue-by-issue approach is likely to produce a 'fairer' answer and is likely to make parties consider carefully before advancing or disputing a particular issue, it should not be thought that it is capable of achieving a 'precise' answer. The estimation of costs, like that of valuation of property, is more of an art than a science. True it is that one can measure certain things (such as pages of witness statements or transcript devoted to a particular issue) but they can only be indicia to be taken into account. It would be dangerous to rely on them as absolutes. Indeed brevity of a document, or cross-examination, may be the result of great care: was it Hazlitt who apologised for the length of a letter, excusing himself on the grounds that he had not had enough time to compose it?[334]

It follows that there is no 'precise' figure of costs which, in theory with perfect measurement tools, one could reach. The best that can be achieved is an estimate which is necessarily going to be somewhat crude."

21-216

This approach is applied by asking a series of questions referred to by Pumfrey LJ in *Monsanto Technology LLC v Cargill International SA (No. 2)*.[335] The questions are first to identify the overall winner, and secondly to ask if there are suitably circumscribed issues on which the winner lost. If there are, then two further questions arise relating to that issue. Should the winner recover its costs of that issue? also, should the winner pay the otherwise unsuccessful party's costs incurred in respect of that issue? Then estimates of the costs of particular issues are made, expressed as a percentage of the receiving party's overall costs and the result is an order that the paying party pays the receiving party X per cent of the receiving party's costs.

21-217

The identification of the overall winner may be obvious but there can be complications. For example, identifying the overall winner of proceedings involving multiple patents in which the outcomes differ may pose problems.[336] In the cases cited in the preceding footnote, the Patents Court applied the guidance of Lord Bingham MR in *Roache v News Group Newspapers*[337] and considered who, as a matter of substance has won. It may be that in multi-patent proceedings an overall winner for the purposes of dealing with costs cannot sensibly be identified.[338] When a large dispute about a portfolio of patents has been split into multiple trials, including technical trials on the patents and a later FRAND trial, the court dealing with the costs of a single technical trial will need to consider whether there is real possibility that the outcome of the outcome of the future trial(s) may affect the merits of the parties' entitlements to costs of the current trial.[339]

21-218

The overall winner is likely (save in the most exceptional circumstances) to be entitled to payment of all their costs which are not or cannot be allocated to a particular issue, which Pumfrey LJ in *Monsanto*[340] referred to as the general costs of the action. The focus then turns to whether there are suitably circumscribed issues on which the winner did not succeed. It is in the nature of patent cases that this

21-219

---

[334] In a separate judgment in the same case Arden LJ attributed the aphorism to *Pascal*—see [46].

[335] [2008] F.S.R. 16.

[336] See, e.g. *Omnipharm v Merial* [2012] EWHC 172 (Pat); *Koninklijke Philips v Nintendo*, Patents Court, Birss J (17 July 2014); *Vringo v ZTE* [2014] EWHC 4475 (Pat); *Merck v Ono* [2015] EWHC 3973 (Pat).

[337] [1998] E.M.L.R. 161

[338] *Vringo v ZTE* [2014] EWHC 4475 (Pat).

[339] See *Unwired Planet v Huawei* [2015] EWHC 3837 and the cases cited in that judgment.

[340] [2008] F.S.R. 16.

is often the case. For those issues the court has to decide whether to deprive the overall winner of its costs on that issue or to go further and award them to the overall loser. In and after *Monsanto* the term "exceptional" or "suitably exceptional"[341] was used to characterise the test to be applied to award costs to the overall loser but that is too stringent a test. The correct test is simply whether it is appropriate to do so in all the circumstances.[342]

21-220   The issues on which the winner has lost can represent substantial costs in the proceedings and the effect of this exercise can lead to a result that the balance of costs to be paid is from the overall winner to the loser. That happened in *Monsanto* itself. For another example, consider *Ratiopharm v Napp*,[343] in which the Patents Court had upheld the validity of the patent in issue but had found that the claimant generics companies' proposed acts would not be infringements. As a commercial matter, the claimants had the declaration they needed. Floyd J nonetheless ordered that Ratiopharm and Sandoz, the claimants, should together pay 20 per cent of the defendant's costs, having failed on validity.

21-221   Each case will be decided on its own facts. For example, on the facts in *SmithKline Beecham Plc v Apotex Europe Ltd*[344] the trial judge had found the patent invalid and not infringed and awarded Apotex 76 per cent of their costs, having regard to certain issues on which Apotex had lost. On appeal the Court of Appeal allowed the appeal on validity, finding the patent valid, but dismissed the appeal on infringement, maintaining the finding of non-infringement. In considering the first instance costs, the Court of Appeal assessed the impact of its judgment on the various issues as well as the effect of s.65[345], and the fact that Apotex were the overall commercial winner[346] because they were free to market their pharmaceutical product. Accordingly the Court of Appeal set aside the trial judge's order and awarded Apotex 16 per cent of their costs at first instance. As to the costs of the appeal, since the majority of the time had been taken up with SmithKline Beecham's successful appeal on validity, albeit that they failed in their infringement action, SmithKline Beecham were awarded 25 per cent of their costs of the appeal. For further examples of the apportionment approach to issue-based costs awards, see the judgments of Kitchin J in *Novartis AG v Johnson & Johnson Medical Ltd (Costs)*,[347] Floyd J in *Schütz v Werit*[348] and the Court of Appeal in *Samsung Electronics Co Ltd v Apple Retail UK Ltd*.[349]

Effect of successful EPO opposition on costs of action in national court

21-222   In *Rambus Inc v Hynix Semiconductor UK Ltd*[350] the claimant had brought infringement proceedings in the UK courts against two different defendants. The defendants disputed infringement and validity, as is usual, but also raised other defences—including a defence under art.82 of the EC Treaty (now art.102 of the

---

341 e.g. Floyd J in *Nokia v Qualcomm* [2008] EWHC 777.
342 See Arnold J in *Hospira v Novartis* [2013] EWHC 886 (Pat), followed by Birss J in *Wobben v Siemens* [2015] EWHC 2863 (Pat).
343 [2009] EWHC 209 (Ch).
344 [2005] F.S.R. 24, [24]–[41].
345 See para.21-196.
346 Arden LJ dissented on this particular point but not as to the result (see [47]).
347 [2009] EWHC 2029 (Pat).
348 [2010] EWHC 1197 (Pat).
349 [2013] EWHC 467 (Pat).
350 [2005] F.S.R. 19.

Treaty on the Functioning of the European Union), and a defence of estoppel and waiver arising out of the parties' involvement with a standardisation body (the "JEDEC" defence). The national proceedings were stayed pending a parallel EPO opposition, which succeeded and resulted in the revocation of the patent in suit. On the return to the UK court, it was common ground that the patent actions should be struck out and that the defendants should have their costs of the infringement and validity issues, but the patentee disputed its entitlement to pay for the art.82 and JEDEC defences. Mann J held that the art.82 and JEDEC defences were reasonable and arguable and neither bound to succeed nor doomed to failure. However, the dismissal of the claim was in the nature of a defeat for the claimant so the claimant should pay the defendants their costs of these issues.

Cost capping

The court has jurisdiction to make an order which caps costs,[351] i.e. which prospectively places a limit on the amount of costs for which a party will be liable if the other party succeeds at trial and obtains on order for costs.   **21-223**

In *Knight v Beyond Properties Pty Ltd*[352] Mann J considered previous authorities, including *King v Telegraph Group*[353] and *Campbell v MGN Ltd*,[354] before deriving the following propositions: **21-224**

(1) It must be established on evidence that there is a real risk of disproportionate or unreasonable costs being incurred.

(2) It must be shown that that risk cannot be satisfactorily provided for by more conventional means (and in particular the usual costs assessment after the trial).

The court may also make an order after trial which caps the costs that can be recovered.[355] However, even after trial there may be practical difficulties in assessing the value of the claim and hence deciding what the cap should be.[356] For instance in *Research in Motion UK Ltd v Visto Corp*[357] the court noted a substantial disparity between the costs incurred by the parties, but felt that its power to do anything about that situation was limited. In a subsequent case between the same parties, and to enable an application for a costs capping order to be considered, Arnold J ordered the parties to exchange information as to the costs incurred to date and their estimated future costs, split according to the patents in suit.[358]   **21-225**

Costs where patent partially valid

Prior to the amendment of s.63(2), if the patentee obtained relief in respect of some claim which is held valid and infringed in a case where one or more the claims   **21-226**

---

[351] CPR Pt 3 rr.3.19–3.21.
[352] [2007] F.S.R. 7.
[353] [2004] EWCA Civ 613.
[354] [2005] 1 W.L.R. 3394, HL.
[355] *Ultraframe (UK) Ltd v Fielding* [2006] EWCA Civ 1660, [2007] 2 All E.R. 983.
[356] See *Research in Motion UK Ltd v Visto Corp* [2008] EWHC 819 (Pat); *Generics (UK) Ltd v Daiichi Pharmaceutical Co Ltd* [2009] F.S.R. 9; *Edwards Lifesciences AG v Cook Biotech Inc (No. 2)* [2009] F.S.R. 28.
[357] [2008] EWHC 89 (Pat).
[358] *Research in Motion UK Ltd v Visto Corp* [2009] F.S.R. 10.

are invalid,[359] no costs would be be awarded to them unless they proved that the specification was framed in good faith and with reasonable skill and knowledge.[360] The same result would not automatically follow today, although the failure to prove the same remains a relevant factor under s.63(2) as amended.

21-227   Where actions are brought upon more than one patent and the claimant is successful as to some but not all of the patents sued on, it is usual for the costs to be apportioned.[361]

Currency in which costs award to be made

21-228   In *Actavis v Novartis*[362] a dispute arose about the currency in which a costs award should be made. The judge had found that Actavis was entitled to 45 per cent of its costs. Actavis asked that that award be made in Euros, since that was the currency in which it had transacted with its solicitors. Alternatively, Actavis asked that the award be made in UK currency but using a conversion rate applicable at the time of assessment. Novartis contended for costs to be awarded in pounds sterling, taking the Euro conversion rate at the time the costs were paid. The currency basis was material, because the Euro:Sterling conversion rate had changed greatly as the proceedings had gone on.

21-229   The judge decided that this was probably a matter for the costs assessment judge but nonetheless recorded that:[363]

> "My strong inclination is towards the view those items of recoverable costs payable by it in Euros or the sterling equivalent of the total Euro amount converted into sterling at the date of the assessment or enforcement."

Conditional fee agreements

21-230   In *Sandvik Intellectual Property AB v Kennametal UK Ltd*[364] the defendant was found to be the commercial victor and entitled to an award of costs. Kennametal's solicitors were acting under a conditional fee agreement (CFA). Under the terms of the CFA, Kennametal's solicitors were entitled to a success fee which amounted to a 35 per cent uplift on their normal rates. The claimant contended that CFAs were a tool to improve access to justice, and that in the circumstances of this litigation between two substantial commercial undertakings, an award of the success fee was inappropriate. It further submitted that none of the policy imperatives which led to the availability of CFAs for litigation was engaged when the parties were of this size, therefore there was no policy reason to support the making of an award including a success fee.

21-231   The Patents Court did not accept the claimant's arguments, finding that the House of Lords' decision in *Campbell v MGN*[365] precluded a suggestion that award of a success fee should be disallowed when the party could have afforded to litigate without a CFA.

---

[359] PA 1977 s.63(1).
[360] PA 1977 s.63(2); and see *Hale v Coombes* (1925) 42 R.P.C. 238, at 350; *Ronson Products Ltd v Lewis & Co* [1963] R.P.C. 103, at 138.
[361] See, e.g. *Hocking v Fraser* (1886) 3 R.P.C. 3; *Brooks v Lamplugh* (1898) 15 R.P.C. 33, at 52.
[362] [2009] EWHC 502 (Ch).
[363] [2009] EWHC 502 (Ch), [34].
[364] [2012] EWHC 245 (Pat).
[365] CPR r.44.2(5)(b), (c).

Effect of Pt 36 Offer

In *Kavanagh Balloons Pty Ltd v Cameron Balloons Ltd*[366] the Court of Appeal **21-232** held that the trial judge does not have a discretion in relation to the costs consequences of a Pt 36 offer. The wording of CPR Pt 36.20 (now Pt 36.17) was quite clear and it required the court to make an order in favour of the offeror, if the offer was not accepted and not beaten, save only in the case in which it would be unjust to make such an order. In *Dyson Ltd v Hoover Ltd (No.2)*[367] Jacob J held that in a situation in which a claimant accepted a Pt 36 offer, the defendant would be ordered to pay costs on the standard basis under the previous version of CPR r.36.13(4), and there was no discretion to award costs on an indemnity basis. It is of note, however, that r.36.13 has since been amended and the new rule r.36.13(4) merely provides that the costs must be "determined by the court".

Summary assessment

The general rule is that summary assessment will be made at the conclusion of **21-233** any hearing which has lasted less than one day.[368] Summary assessment requires that the parties prepare and serve schedules of costs prepared in accordance with the relevant Practice Direction.[369] Given the time and effort often involved in the drawing up of such schedules, however, the parties will often agree not to seek summary assessment.

The summary assessment will be performed by the tribunal hearing the claim, **21-234** hearing or application and is a summary rather than precise exercise. Often the starting point is a comparison of the parties' respective total figures. A line-by-line examination of the individual items contained in the schedule of costs is an inappropriate use of court time and if one or other parties desires such detailed examination the court is likely to defer the matter for detailed assessment by a costs officer. If neither side seeks a detailed assessment, then the court will do its best with the material which is made available and can only adjust figures deposed to by the solicitors concerned if there is a very good reason for doing so.[370]

Detailed assessment

The general rule is that the detailed assessment of costs is not carried out until **21-235** the conclusion of the proceedings, though the court may order it to be carried out immediately.[371] It is not stayed pending an appeal unless the court so orders but where the detailed assessment itself is likely to be highly expensive and time-consuming the court is likely to so order.[372]

---

[366] [2003] EWCA Civ 1952; [2004] F.S.R. 33.
[367] [2002] EWHC 2229 (Ch); [2003] F.S.R. 21.
[368] CPR r.44.6(1); and PD44 §9.2(b).
[369] See also, *Guide to the Summary Assessment of Costs* (2005 edn), *The White Book* (London: Sweet & Maxwell, 2016), para.48GP.17.
[370] *Monsanto Technology LLC v Cargill International SA (No. 2)* [2008] F.S.R. 16.
[371] CPR r.47.1.
[372] CPR r.47.2. See *Lubrizol v Esso (No.6)* [1997] F.S.R. 844, where taxation was estimated to last four to seven weeks as compared to a trial of 13 days—therefore the detailed assessment was stayed pending appeal.

Payments of costs on account

21-236   The court has the power to make an order for payment of costs on account and such an order is normally made.[373] Since the only reason why a party who has succeeded, with costs, is not paid straightaway is the need for a detailed assessment, an interim order will usually be justified.[374] The test is not to find an irreducible minimum sum,[375] rather it is to award a reasonable sum in the circumstances.[376] To find a figure not too much below the likely level of a detailed assessment is an appropriate approach and the other party's costs can be taken into account.[377] The court can make an order for payment on account of costs even without a trial,[378] but may not do so if the reason why there is no trial is because the party seeking costs has chosen to settle the matter and thereby put itself into a position which makes interim payment difficult to assess.[379]

Detailed assessment proceedings

21-237   Detailed assessment proceedings are commenced by the receiving party serving on the paying party a notice of commencement and a copy of the bill of costs[380] within three months after the event giving rise to the right to costs.[381] The paying party may dispute any item in the bill of costs by serving points of dispute within 21 days thereafter.[382] If no points of dispute are served, then the receiving party may obtain a default costs certificate,[383] otherwise the receiving party must file a request for a detailed assessment hearing before a costs officer. The court may make a provisional assessment of costs.[384] It may also issue an interim costs certificate at any time after the receiving party has filed a request for a detailed assessment hearing.[385]

21-238   The receiving party is generally entitled to their costs of the detailed assessment, though the court will have regard, inter alia, to the extent to which it was reasonable to contest particular items.[386]

21-239   In *Bourns Inc v Raychem Corporation*[387] questions arose as to whether and to what extent privilege had been waived during the course of costs assessment proceedings by reason of the production of certain documents in order to support

---

[373]   CPR r.44.2(8). For example in *SmithKline Beecham Plc v Apotex Europe Ltd* [2005] F.S.R. 24 an interim award of £450,000 was made at first instance—see of Jacob LJ's judgment at [41].

[374]   See *Mars UK Ltd v Teknowledge Ltd (No.2)* [1999] 1 P. & T. 26; [2000] F.S.R. 138.

[375]   That phrase had been used by Birss J in *Hospira v Genentech* [2014] EWHC 1668 and variations of it have been used in other cases.

[376]   *Excalibur Ventures v Texas Keystone* [2015] EWHC 566, in which Christopher Clarke LJ (sitting at first instance) reviewed *Hospira v Genentech* [2014] EWHC 1688 and other cases, and rejected the irreducible minimum test. *Excalibur Ventures* was followed by Birss J in *Wobben v Siemens* [2015] EWHC 2863, at [22]–[27].

[377]   *Excalibur Ventures v Texas Keystone* [2015] EWHC 566 and *Wobben v Siemens* [2015] EWHC 2863, [22]–[27].

[378]   *Rambus Inc v Hynix Semiconductor UK Ltd* [2005] F.S.R. 19.

[379]   *Dyson Ltd v Hoover Ltd (No. 4)* [2004] 1 W.L.R. 1264.

[380]   CPR r.47.6(1).

[381]   CPR r.47.7.

[382]   CPR r.47.9.

[383]   CPR r.47.11.

[384]   CPR r.47.15.

[385]   CPR r.47.16(1)

[386]   CPR r.47.20(3).

[387]   [1999] F.S.R. 641. See also *Bourns v Raychem (No.2)* [2000] F.S.R. 841.

the claim for costs. The Court of Appeal held that although on the facts of the case privilege had been waived, it was only for the purposes of the costs assessment proceedings and the waiver did not extend further than those proceedings.

Costs of inspection and experiments

The costs of an inspection are at the discretion of the court.[388] However, if the inspection was necessary and proper, the costs thereof are recoverable even though it was made without an order of the court.[389] The costs of experiments may be disallowed if they are not properly conducted in accordance with the order of the court,[390] or if, at trial, they are found to be of no assistance to the court.

21-240

Costs of product description

In *Taylor v Ishida*[391] the costs of the issue of infringement were awarded on an indemnity basis having regard to the grossly inadequate product description which the defendant had provided.

21-241

Costs of considering independent claims

In *Edwards Lifesciences AG v Cook Biotech Inc* the patentee had been ordered to identify each of the claims said to have independent validity, and in response it had identified all 34 claims of the patent in suit. The court was dissatisfied with this response and ordered that a revised list of such claims should be provided.[392] The patentee then reduced the list to 25, only reducing the number to 10 after expert's reports were substantially complete. The court remained dissatisfied and penalised the patentee in costs accordingly.[393]

21-242

Costs of shorthand notes

The costs of transcripts of the shorthand notes are almost always agreed between the parties before the trial commences. In the past, in default of such an arrangement they were not allowed unless they have been of material assistance to the court in shortening the amount of time the case has taken or otherwise.[394] Given the manner in which modern patent cases are conducted it is likely that—if witnesses are to be examined orally—a shorthand note will almost always be of material assistance in shortening the hearing.

21-243

Costs when action threatened but withdrawn

In *Associated Newspapers Ltd v Impac Ltd*,[395] costs were awarded against a party who had threatened to apply for an interim injunction but withdrew before issuing

21-244

---

[388] *Mitchell v Darley Main Colliery Co* (1883) 10 Q.B.D. 457.
[389] *Ashworth v English Card Clothing Co Ltd* (1904) 21 R.P.C. 353.
[390] *Reitzmann v Grahame-Chapman* (1950) 67 R.P.C. 178, 195.
[391] [2000] F.S.R. 224.
[392] [2008] EWHC 1900 (Pat).
[393] [2009] F.S.R. 29, [6].
[394] See, e.g. *Castner-Kellner Alkali Co v Commercial Development Co Ltd* (1899) 16 R.P.C. 251, at 275; *Palmer Tyre Co Ltd v Pneumatic Tyre Co Ltd* (1889) 6 R.P.C. 451, at 496; *British Westinghouse Electric and Manufacturing Co Ltd v Braulik* (1910) 27 R.P.C. 209, at 233.
[395] [2002] F.S.R. 293, a decision of Master Turner in the QBD.

proceedings. The fact that no action had been issued did not prevent the court for making an appropriate costs order.

Costs of appeal to Patents Court from UKIPO

21-245   The general principle that the unsuccessful party ought to pay the successful party's costs also applies to appeals from the Comptroller.[396] Such costs are to be assessed in accordance with any other proceeding in the High Court.[397] Counsel may be instructed by patent agents to appear and the fees of counsel may be recovered on a detailed assessment.[398]

Several defendants

21-246   Where an action is brought against two defendants and the case against one of them is settled, and the action proceeds against the other and judgment is recovered, then unless a special order as to costs is made, no deduction will be made from the general costs of the action to represent the amount incurred as against the defendant whose case was settled.[399]

21-247   When the costs of an issue raised against or by some of the parties were sought against the other parties, the principles that ought to be applied were the same as those that were applied when costs were sought against a non-party.[400]

21-248   Where one of several parties chooses to sit out the trial, allowing other parties to fight out the issues on its behalf, then the non-participating party may still be ordered to pay the costs of the trial.[401] However, the court will consider whether the non-participating party is an appropriate defendant, whether the real fight is between the parties who contest the issues at trial, and thus whether the non-participating party's stance is justifiable.[402]

21-249   Note that the operation of the cost caps in the IPEC is not affected by the number of parties: the ordinary position is that the recoverable costs remain capped at the same amount regardless of the number of parties.

Parties' own costs

21-250   Parties cannot in general recover their own in-house costs. However, if a litigant in person is a solicitor they can recover costs as if they had employed a solicitor, except in respect of items which the fact of their acting directly rendered unnecessary.[403] Furthermore a litigant in person who has some other professional skill can recover in respect of the time spent exercising that skill. For instance

---

[396] *Omron Tateisi Co's Application* [1981] R.P.C. 125; *Extrude Hone Corp's Patent* [1982] R.P.C. 361; and see now CPR r.44.3(2)(a).

[397] *Extrude Hone Corp's Patent* [1982] R.P.C. 361.

[398] *Reiss Engineering Co Ltd v Harris* [1987] R.P.C. 171.

[399] *Kelly's Directories Ltd v Gavin and Lloyds* [1901] 2 Ch. 763; *Badische Anilin und Soda Fabrik v Hickson* (1906) 23 R.P.C. 149.

[400] *Quadrant Holdings Cambridge Ltd v Quadrant Research Foundation* [1999] F.S.R. 918, citing *Symphony v Hodgson* [1994] Q.B. 179.

[401] See, e.g. *Actavis UK Ltd v Eli Lilly & Company Limited, Dr Reddy's Laboratories Limited* [2010] EWCA Civ 43. Here two actions were heard together, although Actavis chose to discontinue prior to trial with the question of costs being stood over.

[402] *Tamglass Ltd OY v Luoyang North Glass Technology Ltd (No. 2)* [2006] F.S.R. 33.

[403] *London Scottish Benefit Society (The) v Chorley* (1884) 12 QBD 452, 13 QBD 872, CA; considered in *Sisu Capital Fund Ltd v Tucker* [2006] F.S.R. 21.

another professional, such as an accountant or (it is submitted) a patent agent, should be able to recover as a litigant in person for those items which they would have been able to recover had they instructed an independent professional to perform them. Such items may include the cost of any expert advice given by such professional but not the cost of any general assistance in the conduct of the litigation. In addition, the litigant in person can only recover such costs insofar as such items fall within their own professional expertise and require the attention of an expert.[404]

Undertaking to return costs

A common course with regard to costs is for the solicitor to the successful party **21-251** to give an undertaking to return the costs in the event of a successful appeal.[405] In *Ackroyd and Best Ltd v Thomas and Williams*,[406] where the solicitors declined to give the undertaking, Joyce J stayed the payment of costs but refused to stay the taxation.

Interest on costs

The rule is that interest on a judgment or order for the payment of costs runs from **21-252** the date of the judgment or order,[407] overruling an old rule that interest on costs ran from the date of the Master's certificate on taxation.[408] In *Dyson Ltd v Hoover Ltd (No.2)*[409] Jacob J awarded interest on costs of an enquiry running from the mid-point between the commencement of the enquiry and the date it came to an end.

Under CPR Pt 44.2(6)(g), the court may order interest on costs for or until a **21-253** certain date, including a date before judgment. In *Nova Productions Ltd v Mazooma Games Ltd (No. 2)*[410] Kitchin J reviewed the existing authorities,[411] drawing attention to the observation of the Court of Appeal in *Bin Kemie*[412] that "in principle there seems no reason why the court should not [order interest on costs] where a party has had to put up money paying its solicitors and [has] been out of the use of that money in the meantime". He concluded:

"16. In the light of all these authorities, it seems to me that the court has a broad discretion when deciding whether to award interest on costs from a date before judgment. That discretion must be exercised in accordance with the principles set out in CPR 44.3 and the court must take into account all the circumstances of the case, including such matters as the conduct of the parties and the degree to which a party has succeeded. Further, the discretion must be exercised in accordance with the overriding objective of dealing with the case justly. I am unable to accept the submission that interest on costs should only be awarded in a case which is in some way out of the norm. I find no basis for that in the CPR and I believe it would provide an unwar-

---

[404] *Sisu Capital Fund Ltd v Tucker* [2006] F.S.R. 21: see also *Re Nossen's Letter Patent* [1969] 1 W.L.R. 683.
[405] *Ticket Punch Register Co Ltd v Colley's Patents Ltd* (1895) 12 R.P.C. 1, 10.
[406] (1904) 21 R.P.C. 403, 412.
[407] *Hunt v R.M. Douglas (Roofing) Ltd* [1990] 1 A.C. 398; [1988] 3 All E.R. 823, HL.
[408] *K. v K.* [1977] Fam. 39; followed in *Erven Warnink B.V. v J. Townend & Sons (Hull) Ltd* [1982] R.P.C. 511.
[409] [2003] F.S.R. 21.
[410] [2006] R.P.C. 15.
[411] In his review of the law Kitchin J explained that in *Rambus Inc v Hynix Semiconductor UK Ltd* [2005] F.S.R. 19, which appeared to have come to a contrary conclusion as to the Court's approach, *Bin Kemie* had not been cited.
[412] *Bin Kemie AB v Blackburn Chemicals Ltd* [2003] EWCA Civ 889.

ranted fetter on the court's discretion. This conclusion is, in my judgment, supported by the decisions of the Court of Appeal in *Powell*[413] and *Bin Kemie*."

21-254   Applying this approach to the facts, he ordered interest on costs from date at those costs were actually paid at base rate from time to time plus 1 per cent. In *Douglas v Hello! Ltd (No. 7)*[414] Lindsay J ordered the successful party interest over the same period at a rate of base rate form time to time plus 1.5 per cent. The interest rate on costs reverts to the Judgments Act rate from the date of judgment, although the court has power to postpone that date.[415]

21-255   Where the post-judgment hearing dealing with costs is adjourned at the request of a party, interest will ordinarily run from the earlier date.[416]

21-256   In *Dupont Nutrition Biosciences ApS v Novozymes A/S*,[417] the court made an order that interest on costs would be applied at the Judgment Rate from the date at which the Technical Board of Appeal (TBA) at the EPO revoked the patent-in-suit on appeal. The judge held that from that date, the defendant was clear as to the nature of the judgment against them that would be entered. Accordingly, he ordered that interest on costs should run at the Judgment Rate from 14 days after the date of the TBA's appeal judgment. In the absence of any authority, the judge did grant the defendant permission to appeal on the point.[418]

Costs in the Intellectual Property Enterprise Court

21-257   The Intellectual Property Enterprise Court has a distinct approach to award and assessment of costs, centred on a cost caps for each stage of the litigation. The approach to costs in the IPEC is discussed in Ch.20.

8.   MISCELLANEOUS MATTERS

"Earth Closet"/See v Scott-Paine orders

21-258   A longstanding practice in patents actions had been that where a party introduced a new ground of invalidity in respect of a patent, the patentee could consent to revocation on that basis and would not be liable for the costs of the proceedings from the date on which the relevant new ground was raised. Instead, the objecting party would be liable for costs from that point onward. These were known as *"Earth Closet"* orders or *"See v Scott-Paine"* orders, after cases in which they had been made.[419]

21-259   In *Fresenius v Carefusion*[420] the Court of Appeal ruled that such an order should no longer be the ordinary course. The court retains a broad discretion in relation to costs, so that such an order might remain possible if it seemed to the court to be the most appropriate remedy in the circumstances. However, any presumption that such an order was available has been dispelled by the judgment in *Fresenius*.

---

[413] *Powell v Herefordshire Health Authority* [2003] 3 All E.R. 253.
[414] [2004] E.M.L.R. 14.
[415] *Cranway v Playtech* [2009] EWHC 2008 (Pat).
[416] *Sandvik v Kennametal* [2012] EWHC 247 (Pat).
[417] [2013] EWHC 483 (Pat).
[418] See the *Dupont* judgment at [45].
[419] *Baird v Moule's Patent Earth Closet Co Ltd* (1881) L.R. 17 Ch D. 139, and *See v Scott-Paine* (1933) 50 R.P.C. 56.
[420] [2011] EWCA Civ 1288, [2012] R.P.C. 8.

The meaning of "further or other relief"

In *Kirin-Amgen Inc v Transkaryotic Therapies Inc (No.2)*[421] Neuberger J **21-260** considered the meaning of the conventional plea for "further or other relief" which a claimant will usually make in addition to express claims for an injunction, delivery up and an inquiry. He held that this plea did not entitle the patentee to take a defendant by surprise. It does not permit a claimant to seek relief after trial in relation to a claim which had not been pleaded as being alleged to be infringed hitherto. The plea for "further or other relief" will not permit relief for a type of infringement which had not been pleaded hitherto, nor will it permit relief inconsistent with relief already claimed (albeit that express pleas for alternative relief are possible) nor for relief if not supported by the allegations in the pleaded case. Accordingly, he refused to allow the claimant to amend after judgment to include an allegation of infringement of a claim which had not already been dealt with and also refuse to allow various pleas for extra-territorial relief. However, Neuberger J did permit the patentee to pursue an application for a post-expiry injunction. Before the Court of Appeal[422] the only issue arising from this decision was the refusal to allow amendment to plead infringement of the new claim. That appeal was dismissed as a proper exercise of the judge's discretion.[423]

Draft orders

When drawing up a draft order after judgment care should be exercised, when **21-261** an inquiry is directed, that provision be made for the payment of costs to the claimant up to and including the hearing, otherwise the payment of all costs may be delayed until the final account has been taken.[424]

Relief against non-infringers

Where goods infringe a patent, the patentee is entitled to an injunction against a **21-262** carrier or warehouseman found in possession of infringing goods even though that person is not themselves an infringer.[425] A patentee is also entitled to discovery of the names of the suppliers and customers of infringing goods.[426] Such an order may be made against an infringer or any other person who has become mixed up in the tortious activities of the defendant.[427]

Action based on undertaking or contract

If a defendant has given an undertaking or entered into a contract not to infringe **21-263** a patent (e.g. as part of the terms of settlement of a previous action or threatened action) such a bargain can be enforced (subject to its enforceability under EU

---

[421] [2002] R.P.C. 3.
[422] *Kirin-Amgen v Transkaryotic Therapies* [2003] R.P.C. 3.
[423] [2003] R.P.C. 3, [125]–[130].
[424] *Mölnlycke A.B. v Procter & Gamble Ltd* [1993] F.S.R. 154.
[425] See para.19-40.
[426] See paras 19–286 and 19–287. See also, for example, *Eli Lilly & Company Limited v Neopharma Ltd* [2008] F.S.R. 25.
[427] See para.19–301.

competition law) notwithstanding the invalidity of the patent.[428] Such an agreement or undertaking will normally be assumed to subsist for the life of the patent.[429]

Revocation

21-264   Where the decision is that the patent is to be revoked, the normal course is for the patentee to apply for a stay of revocation pending appeal, upon an undertaking to prosecute the appeal with due diligence. By so doing the patentee avoids a number of practical and conceptual problems which might arise if an order for revocation is executed and then sought to be reversed on appeal.[430] If a patentee fails to do so but later applies, they can expect little sympathy from the court.

Publication of judgment

21-265   Article 15 of the IP Enforcement Directive[431] provides as follows:

"Publication of judicial decisions.
    Member States shall ensure that, in legal proceedings instituted for infringement of an intellectual property right, the judicial authorities may order, at the request of the applicant and at the expense of the infringer, appropriate measures for the dissemination of the information concerning the decision, including displaying the decision and publishing it in full or in part. Member States may provide for other additional publicity measures which are appropriate to the particular circumstances, including prominent advertising."

21-266   Article 15 as been implemented in England and Wales by the Practice Direction to CPR Pt 63 para.29.2. An order for publication of the judgment pursuant to art.15 and the Practice Direction was sought in *Vestergaard Frandsen A/S v Bestnet Europe Ltd*,[432] a breach of confidence case As Arnold J records,[433] during the course of the hearing relating to relief in that case, substantial agreement was reached as to the appropriate course. It is to be noted, however, that publication included the display upon the homepage of the defendant's website for a period of one year of a short summary of the outcome of the case and of a hyperlink to the publicly available version of the judgment. The court also indicated that it would be open to the defendants, if they so wished, to add a statement to the effect that they were seeking to appeal the judgment.

21-267   In *Samsung Electronics (UK) Ltd v Apple Inc*,[434] the Court of Appeal upheld the judge's order at first instance. The judge had ordered Apple to publish notices informing the public that Samsung had not infringed its registered community design for a tablet computer. Apple's actions had caused commercial uncertainty and the dissemination order was necessary to dispel it. The test of "commercial

---

[428] *Heginbotham Bros Ltd v Burne* (1939) 56 R.P.C. 399, 407; *Van de Lely (C.) N.V. v Maulden Engineering Co (Beds) Ltd* [1984] F.S.R. 157, (Pat).

[429] *Heginbotham Bros Ltd v Burne* (1939) 56 R.P.C. 399, 407; *Van de Lely (C.) N.V. v Maulden Engineering Co (Beds) Ltd* [1984] F.S.R. 157, (Pat). See also *Bescol (Electric) Ltd v Merlin Mouldings Ltd* (1952) 69 R.P.C. 297.

[430] The position of patents which lapse and are later restored to the register is governed by s.28 but no such provisions exist in relation to revoked patents. Revocation of a UK patent may affect the status of patents in other countries in which it is registered. A problem may also arise in relation to the non-payment of renewal fees for the intervening period.

[431] See para.1-85(6).

[432] [2010] F.S.R. 2.

[433] *Vestergaard Frandsen A/S v Bestnet Europe Ltd* [2010] F.S.R. 2, [114].

[434] [2012] EWCA Civ 1339, [2013] E.C.D.R. 2, [2013] F.S.R. 9.

uncertainty" needing to be dispelled has been applied subsequently in assessing whether a dissemination order is merited: see, for example, *Brundle v Perry*.[435]

Whilst the Directive itself only expressly contemplates the making of such an **21-268** order in favour of a successful rights holder, the courts have made dissemination orders in respect of those who have successfully avoided a finding of infringement (including in *Samsung*), and in *BOS GmbH & Co KG v Cobra UK Automotive Products Division Ltd*[436] the Patents County Court rejected the suggestion that either the Directive or the Court of Appeal in *Samsung* established that a different standard should be applied depending on whether or not it was the rights holder who had won.

---

[435] [2012] EWHC 979 (IPEC).
[436] [2012] EWPCC 44.

CHAPTER 22

REVOCATION PROCEEDINGS

CONTENTS

1. INTRODUCTION

The applicant

Section 72 of the Patents Act 1977 provides for revocation of patent by "any person". There is no requirement that the person applying for revocation should have any particular interest in revoking the patent (contrast the previous position under s.32(4) of the Patents Act 1949). Thus an "off-the-shelf" property company, which had no assets and did not trade, was permitted to pursue revocation proceedings for a pharmaceutical patent, albeit at the same time having to give security for costs,[1] as was a firm of patent agents.[2] The applicant's motive for applying to revoke is irrelevant.[3]   **22-01**

Application by the patent proprietor

Section 72 has also been amended by the Patents Act 2004[4] with effect from 1 October 2005[5] in order to provide that a patentee is included within the expression "any person". Accordingly a patentee may apply to have their own patent revoked.   **22-02**

The grounds available for revocation of a patent

The grounds available to a claimant for revocation of a patent are set out in s.72(1) of the Patents Act 1977. These grounds are dealt with in detail in Chs 2, 10–13 and 15.   **22-03**

---

[1] *Cairnstores Ltd v Aktiebolaget Hassle* [2002] F.S.R. 35.
[2] *Oystertec's Patent* [2003] R.P.C. 29.
[3] *TNS Group Holdings Ltd v Nielsen Media Research Inc* [2009] F.S.R. 23.
[4] PA 2004 s.16, Sch.2 para.18.
[5] The Patents Act 2004 (Commencement No.3 and Transitional Provisions) Order 2005 (SI 2005/2471).

The tribunal

22-04   The application can be made before the High Court, IPEC[6] or before the Comptroller.[7]

No declaration of invalidity

22-05   An action cannot be brought claiming only a declaration that a patent is invalid[8]; the proper course being to claim for revocation. It is probable that a claim would lie for the revocation of a patent which had expired,[9] particularly by way of a defence to a claim for damages for acts committed whilst the patent was in force.

No revocation of an application for a patent

22-06   An action cannot be brought for revocation of an application for a patent.[10] However, in an appropriate case, a party may seek a declaration that their own product was obvious at the priority date of the patent application.[11]

Stay of revocation proceedings in favour of EPO opposition

22-07   Where there are opposition proceedings pending in the European Patent Office in respect of a European patent (UK), it may be appropriate to stay an application for revocation in the national courts (or before the Comptroller)[12] in respect of the same patent pending the outcome of the EPO proceedings. This matter is dealt with in Ch.19, see para.19–12, et seq.

2. BEFORE THE HIGH COURT

Commencement, parties and service

22-08   Where there are no other proceedings in existence between the parties, the application is commenced by the issue of a Pt 7 claim form by the court[13] and by its service upon the defendant. Under the CPR, claims for revocation must be started in the Patents Court or IPEC and are allocated to the multi-track.[14] Since the introduction of the CPR in 1999, an application for revocation is no longer made by petition.

22-09   The person upon whom a claim form should be served is the registered proprietor of the patent. It is customary also to serve any other persons who at the time the claim form is issued appear upon the register as being beneficially interested in the

---

6   CPR r.63.2.
7   PA 2007 s.72(1).
8   PA 1977 s.74(2); *North-Eastern Marine Engineering Co v Leeds Forge Co* (1906) 23 R.P.C. 529; *Traction Corp v Bennett* (1908) 25 R.P.C. 819, 822; cf. *Killen v MacMillan* (1932) 49 R.P.C. 258, 260.
9   *North-Eastern Marine Engineering Co v Leeds Forge Co* (1906) 23 R.P.C. 529, 531. See also *John Summers & Sons Ltd v The Cold Metal Process Co Ltd* (1948) 65 R.P.C. 75, 91.
10   *Arrow Generics v Merck & Co Inc* [2007] F.S.R. 39, [55] and [57].
11   *Arrow Generics v Merck & Co Inc* [2007] F.S.R. 39.
12   The Comptroller has power to stay proceedings under Patents Rules 2007 r.82(1)(f).
13   CPR rr.7.2 and 63.5(a).
14   CPR r.63.1(3).

patent,[15] although not persons who would not have a claim in damages for infringement.[16]

If the registered proprietor of the patent or any other person to be served is a company in administration then the consent of the administrators or the permission of the court is required before proceedings can be issued.[17]   **22-10**

The claim form can be served in the normal way in accordance with the provisions of CPR Pt 6. However, an alternative method of service exists,[18] namely upon the address for service given in the Register, because of the requirement for patentees and those with a registered interest in a patent to give to the Registrar an address for service within the UK.[19] Although the proprietor of a European Patent (UK) is also required to give to the Registrar an address for service within the UK, there may be a delay between the grant of the Patent by the European Patent Office and amendment of the register, and in such circumstances proceedings might still have to be served abroad.   **22-11**

Grounds of invalidity

Where the validity of a patent is challenged, the statement of case must have a separate document attached to and forming part of it headed Grounds of Invalidity (formerly called Particulars of Objections) which must specify the grounds on which validity of the patent is challenged; and include particulars that will clearly define every issue (including any challenge to any claimed priority date) which it is intended to raise.[20] A copy of each document referred to in the Grounds of Invalidity, and where necessary a translation of the document, must be served with the Grounds of Invalidity.[21] The practice as to the detailed contents of the Grounds of Invalidity is the same as in the case of an action for infringement in which the issue of invalidity is raised.[22]   **22-12**

Assignment of patent

Where an assignment has been executed after the claim form has been issued, the assignee will be added as a defendant to the claim. Usually the original defendant will be removed as a party to the action at the same time.[23] However, this will not invariably be the case. In *Teva v Amgen*[24] the party who was recorded as being the registered proprietor had, before the date of commencement of the revocation action, already assigned it to another company in the same corporate group. It was held that the court has the power to retain the former proprietor as a party to the action, notwithstanding the joinder of the new proprietor and updating of the   **22-13**

---

15 See *Avery's Patent* (1887) 36 Ch D. 307; (1887) 4 R.P.C. 152 and 322.
16 *Biogen Inc v Medeva Plc* [1993] R.P.C. 475, 489.
17 Insolvency Act 1986 s.11(3); *Axis Genetics Plc's (in administration) Patent* [2000] F.S.R. 448.
18 CPR r.63.14(2); however the application of this rule is not always straightforward—see *Bullit v Sonim* [2013] EWHC 3367 (IPEC), cf. the position under the old law as set out in *Symbol Technologies Inc v Optican Sensors Europe B.V. (No.1)* [1993] R.P.C. 211.
19 Patents Rules 2007 r.103.
20 CPR Pt 63, Practice Direction—Intellectual Property Claims para.4.2(2).
21 CPR Pt 63, Practice Direction—Intellectual Property Claims para.4.2(3).
22 See Ch.19, para.19–199, et seq.
23 *Haddan's Patent* (1885) 2 R.P.C. 218.
24 *Teva Pharma BV v Amgen, Inc* [2013] EWHC 3711.

register, if it desirable to do so. In that case it was desirable in order to make binding declarations in relation to the patent.

Persons out of jurisdiction

22-14　　The effect of CPR r.63.14(2) is that the requirement to serve out of the jurisdiction is rarely necessary. Under the old rules, where the procedure was by petition, it was held that leave to serve out was not required[25] and providing that the provisions of CPR r.6.33 are met, proceedings can continue to be served out of the United Kingdom without the permission of the court.

Application by counterclaim

22-15　　The defendant in existing proceedings such as an action for infringement who wishes to apply for revocation should make a counterclaim under CPR Pt 20.[26] The grounds available for revocation of the patent are also available as defences to the allegation of infringement.[27] As with a claim under CPR Pt 7, Grounds of Invalidity must be served.[28]

Counterclaim is a claim in its own right

22-16　　A counterclaim for revocation is a claim in its own right[29] and exists independently of the infringement action. Thus, the counterclaim may be proceeded with even though the infringement action by the claimant is stayed, discontinued or dismissed. However, the court will seek to manage both the claim for infringement and the claim for revocation together.[30]

Counterclaim for infringement in response to application to revoke

22-17　　Under the old Rules of the Supreme Court (which applied prior to the introduction of the Civil Procedure Rules in 1999), an application to revoke a patent was made by petition. Consequently, it was not possible to counterclaim for infringement in response to a petition for revocation and separate infringement proceedings had to be instituted and, thereafter, directions sought for the petition for revocation and the infringement action have to be heard together.[31] Under the CPR, the position changed because the application for revocation is no longer made by petition but by Part 7 claim form.[32] Accordingly, a counterclaim under Part 20 for infringement should now be made, where appropriate, in response to a claim for revocation.[33]

Res judicata and estoppel

22-18　　Where a defendant in an action for infringement puts in issue the validity of the patent by way of a defence to the allegation of infringement, but does not

---

[25]　*Napp Laboratories Ltd v Pfizer Inc* [1993] F.S.R. 150.
[26]　CPR r.63.5(b).
[27]　PA 1977 s.74(1).
[28]　CPR Pt 63, Practice Direction—Intellectual Property Claims para.4.2(2).
[29]　CPR, r.20.3(1).
[30]　CPR, r.20.13(2).
[31]　See, e.g. *Genentech Inc's Patent* [1987] R.P.C. 553.
[32]　CPR rr.7.2 and 63.5(a).
[33]　See also CPR r.63.5(b).

counterclaim for its revocation, the question arises whether the validity of the patent can be re-litigated in subsequent proceedings for revocation. Under the old law it was held that the earlier infringement proceedings were not a bar to a subsequent petition to revoke by a petitioner who had the Attorney-General's *fiat* to present the petition on the ground that they were then acting as a member of the public and not as an individual.[34] Now that the necessity for the *fiat* and for a petition have been abolished, it is submitted that if a defendant fails to establish the invalidity of a patent in an infringement action, they will thereafter be debarred from attacking the validity of the patent in a subsequent claim for revocation unless special circumstances exist. Such circumstances might include an allegation of infringement by the patentee which relied upon a broader construction of the patent than that put forward on the previous occasion, thereby making available grounds of invalidity that were not previously arguable.[35]

Likewise, a claimant in an action for revocation of a patent will, if unsuccessful, be estopped from challenging the validity of the patent in a subsequent infringement action, whether by way of defence to the allegation of infringement or by way of counterclaim, and whether the specific grounds of invalidity to be relied upon in the later proceedings are the same or different to those relied upon in the earlier proceedings (unless in the latter case, special circumstances apply, e.g. because the new ground could not with reasonable diligence have been raised).[36] However, in the light of the decision of the Supreme Court in *Virgin v Zodiac*,[37] they will be able to rely upon the fact that the patent has subsequently been revoked, whether by the court or the EPO, on an enquiry as to damages as a defence to the claim for damages. Whether they can rely upon the revocation after judgment in the enquiry, or even after payment of the sums found due, remains an open question.

22-19

No estoppel from a decision of the Comptroller or the EPO

In contrast, where the application for revocation is made before the Comptroller, s.72(5) of the 1977 Act expressly prevents an estoppel arising from his decision. Nor does any estoppel arise from unsuccessful opposition proceedings in the EPO.[38]

22-20

Estoppel on discontinuance

Generally, an estoppel does not arise where an action is discontinued,[39] although the permission of the court will be required before a new action can be commenced against the same defendant if the claimant discontinued after the defendant filed a defence.[40] Thus, if an application to revoke a patent is commenced by

22-21

---

[34] *Shoe Machinery Co Ltd v Cutlan* (1895) 12 R.P.C. 530; *Deeley's Patent* (1895) 12 R.P.C. 192; *Lewis and Stirkler's Patent* (1897) 14 R.P.C. 24; *Jameson's Patent* (1902) 19 R.P.C. 246; and see *Poulton's Patent* (1906) 23 R.P.C. 506; but cf. *Shoe Machinery Co Ltd v Cutlan (No.2)* (1896) 13 R.P.C. 141.

[35] *Agilent Technologies v Waters Corporation*, [2004] EWHC 2992 (Ch), per Pumfrey J, at [46]. See also *Coflexip SA v Stolt Offshore MS Ltd* [2004] F.S.R. 7 (Jacob J) and 34 (CA); *Unilin Beheer BV v Berry Floor NV* [2007] F.S.R. 25; *Virgin Atlantic v Zodiac* [2013] R.P.C 29. see also Ch.19.

[36] In other words, it is submitted that the approach will be the same as in two actions for infringement— see *Chiron v Organon Teknika (No.6)* [1994] F.S.R. 448; and *Chiron v Organon Teknika (No.14)* [1996] F.S.R. 701, CA. See also *Virgin v Zodiac* [2013] R.P.C. 29.

[37] [2013] R.P.C. 29.

[38] *Buehler A.G. v Chronos Richardson Ltd* [1998] R.P.C. 609, CA. See also para.19–188.

[39] See Ch.19.

[40] CPR r.38.7.

claim form and subsequently discontinued, no estoppel will arise against the claimant preventing them from challenging the validity of the patent on another occasion.

Estoppel arising from foreign proceedings

22-22   Issue estoppel may also arise in the case of parties who have previously litigated
abroad.[41]

Estoppel arising in the case of an assignor or licensor

22-23   An estoppel relating to the validity of the patent may also arise in the case of an
assignor of or a licensee under a patent.[42]

Practice before trial

22-24   The practice is regulated by CPR Pt 63 rr.63.5–63.10 and by CPR Pt 63, Practice
Direction—Intellectual Property Claims paras 3–11, and is in most respects similar
to or identical with the practice in actions for infringement.[43]

Security for costs

22-25   Under the previous rules of procedure a respondent residing out of the jurisdiction was not liable to give security for the petitioner's costs.[44] Now that the recipient of a claim for revocation is termed a defendant, the normal rules apply and an
application for security against a defendant will not be entertained.

Application for directions

22-26   CPR r.63.8 and Pt 63, Practice Direction-Intellectual Property Claims para.5.1
apply to claims for revocation, and a case management conference should be applied for once any defences have been served. The case management conference
is the appropriate time to consider whether the proceedings should be expedited or
whether they can be dealt with by way of streamlined procedure although a party
may apply to the court for a streamlined procedure at any time.[45] A standard form
order for directions can be found attached to the Patents Court Guide. The practice
as to directions in a revocation action is largely (if not entirely) the same as in the
case of an action for infringement.

Disclosure of documents and experiments

22-27   The practice as to disclosure of documents, and experiments, are the same as in
the case of an action for infringement.

Amendment of specification

22-28   Section 75 of the 1977 Act applies to claims for revocation as well as to actions
for infringement, and a patentee may apply to amend their specification after

---

41   See para.19-185.
42   See para.16–62.
43   See Ch.19.
44   *Miller's Patent* (1894) 11 R.P.C. 55.
45   See paras 7.6–7.8 of the Patents Court Guide.

revocation proceedings have been commenced. The practice in such applications is dealt with in Ch.15.

The trial

As the onus is on the claimant, normally they will open the case and call their evidence first.[46] However, the court has complete power to give directions as to which party should begin.[47] If the claimant starts, their counsel will open and then call evidence which must prove their case: a defendant need not call evidence and can thereby request the final speech. If the defendant calls evidence, as is usual, the claimant has the right of reply. The nature of the evidence required and the procedure generally at the trial is similar to that at the trial of an action for infringement.[48] Claims for revocation are tried using live witnesses,[49] unless the parties agree to the streamlined trial procedure under which evidence may be given by way of witness statements[50] or unless the court otherwise directs.

22-29

The remedy

If, in any proceedings for revocation, the court decides that the patent is invalid, the court may make an order for the unconditional revocation of the patent or, where the court decides that the patent is invalid but only to a limited extent, the court may make an order that the patent should be revoked unless within a specified time the specification is amended to the satisfaction of the court.[51] The amendment may be made under s.75 of the 1977 Act or, in the case of a European patent (UK), by the European Patent Office.[52] The court does have the power, in exceptional cases, to permit a patent to remain on the register in a partially valid form, i.e. with some claims that have been held to be invalid. However, if adopting this course, the court is likely to also adopt safeguards to protect the public. In *Phillips v Nintendo*[53] the court required the following undertakings of the patentee in return for not requiring deletion of the invalid claims by amendment:

22-30

(a) that it would not assert or commence proceedings based upon the claims found to be invalid against any persons;
(b) that it would not assign the patent;
(c) that it would serve a copy of the order on the Controller General of Patents Trademarks and Designs and would make an application under r.47 of the Patents Rules 2007 to register the order on the Register of Patents; and
(d) that it would not grant any exclusive licence under the claims found to be invalid.

---

[46] As in *Genentech Inc's Patent* [1987] R.P.C. 553 and in *Genentech Inc's (Human Growth Hormone) Patent* [1989] R.P.C. 613. The rule of court which provided that the patentee was entitled to begin in a petition to revoke was abolished when the 1977 Act came into force.
[47] CPR r.29.9.
[48] See Ch.19.
[49] *Gaulard and Gibb's Patent* (1889) 34 Ch D. 396.
[50] See Patents Court Guide, para.7.6.
[51] PA 1977 s.72(4). See Ch.14.
[52] PA 1977 s.72(4A).
[53] [2014] EWHC 3177 (Pat).

22-31   An order for revocation will only be made in open court, and will not be made in chambers even though the patentee consents.[54]

Declarations of invalidity

22-32   Where a court hears a revocation action, finds the patent invalid and orders its revocation, usually there is no issue with the court additionally making a declaration that the patent is invalid.[55] However, on occasions declarations of invalidity are sought when the patentee has consented to revocation before trial and there has been no judicial consideration of the issue of validity. In *ConvaTec v Smith & Nephew*[56] the court held that it would not be appropriate to exercise its discretion to grant a declaration of invalidity, since such a declaration "could be misunderstood as a statement that I had been in a position to form a view that the patent was indeed invalid". The court reached a similar conclusion in *Fresenius Kabi Deutschland GmbH v Carefusion 303, Inc.*[57]

Stay pending appeal

22-33   It is usual to stay the order for revocation pending an appeal.[58] The form of order made in such cases follows that made in *Cincinnati Grinders (Inc) v BSA Tools Ltd*.[59] An undertaking has in older cases been required to the effect that the patentee will not apply to the Comptroller to amend the specification pending the appeal.[60] Such undertakings may have more modern relevance in the light to of the ability to amend centrally in the EPO (see below). An undertaking not to advertise or threaten has also been required.[61] Such orders are otherwise to be filed at the Patent Office forthwith by the person in whose favour they are made.[62]

Certificate of validity

22-34   If any claim whose validity is contested is found to be valid, the court may so certify[63]; and in that case, in any subsequent first instance proceedings the party upholding the validity of the patent, if finally successful, may recover their costs as between solicitor and client.[64] These are taxed on an indemnity basis subject to the presumptions set out in CPR r.48.8(2).

---

[54]   *Clifton's Patent* (1904) 21 R.P.C. 515.
[55]   Or where, as in *Connaught Laboratories Inc's Patent* [1999] F.S.R. 284, the judge had read into the case in the process of preparing for trial and was in a position to form a view about the invalidity of the patent before him.
[56]   *ConvaTec Ltd v Smith & Nephew Healthcare Ltd* [2011] EWHC 3461 (Pat).
[57]   [2011] EWHC 2959 (Pat).
[58]   See, e.g. *Klaber's Patent* (1905) 22 R.P.C. 405; *Waterhouse's Patent* (1906) 23 R.P.C. 470; cf. *Stahlwerk Becker A.G.'s Patent* (1918) 35 R.P.C. 81. See also *Pavel v Sony Corp* [1995] R.P.C. 500, CA.
[59]   (1931) 48 R.P.C. 33, 60.
[60]   *Cincinnati Grinders (Inc) v BSA Tools Ltd* (1931) 48 R.P.C. 33, 60; see also *Le Rasoir Apollo's Patent* (1932) 49 R.P.C. 1, at 15.
[61]   *Amalgamated Carburettors Ltd v Bowden Wire Ltd* (1931) 48 R.P.C. 105, 122; see also *Klaber's Patent* (1905) 22 R.P.C. 405, at 416.
[62]   CPR Pt 63, Practice Direction-Intellectual Property Claims para.14.
[63]   PA 1977 s.65.
[64]   PA 1977 s.65; and CPR r.48.8. It has been held that s.65 does not apply to any appeal in the subsequent proceedings, but this does not prevent the court exercising its discretion to award

Costs

The principles governing the award of costs are the same as in the case of actions for infringement.[65] Thus the provisions of CPR r.44.3 are relevant to patent actions and, as far as it can reasonably do so, the court will adopt an issue based approach where a party has not been successful on all issues, even though such an exercise is necessarily imprecise.[66]   **22-35**

An order for revocation will usually include an order for the defendant to pay the claimant's costs. In a series of older cases, this was ordered even though the order was made by consent and no previous notice of the intention to issue a claim had been given to the patentee (which would enable the latter to surrender their patent).[67] It is doubtful that this would necessarily be the appropriate costs order under the CPR, where the court is required inter alia to take into account the conduct of the parties, including conduct before the proceedings and in particular the extent to which the parties followed the Practice Direction—Pre-Action Conduct or any relevant pre-action protocol.[68]   **22-36**

Appeals

Appeals upon claims for revocation are (with permission) to the Court of Appeal and (with permission) to the Supreme Court as in ordinary actions. In the Court of Appeal, the appellant must file the appellant's notice at the Court of Appeal within such period as may be directed by the lower court or, where the court makes no such direction, within 21 days after the date of the decision of the lower court that the appellant wished to appeal.[69]   **22-37**

Amendment of the patent in the EPO pending appeal

In a case where an order for revocation was stayed and the patent was subsequently amended in opposition proceedings in the European Patent Office while the appeal was pending, the Court of Appeal considered the amended form of the patent on the hearing of the appeal.[70] However, this was prior to the introduction of CPR Pt 63, Practice Direction—Intellectual Property Claims para.11 which now requires that, where there are proceedings before the court in which the validity of a European patent (UK) may be put in issue, the proprietor of a European patent (UK) must serve on all the parties to the proceedings notice of their intention to file a request for amendment of the patent at the EPO at least 28 days prior to filing the same so that appropriate directions may be given by the court under para.11.3 as to the future conduct of the national proceedings.   **22-38**

---

indemnity costs in any event, see *SmithKline Beecham Plc v Apotex Europe Ltd (No.2)* [2005] F.S.R. 24, CA.

[65] See para.21–208, et seq.

[66] See, for example, *Generics (UK) Ltd v Daiichi Pharmaceutical Co Ltd* [2009] F.S.R. 9; *MMI v Cellxion* [2013] 3 Costs LO 387, at [4].

[67] *Aylott's Patent* (1911) 28 R.P.C. 227; *Merryweather's Patent* (1912) 29 R.P.C. 64; *Berry's Patent* (1915) 32 R.P.C. 350.

[68] CPR r.44.2(4) and (5).

[69] CPR, r.52.4(2)

[70] *Palmaz's European Patents* [2000] R.P.C. 631, CA.

22-39   This procedure was not followed in *Samsung v Apple*[71] where between trial and appeal the patentee applied for a central limitation in the EPO seeking a set of claims that had not been considered by the trial judge (notwithstanding that it had made two applications to amend before him, which had been held not to cure the invalidity of the patent as granted). In the light of the application for a central limitation, the patentee contended that the Court of Appeal ought to remit the patent back to the Patents Court for a further trial. The defendant contended that the application for the central limitation was an abuse of process.[72] The Court of Appeal held that the filing and pursuit by the patentee of its central amendment application could not be characterised as an abuse of process or an activity with which the court could properly interfere for any other reason. However, the Court of Appeal also held that whether or not any subsequent attempted reliance on a patent amended pursuant to a central amendment application made after trial was an abuse of process would depend on all the circumstances including whether it would be necessary to remit the case for retrial and if so, what the consequence of that would be. The Court of Appeal accordingly stayed the appeal pending the outcome of the central limitation application. The case then settled and there was no decision about whether any subsequent reliance would have been an abuse.

22-40   The Patents Court followed *Apple v Samsung* in *Rovi Solutions Corp v Virgin Media Ltd*,[73] albeit with some hesitation, in a case where the patentee applied to amend centrally in the EPO shortly before trial. The court granted an adjournment but commented that a patentee could not assume that the self-generated uncertainty from a central amendment application would necessarily always result in an adjournment of the trial. In *Kennametal v Pramet*[74] the court rejected a request for a stay of the order for revocation of a patent after it had been found invalid at trial. Although there was a pending central limitation in the EPO, there had been no attempt to amend the patent in the UK and no appeal was sought against the court's order for revocation. There was therefore no reason to delay revocation of the patent.

3. BEFORE THE IPEC

Jurisdiction

22-41   The IPEC has jurisdiction to hear any action or matter relating to patents over which the High Court would have jurisdiction (except appeals from the Comptroller).[75] This includes an application for revocation of a patent.

Procedure

22-42   An application for revocation in the IPEC is made by claim form in the same way as an application to the High Court.[76] The CPR applies to both the High Court and to the IPEC and the procedure is therefore the same in general terms. However,

---

[71] [2015] R.P.C 3.
[72] Relying on the domestic cases on this points: e.g. *Nikken Kosakusho Works v Pioneer Trading Co* [2005] EWCA Civ 906, [2006] F.S.R. 4 and *Nokia GmbH v IPCom GmbH & Co KG* [2011] EWCA Civ 6, [2011] Bus. L.R. 1488; [2011] F.S.R. 15.
[73] [2014] EWHC 1793 (Pat); [2015] R.P.C. 5.
[74] [2015] R.P.C. 4.
[75] CPR Pt 63.2.
[76] CPR, Pt 7.

CPR Pt 63 Section V (rr.63.17–63.26) and CPR Pt 63, Practice Direction—Intellectual Property Claims paras 27–31 contain modifications of the procedure in respect of claims started in, or transferred to IPEC.[77] For example, the statement of case must set out concisely all the facts and arguments upon which the party serving it relies (CPR r.63.20(1)). The first case management conference is a significant occasion (see para.20-29). Where possible the court will determine the claim solely on the basis of the parties' statements of case and oral submissions (CPR Pt 63, Practice Direction—Intellectual Property Claims para.31.1).

Costs

Unless a party has behaved unreasonably, the court will reserve the costs of all applications to the conclusion of the trial when they will be subject to a summary assessment.[78] The summary assessment will be conducted in accordance with CPR Pt 45 Section IV.[79] Unless a party has behaved in a manner which amounts to an abuse of the court's process or the validity of the patent has been certified by a court in earlier proceedings,[80] costs will be awarded on the basis of a scale of maximum amounts set out in the Costs Practice Direction Section IV[81] and the total award of costs will be subject to a costs cap of £50,000 on the final determination of a claim in relation to liability, after allowing for any set-off.[82] **22-43**

Appeals

Appeals from any final determination of the judge in the IPEC are to the Court of Appeal and the procedure for such appeals is governed by CPR Pt 52. Permission to appeal is required.[83] Such permission may be given by the IPEC or by the Court of Appeal.[84] **22-44**

Time for appealing

On appeal from the IPEC, the appellant's notice must be filed at the Court of Appeal within 21 days after the date on which the court gave its decision, unless an adjournment of the hearing to determine whether to grant permission is granted.[85] Unlike under the old rules,[86] time now runs from the date on which the judge hands down their written judgment. **22-45**

4. BEFORE THE COMPTROLLER

Jurisdiction

The Comptroller has the same power to revoke a patent as the court upon an ap- **22-46**

---

77 CPR r.63.17.
78 CPR r.63.26(1) and (2).
79 CPR r.63.26(3).
80 CPR r.45.30.
81 CPR r.45.31(3).
82 CPR r.45.31(1) and (2).
83 CPR r.52.3(1).
84 CPR r.52.3(2).
85 CPR Pt 52, Practice Direction 52A para.4.1(a).
86 See *Pavel v Sony Corp* [1993] F.S.R. 177.

plication made to him under the 1977 Act.[87] However, a decision of the Comptroller or an appeal from such a decision, does not create an estoppel in proceedings for infringement.[88] There is no restriction as to what the Comptroller can or cannot decide,[89] although it has been suggested that the Comptroller ought only to revoke patents that are clearly invalid.[90]

22-47   If an application to the Comptroller for revocation of a patent has been refused, then the applicant may not make a subsequent application to the court (except by way of appeal or by putting validity in issue in an infringement action) without the leave of the court.[91] If an application to the Comptroller for revocation is still pending, the applicant may not make a subsequent application to revoke to the court without either the agreement of the proprietor or a certificate from the Comptroller that the matters would be more properly dealt with by the court.[92]

22-48   The Comptroller also has a limited jurisdiction to revoke a patent on his own initiative.[93]

Procedure

22-49   An application for revocation is made to the Comptroller in accordance with the Patents Rules 2007 Pt 7 (rr.73–91).[94] The "overriding objective" is now set out in r.74 of the Patents Rules 2007 and the Comptroller is required to give effect to it when he exercising any power given to him by Pt 7 of the 2007 Rules or interprets any rule in that Part.[95] The parties are also required to help the Comptroller to further the overriding objective.[96] The Rules are supported by a number of Tribunal Practice Notices, the objective being to complete inter partes proceedings within 12 months of the date when the proceedings are formally joined by the filing of the counter-statement.[97]

Application and statement

22-50   The application for revocation must be made on Patents Form 2 and must be accompanied by a statement of grounds setting out a concise statement of the facts and grounds on which the claimant relies, and the relief sought.[98] The statement must also be verified by a statement of truth.[99] Further particulars of the statement

---

[87] PA 1977 s.72.
[88] PA 1977 s.72(5).
[89] Thus the Comptroller may decide pure questions of law—see *Petra Fischer's Application* [1997] R.P.C. 899, at 905.
[90] See *Petra Fischer's Application* [1997] R.P.C. 899, at 905.
[91] PA 1977 s.72(6).
[92] PA 1977 s.72(7). See also CPR r.63.11 for the procedure where the Comptroller so certifies.
[93] PA 1977 s.73. Section 73(1) permits the Comptroller to revoke a patent where it appears to him that the invention formed part of the state of the art pursuant to s.2(3) of PA 1977. Section 73(2) permits the Comptroller to revoke where it appears that a UK Patent and an EP (UK) have been granted for the same invention having the same priority date and were filed by the same inventor or his successor in title. In each case the Comptroller must allow the patentee to make observations.
[94] Patent Rules 2007 r.73(1)(a) and Sch.3 Pt 1.
[95] Patents Rules 2007 r.74(3).
[96] Patents Rules 2007 r.74(4).
[97] TPN 6/2007 [2008] R.P.C. 8, para.3.1.
[98] Patents Rules 2007, r.76. See also TPN 1/2000 [2000] R.P.C. 16, [15]–[26].
[99] Patents Rules 2007 r.76(4)(f). See also r.87(5).

may be sought and ordered.[100] Duplicates of all documents should be sent to the Comptroller. Copies of the Form and statement will then be sent by the Comptroller to the proprietor and, at the same time, the Comptroller will specify a period within which the proprietor may file a counter-statement.[101] Normally the Comptroller will allow six weeks.[102] The fact that the applicant's statement does not accompany the application is not necessarily fatal as the Comptroller has a complete discretion to enlarge the times under this rule.[103] The extent to which particulars of any allegation (e.g. prior user) must be given depends on the facts of each case.

Counter-statement

If the proprietor desires to contest the application they must, before the end of the period specified by the Comptroller when sending the Form and statement to them, file a counter-statement in duplicate. The counter-statement must state which of the allegations in the statement of grounds the proprietor admits, which they deny (in which case they must also state their reasons for doing so and any positive case of their own) and which they are unable to admit or deny but require to be proved.[104] Failure to deal with an allegation will be taken as an admission.[105] The counter-statement must also be verified by a statement of truth and be accompanied by a copy of any document to which it refers.[106] The Comptroller sends a copy of the counter-statement to the applicant and specifies a period within which the applicant must file Patents Form 4; if the form is not filed within the specified period, the applicant is deemed to have filed a request for withdrawal of the proceedings.[107] Again, the Comptroller has a complete discretion to allow a counter-statement to be filed late under this rule, although retrospective extensions of time must be supported by reasons and the circumstances must justify the exercise of the Comptroller's discretion.[108]

22-51

Statement and counter-statement to define the issues

The issues must be adequately defined by the statement and counter-statement[109] and not left to be made clear by the witness statements filed at a later stage. In appropriate instances, the parties may be ordered to file supplementary statements to clarify the issues between them.[110] A counter-statement which contains merely a bare denial of the applicant's allegations is not a sufficient compliance with the rules.[111] The counter-statement must set out the facts relied upon and must contain replies in a reasonable manner to each of the matters pleaded in the statement by

22-52

---

[100] *Morgan Refractories Ltd's Patent* [1968] R.P.C. 374.
[101] Patents Rules 2007 r.77(5).
[102] TRN 6/2007 [2008] R.P.C. 8, para.2.5. The Comptroller may extend or shorten any period of time which has been specified under any provision of Pt 7, see Patents Rules 2007 r.81.
[103] See *Morton and Others' Application* (1932) 49 R.P.C. 404; see also Patents Rules 2007 r.108.
[104] Patents Rules 2007 r.78(1) and (2).
[105] Patents Rules 2007 r.78(3).
[106] Patents Rules 2007 rr.78(1)(d) and 79(1).
[107] Patents Rules 2007 rr.80(1) and (1A) and 81A.
[108] Patents Rules 2007 r.108(1) and (6). And see *Norsk Hydro A.S.'s Patent* [1997] R.P.C. 89.
[109] TPN 1/2000 [2000] R.P.C. 16, [15]–[26].
[110] See *Riker Laboratories Inc's Patent* [1997] F.S.R. 714 (a case in the Patents Court).
[111] Patents Rules 2007 r.78. See also (1929) 46 R.P.C., Comptroller's Ruling B; (1932) 49 R.P.C., Comptroller's Ruling A.

way of admission, denial or an offer to amend the specification of the patent.[112] If amendments are offered in the counter-statement and the applicants then wish to rely upon additional matters not pleaded, an application should be made to amend the statement.[113]

22-53   The application and statement may be amended so as to include all documents to which it is desired to refer[114] and all grounds on which it is proposed to rely.[115] However, the addition of new grounds may be refused if made at a very late stage or after unreasonable delay.[116]

Security for costs

22-54   The Comptroller may order security for costs against any person who invokes his litigious jurisdiction, if any of the conditions set out in r.85 of the Patents Rules 2007 are satisfied. Those conditions include provisions relating to a party that is resident outside the jurisdiction or who is a company and there is reason to believe that it will be unable to pay another party's costs if ordered to do so.[117] The amount to be awarded will be decided on a case-by-case basis.[118]

Preliminary Evaluation

22-55   A Preliminary Evaluation similar to those produced by the EPO Boards of Appeal will normally be issued in most patent proceedings before the Comptroller.[119] The aim of the Evaluation is to focus the parties' minds on the key issues by exposing the strength or otherwise of their cases and so lead to more efficient conduct of the proceedings including the hearing. The evaluation may be issued after pleadings or after evidence. A party that ignores the Preliminary Evaluation, or acts unreasonably in the light of it, may be penalised in costs. A Preliminary Evaluation will not constitute a decision and consequently it will not be appealable.[120]

Evidence

22-56   When sending the counter-statement to the applicant, the Comptroller will also specify the periods within which evidence may be filed by the applicant and the proprietor.[121] He may direct evidence to be filed simultaneously or sequentially depending on the circumstances of the case. Usually six weeks is allowed for each round of evidence.[122] Any period specified may be shortened or enlarged at the Comptroller's discretion.[123] In exercise of his case management powers, the

---

112 Patents Rules 2007 r.78. see also *Marshall's Application* [1969] R.P.C. 83.
113 *Horville Engineering Co Ltd's Application* (1969) R.P.C. 266. See also Patents Rules 2007 r.82(1)(e).
114 *Horville Engineering Co Ltd's Application* (1969) R.P.C. 266. See also (1910) 27 R.P.C., Comptroller's Ruling C. And see Patents Rules 2007 r.82(1)(e).
115 *Linotype and Machinery Ltd's Application* (1937) 54 R.P.C. 228; Patents Rules 2007 r.82(1)(e).
116 *Phillips Petroleum Co's Application* [1964] R.P.C. 470.
117 PA 1977 s.107(4) as amended by PA 2004 s.15. See also Patents Rules 2007 r.85.
118 TPN 2/2000 [2000] R.P.C. 16, [16].
119 TPN 3/2009, para.3.1.
120 TPN 3/2009, paras 3.2–3.5.
121 Patents Rules 2007 r.80(1).
122 TPN 3/2009, paras 3.6 and 3.7.
123 Patents Rules 2007 r.81.

Comptroller may also limit the issues on which he requires evidence, or the nature of the evidence.[124]

No further evidence may be filed on either side except by leave of the Comptroller.[125] A degree of latitude is, however, given to admitting further evidence provided that it enables all issues fairly to be brought to the attention of the Comptroller and no undue prejudice is caused to either party.

22-57

A party filing evidence which is unnecessary, or which raise matters not relevant to the issues, may be penalised in costs.[126]

22-58

Form of evidence

Evidence is by witness statement unless the Comptroller requires otherwise.[127] A Witness Statement must include a statement of truth which must be dated and signed by the person making the statement.[128]

22-59

Hearsay evidence

Proceedings are governed by the Civil Evidence Act 1995 which amended the rules on the admissibility of hearsay evidence in civil proceedings. No specific notice is required for hearsay evidence that is contained in written evidence filed in the ordinary course of proceedings before the Comptroller, although the Comptroller may order that further particulars of or relating to the evidence be given to enable the other party to deal properly with it.[129] The various factors that the Comptroller should take into account when considering the weight (if any) to be given to the hearsay evidence include the reasons for the evidence not being adduced by the maker of the original statement, the time that the statement was made, the involvement of multiple hearsay and any other circumstances which might affect the reliability of the evidence.[130]

22-60

Oral evidence and cross-examination

The Comptroller has power to take oral evidence and to allow any witness to be cross-examined on his Witness Statement or other evidence.[131] If cross-examination is desired, the party desiring to cross-examine should give reasonable notice[132] of its request to the other parties and to the Comptroller, who will, if he thinks the request reasonable, inquire of the other party whether he will produce the witnesses for cross-examination without any order for their attendance. Where a party adduces evidence of a statement made by a person otherwise than while giving oral evidence in the proceedings and does not call that person as a witness, the

22-61

---

[124] Patents Rules 2007 r.82(2).
[125] *Bakelite Ltd's Patent* [1958] R.P.C. 152; *Ford Motor Co Ltd's Application* [1968] R.P.C. 220. See also Patents Rules 2007 r.80(2).
[126] *Brand's Application* (1895) 12 R.P.C. 102. See also *Hedges' Application* (1895) 12 R.P.C. 136.
[127] Patents Rules 2007 r.87(3).
[128] Patents Rules 207 rr.87(2) and 87(5)(a).
[129] See the Patent Office Practice Notice on Evidence of 4 January 1999 [1999] R.P.C. 294.
[130] See the Patent Office Practice Notice on Evidence of 4 January 1999 [1999] R.P.C. 294.
[131] Patents Rules 2007 rr.82(1)(d), 82(2), 86(a) and 87(1)(b).
[132] Usually four weeks, but longer if the witness to be cross-examined is abroad—see the Patent Office Practice Notice on Evidence of 4 January 1999 [1999] R.P.C. 294.

Comptroller may, if he thinks fit permit any other party to call and cross-examine that person on his statement.[133]

22-62   The Comptroller has all the powers of a judge of the High Court as regards the attendance and examination of witnesses and the discovery and production of documents, except the power to punish summarily for contempt.[134] The attendance of witnesses may be enforced by witness summons under CPR r.34.3 and privilege can be claimed for documents if the appropriate conditions are satisfied.[135] However, the Comptroller should exercise his discretion to order specific disclosure only where appropriate,[136] given the desire for the Patent Office to provide a forum which is less complicated and expensive than the High Court.[137]

Withdrawal of application

22-63   A party applying to revoke a patent may withdraw some or all of its case during the proceedings, although in such circumstances the Comptroller is likely to make an order that such issues are not to be raised again between the parties in proceedings before the Comptroller, and that they may only be raised in proceedings before the court with the leave of the court.[138] In appropriate circumstances (where the application to revoke was made on rational, non-capricious grounds) it is open to the Comptroller to refuse to accept withdrawal of the application and to go on to make findings as to validity.[139]

Hearing

22-64   The parties, if they so wish, are entitled to a hearing,[140] which will be in public unless the Comptroller, after consultation with the parties represented at the hearing, otherwise directs.[141] In an appropriate case where savings in cost and time are likely to be made, the Comptroller may direct that an issue be heard as a preliminary point[142] or via telephone or video link.[143] Where, in revocation proceedings pursuant to s.33 of the Patents Act 1949, the patentees failed to file a counter-statement notwithstanding repeated extensions of time, it was held that the Comptroller had no duty to consider the merits of the case and the patent was revoked.[144] If a counter-statement is filed but the applicant does not appear at the hearing nor file evidence, then the inference may be drawn that the applicant sees no effective answer to the case made against their application.[145] The old practice of requiring the patentee to open the proceedings has been abolished, and now the right to open is vested in the

---

[133] The Patents Rules 2007 do not contain a rule corresponding to r.103(6) of the 1995 Rules. Nevertheless it is submitted that the Comptroller retains this power under more general provisions of the 2007 Rules, for example r.86(a).

[134] Patents Rules 2007 r.86.

[135] *Cooper Mechanical Joints Ltd's Application* [1958] R.P.C. 459.

[136] See [33]–[37] of TPN 1/2000 [2000] R.P.C. 16.

[137] See *John Guest's Patent* [1987] R.P.C. 259; see also *Osterman's Patent* [1985] R.P.C. 579.

[138] See *Flude's Patent* [1993] R.P.C. 197.

[139] *R. v Comptroller General of Patents* [2002] R.P.C. 46.

[140] See Patents Rules 2007 r.80(4).

[141] Patents Rules 2007 r.84.

[142] Patents Rules 2007 r.82(1)(h). See also *Norsk Hydro A.S.'s Patent* [1997] R.P.C. 89.

[143] Patents Rules 2007 r.82(1)(d). See also TPN 1/2000 [2000] R.P.C. 16, [47].

[144] *Fontaine Converting Works Inc's Patent* [1959] R.P.C. 72.

[145] *Eichengrun's Application* (1932) 49 R.P.C. 435.

party who bears the initial burden of proof.[146] Parties are expected to supply skeleton arguments in advance.[147]

The Comptroller has jurisdiction to accept further submissions after the hearing has taken place but because of the inevitable delay and extra expense that their introduction will cause, the presumption is that the parties have made all their submissions by the end of the hearing.[148]   **22-65**

The decision

When the Comptroller has decided the matter, he must notify all the parties of his decision, including his reasons for making the decision.[149]   **22-66**

Interim decision

It is likely that interim decisions—i.e. decisions that a patent needs amendment— will arise. If so, there does not seem to be any reason why the suggestions made in the past as to the best procedure should not be adopted.[150] However, an appeal should be entered unless all parties agree that a reasonable chance exists of resolving the matters in issue.[151]   **22-67**

Costs

The Comptroller has power to award to any party such costs as he thinks reasonable and any such order may be enforced.[152] This includes the power to award compensatory costs in exceptional circumstances.[153] Guidance as to the approach to be taken and the relevant scale of costs to be applied can be found in TPN 4/2007[154] and in TPN 2/2000.[155]   **22-68**

If an applicant does not succeed in obtaining the full amount of relief asked for, they will not necessarily be deprived of costs[156]; although if, after having been offered by the proprietor substantially all that they ultimately are held entitled to, they persist in forcing the matter to a hearing thet will get no costs.[157] Similarly, if the application is not contested by the proprietor or the proprietor offers to surrender the patent,[158] the Comptroller in awarding costs will consider whether the proceedings might have been avoided if reasonable notice had been given to the applicant before the opposition or application for revocation was lodged.   **22-69**

Where an adjournment is necessary by reason of a party introducing an important   **22-70**

---

[146] TPN 1/2000 [2000] R.P.C. 16, [43].
[147] TPN 1/2000 [2000] R.P.C. 16, [45].
[148] *Interfilta (UK) Ltd's Patent* [2003] R.P.C. 22.
[149] Patents Rules 2007 r.80(6).
[150] *L. Oertling Ltd's Application* [1959] R.P.C. 148; *Du Pont (E.I.)'s War Loss Application* [1962] R.P.C. 228.
[151] *Du Pont de Nemours & Co (Bunting's) Application* [1969] R.P.C. 271.
[152] PA 1977 s.107(1).
[153] See *Rizla's Application* [1993] R.P.C. 365.
[154] [2008] R.P.C. 7.
[155] [2000] R.P.C. 16.
[156] (1910) 27 R.P.C., Comptroller's Ruling H.
[157] (1910) 27 R.P.C., Comptroller's Ruling H.
[158] See para.22-78.

document into the case at a late stage, a special award of costs may also be made.[159] If a party, though successful, overloads the case with unnecessary documents, no costs may be awarded.[160]

Appeal to the Patents Court

22-71   An appeal lies as of right to the Patents Court both from an interlocutory and from a final order of the Comptroller.[161]

Procedure on appeal

22-72   The procedure for an appeal is governed by CPR Pt 52 and its relevant practice direction[162] and guidance as to this can be found in TPN 1/2003 (Revised).[163] An appeal from the Comptroller is a Statutory Appeal and notice of appeal but there are no special provisions for service of the appellant's notice. Thus it must therefore be served within 21 days of the decision, unless a different period is ordered or unless the hearing to determine permission is adjourned.[164] The old system where the appellant had 28 days to file their appellant's notice at Court is no longer in force. Copies of any documents served should also be served on the Comptroller, as well as any respondents, as soon as practicable and in any event within seven days.[165]

22-73   The notice of appeal must state the nature of the decision, and the parts appealed against. A cross-appeal is necessary if a defendant desires to contend that the actual decision of the hearing officer should be varied. Thus, if the Comptroller decides that a patent will be revoked if the specification is not amended, the proprietor may appeal and contend that no amendment is necessary. If the applicant wishes to argue that even if the amendments are made no patent should be granted, a cross-appeal is necessary. If the applicant merely wishes to contend that the decision ought to be affirmed on grounds other than those set out in the decision, they ought to file a respondent's notice.

22-74   The appeal is by way of review, not rehearing.[166] A submission that a rehearing ought to take place in an appeal from the Comptroller because the decision in question had been made without a hearing was rejected in *Halliburton Energy Service Inc's Patent Application*.[167] The applicant had a right to a hearing. The fact that it chose not to exercise that right did not affect the nature of the appeal. Unless the court orders otherwise, evidence at the hearing is the same as that used before the Comptroller and any application to adduce further evidence will be decided under normal CPR principles.[168]

---

[159] See (1929) 46 R.P.C., Comptroller's Ruling B.
[160] *Metallgesellschaft A.G.'s Application* (1934) 51 R.P.C. 368.
[161] PA 1977 s.97.
[162] CPR r.63.16.
[163] [2003] R.P.C. 46.
[164] See CPR r.63.16 and CPR Pt 52.4 and CPR Pt 52 Practice Direction 52A, para.4.1(a) and Practice Direction 52D.
[165] CPR rr.52.4(3) and 63.16(3). See also TPN 1/2003 (Revised) [2003] R.P.C. 46, [7].
[166] CPR r.52.11. See also TPN 1/2003 (Revised) [2003] R.P.C. 46, [10].
[167] [2011] EWHC 2508 (Pat); [2012] R.P.C. 12.
[168] CPR r.52.11(2).

The appellant normally has the right to begin at the hearing, except where there **22-75**
is an appeal and a cross-appeal, then the patentee normally begins.[169]

Costs on appeal

An appellant who abandons an appeal before the hearing will be ordered to pay **22-76**
the costs,[170] and if fresh evidence is permitted on the appeal and the appeal is allowed in consequence, the appellant may be refused costs.[171] An unsuccessful appellant appealing from an ex parte decision of the Comptroller will normally have
to pay the Comptroller's costs of the appeal.[172]

Appeals to Court of Appeal

An appeal lies to the Court of Appeal (with leave from either the Patents Court **22-77**
or the Court of Appeal) from a decision of the Patents Court acting in its appellate
capacity when considering revocation.[173] CPR r.52.13 generally requires the permission of the Court of Appeal in the case of a second tier appeal (which permission
will not be given unless the criteria set out in r.52.13(2) are met), but the Court of
Appeal held in *Smith International Inc v Specialised Petroleum Services*[174] that s.55
of the Access to Justice Act 1999—and thus CPR r.52.13—do not apply to appeals under s.97(3) of the Patents Act 1977.

5. SURRENDER OF PATENT

Effect of surrender

A patentee may at any time by notice to the Comptroller offer to surrender their **22-78**
patent.[175] The effect of surrender is that the patent is deemed to cease to exist as from
the date when notice of the Comptroller's acceptance of the offer is published in
the *Official Journal*. No action for infringement of the patent lies in respect of any
act done before that date.[176] However, licence fees can still be collected for the
period prior to surrender.[177] This is in contrast to revocation which takes effect from
the date of grant, with the effect being that the patent never existed.

When surrender is appropriate

Surrender is appropriate where the patent proprietor no longer wishes to maintain **22-79**
the patent but equally does not accept that the patent is invalid and ought to be
revoked. Thus surrender may be appropriate where, for example, the proprietor
decides that the renewal fees exceed the commercial value of the patent. An offer
to surrender may also be appropriate by way of a compromise of revocation

---

[169] *Johnson & Johnson's Application* [1963] R.P.C. 40.
[170] See *Knight's Application* (1887) Griff.P.C. 35; *Metallgesellschaft A.G.'s Application* (1934) 51
R.P.C. 368.
[171] See *Stubb's Patent* (1884) Griff.P.C. 298; *Chambers' Application* (1915) 32 R.P.C. 416, at 420.
[172] TPN 2/2000 [2000] R.P.C. 16, [19].
[173] PA 1977 s.97(3).
[174] [2006] F.S.R. 25, following *Henry Boot Construction (UK) Ltd v Malmaison Hotel* [2001] Q.B. 388,
CA.
[175] PA 1977 s.29(1).
[176] PA 1977 s.29(3).
[177] Although there can be no compensation for Crown use—see PA 1977 s.29(3).

proceedings, thereby saving the parties (and the court or the Comptroller) the time and cost which such proceedings would inevitably entail. However, owing to the difference in effect between revocation (in which the patent is void ab initio) and surrender (in which it is not)[178] such an offer to surrender will not necessarily be accepted. The practice of the Comptroller in these circumstances is to consider the grounds upon which revocation is contended for, prior to accepting an offer to surrender.[179] Thus, in *Connaught Laboratories Inc's Patent*,[180] the court, when presented with an offer to surrender a patent made on what was to have been the first day of the trial of an action for revocation, refused to allow an offer to surrender to be further processed through the Comptroller and, having considered the grounds of invalidity, revoked the patent instead. In *Dyson Ltd's Patent*[181] there were prior ongoing revocation proceedings before the court. The Comptroller first stayed the application to surrender in order that the court might be informed, and later allowed the patent to be surrendered in the absence of any opposition to surrender or expression of view by the court.[182] In *OR Specific's Patent*,[183] there were parallel revocation proceedings but there had been no opposition to the offer of surrender. The Comptroller still considered it to be desirable to bring the offer of surrender into the same forum as the revocation action so that the appropriate course of action can be considered in the light of all the circumstances of the case. He therefore stayed the surrender proceedings and ordered the proprietor to: (a) notify the court of the offer to surrender, and (b) to notify the Comptroller of the outcome of the court proceedings or any order from the court that the surrender proceedings should continue before the Comptroller, so that he could consider the matter further.

Circumventing s.18(5)

22-80   Surrender cannot be invoked to validate a later filed patent application which would otherwise be refused for duplication under s.18(5) of the 1977 Act.[184]

Procedure

22-81   Where an offer to surrender a patent is made, the offer is advertised by the Comptroller in the *Official Journal*[185] and any person interested (e.g. a licensee) may oppose.[186] The practice on opposition is governed by Pt 7 (rr.73–91) of the Patents Rules 2007.[187] Notice of opposition must be given within four weeks of the advertisement.[188] The proceedings are started when the opponent files in duplicate Patents Form 15 and their statement of grounds which must include a concise statement of the facts and grounds in which the opponent relies and specify the remedy

---

[178] Referred to as the *ex nunc* effect of surrender as opposed to the *ex tunc* effect of revocation.
[179] See the practice referred to in *Connaught Laboratories Inc's Patent* [1999] F.S.R. 284.
[180] [1999] F.S.R. 284.
[181] [2003] R.P.C. 24
[182] See *Dyson Ltd's Patent (No.2)* [2003] R.P.C. 48.
[183] BL O/170/14.
[184] See *IBM's Application* [1983] R.P.C. 283.
[185] Patents Rules 2007 r.75 and Sch.3 Pt 2.
[186] PA 1977 s.29(2).
[187] Patents Rules 2007 r.73(1)(b) and Sch.3 Pt 2.
[188] Patents Rules 2007 r.76(2). This period cannot be extended, see r.108 and Sch.4 Pt 1.

which they seek.[189] The statement must be verified by a statement of truth. The Comptroller must notify the proprietor of the commencement of the opposition. He must also send the Form and statement of grounds to the proprietor and specify a period within which they may file a counter-statement.[190]

If the proprietor wishes to continue with the surrender, they must file a counter-statement in duplicate within the period specified by the Comptroller setting out fully the grounds upon which the opposition is resisted.[191] **22-82**

The Comptroller must then send the counter-statement to the opponent and specify a period within which Patents Form 4 must be filed; if the opponent fails to file the form within the period specified, they will be deemed to have filed a request to withdraw from the proceedings.[192] **22-83**

When sending the counter-statement, the Comptroller will also specify the periods within which evidence may be filed by the parties.[193] **22-84**

The Comptroller may shorten or enlarge any period of time which has been specified under any provision of Pt 7 and an extension may be granted notwithstanding that the period of time specified as expired.[194] **22-85**

The Comptroller must give the parties an opportunity to be heard if they so wish.[195] **22-86**

Costs

The Comptroller may also award costs. The Comptroller's Practice with regard to costs is set out in the Tribunal Practice Notice 4/2007 entitled "Costs in Proceedings before the Comptroller". Costs are normally awarded by reference to a scale. **22-87**

Appeal

An appeal to the Patents Court lies as of right from the decision of the Comptroller.[196] As to the procedure on appeal and any further appeal to the Court of Appeal, see paras 17–206 and 17–207. **22-88**

---

[189] Patents Rules 2007 r.76(4).
[190] Patents Rules 2007 r.77.
[191] Patents Rules 2007 r.78.
[192] Patents Rules 2007 rr.80(1) and (1A) and 81A.
[193] Patents Rules 2007 r.80(1)–(3).
[194] Patents Rules 2007 r.81.
[195] Patents Rules 2007 r.80(4) and (5).
[196] PA 1977 s.97.

CHAPTER 23

DECLARATIONS

CONTENTS

1. INTRODUCTION

Subject to any limitation period, a patentee may start an infringement claim whenever they like. They can choose to start so as to maximise the perceived chance of success. Ordinarily, a patentee will wish to proceed at a time which minimises any damage to their business, but maximises the relief available. **23-01**

None of that provides much reassurance to the would-be entrant into the patentee's market. Such an entrant may often have good reason for seeking to "clear the way", to confirm their freedom to operate, before market entry. Otherwise, the threat of proceedings for patent infringement may hang over them. Parliament has recognised that such a threat may be damaging and indeed may amount to a substantial hindrance to trade. This is part of the rationale behind the actionability of groundless threats (provided for by s.70). **23-02**

For these reasons, the law provides an ability to seek a negative declaration: a binding statement by the court (or the Comptroller) that the applicant's proposed acts do not infringe a specified patent. **23-03**

Declaration of non-infringement under s.71

Section 71 of the Patents Act 1977 therefore contains specific provisions for seeking a declaration of non-infringement from the court or the Comptroller. They allow the applicant to seek such a declaration regardless of whether the patentee has asserted infringement. **23-04**

Developments in the jurisprudence on the court's inherent jurisdiction to grant negative declarations[1] may often mean that a sufficient reassurance may be gained without recourse to s.71. Nevertheless, the statutory route remains a useful one for those who wish to know where they stand before launching a new product or venture. **23-05**

---

[1] See para.23-50, et seq.

Declarations under the inherent jurisdiction of the court

23-06   In addition to the statutory power, the court has an inherent power to grant declarations, including negative declarations. It was previously thought that the court's jurisdiction to grant a negative declaration under its inherent power was limited by a requirement that the proposed defendant must have made a claim of right.[2] Now, it is clear that this view of the law is not correct: a claimant is entitled to seek to clear the way under the inherent jurisdiction too. Nevertheless, the exercise of the jurisdiction remains discretionary, and the s.71 jurisdiction remains important.

CPR Pt 40.20

23-07   The court's power to make declarations under the inherent jurisdiction is now regulated by CPR Pt 40.20:

> "The court may make binding declarations whether or not any other remedy is claimed."

Examples of declarations sought

23-08   The court may, under its inherent jurisdiction, grant any of the following declarations:

(a)   declarations of infringement, and non-infringement, of intellectual property rights;[3]
(b)   declarations of validity and invalidity;[4]
(c)   declarations of essentiality or non-essentiality;[5] and
(d)   declarations of obviousness (e.g. a declaration that a particular product or process was obvious in the light of the state of the art at a particular date).[6]

Commercial importance of declarations

23-09   Actions for declarations, particularly those for declarations of non-infringement, provide a commercially important means of risk management. Although an action will still take time to come to trial, the issues and risks will be clarified as the respective positions of the parties emerge through the various stages of exchange of pleadings and evidence. The applicant seeking the declaration has a motivation to push the action forward.

23-10   There is no reason why, in a suitable case, declarations of non-infringement may not be sought in respect of several alternative products or processes. However, if the number of proposed alternatives were excessive, the court might decline to deal with the application in its entirety. Care must be taken to ensure that the declaration sought is worded so that it can in fact provide the commercial certainty that a party seeks, particularly in a situation where the court is not able to assess the

---

[2]   See para.23-53, et seq.
[3]   See para.23-14, et seq. below for declarations of non-infringement. Declarations of infringement are routinely sought by patentees in infringement actions, although they are seldom strictly necessary. The judgment itself will indicate whether infringement has been established, and the purpose of such a declaration is often commercial rather than legal.
[4]   See para.23-78, et seq.
[5]   These are dealt with in Ch.18, "FRAND".
[6]   See para.23-81, et seq.

proposed product by inspection.[7] In *Gore v Geox*,[8] Jacob LJ (giving the judgment of the Court of Appeal) suggested that rather than wording a declaration broadly so as to encompass all possible future variants, claimants might more usefully describe precisely one product (or process) and then list any proposed variants with respect to that first description.

A declaration may also be sought in relation to a product or process (or proposed **23-11** product or process), which engages only some of the claims of a patent.[9]

Parties to actions for declarations

It is important to ensure that an action for one or more declarations is brought **23-12** against the proper party or parties. That will often be just the proprietor/s of the patent in issue, although other parties may be affected by the declaration/s sought. If so it may be proper that they are joined as parties to the action. In *Teva v Amgen*[10] Arnold J considered the issue of whether Amgen Inc should cease to be a party to three claims relating to the UK designation of a European patent which Amgen Inc had assigned to Amgen Manufacturing Ltd. One submission made by Teva was that Amgen Inc was its "real adversary" in this litigation, and that it was desirable for it to be a party for that reason. Applying the summary of the principles governing declaratory relief given by Aikens LJ in *Rolls-Royce v Unite*,[11] Arnold J held that Teva had a real prospect of successfully claiming declaratory relief against Amgen Inc and that it was therefore desirable that Amgen Inc should remain as a party (see [44]). The key question (see [48]) was Aikens LJ's third enumerated principle from *Rolls-Royce*, namely whether that party will be affected by the court's determination of the issues concerning that right.

Aikens LJ's summary from *Rolls-Royce* was quoted in full by Arnold J (at [44]) **23-13** in *Teva v Amgen*. It provides as follows:

"120. For the purposes of the present case, I think that the principles in the cases can be summarised as follows:

(1)   The power of the court to grant declaratory relief is discretionary.

(2)   There must, in general, be a real and present dispute between the parties before the court as to the existence or extent of a legal right between them. However, the claimant does not need to have a present cause of action against the defendant.

(3)   Each party must, in general, be affected by the court's determination of the issues concerning the legal right in question.

(4)   The fact that the claimant is not a party to the relevant contract in respect of which a declaration is sought is not fatal to an application for a declaration, provided that it is directly affected by the issue (fn: in this respect the cases have undoubtedly 'moved on' from *Meadows*).

(5)   The court will be prepared to give declaratory relief in respect of a 'friendly action' or where there is an 'academic question' if all parties so wish, even on 'private law' issues. This may particularly be so if it is a 'test case', or it may affect a significant number of other cases, and it is in the public interest to decide the issue concerned.

(6)   However, the court must be satisfied that all sides of the argument will be fully and properly

---

[7]   See *Mallory Metallurgical Products v Black Sivalls and Bryson* [1977] R.P.C. 321 (decided under s.66 of the Patents Act 1949). And see para.23-30, et seq.

[8]   *W.L. Gore & Associates GmbH v Geox SpA* [2009] EWCA Civ 794; see in particular [7].

[9]   As was the case, for example, in *Eugen Seitz AG v KHS Corpoplast GmbH and Norgren AG* [2014] EWHC 14 (Ch).

[10]   *Teva Pharma BV and Teva UK Ltd v Amgen, Inc and Amgen Manufacturing Ltd* [2013] EWHC 3711 (Pat).

[11]   *Rolls-Royce plc v Unite the Union* [2009] EWCA Civ 387, [2010] 1 W.L.R. 318, [120].

put. It must therefore ensure that all those affected are either before it or will have their arguments put before the court.

(7) In all cases, assuming that the other tests are satisfied, the court must ask: is this the most effective way of resolving the issues raised? In answering that question it must consider the other options of resolving this issue."

2. DECLARATION OF NON-INFRINGEMENT UNDER S.71

The jurisdiction

23-14   Section 71(1) of the 1977 Act provides as follows:

"**71.**—(1) Without prejudice to the court's jurisdiction to make a declaration or declarator apart from this section, a declaration or declarator that an act does not, or a proposed act would not, constitute an infringement of a patent may be made by the Court or the Comptroller in proceedings between the person doing or proposing to do the act and the proprietor of the patent, notwithstanding that no assertion to the contrary has been made by the proprietor, if it is shown—
(a) that that person has applied in writing to the proprietor for a written acknowledgment to the effect of the declaration or declarator claimed, and has furnished him with full particulars in writing of the act in question; and
(b) that the proprietor has refused or failed to give any such acknowledgment."

Declaration by Comptroller

23-15   It is to be noted that the Comptroller also has jurisdiction to make a declaration under s.71: see, for example, *Tek-Dek Ltd v Flexiteek International A/S*.[12] A declaration made by the Comptroller has the same effect as a declaration by the court. There is one exception: a decision by the Comptroller (or on appeal from him) as to validity does not create an estoppel in a subsequent attack on validity in civil proceedings where infringement is an issue.[13] It is submitted that this merely means that the party alleging invalidity in the subsequent proceedings is not prevented from doing so by the earlier declaration, whatever it may be. Conversely a declaration under s.71, whether made by the court or Comptroller, would be binding against the patentee and all successors in title.

The claimant

23-16   Under the section, any person doing or proposing to do any act may seek a declaration from the court (or the Comptroller) that that act is not or would not be an infringement of a specified patent. It was suggested in *Minnesota Mining and Manufacturing's Patent*[14] that these words therefore precluded the court from considering a purely hypothetical product, in particular one which was devised merely for the purpose of testing the limits of the claim. Pumfrey J rejected this; he held that it would be sufficient for an applicant for a declaration to be able to say "I should like to do this if I can". More recently, Birss J applied the same test in *IPCom v HTC*[15](at [119]) citing Jacob LJ in *Interdigital v Nokia*.[16]

---

[12] BL O/001/14 (3 January 2014).
[13] PA 1977 ss.71(2) and 72(5).
[14] [1999] R.P.C. 135, 152.
[15] [2015] EWHC 1034 (Pat).
[16] [2006] EWCA Civ 1618, [17].

Omnipharm v Merial

The claimant in *Omnipharm v Merial*[17] specialised in the regulatory aspects of   **23-17**
pharmaceutical licensing. Its original claim was started as one for revocation of
Merial's patents. Omnipharm sought to amend its claim so as also to seek declarations of non-infringement. Merial opposed the amendment: it said that Omnipharm
had not shown it was the person proposing to do the acts covered by the declaration sought.

Norris J, hearing the application to amend,[18] held that that was not the appropriate time to decide the issue of whether Omnipharm had properly made out its   **23-18**
entitlement to seek the declarations, provided that (as he found) Omnipharm had a
realistic prospect of establishing its standing at trial. Merial's secondary position,
that the issue of such standing under s.71 should be heard as a preliminary issue,
was also rejected by Norris J, who instead left the issue to be heard at trial.

The trial judge, Floyd J, decided that Omnipharm had satisfied the requirements   **23-19**
of s.71.[19] In his judgment, he made the following observations (at [154]) regarding those requirements:

"i)   The language is in contrast to that of section 72, the section which governs applications for
       revocation of patents. That section confers standing on 'any person': even a 'straw man'
       provided no abuse of process is involved: see *Cairnstores v Hassle* [2002] F.S.R. 564.
 ii)   The language is also in contrast with section 64 which confers a right to continue in certain
       circumstances on a person who either 'does in good faith an act which would constitute an
       infringement of the patent if it were in force' or 'makes in good faith serious and effective
       preparations to do such an act'.
 iii) In *Nokia v Interdigital* [2007] F.S.R. 23 at [17] Jacob LJ said, obiter, 'Section 71 requires no
       claim of right, nor even any intention by the applicant to make or do the acts the subject matter of the declaration he seeks. Normally, of course, the applicant will at least have in mind
       the possibility of doing those acts, but whether he does so or not is irrelevant.'
 iv)   In *3M's Patent* [1999] R.P.C. 135 at 152, Pumfrey J (as he was then) described the proposed
       formulations as 'argumentative' in the sense that they were intended to point up particular difficulties on construction. He considered that it was sufficient for the applicant to be able to say
       'I should like to do this if I can'.
 v)   The section supplements the court's inherent power to grant a declaration where to do so would
       serve a useful purpose. It was enacted at a time when the court's inherent power was thought
       to be subject to jurisdictional constraints, such as the need for an applicant for a declaration
       to show a contrary claim of right. Its object was to allow a defendant to bring a question before
       the court where a patentee was prevaricating, but making no claim of right. Its purpose was
       accordingly to remove jurisdictional constraints, not create them."

The judge went on to hold that the requirement that an applicant should propose   **23-20**
to do an act does not require any investigation into how settled, firm or commercially realistic the proposal is.

In *Filhol v Fairfax*[20] Falconer J seems to have considered that the words "the   **23-21**
person doing or proposing to do the act" in the statute prevented the court from
making declarations about acts of persons other than the claimant. It did not matter in *Filhol*, as he was able to make a declaration under the court's inherent
jurisdiction.

The court can also make declarations under s.71 that certain acts would constitute   **23-22**

---

17   [2011] EWHC 3393 (Pat).
18   [2010] EWHC 3059 (Pat).
19   This issue was not raised on appeal: [2013] EWCA Civ 2.
20   [1990] R.P.C. 293.

indirect infringements under s.60(2). In *Actavis v Lilly*[21] though Arnold J's declarations of non-infringement were reversed on appeal[22] it was not disputed that the court could make declarations in relation to indirect infringement of the UK designation of the Patent at issue, if that was made out.

The defendant

23-23   The defendant to the action will be the patentee. They need not have made any positive assertion of infringement. It is sufficient that he has "refused or failed" to give a written acknowledgement that the relevant acts do not infringe.

Position of exclusive licensee

23-24   It was held in *Chiron Corp v Evans Medical Ltd*[23] that an exclusive licensee was a proper co-defendant in an action for a declaration of non-infringement under the court's inherent jurisdiction. This judgment was reached on the bases that the exclusive licensee had the right to bring an action for damages for infringement under s.67 of the 1977 Act so that it had a real interest in the relief sought, and it had itself made a claim of right. However, s.71(1) expressly refers only to proceedings against the proprietor of the patent. In a suitable case it may be possible to commence proceedings under the section against the patentee and join the exclusive licensee to a further claim under the court's inherent jurisdiction, but only where some useful purpose is served by doing so.[24] Alternatively, it may be argued that "the proprietor" of s.71 may include the holder of an exclusive licence having regard to the terms of s.67(1).

The act

23-25   The "act" referred to appears to refer back to the classes of potentially infringing act set out in s.60; although subss.(1) and (2) do not use the word, it is found in the other subsections and also in s.64. The description to be given will describe the commercial activity intended to be carried out. It will also necessarily have to describe the product or process in relation to which the acts are proposed, since the court will have to decide whether the relevant act is to be performed "in relation to the invention" of the patent in suit.

23-26   The section refers only to patents and it therefore appears that it cannot be invoked in respect of an application for a patent. Since the section is expressly framed as being without prejudice to the court's jurisdiction to make a declaration, though, it is submitted that in an appropriate case this jurisdiction could be invoked. Other than this, no restriction is placed upon the right to seek a declaration. Thus, a declaration could be sought, for example, to the effect that the act is not an infringement by reason of the provisions of s.64 of the 1977 Act[25] as well as the more conventional type of declaration.

23-27   The section is confined to acts within the UK, so that in *PlastusKreativ v Min-*

21   [2015] R.P.C. 6.
22   [2015] EWCA Civ 555.
23   [1996] F.S.R. 863, (Pat).
24   See "Declaration under the court's inherent jurisdiction" at para.23-50, et seq.
25   See para.14–199, et seq.

nesota Mining and Manufacturing[26] the court struck out that part of a claim seeking a declaration under s.71 of the 1977 Act that the French and German equivalents of the European patent (UK) in suit would not be infringed. Insofar as the court in *PlastusKreativ* also struck out the claim for a declaration of non-infringement under the inherent jurisdiction, the judgment would appear to have been overturned by the Court of Appeal's judgments in *Actavis v Lilly*.[27]

Furthermore, it was stressed in *Knorr-Bremse Systems v Haldex Brake Products*[28] (an action for a declaration of non-infringement of certain European patents (UK)) that where the validity of foreign patents is to be put in issue, even if invalidity is not formally pleaded, the UK Court would have to decline jurisdiction on validity and therefore (following *Fort Dodge v Akzo Nobel*)[29] infringement as well, since infringement and validity of an intellectual property right "are so closely interrelated that they should be treated for jurisdiction purposes as one issue or claim".   **23-28**

In *Actavis v Lilly*, the claimant sought declarations in respect of a European (UK) patent and its corresponding French, German, Spanish and Italian designations. The UK declaration was sought under s.71 and/or the court's inherent jurisdiction; the declarations in respect of the foreign designations were sought under the inherent jurisdiction.   **23-29**

Full written particulars

It is a prerequisite to the making of a declaration under the section that the person has applied in writing to the patentee for a written acknowledgment to the effect of the declaration claimed. In doing so, the applicant must supply the patentee with full written particulars of the act in question. The final requirement expressed in the statute is that the patentee has failed to give the acknowledgment sought.   **23-30**

It is preferable that where practicable the description should be accompanied by a sample or drawings of the possible infringement.[30] This will avoid the problem in *Mallory Metallurgical Products v Black Sivalls and Bryson Inc*.[31] The Court of Appeal held in *Mallory* that as there was no actual article before the court, and the description was capable of referring to more than one article, the declaration would be refused as it was not possible to say that no article within that description would infringe the patent. This emphasises the importance of framing the declaration sought in suitably precise language. In *Mallory*, the applicant failed to get its declaration because there was insufficient information to allow the court to conclude that the proposed acts across the breadth of the product description were non-infringing.   **23-31**

In *Generics (UK) Limited t/a Mylan v Yeda Research and Development Co*,[32] the judge's findings on construction were reversed by the Court of Appeal. The Court of Appeal went on to consider the case on infringement under its construction[33] and the claimant had not adduced sufficient evidence to establish infringement, as to which it held the burden.   **23-32**

---

[26] [1995] R.P.C. 438.
[27] [2013] EWCA Civ 517, [2013] R.P.C. 37 (service and jurisdiction over foreign designations); and [2015] EWCA Civ 666 (substantive appeal on infringement). See also para.23–67, et seq.
[28] [2008] F.S.R. 30.
[29] [1998] F.S.R. 222. See also *GAT v Luk* (C-04/03) [2006] F.S.R. 45, [25].
[30] *Minnesota Mining and Manufacturing's Patent* [1999] R.P.C. 135, 153.
[31] [1977] R.P.C. 321.
[32] [2013] EWCA Civ 925, (CA); [2013] Bus L.R. 1329; [2014] R.P.C. 4.
[33] [2013] EWCA Civ 925, (CA); [2013] Bus L.R. 1329; [2014] R.P.C. 4, [106]–[111].

23-33   It would appear to be implicit that the patentee has had sufficient time and opportunity to consider the particulars before they could be said to have failed to give the declaration sought, and that the action cannot be brought until such time has elapsed. However, in *MMD Design & Consultancy Limited's Patent*,[34] a case involving an application made to the Comptroller, the hearing officer held that this was a very strict interpretation and oppressively bureaucratic, and that the section was satisfied if the patentee had had an opportunity to consider his position before he was called upon to respond in the proceedings. This interpretation has not yet been considered by the court. Although in that case, even if the strict interpretation had been correct, it would have been open to the applicant immediately to commence fresh proceedings, and thus no useful purpose would have been served by applying it.

23-34   It is also possible to contemplate a case in which the description is supplemented during the course of the proceedings, where some defect emerges in the original description; if the patentee is still challenging the declaration, it would appear to be needlessly inflexible to construe the section so as to require that the proceedings must be recommenced with a fresh description being first served upon them. Applying the reasoning of Arnold J in *Actavis v Lilly (abuse of process)*,[35] should there be an alleged defect in the claimant's compliance with the prerequisites for seeking a declaration, then it may not be an abuse of process merely to start a fresh, "remedied" action within the currency of the initial, allegedly-defective one.

Confidential product or process

23-35   Where "particulars of the product or process alleged to infringe" are given in the course of infringement proceedings in lieu of disclosure, it has been held that the party serving them was compelled to do so and that therefore they were to be treated as confidential in the same way as documents produced on disclosure.[36] This reasoning would appear not to apply to particulars served under s.71(1)(a) prior to any action. If details of the product or process in question are confidential, this may present a problem in complying with the section. If express confidentiality terms cannot be agreed in advance, it would be prudent to include only non-confidential material in particulars tendered voluntarily, and to incorporate any confidential material in an annex which is offered for inspection only on terms as to confidentiality. The court may subsequently have to decide whether an offer on those terms was reasonable and did in substance furnish full particulars, or whether such a course meant that the requirements of s.71(1)(a) were not in substance satisfied.

Onus

23-36   The burden of proof in a case where a declaration of non-infringement is sought lies on the person seeking the declaration. Thus it is for the applicant for the declaration to prove that the product or process does not infringe the patent.[37]

---

[34] [1989] R.P.C. 131.

[35] [2013] EWHC 3749 (Pat); this application was not subject to appeal.

[36] *Chiron Corp v Evans Medical Ltd (No.2)* [1997] F.S.R. 268.

[37] *Rohm & Haas Co v Collag Ltd* [2001] F.S.R. 28, [30]–[37] (Neuberger J); [2002] F.S.R. 28, 445, at [26]–[28], CA; following *Mallory Metallurgical Products v Black Sivalls and Bryson Inc* [1977]

Putting validity in issue

In an action for a declaration of non-infringement under the section, the validity of the patent may also be put in issue.[38] A potential market entrant who might be an eventual defendant to an infringement action can therefore issue a pre-emptive action for a declaration, but still avail themselves of the usual "squeeze" between validity and infringement. In *Minnesota Mining and Manufacturing's Patent* the applicant benefited from such a squeeze.[39] Pumfrey J revoked the patent in suit and therefore refused the declaration sought (on the ground that in the light of the wide construction of the patent, the particulars were inadequate). However, had the patent been valid on the alternative narrower construction, the particulars would have been adequate and he would have granted the declaration sought.

23-37

Effect of declaration

In *Niche Generics Ltd v Lundbeck A/S*,[40] Pumfrey J explained the effect of a declaration of non-infringement:

23-38

"The declaration merely tells the defendant that if the claimants can demonstrate that the manufacture is according to the process description which forms the subject matter of the declaration, then there is no infringement of the patent. It neither involves a warrant by the claimants that the product sold within the United Kingdom will be manufactured according to that process description, nor does it provide the claimants with an immunity based upon the claimants' own assertion of the manner in which the product is made. It is merely a manner of clearing out of the way issues of construction and substantive law relating to infringement so that the only issue in the future which should arise between the parties is the process used for the manufacture of the defendant's product."

It follows that a declaration of non-infringement does not prevent the patentee from issuing proceedings for infringement in due course where the allegation is that the product or process complained of in the subsequent proceedings is not in accordance with that forming the subject of the declaration. Nevertheless, if it is shown that the product or process is in accordance with that forming the subject of the declaration, then "the action stops at that point".[41]

23-39

Ordering samples to be provided

Where the patentee conceded that a declaration of non-infringement should be granted substantially in the form sought by the claimant but applied for an order that the claimant provide certain samples manufactured during the inspection of the process by the parties, the court treated the application as made under CPR r.25.5 (inspection of property relevant to issues that will arise in relation to anticipated proceedings); but, in the exercise of its discretion, the court refused to grant the relief sought.[42]

23-40

Procedural matters arising under s.71

In the case of a declaration action brought in the High Court no exceptional procedure is laid down, so that the ordinary Civil Procedure Rules will apply.

23-41

R.P.C. 321, CA.
[38] PA 1977 s.74(1)(c), reversing PA 1949 s.66(3).
[39] [1999] R.P.C. 135, 153.
[40] [2004] F.S.R. 20, [24].
[41] *Niche Generics Ltd v Lundbeck A/S* [2004] F.S.R. 20, [25].
[42] *Niche Generics v Lundbeck A/S* [2004] F.S.R. 20.

23-42   Where the action is brought before the Comptroller, rules of procedure are laid down in the Patents Rules 2007 Pt 7 (rr.73–91).[43] However, such an action cannot be brought when proceedings relating to the patent are pending in the court without leave of that court.[44]

23-43   In *Tek-Dek*,[45] the claimant had applied for its declaration but had not supplied evidence that it had sought the necessary written acknowledgment under s.71(1)(a). Also, it had not clearly specified what its proposed acts were. The UKIPO gave a preliminary view that the application did not satisfy the requirements of s.71(1), in response to which the claimant filed an amended statement of case with supporting evidence.

23-44   In response, the defendant made certain applications which were decided as preliminary issues by a UKIPO hearing officer on behalf of the Comptroller.[46] Applications for strike-out and a stay were both refused, so the application for declaration of non-infringement proceeded.

23-45   The defendant subsequently filed its counterstatement, and Tek-Dek sought permission to amend its application in response to the defendant's arguments on construction. The defendant resisted that amendment, but by a decision on the papers[47] it was admitted by the hearing officer. The application for the declaration continued as amended and the hearing officer granted the declaration of non-infringement requested.

Making other claims when seeking a declaration under s.71

23-46   As noted above, it is possible to put validity in issue in the proceedings, and other claims may also be made. In *Demel v Jefferson*,[48] the claimant sought damages for threats, a declaration of non-infringement and revocation; the defendant pleaded justification and counterclaimed for infringement.

Seeking a declaration by counterclaim

23-47   A declaration of non-infringement may also be sought by way of counterclaim; in *Vax v Hoover*,[49] the defendant who had been sued for infringement on one product was permitted to amend at a late stage to add a counterclaim seeking a declaration that a new model did not infringe. A further, more recent, example was *AGA v Occlutech*.[50]

Summary judgment on a declaration for non-infringement.

23-48   Summary judgment is unusual in patent cases; since the court needs to construe the claim as the skilled addressee of the patent would understand it, expert evidence is ordinarily necessary.[51] Nonetheless, in an appropriate case, summary judgment may be given: Birss J awarded summary judgment and a declaration of non-

---

[43] Patent Rules 2009 r.73(1)(a) and Sch.3 Pt 1.
[44] PA 1977 s.74(7).
[45] PA 1977 ss.71(2) and 72(5).
[46] BL O/311/12—decision of J.E. Porter, 10 August 2012.
[47] BL O/120/13—decision of A.C. Howard, 13 March 2013.
[48] [1999] F.S.R. 204.
[49] [1990] R.P.C. 656.
[50] [2015] R.P.C. 12.
[51] As explained by Arnold J in *Starsight Telecast Inc v Virgin Media Ltd* [2014] EWHC 8 (Pat), at [20].

infringement in favour of the defendant in *Nampak v Alpla*.[52] There was a dispute between the parties as to whether expert evidence was necessary; Birss J held that Nampak's submissions in favour of the need for expert evidence were too vague to establish such a need. He went on to construe the relevant claims in the absence of expert evidence, and granted summary judgment. That grant of summary judgment was upheld on appeal.[53]

Costs

No special provisions are made as to costs and therefore the normal principles under which costs are awarded both in the court and before the Comptroller apply.[54] In the UKIPO there may be disputes about whether costs should be ordered off the ordinary scale. In *Wragg v Donnelly*,[55] Mr J. Elbro (for the Comptroller) refused declarations of infringement, having also dismissed the claimant's attacks on the validity of the patent. The defendant sought costs above the ordinary scale: it submitted that since the claimant had sought two non-binding opinions from the UKIPO and both of these had been unfavourable to the claimant, the action should not have been brought. The application for off-scale costs was refused on the grounds that this would act to discourage parties from using the UKIPO's opinion service.

23-49

3. DECLARATIONS UNDER THE COURT'S INHERENT JURISDICTION

A. Declaration of Non-infringement

Relationship with s.71

Section 71 of the 1977 Act expressly provides that its provisions are without prejudice to the court's jurisdiction to make such a declaration in relation to a patent apart from the section. Proceedings for declaratory relief as to non-infringement are a well recognised procedure in appropriate circumstances and the inherent jurisdiction, as well as the jurisdiction under s.71, is well recognised.[56]

23-50

Width of the declaration

In certain circumstances the inherent jurisdiction may enable the court to grant a wider declaration than it can under s.71,[57] including declarations in respect of non-UK designations of European patents.[58] On the other hand, in a case where a declaration of non-infringement of trade mark rights was sought under s.21 of the Trade Marks Act 1994, it was said that, as a matter of discretion, the court may

23-51

---

[52] *Nampak Plastics Europe Ltd v Alpla UK Ltd* [2014] EWHC 2196 (Pat).
[53] [2014] EWCA Civ 1293, [2015] F.S.R. 11; Floyd LJ (with whom Macur and Briggs LJJ agreed).
[54] *Mölnlycke AB v Procter & Gamble Ltd* [1990] R.P.C. 267. *Niche Generics Ltd v Lundbeck A/S* [2004] F.S.R. 20, 392, at [12]–[21]. Note that PA 1949 s.66(2) had special provisions but these have not been re-enacted. For costs before the Comptroller, see generally TPN 2/2000 [2000] R.P.C. 598 and TPN 4/2007 [2008] R.P.C. 7.
[55] *Richard Wragg v Mike Donnelly* BL O/280/10 (9 August 2010).
[56] Per Robert Walker J in *Chiron Corp v Evans Medical Ltd* [1996] F.S.R. 863, at 871 and 872.
[57] *Auchincloss v Agricultural & Veterinary Supplies* [1997] R.P.C. 649; see also *Filhol v Fairfax* [1990] R.P.C 293 referred to at para.23-21.
[58] *Actavis v Lilly (service and jurisdiction over foreign designations)* [2013] EWCA Civ 517, [2013] R.P.C. 37.

decline to grant any wider declaration under the inherent jurisdiction on grounds that it is unnecessary or undesirable.[59]

The Comptroller

23-52   The Comptroller does not have an inherent jurisdiction to grant a declaration of non-infringement and his jurisdiction is limited to that afforded to him by the 1977 Act.

Circumstances under which inherent jurisdiction may be invoked

23-53   In *Unilever Plc v The Procter & Gamble Co*,[60] Robert Walker LJ held that "the court should be particularly wary of granting declarations of non-infringement under the general jurisdiction, because of the existence of the special jurisdiction under s.71 of the 1977 Act and the detailed requirements which it imposes." On that basis, Norris J in *Omnipharm v Merial (amendment)*[61] treated a claim made under both s.71 and the inherent jurisdiction as one whose "real focus is s.71."

23-54   However, *Unilever* was distinguished by the Court of Appeal in *Nokia Corp v Interdigital Technology Corporation*. Carnwath LJ (with whom Waller LJ agreed in this regard) noted at [29]–[31] of *Nokia* that *Unilever* preceded the Court of Appeal's judgment in the *Messier-Dowty* case,[62] and that its authority had thereby been "weakened".

23-55   *Messier-Dowty* was an important development in the jurisprudence concerning the court's power to grant a negative declaration under its inherent jurisdiction. It was submitted in *Messier-Dowty* that there was no cause of action and the court did not have jurisdiction to grant a negative declaration having regard to the earlier decision of the court in *In re Clay: Clay v Booth*.[63] In *In re Clay*, no claim of right had been made against the party seeking the declaration. However Lord Woolf MR (with whom Hale LJ and Lord Mustill agreed) rejected the submission, stating (at [41]):

> "It is not a matter of jurisdiction. It is a matter of discretion. The deployment of negative declarations should be scrutinised and their use rejected where it would serve no useful purpose. However where a negative declaration would help to ensure that the aims of justice are achieved the courts should not be reluctant to grant such declarations. They can and do assist in achieving justice. For example where a patient is not in a position to consent to medical treatment declarations have an important role to play. Without the use of negative declarations, recent extensions in the use of declaratory relief, including the beneficial intervention of the courts in cases concerning mentally incapacitated people would not have been possible. As Sir Thomas Bingham MR said in *Re S (Hospital Patient: Court's Jurisdiction)* [1996] FAM 1, [1995] 3 All E.R. 290 (at p.303) 'any statutory rule, unless framed in terms so wide as to the give the court an almost unlimited discretion, would be bound to impose an element of inflexibility which would in my view be wholly undesirable'. He considered that the different situation he was there considering was 'pre-eminently an area in which the common law should respond to social needs'. So in my judgment the development of the use of declaratory relief in relation to commercial disputes should not be constrained by artificial limits wrongly related to jurisdiction. It should instead be kept within proper bounds by the exercise of the courts' discretion."

---

[59]   *L'Oréal (UK) Ltd v Johnson & Johnson* [2000] F.S.R. 686; see also *Prince Plc v Prince Sports Group Inc* [1998] F.S.R. 21.

[60]   [2000] 1 W.L.R. 2436, 2451.

[61]   [2010] EWHC 3059 (Pat).

[62]   *Messier-Dowty v Sabena* [2000] 1 W.L.R. 2040, [2001] 1 All E.R. 275.

[63]   [1919] 1 Ch. 66.

In *Financial Services Authority v Rourke*[64] Neuberger J (as he then was) further **23-56** explained the court's approach to exercising its discretion as follows:

"It seems to me that, when considering whether to grant a declaration or not, the court should take into account justice to the claimant, justice to the defendant, whether the declaration would serve a useful purpose and whether there are any other special reasons why or why not the court should grant the declaration."

In general terms, the court will be more reluctant to grant a negative declaration **23-57** in favour of a party against whom no claim has been formulated for the obvious reason that there is often no real point in doing so.[65] Furthermore, before a court can properly make a negative declaration, the underlying issue must be sufficiently clearly defined to render it properly justiciable. However, in *Nokia Corporation v InterDigital Technology Corporation*,[66] a case about 3G mobile telephone systems, the Court of Appeal allowed a claim to a negative declaration to be maintained since there were real commercial reasons for doing so.

Thus, although the court will not make purely hypothetical declarations, there is **23-58** no rule of law which makes it necessary to show that the proposed defendant has asserted a "claim of right" against the party seeking a negative declaration. The rule was previously thought to have been established by the decision in the Court of Appeal in *Re Clay*.[67]

The modern approach is as set out in *Messier-Dowty*:[68] it is a matter for the **23-59** court's discretion as to whether to entertain the claim to negative declaratory relief in the circumstances of the particular case.[69] Floyd LJ in *Actavis v Lilly* held, citing *Messier-Dowty*, that "the court has a general jurisdiction to make declarations of non-liability where such a declaration would serve a useful purpose."[70]

The position regarding exercise of the discretion in a patents case had previ- **23-60** ously been considered in *Biogen v Medeva*,[71] where Aldous J summarised the position with regard to the court's discretion as follows:

"The power to make a declaration is a discretionary power which will only be invoked in appropriate circumstances to settle appropriate questions. In particular, I adopt the words of Lord Dunedin, approved by Viscount Kilmuir, L.C. in *Vine v National Dock Labour Board* [1957] A.C. 488 at 500:

'The question must be a real and not a theoretical question; the person raising it must have a real interest to raise it; he must be able to secure a proper contradictor, that is to say, someone presently existing who has a true interest to oppose the declaration sought.'"

The final paragraph is a verbatim quote taken from Lord Dunedin's speech in **23-61**

---

64 [2001] EWHC 704 (Ch), [2002] C.P.Rep. 14.
65 *Nokia Corporation v InterDigital Technology Corporation* [2007] F.S.R. 23, [15].
66 [2007] F.S.R. 23.
67 [1919] 1 Ch. 66.
68 [2000] 1 W.L.R. 2040, [2001] 1 All E.R. 275.
69 See also *Auchincloss v Agricultural & Veterinary Supplies* [1997] R.P.C. 649 where the deputy judge suggested that a claim of right was not an absolute rule of law but more in the nature of a rule of practice; in a case brought under s.71, and where the plaintiffs were contesting the issue anyway, he therefore held that he also had jurisdiction to make a slightly wider declaration by invoking the inherent jurisdiction. This part of his decision was not challenged on appeal ([1998] R.P.C. 397). See also the comments of Lightman J on the inherent jurisdiction in *L'Oréal (UK) Ltd v Johnson & Johnson* [2000] F.S.R. 686, at [13]–[15] (a trade mark case).
70 [2015] EWCA Civ 555, [102].
71 [1993] R.P.C. 475, 489. That part of the judgment where Aldous J said that a person cannot obtain a declaration unless a claim of right has been made against them can no longer be regarded as good law.

Russian Commercial and Industrial Bank v British Bank for Foreign Trade,[72] where he summarised the Scottish rule, and then applied it to the English case before him. It is submitted that this remains useful guidance in relation to the exercise of the court's discretion in relation to an application for a declaration, though the discretion remains complete, as the Court of Appeal in *Messier-Dowty* made clear. Put shortly, if the claimant has sufficient commercial interest in knowing whether the proposed acts constitute infringement, then the declarations would serve a useful purpose and the court will ordinarily exercise its jurisdiction to consider making them.

Evidence of grounds giving rise to claim for declaration must be admissible

23-62   The grounds giving rise to the declaration sought must be made in circumstances in which evidence of it having been made is admissible. In *Unilever v Procter & Gamble*,[73] the relevant statements relied upon were made in the course of "without prejudice" discussions. The claim was struck out as an abuse of the process of the court as the statements made in the course of such discussions could not be used in legal proceedings. Of course, in such a circumstance, it is open to a party to make an open request for a written acknowledgment and then proceed under s.71.

Position of exclusive licensee

23-63   It is permissible in a suitable case to join an exclusive licensee under the patent in suit as a proper co-defendant in an action for a declaration under the court's inherent jurisdiction.[74]

Putting validity in issue

23-64   Section 74(1)(c) of the 1977 Act provides that validity may be brought into dispute in proceedings for a declaration under s.71, but its wording appears not to apply to proceedings brought under the inherent jurisdiction.[75] The point, however, appears academic since a separate claim for revocation can also be made in the same proceedings. Difficulties arising from the procedural rules that preceded the CPR were swept away when the latter was brought into force. There would now appear to be no difficulty in considering both validity and (non-)infringement in the same set of proceedings, whether under s.71 or the court's inherent jurisdiction.

Procedural matters arising under the inherent jurisdiction

23-65   In relation to a declaration that relates to the non-infringement of a patent, the relevant patent and the acts or proposed acts (including the relevant product or process) must be identified and particularised. Just as with declarations under s.71, it is necessary for the claimant to define with precision the declaration which it seeks. Normally this will be by reference to a specific product or process, defined by a product or process description and/or a sample.

---

[72]   [1921] 2 A.C. 438, 448. See also Lord Goff in *Re F* [1990] 2 A.C. 1, at 82.
[73]   [2000] F.S.R. 344, CA; affirming [1999] F.S.R. 849.
[74]   *Chiron Corp v Evans Medical Ltd* [1996] F.S.R. 863. See also para.23-24.
[75]   *OrganonTeknika Ltd v Hoffmann-La Roche A.G.* [1996] F.S.R. 383.

Costs

An action for a declaration under the inherent jurisdiction does not require any special approach in relation to costs. The costs will normally follow the event in the usual manner.

23-66

Declarations of non-infringement in respect of foreign designations

Statutory declarations under s.71 are limited to acts committed in the UK. As such, they are generally restricted to UK patents and UK designations of European patents. Declarations made pursuant to the court's inherent jurisdiction are not subject to such limits: they may be made where they serve a useful purpose.

23-67

Where the validity of one or more foreign designations is placed in issue, jurisdiction lies with the national courts where that designation of the patent was applied for,[76] and the UK court will cede jurisdiction over those designations.

23-68

A claimant may of course apply for a declaration of non-infringement without putting validity in issue. That was the situation in *Actavis v Lilly*: Actavis sought declarations of non-infringement in respect of a European (UK) patent and its corresponding French, German, Spanish and Italian designations. The UK declaration was sought under s.71 and/or the court's inherent jurisdiction; the declarations in respect of the foreign designations were sought under the inherent jurisdiction. Actavis did not put validity in issue and indicated that they would not do so.

23-69

Lilly, the defendant patentee, resisted trial of the foreign designations by the UK court. It submitted that the UK court should decline jurisdiction over the foreign designations on grounds of forum non conveniens. The trial would require an in-depth consideration of the respective foreign laws which the courts in those jurisdictions were better placed to carry out. As well as contesting UK jurisdiction, Lilly contended that Actavis's claim had not been properly served upon it. At first instance,[77] the judge found in favour of Actavis: Lilly's solicitors had consented to service; service had been properly effected (under r.6.9 but not r.63.14), and the court would not decline jurisdiction and stay the claim on grounds of forum non conveniens. Lilly appealed to the Court of Appeal[78] but their appeal was dismissed. The trial of the UK patent and the foreign designations therefore went ahead in the Patents Court, before Arnold J.

23-70

Though the question of jurisdiction had been decided, the question of which jurisdiction's rules should be applied to each issue was still open. Should the court apply its own rules (the lex fori) or those of the "home" jurisdictions of the respective patents (the lex causae or lex loci protectionis)? It was common ground that the substantive questions of infringement fell to be determined under the lex loci protectionis; accordingly, the judge received written expert evidence of French, German,[79] Spanish and Italian law.[80]

23-71

---

[76] art.22(4) of Council Regulation 44/2001/EC (the "Brussels I" Regulation).

[77] [2012] EWHC 3316 (Pat).

[78] [2013] EWCA Civ 517, [2013] R.P.C. 37.

[79] The Düsseldorf court released its judgment on infringement very shortly before the UK trial, and so Actavis withdrew its request for a declaration regarding the German designation from the UK action.

[80] The judge ruled at a pre-trial review that there was to be no oral expert evidence relating to the foreign laws, and therefore no cross-examination: [2014] EWHC 838 (Pat).

23-72   A dispute remained over which rules should be applied to the question of standing: whether the claimants were entitled to request the declarations that they sought. Actavis contended that since it was seeking declarations from the UK court, it need only meet such requirements as were imposed by UK law. The pre-requisites to seeking a declaration were properly matters of "evidence or procedure" within the meaning of art.1(3) of the "Rome II" Regulation,[81] and were therefore excluded from the scope of that regulation.

23-73   As discussed above,[82] the requirements for entitlement to seek a declaration in the UK are not particularly onerous. Indeed, in deciding the appeal in *Actavis v Lilly*, Floyd LJ commented that "English law takes the most relaxed attitude amongst the relevant designated states of what must be shown before a party can apply to the court for a DNI."[83] He went on to explain the more specific requirements demanded of a prospective claimant respectively under French, Spanish and Italian law.

23-74   At trial,[84] the judge determined that it was the more relaxed requirements of the UK (the lex fori) that should be applied to determining Actavis's entitlement to seek the declarations, since the pre-requisites were matters of procedure. He went on to find that in any event Actavis had met the requirements not only in UK law but also under the respective foreign laws. On the substantive issue of infringement, the judge also found for Actavis and granted all the declarations that it had requested.

23-75   Lilly appealed. It did so both on the substantive issue of infringement, and on the question of whether Rome II mandated the application of the lex causae requirements to assess Actavis's entitlement to seek the declarations. The Court of Appeal unanimously reversed the judge on the substantive issue, finding that Actavis's proposed acts would constitute indirect infringement of the patent.

23-76   It was common ground between the parties that there was no material difference between the respective jurisdictions' laws of indirect infringement, and so the Rome II issue did not need to be decided. Floyd LJ (with whom Kitchin and Longmore LJJ agreed) nonetheless dealt with the question, obiter, in the judgment of the Court. On this, the Court of Appeal agreed with the judge: the correct law to be applied to the question of a claimant's entitlement to seek a declaration of non-infringement is that of the lex fori. Such questions were properly to be regarded as procedural within the meaning of art.1(3) of the Rome II Regulation.

23-77   As Floyd LJ noted, the UK has some of the most "relaxed" requirements before a claimant can seek a declaration of non-infringement. This gives rise to the possibility of claimants coming to the UK court to seek a declaration they would not, under the law of the "home" country of the patent, be entitled to request. It remains to be seen whether this will increase the volume of foreign law non-infringement actions with which the UK courts are asked to deal. The requirement that validity must not be placed in issue if the UK court is to retain jurisdiction over foreign designations, of course, remains.

---

[81] European Parliament and Council Regulation 864/2007/EC of 31 July 2007.
[82] See para.23–16, et seq.
[83] [2015] EWCA Civ 555, [110].
[84] [2014] EWHC 1511 (Pat); [2014] 4 All E.R. 331; [2014] 2 All E.R. (Comm) 669; [2015] Bus. L.R. 154; [2015] R.P.C. 6.

B. Declaration of Invalidity

Contrast with an order for revocation

A declaration of invalidity of a patent may also be sought although this is less   **23-78**
common; the appropriate remedy where a patent is invalid is normally an order for
its revocation. Further, s.74(2) of the 1977 Act provides that "no proceedings may
be instituted (whether under this Act or otherwise) seeking only a declaration as to
the validity of a patent". The purpose of this section is to ensure that patents which
are invalid are not merely declared to be invalid but are in fact revoked.[85]

In *Lever-Faberge v Colgate Palmolive*,[86] the patentee defendant intended to al-   **23-79**
low the patent in suit to lapse rather than have it revoked. However, the claimant
sought a positive declaration from the court that the patent was in any event invalid.
Lewison J pointed out that since the introduction of the CPR (and in particular the
requirement for pleadings to be verified by a Statement of Truth) the court was less
reluctant to grant declarations without full investigation of the facts. On the basis
of the pleadings, a witness statement from the claimant's patent attorney and a
consideration of one item of prior art, he granted a declaration that the patent was
invalid on the grounds pleaded in the grounds of invalidity served with the
Particulars of Claim.

In *ConvaTec v Smith & Nephew*,[87] HHJ Birss QC (as he then was, sitting as a   **23-80**
deputy judge of the High Court) considered an application for a declaration of
invalidity. ConvaTec had sued S&N on the UK designation of a European patent
but had dropped their case in relation to that patent before trial, and had agreed to
submit to judgment on revocation. S&N sought a declaration of invalidity, and
whilst the judge considered the request understandable, he did not grant the
declaration. The judge found that it would not be appropriate to exercise his discretion and grant a declaration of invalidity, since such a declaration "could be
misunderstood as a statement that I had been in a position to form a view that the
patent was indeed invalid."[88]

C. Declaration of Obviousness

Where a declaration of obviousness may be appropriate

In an appropriate case, a party may apply to the court for a declaration that its   **23-81**
product was obvious in the light of the state of the art at a particular date ("the
obviousness date"). The commercial advantage of such a declaration is that, if
granted, it follows that the product in question cannot then infringe a valid claim
of any patent with a priority date after the obviousness date. The declaration may
be particularly useful where there is a pending application for a patent and the final
form of the claims is not settled.

---

[85] *Arrow Generics v Merck & Co Inc* [2007] F.S.R. 39, [55].
[86] [2006] F.S.R. 19.
[87] *ConvaTec Ltd v Smith & Nephew Healthcare Ltd* [2011] EWHC 3461 (Pat).
[88] *ConvaTec Ltd v Smith & Nephew Healthcare Ltd* [2011] EWHC 3461 (Pat), [93].

Arrow Generics v Merck & Co Inc

23-82   In *Arrow Generics v Merck & Co Inc*,[89] the defendant was the proprietor of a European patent (UK) ("the 292 patent"). The key idea of the patent was to treat osteoporosis patients with 70mg of alendronate once a week rather than 10mg once a day. The claimant had brought earlier proceedings seeking to revoke that patent in the UK and thereby clear the way for its own product. The patent was duly revoked by the UK Court inter alia on the grounds of lack of novelty and obviousness and the claimant proceeded to make "very substantial" sales of its generic product across Europe.

23-83   Subsequently the European patent was also revoked by the EPO but on the narrow grounds of added matter. However, prior to its revocation the defendant had filed a number of divisional applications. One of the divisional applications (which later became the 904 patent) included a Swiss-type claim in respect of the same key idea as the 292 patent. The 904 application had originally contained a GB designation, but immediately before publication in the European Patent Bulletin the defendant informed the EPO that it was withdrawing the GB designation. The defendant also made it clear that it intended to take action against the claimant in relation to its product in other European countries, not including the UK.

The declarations

23-84   Kitchin J was asked to make a number of declarations, relating both to the 904 patent and to the claimant's product. He held that he had no jurisdiction to make any declarations relating to the validity of the 904 patent because it was never granted in the UK and he did not have jurisdiction to make any declarations in relation to the validity of other European national equivalents of the 904 patent.

23-85   However, the judge held that he did have jurisdiction to allow declarations in relation to the obviousness of the defendant's own product and, in the circumstances, such declarations served a valuable commercial purpose. Further, the judge held that s.74(2) of the 1977 Act did not exclude the claimant's right to such declarations. Accordingly he refused to strike out this part of the claim and allowed it to proceed.

D.   Declarations regarding Supplementary Protection Certificates (SPCs)

23-86   Owing to the uncertainties around the interpretation and application of the SPC Regulation,[90] the court has been asked to make several preliminary references to the CJEU. In *Lilly v Human Genome Sciences*,[91] Warren J heard a request by Lilly that a reference be made before trial on two questions of law. Those questions arose in the context of its claim for a declaration that any application that HGS might make for a SPC based upon Lilly's marketing authorisation for Lilly's own antibody product would be invalid. No such application for a SPC had yet been made, although a pre-emptive declaration was sought. HGS applied to strike out the claim, contending that the court should not exercise its jurisdiction to adjudicate on an

---

[89] [2007] F.S.R. 39.
[90] See Ch.6.
[91] [2012] EWHC 2290 (Pat).

intellectual property right that did not exist: Kitchin J in *Arrow*[92] had held that a declaration should not be made in relation to a patent application as its claims could change during examination, and that reasoning was said by HGS to apply a fortiori here.

Warren J held that the court did in fact have jurisdiction to grant declaratory relief of the sort Lilly requested. He did so whilst explaining that his decision arose from the special legal and factual difficulties arising in that case. The judge was at pains to state that his judgment should not be seen as "opening the gates to actions for declarations concerning SPCs." In fact the action for the declarations was stayed until the Court of Appeal had determined the validity of the underlying patent. **23-87**

In *Generics (UK) v Daiichi Pharmaceutical Co Ltd*,[93] the court heard an application for a declaration of invalidity in respect of a SPC[94] which had been granted in relation to the patent in suit. In the alternative, the claimant sought an order for rectification of the register in respect of the SPC. **23-88**

E.   Other Declarations

The declarations discussed in this chapter do not constitute an exhaustive list of the types of declarations which may be sought in patent cases. It would seem likely that, in future, other circumstances will arise whereby it may be appropriate to seek other types of declaration from the court. Under the relatively liberal approach to the granting of declarations that *Messier-Dowty* heralded, there is scope for creativity in framing claims for declaratory relief. This approach led to the courts making declarations of essentiality to a technical standard[95] and entertaining applications for declarations as to whether licence terms offered in respect of a standards essential patent are fair, reasonable and non-discriminatory (FRAND).[96] These declarations are covered in Ch.18, "FRAND". **23-89**

Examples of other types of declaration which have been sought in other fields of law include declarations as to remedies,[97] a declaration as to facts[98] and a declaration of abuse of dominant position.[99] Interim declarations may also be available in appropriate circumstances and are expressly contemplated by CPR Pt 40.20. **23-90**

Declarations may also prove useful in proceedings against the Crown where no injunction can be granted[100] and in respect of any contravention by Government of the Human Rights Act 1998. The primary remedy in all such cases is declaratory. **23-91**

Jurisdiction to give other declarations in relation to foreign designations

In *Innovia v Frito Lay*,[101] Arnold J heard applications in relation to a patent entitlement dispute. The claimant, Innovia, claimed that Frito Lay had applied for patents by using Innovia's confidential information. The allegations of breach of confidence and the entitlement dispute were closely intertwined. Moreover, the pat- **23-92**

---

[92] [2007] F.S.R. 39, [60].
[93] [2009] R.P.C. 4; see also [2009] R.P.C. 23.
[94] Pursuant to art.15 of Council Regulation No. 1768/92.
[95] *Nokia Corp v Interdigital Technology Corp* [2005] EWCA Civ 614 and [2006] EWCA Civ 1618.
[96] *Unwired Planet v Huawei* [2015] EWHC 1029 (Pat).
[97] *Greenwich Healthcare NHS Trust v Quadrant Housing Trust* [1998] 1 W.L.R. 1749.
[98] *Financial Services Authority v Rourke* [2001] EWHC 704 (Ch), [2002] C.P.Rep. 14.
[99] *SanDisk Corp v Koninklijke Philips Electronics* [2007] F.S.R. 22.
[100] Crown Proceedings Act 1947 s.21.
[101] *Innovia Films Ltd v Frito-Lay North America, Inc* [2012] EWHC 790 (Pat), [2012] R.P.C. 24.

ent applications were not all UK applications but related to several jurisdictions. In response to Innovia's claim, Frito Lay had indicated its intention to dispute the jurisdiction of the UK court, and had issued actions against Innovia in the courts of Texas, USA.

23-93   Frito Lay applied to set aside Innovia's permission to serve its claim upon Frito Lay out of the jurisdiction. Alternatively they sought a stay of the claim: (i) indefinitely, or otherwise (ii) pending determination of Frito Lay's claims against Innovia in Texas.

23-94   Arnold J refused the stay, finding that Frito Lay's submission of forum non conveniens was not properly made out in relation to the European Applications. Under s.12 of the PA77, the UK court had jurisdiction to determine claims in relation to the pending US applications (but would not have had such jurisdiction had the patents already been granted). The grant of those patents in the US between the commencement of the action and the trial would not mean that the UK courts ceded such jurisdiction. Considering the application in the round, Arnold J held that the interests of justice were best served by trying as many claims as was possible within a single dispute in a single forum. The UK court was in the best position to hear such an action, because it also had jurisdiction over the European patent applications. In the result, Arnold J refused Frito Lay's applications and held that the UK court was the appropriate forum for the dispute.

23-95   A further, similar dispute relating to entitlement proceedings and jurisdiction was *Conductive Inkjet Technology v Uni-Pixel*.[102] Roth J heard an application to set aside the claimant's permission to serve its claim out of the jurisdiction. Like *Innovia*, the context was an action for breach of confidence and patent entitlement, in which the defendant was alleged to have applied for patents using the claimant's confidential information. Leave to serve the claim out of the jurisdiction was upheld.

23-96   Roth J held that art.71 of the Brussels I Regulation provides that for a convention within its scope, the rules of jurisdiction *in that convention* shall apply "provided that they are highly predictable, facilitate the sound administration of justice and enable the risk of concurrent proceedings to be minimised and that they ensure, under conditions at least as favourable as those provided for by the regulation, the free movement of judgments in civil and commercial matters and mutual trust in the administration of justice in the European Union".[103]

23-97   Article 3 of the Protocol on Jurisdiction and the Recognition of Decisions in respect of the Right to the Grant of a European Patent was the applicable jurisdictional rule; it provides as follows:

> "**Article 3**
> Subject to Articles 4 and 5, if an applicant for a European patent has his residence or principal place of business outside the Contracting States, and if the party claiming the right to the grant of the European patent has his residence or principal place of business within one of the Contracting States, the courts of the latter State shall have exclusive jurisdiction."

23-98   This provision met the above test from the CJEU's judgment in *TNT*. Accordingly, Roth J found that forum non conveniens was not a doctrine that applied to jurisdiction under art.3 of the Protocol. The claimant's secondary argument, that the

---

[102] *Conductive Inkjet Technology Ltd v Uni-Pixel Displays Inc* [2013] EWHC 2968 (Ch), [2014] F.S.R. 22.

[103] This test arises from the judgment of the CJEU in *TNT Express Nederland v AXA Versicherung* (C-533/08) [2010] E.C.R. I-4107: see *Conductive Inkjet Technology Ltd v Uni-Pixel Displays Inc* [2013] EWHC 2968 (Ch), [2014] F.S.R. 22.

court could nonetheless stay the action on case management grounds, was deprecated as amounting "essentially to forum non conveniens by the backdoor."[104]

---

[104] *Conductive Inkjet Technology*, [91].

CHAPTER 24

ACTION TO RESTRAIN THREATS

CONTENTS

1. HISTORY

Prior to the Patents, Designs and Trade Marks Act 1883 the proprietor of a patent might issue threats of proceedings for infringement without rendering themselves liable for any damage which they might occasion thereby, provided such threats were made bona fide. It was open to an injured person to apply for an injunction to restrain the patentee from continuing to threaten them, although he could be successful only by showing that the statements made were in fact untrue,[1] and that the defendant intended, even after they were found to be untrue, to repeat them.[2] **24-01**

In the case of malicious threats an action for damages lay similar to that of slander of title, when the claimant had to show that the threat made by the defendant amounted to a "malicious attempt to injure the plaintiffs by asserting a claim of right against his own knowledge that it was without any foundation",[3] and that actual damage had resulted from the threats.[4] Such an action could, and may still, be maintained quite independently of any provisions of the Patents Acts.[5] **24-02**

Statutes prior to the Patents Act 1977

Section 32 of the 1883 Act and s.36 of the 1907–1928 Acts gave a statutory right of action, in certain limited cases, to any person who was damaged by groundless threats of infringement proceedings, whether such threats were made bona fide or not.[6] These sections did not apply if an action for infringement was "commenced and prosecuted with due diligence" and it was also held that s.36 of the 1907–1928 Acts had no application where no patents had in fact been sealed.[7] The Patents and Designs Act 1932 repealed s.36 of the 1907–1928 Acts and enacted a new sec- **24-03**

---

[1] *Halsey v Brotherhood* (1880) 15 Ch D. 514; (1881) 19 Ch D. 386.
[2] *Sugg v Bray* (1885) 2 R.P.C. 223, 246.
[3] Per Blackburn J in *Wren v Weild* (1869) L.R. 4 Q.B. 730, at 727. See also *Halsey v Brotherhood* (1881) 19 Ch D. 386, at 388, CA.
[4] See, e.g. *Farr v Weatherhead and Harding* (1932) 49 R.P.C. 262, at 267.
[5] See *Cars v Bland Light Syndicate Ltd* (1911) 28 R.P.C. 33; *Mentmore Manufacturing Co Ltd v Fomento (Sterling Area) Ltd* (1955) 72 R.P.C. 157; *Olin Mathieson Chemical Co v Biorex Laboratories Ltd* [1970] R.P.C. 157.
[6] See, e.g. *Day v Foster* (1890) 7 R.P.C. 54; *Skinner Co v Perry* (1893) 10 R.P.C. 1; *Diamond Coal Cutter Co v Mining Appliances Co* (1915) 32 R.P.C. 569.
[7] See *Ellis Sons Ltd v Pogson* (1923) 40 R.P.C. 62, at 179.

tion in its place which gave a remedy for groundless threats irrespective of whether the person making the threats did or did not have any interest in a patent. That section also revoked the previous statutory defence to an action for threats of commencing and prosecuting an action for infringement with due diligence.

24-04   Section 65 of the Patents Act 1949 substantially re-enacted s.36 of the Act of 1932 but was more clearly drafted. Under s.65, if any person threatened any other person with proceedings for infringement of a patent, any person aggrieved could claim relief. Unless the defendant proved that the acts in respect of which the threats were made constituted an infringement of a patent or of rights arising from the publication of a complete specification in respect of a claim not shown by the plaintiff to be invalid, the plaintiff could obtain a declaration that the threats were unjustifiable, an injunction to restrain their continuance and damages. It was enacted that a mere notification of the existence of a patent did not constitute such a threat.

2.   THREATS UNDER THE PATENTS ACT 1977

24-05   The remedy of an aggrieved party for groundless threats of proceedings for infringement of patents and applications is governed by s.70 of the 1977 Act. As originally enacted, the section substantially re-enacted s.65 of the 1949 Act with one significant limitation on the ambit of an actionable threat[8] and in proceedings under the 1977 Act the case law developed under preceding statutes continued to apply. The Patents Act 2004 introduced various amendments to s.70 because there were concerns that the existing legislation discouraged patent holders from making genuine attempts to settle disputes over infringement.[9] The amendments came into force on 1 January 2005[10] and the transitional provisions provide that for alleged threats made before that date, s.70 has effect as if the amendments had not been made.[11]

24-06   Under s.70 as originally enacted, if any person (whether or not entitled to any right in a patent) threatens another person with proceedings for any infringement of a patent by circulars, advertisements or otherwise, a person aggrieved by the threats (whether or not the person to whom the threats are made) may bring proceedings against the person making the threats, provided that proceedings may not be brought for a threat to bring proceedings for infringement alleged to consist of making or importing a product for disposal or of using a process. The foregoing remains the law under s.70 as amended however a further proviso has been added (now s.70(4)(b)) such that proceedings may not be brought for a threat made to a person, who has made or imported a product for disposal or used a process, to bring proceedings for an infringement alleged to consist of doing anything else in relation to that product or process.

24-07   The claimant may claim relief by way of a declaration, injunction and damages. Under s.70(2) as originally enacted, if the threats and the claimant's status as a person aggrieved are proved, then the claimant can obtain relief unless the defendant proves that the acts in respect of which proceedings were threatened constitute or would constitute an infringement of a patent and the patent alleged to be infringed is not shown by the claimant to be invalid. Again the foregoing remains

---

8   See paras 24-31 to 24-32.
9   See para.3 of *Guidance Note No.2* issued by the Patent Office in relation to the Patents Act 2004; see also Laddie J in *Reckitt Benkiser UK v Home Pairfum Ltd* [2004] F.S.R. 37, a trade mark case.
10   SI 2004/3205.
11   SI 2004/3205 art.9(4).

the law under s.70 as amended, however s.70(2) has been divided into ss.70(2) and (2A) and a further provision has been added (now s.70(2A)(b)) such that even if the claimant shows the patent is invalid, they shall not be entitled to relief if the defendant proves that at the time of making the threats they did not know and had no reason to suspect that the patent was invalid in the relevant respect.

Under s.70(5) of the 1977 Act, as originally enacted, mere notification of the **24-08** existence of a patent did not constitute a threat of proceedings within the meaning of s.70.[12] This provision has been replaced by newly formulated exceptions as follows. Mere provision of factual information about a patent does not constitute a threat.[13] Mere enquiries for the sole purpose of discovering whether or by whom the patent has been infringed by making or importing a product for disposal or using a process do not constitute a threat[14] nor do mere assertions about a patent for the purpose of any enquiries so made.[15]

The amendments to the 1977 Act contained in the 2004 Act have also introduced **24-09** a new defence to an action for threats. The party making the threats has a defence if they can prove that they used their best endeavours, without success, to discover the identity of certain classes of person (see below) and that they notified the person threatened accordingly before or at the time of making the threats.[16] The notification has to identify the endeavours used.[17]

The classes of person whose identities must have been sought depend on the **24-10** nature of the invention and of the alleged infringement. Where the invention is a product, it is the identity of the person who made or imported the product for disposal.[18] Where the invention is a process and the alleged infringement consists of offering it for use, it is the identity of the person who used the process.[19] Where the invention is a process and the alleged infringement is an act falling within s.60(1)(c) of the 1977 Act, it is the identity of the person who used the process to produce the product in question.[20]

The modern law of threats is not confined to patent matters. The Registered **24-11** Design Act 1949 contained a corresponding threats provision (s.26), the Copyright Designs and Patents Act 1988 enacted a threats provision relating to unregistered design right (s.253), the Community Design Regulations 2005[21] enacted similar provisions in relation to Community registered and unregistered designs (reg.2), the Trade Marks Act 1994 enacted a threats provision relating to trade marks (s.21) and the Community Trade Mark Regulations 1996[22] enacted similar provisions in relation to Community Trade Marks (reg.4). Although care must be taken when applying cases decided in relation to one statute to another field since the enactments are not the same, the principles underlying them all correspond in broad terms to one another.

That the principles all correspond in broad terms was confirmed in *Best Buy v* **24-12**

---

[12] See also paras 24-33 to 24-35.
[13] PA 1977 s.70(5)(a).
[14] PA 1977 s.70(5)(b).
[15] PA 1977 s.70(5)(c).
[16] PA 1977 s.70(6).
[17] PA 1977 s.70(6).
[18] PA 1977 s.70(6)(a).
[19] PA 1977 s.70(6)(b).
[20] PA 1977 s.70(6)(c).
[21] SI 2005/2339.
[22] SI 1996/1908.

Worldwide Sales Corporation España.[23] *Best Buy* was concerned with an alleged threat for trade mark infringement, although the principle of law as to what constitutes a threat to bring proceedings was treated as the same for trade marks as for patents.

Reform to the law of threats

24-13   In 2012 the Law Commission was asked to review the law of threats regarding patents, trade marks and design rights by the Department for Business, Innovation and Skills and the Intellectual Property Office. Following the consultation period, the final Report was published on 15 April 2014,[24] which identified 18 separate recommendations. The Law Commission then published an Executive Summary of the final report and outlined the headline reforms and recommendations. Most of these reforms and recommendations apply more to trade marks and design rights than patents. However, of note are the following headlines reforms:

(1) The recommendation that professional advisors, acting on their client's instructions and in their professional capacity, should not be liable for making threats.

(2) The general recommendation that where communications are made for a "legitimate commercial purpose", and if the information provided is necessary for such purposes, they should be excluded from any groundless threats provisions. Part of this recommendation is a suggestion that the statute should provide examples of legitimate commercial purposes.

(3) Finally, the Report recommended that trade marks and design rights law be brought into line with the 1977 Act and include the provision that threats actions cannot be brought where the threat is made to someone who has carried out the primary act, even if the threat refers to other, secondary acts. There is a further recommendation that this should apply to threats regarding intended acts.

24-14   The Government's Response was published on 26 February 2015.[25] The Government accepted outright 15 of the recommendations and three in principle and asked the Law Commission to draft a Bill: the *"Intellectual Property (Unjustified Threats) Bill"*. On 12 October 2015 the Law Commission published a second, final report on this topic, which includes a draft Bill,[26] which incorporates the recommendations. This second Report also made two further recommendations to apply the law of unjustified threats to the Unitary Patent. First, that the 1977 Act should apply to Unitary Patents that have not opted out of the Unitary Patent Court jurisdiction during the transitional period. Secondly, with respect to the test for a threat of infringement proceedings, that the reasonable person in the position of a recipient would understand from such a communication that the person: (1) has a right in a Unitary Patent, European Patent (UK) or national patent; and (2) intends to bring proceedings against another person for infringement of more of those rights by: (i) an act

[23] [2011] EWCA Civ 618; F.S.R. 30.
[24] Law Commission Report No.346, *Patents, Trade Marks and Design Rights: Groundless Threats.*
[25] The Government's Response to the Law Commission's Report (Law Com. No.346) *"Patents, Trade Marks and Design Rights: Groundless Threats"*.
[26] Law Commission Report No.360, *Patents, Trade Marks and Designs: Unjustified Threats.*

done in the UK; or (ii) an act, which if done, would be done in the UK. At the time of writing the Bill has not been enacted.

The relevance of bona fides

It was no defence to an action for threats under s.70, as originally enacted, or under its predecessors, that the threats were made in good faith in the honest belief that the act complained of was an infringement of a valid claim.[27] That aspect of the law has been modified by an amendment introduced by the 2004 Act. Section 70(2A) of the 1977 Act, as amended, now provides that, even if the patent is found invalid, the claimant shall not be entitled to the relief claimed where the defendant proves that at the time of making the threats they did not know and had no reason to suspect that the patent was invalid in the relevant respect.   **24-15**

The right at common law to take proceedings for malicious threats remains unaffected by the statutory provisions as to threats.[28]   **24-16**

Threats made outside the United Kingdom

It is submitted that a threat will be actionable even if made outside the UK provided that the threat is of proceedings within the UK.[29] In this respect, the tort may be likened to authorising a primary act of infringement of copyright which is actionable even if the authorisation is given outside the UK provided that the infringement takes place within the UK.[30]   **24-17**

Where a threat of infringement proceedings in respect of a European patent had been made to retailers both in the UK and in France, it was held to be permissible, on the facts of the case, to look at the reaction of one of the French retailers as evidence of the likely effect of the threat on the retailers within the UK.[31]   **24-18**

Nature of threats

The cause of action given by s.70 is not similar to libel and there is no question of publication; the manner in which the threat was made is, therefore, not material. In *Skinner & Co v Perry*,[32] the claimants complained of two threats—one in the form of a letter to a third party, who had inquired of the defendants whether they thought that the claimants' article of manufacture infringed the defendants' patent; the other contained in a letter from the defendants to the claimants themselves in reply to similar inquiries. It was held that the words "or otherwise" in the section were not to be construed ejusdem generis with the preceding words "circulars, advertisements".[33] In giving judgment for the claimants, Bowen LJ said[34]:   **24-19**

> "Using language in its ordinary sense, it is difficult to see that an intimation ceases to be a threat because it is addressed to a third person in answer to an inquiry, or because it is addressed to the

---

[27] See *Skinner Co v Perry* (1893) 10 R.P.C. 1, at 8.
[28] See the final sentence of para.24-02 and the cases there cited.
[29] The reasoning in *Kenburn Waste Management Ltd v Heinz Bergmann* [2002] F.S.R. 44 (Pumfrey J) and 45 (CA) provides support for this submission.
[30] *ABKCO Music v Music Collection Int* [1995] R.P.C. 657. The decision in *Egg Fillers, etc., Ltd v Holed-Tite Packing Corp* (1934) 51 R.P.C. 9 turned on the wording of RSC Ord.11 r.1.
[31] See *Dimplex (UK) Ltd v De'Longhi Ltd* [1996] F.S.R. 622.
[32] (1893) 10 R.P.C. 1.
[33] See also *Speedcranes Ltd v Thomson* [1978] R.P.C. 221.
[34] (1893) 10 R.P.C. 1, 5.

person himself. We are not dealing with libel or questions of publication—we are dealing with threats. If I threaten a man that I will bring an action against him, I threaten him nonetheless because I address that intimation to himself, and I threaten him nonetheless because I address the intimation to a third person."

24-20   Verbal statements can amount to threats[35] in appropriate cases, even when made in answer to inquiries.[36] A letter by a solicitor before issuing proceedings, or in proposing a compromise, is capable of amounting to a threat within the meaning of the subsection if it conveys an intimation that proceedings would be taken to restrain infringement.[37]

Background to be considered

24-21   Regard has to be had to the background in which the alleged threat was made.[38] The threat of an action for infringement can thus be made indirectly or by implication. It is not necessary to prove that the defendant has in so many words said that it intends to issue proceedings against the claimant for infringement; the threat may be veiled, covert, conditional or future.[39] The meaning and impact of the alleged threats have to be decided in accordance with how they would be understood by the ordinary reader—see *Luna Advertising Co Ltd v Burnham & Co*.[40] In that case a representative of the defendants called on a customer of the plaintiff and stated that a sign exhibited outside the customer's premises was an infringement of his firm's patent and requested that it should be removed. Clauson J granted an interlocutory injunction, and said:

"I think that an interview of this kind ... between business men, although nobody speaks of solicitors and writs, has no real meaning except to convey ... that the threatener has legal rights and means to enforce them ... in the way in which they are naturally enforced, i.e. by legal proceedings."

24-22   The *Luna Advertising* case was followed in *Bowden Controls v Acco Cable Controls Ltd*,[41] where the threat was alleged to have been made in a letter to the claimant's customers which stated that the claimant's product had been found by a German court to infringe a European patent (in Germany) and that the defendant had corresponding patents in all major European countries. The letter then said: "It is the intention of [the defendant] to enforce the rights arising by virtue of these patents in a realistic manner and will carefully ensure all current customers requirements are properly safeguarded". In considering whether to grant an interlocutory injunction, Aldous J said:

"The letter does not explicitly threaten patent proceedings, but states that the first defendant will

---

[35]   See *Kurtz v Spence* (1887) 4 R.P.C. 161; *Ellis Sons Ltd v Pogson* (1932) 49 R.P.C. 62; *Luna Advertising Co Ltd v Burnham Co* (1928) 45 R.P.C. 258; *Farr v Weatherhead and Harding* (1922) 39 R.P.C. 262.

[36]   *Skinner Co v Perry* (1893) 10 R.P.C. 1. But see *Alpi-Pietro E Figlio Co v John Wright Sons (Veneers) Ltd* [1972] R.P.C. 125.

[37]   See, e.g. *Driffield Cake Co v Waterloo Mills Cake Co* (1886) 3 R.P.C. 46; *Kurtz v Spence* (1887) 4 R.P.C. 161; *Combined Weighting, etc., Machine Co v Automatic Weighing Machine Co* (1889) 6 R.P.C. 502; *Day v Foster* (1890) 7 R.P.C. 54, at 58; *Douglass v Pintsch's Patent Lighting Co Ltd* (1897) 14 R.P.C. 673; *Farr v Weatherhead and Harding* (1922) 39 R.P.C. 262; *Luna Advertising Co Ltd v Burnham Co* (1928) 45 R.P.C. 258; *Ellis Sons Ltd v Pogson* (1932) 49 R.P.C. 62; *HVE Electric Ltd v Cuffin Holdings Ltd* [1964] R.P.C. 149.

[38]   *Surridge's Patents Ltd v Trico-Folberth Ltd* (1936) 53 R.P.C. 420, at 423 and 424.

[39]   *F.H. Brundle v Perry* [2014] EWHC 475 (IPEC), [23].

[40]   (1928) 45 R.P.C. 258.

[41]   [1990] R.P.C. 427.

enforce its rights. The fact that it is not explicit that patent proceedings will be taken is in no way conclusive as a threat can be veiled or implied just as much as it can be explicit ..."

The judge went on to decide: 24-23

"He [the reader] would realise that it contained a threat of patent proceedings. He would realise that there is nothing in the letter which explicitly excluded him from the threat. Even if he thought that suppliers did not consider it practical to sue manufacturers, I believe the recipient would consider what was the purpose of the letter. He would conclude that the purpose of the letter was to give him information and a warning. That requires the answer; a warning as to what?"

The principle that the test was to ask how the threat would be perceived by the   24-24
ordinary recipient in the position actual recipient was also followed in *Brain v
Ingledew Brown Bennison*,[42] *L'Oréal (UK) Ltd v Johnson & Johnson*[43] and *Grimme
Landmaschinenfabrik GmbH & Co KG v Scott*.[44] In the latter case it was held to be
no defence that the solicitor's letter in question expressly stated "our client does not
intend to commence proceedings against you" because, in the context, the ordinary
recipient would have read the letter as indicating that the patentee did not at present
intend to commence proceedings against the recipient, but would be likely to do so
in the future if it was successful in its action against another party.

In *Best Buy v Worldwide Sales Corporation España*[45] the question as to whether   24-25
or not a letter (or other communication) constitutes a threat was "to be answered
by reference to what a reasonable person, in the position of the recipient of the letter, with its knowledge of all of the relevant circumstances as at the date the letter
was written, would have understood the writer of the passage to have intended,
when read in the context of the letter as a whole."[46] Although *Best Buy* was not a
case concerned with patents, it is applicable. See, for example, *F.H. Brundle v Perry*
(at [22]).[47]

This principle was applied in *SDL Hair v Next Row*[48] in the Patents County Court   24-26
(as it then was) by Mr Recorder Richard Meade QC. There it was held that even if
individual parts of the letter identified as containing the threat do not, in themselves,
amount to such a threat, the court ought to look at the letter as a whole and consider
whether it contains a threat. The argument that such a letter does not expressly refer
to infringement proceedings was dismissed as being "far too dry and literal an
approach."[49]

In *Olin Mathieson Chemical Co v Biorex Laboratories Ltd*,[50] it was held that   24-27
writing a letter to the Ministry of Health with the object of ensuring that hospitals
would not purchase the defendant's products amounted to a threat.[51]

---

[42] [1997] F.S.R. 511.
[43] [2000] F.S.R. 686 (a trade mark case).
[44] [2010] F.S.R. 11.
[45] [2011] EWCA Civ 618; F.S.R. 30.
[46] *Best Buy v Worldwide Sales Corporation España* [2011] EWCA Civ 618; F.S.R. 30, [18].
[47] [2014] EWHC 475 (IPEC).
[48] [2013] EWPCC 31.
[49] *SDL Hair Ltd v Next Row Ltd; Master Distributor Ltd v SDL Hair Ltd* [2013] EWPCC 31, [102].
[50] [1970] R.P.C. 157.
[51] See also *Willis Bates Ltd v Tilley Lamp Co* (1944) 61 R.P.C. 8; *Alpi Pietro E Figlio Co v John Wright
      Sons (Veneers) Ltd* [1972] R.P.C. 125.

Without prejudice communications

24-28 A threat made at a meeting held "without prejudice" or in "without prejudice" correspondence cannot normally be relied upon to support an action for threats.[52] It would be otherwise if the threat amounted to an abuse of the "without prejudice" rule.[53] In *Kooltrade Ltd v XTS Ltd*[54] Pumfrey J held that it is not an abuse of the rule to issue a threat even if no patent or other relevant right exists. However, if in fact no without prejudice negotiations are in existence, simply marking a threatening letter "without prejudice" will not prevent an action being brought on it.[55]

"Threatens another person"

24-29 Thus, it is not necessary in order that the threat should be actionable that it should have been communicated either directly or through an agent to the person threatened; the words "threaten another person" do not mean only "communicates a threat to any person", but include also the expression of a threat, by circulars, advertisements, or otherwise, "in relation to any person".[56]

Threats as to the future

24-30 Threats that acts to be done in the future will constitute an infringement are actionable.[57]

Threats to manufacturers or importers of products or users of processes

24-31 As originally enacted in the 1977 Act, s.70(4) provided that proceedings may not be brought under the section for a threat to bring proceedings for an infringement alleged to consist of making or importing a product for disposal or of using a process. This subsection meant that threats in respect of making and importing products and using processes were permitted, although threats (even to a manufacturer) in respect of other infringing acts (e.g. selling) were actionable.[58] It was, thus, specific acts of alleged infringement that were excluded by this subsection, not the type of person who can be threatened.

24-32 In *Cavity Trays Ltd v RMC Panel Products Ltd*,[59] Aldous LJ accepted that this division between the acts about which threats could and could not be made was arbitrary. The amendments to s.70(4) of the 1977 Act introduced by the 2004 Act sought to address this issue by adding further acts in respect of which threats could be made. In particular, as amended, s.70(4)(b) now provides that a claim may not be brought in respect of a threat to bring proceedings for an infringement alleged to consist of doing any act in relation to a product or process where the threat in

---

[52] *Unilever Plc v Procter Gamble* [2000] F.S.R. 344; disapproving *Kurtz v Spence* (1887) 4 R.P.C. 161; see also *Schering Corp v Cipla Ltd* [2005] F.S.R. 25.

[53] *Unilever Plc v Procter Gamble* [2000] F.S.R. 344; disapproving *Kurtz v Spence* (1887) 4 R.P.C. 161. See also Laddie J at first instance at [1999] F.S.R. 849.

[54] [2001] F.S.R. 13.

[55] *Kooltrade Limited v XTS* [2001] F.S.R. 13.

[56] *John Summers Sons Ltd v The Cold Metal Process Co* (1948) 65 R.P.C. 75, 96; and see *Bowden Controls v Acco Cable Controls Ltd* [1990] R.P.C. 427.

[57] PA 1977 s.70(1) and (2).

[58] See *Cavity Trays Ltd v RMC Panel Products Ltd* [1996] R.P.C. 361, CA.

[59] [1996] R.P.C. 361, 373.

question is made to a person who has made or imported that product for disposal or used that process. Thus the anomaly has been removed and for example a threat to a manufacturer may now address the sale of products made in infringement.

Factual information, enquiries and mere notification

A mere notification of the existence of a patent did not constitute a threat under the 1977 Act as originally enacted.[60] However, if words were added to the effect that what was complained of constituted an infringement of the patent, this constituted a threat.[61]

24-33

Under the 1977 Act, as amended, the concept of a defence of "mere notification" has been replaced by the wider concept of the mere provision of "factual information about the patent".[62] It is submitted that this will include everything regarded as a mere notification hitherto (since such notifications did no more than provide factual information about the patent) but will also permit further statements to be made. However, a plainly threatening statement such as "We intend to bring proceedings against you for infringement of the patent within 7 days" could be argued to be entirely factual as a statement of the patentee's intention. Nevertheless, such a statement cannot have been intended to fall within the ambit of mere provision of factual information about the patent.

24-34

Sections 70(5)(b) and (c) of the 1977 Act, as amended, also permit the mere making of enquiries for the sole purpose of discovering whether and by whom a patent has been infringed by the making or importing a product for disposal or of using a process and permit assertions to be made about the patent for the purposes of such enquiries. Thus, for example, a party may write to a company selling a product for the sole purpose of enquiring as to the identity of the manufacturer of the product and in the course of such a latter the party may presumably assert that the product infringes the patent.

24-35

General warnings

By s.70(1), in order that a threat may be actionable under the 1977 Act, it must have been directed against "another person". In *Challender v Royle*,[63] Bowen LJ said:

24-36

> "Everybody, it seems to me, has still a right to issue a general warning to pirates not to pirate, and to infringers not to infringe, and to warn the public that the patent to which the patentee is entitled, and under which he claims, is one which he intends to enforce.
>
> But my language must not be misunderstood on this point. It does not follow that because a threat is so worded as in mere language apparently and grammatically to apply only to the future that, therefore, it may not be in any particular case in substance, and, in fact, applicable to what has been done. Supposing, for a moment, that a manufacturer is making and issuing machines which the patentee considers to be infringements of his patent; if with reference to that act done, or to those machines made, the patentee endeavours to guard himself against this section by merely issuing a threat in the air, it seems to me he would not escape if the true gist of what he has done is to apply that threat to a particular person and to a particular act."

---

[60] PA 1977 s.70(5) as originally enacted. See also *Paul Trading Co Ltd v J. Marksmith Co Ltd* (1952) 69 R.P.C. 301; *C. and P. Development Co (London) Ltd v Sisabro Novelty Co Ltd* (1953) 70 R.P.C. 277.

[61] *Finkelstein v Billig* (1930) 47 R.P.C. 516; *C. and P. Development Co (London) Ltd v Sisabro Novelty Co Ltd* (1953) 70 R.P.C. 277.

[62] PA 1977 s.70(5)(a).

[63] (1887) 4 R.P.C. 363, 375.

24-37   Thus, if, by issuing a general warning, it can be shown that a warning finger was pointed against the products of some other specific manufacturer, importer or vendor, the warning becomes an actionable threat.[64]

Information on pending applications

24-38   A person notified of an unpublished UK national patent application and threatened with proceedings may obtain information relating to that application from the Comptroller at the UK Patent Office (now UKIPO) which would otherwise not be available until publication.[65]

24-39   Similarly, a person who can show that the applicant for a European patent "has invoked the rights under the application against him" may obtain information relating to that application from the EPO.[66]

Abuse of monopoly when action pending

24-40   Once an action for infringement has been commenced, s.70 of the 1977 Act provides no remedy for the defendant to that action for any injury suffered by reason of the existence or publication of the action. The courts have, however, sought to prevent such injury when inflicted by an abuse of the patentee's monopoly. Thus, a statement that an action for infringement has been commenced against a specific person, coupled with a general warning against dealing in infringing goods, may constitute a contempt of court if it suggests that the validity of the patent has been determined and that the defendant has in fact infringed,[67] or if it misrepresents what has in fact taken place in proceedings before the court.[68] The general principle is, however, that an application to commit for contempt of court should not be made "unless the thing done is of such a nature as to require the arbitrary and summary interference of the court in order to enable justice to be duly and properly administered without any interruption or interference …".[69] The courts have refused to consider as contempt of court advertisements which referred to certain specified goods as "infringing" goods or goods "offered for sale in infringement" of the letters patent, apparently upon the ground that a patentee was entitled to say: "The patent is a good one; I am going to maintain that it is a good patent and that you are infringing it".[70]

24-41   Similarly, where, having sued the manufacturer of a product, a patentee com-

---

[64] See *Weldrics Ltd v Quasi-Arc Co Ltd* (1922) 39 R.P.C. 323; *Cars v Bland Light Syndicate Ltd* (1911) 28 R.P.C. 33; *Boneham and Hart v Hirst Bros Co Ltd* (1917) 34 R.P.C. 209; *Martin v Selsdon Fountain Pen Co Ltd* (1949) 66 R.P.C. 193, 215; *Alpi Pietro E Figlio Co v John Wright Sons (Veneers) Ltd* [1972] R.P.C. 125, 133.

[65] PA 1977 s.118(4); Patent Rules 2007 r.52.

[66] EPC art.128(2); EPC Rules r.146.

[67] See *Goulard Gibbs v Sir Coutts Lindsay Co Ltd and Ferranti* (1887) 4 R.P.C. 189, at 190; *St Mungo Manufacturing Co Ltd v Hutchinson, Main Co Ltd* (1908) 25 R.P.C. 356, at 360.

[68] See *Gillette Safety Razor Co v A.W. Gamage Ltd* (1906) 24 R.P.C. 1; *Mentmore Manufacturing Co Ltd v Fomento (Sterling Area) Ltd* (1955) 72 R.P.C. 157; *Therm-a-Stor Ltd v Weatherseal Windows Ltd* [1981] F.S.R. 579.

[69] *Hunt v Clarke* (1919) 58 L.J.Q.B. 490, 493. *Re New Gold Coast Exploration Co* [1901] 1 Ch. 860.

[70] See *Haskell Golf Ball Co v Hutchinson and Main* (1904) 21 R.P.C. 497, at 500; see also *Fenner Wilson Co Ltd* (1893) 10 R.P.C. 283; *De Mare's Patent* (1899) 16 R.P.C. 528; *Dunlop Pneumatic Tyre Co Ltd v Suction Cleaners Ltd* (1904) 21 R.P.C. 300; *Mullard Radio Valve Co Ltd v Rothermel Corp Ltd* (1934) 51 R.P.C. 1; *Selsdon Fountain Pen Co Ltd v Miles Martin Pen Co Ltd* (1934) 51 R.P.C. 365, at 367.

mences proceedings against the manufacturer's customers, so as to secure a collateral advantage, such proceedings may be stayed or restrictions placed on the commencement of further actions.[71]

The commencement of proceedings against one party does not prevent a third **24-42** party bringing an action under s.70. Thus, it would appear that an advertisement which stated that an action for infringement had been commenced against a specified person and that others dealing in similar goods would also be proceeded against would be a threat which could be restrained under the provisions of s.70(1).

The claimant

The statutory right of action is not merely limited to the person to whom the **24-43** threats were directly made; any person aggrieved,[72] such as a rival patentee, to whom damage was occasioned by the issue of the threats is entitled to relief. Thus, in *Johnson v Edge*,[73] where circulars were issued to the trade intimating that the articles manufactured and sold by the plaintiff were infringements of the defendant's patent and that proceedings would be taken against any person dealing with such articles, and in consequence injury was done to the plaintiff's business, it was held that the plaintiff was a person aggrieved and could maintain an action, although no threats were made to him personally.[74] However, in *Reymes-Cole v Elite Hosiery Co Ltd*,[75] the defendants were held not to be persons aggrieved as they had ceased to supply the alleged infringing stocking to the recipient of the threat prior to the threat being made. This does not mean that the recipient of an indirect threat needs to prove damage or the likelihood of damage for the claim to succeed, but they must show that the threat was directed at them.[76] Where the threats are made to a limited company, it appears that shareholders and directors are capable of having a sufficient interest to bring a claim.[77]

The defendant

In a normal case the person making the threat will be named as the defendant. **24-44** When the threat complained of is a solicitor's letter, the solicitor's firm has sometimes been named as a defendant (e.g. in *Brain v Ingledew Brown Bennison*[78] the defendant Ingledew Brown Bennison was a firm of solicitors). In *Reckitt Benkiser UK v Home Pairfum Ltd*[79] (a trade mark case) Laddie J considered an application to join the claimant's solicitors, whose letter was said to be a threat, as additional defendants to an existing threats counterclaim. He refused to do so on the ground that although the counterclaim may be prima facie a valid one, the defendant seeking to add the claimant's solicitors had not put forward any reason why

---

[71] *Landi den Hartog BV v Sea Bird Ltd* [1975] F.S.R. 502; *Jacey (Printers) v Norton Wright Group Ltd* [1977] F.S.R. 475.
[72] PA 1977 s.70(1).
[73] (1892) 9 R.P.C. 142.
[74] See, e.g. *Challender v Royle* (1887) 4 R.P.C. 363, at 371; *Kensington and Knightsbridge Electric Lighting Co Ltd v Lane Fox Electrical Co Ltd* (1891) 8 R.P.C. 277; *Douglass v Pintsch's Patent Lighting Co Ltd* (1897) 14 R.P.C. 673; *Hoffnung Co v Salsbury* (1899) 16 R.P.C. 375.
[75] [1965] R.P.C. 102, 112.
[76] See *Brain v Ingledew Brown Bennison Garrett (No.3)* [1997] F.S.R. 511.
[77] See *Brain v Ingledew Brown Bennison Garrett (No.3)* [1997] F.S.R. 511.
[78] See [1995] F.S.R 552; [1996] F.S.R. 341; and [1997] F.S.R. 511.
[79] [2004] EWHC 302 (Pat); [2004] F.S.R. 37.

joinder was being pursued nor had it explained how joinder would be of benefit. The judge held that the attempted joinder was intended to make the solicitors relationship with the claimant uncomfortable and as a result was not legitimate.

24-45 In *Kooltrade v XTS*[80] the importance of a careful choice of defendant was illustrated by the court's refusal to allow joinder of the defendant's directors and solicitors into an action after obtaining judgment against the defendant company (which was unable to meet the damages awarded on an inquiry).

24-46 In *SDL Hair* an issue between the parties was whether an individual acting in the course of employment or an office would be liable under s.70 of the 1977 Act, or whether such an individual would escape as they are not doing it for themselves.[81] There the individual was found to be liable for the threats contained in an email which they had sent for and on behalf of the third defendant in the threats action. However, the judge, as part of this finding, stated that he was unsure why it was necessary to join the individual in question as a defendant.[82]

3. JUSTIFICATION

Justification as a defence to an action for threats

24-47 If there is a patent in existence, the defendant can defend the action on the ground that the acts in respect of which the threats were made constituted an infringement of some claim and can (if so entitled) counterclaim for infringement. The onus then shifts to the claimant who can rebut the allegation of infringement and attack the validity of that claim in the same way as in an action for infringement.[83] It is to be observed, however, that the defendant does not have to be the proprietor of, or entitled to, any right in the patent.

24-48 A new defence of belief of validity has been introduced into the 1977 Act as part of the 2004 Act amendments. Thus even if the patent is found invalid, the defendant has a defence if they prove that at the time of making the threats they did not know and had no reason to suspect that the patent was invalid in the relevant respect.

24-49 In *Sudarshan Chemical Industrie Limited v Clariant Produkte (Deutschland) GmbH*,[84] affirmed by the Court of Appeal,[85] the defendant sought to rely on s.70(2)(A). The patent was held to be invalid and the defence was dismissed at first instance. The defendant appealed to the Court of Appeal. The Court of Appeal considered the submissions of the defendant that, at the time it had made the threat in question, it did not know and had no reason to suspect that the patent was invalid. The defendant relied upon the evidence of the patent attorney responsible for drafting the patent, who wrote the letter which contained the threat. It was accepted that at the time of writing the letter, the patent attorney did not personally know and had no reason to suspect that the patent was invalid. However, the court found that the uninformed patent attorney's knowledge alone was not the relevant knowledge of

[80] [2002] F.S.R. 49.
[81] *SDL Hair Ltd v Next Row Ltd; Master Distributor Ltd v SDL Hair Ltd* [2013] EWPCC 31, [126].
[82] *SDL Hair Ltd v Next Row Ltd; Master Distributor Ltd v SDL Hair Ltd* [2013] EWPCC 31, [130].
[83] PA 1977 s.70(2) and see *John Summers Sons Ltd v The Cold Metal Process Co* (1948) 65 R.P.C. 75.
[84] [2012] EWHC 1569 (Ch).
[85] [2013] EWCA Civ 919.

the company. In dismissing the appeal, Lord Justice Kitchin said[86]:

> "So I consider this is one of those cases where we must look to see whose knowledge was for the purpose of this provision intended to count as the knowledge of the company. Where, as here, a company has secured the grant of a patent and then seeks to enforce it, to limit that knowledge to that of an uninformed patent attorney in the patent department who writes a threatening letter would, in my judgment, be too restrictive. … If a company has applied for and secured the grant of a patent and then it seeks to enforce it, the controlling mind of the company must include at least the mind of the properly informed patent attorney or, put another way, the minds of the patent attorney and inventor."

24-50 Given that a patentee cannot be compelled to waive privilege and that no adverse inference may be drawn against a party who does not waive privilege,[87] the preparation of the evidence to be called by a patentee in order to take advantage of this defence will require some care.

Amendment of patent

24-51 If the specification is amended after the threats and before the action, the issues of infringement and validity must presumably be tried with reference to the amended document and not the specification as it stood at the date when the threats were made.[88]

Where an application has been published but no patent has been granted

24-52 Section 70 applies to a threat of proceedings for infringement of the rights arising under s.69 upon publication of the application for a patent.[89] Such a threat is a threat to bring proceedings when the patent is granted.[90]

24-53 The defence of justification under s.70(2A) is also available, at least in principle, to a person who threatens proceedings for infringement of the rights arising upon publication of an application.[91] However, in order to sustain the defence it must be shown that the act complained of by the threat would, if the patent had been granted on the date of publication of the application, have infringed the patent as granted.[92] Thus, whether or not the defence can be made out is to be tested as at the date of the trial—not at the date when the threat was made—and if the application does not reach grant by the date of trial then the defence will fail.[93] A stay of the action pending the grant (or final refusal) of the patent will not necessarily be available.[94] Thus, a party who has applied for a patent should be cautious about issuing threats unless the patent is likely to reach grant before trial.

---

[86] *Sudarshan Chemical Industrie Limited v Clariant Produkte (Deutschland) GmbH* [2013] EWCA Civ 919, [132].
[87] See *Wentworth v J.C. Lloyd* (1864) 10 H.L.C. 589 and see also *Aldous LJ in Oxford Gene Technology Ltd v Affymetrix Inc (No.2)* [2001] R.P.C. 18 concerning the related question of justification of reasons for amending a patent after grant.
[88] PA 1977 s.75(3). See *Hall v Stepney Spare Motor Wheel Ltd* (1910) 27 R.P.C. 233; (1911) 28 R.P.C. 381. Also see paras 24-52 to 24-53: if the defence of justification is to be tested at the date of trial, then it must be tested on the amended specification.
[89] *Brain v Ingledew Brown Bennison Garrett* [1996] F.S.R. 341, CA.
[90] *Brain v Ingledew Brown Bennison Garrett* [1996] F.S.R. 341, CA.
[91] *Brain v Ingledew Brown Bennison Garrett* [1996] F.S.R. 341, CA. See Aldous LJ at 348 and Hobhouse LJ at 354–355.
[92] PA 1977 s.69(1) and (2)(b).
[93] *Brain v Ingledew Brown Bennison Garrett (No.2)* [1997] F.S.R. 271.
[94] *Brain v Ingledew Brown Bennison Garrett (No.2)* [1997] F.S.R. 271.

24-54   A party who is relying on a patent application being granted before trial must expressly plead an assertion to that effect, but at least for the purposes of successfully resisting an application for summary judgment, the absence of it being pleaded is not fatal.[95] In *Global Flood Defence Systems v Van den Noort Innovations BV*[96] the court found that the claimants had assumed that such an assertion would be pleaded and therefore allowed the defendant to amend to do so.

Certificate of contested validity

24-55   Under the law prior to 1949, it was doubtful whether a certificate of contested validity could be granted in a threats action.[97] The words of the 1977 Act[98] are plainly wide enough to enable this to be done in an appropriate case. Where a certificate of validity has been granted, it is submitted that it would not entitle a patentee to the increased allowance of costs in a subsequent threats action unless the threats action contained a counterclaim for infringement.

4. PROCEDURE

Particulars

24-56   The defendant in an action under s.70 of the 1977 Act is entitled to particulars of the threats upon which the claimant relies.[99] The claimant is entitled, if the defendant seeks to justify, to particulars of the acts which are said to constitute infringement of the patent[100] and if the validity of the patent is put in question the general rules relating to particulars of objections also apply.[101] Where there was a doubt upon which patents the defendants had based their threats, the court ordered that the defendants should deliver to the claimants a list of such patents.[102] Also, where the claimants alleged that the threats were made by the defendants' agents, it was held that the defendants were entitled to particulars of the names of those agents.[103]

If mala fides is relied on

24-57   If, for any reason, it is intended to rely upon mala fides on the part of the defendant, the fact should be brought out at an early stage and not concealed until the actual trial.[104]

---

95 *Global Flood Defence Systems v Van den Noort Innovations BV* [2015] EWHC 153 (IPEC).
96 [2015] EWHC 153 (IPEC).
97 See, e.g. *Crampton v Patents Investments Co* (1888) 5 R.P.C. 382; *Pittevil Co v Brackelsberg Melting Processes Ltd* (1932) 49 R.P.C. 73.
98 PA 1977 s.65; and see PA 1949 s.64; and *Canon K.K.'s Application* [1982] R.P.C. 446.
99 Plainly under the Civil Procedure Rules and established as long ago as *Law v Ashworth* (1890) 7 R.P.C. 86.
100 Again plainly under the Civil Procedure Rules in general and well established before hand—see *Reymes-Cole v Elite Hosiery Co Ltd* [1961] R.P.C. 277.
101 See para.4.2 of the Practice Direction 63—Intellectual Property Claims.
102 *Union Electrical Power, etc., Co v Electrical Storage Co* (1888) 5 R.P.C. 329.
103 *Downson-Taylor Co Ltd v The Drosophore Co Ltd* (1894) 11 R.P.C. 653.
104 For an old authority on the point, see *English and American Machinery Co Ltd v Gare Machine Co Ltd* (1894) 11 R.P.C. 627, at 631.

Right to begin

In *Lewis Falk Ltd v Jacobwitz*,[105] Morton J[106] said: 24-58

"It is for a plaintiff in a 'threats' action first to prove the threat or threats and, once that has been done, the onus shifts to the defendant, and the burden is on him to prove that the acts, in respect of which proceedings are threatened, constitute, or if done would constitute, an infringement of a patent ... If the defendant succeeds in proving this, the burden then shifts again to the plaintiff to prove, if he can, that the patent ... is invalid. In the present case one threat is admitted, and it is, therefore, for the defendant to open his case first."[107]

Interim injunction

The general principles upon which an interim injunction will be granted are those   24-59
set out in the speech of Lord Diplock in *American Cyanamid Co v Ethicon Ltd*.[108]

A claim for unjustified threats is essentially an issue of fact and not law, and as   24-60
a jury-type question it can only be decided at trial.[109] Nevertheless, in accordance
with *American Cyanamid*, the court must be satisfied that it is arguable that an
actionable threat has been made.[110]

Although justification is a defence, the onus is on the maker of the threats to   24-61
justify them and such justification will not usually be a matter which can be resolved
on an interim application unless validity and infringement are admitted.[111]
Consequently, if the claimant shows an arguable case that a threat has been made,
the fact that the defendant intends to justify the threat at trial is unlikely to rebut
the claimant's case that it is arguable that the threat is actionable.

In any event, a plea of justification is not a bar to the granting of an interim   24-62
injunction and there is no analogy to be drawn with trade libel cases where an assertion by a defendant that the threats will be justified is a bar to interlocutory
relief.[112]

Provided that an arguable case is made out, the grant or withholding of interim   24-63
relief will depend upon the ability of either party adequately to be compensated in
monetary terms and ultimately on the balance of convenience. The damage which
can be caused by unjustified threats of proceedings for patent infringement is such
that an interim injunction to restrain such threats represents a valuable remedy. The
provisos in s.70(5) which permit mere provision of factual information and certain
enquiries and the fact that proceedings to restrain threats may not be brought for a
threat alleged to consist of making or importing a product for disposal or of using
a process (and subsequent dealings with relevant products)[113] means that the bal-

---

[105] (1944) 61 R.P.C. 116.

[106] (1944) 61 R.P.C. 116, 118.

[107] See also *John Summers Sons Ltd v The Cold Metal Process Co* (1948) 65 R.P.C. 75; *Pearson v Holden* (1948) 65 R.P.C. 424, at 428.

[108] [1975] A.C. 396. See para.19-77, et seq. See also *Bowden Controls v Acco Cable Controls Ltd* [1990] R.P.C. 427.

[109] See *Brain v Ingledew Brown Bennison Garrett* [1996] F.S.R. 341, CA.

[110] For an example of a case where the plaintiff failed to show a serious issue to be tried with regard to the making of a threat, see *Easycare Inc v Bryan Lawrence Co* [1995] F.S.R. 597.

[111] *Johnson Electric Industrial Manufactory Ltd v Mabuchi-Motor K.K.* [1986] F.S.R. 280.

[112] *HVE Electric Ltd v Cuffin Holdings Ltd* [1964] R.P.C. 149; *Cerosa Ltd v Poseidon Industrie A.B.* [1973] R.P.C. 882; *Johnson Electric Industrial Manufactory v Mabuchi Motor K.K* [1986] F.S.R. 280.

[113] PA 1977 s.70(4).

ance of convenience will usually be in favour of restraining any threats which go outside of these categories.

Summary judgment

24-64   It is submitted that in practice the threshold for obtaining summary judgment in relation to allegations of unjustified threats for patent infringement is, as with other areas of patent law, very high. The test that the court has to apply to a defence advanced under s.70(2A) is whether it lacks reality, and "[i]n so far as that test turns on a point of law or construction in relation to which there was no prospect of further significant evidence at trial, or at least nothing more than the mere possibility that there may be such evidence, the point should be decided."[114]

5. THE RELIEF

Declaration, injunction, damages

24-65   By the terms of s.70(3) of the 1977 Act, the claimant, if successful, is entitled to:

   (1)   a declaration that the threats were unjustifiable;
   (2)   an injunction against the continuance of the threats; and
   (3)   damages.

24-66   A declaration will not, however, be made by consent or in default of defence.[115] Further, the claimant who is threatened with a number of patents will not be entitled to any relief if the defendant can justify the threat in respect of one patent. In *Rosedale Associated Manufacturers Ltd v Carlton Tyre Saving Co Ltd*, Lord Evershed MR said[116]:

> "Prima facie the right to relief which section 65(2) [of the 1949 Act] postulates depends upon the defendant in the action failing to prove that the acts in respect of which the threats were made did or would constitute an infringement of 'a patent.' Prima facie, therefore, the defendant's burden is discharged if he does prove infringement of 'a', that is, any patent."

24-67   The width of the injunction granted will in part depend upon the nature of the threat, and a threat made in intentionally broad terms may give rise to an injunction in correspondingly broad terms.[117]

24-68   The quantum of damage can be assessed by the judge at the trial,[118] but the ordinary form of order directs an inquiry.[119] The measure of damages is that ordinarily applicable in cases of tort and damages can only be recovered if they are the natural and reasonable consequences of the threats,[120] and have to be due to the

---

[114]   *Global Flood Defence Systems v Van den Noort Innovations BV* [2015] EWHC 153 (IPEC), [25].
[115]   *Corn Products Co Ltd v Scholten's Chemische Fabrieken* (1939) 56 R.P.C. 59; *Demuth (R.) Ltd v Inter-Pan Ltd* [1967] R.P.C. 75.
[116]   [1960] R.P.C. 59, 62.
[117]   *Mechanical Services (Trade Engineers) Ltd v Avon Rubber Co Ltd* [1977] R.P.C. 66.
[118]   See, e.g. *Cars v Bland Light Syndicate Ltd* (1911) 28 R.P.C. 33; *Horne v Johnston Bros* (1921) 38 R.P.C. 366.
[119]   See, e.g. *Hoffnung v Salsbury* (1899) 16 R.P.C. 375; *Pittevil Co v Brackelsberg Melting Process Ltd* (1932) 49 R.P.C. 73; *Neild v Rockley* [1986] F.S.R. 3.
[120]   See *Horne v Johnston Bros* (1921) 38 R.P.C. 366, at 372.

threats alone. In *Ungar v Sugg*,[121] Lord Esher MR said:

> "But then what is the liability? It must be for damage done by the threats not damage done by anything else. They (i.e. the defendants) are not liable for the damage which is the result of any rumour getting about in the trade which is not their act. They are liable for the damages caused by their own act—the threats which they have made, and which they have caused to be made known to the people to whom their circulars were given."

Accordingly, a defendant will not be liable for damage caused by threats not authorised to be made by them.[122] Nor will a defendant be liable for losses caused by their issuing of proceedings where their original threatening letters had been ignored.[123]   **24-69**

Damages suffered through the loss of a contract[124] or the breaking off of negotiations for a contract[125] are recoverable. Where the claimant was not inconvenienced by the threat, the court in its discretion made no order in the action.[126] The court retains a discretion to refuse an inquiry if there is no, or at best trivial, damage, although in the normal course of events an inquiry will follow from a finding of liability.[127]   **24-70**

The principles to be applied in determining what damages the party aggrieved ought to be awarded were considered in the enquiry as to damages in *SDL Hair Ltd v Next Row Ltd*[128] following a declaration granted in the main action that three letters and an email which had been sent by the defendants constituted groundless threats of patent infringement. In *SDL* the court found that the defendants were liable for the losses caused by two of the letters, and applied a number of principles from the authorities which relate to damages inquiries in general, including "loss of chance".[129]   **24-71**

Dissemination of judgment

The court's power to order dissemination of judgment is not confined to situations where an intellectual property right has been found to be infringed.[130] Whilst dissemination of judgment orders are not the norm, where commercial uncertainty needs to be dispelled the court may make such an order, including circumstances where the court has found that a party has made unjustifiable threats of bringing patent infringement proceedings.[131]   **24-72**

---

[121] (1892) 9 R.P.C. 114, 118.
[122] *Ungar v Sugg* (1892) 9 R.P.C. 114.
[123] See *Carfiow Products (UK) Ltd v Linwood Securities (Birmingham) Ltd* [1998] R.P.C. 691 —a case involving threats under equivalent provisions in the law of registered designs.
[124] *Skinner Co v Perry* (1894) 11 R.P.C. 406; see also *Hoffnung v Salsbury* (1899) 16 R.P.C. 375.
[125] *Solanite Signs Ltd v Wood* (1933) 50 R.P.C. 315.
[126] *Tudor Accessories Ltd v J.N. Somers Ltd* [1960] R.P.C. 215.
[127] See *Brain v Ingledew Brown Bennison Garrett (No.3)* [1997] F.S.R. 511.
[128] [2014] EWHC 2084 (IPEC).
[129] *SDL Hair Ltd v Next Row Ltd* [2014] EWHC 2084 (IPEC), [31]–[32] and [37]–[40].
[130] *Samsung Electronics (UK) Ltd v Apple Inc* [2012] EWCA Civ 1339; [2013] F.S.R. 9.
[131] *F.H. Brundle v Perry* [2014] EWHC 979 (IPEC), [24].

Settlement

24-73   Like any other proceedings, a threats action may be compromised by settlement. In *Kenburn Waste Management Ltd v Heinz Bergmann*[132] the court had to consider whether English or German law covered the negative obligations in a compromise of a threats claim brought under s.70 of the 1977 Act. It was common ground that the Contracts (Applicable Law) Act 1990 applied. The German defendant contended that German law was applicable because the obligations on him mostly had to be performed in Germany. The court held that nevertheless English law applied essentially because the object of the contract was to achieve results in the UK only (non-communication with the claimant's UK customers), the contract had as its substratum a purely English right of action under s.70 if the 1977 Act and such a claim was only actionable in the United Kingdom.

---

[132] [2002] F.S.R. 44.

CHAPTER 25

USE BY THE CROWN

CONTENTS

1. INTRODUCTION

History

Prior to the Patents, Designs and Trade Marks Act 1883 the Crown was entitled **25-01** to use patented inventions without the assent of or compensation to the patentee,[1] though it was the practice to reward the patentee ex gratia. The exemption of the Crown did not, however, extend to protect contractors who supplied patented articles to the Crown,[2] as distinguished from servants or agents of the Crown, at any rate where such contractors could if they had so wished have instead supplied articles which were not patented.

Present law

Since the Act of 1883, and now under the present law, a patent has the same ef- **25-02** fect against the Crown as against a subject.[3] This, however, is subject to very wide rights of user by the Crown and to an obligation upon the Crown to pay compensation where such rights are exercised, as set out below. By s.3 of the Crown Proceedings Act 1947,[4] a patentee is able to sue the Crown in civil proceedings for infringement, where the Crown uses an invention otherwise than in accordance with its statutory rights.

2. RIGHTS OF USER BY THE CROWN

The acts which may be done: s.55(1)

Any government department and any person authorised in writing by a govern- **25-03** ment department may for the services of the Crown do any of the acts listed in s.55(1) of the Patents Act 1977 in relation to a patented invention without the

---

[1] *Feather v R.* (1865) 6 B. & S. 257.
[2] *Dixon v London Small Arms Co* (1874) L.R. 10 Q.B. 130; (1875) 1 Q.B.D. 384; (1875) 1 App. Cas. 632.
[3] PA 1949 s.21(2); PA 1977 s.129.
[4] As substituted by CDPA 1988 s.303(1), Sch.7 para.4(1).

consent of the proprietor.[5] The listed acts are similar to the infringing acts set out in s.60, the main difference being the qualified right of the Crown to sell a patented product[6] other than for purposes of foreign defence or for production or supply of specified drugs and medicines.[7] In so far as the provisions of s.55 are narrower than s.60, any act by the Crown or any act authorised by the Crown which is not covered by s.55 will constitute an infringing act and the patentee proprietor may sue the Crown in civil proceedings for such infringement.[8] In such circumstances, although damages may be obtainable, no injunction will lie.[9]

Requirment for authorisation to be in writing

25-04   The requirement that the authorisation must be in writing was first introduced by the Patents and Designs Act 1919. It would seem that such written authorisation need not be directed specifically to the use of the particular patent concerned and that a written authorisation or requirement of a department that a contractor should supply apparatus of a certain type is sufficient if it is in fact impossible for the contractor to supply such apparatus without infringing the patent.[10]

25-05   In *Aktiengesellschaft für Aluminium Schweissung v London Aluminium Co Ltd (No.2)*,[11] Sargant J said:

"The origin of the section, of course, is well known; it is to be found undoubtedly in the decision of the House of Lords in *Dixon v London Small Arms Co Ltd*,[12] where it was held that the right of the Crown to use a patented article or process could not extend to contractors who were employed as contractors by the Government. The difficulty that arises is this: In some cases it is clear that the defendants, who were the direct contractors with the Government, were told to use this particular process, and in those cases it is not questioned by counsel for the plaintiffs that no damages can be assessed. The right of the patentees in that case will be under section 29 [now section 55] ... But there are a number of cases where the facts are nothing like so simple, cases where the company, the defendants, have not been contracting directly with the Government, but have been, for instance, supplying persons who themselves were the direct contractors with the Government; in those cases it is said that the protection of the section does not apply and that the patentees accordingly are entitled to the ordinary remedy against the defendant company. It seems to me really that it is impossible to deal as a whole with the various contracts that are now in question. In my judgment, the section is primarily an agency section; that is to say, protection is afforded to the government department, and to any person or persons, contractors or others, who are acting as agents for, or by the express or implied authority of, a government department. In each case it will have to be ascertained, if the parties think fit to fight out each individual case, whether the acts of the defendant company in that particular case were acts done for the purposes of the Crown, and with the authority or by the direction of the Crown. In that case they will not be liable; but where the acts that they have done have not been done by virtue of some express or implied authority from the Crown, then it seems to me they will be liable. It may be in many cases that, where they are sub-contractors, there will have been such a relation between them and their contractors, such a direction given by the Government to the contractors, or such a direct supervision over the employers by the Government, as will amount to

---

5   See *MMI v Cellxion* [2009] EWHC 1533 (Pat), where the court considered (without deciding) whether retrospectively granted permission could render a sale non-infringing which did infringe at the time of sale.
6   PA 1977 s.55(1)(a). In particular the Crown can only sell or offer to sell a product where to do so would be incidental or ancillary to making, using, importing of keeping the product.
7   PA 1977 s.55(1)(b). In contrast the Crown has an unqualified right to sell or offer to sell a product for foreign defence purposes, or for the production or supply of specified drugs or medicines.
8   Crown Proceedings Act 1947 s.21(1).
9   See the proviso to Crown Proceedings Act 1947 s.21(1).
10   See *Pyrene Co Ltd v Webb Lamp Co Ltd* (1920) 37 R.P.C. 57.
11   (1923) 40 R.P.C. 107, 116.
12   (1876) 1 App. Cas. 632.

an implied authority sufficient to make the company in that individual case an agent acting by the authority, and for the purposes, of the Crown."

Timing of authorisation

The authorisation may be given either before or after the patent is granted and either before or after the acts authorised are done.[13] Retrospective authorisation takes away any cause of action which may have existed and substitutes a right of remuneration under s.55(4).[14]   **25-06**

Meaning of "for the services of the Crown"

Use "for the services of the Crown" is use by members of such services in the course of their duties. Thus, the use of patented drugs in the treatment of National Health Service hospital patients has been held to be use for the services of the Crown.[15]   **25-07**

As Diplock LJ (as he then was) said in the Court of Appeal in the *Pfizer* case: **25-08**

"An act is done for 'the services (or service) of the Crown' if it is done for the purpose of the performance of a duty or the exercise of a power which is imposed upon or vested in the executive government of the United Kingdom by statute or by the prerogative. Where there is no explicit agency between the persons performing the act and the executive government, difficult questions may arise as to whether the duty or power, the performance or exercise of which is the purpose of the act, is one which is imposed upon or vested in the executive government of the United Kingdom and not upon some other person or authority; but this problem does not arise where the act is done by an agent for a government department itself."[16]

Section 56(2) of the 1977 Act lists three matters that are included within the meaning of "the services of the Crown", namely the supply of anything for foreign defence purposes,[17] the production or supply of specific drugs and medicines[18] and matter relating to the production or use of atomic energy or research connected therewith.   **25-09**

Henry Brothers (Magherafelt) v Ministry of Defence and Northern Ireland Office[19] was a case under s.36(2) of the Act, whereby a co-proprietor may without the consent of his co-proprietors "for his own benefit" do an act which would otherwise amount to infringement.[20] It was held obiter that the use of an invention relating to prefabricated blast-resistant building structures in a police station in Northern Ireland was use for the Crown's own benefit. It is submitted that such use would also be use "for the services of the Crown".   **25-10**

Meaning of "a patented invention"

The Crown's right to do acts and to authorise others to do acts under s.55(1) of the 1977 Act applies to "a patented invention", and, in this context, a patented   **25-11**

---

[13] PA 1977 s.55(6).
[14] *Dory v Sheffield Health Authority* [1991] F.S.R. 221.
[15] *Pfizer Corp v Minister of Health* [1965] R.P.C. 261; see also *Dory v Sheffield Health Authority* [1991] F.S.R. 221.
[16] [1965] R.P.C. 261, 276.
[17] See PA 1977 s.56(3) as to meaning of foreign defence purposes.
[18] See PA 1977 s.56(4) as to meaning of specified drugs and medicines.
[19] [1999] R.P.C. 442, CA.
[20] Subject to s.55 and s.36(2) itself.

invention means an invention for which a patent has been or is subsequently granted, i.e. it includes an alleged invention that is the subject of a patent application.[21] It also applies to European patents (UK)[22] and applications therefore.[23]

Sale of a patented product to or by the Crown

25-12   The sale of a patented product to a government department for the services of the Crown is a "use" of the patented invention which may be authorised by that department.[24] The Crown may also sell to anybody patented products made pursuant to an authority given by a government department when those products are no longer required for the purpose for which they were made.[25] The purchaser of such products and any person claiming through them may deal with them freely, as though the patent were held by the Crown.[26]

Sale of products forfeited under customs law

25-13   It is a matter of doubt whether purchasers from the Crown of products manufactured in infringement of a patent and forfeited under the laws relating to the customs or excise are entitled to use them without the licence of the patentee.[27] Section 122 of the 1977 Act says:

> "Nothing in this Act shall affect the right of the Crown or of any person deriving title directly or indirectly from the Crown to dispose of or use articles forfeited under the laws relating to customs or excise."

25-14   This section does not confer any rights upon the Crown or persons deriving title from the Crown, but merely states that existing rights are not affected.

Use for foreign defence purposes and health services

25-15   Under s.55(1)(a)(ii) of the 1977 Act[28] the powers exercisable for the services of the Crown in respect of foreign defence and health include the power to sell or offer to sell without qualification in contrast to the more limited powers of sale under s.55(1)(a)(i) in respect of other Crown services which can only be exercised where the sale or offer for sale would be incidental or ancillary to making, using, importing or keeping the patented product.

25-16   The meaning of a sale or supply of anything "for foreign defence purposes" is set out in s.56(3) of the 1977 Act and it includes the sale or supply by the UK Government to a government of any country outside the UK where the thing in question is required for the defence of that country. Sale or supply to the United Nations is also included within the sub-section.

25-17   As regards health, the powers exercisable under s.55(1) are in respects of drugs

---

[21]   PA 1977 s.56(1); see also *American Flange and Manufacturing Co Inc v Van Leer* (1948) 65 R.P.C. 305, at 318.
[22]   PA 1977 s.77.
[23]   PA 1977 s.78.
[24]   *Pfizer Corp v Minister of Health* [1965] R.P.C. 261, (1965) A.C. 512; *Dory v Sheffield Health Authority* [1991] F.S.R. 221.
[25]   PA 1977 s.55(1)(e).
[26]   PA 1977 s.55(8).
[27]   See *British Mutoscope and Biograph Co Ltd v Homer* (1901) 18 R.P.C. 177.
[28]   See also PA 1977 s.55(1)(c) for power to sell drugs and medicines.

and medicines specified in regulations made by the Secretary of State[29] and required for any of the medical, dental or pharmaceutical services specified in s.56(4)(a) of the 1977 Act.

Use during a period of emergency

During a period of emergency very wide powers are conferred on the Crown.[30] In particular during a period of emergency the Crown may do any act which would otherwise constitute an infringement of a patent or the rights arising upon publication of the application for a patent for any of the purposes set out in s.59(1).[31] A "period of emergency" must be declared by Order in Council.[32] **25-18**

Information as to use to be given

Where any use is made of an invention by or with the authority of a government department under s.55(1), then the department must notify the patentee as soon as practicable after the use has begun and the patent has been granted, and must give them such information as to the extent of the use as they may from time to time require, unless it would be contrary to the public interest to do so.[33] **25-19**

Terms of any licence or assignment, etc. to be inoperative

A government department may authorise a licensee of the patentee to make use of the invention for the services of the Crown and in such a case the terms of any licence or agreement (other than one made with a government department) are inoperative as regards such user.[34] Similarly, the patentee may be authorised to use or supply the patented invention for the services of the Crown, notwithstanding the terms of any licence, assignment or agreement which purport to debar them from so doing,[35] and any provisions which restrict or regulate the use of the invention or of any model, document, or information relating to the invention are inoperative.[36] Furthermore, the reproduction or publication of any model or document in connection with such use is not to be deemed an infringement of copyright, design right or topography right.[37] **25-20**

3. THE OBLIGATION TO PAY COMPENSATION

Circumstances in which compensation is payable

If the invention has been recorded by, tried by or on behalf of a government department[38] before the relevant priority date otherwise than in consequence of a **25-21**

---

29 PA 1977 s.56(4)(b).
30 PA 1977 s.59.
31 PA 1977 s.59(2).
32 PA 1977 s.59(3)
33 PA 1977 s.55(7). See *MMI v Cellxion* [2009] EWHC 1533 (Pat).
34 PA 1977 s.57(1). See *No-Nail Cases Proprietary Ltd v No-Nail Boxes Ltd* (1944) 61 R.P.C. 94.
35 PA 1977 s.57(1); overruling *Foster Wheeler Ltd v E. Green & Son Ltd* (1946) 63 R.P.C. 10.
36 PA 1977 s.57(1).
37 PA 1977 s.57(1).
38 See *Re Carbonit A.G.* (1923) 40 R.P.C. 360; *Henry Bros Ltd v The Ministry of Defence* [1997] R.P.C. 693, at 709.

communication made in confidence directly or indirectly from the patentee or a predecessor in title, any use of the invention may be made free of any royalty or other payment.[39] However, if the invention had not been so recorded or tried, any use made after the publication of the application or in consequence of such a communication of the invention is to be on terms to be agreed between the government department and the patentees with the approval of the Treasury or in default of agreement to be settled by the Court,[40] which may refer the whole proceedings or any issue of fact to a Circuit judge discharging the functions of an official referee or an arbitrator.[41]

Validity may be challenged

25-22   In proceedings for the assessment of compensation for Crown user, if the patentee is a party the government department may apply for revocation of the patent and, in any case, may put validity in issue without applying for revocation.[42]

25-23   If the patent is found partially valid, then the court may grant relief in respect of that part of the patent which is found to be valid and to have been used for the services of the Crown.[43] However, the grant of such relief will be subject to the terms of s.58(8) of the 1977 Act, including the discretion contained therein.[44]

25-24   Where an amendment of the specification of the patent has been allowed, then the court may not grant relief by way of compensation in respect of any such use before the decision to allow the amendment unless the court is satisfied that the specification of the patent as published was framed in good faith and with reasonable skill and knowledge and the relief is sought in good faith.[45]

25-25   Where the Crown puts validity in issue and there is also concurrently an action for infringement of the patent against a third party who has also put validity in issue, the Crown proceedings and the action may be ordered to be heard together so far as they raise common issues.[46]

Amount of compensation payable

25-26   The sum payable by way of compensation under s.55(4) of the 1977 Act is in the nature of remuneration payable to the inventor or their successor in title for the use made by the Crown of their invention pursuant to that concurrent right; they are not entitled to compensation under s.55(4) on any other basis, for instance, in their status as a manufacturer for loss of chance to manufacture.[47] However, s.57A of the 1977 Act[48] now provides for compensation to the proprietor or the exclusive licensee for loss of profit resulting from their not being awarded a contract. Compensation is payable only to the extent that such a contract could have been

---

[39]   PA 1977 s.55(3), (9).
[40]   PA 1977 ss.55(4) and 58.
[41]   PA 1977 s.58(12).
[42]   PA 1977 s.74(1)(e).
[43]   PA 1977 s.58(7).
[44]   Cf. PA 1977 s.63(2), as amended in the light of the IP Enforcement Directive art.13(1).
[45]   PA 1977 s.58(6), cf. PA 1977 s.62(3), as amended in the light of the IP Enforcement Directive art.13(1). See also *Electric and Musical Industries' Patent* [1963] R.P.C. 241.
[46]   *Anxionnaz v Ministry of Aviation* [1966] R.P.C. 510.
[47]   *Patchett's Patent* [1967] R.P.C. 237, 246, 251 and 257; see also *Allen & Hanburys (Salbutamol) Patent* [1987] R.P.C. 327, at 328.
[48]   Added by CDPA 1988 s.295 and Sch.5 para.16(1).

fulfilled from their existing manufacturing or other capacity.[49] The amount payable is in addition to any amount payable under ss.55 or 57.[50]

Date from which compensation runs

It is to be noted that compensation is payable in respect of use either from the date of publication of the application or the date of communication of the invention. The reason for this is that the Crown may require that patent to be kept secret,[51] and, if the date of publication were the relevant date, the patentees could thereby be deprived of compensation altogether.

25-27

Interest

The court may also order interest to be paid to the patentee on the compensation sum.[52]

25-28

Compensation payable to exclusive licensee or assignor

An exclusive licensee whose licence was granted for a consideration other than a royalty assessed by reference to use can claim compensation for Crown user,[53] including user by the patentee for the services of the Crown. Similarly, where a patent or the right to apply for a patent has been assigned in consideration of the payment of royalties, the assignor can claim compensation and any sum payable is to be divided between assignor and patentee as may be agreed or be settled by reference to the court.[54] An exclusive licensee whose licence was granted in consideration of the payment of royalties can recover such proportion of any payment made to the patentee as may be agreed or determined by the court.[55]

25-29

Apportionment of compensation between co-owners

Where co-owners of a patent have previously agreed on the proportions in which they will divide any royalties or other proceeds from exploitation of the patent, the court will apportion in those proportions any compensation awarded in respect of Crown use of the patent.[56]

25-30

Factors taken into account in determining terms

Any benefit or compensation that the claimant or their predecessor in title may have received or be entitled to receive directly or indirectly from any government department in respect of the invention is to be taken into account in assessing compensation.[57] Furthermore, the court shall have regard to whether the claimant or their predecessor in title has without reasonable cause failed to comply with a

25-31

---

49 PA 1977 s.57A(2).
50 PA 1977 s.57A(5).
51 PA 1977 s.22; see paras 3-36, 3-88 to 3-90.
52 *Patchett's Patent* [1967] R.P.C. 237.
53 PA 1977 s.57(3)(a).
54 PA 1977 s.57(4).
55 PA 1977 s.57(5), (7), (8).
56 *Patchett's Patent* [1967] R.P.C. 237.
57 PA 1977 s.58(3)(a).

request of the department to use the invention for the services of the Crown on reasonable terms.[58]

4. PROCEDURE IN CASES OF DISPUTE

Jurisdiction of the court

25-32   Under s.58(1) of the 1977 Act, after a patent has been granted for an invention, the court[59] has power to hear and determine any dispute as to—

(a) the exercise by a government department or a person authorised by a government department, of the powers conferred by s.55 of the Act,

(b) terms for the use of the invention for the services of the Crown under that section,

(c) the right of any person to receive any part of a payment made in pursuance of subs.(4) of that section, or

(d) the right of any person to receive a payment under s.57A.

Procedure

25-33   The procedure on a reference of a dispute to the court under s.58 of the 1977 Act is by issue of a claim form.[60] The claim is one under the Patents Act 1977 and, consequently, Section I of CPR Pt 63 applies to it.[61] A dispute may be referred to the court by either party.[62]

Confidential disclosure

25-34   If any question arises as to whether or not an invention has been recorded or tried by a government department and any disclosure would be contrary to the public interest, such disclosure may be made confidentially to the other party's legal representative or to an independent expert mutually agreed on.[63]

Costs in proceedings against the Crown

25-35   In any civil proceedings or arbitration to which the Crown (or a government department) is a party, the court or arbitrator, may make "an order for the payment of costs by or to the Crown".[64]

---

58 PA 1977 s.58(3)(b).
59 The court is defined as meaning the High Court, see PA 1977 s.130(1).
60 CPR rr.63.2 and 63.5.
61 CPR r.63.2.
62 PA 1977 s.58(1).
63 PA 1977 s.58(2).
64 See Administration of Justice (Miscellaneous Provisions) Act 1933 s.7(1) and (2); and see *Patchett's Patent* [1967] R.P.C. 237, at 259.

CHAPTER 26

THE UNIFIED PATENT COURT

CONTENTS

1. INTRODUCTION AND HISTORICAL BACKGROUND

The Unified Patent Court ("UPC") is to be a new court with a more or less pan-European jurisdiction in patent matters. The point of the court is to allow European patent disputes to be tried once and for all in one court instead of the current arrangements in which patents are litigated in parallel in many European states at the same time. The instrument creating the court is the UPC Agreement.[1] The court will start to function when the agreement formally comes into force. That occurs when it has been ratified appropriately. Although the UPC Agreement is not yet in force, it is anticipated that the agreement will come into force quite soon. Indications are that the agreement may come into full effect at the beginning of 2017. While many details concerning how the UPC will function are not yet certain, there is sufficient clarity about many aspects to make it possible to address the UPC in this work in outline. **26-01**

The UPC in summary

The UPC consists of a Court of First Instance and Court of Appeal. The Court of First Instance has a central division, which is seated in Paris with sections in London and Munich. There will also be local or regional divisions. Member States will either have their own local division or participate in a regional division with other Member States. Alternatively, they may choose to have neither, in which case actions for infringements in their territory can be heard in the central division. Where there is a counterclaim for revocation in a local/regional division, the panel of judges at that division will decide whether to send the whole case to the central division; hear the whole case at the local division; or "bifurcate", i.e. hear revocation at the central division and infringement at the local or regional division. There is a mixture of legally qualified judges and technically qualified judges. **26-02**

The UPC has jurisdiction over both types of European patents, which will be referred to as European bundle patents (i.e. European patents which take effect as a bundle of national patents such as the European Patent (UK)) and unitary patents (i.e. the new single European patent which will have pan-European effect pursuant to the UPC Agreement). However, there will be a seven-year transitional period during which proprietors of European bundle patents (but not proprietors of **26-03**

---

[1] EU Document 16351/12.

European unitary patents) can opt out of the exclusive jurisdiction of the UPC. The UPC Administrative Committee may extend this period by a further seven years up to a total of 14 years. Patent owners can file opt-out demands before the UPC opens. The UPC has no jurisdiction over national patents; patents in non-EU Member States (e.g. Switzerland); or non-unitary European patents in non-participating EU states (e.g. the Spanish national designation of a European bundle patent, namely the European Patent (ES)).

26-04   The UPC will be able to grant relief, including injunction, which is immediately valid across the whole of the relevant territory and which can be enforced by means of national laws. This means that patentees no longer have to litigate the issue of infringement on a country-by-country basis; equally, parties attacking validity do not have to do so on a country-by-country basis either.

The previous attempts and the negotiations which led to the UPC

The Community Patent Convention 1973–1989

26-05   The CPC, to which the Member States of the European Community (EC) were signatories, constituted a special agreement within the EPC[2] and had as its object the creation of a Community patent system for the EC with a view to ensuring the free movement within the EC of goods protected by patents. Although signed in December 1975 and revised in December 1989, the Convention was not ratified by all the Member States and did not come into force.[3]

26-06   Under the CPC an application for a European patent designating any EC country would have been deemed to have designated all EC countries and, if the application proceeded to grant, a single "unitary" Community patent would have been granted for the whole of the EC instead of separate European patents for each of the EC countries. Such Community patents would have been of "equal effect" throughout the EC and would have been granted, transferred, revoked or allowed to lapse only in respect of the whole of the EC.[4] Under the transitional provisions of the Convention, during the transitional period (unspecified in duration) an applicant would have been able to opt for separate European patents for designated countries of the EC instead of a Community patent, but after the termination of such transitional period the only European patents which could have been granted in respect of the United Kingdom would have been Community patents. Further, a national patent would have been ineffective to the extent that it covered the same invention as a Community patent.[5]

26-07   The CPC also provided that Community patents would have been subject only to the provisions of the CPC and those provisions of the EPC which are binding upon every European patent.[6] Accordingly, s.86(1) of the 1977 Act provided that:

"all rights, powers, liabilities, obligations and restrictions from time to time created or arising by or under the Community Patent Convention and all remedies and procedures from time to time provided for by or under that Convention shall ... have legal effect in the United Kingdom".

---

[2]   EPC art.142.

[3]   The only Member States to ratify the CPC were France, Germany, Greece, Denmark, Luxembourg, the United Kingdom and the Netherlands. However, the CPC required ratification by all Member States for it to come into force, see CPC (1975) art.98 and art.10 of the Revision Agreement of 1989.

[4]   CPC (1975 and 1989) art.2.

[5]   CPC (1975) art.80; CPC (1989) art.75.

[6]   CPC (1975 and 1989) art.2(3).

In the event, s.86 was never brought into force and the 2004 Act has now amended the 1977 Act so as to repeal s.86 (and ss.87 and 88) altogether.[7]   **26-08**

Council Regulation on the Community Patent and the Common Political Approach

In August 2000 the European Commission put forward a proposal for a Council   **26-09**
Regulation on the Community patent.[8] This initiative has been referred to as the Lisbon strategy. With reference to the CPC, the Commission said:

> "The failure of the [Community Patent] Convention has generally been attributed to the costs of the Community patent, chiefly that of translation, and to the judicial system. Under the Convention, a patent had to be translated into every Community language.[9] Interested parties felt that this requirement was excessive. Under the highly complex judicial system, national judges would have been able to declare a Community patent invalid with effect for the entire territory of the Community.[10] This aspect aroused the distrust of interested parties, who considered it to be a major element of legal uncertainty."

The draft Council Regulation on the Community patent, like the CPC itself, also   **26-10**
ran into difficulties and it was not enacted, despite reaching an important milestone on 7 March 2003, with the adoption of the Council's Common Political Approach.[11] At the Competitiveness Council of Ministers held at Brussels on 11 March 2004, the main sticking point was how to treat infringements of patents arising as a result of mistranslations.[12] In the absence of agreement, the Presidency famously concluded that it would "reflect on how to proceed further".[13]

European Patent Litigation Agreement ("EPLA")

Meanwhile, at the Paris Intergovernmental Conference on 25 June 1999, the   **26-11**
contracting states of the European Patent Organisation had set up a Working Party to present a draft text for an optional protocol to the European Patent Convention which would commit its signatory states to an integrated judicial system, including rules of procedure and a common appeal court. The draft protocol became known as the European Patent Litigation Agreement ("the EPLA"). It proposed a European Patent Court where European patents (that is, patents granted by the European Patent Office) could be litigated. The Agreement was to be voluntary in the sense that contracting states of the EPC could join the Agreement if they wished, but there was to be no obligation upon them to do so.

In January 2006, the Commission issued a Consultation Paper entitled "*Future*   **26-12**
Patent Policy in Europe". The Paper discussed a wide range of issues but two of the key issues were: (1) the EPLA, and (2) the creation of a Community patent. The Commission received over 2500 responses to its Consultation Paper and, in July 2006, it held an Open Hearing in Brussels to discuss them. A clear majority expressed a preference for the implementation of the EPLA in the near term with the Community patent being an objective for the longer term.

---

7   PA 2004 Sch.1 para.6.
8   COM (2000) 412.
9   CPC (1989) art.30(1) and (2).
10 CPC (1989), the Protocol on the Settlement of Litigation concerning the Infringement and Validity of Community Patents arts 15(2) and 19(1).
11 7159/03.
12 See MEMO/04/58 dated 12 March 2004.
13 See MEMO/04/58 dated 12 March 2004.

26-13   On 8 September 2006, Commissioner Charlie McCreevy, European Commissioner for Internal Market and Services, stated in a speech entitled "IPR—Next
Steps" delivered to the Economic and Finance Council of the EU in Helsinki[14] that
he believed the EPLA to be "a goal worth pursuing" and that he wanted to "involve
the Community in the EPLA negotiations and bring them to finality". Subsequently,
on 12 October 2006, the European Parliament passed a resolution supporting the
Commission's participation in the EPLA negotiations.[15]

26-14   However, in the following months, it became clear that some Member States of
the EU wanted a more EU-based scheme than that envisaged by the EPLA, including the creation of a Community patent as part of the scheme. Furthermore, on 1
February 2007 the Legal Service of the European Parliament produced an opinion
which concluded that compliance with the EPLA by Member States of the Community would prima facie constitute a breach of art.292 of the EC Treaty. The
EPLA itself was thereafter considered to be dead, although many of its provisions
were incorporated into the UPC Agreement.

26-15   In April 2007, the Commission published a compromise scheme in a Communication from the Commission to the European Parliament and the Council
entitled "*Enhancing the patent system in Europe*".[16] The compromise scheme was
neither the EPLA nor the EU-based scheme but rather a combination of the two. It
is that scheme which led to the creation of the UPC.

The European and EU Patents Court and the EU Patent[17]

26-16   After several years of discussions and negotiations, the Commission's
compromise scheme was divided into three parts. First, there was a draft agreement for the creation of a European and EU Patents Court to provide a forum where
European patents and EU patents can be litigated. Participation in the Agreement
was to be open to all contracting states of the EPC. Secondly, there was a draft EU
Regulation for the creation of an EU patent. Amongst other things, the draft Regulation set down the substantive patent law applicable to EU patents. Thirdly, there was
a separate draft EU Regulation relating to the language and translation issues. The
hiving-off of these issues into a separate agreement meant that the negotiations on
other matters could continue without being over-shadowed by the problem that had
defied solution for over 35 years. Furthermore, art.118 of the TFEU[18] provides that
the Council of the EU must act unanimously in "establishing language arrangements for the European intellectual property rights". So for this further reason, it
was desirable for the language and translation issues to be dealt with separately.

26-17   In July 2009 the Commission requested an opinion from the European Court of
Justice ("the ECJ") on the compatibility with the EC Treaty of the draft Agreement for the creation of the European and EU Patents Court. The court's opinion
was negative,[19] expressing the view that the draft Agreement was not compatible
with the EU Treaty and FEU Treaty.

---

14   SPEECH/06/485.
15   Resolution P6 TA(2006)0416, Future Action in the field of patents.
16   COM (2007) 165 final.
17   Following the entry into force of the Treaty of Lisbon on 1 December 2009, all references to "the
      Community" are now replaced by references to "the EU". Thus "the Community patent" was now
      referred to as "the EU patent".
18   In force since 1 December 2009, as part of the Treaty of Lisbon.
19   Opinion 1/09 delivered on 8 March 2011.

On 30 June 2010 the Commission adopted a proposal for a Council Regulation **26-18**
on the translation arrangements for the EU patent.[20] By November 2010 it was clear
that the required unanimity could not be achieved within a reasonable timescale.

Enhanced co-operation led to the UPC Agreement

In December 2010 Member States requested that the Commission should make **26-19**
a proposal to use the enhanced co-operation procedure to take the UPC project
forward. Only Spain and Italy did not join in the request. The Commission submitted a proposal to the Council for authorising enhanced co-operation, the European
Parliament gave its consent, and the Council adopted an Authorisation Decision on
10 March 2011. In April 2011 Spain and Italy mounted challenges to the Authorisation Decision, which were unsuccessful.[21] Also in April 2011 the Commission issued proposals for two Regulations, on substantive law and translation
arrangements. These became Regulations 1257/2012 and 1260/2012 (see below).

After a period of intense negotiations, there was agreement between the Heads **26-20**
of State and Governments at the EU Summit in June 2012. On 17 December 2012
the Regulations were adopted. Finally, the UPC Agreement was signed on 19
February 2013.[22] In the language of the UPC Agreement, what had previously been
referred to as a Community or EU patent is now called a European patent with
unitary effect.

The UPC Agreement is between participating EU Member States, not including **26-21**
Spain, Poland or Croatia. The EU itself is not a party and the UPC is not open to
states outside of the European Union. The UPC itself comes into force four months
after the 13th ratification of the Agreement, so long as this includes ratification by
the UK, France and Germany.

Steps after the UPC Agreement was signed

In March 2013 Spain launched challenges to Regulations 1257/2012 and 1260/ **26-22**
2012. Despite these challenges, work on setting up the UPC gathered pace after
March 2013. This work is co-ordinated by an intergovernmental Preparatory
Committee. The work includes finding appropriate premises, building an IT system,
setting up the court's administrative infrastructure, settling the Rules of Procedure,
and recruiting and training judges.

The Spanish challenges to the Regulations were rejected by the TFEU in judg- **26-23**
ments delivered on 5 May 2015.[23]

A protocol to the UPC Agreement was signed on 1 October 2015 to allow for **26-24**
various institutional organisational and financial aspects of the agreement to be
brought into force in advance of the rest of the agreement. This is in order to bring
the whole system into operation smoothly, for example by allowing for the recruit-
ment of judges in advance and the early registration of opt-outs. Also in October
2015 the Preparatory Committee adopted the Rules of Procedure of the UPC. At
about the same time the UK government secured premises at Aldgate for the

---

[20] COM (2010) 350 final.
[21] (C-274/11) and (C-295/11), 16 April 2013.
[22] EU Series 003/2013: Cm 8653.
[23] (C-146/13) and (C-147/13).

London divisions of the court. In early 2016 a draft statutory instrument to give effect to the UPC Agreement was laid before Parliament.

2.   UPC LEGAL INSTRUMENTS

The instruments setting up the UPC

26-25   The key instruments which set up the UPC system are the UPC Agreement, Regulations 1257/2012 and 1260/2012 and the rules for unitary patents adopted in the EPO.

The UPC Agreement

26-26   The UPC Agreement is an intergovernmental agreement signed by almost all EU Member States, including the UK. The Agreement was signed at Brussels on 19 February 2013 and established "a Unified Patent Court for the settlement of disputes relating to European patents and European patents with unitary effect".[24]

26-27   The UPC Agreement sets up the Unified Patent Court itself as an institution with various parts: a Court of First Instance[25], consisting of various divisions; a single Court of Appeal[26], situated in Luxembourg; and a Registry[27], also based on Luxembourg but with sub-registries in all divisions of the Court of First Instance. There is to be a patent mediation and arbitration centre[28] with seats in Ljubljana and Lisbon, and a training centre[29] in Budapest. There will be an Administrative Committee, a Budget Committee and an Advisory Committee.[30] An important role for the Administrative Committee is to appoint the judges for the court.[31] One of the roles of the Advisory Committee is to assist the Administrative Committee in judicial appointments. The UPC Agreement also provides for a Presidium composed of UPC judges which will be responsible for the management of the court.[32]

26-28   The 15 recitals to the UPC agreement provide an indication of the purposes for which the agreement was entered into. From these recitals emerge a number of purposes which can be identified. One is to further European integration, the establishment of the single market and free movement of goods and services (first recital). Another is to address difficulties experienced by small- and medium-sized enterprises in enforcing their patents and defending themselves against unfounded claims (second recital). A third purpose is to ensure the uniformity of the European legal order and the primacy of EU law (eighth, ninth, 10th, 11th, 12th and 13th recitals). The reason that this third purpose receives so much attention in the recitals is partly historical, given the earlier attempts at a Europe-wide patent litigation system such as the EPLA which were outside the EU legal system, and partly a reaction to the clear wish by some negotiating states to ensure that the UPC Agreement did not enlarge the jurisdiction of the CJEU over substantive patent law. A

---

[24]   art.1 UPC Agreement.
[25]   arts 5–8 UPC Agreement.
[26]   art.9 UPC Agreement.
[27]   art.10 UPC Agreement.
[28]   art.35 UPC Agreement.
[29]   art.19 UPC Agreement.
[30]   arts 11–14 UPC Agreement.
[31]   art.16 UPC Agreement.
[32]   art.15(3) of the UPC Statute.

fourth purpose of the agreement, of some importance, is to provide a court system in which European patents having unitary effect can be litigated (see the fourth recital).

Finally, a fifth purpose of the UPC Agreement is to create a single unified court **26-29** across the UPC states. This is an important objective of the agreement. It makes the UPC scheme distinctively different from the regime under the EPC. Although the EPC provides for the same substantive law of patents to apply across the contracting states, that convention says nothing about how the different national court systems should function in order to apply that law. The second recital to the UPC Agreement draws attention to the "significant variations between national court systems" as being something the agreement is intended to address and also relevant in this respect are the fifth, sixth and seventh recitals. By setting up a single unified court system common to all relevant states, the UPC aims to address this by producing a system which not only applies the same substantive law to patents but does so using the same procedure in all UPC states.

The substantive articles of the UPC Agreement are organised into five Parts and **26-30** within these Parts the articles are divided into Chapters. Part I contains general and institutional provisions, Part II (arts 36–39) deals with financial provisions and budgeting for the court, Part III is concerned with organisational and procedural matters, Part IV contains transitional provisions, and Part V contains final provisions. The important provisions for the practice of the court will be in Parts I and III.

Part I Chapters I–III (arts 1–19) deals with general and institutional provisions **26-31** and with judges.

In Part I Chapter IV art.20 of the UPC agreement provides for the primacy of **26-32** European Union law and art.21 for references to the CJEU from the UPC. Article 22 provides a form of *Francovich* damages. Sources of law are set out in art.24. They run in a hierarchy starting from Union law (including Regs 1257/2012 and 1260/2012), and then running down to the UPC Agreement, the EPC, other applicable international agreements, ending finally with national law.

In Part I Chapter V arts 25–28 provide for a law of direct and indirect infringe- **26-33** ment and exceptions to infringement. The provisions for direct (art.25) and indirect (art.26) infringement have the same effect as the corresponding provisions in the 1977 Act, which are themselves in accordance with the relevant parts of the EPC and CPC respectively. Article 27 provides for exceptions to infringement which essentially correspond to the defences available under the 1977 Act in s.60(5) but includes at art.27(k) a defence relating to decompilation and interoperability under Directive 2009/24/EC.[33] Article 28 provides that a right based on a prior use (in the UK a defence under s.64 of the 1977 Act) has the same effect under the UPC Agreement. Article 29 deals with exhaustion and art.30 provides that supplementary protection certificates will work in the same way in the UPC as they do in the national courts. Notable by its omission from the UPC Agreement is any law of accessory liability. The application of national law in this area may give rise to complicated conflict of laws problems before the UPC.

Part I Chapter VI (arts 31–34) deal with the court's international jurisdiction and **26-34** with the competence of the court. These matters are addressed below. Part I Chapter

---

[33] Oddly the draft Statutory Instrument to give effect to the UPC Agreement in the UK (as it stands at the time of writing) appears to contemplate amending the 1977 Act in such a way that national (GB) patents will not be subject to this defence while European and unitary patents will be.

VII provides for the mediation and arbitration centres. While patents can be amended or revoked before the courts of the UPC, that power does not extend to the mediation or arbitration centres.[34]

26-35   Part III (organisation and procedure) is divided into five Chapters. Part III Chapter 1 deals with general provisions, starting with art.40. This article provides for the Statute. General principles applying to the procedure before the court are provided for in arts 42–48. Article 41 provides for Rules of Procedure to be adopted by the Administrative Committee. These matters are addressed below.

26-36   Part III Chapter II deals with the languages of proceedings. The details of the language regime in the UPC have been controversial in some quarters and a complete statement of how the regime will work cannot be made until the Rules of Procedure are finalised. Nevertheless, some aspects are clear. Proceedings in the UPC will be conducted in a language of the proceedings (arts 49 and 50). In the local and regional divisions that language could be an official language of the state hosting the relevant division.[35] In addition to the official language of a state, a state may designate one or more of the official languages of the EPO (i.e. French, German or English) as the language of proceedings in their local or regional division.[36] It is expected that a number of continental European states will take advantage of this option and designate one or more EPO official languages as a possible language of proceedings even though it is not an official language of the state. The language in which the patent was granted may also be used on grounds of convenience and fairness.[37]

26-37   In the Central Division the language of proceedings will be the language in which the patent was granted.[38] In the Court of Appeal the language will generally be the language of the proceedings at first instance[39] but there are exceptions.[40]

26-38   Part III Chapter III (arts 52–55) deals with proceedings before the court, Chapter IV (arts 56–72) deals with the court's powers, Chapter V (arts 73–75) deals with appeals, and Chapter VI (arts 76–82) deals with decisions and enforcement. These matters are addressed below.

The Statute of the UPC

26-39   The Statute of the UPC forms Annex I to the UPC Agreement. It lays down details of the organisation and functioning of the court, including the appointment of judges and provisions about the Registry. The Statute contains the institutional and financial arrangements for the UPC as a functioning institution. By art.40(2) of the UPC Agreement, the Statute may be amended by a decision of the Administrative Committee as long as the amendment does not contradict the UPC Agreement.

---

[34] art.35 of the UPC Agreement.
[35] art.49(1) of the UPC Agreement.
[36] art.49(2) of the UPC Agreement.
[37] art.49(4) and (5) of the UPC Agreement.
[38] art.49(6) of the UPC Agreement.
[39] art.50(1) of the UPC Agreement.
[40] art.50(2)–(3) of the UPC Agreement: by agreement or in exceptional circumstances.

The Unitary Patent Regulation

The Unitary Patent Regulation (Reg.1257/2012)[41] provides for the creation of **26-40** unitary patents. They will be granted by the EPO.[42] In practice before the EPO, an applicant will be able to apply for a unitary patent by making an appropriate designation of the same kind as a designation of states in which a conventional European patent is applied for.

Unitary patents take effect as a single patent providing uniform protection and **26-41** equal effect in all participating Member States of the UPC.[43] Article 5(3) of the Regulation provides that the definition of what amounts to an act of infringement (including exceptions to infringement) applicable to a unitary patent, is the definition provided for in the law applicable to unitary patents in the participating Member State whose national law is applicable to the unitary patent as an object of property in accordance with art.7 (see para.26-43).

Unitary patents can only be amended, transferred, revoked or lapse in respect of **26-42** all states at once. However, they can be licensed in the same way as national patents (for individual states or parts of state). The provision for exhaustion applies across all participating Member States as a whole.[44] The Regulation is expressed to be without prejudice to competition law and the law relating to unfair competition.[45]

As an object of property, a unitary patent is treated as a national patent of a **26-43** particular state defined in art.7 of the Regulation. The article contains a general rule, that the state is the one in which the applicant for the patent had their residence on the date of filing, as long as it is a state within which the patent has unitary effect. There are provisions for cases in which this general rule does not apply and rules for joint applicants.

The Unitary Patent Translation Arrangements Regulation

The Unitary Patent Translation Arrangements Regulation (Reg.1260/2012)[46] **26-44** deals with languages for unitary patents. The general rule is that once the specification for the European patent is published in the appropriate language of the proceedings before the EPO,[47] no further translation will be required in order to bring the patent into effect. However, in the event of a dispute the alleged infringer will be entitled to require the patentee to produce a full translation into a relevant local language.[48] The relevant local language will be an official language of the state in which the alleged infringement took place or the state in which the alleged infringer is domiciled. There are also provisions for further translations to be provided during a transitional period.[49]

---

[41] 31 December 2012 O.J. EU L 361/1.
[42] Reg.1257/2012 arts 9–13. The provisions deal with grant of unitary patents and with renewal fees.
[43] Reg.1257/2012 art.3(2) and art.5.
[44] Reg.1257/2012 art.6.
[45] Reg.1257/2012 art.15.
[46] 31 December 2012 O.J. EU 361/89.
[47] EPC art.14 and in particular art.14(6).
[48] Reg.1260/2012 art.4.
[49] Reg.1260/2012 art.6.

EPO rules relating to Unitary Patent Protection

26-45   In a decision on 15 December 2015 the Select Committee of the Administrative Council of the European Patent Organisation adopted a set of Rules relating to Unitary Patent Protection.[50] They will enter into force on the same date as Regs 1257/2012 and 1260/2012. These EPO rules make the necessary provisions to handle unitary patents and applications for unitary patents in the EPO.

3. UPC PATENTS, COURTS AND JUDGES

Which patents and which cases are within the jurisdiction of the UPC

26-46   As art.1 of the UPC agreement indicates, the UPC deals both with unitary patents and with traditional European patents, that is to say European bundle patents. Subject to the opt-out arrangements, any existing European bundle patent may be litigated in the UPC while opted out patents may be litigated in the existing national court systems. Unitary patents can only be litigated in the UPC.[51] The limitation period for proceedings before the UPC is five years (art.72).

26-47   Article 34 provides that the territorial scope of a decision of the UPC relating to a European patent (as opposed to a unitary patent) covers the territory of those contracting Member States for which the European patent has effect. Multiple national designations of the same European patent can and no doubt will be tried in the UPC at the same time.

26-48   Article 31 provides for the international jurisdiction of the court to be established in accordance with Reg.1215/2012[52] (also known as the "Brussels Regulation (recast)") or, where applicable, the Lugano Convention. Dealing with the detailed provisions of the Brussels Regulation (recast) and Lugano Convention is beyond the scope of this chapter. EU Regulation 542/2014[53] amended the Brussels Regulation (recast), save in relation to Denmark, in order to deal with the UPC as a court common to several Member States.[54]

26-49   Article 32 provides for the types of cases which fall within the exclusive competence of the UPC. The full list in art.31(1) is:

(a)   actions for actual or threatened infringements of patents and supplementary protection certificates and related defences, including counterclaims concerning licences;

(b)   actions for declarations of non-infringement of patents and supplementary protection certificates;

(c)   actions for provisional and protective measures and injunctions;

(d)   actions for revocation of patents and for declaration of invalidity of supplementary protection certificates;

---

[50] SC/D 1/15 e.

[51] By the combined effect of the definitions in art.2, the terms of art.32 (exclusive competence) and the fact that opt-outs in art.83 only apply to bundle patents.

[52] 20 December 2012 O.J. EU L 351.

[53] 29 May 2014 O.J. EU L 163.

[54] It should be noted that Denmark has since 18 January 2007 adopted parallel arrangements having the same effect as the Brussels Regulation. In relation to the recast Regulation, see the Agreement between the European Union and the Kingdom of Denmark on jurisdiction and the recognition and enforcement of judgments in civil and commercial matters published in the Official Journal on 10 July 2015 at L-182/1.

(e)   counterclaims for revocation of patents and for declaration of invalidity of supplementary protection certificates;

(f)   actions for damages or compensation derived from the provisional protection conferred by a published European patent application;

(g)   actions relating to the use of the invention prior to the granting of the patent or to the right based on prior use of the invention;

(h)   actions for compensation for licences on the basis of art.8 of Reg. (EU) No.1257/2012; and

(i)   actions concerning decisions of the European Patent Office in carrying out the tasks referred to in art.9 of Reg. (EU) No.1257/2012.

Article 32(2) provides that national courts shall remain competent for actions **26-50** which do not fall within the exclusive competence of the UPC. It appears therefore that entitlement disputes, including disputes to the ownership of unitary patents, can be dealt with by the national courts.

Opt outs

It will be possible to opt-out of European patents from the UPC (art.83 UPC **26-51** Agreement). Unitary patents cannot be opted out since they have no other court in which they could be tried. The opt-out will be available in the transitional period (an extendable period of seven years). RoP r.5[55] deals with lodging applications for opt-outs and withdrawal of an opt-out. As a result of the October 2015 Protocol, the opt-out mechanism will be in place before the UPC actually starts, allowing anyone who wishes to do so to make sure they have opted-out from the outset. A fee for opt-out had been provisionally set at €80 (as of 5 May 2015) but most recently it has been decided that there be no opt out fee.[56]

The courts of the UPC

The UPC will have first instance local divisions in most signatory states, includ- **26-52** ing the UK, and a central division split into three parts (with the seat of the central division in Paris and then two sections in Munich and London).[57] The UK Government have indicated that London will host a local division of the UPC in addition to the section of the central division. Whether there will be another local division in the UK is not clear. The UPC Court of Appeal will be in Luxembourg.[58]

Article 33 of the UPC Agreement deals with allocation of cases between the divi- **26-53** sions of the first instance courts. The scheme is complicated because different types of action are subject to different rules. The main rules are these:

(a)   actions for infringement (actual or threatened) will generally be started in an applicable local or regional division if there is one;[59]

(b)   actions for infringement can also be started in the central division but only in certain circumstances (see below);

---

55   RoP 18th Draft.
56   Agreed Rules on Court fees and recoverable costs, Preparatory Committee, 25 February 2016.
57   art.7(2) and Annex II of the UPC Agreement.
58   art.9(5) of the UPC Agreement.
59   art.33(1)(a) of the UPC Agreement.

(c)   actions for provisional or protective measures must be started in an applicable local or regional division if there is one;[60]

(d)   a party sued for infringement in a local or regional division may counterclaim for revocation in that division;[61]

(e)   in appropriate cases multiple defendants can be sued in the same action;[62]

(f)   actions for revocation must be brought in the central division as long as no relevant infringement action is in existence already;[63]

(g)   actions for declarations of non-infringement must be brought in the central division as long as no relevant infringement action is in existence already[64]; and

(h)   parties can agree to bring any proceedings (except the special cases about decisions of the EPO[65]) before any division including the central division.[66]

26-54   The main rules determining which local or regional division in which an action for infringement can be brought are that such cases have to be brought either before a division for a UPC state in which the actual or threatened infringement has occurred or may occur[67] or a division for a UPC state in which the defendant has its residence or principal place of business.[68] These rules also apply to provisional or protective measures.

26-55   Further rules determining the correct division are as follows:

(a)   In the absence of a residence or principal place of business in any UPC state, a defendant may be sued in a local or regional division in a UPC state where it has any place of business.[69]

(b)   For actions for infringement or for provisional or protective measures applicable to a UPC state which has no local division and does not participate in a regional division, those actions must be brought in the central division.[70]

(c)   For defendants with no residence or any place of business (principal or otherwise) within the UPC states, they can be sued where the infringement occurs under art.33(1)(a) or in the central division.[71]

26-56   For cases to be started in the central division, the distribution of cases between Paris, Munich and London depends on the subject matter of the patent defined using the WIPO International Patent Classifications.[72] Class F (broadly mechanical engineering) is allocated to Munich, classes A and C (broadly life sciences, chemistry and metallurgy) are allocated to London and the rest are in Paris. Rule 17(3) of the 18th draft of the Rules of Procedure addresses distribution of cases, for

---

[60]   art.33(1) referring to art.32(1)(c) of the UPC Agreement.

[61]   art.33(3) of the UPC Agreement.

[62]   art.33(1)(b) of the UPC Agreement. The action has to relate to the same alleged infringement and there must be a commercial relationship between the defendants.

[63]   art.33(4) of the UPC Agreement.

[64]   art.33(4) of the UPC Agreement.

[65]   art.32(1)(i) of the UPC Agreement.

[66]   art.33(7) of the UPC Agreement.

[67]   art.33(1)(a) of the UPC Agreement.

[68]   art.33(1)(b) of the UPC Agreement.

[69]   art.33(1)(b) of the UPC Agreement.

[70]   art.33(1), last sentence of the UPC Agreement. Note that as paginated in English, the last sentence of this article appears on the next page of the official text.

[71]   art.33(1), penultimate sentence of the UPC Agreement. Note that as paginated in English, the penultimate sentence of this article appears on the next page of the official text.

[72]   See Annex II of the UPC Agreement.

example dealing with patents with more than one classification and actions with more than one patent.

The rule providing that actions for revocation and declarations of non-infringement may be brought in the central division only applies if a relevant infringement action in a local or regional division is not already in existence. A relevant infringement action is one between the same parties on the same patent. If a relevant infringement action exists, then the action for revocation or a declaration must be brought in the same local or regional division.[73]   **26-57**

The circumstances in which an action for infringement may be started in the central division are the following: **26-58**

    (a) if a revocation action on the same patent is already before the central division[74];

    (b) if the UPC state does not host a local division or participate in a regional division[75]; or

    (c) if the defendant has no presence in the UPC states.[76]

The permission to bring infringement cases centrally if the UPC state does not have a local or regional division presumably only has to be satisfied for either the rule about the place in which infringement occurs (art.33(1)(a)) or the rule about residence or place of business of the defendant (art.33(1)(b)). In other words, if the alleged infringements are taking place in a UPC state with no local or regional division then the action can be brought in the central division even though the defendant may be resident in a UPC state which does have a local or regional division (and vice versa). Otherwise the ability of the claimant to choose which court to commence proceedings is unduly impaired.   **26-59**

Once cases have been started there are rules governing transfer. When a counterclaim for revocation is filed in an infringement action in a local or regional division, the court has the option of allowing the whole case (infringement action plus counterclaim) to go forward but could also transfer either the whole case or just the counterclaim to the central division.[77] This could lead to bifurcation (see below).   **26-60**

Actions and counterclaims for revocation can be brought without a party being required to start opposition proceedings before the EPO.[78] Notably in the UPC a party can bring an action for revocation on the day a patent is granted and expect the proceedings to get going immediately. This is unlike the EPO opposition procedure which will not start processing an opposition until the end of the nine-month period within which EPO oppositions can be commenced.[79] In such a case, if the party filed both a UPC revocation claim and EPO opposition, by the time the EPO opposition procedure has started, the UPC revocation claim is likely to be well on the way to a trial.   **26-61**

---

[73] art.33(4) of the UPC Agreement. See also arts 33(5) and 33(6) for what happens if a relevant infringement action then starts.

[74] art.33(5) of the UPC Agreement.

[75] art.33(1), last sentence of the UPC Agreement. Note that as paginated in English, the last sentence of this article appears on the next page of the official text.

[76] art.33(1), penultimate sentence of the UPC Agreement. Note that as paginated in English, the penultimate sentence of this article appears on the next page of the official text.

[77] art.33(3) of the UPC Agreement.

[78] art.33(8) of the UPC Agreement.

[79] art.99(1) of the EPC.

The judges of the UPC

26-62 The court will have a pool of judges composed of both legally qualified judges and technically qualified judges.[80] Legally qualified judges possess the qualifications required for appointment to judicial offices in a UPC state[81] while technically qualified judges have a university degree and proven expertise in a field of technology (and proven knowledge of civil law and procedure relevant in patent litigation).[82] The allocation of judges will be based on their legal or technical expertise, linguistic skills and relevant experience.[83]

26-63 Both kinds of judge can be either full-time or part-time.[84] Being a judge of the UPC does not prevent the exercise of other judicial functions at a national level.[85] Therefore it may be possible for a legally qualified judge to retain their status as a national judge and at the same time be a "full time" first instance judge of the UPC.

26-64 Local divisions will sit in panels of three legally qualified judges[86] with a fourth technical qualified judge in certain circumstances.[87] The panels are always multi-national in nature. There will be at least one legally qualified judge who is a national of the relevant state and at least one legally qualified judge who is a national of a different state but the nationality of the third judge depends on a criterion based on the number of patent cases tried in that state over time.[88] The rule for regional divisions is similar in that there will be two legally qualified judges from the region while the third legally qualified judge must come from outside the region.[89] The panel in the central division consists of two legally qualified judges from different states and a technically qualified judge with qualifications and experience in the field of technology concerned.[90]

26-65 The parties will always have the option of agreeing to have their case tried at first instance by a single judge.[91]

26-66 The Court of Appeal will sit as a panel of five judges, three legally qualified judges from three different states, and two technically qualified with experience in the field of technology concerned.[92]

26-67 In both the Court of First Instance and the Court of Appeal, one judge of the panel shall act as judge-rapporteur.[93] The role of the judge-rapporteur is discussed below.

[80] art.18 of the UPC Agreement.
[81] art.15(2) of the UPC Agreement.
[82] art.15(3) of the UPC Agreement.
[83] art.18(3), UPC Agreement.
[84] This is never stated in terms in the UPC Agreement but art.3 of the Statute makes it clear.
[85] art.17(3) of the UPC Agreement.
[86] art.8(1) of the UPC Agreement.
[87] art.8(5) of the UPC Agreement. The circumstances include by request of the parties or the judges and if validity is put in issue (art.33(3)(a)).
[88] art.8(2) and (3) of the UPC Agreement.
[89] art.8(4) of the UPC Agreement.
[90] art.8(6) of the UPC Agreement.
[91] art.8(7) of the UPC Agreement.
[92] art.9 of the UPC Agreement.
[93] arts 19(5) and 21(4) of the Statute.

4. PROCEDURE BEFORE THE UPC

Parties and representation

The UPC Agreement deals with who may be a party to proceedings before the **26-68**
court in arts 46 and 47. The main provisions are these. Any natural or legal person
or equivalent body able to initiate proceedings in accordance with its national law
can do so before the UPC. The patentee is entitled to bring proceedings. Exclusive
licensees can bring actions as long as the patentee could do so. Non-exclusive
licensees can also bring actions as long as the licence permits it. Licensees must
give notice to the patentee and the patentee is entitled to join in the proceedings. If
validity is in issue, the patentee obviously should be a party and this is achieved by
providing that any action or counterclaim for revocation has to be against the
patentee. Article 47(6) provides that any other person who "is concerned by a patent" may bring actions in accordance with the Rules of Procedure. This rule may
prohibit actions for revocation brought by a straw man, since such a claimant would
not truly be concerned by the patent.

The UPC Agreement deals with representation in art.48. The effect of the article **26-69**
is that parties must be represented by an appropriate professional. The UPC will
have no litigants in person. Any lawyer authorised to practice in a UPC state may
represent a party in the UPC. No distinction is made relating to the location of divisions and so lawyers from one UPC state may represent clients before the local or
regional divisions in other UPC states.

Also under art.48, European Patent Attorneys entitled to act before the EPO **26-70**
under art.134 EPC may also represent parties before the UPC if they have "appropriate" qualifications such as a European Patent Litigation Certificate. The current proposals relating to existing European Patent Attorneys are expansive, in that
the majority of existing UK qualified European Patent Attorneys are likely to fall
within the provisions allowing them to represent parties before the UPC.

Article 48(5) provides for a wide form of legal privilege for all representatives, **26-71**
including lawyers and European Patent Attorneys. The privilege includes both attorney client and litigation privilege.[94]

Proceedings before the UPC

The UPC Agreement contains articles which provide for the following general **26-72**
principles which will be applicable to all proceedings before the court. The court
will deal with litigation in ways which are proportionate to the importance and
complexity of the dispute.[95] The court will ensure that the rules, procedures and
remedies will be used in a fair and equitable manner and do not distort
competition.[96] The court will actively manage cases in accordance with the Rules
of Procedure without impairing the freedom of the parties to determine the subject
matter of, and the supporting evidence for, their case.[97] The proceedings will be
public. That is subject to the court's power to make the proceedings confidential if

[94] See the 18th draft RoP rr.287 and 288.
[95] art.42(1) of the UPC Agreement.
[96] art.42(2) of the UPC Agreement.
[97] art.43 of the UPC Agreement.

appropriate, to the extent necessary.[98] Parties have a right to a hearing before an order is made unless this is incompatible with effective enforcement.[99]

26-73   The 18th draft Rules of Procedure ("RoP") has a significant preamble, as follows:

"1.   The Court shall conduct proceedings in accordance with the Agreement, the Statute and these Rules. In the event of a conflict between the provisions of the Agreement and/or the Statute on the one hand and of the Rules on the other hand, the provisions of the Agreement and/or the Statute shall prevail.
2.   The Rules shall be applied and interpreted in accordance with Articles 41(3), 42 and 52(1) of the Agreement on the basis of the principles of proportionality, flexibility, fairness and equity.
3.   Proportionality shall be ensured by giving due consideration to the nature and complexity of each action and its importance.
4.   Flexibility shall be ensured by applying all procedural rules in a flexible and balanced manner with the required level of discretion for the judges to organise the proceedings in the most efficient and cost effective manner.
5.   Fairness and equity shall be ensured by having regard to the legitimate interests of all parties.
6.   In accordance with these principles, the Court shall apply and interpret the Rules in a way which shall ensure decisions of the highest quality.
7.   In accordance with these principles, proceedings shall be conducted in a way which will normally allow the final oral hearing on the issues of infringement and validity at first instance to take place within one year whilst recognising that complex actions may require more time and procedural steps and simple actions less time and fewer procedural steps. Decisions on costs and/or damages may take place at the same time or as soon as practicable thereafter. Case management shall be organised in accordance with these objectives. Parties shall cooperate with the Court and set out their full case as early as possible in the proceedings.
8.   The Court shall endeavour to ensure consistent application and interpretation of these Rules by all first instance divisions and the Court of Appeal. Due consideration shall also be given to this objective in any decision concerning leave to appeal against procedural orders."

26-74   The seventh and eight preambles contain some significant points. The seventh preamble identifies objectives which case management will be organised to achieve. The main one is to have the final oral hearing on the issues of infringement and validity at first instance to take place within one year. This is clearly achievable—after all the Patents Court and IPEC are both able to do this for many cases—but it can be challenging. The preamble expressly recognises this by referring to the idea that complex actions may require more time and procedural steps, whereas simple actions may require less time and fewer procedural steps.

26-75   The seventh preamble also refers to the idea that parties will co-operate with the court and set out their full case as early as possible. From an English perspective, although the traditional mode of conducting patent litigation in the Patents Court does not involve setting out a party's full case at the start, experience in the IPEC demonstrates that this can be done successfully.

26-76   The eighth preamble is aimed at ensuring that the UPC operates as a unified court system. This is a reflection of one of the purposes of the UPC, reflected in the second recital to the UPC Agreement. If the English local division of the UPC remains just like the Patents Court while the local divisions in France, Germany and the Netherlands remain just like their existing national courts, the UPC will not be a single unified court. This eighth recital recognises that the Court of Appeal will have a role to play in aligning the procedures applied in the first instance courts so that, for example, different divisions do not develop idiosyncratic local practices. Appeals from procedural decisions made at first instance (including case management decisions) are possible but might only reach the Court of Appeal along with

[98]   art.45 of the UPC Agreement.
[99]   art.56 of the UPC Agreement.

an appeal against the main decision made at trial. By then it may be too late. In order to further the objective articulated in the eighth preamble, the Court of Appeal may need to give permission to hear such a procedural appeal at an earlier stage. This is referred to in the 18th draft Rules of Procedure as a "discretionary review".[100]

Following some general matters in rr.1–9, the rules in the 18th draft Rules of Procedure are grouped into six parts. Part 1 deals with the first instance court procedure, Part 2 deals with evidence, Part 3 concerns provisional measures, Part 4 deals with procedures before the Court of Appeal, Part 5 consists of general provisions, and Part 6 with fees and legal aid. No general distinction is drawn in the Rules of Procedure between the procedures applicable in local, regional or central divisions.   **26-77**

The proceedings before both the Court of First Instance and the Court of Appeal consist of three phases: a written procedure, an interim procedure and an oral procedure.[101] The written procedure involves the filing and exchange of written pleadings by all parties. When a case starts it is assigned to a panel of judges and one of them is appointed to be the judge-rapporteur for the case.[102]   **26-78**

Court fees will be due. They consist of a fixed fee, combined with a value based fee above a pre-defined level.[103] The fees are set by a table referred to in r.370 of the Rules of Procedure.[104] The fees will be much higher than court fees in English courts but they will be broadly comparable to court fees levied in Germany. For example, there is to be a fixed fee of €11,000 for an infringement action together with a further value based fee ranging from zero for infringement actions with a value below €500,000, up to a fee of €325,000 for actions with a value over €350 million. Fees may be reduced in various circumstances. The fees will be the UPC's main source of funding and by the end of its first seven years the court is expected to be self-financing.[105]   **26-79**

The written procedure at first instance (Part 1 Chapter 1 of the Rules of Procedure)

The Rules of Procedure ("RoP") set out the details and distinguish between the different forms of action (infringement[106], revocation[107], declaration of non-infringement,[108] etc.). However, although the RoP contains different provisions for each form of action, the essential structure of the written procedure is the same in each case. The rules set out for infringement actions are often applied mutatis mutandis by the provisions relating to other forms of action.   **26-80**

The action begins with the filing and service of a Statement of Claim. The defendant may serve a Statement of Defence. In an infringement action the State-   **26-81**

---

[100] RoP 18th Draft rr.220(3) and (4). See also r.333(5) which provides that a decision by the first instance panel on a review of a case management decision of the judge-rapporteur is a procedural decision for the purposes of r.220(2), which therefore brings it within the ambit of the discretionary review procedure before the Court of Appeal.

[101] art.52 of the UPC Agreement.

[102] RoP 18th Draft r.18 for infringement actions, applied mutatis mutandis for other actions at first instance. Rule 231 has the same effect in the Court of Appeal.

[103] art.36 of the UPC Agreement.

[104] Agreed Rules on Court Fees and Recoverable Costs, Preparatory Committee, 25 February 2016.

[105] art.37(4) of the UPC Agreement.

[106] RoP 18th Draft rr.12–41.

[107] RoP 18th Draft rr.42–60.

[108] RoP 18th Draft rr.61–74.

ment of Defence can include a Counterclaim for Revocation. The claimant can reply with a Defence to the Counterclaim for Revocation and Reply to the Statement of Defence. The defendant may retort with a Rejoinder to the Reply.

26-82   The rules require the statements to set out the party's case in detail. For an infringement action[109] this will include instances of the alleged infringements or threatened infringements relied on, identification of which patent claims are alleged to be infringed and an explanation why the facts amount to infringement. The latter will include arguments of law and where appropriate an explanation of the proposed claim interpretation.[110]

26-83   In general what is required in written pleadings by the RoP is very similar to what is required in the IPEC. This includes providing evidence which will be relied on if it is available and an indication of any further evidence which will be offered in support.[111] This means, for example, that a party need not produce an expert's report at the outset but can indicate in its statement that such a report will be offered in support in due course.

26-84   If disputes arise during the written procedure, they will be resolved by the judge-rapporteur. Following exchange of written pleadings the judge-rapporteur shall inform the parties of the date on which the written procedure will be closed.[112] Further written pleadings may be permitted, on a reasoned request lodged before that date.[113]

Transfer under art.33 of the UPC Agreement and bifurcation

26-85   One question which may arise is whether the action should be transferred to a different division under art.33 of the UPC Agreement. This is decided by the panel of judges and is to be dealt with as soon as practicable after the closure of the written procedure or earlier if appropriate.[114] It could lead to the bifurcation of the issues of infringement and validity. In an infringement action before a local division in which the defendant has brought a counterclaim for revocation, it is open to the panel to transfer the revocation action to the central division and if taking that course it may then proceed with the infringement action or it may suspend it, pending resolution of the validity issue by the central division.

26-86   The possibility of bifurcation of patent proceedings was and remains one of the controversial elements in the negotiations concerning the UPC Agreement and the RoP. The extent to which it occurs in practice, and the consequences if it does, remain to be seen. What is clear however is that bifurcation is possible in the UPC and in that respect the UPC is no different from the English courts, which can already manage a case so as to decide these issues separately if appropriate (see paras 19-342 to 19-347). A lesson from the IPEC is that patent cases can be dealt with in a timely and cost effective manner without any need to try the issues of infringement and validity separately.

26-87   Rule 118(2) deals with a decision on the merits in infringement proceedings by a local or regional division when a revocation action is pending between the same parties before the central division, e.g. following bifurcation or an opposition is

---

[109] RoP 18th Draft r.13.
[110] RoP 18th Draft r.13(1)(n).
[111] RoP 18th Draft, e.g. for the infringement Statement of Claim r.13(1)(m).
[112] RoP 18th Draft, for the infringement action r.35.
[113] RoP 18th Draft, for the infringement action r.36.
[114] RoP 18th Draft, for the infringement action r.37.

pending before the EPO. The local or regional division:

"(a) may render its decision on the merits of the infringement claim, including its orders, under the condition subsequent pursuant to Article 56(1) of the Agreement that the patent is not held to be wholly or partially invalid by the final decision in the revocation proceedings or a final decision of the European Patent Office or under any other term or condition; or

(b) may stay the infringement proceedings pending a decision in the revocation procedure or a decision of the European Patent Office and shall stay the infringement proceedings if it is of the view that there is a high likelihood that the relevant claims of the patent will be held to be invalid on any ground by the final decision in the revocation proceedings or of the European Patent Office where such decision of the European Patent Office may be expected to be given rapidly."

The reference in r.118(2)(a) to a "condition subsequent" means that, for example, **26-88** an injunction granted following the infringement trial would be made expressly subject to the future revocation of the patent. It is difficult to imagine why a local or regional division in those circumstances would not make the order conditional in that sense. Rule 118(4) permits a party to apply to the court within two months if the patent is revoked when an order under r.118(2)(a) has been made.

Although its place in the rules suggests that the reference in r.118(2)(b) to a stay **26-89** could be to a stay ordered at the end of an infringement trial, nevertheless it clearly has a wider ambit since in a suitable case such a stay could be ordered earlier in the proceedings (see, e.g. art.33(3)(b)).

Provisional and protective measures

Provisional and protective measures can be obtained in the UPC in appropriate **26-90** cases (arts 60–62). The measures include interim injunctions, asset freezing orders and evidence preservation orders, including those like the French "saisie" which involve inspection of a defendant's premises and removal of evidence. The rules governing these measures are in the RoP Part 2 Chapter 4 and 5, and the RoP Part 3 (rr.192–213). Where appropriate the order may be made without notice to the defendant.

The court also has to power to make evidence gathering orders. It can order a **26-91** party to produce evidence (art.59 of the UPC Agreement and RoP r.170(3)(a)). The court can order experiments (r.201) including experiments to be conducted in the presence of the parties and their experts,[115] and letters rogatory (r.202).

The interim procedure at first instance (Part 1 Chapter 2 of the Rules of Procedure)

The interim procedure is governed by rr.101–110 (see also art.52(2) of the UPC **26-92** Agreement). The purpose of the interim procedure is for the judge-rapporteur to make all necessary preparations for the oral hearing.

Various procedural remedies familiar to English lawyers are available in the **26-93** interim procedure of the UPC, for example security for costs (art.69(4) and rr.158–159). Mentioned already are the UPC's powers to order a party to produce evidence (art.59 and r.196) and to inspect premises (art.60 and r.199). The UPC's power to require production of evidence is wide enough to include the power to require one party to search for and produce documents relevant to an issue. Thus disclosure (discovery) of documents in the UPC is possible but will not be automatic and will

---

[115] RoP r.201(6).

be kept under the control of the court, as in the IPEC. In a manner similar to CPR Ord.31.22, under the RoP r.196(2) the use to which evidence ordered to be produced can be put will normally only be for the proceedings.

26-94 Importantly the RoP include provisions whereby compliance with orders can be made subject to sanctions (e.g. rr.190(4) and 196(3)). The RoP make clear that the court can make compliance with an order within a time limit subject to a sanction of judgment by default (rr.355–357). The rules provide expressly that certain orders can be enforced in this way: they are orders to provide clarification, answer questions or produce evidence in preparation for the interim conference (r.103), and orders for security for costs (r.158(4)). Thus the UPC court is able to enforce procedural compliance with a scheme similar to the English "unless order".

26-95 The interim procedure is likely to include an interim conference (rr.104–106). In order to prepare for the oral hearing, the aim of the interim conference is to enable the judge-rapporteur to perform a number of tasks, very similar to the tasks of the enterprise judge sitting at the case management conference in the IPEC. The main tasks defined in r.104 are to:

"(a)   identify main issues and determine which relevant facts are in dispute;
(b)   where appropriate, clarify the position of the parties as regards those issues and facts;
(c)   establish a schedule for the further progress of the proceedings;
    [...]
(e)   where appropriate, issue orders regarding production of further pleadings, documents, experts (including court experts), experiments, inspections, further written evidence, the matters to be the subject of oral evidence and the scope of questions to be put to the witnesses;
(f)   where appropriate, but only in the presence of the parties, hold preparatory discussions with witnesses and experts with a view to properly preparing for the oral hearing;
(g)   make any other decision or order as he deems necessary for the preparation of the oral hearing including, after consultation with the presiding judge, an order for a separate hearing of witnesses and experts before the panel;
(h)   set a date for any separate hearing pursuant to point (g) of this Rule and confirm the date for the oral hearing;
    [...]"

26-96 When considered by comparison with the procedure in IPEC, these matters are fairly self-explanatory. Just as in the IPEC, the sort of evidence employed in English courts will be available in the UPC but it will be kept under tight judicial control. One notable option is to arrange for a separate hearing to deal with oral testimony from witnesses or experts. This may lead to a trial process akin to that of the Patents Court in which the main oral submissions (which take place in closing) often occur at a date a few days after the hearing of the witnesses. The RoP allow for a scheme of this kind to be organised.

26-97 Also in r.104 are some aspects of the UPC interim conference which are not directly concerned with preparation for the oral hearing but are reasonably self-explanatory:

"*[...]*
(d)   explore with the parties the possibilities to settle the dispute or to make use of the facilities of the Centre;
    [...]
(i)   decide the value of the particular dispute which value may, in exceptional cases, differ as between the parties depending upon the parties' individual circumstances;
(j)   order the parties to submit, in advance of the decision at the oral hearing, a preliminary estimate of the legal costs that they will seek to recover.
    [...]"

The judge-rapporteur may refer any matter to the full panel.[116] A party dissatisfied with any decisions or orders of the judge-rapporteur can refer the matter to the panel for a review under r.333.[117] Decisions of the panel may be appealed to the Court of Appeal provided leave is given (see para.26-76).   **26-98**

The interim procedure will be closed when the judge-rapporteur considers the case is ready for the oral hearing.[118]   **26-99**

Evidence in the UPC (Part 2 of the Rules of Procedure)

Article 53 UPC Agreement and Part 2 of the Rules of Procedure deal with evidence. These provisions show that the UPC has an open approach to evidence in the sense that anything which would be considered admissible evidence in an English court will be admissible in the UPC. That includes experiments and also oral evidence from witnesses. However, like the IPEC, the judges in the UPC have the powers and a mandate in the rules to keep evidence under control.   **26-100**

A key tool in English courts is the cross-examination of one party's witness by a representative of the other party. Cross-examination of witnesses is permissible in the UPC, provided always that it is under the control of the court and limited to what is necessary (art.53(2) and RoP r.112(4)). The IPEC provides an example of the conduct of cross-examination under the control of the court.   **26-101**

The oral procedure at first instance (Part 1 Chapter 3 of the Rules of Procedure)

The oral hearing is before the panel of judges, one of whom will be the presiding judge. The presiding judge may be the same individual who was the judge-rapporteur in the written and interim phases. The oral hearing will consist of hearing the oral submissions of the parties. It will also include hearing any fact or expert witnesses if that has been ordered during the interim procedure.[119] The rules provide that the presiding judge may provide a preliminary introduction to the action.[120] This permits but does not require the court to inform the parties at the start of the oral hearing as to which issues the court regards as important.   **26-102**

Rule 113 provides that the presiding judge will endeavour to complete the oral hearing in one day, can set time limits for oral submissions and can truncate them if appropriate.[121] Oral testimony shall be limited to the issues.[122]   **26-103**

The decision at first instance (Part 1 Chapter 3 of the Rules of Procedure)

Rule 118(6) provides that the court will give the decision on the merits as soon as possible after the closure of the oral hearing, endeavouring to do so in writing within six weeks. The decision will give reasons. Alternatively the court may give its decision orally immediately after the closure of the oral hearing and provide reasons later.[123] Dissenting opinions are possible.[124]   **26-104**

---

116 RoP 18th Draft r.102(1).
117 RoP 18th Draft r.102(2).
118 RoP 18th Draft r.110.
119 RoP 18th Draft r.112(2)(b).
120 RoP 18th Draft r.112(3).
121 RoP 18th Draft r.113(3).
122 RoP 18th Draft r.113(2).
123 RoP 18th Draft r.118(7).

Final remedies

26-105 The remedies which may be ordered by the court include permanent injunctions (art.63 of the UPC Agreement), corrective measures such as declarations and orders for delivery up (art.64), complete revocation or partial revocation with amendment (art.65), disclosure of information about the infringing products or process (art.67), damages (art.68), and legal costs (art.69). Dissemination of the judgment is also available as a remedy (art.80) but it is to be hoped that a scheme for publishing full copies of all judgments of the UPC will be in place in any event.[125]

26-106 Article 63(2) provides that where appropriate, compliance with an injunction shall be subject to a recurring penalty. Although not generally ordered in the UK, orders of this kind are commonly made in other European states. Whether a patentee who obtained an injunction and wanted to enforce it in the UK would be required to limit that enforcement to a recurring penalty payment remains to be seen.

26-107 The way the provision in the UP Agreement on damages (art.68) is drafted is clearly intended to mirror art.13 of the Enforcement Directive.[126] So damages are compensatory not punitive and an account of profits is available.

26-108 The Rules of Procedure contain provisions dealing with the assessment of damages[127] and costs.[128] Interim awards of damages are also available.[129] Liability for the court fees is dealt with as part of legal costs.[130]

26-109 Costs in the UPC are subject to caps. The cost caps are set out in agreed rules on court fees and recoverable costs.[131] These propose a lowest cap of €38,000 for actions with a value up to €250,000 and a highest cap of €2 million for actions with a value up to €50 million. There is scope for exceeding the caps in cases of particular complexity and to lower them if one party is a micro-enterprise, SME, non-profit organisation, university, public research organisation or natural person.

Enforcement of orders of the UPC

26-110 Article 82 of the UPC Agreement provides that decisions and orders of the court will be enforceable in any UPC state. The relevant rule is r.354. The enforcement procedures are governed by the laws of the UPC state in which enforcement takes place: see art.82(3). Article 82(3) also states:

> "*[...]* Any decision of the Court shall be enforced under the same conditions as a decision given in the Contracting Member State where the enforcement takes place."

26-111 Schedule A4 para.4 of the draft Statutory Instrument which the UK proposes to enact in order to give effect to the UPC Agreement provides that an order of the UPC is to have the same force and effect as if the order had originally been made by the High Court (if it is being enforced in England and Wales). While this is no

---

124 RoP 18th Draft r.350(3).
125 r.19 of the EPO Rules on Unitary Patent Protection provides that any decision of the UPC forwarded to the EPO will be kept on file at the EPO where it shall be open to inspection.
126 Directive 2004/48/EC OJ C 32, 5 February 2005, p.15.
127 RoP 18th Draft Part 1 Chapter 4 rr.125–144.
128 RoP 18th Draft Part 1 Chapter 4 rr.150–157.
129 RoP 18th Draft r.119.
130 RoP 18th Draft r.150.
131 Published by the Preparatory Committee on 25 February 2016.

doubt what the framers of the UPC intended, it illustrates the potentially far reaching effects of the UPC. In a proper case a local division located in a UPC state outside the UK will make orders covering the UK. The order could be an injunction (which may or may not contain a recurring penalty under art.63(2)) but could also be an ex parte "saisie" order to preserve evidence (art.60 of the UPC Agreement, RoP rr.192–198). Such an order is akin to a search or Anton Piller order. The search may relate to premises in the UK. The effect of Sch.A4 para.4 of the draft Statutory Instrument must be that breach of such an order will be enforceable, among other ways, by committal for contempt of court.

Court of Appeal

Appeal to the Court of Appeal can be on points of law and matters of fact **26-112** (art.73(3) of the UPC Agreement). New facts and evidence may only be admitted before the Court of Appeal if their submission at first instance could not reasonably have been expected during proceedings before the Court of First Instance (art.73(4) of the UPC Agreement).

The procedure before the Court of Appeal has the same overall structure as the **26-113** procedure at first instance, with three phases: written, interim and oral. There is a judge-rapporteur at the written and interim phase and a presiding judge at the oral phase.

Although it is within the powers of the Court of Appeal,[132] the scheme of the UPC **26-114** and Rules of Procedure are designed to discourage the court from referring cases back to the first instance, thereby avoiding the sort of inordinate delays which can occur with that process in the EPO. Referral back is only to be ordered in exceptional circumstances.[133] This is an important provision in order to ensure that the UPC provides certainty within a reasonable time scale. Further considerations are that first instance court is not obliged to decide all the issues before it but only those necessary to reach a decision and also the limited scope for fresh evidence or facts on appeal. It is submitted that one possible way in which an appropriate balance between these various factors may be reached is for the first instance court to decide all factual issues before it which at that stage can be seen to depend on hearing oral evidence. As long as that is done, the Court of Appeal will be in a position to decide those issues as an appellate court and decide afresh any issues which did not involve oral evidence. Oral evidence would then only be needed on appeal in the unusual circumstances of art.73(4).

---

[132] RoP 18th Draft r.242.
[133] art.75 of the UPC Agreement, RoP 18th Draft r.242(2)(b).

APPENDICES

PATENTS ACT 1977

(1977 C.37 AS AMENDED)

An Act to establish a new law of patents applicable to future patents and applications for patents; to amend the law of patents applicable to existing patents and applications for patents; to give effect to certain international conventions on patents; and for connected purposes.

[29th July 1977]

ARRANGEMENT OF SECTIONS

PART I NEW DOMESTIC LAW

Patentability

[893]

General

Textual additions and amendments to the 1977 Act are printed in bold, while the original version appears within square brackets and in italics.

PART I – NEW DOMESTIC LAW

Patentability

Patentable inventions

AppA-01   **1.**—(1)   A patent may be granted only for an invention in respect of which the following conditions are satisfied, that is to say—

(a)   the invention is new;

(b)   it involves an inventive step;

    (c)   it is capable of industrial application;

    (d)   the grant of a patent for it is not excluded by subsections (2) and (3) **or section 4A** below; and references in this Act to a patentable invention shall be construed accordingly.

(2)   It is hereby declared that the following (among other things) are not inventions for the purposes of this Act, that is to say, anything which consists of—

    (a)   a discovery, scientific theory or mathematical method;

    (b)   a literary, dramatic, musical or artistic work or any other aesthetic creation whatsoever;

    (c)   a scheme, rule or method for performing a mental act, playing a game, or doing business, or a program for a computer;

    (d)   the presentation of information; but the foregoing provision shall prevent anything from being treated as an invention for the purposes of this Act only to the extent that a patent or application for a patent relates to that thing as such.

[*(3)   A patent shall not be granted—*

    (a)   for an invention the publication or exploitation of which would be generally expected to encourage offensive, immoral or anti-social behaviour;

    (b)   for any variety of animal or plant or any essentially biological process for the production of animals or plants, not being a micro-biological process or the product of such a process.

(4)   For the purposes of subsection (3) above behaviour shall not be regarded as offensive, immoral or anti-social only because it is prohibited by any law in force in the United Kingdom or any part of it.]

(3)   A patent shall not be granted for an invention the commercial exploitation of which would be contrary to public policy or morality.

(4)   For the purposes of subsection (3) above exploitation shall not be regarded as contrary to public policy or morality only because it is prohibited by any law in force in the United Kingdom or any part of it.

(5)   The Secretary of State may by order vary the provisions of subsection (2) above for the purpose of maintaining them in conformity with developments in science and technology; and no such order shall be made unless a draft of the order has been laid before, and approved by resolution of, each House of Parliament.

Notes

    Subsection (1) amended by Patents Act 2004 (c.16) s.16 and Sch.2 para.2, with effect from 13 December 2007 (SI 2007/3396).

    Subsections (3) and (4) substituted by Patents Regulations 2000 (SI 2000/2037) reg.3, with effect from 28 July 2000, subject to transitional provisions contained in reg.9 which provide that the amendments apply to applications for patents made on or after that date (and to patents granted in pursuance of such applications).

Novelty

    2.—(1)   An invention shall be taken to be new if it does not form part of the state of the art.   **AppA-02**

(2)   The state of the art in the case of an invention shall be taken to comprise all matter (whether a product, a process, information about either, or anything else) which has at any time before the priority date of that invention been made available to the public (whether in the United Kingdom or elsewhere) by written or oral description, by use or in any other way.

(3) The state of the art in the case of an invention to which an application for a patent or a patent relates shall be taken also to comprise matter contained in an application for another patent which was published on or after the priority date of that invention, if the following conditions are satisfied, that is to say—

    (a) that matter was contained in the application for that other patent both as filed and as published; and

    (b) the priority date of that matter is earlier than that of the invention.

(4) For the purposes of this section the disclosure of matter constituting an invention shall be disregarded in the case of a patent or an application for a patent if occurring later than the beginning of the period of six months immediately preceding the date of filing the application for the patent and either—

    (a) the disclosure was due to, or made in consequence of, the matter having been obtained unlawfully or in breach of confidence by any person—

        (i) from the inventor or from any other person to whom the matter was made available in confidence by the inventor or who obtained it from the inventor because he or the inventor believed that he was entitled to obtain it; or

        (ii) from any other person to whom the matter was made available in confidence by any person mentioned in subparagraph (i) above or in this sub-paragraph or who obtained it from any person so mentioned because he or the person from whom he obtained it believed that he was entitled to obtain it;

    (b) the disclosure was made in breach of confidence by any person who obtained the matter in confidence form the inventor or from any other person to whom it was made available, or who obtained it, from the inventor; or

    (c) the disclosure was due to, or made in consequence of the inventor displaying the invention at an international exhibition and the applicant states, on filing the application, that the invention has been so displayed and also, within the prescribed period, files written evidence in support of the statement complying with any prescribed conditions.

(5) In this section references to the inventor include references to any proprietor of the invention for the time being.

[(6) In the case of an invention consisting of a substance or composition for use in a method of treatment of the human or animal body by surgery or therapy or of diagnosis practised on the human or animal body, the fact that the substance or composition forms part of the state of the art shall not prevent the invention from being taken to be new if the use of the substance or composition in any such method does not form part of the state of the art.]

Note

Subsection (6) repealed by Patents Act 2004 (c.16) s.16, Sch.2 para.3 and Sch.3, with effect from 13 December 2007 (SI 2007/3396).

Inventive step

AppA-03   **3.** An invention shall be taken to involve an inventive step if it is not obvious to a person skilled in the art, having regard to any matter which forms part of the state of the art by virtue only of section 2(2) above (and disregarding section 2(3) (above).

Industrial application

4.—(1) [*Subject to subsection (2) below,*] an invention shall be taken to be capable of industrial application if it can be made or used in any kind of industry, including agriculture.

[*(2)   An invention of a method of treatment of the human or animal body by surgery or therapy or of diagnosis practised on the human or animal body shall not be taken to be capable of industrial application.*

(3)   Subsection (2) above shall not prevent a product consisting of a substance or composition being treated as capable of industrial application merely because it is invented for use in any such method.]

AppA-04

Notes

Subsection (1) amended by Patents Act 2004 (c.16) s.16, Sch.2 para.4, with effect from 13 December 2007 (SI 2007/3396).

Subsections (2) and (3) repealed by Patents Act 2004 (c.16) s.16, Sch.2 para.4 and Sch.3, with effect from 13 December 2007 (SI 2007/3396).

Methods of treatment or diagnosis

4A.—**(1)   A patent shall not be granted for the invention of—**
   (a)   a method of treatment of the human or animal body by surgery or therapy, or
   (b)   a method of diagnosis practised on the human or animal body.

(2)   Subsection (1) above does not apply to an invention consisting of a substance or composition for use in any such method.

(3)   In the case of an invention consisting of a substance or composition for use in any such method, the fact that the substance or composition forms part of the state of the art shall not prevent the invention from being taken to be new if the use of the substance or composition in any such method does not form part of the state of the art.

(4)   In the case of an invention consisting of a substance or composition for a specific use in any such method, the fact that the substance or composition forms part of the state of the art shall not prevent the invention from being taken to be new if that specific use does not form part of the state of the art.

AppA-04A

Note

Section 4A inserted by Patents Act 2004 (c.16) s.1, with effect from 13 December 2007 (SI 2007/3396).

Priority date

5.—(1)   For the purposes of this Act the priority date of an invention to which an application for a patent relates and also of any matter (whether or not the same as the invention) contained in any such application is, except as provided by the following provisions of this Act, the date of filing the application.

(2)   If in or in connection with an application for a patent (the application in suit) a declaration is made, whether by the applicant or any predecessor in title of his, complying with the relevant requirements of rules and specifying one or more

AppA-05

earlier relevant applications for the purposes of this section made by the applicant or a predecessor in title of his and [*each having a date of filing during the period of twelve months immediately preceding the date of filing the application in suit*] **the application in suit has a date of filing during the period allowed under subsection (2A)(a) or (b) below**, then—

    (a) if an invention to which the application in suit relates is supported by matter disclosed in the earlier relevant application or applications, the priority date of that invention shall instead of being the date of filing the application in suit be the date of filing the relevant application in which the matter was disclosed or, if it was disclosed in more than one relevant application, the earliest of them;

    (b) the priority date of any matter contained in the application in suit which was also disclosed in the earlier relevant application or applications shall be the date of filing the relevant application in which that matter was disclosed or, if it was disclosed in more than one relevant application, the earliest of them.

  (2A) **The periods are—**

    (a) **the period of twelve months immediately following the date of filing of the earlier specified relevant application, or if there is more than one, of the earliest of them; and**

    (b) **where the comptroller has given permission under subsection (2B) below for a late declaration to be made under subsection (2) above, the period commencing immediately after the end of the period allowed under paragraph (a) above and ending at the end of the prescribed period.**

  (2B) **The applicant may make a request to the comptroller for permission to make a late declaration under subsection (2) above.**

  (2C) **The comptroller shall grant a request made under subsection (2B) above if, and only if—**

    (a) **the request complies with the relevant requirements of rules; and**

    (b) **the comptroller is satisfied that the applicant's failure to file the application in suit within the period allowed under subsection (2A)(a) above was unintentional.**

  (3) Where an invention or other matter contained in the application in suit was also disclosed in two earlier relevant applications filed by the same applicant as in the case of the application in suit or a predecessor in title of his and the second of those relevant applications was specified in or in connection with the application in suit, the second of those relevant applications shall, so far as concerns that invention or matter, be disregarded unless—

    (a) it was filed in or in respect of the same country as the first; and

    (b) not later than the date of filing the second, the first (whether or not so specified) was unconditionally withdrawn, or was abandoned or refused, without—

        (i) having been made available to the public (whether in the United Kingdom or elsewhere);

        (ii) leaving any rights outstanding; and

        (iii) having served to establish a priority date in relation to another application, wherever made.

  (4) The foregoing provisions of this section shall apply for determining the priority date of an invention for which a patent has been granted as they apply for

determining the priority date of an invention to which an application for that patent relates.

(5)   In this section "relevant application" means any of the following applications which has a date of filing, namely—

    (a)   an application for a patent under this Act;

  (aa) **an application in or for a country (other than the United Kingdom) which is a member of the World Trade Organisation for protection in respect of an invention which, in accordance with the law of that country or a treaty or international obligation to which it is a party, is equivalent to an application for a patent under this Act;**

    (b)   an application in or for a convention country (specified under section 90 below) for protection in respect of an invention or an application which, in accordance with the law of a convention country or a treaty or international convention to which a convention country is a party, is equivalent to **an application for a patent under this Act** [*such an application*].

[*(6)   References in subsection (5) above to a convention country include references to a country, other than the United Kingdom, which is a member of the World Trade Organisation.*]

Notes

Subsection (2) amended and subss.(2A)–(2C) inserted by Regulatory Reform (Patents) Order 2004 (SI 2004/2357) art.3, with effect from 1 January 2005, subject to transitional provisions contained in arts 20–23 of that Order.

Subsection (5)(aa) inserted, subs.5(b) amended and subs.(6) repealed by Intellectual Property Act 2014 Sch.1 with effect from 1 October 2014.

Disclosure of matter, etc., between earlier and later applications

6.—(1)   It is hereby declared for the avoidance of doubt that where an application (the application in suit) is made for a patent and a declaration is made in accordance with section 5(2) above in or in connection with that application specifying an earlier relevant application, the application in suit and any patent granted in pursuance of it shall not be invalidated by reason only of relevant intervening acts.   **AppA-06**

(2)   In this section—

"relevant application" has the same meaning as in section 5 above; and
"relevant intervening acts" means acts done in relation to matter disclosed in an earlier relevant application between the dates of the earlier relevant application and the application in suit, as for example, filing another application for the invention for which the earlier relevant application was made, making information available to the public about that invention or that matter or working that invention, but disregarding any application, or the disclosure to the public of matter contained in any application, which is itself to be disregarded for the purposes of section 5(3) above.

Right to apply for and obtain a patent and be mentioned as inventor

Right to apply for and obtain a patent

7.—(1)   Any person may make an application for a patent either alone or jointly with another.   **AppA-07**

(2)   A patent for an invention may be granted—

(a)　primarily to the inventor or joint inventors;

(b)　in preference to the foregoing, to any person or persons who, by virtue of an enactment or rule of law, or any foreign law or treaty or international convention, or by virtue of any enforceable term of any agreement entered into with the inventor before the making of the invention, was or were at the time of the making of the invention entitled to the whole of the property in it (other than equitable interests) in the United Kingdom;

(c)　in any event, to the successor or successors in title of any person or person mentioned in paragraph (a) or (b) above or any person so mentioned and the successor or successors in title of another person so mentioned;

and to no other person.

(3)　In this Act "inventor" in relation to an invention means the actual deviser of the invention and "joint inventor" shall be construed accordingly.

(4)　Except so far as the contrary is established, a person who makes an application for a patent shall be taken to be the person who is entitled under subsection (2) above to be granted a patent and two or more persons who make such an application jointly shall be taken to be the persons so entitled.

Determination before grant of questions about entitlement to patents, etc.

AppA-08　　**8.**—(1)　At any time before a patent has been granted for an invention (whether or not an application has been made for it)—

(a)　any person may refer to the comptroller the question whether he is entitled to be granted (alone or with any other persons) a patent for that invention or has or would have any right in or under any patent so granted or any application for such a patent; or

(b)　any of two or more co-proprietors of an application for a patent for that invention may so refer the question whether any right in or under the application should be transferred or granted to any other person;

and the comptroller shall determine the question and may make such order as he thinks fit to give effect to the determination.

(2)　Where a person refers a question relating to an invention under subsection (1)(a) above to the comptroller after an application for a patent for the invention has been filed and before a patent is granted in pursuance of the application, then, unless the application is refused or withdrawn before the reference is disposed of by the comptroller, the comptroller may, without prejudice to the generality of subsection (1) above and subject to subsection (6) below,—

(a)　order that the application shall proceed in the name of that person, either solely or jointly with that of any other applicant, instead of in the name of the applicant or any specified applicant;

(b)　where the reference was made by two or more persons, order that the application shall proceed in all their names jointly;

(c)　refuse to grant a patent in pursuance of the application or order the application to be amended so as to exclude any of the matter in respect of which the question was referred;

(d)　make an order transferring or granting any licence or other right in or under the application and give directions to any person for carrying out the provisions of any such order.

(3)　Where a question is referred to the comptroller under subsection (1)(a) above and—

(a) the comptroller orders an application for a patent for the invention to which the question relates to be so amended;

(b) any such application is refused under subsection (2)(c) above before the comptroller has disposed of the reference (whether the reference was made before or after the publication of the application); or

(c) any such application is refused under any other provision of this Act or is withdrawn before the comptroller has disposed of the reference, [*but after the publication of the application*] **(whether the application is refused or withdrawn before or after its publication)**;

the comptroller may order that any person by whom the reference was made may within the prescribed period make a new application for a patent for the whole or part of any matter comprised in the earlier application or, as the case may be, for all or any of the matter excluded from the earlier application, subject in either case to section 76 below, and in either case that, if such a new application is made, it shall be treated as having been filed on the date of filing the earlier application.

(4) Where a person refers a question under subsection (1)(b) above relating to an application, any order under subsection (1) above may contain directions to any person for transferring or granting any right in or under the application.

(5) If any person to whom directions have been given under subsection (2)(d) or (4) above fails to do anything necessary for carrying out any such directions within 14 days after the date of the directions, the comptroller may, on application made to him by any person in whose favour or on whose reference the directions were given, authorise him to do that thing on behalf of the person to whom the directions were given.

(6) Where on a reference under this section it is alleged that, by virtue of any transaction, instrument or event relating to an invention or an application for a patent, any person other than the inventor or the applicant for the patent has become entitled to be granted (whether alone or with any other persons) a patent for the invention or has or would have any right in or under any patent so granted or any application for any such patent, an order shall not be made under subsection (2)(a), (b) or (d) above on the reference unless notice of the reference is given to the applicant and any such person, except any of them who is a party to the reference.

(7) If it appears to the comptroller on a reference of a question under this section that the question involves matters which would more properly be determined by the court, he may decline to deal with it and, without prejudice to the court's jurisdiction to determine any such question and make a declaration, or any declaratory jurisdiction of the court in Scotland, the court shall have jurisdiction to do so.

(8) No directions shall be given under this section so as to affect the mutual rights or obligations of trustees or of the personal representatives of deceased persons, or their rights or obligations as such.

Note

Subsection (3) amended by Patents Act 2004 (c.16) s.6(1), with effect from 1 January 2005 (SI 2004/3205), subject to transitional provisions contained in art.9 of that Order.

Determination after grant of questions referred before grant

9. If a question with respect to a patent or application is referred by any person to the comptroller under section 8 above, whether before or after the making of an application for the patent, and is not determined before the time when the application is first in order for a grant of a patent in pursuance of the application, that fact AppA-09 shall not prevent the grant of a patent, but on its grant that person shall be treated as having referred to the comptroller under section 37 below any question mentioned in that section which the comptroller thinks appropriate.

Handling of application by joint applicants

AppA-10   **10.**   If any dispute arises between joint applicants for a patent whether or in what manner the application should be proceeded with, the comptroller may, on a request made by any of the parties, give such directions as he thinks fit for enabling the application to proceed in the name of one or more of the parties alone or for regulating the manner in which it shall be proceeded with, or for both those purposes, according as the case may require.

Effect of transfer of application under s. 8 or 10

AppA-11   **11.**—(1)   Where an order is made or directions are given under section 8 or 10 above that an application for a patent shall proceed in the name of one or some of the original applicants (whether or not it is also to proceed in the name of some other person), any licenses or other rights in or under the application shall, subject to the provisions of the order and any directions under either of those sections, continue in force and be treated as granted by the persons in whose name the application is to proceed.

(2)   Where an order is made or directions are given under section 8 above that an application for a patent shall proceed in the name of one or more persons none of whom was an original applicant (on the ground that the original applicant or applicants was or were not entitled to be granted the patent), any licences or other rights in or under the application shall, subject to the provisions of the order and any directions under that section and subject to subsection (3) below, lapse on the registration of that person or those persons as the applicant or applicants or, where the application has not been published, on the making of the order.

(3)   If before registration of a reference under section 8 above resulting in the making of any order mentioned in subsection (2) above—

    (a)   the original applicant or any of the applicants, acting in good faith, worked the invention in question in the United Kingdom or made effective and serious preparations to do so; or

    (b)   a licensee of the applicant, acting in good faith, worked the invention in the United Kingdom or made effective and serious preparations to do so;

that or those original applicant or applicants or the licensee shall, on making a request within the prescribed period to the person in whose name the application is to proceed, be entitled to be granted a licence (but not an exclusive licence) to continue working or, as the case may be, to work the invention.

(3A)   If, before registration of a reference under section 8 above resulting in the making of an order under subsection (3) of that section, the condition in subsection (3)(a) or (b) above is met, the original applicant or any of the applicants or the licensee shall, on making a request within the prescribed period to the new applicant, be entitled to be granted a licence (but not an exclusive licence) to continue working or, as the case may be, to work the invention so far as it is the subject of the new application.

(4)   [*Any such licence*] **A licence under subsection (3) or (3A) above** shall be granted for a reasonable period and on reasonable terms.

(5)   Where an order is made as mentioned in subsection (2) **or (3A)** above, the

person in whose name the application is to proceed **or, as the case may be, who makes the new application** or any person claiming that he is entitled to be granted any such licence may refer to the comptroller the question whether the latter is so entitled and whether any such period is or terms are reasonable, and the comptroller shall determine the question and may, if he considers it appropriate, order the grant of such a licence.

Note

Subsection (3A) inserted and subss.(4) and (5) amended by Patents Act 2004 (c.16) s.6(2), (3), (4), with effect from 1 January 2005 (SI 2004/3205), subject to transitional provisions contained in art.9 of that Order.

Determination of questions about entitlement to foreign and convention patents, etc.

12.—(1) At any time before a patent is granted for an invention in pursuance   AppA-12
of an application made under the law of any country other than the United Kingdom or under any treaty or international convention (whether or not the application has been made)—

    (a)   any person may refer to the comptroller the question whether he is entitled to be granted (alone or with any other persons) any such patent for that invention or has or would have any right in or under any such patent or an application for such a patent; or

    (b)   any of two or more co-proprietors of an application for such a patent for that invention may so refer the question whether any right in or under the application should be transferred or granted to any other person;

and the comptroller shall determine the question so far as he is able to and may make such order as he thinks fit to give effect to the determination.

    (2) If it appears to the comptroller on a reference of a question under this section that the question involves matters which would more properly be determined by the court, he may decline to deal with it and, without prejudice to the court's jurisdiction to determine any such question and make a declaration, or any declaratory jurisdiction of the court in Scotland, the court shall have jurisdiction to do so.

    (3) Subsection (1) above, in its application to a European patent and an application for any such patent, shall have effect subject to section 82 below.

    (4) Section 10 above, except so much of it as enables the comptroller to regulate the manner in which an application is to proceed, shall apply to disputes between joint applicants for any such patent as is mentioned in subsection (1) above as it applies to joint applicants for a patent under this Act.

    (5) Section 11 above shall apply in relation to—

    (a)   any orders made under subsection (1) above and any directions given under section 10 above by virtue of subsection (4) above; and

    (b)   any orders made and directions given by the relevant convention court with respect to a question corresponding to any question which may be determined under subsection (1) above;

as it applies to orders made and directions given apart from this section under section 8 or 10 above.

    (6) In the following cases, that is to say—

    (a)   where an application for a European patent (UK) is refused or withdrawn, or the designation of the United Kingdom in the application is withdrawn, **whether before or** after publication of the application but before a question relating to the right to the patent has been referred to the comptroller under subsection (1) above or before proceedings relating to that right have begun before the relevant convention court;

    (b)   where an application has been made for a European patent (UK) and on a reference under subsection (1) above or any such proceedings as are mentioned in paragraph (a) above, the comptroller, the court or the relevant convention court determines by a final decision (whether before or after publication of the application) that a person other than the applicant has the right to the patent, but that person requests the European Patent Office that the application for the patent should be refused; or

    (c)   where an international application for a patent (UK) is withdrawn, or the designation of the United Kingdom in the application is withdrawn, whether before or after the making of any reference under subsection (1) above [*but after*] **or the** publication of the application; the comptroller may order that any person (other than the applicant) appearing to him to be entitled to be granted a patent under the Act may within the prescribed period make an application for such a patent for the whole or part of any matter comprised in the earlier application (subject, however, to section 76 below) and that if the application for a patent under this Act is filed, it shall be treated as having been filed on the date of filing the earlier application.

    (7)   In this section—

    (a)   references to a patent and an application for a patent include respectively references to protection in respect of an invention and an application which, in accordance with the law of any country other than the United Kingdom or any treaty or international convention, is equivalent to an application for a patent or for such protection; and

    (b)   a decision shall be taken to be final for the purposes of this section when the time for appealing from it has expired without an appeal being brought or, where an appeal is brought, when it is finally disposed of.

Note

    Subsection (6) amended by Patents Act 2004 (c.16) s.16 and Sch.2 para.5, with effect from 1 January 2005 (SI 2004/3205), subject to transitional provisions contained in art.9 of that Order.

Mention of inventor

AppA-13   **13.**—(1)   The inventor or joint inventors of an invention shall have a right to be mentioned as such in any patent granted for the invention and shall also have a right to be so mentioned if possible in any published application for a patent for the invention and, if not so mentioned, a right to be so mentioned in accordance with rules in a prescribed document.

    (2)   Unless he has already given the Patent Office the information hereinafter mentioned, an applicant for a patent shall within the prescribed period file with the Patent Office a statement—

    (a)   identifying the person or persons whom he believes to be the inventor or inventors; and

(b)   where the applicant is not the sole inventor or the applicants are not the
joint inventors, indicating the derivation of his or their right to be
granted the patent;

and, if he fails to do so, the application shall be taken to be withdrawn.

(3)   Where a person has been mentioned as sole or joint inventor in pursuance
of this section, any other person who alleges that the former ought not to have been
so mentioned may at any time apply to the comptroller for a certificate to that effect, and the comptroller may issue such a certificate; and if he does so, he shall accordingly rectify any undistributed copies of the patent and of any documents
prescribed for the purposes of subsection (1) above.

Applications

Making of an application

14.—(1)   Every application for a patent—   AppA-14

(a)   shall be made in the prescribed form and shall be filed at the Patent Office in the prescribed manner; [*and*

(b)   *shall be accompanied by the fee prescribed for the purposes of this
subsection (hereafter in this Act referred to as the filing fee).*]

**(1A)   Where an application for a patent is made, the fee prescribed for the
purposes of this subsection ("the application fee") shall be paid not later than
the end of the period prescribed for the purposes of section 15(10)(c) below.**

(2)   Every application for a patent shall contain—

(a)   a request for the grant of a patent;

(b)   a specification containing a description of the invention, a claim or
claims and any drawing referred to in the description or any claim; and

(c)   an abstract;

but the foregoing provision shall not prevent an application being initiated by documents complying with section 15(1) below.

(3)   The specification of an application shall disclose the invention in a manner which is clear enough and complete enough for the invention to be performed
by a person skilled in the art.

[*(4)   Without prejudice to subsection (3) above, rules may prescribe the
circumstances in which the specification of an application which requires for its
performance the use of a micro-organism is to be treated for the purposes of this
Act as complying with that subsection.*]

(5)   The claim or claims shall—

(a)   define the matter for which the applicant seeks protection;

(b)   be clear and concise;

(c)   be supported by the description; and

(d)   relate to one invention or to a group of inventions which are so linked
as to form a single inventive concept.

(6)   Without prejudice to the generality of subsection (5)(d) above, rules may
provide for treating two or more inventions as being so linked as to form a single
inventive concept for the purposes of this Act.

(7)   The purpose of the abstract is to give technical information and on publication it shall not form part of the state of the art by virtue of section 2(3) above, and
the comptroller may determine whether the abstract adequately fulfils its purpose
and, if it does not, may reframe it so that it does.

[*(8)   Rules may require a person who has made an application for a patent for an invention which requires for its performance the use of a micro-organism not to impose or maintain in the prescribed circumstances any restrictions on the availability to the public of samples of the micro-organism and the uses to which they may be put, subject, however, to any prescribed exceptions, and rules may provide that in the event of a contravention of any provision included in the rules by virtue of this subsection the specification shall be treated for the purposes of this Act as not disclosing the invention in a manner required by subsection (3) above.]*

(9)   An application for a patent may be withdrawn at any time before the patent is granted and any withdrawal of such an application may not be revoked.

(10)   Subsection (9) above does not affect the power of the comptroller under section 117(1) below to correct an error or mistake in a withdrawal of an application for a patent.

Notes

Subsection (1) amended and subs.(1A) and (10) inserted by Regulatory Reform (Patents) Order 2004 (SI 2004/2357) art.4, with effect from 1 January 2005, subject to transitional provisions contained in arts 20–23 of that Order.

Subsections (4) and (8) repealed by CDPA 1988 (c.48) s.303(2) and Sch.8, with effect from 7 January 1991 (SI 1990/2168).

[Date of filing application

AppA-15   *15.—(1)   The date of filing an application for a patent shall, subject to the following provisions of this Act, be taken to be the earliest date on which the following conditions are satisfied in relation to the application, that is to say—*

(a)   *the documents filed at the Patent Office contain an indication that a patent is sought in pursuance of the application;*

(b)   *those documents identify the applicant or applicants for the patent;*

(c)   *those documents contain a description of the invention for which a patent is sought (whether or not the description complies with the other provisions of this Act and with any relevant rules); and*

(d)   *the applicant pays the filing fee.*

(2)   If any drawing referred to in any such application is filed later than the date which by virtue of subsection (1) above is to be treated as the date of filing the application, but before the beginning of the preliminary examination of the application under section 17 below, the comptroller shall give the applicant an opportunity of requesting within the prescribed period that the date on which the drawing is filed shall be treated for the purposes of this Act as the date of filing the application, and—

(a)   *if the applicant makes any such request, the date of filing the drawing shall be so treated; but*

(b)   *otherwise any reference to the drawing in the application shall be treated as omitted.*

(3)   If on the preliminary examination of an application under section 17 below it is found that any drawing referred to in the application has not been filed, then—

(a)   *if the drawing is subsequently filed within the prescribed period, the date on which it is filed shall be treated for the purposes of this Act as the date of filing the application; but*

(b)   *otherwise any reference to the drawing in the application shall be treated as omitted.*

*(3A)   **Nothing in subsection (2) or (3) above shall be construed as affecting***

the power of the comptroller under section 117(1) below to correct errors or mistakes with respect to the filing of drawings.

(4) Where, after an application for a patent has been filed and before the patent is granted, a new application is filed by the original applicant or his successor in title in accordance with rules in respect of any part of the matter contained in the earlier application and the conditions mentioned in subsection (1) above are satisfied in relation to the new application (without the newapplication contravening section 76 below) the new application shall be treated as having, as its date of filing, the date of filing the earlier application.

(5) An application which has a date of filing by virtue of the foregoing provisions of this section shall be taken to be withdrawn at the end of the relevant prescribed period, unless before that end the applicant—

(a) files at the Patent Office one or more claims for the purposes of the application and also the abstract; and

(b) makes a request for a preliminary examination and search under the following provisions of this Act and pays the search fee.]

Note

Subsection (3A) inserted by CDPA 1988 (c.48) s.295 and Sch.5 para.2, with effect from 7 January 1991 (SI 1990/2168), subject to savings contained in Sch.5 para.2(2) of that Act.

Date of filing application

15.—**(1)** Subject to the following provisions of this Act, the date of filing an application for a patent shall be taken to be the earliest date on which documents filed at the Patent Office to initiate the application satisfy the following conditions—

    (a)   the documents indicate that a patent is sought;

    (b)   the documents identify the person applying for a patent or contain information sufficient to enable that person to be contacted by the Patent Office; and

    (c)   the documents contain either—

        (i)   something which is or appears to be a description of the invention for which a patent is sought; or

        (ii)   a reference, complying with the relevant requirements of rules, to an earlier relevant application made by the applicant or a predecessor in title of his.

(2) It is immaterial for the purposes of subsection (1)(c)(i) above—

    (a)   whether the thing is in, or is accompanied by a translation into, a language accepted by the Patent Office in accordance with rules;

    (b)   whether the thing otherwise complies with the other provisions of this Act and with any relevant rules.

(3) Where documents filed at the Patent Office to initiate an application for a patent satisfy one or more of the conditions specified in subsection (1) above, but do not satisfy all those conditions, the comptroller shall as soon as practicable after the filing of those documents notify the applicant of what else must be filed in order for the application to have a date of filing.

(4) Where documents filed at the Patent Office to initiate an application for a patent satisfy all the conditions specified in subsection (1) above, the comptroller shall as soon as practicable after the filing of the last of those documents notify the applicant of—

    (a)   the date of filing the application, and

    (b)   the requirements that must be complied with, and the periods within which they are required by this Act or rules to be complied with, if the application is not to be treated as having been withdrawn.

(5)   Subsection (6) below applies where—

    (a)   an application has a date of filing by virtue of subsection (1) above;

    (b)   within the prescribed period the applicant files at the Patent Office—

        (i)   a drawing, or

        (ii)   part of the description of the invention for which a patent is sought, and

    (c)   that drawing or that part of the description was missing from the application at the date of filing.

(6)   Unless the applicant withdraws the drawing or the part of the description filed under subsection (5)(b) above ("the missing part") before the end of the prescribed period—

    (a)   the missing part shall be treated as included in the application; and

    (b)   the date of filing the application shall be the date on which the missing part is filed at the Patent Office.

(7)   Subsection (6)(b) above does not apply if—

    (a)   on or before the date which is the date of filing the application by virtue of subsection (1) above a declaration is made under section 5(2) above in or in connection with the application;

    (b)   the applicant makes a request for subsection (6)(b) above not to apply; and

    (c)   the request complies with the relevant requirements of rules and is made within the prescribed period.

(8)   Subsections (6) and (7) above do not affect the power of the comptroller under section 117(1) below to correct an error or mistake.

(9)   Where, after an application for a patent has been filed and before the patent is granted—

    (a)   a new application is filed by the original applicant or his successor in title in accordance with rules in respect of any part of the matter contained in the earlier application, and

    (b)   the conditions mentioned in subsection (1) above are satisfied in relation to the new application (without the new application contravening section 76 below), the new application shall be treated as having, as its date of filing, the date of filing the earlier application.

(10)   Where an application has a date of filing by virtue of this section, the application shall be treated as having been withdrawn if any of the following applies—

    (a)   the applicant fails to file at the Patent Office, before the end of the prescribed period, one or more claims and the abstract;

    (b)   where a reference to an earlier relevant application has been filed as mentioned in subsection (1)(c)(ii) above—

        (i)   the applicant fails to file at the Patent Office, before the end of the prescribed period, a description of the invention for which the patent is sought;

      (ii) the applicant fails to file at the Patent Office, before the end of the prescribed period, a copy of the application referred to, complying with the relevant requirements of rules;

    (c) the applicant fails to pay the application fee before the end of the prescribed period;

    (d) the applicant fails, before the end of the prescribed period, to make a request for a search under section 17 below and pay the search fee.

(11)   In this section "relevant application" has the meaning given by section 5(5) above.

Note

New s.15 substituted, together with s.15A, for original s.15 by Regulatory Reform (Patents) Order 2004 (SI 2004/2357) art.5, with effect from 1 January 2005, subject to transitional provisions contained in arts 20–23 of that Order.

Preliminary examination

15A.—(1) The comptroller shall refer an application for a patent to an examiner for a preliminary examination if—   AppA-15

    (a) the application has a date of filing;

    (b) the application has not been withdrawn or treated as withdrawn; and

    (c) the application fee has been paid.

(2)   On a preliminary examination of an application the examiner shall—

    (a) determine whether the application complies with those requirements of this Act and the rules which are designated by the rules as formal requirements for the purposes of this Act; and

    (b) determine whether any requirements under section 13(2) or 15(10) above remain to be complied with.

(3)   The examiner shall report to the comptroller his determinations under subsection (2) above.

(4)   If on the preliminary examination of an application it is found that—

    (a) any drawing referred to in the application, or

    (b) part of the description of the invention for which the patent is sought, is missing from the application, then the examiner shall include this finding in his report under subsection (3) above.

(5)   Subsections (6) to (8) below apply if a report is made to the comptroller under subsection (3) above that not all the formal requirements have been complied with.

(6)   The comptroller shall specify a period during which the applicant shall have the opportunity—

    (a) to make observations on the report, and

    (b) to amend the application so as to comply with those requirements (subject to section 76 below).

(7)   The comptroller may refuse the application if the applicant fails to amend the application as mentioned in subsection (6)(b) above before the end of the period specified by the comptroller under that subsection.

(8)   Subsection (7) above does not apply if—

    (a) the applicant makes observations as mentioned in subsection (6)(a) above before the end of the period specified by the comptroller under that subsection, and

(b) as a result of the observations, the comptroller is satisfied that the formal requirements have been complied with.

(9) If a report is made to the comptroller under subsection (3) above—

(a) that any requirement of section 13(2) or 15(10) above has not been complied with; or

(b) that a drawing or part of the description of the invention has been found to be missing, then the comptroller shall notify the applicant accordingly.

Note

Section 15A substituted, together with new s.15, for original s.15 by Regulatory Reform (Patents) Order 2004 (SI 2004/2357) art.5, with effect from 1 January 2005, subject to transitional provisions contained in arts 20–23 of that Order.

Publication of application

AppA-16   **16.**—(1)   Subject to section 22 below **and to any prescribed restrictions**, where an application has a date of filing, then, as soon as possible after the end of the prescribed period, the comptroller shall, unless the application is withdrawn or refused before preparations for its publication have been completed by the Patent Office, publish it as filed (including not only the original claims but also any amendments of those claims and new claims subsisting immediately before the completion of those preparations) and he may, if so requested by the applicant, publish it as aforesaid during that period, and in either event shall advertise the fact and date of its publication in the journal.

(2)   The comptroller may omit from the specification of a published application for a patent any matter—

(a)   which in his opinion disparages any person in a way likely to damage him, or

(b)   the publication or exploitation of which would in his opinion be generally expected to encourage offensive, immoral or anti-social behaviour.

Note

Subsection (1) amended by Patents Act 2004 (c.16) s.16 and Sch.2 para.6, with effect from 1 October 2005 (SI 2005/2471).

Examination and search

[Preliminary examination and search] Search

AppA-17   *17.*—[*(1)   Where an application for a patent has a date of filing and is not withdrawn, and before the end of the prescribed period—*

(a)   a request is made by the applicant to the Patent Office in the prescribed form for a preliminary examination and a search; and

(b)   the prescribed fee is paid for the examination and search (the search fee); the comptroller shall refer the application to an examiner for a preliminary examination and search, except that he shall not refer the application for a search until it includes one or more claims.]

(1)   The comptroller shall refer an application for a patent to an examiner for a search if, and only if—

(a)   the comptroller has referred the application to an examiner for a preliminary examination under section 15A(1) above;

[910]

(b) the application has not been withdrawn or treated as withdrawn;

(c) before the end of the prescribed period—

    (i) the applicant makes a request to the Patent Office in the prescribed form for a search; and

    (ii) the fee prescribed for the search ("the search fee") is paid;

(d) the application includes—

    (i) a description of the invention for which a patent is sought; and

    (ii) one or more claims; and

(e) the description and each of the claims comply with the requirements of rules as to language.

[*(2) On a preliminary examination of an application the examiner shall determine whether the application complies with those requirements of this Act and the rules which are designated by the rules as formal requirements for the purposes of this Act and shall report his determination to the comptroller.*

(3) If it is reported to the comptroller under subsection (2) above that not all the formal requirements are complied with, he shall give the applicant an opportunity to make observations on the report and to amend the application within a specified period (subject to section 15(5) above) so as to comply with those requirements (subject, however, to section 76 below), and if the applicant fails to do so the comptroller may refuse the application.]

(4) Subject to subsections (5) and (6) below, on a search requested under this section, the examiner shall make such investigation as in his opinion is reasonably practicable and necessary for him to identify the documents which he thinks will be needed to decide, on a substantive examination under section 18 below, whether the invention for which a patent is sought is new and involves an inventive step.

(5) On any such search the examiner shall determine whether or not the search would serve any useful purpose on the application as for the time being constituted and—

(a) if he determines that it would serve such a purpose in relation to the whole or part of the application, he shall proceed to conduct the search so far as it would serve such a purpose and shall report on the results of the search to the comptroller; and

(b) if he determines that the search would not serve such a purpose in relation to the whole part of the application, he shall report accordingly to the comptroller;

and in either event the applicant shall be informed of the examiner's report.

(6) If it appears to the examiner, either before or on conducting a search under this section, that an application relates to two or more inventions, but that they are not so linked as to form a single inventive concept, he shall initially only conduct a search in relation to the first invention specified in the claims of the application, but may proceed to conduct a search in relation to another invention so specified if the applicant pays the search fee in respect of the application so far as it relates to that other invention.

(7) After a search has been requested under this section for an application the comptroller may at any time refer the application to an examiner for a supplementary search, and [*subsection 4 above*] **subsections (4) and (5) above** shall apply in relation to a supplementary search as [*it applies*] **they apply** in relation to any other search under this section.

(8) A reference for a supplementary search in consequence of—

(a) an amendment of the application made by the applicant under section 18(3) or 19(1) below, or

(b) a correction of the application, or of a document filed in connection with the application, under section 117 below, shall be made only on payment of the prescribed fee, unless the comptroller directs otherwise.

Notes

Provision heading and subs.(1) substituted and subss.(2) and (3) repealed by Regulatory Reform (Patents) Order 2004 (SI 2004/2357) art.6, with effect from 1 January 2005, subject to transitional provisions contained in arts 20–23 of that Order.

Subsection (7) amended and subs.(8) inserted by CDPA 1988 (c.48) s.295 and Sch.5 para.3, with effect from 7 January 1991 (SI 1990/2168).

Substantive examination and grant or refusal of patent

AppA-18   **18.**—(1)   Where the conditions imposed by section 17(1) above for the comptroller to refer an application to an examiner for a [*preliminary examination and*] search are satisfied and at the time of the request under that subsection or within the prescribed period—

(a) a request is made by the applicant to the Patent Office in the prescribed form for a substantive examination; and

(b) the prescribed fee is paid for the examination;

the comptroller shall refer the application to an examiner for a substantive examination; and if no such request is made or the prescribed fee is not paid within that period, the application shall be treated as having been withdrawn at the end of that period.

(1A)   If the examiner forms the view that a supplementary search under section 17 above is required for which a fee is payable, he shall inform the comptroller, who may decide that the substantive examination should not proceed until the fee is paid; and if he so decides, then unless within such period as he may allow—

(a) the fee is paid, or

(b) the application is amended so as to render the supplementary search unnecessary, he may refuse the application.

(2)   On a substantive examination of an application the examiner shall investigate, to such extent as he considers necessary in view of any examination **carried out under section 15A above** and search carried out under section 17 above, whether the application complies with the requirements of this Act and the rules and shall determine that question and report his determination to the comptroller.

(3)   If the examiner reports that any of those requirements are not complied with, the comptroller shall give the applicant an opportunity within a specified period to make observations on the report and to amend the application so as to comply with those requirements (subject, however, to section 76 below), and if the applicant fails to satisfy the comptroller that those requirements are complied with, or to amend the application so as to comply with them, the comptroller may refuse the application.

(4)   If the examiner reports that the application, whether as originally filed or as amended in pursuance of [*section 17*] **section 15A above**, this section or section 19 below, complies with those requirements at any time before the end of the

prescribed period, the comptroller shall notify the applicant of that fact and, subject to subsection (5) and sections 19 and 22 below and on payment within the prescribed period of any fee prescribed for the grant, grant him a patent.

(5) Where two or more applications for a patent for the same invention having the same priority date are filed by the same applicant or his successor in title, the comptroller may on that ground refuse to grant a patent in pursuance of more than one of the applications.

Notes

Subsections (1), (2) and (4) amended by Regulatory Reform (Patents) Order 2004 (SI 2004/2357) art.7, with effect from 1 January 2005, subject to transitional provisions contained in arts 20–23 of that Order.

Subsection (1A) inserted by CDPA 1988 (c.48) s.295 and Sch.5 para.4, with effect from 7 January 1991 (SI 1990/2168).

General power to amend application before grant

19.—(1) At any time before a patent is granted in pursuance of an application the applicant may, in accordance with the prescribed conditions and subject to section 76 below, amend the application of his own volition.   **AppA-19**

(2) The comptroller may, without an application being made to him for the purpose, amend the specification and abstract contained in an application for a patent so as to acknowledge a registered trade mark.

Failure of application

20.—(1) If it is not determined that an application for a patent complies before the end of the prescribed period with all the requirements of this Act and the rules, the application shall be treated as having been refused by the comptroller at the end of that period, and section 97 below shall apply accordingly.   **AppA-20**

(2) If at the end of that period an appeal to the court is pending in respect of the application or the time within which such an appeal could be brought has not expired, that period—

(a) where such an appeal is pending, or is brought within the said time or before the expiration of any extension of that time granted (in the case of a first extension) on an application made within that time or (in the case of a subsequent extension) on an application made before the expiration of the last previous extension, shall be extended until such date as the court may determine;

(b) Where no such appeal is pending or is so brought, shall continue until the end of the said time or, if any extension of that time is so granted, until the expiration of the extension or last extension so granted.

Reinstatement of applications

20A.—(1) Subsection (2) below applies where an application for a patent is refused, or is treated as having been refused or withdrawn, as a direct consequence of a failure by the applicant to comply with a requirement of this Act or rules within a period which is—   **AppA-20**

(a) set out in this Act or rules, or

(b) specified by the comptroller.

(2) Subject to subsection (3) below, the comptroller shall reinstate the application if, and only if—

(a) the applicant requests him to do so;
(b) the request complies with the relevant requirements of rules; and
(c) he is satisfied that the failure to comply referred to in subsection (1) above was unintentional.

(3) The comptroller shall not reinstate the application if—
   (a) an extension remains available under this Act or rules for the period referred to in subsection (1) above; or
   (b) the period referred to in subsection (1) above is set out or specified—
      (i) in relation to any proceedings before the comptroller;
      (ii) for the purposes of section 5(2A)(b) above; or
      (iii) for the purposes of a request under this section or section 117B below.

(4) Where the application was made by two or more persons jointly, a request under subsection (2) above may, with the leave of the comptroller, be made by one or more of those persons without joining the others.

(5) If the application has been published under section 16 above, then the comptroller shall publish notice of a request under subsection (2) above in the prescribed manner.

(6) The reinstatement of an application under this section shall be by order.

(7) If an application is reinstated under this section the applicant shall comply with the requirement referred to in subsection (1) above within the further period specified by the comptroller in the order reinstating the application.

(8) The further period specified under subsection (7) above shall not be less than two months.

(9) If the applicant fails to comply with subsection (7) above the application shall be treated as having been withdrawn on the expiry of the period specified under that subsection.

Note

Section 20A inserted, together with s.20B, by Regulatory Reform (Patents) Order 2004 (SI 2004/2357) art.8, with effect from 1 January 2005, subject to transitional provisions contained in arts 20–23 of that Order.

Effect of reinstatement under section 20A

AppA-20B

20B.—(1) The effect of reinstatement under section 20A of an application for a patent is as follows.

(2) Anything done under or in relation to the application during the period between termination and reinstatement shall be treated as valid.

(3) If the application has been published under section 16 above before its termination anything done during that period which would have constituted an infringement of the rights conferred by publication of the application if the termination had not occurred shall be treated as an infringement of those rights—
   (a) if done at a time when it was possible for the period referred to in section 20A(1) above to be extended, or
   (b) if it was a continuation or repetition of an earlier act infringing those rights.

[914]

(4) If the application has been published under section 16 above before its termination and, after the termination and before publication of notice of the request for its reinstatement, a person—

  (a) began in good faith to do an act which would have constituted an infringement of the rights conferred by publication of the application if the termination had not taken place, or

  (b) made in good faith effective and serious preparations to do such an act, he has the right to continue to do the act or, as the case may be, to do the act, notwithstanding the reinstatement of the application and the grant of the patent; but this right does not extend to granting a licence to another person to do the act.

(4A) The right conferred by subsection (4) does not become exercisable until the end of the period during which a request may be made under this Act, or under the rules, for an extension of the period referred to in section 20A(1).

(5) If the act was done, or the preparations were made, in the course of a business, the person entitled to the right conferred by subsection (4) above may—

  (a) authorise the doing of that act by any partners of his for the time being in that business, and

  (b) assign that right, or transmit it on death (or in the case of a body corporate on its dissolution), to any person who acquires that part of the business in the course of which the act was done or the preparations were made.

(6) Where a product is disposed of to another in exercise of a right conferred by subsection (4) or (5) above, that other and any person claiming through him maydeal with the product in the same way as if it had been disposed of by the applicant.

(6A) The above provisions apply in relation to the use of a patented invention for the services of the Crown as they apply in relation to infringement of the rights conferred by publication of the application for a patent (or, as the case may be, infringement of the patent).

"Patented invention" has the same meaning as in section 55 below.

(7) In this section "termination", in relation to an application, means—

  (a) the refusal of the application, or

  (b) the application being treated as having been refused or withdrawn.

Notes

Section 20B inserted, together with s.20A, by Regulatory Reform (Patents) Order 2004 (SI 2004/2357) art.8, with effect from 1 January 2005, subject to transitional provisions contained in arts 20–23 of that Order.

Subsection (4A) inserted by Intellectual Property Act 2014 (c.18) Sch.1 para.2 with effect from 1 October 2014

Subsection (6A) inserted by Patents Act 2004 (c.16) s.17(2) and Sch.2 para.7, with effect from 1 January 2005.

Observations by third party on patentability

21.—(1) Where an application for a patent has been published but a patent has not been granted to the applicant, any other person may make observations in writing to the comptroller on the question whether the invention is a patentable invention, stating reasons for the observations, and the comptroller shall consider the observations in accordance with rules.   AppA-21

(2)   It is hereby declared that a person does not become a party to any proceedings under this Act before the comptroller by reason only that he makes observations under this section.

Security and safety

Information prejudicial to [defence of realm] national security or safety of public

AppA-22   **22.**—(1)   Where an application for a patent is filed in the Patent Office (whether under this Act or any treaty or international convention to which the United Kingdom is a party and whether before or after the appointed day) and it appears to the comptroller that the application contains information of a description notified to him by the Secretary of State as being information the publication of which might be prejudicial to [*the defence of the realm*], **national security** the comptroller may give directions prohibiting or restricting the publication of that information or its communication to any specified person or description of persons.

(2)   If it appears to the comptroller that any application so filed contains information the publication of which might be prejudicial to the safety of the public, he may give directions prohibiting or restricting the publication of that information or its communication to any specified person or description of persons until the end of a period not exceeding three months from the end of the period prescribed for the purposes of section 16 above.

(3)   While directions are in force under this section with respect to an application—

    (a)   if the application is made under this Act, it may proceed to the stage where it is in order for the grant of a patent, but it shall not be published and that information shall not be so communicated and no patent shall be granted in pursuance of the application;

    (b)   if it is an application for a European patent, it shall not be sent to the European Patent Office; and

    (c)   if it is an international application for a patent, a copy of it shall not be sent to the International Bureau or any international searching authority appointed under the Patent Co-operation Treaty.

(4)   Subsection (3)(b) above shall not prevent the comptroller from sending the European Patent Office any information which it is his duty to send that office under the European Patent Convention.

(5)   Where the comptroller gives directions under this section with respect to any application, he shall give notice of the application and of the directions to the Secretary of State, and the following provisions shall then have effect:—

    (a)   The Secretary of State shall, on receipt of the notice, consider whether the publication of the application or the publication or communication of the information in question would be prejudicial to [*the defence of the realm*] **national security** or the safety of the public;

    (b)   if the Secretary of State determines under paragraph (a) above that the publication of the application or the publication or communication of that information would be prejudicial to the safety of the public, he shall notify the comptroller who shall continue his directions under subsection (2) above until they are revoked under paragraph (e) below;

    (c)   if the Secretary of State determines under paragraph (a) above that the publication of the application or the publication or communication of that information would be prejudicial to [*the defence of the realm*] **national security** or the safety of the public, he shall (unless a notice under paragraph (d) below has previously been given by the Secretary of State to the comptroller) reconsider that question during the period of nine months from the date of filing the application and at least once in every subsequent period of twelve months;

(d) if on consideration of an application at any time it appears to the Secretary of State that the publication of the application or the publication or communication of the information contained in it would not, or would no longer, be prejudicial to [*the defence of the realm*] **national security** or the safety of the public, he shall give notice to the comptroller to that effect; and

(e) on receipt of such a notice the comptroller shall revoke the directions and may, subject to such conditions (if any) as he thinks fit, extend the time for doing anything required or authorised to be done by or under this Act in connection with the application, whether or not that time has previously expired.

(6) The Secretary of State may do the following for the purpose of enabling him to decide the question referred to in subsection (5)(c) above—

(a) where the application contains information relating to the production or use of atomic energy or research into matters connected with such production or use, he may at any time do one or both of the following, that is to say, [*inspect and authorise the United Kingdom Atomic Energy Authority to inspect the application and any documents sent to the comptroller in connection with it*];

    (i) **inspect the application and any documents sent to the comptroller in connection with it;**

    (ii) **authorise a government body with responsibility for the production of atomic energy or for research into matters connected with its production or use, or a person appointed by such a government body, to inspect the application and any documents sent to the comptroller in connection with it; and**

(b) in any other case, he may at any time after (or, with the applicant's consent, before) the end of the period prescribed for the purposes of section 16 above inspect the application and any such documents;

and where [*that Authority are authorised under paragraph (a) above they shall as soon as practicable report on their inspection to the Secretary of State.*] **a government body or a person appointed by a government body carries out an inspection which the body or person is authorised to carry out under paragraph (a) above, the body or (as the case may be) the person shall report on the inspection to the Secretary of State as soon as practicable.**

(7) Where directions have been given under this section in respect of an application for a patent for an invention and, before the directions are revoked, that prescribed period expires and the application is brought in order for the grant of a patent then—

(a) if while the directions are in force the invention is worked by (or with the written authorisation of or to the order of) a government department, the provisions of sections 55 to 59 below shall apply as if—

    (i) the working were use made by section 55;

    (ii) the application had been published at the end of that period; and

    (iii) a patent had been granted for the invention at the time the application is brought in order for the grant of a patent (taking the terms of the patent to be those of the application as it stood at the time it was so brought in order); and

(b)   if it appears to the Secretary of State that the applicant for the patent has suffered hardship by reason of the continuance in force of the directions, the Secretary of State may, with the consent of the Treasury, make such payment (if any) by way of compensation to the applicant as appears to the Secretary of State and the Treasury to be reasonable having regard to the inventive merit and utility of the invention, the purpose for which it is designed and any other relevant circumstances.

(8)   Where a patent is granted in pursuance of an application in respect of which directions have been given under this section, no renewal fees shall be payable in respect of any period during which those directions were in force.

(9)   A person who fails to comply with any direction under this section shall be liable—

(a)   on summary conviction, to a fine not exceeding [*£1,000*] **the prescribed sum**; or

(b)   on conviction on indictment, to imprisonment for a term not exceeding two years or a fine, or both.

Notes

Provision heading and subss.(1), (5) and (6) amended by Patents Act 2004 (c.16) s.16 and Sch.2 para.8, with effect from 1 January 2005 (SI 2004/3205).

Subsection (9)(a) amended by Magistrates' Courts Act 1980 (c.43) s.32(2).

Restrictions on applications abroad by United Kingdom residents

AppA-23   **23.**—(1)   Subject to the following provisions of this section, no person resident in the United Kingdom shall, without written authority granted by the comptroller, file or cause to be filed outside the United Kingdom an application for a patent for an invention **if subsection (1A) below applies to that application,** unless—

(a)   an application for a patent for the same invention has been filed in the Patent Office (whether before, on or after the appointed day) not less than six weeks before the application outside the United Kingdom; and

(b)   either no directions have been given under section 22 above in relation to the application in the United Kingdom or all such directions have been revoked.

(1A)   This subsection applies to an application if—

(a)   the application contains information which relates to military technology or for any other reason publication of the information might be prejudicial to national security; or

(b)   the application contains information the publication of which might be prejudicial to the safety of the public.

(2)   Subsection (1) above does not apply to an application for a patent for an invention for which an application for a patent has first been filed (whether before or after the appointed day) in a country outside the United Kingdom by a person resident outside the United Kingdom.

(3)   A person who files or causes to be filed an application for the grant of a patent in contravention of this section shall be liable—

(a)   on summary conviction, to a fine not exceeding [*£1,000*] **the prescribed sum**; or

(b)   on conviction on indictment, to imprisonment for a term not exceeding two years or a fine, or both.

(3A)   A person is liable under subsection (3) above only if—

    (a)   he knows that filing the application, or causing it to be filed, would contravene this section; or

    (b)   he is reckless as to whether filing the application, or causing it to be filed, would contravene this section.

(4)   In this section—

    (a)   any reference to an application for a patent includes a reference to an application for other protection for an invention;

    (b)   any reference to either kind of application is a reference to an application under this Act, under the law of any country other than the United Kingdom or under any treaty or international convention to which the United Kingdom is a party.

Notes

Subsection (1) amended and subss.(1A) and (3A) inserted by Patents Act 2004 (c.16) s.7, with effect from 1 January 2005 (SI 2004/3205).

Subsection (3)(a) amended by Magistrates' Courts Act 1980 (c.43) s.32(2).

Provisions as to patents after grant

Publication and certificate of grant

24.—(1)   As soon as practicable after a patent has been granted under this Act the comptroller shall publish in the journal a notice that it has been granted.   **AppA-24**

(2)   The comptroller shall, as soon as practicable after he publishes a notice under subsection (1) above, send the proprietor of the patent a certificate in the prescribed form that the patent has been granted to the proprietor.

(3)   The comptroller shall, at the same time as he publishes a notice under subsection (1) above in relation to a patent publish the specification of the patent, the names of the proprietor and (if different) the inventor and any other matters constituting, or relating to the patent which, in the comptroller's opinion it is desirable to publish.

(4)   Subsection (3) above shall not require the comptroller to identify as inventor a person who has waived his right to be mentioned as inventor in any patent granted for the invention.

Note

Subsection (4) inserted by Patents Act 2004 (c.16) s.16 and Sch.2, para.9, with effect from 1 October 2005 (SI 2005/2471).

Term of patent

25.—(1)   A patent under this Act shall be treated for the purposes of the following provisions of this Act as having been granted, and shall take effect, on the date on which notice of its grant is published in the journal and, subject to subsection (3) below, shall continue in force until the end of the period of 20 years beginning with the date of filing the application for the patent or with such other date as may be prescribed.   **AppA-25**

(2)   A rule prescribing any such other date under this section shall not be made

unless a draft of the rule has been laid before, and approved by resolution of, each House of Parliament.

[*(3)   A patent shall cease to have effect at the end of the period prescribed for the payment of any renewal fee if it is not paid within that period.*]

(3)   Where any renewal fee in respect of a patent is not paid by the end of the period prescribed for payment (the "prescribed period") the patent shall cease to have effect at the end of such day, in the final month of that period, as may be prescribed.

(4)   If during [*the period of six months immediately following the end of the prescribed period*] **the period ending with the sixth month after the month in which the prescribed period ends** the renewal fee and any prescribed additional fee are paid, the patent shall be treated for the purposes of this Act as if it had never expired, and accordingly—

    (a)   anything done under or in relation to it during that further period shall be valid;

    (b)   an act which would constitute an infringement of it if it had not expired shall constitute such an infringement; and

    (c)   an act which would constitute the use of the patented invention for the services of the Crown if the patent had not expired shall constitute that use.

(5)   Rules shall include provision requiring the comptroller to notify the registered proprietor of a patent that a renewal fee has not been received from him in the Patent Office before the end of the prescribed period and before the framing of the notification.

Note

Subsection (3) substituted and subs.(4) amended by Patents Act 2004 (c.16) s.8, with effect from 1 October 2005 (SI 2005/2471), subject to transitional provisions contained in art.3 of that Order.

Patent not to be impugned for lack of unity

AppA-26   **26.**   No person may in any proceeding object to a patent or to an amendment of a specification of a patent on the ground that the claims contained in the specification of the patent, as they stand or, as the case may be, as proposed to be amended, relate—

    (a)   to more than one invention; or

    (b)   to a group of inventions which are not so linked as to form a single inventive concept.

General power to amend specification after grant

AppA-27   **27.**—(1)   Subject to the following provisions of this section and to section 76 below, the comptroller may, on an application made by the proprietor of a patent, allow the specification of the patent to be amended subject to such conditions, if any, as he thinks fit.

(2)   No such amendments shall be allowed under this section where there are pending before the court or the comptroller proceedings in which the validity of the patent may be put in issue.

(3)   An amendment of a specification of a patent under this section shall have effect and be deemed always to have had effect from the grant of the patent.

(4)   The comptroller may, without an application being made to him for the

purpose, amend the specification of a patent so as to acknowledge a registered trademark.

(5)   A person may give notice to the comptroller of his opposition to an application under this section by the proprietor of a patent, and if he does so the comptroller shall notify the proprietor and consider the opposition in deciding whether to grant the application.

(6)   In considering whether or not to allow an application under this section, the comptroller shall have regard to any relevant principles applicable under the European Patent Convention.

Note

Subsection (6) inserted by Patents Act 2004 (c.16) s.2(1), with effect from 13 December 2007 (SI 2007/3396).

Restoration of lapsed patents

28.—[*(1)   Where a patent has ceased to have effect by reason of a failure to pay*   AppA-28
*any renewal fee within the prescribed period, an application for the restoration of
the patent may be made to the comptroller under this section within one year from
the date on which the patent ceased to have effect.*]

**(1)   Where a patent has ceased to have effect by reason of a failure to pay
any renewal fee, an application for the restoration of the patent may be made
to the comptroller within the prescribed period.**

**(1A)   Rules prescribing that period may contain such transitional provisions and savings as appear to the Secretary of State to be necessary or
expedient.**

(2)   An application under this section may be made by the person who was the proprietor of the patent or by any other person who would have been entitled to the patent if it had not ceased to have effect; and where the patent was held by two or more persons jointly, the application may, with the leave of the comptroller, be made by one or more of them without joining the others.

**(2A)   Notice of the application shall be published by the comptroller in the
prescribed manner.**

[*(3)   If the comptroller is satisfied that—*

  (a)   *the proprietor of the patent took reasonable care to see that any
        renewal fee was paid within the prescribed period or that that fee and
        any prescribed additional fee were paid within the six months immediately following the end of that period,* [*and*

  (b)   *those fees were not so paid because of circumstances beyond his
        control,*]

*the comptroller shall by order restore the patent on payment of any unpaid renewal
fee and any prescribed additional fee.*]

**(3)   If the comptroller is satisfied that the failure of the proprietor of the
patent—**

  (a)   to pay the renewal fee within the prescribed period; or

  **(b)   to pay that fee and any prescribed additional fee [*within the period
          of six months immediately following the end of that period*] within
          the period ending with the sixth month after the month in which
          the prescribed period ended, was unintentional, the comptroller
          shall by order restore the patent on payment of any unpaid
          renewal fee and any prescribed additional fee.**

(4)   An order under this section may be made subject to such conditions as the comptroller thinks fit (including a condition requiring compliance with any provisions of the rules relating to registration which have not been complied with), and if the proprietor of the patent does not comply with any condition of such an order the comptroller may revoke the order and give such directions consequential on the revocation as he thinks fit.

[(5)   *Where an order is made under this section and, between the end of the period of six months beginning with the date when the patent concerned ceased to have effect and the date of the application under this section,—*

(a)   *a person continued to do or did again an act which would have constituted an infringement of the patent if it had not expired and which he first did before the end of that period, that act shall constitute such an infringement; or*

(b)   *a person began in good faith to do an act which would constitute an infringement of the patent if it had been in force or made in good faith effective and serious preparations to do such an act, he shall, after the order comes into force, have the rights conferred by subsection (6) below.*

(6)   *Any such person shall have the right—*

(a)   *to continue to do or, as the case may be, to do that act himself; and*

(b)   *if it was done or preparations had been made to do it in the course of a business, to assign the right to do it or to transmit that right on his death or, in the case of a body corporate on its dissolution, to any person who acquires that part of the business in the course of which the act was done or preparations had been made to do it, or to authorise it to be done by any partners of his for the time being in that business;*

and the doing of that act by virtue of this subsection shall not amount to an infringement of the patent concerned.

(7)   *The rights mentioned in subsection (6) above shall not include the right to grant a licence to any person to do an act so mentioned.*

(8)   *Where a patented product is disposed of by any person to another in exercise of a right conferred by subsection (6) above, that other and any other person claiming through him shall be entitled to deal with the product in the same way as if it had been disposed of by a sole registered proprietor.*

(9)   *Subsections (5) to (7) above shall apply in relation to an act which would constitute the use of a patented invention for the services of the Crown if the patent had been in force as they apply in relation to an act which would constitute an infringement of the patent if it had been in force, and subsection (8) above shall apply accordingly to the disposal of a patented product in the exercise of a right conferred by subsection (6) above as applied by the foregoing provision.*]

Notes

Subsections (1), (1A) substituted for original subs.(1), subs.(2A) inserted, subs.(3) amended and subss.(5)–(9) repealed by CDPA 1988 (c.48) s.295 and Sch.5, para.6, with effect from 7 January 1991 (SI 1990/2168).

Subsection (3) substituted by Regulatory Reform (Patents) Order 2004 (SI 2004/2357) art.9, with effect from 1 January 2005, subject to transitional provisions contained in arts 20–23 of that Order.

Subsection (3)(b) amended by Patents Act 2004 (c.16) s.8(3), with effect from 1 October 2005 (SI 2005/2471), subject to transitional provisions contained in art.3 of that Order.

Effect of order for restoration of patent

28A.—(1)   The effect of an order for the restoration of a patent is as follows.   AppA-28A

(2)   Anything done under or in relation to the patent during the period between expiry and restoration shall be treated as valid.

(3)   Anything done during that period which would have constituted an infringement if the patent had not expired shall be treated as an infringement—

- (a)   if done at a time when it was possible for the patent to be renewed under section 25(4), or
- (b)   if it was a continuation or repetition of an earlier infringing act.

(4)   If after it was no longer possible for the patent to be so renewed, and before publication of notice of the application for restoration, a person—

- (a)   began in good faith to do an act which would have constituted an infringement of the patent if it had not expired, or
- (b)   made in good faith effective and serious preparations to do such an act, he has the right to continue to do the act or, as the case may be, to do the act, notwithstanding the restoration of the patent; but this right does not extend to granting a licence to another person to do the act.

(5)   If the act was done, or the preparations were made, in the course of a business, the person entitled to the right conferred by subsection (4) may—

- (a)   authorise the doing of that act by any partners of his for the time being in that business, and
- (b)   assign that right, or transmit it on death (or in the case of a body corporate on its dissolution), to any person who acquires that part of the business in the course of which the act was done or the preparations were made.

(6)   Where a product is disposed of to another in exercise of the rights conferred by subsection (4) or (5), that other and any person claiming through him may deal with the product in the same way as if it had been disposed of by the registered proprietor of the patent.

(7)   The above provisions apply in relation to the use of a patent for the services of the Crown as they apply in relation to infringement of the patent.

Note

Section 28A inserted by CDPA 1988 (c.48) s.295 and Sch.5 para.7, with effect from 7 January 1991 (SI 1990/2168).

Surrender of patents

29.—(1)   The proprietor of a patent may at any time by notice given to the   AppA-29 comptroller offer to surrender his patent.

(2)   A person may give notice to the comptroller of his opposition to the surrender of a patent under this section, and if he does so the comptroller shall notify the proprietor of the patent and determine the question.

(3)   If the comptroller is satisfied that the patent may properly be surrendered, he may accept the offer and, as from the date when notice of his acceptance is published in the journal, the patent shall cease to have effect, but no action for infringement shall lie in respect of any act done before that date and no right to compensation shall accrue for any use of the patented invention before that date for the services of the Crown.

Property in patents and applications, and registration

Nature of, and transactions in, patents and applications for patents

AppA-30   **30.**—(1)   Any patent or application for a patent is personal property (without being a thing in action), and any patent or any such application and rights in or under it may be transferred, created or granted in accordance with subsections (2) to (7) below.

(2)   Subject to section 36(3) below, any patent or any such application, or any right in it, may be assigned or mortgaged.

(3)   Any patent or any such application or right shall vest by operation of law in the same way as any other personal property and may be vested by an assent of personal representatives.

(4)   Subject to section 36(3) below, a licence may be granted under any patent or any such application for working the invention which is the subject of the patent or the application; and—

    (a)   to the extent that the licence so provides, a sub-licence may be granted under any such licence and any such licence or sub-licence may be assigned or mortgaged; and

    (b)   any such licence or sub-licence shall vest by operation of law in the same way as any other personal property and may be vested by an assent of personal representatives.

(5)   Subsections (2) to (4) above shall have effect subject to the following provisions of this Act.

(6)   Any of the following transactions, that is to say—

    (a)   any assignment or mortgage of a patent or any such application, or any right in a patent or any such application;

    (b)   any assent relating to any patent or any such application or right; shall be void unless it is in writing and is signed by or on behalf of [*the parties to the transaction*] **the assignor or mortgagor** (or, in the case of an assent or other transaction by a personal representative, by or on behalf of the personal representative) [*or in the case of a body corporate is so signed or is under the seal of that body.*]

(6A)   If a transaction mentioned in subsection (6) above is by a body corporate, references in that subsection to such a transaction being signed by or on behalf of the assignor or mortgagor shall be taken to include references to its being under the seal of the body corporate.

(7)   An assignment of a patent or any such application or a share in it, and an exclusive licence granted under any patent or any such application, may confer on the assignee or licensee the right of the assignor or licensor to bring proceedings by virtue of section 61 or 69 below for a previous infringement or to bring proceedings under section 58 below for a previous act.

Note

Subsection (6) amended and subs.(6A) inserted by Regulatory Reform (Patents) Order 2004 (SI 2004/2357) art.10, with effect from 1 January 2005, subject to transitional provisions contained in arts 20–23 of that Order.

Nature of, and transactions in, patents and applications for patents in Scotland

AppA-31   **31.**—(1)   Section 30 above shall not extend to Scotland, but instead the following provisions of this section shall apply there.

(2)   Any patent or application for a patent, and any right in or under any patent or any such application, is incorporeal moveable property, and the provisions of the following subsections and of section 36(3) below shall apply to any grant of licences, assignations and securities in relation to such property.

(3)   Any patent or any such application, or any right in it, may be assigned and security may be granted over a patent or any such application or right.

(4)   A licence may be granted, under any patent or any application for a patent, for working the invention which is the subject of the patent or the application.

(5)   To the extent that any licence granted under subsection (4) above so provides, a sub-licence may be granted under any such licence and any such licence or sub-licence may be assigned and security may be granted over it.

(6)   Any assignation or grant of security under this section may be carried out by writing [*probative or holograph of the parties to the transaction*] **subscribed in accordance with the Requirements of Writing (Scotland) Act 1995.**

(7)   An assignation of a patent or application for a patent or a share in it, and an exclusive licence granted under any patent or any such application, may confer on the assignee or licensee the right of the assignor or licensor to bring proceedings by virtue of section 61 or 69 below for a previous infringement or to bring proceedings under section 58 below for a previous act.

Note

Subsection (6) amended by Requirements of Writing (Scotland) Act 1995 (c.7) s.14(1) and Sch.4 para.49, with effect from 1 August 1995, subject to savings specified in s.14(3) of that Act.

[Register of patents, etc.

32.—(1)   There shall continue to be a register kept at the Patent Office and   **AppA-32**
known as the register of patents which shall comply with rules made by virtue of this section and shall be kept in accordance with such rules; and in this Act, except so far as the context otherwise requires—

> *"register," as a noun, means the register of patents;*
> *"register", as a verb, means, in relation to any thing, to register or register particulars, or enter notice, of that thing in the register and, in relation to a person, means to enter his name in the register;*
> *and cognate expressions shall be construed accordingly.*

(2)   Without prejudice to any other provision of this Act or rules, rules may make provision with respect to the following matters, including provision imposing requirements as to any of those matters, that is to say—

> *(a)   the registration of patents and of published applications for patents;*
> *(b)   the registration of transactions, instruments or events affecting rights in or under patents and applications;*
> *(c)   the furnishing to the comptroller of any prescribed documents or description of documents in connection with any matter which is required to be registered;*
> *(d)   the correction of errors in the register and in any documents filed at the Patent Office in connection with registration;*
> *(e)   making the register or entries or reproductions of entries in it available for inspection by the public;*
> *(f)   supplying certified copies of any such entries or reproductions to persons requiring them; and*

Register of patents, etc.

32.—(1)   The comptroller shall maintain the register of patents, which shall
comply with rules made by virtue of this section and shall be kept in accordance with such rules.

(2)   Without prejudice to any other provision of this Act or rules, rules may
make provision with respect to the following matters, including provision
imposing requirements as to any of those matters—

    (a)   the registration of patents and of published applications for
        patents;

    (b)   the registration of transactions, instruments or events affecting
        rights in or under patents and applications;

  [(ba)   the entering on the register of notices concerning opinions issued,
        or to be issued, under section 74A below;]

    (c)   the furnishing to the comptroller of any prescribed documents or
        description of documents in connection with any matter which is
        required to be registered;

    (d)   the correction of errors in the register and in any documents filed
        at the Patents Office in connection with registration; and(e) the
        publication and advertisement of anything done under this Act or
        rules in relation to the register.

(3)   Notwithstanding anything in subsection (2)(b) above, no notice of any
trust, whether express, implied or constructive, shall be entered in the register
and the comptroller shall not be affected by any such notice.

(4)   The register need not be kept in documentary form.

(5)   Subject to rules, the public shall have a right to inspect the register at
the Patent Office at all convenient times.

(6)   Any person who applies for a certified copy of an entry in the register
or a certified extract from the register shall be entitled to obtain such a copy
or extract on payment of a fee prescribed in relation to certified copies and
extracts; and rules may provide that any person who applies for an uncertified copy or extract shall be entitled to such a copy or extract on payment of a
fee prescribed in relation to uncertified copies and extracts.

(7)   Applications under subsection (6) above or rules made by virtue of that
subsection shall be made in such manner as may be prescribed.

(8)   In relation to any portion of the register kept otherwise than in
documentary form—

    (a)   the right of inspection conferred by subsection (5) above is a right
        to inspect the material on the register; and

    (b)   the right to a copy or extract conferred by subsection (6) above or
        rules is a right to a copy or extract in a form in which it can be
        taken away and in which it is visible and legible.

(9)   [*Subject to subsection (12) below,*] the register shall be prima facie
evidence of anything required or authorised by this Act or rules to be
registered and in Scotland shall be sufficient evidence of any such thing.

(10)   A certificate purporting to be signed by the comptroller and certifying that any entry which he is authorised by this Act or rules to make has or has not been made, or that any other thing which he is so authorised to do has or has not been done, shall be prima facie evidence, and in Scotland shall be sufficient evidence, of the matters so certified.

(11)   Each of the following, that is to say—

    (a)   a copy of an entry in the register or an extract from the register which is supplied under subsection (6) above;

    (b)   a copy of any document kept in the Patent Office or an extract from any such document, any specification of a patent or any application for a patent which has been published, which purports to be a certified copy or a certified extract shall [, *subject to subsection (12) below,*] be admitted in evidence without further proof and without production of any original; and in Scotland such evidence shall be sufficient evidence.

[*(12)   In the application of this section to England and Wales nothing in it shall be taken as detracting from section 69 or 70 of the Police and Criminal Evidence Act 1984 or any provision made by virtue of either of them.*]

(13)   In this section "certified copy" and "certified extract" mean a copy and extract certified by the comptroller and sealed with the seal of the Patent Office.

(14)   In this Act, except so far as the context otherwise requires—

"register" as a noun, means the register of patents;

"register" as a verb, means, in relation to any thing, to register or register particulars, or enter notice, of that thing in the register and, in relation to a person, means to enter his name in the register;

and cognate expressions shall be construed accordingly.

Notes

Section 32 substituted by Patents, Designs and Marks Act 1986 (c.39) s.1 and Sch.1 para.4, with effect from 1 January 1989 (SI 1988/1824).

Subsection (2)(ba) inserted by Patents Act 2004 (c.16) s.13(3), with effect from 1 October 2005 (SI 2005/2471).

Subsections (9) and (11) amended by Criminal Justice Act 2003 (c.44) s.332 and Sch.37 Pt 6, with effect from 4 April 2005 (SI 2005/950).

Subsection (12) repealed by Youth Justice and Criminal Evidence Act 1999 (c.23) s.67 and Sch.6.

Effect of registration, etc., on rights in patents

33.—(1)   Any person who claims to have acquired the property in a patent or   AppA-33
application for a patent by virtue of any transaction, instrument or event to which this section applies shall be entitled as against any other person who claims to have acquired that property by virtue of an earlier transaction, instrument or event to which this section applies, if, at the time of the later transaction, instrument or event—

    (a)   the earlier transaction, instrument or event was not registered, or

    (b)   in the case of any application which has not been published, notice of the earlier transaction, instrument or event had not been given to the comptroller, and

    (c)   in any case, the person claiming under the later transaction, instrument or event, did not know of the earlier transaction, instrument or event.

(2)   Subsection (1) above shall apply equally to the case where any person claims to have acquired any right in or under a patent or application for a patent, by virtue of a transaction, instrument or event to which this section applies, and that right is incompatible with any such right acquired by virtue of an earlier transaction, instrument or event to which this section applies.

(3)   This section applies to the following transactions, instruments and events:—

    (a)   the assignment or assignation of a patent or application for a patent, or a right in it;

    (b)   the mortgage of a patent or application or the granting of security over it;

    (c)   the grant, assignment or assignation of a licence or sub-licence or mortgage of a licence or sub-licence under a patent or application;

    (d)   the death of the proprietor or one of the proprietors of any such patent or application or any person having a right in or under a patent or application and the vesting by an assent of personal representatives of a patent, application or any such right; and

    (e)   any order or directions of a court or other competent authority—

        (i)   transferring a patent or application or any right in or under it to any person; or (ii) that an application should proceed in the name of any person;

and in either case the event by virtue of which the court or authority had power to make any such order to give any such directions.

(4)   Where an application for the registration of a transaction, instrument or event has been made, but the transaction, instrument or event has not been registered, then, for the purposes of subsection (1)(a) above, registration of the application shall be treated as registration of the transaction, instrument or event.

Rectification of register

AppA-34   **34.**—(1)   The court may, on the application of any person aggrieved, order the register to be rectified by the making, or the variation or deletion, of any entry in it.

(2)   In proceedings under this section the court may determine any question which it may be necessary or expedient to decide in connection with the rectification of the register.

(3)   Rules of court may provide for the notification of any application under this section to the comptroller and for his appearance on the application and for giving effect to any order of the court on the application.

[Evidence of register, documents, etc.

AppA-35   **35.**—(1)   *The register shall be prima facie evidence of anything required or authorised by this Act or rules to be registered and in Scotland shall be admissible and sufficient evidence of any such thing.*

(2)   A certificate purporting to be signed by the comptroller and certifying that any entry which he is authorised by this Act or rules to make has or has not been made, or that any other thing which he is so authorised to do has or has not been done, shall be prima facie evidence, and in Scotland shall be admissible, and sufficient evidence, of the matters so certified.

(3)   Each of the following, that is to say—

    (a)   a copy of any entry in the register or of any document kept in the Pat-

ent Office, any specification of a patent or any application for a patent which has been published;

(b) a document reproducing in legible form an entry made in the register otherwise than in legible form; or

(c) an extract from the register or of any document mentioned in paragraph (a) or (b) above; purporting to be certified by the comptroller and to be sealed with the seal of the Patent Office shall be admitted in evidence without further proof and without production of the original, and in Scotland such evidence shall be sufficient evidence.]

Note

Section 35 repealed by Patents, Designs and Marks Act 1986 (c.39) s.3 and Sch.3 Pt 1 para.1, with effect from 1 January 1989 (SI 1988/1824).

Co-ownership of patents and applications for patents

36.—(1) Where a patent is granted to two or more persons, each of them shall, subject to any agreement to the contrary, be entitled to an equal undivided share in the patent.

AppA-36

(2) Where two or more persons are proprietors of a patent, then, subject to the provisions of this section and subject to any agreement to the contrary—

    (a) each of them shall be entitled, by himself or his agents, to do in respect of the invention concerned, for his own benefit and without the consent of or the need to account to the other or others, any act which would apart from this subsection and section 55 below, amount to an infringement of the patent concerned; and

    (b) any such act shall not amount to an infringement of the patent concerned.

(3) Subject to the provisions of section 8 and 12 above and section 37 below and to any agreement for the time being in force, where two or more persons are proprietors of a patent one of them shall not without the consent of the other or others

    (a) amend the specification of the patent or apply for such an amendment to be allowed or for the patent to be revoked, or

    (b) grant a licence under the patent or assign or mortgage a share in the patent or in Scotland cause or permit security to be granted over it.

(4) Subject to the provisions of those sections, where two or more persons are proprietors of a patent, anyone else may supply one of those persons with the means, relating to an essential element of the invention, for putting the invention into effect, and the supply of those means by virtue of this subsection shall not amount to an infringement of the patent.

(5) Where a patented product is disposed of by any of two or more proprietors to any person, that person and any other person claiming through him shall be entitled to deal with the product in the same way as if it had been disposed of by a sole registered proprietor.

(6) Nothing in subsection (1) or (2) above shall affect the mutual rights or obligations of trustees or of the personal representatives of a deceased person, or their rights or obligations as such.

(7) The foregoing provisions of this section shall have effect in relation to an application for a patent which is filed as they have effect in relation to a patent and—

    (a) references to a patent and a patent being granted shall accordingly include references respectively to any such application and to the application being filed; and

    (b)   the reference in subsection (5) above to a patented product shall be construed accordingly.

Note

Subsection (3) amended by Patents Act 2004 (c.16) s.9, with effect from 1 October 2005 (SI 2005/2471).

Determination of right to patent after grant

AppA-37   **37.**—[*(1)   After a patent has been granted for an invention—*

    (a)   any person may refer to the comptroller the question whether he is the true proprietor of the patent or whether the patent should have beengranted to him (in either case alone or jointly with any other persons) or whether the patent or any right in or under it should be transferred to him (alone or jointly with any other persons); and

    (b)   any of two or more persons registered as joint proprietors of the patent may refer to the comptroller the question whether any right in or under the patent should be transferred or granted to any other person;and the comptroller shall determine the question and make such order as he thinks fit to give effect to the determination.]

(1)   After a patent has been granted for an invention any person having or claiming a proprietary interest in or under the patent may refer to the comptroller the question—

    (a)   who is or are the true proprietor or proprietors of the patent,

    (b)   whether the patent should have been granted to the person or persons to whom it was granted, or

    (c)   whether any right in or under the patent should be transferred or granted to any other person or persons;

and the comptroller shall determine the question and make such order as he thinks fit to give effect to the determination.

(2)   Without prejudice to the generality of subsection (1) above, an order under that subsection may contain provision—

    (a)   directing that the person by whom the reference is made under that subsection shall be included (whether or not to the exclusion of any other person) among the persons registered as proprietors of the patent;

    (b)   directing the registration of a transaction, instrument or event by virtue of which that person has acquired any right in or under the patent;

    (c)   granting any licence or other right in or under the patent;

    (d)   directing the proprietor of the patent or any person having any right in or under the patent to do anything specified in the order as necessary to carry out the other provisions of the order.

(3)   If any person to whom directions have been given under subsection (2)(d) above fails to do anything necessary for carrying out any such directions within 14 days after the date of the order containing the directions, the comptroller may, on application made to him by any person in whose favour or on whose reference the order containing the directions was made, authorise him to do that thing on behalf of the person to whom the directions were given.

(4)   Where the comptroller finds on a reference under [*subsection (1)(a) above*]

this section that the patent was granted to a person not entitled to be granted that patent (whether alone or with other persons) and on an application made under section 72 below makes an order on that ground for the conditional or unconditional revocation of the patent, the comptroller may order that the person by whom the application was made or his successor in title may, subject to section 76 below, make a new application for a patent—

    (a)   in the case of unconditional revocation, for the whole of the matter comprised in the specification of that patent; and

    (b)   in the case of conditional revocation, for the matter which in the opinion of the comptroller should be excluded from that specification by amendment under section 75 below: and where such a new application is made, it shall be treated as having been filed on the date of filing the application for the patent to which the reference relates.

(5)   On any such reference no order shall be made under this section transferring the patent to which the reference relates on the ground that the patent was granted to a person not so entitled, and no order shall be made under subsection (4) above on that ground, if the reference was made after **the second anniversary of** [*the end of the period of two years beginning with*] the date of the grant, unless it is shown that any person registered as a proprietor of the patent knew at the time of the grant or, as the case may be, of the transfer of the patent to him that he was not entitled to the patent.

(6)   An order under this section shall not be so made as to affect the mutual rights or obligations of trustees or of the personal representatives of a deceased person, or their rights or obligations as such.

(7)   Where a question is referred to the comptroller under [*subsection (1)(a) above*] **this section** an order shall not be made by virtue of subsection (2) or under subsection (4) above on the reference unless notice of the reference is given to all persons registered as proprietor of the patent or as having a right in or under the patent except those who are parties to the reference.

(8)   If it appears to the comptroller on a reference under [*subsection (1) above*] **this section** that the question referred to him would more properly be determined by the court, he may decline to deal with it and, without prejudice to the court's jurisdiction to determine any such question and make a declaration, or any declaratory jurisdiction of the court in Scotland, the court shall have jurisdiction to do so.

(9)   The court shall not in the exercise of any such declaratory jurisdiction determine a question whether a patent was granted to a person not entitled to be granted the patent if the proceedings in which the jurisdiction is invoked were commenced after the end of the period of two years beginning with the date of the grant of the patent, unless it is shown that any person registered as a proprietor of the patent knew at the time of the grant or, as the case may be, of the transfer of the patent to him that he was not entitled to the patent.

Note

   Subsection (1) substituted and subs.(4), (7) and (8) amended by CDPA 1988 (c.48) s.295 and Sch.5 para.9, with effect from 7 January 1991 (SI 1990/2168).

   Subsection (5) amended by Intellectual Property Act 2014 (c.18) Sch.1 para.3(1)(a) with effect from 1 October 2014

Effect of transfer of patent under s. 37

38.—(1)   Where an order is made under section 37 above that a patent shall be transferred from any person or persons (the old proprietor or proprietors) to one or   AppA-38 more persons (whether or not including an old proprietor), then, except in a case falling within subsection (2) below, any licences or other rights granted or created by the old proprietor or proprietors shall, subject to section 33 above and to the provisions of the order, continue in force and be treated as granted by the person or persons to whom the patent is ordered to be transferred (the new proprietor or proprietors).

(2)   Where an order is so made that a patent shall be transferred from the old proprietor or proprietors to one or more persons none of whom was an old proprietor (on the ground that the patent was granted to a person not entitled to be granted the patent), any licences or other rights in or under the patent shall, subject to the provisions of the order and subsection (3) below, lapse on the registration of that person or those persons as the new proprietor or proprietors of the patent.

(3)   Where an order is so made that a patent shall be transferred as mentioned in subsection (2) above or that a person other than an old proprietor may make a new application for a patent and before the reference of the question under that section resulting in the making of any such order is registered, the old proprietor or proprietors or a licensee of the patent, acting in good faith, worked the invention in question in the United Kingdom or made effective and serious preparations to do so, the old proprietor or proprietors or the licensee shall, on making a request to the new proprietor or proprietors **or, as the case may be, the new applicant** within the prescribed period, be entitled to be granted a licence (but not an exclusive licence) to continue working or, as the case may be, to work the invention, so far as it is the subject of the new application.

(4)   Any such licence shall be granted for a reasonable period and on reasonable terms.

(5)   The new proprietor or proprietors of the patent **or, as the case may be, the new applicant** or any person claiming that he is entitled to be granted any such licence may refer to the comptroller the question whether that person is so entitled and whether any such period is or terms are reasonable, and the comptroller shall determine the question and may, if he considers it appropriate, order the grant of such a licence.

Note

Subsections (3) and (5) amended by Patents Act 2004 (c.16) s.16 and Sch.2 para.10, with effect from 1 January 2005 (SI 2004/3205).

Employees' inventions

Right to employees' inventions

AppA-39   **39.**—(1)   Notwithstanding anything in any rule of law, an invention made by an employee shall, as between him and his employer, be taken to belong to his employer for the purposes of this Act and all other purposes if—

   (a)   it was made in the course of the normal duties of the employee or in the course of duties falling outside his normal duties, but specifically assigned to him, and the circumstances in either case were such that an invention might reasonably be expected to result from the carrying out of his duties; or

   (b)   the invention was made in the course of the duties of the employee and, at the time of making the invention, because of the nature of his duties and the particular responsibilities arising from the nature of his duties he had a special obligation to further the interests of the employer's undertaking.

(2) Any other invention made by an employee shall, as between him and his employer, be taken for those purposes to belong to the employee.

(3) Where by virtue of this section an invention belongs, as between him and his employer, to an employee, nothing done—

(a) by or on behalf of the employee or any person claiming under him for the purposes of pursuing an application for a patent, or

(b) by any person for the purpose of performing or working the invention, shall be taken to infringe any copyright or design right to which, as between him and his employer, his employer is entitled in any model or document relating to the invention.

Note

Subsection (3) inserted by CDPA 1988 (c.48) s.295 and Sch.5 para.11, with effect from 7 January 1991 (SI 1990/2168).

Compensation of employees for certain inventions

40.—[(1) Where it appears to the court or the comptroller on an application AppA-40
made by an employee within the prescribed period that the employee has made an invention belonging to the employer for which a patent has been granted, that the patent is (having regard among other things to the size and nature of the employer's undertaking) of outstanding benefit to the employer and that by reason of those facts it is just that the employee should be awarded compensation to be paid by the employer, the court or the comptroller may award him such compensation of an amount determined under section 41 below.]

(1) Where it appears to the court or the comptroller on an application made by an employee within the prescribed period that—

(a) the employee has made an invention belonging to the employer for which a patent has been granted,

(b) having regard among other things to the size and nature of the employer's undertaking, the invention or the patent for it (or the combination of both) is of outstanding benefit to the employer, and

(c) by reason of those facts it is just that the employee should be awarded compensation to be paid by the employer, the court or the comptroller may award him such compensation of an amount determined under section 41 below.

(2) Where it appears to the court or the comptroller on an application made by an employee within the prescribed period that—

(a) a patent has been granted for an invention made by and belonging to the employee;

(b) his rights in the invention, or in any patent or application for a patent for the invention, have since the appointed day been assigned to the employer or an exclusive licence under the patent or application has since the appointed day been granted to the employer;

(c) the benefit derived by the employee from the contract of assignment, assignation or grant or any ancillary contract ("the relevant contract") is inadequate in relation to the benefit derived by the employer from [*the patent*] **the invention or the patent for it (or both)**; and

(d) by reason of those facts it is just that the employee should be awarded compensation to be paid by the employer in addition to the benefit derived from the relevant contract;

the court or the comptroller may award him such compensation of an amount determined under section 41 below.

(3) Subsections (1) and (2) above shall not apply to the invention of an employee where a relevant collective agreement provides for the payment of compensation in respect of inventions of the same description as that invention to employees of the same description as that employee.

(4) Subsection (2) above shall have effect notwithstanding anything in the relevant contract or any agreement applicable to the invention (other than any such collective agreement).

(5) If it appears to the comptroller on an application under this section that the application involves matters which would more properly be determined by the court, he may decline to deal with it.

(6) In this section—

"the prescribed period", in relation to proceedings before the court, means the period prescribed by rules of court, and "relevant collective agreement" means a collective agreement within the meaning of [*the Trade Union and Labour Relations Act 1974*] **the Trade Union and Labour Relations (Consolidation) Act 1992**, made by or on behalf of a trade union to which the employee belongs, and by the employer or an employers' association to which the employer belongs which is in force at the time of the making of the invention.

(7) References in this section to an invention belonging to an employer or employee are references to it so belonging as between the employer and the employee.

Notes

Subsection (1) substituted and subs.(2) amended by Patents Act 2004 (c.16) s.10(1), (2), with effect from 1 January 2005 (SI 2004/3205), subject to savings contained in s.10(8) of that Act.

Subsection (6) amended by Trade Union and Labour Relations (Consolidation) Act 1992 (c.52) s.300(2) and Sch.2 para.9.

Amount of compensation

AppA-41   **41.**—[*(1) An award of compensation to an employee under section 40(1) or (2) above in relation to a patent for an invention shall be such as will secure for the employee a fair share (having regard to all the circumstances) of the benefit which the employer has derived, or may reasonably be expected to derive, from the patent or from the assignment, assignation or grant to a person connected with the employer of the property or any right in the invention or the property in, or any right in or under, an application for that patent.*]

(1) **An award of compensation to an employee under section 40(1) or (2) above shall be such as will secure for the employee a fair share (having regard to all the circumstances) of the benefit which the employer has derived, or may reasonably be expected to derive, from any of the following—**

(a)   **the invention in question;**
(b)   **the patent for the invention;**
(c)   **the assignment, assignation or grant of—**
(i)   **the property or any right in the invention, or**

[934]

> **(ii)** **the property in, or any right in or under, an application for the patent, to a person connected with the employer.**

(2)   For the purposes of subsection (1) above the amount of any benefit derived or expected to be derived by an employer from the assignment, assignation or grant of—

> (a)   the property in, or any right in or under, a patent for the invention or an application for such a patent; or
>
> (b)   the property or any right in the invention;

to a person connected with him shall be taken to be the amount which could reasonably be expected to be so derived by the employer if that person had not been connected with him.

(3)   Where the Crown or a Research Council in its capacity as employer assigns or grants the property in, or any right in or under, an invention, patent or application for a patent to a body having among its functions that of developing or exploiting inventions resulting from public research and does so for no consideration or only a nominal consideration, any benefit derived from the invention, patent or application by that body shall be treated for the purposes of the foregoing provisions of this section as so derived by the Crown or, as the case may be, Research Council.

In this subsection "Research Council" means a body which is a Research Council for the purposes of the Science and Technology Act 1965 **or the Arts and Humanities Research Council (as defined by section 1 of the Higher Education Act 2004).**

(4)   In determining the fair share of the benefit to be secured for an employee in respect of [*a patent for*] an invention which has always belonged to an employer, the court or the comptroller shall, among other things, take the following matters into account, that is to say—

> (a)   the nature of the employee's duties, his remuneration and the other advantages he derives or has derived from his employment or has derived in relation to the invention under this Act;
>
> (b)   the effort and skill which the employee has devoted to making the invention;
>
> (c)   the effort and skill which any other person has devoted to making the invention jointly with the employee concerned, and the advice and other assistance contributed by any other employee who is not a joint inventor of the invention; and
>
> (d)   the contribution made by the employer to the making, developing and working of the invention by the provision of advice, facilities and other assistance, by the provision of opportunities and by his managerial and commercial skill and activities.

(5)   In determining the fair share of the benefit to be secured for an employee in respect of [*a patent for*] an invention which originally belonged to him, the court or the comptroller shall, among other things, take the following matters into account, that is to say—

> (a)   any conditions in a licence or licences granted under this Act or otherwise in respect of the invention or the patent **for it;**
>
> (b)   the extent to which the invention was made jointly by the employee with any other person; and
>
> (c)   the contribution made by the employer to the making, developing and working of the invention as mentioned in subsection (4)(d) above.

(6) Any order for the payment of compensation under section 40 above may be an order for the payment of a lump sum or for periodical payment, or both.

(7) Without prejudice to [*section 32 of the Interpretation Act 1889 (which provides that a statutory power may in general be exercised from time to time),*] **section 12 or section 14 of the Interpretation Act 1978**, the refusal of the court or the comptroller to make any such order on an application made by an employee under section 40 above shall not prevent a further application being made under that section by him or any successor in title of his.

(8) Where the court or the comptroller has made any such order, the court or he may on the application of either the employer or the employee vary or discharge it or suspend any provision of the order and revive any provision so suspended, and section 40(5) above shall apply to the application as it applies to an application under that section.

(9) In England and Wales any sums awarded by the comptroller under section 40 above shall, if **the county court** [*a county court*] so orders, be recoverable [*by execution issued from the county court*] **under section 85 of the County Courts Act 1984** or otherwise as if they were payable under an order of that court.

(10) In Scotland an order made under section 40 above by the comptroller for the payment of any sums may be enforced in like manner as [*a recorded decree arbitral*] **an extract registered decree arbitral bearing a warrant for execution issued by the sheriff court of any sheriffdom in Scotland.**

(11) In Northern Ireland an order made under section 40 above by the comptroller for the payment of any sums may be enforced as if it were a money judgment.

Notes

Subsection (1) substituted and subss.(4) and (5) amended by Patents Act 2004 (c.16) s.10(3), (4), (5), with effect from 1 January 2005 (SI 2004/3205), subject to savings contained in s.10(8) of that Act.

Subsection (3) amended by Higher Education Act 2004 (c.8) s.49 and Sch.6 para.5, with effect from 16 December 2004 (SI 2004/3255).

Subsection (7) amended by Interpretation Act 1978 (c.30) s.25.

Subsection (9) reference to "the county court" amended by Crime and courts Act 2013 (c.22) Sch 9(3) para.52(1)(b) with effect from 22 April 2014.

Subsection (9) reference to s.85 of the County Courts Act 1984 amended by Tribunals, Courts and Enforcement Act 2007 s.62(3), Sch.13 paras 39, 40, as from 6 April 2014.

Subsection (10) amended by Patents Act 2004 (c.16) s.16 and Sch.2 para.11, Sch.3, with effect from 1 January 2005 (SI 2004/3205).

Enforceability of contracts relating to employees' inventions

AppA-42 **42.**—(1) This section applies to any contract (whenever made) relating to inventions made by an employee, being a contract entered into by him—

    (a) with the employer (alone or with another); or

    (b) with some other person at the request of the employer or in pursuance of the employee's contract of employment.

(2) Any term in a contract to which this section applies which diminishes the employee's rights in inventions of any description made by him after the appointed day and the date of the contract, or in or under patents for those inventions or applications for such patents, shall be unenforceable against him to the extent that it diminishes his rights in an invention of that description so made, or in or under a patent for such an invention or an application for any such patent.

(3) Subsection (2) above shall not be construed as derogating from any duty

of confidentiality owed to his employer by an employee by virtue of any rule of law or otherwise.

(4)   This section applies to any arrangement made with a Crown employee by or on behalf of the Crown as his employer as it applies to any contract made between an employee and an employer other than the Crown, and for the purposes of this section "Crown employee" means a person employed under or for the purposes of a Government department or any officer or body exercising on behalf of the Crown functions conferred by any enactment **or a person serving in the naval, military or air forces of the Crown.**

Note

Subsection (4) amended by Armed Forces Act 1981 (c.55) s.22.

Supplementary

43.—(1)   Sections 39 to 42 above shall not apply to an invention made before the appointed day.   AppA-43

(2)   Sections 39 to 42 above shall not apply to an invention made by an employee unless at the time he made the invention one of the following conditions was satisfied in his case, that is to say—

(a)   he was mainly employed in the United Kingdom; or

(b)   he was not mainly employed anywhere or his place of employment could not be determined, but his employer had a place of business in the United Kingdom to which the employee was attached, whether or not he was also attached elsewhere.

(3)   In sections 39 to 42 above and this section, except so far as the context otherwise requires, references to the making of an invention by an employee are references to his making it alone or jointly with any other person, but do not include references to his merely contributing advice or other assistance in the making of an invention by another employee.

(4)   Any references [*in sections 40 to 42*] **in sections 39 to 42** above to a patent and to a patent being granted are respectively references to a patent or other protection and to its being granted whether under the law of the United Kingdom or the law in force in any other country or under any treaty or international convention.

(5)   For the purposes of section 40 and 41 above the benefit derived or expected to be derived by an employer from [*a patent*] **an invention or patent** shall, where he dies before any award is made under section 40 above in respect of [*the patent*] **it**, include any benefit derived or expected to be derived from [*the patent*] **it** by his personal representatives or by any person in whom it was vested by their assent.

(5A)   For the purposes of sections 40 and 41 above the benefit derived or expected to be derived by an employer from an invention shall not include any benefit derived or expected to be derived from the invention after the patent for it has expired or has been surrendered or revoked.

(6)   Where an employee dies before an award is made under section 40 above in respect of a patented invention made by him, his personal representatives or their successors in title may exercise his right to make or proceed with an application for compensation under subsection (1) or (2) of that section.

(7)   In sections 40 and 41 above and this section "benefit" means benefit in money or money's worth.

(8)   Section 533 of the Income and Corporation Taxes Act 1970 (definition of connected persons) shall apply for determining for the purposes of section 41(2) above whether one person is connected with another as it applies for determining that question for the purposes of the Tax Acts.

Notes

Subsection (4) amended by CDPA 1988 (c.48) s.295 and Sch.5 para.11, with effect from 7 January 1991 (SI 1990/2168).

Subsection (5) amended and subs.(5A) inserted by Patents Act 2004 (c.16) s.10(6), (7), with effect from 1 January 2005 (SI 2004/3205), subject to savings contained in s.10(8) of that Act.

Contracts as to patented products, etc.

[Avoidance of certain restrictive conditions

AppA-44   *44.—(1)   Subject to the provisions of this section, any condition or term of a contract for the supply of a patented product or of a licence to work a patented invention, or of a contract relating to any such supply or licence, shall be void in so far it purports—*

   (a)   in the case of a contract for supply, to require the person supplied to acquire from the supplier, or his nominee, or prohibit him from acquiring from any specified person, or from acquiring except from the supplier or his nominee, anything other than the patented product;

   (b)   in the case of a licence to work a patented invention, to require the licensee to acquire from the licensor or his nominee, or prohibit him from acquiring from any specified person, or from acquiring except from the licensor or his nominee, anything other than the product which is the patented invention or (if it is a process) other than any product obtained directly by means of the process or to which the process has been applied;

   (c)   in either case, to prohibit the person supplied or licensee from using articles (whether patented products or not) which are not supplied by, or any patented process which does not belong to, the supplier or licensor, or his nominee, or to restrict the right of the person supplied or licensee to use any such articles or process.

   (2)   Subsection (1) above applies to contracts and licences whether made or granted before or after the appointed day, but not to those made or granted before 1st January 1950.

   (3)   In proceedings against any person for infringement of a patent it shall be a defence to prove that at the time of the infringement there was in force a contract relating to the patent made by or with the consent of the plaintiff or pursuer or a licence under the patent granted by him or with his consent and containing in either case a condition or term void by virtue of this section.

   (4)   A condition or term of a contract or licence shall not be void by virtue of this section if—

   (a)   at the time of the making of the contract or granting of the licence the supplier or licensor was willing to supply the product, or grant a licence to work the invention, as the case may be, to the person supplied or licensee, on reasonable terms specified in the contract or licence and without any such condition or term as is mentioned in subsection (1) above; and

[938]

(b) the person supplied or licensee is entitled under the contract or licence to relieve himself of his ability to observe the condition or term on giving to the other party three months' notice in writing and subject to payment to that other party of such compensation (being, in the case of a contract to supply, a lump sum or rent for the residue of the term of the contract and, in the case of a licence, a royalty for the residue of the term of the licence) as may be determined by an arbitrator or arbiter appointed by the Secretary of State.

(5) If in any proceeding it is alleged that any condition or term of a contract or licence is void by virtue of this section it shall lie on the supplier or licensor to prove the matters set out in paragraph (a) of subsection (4) above.

(6) A condition or term of a contract or licence shall not be void by virtue of this section by reason only that it prohibits any person from selling goods other than those supplied by a specific person or, in the case of a contract for the hiring of or licence to use a patented product, that it reserves to the bailor (or, in Scotland, hirer) or licensor, or his nominee, the right to supply such new parts of the patented product as may be required to put or keep it in repair.]

Note

Section 44 repealed by Competition Act 1998 (c.41) ss.70, 74 and Sch.14, with effect from 1 March 2000 (SI 2000/344), subject to savings contained in SI 2000/311 art.3.

[Determination of parts of certain contracts

45.—*(1) Any contract for the supply of a patented product or licence to work* AppA-45 *a patented invention, or contract relating to any such supply or licence, may at any time after the patent or all the patents by which the product or invention was protected at the time of the making of the contract or granting of the licence has or have ceased to be in force, and notwithstanding anything to the contrary in the contract or licence or in any other contract, be determined, to the extent (and only to the extent) that the contract or licence relates to the product or invention, by either party on giving three months' notice in writing to the other party.*

(2) In subsection (1) above "patented product" and "patented invention" include respectively a product and an invention which is the subject of an application for a patent, and that subsection shall apply in relation to a patent by which any such product or invention was protected and which was granted after the time of the making of the contract or granting of the licence in question, on an application which had been filed before that time, as it applies to a patent in force at that time.

(3) If, on an application under this subsection made by either party to a contract or licence falling within subsection (1) above, the court is satisfied that, in consequence of the patent or patents concerned ceasing to be in force, it would be unjust to require the applicant to continue to comply with all terms and conditions of the contract or licence, it may make such order varying those terms or conditions, as, having regard to all the circumstances of the case, it thinks just as between the parties.

(4) Without prejudice to any other right of recovery, nothing in subsection (1) above shall be taken to entitle any person to recover property bailed under a hire-purchase agreement (within the meaning of the Consumer Credit Act 1974).

(5) The foregoing provisions of this section apply to contracts and licences whether made before or after the appointed day.

(6) The provisions of this section shall be without prejudice to any rule of law relating to the frustration of contracts and any right of determining a contract or licence exercisable apart from this section.]

Note

Section 45 repealed by Competition Act 1998 (c.41) ss.70, 74 and Sch.14, with effect from 1 March 2000 (SI 2000/344), subject to savings contained in SI 2000/311 art.3.

Licences of right and compulsory licences

Patentee's application for entry in register that licences are available as of right

AppA-46   **46.**—(1) At any time after the grant of a patent its proprietor may apply to the comptroller for an entry to be made in the register to the effect that licences under the patent are to be available as of right.

(2) Where such an application is made, the comptroller shall give notice of the application to any person registered as having a right in or under the patent and, if satisfied that the proprietor of the patent is not precluded by contract from granting licences under the patent, shall make that entry.

(3) Where such an entry is made in respect of a patent—

    (a) any person shall, at any time after the entry is made, be entitled as of right to a licence under the patent on such terms as may be settled by agreement or, in default of agreement, by the comptroller on the application of the proprietor of the patent or the person requiring the licence;

    (b) the comptroller may, on the application of the holder of any licence granted under the patent before the entry was made, order the licence to be exchanged for a licence of right on terms so settled;

    (c) if in proceedings for infringement of the patent (otherwise than by the importation of any article **from a country which is not a member State of the European Economic Community**) the defendant or defender undertakes to take a licence on such terms, no injunction or interdict shall be granted against him and the amount (if any) recoverable against him by way of damages shall not exceed double the amount which would have been payable by him as licensee if such a licence on those terms had been granted before the earliest infringement;

    [*(d) the renewal fee payable in respect of the patent after the date of the entry shall be half the fee which would be payable if the entry had not been made.*]

    (d) if the expiry date in relation to a renewal fee falls after the date of the entry, that fee shall be half the fee which would be payable had the entry not been made.

(3A) An undertaking under subsection (3)(c) above may be given at any time before final order in the proceedings, without any admission of liability.

(3B) For the purposes of subsection (3)(d) above the expiry date in relation to a renewal fee is the day at the end of which, by virtue of section 25(3) above, the patent in question ceases to have effect if that fee is not paid.

(4) The licensee under a licence of right may (unless, in the case of a licence the terms of which are settled by agreement, the licence otherwise expressly

provides) request the proprietor of the patent to take proceedings to prevent any infringement of the patent; and if the proprietor refuses or neglects to do so within two months after being so requested, the licensee may institute proceedings for the infringement in his own name as if he were proprietor, making the proprietor a defendant or defender.

(5)   A proprietor so added as defendant or defender shall not be liable for any costs or expenses unless he enters an appearance and takes part in the proceedings.

Notes

Subsection (3)(c) amended and subs.(3A) inserted by CDPA 1988 (c.48) s.295 and Sch.5 para.12(2), (3), with effect from 1 August 1989 (SI 1989/816).

Subsection (3)(d) substituted and subs.(3B) inserted by Patents Act 2004 (c.16) s.8(4)(a), (b), with effect from 1 October 2005 (SI 2005/2471).

Cancellation of entry made under s. 46

47.—(1)   At any time after an entry has been made under section 46 above in respect of a patent, the proprietor of the patent may apply to the comptroller for cancellation of the entry.   **AppA-47**

(2)   Where such an application is made and the balance paid of all renewal fees which would have been payable if the entry had not been made, the comptroller may cancel the entry, if satisfied that there is no existing licence under the patent or that all licensees under the patent consent to the application.

(3)   Within the prescribed period after an entry has been made under section 46 above in respect of a patent, any person who claims that the proprietor of the patent is, and was at the time of the entry, precluded by a contract in which the claimant is interested from granting licences under the patent may apply to the comptroller for cancellation of the entry.

(4)   Where the comptroller is satisfied, on an application under subsection (3) above, that the proprietor of the patent is and was so precluded, he shall cancel the entry; and the proprietor shall then be liable to pay, within a period specified by the comptroller, a sum equal to the balance of all renewal fees which would have been payable if the entry had not been made, and the patent shall cease to have effect at the expiration of that period if that sum is not so paid.

(5)   Where an entry is cancelled under this section, the rights and liabilities of the proprietor of the patent shall afterwards be the same as if the entry had not been made.

(6)   Where an application has been made under this section, then—

(a)   in the case of an application under subsection (1) above, any person, and

(b)   in the case of an application under subsection (3) above, the proprietor of the patent, may within the prescribed period give notice to the comptroller of opposition to the cancellation; and the comptroller shall, in considering the application, determine whether the opposition is justified.

[Compulsory licences

48.—*(1)   At any time after the expiration of three years, or of such other period as may be prescribed, from the date of the grant of a patent, any person may apply to the comptroller on one or more of the grounds specified in subsection (3) below—*   **AppA-48**

(a) for a licence under a patent,

(b) for an entry to be made in the register to the effect that licences under the patent are to be available as of right, or

(c) where the applicant is a government department, for the grant to any person specified in the application of a licence under the patent.

(2) A rule prescribing any such other period under subsection (1) above shall not be made unless a draft of the rule has been laid before, and approved by resolution of, each House of Parliament.

(3) The grounds are:

(a) where the patented invention is capable of being commercially worked in the United Kingdom, that it is not being so worked or is not being so worked to the fullest extent that is reasonably practicable;

(b) where the patented invention is a product, that a demand for the product in the United Kingdom—

(i) is not being met on reasonable terms, or

(ii) is being met to a substantial extent by importation;

(c) where the patented invention is capable of being commercially worked in the United Kingdom, that it is being prevented or hindered from being so worked—

(i) where the invention is a product, by the importation of the product,

(ii) where the invention is a process, by the importation of a product obtained directly by means of the process or to which the process has been applied;

(d) that by reason of the refusal of the proprietor of the patent to grant a licence or licences on reasonable terms—

(i) a market for the export of any patented product made in the United Kingdom is not being supplied, or

(ii) the working or efficient working in the United Kingdom of any other patented invention which makes a substantial contribution to the art is prevented or hindered, or

(iii) the establishment or development of commercial or industrial activities in the United Kingdom is unfairly prejudiced;

(e) that by reason of conditions imposed by the proprietor of the patent on the grant of licences under the patent, or on the disposal or use of the patented product or on the use of the patented process, the manufacture, use or disposal of materials not protected by the patent, or the establishment or development of commercial or industrial activities in the United Kingdom, is unfairly prejudiced.

(4) Subject to the provisions of subsections (5) to(7) below, if he is satisfied that any of those grounds are established, the comptroller may—

(a) where the application is under subsection (1)(a) above, order the grant of licence to the applicant on such terms as the comptroller thinks fit;

(b) where the application is under subsection (1)(b) above, make such an entry as is there mentioned;

(c) where the applications is under subsection (1)(c) above, order the grant of a licence to the person specified in the application on such terms as the comptroller thinks fit.

(5) Where the application is made on the ground that the patented inventionis not being commercially worked in the United Kingdom or is not being so worked

to the fullest extent that is reasonably practicable, and it appears to the comptroller that the time which has elapsed since the publication in the journal of a notice of the grant of the patent has for any reason been insufficient to enable the invention to be so worked, he may by order adjourn the application for such period as will in his opinion give sufficient time for the invention to be so worked.

(6)   No entry shall be made in the register under this section on the ground mentioned in subsection (3)(d)(i) above, and any licence granted under this section on that ground shall contain such provisions as appear to the comptroller to be expedient for restricting the countries in which any product concerned may be disposed of or used by the licensee.

(7)   No order or entry shall be made under this section in respect of a patent (the patent concerned) on the ground mentioned in subsection (3)(d)(ii) above unless the comptroller is satisfied that the proprietor of the patent for the other invention is able and willing to grant to the proprietor of the patent concerned and his licensees a licence under the patent for the other invention on reasonable terms.

(8)   An application may be made under this section in respect of a patent notwithstanding that the applicant is already the holder of a licence under the patent; and no person shall be estopped or barred from alleging any of the matters specified in subsection (3) above by reason of any admission made by him, whether in such a licence or otherwise, or by reason of his having accepted such a licence.]

Compulsory licences: general

48.—(1)   At any time after the expiration of three years, or of such other period as may be prescribed, from the date of the grant of a patent, any person may apply to the comptroller on one or more of the relevant grounds— AppA-48A

    (a)   for a licence under the patent;

    (b)   for an entry to be made in the register to the effect that licences under the patent are to be available as of right; or

    (c)   where the applicant is a government department, for the grant to any person specified in the application of a licence under the patent.

(2)   Subject to sections 48A and 48B below, if he is satisfied that any of the relevant grounds are established, the comptroller may—

    (a)   where the application is under subsection (1)(a) above, order the grant of a licence to the applicant on such terms as the comptroller thinks fit;

    (b)   where the application is under subsection (1)(b) above, make such an entry as is there mentioned;

    (c)   where the application is under subsection (1)(c) above, order the grant of a licence to the person specified in the application on such terms as the comptroller thinks fit.

(3)   An application may be made under this section in respect of a patent even though the applicant is already the holder of a licence under the patent; and no person shall be estopped or barred from alleging any of the matters specified in the relevant grounds by reason of any admission made by him, whether in such a licence or otherwise, or by reason of his having accepted a licence.

(4)   In this section "the relevant grounds" means—

    (a)   in the case of an application made in respect of a patent whose proprietor is a WTO proprietor, the grounds set out in section 48A(1) below;

[943]

(b)   in any other case, the grounds set out in section 48B(1) below.

(5)   A proprietor is a WTO proprietor for the purposes of this section and sections 48A, 48B, 50 and 52 below if—

(a)   he is a national of, or is domiciled in, a country which is a member of the World Trade Organisation; or

(b)   he has a real and effective industrial or commercial establishment in such a country.

(6)   A rule prescribing any such other period under subsection (1) above shall not be made unless a draft of the rule has been laid before, and approved by resolution of, each House of Parliament.

Note

Section 48 substituted by Patents and Trade Marks (World Trade Organisation) Regulations 1999 (SI 1999/1899) reg.4, with effect from 29 July 1999, subject to transitional provisions contained in reg.8 of those Regulations.

Compulsory licences: WTO proprietors

AppA-
48A

48A.—(1)   In the case of an application made under section 48 above in respect of a patent whose proprietor is a WTO proprietor, the relevant grounds are—

(a)   where the patented invention is a product, that a demand in the United Kingdom for that product is not being met on reasonable terms;

(b)   that by reason of the refusal of the proprietor of the patent concerned to grant a licence or licences on reasonable terms—

(i)   the exploitation in the United Kingdom of any other patented invention which involves an important technical advance of considerable economic significance in relation to the invention for which the patent concerned was granted is prevented or hindered, or

(ii)   the establishment or development of commercial or industrial activities in the United Kingdom is unfairly prejudiced;

(c)   that by reason of conditions imposed by the proprietor of the patent concerned on the grant of licences under the patent, or on the disposal or use of the patented product or on the use of the patented process, the manufacture, use or disposal of materials not protected by the patent, or the establishment or development of commercial or industrial activities in the United Kingdom, is unfairly prejudiced.

(2)   No order or entry shall be made under section 48 above in respect of a patent whose proprietor is a WTO proprietor unless—

(a)   the applicant has made efforts to obtain a licence from the proprietor on reasonable commercial terms and conditions; and

(b)   his efforts have not been successful within a reasonable period.

(3)   No order or entry shall be so made if the patented invention is in the field of semi-conductor technology.

(4)   No order or entry shall be made under section 48 above in respect of a patent on the ground mentioned in subsection (1)(b)(i) above unless the comptroller is satisfied that the proprietor of the patent for the other invention is able and willing to grant the proprietor of the patent concerned and his

licensees a licence under the patent for the other invention on reasonable terms.

(5) A licence granted in pursuance of an order or entry so made shall not be assigned except to a person to whom the patent for the other invention is also assigned.

(6) A licence granted in pursuance of an order or entry made under section 48 above in respect of a patent whose proprietor is a WTO proprietor—

    (a) shall not be exclusive;

    (b) shall not be assigned except to a person to whom there is also assigned the part of the enterprise that enjoys the use of the patented invention, or the part of the goodwill that belongs to that part;

    (c) shall be predominantly for the supply of the market in the United Kingdom;

    (d) shall include conditions entitling the proprietor of the patent concerned to remuneration adequate in the circumstances of the case, taking into account the economic value of the licence; and

    (e) shall be limited in scope and in duration to the purpose for which the licence was granted.

Note

Section 48A inserted by Patents and Trade Marks (World Trade Organisation) Regulations 1999 (SI 1999/1899) reg.4, with effect from 29 July 1999, subject to transitional provisions contained in reg.8 of those Regulations.

Compulsory licences: other cases

48B.—(1) In the case of an application made under section 48 above in respect of a patent whose proprietor is not a WTO proprietor, the relevant grounds are—   AppA-48B

    (a) where the patented invention is capable of being commercially worked in the United Kingdom, that it is not being so worked or is not being so worked to the fullest extent that is reasonably practicable;

    (b) where the patented invention is a product, that a demand for the product in the United Kingdom—

        (i) is not being met on reasonable terms, or

        (ii) is being met to a substantial extent by importation from a country which is not a member State;

    (c) where the patented invention is capable of being commercially worked in the United Kingdom, that it is being prevented or hindered from being so worked—

        (i) where the invention is a product, by the importation of the product from a country which is not a member State,

        (ii) where the invention is a process, by the importation from such a country of a product obtained directly by means of the process or to which the process has been applied;

    (d) that by reason of the refusal of the proprietor of the patent to grant a licence or licences on reasonable terms—

        (i) a market for the export of any patented product made in the United Kingdom is not being supplied, or

        (ii) the working or efficient working in the United Kingdom of any other patented invention which makes a substantial contribution to the art is prevented or hindered, or

(iii) the establishment or development of commercial or industrial activities in the United Kingdom is unfairly prejudiced;

(e) that by reason of conditions imposed by the proprietor of the patent on the grant of licences under the patent, or on the disposal or use of the patented product or on the use of the patented process, the manufacture, use or disposal of materials not protected by the patent, or the establishment or development of commercial or industrial activities in the United Kingdom, is unfairly prejudiced.

(2) Where—

(a) an application is made on the ground that the patented invention is not being commercially worked in the United Kingdom or is not being so worked to the fullest extent that is reasonably practicable; and

(b) it appears to the comptroller that the time which has elapsed since the publication in the journal of a notice of the grant of the patent has for any reason been insufficient to enable the invention to be so worked, he may by order adjourn the application for such period as will in his opinion give sufficient time for the invention to be so worked.

(3) No order or entry shall be made under section 48 above in respect of a patent on the ground mentioned in subsection (1)(a) above if—

(a) the patented invention is being commercially worked in a country which is a member State; and

(b) demand in the United Kingdom is being met by importation from that country.

(4) No entry shall be made in the register under section 48 above on the ground mentioned in subsection (1)(d)(i) above, and any licence granted under section 48 above on that ground shall contain such provisions as appear to the comptroller to be expedient for restricting the countries in which any product concerned may be disposed of or used by the licensee.

(5) No order or entry shall be made under section 48 above in respect of a patent on the ground mentioned in subsection (1)(d)(ii) above unless the comptroller is satisfied that the proprietor of the patent for the other invention is able and willing to grant to the proprietor of the patent concerned and his licensees a licence under the patent for the other invention on reasonable terms.

Note

Section 48B inserted by Patents and Trade Marks (World Trade Organisation) Regulations 1999 (SI 1999/1899) reg.5, with effect from 29 July 1999, subject to transitional provisions contained in reg.8 of those Regulations.

Provisions about licences under s. 48

49.—(1) Where the comptroller is satisfied, on an application made under section 48 above in respect of a patent, that the manufacture, use or disposal of materials not protected by the patent is unfairly prejudiced by reason of conditions imposed by the proprietor of the patent on the grant of licences under the patent, or on the disposal or use of the patented product or the use of the patented process,

[946]

he may (subject to the provisions of that section) order the grant of licences under the patent to such customers of the applicant as he thinks fit as well as to the applicant.

(2)   Where an application under section 48 above is made in respect of a patent by a person who holds a licence under the patent, the comptroller—

(a)   may, if he orders the grant of a licence to the applicant, order the existing licence to be cancelled, or

(b)   may, instead of ordering the grant of a licence to the applicant, order the existing licence to be amended.

[*(3)   Where, on an application under section 48 above in respect of a patent, the comptroller orders the grant of a licence, he may direct that the licence shall operate—*

(a)   to deprive the proprietor of the patent of any right he has to work the invention concerned or grant licences under the patent:

(b)   to revoke all existing licences granted under the patent.]

(4)   Section 46(4) and (5) above shall apply to a licence granted in pursuance of an order under section 48 above and to a licence granted by virtue of an entry, under that section as it applies to a licence granted by virtue of an entry under section 46 above.

Note

Subsection (3) repealed by CDPA 1988 (c.48) s.295 and Sch.5 para.13, with effect from 1 August 1989 (SI 1989/816).

Exercise of powers on applications under s. 48

50.—(1)   The powers of the comptroller on an application under section 48 above in respect of a patent **whose proprietor is not a WTO proprietor** shall be exercised with a view to securing the following general purposes:— AppA-50

(a)   that inventions which can be worked on a commercial scale in the United Kingdom and which should in the public interest be so worked shall be worked there without undue delay and to the fullest extent that is reasonably practicable;

(b)   that the inventor or other person beneficially entitled to a patent shall receive reasonable remuneration having regard to the nature of the invention;

(c)   that the interests of any person for the time being working or developing an invention in the United Kingdom under the protection of a patent shall not be unfairly prejudiced.

(2)   Subject to subsection (1) above, the comptroller shall, in determining whether to make an order or entry in pursuance of [*such an application*] **any application under section 48 above**, take account of the following matters, that is to say—

(a)   the nature of the invention, the time which has elapsed since the publication in the journal of a notice of the grant of the patent and the measures already taken by the proprietor of the patent or any licensee to make full use of the invention;

(b)   the ability of any person to whom a licence would be granted under the order concerned to work the invention to the public advantage; and

(c)   the risks to be undertaken by that person in providing capital and working the invention if the application for an order is granted.

but shall not be required to take account of matters subsequent to the making of the application.

Note

Subsections (1) and (2) amended by Patents and Trade Marks (World Trade Organisation) Regulations 1999 (SI 1999/1899) reg.7, with effect from 29 July 1999, subject to transitional provisions contained in reg.8 of those Regulations.

Powers exercisable following merger and market investigations

AppA-
50A

50A.—(1) Subsection (2) below applies where—

(a) section 41(2), 55(2), 66(6), 75(2), 83(2), 138(2), 147(2), 147A(2) or 160(2) of, or paragraph 5(2) or 10(2) of Schedule 7 to, the Enterprise Act 2002 (powers to take remedial action following merger or market investigations) applies;

(b) the Competition and Markets Authority [*Competition Commission*] or (as the case may be) the Secretary of State considers that it would be appropriate to make an application under this section for the purpose of remedying, mitigating or preventing a matter which cannot be dealt with under the enactment concerned; and

(c) the matter concerned involves—

   (i) conditions in licences granted under a patent by its proprietor restricting the use of the invention by the licensee or the right of the proprietor to grant other licences; or

   (ii) a refusal by the proprietor of a patent to grant licences on reasonable terms.

(2) The Competition and Markets Authority [*Competition Commission*] or (as the case may be) the Secretary of State may apply to the comptroller to take action under this section.

(3) Before making an application the Competition and Markets Authority [*Competition Commission*] or (as the case may be) the Secretary of State shall publish, in such manner as it or he thinks appropriate, a notice describing the nature of the proposed application and shall consider any representations which may be made within 30 days of such publication by persons whose interests appear to it or him to be affected.

(4) The comptroller may, if it appears to him on an application under this section that the application is made in accordance with this section, by order cancel or modify any condition concerned of the kind mentioned in subsection (1)(c)(i) above or may, instead or in addition, make an entry in the register to the effect that licences under the patent are to be available as of right.

(5) References in this section to the Competition and Markets Authority are references to a CMA group except where—

(a) section 75(2) of the Enterprise Act 2002 applies; or

(b) any other enactment mentioned in subsection (1)(a) above applies and the functions of the Competition and Markets Authority under that enactment are being performed by the CMA Board by virtue of section 34C(3) or 133A(2) of the Enterprise Act 2002.

[*(5) References in this section to the Competition Commission shall, in cases where section 75(2) of the Enterprise Act 2002 applies, be read as references to the Office of Fair Trading.*]

(6) References in section 35, 36, 47, 63, 134, 141 or 141A of the Enterprise

[948]

Act 2002 (questions to be decided by the Competition and Markets Authority [*Competition Commission*] in its reports) to taking action under section 41(2), 55, 66, 138, 147 or 147A shall include references to taking action under subsection (2) above.

(7) Action taken by virtue of subsection (4) above in consequence of an application under subsection (2) above where an enactment mentioned in subsection (1)(a) above applies shall be treated, for the purposes of sections 91(3), 92(1)(a), 162(1) and 166(3) of the Enterprise Act 2002 (duties to register and keep under review enforcement orders etc.), as if it were the making of an enforcement order (within the meaning of the Part concerned) under the relevant power in Part 3 or (as the case may be) 4 of that Act.

(8) In subsection (5) "CMA Board" and "CMA group" have the same meaning as in Schedule 4 to the Enterprise and Regulatory Reform Act 2013.

Note

Section 50A inserted by Enterprise Act 2002 (c.40) s.278 and Sch.25 para.8(2), with effect from 20 June 2003, subject to savings contained in SI 2003/1397 arts 8–12.

Subsection (1), insertion of s.147A(2) by Enterprise and Regulatory Reform Act 2013 (Competition) (Consequential, Transitional and Saving Provisions) Order (SI 2014/892) Sch.1(2) para.32(2) with effect from 1 April 2014.

Subsections (2) and (3), amended by Enterprise and Regulatory Reform Act 2013 (Competition) (Consequential, Transitional and Saving Provisions) Order (SI 2014/892) Sch.1(2) para.32(3) with effect from 1 April 2014.

Subsection (5) subsitutued by Enterprise and Regulatory Reform Act 2013 (Competition) (Consequential, Transitional and Saving Provisions) Order (SI 2014/892) Sch.1(2) para.32(4) with effect from 1 April 2014.

Subsection (6) amended by Enterprise and Regulatory Reform Act 2013 (Competition) (Consequential, Transitional and Saving Provisions) Order (SI 2014/892) Sch.1(2) para.32(5)(a), (b), (c) with effect from 1 April 2014.

Subsection (8) added by Enterprise and Regulatory Reform Act 2013 (Competition) (Consequential, Transitional and Saving Provisions) Order (SI 2014/892) Sch.1(2) para.32(6) with effect from 1 April 2014.

[Application by Crown in cases of monopoly or merger

51.—*(1) Where, on a reference under section 50 or 51 of the Fair Trading Act 1973 (the 1973 Act), a report of the Monopolies and Mergers Commission (the Commission), as laid before Parliament, contains conclusions to the effect—* AppA-51

    (a) that a monopoly situation (within the meaning of the 1973 Act) exists in relation to a description of goods which consist of or include patented products or in relation to a description of services in which a patented product or process is used, and

    (b) that facts found by the Commission in pursuance of their investigations under section 49 of the 1973 Act operate, or may be expected to operate, against the public interest, the appropriate Minister or Ministers may, subject to subsection (3) below, apply to the comptroller for relief under subsection (4) below in respect of the patent.

  (2) Where, on a reference under section 64 or 75 of the 1973 Act, a report of the Commission, as laid before Parliament, contains conclusions to the effect—

    (a) that a merger situation qualifying for investigation has been created;

    (b) that one of the elements which constitute the creation of that situation is that the condition specified in section 64(2) or (3) of the 1973 Act prevails (or does so to a greater extent) in respect of a description of goods which consist of or include patented products or in respect of a

description of services in which a patented product or process is used; and

(c) *that the creation of that situation, or particular elements in or consequences of it specified in the report, operate, or may be expected to operate, against the public interest, the Secretary of State may, subject to subsection (3) below, apply to the comptroller for relief under subsection (5) below in respect of the patent.*

(2A) *Where—*

(a) *on a reference under section 5 of the Competition Act 1980, a report of the Commission, as laid before Parliament, contains conclusions to the effect that—*

(i) *any person was engaged in an anti-competitive practicein relation to a description of goods which consist of or include patented products or in relation to a description of services in which a patented product or process is used, and*

(ii) *that practice operated or might be expected to operate against the public interest; or*

(b) *on a reference under section 11 of that Act, such a report contains conclusions to the effect that—*

(i) *any person is pursuing a course of conduct in relation to such a description of goods or services, and*

(ii) *that course of conduct operates against the public interest, the appropriate Minister or Ministers may, subject to subsection (3) below, apply to the comptroller for relief under subsection (5A) below in respect of the patent.*

(3) *Before making an application under [subsection (1) or (2)] subsection (1), (2) or (2A) above, the appropriate Minister or Ministers shall publish, in such manner as he or they think appropriate, a notice describing the nature of the proposed application, and shall consider any representations which, within the period of thirty days from the date of publication of the notice, may be made to him or them by persons whose interests appear to the appropriate Minister or Ministers to be likely to be affected by the proposed application.*

(4) *If on an application under subsection (1) above it appears to the comptroller that the facts specified in the Commission's report as being those which, in the Commission's opinion, operate or may be expected to operate against the public interest include—*

(a) *any conditions in a licence or licences granted under the patent by its proprietor restricting the use of the invention concerned by the licensee or the right of the proprietor to grant other licences under the patent, or*

(b) *a refusal by the proprietor to grant licences under the patent on reasonable terms;*

the comptroller may by order cancel or modify any such condition or may, instead or in addition, make an entry in the register to the effect that licences under the patent are to be available as of right.

(5) *If on an application under subsection (2) above it appears to the comptroller that the particular matters indicated in the Commission's report as being those which, in the Commission's opinion, operate or may be expected to operate against the public interest (whether those matters are so indicated in pursuance of a requirement imposed under section 69(4) or 75(3) of the 1973 Act or otherwise)*

include any such condition or refusal as is mentioned in paragraph (a) or (b) of subsection (4) above, the comptroller may by order cancel or modify any such condition or may, instead or in addition, make an entry in the register to the effect that licences under the patent are to be available as of right.

(5A) If on an application under subsection (2A) above it appears to the comptroller that the practice of course of conduct in question involved or involves the imposition of any such condition as is mentioned in paragraph (a) of subsection (4) above or such a refusal as is mentioned in paragraph (b) of that subsection, the comptroller may by order cancel or modify any such condition or may, instead or in addition, make an entry in the register to the effect that licences under the patent are to be available as of right.

(6)   In this section "the appropriate Minister or Ministers", in relation to a report of the Commission, means the Minister or Ministers to whom the report is made.]

Note

Subsections (2A) and (5A) inserted and subs.(3) amended by Competition Act 1980 (c.21) s.14.

Powers exercisable in consequence of report of [*Monopolies and Mergers Commission*] [*Competition Commission*] **Competition and Markets Authority**

51.—(1)   **Where a report of the** [*Monopolies and Mergers Commission*] [*Competition Commission*] **Competition and Markets Authority has been laid before Parliament containing conclusions to the effect—**

[*(a)   **on a monopoly reference, that a monopoly situation exists and facts found by the Commission operate or may be expected to operate against the public interest,***

*(b)   **on a merger reference, that a merger situation qualifying for investigation has been created and the creation of the situation, or particular elements in or consequences of it specified in the report, operate or may be expected to operate against the public interest,***]

(c)   **on a competition reference, that a person was engaged in an anticompetitive practice which operated or may be expected to operate against the public interest, or**

(d)   **on a reference under section 11 of the Competition Act 1980** (reference of public bodies and certain other persons), that a person is pursuing a course of conduct which operates against the public interest, the appropriate Minister or Ministers may apply to the comptroller to take action under this section.

(2)   Before making an application the appropriate Minister or Ministers shall publish, in such manner as he or they think appropriate, a notice describing the nature of the proposed application and shall consider any representations which may be made within 30 days of such publication by persons whose interests appear to him or them to be affected.

(3)   If on an application under this section it appears to the comptroller that the matters specified in the Competition and Markets Authority's report as being those which in the opinion of the Competition and Markets Authority [*Commission's report as being those which in the Commission's opinion*] operate, or operated or may be expected to operate, against the public interest include—

(a)   conditions in licences granted under a patent by its proprietor restricting the use of the invention by the licensee or the right of the proprietor to grant other licences, or

(b) a refusal by the proprietor of a patent to grant licences on reasonable terms.

he may by order cancel or modify any such condition or may, instead or in addition, make an entry in the register to the effect that licences under the patent are to be available as of right.

(4) In this section "the appropriate Minister or Ministers" means the Minister or Ministers to whom the report of the Competition and Markets Authority [*Commission*] was made.

Notes

Section 51 substituted by CDPA 1988 (c.48) s.295 and Sch.5 para.14.

Subsection (1) amended to refer to Competition and Markets Authority by Enterprise and Regulatory Reform Act 2013 (Competition) (Consequential, Transitional and Saving Provisions) Order (SI 2014/892) Sch.1(2) para.33(2) with effect from 1 April 2014. The heading of this section has been amended accordingly. The previous amendments to refer to the Competition Commission derived from the Competition Act 1998 (Competition Commission) Transitional, Consequential and Supplemental Provisions Order 1999 (SI 1999/506) art.17.

Subsection (1)(a) repealed by Enterprise Act 2002 (c.40) s.278, Sch.25 para.8(3) and Sch.26, with effect from 20 June 2003 (SI 2003/1397), subject to savings contained in arts 3–12.

Subsection (1)(b) repealed by Enterprise Act 2002 (c.40) s.278, Sch.25 para.8(3), and Sch.26, with effect from 20 June 2003 (SI 2003/1397), subject to savings contained in arts 3–12, and with effect from 29 December 2004 (SI 2004/3233), subject to savings contained in arts 3–5.

Subsection (3) amended by Enterprise and Regulatory Reform Act 2013 (Competition) (Consequential, Transitional and Saving Provisions) Order (SI 2014/892) Sch.1(2) para.33(3) with effect from 1 April 2014.

Subsection (4) amended by Enterprise and Regulatory Reform Act 2013 (Competition) (Consequential, Transitional and Saving Provisions) Order (SI 2014/892) Sch.1(2) para.33(4) with effect from 1 April 2014.

[Opposition, appeal and arbitration

AppA-52   **52.**—*(1)   The proprietor of the patent concerned or any other person wishing to oppose an application under sections 48 to 51 above may, in accordance with rules, give to the comptroller notice of opposition; and the comptroller shall consider the opposition in deciding whether to grant the application.*

(2)   Where an appeal is brought from an order made by the comptroller in pursuance of an application under sections 48 to 51 above or from a decision of his to make an entry in the register in pursuance of such an application or from a refusal of his to make such an order or entry, the Attorney General, Lord Advocate or Attorney General for Northern Ireland, or such other counsel as any of them may appoint, shall be entitled to appear and be heard.

(3)   Where an application under sections 48 to 51 above is opposed under subsection (1) above, and either—

(a)   the parties consent, or

(b)   the proceedings require a prolonged examination of documents or any scientific or local investigation which cannot in the opinion of the comptroller conveniently be made before him, the comptroller may at any time order the whole proceedings, or any question or issue of fact arising in them, to be referred to an arbitrator or arbiter agreed on by the parties or, in default of agreement, appointed by the comptroller.

(4)   Where the whole proceedings are so referred, section 21 of the Arbitration Act 1950 or, as the case may be, section 22 of the Arbitration Act (Northern

*Ireland) 1937 (statement of cases by arbitrators) shall not apply to the arbitation;
but unless the parties otherwise agree before the award of the arbitrator or arbiter
is made, an appeal shall lie from the award to the court.*

*(5)   Where a question or issue of fact is so referred, the arbitrator or arbiter
shall report his findings to the comptroller.*]

Opposition, appeal and arbitration

52.—(1)   The proprietor of the patent concerned or any other person wishing to oppose an application under sections 48 to 51 above may, in accordance with rules, give to the comptroller notice of opposition; and the comptroller shall consider any opposition in deciding whether to grant the application.

(2)   Where an order or entry has been made under section 48 above in
respect of a patent whose proprietor is a WTO proprietor—

- (a)   the proprietor or any other person may, in accordance with rules,
  apply to the comptroller to have the order revoked or the entry
  cancelled on the grounds that the circumstances which led to the
  making of the order or entry have ceased to exist and are unlikely
  to recur;
- (b)   any person wishing to oppose an application under paragraph (a)
  above may, in accordance with rules, give to the comptroller notice
  of opposition; and
- (c)   the comptroller shall consider any opposition in deciding whether
  to grant the application.

(3)   If it appears to the comptroller on an application under subsection
(2)(a) above that the circumstances which led to the making the order or entry
have ceased to exist and are unlikely to recur, he may—

- (a)   revoke the order or cancel the entry; and
- (b)   terminate any licence granted to a person in pursuance of the
  order or entry subject to such terms and conditions as he thinks
  necessary for the protection of the legitimate interests of that
  person.

(4)   Where an appeal is brought—

- (a)   from an order made by the comptroller in pursuance of an application under sections 48 to 51 above;
- (b)   from a decision of his to make an entry in the register in pursuance of such an application;
- (c)   from a revocation or cancellation made by him under subsection
  (3) above; or
- (d)   from a refusal of his to make such an order, entry, revocation or
  cancellation, the Attorney General, the appropriate Law Officer
  within the meaning of section 4A of the Crown Suits (Scotland) Act
  1857 or the Attorney General for Northern Ireland, or such other
  person who has a right of audience [*such other counsel*] as any of
  them may appoint, shall be entitled to appear and be heard.

(5)   Where an application under sections 48 to 51 above or subsection (2)
above is opposed, and either—

- (a)   the parties consent, or
- (b)   the proceedings require a prolonged examination of documents or
  any scientific or local investigation which cannot in the opinion of
  the comptroller conveniently be made before him, the comptrol-

ler may at any time order the whole proceedings, or any question or issue of fact arising in them, to be referred to an arbitrator or arbiter agreed on by the parties or, in default of agreement, appointed by the comptroller.

(6)   Where the whole proceedings are so referred, unless the parties otherwise agree before the award of the arbitrator or arbiter is made, an appeal shall lie from the award to the court.

(7)   Where a question or issue of fact is so referred, the arbitrator or arbiter shall report his findings to the comptroller.

Note

Section 52 substituted by Patents and Trade Marks (World Trade Organisation) Regulations 1999 (SI 1999/1899) reg.6, with effect from 29 July 1999, subject to transitional provisions contained in reg.8 of those Regulations.

Subsection (4) amended by Intellectual Property Act 2014 (c.18) Sch. 1 para.4(1) with effect from 1 October 2014.

Compulsory licences; supplementary provisions

AppA-53   **53.**—[*(1)   Without prejudice to section 86 below (by virtue of which the Community Patent Convention has effect in the United Kingdom), sections 48 to 51 above shall have effect subject to any provision of that convention relatingto the grant of compulsory licences for lack or insufficiency of exploitation, as that provision applies by virtue of that section.*]

(2)   In any proceedings on an [*application made in relation to a patent under sections 48 to 51 above*] **application made under section 48 above in respect of a patent**, any statement with respect to any activity in relation to the patented invention, or with respect to the grant or refusal of licences under the patent, contained in a report of the [*Monopolies and Mergers Commission*] [*Competition Commission*] **Competition and Markets Authority** laid before Parliament under Part VII of the Fair Trading Act 1973 **or section 17 of the Competition Act 1980 or published under Part 3 or 4 of the Enterprise Act 2002** shall be prima facie evidence of the matters stated, and in Scotland shall be sufficient evidence of those matters.

(3)   The comptroller may make an entry in the register under sections 48 to 51 above notwithstanding any contract which would have precluded the entry on the application of the proprietor of the patent under section 46 above.

(4)   An entry made in the register under sections 48 to 51 above shall for all purposes have the same effect as an entry made under section 46 above.

(5)   No order or entry shall be made in pursuance of an application under sections 48 to 51 above which would be at variance with any treaty or international convention to which the United Kingdom is a party.

Notes

Subsection (1) repealed by Patents Act 2004 (c.16) s.16, Sch.2 para.12 and Sch.3, with effect from 1 January 2005 (SI 2004/3205).

Subsection (2) amended by CDPA 1988 (c.48) s.295 and Sch.5 para.15, with effect from 1 August 1989 (SI 1989/816); Competition Act 1998 (Competition Commission) Transitional, Consequential and Supplemental Provisions Order 1999 (SI 1999/506) art.17; Enterprise Act 2002 (c.40) s.278 and Sch.25 para.8(4), subject to savings contained in SI 2003/1397 arts 3–12.

Subsection (2) amended by Enterprise and Regulatory Reform Act 2013 (Competition) (Consequential, Transitional and Saving Provisions) Order (SI 2014/892) Sch.1(2) para.34 with effect from 1 April 2014.

Special provisions where patented invention is being worked abroad

54.—(1)   Her Majesty may by Order in Council provide that the comptroller may not (otherwise than for purposes of the public interest) make an order or entry in respect of a patent in pursuance of an application under sections 48 to 51 above if the invention concerned is being commercially worked in any relevant country specified in the Order and demand in the United Kingdom for any patented product resulting from that working is being met by importation from that country.

AppA-54

(2)   In subsection (1) above "relevant country" means a country other than a member state **or a member of the World Trade Organisation** whose law in the opinion of Her Majesty in Council incorporates or will incorporate provisions treating the working of an invention in, and importation from, the United Kingdom in a similar way to which the Order in Council would (if made) treat the working of an invention in, and importation from, the country.

Note

Subsection (2) amended by Patents and Trade Marks (World Trade Organisation) Regulations 1999 (SI 1999/1899) reg.7, with effect from 29 July 1999, subject to transitional provisions contained in reg.8 of those Regulations.

Use of patented inventions for services of the Crown

Use of patented inventions for services of the Crown

55.—(1)   Notwithstanding anything in this Act, any government department and any person authorised in writing by a government department may, for the services of the Crown and in accordance with this section, do any of the following acts in the United Kingdom in relation to a patented invention without the consent of the proprietor of the patent, that is to say—

AppA-55

  (a)   where the invention is a product, may—
    (i)   make, use, import or keep the product, or sell or offer to sell it where to do so would be incidental or ancillary to making, using, importing or keeping it; or
    (ii)   in any event, sell or offer to sell it for foreign defence purposes or for the production or supply of specified drugs and medicines, or dispose or offer to dispose of it (otherwise than by selling it) for any purpose whatever;
  (b)   where the invention is a process, may use it or do in relation to any product obtained directly by means of the process anything mentioned in paragraph (a) above;
  (c)   without prejudice to the foregoing, where the invention or any product obtained directly by means of the invention is a specified drug or medicine, may sell or offer to sell the drug or medicine;
  (d)   may supply or offer to supply to any person any of the means, relating to an essential element of the invention, for putting the invention into effect;
  (e)   may dispose or offer to dispose of anything which was made, used, imported or kept in the exercise of the powers conferred by this section and which is no longer required for the purpose for which it was

made, used, imported or kept (as the case may be), and anything done by virtue of this subsection shall not amount to an infringement of the patent concerned.

(2) Any act done in relation to an invention by virtue of this section is in the following provisions of this section referred to as use of the invention; and "use", in relation to an invention, in sections 56 to 58 below shall be construed accordingly.

(3) So far as the invention has before its priority date been duly recorded by or tried by or on behalf of a government department or the United Kingdom Atomic Energy Authority otherwise than in consequence of a relevant communication made in confidence, any use of the invention by virtue of this section may be made free of any royalty or other payment to the proprietor.

(4) So far as the invention has not been so recorded or tried, any use of it made by virtue of this section at any time either—

(a) after the publication of the application for the patent for the invention; or

(b) without prejudice to paragraph (a) above, in consequence of a relevant communication made after the priority date of the invention otherwise than in confidence;

shall be made on such terms as may be agreed either before or after the use by the government department and the proprietor of the patent with the approval of the Treasury or as may in default of agreement be determined by the court on a reference under section 58 below.

(5) Where an invention is used by virtue of this section at any time after publication of an application for a patent for the invention but before such a patent is granted, and the terms for its use agreed or determined as mentioned in subsection (4) above include terms as to payment for the use, then (notwithstanding anything in those terms) any such payment shall be recoverable only—

(a) after such a patent is granted; and

(b) if (apart from this section) the use would, if the patent had been granted on the date of the publication of the application, have infringed not only the patent but also the claims (as interpreted by the description and any drawings referred to in the description or claims) in the form in which they were contained in the application immediately before the preparations for its publication were completed by the Patent Office.

(6) The authority of a government department in respect of an invention may be given under this section before or after the patent is granted and either before or after the use in respect of which the authority is given is made, and may be given to any person whether or not he is authorised directly or indirectly by the proprietor of the patent to do anything in relation to the invention.

(7) Where any use of an invention is made by or with the authority of a government department under this section, then, unless it appears to the department that it would be contrary to the public interest to do so, the department shall notify the proprietor of the patent as soon as practicable after the second of the following events, that is to say, the use is begun and the patent is granted, and furnish him with such information as to the extent of the use as he may from time to time require.

(8) A person acquiring anything disposed of in the exercise of powers conferred by this section, and any person claiming through him, may deal with it in the same manner as if the patent were held on behalf of the Crown.

(9) In this section "relevant communication" in relation to an invention, means

a communication of the invention directly or indirectly by the proprietor of the patent or any person from whom he derives title.

(10)   Subsection (4) above is without prejudice to any rule of law relating to the confidentiality of information.

(11)   In the application of this section to Northern Ireland, the reference in subsection (4) above to the Treasury shall, where the government department referred to in that subsection is a department of the Government of Northern Ireland, be construed as a reference to the Department of Finance for Northern Ireland.

Interpretation, etc., of provisions about Crown use

56.—(1)   Any reference in section 55 above to a patented invention, in rela-   AppA-56
tion to any time, is a reference to an invention for which a patent has before that time been, or is subsequently, granted.

(2)   In this Act, except so far as the context otherwise requires, "the services of the Crown" includes—

    (a)   the supply of anything for foreign defence purposes;

    (b)   the production or supply of specified drugs and medicines; and

    (c)   such purposes relating to the production or use of atomic energy or research into matters connected therewith as the Secretary of State thinks necessary or expedient;

and "use for the services of the Crown" shall be construed accordingly.

(3)   In section 55(1)(a) above and subsection (2)(a) above, references to a sale or supply of anything for foreign defence purposes are references to a sale or supply of the thing—

    (a)   to the government of any country outside the United Kingdom, in pursuance of an agreement or arrangement between Her Majesty's Government in the United Kingdom and the government of that country, where the thing is required for the defence of that country or of any other country whose government is party to any agreement or arrangement with Her Majesty's Government in respect of defence matters; or

    (b)   to the United Nations, or to the government of any country belonging to that organisation, in pursuance of an agreement or arrangement between Her Majesty's Government and that organisation or government, where the thing is required for any armed forces operating in pursuance of a resolution of that organisation or any organ of that organisation.

(4)   For the purposes of section 55(1)(a) and (c) above and subsection (2)(b) above, specified drugs and medicines are drugs and medicines which are both—

    (a)   required **for the provision of**—

        (ai)   **primary medical services under [*Part 1 of the National Health Service Act 1977*], the National Health Service Act 2006, the National Health Service (Wales) Act 2006, Part 1 of the National Health Service (Scotland) Act 1978 or any corresponding provisions of the law in force in Northern Ireland or the Isle of Man or primary dental services under [*Part 1 of the National Health Service Act 1977*], the National Health Service Act 2006, the National Health Service (Wales) Act 2006 or any corresponding provisions of the law in force in Northern Ireland or the Isle of Man, or**

[957]

(i)   **pharmaceutical services, general medical services or general dental services under [*Part II of the National Health Service Act 1977*] Chapter 1 of Part 7 of the National Health Service Act 2006 or Chapter 1 of Part 7 of the National Health Service (Wales) Act 2006 (in the case of pharmaceutical services), [*Part IV of the National Health Service (Scotland) Act 1947*], Part II of the National Health Service (Scotland) Act 1978 (in the case of pharmaceutical services or general dental services), or the corresponding provisions of the law in force in Northern Ireland or the Isle of Man, or**

(ii)   **personal medical services or personal dental services provided in accordance with arrangements made under [*section 28C of the 1977 Act*,] section 17C of the 1978 Act (in the case of personal dental services), or thecorresponding provisions of the law in force in Northern Ireland or the Isle of Man, or**

(iii)   **local pharmaceutical services provided under a pilot scheme established under [*section 28 of the Health and Social Care Act 2001*] section 134 of the National Health Service Act 2006, or section 92 of the National Health Service (Wales) Act 2006, or an LPS scheme established under [*Schedule 8A to the National Health Service Act 1977 (c. 49)*] Schedule 12 to the National Health Service Act 2006, or Schedule 7 to the National Health Service (Wales) Act 2006, or under any corresponding provision of the law in force in the Isle of Man, or**

(iiia)   **pharmaceutical care services under Part 1 of the National Health Service (Scotland) Act 1978 and**

(b)   specified for the purposes of this subsection in regulations made by the Secretary of State.

Note

Subsection (4) amended by National Health Service (Scotland) Act 1978 (c.29) Sch.16; National Health Service (Primary Care) Act 1997 (c.46) s.41 and Sch.2 para.2; Health and Social Care Act 2001 (c.15) s.67 and Sch.5 para.4, with effect from 1 July 2002 in relation to Wales, SI 2002/1475 and 1 January 2003, in relation to England, SI 2003/53; Health and Social Care (Community Health and Standards) Act 2003 s.184 and Sch.11 para.6; Primary Medical Services (Scotland) Act 2004 (Consequential Modifications) Order 2004 (SI 2004/957) Sch. para.2. Smoking, Health and Social Care (Scotland) Act 2005 (Consequential Modifications) (England, Wales and Northern Ireland) Order 2006 (SI 2006/1056) Sch. Pt.1 para.(2); National Health Service (Consequential Provisions) Act 2006 s.2, Sch.1 para.58, with effect from 1 March 2007.

Rights of third parties in respect of Crown use

AppA-57   **57.**—(1) In relation to—

(a)   any use made for the services of the Crown of an invention by a government department, or a person authorised by a government department, by virtue of section 55 above, or

(b)   anything done for the services of the Crown to the order of a government department by the proprietor of a patent in respect of a patented invention or by the proprietor of an application in respect of an invention for which an application for a patent has been filed and is still pending, the provisions of any licence, assignment, assignation or agreement to which this subsection applies shall be of no effect so far as those provisions restrict or regulate the working of the invention, or the use of any model, document or information relating to it, or provide for the making of payments in respect of, or calculated by reference to, such working or use; and the reproduction or publication of any model or document in connection with the said working or use shall not be deemed to be an infringement of any copyright **or design right** subsisting in the model or document **or of any topography right.**

(2)   Subsection (1) above applies to a licence, assignment, assignation or agreement which is made, whether before or after the appointed day, between (on the one hand) any person who is a proprietor of or an applicant for the patent, or anyone who derives title from any such person or from whom such person derives title, and (on the other hand) any person whatever other than a government department.

(3)   Where an exclusive licence granted otherwise than for royalties or other benefits determined by reference to the working of the invention is in force under the patent or application concerned, then—

    (a)   in relation to anything done in respect of the invention which, but for the provisions of this section and section 55 above, would constitute an infringement of the rights of the licensee, subsection (4) of that section shall have effect as if for the reference to the proprietor of the patent there were substituted a reference to the licensee; and

    (b)   in relation to anything done in respect of the invention by the licensee by virtue of an authority given under that section, that section shall have effect as if the said subsection (4) were omitted.

(4)   Subject to the provisions of subsection (3) above, where the patent, or the right to the grant of the patent, has been assigned to the proprietor of the patent on application in consideration of royalties or other benefits determined by reference to the working of the invention, then—

    (a)   in relation to any use of the invention by virtue of section 55 above, subsection (4) of that section shall have effect as if the reference to the proprietor of the patent included a reference to the assignor, and any sum payable by virtue of that subsection shall be divided between the proprietor of the patent or application and the assignor in such proportion as may be agreed on by them or as may in default of agreement be determined by the court on a reference under section 58 below; and

    (b)   in relation to any act done in respect of the invention for the services of the Crown by the proprietor of the patent or application to the order of a government department, section 55(4) above shall have effect as if that act were use made by virtue of an authority given under that section.

(5)   Where section 55(4) above applies to any use of an invention and a person holds an exclusive licence under the patent or application concerned (other than such a licence as is mentioned in subsection (3) above) authorising him to work the invention, then subsections (7) and (8) below shall apply.

(6)   In those subsections "the section 55(4)" payment means such payment (if any) as the proprietor of the patent or application and the department agree under section 55 above, or the court determines under section 58 below, should be made by the department to the proprietor in respect of the use of the invention.

(7) The licensee shall be entitled to recover from the proprietor of the patent or application such part (if any) of the section 55(4) payment as may be agreed on by them or as may in default of agreement be determined by the court under section 58 below to be just having regard to any expenditure incurred by the licensee—

(a) in developing the invention, or

(b) in making payments to the proprietor in consideration of the licence, other than royalties or other payments determined by reference to the use of the invention.

(8) Any agreement by the proprietor of the patent or application and the department under section 55(4) above as to the amount of the section 55(4) payment shall be of no effect unless the licensee consents to the agreement; and any determination by the court under section 55(4) above as to the amount of that payment shall be of no effect unless the licensee has been informed of the reference to the court and is given an opportunity to be heard.

(9) Where any models, documents or information relating to an invention are used in connection with any use of the invention which falls within subsection (1)(a) above, or with anything done in respect of the invention which falls within subsection (1)(b) above, subsection (4) of section 55 above shall (whether or not it applies to any such use of the invention) apply to the use of the models, documents or information as if for the reference in it to the proprietor of the patent there were substituted a reference to the person entitled to the benefit of any provision of an agreement which is rendered inoperative by this section in relation to that use; and in section 58 below the references to terms for the use of an invention shall be construed accordingly.

(10) Nothing in this section shall be construed as authorising the disclosure to a government department or any other person of any model, document or information to the use of which this section applies in contravention of any such licence, assignment, assignation or agreement as is mentioned in this section.

Notes

Subsection (1) amended by CDPA 1988 (c.48) s.303(1) and Sch.7 para.20, with effect from 1 August 1989.

Subsection (1) amended by Semiconductor Products (Protection of Topography) Regulations 1987 (SI 1987/1497) reg.9(2), Sch. Table B.

Compensation for loss of profit

AppA-
57A

57A.—(1) Where use is made of an invention for the services of the Crown, the government department concerned shall pay—

(a) **to the proprietor of the patent, or**

(b) **if there is an exclusive licence in force in respect of the patent, to the exclusive licensee, compensation for any loss resulting from his not being awarded a contract to supply the patented product or, as the case may be, to perform the patented process or supply a thing made by means of the patented process.**

(2) Compensation is payable only to the extent that such a contract could have been fulfilled from his existing manufacturing or other capacity; but is payable notwithstanding the existence of circumstances rendering him ineligible for the award of such a contract.

(3) In determining the loss, regard shall be had to the profit which would have been made on such a contract and to the extent to which any manufacturing or other capacity was under-used.

(4)   No compensation is payable in respect of any failure to secure contracts to supply the patented product or, as the case may be, to perform the patented process or supply a thing made by means of the patented process, otherwise than for the services of the Crown.

(5)   The amount payable shall, if not agreed between the proprietor or licensee and the government department concerned with the approval of the Treasury, be determined by the court on a reference under section 58, and is in addition to any amount payable under section 55 or 57.

(6)   In this section "the government department concerned", in relation to any use of an invention for the services of the Crown, means the government department by whom or on whose authority the use was made.

(7)   In the application of this section to Northern Ireland, the reference in subsection (5) above to the Treasury shall, where the government department concerned is a department of the Government of Northern Ireland, be construed as a reference to the Department of Finance and Personnel.

Note

Section 57A inserted by CDPA 1988 (c.48) s.295 and Sch.5 para.16, with effect from 1 August 1989, SI 1989/816.

References of disputes as to Crown use

58.—[*(1)   Any dispute as to the exercise by a government department or a person authorised by a government department of the powers conferred by section 55 above, or as to terms for the use of an invention for the services of the Crown thereunder, or as to the right of any person to receive any part of a payment made or agreed to be made in pursuance of subsection (4) of that section or determined by the court in pursuance of that subsection and this section, may be referred to the court by either party to the dispute after a patent has been granted for the invention.*]   AppA-58

(1)   Any dispute as to—
   (a)   the exercise by a government department, or a person authorised by a government department, of the powers conferred by section 55 above,
   (b)   terms for the use of an invention for the services of the Crown under that section,
   (c)   the right of any person to receive any part of a payment made in pursuance of subsection (4) of that section, or
   (d)   the right of any person to receive a payment under section 57A, may be referred to the court by either party to the dispute after a patent has been granted for the invention.

(2)   If in such proceedings any question arises whether an invention has been recorded or tried as mentioned in section 55 above, and the disclosure of any document recording the invention, or of any evidence of the trial thereof, would in the opinion of the department be prejudicial to the public interest, the disclosure may be made confidentially to **the other party's legal representative** [*counsel for the other party*] or to an independent expert mutually agreed upon.

(3)   In determining under this section any dispute between a government department and any person as to the terms for the use of an invention for the services of the Crown, the court shall have regard—
   (a)   to any benefit or compensation which that person or any person from

whom he derives title may have received or may be entitled to receive directly or indirectly from any government department in respect of the invention in question;

    (b)   to whether that person or any person from whom he derives title has in the court's opinion without reasonable cause failed to comply with a request of the department to use the invention for the services of the Crown on reasonable terms.

(4)   In determining whether or not to grant any relief [*under this section*] **under subsection (1)(a), (b) or (c) above,** and the nature and extent of the relief granted the court shall, subject to the following provisions of this section, apply the principles applied by the court immediately before the appointed day to the granting of relief under section 48 of the 1949 Act.

(5)   On a reference under this section the court may refuse to grant relief by way of compensation in respect of the use of an invention for the services of the Crown during any further period specified under section 25(4) above, but before the payment of the renewal fee and any additional fee prescribed for the purposes of that section.

(6)   Where an amendment of the specification of a patent has been allowed under any of the provisions of this Act, the court shall not grant relief by way of compensation under this section in respect of any such use before the decision to allow the amendment unless the court is satisfied that

    (a)   the specification of the patent as published was framed in good faith and with reasonable skill and knowledge, **and**

    (b)   the relief is sought in good faith.

(7)   If the validity of a patent is put in issue in proceedings under this section and it is found that the patent is only partially valid, the court may, subject to subsection (8) below, grant relief to the proprietor of the patent in respect of that part of the patent which is found to be valid and to have been used for the services of the Crown.

(8)   Where in any such proceedings it is found that a patent is only partially valid, the court shall not grant relief by way of compensation, costs or expenses except where the proprietor of the patent proves that

    (a)   the specification of the patent was framed in good faith and with reasonable skill and knowledge, and

    (b)   the relief is sought in good faith, and

in that event the court may grant relief in respect of that part of the patent which is valid and has been so used, subject to the discretion of the court as to costs and expenses and as to the date from which compensation should be awarded.

(9)   As a condition of any such relief the court may direct that the specification of the patent shall be amended to its satisfaction upon an application made for that purpose under section 75 below, and an application may be so made accordingly, whether or not all other issues in the proceedings have been determined.

(9A)   The court may also grant such relief in the case of a European patent (UK) on condition that the claims of the patent are limited to its satisfaction by the European Patent Office at the request of the proprietor.

(10)   In considering the amount of any compensation for the use of an invention for the services of the Crown after publication of an application for a patent for the invention and before such a patent is granted, the court shall consider whether or not it would have been reasonable to expect, from a consideration of the application as published under section 16 above, that a patent would be granted

conferring on the proprietor of the patent protection for an act of the same description as that found to constitute that use, and if the court finds that it would not have been reasonable, it shall reduce the compensation to such amount as it thinks just.

(11) Where by virtue of a transaction, instrument or event to which section 33 above applies a person becomes the proprietor or one of the proprietors or an exclusive licensee of a patent (the new proprietor or licensee) and a government department or a person authorised by a government department subsequently makes use under section 55 above of the patented invention, the new proprietor or licensee shall not be entitled to any compensation under section 55(4) above (as it stands or as modified by section 57(3) above) , or to any compensation under section 57A above, in respect of a subsequent use of the invention before the transaction, instrument or event is registered unless—

(a) the transaction, instrument or event is registered within the period of six months beginning with its date; or

(b) the court is satisfied that it was not practicable to register the transaction, instrument or event before the end of that period and that it was registered as soon as practicable thereafter.

(12) In any proceedings under this section the court may at any time order the whole proceedings or any question or issue of fact arising in them to be referred, on such terms as the court may direct, to a Circuit judge discharging the functions of an official referee or an arbitrator in England and Wales or Northern Ireland, or to an arbiter in Scotland; and references to the court in the foregoing provisions of this section shall be construed accordingly.

(13) One of two or more joint proprietors of a patent or application for a patent may without the concurrence of the others refer a dispute to the court under this section, but shall not do so unless the others are made parties to the proceedings; but any of the others made a defendant or defender shall not be liable for any costs or expenses unless he enters an appearance and takes part in the proceedings.

Notes

Subsection (1) substituted and subss.(4) and (11) amended by CDPA 1988 (c.48) s.295 and Sch.5 para.16, with effect from 1 August 1989, SI 1989/816.

Subsection (2) amended by Intellectual Property Act 2014 (c.18) Sch.1 para.4(2) with effect from 1 October 2014.

Subsections (6) and (8) amended and subs.(9A) inserted by Patents Act 2004 (c.16) ss.2(2), 3(2), with effect from 13 December 2007, SI 2007/3396.

Special provisions as to Crown use during emergency

59.—(1) During any period of emergency within the meaning of this section the powers exercisable in relation to an invention by a government department or a person authorised by a government department under section 55 above shall include power to use the invention for any purpose which appears to the department necessary or expedient— **AppA-59**

(a) for the efficient prosecution of any war in which Her Majesty may be engaged;

(b) for the maintenance of supplies and services essential to the life of the community;

(c) for securing a sufficiency of supplies and services essential to the wellbeing of the community;

(d) for promoting the productivity of industry, commerce and agriculture;

(e) for fostering and directing exports and reducing imports, or imports of any classes, from all or any countries and for redressing the balance of trade;

(f) generally for ensuring that the whole resources of the community are available for use, and are used, in a manner best calculated to serve the interests of the community; or

(g) for assisting the relief of suffering and the restoration and distribution of essential supplies and services in any country or territory outside the United Kingdom which is in grave distress as the result of war;

and any reference in this Act to the services of the Crown shall as respects any period of emergency, include a reference to those purposes.

(2) In this section the use of an invention includes, in addition to any act constituting such use by virtue of section 55 above, any act which would, apart from that section and this section, amount to an infringement of the patent concerned or, as the case may be, give rise to a right under section 69 below to bring proceedings in respect of the application concerned, and any reference in this Act to "use for the services of the Crown" shall, as respects any period of emergency, be construed accordingly.

(3) In this section "period of emergency" means any period beginning with such date as may be declared by Order in Council to be the commencement, and ending with such date as may be so declared to be the termination, of a period of emergency for the purposes of this section.

(4) A draft of an Order under this section shall not be submitted to Her Majesty unless it has been laid before, and approved by resolution of, each House of Parliament.

Infringement

Meaning of infringement

AppA-60   **60.**—(1) Subject to the provisions of this section, a person infringes a patent for an invention if, but only if, while the patent is in force, he does any of the following things in the United Kingdom in relation to the invention without the consent of the proprietor of the patent, that is to say—

(a) where the invention is a product, he makes, disposes of, offers to dispose of, uses or imports the product or keeps it whether for disposal or otherwise;

(b) where the invention is a process, he uses the process or he offers it for use in the United Kingdom when he knows, or it is obvious to a reasonable person in the circumstances, that its use there without the consent of the proprietor would be an infringement of the patent;

(c) where the invention is a process, he disposes of, offers to dispose of, uses or imports any product obtained directly by means of that process or keeps any such product whether for disposal or otherwise.

(2) Subject to the following provisions of this section, a person (other than the proprietor of the patent) also infringes a patent for an invention if, while the patent is in force and without the consent of the proprietor, he supplies or offers to supply in the United Kingdom a person other than a licensee or other person entitled to work the invention with any of the means, relating to an essential element of the invention, for putting the invention into effect when he knows, or it is obvious to a reasonable person in the circumstances, that those means are suitable for putting, and are intended to put, the invention into effect in the United Kingdom.

(3) Subsection (2) above shall not apply to the supply or offer of a staple commercial product unless the supply or the offer is made for the purpose of inducing the person supplied or, as the case may be, the person to whom the offer is made to do an act which constitutes an infringement of the patent by virtue of subsection (1) above.

[(4) *Without prejudice to section 86 below, subsections (1) and (2) above shall not apply to any act which, under any provision of the Community Patent Convention relating to the exhaustion of the rights of the proprietor of a patent, as that provision applies by virtue of that section, cannot be prevented by the proprietor of the patent.*]

(5) An act which, apart from this subsection, would constitute an infringement of a patent for an invention shall not do so if—

    (a)   it is done privately and for purposes which are not commercial;

    (b)   it is done for experimental purposes relating to the subject-matter of the invention;

    (c)   it consists of the extemporaneous preparation in a pharmacy of a medicine for an individual in accordance with a prescription given by a registered medical or dental practitioner or consists of dealing with a medicine so prepared;

    (d)   it consists of the use, exclusively for the needs of a relevant ship, of a product or process in the body of such a ship or in its machinery, tackle, apparatus or other accessories, in a case where the ship has temporarily or accidentally entered the internal or territorial waters of the United Kingdom;

    (e)   it consists of the use of a product or process in the body or operation of a relevant aircraft, hovercraft or vehicle which has temporarily or accidentally entered or is crossing the United Kingdom (including the air space above it and its territorial waters) or the use of accessories for such a relevant aircraft, hovercraft or vehicle;

    (f)   it consists of the use of an exempted aircraft which has lawfully entered or is lawfully crossing the United Kingdom as aforesaid or of the importation into the United Kingdom, or the use or storage there, of any part or accessory for such an aircraft.

    (g)   it consists of the use by a farmer of the product of his harvest for propagation or multiplication by him on his own holding, where there has been a sale of plant propagating material to the farmer by the proprietor of the patent or with his consent for agricultural use;

    (h)   it consists of the use of an animal or animal reproductive material by a farmer for an agricultural purpose following a sale to the farmer, by the proprietor of the patent or with his consent, of breeding stock or other animal reproductive material which constitutes or contains the patented invention.

    (i)   it consists of—

        (i)   an act done in conducting a study, test or trial which is necessary for and is conducted with a view to the application of paragraphs 1 to 5 of article 13 of Directive 1001/82/EC or paragraphs 1 to 4 of article 10 of Directive 2001/83/EC, or

        (ii)   any other act which is required for the purpose of the application of those paragraphs.

(6) For the purposes of subsection (2) above a person who does an act in rela-

tion to an invention which is prevented only by virtue of paragraph (a), (b) or (c) of subsection (5) above from constituting an infringement of a patent for the invention shall not be treated as a person entitled to work the invention, but—

    (a)   the reference in that subsection to a person entitled to work an invention includes a reference to a person so entitled by virtue of section 55 above, and

    (b)   a person who by virtue of **section 20B(4) or (5) above or** [*section 28(6)*] **section 28A(4) or (5)** above or section 64 below **or section 117A(4) or (5) below** is entitled to do an act in relation to the invention without it constituting such an infringement shall, so far as concerns that act, be treated as a person entitled to work the invention.

  (6A)   Schedule A1 contains—

    (a)   **provisions restricting the circumstances in which subsection (5)(g) applies; and**

    (b)   **provisions which apply where an act would constitute an infringement of a patent but for subsection (5)(g).**

  (6B)   **For the purposes of subsection (5)(h), use for an agricultural purpose—**

    (a)   **includes making an animal or animal reproductive material available for the purposes of pursuing the farmer's agricultural activity; but**

    (b)   **does not include sale within the framework, or for the purposes, of a commercial reproduction activity.**

  (6C)   **In paragraphs (g) and (h) of subsection (5) "sale" includes any other form of commercialisation.**

  (6D)   **For the purposes of subsection (5)(b), anything done in or for the purposes of a medicinal product assessment which would otherwise constitute an infringement of a patent for an invention is to be regarded as done for experimental purposes relating to the subject-matter of the invention.**

  (6E)   **In subsection (6D), "*medicinal product assessment*" means any testing, course of testing or other activity undertaken with a view to providing data for any of the following purposes—**

    (a)   **obtaining or varying an authorisation to sell or supply, or offer to sell or supply, a medicinal product (whether in the United Kingdom or elsewhere);**

    (b)   **complying with any regulatory requirement imposed (whether in the United Kingdom or elsewhere) in relation to such an authorisation;**

    (c)   **enabling a government or public authority (whether in the United Kingdom or elsewhere), or a person (whether in the United Kingdom or elsewhere) with functions of—**

        (i)   **providing health care on behalf of such a government or public authority, or**

        (ii)   **providing advice to, or on behalf of, such a government or public authority about the provision of health care,**

    to carry out an assessment of suitability of a medicinal product for human use for the purpose of determining whether to use it, or recommend its use, in the provision of health care.

  (6F)   **In subsection (6E) and this subsection—**

    "medicinal product" means a medicinal product for human use or a veterinary medicinal product;

"medicinal product for human use" has the meaning given by article 1 of Directive 2001/83/EC [9];

"veterinary medicinal product" has the meaning given by article 1 of Directive 2001/82/EC [10].

(6G)   Nothing in subsections (6D) to (6F) is to be read as affecting the application of subsection (5)(b) in relation to any act of a kind not falling within subsection (6D).

(7)   In this section—

"relevant ship" and "relevant aircraft, hovercraft or vehicle" mean respectively a ship and an aircraft, hovercraft or vehicle registered in, or belonging to, any country, other than the United Kingdom, which is a party to the Convention for the Protection of Industrial Property signed at Paris on 20th March 1883 **or which is a member of the World Trade Organisation**; and

"exempted aircraft" means an aircraft to which section [*53*] **89** of the Civil Aviation Act [*1949*] **1982** (aircraft exempted from seizure in respect of patent claims) applies.

"Directive 2001/82/EC" means Directive 2001/82/EC of the European Parliament and of the Council on the Community code relating to veterinary medicinal products as amended by Directive 2004/28/EC of the European Parliament and of the Council [*Directive 2004/28 of the European Parliament and of the Council*]**;**

"Directive 2001/83/EC" means Directive 2001/83/EC of the European Parliament and of the Council on the Community code relating to medicinal products for human use, as amended by Directive 2002/98/EC of the European Parliament and of the Council, by Commission Directive 2003/63/EC and by Directives 2004/24/EC and 2004/27/EC of the European Parliament and of the Council.

Notes

Subsection (4) repealed by Patents Act 2004 (c.16) s.16, Sch.2 para.13 and Sch.3, with effect from 1 January 2005, SI 2004/3205.

Subsection (5) amended by Patents Regulations 2000 (SI 2000/2037) reg.4, subject to transitional provisions contained in reg.9, with effect from 28 July 2000, subject to transitional provisions contained in reg.9 which provide that the amendments apply to applications for patents made on or after that date (and to patents granted in pursuance of such applications).

Subsection (5)(i) inserted by Medicines (Marketing Authorisations Etc.) Amendment Regulation 2005 (SI 2005/2579) para.3, with effect from 30 October 2005.

Subsection (6) amended by CDPA 1988 (c.48) s.295 and Sch.5 para.8, with effect from 7 January 1991, SI 1991/2168; Regulatory Reform (Patents) Order 2004 (SI 2004/2357) art.11, with effect from 1 January 2005, subject to transitional provisions contained in arts 20–23 of that Order.

Subsections (6A), (6B) and (6C) inserted by Patents Regulations 2000 (SI 2000/2037) reg.4, with effect from 28 July 2000, subject to transitional provisions contained in reg.9 which provide that the amendments apply to applications for patents made on or after that date (and to patents granted in pursuance of such applications).

Subsections (6D), (6E), (6F), and (6G) inserted by Legislative Reform (Patents) Order (SI 2014/1997) art.2 with effect from 1 October 2014.

Subsection (7) amended by Civil Aviation Act 1982 (c.16) Sch.15 para.19; Patents and Trademarks (World Trade Organisation) Regulations 1999 (SI 1999/1899) reg.7; and Medicines (Marketing Authorisations Etc.) Amendment Regulation 2005 (SI 2005/2579) para.3, with effect from 30 October 2005.

Subsection (7) reference to Directive 2004/28 was amended to refer to Directive 2004/28/EC by the Intellectual Property Act 2014 (c.18) Sch.1 para.5 with effect from 1 October 2014.

Proceedings for infringement of patent

AppA-61   **61.**—(1)   Subject to the following provisions of this Part of this Act, civil proceedings may be brought in the court by the proprietor of a patent in respect of any act alleged to infringe the patent and (without prejudice to any other jurisdiction of the court) in those proceedings a claim may be made—

(a) for an injunction or interdict restraining the defendant or defender from any apprehended acts of infringement;

(b) for an order for him to deliver up or destroy any patented product in relation to which the patent is infringed or any article in which that product is inextricably comprised;

(c) for damages in respect of the infringement;

(d) for an account of the profits derived by him from the infringement;

(e) for a declaration or declarator that the patent is valid and has been infringed by him.

(2)   The court shall not, in respect of the same infringement, both award the proprietor of a patent damages and order that he shall be given an account of the profits.

(3)   The proprietor of a patent and any other person may by agreement with each other refer to the comptroller the question whether that other person has infringed the patent and on the reference of the proprietor of the patent may make any claim mentioned in subsection (1)(c) or (e) above.

(4)   Except so far as the context requires, in the following provisions of this Act—

(a) any reference to proceedings for infringement and the bringing of such proceedings includes a reference to a reference under subsection (3) above and the making of such a reference;

(b) any reference to a [*plaintiff*] **claimant** or pursuer includes a reference to the proprietor of the patent; and

(c) any reference to a defendant or defender includes a reference to any other party to the reference.

(5)   If it appears to the comptroller on a reference under subsection (3) above that the question referred to him would more properly be determined by the court, he may decline to deal with it and the court shall have jurisdiction to determine the question as if the reference were proceedings brought in the court.

(6)   Subject to the following provisions of this Part of this Act, in determining whether or not to grant any kind of relief claimed under this section and the extent of the relief granted the court or the comptroller shall apply the principles applied by the court in relation to that kind of relief immediately before the appointed day.

(7)   **If the comptroller awards any sum by way of damages on a reference under subsection (3) above, then—**

(a) **in England and Wales, the sum shall be recoverable, if the county court [*a county court*] so orders, [*by execution issued from the county court*] under section 85 of the County Courts Act 1984 or otherwise as if it were payable under an order of that court;**

(b) **in Scotland, payment of the sum may be enforced in like manner as an extract registered decree arbitral bearing a warrant for execution issued by the sheriff court of any sheriffdom in Scotland;**

(c) **in Northern Ireland, payment of the sum may be enforced as if it were a money judgment.**

Note

Subsection (4) amended and subs.(7) inserted by Patents Act 2004 (c.16) s.11, Sch.2 para.14, with effect from 1 January 2005, SI 2004/3205.

Subsection (7) reference to s.85 of the County Courts Act 1984 amended by the Tribunals, Courts and Enforcement Act 2007 s.62(3), Sch.13 para.41, as from 22 April 2014 subject to savings and transitional provisions.

Subsection (7) amended to refer to the county court by Tribunals, Courts and Enforcement Act 2007 (c.15) Sch.13 para.41 with effect from 6 April 2014.

Restrictions on recovery of damages for infringement

62.—(1)   In proceedings for infringement of a patent damages shall not be   AppA-62
awarded, and no order shall be made for an account of profits, against a defendant
or defender who proves that at the date of the infringement he was not aware, and
had no reasonable grounds for supposing, that the patent existed; and a person shall
not be taken to have been so aware or to have had reasonable grounds for so supposing by reason only of the application to a product of the word "patent" or
"patented," or any word or words expressing or implying that a patent has been
obtained for the product, unless the number of the patent accompanied the word or
words in question.

**(1A)   The reference in subsection (1) to a relevant internet link is a refer-
ence to an address of a posting on the internet—**

    (a)   which is accessible to the public free of charge, and

    (b)   which clearly associates the product with the number of the patent.

(2)   In proceedings for infringement of a patent the court or the comptroller
may, if it or he thinks fit, refuse to award any damages or make any such order in
respect of an infringement committed during [*any further period specified under*]
the further period specified in section 25(4) above, but before the payment of the
renewal fee and any additional fee prescribed for the purposes of that subsection.

(3)   Where an amendment of the specification of a patent has been allowed
under any of the provisions of this Act, [*no damages shall be awarded in proceedings for an infringement of the patent committed before the decision to allow the
amendment unless the court or the comptroller is satisfied that*

    *(a)   the specification of the patent as published was framed in good faith
and with reasonable skill and knowledge, and*

    (b)   the proceedings are brought in good faith.]
**the court or the comptroller shall, when awarding damages or making an
order for an account of profits in proceedings for an infringement of the patent committed before the decision to allow the amendment, take into account
the following—**

    **(a)   whether at the date of infringement the defendant or defender
knew, or had reasonable grounds to know, that he was infringing
the patent;**

    **(b)   whether the specification of the patent as published was framed in
good faith and with reasonable skill and knowledge;**

    (c)   whether the proceedings are brought in good faith.

Notes

Subsection (1A) inserted by Intellectual Property Act 2014 (c.18) Pt 2 s.15(2) with effect from 1
October 2014 subject to transitional provisions specified in SI 2014/2330 art.5.

Subsection (2) amended by Patents Act 2004 (c.16) s.16 and Sch.2 para.15, with effect from 1 October
2005, SI 2005/2471.

Subsection (3) prospectively amended to insert subs.(3)(b) as shown within the square brackets by Patents Act 2004 (c.16) s.2, as from a day to be appointed; and amended by omission of all the words in square brackets and insertion of the words in bold by the Intellectual Property (Enforcement, etc) Regulations 2006 (SI 2006/1028) reg.2(2), Sch.2 para.2, with effect from 29 April 2006.

Relief for infringement of partially valid patent

AppA-63   **63.**—(1)   If the validity of a patent is put in issue in proceedings for infringement of the patent and it is found that the patent is only partially valid, the court or the comptroller may, subject to subsection (2) below, grant relief in respect of that part of the patent which is found to be valid and infringed.

(2)   Where in any such proceedings it is found that a patent is only partially valid, the court or the comptroller shall [*not grant relief by way of damages, costs or expenses, except where the* [*plaintiff*] **claimant** *or pursuer proves that*

> *(a)   the specification for the patent was framed in good faith and with reasonable skill and knowledge, and*
>
> **(b)   the proceedings are brought in good faith, and**

in that event the court or the comptroller may grant relief in respect of that part of the patent which is valid and infringed, subject to the discretion of the court or the comptroller as to costs or expenses and as to the date from which damages should be reckoned.]

when awarding damages, costs or expenses or making an order for an account of profits, take into account the following—

> **(a)   whether at the date of the infringement the defendant or defender knew, or had reasonable grounds to know, that he was infringing the patent;**
>
> **(b)   whether the specification of the patent was framed in good faith and with reasonable skill and knowledge;**
>
> **(c)   whether the proceedings are brought in good faith;**

and any relief granted shall be subject to the discretion of the court or the comptroller as to costs or expenses and as to the date from which damages or an account should be reckoned.

(3)   As a condition of relief under this section the court or the comptroller may direct that the specification of the patent shall be amended to its or his satisfaction upon an application made for that purpose under section 75 below, and an application may be so made accordingly, whether or not all other issues in the proceedings have been determined.

(4)   The court or the comptroller may also grant relief under this section in the case of a European patent (UK) on condition that the claims of the patent are limited to its or his satisfaction by the European Patent Office at the request of the proprietor.

Notes

Subsection (2) amended to substitute "claimant" for "plaintiff" by Patents Act 2004 (c.16) s.16 and Sch.2 para.16, with effect from 1 January 2005, SI 2004/3205; prospectively amended to insert subs.2(b) as shown within square brackets by Patents Act 2004 (c.16) ss.2(4), 3(1), as from a day to be appointed; and amended by omission of all the words in square brackets and insertion of the words in bold by the Intellectual Property (Enforcement, etc) Regulations 2006 (SI 2006/1028) reg.2(2), Sch.2 para.3, with effect from 29 April 2006.

Subsection (4) inserted by Patents Act 2004 (c.16) s.3(1), with effect from 13 December 2007, SI 2007/3396.

[Right to continue use begun before priority date

64.—(1) Where a patent is granted for an invention, a person who in the United AppA-64
Kingdom before the priority date of the invention does in good faith an act which would constitute an infringement of the patent if it were in force, or makes in good faith effective and serious preparations to do such an act, shall have the rights conferred by subsection (2) below.

(2) Any such person shall have the right—

(a) to continue to do or, as the case may be, to do that act himself; and

(b) if it was done or preparations had been made to do it in the course of a business, to assign the right to do it or to transmit that right on his death or, in the case of a body corporate on its dissolution, to any person who acquires that part of the business in the course of which the act was done or preparations had been made to do it, or to authorise it to be done by any partners of his for the time being in that business;

and the doing of that act by virtue of this subsection shall not amount to an infringement of the patent concerned.

(3) The right mentioned in subsection (2) above shall not include the right to grant a licence to any person to do an act so mentioned.

(4) Where a patented product is disposed of by any person to another in exercise of a right conferred by subsection (2) above, that other and any person claiming through him shall be entitled to deal with the product in the same way as if it had been disposed of by a sole registered proprietor.]

Right to continue use begun before priority date

64.—(1) Where a patent is granted for an invention, a person who in the AppA-64A
United Kingdom before the priority date of the invention—

(a) does in good faith an act which would constitute an infringement of the patent if it were in force, or

(b) makes in good faith effective and serious preparations to do such an act, has the right to continue to do the act or, as the case may be, to do the act, notwithstanding the grant of the patent; but this right does not extend to granting a licence to another person to do the act.

(2) If the act was done, or the preparations were made, in the course of a business, the person entitled to the right conferred by subsection (1) may—

(a) authorise the doing of that act by any partners of his for the time being in that business, and

(b) assign that right, or transmit it on death (or in the case of a body corporate on its dissolution), to any person who acquires that part of the business in the course of which the act was done or the preparations were made.

(3) Where a product is disposed of to another in exercise of the rights conferred by subsection (1) or (2), that other and any person claiming through him may deal with the product in the same way as if it had been disposed of by the registered proprietor of the patent.

Note

Section 64 substituted by CDPA 1988 (c.48) s.295 and Sch.5 para.17, with effect from 7 January 1991, SI 1990/2168.

Certificate of contested validity of patent

AppA-65   **65.**—(1)   If in any proceedings before the court or the comptroller the validity of a patent to any extent is contested and that patent is found by the court or the comptroller to be wholly or partially valid, the court or the comptroller may certify the finding and the fact that the validity of the patent was so contested.

(2)   Where a certificate is granted under this section, then, if in any subsequent proceedings before the court or the comptroller for infringement of the patent concerned or for revocation of the patent a final order or judgment or interlocutor is made or given in favour of the party relying on the validity of the patent as found in the earlier proceedings, that party shall, unless the court or the comptroller otherwise directs, be entitled to his costs or expenses as between solicitor and own client (other than the costs or expenses of any appeal in the subsequent proceedings).

Proceedings for infringement by a co-owner

AppA-66   **66.**—(1)   In the application of section 60 above to a patent of which there are two or more proprietors the reference to the proprietor shall be construed—

     (a)   in relation to any act, as a reference to that proprietor or those proprietors who, by virtue of section 36 above or any agreement referred to in that section, is or are entitled to do that act without its amounting to an infringement; and

     (b)   in relation to any consent, as a reference to that proprietor or those proprietors who, by virtue of section 36 above or any such agreement, is or are the proper person or persons to give the requisite consent.

(2)   One of two or more joint proprietors of a patent may without the concurrence of the others bring proceedings in respect of an act alleged to infringe the patent, but shall not do so unless the others are made parties to the proceedings, but any of the others made a defendant or defender shall not be liable for any costs or expenses unless he enters an appearance and takes part in the proceedings.

Proceedings for infringement by exclusive licensee

AppA-67   **67.**—(1)   Subject to the provisions of this section, the holder of an exclusive licence under a patent shall have the same right as the proprietor of the patent to bring proceedings in respect of any infringement of the patent committed after the date of the licence; and references to the proprietor of the patent in the provisions of this Act relating to infringement shall be construed accordingly.

(2)   In awarding damages or granting any other relief in any such proceedings the court or the comptroller shall take into consideration any loss suffered or likely to be suffered by the exclusive licensee as such as a result of the infringement, or, as the case may be, the profits derived from the infringement, so far as it constitutes an infringement of the rights of the exclusive licensee as such.

(3)   In any proceedings taken by an exclusive licensee by virtue of this section the proprietor of the patent shall be made a party to the proceedings, but if made a

defendant or defender shall not be liable for any costs or expenses unless he enters an appearance and takes part in the proceedings.

Effect of non-registration on infringement proceedings

68. Where by virtue of a transaction, instrument or event to which section 33 above applies a person becomes the proprietor or one of the proprietors or an exclusive licensee of a patent and the patent is subsequently infringed [, *the court or the comptroller shall not award him damages or order that he be given an account of the profits in respect of such a subsequent infringement occurring*] before the transaction, instrument or event is registered, **in proceedings for such an infringement, the court or comptroller shall not award him costs or expenses** unless—

   (a) the transaction, instrument or event is registered within the period of six months beginning with its date; or

   (b) the court or the comptroller is satisfied that it was not practicable to register the transaction, instrument or event before the end of that period and that it was registered as soon as practicable thereafter.

Note

Section 68 amended by the Intellectual Property (Enforcement, etc) Regulations 2006 (SI 2006/1028) reg.2(2), Sch.2 para.4, with effect from 29 April 2006.

Infringement of rights conferred by publication of application

69.—(1) Where an application for a patent for an invention is published, then, subject to subsections (2) and (3) below, the applicant shall have, as from the publication and until the grant of the patent, the same right as he would have had, if the patent had been granted on the date of the publication of the application, to bring proceedings in the court or before the comptroller for damages in respect of any act which would have infringed the patent; and (subject to subsections (2) and (3) below) references in sections 60 to 62 and 66 to 68 above to a patent and the proprietor of a patent shall be respectively construed as including references to any such application and the applicant, and references to a patent being in force, being granted, being valid or existing shall be construed accordingly.

(2) The applicant shall be entitled to bring proceedings by virtue of this section in respect of any act only—

   (a) after the patent has been granted; and

   (b) if the act would, if the patent had been granted on the date of the publication of the application, have infringed not only the patent, but also the claims (as interpreted by the description and any drawings referred to in the description or claims) in the form in which they were contained in the application immediately before the preparations for its publication were completed by the Patent Office.

(3) Section 62(2) and (3) above shall not apply to an infringement of the rights conferred by this section, but in considering the amount of any damages for such an infringement, the court or the comptroller shall consider whether or not it would have been reasonable to expect, from a consideration of the application as published under section 16 above, that a patent would be granted conferring on the proprietor of the patent protection from an act of the same description as that found to infringe those rights, and if the court or the comptroller finds that it would not have

been reasonable, it or he shall reduce the damages to such an amount as it or he thinks just.

Remedy for groundless threats of infringement proceedings

AppA-70   **70.**—(1)   Where a person (whether or not the proprietor of, or entitled to any right in, a patent) by circulars, advertisements or otherwise threatens another person with proceedings for any infringement of a patent, a person aggrieved by the threats (whether or not he is the person to whom the threats are made) may, subject to subsection (4) below, bring proceedings in the court against the person making the threats, claiming any relief mentioned in subsection (3) below.

[*(2)   In any such proceedings the plaintiff or pursuer shall, if he proves that the threats were so made and satisfies the court that he is a person aggrieved by them, be entitled to the relief claimed unless—*

(a)   *the defendant or defender proves that the acts in respect of which proceedings were threatened constitute or, if done, would constitute an infringement of a patent; and*

(b)   *the patent alleged to be infringed is not shown by the plaintiff or pursuer to be invalid in a relevant respect.*]

(2)   In any such proceedings the claimant or pursuer shall, subject to subsection (2A) below, be entitled to the relief claimed if he proves that the threats were so made and satisfies the court that he is a person aggrieved by them.

(2A)   If the defendant or defender proves that the acts in respect of which proceedings were threatened constitute or, if done, would constitute an infringement of a patent—

(a)   **the claimant or pursuer shall be entitled to the relief claimed only if he shows that the patent alleged to be infringed is invalid in a relevant respect;**

(b)   **even if the claimant or pursuer does show that the patent is invalid in a relevant respect, he shall not be entitled to the relief claimed if the defendant or defender proves that at the time of making the threats he did not know, and had no reason to suspect, that the patent was invalid in that respect.**

(3)   The said relief is—

(a)   a declaration or declarator to the effect that the threats are unjustifiable;

(b)   an injunction or interdict against the continuance of the threats; and

(c)   damages in respect of any loss which the [*plaintiff*] **claimant** or pursuer has sustained by the threats.

[*(4)   Proceedings may not be brought under this section for a threat to bring proceedings for an infringement alleged to consist of making or importing a product for disposal or of using a process.*]

(4)   Proceedings may not be brought under this section for—

(a)   **a threat to bring proceedings for an infringement alleged to consist of making or importing a product for disposal or of using a process, or**

(b)   **a threat, made to a person who has made or imported a product for disposal or used a process, to bring proceedings for an infringement alleged to consist of doing anything else in relation to that product or process.**

[*(5)   It is hereby declared that a mere notification of the existence of a patent does not constitute a threat of proceedings within the meaning of this section.*]

(5)   For the purposes of this section a person does not threaten another person with proceedings for infringement of a patent if he merely—

    (a)   provides factual information about the patent,

    (b)   makes enquiries of the other person for the sole purpose of discovering whether, or by whom, the patent has been infringed as mentioned in subsection (4)(a) above, or

    (c)   makes an assertion about the patent for the purpose of any enquiries so made.

(6)   In proceedings under this section for threats made by one person (A) to another (B) in respect of an alleged infringement of a patent for an invention, it shall be a defence for A to prove that he used his best endeavours, without success, to discover—

    (a)   where the invention is a product, the identity of the person (if any) who made or (in the case of an imported product) imported it for disposal;

    (b)   where the invention is a process and the alleged infringement consists of offering it for use, the identity of a person who used the process;

    (c)   where the invention is a process and the alleged infringement is an act falling within section 60(1)(c) above, the identity of the person who used the process to produce the product in question;

and that he notified B accordingly, before or at the time of making the threats, identifying the endeavours used.

Note

Subsections (2) and (2A) substituted for original subs.(2), subs.(3) amended, subss.(4) and (5) substituted and subs.(6) inserted by Patents Act 2004 (c.16) ss.12, 16 and Sch.2 para.17, with effect from 1 January 2005, SI 2004/3205, subject to transitional provisions contained in art.9 of that Order.

Declaration or declarator as to non-infringement

71.—(1)   Without prejudice to the court's jurisdiction to make a declaration or declarator apart from this section, a declaration or declarator that an act does not, or a proposed act would not, constitute an infringement of a patent may be made by the court or the comptroller in proceedings between the person doing or proposing to do the act and the proprietor of the patent, notwithstanding that no assertion to the contrary has been made by the proprietor, if it is shown—   AppA-71

    (a)   that that person has applied in writing to the proprietor for a written acknowledgement to the effect of the declaration or declarator claimed, and has furnished him with full particulars in writing of the act in question; and

    (b)   that the proprietor has refused or failed to give any such acknowledgement.

(2)   Subject to section 72(5) below, a declaration made by the comptroller under this section shall have the same effect as a declaration or declarator by the court.

Revocation of patents

Power to revoke patents on application

AppA-72   **72.**—(1)   Subject to the following provisions of this Act, the court or the comptroller may [*on the application of any person*] by order revoke a patent for an invention **on the application of any person (including the proprietor of the patent)** on (but only on) any of the following grounds, that is to say—

    (a)   the invention is not a patentable invention;

    [*(b)   the patent was granted to a person who was not the only person entitled under section 7(2) above to be granted that patent or to two or more persons who were not the only persons so entitled;*]

    (b)   that the patent was granted to a person who was not entitled to be granted that patent;

    (c)   the specification of the patent does not disclose the invention clearly enough and completely enough for it to be performed by a person skilled in the art;

    (d)   the matter disclosed in the specification of the patent extends beyond that disclosed in the application for the patent, as filed, or, if the patent was granted on a new application filed under section 8(3), 12, or 37(4) above or as mentioned in [*section 15(4)*] **section 15(9)** above, in the earlier application, as filed;

    (e)   the protection conferred by the patent has been extended by an amendment which should not have been allowed.

(2)   An application for the revocation of a patent on the ground mentioned in subsection (1)(b) above—

    (a)   may only be made by a person found by the court in an action for a declaration or declarator, or found by the court or the comptroller on a reference under section 37 above, to be entitled to be granted that patent or to be granted a patent for part of the matter comprised in the specification of the patent sought to be revoked; and

    (b)   may not be made if that action was commenced or that reference was made after **the second anniversary of** [*the end of the period of two years beginning with*] the date of the grant of the patent sought to be revoked, unless it is shown that any person registered as a proprietor of the patent knew at the time of the grant or of the transfer of the patent to him that he was not entitled to the patent.

[*(3)   Rules under section 14(4) and (8) above shall, with any necessary modifications, apply for the purposes of subsection (1)(c) above as they apply for the purposes of section 14(3) above.*]

(4)   An order under this section may be an order for the unconditional revocation of the patent or, where the court or the comptroller determines that one of the grounds mentioned in subsection (1) above has been established, but only so as to invalidate the patent to a limited extent, an order that the patent should be revoked unless within a specified time the specification is amended [*under section 75 below*] to the satisfaction of the court or the comptroller, as the case may be.

(4A)   The reference in subsection (4) above to the specification being amended is to its being amended under section 75 below and also, in the case

of a European patent (UK), to its being amended under any provision of the European Patent Convention under which the claims of the patent may be limited by amendment at the request of the proprietor.

(5) A decision of the comptroller or on appeal from the comptroller shall not estop any party to civil proceedings in which infringement of a patent is in issue from alleging invalidity of the patent on any of the grounds referred to in subsection (1) above, whether or not any of the issues involved were decided in the said decision.

(6) Where the comptroller refuses to grant an application made to him by any person under this section, no application (otherwise than by way of appeal or by way of putting validity in issue in proceedings for infringement) may be made to the court by that person under this section in relation to the patent concerned, without the leave of the court.

(7) Where the comptroller has not disposed of an application made to him under this section, the applicant may not apply to the court under this section in respect of the patent concerned unless either—

    (a)   the proprietor of the patent agrees that the applicant may so apply, or

    (b)   the comptroller certifies in writing that it appears to him that the question whether the patent should be revoked is one which would more properly be determined by the court.

Notes

Subsection (1) amended by Patents Act 2004 (c.16) s.16 and Sch.2 para.18, with effect from 1 October 2005, SI 2005/2471.

Subsection (1)(b) substituted by CDPA 1988 (c.48) s.295 and Sch.5 para.18, with effect from 7 January 1991, SI 1990/2168.

Subsection (1)(d) amended by Regulatory Reform (Patents) Order SI 2004/2357 art.12, with effect from 1 January 2005, subject to transitional provisions contained in arts 20–23 of that Order.

Subsection (2)(b) amended by Intellectual Property Act 2014 (c.18) Sch.1 para.3(1)(b) with effect from 1 October 2014.

Subsection (3) repealed by CDPA 1988 s.303(2) and Sch.8, with effect from 1 August 1988, SI 1989/816.

Subsection (4) amended and subs.(4A) inserted by Patents Act 2004 (c.16) s.4, with effect from 13 December 2007, SI 2007/3396.

Comptroller's power to revoke patents on his own initiative

73.—(1) If it appears to the comptroller that an invention for which a patent   **AppA-73** has been granted formed part of the state of the art by virtue only of section 2(3) above, he may on his own initiative by order revoke the patent, but shall not do so without giving the proprietor of the patent an opportunity of making any observations and of amending the specification of the patent so as to exclude any matter which formed part of the state of the art as aforesaid without contravening section 76 below.

(1A) Where the comptroller issues an opinion under section 74A that section 1(1)(a) or (b) is not satisfied in relation to an invention for which there is a patent, the comptroller may revoke the patent.

(1B) The power under subsection (1A) may not be exercised before—

    (a)   the end of the period in which the proprietor of the patent may apply under the rules (by virtue of section 74B) for a review of the opinion, or

    (b)   if the proprietor applies for a review, the decision on the review is

made (or, if there is an appeal against that decision, the appeal is determined).

(1C)   The comptroller shall not exercise the power under subsection (1A) without giving the proprietor of the patent an opportunity to make any observations and to amend the specification of the patent without contravening section 76.

[*(2)   If it appears to the comptroller that a patent under this Act and a European patent (UK) have been granted for the same invention having the same priority date and that the applications for both patents were filed by the same applicant or his successor in title, the comptroller may, on his own initiative but only after the relevant date, consider whether to revoke the patent granted under this Act and may, after giving the proprietor of the patent an opportunity of making any observations and of amending the specification of the patent, revoke the patent.*]

(2)   If it appears to the comptroller that a patent under this Act and a European patent (UK) have been granted for the same invention having the same priority date, and that the applications for the patents were filed by the same applicant or his successor in title, he shall give the proprietor of the patent under this Act an opportunity of making observations and of amending the specification of the patent, and if the proprietor fails to satisfy the comptroller that there are not two patents in respect of the same invention, or to amend the specification so as to prevent there being two patents in respect of the same invention, the comptroller shall revoke the patent.

[*(3)   In this section "the relevant date" means whichever of the following dates is relevant, that is to say—*

(a)   the date on which the period for filing an opposition to patent under the European Patent Convention expires without an opposition being filed;

(b)   the date when any opposition proceedings under that convention are finally disposed of by a decision to maintain the European patent;

(c)   if later than either of the foregoing dates, the date when the patent under this Act is granted.]

(3)   The comptroller shall not take action under subsection (2) above before—

(a)   the end of the period for filing an opposition to the European patent (UK) under the European Patent Convention, or

(b)   if later, the date on which opposition proceedings are finally disposed of;

and he shall not then take any action if the decision is not to maintain the European patent or if it is amended so that there are not two patents in respect of the same invention.

(4)   The comptroller shall not take action under subsection (2) above if the European patent (UK) has been surrendered under section 29(1) above before the date on which by virtue of section 25(1) above the patent under this Act is to be treated as having been granted or, if proceedings for the surrender of the European patent (UK) have been begun before that date, until those proceedings are finally disposed of; and he shall not then take any action if the decision is to accept the surrender of the European patent.

Note

Subsections (1A), (1B), and (1C) inserted by Intellectual Property Act 2014 (c.18) Pt 2 s.16(4) with effect from 1 October 2014 subject to transitional provisions specified in SI 2014/2330 art.6

Subsections (2)–(4) substituted for original subss.(2) and (3) by CDPA 1988 (c.48) s.295 and Sch.5 para.19, with effect from 7 January 1991, SI 1990/2168.

Putting validity in issue

Proceedings in which validity of patent may be put in issue

74.—(1)   Subject to the following provisions of this section, the validity of a   AppA-74
patent may be put in issue—

   (a)   by way of defence, in proceedings for infringement of the patent under
         section 61 above or proceedings under section 69 above for infringe-
         ment of rights conferred by the publication of an application;
   (b)   in proceedings under section 70 above;
   (c)   in proceedings in which a declaration in relation to the patent is sought
         under section 71 above;
   (d)   in proceedings before the court or the comptroller under section 72
         above for the revocation of the patent; (e) in proceedings under sec-
         tion 58 above.

   (2)   The validity of a patent may not be put in issue in any other proceedings
and, in particular, no proceedings may be instituted (whether under this Act or
otherwise) seeking only a declaration as to the validity or invalidity of a patent.

   (3)   The only grounds on which the validity of a patent may be put in issue
(whether the proceedings for revocation under section 72 above or otherwise) are
the grounds on which the patent may be revoked under that section.

   (4)   No determination shall be made in any proceedings mentioned in subsection (1) above on the validity of a patent which any person puts in issue on the
ground mentioned in section 72(1)(b) above unless—

   (a)   it has been determined in entitlement proceedings commenced by that
         person or in the proceedings in which the validity of the patent is in
         issue that the patent should have been granted to him and not some
         other person; and
   (b)   except where it had been so determined in entitlement proceedings, the
         proceedings in which the validity of the patent is in issue are com-
         menced **on or before the second anniversary of** [*before the end of the
         period of two years beginning with*] the date of the grant of the patent
         or it is shown that any person registered as a proprietor of the patent
         knew at the time of the grant or of the transfer of the patent to him that
         he was not entitled to the patent.

   (5)   Where the validity of a patent is put in issue by way of defence or
counterclaim the court or the comptroller shall, if it or he thinks it just to do so, give
the defendant an opportunity to comply with the condition in subsection (4)(a)
above.

   (6)   In subsection (4) above "entitlement proceedings," in relation to a patent,
means a reference under [*section 37(1)(a) above*] **section 37(1) above** on the
ground that the patent was granted to a person not entitled to it or proceedings for
a declaration or declarator that it was so granted.

   (7)   Where proceedings with respect to a patent are pending in the court under
any provision of this Act mentioned in subsection (1) above, no proceedings may
be instituted without the leave of the court before the comptroller with respect to
that patent under section 61(3), 69, 71 or 72 above.

   (8)   It is hereby declared that for the purposes of this Act the validity of a patent is not put in issue merely because

[979]

(a) the comptroller is considering its validity in order to decide whether to revoke it under section 73 above, **or**

(b) its validity is being considered in connection with an opinion under section 74A below or a review of such an opinion.

Notes

Subsection (4)(b) amended by Intellectual Property Act 2014 (c.18) Sch.1 para.3(2) with effect from 1 October 2014.

Subsection (6) amended by CDPA 1988 (c.48) s.295 and Sch.5 para.10, with effect from 7 January 1991, SI 1990/2168.

Subsection (8) amended by Patents Act 2004 (c.16) s.13(2), with effect from 1 October 2005, SI 2005/2471.

Opinions by Patent Office

Opinions on matters prescribed in the rules [*as to validity or infringement*]

AppA-74A

74A.—(1) The proprietor of a patent or any other person may request the comptroller to issue an opinion on a prescribed matter in relation to a patent.
[*an opinion—*

(a) *as to whether a particular act constitutes, or (if done) would constitute, an infringement of the patent;*

(b) *as to whether, or to what extent, the invention in question is not patentable because the condition in section 1(1)(a) or (b) above is not satisfied.*]

(2) Subsection (1) above applies even if the patent has expired or has been surrendered.

(3) The comptroller shall issue an opinion if requested to do so under subsection (1) above, but shall not do so—

(a) in such circumstances as may be prescribed, or

(b) if for any reason he considers it inappropriate in all the circumstances to do so.

(4) An opinion under this section shall not be binding for any purposes.

(5) An opinion under this section shall be prepared by an examiner.

(6) In relation to a decision of the comptroller whether to issue an opinion under this section—

(a) for the purposes of section 101 below, only the person making the request under subsection (1) above shall be regarded as a party to a proceeding before the comptroller; and

(b) no appeal shall lie at the instance of any other person.

Note

Section 74A inserted together with s.74B, by Patents Act 2004 (c.16) s.13(1), with effect from 1 October 2005, SI 2005/2471.

Heading and subsection (1) amended by Intellectual Property Act 2014 (c.18) Pt 2 s.16(1) with effect from 1 October 2014.

Reviews of opinions under section 74A

AppA-74B

74B.—(1) Rules may make provision for a review before the comptroller, on an application by the proprietor or an exclusive licensee of the patent in question, of an opinion under section 74A above.

(2) The rules may, in particular—

(a) prescribe the circumstances in which, and the period within which, an application may be made;

(b) provide that, in prescribed circumstances, proceedings for a review may not be brought or continued where other proceedings have been brought;

[(c) *make provision under which, in prescribed circumstances, proceedings on a review are to be treated for prescribed purposes as if they were proceedings under section 61(1)(c) or (e), 71(1) or 72(1)(a) above;*]

(d) provide for there to be a right of appeal against a decision made on a review only in prescribed cases.

Note

Section 74B inserted together with s.74A, by Patents Act 2004 (c.16) s.13(1), with effect from 1 October 2005, SI 2005/2471.

Subsection (2)(c) repealed by Intellectual Property Act 2014 (c.18) Pt 2 s.16(2) with effect from 1 October 2014.

General provisions as to amendment of patents and applications

Amendment of patent in infringement or revocation proceedings

75.—(1) In any proceedings before the court or the comptroller in which the validity of a patent [*is*] **may be** put in issue the court or, as the case may be, the comptroller may, subject to section 76 below, allow the proprietor of the patent to amend the specification of the patent in such manner, and subject to such terms as to advertising the proposed amendment and as to costs, expenses or otherwise, as the court or comptroller thinks fit. **AppA-75**

(2) A person may give notice to the court or the comptroller of his opposition to an amendment proposed by the proprietor of the patent under this section, and if he does so the court or the comptroller shall notify the proprietor and consider the opposition in deciding whether the amendment or any amendment should be allowed.

(3) An amendment of a specification of a patent under this section shall have effect and be deemed always to have had effect from the grant of the patent.

(4) Where an application for an order under this section is made to the court, the applicant shall notify the comptroller, who shall be entitled to appear and be heard and shall appear if so directed by the court.

(5) In considering whether or not to allow an amendment proposed under this section, the court or the comptroller shall have regard to any relevant principles applicable under the European Patent Convention.

Notes

Subsection (1) amended by Patents Act 2004 (c.16) s.16 and Sch.2 para.19, with effect from 1 January 2005, SI 2004/3205, subject to transitional provisions contained in art.9 of that Order.

Subsection (5) inserted by Patents Act 2004 (c.16) s.2(5), with effect from 13 December 2007, SI 2007/3396.

Amendments of applications and patents not to include added matter

76.—[(1) *An application for a patent (the later application) shall not be allowed to be filed under section 8(3), 12 or 37(4) above or as mentioned in section* **AppA-76**

15(4) above, in respect of any matter disclosed in an earlier application or the specification of a patent which has been granted, if the later application discloses matter which extends beyond that disclosed in the earlier application, as filed, or the application for the patent, as filed.

(2)   No amendment of an application or the specification of a patent shall be allowed under any of the provisions of this Act to which this subsection applies if it—

    (a)   results in the application or specification disclosing any such matter, or

    (b)   (where a patent has been granted) extends the protection conferred by the patent.

(3)   Subsection (2) above applies to the following provisions of this Act, namely, section 17(3), 18(3) 19(1) 27(1), 73 and 75.]

Amendments of applications and patents not to include added matter

AppA-7
6AA

76.—(1)   An application for a patent which—

    (a)   is made in respect of matter disclosed in an earlier application, or in the specification of a patent which has been granted, and

    (b)   discloses additional matter, that is, matter extending beyond that disclosed in the earlier application, as filed, or the application for the patent, as filed, may be filed under section 8(3), 12 or 37(4) above, or as mentioned in [section 15(4)] section 15(9) above, but shall not be allowed to proceed unless it is amended so as to exclude the additional matter.

(1A)   Where, in relation to an application for a patent—

    (a)   a reference to an earlier relevant application has been filed as mentioned in section 15(1)(c)(ii) above; and

    (b)   the description filed under section 15(10)(b)(i) above discloses additional matter, that is, matter extending beyond that disclosed in the earlier relevant application, the application shall not be allowed to proceed unless it is amended so as to exclude the additional matter.

(2)   No amendment of an application for a patent shall be allowed under [section 17(3)] section 15A(6), 18(3) or 19(1) if it results in the application disclosing matter extending beyond that disclosed in the application as filed.

(3)   No amendment of the specification of a patent shall be allowed under section 27(1), 73 or 75 if it—

    (a)   results in the specification disclosing additional matter, or

    (b)   extends the protection conferred by the patent.

(4)   In subsection (1A) above "relevant application" has the meaning given by section 5(5) above.

Notes

Section 76 substituted by CDPA 1988 (c.48) s.295 and Sch.5 para.20, with effect from 7 January 1991 SI 1990/2168.

Subsections (1) and (2) amended and subss.(1A) and (4) inserted by Regulatory Reform (Patents) Order 2004 (SI 2004/2357) art.13, with effect from 1 January 2005, subject to transitional provisions contained in arts 20–23 of that Order.

PATENTS ACT 1977

Biotechnological inventions

76A.—(1) Any provision of, or made under, this Act is to have effect in
relation to a patent or an application for a patent which concerns a biotechnological invention, subject to the provisions of Schedule A2.

AppA-76A

(2) Nothing in this section or Schedule A2 is to be read as affecting the application of any provision in relation to any other kind of patent or application for a patent.

Note

Section 76A inserted by Patents Regulations 2000 (SI 2000/2037), reg.5, with effect from 28 July
2000, subject to transitional provisions contained in reg.9 which provide that the amendments apply to
applications for patents made on or after that date (and to patents granted in pursuance of such
applications).

PART II – PROVISIONS ABOUT INTERNATIONAL CONVENTIONS

European patents and patent applications

Effect of European patent (UK)

77.—(1) Subject to the provisions of this Act, a European patent (UK) shall,
as from the publication of the mention of its grant in the European Patent Bulletin,
be treated for the purposes of Parts I and III of this Act as if it were a patent under
this Act granted in pursuance of an application made under this Act and as if notice
of the grant of the patent had, on the date of that publication, been published under
section 24 above in the journal; and—

AppA-77

    (a)   the proprietor of a European patent (UK) shall accordingly as respects
        the United Kingdom have the same rights and remedies, subject to the
        same conditions, as the proprietor of a patent under this Act;

    (b)   references in Parts I and III of this Act to a patent shall be construed
        accordingly; and

    (c)   any statement made and any certificate filed for the purposes of the
        provision of the convention corresponding to section 2(4)(c) above
        shall be respectively treated as a statement made and written evidence
        filed for the purposes of the said paragraph (c).

(2) Subsection (1) above shall not affect the operation in relation to a European
patent (UK) of any provisions of the European Patent Convention relating to the
amendment or revocation of such a patent in proceedings before the European Patent Office.

*[(3) Sections 58(7) to (9) and 63 above shall apply to the case where, after
proceedings for the infringement of a European patent have been commenced
before the court or the comptroller but have not been finally disposed of, it is
established in proceedings before the European Patent Office that the patent is only
partially valid as those provisions apply to proceedings in which the validity of a
patent is put in issue and in which it is found that the patent is only partially valid.]*

(3) Where in the case of a European patent (UK)—

    (a)   proceedings for infringement, or proceedings under section 58
        above, have been commenced before the court or the comptroller
        and have not been finally disposed of, and

    (b)   it is established in proceedings before the European Patent Office
        that the patent is only partially valid, the provisions of section 63

[983]

or, as the case may be, of subsections (7) to (9) of section 58 apply as they apply to proceedings in which the validity of a patent is put in issue and in which it is found that the patent is only partially valid.

[*(4)   Subject to subsection (6) below, where a European patent (UK) is amended or revoked in accordance with the European Patent Convention, the amendment shall be treated for the purposes of Parts I and III of this Act as if it had been made, or as the case may be the patent shall be treated for those purposes as having been revoked, under this Act.*]

(4)   Where a European patent (UK) is amended in accordance with the European Patent Convention, the amendment shall have effect for the purposes of Parts I and III of this Act as if the specification of the patent had been amended under this Act; but subject to subsection (6)(b) below.

(4A)   Where a European patent (UK) is revoked in accordance with the European Patent Convention, the patent shall be treated for the purposes of Parts I and III of this Act as having been revoked under this Act.

(5)   Where—

    (a)   under the European Patent Convention a European patent (UK) is revoked for failure to observe a time limit and is subsequently restored **or is revoked by the Board of Appeal and is subsequently restored by the Enlarged Board of Appeal**; and

    (b)   between revocation and publication of the fact that it has been restored a person begins in good faith to do an act which would, apart from section 55 above, constitute an infringement of the patent or makes in good faith effective and serious preparations to do such an act;

he shall have the rights conferred by [*section 28(6) above, and subsections (8) and (9) of that section shall apply accordingly*] **section 28A(4) and (5) above, and subsections (6) and (7) of that section shall apply accordingly.**

(5A)   Where, under the European Patent Convention, a European patent (UK) is revoked and subsequently restored (including where it is revoked by the Board of Appeal and subsequently restored by the Enlarged Board of Appeal), any fee that would have been imposed in relation to the patent after the revocation but before the restoration is payable within the prescribed period following the restoration.

[*(6)   While this subsection is in force—*

    (a)   subsection (1) above shall not apply to a European patent (UK) the specification of which was published in French or German, unless a translation of the specification into English is filed at the Patent Office and the prescribed fee is paid before the end of the prescribed period;

    (b)   subsection (4) above shall not apply to an amendment made in French or German unless [*a translation of the amendment into English*] ***a translation into English of the specification as amended*** *is filed at the Patent Office and the prescribed fee is paid before the end of the prescribed period.*]

(7)   Where [*a translation of a specification or amendment into English is not filed in accordance with subsection (6)(a) or (b) above*] **such a translation is not filed**, the patent shall be treated as always having been void.

(8)   The comptroller shall publish any translation filed at the Patent Office under subsection (6) above.

(9)   Subsection (6) above shall come into force on a day appointed for the purpose by rules and shall cease to have effect on a day so appointed, without prejudice, however, to the power to bring it into force again.

Note

Subsection (3) substituted, subss.(4) and (4A) substituted for original subs.(4) and subss.(6) and (7) amended by CDPA 1988 (c.48) s.295 and Sch.5 para.21, with effect from 7 January 1991, SI 1990/2168.

Subsection (5) amended by CDPA 1988 (c.48) s.295 and Sch.5 para.8(b), with effect from 7 January 1991, SI 1990/2168.

Subsection (5)(a) amended by Patents Act 2004 (c.16) s.5 and Sch.1 para.2, with effect from 13 December 2007, SI 2007/3396.

Subsection (5A) inserted by Intellectual Property Act 2014 (c.18) Sch.1 para.6 with effect from 1 October 2014 subject to transitional provisions specified in SI 2014/2330 art.8.

Subsection (6) ceased to have effect by Patents Rules 2007 (SI 2007/3291) r.56(9), with effect from 1 May 2008, being the date on which the London Agreement (referred to in r.56(10) of those Rules) came into force.

Effect of filing an application for a European patent (UK)

78.—(1)   Subject to the provisions of this Act, an application for a European   AppA-78
patent (UK) having a date of filing under the European Patent Convention shall be treated for the purposes of the provisions of this Act to which this section applies as an application for a patent under this Act having that date as its date of filing and having the other incidents listed in subsection (3) below, but subject to the modifications mentioned in the following provisions of this section.

(2)   This section applies to the following provisions of this Act—
   section 2(3) and so much of section 14(7) as relates to section 2(3);
   section 5; section 6; so much of section 13(3) as relates to an application for and issue of a certificate under that subsection;
   sections 30 to 33;
   section 36;
   sections 55 to 69; section 74, so far as relevant to any of the provisions mentioned above;
   section 111; and section 125.

(3)   The incidents referred to in subsection (1) above in relation to an application for a European patent (UK) are as follows—
   (a)   any declaration of priority made in connection with the application under the European Patent Convention shall be treated for the purposes of this Act as a declaration made under section 5(2) above;
   (b)   where a period of time relevant to priority is extended under that convention, the period of twelve months [*specified in section 5(2)*] **allowed under section 5(2A)(a)** above shall be so treated as altered correspondingly;
   (c)   where the date of filing an application is re-dated under that convention to a later date, that date shall be so treated as the date of filing the application;
   (d)   the application, if published in accordance with that convention, shall, subject to subsection (7) and section 79 below, be so treated as published under section 16 above;
   (e)   any designation of the inventor under that convention or any statement under it indicating the origin of the right to a European patent

[985]

shall be treated for the purposes of section 13(3) above as a statement filed under section 13(2) above;

    (f)   registration of the application in the register of European patents shall be treated as registration under this Act.

(4)   Rules under section 32 above may not impose any requirements as to the registration of applications for European patents (UK) but may provide for the registration of copies of entries relating to such applications in the European register of patents.

[(5)   Subsections (1) to (3) above shall cease to apply to an application for a European patent (UK) when the application is refused or withdrawn or deemed to be withdrawn, or the designation of the United Kingdom in the application is withdrawn or deemed to be withdrawn, but if the rights of the applicant are re-established under the European Patent Convention, subsections (1) to (3) above shall as from the re-establishment of those rights again apply to the application.]

(5)   Subsections (1) to (3) above shall cease to apply to an application for a European patent (UK), except as mentioned in subsection (5A) below, if—

    (a)   the application is refused or withdrawn or deemed to be withdrawn, or

    (b)   the designation of the United Kingdom in the application is withdrawn or deemed to be withdrawn, but shall apply again if the rights of the applicant are re-established under the European Patent Convention, as from their re-establishment.

(5A)   The occurrence of any of the events mentioned in subsection (5)(a) or (b) shall not affect the continued operation of section 2(3) above in relation to matter contained in application for a European patent (UK) which by virtue of that provision has become part of the state of the art as regards other inventions [; and the occurrence of any event mentioned in subsection (5)(b) shall not prevent matter contained in an application for a European patent (UK) becoming part of the state of the art by virtue of section 2(3) above as regards other inventions where the event occurs before the publication of that application.]

[(6)   Where between those subsections ceasing to apply to any such application and the re-establishment of the rights of the applicant a person begins in good faith to do an act which would, apart from section 55 above, constitute an infringement of the application if those subsections then applied, or makes in good faith effective and serious preparations to do such an act, he shall have the rights conferred by [section 28(6) above, and section 28(8) and (9) above shall apply to the exercise of any such right accordingly] **section 28A(4) and (5) above, and** *subsections (6) and (7) of that section shall apply accordingly.]*

(6)   Where, between subsections (1) to (3) above ceasing to apply to an application for a European patent (UK) and the re-establishment of the rights of the applicant, a person—

    (a)   begins in good faith to do an act which would constitute an infringement of the rights conferred by publication of the application if those subsections then applied, or

    (b)   makes in good faith effective and serious preparations to do such an act, he shall have the right to continue to do the act or, as the case may be, to do the act, notwithstanding subsections (1) to (3) applying again and notwithstanding the grant of the patent.

(6A) Subsections **(5)** and **(6)** of section **20B** above have effect for the purposes of subsection **(6)** above as they have effect for the purposes of that section and as if the references to subsection **(4)** of that section were references to subsection **(6)** above.

(6B) Subject to subsection **(6A)** above, the right conferred by subsection **(6)** above does not extend to granting a licence to another person to do the act in question.

(6C) Subsections **(6)** to **(6B)** above apply in relation to the use of a patented invention for the services of the Crown as they apply in relation to an infringement of the rights conferred by publication of the application (or, as the case may be, infringement of the patent).

"Patented invention" has the same meaning as in section 55 above.

(7)   While this subsection is in force, an application for a European patent (UK) published by the European Patent Office under the European Patent Convention in French or German shall be treated for the purposes of sections 55 and 69 above as published under section 16 above when a translation into English of the claims of the specification of the application has been filed at and published by the Patent Office and the prescribed fee has been paid, but an applicant—

    (a)   may recover a payment by virtue of section 55(5) above in respect of the use of the invention in question before publication of that translation; or

    (b)   may bring proceedings by virtue of section 69 above in respect of an act mentioned in that section which is done before publication of that translation;

if before that use or the doing of that act he has sent by post or delivered to the government department who made use or authorised the use of the invention, or, as the case may be, to the person alleged to have done the act, a translation into English of those claims.

(8)   Subsection (7) above shall come into force on a day appointed for the purpose by rules and shall cease to have effect on a day so appointed, without prejudice, however, to the power to bring it into force again.

Notes

    Subsection (3) amended by Regulatory Reform (Patents) Order 2004 (SI 2004/2357) art.14, with effect from 1 January 2005, subject to transitional provisions contained in arts 20–23 of that Order.

    Subsections (5) and (5A) substituted for original subs.(5) and subs.(6) amended by CDPA 1988 (c.48) s.294 and Sch.5 paras 8, 22, with effect from 7 January 1991, SI 1990/2168.

    Subsection (5A) amended by insertion of the words in bold and in square brackets by Patents Act 2004 (c.16) s.5 and Sch.1 para.3(2), with effect from 13 December 2007, SI 2007/3396, subject to transitional provisions contained in art.3 of that Order.

    Subsections.(6), (6A), (6B) and (6C) substituted for original subs.(6) by Patents Act 2004 (c.16) s.5 and Sch.1 para.3(3), with effect from 13 December 2007, SI 2007/3396.

Operation of s. 78 in relation to certain European patent applications

79.—(1)   Subject to the following provisions of this section, section 78 above, in its operation in relation to an international application for a patent (UK) which is treated by virtue of the European Patent Convention as an application for a European patent (UK), shall have effect as if any reference in that section to anything done in relation to the application under the European Patent Conven-   AppA-79

PATENTS ACT 1977

tion included a reference to the corresponding thing done under the Patent Co-operation Treaty.

(2) Any such international application which is published under that treaty shall be treated for the purposes of section 2(3) above as published only when a copy of the application has been supplied to the European Patent Office in English, French or German and the relevant fee has been paid under that convention.

(3) Any such international application which is published under that treaty in a language other than English, French or German shall, subject to section 78(7) above, be treated for the purposes of sections 55 and 69 above as published only when it is re-published in English, French or German by the European Patent Office under that convention.

Authentic text of European patents and patent applications

AppA-80   **80.**—(1)   Subject to subsection (2) below, the text of a European patent or application for such a patent in the language of the proceedings, that is to say, the language in which proceedings relating to the patent or the application are to be conducted before the European Patent Office, shall be the authentic text for the purposes of any domestic proceedings, that is to say, any proceedings relating to the patent or application before the comptroller or the court.

(2) Where the language of the proceedings is French or German, a translation into English of the specification of the patent under section 77 above or of the claims of the application under section 78 above shall be treated as the authentic text for the purpose of any domestic proceedings, other than proceedings for the revocation of the patent, if the patent or application as translated into English confers protection which is narrower than that conferred by it in French or German.

(3) If any such translation results in a European patent or application conferring the narrower protection, the proprietor of or applicant for the patent may file a corrected translation with the Patent Office and, if he pays the prescribed fee within the prescribed period, the Patent Office shall publish it, but—

   (a) any payment for any use of the invention which (apart from section 55 above) would have infringed the patent as correctly translated, but not as originally translated, or in the case of an application would have infringed it as aforesaid if the patent had been granted, shall not be recoverable under that section,

   (b) the proprietor or applicant shall not be entitled to bring proceedings in respect of an act which infringed the patent as correctly translated, but not as originally translated, or in the case of an application would have infringed it as aforesaid if the patent had been granted, unless before that use or the doing of the act the corrected translation has been published by the Patent Office or the proprietor or applicant has sent the corrected translation by post or delivered it to the government department who made use or authorised use of the invention or, as the case may be, to the person alleged to have done that act.

   [(4)   Where a correction of a translation is published under subsection (3) above and before it is so published a person begins in good faith to do an act which would not constitute an infringement of the patent or application as originally translated but would (apart from section 55 above) constitute an infringement of it under the amended translation, or makes in good faith effective and serious preparations to do such an act, he shall have the rights conferred by [section 28(6)

[988]

above, and section 28(8) and (9) above shall apply to the exercise of any such right accordingly] **section 28A(4) and (5) above, and subsections (6) and (7) of that section shall apply accordingly.]**

(4)   Where a correction of a translation is published under subsection (3) above and before it is so published a person—

(a)   begins in good faith to do an act which would not constitute an infringement of the patent as originally translated, or of the rights conferred by publication of the application as originally translated, but would do so under the amended translation, or

(b)   makes in good faith effective and serious preparations to do such an act, he shall have the right to continue to do the act or, as the case may be, to do the act, notwithstanding the publication of the corrected translation and notwithstanding the grant of the patent.

(5)   Subsections (5) and (6) of section 28A above have effect for the purposes of subsection (4) above as they have effect for the purposes of that section and as if—

(a)   the references to subsection (4) of that section were references to subsection (4) above;

(b)   the reference to the registered proprietor of the patent included a reference to the applicant.

(6)   Subject to subsection (5) above, the right conferred by subsection (4) above does not extend to granting a licence to another person to do the act in question.

(7)   Subsections (4) to (6) above apply in relation to the use of a patented invention for the services of the Crown as they apply in relation to an infringement of the patent or of the rights conferred by the publication of the application.

"Patented invention" has the same meaning as in section 55 above.

Notes

Subsection (4) amended by CDPA 1988 (c.48) s.295 and Sch.5 para.8, with effect from 7 January 1991, SI 1990/2168.

Subsections (4)–(7) substituted for original subs.(4) by Patents Act 2004 (c.16) s.5 and Sch.1 para.4, with effect from 13 December 2007, SI 2007/3396.

Conversion of European patent applications

81.—(1)   The comptroller may direct that on compliance with the relevant AppA-81
conditions mentioned in subsection (2) below an application for a European patent (UK) shall be treated as an application for a patent under this Act [*in the following cases:—*

(a)   *where the application is deemed to be withdrawn under the provisions of the European Patent Convention relating to the restriction of the processing of applications;*

(b)   *where under the convention the application is deemed to be withdrawn because it has not, within the period required by the convention, been received by the European Patent Office.*]

where the application is deemed to be withdrawn under the provisions of the European Patent Convention relating to the time for forwarding applications

to the European Patent Office.

(2) The relevant conditions referred to above are [*that*—

    (a) *in the case of an application falling within subsection (1)(a) above, the European Patent Office transmits a request of the applicant to the Patent Office that his application should be converted into an application under this Act, together with a copy of the files relating to the application.*]

    (b) *in the case of an application falling within subsection (1)(b) above*] **that**—

        (i) the applicant requests the comptroller within the relevant prescribed period (where the application was filed with the Patent Office) to give a direction under this section, or

        (ii) the central industrial property office of a country which is party to the convention, other than the United Kingdom, with which the application was filed transmits within the relevant prescribed period a request that the application should be converted into an application under this Act, together with a copy of the application; and

    (c) [*in either case*] **that** the applicant within the relevant prescribed period pays the [*filing fee*] **application fee** and if the application is in a language other than English, files a translation into English of the application and of any amendments previously made in accordance with the convention.

(3) Where an application for a European patent falls to be treated as an application for a patent under this Act by virtue of a direction under this section—

    (a) the date which is the date of filing the application under the European Patent Convention shall be treated as its date of filing for the purposes of this Act, but if that date is re-dated under the convention to a later date, that later date shall be treated for those purposes as the date of filing the application;

    (b) if the application satisfies a requirement of the convention corresponding to any of the requirements of this Act or rules designated as formal requirements, it shall be treated as satisfying that formal requirement;

    (c) any document filed with the European Patent Office under any provision of the convention corresponding to any of the following provisions of this Act, that is to say, sections 2(4)(c), 5, 13(2) and 14, or any rule made for the purposes of any of those provisions, shall be treated as filed with the Patent Office under that provision or rule; and

    (d) the comptroller shall refer the application for only so much of the examination and search required by sections **15A**, 17 and 18 above as he considers appropriate in view of any examination and search carried out under the convention, and those sections shall apply with any necessary modifications accordingly.

Notes

Subsection (1) amended by Patents Act 2004 (c.16) s.5 and Sch.1 para.5,with effect from 13 December 2007, SI 2007/3396.

Subsection (2) amended by Regulatory Reform (Patents) Order 2004 (SI 2004/2357) art.15, with effect from 1 January 2005, subject to transitional provisions contained in arts 20–23 of that Order;

amended by Patents Act 2004 (c.16) s.5 and Sch.1 para.5(3), with effect from 13 December 2007, SI 2007/3396.

Subsection (3) amended by Regulatory Reform (Patents) Order 2004 (SI 2004/2357) art.15, with effect from 1 January 2005, subject to transitional provisions contained in arts 20–23 of that Order.

Jurisdiction to determine questions as to right to a patent

82.—(1) The court shall not have jurisdiction to determine a question to which this section applies except in accordance with the following provisions of this section. **AppA-82**

(2) Section 12 above shall not confer jurisdiction on the comptroller to determine a question to which this section applies except in accordance with the following provisions of this section.

(3) This section applies to a question arising before the grant of a European patent whether a person has a right to be granted a European patent, or a share in any such patent, and in this section "employer-employee question" means any such question between an employer and an employee, or their successors in title, arising out of an application for a European patent for an invention made by the employee.

(4) The court and the comptroller shall have jurisdiction to determine any question to which this section applies, other than an employer-employee question, if either of the following conditions is satisfied, that is to say—

    (a) the applicant has his residence or principal place of business in the United Kingdom; or

    (b) the other party claims that the patent should be granted to him and he has his residence or principal place of business in the United Kingdom and the applicant does not have his residence or principal place of business in any of the relevant contracting states;

and also if in either of those cases there is no written evidence that the parties have agreed to submit to the jurisdiction of the competent authority of a relevant contracting state other than the United Kingdom.

(5) The court and the comptroller shall have jurisdiction to determine an employer-employee question if either of the following conditions is satisfied, that is to say—

    (a) the employee is mainly employed in the United Kingdom; or

    (b) the employee is not mainly employed anywhere or his place of main employment cannot be determined, but the employer has a place of business in the United Kingdom to which the employee is attached (whether or not he is also attached elsewhere);

and also if in either of those cases there is no written evidence that the parties have agreed to submit to the jurisdiction of the competent authority of a relevant contracting state other than the United Kingdom or, where there is such evidence of such an agreement, if the [*proper law of*] **law applicable to** the contract of employment does not recognise the validity of the agreement.

(6) Without prejudice to subsections (2) to (5) above, the court and the comptroller shall have jurisdiction to determine any question to which this section applies if there is written evidence that the parties have agreed to submit to the jurisdiction of the court or the comptroller, as the case may be, and, in the case of an employer-employee question, the [*proper law of*] **law applicable to** the contract of employment recognises the validity of the agreement.

(7)   If, after proceedings to determine a question to which this section applies have been brought before the competent authority of a relevant contracting state other than the United Kingdom, proceedings are begun before the court or a reference is made to the comptroller under section 12 above to determine that question, the court or the comptroller, as the case may be, shall stay or sist the proceedings before the court or the comptroller unless or until the competent authority of that other state either—

(a)   determines to decline jurisdiction and no appeal lies from the determination or the time for appealing expires, or

(b)   makes a determination which the court or the comptroller refuses to recognise under section 83 below.

(8)   References in this section to the determination of a question include respectively references to—

(a)   the making of a declaration or the grant of a declarator with respect to that question (in the case of the court); and

(b)   the making of an order under section 12 above in relation to that question (in the case of the court or the comptroller).

(9)   In this section and section 83 below "relevant contracting state" means a country which is a party to the European Patent Convention and has not exercised its right under the convention to exclude the application of the protocol to the convention known as the Protocol on Recognition.

Note

Subsections (5) and (6) amended by Contracts (Applicable Law) Act 1990 (c.36) s.5 and Sch.4 para.3.

Effect of patent decisions of competent authorities of other states

AppA-83   **83.**—(1)   A determination of a question to which section 82 above applies by the competent authority of a relevant contracting state other than the United Kingdom shall, if no applies lies from the determination or the time for appealing has expired, be recognised in the United Kingdom as if it had been made by the court or the comptroller unless the court or he refuses to recognise it under subsection (2) below.

(2)   The court or the comptroller may refuse to recognise any such determination that the applicant for a European patent had no right to be granted the patent, or any share in it, if either—

(a)   the applicant did not contest the proceedings in question because he was not notified of them at all or in the proper manner or was not notified of them in time for him to contest the proceedings; or

(b)   the determination in the proceedings in question conflicts with the determination of the competent authority of any relevant contracting state in proceedings instituted earlier between the same parties as in the proceedings in question.

[Patent agents and other representatives

AppA-84   *84.—(1)   No individual shall carry on for gain in the United Kingdom, alone or in partnership with any other person, the business of acting as agent or other representative of other persons for the purpose of conducting proceedings in connection with such patents before the European Patent Office or the comptroller, or* hold himself out or permit himself to be held out as so carrying on such a business, unless he satisfies the condition that his name and that of each of his partners appears on the European list.

(2)   Subsection (1) above shall not prohibit a barrister, advocate or solicitor of any part of the United Kingdom from conducting or otherwise taking part in any proceedings in connection with European patents before the European Patent Office or the comptroller to the same extent as he is entitled to take part in the corresponding proceedings in connection with patents under this Act before the Patent Office or the comptroller.

(3)   A body corporate shall not for gain act or describe itself or hold itself out as entitled to act as agent or other representative of other persons for any purpose mentioned in subsection (1) above unless permitted to do so under the European Patent Convention.

(3A)   In so far as it imposes any prohibition in relation to the business of acting as agent of other persons for the purpose of conducting proceedings before the comptroller in connection with European patents (UK) to which section 77(1) above for the time being applies—

   (a)   subsection (1) above does not apply to any individual who carries on such a business alone if he is registered as a patent agent in the register of patent agents, or to an individual who carries on such a business in partnership if he and each of his partners is so registered; and

   (b)   subsection (3) above does not apply to any body corporate which satisfies the condition specified in paragraph (a) or (b) of section 114(2) below (as the case may require).

(4)   Any person who contravenes subsection (1) or (3) above shall be liable on summary conviction to a fine not exceeding £1,000.

(5)   Proceedings for an offence under this section may be begun at any time within twelve months from the date of the offence.

(6)   A person who does any act mentioned in subsection (1) above, but satisfies the condition mentioned in that subsection, shall not be treated as contravening section 114 below so long as he does not describe himself as a patent agent without qualification and does not hold himself out or permit himself to be held out as carrying on any business other than one mentioned in that subsection.

(7)   In this section "the European list" means the list of professional representatives maintained by the European Patent Office in pursuance of the European Patent Convention.]

Note

Section 84 repealed by CDPA 1988 (c.48) s.303(2) and Sch.8, with effect from 13 August 1990, SI 1990/1400.

[European patent attorneys

85.—*(1)   For the avoidance of doubt, it is hereby declared that any person whose name appears on the European list shall not be guilty of an offence under section 21 of the Solicitors Act 1974 or Article 22 of the Solicitors (Northern Ireland) Order 1976 by reason only of his describing himself as a European patent attorney.* AppA-85

(2)   *A person whose name appears on the European list shall not be guilty of an offence under any of the enactments mentioned in subsection (3) below by reason only for the preparation by him of any document (other than a deed) for use in proceedings before the comptroller under this Act, in relation to a European patent or application for such a patent.*

(3)   *The enactments referred to in subsection (2) above (which prohibit the preparation for reward of certain instruments or writs by persons not legally qualified) are—*

(a)   *section 22 of the Solicitors Act 1974;*

(b)   *section 39 of the Solicitors (Scotland) Act 1933; and*

(c)   *Article 23 of the Solicitors (Northern Ireland) Order 1976.*

(4)   *In this section "the European list" means the list of professional representatives maintained by the European Patent Office in pursuance of the European Patent Convention.*]

Note

Section 85 repealed by CDPA 1988 (c.48) s.303(2) and Sch.8, with effect from 13 August 1990, SI 1990/1400.

Community patents

[Implementation of Community Patent Convention

AppA-86   **86.**—*(1)   All rights, powers, liabilities, obligations and restrictions from time to time created or arising by or under the Community Patent Convention and all remedies and procedures from time to time provided for by or under that convention shall by virtue of this section have legal effect in the United Kingdom and shall be used there, be recognised and available in law and be enforced, allowed and followed accordingly.*

(2)   *The Secretary of State may by regulations make provision—*

(a)   *for implementing any obligations imposed by that convention on a domestic institution or enabling any such obligation to be implemented or enabling any rights or powers conferred on any such institution to be exercised; and*

(b)   *otherwise for giving effect to subsection (1) above and dealing with matters arising out of its commencement or operation.*

(3)   *Regulations under this section may include any incidental, consequential, transitional or supplementary provision appearing to the Secretary of State to be necessary or expedient, including provision amending any enactment, whenever passed, other than an enactment contained in this Part of this Act, and provision for the application of any provision of the regulations outside the United Kingdom.*

(4)   *Sections 12, 73(2), 77 to 80, 82 and 83 above shall not apply to any application for a European Patent which under the Community Patent Convention is treated as an application for a Community patent, or to a Community patent (since any such application or patent falls within the foregoing provisions of this section).*

(5)   *In this section "domestic institution" means the court, the comptroller or the Patent Office, as the case may require.*]

Note

Section 86 repealed by Patents Act 2004 (c.16) s.5 and Sch.1 para.6, Sch.3, with effect from 1 January 2005, SI 2004/3205.

[Decisions on Community Patent Convention

87.—*(1)   For the purposes of all legal proceedings, including proceedings*   AppA-87
*before the comptroller, any question as to the meaning or effect of the Community
Patent Convention, or as to the validity, meaning and effect of any instrument made
under or in implementation of that convention by any relevant convention institution shall be treated as a question of law (and if not referred to the relevant convention court, be for determination as such in accordance with the principles laid down
by and any relevant decision of that court).*

(2)   In this section—

"relevant convention institution" means any institution established by or having functions under the Community Patent Convention, not being an institution of the United Kingdom or any other member state , and
"relevant convention court" does not include—
   (a)   the European Patent Office or any of its departments; or
   (b)   a court of the United Kingdom or of any other member state.]

Note

Section 87 repealed by Patents Act 2004 (c.16) s.5 and Sch.1 para.6, Sch.3, with effect from 1 January 2005, SI 2004/3205.

[Jurisdiction in legal proceedings in connection with Community Patent Convention

88.—*(1)   For the purposes of the application in the United Kingdom of Article*   AppA-88
*69 of the Community Patent Convention (residence of a party as founding jurisdiction in actions for infringement, etc.) the residence of a party shall be determined
in accordance with the following provisions of this section until such date as the
Secretary of State may by order appoint for the repeal of those provisions.*

*(2)   For the purpose of determining whether a person is resident in any part of
the United Kingdom the court shall apply the law of that part of the United
Kingdom.*

*(3)   A company within the meaning of the Companies Act 1948 shall be treated
for the purposes of subsection (2) above as resident in that part of the United
Kingdom where its registered office is situated or where it has a principal place
of business.*

*(4)   Any other body corporate or any unincorporated body of persons shall be
so treated as resident in that part of the United Kingdom where it has a principal
place of business.*

*(5)   Where any body has a principal place of business in two or more parts of
the United Kingdom it shall be so treated as resident in all those parts.*

*(6)   If the court determines that a person is not resident in the United Kingdom,
then, in order to determine whether he is resident in a country which is a party to
the Community Patent Convention the court shall, except in a case falling within
subsection (7) below, apply the law which would be applied by the courts of that
country in order to found jurisdiction under that convention.*

*(7)   The question whether a person is to be taken for the purposes of this sec-
tion as resident in the United Kingdom or any other country shall be determined
in accordance with the law of that country of which he is a citizen if by that law
his residence depends on that of another person or on the location of an authority.]*

Note

Section 88 repealed by CDPA 1988 (c.48) s.295 and Sch.5 para.23, with effect from 7 January 1991,
SI 1990/2168.

Unified Patent Court

Implementation of Agreement on a Unified Patent Court

AppA-
88A

**88A.—(1)   The Secretary of State may by order make provision for giving
effect in the United Kingdom to the provisions of the Agreement on a Unified
Patent Court made in Brussels on 19 February 2013.**

(2)   An order under this section may, in particular, make provision—

> **(a)   to confer jurisdiction on a court, remove jurisdiction from a court
> or vary the jurisdiction of a court;**

> **(b)   to require the payment of fees.**

**(3)   An order under this section may also make provision for varying the
application of specified provisions of this Act so that they correspond to provision made by the Agreement.**

(4)   An order under this section may—

> **(a)   make provision which applies generally or in relation only to speci-
> fied cases;**

> **(b)   make different provision for different cases.**

**(5)   An order under this section may amend this Act or any other
enactment.**

**(6)   An order under this section may not be made unless a draft of the order
has been laid before, and approved by resolution of, each House of Parliament.**

**(7)   The meaning of court in this section is not limited by the definition of
that expression in section 130(1).**

Note

Section 88A added by Intellectual Property Act 2014 (c.18) Pat 2 s.17 with effect from 1 October
2014.

Designation as international organisation of which UK is member

AppA-
88B

**88B   The Unified Patent Court is to be treated for the purposes of section
1 of the International Organisations Act 1968 (organisations of which the
United Kingdom is a member) as an organisation to which that section applies.**

[996]

Note

Section 88B added by Intellectual Property Act 2014 (c.18) Pat 2 s.17 with effect from 1 October 2014.

International applications for patents

[Effect of filing international application for a patent

89.—*(1)   Subject to the provisions of this Act, an international application for a patent (UK) for which a date of filing has been accorded (whether by the Patent Office or by any other body) under the Patent Co-operation Treaty (in this section referred to as the Treaty) shall, until this subsection ceases to apply to the application, be treated for the purposes of Parts I and III of this Act as an application for a patent under this Act having that date as its date of filing and—* AppA-89

    (a)   the application, if published in accordance with the Treaty and if it satisfies relevant conditions, shall be so treated as published under section 16 above, subject, however, to subsection (7) below;

    (b)   where the date of filing an application is re-dated under the Treaty to a later date, that date shall be so treated as the date of filing the application;

    (c)   any declaration of priority made under the Treaty shall be so treated as a declaration made under section 5(2) above;

    (d)   where a period of time relevant to priority is extended under the Treaty, the period of twelve months specified in section 5(2) above shall be treated as altered correspondingly;

    (e)   any statement of the name of the inventor under the Treaty shall be so treated as a statement filed under section 13(2) above; and

    (f)   an amendment of the application made in accordance with the Treaty shall, if it satisfies the relevant conditions, be so treated as made under this Act.

(2)   Accordingly, until subsection (1) above ceases to apply to an application filed or published in accordance with the Treaty, the applicant shall, subject to subsection (7) below, have the same rights and remedies in relation to the application as an applicant for a patent under this Act has in relation to a filed or, as the case may be, a published application for such a patent.

(3)   Notwithstanding anything in subsection (1) above, the provisions of the Treaty and not those of this Act relating to publication, search, examination and amendment shall apply to any such application until all the relevant conditions are satisfied and, if those conditions are not satisfied before the end of the prescribed period, the application shall be taken to be withdrawn.

(3A)   If the relevant conditions are satisfied with respect to an application which is amended in accordance with the Treaty and the relevant conditions are not satisfied with respect to any amendment, that amendment shall be disregarded.

(4)   The relevant conditions—

    (a)   in the case of an application, are that a copy of the application and, if it is not in English, a translation into English have been filed at the Patent Office and the filing fee has been paid to the Patent Office by the applicant; and

    (b)   in the case of an amendment, are that a copy of the amendment and, if it is not in English, a translation into English have been filed at the Patent Office.

(4A) In subsection (4)(a) "a copy of the application" includes a copy of the application published in accordance with the Treaty in a language other than that in which it was filed.

(5) The comptroller shall on payment of the prescribed fee publish any translation filed at the Patent Office under subsection (4) above.

(6) Before the relevant conditions are satisfied, subsection (1) above shall not operate so as to secure that an international application for a patent (UK) is to be treated for the purposes of section 8 above as an application for a patent under this Act and shall not affect the application of section 12 above to an invention for which an international application of a patent is made or proposed to be made, but when the relevant conditions are satisfied the international application shall be so treated and accordingly section 12 above shall not apply to it

(7) For the purposes of sections 55 and 69 above an international application for a patent (UK) published in accordance with the Treaty—

    (a) shall, if published in English, be treated as published under section 16 above on its publication in accordance with the Treaty;

    (b) shall, if published in any other language and if the relevant conditions are satisfied, be treated as published under section 16 above on the publication of a translation of the application under subsection (5) above;

but, if the application is published in a language other than English, the applicant may recover a payment by virtue of section 55 above in respect of the use of the invention in question before publication of that translation, or may bring proceedings by virtue of section 69 above in respect of an act mentioned in that section which is done before publication of that translation, if before that use or the doing of that act he has sent by post or delivered to the government department who made use or authorised the use of the invention, or, as the case may be, to the person alleged to have done the act, a translation into English of the specification of the application.

(8) Subsection (1) above shall cease to apply to an international application for a patent (UK) if—

    (a) the application is withdrawn or deemed to be withdrawn; or

    (b) the designation of the United Kingdom in the application is withdrawn or deemed to be withdrawn;

except where the application or the designation of the United Kingdom in the application is deemed to be withdrawn under the Treaty because of an error or omission in the Patent Office or any other institution having functions under the Treaty or of an application not being received by the International Bureau, owing to circumstances outside the applicant's control, before the end of the time limited for that purpose by the Treaty.

(9) Where the relevant conditions are satisfied before the end of the prescribed period, the comptroller shall refer the application for so much of the examination and search as is required by sections 17 and 18 above as he considers appropriate in view of any examination and search carried out under the Treaty, and those sections shall apply with any necessary modifications accordingly.

[(10) The foregoing provisions of this section shall not apply to an international application for a patent (UK) which is treated by virtue of the European Patent Convention as an application for a European patent (UK) or which contains an indication that the applicant wishes to obtain a European patent (UK).]

(10) The foregoing provisions of this section do not apply to anapplication

which falls to be treated as an international application for a patent (UK) by reason only of its containing an indication that the applicant wishes to obtain a European patent (UK); but without prejudice to the application of those provisions to an application which also separately designates the United Kingdom.

(11)   If an international application for a patent which purports to designate the United Kingdom is refused a filing date under the Treaty and the comptroller determines that the refusal was caused by an error or omission in the Patent Office or any other institution having functions under the Treaty; he may direct that that application shall be treated as an application under this Act.]

Note

Subsections (3A) and (4A) inserted and subs.(10) substituted by CDPA 1988 (c.48) s.295 and Sch.5 para.24 and deemed always to have had effect, SI 1990/2168.

Effect of international application for patent

89.—**(1)   An international application for a patent (UK) for which a date of filing has been accorded under the Patent Co-operation Treaty shall, subject to—** AppA-89AA

section 89A (international and national phases of application), and section 89B (adaptation of provisions in relation to international application), be treated for the purposes of Parts I and III of this Act as an application for a patent under this Act.

(2)   If the application, or the designation of the United Kingdom in it, is withdrawn or (except as mentioned in subsection (3)) deemed to be withdrawn under the Treaty, it shall be treated as withdrawn under this Act.

(3)   An application shall not be treated as withdrawn under this Act if it, or the designation of the United Kingdom in it, is deemed to be withdrawn under the Treaty—

   (a)   because of an error or omission in an institution having functions under the Treaty, or

   (b)   because, owing to circumstances outside the applicant's control, a copy of the application was not received by the International Bureau before the end of the time limited for that purpose under the Treaty, or in such other circumstances as may be prescribed.

[(4)   For the purposes of the above provisions an application shall not be treated as an international application for a patent (UK) by reason only of its containing an indication that the applicant wishes to obtain a European patent (UK), but an application shall be so treated if it also separately designates the United Kingdom.]

(5)   If an international application for a patent which designates the United Kingdom is refused a filing date under the Treaty and the comptroller determines that the refusal was caused by an error or omission in an institution having functions under the Treaty, he may direct that the application shall be treated as an application under this Act, having such date of filing as he may direct.

Note

Section 89 substituted, together with ss.89A, 89B, for original s.89 by CDPA 1988 (c.48) Sch.5 para.25, with effect from 5 January 1991, SI 1990/2168.

Subsection (4) repealed by Patents Act 2004 (c.16) s.5 and Sch.1 para.7, Sch.3, with effect from 1 January 2005, SI 2004/3205.

International and national phases of application

AppA-
89A

89A.—(1) The provisions of the Patent Co-operation Treaty relating to publication, search, examination and amendment, and not those of this Act, apply to an international application for a patent (UK) during the international phase of the application.

(2) The international phase of the application means the period from the filing of the application in accordance with the Treaty until the national phase of the application begins.

(3) The national phase of the application begins—

(a) when the prescribed period expires, provided any necessary translation of the application into English has been filed at the Patent Office and the prescribed fee has been paid by the applicant; or

(b) on the applicant expressly requesting the comptroller to proceed earlier with the national phase of the application, filing at the Patent Office—

(i) a copy of the application, if none has yet been sent to the Patent Office in accordance with the Treaty, and

(ii) any necessary translation of the application into English, and paying the prescribed fee.

For this purpose a "copy of the application" includes a copy published in accordance with the Treaty in a language other than that in which it was originally filed.

(4) If the prescribed period expires without the conditions mentioned in subsection (3)(a) being satisfied, the application shall be taken to be withdrawn.

(5) Where during the international phase the application is amended in accordance with the Treaty, the amendment shall be treated as made under this Act if—

(a) when the prescribed period expires, any necessary translation of the amendment into English has been filed at the Patent Office, or

(b) where the applicant expressly requests the comptroller to proceed earlier with the national phase of the application, there is then filed at the Patent Office—

(i) a copy of the amendment, if none has yet been sent to the Patent Office in accordance with the Treaty, and

(ii) any necessary translation of the amendment into English; otherwise the amendment shall be disregarded.

(6) The comptroller shall on payment of the prescribed fee publish any translation filed at the Patent Office under subsection (3) or (5) above.

Note

Section 89A substituted, together with ss.89, 89B, for original s.89 by CDPA 1988 (c.48) s.295 and Sch.5 para.25 with effect from 7 January 1991, SI 1990/2168.

Adaptation of provisions in relation to international application

AppA-
89B

89B.—(1) Where an international application for a patent (UK) is accorded a filing date under the Patent Co-operation Treaty—

    (a)   that date, or if the application is re-dated under the Treaty to a later date that later date, shall be treated as the date of filing the application under this Act,

    (b)   any declaration of priority made under the Treaty shall be treated as made under section 5(2) above, and where in accordance with the Treaty any extra days are allowed, the period of 12 months [*specified in section 5(2)*] allowed under section 5(2A)(a) above shall be treated as altered accordingly, and

    (c)   any statement of the name of the inventor under the Treaty shall be treated as a statement filed under section 13(2) above.

(2)   If the application, not having been published under this Act, is published in accordance with the Treaty it shall be treated, for purposes other than those mentioned in subsection (3), as published under section 16 above when the [*conditions mentioned in section 89A(3)(a) are complied with*] national phase of the application begins or, if later, when published in accordance with the Treaty.

(3)   For the purposes of section 55 (use of invention for service of the Crown) and section 69 (infringement of rights conferred by publication) the application, not having been published under this Act, shall be treated as published under section 16 above—

    (a)   if it is published in accordance with the Treaty in English, on its being so published; and

    (b)   if it is so published in a language other than English—

        (i)   on the publication of a translation of the application in accordance with section 89A(6) above, or

        (ii)   on the service by the applicant of a translation into English of the specification of the application on the government department concerned or, as the case may be, on the person committing the infringing act.

The reference in paragraph (b)(ii) to the service of a translation on a government department or other person is to its being sent by post or delivered to that department or person.

(4)   During the international phase of the application, section 8 above does not apply (determination of questions of entitlement in relation to application under this Act) and section 12 above (determination of entitlement in relation to foreign and convention patents) applies notwithstanding the application; but after the end of the international phase, section 8 applies and section 12 does not.

(5)   When the national phase begins the comptroller shall refer the application for so much of the examination and search [*under section*] under sections 15A, 17 and 18 above as he considers appropriate in view of any examination or search carried out under the Treaty.

Notes

    Section 89B substituted, together with ss.89, 89A, for original s.89 by CDPA 1988 (c.48) s.295 and Sch.5 para.25, with effect from 7 January 1991, SI 1990/2168.

    Subsections (1) and (5) amended by Regulatory Reform (Patents) Order 2004 (SI 2004/2357) art.16, with effect from 1 January 2005, subject to transitional provisions contained in arts 20–23 of that Order.

Subsection (2) amended by Patents Act 2004 (c.16) s.5 and Sch.1 para.8, with effect from 1 January 2005, SI 2004/3205, subject to transitional provisions contained in art.9 of that Order.

Convention countries

Orders in Council as to convention countries

AppA-90   **90.**—(1)   Her Majesty may with a view to the fulfilment of a treaty or international convention, arrangement or engagement, by Order in Council declare that any country specified in the Order is a convention country for the purposes of section 5 above.

(2)   Her Majesty may Order in Council direct that any of the Channel Islands, any colony [*or any British protectorate or protected state*] shall be taken to be a convention country for those purposes.

(3)   For the purposes of subsection (1) above every colony, protectorate, and territory subject to the authority or under the suzerainty of another country, and every territory administered by another country under the trusteeship system of the United Nations shall be taken to be a country in the case of which a declaration may be made under that subsection.

Note

Subsection (2) amended by Statute Law (Repeals) Act 1986 (c.12) s.1 and Sch.1 Pt VI.

Miscellaneous

Evidence of conventions and instruments under conventions

AppA-91   **91.**—(1)   Judicial notice shall be taken of the following, that is to say—

    (a)   the European Patent Convention, the Community Patent Convention and the Patent Co-operation Treaty (each of which is hereafter in this section referred to as the relevant convention);

    (b)   any bulletin, journal or gazette published under the relevant convention and the register of European [*or Community patents kept under it;*] **patents kept under the European Patent Convention** and

    (c)   any decision of, or expression of opinion by, the relevant convention court on any question arising under or in connection with the relevant convention.

(2)   Any document mentioned in subsection (1)(b) above shall be admissible as evidence of any instrument or other act thereby communicated of any convention institution.

(3)   Evidence of any instrument issued under the relevant convention by any such institution, including any judgment or order or the relevant convention court, or of any document in the custody of any such institution or reproducing in legible form any information in such custody otherwise than in legible form, of any entry in or extract from such a document, may be given in any legal proceedings by production of a copy certified as a true copy by an official of that institution; and any document purporting to be such a copy shall be received in evidence without proof of the official position or handwriting of the person signing the certificate.

(4)   Evidence of any such instrument may also be given in any legal proceedings—

    (a)   by production of a copy purporting to be printed by the Queen's Printer;

(b) where the instrument is in the custody of a government department, by production of a copy certified on behalf of the department to be a true copy by an officer of the department generally or specially authorised to do so;

and any document purporting to be such a copy as is mentioned in paragraph (b) above of an instrument in the custody of a department shall be received in evidence without proof of the official position or handwriting of the person signing the certificate, or of his authority to do so, or of the document being in the custody of the department.

(5) In any legal proceedings in Scotland evidence of any matter given in a manner authorised by this section shall be sufficient evidence of it.

(6) In this section—

"convention institution" means an institution established by or having functions under the relevant convention;

"relevant convention court" does not include a court of the United Kingdom or of any other country which is a party to the relevant convention; and

"legal proceedings," in relation to the United Kingdom, includes proceedings before the comptroller.

Note

Subsection (1) amended by Patents Act 2004 (c.16) s.16 and Sch.2 para.20, with effect from 1 January 2005, SI 2004/3205.

Obtaining evidence for proceedings under the European Patent Convention

92.—(1) Sections 1 to 3 of the Evidence (Proceedings in Other Jurisdictions) **AppA-92** Act 1975 (provisions enabling United Kingdom courts to assist in obtaining evidence for foreign courts) shall apply for the purpose of proceedings before a relevant convention court under the European Patent Convention as they apply for the purpose of civil proceedings in a court exercising jurisdiction in a country outside the United Kingdom.

(2) In the application of those sections by virtue of this section any reference to the High Court, the Court of Session or the High Court of Justice in Northern Ireland shall include a reference to the comptroller.

(3) Rules under this Act may include provision—

(a) as to the manner in which an application under section 1 of the said Act of 1975 is to be made to the comptroller for the purpose of proceedings before a relevant convention court under the European Patent Convention; and

(b) subject to the provisions of that Act, as to the circumstances in which an order can be made under section 2 of that Act on any such application.

(4) Rules of court and rules under this Act may provide for an officer of the European Patent Office to attend the hearing of an application under section 1 of that Act before the court or the comptroller, as the case may be, and examine the witnesses or request the court or comptroller to put specified questions to the witnesses.

(5) Section 1(4) of the Perjury Act 1911 and [*section 1(4) of the Perjury Act (Northern Ireland) 1946*] **Article 3(4) of the Perjury (Northern Ireland) Order 1979** (statements made for the purposes, among others, of judicial proceedings in

a tribunal of a foreign state) shall apply in relation to proceedings before a relevant convention court under the European Patent Convention as they apply to a judicial proceeding in a tribunal of a foreign state.

Note

Subsection (5) amended by Perjury (Northern Ireland) Order 1979 (SI 1979/1714) art.19(1) and Sch.1 para.28.

Enforcement of orders for costs

AppA-93   **93.**   If the European Patent Office orders the payment of costs in any proceedings before it—

    (a)   in England and Wales the costs shall, if **the county court** [*a county court*] so orders, be recoverable [*by execution issued from the county court*] **under section 85 of the County Courts Act 1984** or otherwise as if they were payable under an order of that court;

    (b)   in Scotland the order may be enforced in like manner as [*a recorded decree arbitral*] **an extract registered decree arbitral bearing a warrant for execution issued by the sheriff court of any sheriffdom in Scotland**;

    (c)   in Northern Ireland the order may be enforced as if it were a money judgment.

Notes

Subsection (a) reference to s.85 of the County Courts Act 1984 amended by the Tribunals, Courts and Enforcement Act 2007 s.62(3), Sch.13 para.41, as from 22 April 2014 subject to savings and transitional provisions.

Subsection (a) amended to refer to the county court by Tribunals, Courts and Enforcement Act 2007 (c.15) Sch.13 para.41 with effect from 6 April 2014.

Subsection (b) amended by Debtors (Scotland) Act 1987 (c.18) s.108(1) and Sch.6 paras 1, 20.

Communication of information to the European Patent Office, etc.

AppA-94   **94.**   It shall not be unlawful by virtue of any enactment to communicate the following information in pursuance of the European Patent Convention to the European Patent Office or the competent authority of any country which is party to the Convention, that is to say—

    (a)   information in the files of the court which, in accordance with rules of court, the court authorises to be so communicated;

    (b)   information in the files of the Patent Office which, in accordance with rules under this Act, the comptroller authorises to be so communicated.

Financial provisions

AppA-95   **95.**—(1)   There shall be paid out of moneys provided by Parliament any sums required by any Minister of the Crown or government department to meet any financial obligation of the United Kingdom under the European Patent Convention, [*the Community Patent Convention*] or the Patent Co-operation Treaty.

    (2)   Any sums received by any Minister of the Crown or government department in pursuance of [*either of those conventions*] **that convention** or that treaty shall be paid into the Consolidated Fund.

Note

Subsections (1) and (2) amended by Patents Act 2004 (c.16) s.16 and Sch.2 para.21, with effect from 1 January 2005, SI 2004/3205.

<h3 style="text-align:center">PART III – MISCELLANEOUS AND GENERAL</h3>

Legal Proceedings

[The Patents Court

96.—*(1)   There shall be constituted, as part of the Chancery Division of the*   AppA-96
High Court, a Patents Court to take such proceedings relating to patents and other matters as may be prescribed by rules of court.

(2)   The judges of the Patents Court shall be such of the puisne judges of the High Court as the Lord Chancellor may from time to time nominate.

(3)   The foregoing provisions of this section shall not be taken as prejudicing the provisions of the Supreme Court of Judicature (Consolidation) Act 1925 which enable the whole jurisdiction of the High Court to be exercised by any judge of that court.

(4)   Rules of court shall make provision for the appointment of scientific advisers to assist the Patents Court in proceedings under this Act and for regulating the functions of such advisers.

(5)   The remuneration of any such adviser shall be determined by the Lord Chancellor with the consent of the Minister for the Civil Service and shall be defrayed out of moneys provided by Parliament.]

Note

Section 96 repealed by Senior Courts Act (formerly Supreme Courts Act) 1981 (c.54) s.152(4) and Sch.4.

Appeals from the comptroller

97.—(1)   Except as provided by subsection (4) below, an appeal shall lie to the   AppA-97
Patents Court from any decision of the comptroller under this Act or rules except any of the following decisions, that is to say—

(a)   a decision falling within section 14(7) above;

(b)   a decision under section 16(2) above to omit matter from a specification;

(c)   a decision to give directions under subsection (1) or (2) of section 22 above;

(d)   a decision under rules which is excepted by rules from the right of appeal conferred by this section.

(2)   For the purpose of hearing appeals under this section the Patents Court may consist of one or more judges of that court in accordance with directions given by [*or on behalf of the Lord Chancellor*] **the Lord Chief of Justice of England and Wales after consulting the Lord Chancellor** [*and the Patents Court shall not be treated as a divisional court for the purposes of section 31(1)(f) of the Supreme Court of Judicature (Consolidation) Act 1925 (appeals from divisional courts).*]

(3)   An appeal shall not lie to the Court of Appeal from a decision of the Patents Court on appeal from a decision of the comptroller under this Act or rules—

(a)   except where the comptroller's decision was given under section 8, 12, 18, 20, 27, 37, 40, 61, 72, 73 or 75 above; or

[1005]

(b) except where the ground of appeal is that the decision of the Patents Court is wrong in law; but an appeal shall only lie to the Court of Appeal under this section if leave to appeal is given by the Patents Court or the Court of Appeal.

(4) The Lord Chief Justice may nominate a judicial office holder (as defined in section 109(4) of the Constitutional Reform Act 2005) to exercise his functions under subsection (2).

(4) An appeal shall lie to the Court of Session from any decision of the comptroller in proceedings which under rules are held in Scotland, except any decision mentioned in paragraphs (a) to (d) of subsection (1) above.

(5) An appeal shall not lie to the Inner House of the Court of Session from a decision of an Outer House judge on appeal from a decision of the comptroller under this Act or rules—

(a) except where the comptroller's decision was given under section 8, 12, 18, 20, 27, 37, 40, 61, 72, 73 or 75 above; or

(b) except where the ground of appeal is that the decision of the Outer House judge is wrong in law.

Notes

Subsection (2) amended by Senior Courts Act 1981 (c.54) s.152(4) and Sch.7; amended by Constitutional Reform Act 2005 (c.4) s.15 and Sch.4 Pt 1 para.91(2), with effect from 3 April 2006, SI 2006/1014.

Subsection (4) inserted by Constitutional Reform Act 2005 (c.4) s.15 and Sch.4 Pt 1 para.91(3), with effect from 3 April 2006, SI 2006/1014.

Proceedings in Scotland

AppA-98 **98.**—(1) In Scotland proceedings relating primarily to patents (other than proceedings before the comptroller) shall be competent in the Court of Session only and any jurisdiction of the sheriff court relating to patents is hereby abolished except in relation to questions which are incidental to the issue in proceedings which are otherwise competent there.

(2) The remuneration of any assessor appointed to assist the court in proceedings under this Act in the Court of Session shall be determined by the Lord President of the Court of Session with the consent of the [*Minister for the Civil Service*] **Treasury** and shall be defrayed out of moneys provided by Parliament.

Note

Word substituted by Transfer of Functions (Minister for the Civil Service and Treasury) Order 1981 (SI 1981/1670) arts 2(2) and 3(5).

General powers of the court

AppA-99 **99.** The court may, for the purpose of determining any question in the exercise of its original or appellate jurisdiction under this Act or any treaty or international convention to which the United Kingdom is a party, make any order or exercise any other power which the comptroller could have made or exercised for the purpose of determining that question.

Power of Patents Court to order report

AppA-99A **99A.**—(1) **Rules of court shall make provision empowering the Patents Court in any proceedings before it under this Act, on or without the applica-**

tion of any party, to order the Patent Office to inquire into and report on any question of fact or opinion.

(2) Where the court makes such an order on the application of a party, the fee payable to the Patent Office shall be at such rate as may be determined in accordance with rules of court and shall be costs of the proceedings unless otherwise ordered by the court.

(3) Where the court makes such an order of its own motion, the fee payable to the Patent Office shall be at such rate as may be determined by the Lord Chancellor with the approval of the Treasury and shall be paid out of money provided by Parliament.

Note

Section 99A inserted by CDPA 1988 (c.48) s.295 and Sch.5 para.26, with effect from 7 January 1991, SI 1990/2168.

Power of Court of Session to order report

99B.—(1) In any proceedings before the Court of Session under this Act the court may, either of its own volition or on the application of any party, order the Patent Office to inquire into and report on any question of fact or opinion.   AppA-99B

(2) Where the court makes an order under subsection (1) above of its own violation the fee payable to the Patent Office shall be at such rate as may be determined by the Lord President of the Court of Session with the consent of the Treasury and shall be defrayed out of moneys provided by Parliament.

(3) Where the court makes an order under subsection (1) above on the application of a party, the fee payable to the Patent Office shall be at such rate as may be provided for in rules of court and shall be treated as expenses in the cause.

Note

Section 99B inserted by CDPA 1988 (c.48) s.295 and Sch.5 para.26, with effect from 7 January 1991, SI 1990/2168.

Burden of proof in certain cases

100.—(1) If the invention for which a patent is granted is a process for obtaining a new product, the same product produced by a person other than the proprietor of the patent or a licensee of his shall, unless the contrary is proved, be taken in any proceedings to have been obtained by that process.   AppA-100

(2) In considering whether a party has discharged the burden imposed upon him by this section, the court shall not require him to disclose any manufacturing or commercial secrets if it appears to the court that it would be unreasonable to do so.

Exercise of comptroller's discretionary powers

101. Without prejudice to any rule of law, the comptroller shall give any party to a proceeding before him an opportunity of being heard before exercising adversely to that party any discretion vested in the comptroller by this Act or rules.   AppA-101

[Right of audience in patent proceedings

102.—(1)   Any party to any proceedings before the comptroller under this Act or any treaty or international convention to which the United Kingdom is a party, may appear before the comptroller in person or be represented by counsel or a solicitor (of any part of the United Kingdom) or a patent agent or, subject to rules under section 115 below, by any other person whom he desires to represent him.

(2)   Subsection (1) above, in its application to proceedings under any such treaty or convention, shall have effect subject to section 84(1) or (3) above.

(3)   Without prejudice to the right of counsel to appear before the High Court, a member of the Bar of England and Wales who is not in actual practice, a solicitor of the Supreme Court and a patent agent shall each have the right to appear and be heard on behalf of any party to an appeal under this Act from the comptroller to the Patents Court.]

Right of audience, etc. in proceedings before comptroller

102.—(1)   A party to proceedings before the comptroller under this Act, or under any treaty or international convention to which the United Kingdom is a party, may appear before the comptroller in person or be represented by any person whom he desires to represent him.

(2)   No offence is committed under the enactments relating to the preparation of documents by persons not legally qualified by reason only of the preparation by any person of a document, other than a deed, for use in such proceedings.

(2A)   For the purposes of subsection (2), as it has effect in relation to England and Wales, "the enactment relating to the preparation of documents by persons not qualified" means section 14 of the Legal Services Act 2007 (offence to carry on a reserved legal activity if not entitled) as it applies in relation to an activity which amounts to the carrying on of reserved instrument activities within the meaning of that Act.

(3)   Subsection (1) has effect subject to rules made under section 281 of the Copyright, Designs and Patents Act 1988 (power of comptroller to refuse to recognise certain agents).

(4)   In its application to proceedings in relation to applications for, or otherwise in connection with, European patents, this section has effect subject to any restrictions imposed by or under the European Patent Convention.

[*(5)   Nothing in this section shall be taken to limit the right to draw or prepare deeds given to a registered patent agent by section 68 of the Courts and Legal Services Act 1990.*]

(5)   Nothing in this section is to be taken to limit any entitlement to prepare deeds conferred on a registered patent attorney by virtue of the Legal Services Act 2007.

Notes

Section 102 substituted, together with s.102A, for original s.102 by CDPA 1988 (c.48) s.295 and Sch.5 para.27, with effect from 13 August 1990, SI 1990/1400.

Subsection (2A) inserted by Legal Services Act 2007 (c.29) s.208(1), Sch.21 para.40, with effect from 1 January 2010, SI 2009/3250.

Subsection (5) as shown in square brackets inserted by Courts and the Legal Services Act 1990 (c.41) s.125(3) and Sch.18 para.20; new subs.(5) substituted for old subs.(5) by Legal Services Act 2007 (c.41) s.208(1), Sch.21 para.40, with effect from 1 January 2010, SI 2009/3250.

[Right of audience, etc., in proceedings on appeal from the comptroller

102A.—*(1)* *A solicitor of the [Supreme Court] Senior Courts or (in the ap-* AppA-102 *plication of this section to Northern Ireland) of the Court of Judicature may appear and be heard on behalf of any party to an appeal under this Act from the comptroller to the Patents Court.*

(2) *A registered patent agent or a member of the Bar not in actual practice may do, in or in connection with proceedings on an appeal under this Act from the comptroller to the Patents Court, anything which a solicitor of the [Supreme Court] Senior Courts or of the Court of Judicature might do, other than prepare a deed.*

(3) *The Lord Chancellor may, with the concurrence of the Lord Chief Justice of England and Wales, by regulations—*

    (a) *provide that the right conferred by subsection (2) shall be subject to such conditions and restrictions as appear to the Lord Chancellor to be necessary or expedient, and*

    (b) *apply to persons exercising that right such statutory provisions, rules of court and other rules of law and practice applying to solicitors as may be specified in the regulations; and different provision may be made for different descriptions of proceedings.*

(4) *Regulations under this section shall be made by statutory instrument which shall be subject to annulment in pursuance of a resolution of either House of Parliament.*

(5) *This section is without prejudice to the right of counsel to appear before the High Court.*

(6) *Nothing in this section shall be taken to limit the right to draw or prepare deeds given to a registered patent agent by section 68 of the Courts and Legal Services Act 1990.*

(7) *The Lord Chief Justice may nominate a judicial office holder (as defined in section 109(4) of the Constitutional Reform Act 2005) to exercise his functions under this section.*]

Notes

    Section 102A inserted, together with s.102, for original s.102 by CDPA 1988 (c.48) s.295 and Sch.5 para.27, with effect from 13 August 1990, SI 1990/1400.

    Subsections (1) and (2) amended by Constitutional Reform Act 2005 (c.4) s.59, Sch.11 Pt 4 para.23, with effect from 1 October 2009.

    Subsections (3) amended by Constitutional Reform Act 2005 (c.4) s.15 and Sch.4 Pt 1 para.92, with effect from 3 April 2006, SI 2006/1014.

    Subsection (6) inserted by Courts and the Legal Services Act 1990 (c.41) s.125(3) and Sch.18 para.20.

    Subsection (7) inserted by Constitutional Reform Act 2005 (c.4) s.15 and Sch.4 Pt 1 para.92, with effect from 3 April 2006, SI 2006/1014.

    Section 102A repealed by the Legal Services Act 2007 s.210, Sch.23, with effect from 1 January 2010, SI 2009/3250.

Extension of privilege for communications with solicitors relating to patent proceedings

103.—(1)   It is hereby declared that the rule of law which confers privilege from   AppA-103 disclosure in legal proceedings in respect of communications made with a solicitor or a person acting on his behalf, or in relation to information obtained or supplied for submission to a solicitor or a person acting on his behalf, for the purpose of any pending or contemplated proceedings before a court in the United Kingdom extends to such communications so made for the purpose of any pending or contemplated—

(a) proceedings before the comptroller under this Act or any of the relevant conventions, or

(b) proceedings before the relevant convention court under any of those conventions.

(2) In this section—

"legal proceedings" includes proceedings before the comptroller; the references to legal proceedings and pending or contemplated proceedings include references to applications for a patent or a European patent and to international applications for a patent; and "the relevant conventions" means the European Patent Convention,

[*the Community Patent Convention*] and the Patent Co-operation Treaty.

(3) This section shall not extend to Scotland.

Note

Subsection (2) amended by Patents Act 2004 (c.16) s.16 and Sch.2 para.22 Sch.3, with effect from 1 January 2005, SI 2004/3205.

[Privilege for communications with patent agents relating to patent proceedings

AppA-104

104.—(1) This section applies to any communication made for the purpose of any pending or contemplated patent proceedings, being either—

(a) a communication between the patent agent of a party to those proceedings and that party or any other person; or

(b) a communication between a party to those proceedings and a person other than his patent agent made for the purpose of obtaining, or in response to a request for, information which that party is seeking for the purpose of submitting it to his patent agent.

(2) For the purposes of subsection (1) above a communication made by or to a person acting—

(i) on behalf of a patent agent; or

(ii) on behalf of a party to any pending or contemplated proceedings, shall be treated as made by or to that patent agent or party, as the case may be.

(3) In any legal proceedings other than criminal proceedings a communication to which this section applies shall be privileged from disclosure in like manner as if any proceedings before the comptroller or the relevant convention court for the purpose of which the communication was made were proceedings before the court (within the meaning of this Act) and the patent agent in question had been the solicitor of the party concerned.

(4) In this section—

"legal proceedings" includes proceedings before the comptroller;

"patent agent" means an individual registered as a patent agent in the register of patent agents, a company lawfully practising as a patent agent in the United Kingdom or a person who satisfies the condition mentioned in sec-

tion 84(1) or (3) above;

"patent proceedings" means proceedings under this Act or any of the relevant conventions before the court, the comptroller or the relevant convention court, whether contested or uncontested and including an application for a patent;

"party", in relation to any contemplated proceedings, means a prospective party to the proceedings; and

"the relevant conventions" means the European Patent Convention, the Community Patent Convention and the Patent Co-operation Treaty.

(5)   This section shall not extend to Scotland.]

Note

Section 104 repealed by CDPA 1988 (c.48) s.303(2) and Sch.8, with effect from 13 August 1990, SI 1990/1400.

Extension of privilege in Scotland for communications relating to patent proceedings

105.—(1)   It is hereby declared that in Scotland the rules of law which confer privilege from disclosure in legal proceedings in respect of communications, reports or other documents (by whomsoever made) made for the purpose of any pending or contemplated proceedings in a court in the United Kingdom extends to communications, reports or other documents made for the purpose of patent proceedings [within the meaning of section 104 above].

(2)   In this section—

"patent proceedings" means proceedings under this Act or any of the relevant conventions, before the court, the comptroller or the relevant convention court, whether contested or uncontested and including an application for a patent; and "the relevant conventions" means the European Patent Convention, [*the Community Patent Convention*] and the Patent Co-operation Treaty.

AppA-105

Notes

Subsection (1) numbered as such and amended, and subs.(2) inserted by CDPA 1988 (c.48) s.303 and Sch.7 para.21, Sch.8, with effect from 13 August 1990, SI 1990/1400.
Subsection (2) amended by Patents Act 2004 (c.16) s.16 and Sch.2 para.22, Sch.3, with effect from 1 January 2005, SI 2004/3205, subject to transitional provisions contained in art.9 of that Order.

Costs and expenses in proceedings before the Court [under s. 40]

106.—(1)   In [*proceedings before the court under section 40 above (whether on an application or on appeal to the court)*] **proceedings to which this section applies**, the court, in determining whether to award costs or expenses to any party and what costs or expenses to award, shall have regard to all the relevant circumstances, including the financial position of the parties.

(1A)   This section applies to proceedings before the court (including proceedings on an appeal to the court) which are—

    (a)   proceedings under section 40;

    (b)   proceedings for infringement;

    (c)   proceedings under section 70; or

    (d)   proceedings on an application for a declaration or declarator under section 71.

(2)   If in any such proceedings the Patents Court directs that any costs of one

AppA-106

party shall be paid by another party, the court may settle the amount of the costs by fixing a lump sum or may direct that the costs shall be taxed on a scale specified by the court, being a scale of costs prescribed by [*the Rules of the Supreme Court or by the County Court Rules*] **rules of court**.

Notes

Provision heading and subs.(1) amended and subs.(1A) inserted by Patents Act 2004 (c.16) ss.14, 16 and Sch.3, with effect from 1 January 2005, SI 2004/3205, subject to savings contained in s.14(4) of that Act which provide that the amendments apply in relation to proceedings commenced on or after 1 January 2005.

Subsection (2) amended by Constitutional Reform Act 2005 (c.4) Sch.11 Pt 4 para.23, with effect from 1 October 2009.

Costs and expenses in proceedings before the comptroller

AppA-107

107.—(1) The comptroller may, in proceedings before him under this Act, by order award to any party such costs or, in Scotland, such expenses as he may consider reasonable and direct how and by what parties they are to be paid.

(2) In England and Wales any costs awarded under this section shall, if **the count court** [*a county court*] so orders, be recoverable [*by execution issued from the county court*] under **section 85 of the County Courts Act 1984** or otherwise as if they were payable under an order of that court.

(3) In Scotland any order under this section for the payment of expenses may be enforced in like manner as [*a recorded decree arbitral*] **an extract registered decree arbitral bearing a warrant for execution issued by the sheriff court of any sheriffdom in Scotland.**

[*(4)   If any of the following persons, that is to say—*
   (a)   any person by whom a reference is made to the comptroller under section 8, 12 or 37 above;
   (b)   any person by whom an application is made to the comptroller for the revocation of a patent;
   (c)   any person by whom notice of opposition is given to the comptroller under section 27(5), 29(2), 47(6), or 52(1) above, or section 117(2) below; neither resides nor carries on business in the United Kingdom, the comptroller may require him to give security for the costs or expenses of the proceedings and in default of such security being given may treat the reference of application as abandoned.]

(4) **The comptroller may make an order for security for costs or expenses against any party to proceedings before him under this Act if—**
   (a) **the prescribed conditions are met, and**
   (b) **he is satisfied that it is just to make the order, having regard to all the circumstances of the case; and in default of the required security being given the comptroller may treat the reference, application or notice in question as abandoned.**

(5) In Northern Ireland any order under this section for the payment of costs may be enforced as if it were a money judgment.

Notes

Subsection (2) reference to s.85 of the County Courts Act 1984 amended by the Tribunals, Courts and Enforcement Act 2007 s.62(3), Sch.13 para.41, as from 22 April 2014 subject to savings and transitional provisions.

Subsection (2) amended to refer to the county court by Tribunals, Courts and Enforcement Act 2007 (c.15) Sch.13 para.41 with effect from 6 April 2014.

Subsection (3) amended by Debtors (Scotland) Act 1987 (c.18) s.108(1) and Sch.6 para.20.

Subsection (4) substituted by Patents Act 2004 (c.16) s.15, with effect from 1 October 2005, SI 2005/2471, subject to the transitional provisions contained in art.3 of that Order which provide that the amendments apply in respect of proceedings commenced on or after 1 October 2005.

Licences granted by order of comptroller

108. Any order for the grant of a licence under section 11, 38, 48 or 49 above shall, without prejudice to any other method of enforcement, have effect as if it were a deed, executed by the proprietor of the patent and all other necessary parties, granting a licence in accordance with the order. AppA-108

Offences

Falsification of register etc.

109. If a person makes or causes to be made a false entry in any register kept under this Act, or a writing falsely purporting to be a copy or reproduction of an entry in any such register, or produces or tenders or causes to be produced or tendered in evidence any such writing, knowing the entry or writing to be false, he shall be liable— AppA-109

    (a)   on summary conviction, to a fine not exceeding [*£1,000*] **the prescribed sum;**

    (b)   on conviction on indictment, to imprisonment for a term not exceeding two years or a fine, or both.

Note

Subsection (a) amended by Magistrates' Courts Act 1980 (c.43) s.32(2).

Unauthorised claim of patent rights

110.—(1) If a person falsely represents that anything disposed of by him for value is a patented product he shall, subject to the following provisions of this section, be liable on summary conviction to a fine not exceeding [*£200*] **level 3 on the standard scale.** AppA-110

(2) For the purposes of subsection (1) above a person who for value disposes of an article having stamped, engraved or impressed on it or otherwise applied to it the word "patent" or "patented" or anything expressing or implying that the article is a patented product, shall be taken to represent that the article is a patented product.

(3) Subsection (1) above does not apply where the representation is made in respect of a product after the patent for that product or, as the case may be, the process in question has expired or been revoked and before the end of a period which is reasonably sufficient to enable the accused to take steps to ensure that the representation is not made (or does not continue to be made).

(4) In proceedings for an offence under this section it shall be a defence for the accused to prove that he used diligence to prevent the commission of the offence.

Note

Subsection (1) amended by Criminal Justice Act 1982 (c.48) ss.37, 39, 46 and Sch.2.

Unauthorised claim that patent has been applied for

AppA-
111

111.—(1)   If a person represents that a patent has been applied for in respect of any article disposed of for value by him and—

(a)   no such application has been made, or

(b)   any such application has been refused or withdrawn.

he shall, subject to the following provisions of this section, be liable on summary conviction to a fine not exceeding [£200] **level 3 on the standard scale.**

(2)   Subsection (1)(b) above does not apply where the representation is made (or continues to be made) before the expiry of a period which commences with the refusal or withdrawal and which is reasonably sufficient to enable the accused to take steps to ensure that the representation is not made (or does not continue to be made).

(3)   For the purposes of subsection (1) above person who for value disposes of an article having stamped, engraved or impressed on it or otherwise applied to it the words "patent applied for" or "patent pending," or anything expressing or imply-ing that a patent has been applied for in respect of the article, shall be taken to represent that such a patent has been applied for in respect of it.

(4)   In any proceedings for an offence under this section it shall be a defence for the accused to prove that he used due diligence to prevent the commission of such an offence.

Note

Subsection (1) amended by Criminal Justice Act 1982 (c.48) ss.37, 39, 46 and Sch.2.

Misuse of title "Patent Office"

AppA-
112

112.   If any person uses on his place of business, or any document issued by him, or otherwise, the words "Patent Office" or on any other words suggesting that his place of business is, or is officially connected with, the Patent Office, he shall be liable on summary conviction to a fine not exceeding [£500] **level 4 on the standard scale.**

Note

Section 112 amended by Criminal Justice Act 1982 (c.48) ss.37, 39, 46 and Sch.2.

Offences by corporations

AppA-
113

113.—(1)   Where an offence under this Act which has been committed by a body corporate is proved to have been committed with the consent or connivance of, or to be attributable to any neglect on the part of, a director, manager, secretary or other similar officer of the body corporate, or any person who was purporting to act in any such capacity, he, as well as the body corporate, shall be guilty of that offence and shall be liable to be proceeded against and punished accordingly.

(2)   Where the affairs of a body corporate are managed by its members, subsec-tion (1) above shall apply in relation to the acts and defaults of a member in con-

nection with his functions of management as if he were a director of the body corporate.

Patent agents

[Restrictions on practice as patent agent

114.—(1)   *An individual shall not, either alone or in partnership with any other person, practise, describe himself or hold himself out as a patent agent, or permit himself to be so described or held out, unless he is registered as a patent agent in the register of patent agents or (as the case may be) unless he and all his partners are so registered.*

AppA-114

(2)   *A body corporate shall not practise, describe itself or hold itself out or permit itself to be described or held out as mentioned in subsection (1) above unless—*

  (a)   *in the case of a company within the meaning of the Companies Act 1948 which began to carry on business as a patent agent before 17th November 1917, a director or the manager of the company is registered as a patent agent in the register of patent agents and the name of that director or manager is mentioned as being so registered in all professional advertisements, circulars or letters issued by or with the consent of the company in which the name of the company appears;*

  (b)   *in any other case, every director or, where the body's affairs are managed by its members, every member of the body and in any event, if it has a manager who is not a director or member, that manager, is so registered.*

(2A)   *Notwithstanding the definition of "patent agent" in section 130(1) below, subsections (1) and (2) above do not impose any prohibition in relation to the business of acting as agent for other persons for the purpose of conducting proceedings before the comptroller in connection with European patents (UK) to which section 77(1) above for the time being applies.*

(3)   *Any person who contravenes the provisions of this section shall be liable on summary conviction to a fine not exceeding £1,000.*

(4)   *Proceedings for an offence under this section may be begun at any time within twelve months from the date of the offence.*

(5)   *This section shall not be construed as prohibiting solicitors from taking such part in proceedings relating to patents and applications for patents as has heretofore been taken by solicitors and, in particular, shall not derogate from the provisions of section 102 above as it applies to solicitors.*

(6)   *A patent agent shall not be guilty of an offence under section 22 of the Solicitors Act 1974 or section 39 of the Solicitors (Scotland) Act 1933 (which prohibit the preparation for reward of certain instruments or writs by persons not legally qualified) by reason only of the preparation by him for use in proceedings under this Act before the comptroller or on appeal under this Act to the Patents Court from the comptroller of any document other than a deed.*

(7)   *For Article 23(2)(d) of the Solicitors (Northern Ireland) Order 1976 there shall be substituted the following paragraph—*

"(d)   a patent agent within the meaning of the Patents Act 1977 preparing, for use in proceedings under that Act or the Patents Act 1949 before the comptroller (as

[1015]

*defined in the former Act) or on appeal under either of those Acts to the Patents
Court from the comptroller, any document other than a deed;".*]

Note

Section 114 repealed by CDPA 1988 (c.48) s.303(2) and Sch.8, with effect from 13 August 1990,
SI 1990/1400.

[Power of comptroller to refuse to deal with certain agents

AppA-
115

*115.—(1)   Rules may authorise the comptroller to refuse to recognise as agent
in respect of any business under this Act—*

  (a)   *any individual whose name has been erased from, and not restored to,
the register of patent agents, or who is for the time being suspended
from acting as a patent agent;*
  (b)   *any person who has been convicted of an offence under section 114
above or section 88 of the 1949 Act (which is replaced by section 114);*
  (c)   *any person who is found by the Secretary of State to have been
convicted of any offence or to have been guilty of any such misconduct
as, in the case of an individual registered in the register of patent
agents, would render him liable to have his name erased from it;*
  (d)   *any person, not being registered as a patent agent, who in the opinion
of the comptroller is engaged wholly or mainly in acting as agent in
applying for patents in the United Kingdom or elsewhere in the name
or for the benefit of a person by whom he is employed;*
  (e)   *any company or firm, if any person whom the comptroller could refuse
to recognise as agent in respect of any business under this Act is acting as director or manager of the company or is a partner in the firm.*

*(2)   The comptroller shall refuse to recognise as agent in respect of any busi-
ness under this Act any person who neither resides nor has a place of business in
the United Kingdom.*

*(3)   Rules may authorise the comptroller to refuse to recognise as agent or other
representative for the purpose of applying for European patents any person who
does not satisfy the condition mentioned in section 84(1) above and does not fall
within the exemption in subsection (2) of that section.*]

Note

Section 115 repealed by CDPA 1988 (c.48) s.303(2) and Sch.8, with effect from 13 August 1990,
SI 1990/1400.

Immunity of department

Immunity of department as regards official acts

AppA-
116

116.   Neither the Secretary of State nor any officer of his—

  (a)   shall be taken to warrant the validity of any patent granted under this
Act or any treaty or international convention to which the United
Kingdom is a party; or
  (b)   shall incur any liability by reason of or in connection with any
examination or investigation required or authorised by this Act or any

such treaty or convention, or any report or other proceedings consequent on any such examination or investigation.

Administrative provisions

Correction of errors in patents and applications

117.—(1)   The comptroller may, subject to any provision of rules, correct any error of translation or transcription, clerical error or mistake in any specification of a patent or application for a patent or any document filed in connection with a patent or such an application.

(2)   Where the comptroller is requested to correct such an error or mistake, any person may in accordance with rules give the comptroller notice of opposition to the request and the comptroller shall determine the matter.

(3)   **Where the comptroller is requested to correct an error or mistake in a withdrawal of an application for a patent, and—**
  (a)   **the application was published under section 16 above; and**
  (b)   **details of the withdrawal were published by the comptroller; the comptroller shall publish notice of such a request in the prescribed manner.**

(4)   **Where the comptroller publishes a notice under subsection (3) above, the comptroller may only correct an error or mistake under subsection (1) above by order.**

AppA-117

Note

Subsections (3) and (4) inserted by Regulatory Reform (Patents) Order 2004 (SI 2004/2357) art.17, with effect from 1 January 2005, subject to transitional provisions contained in arts 20–23 of that Order.

Effect of resuscitating a withdrawn application under section 117

117A.—(1)   **Where—**
  (a)   **the comptroller is requested to correct an error or mistake in a withdrawal of an application for a patent; and**
  (b)   **an application has been resuscitated in accordance with that request, the effect of that resuscitation is as follows.**

(2)   **Anything done under or in relation to the application during the period between the application being withdrawn and its resuscitation shall be treated as valid.**

(3)   **If the comptroller has published notice of the request as mentioned in section 117(3) above, anything done during that period which would have constituted an infringement of the rights conferred by publication of the application if the application had not been withdrawn shall be treated as an infringement of those rights if it was a continuation or repetition of an earlier act infringing those rights.**

(4)   **If the comptroller has published notice of the request as mentioned in section 117(3) above and, after the withdrawal of the application and before publication of the notice, a person—**
  (a)   **began in good faith to do an act which would have constituted an infringement of the rights conferred by publication of the application if the withdrawal had not taken place, or**

AppA-117

(b)   made in good faith effective and serious preparations to do such an act, he has the right to continue to do the act or, as the case may be, to do the act, notwithstanding the resuscitation of the application and the grant of the patent; but this right does not extend to granting a licence to another person to do the act.

(5)   If the act was done, or the preparations were made, in the course of a business, the person entitled to the right conferred by subsection (4) above may—

(a)   authorise the doing of that act by any partners of his for the time being in that business, and

(b)   assign that right, or transmit it on death (or in the case of a body corporate on its dissolution), to any person who acquires that part of the business in the course of which the act was done or the preparations were made.

(6)   Where a product is disposed of to another in exercise of a right conferred by subsection (4) or (5) above, that other and any person claiming through him may deal with the product in the same way as if it had been disposed of by the applicant.

(7)   The above provisions apply in relation to the use of a patented invention for the services of the Crown as they apply in relation to infringement of the rights conferred by publication of the application for a patent (or, as the case may be, infringement of the patent).

"Patented invention" has the same meaning as in section 55 above.

Note

Section 117A inserted by Regulatory Reform (Patents) Order 2004 (SI 2004/2357) art.18, with effect from 1 January 2005, subject to transitional provisions contained in arts 20–23 of that Order.

Subsection (7) inserted by Patents Act 2004 (c.16) s.17(2) and Sch.2 para.23, with effect from 1 January 2005, SI 2004/3205.

Extension of time limits specified by comptroller

AppA-1 17B

117B.—(1)   Subsection (2) below applies in relation to a period if it is specified by the comptroller in connection with an application for a patent, or a patent.

(2)   Subject to subsections (4) and (5) below, the comptroller shall extend a period to which this subsection applies if—

(a)   the applicant or the proprietor of the patent requests him to do so; and

(b)   the request complies with the relevant requirements of rules.

(3)   An extension of a period under subsection (2) above expires—

(a)   at the end of the period prescribed for the purposes of this subsection, or

(b)   if sooner, at the end of the period prescribed for the purposes of section 20 above.

(4)   If a period has already been extended under subsection (2) above—

(a)   that subsection does not apply in relation to it again;

(b)   the comptroller may further extend the period subject to such conditions as he thinks fit.

(5) Subsection (2) above does not apply to a period specified in relation to proceedings before the comptroller.

Note

Section 117B inserted by Regulatory Reform (Patents) Order 2004 (SI 2004/2357) art.18, with effect from 1 January 2005, subject to transitional provisions contained in arts 20–23 of that Order.

Information about patent applications and patents, and inspection of documents

118.—(1)   After publication of an application for a patent in accordance with   AppA-118
section 16 above the comptroller shall on a request being made to him in the
prescribed manner and on payment of the prescribed fee (if any) give the person
making the request such information, and permit him to inspect such documents,
relating to the application or any patent granted in pursuance of the application as
may be specified in the request, subject, however, to any prescribed restrictions.

(2)   Subject to the following provisions of this section, until an application for
a patent is so published documents or information constituting or relating to the application
shall not, without the consent of the applicant, be published or communicated
to any person by the comptroller.

(3)   Subsection (2) above shall not prevent the comptroller from—

    (a)   sending the European Patent Office information which it is his duty to
send that office in accordance with any provision of the European Patent Convention; [*or*]

    **(aa)   sending any patent office outside the United Kingdom such
information about unpublished applications for patents as that office requests; or**

    (b)   publishing or communicating to others any prescribed bibliographic
information about an unpublished application for a patent;

nor shall that subsection prevent the Secretary of State from inspecting or authorising
the inspection of an application for a patent or any connected documents under
[*section 22(6)(a) above*] **section 22(6) above.**

**(3A)   Information may not be sent to a patent office in reliance on subsection (3)(aa) otherwise than in accordance with the working arrangements that
the comptroller has made for that purpose with that office.**

**(3B)   Those arrangements must include provision for ensuring that the
confidentiality of information of the kind referred to in subsection (3)(aa) sent
by the comptroller to the patent office in question is protected.**

**(3C)   The reference in subsection (3)(aa) to a patent office is to an organisation which carries out, in relation to patents, functions of the kind carried out
at the Patent Office.**

(4)   Where a person is notified that an application for a patent has been made,
but not published in accordance with section 16 above, and that the applicant will,
if the patent is granted, bring proceedings against that person in the event of his doing
an act specified in the notification after the application is so published, that
person may make a request under subsection (1) above, notwithstanding that the application
has not been published, and that subsection shall apply accordingly.

(5)   Where an application for a patent is filed, but not published, and a new application
is filed in respect of any part of the subject-matter of the earlier application
(either in accordance with rules or in pursuance of an order under section 8

[1019]

above) and is published, any person may make a request under subsection (1) above relating to the earlier application and on payment of the prescribed fee the comptroller shall give him such information and permit him to inspect such documents as could have been given or inspected if the earlier application had been published.

Notes

Subsection (3) amended by CDPA 1988 (c.48) s.295 and Sch.5 para.28, with effect from 7 January 1991, SI 1990/2168.

Subsection (3) amended by Intellectual Property Act 2014 (c.18) Pat 2 s.18(1) with effect from 1 October 2014 subject to transitional provisions specified in SI 2014/2330 art.4.

Subsections (3A) and (3B) inserted by Intellectual Property Act 2014 (c.18) Pat 2 s.18(2) with effect from 1 October 2014 subject to transitional provisions specified in SI 2014/2330 art.4.

Subsection (3C) inserted by Intellectual Property Act 2014 (c.18) Pat 2 s.18(3) with effect from 1 October 2014 subject to transitional provisions specified in SI 2014/2330 art.4.

[Copyright in documents made available electronically for inspection under section 118(1)

AppA-1
18A

118A.—(1) *This section applies to documents made available for inspection under section 118(1).*

(2) *Any copyright in the documents is not infringed by—*

    (a) *the making available to the public of the documents by electronic transmission in such a way that members of the public may access the documents from a place and at a time individually chosen by them, or*

    (b) *copying the documents for the purpose of facilitating the making available to the public of the documents as mentioned in paragraph (a).*

(3) *Nothing in this section is to be read as affecting the generality of any provision made by Chapter 3 of Part 1 of the Copyright, Designs and Patents Act 1988.*]

Notes

Section 118A inserted by Patents Act (Amendment) Regulations 2011/2059 reg.2 with effect from 1 October 2011.

Section 118A repealed by Copyright (Public Administration) Regulations 2014/1385 reg.3(1) with effect from 1 June 2014.

Service by post

AppA-
119

119. Any notice required or authorised to be given by this Act or rules, and any application or other document so authorised or required to be made or filed, may be given, made or filed by post.

Hours of business and excluded days

AppA-
120

120.—(1) [*Rules may specify*] **The comptroller may give directions specifying** the hour at which the Patent Office shall be taken to be closed on any day for purposes of the transaction by the public of business under this Act or of any class of such business, [*and may specify*] **and the directions may specify** days as excluded days for any such purposes.

(2) Any business done under this Act on any day after the hour so specified in relation to business of that class, or on a day which is an excluded day in relation to business of that class, shall be taken to have been done on the next following day not being an excluded day; and where the time for doing anything under this Act

expires on an excluded day that time shall be extended to the next following day not being an excluded day.

(3) Directions under this section shall be published in the prescribed manner.

Note

Subsection (1) amended and subs.(3) inserted by Patents Act 2004 (c.16) s.16 and Sch.2 para.24, with effect from 22 September 2004, SI 2004/2177, subject to transitional provisions contained in arts 6–8 of that Order.

Comptroller's annual report

121. Before the [*1st June*] **1st December** in every [*year*] **financial year** the comptroller shall cause to be laid before both Houses of Parliament a report with respect to the execution of this Act and the discharge of his functions under the European Patent Convention, [*the Community Patent Convention*] and the Patent Co-operation Treaty, and every such report shall include an account of all fees, salaries and allowances, and other money received and paid by him under this Act, [*those conventions*] **that convention** and that treaty during the previous [*year*] **financial year.** AppA-121

Note

Amended by Patents Act 2004 (c.16) s.16 and Sch.2 para.25, Sch.3, with effect from 1 January 2005, SI 2004/3205.

Supplemental

Crown's right to sell forfeited articles

122. Nothing in this Act affects the right of the Crown or any person deriving title directly or indirectly from the Crown to dispose of or use articles forfeited under the laws relating to customs or excise. AppA-122

Rules

123.—(1) The Secretary of State may make such rules as he thinks expedient for regulating the business of the Patent Office in relation to patents and applications for patents (including European patents, applications for European patents and international applications for patents) and for regulating all matters placed by this Act under the direction or control of the comptroller; and in this Act, except so far as the context otherwise requires, "prescribed" means prescribed by rules and "rules" means rules made under this section. AppA-123

(2) Without prejudice to the generality of subsection (1) above, rules may make provision—

    (a) prescribing the form and contents of applications for patents and other documents which may be filed at the Patent Office and requiring copies to be furnished of any such documents;

    (b) regulating the procedure to be followed in connection with any proceeding or other matter before the comptroller or the Patent Office and authorising the rectification or irregularities of procedure;

(c) requiring fees to be paid in connection with any such proceeding or matter or in connection with the provision of any service by the Patent Office and providing for the remission of fees in the prescribed circumstances;

(d) regulating the mode of giving evidence in any such proceeding and empowering the comptroller to compel the attendance of witnesses and the discovery of and production of documents;

(e) requiring the comptroller to advertise any proposed amendments of patents and any other prescribed matters, including any prescribed steps in any such proceeding;

(f) requiring the comptroller to hold proceedings in Scotland in such circumstances as may be specified in the rules where there is more than one party to proceedings under section 8, 12, 37, 40(1) or (2), 41(8), 61(3), 71 or 72 above;

(g) providing for the appointment of advisers to assist the comptroller in any proceedings before him;

(h) prescribing time limits for doing anything required to be done in connection with any such proceeding by this Act or the rules and providing for the alteration of any period of time specified in this Act or the rules;

[*(i) giving effect to the right of an inventor of an invention to be mentioned in an application for a patent for the invention;*]

(i) giving effect to an inventor's rights to be mentioned conferred by section 13, and providing for an inventor's waiver of any such right to be subject to acceptance by the comptroller;

(j) without prejudice to any other provision of this Act, requiring and regulating the translation of documents in connection with an application for a patent or a European patent or an international application for a patent and the filing and authentication of any such translations;

[*(k) requiring the keeping of a register of patent agents and regulating the registration of patent agents and authorising in prescribed cases the erasure from the register of patent agents of the name of any person registered therein or the suspension of the right of any such person to act as a patent agent;*]

(l) providing for the publication and sale of documents in the Patent Office and of information about such documents.

(2A) The comptroller may set out in directions any forms the use of which is required by rules; and any such directions shall be published in the prescribed manner.

(3) Rules may make different provision for different cases.

(3A) It is hereby declared that rules—

(a) authorising the rectification of irregularities of procedure, or

(b) providing for the alteration of any period of time, may authorise the comptroller to extend or further extend any period notwithstanding that the period has already expired.

[*(4) Rules prescribing fees shall not be made except with the consent of the Treasury.*]

[*(5) The remuneration of any adviser appointed under rules to assist the comptroller in any proceeding shall be determined by the Secretary of State with the consent of the Minister for the Civil Service and shall be defrayed out of moneys provided by Parliament.*]

(6) Rules shall provide for the publication by the comptroller of a journal; (in this Act referred to as "the journal") containing particulars of applications for and grants of patents, and of other proceedings under this Act.

(7) Rules shall require or authorise the comptroller to make arrangements for the publication of reports of cases relating to patents, trade marks [*and registered designs*] **registered designs or design right** decided by him and of cases relating to patents (whether under this Act or otherwise) trade marks, registered designs [*and copyright*] **copyright and design right** decided by any court or body (whether in the United Kingdom or elsewhere).

Notes

Subsection (2)(k) repealed by CDPA 1988 (c.48) s.303(2) and Sch.8, with effect from 13 August 1990, SI 1990/1400.

Subsection (2)(i) substituted by Patents Act 2004 (c.16) s.16 and Sch.2 para.26(2), with effect from 1 October 2005, SI 2005/2471.

Subsection (3A) inserted by CDPA 1988 (c.48) s.295 and Sch.5 para.29, with effect from 15 November 1988.

Subsection (2A) inserted and subss.(4) and (5) repealed by Patents Act 2004 (c.16) s.16 and Sch.2 para.26(3), (4), Sch.3, with effect from 22 September 2004, SI 2004/2177, subject to transitional provisions contained in arts 6–8 of that Order.

Subsection (7) amended by CDPA 1988 (c.48) s.303(1) and Sch.7, para.22, with effect from 1 August 1989, SI 1989/816.

Rules, regulations and orders; supplementary

124.—(1)   Any power conferred on the Secretary of State by this Act to make rules, regulations or orders shall be exercisable by statutory instrument.　　AppA-124

(2)   Any Order in Council and any statutory instrument containing an order, rules or regulations under this Act, other than an order or rule required to be laid before Parliament in draft or an order under section 132(5) below, shall be subject to annulment in pursuance of a resolution of either House of Parliament.

(3)   Any Order in Council or order under any provision of this Act may be varied or revoked by a subsequent order.

Use of electronic communications

124A.—(1)   **The comptroller may [*make*] give directions as to the form and manner in which documents to be delivered to the comptroller—**　　AppA-124A
  (a)   in electronic form; or
  (b)   using electronic communications, are to be delivered to him.

(2)   **A direction under subsection (1) may provide that in order for a document to be delivered in compliance with the direction it shall be accompanied by one or more additional documents specified in the direction.**

(3)   **[*If a document to which a direction under subsection (1)*] Subject to subsections (14) and (15), if a document to which a direction under subsection (1) or (2) applies is delivered to the comptroller in a form or manner which does not comply with the direction the comptroller may treat the document as not having been delivered.**

(4)   **Subsection (5) applies in relation to a case where—**
  (a)   a document is delivered using electronic communications, and

(b) there is a requirement for a fee to accompany the document.

(5) The comptroller may [*make*] give directions specifying—

(a) how the fee shall be paid; and

(b) when the fee shall be deemed to have been paid.

(6) The comptroller may [*make*] give directions specifying that a person who delivers a document to the comptroller in electronic form or using electronic communications cannot treat the document as having been delivered unless its delivery has been acknowledged.

(7) The comptroller may [*make*] give directions specifying how a time of delivery is to be accorded to a document delivered to him in electronic form or using electronic communications.

(8) A direction under this section may be given—

(a) generally;

(b) in relation to a description of cases specified in the direction;

(c) in relation to a particular person or persons.

[(9) In a case falling within subsection (8)(a) or (b), the direction must be published in such manner as the comptroller considers appropriate for the purpose of bringing it to the attention of the persons affected by it.

(10) In a case falling within subsection (8)(c), the direction must be notified to that person or those persons in such manner as may be agreed between that person or those persons and the comptroller.]

(11) A direction under this section may be varied or revoked by a subsequent direction under this section.

[(12) A direction under this section may include incidental, supplementary, saving and transitional provisions.

(13) Where the comptroller delivers a document using electronic communications then, unless the contrary intention has been specified by the comptroller, the delivery is deemed to be effected by the comptroller properly addressing and transmitting the electronic communication.

(14) Where the comptroller makes a direction under this section which applies in addition to or in place of rules, to the extent that the direction applies—

(a) "prescribed" in this Act includes prescribed by the direction;

(b) references in this Act to compliance with rules or requirements of rules include compliance with the direction or requirements of the direction.

(15) In this section—

(a) references to a document include anything that is or may be embodied in paper form;

(b) references to delivery to the comptroller include delivery at, in, with or to the Patent Office;

(c) references to delivery by the comptroller include delivery by the Patent Office; and cognate expressions must be construed accordingly.]

(13) The delivery using electronic communications to any person by the comptroller of any document is deemed to be effected, unless the comptroller has otherwise specified, by transmitting an electronic communication containing the document to an address provided or made available to the comptroller by that person as an address of his for the receipt of electronic communications; and unless the contrary is proved such delivery is deemed to be effected immediately upon the transmission of the communication.

(14) A requirement of this Act that something must be done in the prescribed manner is satisfied in the case of something that is done—

    (a)   using a document in electronic form, or

    (b)   using electronic communications, only if the directions under this section that apply to the manner in which it is done are complied with.

(15) In the case of an application made as mentioned in subsection (14)(a) or (b) above, a reference in this Act to the application not having been made in compliance with rules or requirements of this Act includes a reference to its not having been made in compliance with any applicable directions under this section.

(16) This section applies—

    (a)   to delivery at, in, with or to the Patent Office as it applies to delivery to the comptroller; and

    (b)   to delivery by the Patent Office as it applies to delivery by the comptroller.

Notes

Section 124A inserted by Patents Act 1977 (Electronic Communications) Order 2003 (SI 2003/512) art.2.

Subsections (1), (3), (5), (6), (7) amended, subsections (9), (10), (12) repealed, and subsections (13) to (15) substituted by Registered Designs Act 1949 and Patents Act 1977 (Electronic Communications) Order 2006 (SI 2006/1229), with effect from 1 October 2006.

Extent of invention

125.—(1) For the purposes of this Act an invention for a patent for which an application has been made or for which a patent has been granted shall, unless the context otherwise requires, be taken to be that specified in a claim of the specification of the application or patent, as the case may be, as interpreted by the description and any drawings contained in that specification, and the extent of the protection conferred by a patent or application for a patent shall be determined accordingly.   **AppA-125**

(2) It is hereby declared for the avoidance of doubt that where more than one invention is specified in any such claim, each invention may have a different priority date under section 5 above.

(3) The Protocol on the Interpretation of Article 69 of the European Patent Convention (which Article contains a provision corresponding to subsection (1) above) shall, as for the time being in force, apply for the purposes of subsection (1) above as it applies for the purposes of that Article.

Disclosure of invention by specification: availability of samples of [micro-organisms] biological material

125A.—(1) Provision may be made by rules prescribing the circumstances in which the specification of an application for a patent, or of a patent, for an invention which [*requires for its performance the use of a micro-organism*] involves the use of or concerns biological material is to be treated as disclosing the invention in a manner which is clear enough and complete enough for the invention to be performed by a person skilled in the art.   **AppA-125A**

(2) The rules may in particular require the applicant or patentee—

(a) to take such steps as may be prescribed for the purposes of making available to the public samples of the [*micro-organism*] biological material, and

(b) not to impose or maintain restrictions on the uses to which such samples may be put, except as may be prescribed.

(3) The rules may provide that, in such cases as may be prescribed, samples need only be made available to such persons or descriptions of persons as may be prescribed; and the rules may identify a description of persons by reference to whether the comptroller has given his certificate as to any matter.

(4) An application for revocation of the patent under section 72(1)(c) above may be made if any of the requirements of the rules cease to be complied with.

Notes

Section 125A inserted by CDPA 1988 (c.48) s.295 and CSch.5 para.30, with effect from 7 January 1991, SI 1990/2168.

Provision heading and subss.(1) and (2) amended by Patents Regulations 2000 (SI 2000/2037) reg.6, with effect from 28 July 2000, subject to transitional provisions contained in reg.9 which provide that the amendments apply to applications for patents made on or after that date (and to patents granted in pursuance of such applications).

[Stamp duty

AppA-126

126.—(1) An instrument relating to a Community patent or to an application for a European patent shall not be chargeable with stamp duty by reason only of all or any of the provisions of the Community Patent Convention mentioned in subsection (2) below.

(2) The said provisions are—

(a) Article 2.2 (Community patent and application for European patent in which the contracting states are designated to have effect throughout the territories to which the Convention applies);

(b) Article 39.1(c) (Community patent treated as national patent of contracting state in which applicant's representative has place of business);

(c) Article 39.1(c) as applied by Article 44 to an application for a European patent in which the contracting states are designated.]

Note

Section 126 repealed by Finance Act 2000 (c.17) s.156, Sch.40 Pt III, with effect in relation to instruments executed on or after 28 March 2000.

Existing patents and applications

AppA-127

127.—(1) No application for a patent may be made under the 1949 Act on or after the appointed day.

(2) Schedule 1 to this Act shall have effect for securing that certain provisions of the 1949 Act shall continue to apply on and after the appointed day to—

(a) a patent granted before that day;

(b) an application for a patent which is filed before that day, and which is accompanied by a complete specification or in respect of which a complete specification is filed before that day;

(c) a patent granted in pursuance of such an application.

(3)   Schedule 2 to this Act shall have effect for securing that (subject to the provisions of that Schedule) certain provisions of this Act shall apply on and after the appointed day to any patent and application to which subsection (2) above relates, but, except as provided by the following provisions of this Act, this Act shall not apply to any such patent or application.

(4)   An application for a patent which is made before the appointed day, but which does not comply with subsection (2)(b) above, shall be taken to have been abandoned immediately before that day, but, notwithstanding anything in section 5(3) above, the application may nevertheless serve to establish a priority date in relation to a later application for a patent under this Act if the date of filing the abandoned application falls within the period of fifteen months immediately preceding the filing of the later application.

(5)   Schedule 3 to this Act shall have effect for repealing certain provisions of the 1949 Act.

(6)   The transitional provisions and savings in Schedule 4 to this Act shall have effect.

(7)   In Schedules 1 to 4 to this Act "existing patent" means a patent mentioned in subsection (2)(a) and (c) above, "existing application" means an application mentioned in subsection (2)(b) above, and expressions used in the 1949 Act and those Schedules have the same meanings in those Schedules as in that Act.

Priorities between patents and applications under 1949 Act and this Act

128.—(1)   The following provisions of this section shall have effect for the purpose of resolving questions of priority arising between patents and applications for patents under the 1949 Act and patents and applications for patents under this Act.

AppA-128

(2)   A complete specification under the 1949 Act shall be treated for the purposes of sections 2(3) and 5(2) above—

  (a)   if published under that Act, as a published application for a patent under this Act;

  (b)   if it has a date of filing under that Act, as an application for a patent under this Act which has a date of filing under this Act; and in the said section 2(3), as it applies by virtue of this subsection in relation to any such specification, the words "both as filed and" shall be omitted.

(3)   In section 8(1), (2) and (4) of the 1949 Act (search for anticipation by prior claim) the references to any claim of a complete specification, other than the applicant's, published and filed as mentioned in section 8(1) shall include references to any claim contained in an application made and published under this Act or in the specification of a patent granted under this Act, being a claim in respect of an invention having a priority date earlier than the date of filing the complete specification under the 1949 Act.

(4)   In section 32(1)(a) of the 1949 Act (which specifies, as one of the grounds of revoking a patent, that the invention was claimed in a valid claim of earlier priority date contained in the complete specification of another patent), the reference to such a claim shall include a reference to a claim contained in the specification of a patent granted under this Act (a new claim) which satisfies the following conditions-

  (a)   the new claim must be in respect of an invention having an earlier priority date than that of the relevant claim of the complete specification of the patent sought to be revoked; and

(b)   the patent containing the new claim must be wholly valid or be valid in those respects which have a bearing on that relevant claim.

(5)   For the purposes of this section and the provisions of the 1949 Act mentioned in this section the date of filing an application for a patent under that Act and the priority date of a claim of a complete specification under that Act shall be determined in accordance with the provisions of that Act, and the priority date for an invention which is the subject of a patent or application for a patent under this Act shall be determined in accordance with the provisions of this Act.

EU compulsory licences

AppA-1
28A

128A.—(1)   In this Act an "EU compulsory licence" means a compulsory licence granted under Regulation (EC) No 816/2006 of the European Parliament and of the Council of 17 May 2006 on compulsory licensing of patents relating to the manufacture of pharmaceutical products for export to countries with public health problems (referred to in this Act as "the Compulsory Licensing Regulation").

(2)   In the application to EU compulsory licences of the provisions of this Act listed in subsection (3)—

(a)   references to a licence under a patent,

(b)   references to a right under a patent, and

(c)   references to a proprietary interest under a patent, include an EU compulsory licence.

(3)   The provisions referred to in subsection (2) are—

sections 32 and 33 (registration of patents etc);

section 37 (determination of right to patent after grant);

section 38 (effect of transfer etc of patent under section 37), apart from subsection (2) and subsections (3) to (5) so far as relating to subsection (2);

section 41 (amount of compensation);

section 46(2) (notice of application for entry that licences are available as of right);

section 57(1) and (2) (rights of third parties in respect of Crown use).

(4)   In the following provisions references to this Act include the Compulsory Licensing Regulation—

sections 97 to 99B, 101 to 103, 105 and 107 (legal proceedings);

section 119 (service by post);

section 120 (hours of business and excluded days);

section 121 (comptroller's annual report);

section 123 (rules);

section 124A (use of electronic communications);

section 130(8) (disapplication of Part 1 of Arbitration Act 1996).

(5)   In section 108 (licences granted by order of comptroller) the reference to a licence under section 11, 38, 48 or 49 includes an EU compulsory licence.

(6)   References in this Act to the Compulsory Licensing Regulation are to that Regulation as amended from time to time.

Notes

Section 128A inserted by the Patents (Compulsory Licensing and Supplementary Protection Certificates) Regulations 2007 (SI 2007/3293) reg.2(1), with effect from 17 December 2007.

Regulation (EC) No 816/2006 of the European Parliament and of the Council of 17 May 2006 on compulsory licensing of patents relating to the manufacture of pharmaceutical products for export to countries with public health problems, see [2006] O.J. L157/1.

Supplementary protection certificates

128B.—(1) Schedule 4A contains provision about the application of this Act in relation to supplementary protection certificates and other provision about such certificates. AppA-128B

(2) In this Act a "supplementary protection certificate" means a certificate issued under—

    (a) Regulation (EC) No 469/2009 of the European Parliament and of the Council of 6th May 2009 concerning the supplementary protection certificate for medicinal products [*Council Regulation (EEC) No 1768/92 of 18 June 1992 concerning the creation of a supplementary protection certificate for medicinal products,*] **or**

    (b) Regulation (EC) No 1610/96 of the European Parliament and of the Council of 23 July 1996 concerning the creation of a supplementary protection certificate for plant protection products.

Notes

Section 128B inserted by the Patents (Compulsory Licensing and Supplementary Protection Certificates) Regulations 2007 (SI 2007/3293) reg.2(2), with effect from 17 December 2007.

Council Regulation (EEC) No 1768/92 of 18 June 1992 concerning the creation of a supplementary protection certificate for medicinal products, see [1992] O.J. L182/1.

Regulation (EC) No 1610/96 of the European Parliament and of the Council of 23 July 1996 concerning the creation of a supplementary protection certificate for plant protection products, see [1996] O.J. L198/30.

Subsection (2)(a) amended by Patents (Supplementary Protection Certificates) Regulations 2014/2411 reg.2(2) with effect from 1 October 2014.

Application of Act to Crown

129. This Act does not affect Her Majesty in her private capacity but, subject to that, it binds the Crown. AppA-129

Interpretation

130.—(1) In this Act, except so far as the context otherwise requires— AppA-130

    "application fee" means the fee prescribed for the purposes of section 14(1A) above;

    "application for a European patent (UK)" and **(subject to subsection (4A) below)** "international application for a patent (UK)" each mean an application of the relevant description which, on its date of filing, designates the United Kingdom;

    "appointed day", in any provision of this Act, means the day appointed under section 132 below for the coming into operation of that provision;

    "biological material" means any material containing genetic information and capable of reproducing itself or being reproduced in a biological system;

    "biotechnological invention" means an invention which concerns a product consisting of or containing biological material or a process by means of which biological material is produced, processed or used;

"Community Patent Convention" means the Convention for the European Patent for the Common Market [*and "Community patent" means a patent granted under that convention*];

"comptroller" means the Comptroller-General of Patents, Designs and Trade Marks;

"Convention on International Exhibitions" means the Convention relating to International Exhibitions signed in Paris on 22nd November 1928, as amended or supplemented by any protocol to that convention which is for the time being in force;

"court" means

[*(a) as respects England and Wales, the High Court;*]

(a) **as respects England and Wales, the High Court** [*or any patents county court having jurisdiction by virtue of an order under section 287 of the Copyright, Designs and Patents Act 1988*].

(b) as respects Scotland, the Court of Session;

(c) as respects Northern Ireland, the High Court in Northern Ireland;

"date of filing" means—

(a) in relation to an application for a patent made under this Act, the date which is the date of filing that application by virtue of section 15 above; and

(b) in relation to any other application the date which, under the law of the country where the application was made or in accordance with the terms of a treaty or convention to which that country is a party, is to be treated as the date of filing that application or is equivalent to the date of filing an application in that country (whatever the outcome of the application);

"designate" in relation to an application or a patent, means designate the country or countries (in pursuance of the European Patent Convention or the Patent Co-operation Treaty) in which protection is sought for the invention which is the subject of the application or patent **and includes a reference to a country being treated as designated in pursuance of the convention or treaty**;

"electronic communication" has the same meaning as in the Electronic Communications Act 2000;

"employee" means a person who works or (where the employment has ceased) worked under a contract of employment or in employment under or for the purposes of a government department **or a person who serves (or served) in the naval, military or air forces of the Crown;**

"employer", in relation to an employee, means the person by whom the employee is or was employed;

"European Patent Convention" means the Convention on the Grant of European Patents, "European patent" means a patent granted under that convention, "European patent (UK)" means a European patent designating the United Kingdom, "European Patent Bulletin" means the bulletin of that name published under that convention, and "European Patent Office" means the office of that name established by that convention;

"exclusive licence" means a licence from the proprietor of or applicant for a patent conferring on the licensee, or on him and persons authorised by him, to the exclusion of all other persons (including the proprietor or applicant), any right in respect of the invention to which the patent or application relates, and

"exclusive licensee" and "non-exclusive licence" shall be construed accordingly;

["filing fee" means the fee prescribed for the purposes of section 14 above;]

"formal requirements" means those requirements designated as such by rules made for the purposes of [*section 17*] **section 15A** above;

"international application for a patent" means an application made under the Patent Co-operation Treaty;

"International Bureau" means the secretariat of the World Intellectual Property Organisation established by a convention signed at Stockholm on 14th July 1967;

"international exhibition" means an official or officially recognised international exhibition falling within the terms of the Convention of International Exhibitions or falling within the terms of any subsequent treaty or convention replacing that convention;

"inventor" has the meaning assigned to it by section 7 above;

"journal" has the meaning assigned to it by section 123(6) above; "mortgage" when used as a noun, includes a charge for securing money or money's worth and, when used as a verb, shall be construed accordingly;

"1949 Act" means the Patents Act 1949;

"patent" means a patent under this Act;

["patent agent" means a person carrying on for gain in the United Kingdom the business of acting as agent for other persons for the purpose of applying for or obtaining patents (other than Europeanpatents) in the United Kingdom or elsewhere or for the purpose of conducting proceedings in connection with such patents before the comptroller—

> *(a)   in relation to applications for, or otherwise in connection with, such patents, or*
>
> *(b)   in connection with European patents (UK) to which section 77(1) above for the time being applies;]*

"Patent Co-operation Treaty" means the treaty of that name signed at Washington on 19th June 1970;

"patented invention" means an invention for which a patent is granted and "patented process" shall be construed accordingly;

"patented product" means a product which is a patented invention or, in relation to a patented process, a product obtained directly by means of the process or to which the process has been applied;

"prescribed" and "rules" have the meanings assigned to them by section 123 above;

"priority date" means the date determined as such under section 5 above;

"published" means made available to the public (whether in the United Kingdom or elsewhere) and a document shall be taken to be published under any provision of this Act if it can be inspected as of right at any place in the United Kingdom by members of the public, whether on payment of a fee or not; and

"republished" shall be construed accordingly;

"register" and cognate expressions have the meanings assigned to them by section 32 above;

"relevant convention court", in relation to any proceedings under the European Patent Convention, [*the Community Patent Convention*] or the Patent Co-operation Treaty, means that court or other body which under that convention or treaty has jurisdiction over those proceedings, including (where it has such jurisdiction) any department of the European Patent Office;

"right", in relation to any patent or application, includes an interest in the patent or application and, without prejudice to the foregoing, any reference to a right in a patent includes a reference to a share in the patent;

"search fee" means the fee prescribed for the purposes of [*section 17 above*] **section 17(1) above**;

"services of the Crown" and "use for the services of the Crown" have the meanings assigned to them by section 56(2) above, including, as respects any period of emergency within the meaning of section 59 above, the meanings assigned to them by the said section 59.

(2) Rules may provide for stating in the journal that an exhibition falls within the definition of international exhibition in subsection (1) above and any such statement shall be conclusive evidence that the exhibition falls within that definition.

(3) For the purposes of this Act matter shall be taken to have been disclosed in any relevant application within the meaning of section 5 above or in the specification of a patent if it was either claimed or disclosed (otherwise than by way of disclaimer or acknowledgment of prior art) in that application or specification.

(4) References in this Act to an application for a patent, as filed, are references to such an application in the state it was on the date of filing.

(4A) An international application for a patent is not, by reason of being treated by virtue of the European Patent Convention as an application for a European patent (UK), to be treated also as an international application for a patent (UK).

(5) References in this Act to an application for a patent being published are references to its being published under section 16 above.

(5A) References in this Act to the amendment of a patent or its specification (whether under this Act or by the European Patent Office) include, in particular, limitation of the claims (as interpreted by the description and any drawings referred to in the description or claims).

(6) References in this Act to any of the following conventions, that is to say—

(a) The European Patent Convention;

(b) The Community Patent Convention;

(c) The Patent Co-operation Treaty;

are references to that convention or any other international convention or agreement replacing it, as amended or supplemented by any convention or international agreement (including in either case any protocol or annex), or in accordance with the terms of any such convention or agreement, and include references to any instrument made under any such convention or agreement.

(7) Whereas by a resolution made, on the signature of the Community Patent Convention the governments of the member states of the European Economic Community resolved to adjust their laws relating to patents so as (among other things) to bring those laws into conformity with the corresponding provisions of the European Patent Convention, the Community Patent Convention and the Patent Co-operation Treaty, it is hereby declared that the following provisions of this Act, that is to say, sections 1(1) to (4), 2 to 6, 14(3), (5) and (6), 37(5), 54, 60, 69, 72(1) and (2), 74(4), 82, 83, [*88(6)* and (7),] 100 and 125, are so framed as to have, as nearly as practicable, the same effects in the United Kingdom as the corresponding provisions of the European Patent Convention, the Community Patent Convention and

the Patent Co-operation Treaty have in the territories to which those Conventions apply.

(8) [*The Arbitration Act 1950*] **Nothing in any of sections 1 to 15 of and schedule 1 to the Arbitration (Scotland) Act 2010 or Part I of the Arbitration Act 1996 applies** [*shall not apply*] to any proceedings before the comptroller under this Act.

(9) Except so far as the context otherwise requires, any reference in this Act to any enactment shall be construed as a reference to that enactment as amended or extended by or under any other enactment, including this Act.

Notes

Subsection (1) amended as follows: definition "application fee" inserted by Regulatory Reform (Patents) Order 2004 (SI 2004/2357) art.19, with effect from 1 January 2005, subject to transitional provisions contained in arts 20–23 of that Order; definitions "application for a European Patent (UK)" and "international application for a patent (UK)" amended by Patents Act 2004 (c.16) s.5 and Sch.1 para.9(2)(a), with effect from 1 January 2005, SI 2004/3205; definitions "biological material" and "biotechnological invention" inserted by Patents Regulations 2000 (SI 2000/2037) reg.7, with effect from 28 July 2000, subject to transitional provisions contained in reg.9 which provide that the amendments apply to applications for patents made on or after that date (and to patents granted in pursuance of such applications); definition "Community patent" repealed by Patents Act 2004 (c.16) s.16 and Sch.2 para.27(a), Sch.3, with effect from 1 January 2005, SI 2004/3205; definition "court" amended by CDPA 1988 (c.48) s.303(1) and Sch.7 para.23, with effect from 1 August 1989, SI 1989/816; definition of "court" amended again by Crime and Courts Act 2013 c.22 Sch.9(2) para.27 with effect from 1 October 2013 subject to savings and transitional provisions; definition "designate" amended for the purposes of the Patent Co-operation Treaty only by Patents Act 2004 (c.16) s.5 and Sch.1 para.9(2)(b), with effect from 1 January 2005, SI 2004/3205 and for the purposes of the European Patent Convention by Patents Act 2004 (c.16) s.5 and Sch.1 para.9(2)(b), with effect from 13 December 2007, SI 2007/3396; definition "electronic communication" inserted by Patents Act 1977 (Electronic Communications) Order 2003 (SI 2003/512) art.3, definition "employee" amended by Armed Forces Act 1981 (c.55) s.22, definition "filing fee" repealed by Regulatory Reform (Patents) Order 2004 (SI 2004/2357) art.19, with effect from 1 January 2005, subject to transitional provisions contained in arts 20–23 of that Order; definition "formal requirements" amended by Intellectual Property (Enforcement, etc) Regulations 2006 (SI 2006/1028) reg.2(2), Sch.2 para.5(1), with effect from 29 April 2006, subject to Sch.2 para.5(2) which provides that the amendment does not apply to an application for a patent to which arts 20, 21 or 22 of Regulatory Reform (Patents) Order 2004 applies (SI 2004/2357); definition "patent agent" repealed by CDPA 1988 (c.48) s.303(2) and Sch.8, with effect from 13 August 1990, SI 1990/1400; definition "relevant convention court" amended by Patents Act 2004 (c.16) s.16 and Sch.2 para.27(b), Sch.3, with effect from 1 January 2005, SI 2004/3205; definition "search fee" amended by CDPA 1988 (c.48) s.295 and Sch.5 para.5, with effect from 7 January 1991, SI 1990/2168.

Subsection (4A) inserted by Patents Act 2004 (c.16) s.16 and Sch.1 para.9(3), with effect from 1 January 2005, SI 2004/3205.

Subsection (5A) inserted by Patents Act 2004 (c.16) s.16 and Sch.1 para.9(4), with effect from 13 December 2007, SI 2007/3396.

Subsection (7) amended by CDPA 1988 (c.48) s.303(2) and Sch.8, with effect from 1 August 1989, SI 1989/816.

Subsection (8) amended by Arbitration Act 1996 (c.23) s.107(1) and Sch.3 para.33.

Subsection (8) amended by Arbitration (Scotland) Act 2010 (Consequential Amendments) Order (SI 2010/220) Sch.1 para.5 with effect from 5 June 2010.

Northern Ireland

131. In the application of this Act to Northern Ireland— AppA-13
  (a) "enactment" includes an enactment of the Parliament of Northern Ireland and a Measure of the Northern Ireland Assembly;
  (b) any reference to a government department includes a reference to a Department of the Government of Northern Ireland;
  (c) any reference to the Crown includes a reference to the Crown in right of Her Majesty's Government in Northern Ireland;

(d) any reference to the [*Companies Act 1948*] **Companies Act 1985** includes a reference to the corresponding enactments in force in Northern Ireland; and

[*(e) the Arbitration Act (Northern Ireland) 1937 shall apply in relation to an arbitration in pursuance of this Act as if this Act related to a matter in respect of which the Parliament of Northern Ireland had power to make laws.*]

(f) **any reference to a claimant includes a reference to a plaintiff.**

Notes

Subsection (d) amended by Companies Consolidation (Consequential Provisions) Act 1985 (c.9) s.30 and Sch.2 para.1.

Subsection (e) repealed by Arbitration Act 1996 (c.23) s.107(2) and Sch.4.

Paragraph (f) inserted by Patents Act 2004 (c.16) s.16 and Sch.2 para.28, with effect from 1 January 2005, SI 2004/3205.

Scotland

AppA-1
31A

131A. In the application of this Act to Scotland—

(a) **"enactment" includes an enactment comprised in, or in an instrument made under, an Act of the Scottish Parliament;**

(b) **any reference to a government department includes a reference to any part of the Scottish Administration; and**

(c) **any reference to the Crown includes a reference to the Crown in right of the Scottish Administration.**

Note

Section 131A inserted by Scotland Act 1998 (Consequential Modifications) (No.2) Order 1999 (SI 1999/1820) art.4 and Sch.2 para.58.

Short title, extent, commencement, consequential amendments and repeals

AppA-
132

132.—(1) This Act may be cited as the Patents Act 1977.

(2) This Act shall extend to the Isle of Man, subject to any modifications contained in an Order made by Her Majesty in Council, and accordingly, subject to any such order, references in this Act to the United Kingdom shall be construed as including references to the Isle of Man.

(3) For the purposes of this Act the territorial waters of the United Kingdom shall be treated as part of the United Kingdom.

(4) This Act applies to acts done in an area designated by order under section 1(7) of the Continental Shelf Act 1964, [*in connection with the exploration of the sea bed or subsoil or exploitation of their natural resources*], **or specified by Order under** [*section 22(5) of the Oil and Gas (Enterprise) Act 1982*] **section 10(8) of the Petroleum Act 1998 in connection with any activity falling within** [*section 23(2)*] **section 11(2) of that Act**, as it applies to acts done in the United Kingdom.

(5) This Act (except sections 77(6), (7) and (9), 78(7) and (8), this subsection and the repeal of section 41 of the 1949 Act) shall come into operation on such day as may be appointed by the Secretary of State by order, and different days may be appointed under this subsection for different purposes.

(6) The consequential amendments in Schedule 5 shall have effect.

(7) Subject to the provisions of Schedule 4 to this Act, the enactments speci-

fied in Schedule 6 to this Act (which include certain enactments which were spent before the passing of this Act) are hereby repealed to the extent specified in column 3 of that Schedule.

Note

Subsection (4) amended by Oil and Gas (Enterprise) Act 1982 (c.23) Sch.3 para.39; Petroleum Act 1998 (c.26) s.50 and Sch.4 para.14, with effect from 15 February 1999, SI 1999/161.

SCHEDULES

[Schedules 1–4 are not reproduced here.]

SCHEDULE 4A

SUPPLEMENTARY PROTECTION CERTIFICATES

Reference to patents etc.

1.—(1) In the application to supplementary protection certificates of the provisions of this Act listed in sub-paragraph (2)—
- (a) references to a patent are to a supplementary protection certificate;
- (b) references to an application or the applicant for a patent are to an application or the applicant—
  - (i) for a supplementary protection certificate, or
  - (ii) for an extension of the duration of a supplementary protection certificate;
- (c) references to the proprietor of a patent are to the holder of a supplementary protection certificate;
- (d) references to the specification of a patent are to the text of a supplementary protection certificate;
- (e) references to a patented product or an invention (including a patented invention) are to a product for which a supplementary protection certificate has effect;
- (f) references to a patent having expired or having been revoked are to a supplementary protection certificate having lapsed or having been declared invalid;
- (g) references to proceedings for the revocation of a patent are to proceedings—
  - (i) for a decision that a supplementary protection certificate has lapsed, or
  - (ii) for a declaration that a supplementary protection certificate is invalid;
- (h) references to the issue of the validity of a patent include the issue of whether a supplementary protection certificate has lapsed or is invalid.

(2) The provisions referred to in sub-paragraph (1) are—
section 14(1), (9) and (10) (making of application);
section 19(1) (general power to amend application before grant);
sections 20A and 20B (reinstatement of applications);
section 21 (observations by third party on patentability);
section 27 (general power to amend specification after grant);
section 29 (surrender of patents);
sections 30 to 36, 37(1) to (3) and (5) to (9) and 38 (property in patents and applications, and registration);
sections 39 to 59 (employees' inventions, licences of right and compulsory licences and use of patented inventions for services of the Crown);
sections 60 to 71 (infringement);
section 74(1) and (7) (proceedings in which validity of patent may be put in issue);
section 74A and 74B (opinions by the Patent Office);
section 75 (amendment of patent in infringement or revocation proceedings);
sections 103 and 105 (privilege for communications relating to patent proceedings);
section 108 (licences granted by order of comptroller); sections 110 and 111 (unauthorised claim of patent rights or that patent has been applied for);
section 116 (immunity of department as regards official acts);
sections 117 to 118 (administrative provisions);
section 123 (rules); section 130 (interpretation).

2.—(1)   In the case of the provisions of this Act listed in sub-paragraph (2), paragraph 1 applies in relation to an application for a supplementary protection certificate only if the basic patent expires before the certificate is granted.

(2)   The provisions referred to in sub-paragraph (1) are—
section 20B(3) to (6A) (effect of reinstatement under section 20A); section 55(5) and (7) (use of patented inventions for services of the Crown);
section 58(10) (disputes as to Crown use); section 69 (infringement of rights conferred by publication of application); section 117A(3) to (7) (effect of resuscitating a withdrawn application under section 117).

References to this Act etc.

3. —(1)   In the provisions of this Act listed in sub-paragraph (2)—
    (a)   references to this Act include the Medicinal Products Regulation and the Plant Protection Products Regulation, and
    (b)   references to a provision of this Act include any equivalent provision of the Medicinal Products Regulation and the Plant Protection Products Regulation.

(2)   The provisions referred to in sub-paragraph (1) are—
sections 20A and 20B (reinstatement of applications);
section 21 (observations by third party on patentability);
section 69 (infringement of rights conferred by publication of application);
section 74(1) and (7) (proceedings in which validity of patent may be put in issue);
sections 97 to 99B, 101 to 103, 105 and 107 (legal proceedings);
section 116 (immunity of department as regards official acts);
sections 117 and 118 to 121 (administrative provisions);
section 122 (Crown's right to sell forfeited articles);
section 123 (rules);
section 124A (use of electronic communications); section 130 (interpretation).

Other references

4.—(1)   In the application of section 21(1) (observations by third party on patentability) to supplementary protection certificates, the reference to the question whether the invention is a patentable invention is to the question whether the product is one for which a supplementary protection certificate may have effect.

(2)   In the application of section 69(2) (conditions for infringement of rights conferred by publication of application) to supplementary protection certificates, the condition in paragraph (b) is that the act would, if the certificate had been granted on the date of the publication of the application, have infringed not only the certificate as granted but also the certificate for which the application was made.

Fees

5.   A supplementary protection certificate does not take effect unless—
    (a)   the prescribed fee is paid before the end of the prescribed period, or
    (b)   the prescribed fee and any prescribed additional fee are paid before the end of the period of six months beginning immediately after the prescribed period.

Interpretation

6.—(1)   Expressions used in this Act that are defined in the Medicinal Products Regulation or the Plant Protection Products Regulation have the same meaning as in that Regulation.

(2)   References in this Act to, or to a provision of, the Medicinal Products Regulation or the Plant Protection Products Regulation are to that Regulation or that provision as amended from time to time.

7.   In this Act—
    (a)   "the Medicinal Products Regulation" means Regulation (EC) No 469/2009 of the European Parliament and of the Council of 6th May 2009 concerning the supplementary protection certificate for medicinal products [*Council Regulation (EEC) No 1768/92 of 18 June 1992 concerning the creation of a supplementary protection certificate for medicinal products,*] **and**
    (b)   "the Plant Protection Products Regulation" means Regulation (EC) No 1610/96 of the European Parliament and of the Council of 23 July 1996 concerning the creation of a supplementary protection certificate for plant protection products.".

8.—(1)   A reference (express or implied) in this Act to the Medicinal Products Regulation, or a provision of it, is to be read as being or (subject to context) including a reference to the old Regulation, or the corresponding provision of the old Regulation, in relation to times, circumstances or purposes in relation to which the old Regulation, or that provision, had effect.

(2)   Other than in relation to times, circumstances or purposes referred to in subparagraph (1), anything done, or having effect as if done, under (or for the purposes of or in reliance on) the old Regulation or a provision of the old Regulation and in force or effective immediately before 1st October 2014 (the day on which the Patents (Supplementary Protection Certificates) Regulations 2014 came into force) has effect on or after that date for the purposes of this Act as if done under (or for the purpose of or in reliance on) the Medicinal Products Regulation or the corresponding provision of it.

(3)   In this paragraph "the old Regulation" means Council Regulation (EEC) No 1768/92 of 18th June 1992 concerning the creation of a supplementary protection certificate for medicinal products.

Notes

Schedule 4A inserted by the Patents (Compulsory Licensing and Supplementary Protection Certificates) Regulations 2007 (SI 2007/3293) Reg.2(3), with effect from 17 December 2007.

Council Regulation (EEC) No 1768/92 of 18 June 1992 concerning the creation of a supplementary protection certificate for medicinal products, see O.J. No L.182, 2.7.92, p.1.

Regulation (EC) No 1610/96 of the European Parliament and of the Council of 23 July 1996 concerning the creation of a supplementary protection certificate for plant protection products, see O.J. No L.198, 8.8.96, p.30.

Reference to s.74A and 74B inserted by Intellectual Property Act 2014 (c.18) Pt 2 s.16(3).

Paragraph 7 (a) amended by Patents (Supplementary Protection Certificates) Regulations (SI 2014/2411) reg.2(3)(a) with effect from 1 October 2014.

Paragraph 8 inserted by Patents (Supplementary Protection Certificates) Regulations (SI 2014/2411) reg.2(3)(b) with effect from 1 October 2014.

[Schedules 5 to 6 are not reproduced here.]

SCHEDULE A1

DEROGATION FROM PATENT PROTECTION IN RESPECT OF BIOTECHNOLOGICAL INVENTIONS

Section 60(5)(g)

Interpretation

1.—(1)   In this Schedule —   AppA-13

"Council Regulation" means Council Regulation (EC) No. 2100/94 of 27th July 1994 on Community plant variety rights;

"farmer's own holding" means any land which a farmer actually exploits for plant growing, whether as his property or otherwise managed under his own responsibility and on his own account;

"the gazette" means the gazette published under section 34 of the Plant Variety and Seeds Act 1964;

"protected material" means plant propagating material which incorporates material subject to a patent;

"relevant activity" means the use by a farmer of the product of his harvest for propagation or multiplication by him on his own holding, where the product of the harvest constitutes or contains protected material;

"relevant rights holder" means the proprietor of a patent to which protected material is subject; "seed" includes seed potatoes;

"seed year" means the period from 1st July in one year to 30th June in the following year, both dates inclusive.

PATENTS ACT 1977

Specified species

2. Section 60(5)(g) applies only to varieties of the following plant species and groups:

Name	Common Name
Fodder plants	
Cicer *arietinum* L.	Chickpea milkvetch.
Lupinus luteus L.	Yellow lupin
Medicago sativa L.	Lucerne
Pisum sativum L. (partim)	Field pea
Trifolium alexandrinum L.	Berseem/Egyptian clover
Trifolium resupinatum L.	Persian clover
Vicia faba	Field bean
Vicia sativa L.	Common vetch
Cereals	Oats
Avena sativa	Oats
Hordeum vulgare L.	Barley
Oryza sativa L.	Rice
Phalaris canariensis L.	Canary grass
Secale cereale L.	Rye
X *Triticosecale* Wittm.	Triticale
Triticum aestivum L. emend. Fiori et Paol	
Triticum durum Desf.	Durum wheat
Triticum spelta L.	Spelt wheat
Potatoes	
Solanum tuberosum	Potatoes
Oil and fibre plants	
Brassica napus L. (partim)	Swede rape
Brassica rapa L. (partim)	Turnip rape
Linum usitatissimum	Linseed with the exclusion of flax

Liability to pay equitable remuneration

3.—(1) If a farmer's use of protected material is authorised by section 60(5)(g), he shall, at the time of the use, become liable to pay the relevant rights holder equitable remuneration.

(2) That remuneration must be sensibly lower than the amount charged for the production of protected material of the same variety in the same area with the holder's authority.

(3) Remuneration is to be taken to be sensibly lower if it would be taken to be sensibly lower within the meaning of Article 14(3) fourth indent of the Council Regulation.

Exemption for small farmers

4.—(1) Paragraph 3 does not apply to a farmer who is considered to be a small farmer for the purposes of Article 14(3) third indent of the Council Regulation.

(2) It is for a farmer who claims to be a small farmer to prove that he is such a farmer.

Information to be supplied by farmer

5.—(1) At the request of a relevant rights holder ("H"), a farmer must tell H—
   (a) his name and address;
   (b) whether he has performed a relevant activity; and

[1038]

(c)   if he has performed such an activity, the address of the holding on which he performed it.

(2)   If the farmer has performed such an activity, he must tell H whether he is—
    (a)   liable to pay remuneration as a result of paragraph 3; or
    (b)   not liable because he is a small farmer.

(3)   If the farmer has told H that he is liable to pay remuneration as a result of paragraph 3, he must tell H—
    (a)   the amount of the protected material used;
    (b)   whether the protected material has been processed for planting; and
    (c)   if it has, the name and address of the person who processed it.

(4)   The farmer must comply with sub-paragraphs (2) and (3) when complying with sub-paragraph (1).

(5)   If the farmer has told H that he is liable to pay remuneration as a result of paragraph 3, he must (if H asks him to do so) tell H—
    (a)   whether he used any protected material with the authority of H within the same seed year; and
    (b)   if he did, the amount used and the name and address of the person who supplied it.

Information to be supplied by seed processor

6.—(1)   On the request of a relevant rights holder, a seed processor shall supply the following information—
    (a)   the name and address of the seed processor;
    (b)   the address of the seed processor's principal place of business; and
    (c)   whether the seed processor has processed seed of a species specified in paragraph 2 above.

(2)   If the seed processor has processed seed of a species specified in paragraph 2 above he shall also supply the following information with the information referred to in sub-paragraph (1)—
    (a)   the name and address of the person for whom the processing was carried out;
    (b)   the amount of seed resulting from the processing;
    (c)   the date processing commenced;
    (d)   the date processing was completed;
    (e)   the place where processing was carried out.

Information to be supplied by relevant rights holder

7.   On the request of a farmer or a seed processor a relevant rights holder shall supply the following information—
    (a)   his name and address; and
    (b)   the amount of royalty charged for certified seed of the lowest certification category for seed containing that protected material.

Period in respect of which inquiry may be made

8.   A request may be made under paragraphs 5, 6 and 7 in respect of the current seed year and the three preceding seed years.

Restriction on movement for processing from the holding

9.   No person shall remove or cause to be removed from a holding protected material in order to process it unless—
    (a)   he has the permission of the relevant rights holder in respect of that protected material;
    (b)   he has taken measures to ensure that the same protected material is returned from processing as is sent for processing and the processor has undertaken to him that the processor has taken measures to ensure that the same protected material is returned from processing as is sent for processing; or
    (c)   he has the protected material processed by a seed processor on the list of processors referred to in the gazette as being permitted to process seed away from a holding.

Confidentiality

10.—(1)   A person who obtains information pursuant to this Schedule shall owe an obligation of confidence in respect of the information to the person who supplied it.

(2)   Sub-paragraph (1) shall not have effect to restrict disclosure of information—

(a) for the purposes of, or in connection with, establishing the amount to be paid to the holder of rights pursuant to paragraph 3 and obtaining payment of that amount,

(b) for the purposes of, or in connection with, establishing whether a patent has been infringed, or

(c) for the purposes of, or in connection with, any proceedings for the infringement of a patent.

Formalities

11.—(1) A request for information under this Schedule, and any information given in response to such a request, must be in writing.

(2) Information requested under this Schedule must be given—

(a) within 28 days; or

(b) if the request specifies a longer period, within the specified period.

Remedies

12.—(1) If, in response to a request under this Schedule, a person—

(a) knowingly fails to provide information which he is required by this Schedule to give, or

(b) refuses to provide any such information, the court may order him to provide it.

(2) Sub-paragraph (1) does not affect any of the court's other powers to make orders.

(3) A person who knowingly provides false information in response to a request under this Schedule is liable in damages to the person who made the request.

(4) In any action for damages under sub-paragraph (3) the court must have regard, in particular to—

(a) how flagrant the defendant was in providing the false information, and

(b) any benefit which accrued to him as a result of his providing false information, and shall award such additional damages as the justice of the case may require.

SCHEDULE A2

BIOTECHNOLOGICAL INVENTIONS

Section 76(a)

AppA-135

1. An invention shall not be considered unpatentable solely on the ground that it concerns—

(a) a product consisting of or containing biological material; or

(b) a process by which biological material is produced, processed or used.

2. Biological material which is isolated from its natural environment or produced by means of a technical process may be the subject of an invention even if it previously occurred in nature.

3. The following are not patentable inventions—

(a) the human body, at the various stages of its formation and development, and the simple discovery of one of its elements, including the sequence or partial sequence of a gene;

(b) processes for cloning human beings;

(c) processes for modifying the germ line genetic identity of human beings;

(d) uses of human embyos for industrial or commercial purposes;

(e) processes for modifying the genetic identity of animals which are likely to cause them suffering without any substantial medical benefit to man or animal, and also animals resulting from such processes;

(f) any variety of animal or plant or any essentially biological process for the production of animals or plants, not being a micro-biological or other technical process or the product of such a process.

4. Inventions which concern plants or animals may be patentable if the technical feasibility of the invention is not confined to a particular plant or animal variety.

5. An element isolated from the human body or otherwise produced by means of a technical process, including the sequence or partial sequence of a gene, may constitute a patentable invention, even if the structure of that element is identical to that of a natural element.

6. The industrial application of a sequence or partial sequence of a gene must be disclosed in the patent application as filed.

7. The protection conferred by a patent on a biological material possessing specific characteristics as a result of the invention shall extend to any biological material derived from that biological material through propagation or multiplication in an identical or divergent form and possessing those same characteristics.

8.   The protection conferred by a patent on a process that enables a biological material to be produced possessing specific characteristics as a result of the invention shall extend to biological material directly obtained through that process and to any other biological material derived from the directly obtained biological material through propagation or multiplication in an identical or divergent form and possessing those same characteristics.

9.   The protection conferred by a patent on a product containing or consisting of genetic information shall extend to all material, save as provided for in paragraph 3(a) above, in which the product is incorporated and in which the genetic information is contained and performs its function.

10.   The protection referred to in paragraphs 7, 8 and 9 above shall not extend to biological material obtained from the propagation or multiplication of biological material placed on the market by the proprietor of the patent or with his consent, where the multiplication or propagation necessarily results from the application for which thebiological material was marketed, provided that the material obtained is not subsequently used for other propagation or multiplication.

11.—(1)   In this Schedule:

"essentially biological process" means a process for the production of animals and plants which consists entirely of natural phenomena such as crossing and selection;

"microbiological process" means any process involving or performed upon or resulting in microbiological material;

"plant variety" means a plant grouping within a single botanical taxon of the lowest known rank, which grouping can be:

(a)   defined by the expression of the characteristics that results from a given genotype or combination of genotypes; and

(b)   distinguished from any other plant grouping by the expression of at least one of the said characteristics; and

(c)   considered as a unit with regard to its suitability for being propagated unchanged.

Note

Schedules A1 and A2 inserted by Patents Regulations 2000 (SI 2000/2037) reg.8 and Schs 1 and 2, with effect from 28 July 2000, subject to transitional provisions contained in reg.9 which provide that the amendments apply to applications for patents made on or after that date (and to patents granted in pursuance of such applications).

EUROPEAN PATENT CONVENTION (EXTRACTS)

Convention on the Grant of European Patents (European Patent Convention) of 5 October 1973 as revised by the Act revising Article 63 EPC of 17 December 1991 and the Act revising the EPC of 29 November 2000

PREAMBLE

The Contracting States,

DESIRING to strengthen co-operation between the States of Europe in respect of the protection of inventions,

DESIRING that such protection may be obtained in those States by a single procedure for the grant of patents and by the establishment of certain standard rules governing patents so granted,

DESIRING, for this purpose, to conclude a Convention which establishes a European Patent Organisation and which constitutes a special agreement within the meaning of Article 19 of the Convention for the Protection of Industrial Property, signed in Paris on 20 March 1883 and last revised on 14 July 1967, and a regional patent treaty within the meaning of Article 45, paragraph 1, of the Patent Cooperation Treaty of 19 June 1970,

HAVE AGREED on the following provisions:

PART I.

GENERAL AND INSTITUTIONAL PROVISIONS

CHAPTER I

GENERAL PROVISIONS

Article 1

European law for the grant of patents

AppB-01   A system of law, common to the Contracting States, for the grant of patents for invention is established by this Convention.

Article 2

European patent

AppB-02   **(1)**   Patents granted under this Convention shall be called European patents.

(2)   The European patent shall, in each of the Contracting States for which it is granted, have the effect of and be subject to the same conditions as a national patent granted by that State, unless this Convention provides otherwise.

Article 3

Territorial effect

The grant of a European patent may be requested for one or more of the Contracting States.

AppB-03

Article 4

European Patent Organisation

(1) A European Patent Organisation, hereinafter referred to as the Organisation,
is established by this Convention. It shall have administrative and financial
autonomy.
(2) The organs of the Organisation shall be:
  (a) the European Patent Office;
  (b) the Administrative Council.
(3) The task of the Organisation shall be to grant European patents. This shall be
carried out by the European Patent Office supervised by the Administrative Council.

AppB-04

Article 4a

Conference of ministers of the Contracting States

A conference of ministers of the Contracting States responsible for patent matters shall meet at least every five years to discuss issues pertaining to the Organisation and to the European patent system.

AppB-05

CHAPTER II

THE EUROPEAN PATENT ORGANISATION

[Articles 5–13 are not reproduced here.]

AppB-06

Article 14

Languages of the European Patent Office, European patent applications and other documents

(1) The official languages of the European Patent Office shall be English, French
and German.
(2) A European patent application shall be filed in one of the official languages
or, if filed in any other language, translated into one of the official languages in accordance with the Implementing Regulations. Throughout the proceedings before
the European Patent Office, such translation may be brought into conformity with
the application as filed. If a required translation is not filed in due time, the application shall be deemed to be withdrawn.
(3) The official language of the European Patent Office in which the European patent application is filed or into which it is translated shall be used as the language
of the proceedings in all proceedings before the European Patent Office, unless the
Implementing Regulations provide otherwise.
(4) Natural or legal persons having their residence or principal place of business
within a Contracting State having a language other than English, French or Ger-

AppB-07

man as an official language, and nationals of that State who are resident abroad, may file documents which have to be filed within a time limit in an official language of that State. They shall, however, file a translation in an official language of the European Patent Office in accordance with the Implementing Regulations. If any document, other than those documents making up the European patent application, is not filed in the prescribed language, or if any required translation is not filed in due time, the document shall be deemed not to have been filed.

(5) European patent applications shall be published in the language of the proceedings.

(6) Specifications of European patents shall be published in the language of the proceedings and shall include a translation of the claims in the other two official languages of the European Patent Office.

(7) The following shall be published in the three official languages of the European Patent Office:

    (a)   the European Patent Bulletin;

    (b)   the Official Journal of the European Patent Office.

(8) Entries in the European Patent Register shall be made in the three official languages of the European Patent Office. In cases of doubt, the entry in the language of the proceedings shall be authentic.

Article 15

Departments entrusted with the procedure

AppB-08   To carry out the procedures laid down in this Convention, the following shall be set up within the European Patent Office:

    (a)   a Receiving Section;

    (b)   Search Divisions;

    (c)   Examining Divisions;

    (d)   Opposition Divisions;

    (e)   a Legal Division;

    (f)   Boards of Appeal;

    (g)   an Enlarged Board of Appeal.

Article 16

Receiving Section

AppB-09   The Receiving Section shall be responsible for the examination on filing and the examination as to formal requirements of European patent applications.

Article 17

Search Divisions

AppB-10   The Search Divisions shall be responsible for drawing up European search reports.

Article 18
Examining Divisions

(1) The Examining Divisions shall be responsible for the examination of AppB-11
European patent applications.
(2) An Examining Division shall consist of three technically qualified examiners.
However, before a decision is taken on a European patent application, its examination shall, as a general rule, be entrusted to one member of the Examining Division.
Oral proceedings shall be before the Examining Division itself. If the Examining
Division considers that the nature of the decision so requires, it shall be enlarged
by the addition of a legally qualified examiner. In the event of parity of votes, the
vote of the Chairman of the Examining Division shall be decisive.

Article 19
Opposition Divisions

(1) The Opposition Divisions shall be responsible for the examination of opposi- AppB-12
tions against any European patent.
(2) An Opposition Division shall consist of three technically qualified examiners, at least two of whom shall not have taken part in the proceedings for grant of
the patent to which the opposition relates. An examiner who has taken part in the
proceedings for the grant of the European patent may not be the Chairman. Before
a decision is taken on the opposition, the Opposition Division may entrust the
examination of the opposition to one of its members. Oral proceedings shall be
before the Opposition Division itself. If the Opposition Division considers that the
nature of the decision so requires, it shall be enlarged by the addition of a legally
qualified examiner who shall not have taken part in the proceedings for grant of the
patent. In the event of parity of votes, the vote of the Chairman of the Opposition
Division shall be decisive.

Article 20
Legal Division

(1) The Legal Division shall be responsible for decisions in respect of entries in AppB-13
the Register of European Patents and in respect of registration on, and deletion from,
the list of professional representatives.
(2) Decisions of the Legal Division shall be taken by one legally qualified
member.

Article 21
Boards of Appeal

(1) The Boards of Appeal shall be responsible for the examination of appeals from AppB-14
decisions of the Receiving Section, the Examining Divisions and Opposition Divisions, and the Legal Division.
(2) For appeals from decisions of the Receiving Section or the Legal Division, a
Board of Appeal shall consist of three legally qualified members.
(3) For appeals from a decision of an Examining Division, a Board of Appeal
shall consist of:

    (a)   two technically qualified members and one legally qualified member, when the decision concerns the refusal of a European patent application or the grant, limitation or revocation of a European patent, and was taken by an Examining Division consisting of less than four members;

    (b)   three technically and two legally qualified members, when the decision was taken by an Examining Division consisting of four members, or when the Board of Appeal considers that the nature of the appeal so requires;

    (c)   three legally qualified members in all other cases.

(4)   For appeals from a decision of an Opposition Division, a Board of Appeal shall consist of:

    (a)   two technically qualified members and one legally qualified member, when the decision was taken by an Opposition Division consisting of three members;

    (b)   three technically and two legally qualified members, when the decision was taken by an Opposition Division consisting of four members, or when the Board of Appeal considers that the nature of the appeal so requires.

Article 22

Enlarged Board of Appeal

AppB-15 **(1)**   The Enlarged Board of Appeal shall be responsible for:

    (a)   deciding on points of law referred to it by Boards of Appeal under Article 112;

    (b)   giving opinions on points of law referred to it by the President of the European Patent Office under Article 112;

    (c)   deciding on petitions for review of decisions of the Boards of Appeal under Article 112a.

(2)   In proceedings under paragraph 1(a) and (b), the Enlarged Board of Appeal shall consist of five legally and two technically qualified members. In proceedings under paragraph 1(c), the Enlarged Board of Appeal shall consist of three or five members as laid down in the Implementing Regulations. In all proceedings, a legally qualified member shall be the Chairman.

Article 23

Independence of the members of the Boards

AppB-16 **(1)**   The members of the Enlarged Board of Appeal and of the Boards of Appeal shall be appointed for a term of five years and may not be removed from office during this term, except if there are serious grounds for such removal and if the Administrative Council, on a proposal from the Enlarged Board of Appeal, takes a decision to this effect. Notwithstanding sentence 1, the term of office of members of the Boards shall end if they resign or are retired in accordance with the Service Regulations for permanent employees of the European Patent Office.

(2)   The members of the Boards may not be members of the Receiving Section, Examining Divisions, Opposition Divisions or Legal Division.

(3)   In their decisions the members of the Boards shall not be bound by any instructions and shall comply only with the provisions of this Convention.

(4) The Rules of Procedure of the Boards of Appeal and the Enlarged Board of Appeal shall be adopted in accordance with the Implementing Regulations. They shall be subject to the approval of the Administrative Council.

Article 24

Exclusion and objection

(1) Members of the Boards of Appeal or of the Enlarged Board of Appeal may not take part in a case in which they have any personal interest, or if they have previously been involved as representatives of one of the parties, or if they participated in the decision under appeal.   AppB-17

(2) If, for one of the reasons mentioned in paragraph 1, or for any other reason, a member of a Board of Appeal or of the Enlarged Board of Appeal considers that he should not take part in any appeal, he shall inform the Board accordingly.

(3) Members of a Board of Appeal or of the Enlarged Board of Appeal may be objected to by any party for one of the reasons mentioned in paragraph 1, or if suspected of partiality. An objection shall not be admissible if, while being aware of a reason for objection, the party has taken a procedural step. An objection may not be based upon the nationality of members.

(4) The Boards of Appeal and the Enlarged Board of Appeal shall decide as to the action to be taken in the cases specified in paragraphs 2 and 3, without the participation of the member concerned. For the purposes of taking this decision the member objected to shall be replaced by his alternate.

Article 25

Technical opinion

At the request of the competent national court hearing an infringement or revocation action, the European Patent Office shall be obliged, on payment of an appropriate fee, to give a technical opinion concerning the European patent which is the subject of the action. The Examining Division shall be responsible for issuing such opinions.   AppB-18

[Articles 26–36 are not reproduced here.]   AppB-19

CHAPTER V

FINANCIAL PROVISIONS

[Articles 37–51 are not reproduced here.]   AppB-20

PART II

SUBSTANTIVE PATENT LAW

CHAPTER I

PATENTABILITY

Article 52

Patentable inventions

AppB-21 **(1)** European patents shall be granted for any inventions, in all fields of technology, provided that they are new, involve an inventive step and are susceptible of industrial application.

(2) The following in particular shall not be regarded as inventions within the meaning of paragraph 1:
   (a) discoveries, scientific theories and mathematical methods;
   (b) aesthetic creations;
   (c) schemes, rules and methods for performing mental acts, playing games or doing business, and programs for computers;
   (d) presentations of information.

(3) Paragraph 2 shall exclude the patentability of the subject-matter or activities referred to therein only to the extent to which a European patent application or European patent relates to such subject-matter or activities as such.

Article 53

Exceptions to patentability

AppB-22 European patents shall not be granted in respect of:
   (a) inventions the commercial exploitation of which would be contrary to "ordre public" or morality; such exploitation shall not be deemed to be so contrary merely because it is prohibited by law or regulation in some or all of the Contracting States;
   (b) plant or animal varieties or essentially biological processes for the production of plants or animals; this provision shall not apply to microbiological processes or the products thereof;
   (c) methods for treatment of the human or animal body by surgery or therapy and diagnostic methods practised on the human or animal body; this provision shall not apply to products, in particular substances or compositions, for use in any of these methods.

Article 54

Novelty

AppB-23 **(1)** An invention shall be considered to be new if it does not form part of the state of the art.

(2) The state of the art shall be held to comprise everything made available to the public by means of a written or oral description, by use, or in any other way, before the date of filing of the European patent application.

(3) Additionally, the content of European patent applications as filed, the dates of filing of which are prior to the date referred to in paragraph 2 and which were published on or after that date, shall be considered as comprised in the state of the art.

(4) Paragraphs 2 and 3 shall not exclude the patentability of any substance or composition, comprised in the state of the art, for use in a method referred to in Article 53(c), provided that its use for any such method is not comprised in the state of the art.

(5) Paragraphs 2 and 3 shall also not exclude the patentability of any substance or composition referred to in paragraph 4 for any specific use in a method referred to in Article 53(c), provided that such use is not comprised in the state of the art.

Article 55

Non-prejudicial disclosures

(1) For the application of Article 54, a disclosure of the invention shall not be taken into consideration if it occurred no earlier than six months preceding the filing of the European patent application and if it was due to, or in consequence of: AppB-24

  (a) an evident abuse in relation to the applicant or his legal predecessor, or

  (b) the fact that the applicant or his legal predecessor has displayed the invention at an official, or officially recognised, international exhibition falling within the terms of the Convention on international exhibitions signed at Paris on 22 November 1928 and last revised on 30 November 1972.

(2) In the case of paragraph 1(b), paragraph 1 shall apply only if the applicant states, when filing the European patent application, that the invention has been so displayed and files a supporting certificate within the time limit and under the conditions laid down in the Implementing Regulations.

Article 56

Inventive step

An invention shall be considered as involving an inventive step if, having regard to the state of the art, it is not obvious to a person skilled in the art. If the state of the art also includes documents within the meaning of Article 54, paragraph 3, these documents shall not be considered in deciding whether there has been an inventive step.   AppB-25

Article 57

Industrial application

An invention shall be considered as susceptible of industrial application if it can be made or used in any kind of industry, including agriculture.   AppB-26

CHAPTER II

PERSONS ENTITLED TO APPLY FOR AND OBTAIN A EUROPEAN PATENT—MENTION OF THE INVENTOR

Article 58

Entitlement to file a European patent application

A European patent application may be filed by any natural or legal person, or any body equivalent to a legal person by virtue of the law governing it.   AppB-27

Article 59

Multiple applicants

AppB-28   A European patent application may also be filed either by joint applicants or by two or more applicants designating different Contracting States.

Article 60

Right to a European patent

AppB-29   **(1)**   The right to a European patent shall belong to the inventor or his successor in title. If the inventor is an employee, the right to a European patent shall be determined in accordance with the law of the State in which the employee is mainly employed; if the State in which the employee is mainly employed cannot be determined, the law to be applied shall be that of the State in which the employer has the place of business to which the employee is attached.

(2)   If two or more persons have made an invention independently of each other, the right to a European patent therefor shall belong to the person whose European patent application has the earliest date of filing, provided that this first application has been published.

(3)   In proceedings before the European Patent Office, the applicant shall be deemed to be entitled to exercise the right to a European patent.

Article 61

European patent applications filed by non-entitled persons

AppB-30   **(1)**   If by a final decision it is adjudged that a person other than the applicant is entitled to the grant of the European patent, that person may, in accordance with the Implementing Regulations:

(a)   prosecute the European patent application as his own application in place of the applicant;

(b)   file a new European patent application in respect of the same invention; or

(c)   request that the European patent application be refused.

(2)   Article 76, paragraph 1, shall apply mutatis mutandis to a new European patent application filed under paragraph 1(b).

Article 62

Right of the inventor to be mentioned

AppB-31   The inventor shall have the right, vis-à-vis the applicant for or proprietor of a European patent, to be mentioned as such before the European Patent Office.

CHAPTER III

EFFECTS OF THE EUROPEAN PATENT AND THE EUROPEAN PATENT APPLICATION

Article 63

Term of the European patent

(1)   The term of the European patent shall be 20 years from the date of filing of the application.   AppB-32

(2)   Nothing in the preceding paragraph shall limit the right of a Contracting State to extend the term of a European patent, or to grant corresponding protection which follows immediately on expiry of the term of the patent, under the same conditions as those applying to national patents:

    (a)   in order to take account of a state of war or similar emergency conditions affecting that State;

    (b)   if the subject-matter of the European patent is a product or a process for manufacturing a product or a use of a product which has to undergo an administrative authorisation procedure required by law before it can be put on the market in that State.

(3)   Paragraph 2 shall apply mutatis mutandis to European patents granted jointly for a group of Contracting States in accordance with Article 142.

(4)   A Contracting State which makes provision for extension of the term or corresponding protection under paragraph 2(b) may, in accordance with an agreement concluded with the Organisation, entrust to the European Patent Office tasks associated with implementation of the relevant provisions.

Article 64

Rights conferred by a European patent

(1)   A European patent shall, subject to the provisions of paragraph 2, confer on its proprietor from the date on which the mention of its grant is published in the European Patent Bulletin, in each Contracting State in respect of which it is granted, the same rights as would be conferred by a national patent granted in that State.   AppB-33

(2)   If the subject-matter of the European patent is a process, the protection conferred by the patent shall extend to the products directly obtained by such process.

(3)   Any infringement of a European patent shall be dealt with by national law.

Article 65

Translation of the European patent

(1)   Any Contracting State may, if the European patent as granted, amended or limited by the European Patent Office is not drawn up in one of its official languages, prescribe that the proprietor of the patent shall supply to its central industrial property office a translation of the patent as granted, amended or limited in one of its official languages at his option or, where that State has prescribed the use of one specific official language, in that language. The period for supplying the translation shall end three months after the date on which the mention of the grant,   AppB-34

[1051]

maintenance in amended form or limitation of the European patent is published in the European Patent Bulletin, unless the State concerned prescribes a longer period.

(2) Any Contracting State which has adopted provisions pursuant to paragraph 1 may prescribe that the proprietor of the patent must pay all or part of the costs of publication of such translation within a period laid down by that State.

(3) Any Contracting State may prescribe that in the event of failure to observe the provisions adopted in accordance with paragraphs 1 and 2, the European patent shall be deemed to be void ab initio in that State.

Article 66

Equivalence of European filing with national filing

AppB-35   A European patent application which has been accorded a date of filing shall, in the designated Contracting States, be equivalent to a regular national filing, where appropriate with the priority claimed for the European patent application.

Article 67

Rights conferred by a European patent application after publication

AppB-36   **(1)**   A European patent application shall, from the date of its publication, provisionally confer upon the applicant the protection provided for by Article 64, in the Contracting States designated in the application.

(2)   Any Contracting State may prescribe that a European patent application shall not confer such protection as is conferred by Article 64. However, the protection attached to the publication of the European patent application may not be less than that which the laws of the State concerned attach to the compulsory publication of unexamined national patent applications. In any event, each State shall ensure at least that, from the date of publication of a European patent application, the applicant can claim compensation reasonable in the circumstances from any person who has used the invention in that State in circumstances where that person would be liable under national law for infringement of a national patent.

(3)   Any Contracting State which does not have as an official language the language of the proceedings may prescribe that provisional protection in accordance with paragraphs 1 and 2 above shall not be effective until such time as a translation of the claims in one of its official languages at the option of the applicant or, where that State has prescribed the use of one specific official language, in that language:

    (a)   has been made available to the public in the manner prescribed by national law, or

    (b)   has been communicated to the person using the invention in the said State.

(4)   The European patent application shall be deemed never to have had the effects set out in paragraphs 1 and 2 when it has been withdrawn, deemed to be withdrawn or finally refused. The same shall apply in respect of the effects of the European patent application in a Contracting State the designation of which is withdrawn or deemed to be withdrawn.

Article 68

Effect of revocation or limitation of the European patent

The European patent application and the resulting European patent shall be AppB-37
deemed not to have had, from the outset, the effects specified in Articles 64 and 67,
to the extent that the patent has been revoked or limited in opposition, limitation
or revocation proceedings.

Article 69

Extent of protection

(1) The extent of the protection conferred by a European patent or a European pat- AppB-38
ent application shall be determined by the claims. Nevertheless, the description and
drawings shall be used to interpret the claims.
(2) For the period up to grant of the European patent, the extent of the protection
conferred by the European patent application shall be determined by the claims
contained in the application as published. However, the European patent as granted
or as amended in opposition, limitation or revocation proceedings shall determine
retroactively the protection conferred by the application, in so far as such protection is not thereby extended.

Article 70

Authentic text of a European patent application or European patent

(1) The text of a European patent application or a European patent in the language AppB-39
of the proceedings shall be the authentic text in any proceedings before the
European Patent Office and in any Contracting State.
(2) If, however, the European patent application has been filed in a language
which is not an official language of the European Patent Office, that text shall be
the application as filed within the meaning of this Convention.
(3) Any Contracting State may provide that a translation into one of its official
languages, as prescribed by it according to this Convention, shall in that State be
regarded as authentic, except for revocation proceedings, in the event of the
European patent application or European patent in the language of the translation
conferring protection which is narrower than that conferred by it in the language
of the proceedings.
(4) Any Contracting State which adopts a provision under paragraph 3:
  (a) shall allow the applicant for or proprietor of the patent to file a corrected
       translation of the European patent application or European patent. Such cor-
       rected translation shall not have any legal effect until any conditions
       established by the Contracting State under Article 65, paragraph 2, or
       Article 67, paragraph 3, have been complied with;
  (b) may prescribe that any person who, in that State, in good faith has used or
       has made effective and serious preparations for using an invention the use
       of which would not constitute infringement of the application or patent in
       the original translation, may, after the corrected translation takes effect,
       continue such use in the course of his business or for the needs thereof
       without payment.

CHAPTER IV

THE EUROPEAN PATENT APPLICATION AS AN OBJECT OF PROPERTY

Article 71

Transfer and constitution of rights

AppB-40   A European patent application may be transferred or give rise to rights for one or more of the designated Contracting States.

Article 72

Assignment

AppB-41   An assignment of a European patent application shall be made in writing and shall require the signature of the parties to the contract.

Article 73

Contractual licensing

AppB-42   A European patent application may be licensed in whole or in part for the whole or part of the territories of the designated Contracting States.

Article 74

Law applicable

AppB-43   Unless this Convention provides otherwise, the European patent application as an object of property shall, in each designated Contracting State and with effect for such State, be subject to the law applicable in that State to national patent applications.

PART III

THE EUROPEAN PATENT APPLICATION

CHAPTER 1

FILING AND REQUIREMENTS OF THE EUROPEAN PATENT APPLICATION

Article 75

Filing of a European patent application

AppB-44   (1)   A European patent application may be filed:
   (a)   with the European Patent Office, or
   (b)   if the law of a Contracting State so permits, and subject to

Article 76, paragraph 1, with the central industrial property office or other competent authority of that State. Any application filed in this way shall have the same effect as if it had been filed on the same date with the European Patent Office.

(2) Paragraph 1 shall not preclude the application of legislative or regulatory provisions which, in any Contracting State:
- (a) govern inventions which, owing to the nature of their subject-matter, may not be communicated abroad without the prior authorisation of the competent authorities of that State, or
- (b) prescribe that any application is to be filed initially with a national authority, or make direct filing with another authority subject to prior authorisation

Article 76

European divisional applications

(1) A European divisional application shall be filed directly with the European Patent Office in accordance with the Implementing Regulations. It may be filed only in respect of subject-matter which does not extend beyond the content of the earlier application as filed; in so far as this requirement is complied with, the divisional application shall be deemed to have been filed on the date of filing of the earlier application and shall enjoy any right of priority. `AppB-45`

(2) All the Contracting States designated in the earlier application at the time of filing of a European divisional application shall be deemed to be designated in the divisional application.

Article 77

Forwarding of European patent applications

(1) The central industrial property office of a Contracting State shall forward to the European Patent Office any European patent application filed with it or any other competent authority in that State, in accordance with the Implementing Regulations. `AppB-46`

(2) A European patent application the subject of which has been made secret shall not be forwarded to the European Patent Office.

(3) A European patent application not forwarded to the European Patent Office in due time shall be deemed to be withdrawn.

Article 78

Requirements of a European patent application

(1) A European patent application shall contain: `AppB-47`
- (a) a request for the grant of a European patent;
- (b) a description of the invention;
- (c) one or more claims;
- (d) any drawings referred to in the description or the claims;
- (e) an abstract, and satisfy the requirements laid down in the Implementing Regulations.

(2) A European patent application shall be subject to the payment of the filing fee and the search fee. If the filing fee or the search fee is not paid in due time, the application shall be deemed to be withdrawn.

Article 79
Designation of Contracting States

AppB-48 **(1)** All the Contracting States party to this Convention at the time of filing of the European patent application shall be deemed to be designated in the request for grant of a European patent.
(2) The designation of a Contracting State may be subject to the payment of a designation fee.
(3) The designation of a Contracting State may be withdrawn at any time up to the grant of the European patent.

Article 80
Date of filing

AppB-49 The date of filing of a European patent application shall be the date on which the requirements laid down in the Implementing Regulations are fulfilled.

Article 81
Designation of the inventor

AppB-50 The European patent application shall designate the inventor. If the applicant is not the inventor or is not the sole inventor, the designation shall contain a statement indicating the origin of the right to the European patent.

Article 82
Unity of invention

AppB-51 The European patent application shall relate to one invention only or to a group of inventions so linked as to form a single general inventive concept.

Article 83
Disclosure of the invention

AppB-52 The European patent application shall disclose the invention in a manner sufficiently clear and complete for it to be carried out by a person skilled in the art.

Article 84
Claims

AppB-53 The claims shall define the matter for which protection is sought. They shall be clear and concise and be supported by the description.

Article 85
Abstract

AppB-54 The abstract shall serve the purpose of technical information only; it may not be taken into account for any other purpose, in particular for interpreting the scope of the protection sought or applying Article 54, paragraph 3.

Article 86

Renewal fees for the European patent application

(1) Renewal fees for the European patent application shall be paid to the European   AppB-55
Patent Office in accordance with the Implementing Regulations. These fees shall
be due in respect of the third year and each subsequent year, calculated from the
date of filing of the application. If a renewal fee is not paid in due time, the application shall be deemed to be withdrawn.

(2) The obligation to pay renewal fees shall terminate with the payment of the
renewal fee due in respect of the year in which the mention of the grant of the
European patent is published in the European Patent Bulletin.

CHAPTER II

PRIORITY

Article 87

Priority right

(1) Any person who has duly filed, in or for   AppB-56
    (a)   any State party to the Paris Convention for the Protection of Industrial
        Property or
    (b)   any Member of the World Trade Organization,
an application for a patent, a utility model or a utility certificate, or his successor
in title, shall enjoy, for the purpose of filing a European patent application in respect
of the same invention, a right of priority during a period of twelve months from the
date of filing of the first application.

(2) Every filing that is equivalent to a regular national filing under the national law
of the State where it was made or under bilateral or multilateral agreements, including this Convention, shall be recognised as giving rise to a right of priority.

(3) A regular national filing shall mean any filing that is sufficient to establish the
date on which the application was filed, whatever the outcome of the application
may be.

(4) A subsequent application in respect of the same subject-matter as a previous
first application and filed in or for the same State shall be considered as the first application for the purposes of determining priority, provided that, at the date of filing the subsequent application, the previous application has been withdrawn,
abandoned or refused, without being open to public inspection and without leaving any rights outstanding, and has not served as a basis for claiming a right of
priority. The previous application may not thereafter serve as a basis for claiming
a right of priority.

(5) If the first filing has been made with an industrial property authority which is
not subject to the Paris Convention for the Protection of Industrial Property or the
Agreement Establishing the World Trade Organization, paragraphs 1 to 4 shall apply if that authority, according to a communication issued by the President of the
European Patent Office, recognises that a first filing made with the European Patent Office gives rise to a right of priority under conditions and with effects
equivalent to those laid down in the Paris Convention.

Article 88

Claiming priority

AppB-57 **(1)** An applicant desiring to take advantage of the priority of a previous application shall file a declaration of priority and any other document required, in accordance with the Implementing Regulations.

(2) Multiple priorities may be claimed in respect of a European patent application, notwithstanding the fact that they originated in different countries. Where appropriate, multiple priorities may be claimed for any one claim. Where multiple priorities are claimed, time limits which run from the date of priority shall run from the earliest date of priority.

(3) If one or more priorities are claimed in respect of a European patent application, the right of priority shall cover only those elements of the European patent application which are included in the application or applications whose priority is claimed.

(4) If certain elements of the invention for which priority is claimed do not appear among the claims formulated in the previous application, priority may nonetheless be granted, provided that the documents of the previous application as a whole specifically disclose such elements.

Article 89

Effect of priority right

AppB-58 The right of priority shall have the effect that the date of priority shall count as the date of filing of the European patent application for the purposes of Article 54, paragraphs 2 and 3, and Article 60, paragraph 2.

PART IV

PROCEDURE UP TO GRANT

Article 90

Examination on filing and examination as to formal requirements

AppB-59 **(1)** The European Patent Office shall examine, in accordance with the Implementing Regulations, whether the application satisfies the requirements for the accordance of a date of filing.

(2) If a date of filing cannot be accorded following the examination under paragraph 1, the application shall not be dealt with as a European patent application.

(3) If the European patent application has been accorded a date of filing, the European Patent Office shall examine, in accordance with the Implementing Regulations, whether the requirements in Articles 14, 78 and 81, and, where applicable, Article 88, paragraph 1, and Article 133, paragraph 2, as well as any other requirement laid down in the Implementing Regulations, have been satisfied.

(4) Where the European Patent Office in carrying out the examination under paragraphs 1 or 3 notes that there are deficiencies which may be corrected, it shall give the applicant an opportunity to correct them.

(5) If any deficiency noted in the examination under paragraph 3 is not corrected, the European patent application shall be refused unless a different legal consequence is provided for by this Convention. Where the deficiency concerns the right of priority, this right shall be lost for the application.

Article 91

[Deleted.] AppB-60

Article 92
Drawing up of the European search report

The European Patent Office shall, in accordance with the Implementing Regulations, draw up and publish a European search report in respect of the European patent application on the basis of the claims, with due regard to the description and any drawings. AppB-61

Article 93
Publication of the European patent application

1) The European Patent Office shall publish the European patent application as soon as possible AppB-62
    (a) after the expiry of a period of eighteen months from the date of filing or, if priority has been claimed, from the date of priority, or
    (b) at the request of the applicant, before the expiry of that period.
(2) The European patent application shall be published at the same time as the specification of the European patent when the decision to grant the patent becomes effective before the expiry of the period referred to in paragraph 1(a).

Article 94
Examination of the European patent application

(1) The European Patent Office shall, in accordance with the Implementing Regulations, examine on request whether the European patent application and the invention to which it relates meet the requirements of this Convention. The request shall not be deemed to be filed until the examination fee has been paid. AppB-63
(2) If no request for examination has been made in due time, the application shall be deemed to be withdrawn.
(3) If the examination reveals that the application or the invention to which it relates does not meet the requirements of this Convention, the Examining Division shall invite the applicant, as often as necessary, to file his observations and, subject to Article 123, paragraph 1, to amend the application.
(4) If the applicant fails to reply in due time to any communication from the Examining Division, the application shall be deemed to be withdrawn.

Article 95

[Deleted.] AppB-64

Article 96

[Deleted.] AppB-65

Article 97

Grant or refusal

AppB-66 **(1)** If the Examining Division is of the opinion that the European patent application and the invention to which it relates meet the requirements of this Convention, it shall decide to grant a European patent, provided that the conditions laid down in the Implementing Regulations are fulfilled.

(2) If the Examining Division is of the opinion that the European patent application or the invention to which it relates does not meet the requirements of this Convention, it shall refuse the application unless this Convention provides for a different legal consequence.

(3) The decision to grant a European patent shall take effect on the date on which the mention of the grant is published in the European Patent Bulletin.

Article 98

Publication of the specification of the European patent

AppB-67 The European Patent Office shall publish the specification of the European patent as soon as possible after the mention of the grant of the European patent has been published in the European Patent Bulletin.

PART V

OPPOSITION AND LIMITATION PROCEDURE

Article 99

Opposition

AppB-68 **(1)** Within nine months of the publication of the mention of the grant of the European patent in the European Patent Bulletin, any person may give notice to the European Patent Office of opposition to that patent, in accordance with the Implementing Regulations. Notice of opposition shall not be deemed to have been filed until the opposition fee has been paid.

(2) The opposition shall apply to the European patent in all the Contracting States in which that patent has effect.

(3) Opponents shall be parties to the opposition proceedings as well as the proprietor of the patent.

(4) Where a person provides evidence that in a Contracting State, following a final decision, he has been entered in the patent register of such State instead of the previous proprietor, such person shall, at his request, replace the previous proprietor in respect of such State. Notwithstanding Article 118, the previous proprietor and the person making the request shall not be regarded as joint proprietors unless both so request.

Article 100

Grounds for opposition

AppB-69 Opposition may only be filed on the grounds that:

(a) the subject-matter of the European patent is not patentable under Articles 52 to 57;

(b) the European patent does not disclose the invention in a manner sufficiently clear and complete for it to be carried out by a person skilled in the art;

(c) the subject-matter of the European patent extends beyond the content of the application as filed, or, if the patent was granted on a divisional application or on a new application filed under Article 61, beyond the content of the earlier application as filed.

Article 101

Examination of the opposition—Revocation or maintenance of the European patent

(1) If the opposition is admissible, the Opposition Division shall examine, in ac-   AppB-70
cordance with the Implementing Regulations, whether at least one ground for opposition under Article 100 prejudices the maintenance of the European patent. During this examination, the Opposition Division shall invite the parties, as often as necessary, to file observations on communications from another party or issued by itself.

(2) If the Opposition Division is of the opinion that at least one ground for opposition prejudices the maintenance of the European patent, it shall revoke the patent. Otherwise, it shall reject the opposition.

(3) If the Opposition Division is of the opinion that, taking into consideration the amendments made by the proprietor of the European patent during the opposition proceedings, the patent and the invention to which it relates

(a) meet the requirements of this Convention, it shall decide to maintain the patent as amended, provided that the conditions laid down in the Implementing Regulations are fulfilled;

(b) do not meet the requirements of this Convention, it shall revoke the patent.

Article 102

[Deleted.]   AppB-71

Article 103

Publication of a new specification of the European patent

If the European patent is maintained as amended under Article 101, paragraph   AppB-72
3(a), the European Patent Office shall publish a new specification of the European patent as soon as possible after the mention of the opposition decision has been published in the European Patent Bulletin.

Article 104

Costs

(1) Each party to the opposition proceedings shall bear the costs it has incurred,   AppB-73
unless the Opposition Division, for reasons of equity, orders, in accordance with the Implementing Regulations, a different apportionment of costs.

(2) The procedure for fixing costs shall be laid down in the Implementing Regulations.

(3) Any final decision of the European Patent Office fixing the amount of costs shall be dealt with, for the purpose of enforcement in the Contracting States, in the same way as a final decision given by a civil court of the State in which enforcement is to take place. Verification of such decision shall be limited to its authenticity.

Article 105

Intervention of the assumed infringer

AppB-74 **(1)** Any third party may, in accordance with the Implementing Regulations, intervene in opposition proceedings after the opposition period has expired, if the third party proves that

(a) proceedings for infringement of the same patent have been instituted against him, or

(b) following a request of the proprietor of the patent to cease alleged infringement, the third party has instituted proceedings for a ruling that he is not infringing the patent.

(2) An admissible intervention shall be treated as an opposition.

Article 105a

Request for limitation or revocation

AppB-75 **(1)** At the request of the proprietor, the European patent may be revoked or be limited by an amendment of the claims. The request shall be filed with the European Patent Office in accordance with the Implementing Regulations. It shall not be deemed to have been filed until the limitation or revocation fee has been paid.

(2) The request may not be filed while opposition proceedings in respect of the European patent are pending.

Article 105b

Limitation or revocation of the European patent

AppB-76 **(1)** The European Patent Office shall examine whether the requirements laid down in the Implementing Regulations for limiting or revoking the European patent have been met.

(2) If the European Patent Office considers that the request for limitation or revocation of the European patent meets these requirements, it shall decide to limit or revoke the European patent in accordance with the Implementing Regulations. Otherwise, it shall reject the request.

(3) The decision to limit or revoke the European patent shall apply to the European patent in all the Contracting States in respect of which it has been granted. It shall take effect on the date on which the mention of the decision is published in the European Patent Bulletin.

Article 105c

Publication of the amended specification of the European patent

If the European patent is limited under Article 105b, paragraph 2, the European   AppB-77
Patent Office shall publish the amended specification of the European patent as soon
as possible after the mention of the limitation has been published in the European
Patent Bulletin.

PART VI

APPEALS PROCEDURE

Article 106

Decisions subject to appeal

(1)   An appeal shall lie from decisions of the Receiving Section, Examining Divi-   AppB-78
sions, Opposition Divisions and the Legal Division. It shall have suspensive effect.
(2)   A decision which does not terminate proceedings as regards one of the parties can only be appealed together with the final decision, unless the decision allows a separate appeal.
(3)   The right to file an appeal against decisions relating to the apportionment or
fixing of costs in opposition proceedings may be restricted in the Implementing
Regulations.

Article 107

Persons entitled to appeal and to be parties to appeal proceedings

Any party to proceedings adversely affected by a decision may appeal. Any other   AppB-79
parties to the proceedings shall be parties to the appeal proceedings as of right.

Article 108

Time limit and form

Notice of appeal shall be filed, in accordance with the Implementing Regula-   AppB-80
tions, at the European Patent Office within two months of notification of the
decision. Notice of appeal shall not be deemed to have been filed until the fee for
appeal has been paid. Within four months of notification of the decision, a statement setting out the grounds of appeal shall be filed in accordance with the
Implementing Regulations.

Article 109

Interlocutory revision

(1)   If the department whose decision is contested considers the appeal to be   AppB-81
admissible and well founded, it shall rectify its decision. This shall not apply where
the appellant is opposed by another party to the proceedings.
(2)   If the appeal is not allowed within three months of receipt of the statement of
grounds, it shall be remitted to the Board of Appeal without delay, and without comment as to its merit.

Article 110

Examination of appeals

AppB-82   If the appeal is admissible, the Board of Appeal shall examine whether the appeal is allowable. The examination of the appeal shall be conducted in accordance with the Implementing Regulations.

Article 111

Decision in respect of appeals

AppB-83   **(1)**   Following the examination as to the allowability of the appeal, the Board of Appeal shall decide on the appeal. The Board of Appeal may either exercise any power within the competence of the department which was responsible for the decision appealed or remit the case to that department for further prosecution.

(2)   If the Board of Appeal remits the case for further prosecution to the department whose decision was appealed, that department shall be bound by the ratio decidendi of the Board of Appeal, in so far as the facts are the same. If the decision under appeal was taken by the Receiving Section, the Examining Division shall also be bound by the ratio decidendi of the Board of Appeal.

Article 112

Decision or opinion of the Enlarged Board of Appeal

AppB-84   **(1)**   In order to ensure uniform application of the law, or if a point of law of fundamental importance arises:

    (a)   the Board of Appeal shall, during proceedings on a case and either of its own motion or following a request from a party to the appeal, refer any question to the Enlarged Board of Appeal if it considers that a decision is required for the above purposes. If the Board of Appeal rejects the request, it shall give the reasons in its final decision;

    (b)   the President of the European Patent Office may refer a point of law to the Enlarged Board of Appeal where two Boards of Appeal have given different decisions on that question.

(2)   In the cases referred to in paragraph 1(a) the parties to the appeal proceedings shall be parties to the proceedings before the Enlarged Board of Appeal.

(3)   The decision of the Enlarged Board of Appeal referred to in paragraph 1(a) shall be binding on the Board of Appeal in respect of the appeal in question.

Article 112a

Petition for review by the Enlarged Board of Appeal

AppB-85   **(1)**   Any party to appeal proceedings adversely affected by the decision of the Board of Appeal may file a petition for review of the decision by the Enlarged Board of Appeal.

(2)   The petition may only be filed on the grounds that:

    (a)   a member of the Board of Appeal took part in the decision in breach of Article 24, paragraph 1, or despite being excluded pursuant to a decision under Article 24, paragraph 4;

(b)   the Board of Appeal included a person not appointed as a member of the Boards of Appeal;

(c)   a fundamental violation of Article 113 occurred;

(d)   any other fundamental procedural defect defined in the Implementing Regulations occurred in the appeal proceedings; or

(e)   a criminal act established under the conditions laid down in the Implementing Regulations may have had an impact on the decision.

(3)   The petition for review shall not have suspensive effect.

(4)   The petition for review shall be filed in a reasoned statement, in accordance with the Implementing Regulations. If based on paragraph 2(a) to (d), the petition shall be filed within two months of notification of the decision of the Board of Appeal. If based on paragraph 2(e), the petition shall be filed within two months of the date on which the criminal act has been established and in any event no later than five years from notification of the decision of the Board of Appeal. The petition shall not be deemed to have been filed until after the prescribed fee has been paid.

(5)   The Enlarged Board of Appeal shall examine the petition for review in accordance with the Implementing Regulations. If the petition is allowable, the Enlarged Board of Appeal shall set aside the decision and shall re-open proceedings before the Boards of Appeal in accordance with the Implementing Regulations.

(6)   Any person who, in a designated Contracting State, has in good faith used or made effective and serious preparations for using an invention which is the subject of a published European patent application or a European patent in the period between the decision of the Board of Appeal and publication in the European Patent Bulletin of the mention of the decision of the Enlarged Board of Appeal on the petition, may without payment continue such use in the course of his business or for the needs thereof.

PART VII

COMMON PROVISIONS

CHAPTER I

COMMON PROVISIONS GOVERNING PROCEDURE

Article 113

Right to be heard and basis of decisions

(1)   The decisions of the European Patent Office may only be based on grounds or evidence on which the parties concerned have had an opportunity to present their comments.   AppB-86

(2)   The European Patent Office shall examine, and decide upon, the European patent application or the European patent only in the text submitted to it, or agreed, by the applicant or the proprietor of the patent.

Article 114

Examination by the European Patent Office of its own motion

AppB-87 **(1)** In proceedings before it, the European Patent Office shall examine the facts of its own motion; it shall not be restricted in this examination to the facts, evidence and arguments provided by the parties and the relief sought.

(2) The European Patent Office may disregard facts or evidence which are not submitted in due time by the parties concerned.

Article 115

Observations by third parties

AppB-88 In proceedings before the European Patent Office, following the publication of the European patent application, any third party may, in accordance with the Implementing Regulations, present observations concerning the patentability of the invention to which the application or patent relates. That person shall not be a party to the proceedings.

Article 116

Oral proceedings

AppB-89 **(1)** Oral proceedings shall take place either at the instance of the European Patent Office if it considers this to be expedient or at the request of any party to the proceedings. However, the European Patent Office may reject a request for further oral proceedings before the same department where the parties and the subject of the proceedings are the same.

(2) Nevertheless, oral proceedings shall take place before the Receiving Section at the request of the applicant only where the Receiving Section considers this to be expedient or where it intends to refuse the European patent application.

(3) Oral proceedings before the Receiving Section, the Examining Divisions and the Legal Division shall not be public.

(4) Oral proceedings, including delivery of the decision, shall be public, as regards the Boards of Appeal and the Enlarged Board of Appeal, after publication of the European patent application, and also before the Opposition Divisions, in so far as the department before which the proceedings are taking place does not decide otherwise in cases where admission of the public could have serious and unjustified disadvantages, in particular for a party to the proceedings.

Article 117

Means and taking of evidence

AppB-90 **(1)** In proceedings before the European Patent Office the means of giving or obtaining evidence shall include the following:

(a) hearing the parties;
(b) requests for information;
(c) production of documents;
(d) hearing witnesses;
(e) opinions by experts;
(f) inspection;

[1066]

(g)   sworn statements in writing.

(2)   The procedure for taking such evidence shall be laid down in the Implementing Regulations.

Article 118

Unity of the European patent application or European patent

Where the applicants for or proprietors of a European patent are not the same in respect of different designated Contracting States, they shall be regarded as joint applicants or proprietors for the purposes of proceedings before the European Patent Office. The unity of the application or patent in these proceedings shall not be affected; in particular the text of the application or patent shall be uniform for all designated Contracting States, unless this Convention provides otherwise. **AppB-91**

Article 119

Notification

Decisions, summonses, notices and communications shall be notified by the European Patent Office of its own motion in accordance with the Implementing Regulations. Notification may, where exceptional circumstances so require, be effected through the intermediary of the central industrial property offices of the Contracting States. **AppB-92**

Article 120

Time limits

The Implementing Regulations shall specify: **AppB-93**
(a)   the time limits which are to be observed in proceedings before the European Patent Office and are not fixed by this Convention;
(b)   the manner of computation of time limits and the conditions under which time limits may be extended;
(c)   the minima and maxima for time limits to be determined by the European Patent Office.

Article 121

Further processing of the European patent application

(1)   If an applicant fails to observe a time limit vis-à-vis the European Patent Office, he may request further processing of the European patent application. **AppB-94**

(2)   The European Patent Office shall grant the request, provided that the requirements laid down in the Implementing Regulations are met. Otherwise, it shall reject the request.

(3)   If the request is granted, the legal consequences of the failure to observe the time limit shall be deemed not to have ensued.

(4)   Further processing shall be ruled out in respect of the time limits in Article 87, paragraph 1, Article 108 and Article 112a, paragraph 4, as well as the time limits for requesting further processing or re-establishment of rights. The Implementing Regulations may rule out further processing for other time limits.

Article 122

Re-establishment of rights

AppB-95 **(1)** An applicant for or proprietor of a European patent who, in spite of all due care required by the circumstances having been taken, was unable to observe a time limit vis-à-vis the European Patent Office shall have his rights re-established upon request if the non-observance of this time limit has the direct consequence of causing the refusal of the European patent application or of a request, or the deeming of the application to have been withdrawn, or the revocation of the European patent, or the loss of any other right or means of redress.

(2) The European Patent Office shall grant the request, provided that the conditions of paragraph 1 and any other requirements laid down in the Implementing Regulations are met. Otherwise, it shall reject the request.

(3) If the request is granted, the legal consequences of the failure to observe the time limit shall be deemed not to have ensued.

(4) Re-establishment of rights shall be ruled out in respect of the time limit for requesting re-establishment of rights. The Implementing Regulations may rule out re-establishment for other time limits.

(5) Any person who, in a designated Contracting State, has in good faith used or made effective and serious preparations for using an invention which is the subject of a published European patent application or a European patent in the period between the loss of rights referred to in paragraph 1 and publication in the European Patent Bulletin of the mention of re-establishment of those rights, may without payment continue such use in the course of his business or for the needs thereof.

(6) Nothing in this Article shall limit the right of a Contracting State to grant re-establishment of rights in respect of time limits provided for in this Convention and to be observed vis-à-vis the authorities of such State.

Article 123

Amendments

AppB-96 **(1)** The European patent application or European patent may be amended in proceedings before the European Patent Office, in accordance with the Implementing Regulations. In any event, the applicant shall be given at least one opportunity to amend the application of his own volition.

(2) The European patent application or European patent may not be amended in such a way that it contains subject-matter which extends beyond the content of the application as filed.

(3) The European patent may not be amended in such a way as to extend the protection it confers.

Article 124

Information on prior art

AppB-97 **(1)** The European Patent Office may, in accordance with the Implementing Regulations, invite the applicant to provide information on prior art taken into consideration in national or regional patent proceedings and concerning an invention to which the European patent application relates.

(2) If the applicant fails to reply in due time to an invitation under paragraph 1, the European patent application shall be deemed to be withdrawn.

Article 125

Reference to general principles

In the absence of procedural provisions in this Convention, the European Patent Office shall take into account the principles of procedural law generally recognised in the Contracting States.

AppB-98

Article 126

[Deleted.]

AppB-99

CHAPTER II

INFORMATION TO THE PUBLIC OR TO OFFICIAL AUTHORITIES

Article 127

European Patent Register

The European Patent Office shall keep a European Patent Register, in which the particulars specified in the Implementing Regulations shall be recorded. No entry shall be made in the European Patent Register before the publication of the European patent application. The European Patent Register shall be open to public inspection.

AppB-100

Article 128

Inspection of files

(1) Files relating to European patent applications which have not yet been published shall not be made available for inspection without the consent of the applicant.

AppB-101

(2) Any person who can prove that the applicant has invoked the rights under the European patent application against him may obtain inspection of the files before the publication of that application and without the consent of the applicant.

(3) Where a European divisional application or a new European patent application filed under Article 61, paragraph 1, is published, any person may obtain inspection of the files of the earlier application before the publication of that application and without the consent of the applicant.

(4) After the publication of the European patent application, the files relating to the application and the resulting European patent may be inspected on request, subject to the restrictions laid down in the Implementing Regulations.

(5) Even before the publication of the European patent application, the European Patent Office may communicate to third parties or publish the particulars specified in the Implementing Regulations.

Article 129

Periodical publications

AppB-
102

The European Patent Office shall periodically publish:
  (a) a European Patent Bulletin containing the particulars the publication of which is prescribed by this Convention, the Implementing Regulations or the President of the European Patent Office;
  (b) an Official Journal containing notices and information of a general character issued by the President of the European Patent Office, as well as any other information relevant to this Convention or its implementation.

Article 130

Exchange of information

AppB-
103

(1) Unless this Convention or national laws provide otherwise, the European Patent Office and the central industrial property office of any Contracting State shall, on request, communicate to each other any useful information regarding European or national patent applications and patents and any proceedings concerning them.
(2) Paragraph 1 shall apply to the communication of information by virtue of working agreements between the European Patent Office and
  (a) the central industrial property offices of other States;
  (b) any intergovernmental organisation entrusted with the task of granting patents;
  (c) any other organisation.
(3) Communications under paragraphs 1 and 2(a) and (b) shall not be subject to the restrictions laid down in Article 128. The Administrative Council may decide that communications under paragraph 2(c) shall not be subject to such restrictions, provided that the organisation concerned treats the information communicated as confidential until the European patent application has been published.

Article 131

Administrative and legal co-operation

AppB-
104

(1) Unless this Convention or national laws provide otherwise, the European Patent Office and the courts or authorities of Contracting States shall on request give assistance to each other by communicating information or opening files for inspection. Where the European Patent Office makes files available for inspection by courts, Public Prosecutors' Offices or central industrial property offices, the inspection shall not be subject to the restrictions laid down in Article 128.
(2) At the request of the European Patent Office, the courts or other competent authorities of Contracting States shall undertake, on behalf of the Office and within the limits of their jurisdiction, any necessary enquiries or other legal measures.

Article 132

Exchange of publications

AppB-
105

(1) The European Patent Office and the central industrial property offices of the Contracting States shall despatch to each other on request and for their own use one or more copies of their respective publications free of charge.

[1070]

(2) The European Patent Office may conclude agreements relating to the exchange or supply of publications.

CHAPTER III

REPRESENTATION

Article 133

General principles of representation

(1) Subject to paragraph 2, no person shall be compelled to be represented by a professional representative in proceedings established by this Convention.   AppB-106

(2) Natural or legal persons not having their residence or principal place of business in a Contracting State shall be represented by a professional representative and act through him in all proceedings established by this Convention, other than in filing a European patent application; the Implementing Regulations may permit other exceptions.

(3) Natural or legal persons having their residence or principal place of business in a Contracting State may be represented in proceedings established by this Convention by an employee, who need not be a professional representative but who shall be authorised in accordance with the Implementing Regulations. The Implementing Regulations may provide whether and under what conditions an employee of a legal person may also represent other legal persons which have their principal place of business in a Contracting State and which have economic connections with the first legal person.

(4) The Implementing Regulations may lay down special provisions concerning the common representation of parties acting in common.

Article 134

Representation before the European Patent Office

(1) Representation of natural or legal persons in proceedings established by this Convention may only be undertaken by professional representatives whose names appear on a list maintained for this purpose by the European Patent Office.   AppB-107

(2) Any natural person who
  (a) is a national of a Contracting State,
  (b) has his place of business or employment in a Contracting State and
  (c) has passed the European qualifying examination may be entered on the list of professional representatives.

(3) During a period of one year from the date on which the accession of a State to this Convention takes effect, entry on that list may also be requested by any natural person who
  (a) is a national of a Contracting State,
  (b) has his place of business or employment in the State having acceded to the Convention and
  (c) is entitled to represent natural or legal persons in patent matters before the central industrial property office of that State. Where such entitlement is not conditional upon the requirement of special professional qualifications, the person shall have regularly so acted in that State for at least five years.

[1071]

(4) Entry shall be effected upon request, accompanied by certificates indicating that the conditions laid down in paragraph 2 or 3 are fulfilled.

(5) Persons whose names appear on the list of professional representatives shall be entitled to act in all proceedings established by this Convention.

(6) For the purpose of acting as a professional representative, any person whose name appears on the list of professional representatives shall be entitled to establish a place of business in any Contracting State in which proceedings established by this Convention may be conducted, having regard to the Protocol on Centralisation annexed to this Convention. The authorities of such State may remove that entitlement in individual cases only in application of legal provisions adopted for the purpose of protecting public security and law and order. Before such action is taken, the President of the European Patent Office shall be consulted.

(7) The President of the European Patent Office may grant exemption from:

   (a) the requirement of paragraphs 2(a) or 3(a) in special circumstances;

   (b) the requirement of paragraph 3(c), second sentence, if the applicant furnishes proof that he has acquired the requisite qualification in another way.

(8) Representation in proceedings established by this Convention may also be undertaken, in the same way as by a professional representative, by any legal practitioner qualified in a Contracting State and having his place of business in that State, to the extent that he is entitled in that State to act as a professional representative in patent matters. Paragraph 6 shall apply mutatis mutandis.

Article 134a

Institute of Professional Representatives before the European Patent Office

AppB-
108

(1) The Administrative Council shall be competent to adopt and amend provisions governing:

   (a) the Institute of Professional Representatives before the European Patent Office, hereinafter referred to as the Institute;

   (b) the qualifications and training required of a person for admission to the European qualifying examination and the conduct of such examination;

   (c) the disciplinary power exercised by the Institute or the European Patent Office in respect of professional representatives;

   (d) the obligation of confidentiality on the professional representative and the privilege from disclosure in proceedings before the European Patent Office in respect of communications between a professional representative and his client or any other person.

(2) Any person entered on the list of professional representatives referred to in Article 134, paragraph 1, shall be a member of the Institute.

PART VIII

IMPACT ON NATIONAL LAW

CHAPTER I

CONVERSION INTO A NATIONAL PATENT APPLICATION

Article 135

Request for conversion

(1) The central industrial property office of a designated Contracting State shall, at the request of the applicant for or proprietor of a European patent, apply the procedure for the grant of a national patent in the following circumstances:

    (a) where the European patent application is deemed to be withdrawn under Article 77, paragraph 3;

    (b) in such other cases as are provided for by the national law, in which the European patent application is refused or withdrawn or deemed to be withdrawn, or the European patent is revoked under this Convention.

(2) In the case referred to in paragraph 1(a), the request for conversion shall be filed with the central industrial property office with which the European patent application has been filed. That office shall, subject to the provisions governing national security, transmit the request directly to the central industrial property offices of the Contracting States specified therein.

(3) In the cases referred to in paragraph 1(b), the request for conversion shall be submitted to the European Patent Office in accordance with the Implementing Regulations. It shall not be deemed to be filed until the conversion fee has been paid. The European Patent Office shall transmit the request to the central industrial property offices of the Contracting States specified therein.

(4) The effect of the European patent application referred to in Article 66 shall lapse if the request for conversion is not submitted in due time.

AppB-109

Article 136

[Deleted.]

AppB-110

Article 137

Formal requirements for conversion

(1) A European patent application transmitted in accordance with Article 135, paragraph 2 or 3, shall not be subjected to formal requirements of national law which are different from or additional to those provided for in this Convention.

(2) Any central industrial property office to which the European patent application is transmitted may require that the applicant shall, within a period of not less than two months:

    (a) pay the national application fee; and

    (b) file a translation of the original text of the European patent application in an official language of the State in question and, where appropriate, of the text as amended during proceedings before the European Patent Office which the applicant wishes to use as the basis for the national procedure.

AppB-111

CHAPTER II

REVOCATION AND PRIOR RIGHTS

Article 138

Revocation of European patents

AppB-
112

(1) Subject to Article 139, a European patent may be revoked with effect for a Contracting State only on the grounds that:

  (a) the subject-matter of the European patent is not patentable under Articles 52 to 57;
  (b) the European patent does not disclose the invention in a manner sufficiently clear and complete for it to be carried out by a person skilled in the art;
  (c) the subject-matter of the European patent extends beyond the content of the application as filed or, if the patent was granted on a divisional application or on a new application filed under Article 61, beyond the content of the earlier application as filed;
  (d) the protection conferred by the European patent has been extended; or
  (e) the proprietor of the European patent is not entitled under Article 60, paragraph 1.

(2) If the grounds for revocation affect the European patent only in part, the patent shall be limited by a corresponding amendment of the claims and revoked in part.

(3) In proceedings before the competent court or authority relating to the validity of the European patent, the proprietor of the patent shall have the right to limit the patent by amending the claims. The patent as thus limited shall form the basis for the proceedings.

Article 139

Prior rights and rights arising on the same date

AppB-
113

(1) In any designated Contracting State a European patent application and a European patent shall have with regard to a national patent application and a national patent the same prior right effect as a national patent application and a national patent.

(2) A national patent application and a national patent in a Contracting State shall have with regard to a European patent designating that Contracting State the same prior right effect as if the European patent were a national patent.

(3) Any Contracting State may prescribe whether and on what terms an invention disclosed in both a European patent application or patent and a national application or patent having the same date of filing or, where priority is claimed, the same date of priority, may be protected simultaneously by both applications or patents.

CHAPTER III

MISCELLANEOUS EFFECTS

Article 140
National utility models and utility certificates

Articles 66, 124, 135, 137 and 139 shall apply to utility models and utility certificates and to applications for utility models and utility certificates registered or deposited in the Contracting States whose laws make provision for such models or certificates. AppB-114

Article 141
Renewal fees for European patents

(1) Renewal fees for a European patent may only be imposed for the years which follow that referred to in Article 86, paragraph 2. AppB-115
(2) Any renewal fees falling due within two months of the publication in the European Patent Bulletin of the mention of the grant of the European patent shall be deemed to have been validly paid if they are paid within that period. Any additional fee provided for under national law shall not be charged.

PART IX

SPECIAL AGREEMENTS

[Articles 142–149a are not reproduced here.] AppB-116

PART X

INTERNATIONAL APPLICATIONS UNDER THE PATENT COOPERATION TREATY—EURO-PCT APPLICATIONS

Article 150
Application of the Patent Cooperation Treaty

(1) The Patent Cooperation Treaty of 19 June 1970, hereinafter referred to as the PCT, shall be applied in accordance with the provisions of this Part. AppB-117
(2) International applications filed under the PCT may be the subject of proceedings before the European Patent Office. In such proceedings, the provisions of the PCT and its Regulations shall be applied, supplemented by the provisions of this Convention. In case of conflict, the provisions of the PCT or its Regulations shall prevail.

Article 151

The European Patent Office as a receiving Office

AppB-
118

The European Patent Office shall act as a receiving Office within the meaning of the PCT, in accordance with the Implementing Regulations. Article 75, paragraph 2, shall apply.

Article 152

The European Patent Office as an International Searching Authority or International Preliminary Examining Authority

AppB-
119

The European Patent Office shall act as an International Searching Authority and International Preliminary Examining Authority within the meaning of the PCT, in accordance with an agreement between the Organisation and the International Bureau of the World Intellectual Property Organization, for applicants who are residents or nationals of a State party to this Convention. This agreement may provide that the European Patent Office shall also act for other applicants.

Article 153

The European Patent Office as designated Office or elected Office

AppB-
120

(1) The European Patent Office shall be
   (a) a designated Office for any State party to this Convention in respect of which the PCT is in force, which is designated in the international application and for which the applicant wishes to obtain a European patent, and
   (b) an elected Office, if the applicant has elected a State designated pursuant to letter (a).

(2) An international application for which the European Patent Office is a designated or elected Office, and which has been accorded an international date of filing, shall be equivalent to a regular European application (Euro-PCT application).

(3) The international publication of a Euro-PCT application in an official language of the European Patent Office shall take the place of the publication of the European patent application and shall be mentioned in the European Patent Bulletin.

(4) If the Euro-PCT application is published in another language, a translation into one of the official languages shall be filed with the European Patent Office, which shall publish it. Subject to Article 67, paragraph 3, the provisional protection under Article 67, paragraphs 1 and 2, shall be effective from the date of that publication.

(5) The Euro-PCT application shall be treated as a European patent application and shall be considered as comprised in the state of the art under Article 54, paragraph 3, if the conditions laid down in paragraph 3 or 4 and in the Implementing Regulations are fulfilled.

(6) The international search report drawn up in respect of a Euro-PCT application or the declaration replacing it, and their international publication, shall take the place of the European search report and the mention of its publication in the European Patent Bulletin.

(7) A supplementary European search report shall be drawn up in respect of any Euro-PCT application under paragraph 5. The Administrative Council may decide that the supplementary search report is to be dispensed with or that the search fee is to be reduced.

Article 154

[Deleted.]   AppB-121

Article 155

[Deleted.]   AppB-122

Article 156

[Deleted.]   AppB-123

Article 157

[Deleted.]   AppB-124

Article 158

[Deleted.]   AppB-125

PART XI

TRANSITIONAL PROVISIONS

[Deleted.]   AppB-126

PART XII

FINAL PROVISIONS

Article 164

Implementing Regulations and Protocols

(1) The Implementing Regulations, the Protocol on Recognition, the Protocol on   AppB-127
Privileges and Immunities, the Protocol on Centralisation, the Protocol on the
Interpretation of Article 69 and the Protocol on Staff Complement shall be integral
parts of this Convention.
(2) In case of conflict between the provisions of this Convention and those of the
Implementing Regulations, the provisions of this Convention shall prevail.

Article 165

Signature—Ratification

(1) This Convention shall be open for signature until 5 April 1974 by the States   AppB-128
which took part in the Inter-Governmental Conference for the setting up of a
European System for the Grant of Patents or were informed of the holding of that
conference and offered the option of taking part therein.
(2) This Convention shall be subject to ratification; instruments of ratification shall
be deposited with the Government of the Federal Republic of Germany.

Article 166
Accession

AppB-129

(1) This Convention shall be open to accession by:
  (a) the States referred to in Article 165, paragraph 1;
  (b) any other European State at the invitation of the Administrative Council.
(2) Any State which has been a party to the Convention and has ceased to be so as a result of the application of Article 172, paragraph 4, may again become a party to the Convention by acceding to it.
(3) Instruments of accession shall be deposited with the Government of the Federal Republic of Germany.

Article 167

AppB-130

[Deleted.]

Article 168
Territorial field of application

AppB-131

(1) Any Contracting State may declare in its instrument of ratification or accession, or may inform the Government of the Federal Republic of Germany by written notification at any time thereafter, that this Convention shall be applicable to one or more of the territories for the external relations of which it is responsible. European patents granted for that Contracting State shall also have effect in the territories for which such a declaration has taken effect.
(2) If the declaration referred to in paragraph 1 is contained in the instrument of ratification or accession, it shall take effect on the same date as the ratification or accession; if the declaration is notified after the deposit of the instrument of ratification or accession, such notification shall take effect six months after the date of its receipt by the Government of the Federal Republic of Germany.
(3) Any Contracting State may at any time declare that the Convention shall cease to apply to some or to all of the territories in respect of which it has given notification pursuant to paragraph 1. Such declaration shall take effect one year after the date on which the Government of the Federal Republic of Germany received notification thereof.

Article 169
Entry into force

AppB-132

(1) This Convention shall enter into force three months after the deposit of the last instrument of ratification or accession by six States on whose territory the total number of patent applications filed in 1970 amounted to at least 180 000 for all the said States.
(2) Any ratification or accession after the entry into force of this Convention shall take effect on the first day of the third month after the deposit of the instrument of ratification or accession.

Article 170
Initial contribution

(1) Any State which ratifies or accedes to this Convention after its entry into force shall pay to the Organisation an initial contribution, which shall not be refunded.
(2) The initial contribution shall be 5% of an amount calculated by applying the percentage obtained for the State in question, on the date on which ratification or accession takes effect, in accordance with the scale provided for in Article 40, paragraphs 3 and 4, to the sum of the special financial contributions due from the other Contracting States in respect of the accounting periods preceding the date referred to above.
(3) In the event that special financial contributions were not required in respect of the accounting period immediately preceding the date referred to in paragraph 2, the scale of contributions referred to in that paragraph shall be the scale that would have been applicable to the State concerned in respect of the last year for which financial contributions were required.

AppB-133

Article 171
Duration of the Convention

The present Convention shall be of unlimited duration.

AppB-134

Article 172
Revision

(1) This Convention may be revised by a Conference of the Contracting States.
(2) The Conference shall be prepared and convened by the Administrative Council. The Conference shall not be validly constituted unless at least three-quarters of the Contracting States are represented at it. Adoption of the revised text shall require a majority of three-quarters of the Contracting States represented and voting at the Conference. Abstentions shall not be considered as votes.
(3) The revised text shall enter into force when it has been ratified or acceded to by the number of Contracting States specified by the Conference, and at the time specified by that Conference.
(4) Such States as have not ratified or acceded to the revised text of the Convention at the time of its entry into force shall cease to be parties to this Convention as from that time.

AppB-135

Article 173
Disputes between Contracting States

(1) Any dispute between Contracting States concerning the interpretation or application of the present Convention which is not settled by negotiation shall be submitted, at the request of one of the States concerned, to the Administrative Council, which shall endeavour to bring about agreement between the States concerned.
(2) If such agreement is not reached within six months from the date when the dispute was referred to the Administrative Council, any one of the States concerned may submit the dispute to the International Court of Justice for a binding decision.

AppB-136

Article 174

Denunciation

AppB-
137

Any Contracting State may at any time denounce this Convention. Denunciation shall be notified to the Government of the Federal Republic of Germany. It shall take effect one year after the date of receipt of such notification.

Article 175

Preservation of acquired rights

AppB-
138

(1) In the event of a State ceasing to be party to this Convention in accordance with Article 172, paragraph 4, or Article 174 rights already acquired pursuant to this Convention shall not be impaired.

(2) A European patent application which is pending when a designated State ceases to be party to the Convention shall be processed by the European Patent Office, as far as that State is concerned, as if the Convention in force thereafter were applicable to that State.

(3) Paragraph 2 shall apply to European patents in respect of which, on the date mentioned in that paragraph, an opposition is pending or the opposition period has not expired.

(4) Nothing in this Article shall affect the right of any State that has ceased to be a party to this Convention to treat any European patent in accordance with the text to which it was a party.

Article 176

Financial rights and obligations of former Contracting States

AppB-
139

(1) Any State which has ceased to be a party to this Convention in accordance with Article 172, paragraph 4, or Article 174, shall have the special financial contributions which it has paid pursuant to Article 40, paragraph 2, refunded to it by the Organisation only at the time when and under the conditions whereby the Organisation refunds special financial contributions paid by other States during the same accounting period.

(2) The State referred to in paragraph 1 shall, even after ceasing to be a party to this Convention, continue to pay the proportion pursuant to Article 39 of renewal fees in respect of European patents remaining in force in that State, at the rate current on the date on which it ceased to be a party.

Article 177

Languages of the Convention

AppB-
140

(1) This Convention, drawn up in a single original, in the English, French and German languages, shall be deposited in the archives of the Government of the Federal Republic of Germany, the three texts being equally authentic.

(2) The texts of this Convention drawn up in official languages of Contracting States other than those specified in paragraph 1 shall, if they have been approved by the Administrative Council, be considered as official texts. In the event of disagreement on the interpretation of the various texts, the texts referred to in paragraph 1 shall be authentic.

Article 178

Transmission and notifications

(1) The Government of the Federal Republic of Germany shall draw up certified true copies of this Convention and shall transmit them to the Governments of all signatory or acceding States. `AppB-141`
(2) The Government of the Federal Republic of Germany shall notify to the Governments of the States referred to in paragraph 1:
  (a) the deposit of any instrument of ratification or accession;
  (b) any declaration or notification received pursuant to Article 168;
  (c) any denunciation received pursuant to Article 174 and the date on which such denunciation comes into force.
(3) The Government of the Federal Republic of Germany shall register this Convention with the Secretariat of the United Nations.

IN WITNESS WHEREOF, the Plenipotentiaries authorised thereto, having presented their Full Powers, found to be in good and due form, have signed this Convention.
  Done at Munich this fifth day of October one thousand nine hundred and seventy-three

Protocol on Jurisdiction and the Recognition of Decisions in respect of the Right to the Grant of a European Patent (Protocol on Recognition) of 5 October 1973 `AppB-142`

SECTION I

Jurisdiction

Article 1

(1) The courts of the Contracting States shall, in accordance with Articles 2 to 6, have jurisdiction to decide claims, against the applicant, to the right to the grant of a European patent in respect of one or more of the Contracting States designated in the European patent application. `AppB-142`
(2) For the purposes of this Protocol, the term "courts" shall include authorities which, under the national law of a Contracting State, have jurisdiction to decide the claims referred to in paragraph 1. Any Contracting State shall notify the European Patent Office of the identity of any authority on which such a jurisdiction is conferred, and the European Patent Office shall inform the other Contracting States accordingly.
(3) For the purposes of this Protocol, the term "Contracting State" refers to a Contracting State which has not excluded application of this Protocol pursuant to Article 167 of the Convention.

Article 2

Subject to Articles 4 and 5, if an applicant for a European patent has his residence or principal place of business within one of the Contracting States, proceedings shall be brought against him in the courts of that Contracting State. `AppB-143`

Article 3

AppB-
144

Subject to Articles 4 and 5, if an applicant for a European patent has his residence or principal place of business outside the Contracting States, and if the party claiming the right to the grant of the European patent has his residence or principal place of business within one of the Contracting States, the courts of the latter State shall have exclusive jurisdiction.

Article 4

AppB-
145

Subject to Article 5, if the subject-matter of a European patent application is the invention of an employee, the courts of the Contracting State, if any, whose law determines the right to the European patent pursuant to Article 60, paragraph 1, second sentence, of the Convention, shall have exclusive jurisdiction over proceedings between the employee and the employer.

Article 5

AppB-
146

(1) If the parties to a dispute concerning the right to the grant of a European patent have concluded an agreement, either in writing or verbally with written confirmation, to the effect that a court or the courts of a particular Contracting State shall decide on such a dispute, the court or courts of that State shall have exclusive jurisdiction.
(2) However, if the parties are an employee and his employer, paragraph 1 shall only apply in so far as the national law governing the contract of employment allows the agreement in question.

Article 6

AppB-
147

In cases where neither Articles 2 to 4 nor Article 5, paragraph 1, apply, the courts of the Federal Republic of Germany shall have exclusive jurisdiction.

Article 7

AppB-
148

The courts of Contracting States before which claims referred to in Article 1 are brought shall of their own motion decide whether or not they have jurisdiction pursuant to Articles 2 to 6.

Article 8

AppB-
149

(1) In the event of proceedings based on the same claim and between the same parties being brought before courts of different Contracting States, the court to which a later application is made shall of its own motion decline jurisdiction in favour of the court to which an earlier application was made.

(2) In the event of the jurisdiction of the court to which an earlier application is made being challenged, the court to which a later application is made shall stay the proceedings until the other court takes a final decision.

SECTION II

Recognition

Article 9

(1) Subject to the provisions of Article 11, paragraph 2, final decisions given in any Contracting State on the right to the grant of a European patent in respect of one or more of the Contracting States designated in the European patent application shall be recognised without requiring a special procedure in the other Contracting States.
(2) The jurisdiction of the court whose decision is to be recognised and the validity of such decision may not be reviewed.

AppB-150

Article 10

Article 9, paragraph 1, shall not be applicable where:
  (a) an applicant for a European patent who has not contested a claim proves that the document initiating the proceedings was not notified to him regularly and sufficiently early for him to defend himself; or
  (b) an applicant proves that the decision is incompatible with another decision given in a Contracting State in proceedings between the same parties which were started before those in which the decision to be recognised was given.

AppB-151

Article 11

(1) In relations between any Contracting States the provisions of this Protocol shall prevail over any conflicting provisions of other agreements on jurisdiction or the recognition of judgments.
(2) This Protocol shall not affect the implementation of any agreement between a Contracting State and a State which is not bound by the Protocol.

AppB-152

Protocol on Privileges and Immunities of the European Patent Organisation (Protocol on Privileges and Immunities) of 5 October 1973

[The Protocol is not reproduced here.]

AppB-153

Protocol on the Centralisation of the European Patent System and on its Introduction (Protocol on Centralisation) of 5 October 1973 as revised by the Act revising the EPC of 29 November 2000

[The Protocol is not reproduced here.]

AppB-154

AppB-
155

Protocol on the Staff Complement of the European Patent Office at The Hague (Protocol on Staff Complement) of 29 November 2000

Protocol on the Interpretation of Article 69 EPC of 5 October 1973 as revised by the Act revising the EPC of 29 November 2000

Article 1

General principles

AppB-
156

Article 69 should not be interpreted as meaning that the extent of the protection conferred by a European patent is to be understood as that defined by the strict, literal meaning of the wording used in the claims, the description and drawings being employed only for the purpose of resolving an ambiguity found in the claims. Nor should it be taken to mean that the claims serve only as a guideline and that the actual protection conferred may extend to what, from a consideration of the description and drawings by a person skilled in the art, the patent proprietor has contemplated. On the contrary, it is to be interpreted as defining a position between these extremes which combines a fair protection for the patent proprietor with a reasonable degree of legal certainty for third parties.

Article 2

Equivalents

AppB-
157

For the purpose of determining the extent of protection conferred by a European patent, due account shall be taken of any element which is equivalent to an element specified in the claims.

[The Protocol is not reproduced here.]

COMMUNITY PATENT CONVENTION (EXTRACTS)
Done at Luxembourg on 15 December 1989 89/695/EEC

PART II.

SUBSTANTIVE PATENT LAW

CHAPTER II.

EFFECTS OF THE COMMUNITY PATENT AND THE EUROPEAN PATENT APPLICATION

Article 25

Prohibition of direct use of the invention

A Community patent shall confer on its proprietor the right to prevent all third parties not having his consent: **AppC-01**

(a) from making, offering, putting on the market or using a product which is the subject-matter of the patent, or importing or stocking the product for these purposes;

(b) from using a process which is the subject-matter of the patent or, when the third party knows, or it is obvious in the circumstances, that the use of the process is prohibited without consent of the proprietor of the patent, from offering the process for use within the territories of the Contracting States;

(c) from offering, putting on the market, using, or importing or stocking for these purposes of the product obtained directly by a process which is the subject-matter of the patent.

Article 26

Prohibition of indirect use of the invention

1. A Community patent shall also confer on its proprietor the right to prevent all third parties not having his consent from supplying or offering to supply within the territories of the Contracting States a person, other than a party entitled to exploit the patented invention, with means, relating to an essential element of that invention, for putting it into effect therein, when the third party knows, or it is obvious in the circumstances, that these means are suitable and intended for putting that invention into effect. **AppC-02**

2. Paragraph 1 shall not apply when the means are staple commercial products, except when the third party induces the person supplied to commit acts prohibited by Article 25.

3. Persons performing the acts referred to in Article 27(a) to (c) shall not be considered to be parties entitled to exploit the invention within the meaning of paragraph 1.

Article 27

Limitation of the effects of the Community patent

AppC-03   The rights conferred by a Community patent shall not extend to:

     (a)   acts done privately and for non-commercial purposes;

     (b)   acts done for experimental purposes relating to the subject-matter of the patented invention;

     (c)   the extemporaneous preparation for individual cases in a pharmacy of a medicine in accordance with a medical prescription nor acts concerning the medicine so prepared;

     (d)   the use on board vessels of the countries of the Union of Paris for the Protection of Industrial Property, other than the Contracting States, of the patented invention, in the body of the vessel, in the machinery, tackle, gear and other accessories, when such vessels temporarily or accidentally enter the waters of Contracting States, provided that the invention is used there exclusively for the needs of the vessel;

     (e)   the use of the patented invention in the construction or operation of aircraft or land vehicles of countries of the Union of Paris for the Protection of Industrial Property, other than the Contracting States, or of accessories to such aircraft or land vehicles, when these temporarily or accidentally enter the territory of Contracting States;

     (f)   the acts specified in Article 27 of the Convention on International Civil Aviation of December 7, 1944, where these acts concern the aircraft of a State, other than the Contracting States, benefiting from the provisions of that Article.

Article 28

Exhaustion of the rights conferred by the Community patent

AppC-04   The rights conferred by a Community patent shall not extend to acts concerning a product covered by that patent which are done within the territories of the Contracting States after that product has been put on the market in one of these States by the proprietor of the patent or with his express consent, unless there are grounds which, under Community law, would justify the extension to such acts of the rights conferred by the patent.

     [...]

Article 32

Rights conferred by a European patent application after publication

AppC-05 **1.** Compensation reasonable in the circumstances may be claimed from a third party who, in the period between the date of publication of a European patent application in which the Contracting States are designated and the date of publication of the mention of the grant of the European patent, has made any use of the invention which, after that period, would be prohibited by virtue of the Community patent.

2. Any Contracting State which does not have as an official language the language of the proceedings of a European patent application in which the Contracting States are designated may prescribe that such application shall not confer, in respect of use of the invention within its territory, the right referred to in paragraph 1 until such time as the applicant, at his option, has:

(a) supplied a translation of the claims in one of its official languages to the competent authority of that State and the translation has been published in accordance with the law of that State; or

(b) communicated such a translation to the person using the invention within that State.

3. Any Contracting State referred to in paragraph 2 may prescribe that, where the applicant avails himself of the option provided for in sub-paragraph 2(b), the right conferred by the application in respect of use of the invention within the territory of the State concerned may be invoked only if the applicant supplies a copy of the translation to the competent authority of that State within 15 days after it has been communicated to the person using the invention within that State. The Contracting State may prescribe that the authority shall publish the translation, in accordance with the law of that State.

4. Any Contracting State which adopts a provision under paragraph 2 may prescribe that, where the translation of the claims is defective, any person who, in that State, has used or made effective and serious preparations for using the invention the use of which would not constitute infringement of the application in the original translation of the claims shall be liable for reasonable compensation in accordance with paragraph 1 only from the moment when the corrected translation of the claims has been published or has been received by him, unless it is established that he did not act in good faith, in which case he shall be liable for reasonable compensation in accordance with paragraph 1 from the moment when the requirements of paragraph 2 were fulfilled.

[...]

Article 35
Burden of proof

1. If the subject-matter of a Community patent is a process for obtaining a new product, the same product when produced by any other party shall, in the absence of proof to the contrary, be deemed to have been obtained by the patented process. **AppC-06**

2. In the adduction of proof to the contrary, the legitimate interests of the defendant in protecting his manufacturing and business secrets shall be taken into account.

REGULATION 469/2009 OF THE EUROPEAN PARLIAMENT AND COUNCIL

Regulation (EC) No 469/2009 Of The European Parliament And Of The Council Of 6 May 2009 Concerning The Supplementary Protection Certificate For Medicinal Products (Codified Version)

THE EUROPEAN PARLIAMENT AND THE COUNCIL OF THE EUROPEAN UNION,

Having regard to the Treaty establishing the European Community, and in particular Article 95 thereof,

Having regard to the proposal from the Commission,

Having regard to the opinion of the European Economic and Social Committee[1],

Acting in accordance with the procedure laid down in Article 251 of the Treaty[2]

Whereas:

(1)   Council Regulation (EEC) No 1768/92 of 18 June 1992 concerning the creation of a supplementary protection certificate for medicinal products[3] has been substantially amended several times[4]. In the interests of clarity and rationality the said Regulation should be codified.

(2)   Pharmaceutical research plays a decisive role in the continuing improvement in public health.

(3)   Medicinal products, especially those that are the result of long, costly research will not continue to be developed in the Community and in Europe unless they are covered by favourable rules that provide for sufficient protection to encourage such research.

(4)   At the moment, the period that elapses between the filing of an application for a patent for a new medicinal product and authorisation to place the medicinal product on the market makes the period of effective protection under the patent insufficient to cover the investment put into the research.

(5)   This situation leads to a lack of protection which penalises pharmaceutical research.

(6)   There exists a risk of research centres situated in the Member States relocating to countries that offer greater protection.

---

[1]   OJ C 77, 31.3.2009, p. 42.
[2]   Opinion of the European Parliament of 21 October 2008 (not yet published in the Official Journal) and Council Decision of 6 April 2009.
[3]   OJ L 182, 2.7.1992, p. 1.
[4]   See Annex I. (Editorial note: Annex I is not reproduced here.)

(7) A uniform solution at Community level should be provided for, thereby preventing the heterogeneous development of national laws leading to further disparities which would be likely to create obstacles to the free movement of medicinal products within the Community and thus directly affect the functioning of the internal market.

(8) Therefore, the provision of a supplementary protection certificate granted, under the same conditions, by each of the Member States at the request of the holder of a national or European patent relating to a medicinal product for which marketing authorisation has been granted is necessary. A regulation is therefore the most appropriate legal instrument.

(9) The duration of the protection granted by the certificate should be such as to provide adequate effective protection. For this purpose, the holder of both a patent and a certificate should be able to enjoy an overall maximum of 15 years of exclusivity from the time the medicinal product in question first obtains authorisation to be placed on the market in the Community.

(10) All the interests at stake, including those of public health, in a sector as complex and sensitive as the pharmaceutical sector should nevertheless be taken into account. For this purpose, the certificate cannot be granted for a period exceeding five years. The protection granted should furthermore be strictly confined to the product which obtained authorisation to be placed on the market as a medicinal product.

(11) Provision should be made for appropriate limitation of the duration of the certificate in the special case where a patent term has already been extended under a specific national law,

HAVE ADOPTED THIS REGULATION:

Article 1

Definitions

For the purposes of this Regulation, the following definitions shall apply: AppD-01

(a) 'medicinal product' means any substance or combination of substances presented for treating or preventing disease in human beings or animals and any substance or combination of substances which may be administered to human beings or animals with a view to making a medical diagnosis or to restoring, correcting or modifying physiological functions in humans or in animals;

(b) 'product' means the active ingredient or combination of active ingredients of a medicinal product;

(c) 'basic patent' means a patent which protects a product as such, a process to obtain a product or an application of a product, and which is designated by its holder for the purpose of the procedure for grant of a certificate;

(d) 'certificate' means the supplementary protection certificate;

(e) 'application for an extension of the duration' means an application for an extension of the duration of the certificate pursuant to Article 13(3) of this Regulation and Article 36 of Regulation (EC) No 1901/2006 of the

European Parliament and of the Council of 12 December 2006 on medicinal products for paediatric use[5].

Article 2

Scope

AppD-02 Any product protected by a patent in the territory of a Member State and subject, prior to being placed on the market as a medicinal product, to an administrative authorisation procedure as laid down in Directive 2001/83/EC of the European Parliament and of the Council of 6 November 2001 on the Community code relating to medicinal products for human use[6] or Directive 2001/82/EC of the European Parliament and of the Council of 6 November 2001 on the Community code relating to veterinary medicinal products[7] may, under the terms and conditions provided for in this Regulation, be the subject of a certificate.

Article 3

Conditions for obtaining a certificate

AppD-03 A certificate shall be granted if, in the Member State in which the application referred to in Article 7 is submitted and at the date of that application:
  (a) the product is protected by a basic patent in force;
  (b) a valid authorisation to place the product on the market as a medicinal product has been granted in accordance with Directive 2001/83/EC or Directive 2001/82/EC, as appropriate;
  (c) the product has not already been the subject of a certificate;
  (d) the authorisation referred to in point (b) is the first authorisation to place the product on the market as a medicinal product.

Article 4

Subject matter of protection

AppD-04 Within the limits of the protection conferred by the basic patent, the protection conferred by a certificate shall extend only to the product covered by the authorisation to place the corresponding medicinal product on the market and for any use of the product as a medicinal product that has been authorised before the expiry of the certificate.

Article 5

Effects of the certificate

AppD-05 Subject to the provisions of Article 4, the certificate shall confer the same rights as conferred by the basic patent and shall be subject to the same limitations and the same obligations.

---

5 OJ L 378, 27.12.2006, p. 1.
6 OJ L 311, 28.11.2001, p. 67.
7 OJ L 311, 28.11.2001, p. 1.

Article 6

Entitlement to the certificate

The certificate shall be granted to the holder of the basic patent or his successor in title. **AppD-06**

Article 7

Application for a certificate

1. The application for a certificate shall be lodged within six months of the date on which the authorisation referred to in Article 3(b) to place the product on the market as a medicinal product was granted. **AppD-07**

2. Notwithstanding paragraph 1, where the authorisation to place the product on the market is granted before the basic patent is granted, the application for a certificate shall be lodged within six months of the date on which the patent is granted.

3. The application for an extension of the duration may be made when lodging the application for a certificate or when the application for the certificate is pending and the appropriate requirements of Article 8(1)(d) or Article 8(2), respectively, are fulfilled.

4. The application for an extension of the duration of a certificate already granted shall be lodged not later than two years before the expiry of the certificate.

5. Notwithstanding paragraph 4, for five years following the entry into force of Regulation (EC) No 1901/2006, the application for an extension of the duration of a certificate already granted shall be lodged not later than six months before the expiry of the certificate.

Article 8

Content of the application for a certificate

1. The application for a certificate shall contain: **AppD-08**

  (a) a request for the grant of a certificate, stating in particular:

    (i) the name and address of the applicant;

    (ii) if he has appointed a representative, the name and address of the representative;

    (iii) the number of the basic patent and the title of the invention;

    (iv) the number and date of the first authorisation to place the product on the market, as referred to in Article 3(b) and, if this authorisation is not the first authorisation for placing the product on the market in the Community, the number and date of that authorisation;

  (b) a copy of the authorisation to place the product on the market, as referred to in Article 3(b), in which the product is identified, containing in particular the number and date of the authorisation and the summary of the product characteristics listed in Article 11 of Directive 2001/83/EC or Article 14 of Directive 2001/82/EC;

  (c) if the authorisation referred to in point (b) is not the first authorisation for placing the product on the market as a medicinal product in the Community, information regarding the identity of the product thus authorised and the legal provision under which the authorisation procedure took place, together with a copy of the notice publishing the authorisation in the appropriate official publication;

(d) where the application for a certificate includes a request for an extension of the duration:

  (i) a copy of the statement indicating compliance with an agreed completed paediatric investigation plan as referred to in Article 36(1) of Regulation (EC) No 1901/2006;

  (ii) where necessary, in addition to the copy of the authorisation to place the product on the market as referred to in point (b), proof of possession of authorisations to place the product on the market of all other Member States, as referred to in Article 36(3) of Regulation (EC) No 1901/2006.

2. Where an application for a certificate is pending, an application for an extended duration in accordance with Article 7(3) shall include the particulars referred to in paragraph 1(d) of this Article and a reference to the application for a certificate already filed.

3. The application for an extension of the duration of a certificate already granted shall contain the particulars referred to in paragraph 1(d) and a copy of the certificate already granted.

4. Member States may provide that a fee is to be payable upon application for a certificate and upon application for the extension of the duration of a certificate.

Article 9
Lodging of an application for a certificate

AppD-09 1. The application for a certificate shall be lodged with the competent industrial property office of the Member State which granted the basic patent or on whose behalf it was granted and in which the authorisation referred to in Article 3(b) to place the product on the market was obtained, unless the Member State designates another authority for the purpose.

The application for an extension of the duration of a certificate shall be lodged with the competent authority of the Member State concerned.

2. Notification of the application for a certificate shall be published by the authority referred to in paragraph 1. The notification shall contain at least the following information:

(a) the name and address of the applicant;
(b) the number of the basic patent;
(c) the title of the invention;
(d) the number and date of the authorisation to place the product on the market, referred to in Article 3(b), and the product identified in that authorisation;
(e) where relevant, the number and date of the first authorisation to place the product on the market in the Community;
(f) where applicable, an indication that the application includes an application for an extension of the duration.

(3) Paragraph 2 shall apply to the notification of the application for an extension of the duration of a certificate already granted or where an application for a certificate is pending. The notification shall additionally contain an indication of the application for an extended duration of the certificate.

[1092]

Article 10

Grant of the certificate or rejection of the application for a certificate

1. Where the application for a certificate and the product to which it relates meet the conditions laid down in this Regulation, the authority referred to in Article 9(1) shall grant the certificate. **AppD-10**

2. The authority referred to in Article 9(1) shall, subject to paragraph 3, reject the application for a certificate if the application or the product to which it relates does not meet the conditions laid down in this Regulation.

3. Where the application for a certificate does not meet the conditions laid down in Article 8, the authority referred to in Article 9(1) shall ask the applicant to rectify the irregularity, or to settle the fee, within a stated time.

4. If the irregularity is not rectified or the fee is not settled under paragraph 3 within the stated time, the authority shall reject the application.

5. Member States may provide that the authority referred to in Article 9(1) is to grant certificates without verifying that the conditions laid down in Article 3(c) and (d) are met.

6. Paragraphs 1 to 4 shall apply mutatis mutandis to the application for an extension of the duration.

Article 11

Publication

1. Notification of the fact that a certificate has been granted shall be published by the authority referred to in Article 9(1). The notification shall contain at least the following information: **AppD-11**

(a) the name and address of the holder of the certificate;

(b) the number of the basic patent;

(c) the title of the invention;

(d) the number and date of the authorisation to place the product on the market referred to in Article 3(b) and the product identified in that authorisation;

(e) where relevant, the number and date of the first authorisation to place the product on the market in the Community;

(f) the duration of the certificate.

2. Notification of the fact that the application for a certificate has been rejected shall be published by the authority referred to in Article 9(1). The notification shall contain at least the information listed in Article 9(2).

3. Paragraphs 1 and 2 shall apply to the notification of the fact that an extension of the duration of a certificate has been granted or of the fact that the application for an extension has been rejected.

Article 12

Annual fees

Member States may require that the certificate be subject to the payment of annual fees. **AppD-12**

Article 13

Duration of the certificate

AppD-13 **1.** The certificate shall take effect at the end of the lawful term of the basic patent for a period equal to the period which elapsed between the date on which the application for a basic patent was lodged and the date of the first authorisation to place the product on the market in the Community, reduced by a period of five years.

2. Notwithstanding paragraph 1, the duration of the certificate may not exceed five years from the date on which it takes effect.

3. The periods laid down in paragraphs 1 and 2 shall be extended by six months in the case where Article 36 of Regulation (EC) No 1901/2006 applies. In that case, the duration of the period laid down in paragraph 1 of this Article may be extended only once.

4. Where a certificate is granted for a product protected by a patent which, before 2 January 1993, had its term extended or for which such extension was applied for, under national law, the term of protection to be afforded under this certificate shall be reduced by the number of years by which the term of the patent exceeds 20 years.

Article 14

Expiry of the certificate

AppD-14 The certificate shall lapse:

(a) at the end of the period provided for in Article 13;

(b) if the certificate holder surrenders it;

(c) if the annual fee laid down in accordance with Article 12 is not paid in time;

(d) if and as long as the product covered by the certificate may no longer be placed on the market following the withdrawal of the appropriate authorisation or authorisations to place on the market in accordance with Directive 2001/83/EC or Directive 2001/82/EC. The authority referred to in Article 9(1) of this Regulation may decide on the lapse of the certificate either of its own motion or at the request of a third party.

Article 15

Invalidity of the certificate

AppD-15 **1.** The certificate shall be invalid if:

(a) it was granted contrary to the provisions of Article 3;

(b) the basic patent has lapsed before its lawful term expires;

(c) the basic patent is revoked or limited to the extent that the product for which the certificate was granted would no longer be protected by the claims of the basic patent or, after the basic patent has expired, grounds for revocation exist which would have justified such revocation or limitation.

2. Any person may submit an application or bring an action for a declaration of invalidity of the certificate before the body responsible under national law for the revocation of the corresponding basic patent.

Article 16

Revocation of an extension of the duration

1. The extension of the duration may be revoked if it was granted contrary to the   AppD-16
provisions of Article 36 of Regulation (EC) No 1901/2006.
2. Any person may submit an application for revocation of the extension of the
duration to the body responsible under national law for the revocation of the corresponding basic patent.

Article 17

Notification of lapse or invalidity

1. If the certificate lapses in accordance with point (b), (c) or (d) of Article 14,   AppD-17
or is invalid in accordance with Article 15, notification thereof shall be published
by the authority referred to in Article 9(1).
2. If the extension of the duration is revoked in accordance with Article 16,
notification thereof shall be published by the authority referred to in Article 9(1).

Article 18

Appeals

The decisions of the authority referred to in Article 9(1) or of the bodies referred   AppD-18
to in Articles 15(2) and 16(2) taken under this Regulation shall be open to the same
appeals as those provided for in national law against similar decisions taken in
respect of national patents.

Article 19

Procedure

1. In the absence of procedural provisions in this Regulation, the procedural provi-   AppD-19
sions applicable under national law to the corresponding basic patent shall apply
to the certificate, unless the national law lays down special procedural provisions
for certificates.
2. Notwithstanding paragraph 1, the procedure for opposition to the granting of
a certificate shall be excluded.

Article 20

Additional provisions relating to the enlargement of the Community

Without prejudice to the other provisions of this Regulation, the following provi-   AppD-20
sions shall apply:
  (a) any medicinal product protected by a valid basic patent and for which the
      first authorisation to place it on the market as a medicinal product was
      obtained after 1 January 2000 may be granted a certificate in Bulgaria,
      provided that the application for a certificate was lodged within six months
      from 1 January 2007;
  (b) any medicinal product protected by a valid basic patent in the Czech

Republic and for which the first authorisation to place it on the market as a medicinal product was obtained:

(i)   in the Czech Republic after 10 November 1999 may be granted a certificate, provided that the application for a certificate was lodged within six months of the date on which the first market authorisation was obtained;

(ii) in the Community not earlier than six months prior to 1 May 2004 may be granted a certificate, provided that the application for a certificate was lodged within six months of the date on which the first market authorisation was obtained;

(c) any medicinal product protected by a valid basic patent and for which the first authorisation to place it on the market as a medicinal product was obtained in Estonia prior to 1 May 2004 may be granted a certificate, provided that the application for a certificate was lodged within six months of the date on which the first market authorisation was obtained or, in the case of those patents granted prior to 1 January 2000, within the six months provided for in the Patents Act of October 1999;

(d) any medicinal product protected by a valid basic patent and for which the first authorisation to place it on the market as a medicinal product was obtained in Cyprus prior to 1 May 2004 may be granted a certificate, provided that the application for a certificate was lodged within six months of the date on which the first market authorisation was obtained; notwithstanding the above, where the market authorisation was obtained before the grant of the basic patent, the application for a certificate must be lodged within six months of the date on which the patent was granted;

(e) any medicinal product protected by a valid basic patent and for which the first authorisation to place it on the market as a medicinal product was obtained in Latvia prior to 1 May 2004 may be granted a certificate. In cases where the period provided for in Article 7(1) has expired, the possibility of applying for a certificate shall be open for a period of six months starting no later than 1 May 2004;

(f) any medicinal product protected by a valid basic patent applied for after 1 February 1994 and for which the first authorisation to place it on the market as a medicinal product was obtained in Lithuania prior to 1 May 2004 may be granted a certificate, provided that the application for a certificate was lodged within six months from 1 May 2004;

(g) any medicinal product protected by a valid basic patent and for which the first authorisation to place it on the market as a medicinal product was obtained after 1 January 2000 may be granted a certificate in Hungary, provided that the application for a certificate was lodged within six months from 1 May 2004;

(h) any medicinal product protected by a valid basic patent and for which the first authorisation to place it on the market as a medicinal product was obtained in Malta prior to 1 May 2004 may be granted a certificate. In cases where the period provided for in Article 7(1) has expired, the possibility of applying for a certificate shall be open for a period of six months starting no later than 1 May 2004;

(i) any medicinal product protected by a valid basic patent and for which the first authorisation to place it on the market as a medicinal product was obtained after 1 January 2000 may be granted a certificate in Poland,

[1096]

provided that the application for a certificate was lodged within six months starting no later than 1 May 2004;

(j) any medicinal product protected by a valid basic patent and for which the first authorisation to place it on the market as a medicinal product was obtained after 1 January 2000 may be granted a certificate in Romania. In cases where the period provided for in Article 7(1) has expired, the possibility of applying for a certificate shall be open for a period of six months starting no later than 1 January 2007;

(k) any medicinal product protected by a valid basic patent and for which the first authorisation to place it on the market as a medicinal product was obtained in Slovenia prior to 1 May 2004 may be granted a certificate, provided that the application for a certificate was lodged within six months from 1 May 2004, including in cases where the period provided for in Article 7(1) has expired;

(l) any medicinal product protected by a valid basic patent and for which the first authorisation to place it on the market as a medicinal product was obtained in Slovakia after 1 January 2000 may be granted a certificate, provided that the application for a certificate was lodged within six months of the date on which the first market authorisation was obtained or within six months of 1 July 2002 if the market authorisation was obtained before that date.

Article 21

Transitional provisions

1. This Regulation shall not apply to certificates granted in accordance with the national legislation of a Member State before 2 January 1993 or to applications for a certificate filed in accordance with that legislation before 2 July 1992. `AppD-21`

With regard to Austria, Finland and Sweden, this Regulation shall not apply to certificates granted in accordance with their national legislation before 1 January 1995.

2. This Regulation shall apply to supplementary protection certificates granted in accordance with the national legislation of the Czech Republic, Estonia, Cyprus, Latvia, Lithuania, Malta, Poland, Slovenia and Slovakia prior to 1 May 2004 and the national legislation of Romania prior to 1 January 2007.

Article 22

Repeal

Regulation (EEC) No 1768/92, as amended by the acts listed in Annex I, is repealed. `AppD-22`

References to the repealed Regulation shall be construed as references to this Regulation and shall be read in accordance with the correlation table in Annex II.

Article 23

Entry into force

This Regulation shall enter into force on the 20th day following its publication in the Official Journal of the European Union. `AppD-23`

This Regulation shall be binding in its entirety and directly applicable in all Member States.

Done at Strasbourg, 6 May 2009.

For the European Parliament The President H-G. PÖTTERING

For the Council The President J. KOHOUT

[Annex I and II are not reproduced here]

REGULATION 1610/96 OF THE EUROPEAN PARLIAMENT AND OF THE COUNCIL

Regulation (EC) No 1610/96 Of The European Parliament And Of The Council Of 23 July 1996 Concerning The Creation Of A Supplementary Protection Certificate For Plant Protection Products

THE EUROPEAN PARLIAMENT AND THE COUNCIL OF THE EUROPEAN UNION,

Having regard to the Treaty establishing the European Community, and in particular Article 100a thereof,

Having regard to the proposal from the Commission[1],

Having regard to the opinion of the Economic and Social Committee[2], Acting in accordance with the procedure referred to in Article 189b of the Treaty[3],

(1) Whereas research into plant protection products contributes to the continuing improvement in the production and procurement of plentiful food of good quality at affordable prices;

(2) Whereas plant protection research contributes to the continuing improvement in crop production;

(3) Whereas plant protection products, especially those that are the result of long, costly research, will continue to be developed in the Community and in Europe if they are covered by favourable rules that provide for sufficient protection to encourage such research;

(4) Whereas the competitiveness of the plant protection sector, by the very nature of the industry, requires a level of protection for innovation which is equivalent to that granted to medicinal products by Council Regulation (EEC) No 1768/92 of 18 June 1992 concerning the creation of a supplementary protection certificate for medicinal products[4];

(5) Whereas, at the moment, the period that elapses between the filing of an application for a patent for a new plant protection product and authorization to place the said plant protection product on the market makes the period of effective protection under the patent insufficient to cover the investment put into the research and to generate the resources needed to maintain a high level of research;

---

[1] OJ C 390, 31. 12. 1994, p. 21 and OJ C 335, 13. 12. 1995, p. 15.
[2] OJ No C 155, 21. 6. 1995, p. 14.
[3] Opinion of the European Parliament of 15 June 1995 (OJ C 166, 3. 7. 1995, p. 89), common position of the Council of 27 November 1995 (OJ C 353, 30. 12. 1995, p. 36) and decision of the European Parliament of 12 March 1996 (OJ C 96, 1. 4. 1996, p. 30).
[4] OJ No L 182, 2. 7. 1992, p. 1.

(6) Whereas this situation leads to a lack of protection which penalizes plant protection research and the competitiveness of the sector;

(7) Whereas one of the main objectives of the supplementary protection certificate is to place European industry on the same competitive footing as its North American and Japanese counterparts;

(8) Whereas, in its Resolution of 1 February 1993[5] on a Community programme of policy and action in relation to the environment and sustainable development, the Council adopted the general approach and strategy of the programme presented by the Commission, which stressed the interdependence of economic growth and environmental quality; whereas improving protection of the environment means maintaining the economic competitiveness of industry; whereas, accordingly, the issue of a supplementary protection certificate can be regarded as a positive measure in favour of environmental protection;

(9) Whereas a uniform solution at Community level should be provided for, thereby preventing the heterogeneous development of national laws leading to further disparities which would be likely to hinder the free movement of plant protection products within the Community and thus directly affect the functioning of the internal market; whereas this is in accordance with the principle of subsidiarity as defined by Article 3b of the Treaty;

(10) Whereas, therefore, there is a need to create a supplementary protection certificate granted, under the same conditions, by each of the Member States at the request of the holder of a national or European patent relating to a plant protection product for which marketing authorization has been granted is necessary; whereas a Regulation is therefore the most appropriate legal instrument;

(11) Whereas the duration of the protection granted by the certificate should be such as to provide adequate, effective protection; whereas, for this purpose, the holder of both a patent and a certificate should be able to enjoy an overall maximum of fifteen years of exclusivity from the time the plant protection product in question first obtains authorization to be placed on the market in the Community;

(12) Whereas all the interests at stake in a sector as complex and sensitive as plant protection must nevertheless be taken into account; whereas, for this purpose, the certificate cannot be granted for a period exceeding five years;

(13) Whereas the certificate confers the same rights as those conferred by the basic patent; whereas, consequently, where the basic patent covers an active substance and its various derivatives (salts and esters), the certificate confers the same protection;

(14) Whereas the issue of a certificate for a product consisting of an active substance does not prejudice the issue of other certificates for derivatives (salts and esters) of the substance, provided that the derivatives are the subject of patents specifically covering them;

(15) Whereas a fair balance should also be stuck with regard to the determination of the transitional arrangements; whereas such arrangements should enable the Community plant protection industry to catch up to some extent with its main competitors, while making sure that the arrangements do not compromise the achievement of other legitimate objectives concerning the agricultural policy and environment protection policy pursued at both national and Community level;

---

[5]   OJ No C 138, 17. 5. 1993, p. 1.

(16) Whereas only action at Community level will enable the objective, which consists in ensuring adequate protection for innovation in the field of plant protection, while guaranteeing the proper functioning of the internal market for plant protection products, to be attained effectively;

(17) Whereas the detailed rules in recitals 12, 13 and 14 and in Articles 3(2), 4, 8(1)(c) and 17(2) of this Regulation are also valid, mutatis mutandis, for the interpretation in particular of recital 9 and Articles 3, 4, 8(1)(c) and 17 of Council Regulation (EEC) No 1768/92,

HAVE ADOPTED THIS REGULATION:

Article 1

Definitions

For the purposes of this Regulation, the following definitions shall apply:　　AppE-01

1. 'plant protection products': active substances and preparations containing one or more active substances, put up in the form in which they are supplied to the user, intended to:
   - (a) protect plants or plant products against all harmful organisms or prevent the action of such organisms, in so far as such substances or preparations are not otherwise defined below;
   - (b) influence the life processes of plants, other than as a nutrient (e.g. plant growth regulators);
   - (c) preserve plant products, in so far as such substances or products are not subject to special Council or Commission provisions on preservatives;
   - (d) destroy undesirable plants; or
   - (e) destroy parts of plants, check or prevent undesirable growth of plants;
2. 'substances': chemical elements and their compounds, as they occur naturally or by manufacture, including any impurity inevitably resulting from the manufacturing process;
3. 'active substances': substances or micro-organisms including viruses, having general or specific action:
   - (a) against harmful organisms; or
   - (b) on plants, parts of plants or plant products;
4. 'preparations': mixtures or solutions composed of two or more substances, of which at least one is an active substance, intended for use as plant protection products;
5. 'plants': live plants and live parts of plants, including fresh fruit and seeds;
6. 'plant products': products in the unprocessed state or having undergone only simple preparation such as milling, drying or pressing, derived from plants, but excluding plants themselves as defined in point 5;
7. 'harmful organisms': pests of plants or plant products belonging to the animal or plant kingdom, and also viruses, bacteria and mycoplasmas and other pathogens;
8. 'product': the active substance as defined in point 3 or combination of active substances of a plant protection product;
9. 'basic patent': a patent which protects a product as defined in point 8 as such, a preparation as defined in point 4, a process to obtain a product or an

application of a product, and which is designated by its holder for the purpose of the procedure for grant of a certificate;

10. 'certificate': the supplementary protection certificate.

Article 2

Scope

AppE-02   Any product protected by a patent in the territory of a Member State and subject, prior to being placed on the market as a plant protection product, to an administrative authorization procedure as laid down in Article 4 of Directive 91/414/EEC[6], or pursuant to an equivalent provision of national law if it is a plant protection product in respect of which the application for authorization was lodged before Directive 91/414/EEC was implemented by the Member State concerned, may, under the terms and conditions provided for in this Regulation, be the subject of a certificate.

Article 3

Conditions for obtaining a certificate

AppE-03   **1.**   A certificate shall be granted if, in the Member State in which the application referred to in Article 7 is submitted, at the date of that application:

(a)   the product is protected by a basic patent in force;

(b)   a valid authorization to place the product on the market as a plant protection product has been granted in accordance with Article 4 of Directive 91/414/EEC or an equivalent provision of national law;

(c)   the product has not already been the subject of a certificate;

(d)   the authorization referred to in (b) is the first authorization to place the product on the market as a plant protection product.

2.   The holder of more than one patent for the same product shall not be granted more than one certificate for that product. However, where two or more applications concerning the same product and emanating from two or more holders of different patents are pending, one certificate for this product may be issued to each of these holders.

Article 4

Subject-matter of protection

AppE-04   Within the limits of the protection conferred by the basic patent, the protection conferred by a certificate shall extend only to the product covered by the authorizations to place the corresponding plant protection product on the market and for any use of the product as a plant protection product that has been authorized before the expiry of the certificate.

---

[6]   OJ L 230, 19. 8. 1991, p. 1. Directive as last amended by Directive 95/36/EC (OJ L 172, 22. 7. 1995, p. 8).

Article 5

Effects of the certificate

Subject to Article 4, the certificate shall confer the same rights as conferred by the basic patent and shall be subject to the same limitations and the same obligations.

AppE-05

Article 6

Entitlement to the certificate

The certificate shall be granted to the holder of the basic patent or his successor in title.

AppE-06

Article 7

Application for a certificate

1.   The application for a certificate shall be lodged within six months of the date on which the authorization referred to in Article 3(1)(b) to place the product on the market as a plant protection product was granted.
2.   Notwithstanding paragraph 1, where the authorization to place the product on the market is granted before the basic patent is granted, the application for a certificate shall be lodged within six months of the date on which the patent is granted.

AppE-07

Article 8

Content of the application for a certificate

1.   The application for a certificate shall contain:
   (a)   a request for the grant of a certificate, stating in particular:
      (i)   the name and address of the applicant;
      (ii)   the name and address of the representative, if any;
      (iii) the number of the basic patent and the title of the invention;
      (iv)   the number and date of the first authorization to place the product on the market, as referred to in Article 3(1)(b) and, if this authorization is not the first authorization to place the product on the market in the Community, the number and date of that authorization;
   (b)   a copy of the authorization to place the product on the market, as referred to in Article 3(1)(b), in which the product is identified, containing in particular the number and date of the authorization and the summary of the product characteristics listed in Part A.I (points 1-7) or B.I (points 1-7) of Annex II to Directive 91/414/EEC or in equivalent national laws of the Member State in which the application was lodged;
   (c)   if the authorization referred to in (b) is not the first authorization to place the product on the market as a plant protection product in the Community, information regarding the identity of the product thus authorized and the legal provision under which the authorization procedure took place, together with a copy of the notice publishing the authorization in the appropriate official publication or, failing such a notice, any other document proving that

AppE-08

the authorization has been issued, the date on which it was issued and the identity of the product authorized.

2. Member States may require a fee to be payable upon application for a certificate.

Article 9

Lodging of an application for a certificate

AppE-09 **1.** The application for a certificate shall be lodged with the competent industrial property office of the Member State which granted the basic patent or on whose behalf it was granted and in which the authorization referred to in Article 3(1)(b) to place the product on the market was obtained, unless the member State designates another authority for the purpose.

2. Notification of the application for a certificate shall be published by the authority referred to in paragraph 1. The notification shall contain at least the following information:

    (a)   the name and address of the applicant;

    (b)   the number of the basic patent;

    (c)   the title of the invention;

    (d)   the number and date of the authorization to place the product on the market, referred to in Article 3(1)(b), and the product identified in that authorization;

    (e)   where relevant, the number and date of the first authorization to place the product on the market in the Community.

Article 10

Grant of the certificate or rejection of the application

AppE-10 **1.** Where the application for a certificate and the product to which it relates meet the conditions laid down in this Regulation, the authority referred to in Article 9(1) shall grant the certificate.

2. The authority referred to in Article 9(1) shall, subject to paragraph 3, reject the application for a certificate if the application or the product to which it relates does not meet the conditions laid down in this Regulation.

3. Where the application for a certificate does not meet the conditions laid down in Article 8, the authority referred to in Article 9(1) shall ask the applicant to rectify the irregularity, or to settle the fee, within a stated time.

4. If the irregularity is not rectified or the fee is not settled under paragraph 3 within the stated time, the application shall be rejected.

5. Member States may provide that the authority referred to in Article 9(1) is to grant certificates without verifying that the conditions laid down in Article 3(1)(c) and (d) are met.

Article 11

Publication

AppE-11 **1.** Notification of the fact that a certificate has been granted shall be published by the authority referred to in Article 9(1). The notification shall contain at least the following information:

(a) the name and address of the holder of the certificate;
(b) the number of the basic patent;
(c) the title of the invention;
(d) the number and date of the authorization to place the product on the market referred to in Article 3(1)(b) and the product identified in that authorization;
(e) where relevant, the number and date of the first authorization to place the product on the market in the Community;
(f) the duration of the certificate.

2. Notification of the fact that the application for a certificate has been rejected shall be published by the authority referred to in Article 9(1). The notification shall contain at least the information listed in Article 9(2).

Article 12

Annual fees

Member States may require the certificate to be subject to the payment of an-   **AppE-12**
nual fees.

Article 13

Duration of the certificate

1. The certificate shall take effect at the end of the lawful term of the basic pat-   **AppE-13**
ent for a period equal to the period which elapsed between the date on which the application for a basic patent was lodged and the date of the first authorization to place the product on the market in the Community, reduced by a period of five years.
2. Notwithstanding paragraph 1, the duration of the certificate may not exceed five years from the date on which it takes effect.
3. For the purposes of calculating the duration of the certificate, account shall be taken of a provisional first marketing authorization only if it is directly followed by a definitive authorization concerning the same product.

Article 14

Expiry of the certificate

The certificate shall lapse: **AppE-14**
(a) at the end of the period provided for in Article 13;
(b) if the certificate-holder surrenders it;
(c) if the annual fee laid down in accordance with Article 12 is not paid in time;
(d) if and as long as the product covered by the certificate may no longer be placed on the market following the withdrawal of the appropriate authorization or authorizations to place it on the market in accordance with Article 4 of Directive 91/414/EEC or equivalent provisions of national law. The authority referred to in Article 9(1) may decide on the lapse of the certificate either on its own initiative or at the request of a third party.

Article 15

Invalidity of the certificate

AppE-15 **1.**   The certificate shall be invalid if:

(a)   it was granted contrary to the provisions of Article 3;

(b)   the basic patent has lapsed before its lawful term expires;

(c)   the basic patent is revoked or limited to the extent that the product for which the certificate was granted would no longer be protected by the claims of the basic patent or, after the basic patent has expired, grounds for revocation exist which would have justified such revocation or limitation.

2.   Any person may submit an application or bring an action for a declaration of invalidity of the certificate before the body responsible under national law for the revocation of the corresponding basic patent.

Article 16

Notification of lapse or invalidity

AppE-16   If the certificate lapses in accordance with Article 14(b)(c) or (d) or is invalid in accordance with Article 15, notification thereof shall be published by the authority referred to in Article 9(1).

Article 17

Appeals

AppE-17 **1.**   The decisions of the authority referred to in Article 9(1) or of the body referred to in Article 15(2) taken under this Regulation shall be open to the same appeals as those provided for in national law against similar decisions taken in respect of national patents.

2.   The decision to grant the certificate shall be open to an appeal aimed at rectifying the duration of the certificate where the date of the first authorization to place the product on the market in the Community, contained in the application for a certificate as provided for in Article 8, is incorrect.

Article 18

Procedure

AppE-18 **1.**   In the absence of procedural provisions in this Regulation, the procedural provisions applicable under national law to the corresponding basic patent and, where appropriate, the procedural provisions applicable to the certificates referred to in Regulation (EEC) No 1768/92, shall apply to the certificate, unless national law lays down special procedural provisions for certificates as referred to in this Regulation.

2.   Notwithstanding paragraph 1, the procedure for opposition to the granting of a certificate shall be excluded.

TRANSITIONAL PROVISIONS

Article 19

1. Any product which, on the date on which this Regulation enters into force, is AppE-19 protected by a valid basic patent and for which the first authorization to place it on the market as a plant protection product in the Community was obtained after 1 January 1985 under Article 4 of Directive 91/414/EEC or an equivalent national provision may be granted a certificate.
2. An application made under paragraph 1 for a certificate shall be submitted within six months of the date on which this Regulation enters into force.

Article 20

In those Member States whose national law did not, on 1 January 1990, provide AppE-20 for the patentability of plant protection products, this Regulation shall apply from 2 January 1998.

Article 19 shall not apply in those Member States.

FINAL PROVISION

Article 21
Entry into force

This Regulation shall enter into force six months after its publication in the Of- AppE-21 ficial Journal of the European Communities.

This Regulation shall be binding in its entirety and directly applicable in all Member States.

Done at Brussels, 23 July 1996.

For the European Parliament The President K. HÄNSCH
For the Council The President M. LOWRY

DIRECTIVE 2004/48/EC OF THE EUROPEAN PARLIAMENT AND OF THE COUNCIL

Directive 2004/48/EC of the European Parliament and of the Council of 29 April 2004 on the enforcement of intellectual property rights

THE EUROPEAN PARLIAMENT AND THE COUNCIL OF THE EURO-PEAN UNION,

Having regard to the Treaty establishing the European Community, and in particular Article 95 thereof,

Having regard to the proposal from the Commission,

Having regard to the opinion of the European Economic and Social Committee[1],

After consulting the Committee of the Regions,

Acting in accordance with the procedure referred to in Article 251 of the Treaty[2],

Whereas:

(1) The achievement of the internal market entails eliminating restrictions on freedom of movement and distortions of competition, while creating an environment conducive to innovation and investment. In this context, the protection of intellectual property is an essential element for the success of the internal market. The protection of intellectual property is important not only for promoting innovation and creativity, but also for developing employment and improving competitiveness.

(2) The protection of intellectual property should allow the inventor or creator to derive a legitimate profit from his/her invention or creation. It should also allow the widest possible dissemination of works, ideas and new knowhow. At the same time, it should not hamper freedom of expression, the free movement of information, or the protection of personal data, including on the Internet.

(3) However, without effective means of enforcing intellectual property rights, innovation and creativity are discouraged and investment diminished. It is therefore necessary to ensure that the substantive law on intellectual property, which is nowadays largely part of the acquis communautaire, is applied effectively in the Community. In this respect, the means of enforcing intellectual property rights are of paramount importance for the success of the internal market.

(4) At international level, all Member States, as well as the Community itself as regards matters within its competence, are bound by the Agreement on trade-related aspects of intellectual property (the TRIPS Agreement), approved, as part

---

[1]   OJ C 32, 5.2.2004, p. 15.

[2]   Opinion of the European Parliament of 9 March 2004 (not yet published in the Official Journal) and Council Decision of 26 April 2004.

of the multilateral negotiations of the Uruguay Round, by Council Decision 94/800/EC[3] and concluded in the framework of the World Trade Organisation.

(5) The TRIPS Agreement contains, in particular, provisions on the means of enforcing intellectual property rights, which are common standards applicable at international level and implemented in all Member States. This Directive should not affect Member States' international obligations, including those under the TRIPS Agreement.

(6) There are also international conventions to which all Member States are parties and which also contain provisions on the means of enforcing intellectual property rights. These include, in particular, the Paris Convention for the Protection of Industrial Property, the Berne Convention for the Protection of Literary and Artistic Works, and the Rome Convention for the Protection of Performers, Producers of Phonograms and Broadcasting Organisations.

(7) It emerges from the consultations held by the Commission on this question that, in the Member States, and despite the TRIPS Agreement, there are still major disparities as regards the means of enforcing intellectual property rights. For instance, the arrangements for applying provisional measures, which are used in particular to preserve evidence, the calculation of damages, or the arrangements for applying injunctions, vary widely from one Member State to another. In some Member States, there are no measures, procedures and remedies such as the right of information and the recall, at the infringer's expense, of the infringing goods placed on the market.

(8) The disparities between the systems of the Member States as regards the means of enforcing intellectual property rights are prejudicial to the proper functioning of the Internal Market and make it impossible to ensure that intellectual property rights enjoy an equivalent level of protection throughout the Community. This situation does not promote free movement within the internal market or create an environment conducive to healthy competition.

(9) The current disparities also lead to a weakening of the substantive law on intellectual property and to a fragmentation of the internal market in this field. This causes a loss of confidence in the internal market in business circles, with a consequent reduction in investment in innovation and creation. Infringements of intellectual property rights appear to be increasingly linked to organised crime. Increasing use of the Internet enables pirated products to be distributed instantly around the globe. Effective enforcement of the substantive law on intellectual property should be ensured by specific action at Community level. Approximation of the legislation of the Member States in this field is therefore an essential prerequisite for the proper functioning of the internal market.

(10) The objective of this Directive is to approximate legislative systems so as to ensure a high, equivalent and homogeneous level of protection in the internal market.

(11) This Directive does not aim to establish harmonised rules for judicial cooperation, jurisdiction, the recognition and enforcement of decisions in civil and commercial matters, or deal with applicable law. There are Community instruments which govern such matters in general terms and are, in principle, equally applicable to intellectual property.

---

[3] OJ L 336, 23.12.1994, p. 1.

(12) This Directive should not affect the application of the rules of competition, and in particular Articles 81 and 82 of the Treaty. The measures provided for in this Directive should not be used to restrict competition unduly in a manner contrary to the Treaty.

(13) It is necessary to define the scope of this Directive as widely as possible in order to encompass all the intellectual property rights covered by Community provisions in this field and/or by the national law of the Member State concerned. Nevertheless, that requirement does not affect the possibility, on the part of those Member States which so wish, to extend, for internal purposes, the provisions of this Directive to include acts involving unfair competition, including parasitic copies, or similar activities.

(14) The measures provided for in Articles 6(2), 8(1) and 9(2) need to be applied only in respect of acts carried out on a commercial scale. This is without prejudice to the possibility for Member States to apply those measures also in respect of other acts. Acts carried out on a commercial scale are those carried out for direct or indirect economic or commercial advantage; this would normally exclude acts carried out by end consumers acting in good faith.

(15) This Directive should not affect substantive law on intellectual property, Directive 95/46/EC of 24 October 1995 of the European Parliament and of the Council on the protection of individuals with regard to the processing of personal data and on the free movement of such data[4], Directive 1999/93/EC of the European Parliament and of the Council of 13 December 1999 on a Community framework for electronic signatures[5] and Directive 2000/31/EC of the European Parliament and of the Council of 8 June 2000 on certain legal aspects of information society services, in particular electronic commerce, in the internal market[6].

(16) The provisions of this Directive should be without prejudice to the particular provisions for the enforcement of rights and on exceptions in the domain of copyright and related rights set out in Community instruments and notably those found in Council Directive 91/250/EEC of 14 May 1991 on the legal protection of computer programs[7] or in Directive 2001/29/EC of the European Parliament and of the Council of 22 May 2001 on the harmonisation of certain aspects of copyright and related rights in the information society[8].

(17) The measures, procedures and remedies provided for in this Directive should be determined in each case in such a manner as to take due account of the specific characteristics of that case, including the specific features of each intellectual property right and, where appropriate, the intentional or unintentional character of the infringement.

(18) The persons entitled to request application of those measures, procedures and remedies should be not only the rightholders but also persons who have a direct interest and legal standing in so far as permitted by and in accordance with the applicable law, which may include professional organisations in charge of the

---

[4] OJ L 281, 23.11.1995, p. 31. Directive as amended by Regulation (EC) No 1882/2003 (OJ L 284, 31.10.2003, p. 1).

[5] OJ L 13, 19.1.2000, p. 12.

[6] OJ L 178, 17.7.2000, p. 1.

[7] OJ L 122, 17.5.1991, p. 42. Directive as amended by Directive 93/98/EEC (OJ L 290, 24.11.1993, p. 9).

[8] OJ L 167, 22.6.2001, p. 10.

management of those rights or for the defence of the collective and individual interests for which they are responsible.

(19) Since copyright exists from the creation of a work and does not require formal registration, it is appropriate to adopt the rule laid down in Article 15 of the Berne Convention, which establishes the presumption whereby the author of a literary or artistic work is regarded as such if his/her name appears on the work. A similar presumption should be applied to the owners of related rights since it is often the holder of a related right, such as a phonogram producer, who will seek to defend rights and engage in fighting acts of piracy.

(20) Given that evidence is an element of paramount importance for establishing the infringement of intellectual property rights, it is appropriate to ensure that effective means of presenting, obtaining and preserving evidence are available. The procedures should have regard to the rights of the defence and provide the necessary guarantees, including the protection of confidential information. For infringements committed on a commercial scale it is also important that the courts may order access, where appropriate, to banking, financial or commercial documents under the control of the alleged infringer.

(21) Other measures designed to ensure a high level of protection exist in certain Member States and should be made available in all the Member States. This is the case with the right of information, which allows precise information to be obtained on the origin of the infringing goods or services, the distribution channels and the identity of any third parties involved in the infringement.

(22) It is also essential to provide for provisional measures for the immediate termination of infringements, without awaiting a decision on the substance of the case, while observing the rights of the defence, ensuring the proportionality of the provisional measures as appropriate to the characteristics of the case in question and providing the guarantees needed to cover the costs and the injury caused to the defendant by an unjustified request. Such measures are particularly justified where any delay would cause irreparable harm to the holder of an intellectual property right.

(23) Without prejudice to any other measures, procedures and remedies available, rightholders should have the possibility of applying for an injunction against an intermediary whose services are being used by a third party to infringe the rightholder's industrial property right. The conditions and procedures relating to such injunctions should be left to the national law of the Member States. As far as infringements of copyright and related rights are concerned, a comprehensive level of harmonisation is already provided for in Directive 2001/29/EC. Article 8(3) of Directive 2001/29/EC should therefore not be affected by this Directive.

(24) Depending on the particular case, and if justified by the circumstances, the measures, procedures and remedies to be provided for should include prohibitory measures aimed at preventing further infringements of intellectual property rights. Moreover there should be corrective measures, where appropriate at the expense of the infringer, such as the recall and definitive removal from the channels of commerce, or destruction, of the infringing goods and, in appropriate cases, of the materials and implements principally used in the creation or manufacture of these goods. These corrective measures should take account of the interests of third parties including, in particular, consumers and private parties acting in good faith.

(25) Where an infringement is committed unintentionally and without negligence and where the corrective measures or injunctions provided for by this Directive would be disproportionate, Member States should have the option of providing for the possibility, in appropriate cases, of pecuniary compensation being awarded to the injured party as an alternative measure. However, where the commercial use of counterfeit goods or the supply of services would constitute an infringement of law other than intellectual property law or would be likely to harm consumers, such use or supply should remain prohibited.

(26) With a view to compensating for the prejudice suffered as a result of an infringement committed by an infringer who engaged in an activity in the knowledge, or with reasonable grounds for knowing, that it would give rise to such an infringement, the amount of damages awarded to the rightholder should take account of all appropriate aspects, such as loss of earnings incurred by the rightholder, or unfair profits made by the infringer and, where appropriate, any moral prejudice caused to the rightholder. As an alternative, for example where it would be difficult to determine the amount of the actual prejudice suffered, the amount of the damages might be derived from elements such as the royalties or fees which would have been due if the infringer had requested authorisation to use the intellectual property right in question. The aim is not to introduce an obligation to provide for punitive damages but to allow for compensation based on an objective criterion while taking account of the expenses incurred by the rightholder, such as the costs of identification and research.

(27) To act as a supplementary deterrent to future infringers and to contribute to the awareness of the public at large, it is useful to publicise decisions in intellectual property infringement cases.

(28) In addition to the civil and administrative measures, procedures and remedies provided for under this Directive, criminal sanctions also constitute, in appropriate cases, a means of ensuring the enforcement of intellectual property rights.

(29) Industry should take an active part in the fight against piracy and counterfeiting. The development of codes of conduct in the circles directly affected is a supplementary means of bolstering the regulatory framework. The Member States, in collaboration with the Commission, should encourage the development of codes of conduct in general. Monitoring of the manufacture of optical discs, particularly by means of an identification code embedded in discs produced in the Community, helps to limit infringements of intellectual property rights in this sector, which suffers from piracy on a large scale. However, these technical protection measures should not be misused to protect markets and prevent parallel imports.

(30) In order to facilitate the uniform application of this Directive, it is appropriate to provide for systems of cooperation and the exchange of information between Member States, on the one hand, and between the Member States and the Commission on the other, in particular by creating a network of correspondents designated by the Member States and by providing regular reports assessing the application of this Directive and the effectiveness of the measures taken by the various national bodies.

(31) Since, for the reasons already described, the objective of this Directive can best be achieved at Community level, the Community may adopt measures, in accordance with the principle of subsidiarity as set out in Article 5 of the Treaty. In accordance with the principle of proportionality as set out in that Article, this Directive does not go beyond what is necessary in order to achieve that objective.

(32) This Directive respects the fundamental rights and observes the principles recognised in particular by the Charter of Fundamental Rights of the European Union. In particular, this Directive seeks to ensure full respect for intellectual property, in accordance with Article 17(2) of that Charter,

HAVE ADOPTED THIS REGULATION:

CHAPTER I

OBJECTIVE AND SCOPE

Article 1
Subject matter

This Directive concerns the measures, procedures and remedies necessary to ensure the enforcement of intellectual property rights. For the purposes of this Directive, the term 'intellectual property rights' includes industrial property rights. AppF-01

Article 2
Scope

1. Without prejudice to the means which are or may be provided for in Community or national legislation, in so far as those means may be more favourable for rightholders, the measures, procedures and remedies provided for by this Directive shall apply, in accordance with Article 3, to any infringement of intellectual property rights as provided for by Community law and/or by the national law of the Member State concerned. AppF-02

2. This Directive shall be without prejudice to the specific provisions on the enforcement of rights and on exceptions contained in Community legislation concerning copyright and rights related to copyright, notably those found in Directive 91/250/EEC and, in particular, Article 7 thereof or in Directive 2001/29/EC and, in particular, Articles 2 to 6 and Article 8 thereof.

3. This Directive shall not affect:

(a) the Community provisions governing the substantive law on intellectual property, Directive 95/46/EC, Directive 1999/93/EC or Directive 2000/31/EC, in general, and Articles 12 to 15 of Directive 2000/31/EC in particular;

(b) Member States' international obligations and notably the TRIPS Agreement, including those relating to criminal procedures and penalties;

(c) any national provisions in Member States relating to criminal procedures or penalties in respect of infringement of intellectual property rights.

CHAPTER II

MEASURES, PROCEDURES AND REMEDIES

SECTION 1

General provisions

Article 3

General obligation

AppF-03 1. Member States shall provide for the measures, procedures and remedies necessary to ensure the enforcement of the intellectual property rights covered by this Directive. Those measures, procedures and remedies shall be fair and equitable and shall not be unnecessarily complicated or costly, or entail unreasonable time-limits or unwarranted delays.

2. Those measures, procedures and remedies shall also be effective, proportionate and dissuasive and shall be applied in such a manner as to avoid the creation of barriers to legitimate trade and to provide for safeguards against their abuse.

Article 4

Persons entitled to apply for the application of the measures, procedures and remedies

AppF-04 Member States shall recognise as persons entitled to seek application of the measures, procedures and remedies referred to in this chapter:

(a) the holders of intellectual property rights, in accordance with the provisions of the applicable law;

(b) all other persons authorised to use those rights, in particular licensees, in so far as permitted by and in accordance with the provisions of the applicable law;

(c) intellectual property collective rights-management bodies which are regularly recognised as having a right to represent holders of intellectual property rights, in so far as permitted by and in accordance with the provisions of the applicable law;

(d) professional defence bodies which are regularly recognised as having a right to represent holders of intellectual property rights, in so far as permitted by and in accordance with the provisions of the applicable law.

Article 5

Presumption of authorship or ownership

AppF-05 For the purposes of applying the measures, procedures and remedies provided for in this Directive,

(a) for the author of a literary or artistic work, in the absence of proof to the contrary, to be regarded as such, and consequently to be entitled to institute infringement proceedings, it shall be sufficient for his/her name to appear on the work in the usual manner;

(b) the provision under (a) shall apply mutatis mutandis to the holders of rights related to copyright with regard to their protected subject matter.

SECTION 2

Evidence

Article 6

Evidence

1. Member States shall ensure that, on application by a party which has presented reasonably available evidence sufficient to support its claims, and has, in substantiating those claims, specified evidence which lies in the control of the opposing party, the competent judicial authorities may order that such evidence be presented by the opposing party, subject to the protection of confidential information. For the purposes of this paragraph, Member States may provide that a reasonable sample of a substantial number of copies of a work or any other protected object be considered by the competent judicial authorities to constitute reasonable evidence. **AppF-06**

2. Under the same conditions, in the case of an infringement committed on a commercial scale Member States shall take such measures as are necessary to enable the competent judicial authorities to order, where appropriate, on application by a party, the communication of banking, financial or commercial documents under the control of the opposing party, subject to the protection of confidential information.

Article 7

Measures for preserving evidence

1. Member States shall ensure that, even before the commencement of proceedings on the merits of the case, the competent judicial authorities may, on application by a party who has presented reasonably available evidence to support his/her claims that his/her intellectual property right has been infringed or is about to be infringed, order prompt and effective provisional measures to preserve relevant evidence in respect of the alleged infringement, subject to the protection of confidential information. Such measures may include the detailed description, with or without the taking of samples, or the physical seizure of the infringing goods, and, in appropriate cases, the materials and implements used in the production and/or distribution of these goods and the documents relating thereto. Those measures shall be taken, if necessary without the other party having been heard, in particular where any delay is likely to cause irreparable harm to the rightholder or where there is a demonstrable risk of evidence being destroyed. **AppF-07**

Where measures to preserve evidence are adopted without the other party having been heard, the parties affected shall be given notice, without delay after the execution of the measures at the latest. A review, including a right to be heard, shall take place upon request of the parties affected with a view to deciding, within a reasonable period after the notification of the measures, whether the measures shall be modified, revoked or confirmed.

2. Member States shall ensure that the measures to preserve evidence may be subject to the lodging by the applicant of adequate security or an equivalent assurance intended to ensure compensation for any prejudice suffered by the defendant as provided for in paragraph 4.

3. Member States shall ensure that the measures to preserve evidence are revoked or otherwise cease to have effect, upon request of the defendant, without prejudice to the damages which may be claimed, if the applicant does not institute, within a reasonable period, proceedings leading to a decision on the merits of the case before the competent judicial authority, the period to be determined by the judicial authority ordering the measures where the law of a Member State so permits or, in the absence of such determination, within a period not exceeding 20 working days or 31 calendar days, whichever is the longer.

4. Where the measures to preserve evidence are revoked, or where they lapse due to any act or omission by the applicant, or where it is subsequently found that there has been no infringement or threat of infringement of an intellectual property right, the judicial authorities shall have the authority to order the applicant, upon request of the defendant, to provide the defendant appropriate compensation for any injury caused by those measures.

5. Member States may take measures to protect witnesses' identity.

SECTION 3

Right of information

Article 8

Right of information

AppF-08 **1.** Member States shall ensure that, in the context of proceedings concerning an infringement of an intellectual property right and in response to a justified and proportionate request of the claimant, the competent judicial authorities may order that information on the origin and distribution networks of the goods or services which infringe an intellectual property right be provided by the infringer and/or any other person who:

    (a) was found in possession of the infringing goods on a commercial scale;

    (b) was found to be using the infringing services on a commercial scale;

    (c) was found to be providing on a commercial scale services used in infringing activities;

        or

    (d) was indicated by the person referred to in point (a), (b) or (c) as being involved in the production, manufacture or distribution of the goods or the provision of the services.

2. The information referred to in paragraph 1 shall, as appropriate, comprise:

    (a) the names and addresses of the producers, manufacturers, distributors, suppliers and other previous holders of the goods or services, as well as the intended wholesalers and retailers;

    (b) information on the quantities produced, manufactured, delivered, received or ordered, as well as the price obtained for the goods or services in question.

3. Paragraphs 1 and 2 shall apply without prejudice to other statutory provisions which:

    (a) grant the rightholder rights to receive fuller information;

    (b) govern the use in civil or criminal proceedings of the information communicated pursuant to this Article;

    (c) govern responsibility for misuse of the right of information; or

(d) afford an opportunity for refusing to provide information which would force the person referred to in paragraph 1 to admit to his/her own participation or that of his/her close relatives in an infringement of an intellectual property right;

or

(e) govern the protection of confidentiality of information sources or the processing of personal data.

SECTION 4

Provisional and precautionary measures

Article 9

Provisional and precautionary measures

1. Member States shall ensure that the judicial authorities may, at the request of the applicant: AppF-09

(a) issue against the alleged infringer an interlocutory injunction intended to prevent any imminent infringement of an intellectual property right, or to forbid, on a provisional basis and subject, where appropriate, to a recurring penalty payment where provided for by national law, the continuation of the alleged infringements of that right, or to make such continuation subject to the lodging of guarantees intended to ensure the compensation of the rightholder; an interlocutory injunction may also be issued, under the same conditions, against an intermediary whose services are being used by a third party to infringe an intellectual property right; injunctions against intermediaries whose services are used by a third party to infringe a copyright or a related right are covered by Directive 2001/29/EC;

(b) order the seizure or delivery up of the goods suspected of infringing an intellectual property right so as to prevent their entry into or movement within the channels of commerce.

2. In the case of an infringement committed on a commercial scale, the Member States shall ensure that, if the injured party demonstrates circumstances likely to endanger the recovery of damages, the judicial authorities may order the precautionary seizure of the movable and immovable property of the alleged infringer, including the blocking of his/her bank accounts and other assets. To that end, the competent authorities may order the communication of bank, financial or commercial documents, or appropriate access to the relevant information.

3. The judicial authorities shall, in respect of the measures referred to in paragraphs 1 and 2, have the authority to require the applicant to provide any reasonably available evidence in order to satisfy themselves with a sufficient degree of certainty that the applicant is the rightholder and that the applicant's right is being infringed, or that such infringement is imminent.

4. Member States shall ensure that the provisional measures referred to in paragraphs 1 and 2 may, in appropriate cases, be taken without the defendant having been heard, in particular where any delay would cause irreparable harm to the rightholder. In that event, the parties shall be so informed without delay after the execution of the measures at the latest.

A review, including a right to be heard, shall take place upon request of the defendant with a view to deciding, within a reasonable time after notification of the measures, whether those measures shall be modified, revoked or confirmed.

5. Member States shall ensure that the provisional measures referred to in paragraphs 1 and 2 are revoked or otherwise cease to have effect, upon request of the defendant, if the applicant does not institute, within a reasonable period, proceedings leading to a decision on the merits of the case before the competent judicial authority, the period to be determined by the judicial authority ordering the measures where the law of a Member State so permits or, in the absence of such determination, within a period not exceeding 20 working days or 31 calendar days, whichever is the longer.

6. The competent judicial authorities may make the provisional measures referred to in paragraphs 1 and 2 subject to the lodging by the applicant of adequate security or an equivalent assurance intended to ensure compensation for any prejudice suffered by the defendant as provided for in paragraph 7.

7. Where the provisional measures are revoked or where they lapse due to any act or omission by the applicant, or where it is subsequently found that there has been no infringement or threat of infringement of an intellectual property right, the judicial authorities shall have the authority to order the applicant, upon request of the defendant, to provide the defendant appropriate compensation for any injury caused by those measures.

SECTION 5
Measures resulting from a decision on the merits of the case

Article 10
Corrective measures

AppF-10 **1.** Without prejudice to any damages due to the rightholder by reason of the infringement, and without compensation of any sort, Member States shall ensure that the competent judicial authorities may order, at the request of the applicant, that appropriate measures be taken with regard to goods that they have found to be infringing an intellectual property right and, in appropriate cases, with regard to materials and implements principally used in the creation or manufacture of those goods. Such measures shall include:

    (a)   recall from the channels of commerce;
    (b)   definitive removal from the channels of commerce; or
    (c)   destruction.

2. The judicial authorities shall order that those measures be carried out at the expense of the infringer, unless particular reasons are invoked for not doing so.

3. In considering a request for corrective measures, the need for proportionality between the seriousness of the infringement and the remedies ordered as well as the interests of third parties shall be taken into account.

Article 11
Injunctions

AppF-11 Member States shall ensure that, where a judicial decision is taken finding an infringement of an intellectual property right, the judicial authorities may issue against the infringer an injunction aimed at prohibiting the continuation of the infringement. Where provided for by national law, non-compliance with an injunction shall, where appropriate, be subject to a recurring penalty payment, with a view to ensuring compliance. Member States shall also ensure that rightholders are in a position to apply for an injunction against intermediaries whose services are used by a third party to infringe an intellectual property right, without prejudice to Article 8(3) of Directive 2001/29/EC.

Article 12

Alternative measures

Member States may provide that, in appropriate cases and at the request of the person liable to be subject to the measures provided for in this section, the competent judicial authorities may order pecuniary compensation to be paid to the injured party instead of applying the measures provided for in this section if that person acted unintentionally and without negligence, if execution of the measures in question would cause him/her disproportionate harm and if pecuniary compensation to the injured party appears reasonably satisfactory. AppF-12

SECTION 6

Damages and legal costs

Article 13

Damages

1. Member States shall ensure that the competent judicial authorities, on application of the injured party, order the infringer who knowingly, or with reasonable grounds to know, engaged in an infringing activity, to pay the rightholder damages appropriate to the actual prejudice suffered by him/her as a result of the infringement. AppF-13

When the judicial authorities set the damages:

(a) they shall take into account all appropriate aspects, such as the negative economic consequences, including lost profits, which the injured party has suffered, any unfair profits made by the infringer and, in appropriate cases, elements other than economic factors, such as the moral prejudice caused to the rightholder by the infringement;

   or

(b) as an alternative to (a), they may, in appropriate cases, set the damages as a lump sum on the basis of elements such as at least the amount of royalties or fees which would have been due if the infringer had requested authorisation to use the intellectual property right in question.

2. Where the infringer did not knowingly, or with reasonable grounds know, engage in infringing activity, Member States may lay down that the judicial authorities may order the recovery of profits or the payment of damages, which may be pre-established.

Article 14

Legal costs

AppF-14   Member States shall ensure that reasonable and proportionate legal costs and other expenses incurred by the successful party shall, as a general rule, be borne by the unsuccessful party, unless equity does not allow this.

SECTION 7

Publicity measures

Article 15

Publication of judicial decisions

AppF-15   Member States shall ensure that, in legal proceedings instituted for infringement of an intellectual property right, the judicial authorities may order, at the request of the applicant and at the expense of the infringer, appropriate measures for the dissemination of the information concerning the decision, including displaying the decision and publishing it in full or in part. Member States may provide for other additional publicity measures which are appropriate to the particular circumstances, including prominent advertising.

CHAPTER III

SANCTIONS BY MEMBER STATES

Article 16

Sanctions by Member States

AppF-16   Without prejudice to the civil and administrative measures, procedures and remedies laid down by this Directive, Member States may apply other appropriate sanctions in cases where intellectual property rights have been infringed.

CHAPTER IV

CODES OF CONDUCT AND ADMINISTRATIVE COOPERATION

Article 17

Codes of conduct

AppF-17   Member States shall encourage:
(a)   the development by trade or professional associations or organisations of codes of conduct at Community level aimed at contributing towards the enforcement of the intellectual property rights, particularly by recommending the use on optical discs of a code enabling the identification of the origin of their manufacture;
(b)   the submission to the Commission of draft codes of conduct at national and Community level and of any evaluations of the application of these codes of conduct.

Article18

Assessment

1. Three years after the date laid down in Article 20(1), each Member State shall   AppF-18
submit to the Commission a report on the implementation of this Directive.

On the basis of those reports, the Commission shall draw up a report on the application of this Directive, including an assessment of the effectiveness of the measures taken, as well as an evaluation of its impact on innovation and the development of the information society. That report shall then be transmitted to the European Parliament, the Council and the European Economic and Social Committee. It shall be accompanied, if necessary and in the light of developments in the Community legal order, by proposals for amendments to this Directive.

2. Member States shall provide the Commission with all the aid and assistance it may need when drawing up the report referred to in the second subparagraph of paragraph 1.

Article 19

Exchange of information and correspondents

For the purpose of promoting cooperation, including the exchange of informa- AppF-19
tion, among Member States and between Member States and the Commission, each Member State shall designate one or more national correspondents for any question relating to the implementation of the measures provided for by this Directive. It shall communicate the details of the national correspondent(s) to the other Member States and to the Commission.

CHAPTER V

FINAL PROVISIONS

Article 20

Implementation

1. Member States shall bring into force the laws, regulations and administrative   AppF-20
provisions necessary to comply with this Directive by 29 April 2006. They shall forthwith inform the Commission thereof.

When Member States adopt these measures, they shall contain a reference to this Directive or shall be accompanied by such reference on the occasion of their official publication. The methods of making such reference shall be laid down by Member States.

2. Member States shall communicate to the Commission the texts of the provisions of national law which they adopt in the field governed by this Directive.

Article 21

Entry into force

This Directive shall enter into force on the 20th day following that of its publica- AppF-21
tion in the Official Journal of the European Union.

Article 22

Addressees

AppF-22   This Directive is addressed to the Member States.

Done at Strasbourg, 29 April 2004.

For the European Parliament The President P. COXM.

For the Council The President McDOWELL

APPENDIX G

AGREEMENT ON A UNIFIED PATENT COURT

THE CONTRACTING MEMBER STATES,

CONSIDERING that cooperation amongst the Member States of the European Union in the field of patents contributes significantly to the integration process in Europe, in particular to the establishment of an internal market within the European Union characterised by the free movement of goods and services and the creation of a system ensuring that competition in the internal market is not distorted;

CONSIDERING that the fragmented market for patents and the significant variations between national court systems are detrimental for innovation, in particular for small and medium sized enterprises which have difficulties to enforce their patents and to defend themselves against unfounded claims and claims relating to patents which should be revoked;

CONSIDERING that the European Patent Convention ("EPC") which has been ratified by all Member States of the European Union provides for a single procedure for granting European patents by the European Patent Office;

CONSIDERING that by virtue of Regulation (EU) No 1257/2012[1], patent proprietors can request unitary effect of their European patents so as to obtain unitary patent protection in the Member States of the European Union participating in the enhanced cooperation;

WISHING to improve the enforcement of patents and the defence against unfounded claims and patents which should be revoked and to enhance legal certainty by setting up a Unified Patent Court for litigation relating to the infringement and validity of patents;

CONSIDERING that the Unified Patent Court should be devised to ensure expeditious and high quality decisions, striking a fair balance between the interests of right holders and other parties and taking into account the need for proportionality and flexibility;

CONSIDERING that the Unified Patent Court should be a court common to the Contracting Member States and thus part of their judicial system, with exclusive competence in respect of European patents with unitary effect and European patents granted under the provisions of the EPC;

CONSIDERING that the Court of Justice of the European Union is to ensure the uniformity of the Union legal order and the primacy of European Union law;

RECALLING the obligations of the Contracting Member States under the Treaty on European Union (TEU) and the Treaty on the Functioning of the European Union (TFEU), including the obligation of sincere cooperation as set out in Article 4(3) TEU and the obligation to ensure through the Unified Patent Court the full ap-

---

[1] Regulation (EU) No 1257/2012 of the European Parliament and of the Council of 17 December 2012 implementing enhanced cooperation in the area of the creation of unitary patent protection (OJEU L 361, 31.12.2012, p. 1) including any subsequent amendments.

plication of, and respect for, Union law in their respective territories and the judicial protection of an individual's rights under that law;

CONSIDERING that, as any national court, the Unified Patent Court must respect and apply Union law and, in collaboration with the Court of Justice of the European Union as guardian of Union law, ensure its correct application and uniform interpretation; the Unified Patent Court must in particular cooperate with the Court of Justice of the European Union in properly interpreting Union law by relying on the latter's case law and by requesting preliminary rulings in accordance with Article 267 TFEU;

CONSIDERING that the Contracting Member States should, in line with the case law of the Court of Justice of the European Union on non-contractual liability, be liable for damages caused by infringements of Union law by the Unified Patent Court, including the failure to request preliminary rulings from the Court of Justice of the European Union;

CONSIDERING that infringements of Union law by the Unified Patent Court, including the failure to request preliminary rulings from the Court of Justice of the European Union, are directly attributable to the Contracting Member States and infringement proceedings can therefore be brought under Article 258, 259 and 260 TFEU against any Contracting Member State to ensure the respect of the primacy and proper application of Union law;

RECALLING the primacy of Union law, which includes the TEU, the TFEU, the Charter of Fundamental Rights of the European Union, the general principles of Union law as developed by the Court of Justice of the European Union, and in particular the right to an effective remedy before a tribunal and a fair and public hearing within a reasonable time by an independent and impartial tribunal, the case law of the Court of Justice of the European Union and secondary Union law;

CONSIDERING that this Agreement should be open to accession by any Member State of the European Union; Member States which have decided not to participate in the enhanced cooperation in the area of the creation of unitary patent protection may participate in this Agreement in respect of European patents granted for their respective territory;

CONSIDERING that this Agreement should enter into force on 1 January 2014 or on the first day of the fourth month after the 13th deposit, provided that the Contracting Member States that will have deposited their instruments of ratification or accession include the three States in which the highest number of European patents was in force in the year preceding the year in which the signature of the Agreement takes place, or on the first day of the fourth month after the date of entry into force of the amendments to Regulation (EU) No 1215/2012[2] concerning its relationship with this Agreement, whichever is the latest,

HAVE AGREED AS FOLLOWS:

PART I

GENERAL AND INSTITUTIONAL PROVISIONS

---

[2] Regulation (EU) No 1215/2012 of the European Parliament and of the Council of 12 December 2012 on jurisdiction and the recognition and enforcement of judgments in civil and commercial matters (OJEU L 351, 20.12.2012, p. 1) including any subsequent amendments.

CHAPTER I

GENERAL PROVISIONS

Article 1

Unified Patent Court

A Unified Patent Court for the settlement of disputes relating to European patents and European patents with unitary effect is hereby established.

The Unified Patent Court shall be a court common to the Contracting Member States and thus subject to the same obligations under Union law as any national court of the Contracting Member States.

AppG-01

Article 2

Definitions

For the purposes of this Agreement:

AppG-02

(a) "Court" means the Unified Patent Court created by this Agreement.
(b) "Member State" means a Member State of the European Union.
(c) "Contracting Member State" means a Member State party to this Agreement.
(d) "EPC" means the Convention on the Grant of European Patents of 5 October 1973, including any subsequent amendments.
(e) "European patent" means a patent granted under the provisions of the EPC, which does not benefit from unitary effect by virtue of Regulation (EU) No 1257/2012.
(f) "European patent with unitary effect" means a patent granted under the provisions of the EPC which benefits from unitary effect by virtue of Regulation (EU) No 1257/2012.
(g) "Patent" means a European patent and/or a European patent with unitary effect.
(h) "Supplementary protection certificate" means a supplementary protection certificate granted under Regulation (EC) No 469/2009[3] or under Regulation (EC) No 1610/96[4].
(i) "Statute" means the Statute of the Court as set out in Annex I, which shall be an integral part of this Agreement.
(j) "Rules of Procedure" means the Rules of Procedure of the Court, as established in accordance with Article 41.

---

[3] Regulation (EC) No 469/2009 of the European Parliament and of the Council of 6 May 2009 concerning the supplementary protection certificate for medicinal products, (OJEU L 152, 16.6.2009, p.1) including any subsequent amendments.
[4] Regulation (EC) No 1610/96 of the European Parliament and of the Council of 23 July 1996 concerning the creation of a supplementary certificate for plant protection products, (OJEC L 198, 8.8.1996, p.30) including any subsequent amendments.

Article 3

Scope of application

AppG-03   This Agreement shall apply to any:
  (a)   European patent with unitary effect;
  (b)   supplementary protection certificate issued for a product protected by a patent;
  (c)   European patent which has not yet lapsed at the date of entry into force of this Agreement or was granted after that date, without prejudice to Article 83; and
  (d)   European patent application which is pending at the date of entry into force of this Agreement or which is filed after that date, without prejudice to Article 83.

Article 4

Legal status

AppG-04   **(1)**   The Court shall have legal personality in each Contracting Member State and shall enjoy the most extensive legal capacity accorded to legal persons under the national law of that State.
(2)   The Court shall be represented by the President of the Court of Appeal who shall be elected in accordance with the Statute.

Article 5

Liability

AppG-05   **(1)**   The contractual liability of the Court shall be governed by the law applicable to the contract in question in accordance with Regulation (EC) No. 593/2008[5] (Rome I), where applicable, or failing that in accordance with the law of the Member State of the court seized.
(2)   The non-contractual liability of the Court in respect of any damage caused by it or its staff in the performance of their duties, to the extent that it is not a civil and commercial matter within the meaning of Regulation (EC) No. 864/2007[6] (Rome II), shall be governed by the law of the Contracting Member State in which the damage occurred. This provision is without prejudice to the application of Article 22.
(3)   The court with jurisdiction to settle disputes under paragraph 2 shall be a court of the Contracting Member State in which the damage occurred.

---

[5]   Regulation (EC) No 593/2008 of the European Parliament and of the Council of 17 June 2008 on the law applicable to contractual obligations (Rome I) (OJEU L 177, 4.7.2008, p. 6) including any subsequent amendments.
[6]   Regulation (EC) No 864/2007 of the European Parliament and of the Council of 11 July 2007 on the law applicable to non-contractual obligations (Rome II) (OJEU L 199, 31.7.2007, p. 40) including any subsequent amendments.

CHAPTER II

INSTITUTIONAL PROVISIONS

Article 6

The Court

(1) The Court shall comprise a Court of First Instance, a Court of Appeal and a   AppG-06
Registry.
(2) The Court shall perform the functions assigned to it by this Agreement.

Article 7

The Court of First Instance

(1) The Court of First Instance shall comprise a central division as well as local   AppG-07
and regional divisions.
(2) The central division shall have its seat in Paris, with sections in London and
Munich. The cases before the central division shall be distributed in accordance
with Annex II, which shall form an integral part of this Agreement.
(3) A local division shall be set up in a Contracting Member State upon its request
in accordance with the Statute. A Contracting Member State hosting a local division shall designate its seat.
(4) An additional local division shall be set up in a Contracting Member State
upon its request for every one hundred patent cases per calendar year that have been
commenced in that Contracting Member State during three successive years prior
to or subsequent to the date of entry into force of this Agreement. The number of
local divisions in one Contracting Member State shall not exceed four.
(5) A regional division shall be set up for two or more Contracting Member
States, upon their request in accordance with the Statute. Such Contracting Member
States shall designate the seat of the division concerned. The regional division may
hear cases in multiple locations.

Article 8

Composition of the panels of the Court of First Instance

(1) Any panel of the Court of First Instance shall have a multinational   AppG-08
composition. Without prejudice to paragraph 5 of this Article and to Article
33(3)(a), it shall sit in a composition of three judges.
(2) Any panel of a local division in a Contracting Member State where, during a
period of three successive years prior or subsequent to the entry into force of this
Agreement, less than fifty patent cases per calendar year on average have been commenced shall sit in a composition of one legally qualified judge who is a national
of the Contracting Member State hosting the local division concerned and two
legally qualified judges who are not nationals of the Contracting Member State
concerned and are allocated from the Pool of Judges in accordance with Article
18(3) on a case by case basis.
(3) Notwithstanding paragraph 2, any panel of a local division in a Contracting
Member State where, during a period of three successive years prior or subsequent
to the entry into force of this Agreement, fifty or more patent cases per calendar year

on average have been commenced, shall sit in a composition of two legally qualified judges who are nationals of the Contracting Member State hosting the local
division concerned and one legally qualified judge who is not a national of the
Contracting Member State concerned and is allocated from the Pool of Judges in
accordance with Article 18(3). Such third judge shall serve at the local division on
a long term basis, where this is necessary for the efficient functioning of divisions
with a high work load.

(4) Any panel of a regional division shall sit in a composition of two legally qualified judges chosen from a regional list of judges, who shall be nationals of the
Contracting Member States concerned, and one legally qualified judge who shall
not be a national of the Contracting Member States concerned and who shall be allocated from the Pool of Judges in accordance with Article 18(3).

(5) Upon request by one of the parties, any panel of a local or regional division
shall request the President of the Court of First Instance to allocate from the Pool
of Judges in accordance with Article 18(3) an additional technically qualified judge
with qualifications and experience in the field of technology concerned. Moreover,
any panel of a local or regional division may, after having heard the parties, submit
such request on its own initiative, where it deems this appropriate.

In cases where such a technically qualified judge is allocated, no further technically qualified judge may be allocated under Article 33(3)(a).

(6) Any panel of the central division shall sit in a composition of two legally
qualified judges who are nationals of different Contracting Member States and one
technically qualified judge allocated from the Pool of Judges in accordance with
Article 18(3) with qualifications and experience in the field of technology
concerned. However, any panel of the central division dealing with actions under
Article 32(1)(i) shall sit in a composition of three legally qualified judges who are
nationals of different Contracting Member States.

(7) Notwithstanding paragraphs 1 to 6 and in accordance with the Rules of
Procedure, parties may agree to have their case heard by a single legally qualified
judge.

(8) Any panel of the Court of First Instance shall be chaired by a legally qualified judge.

Article 9

The Court of Appeal

AppG-09 **(1)** Any panel of the Court of Appeal shall sit in a multinational composition of
five judges. It shall sit in a composition of three legally qualified judges who are
nationals of different Contracting Member States and two technically qualified
judges with qualifications and experience in the field of technology concerned.
Those technically qualified judges shall be assigned to the panel by the President
of the Court of Appeal from the pool of judges in accordance with Article 18.

(2) Notwithstanding paragraph 1, a panel dealing with actions under Article
32(1)(i) shall sit in a composition of three legally qualified judges who are nationals of different Contracting Member States.

(3) Any panel of the Court of Appeal shall be chaired by a legally qualified judge.

(4) The panels of the Court of Appeal shall be set up in accordance with the
Statute.

(5) The Court of Appeal shall have its seat in Luxembourg.

Article 10

The Registry

(1) A Registry shall be set up at the seat of the Court of Appeal. It shall be man- AppG-10
aged by the Registrar and perform the functions assigned to it in accordance with
the Statute. Subject to conditions set out in this Agreement and the Rules of
Procedure, the register kept by the Registry shall be public.

(2) Sub-registries shall be set up at all divisions of the Court of First Instance.

(3) The Registry shall keep records of all cases before the Court. Upon filing, the
sub-registry concerned shall notify every case to the Registry.

(4) The Court shall appoint the Registrar in accordance with Article 22 of the
Statute and lay down the rules governing the Registrar's service.

Article 11

Committees

An Administrative Committee, a Budget Committee and an Advisory Commit- AppG-11
tee shall be set up in order to ensure the effective implementation and operation of
this Agreement. They shall in particular exercise the duties foreseen by this Agreement and the Statute.

Article 12

The Administrative Committee

(1) The Administrative Committee shall be composed of one representative of AppG-12
each Contracting Member State. The European Commission shall be represented
at the meetings of the Administrative Committee as observer.

(2) Each Contracting Member State shall have one vote.

(3) The Administrative Committee shall adopt its decisions by a majority of three
quarters of the Contracting Member States represented and voting, except where
this Agreement or the Statute provides otherwise.

(4) The Administrative Committee shall adopt its rules of procedure.

(5) The Administrative Committee shall elect a chairperson from among its
members for a term of three years. That term shall be renewable.

Article 13

The Budget Committee

(1) The Budget Committee shall be composed of one representative of each AppG-13
Contracting Member State.

(2) Each Contracting Member State shall have one vote.

(3) The Budget Committee shall take its decisions by a simple majority of the
representatives of the Contracting Member States. However, a majority of three-
quarters of the representatives of Contracting Member States shall be required for
the adoption of the budget.

(4) The Budget Committee shall adopt its rules of procedure.

(5) The Budget Committee shall elect a chairperson from among its members for
a term of three years. That term shall be renewable.

Article 14

The Advisory Committee

AppG-14 **(1)** The Advisory Committee shall:
    (a) assist the Administrative Committee in the preparation of the appointment of judges of the Court;
    (b) make proposals to the Presidium referred to in Article 15 of the Statute on the guidelines for the training framework for judges referred to in Article 19; and
    (c) deliver opinions to the Administrative Committee concerning the requirements for qualifications referred to in Article 48(2).

(2) The Advisory Committee shall comprise patent judges and practitioners in patent law and patent litigation with the highest recognised competence. They shall be appointed, in accordance with the procedure laid down in the Statute, for a term of six years. That term shall be renewable.

(3) The composition of the Advisory Committee shall ensure a broad range of relevant expertise and the representation of each of the Contracting Member States. The members of the Advisory Committee shall be completely independent in the performance of their duties and shall not be bound by any instructions.

(4) The Advisory Committee shall adopt its rules of procedure.

(5) The Advisory Committee shall elect a chairperson from among its members for a term of three years. That term shall be renewable.

CHAPTER III

JUDGES OF THE COURT

Article 15

Eligibility criteria for the appointment of judges

AppG-15 **(1)** The Court shall comprise both legally qualified judges and technically qualified judges. Judges shall ensure the highest standards of competence and shall have proven experience in the field of patent litigation.

(2) Legally qualified judges shall possess the qualifications required for appointment to judicial offices in a Contracting Member State.

(3) Technically qualified judges shall have a university degree and proven expertise in a field of technology. They shall also have proven knowledge of civil law and procedure relevant in patent litigation.

Article 16

Appointment procedure

AppG-16 **(1)** The Advisory Committee shall establish a list of the most suitable candidates to be appointed as judges of the Court, in accordance with the Statute.

(2) On the basis of that list, the Administrative Committee shall appoint the judges of the Court acting by common accord.

(3) The implementing provisions for the appointment of judges are set out in the Statute.

Article 17

Judicial independence and impartiality

(1) The Court, its judges and the Registrar shall enjoy judicial independence. In the performance of their duties, the judges shall not be bound by any instructions.   AppG-17
(2) Legally qualified judges, as well as technically qualified judges who are full-time judges of the Court, may not engage in any other occupation, whether gainful or not, unless an exception is granted by the Administrative Committee.
(3) Notwithstanding paragraph 2, the exercise of the office of judges shall not exclude the exercise of other judicial functions at national level.
(4) The exercise of the office of technically qualified judges who are part-time judges of the Court shall not exclude the exercise of other functions provided there is no conflict of interest.
(5) In case of a conflict of interest, the judge concerned shall not take part in proceedings. Rules governing conflicts of interest are set out in the Statute.

Article 18

Pool of Judges

(1) A Pool of Judges shall be established in accordance with the Statute.   AppG-18
(2) The Pool of Judges shall be composed of all legally qualified judges and technically qualified judges from the Court of First Instance who are full-time or part-time judges of the Court. The Pool of Judges shall include at least one technically qualified judge per field of technology with the relevant qualifications and experience. The technically qualified judges from the Pool of Judges shall also be available to the Court of Appeal.
(3) Where so provided by this Agreement or the Statute, the judges from the Pool of Judges shall be allocated to the division concerned by the President of the Court of First Instance. The allocation of judges shall be based on their legal or technical expertise, linguistic skills and relevant experience. The allocation of judges shall guarantee the same high quality of work and the same high level of legal and technical expertise in all panels of the Court of First Instance.

Article 19

Training framework

(1) A training framework for judges, the details of which are set out in the Statute,   AppG-19
shall be set up in order to improve and increase available patent litigation expertise and to ensure a broad geographic distribution of such specific knowledge and experience. The facilities for that framework shall be situated in Budapest.
(2) The training framework shall in particular focus on:
  (a) internships in national patent courts or divisions of the Court of First Instance hearing a substantial number of patent litigation cases;
  (b) improvement of linguistic skills;
  (c) technical aspects of patent law;
  (d) the dissemination of knowledge and experience in civil procedure for technically qualified judges;
  (e) the preparation of candidate-judges.

(3)   The training framework shall provide for continuous training. Regular meetings shall be organised between all judges of the Court in order to discuss developments in patent law and to ensure the consistency of the Court's case law.

CHAPTER IV

THE PRIMACY OF UNION LAW, LIABILITY AND RESPONSIBILITY OF THE CONTRACTING MEMBER STATES

Article 20

Primacy of and respect for Union law

AppG-20   The Court shall apply Union law in its entirety and shall respect its primacy.

Article 21

Requests for preliminary rulings

AppG-21   As a court common to the Contracting Member States and as part of their judicial system, the Court shall cooperate with the Court of Justice of the European Union to ensure the correct application and uniform interpretation of Union law, as any national court, in accordance with Article 267 TFEU in particular. Decisions of the Court of Justice of the European Union shall be binding on the Court.

Article 22

Liability for damage caused by infringements of Union law

AppG-22   (1)   The Contracting Member States are jointly and severally liable for damage resulting from an infringement of Union law by the Court of Appeal, in accordance with Union law concerning non-contractual liability of Member States for damage caused by their national courts breaching Union law.

(2)   An action for such damages shall be brought against the Contracting Member State where the claimant has its residence or principal place of business or, in the absence of residence or principal place of business, place of business, before the competent authority of that Contracting Member State. Where the claimant does not have its residence, or principal place of business or, in the absence of residence or principal place of business, place of business in a Contracting Member State, the claimant may bring such an action against the Contracting Member State where the Court of Appeal has its seat, before the competent authority of that Contracting Member State.

The competent authority shall apply the lex fori, with the exception of its private international law, to all questions not regulated by Union law or by this Agreement. The claimant shall be entitled to obtain the entire amount of damages awarded by the competent authority from the Contracting Member State against which the action was brought.

(3)   The Contracting Member State that has paid damages is entitled to obtain proportional contribution, established in accordance with the method laid down in Article 37(3) and (4), from the other Contracting Member States. The detailed rules governing the Contracting Member States' contribution under this paragraph shall be determined by the Administrative Committee.

Article 23

Responsibility of the Contracting Member States

Actions of the Court are directly attributable to each Contracting Member State individually, including for the purposes of Articles 258, 259 and 260 TFEU, and to all Contracting Member States collectively.

AppG-23

CHAPTER V

SOURCES OF LAW AND SUBSTANTIVE LAW

Article 24

Sources of law

(1)   In full compliance with Article 20, when hearing a case brought before it under this Agreement, the Court shall base its decisions on:

AppG-24

   (a)   Union law, including Regulation (EU) No 1257/2012 and Regulation (EU) No 1260/2012[7];
   (b)   this Agreement;
   (c)   the EPC;
   (d)   other international agreements applicable to patents and binding on all the Contracting Member States; and
   (e)   national law.

(2)   To the extent that the Court shall base its decisions on national law, including where relevant the law of non-contracting States, the applicable law shall be determined:

   (a)   by directly applicable provisions of Union law containing private international law rules, or
   (b)   in the absence of directly applicable provisions of Union law or where the latter do not apply, by international instruments containing private international law rules; or
   (c)   in the absence of provisions referred to in points (a) and (b), by national provisions on private international law as determined by the Court.

(3)   The law of non-contracting States shall apply when designated by application of the rules referred to in paragraph 2, in particular in relation to Articles 25 to 28, 54, 55, 64, 68 and 72.

Article 25

Right to prevent the direct use of the invention

A patent shall confer on its proprietor the right to prevent any third party not having the proprietor's consent from the following:

AppG-25

   (a)   making, offering, placing on the market or using a product which is the subject matter of the patent, or importing or storing the product for those purposes;

---

[7]   Council Regulation (EU) No 1260/2012 of 17 December 2012 implementing enhanced cooperation in the area of the creation of unitary patent protection with regard to the applicable translation arrangements (OJEU L 361, 31.12.2012, p. 89) including any subsequent amendments.

(b) using a process which is the subject matter of the patent or, where the third party knows, or should have known, that the use of the process is prohibited without the consent of the patent proprietor, offering the process for use within the territory of the Contracting Member States in which that patent has effect;

(c) offering, placing on the market, using, or importing or storing for those purposes a product obtained directly by a process which is the subject matter of the patent.

Article 26

Right to prevent the indirect use of the invention

AppG-26 **(1)** A patent shall confer on its proprietor the right to prevent any third party not having the proprietor's consent from supplying or offering to supply, within the territory of the Contracting Member States in which that patent has effect, any person other than a party entitled to exploit the patented invention, with means, relating to an essential element of that invention, for putting it into effect therein, when the third party knows, or should have known, that those means are suitable and intended for putting that invention into effect.

(2) Paragraph 1 shall not apply when the means are staple commercial products, except where the third party induces the person supplied to perform any of the acts prohibited by Article 25.

(3) Persons performing the acts referred to in Article 27(a) to (e) shall not be considered to be parties entitled to exploit the invention within the meaning of paragraph 1.

Article 27

Limitations of the effects of a patent

AppG-27 The rights conferred by a patent shall not extend to any of the following:

(a) acts done privately and for non-commercial purposes;

(b) acts done for experimental purposes relating to the subject matter of the patented invention;

(c) the use of biological material for the purpose of breeding, or discovering and developing other plant varieties;

(d) the acts allowed pursuant to Article 13(6) of Directive 2001/82/EC[8] or Article 10(6) of Directive 2001/83/EC[9] in respect of any patent covering the product within the meaning of either of those Directives;

(e) the extemporaneous preparation by a pharmacy, for individual cases, of a medicine in accordance with a medical prescription or acts concerning the medicine so prepared;

(f) the use of the patented invention on board vessels of countries of the International Union for the Protection of Industrial Property (Paris Union)

---

[8] Directive 2001/82/EC of the European Parliament and of the Council of 6 November 2001 on the Community code relating to veterinary medicinal products (OJEC L 311, 28.11.2001, p. 1) including any subsequent amendments.

[9] Directive 2001/83/EC of the European Parliament and of the Council of 6 November 2001 on the Community code relating to medicinal products for human use (OJEC L 311, 28.11.2001, p. 67) including any subsequent amendments.

or members of the World Trade Organisation, other than those Contracting Member States in which that patent has effect, in the body of such vessel, in the machinery, tackle, gear and other accessories, when such vessels temporarily or accidentally enter the waters of a Contracting Member State in which that patent has effect, provided that the invention is used there exclusively for the needs of the vessel;

(g) the use of the patented invention in the construction or operation of aircraft or land vehicles or other means of transport of countries of the International Union for the Protection of Industrial Property (Paris Union) or members of the World Trade Organisation, other than those Contracting Member States in which that patent has effect, or of accessories to such aircraft or land vehicles, when these temporarily or accidentally enter the territory of a Contracting Member State in which that patent has effect;

(h) the acts specified in Article 27 of the Convention on International Civil Aviation of 7 December 1944[10], where these acts concern the aircraft of a country party to that Convention other than a Contracting Member State in which that patent has effect;

(i) the use by a farmer of the product of his harvest for propagation or multiplication by him on his own holding, provided that the plant propagating material was sold or otherwise commercialised to the farmer by or with the consent of the patent proprietor for agricultural use. The extent and the conditions for this use correspond to those under Article 14 of Regulation (EC) No. 2100/94[11];

(j) the use by a farmer of protected livestock for an agricultural purpose, provided that the breeding stock or other animal reproductive material were sold or otherwise commercialised to the farmer by or with the consent of the patent proprietor. Such use includes making the animal or other animal reproductive material available for the purposes of pursuing the farmer's agricultural activity, but not the sale thereof within the framework of, or for the purpose of, a commercial reproductive activity;

(k) the acts and the use of the obtained information as allowed under Articles 5 and 6 of Directive 2009/24/EC[12], in particular, by its provisions on decompilation and interoperability; and

(l) the acts allowed pursuant to Article 10 of Directive 98/44/EC[13].

Article 28

Right based on prior use of the invention

Any person, who, if a national patent had been granted in respect of an invention, would have had, in a Contracting Member State, a right based on prior use of

AppG-28

---

[10] International Civil Aviation Organization (ICAO), '*Chicago Convention*', Document 7300/9 (9th edition, 2006).

[11] Council Regulation (EC) No 2100/94 of 27 July 1994 on Community plant variety rights (OJEC L 227, 1.9.1994, p. 1) including any subsequent amendments.

[12] Directive 2009/24/EC of the European Parliament and of the Council of 23 April 2009 on the legal protection of computer programs (OJEU L 111, 05/05/2009, p. 16) including any subsequent amendments.

[13] Directive 98/44/EC of the European Parliament and of the Council of 6 July 1998 on the legal protection of biotechnological inventions (OJEC L 213, 30.7.1998, p. 13) including any subsequent amendments.

that invention or a right of personal possession of that invention, shall enjoy, in that Contracting Member State, the same rights in respect of a patent for the same invention.

Article 29

Exhaustion of the rights conferred by a European patent

AppG-29   The rights conferred by a European patent shall not extend to acts concerning a product covered by that patent after that product has been placed on the market in the European Union by, or with the consent of, the patent proprietor, unless there are legitimate grounds for the patent proprietor to oppose further commercialisation of the product.

Article 30

Effects of supplementary protection certificates

AppG-30   A supplementary protection certificate shall confer the same rights as conferred by the patent and shall be subject to the same limitations and the same obligations.

CHAPTER VI

INTERNATIONAL JURISDICTION AND COMPETENCE

Article 31

International jurisdiction

AppG-31   The international jurisdiction of the Court shall be established in accordance with Regulation (EU) No 1215/2012 or, where applicable, on the basis of the Convention on jurisdiction and the recognition and enforcement of judgments in civil and commercial matters (Lugano Convention)[14].

Article 32

Competence of the Court

AppG-32 **(1)**   The Court shall have exclusive competence in respect of:
  (a)   actions for actual or threatened infringements of patents and supplementary protection certificates and related defences, including counterclaims concerning licences;
  (b)   actions for declarations of non-infringement of patents and supplementary protection certificates;
  (c)   actions for provisional and protective measures and injunctions;
  (d)   actions for revocation of patents and for declaration of invalidity of supplementary protection certificates;
  (e)   counterclaims for revocation of patents and for declaration of invalidity of supplementary protection certificates;

---

[14]   Convention on jurisdiction and the recognition and enforcement of judgments in civil and commercial matters, done at Lugano on 30 October 2007, including any subsequent amendments.

(f)   actions for damages or compensation derived from the provisional protection conferred by a published European patent application;

(g)   actions relating to the use of the invention prior to the granting of the patent or to the right based on prior use of the invention;

(h)   actions for compensation for licences on the basis of Article 8 of Regulation (EU) No 1257/2012; and

(i)   actions concerning decisions of the European Patent Office in carrying out the tasks referred to in Article 9 of Regulation (EU) No 1257/2012.

(2)   The national courts of the Contracting Member States shall remain competent for actions relating to patents and supplementary protection certificates which do not come within the exclusive competence of the Court.

Article 33

Competence of the divisions of the Court of First Instance

(1)   Without prejudice to paragraph 7 of this Article, actions referred to in Article 32(1)(a), (c), (f) and (g) shall be brought before: AppG-33

(a)   the local division hosted by the Contracting Member State where the actual or threatened infringement has occurred or may occur, or the regional division in which that Contracting Member State participates; or

(b)   the local division hosted by the Contracting Member State where the defendant or, in the case of multiple defendants, one of the defendants has its residence, or principal place of business, or in the absence of residence or principal place of business, its place of business, or the regional division in which that Contracting Member State participates. An action may be brought against multiple defendants only where the defendants have a commercial relationship and where the action relates to the same alleged infringement.

Actions referred to in Article 32(1)(h) shall be brought before the local or regional division in accordance with point (b) of the first subparagraph.

Actions against defendants having their residence, or principal place of business or, in the absence of residence or principal place of business, their place of business, outside the territory of the Contracting Member States shall be brought before the local or regional division in accordance with point (a) of the first subparagraph or before the central division.

If the Contracting Member State concerned does not host a local division and does not participate in a regional division, actions shall be brought before the central division.

(2)   If an action referred to in Article 32(1)(a), (c), (f), (g) or (h) is pending before a division of the Court of First Instance, any action referred to in Article 32(1)(a), (c), (f), (g) or (h) between the same parties on the same patent may not be brought before any other division.

If an action referred to in Article 32(1)(a) is pending before a regional division and the infringement has occurred in the territories of three or more regional divisions, the regional division concerned shall, at the request of the defendant, refer the case to the central division.

In case an action between the same parties on the same patent is brought before several different divisions, the division first seized shall be competent for the whole case and any division seized later shall declare the action inadmissible in accordance with the Rules of Procedure.

(3) A counterclaim for revocation as referred to in Article 32(1)(e) may be brought in the case of an action for infringement as referred to in Article 32(1)(a). The local or regional division concerned shall, after having heard the parties, have the discretion either to:

- (a) proceed with both the action for infringement and with the counterclaim for revocation and request the President of the Court of First Instance to allocate from the Pool of Judges in accordance with Article 18(3) a technically qualified judge with qualifications and experience in the field of technology concerned.
- (b) refer the counterclaim for revocation for decision to the central division and suspend or proceed with the action for infringement; or
- (c) with the agreement of the parties, refer the case for decision to the central division.

(4) Actions referred to in Article 32(1)(b) and (d) shall be brought before the central division. If, however, an action for infringement as referred to in Article 32(1)(a) between the same parties relating to the same patent has been brought before a local or a regional division, these actions may only be brought before the same local or regional division.

(5) If an action for revocation as referred to in Article 32(1)(d) is pending before the central division, an action for infringement as referred to in Article 32(1)(a) between the same parties relating to the same patent may be brought before any division in accordance with paragraph 1 of this Article or before the central division. The local or regional division concerned shall have the discretion to proceed in accordance with paragraph 3 of this Article.

(6) An action for declaration of non-infringement as referred to in Article 32(1)(b) pending before the central division shall be stayed once an infringement action as referred to in Article 32(1)(a) between the same parties or between the holder of an exclusive licence and the party requesting a declaration of non-infringement relating to the same patent is brought before a local or regional division within three months of the date on which the action was initiated before the central division.

(7) Parties may agree to bring actions referred to in Article 32(1)(a) to (h) before the division of their choice, including the central division.

(8) Actions referred to in Article 32(1)(d) and (e) can be brought without the applicant having to file notice of opposition with the European Patent Office.

(9) Actions referred to in Article 32(1)(i) shall be brought before the central division.

(10) A party shall inform the Court of any pending revocation, limitation or opposition proceedings before the European Patent Office, and of any request for accelerated processing before the European Patent Office. The Court may stay its proceedings when a rapid decision may be expected from the European Patent Office.

Article 34

Territorial scope of decisions

AppG-34   Decisions of the Court shall cover, in the case of a European patent, the territory of those Contracting Member States for which the European patent has effect.

CHAPTER VII

PATENT MEDIATION AND ARBITRATION

Article 35

Patent mediation and arbitration centre

(1)   A patent mediation and arbitration centre ("the Centre") is hereby established. **AppG-35**
It shall have its seats in Ljubljana and Lisbon.
(2)   The Centre shall provide facilities for mediation and arbitration of patent
disputes falling within the scope of this Agreement. Article 82 shall apply mutatis
mutandis to any settlement reached through the use of the facilities of the Centre,
including through mediation. However, a patent may not be revoked or limited in
mediation or arbitration proceedings.
(3)   The Centre shall establish Mediation and Arbitration Rules.
(4)   The Centre shall draw up a list of mediators and arbitrators to assist the parties in the settlement of their dispute.

PART II

FINANCIAL PROVISIONS

Article 36

Budget of the Court

(1)   The budget of the Court shall be financed by the Court's own financial **AppG-36**
revenues and, at least in the transitional period referred to in Article 83 as necessary, by contributions from the Contracting Member States. The budget shall be
balanced.
(2)   The Court's own financial revenues shall comprise court fees and other
revenues.
(3)   Court fees shall be fixed by the Administrative Committee. They shall consist
of a fixed fee, combined with a value-based fee above a pre-defined ceiling. The
Court fees shall be fixed at such a level as to ensure a right balance between the
principle of fair access to justice, in particular for small and medium-sized
enterprises, micro-entities, natural persons, non-profit organisations, universities and
public research organisations and an adequate contribution of the parties for the
costs incurred by the Court, recognising the economic benefits to the parties
involved, and the objective of a self-financing Court with balanced finances. The
level of the Court fees shall be reviewed periodically by the Administrative
Committee. Targeted support measures for small and medium-sized enterprises and
micro entities may be considered.
(4)   If the Court is unable to balance its budget out of its own resources, the
Contracting Member States shall remit to it special financial contributions.

Article 37

Financing of the Court

AppG-37 **(1)** The operating costs of the Court shall be covered by the budget of the Court, in accordance with the Statute.

Contracting Member States setting up a local division shall provide the facilities necessary for that purpose. Contracting Member States sharing a regional division shall provide jointly the facilities necessary for that purpose. Contracting Member States hosting the central division, its sections or the Court of Appeal shall provide the facilities necessary for that purpose. During an initial transitional period of seven years starting from the date of the entry into force of this Agreement, the Contracting Member States concerned shall also provide administrative support staff, without prejudice to the Statute of that staff.

(2) On the date of entry into force of this Agreement, the Contracting Member States shall provide the initial financial contributions necessary for the setting up of the Court.

(3) During the initial transitional period of seven years, starting from the date of the entry into force of this Agreement, the contribution by each Contracting Member State having ratified or acceded to the Agreement before the entry into force thereof shall be calculated on the basis of the number of European patents having effect in the territory of that State on the date of entry into force of this Agreement and the number of European patents with respect to which actions for infringement or for revocation have been brought before the national courts of that State in the three years preceding entry into force of this Agreement.

During the same initial transitional period of seven years, for Member States which ratify, or accede to, this Agreement after the entry into force thereof, the contributions shall be calculated on the basis of the number of European patents having effect in the territory of the ratifying or acceding Member State on the date of the ratification or accession and the number of European patents with respect to which actions for infringement or for revocation have been brought before the national courts of the ratifying or acceding Member State in the three years preceding the ratification or accession.

(4) After the end of the initial transitional period of seven years, by which the Court is expected to have become self-financing, should contributions by the Contracting Member States become necessary, they shall be determined in accordance with the scale for the distribution of annual renewal fees for European patents with unitary effect applicable at the time the contribution becomes necessary.

Article 38

Financing of the training framework for judges

AppG-38 The training framework for judges shall be financed by the budget of the Court.

Article 39

Financing of the Centre

AppG-39 The operating costs of the Centre shall be financed by the budget of the Court.

PART III

ORGANISATION AND PROCEDURAL PROVISIONS

CHAPTER I

GENERAL PROVISIONS

Article 40
Statute

(1) The Statute shall lay down the details of the organisation and functioning of the Court.
(2) The Statute is annexed to this Agreement. The Statute may be amended by decision of the Administrative Committee, on the basis of a proposal of the Court or a proposal of a Contracting Member State after consultation with the Court. However, such amendments shall not contradict or alter this Agreement.
(3) The Statute shall guarantee that the functioning of the Court is organised in the most efficient and cost-effective manner and shall ensure equitable access to justice.

AppG-40

Article 41
Rules of Procedure

(1) The Rules of Procedure shall lay down the details of the proceedings before the Court. They shall comply with this Agreement and the Statute.
(2) The Rules of Procedure shall be adopted by the Administrative Committee on the basis of broad consultations with stakeholders. The prior opinion of the European Commission on the compatibility of the Rules of Procedure with Union law shall be requested.

The Rules of Procedure may be amended by a decision of the Administrative Committee, on the basis of a proposal from the Court and after consultation with the European Commission. However, such amendments shall not contradict or alter this Agreement or the Statute.
(3) The Rules of Procedure shall guarantee that the decisions of the Court are of the highest quality and that proceedings are organised in the most efficient and cost effective manner. They shall ensure a fair balance between the legitimate interests of all parties. They shall provide for the required level of discretion of judges without impairing the predictability of proceedings for the parties.

AppG-41

Article 42
Proportionality and fairness

(1) The Court shall deal with litigation in ways which are proportionate to the importance and complexity thereof.
(2) The Court shall ensure that the rules, procedures and remedies provided for in this Agreement and in the Statute are used in a fair and equitable manner and do not distort competition.

AppG-42

Article 43

Case management

AppG-43 The Court shall actively manage the cases before it in accordance with the Rules of Procedure without impairing the freedom of the parties to determine the subject-matter of, and the supporting evidence for, their case.

Article 44

Electronic procedures

AppG-44 The Court shall make best use of electronic procedures, such as the electronic filing of submissions of the parties and stating of evidence in electronic form, as well as video conferencing, in accordance with the Rules of Procedure.

Article 45

Public proceedings

AppG-45 The proceedings shall be open to the public unless the Court decides to make them confidential, to the extent necessary, in the interest of one of the parties or other affected persons, or in the general interest of justice or public order.

Article 46

Legal capacity

AppG-46 Any natural or legal person, or any body equivalent to a legal person entitled to initiate proceedings in accordance with its national law, shall have the capacity to be a party to the proceedings before the Court.

Article 47

Parties

AppG-47 (1) The patent proprietor shall be entitled to bring actions before the Court.

(2) Unless the licensing agreement provides otherwise, the holder of an exclusive licence in respect of a patent shall be entitled to bring actions before the Court under the same circumstances as the patent proprietor, provided that the patent proprietor is given prior notice.

(3) The holder of a non-exclusive licence shall not be entitled to bring actions before the Court, unless the patent proprietor is given prior notice and in so far as expressly permitted by the licence agreement.

(4) In actions brought by a licence holder, the patent proprietor shall be entitled to join the action before the Court.

(5) The validity of a patent cannot be contested in an action for infringement brought by the holder of a licence where the patent proprietor does not take part in the proceedings. The party in an action for infringement wanting to contest the validity of a patent shall have to bring actions against the patent proprietor.

(6) Any other natural or legal person, or any body entitled to bring actions in accordance with its national law, who is concerned by a patent, may bring actions in accordance with the Rules of Procedure.

(7) Any natural or legal person, or any body entitled to bring actions in accordance with its national law and who is affected by a decision of the European Patent Office in carrying out the tasks referred to in Article 9 of Regulation (EU) No 1257/2012 is entitled to bring actions under Article 32(1)(i).

Article 48

Representation

(1) Parties shall be represented by lawyers authorised to practise before a court of a Contracting Member State.   AppG-48

(2) Parties may alternatively be represented by European Patent Attorneys who are entitled to act as professional representatives before the European Patent Office pursuant to Article 134 of the EPC and who have appropriate qualifications such as a European Patent Litigation Certificate.

(3) The requirements for qualifications pursuant to paragraph 2 shall be established by the Administrative Committee. A list of European Patent Attorneys entitled to represent parties before the Court shall be kept by the Registrar.

(4) Representatives of the parties may be assisted by patent attorneys, who shall be allowed to speak at hearings of the Court in accordance with the Rules of Procedure.

(5) Representatives of the parties shall enjoy the rights and immunities necessary for the independent exercise of their duties, including the privilege from disclosure in proceedings before the Court in respect of communications between a representative and the party or any other person, under the conditions laid down in the Rules of Procedure, unless such privilege is expressly waived by the party concerned.

(6) Representatives of the parties shall be obliged not to misrepresent cases or facts before the Court either knowingly or with good reasons to know.

(7) Representation in accordance with paragraphs 1 and 2 of this Article shall not be required in proceedings under Article 32(1)(i).

CHAPTER II

LANGUAGE OF PROCEEDINGS

Article 49

Language of proceedings at the Court of First Instance

(1) The language of proceedings before any local or regional division shall be an official European Union language which is the official language or one of the official languages of the Contracting Member State hosting the relevant division, or the official language(s) designated by Contracting Member States sharing a regional division.   AppG-49

(2) Notwithstanding paragraph 1, Contracting Member States may designate one or more of the official languages of the European Patent Office as the language of proceedings of their local or regional division.

(3) The parties may agree on the use of the language in which the patent was granted as the language of proceedings, subject to approval by the competent panel.

If the panel does not approve their choice, the parties may request that the case be referred to the central division.

(4) With the agreement of the parties the competent panel may, on grounds of convenience and fairness, decide on the use of the language in which the patent was granted as the language of proceedings.

(5) At the request of one of the parties and after having heard the other parties and the competent panel, the President of the Court of First Instance may, on grounds of fairness and taking into account all relevant circumstances, including the position of parties, in particular the position of the defendant, decide on the use of the language in which the patent was granted as language of proceedings. In this case the President of the Court of First Instance shall assess the need for specific translation and interpretation arrangements.

(6) The language of proceedings at the central division shall be the language in which the patent concerned was granted.

Article 50

Language of proceedings at the Court of Appeal

AppG-50 **(1)** The language of proceedings before the Court of Appeal shall be the language of proceedings before the Court of First Instance.

(2) Notwithstanding paragraph 1 the parties may agree on the use of the language in which the patent was granted as the language of proceedings.

(3) In exceptional cases and to the extent deemed appropriate, the Court of Appeal may decide on another official language of a Contracting Member State as the language of proceedings for the whole or part of the proceedings, subject to agreement by the parties.

Article 51

Other language arrangements

AppG-51 **(1)** Any panel of the Court of First Instance and the Court of Appeal may, to the extent deemed appropriate, dispense with translation requirements.

(2) At the request of one of the parties, and to the extent deemed appropriate, any division of the Court of First Instance and the Court of Appeal shall provide interpretation facilities to assist the parties concerned at oral proceedings.

(3) Notwithstanding Article 49(6), in cases where an action for infringement is brought before the central division, a defendant having its residence, principal place of business or place of business in a Member State shall have the right to obtain, upon request, translations of relevant documents in the language of the Member State of residence, principal place of business or, in the absence of residence or principal place of business, place of business, in the following circumstances:

    (a) jurisdiction is entrusted to the central division in accordance with Article 33(1) third or fourth subparagraph, and

    (b) the language of proceedings at the central division is a language which is not an official language of the Member State where the defendant has its residence, principal place of business or, in the absence of residence or principal place of business, place of business, and

    (c) the defendant does not have proper knowledge of the language of the proceedings.

CHAPTER III

PROCEEDINGS BEFORE THE COURT

Article 52

Written, interim and oral procedures

(1) The proceedings before the Court shall consist of a written, an interim and an oral procedure, in accordance with the Rules of Procedure. All procedures shall be organized in a flexible and balanced manner. AppG-52

(2) In the interim procedure, after the written procedure and if appropriate, the judge acting as Rapporteur, subject to a mandate of the full panel, shall be responsible for convening an interim hearing. That judge shall in particular explore with the parties the possibility for a settlement, including through mediation, and/or arbitration, by using the facilities of the Centre referred to in Article 35.

(3) The oral procedure shall give parties the opportunity to explain properly their arguments. The Court may, with the agreement of the parties, dispense with the oral hearing.

Article 53

Means of evidence

(1) In proceedings before the Court, the means of giving or obtaining evidence shall include in particular the following: AppG-53
   (a)   hearing the parties;
   (b)   requests for information;
   (c)   production of documents;
   (d)   hearing witnesses;
   (e)   opinions by experts;
   (f)   inspection;
   (g)   comparative tests or experiments;
   (h)   sworn statements in writing (affidavits).

(2) The Rules of Procedure shall govern the procedure for taking such evidence. Questioning of witnesses and experts shall be under the control of the Court and be limited to what is necessary.

Article 54

Burden of proof

Without prejudice to Article 24(2) and (3), the burden of the proof of facts shall be on the party relying on those facts. AppG-54

Article 55

Reversal of burden of proof

(1) Without prejudice to Article 24(2) and (3), if the subject-matter of a patent is a process for obtaining a new product, the identical product when produced without the consent of the patent proprietor shall, in the absence of proof to the contrary, be deemed to have been obtained by the patented process. AppG-55

(2) The principle set out in paragraph 1 shall also apply where there is a substantial likelihood that the identical product was made by the patented process and the patent proprietor has been unable, despite reasonable efforts, to determine the process actually used for such identical product.

(3) In the adduction of proof to the contrary, the legitimate interests of the defendant in protecting its manufacturing and trade secrets shall be taken into account.

CHAPTER IV

POWERS OF THE COURT

Article 56

The general powers of the Court

AppG-56 **(1)** The Court may impose such measures, procedures and remedies as are laid down in this Agreement and may make its orders subject to conditions, in accordance with the Rules of Procedure.

(2) The Court shall take due account of the interest of the parties and shall, before making an order, give any party the opportunity to be heard, unless this is incompatible with the effective enforcement of such order.

Article 57

Court experts

AppG-57 **(1)** Without prejudice to the possibility for the parties to produce expert evidence, the Court may at any time appoint court experts in order to provide expertise for specific aspects of the case. The Court shall provide such expert with all information necessary for the provision of the expert advice.

(2) To this end, an indicative list of experts shall be drawn up by the Court in accordance with the Rules of Procedure. That list shall be kept by the Registrar.

(3) The court experts shall guarantee independence and impartiality. Rules governing conflicts of interest applicable to judges set out in Article 7 of the Statute shall by analogy apply to court experts.

(4) Expert advice given to the Court by court experts shall be made available to the parties which shall have the possibility to comment on it.

Article 58

Protection of confidential information

AppG-58 To protect the trade secrets, personal data or other confidential information of a party to the proceedings or of a third party, or to prevent an abuse of evidence, the Court may order that the collection and use of evidence in proceedings before it be restricted or prohibited or that access to such evidence be restricted to specific persons.

Article 59

Order to produce evidence

(1) At the request of a party which has presented reasonably available evidence sufficient to support its claims and has, in substantiating those claims, specified evidence which lies in the control of the opposing party or a third party, the Court may order the opposing party or a third party to present such evidence, subject to the protection of confidential information. Such order shall not result in an obligation of self-incrimination.

(2) At the request of a party the Court may order, under the same conditions as specified in paragraph 1, the communication of banking, financial or commercial documents under the control of the opposing party, subject to the protection of confidential information.

AppG-59

Article 60

Order to preserve evidence and to inspect premises

(1) At the request of the applicant which has presented reasonably available evidence to support the claim that the patent has been infringed or is about to be infringed the Court may, even before the commencement of proceedings on the merits of the case, order prompt and effective provisional measures to preserve relevant evidence in respect of the alleged infringement, subject to the protection of confidential information.

(2) Such measures may include the detailed description, with or without the taking of samples, or the physical seizure of the infringing products, and, in appropriate cases, the materials and implements used in the production and/or distribution of those products and the documents relating thereto.

(3) The Court may, even before the commencement of proceedings on the merits of the case, at the request of the applicant who has presented evidence to support the claim that the patent has been infringed or is about to be infringed, order the inspection of premises. Such inspection of premises shall be conducted by a person appointed by the Court in accordance with the Rules of Procedure.

(4) At the inspection of the premises the applicant shall not be present itself but may be represented by an independent professional practitioner whose name has to be specified in the Court's order.

(5) Measures shall be ordered, if necessary without the other party having been heard, in particular where any delay is likely to cause irreparable harm to the proprietor of the patent, or where there is a demonstrable risk of evidence being destroyed.

(6) Where measures to preserve evidence or inspect premises are ordered without the other party in the case having been heard, the parties affected shall be given notice, without delay and at the latest immediately after the execution of the measures. A review, including a right to be heard, shall take place upon request of the parties affected with a view to deciding, within a reasonable period after the notification of the measures, whether the measures are to be modified, revoked or confirmed.

(7) The measures to preserve evidence may be subject to the lodging by the applicant of adequate security or an equivalent assurance intended to ensure

AppG-60

compensation for any prejudice suffered by the defendant as provided for in paragraph 9.

(8) The Court shall ensure that the measures to preserve evidence are revoked or otherwise cease to have effect, at the defendant's request, without prejudice to the damages which may be claimed, if the applicant does not bring, within a period not exceeding 31 calendar days or 20 working days, whichever is the longer, action leading to a decision on the merits of the case before the Court.

(9) Where the measures to preserve evidence are revoked, or where they lapse due to any act or omission by the applicant, or where it is subsequently found that there has been no infringement or threat of infringement of the patent, the Court may order the applicant, at the defendant's request, to provide the defendant with appropriate compensation for any damage suffered as a result of those measures.

Article 61

Freezing orders

AppG-61 **(1)** At the request of the applicant which has presented reasonably available evidence to support the claim that the patent has been infringed or is about to be infringed the Court may, even before the commencement of proceedings on the merits of the case, order a party not to remove from its jurisdiction any assets located therein, or not to deal in any assets, whether located within its jurisdiction or not.

(2) Article 60(5) to (9) shall apply by analogy to the measures referred to in this Article.

Article 62

Provisional and protective measures

AppG-62 **(1)** The Court may, by way of order, grant injunctions against an alleged infringer or against an intermediary whose services are used by the alleged infringer, intended to prevent any imminent infringement, to prohibit, on a provisional basis and subject, where appropriate, to a recurring penalty payment, the continuation of the alleged infringement or to make such continuation subject to the lodging of guarantees intended to ensure the compensation of the right holder.

(2) The Court shall have the discretion to weigh up the interests of the parties and in particular to take into account the potential harm for either of the parties resulting from the granting or the refusal of the injunction.

(3) The Court may also order the seizure or delivery up of the products suspected of infringing a patent so as to prevent their entry into, or movement, within the channels of commerce. If the applicant demonstrates circumstances likely to endanger the recovery of damages, the Court may order the precautionary seizure of the movable and immovable property of the alleged infringer, including the blocking of the bank accounts and of other assets of the alleged infringer.

(4) The Court may, in respect of the measures referred to in paragraphs 1 and 3, require the applicant to provide any reasonable evidence in order to satisfy itself with a sufficient degree of certainty that the applicant is the right holder and that the applicant's right is being infringed, or that such infringement is imminent.

(5) Article 60(5) to (9) shall apply by analogy to the measures referred to in this Article.

Article 63

Permanent injunctions

(1) Where a decision is taken finding an infringement of a patent, the Court may AppG-63 grant an injunction against the infringer aimed at prohibiting the continuation of the infringement. The Court may also grant such injunction against an intermediary whose services are being used by a third party to infringe a patent.

(2) Where appropriate, non-compliance with the injunction referred to in paragraph 1 shall be subject to a recurring penalty payment payable to the Court.

Article 64

Corrective measures in infringement proceedings

(1) Without prejudice to any damages due to the injured party by reason of the AppG-64 infringement, and without compensation of any sort, the Court may order, at the request of the applicant, that appropriate measures be taken with regard to products found to be infringing a patent and, in appropriate cases, with regard to materials and implements principally used in the creation or manufacture of those products.

(2) Such measures shall include:
  (a) a declaration of infringement;
  (b) recalling the products from the channels of commerce;
  (c) depriving the product of its infringing property;
  (d) definitively removing the products from the channels of commerce; or
  (e) the destruction of the products and/or of the materials and implements concerned.

(3) The Court shall order that those measures be carried out at the expense of the infringer, unless particular reasons are invoked for not doing so.

(4) In considering a request for corrective measures pursuant to this Article, the Court shall take into account the need for proportionality between the seriousness of the infringement and the remedies to be ordered, the willingness of the infringer to convert the materials into a non-infringing state, as well as the interests of third parties.

Article 65

Decision on the validity of a patent

(1) The Court shall decide on the validity of a patent on the basis of an action for AppG-65 revocation or a counterclaim for revocation.

(2) The Court may revoke a patent, either entirely or partly, only on the grounds referred to in Articles 138(1) and 139(2) of the EPC.

(3) Without prejudice to Article 138(3) of the EPC, if the grounds for revocation affect the patent only in part, the patent shall be limited by a corresponding amendment of the claims and revoked in part.

(4) To the extent that a patent has been revoked it shall be deemed not to have had, from the outset, the effects specified in Articles 64 and 67 of the EPC.

(5) Where the Court, in a final decision, revokes a patent, either entirely or partly, it shall send a copy of the decision to the European Patent Office and, with respect to a European patent, to the national patent office of any Contracting Member State concerned.

Article 66

Powers of the Court concerning decisions of the European Patent Office

AppG-66 **(1)** In actions brought under Article 32(1)(i), the Court may exercise any power entrusted on the European Patent Office in accordance with Article 9 of Regulation (EU) No 1257/2012, including the rectification of the Register for unitary patent protection.

(2) In actions brought under Article 32(1)(i) the parties shall, by way of derogation from Article 69, bear their own costs.

Article 67

Power to order the communication of information

AppG-67 **(1)** The Court may, in response to a justified and proportionate request of the applicant and in accordance with the Rules of Procedure, order an infringer to inform the applicant of:

    (a) the origin and distribution channels of the infringing products or processes;

    (b) the quantities produced, manufactured, delivered, received or ordered, as well as the price obtained for the infringing products; and

    (c) the identity of any third person involved in the production or distribution of the infringing products or in the use of the infringing process.

(2) The Court may, in accordance with the Rules of Procedure, also order any third party who:

    (a) was found in the possession of the infringing products on a commercial scale or to be using an infringing process on a commercial scale;

    (b) was found to be providing on a commercial scale services used in infringing activities; or

    (c) was indicated by the person referred to in points (a) or (b) as being involved in the production, manufacture or distribution of the infringing products or processes or in the provision of the services, to

provide the applicant with the information referred to in paragraph 1.

Article 68

Award of damages

AppG-68 **(1)** The Court shall, at the request of the injured party, order the infringer who knowingly, or with reasonable grounds to know, engaged in a patent infringing activity, to pay the injured party damages appropriate to the harm actually suffered by that party as a result of the infringement.

(2) The injured party shall, to the extent possible, be placed in the position it would have been in if no infringement had taken place. The infringer shall not benefit from the infringement. However, damages shall not be punitive.

(3) When the Court sets the damages:

    (a) it shall take into account all appropriate aspects, such as the negative economic consequences, including lost profits, which the injured party has suffered, any unfair profits made by the infringer and, in appropriate cases, elements other than economic factors, such as the moral prejudice caused to the injured party by the infringement; or

    (b) as an alternative to point (a), it may, in appropriate cases, set the damages as a lump sum on the basis of elements such as at least the amount of the royalties or fees which would have been due if the infringer had requested authorisation to use the patent in question.

(4) Where the infringer did not knowingly, or with reasonable grounds to know, engage in the infringing activity, the Court may order the recovery of profits or the payment of compensation.

Article 69

Legal costs

(1) Reasonable and proportionate legal costs and other expenses incurred by the successful party shall, as a general rule, be borne by the unsuccessful party, unless equity requires otherwise, up to a ceiling set in accordance with the Rules of Procedure. AppG-69

(2) Where a party succeeds only in part or in exceptional circumstances, the Court may order that costs be apportioned equitably or that the parties bear their own costs.

(3) A party should bear any unnecessary costs it has caused the Court or another party.

(4) At the request of the defendant, the Court may order the applicant to provide adequate security for the legal costs and other expenses incurred by the defendant which the applicant may be liable to bear, in particular in the cases referred to in Articles 59 to 62.

Article 70

Court fees

(1) Parties to proceedings before the Court shall pay court fees. AppG-70

(2) Court fees shall be paid in advance, unless the Rules of Procedure provide otherwise. Any party which has not paid a prescribed court fee may be excluded from further participation in the proceedings.

Article 71

Legal aid

(1) A party who is a natural person and who is unable to meet the costs of the proceedings, either wholly or in part, may at any time apply for legal aid. The conditions for granting of legal aid shall be laid down in the Rules of Procedure. AppG-71

(2) The Court shall decide whether legal aid should be granted in full or in part, or whether it should be refused, in accordance with the Rules of Procedure.

(3) On a proposal from the Court, the Administrative Committee shall set the level of legal aid and the rules on bearing the costs thereof.

Article 72

Period of limitation

Without prejudice to Article 24(2) and (3), actions relating to all forms of financial compensation may not be brought more than five years after the date on AppG-72 which the applicant became aware, or had reasonable grounds to become aware, of the last fact justifying the action.

CHAPTER V

APPEALS

Article 73

Appeal

AppG-73 **(1)** An appeal against a decision of the Court of First Instance may be brought before the Court of Appeal by any party which has been unsuccessful, in whole or in part, in its submissions, within two months of the date of the notification of the decision.

(2) An appeal against an order of the Court of First Instance may be brought before the Court of Appeal by any party which has been unsuccessful, in whole or in part, in its submissions:

    (a) for the orders referred to in Articles 49(5), 59 to 62 and 67 within 15 calendar days of the notification of the order to the applicant ;

    (b) for other orders than the orders referred to in point (a):

        (i) together with the appeal against the decision, or

        (ii) where the Court grants leave to appeal, within 15 days of the notification of the Court's decision to that effect.

(3) The appeal against a decision or an order of the Court of First Instance may be based on points of law and matters of fact.

(4) New facts and new evidence may only be introduced in accordance with the Rules of Procedure and where the submission thereof by the party concerned could not reasonably have been expected during proceedings before the Court of First Instance.

Article 74

Effects of an appeal

AppG-74 **(1)** An appeal shall not have suspensive effect unless the Court of Appeal decides otherwise at the motivated request of one of the parties. The Rules of Procedure shall guarantee that such a decision is taken without delay.

(2) Notwithstanding paragraph 1, an appeal against a decision on actions or counterclaims for revocation and on actions based on Article 32(1)(i) shall always have suspensive effect.

(3) An appeal against an order referred to in Articles 49(5), 59 to 62 or 67 shall not prevent the continuation of the main proceedings. However, the Court of First Instance shall not give a decision in the main proceedings before the decision of the Court of Appeal concerning an appealed order has been given.

Article 75

Decision on appeal and referral back

AppG-75 **(1)** If an appeal pursuant to Article 73 is well-founded, the Court of Appeal shall revoke the decision of the Court of First Instance and give a final decision. The

Court of Appeal may in exceptional cases and in accordance with the Rules of Procedure refer the case back to the Court of First Instance for decision.

(2) Where a case is referred back to the Court of First Instance pursuant to paragraph 1, the Court of First Instance shall be bound by the decision of the Court of Appeal on points of law.

CHAPTER VI

DECISIONS

Article 76

Basis for decisions and right to be heard

(1) The Court shall decide in accordance with the requests submitted by the parties and shall not award more than is requested.   AppG-76

(2) Decisions on the merits may only be based on grounds, facts and evidence, which were submitted by the parties or introduced into the procedure by an order of the Court and on which the parties have had an opportunity to present their comments.

(3) The Court shall evaluate evidence freely and independently.

Article 77

Formal requirements

(1) Decisions and orders of the Court shall be reasoned and shall be given in writing in accordance with the Rules of Procedure.   AppG-77

(2) Decisions and orders of the Court shall be delivered in the language of proceedings.

Article 78

Decisions of the Court and dissenting opinions

(1) Decisions and orders of the Court shall be taken by a majority of the panel, in accordance with the Statute. In case of equal votes, the vote of the presiding judge shall prevail.   AppG-78

(2) In exceptional circumstances, any judge of the panel may express a dissenting opinion separately from the decision of the Court.

Article 79

Settlement

The parties may, at any time in the course of proceedings, conclude their case by way of settlement, which shall be confirmed by a decision of the Court. A patent may not be revoked or limited by way of settlement.   AppG-79

Article 80

Publication of decisions

AppG-80   The Court may order, at the request of the applicant and at the expense of the infringer, appropriate measures for the dissemination of information concerning the Court's decision, including displaying the decision and publishing it in full or in part in public media.

Article 81

Rehearing

AppG-81 **(1)**   A request for rehearing after a final decision of the Court may exceptionally be granted by the Court of Appeal in the following circumstances:

    (a)   on discovery of a fact by the party requesting the rehearing, which is of such a nature as to be a decisive factor and which, when the decision was given, was unknown to the party requesting the rehearing; such request may only be granted on the basis of an act which was held, by a final decision of a national court, to constitute a criminal offence; or

    (b)   in the event of a fundamental procedural defect, in particular when a defendant who did not appear before the Court was not served with the document initiating the proceedings or an equivalent document in sufficient time and in such a way as to enable him to arrange for the defence.

(2)   A request for a rehearing shall be filed within 10 years of the date of the decision but not later than two months from the date of the discovery of the new fact or of the procedural defect. Such request shall not have suspensive effect unless the Court of Appeal decides otherwise.

(3)   If the request for a rehearing is well-founded, the Court of Appeal shall set aside, in whole or in part, the decision under review and re-open the proceedings for a new trial and decision, in accordance with the Rules of Procedure.

(4)   Persons using patents which are the subject-matter of a decision under review and who act in good faith should be allowed to continue using such patents.

Article 82

Enforcement of decisions and orders

AppG-82 **(1)**   Decisions and orders of the Court shall be enforceable in any Contracting Member State. An order for the enforcement of a decision shall be appended to the decision by the Court.

(2)   Where appropriate, the enforcement of a decision may be subject to the provision of security or an equivalent assurance to ensure compensation for any damage suffered, in particular in the case of injunctions.

(3)   Without prejudice to this Agreement and the Statute, enforcement procedures shall be governed by the law of the Contracting Member State where the enforcement takes place. Any decision of the Court shall be enforced under the same conditions as a decision given in the Contracting Member State where the enforcement takes place.

(4)   If a party does not comply with the terms of an order of the Court, that party may be sanctioned with a recurring penalty payment payable to the Court. The individual penalty shall be proportionate to the importance of the order to be enforced and shall be without prejudice to the party's right to claim damages or security.

PART IV

TRANSITIONAL PROVISIONS

Article 83
Transitional regime

(1) During a transitional period of seven years after the date of entry into force of this Agreement, an action for infringement or for revocation of a European patent or an action for infringement or for declaration of invalidity of a supplementary protection certificate issued for a product protected by a European patent may still be brought before national courts or other competent national authorities.

AppG-83

(2) An action pending before a national court at the end of the transitional period shall not be affected by the expiry of this period.

(3) Unless an action has already been brought before the Court, a proprietor of or an applicant for a European patent granted or applied for prior to the end of the transitional period under paragraph 1 and, where applicable, paragraph 5, as well as a holder of a supplementary protection certificate issued for a product protected by a European patent, shall have the possibility to opt out from the exclusive competence of the Court. To this end they shall notify their opt-out to the Registry by the latest one month before expiry of the transitional period. The opt-out shall take effect upon its entry into the register.

(4) Unless an action has already been brought before a national court, proprietors of or applicants for European patents or holders of supplementary protection certificates issued for a product protected by a European patent who made use of the opt-out in accordance with paragraph 3 shall be entitled to withdraw their opt-out at any moment. In this event they shall notify the Registry accordingly. The withdrawal of the opt-out shall take effect upon its entry into the register.

(5) Five years after the entry into force of this Agreement, the Administrative Committee shall carry out a broad consultation with the users of the patent system and a survey on the number of European patents and supplementary protection certificates issued for products protected by European patents with respect to which actions for infringement or for revocation or declaration of invalidity are still brought before the national courts pursuant to paragraph 1, the reasons for this and the implications thereof. On the basis of this consultation and an opinion of the Court, the Administrative Committee may decide to prolong the transitional period by up to seven years.

PART V

FINAL PROVISIONS

Article 84

Signature, ratification and accession

AppG-84 **(1)** This Agreement shall be open for signature by any Member State on 19 February 2013.

(2) This Agreement shall be subject to ratification in accordance with the respective constitutional requirements of the Member States. Instruments of ratification shall be deposited with the General Secretariat of the Council of the European Union (hereinafter referred to as "the depositary").

(3) Each Member State having signed this Agreement shall notify the European Commission of its ratification of the Agreement at the time of the deposit of its ratification instrument pursuant to Article 18(3) of Regulation (EU) No 1257/2012.

(4) This Agreement shall be open to accession by any Member State. Instruments of accession shall be deposited with the depositary.

Article 85

Functions of the depositary

AppG-85 **(1)** The depositary shall draw up certified true copies of this Agreement and shall transmit them to the governments of all signatory or acceding Member States.

(2) The depositary shall notify the governments of the signatory or acceding Member States of:

    (a) any signature ;

    (b) the deposit of any instrument of ratification or accession ;

    (c) the date of entry into force of this Agreement.

(3) The depositary shall register this Agreement with the Secretariat of the United Nations.

Article 86

Duration of the Agreement

AppG-86 This Agreement shall be of unlimited duration.

Article 87

Revision

AppG-87 **(1)** Either seven years after the entry into force of this Agreement or once 2000 infringement cases have been decided by the Court, whichever is the later point in time, and if necessary at regular intervals thereafter, a broad consultation with the users of the patent system shall be carried out by the Administrative Committee on the functioning, efficiency and cost-effectiveness of the Court and on the trust and confidence of users of the patent system in the quality of the Court's decisions. On the basis of this consultation and an opinion of the Court, the Administrative Committee may decide to revise this Agreement with a view to improving the functioning of the Court.

(2) The Administrative Committee may amend this Agreement to bring it into line with an international treaty relating to patents or Union law.

(3)   A decision of the Administrative Committee taken on the basis of paragraphs 1 and 2 shall not take effect if a Contracting Member State declares within twelve months of the date of the decision, on the basis of its relevant internal decision-making procedures, that it does not wish to be bound by the decision. In this case, a Review Conference of the Contracting Member States shall be convened.

Article 88

Languages of the Agreement

(1)   This Agreement is drawn up in a single original in the English, French and German languages, each text being equally authentic.   **AppG-88**

(2)   The texts of this Agreement drawn up in official languages of Contracting Member States other than those specified in paragraph 1 shall, if they have been approved by the Administrative Committee, be considered as official texts. In the event of divergences between the various texts, the texts referred to in paragraph 1 shall prevail.

Article 89

Entry into force

(1)   This Agreement shall enter into force on 1 January 2014 or on the first day   **AppG-89** of the fourth month after the deposit of the thirteenth instrument of ratification or accession in accordance with Article 84, including the three Member States in which the highest number of European patents had effect in the year preceding the year in which the signature of the Agreement takes place or on the first day of the fourth month after the date of entry into force of the amendments to Regulation (EU) No 1215/2012 concerning its relationship with this Agreement, whichever is the latest.

(2)   Any ratification or accession after the entry into force of this Agreement shall take effect on the first day of the fourth month after the deposit of the instrument of ratification or accession.

In witness whereof the undersigned, being duly authorised thereto, have signed this Agreement,

Done at Brussels on 19 February 2013 in English, French and German, all three texts being equally authentic, in a single copy which shall be deposited in the archives of the General Secretariat of the Council of the European Union.

ANNEX I

Statute of the Unified Patent Court

Article 1

Scope of the Statute

This Statute contains institutional and financial arrangements for the Unified Pat-   **AppG-90** ent Court as established under Article 1 of the Agreement.

CHAPTER I — JUDGES

Article 2

Eligibility of judges

(1)   Any person who is a national of a Contracting Member State and fulfils the conditions set out in Article 15 of the Agreement and in this Statute may be appointed as a judge.

(2)   Judges shall have a good command of at least one official language of the European Patent Office.

(3)   Experience with patent litigation which has to be proven for the appointment pursuant to Article 15(1) of the Agreement may be acquired by training under Article 11(4)(a) of this Statute.

Article 3

Appointment of judges

(1)   Judges shall be appointed pursuant to the procedure set out in Article 16 of the Agreement.

(2)   Vacancies shall be publicly advertised and shall indicate the relevant eligibility criteria as set out in Article 2. The Advisory Committee shall give an opinion on candidates' suitability to perform the duties of a judge of the Court. The opinion shall comprise a list of most suitable candidates. The list shall contain at least twice as many candidates as there are vacancies. Where necessary, the Advisory Committee may recommend that, prior to the decision on the appointment, a candidate judge receive training in patent litigation pursuant to Article 11(4)(a).

(3)   When appointing judges, the Administrative Committee shall ensure the best legal and technical expertise and a balanced composition of the Court on as broad a geographical basis as possible among nationals of the Contracting Member States.

(4)   The Administrative Committee shall appoint as many judges as are needed for the proper functioning of the Court. The Administrative Committee shall initially appoint the necessary number of judges for setting up at least one panel in each of the divisions of the Court of First Instance and at least two panels in the Court of Appeal.

(5)   The decision of the Administrative Committee appointing full-time or part-time legally qualified judges and full-time technically qualified judges shall state the instance of the Court and/or the division of the Court of First Instance for which each judge is appointed and the field(s) of technology for which a technically qualified judge is appointed.

(6)   Part-time technically qualified judges shall be appointed as judges of the Court and shall be included in the Pool of Judges on the basis of their specific qualifications and experience. The appointment of these judges to the Court shall ensure that all fields of technology are covered.

Article 4

Judges' term of office

(1)   Judges shall be appointed for a term of six years, beginning on the date laid down in the instrument of appointment. They may be re-appointed.

(2)   In the absence of any provision regarding the date, the term shall begin on the date of the instrument of appointment.

Article 5

Appointment of the members of the Advisory Committee

(1)   Each Contracting Member State shall propose a member of the Advisory Committee who fulfils the requirements set out in Article 14(2) of the Agreement.

(2)   The members of the Advisory Committee shall be appointed by the Administrative Committee acting by common accord.

Article 6

Oath

Before taking up their duties judges shall, in open court, take an oath to perform their duties impartially and conscientiously and to preserve the secrecy of the deliberations of the Court.

Article 7

Impartiality

(1)   Immediately after taking their oath, judges shall sign a declaration by which they solemnly undertake that, both during and after their term of office, they shall respect the obligations arising therefrom, in particular the duty to behave with integrity and discretion as regards the acceptance, after they have ceased to hold office, of certain appointments or benefits.

(2)   Judges may not take part in the proceedings of a case in which they:
  (a)   have taken part as adviser;
  (b)   have been a party or have acted for one of the parties;
  (c)   have been called upon to pronounce as a member of a court, tribunal, board of appeal, arbitration or mediation panel, a commission of inquiry or in any other capacity;
  (d)   have a personal or financial interest in the case or in relation to one of the parties; or
  (e)   are related to one of the parties or the representatives of the parties by family ties.

(3)   If, for some special reason, a judge considers that he or she should not take part in the judgement or examination of a particular case, that judge shall so inform the President of the Court of Appeal accordingly or, in the case of judges of the Court of First Instance, the President of the Court of First Instance. If, for some special reason, the President of the Court of Appeal or, in the case of judges of the Court of First Instance, the President of the Court of First Instance considers that a judge should not sit or make submissions in a particular case, the President of the Court of Appeal or the President of the Court of First Instance shall justify this in writing and notify the judge concerned accordingly.

(4)   Any party to an action may object to a judge taking part in the proceedings on any of the grounds listed in paragraph 2 or where the judge is suspected, with good reason, of partiality.

(5) Any difficulty arising as to the application of this Article shall be settled by decision of the Presidium, in accordance with the Rules of Procedure. The judge concerned shall be heard but shall not take part in the deliberations.

Article 8
Immunity of judges

(1) The judges shall be immune from legal proceedings. After they have ceased to hold office, they shall continue to enjoy immunity in respect of acts performed by them in relation to their official capacity.

(2) The Presidium may waive the immunity.

(3) Where immunity has been waived and criminal proceedings are instituted against a judge, that judge shall be tried, in any of the Contracting Member States, only by the court competent to judge the members of the highest national judiciary.

(4) The Protocol on the privileges and immunities of the European Union shall apply to the judges of the Court, without prejudice to the provisions relating to immunity from legal proceedings of judges which are set out in this Statute.

Article 9
End of duties

(1) Apart from replacement after expiry of a judge's term pursuant to Article 4, or death, the duties of a judge shall end when that judge resigns.

(2) Where a judge resigns, the letter of resignation shall be addressed to the President of the Court of Appeal or, in the case of judges of the Court of First Instance, the President of the Court of First Instance for transmission to the Chairman of the Administrative Committee.

(3) Save where Article 10 applies, a judge shall continue to hold office until that judge's successor takes up his or her duties.

(4) Any vacancy shall by filled by the appointment of a new judge for the remainder of his or her predecessor's term.

Article 10
Removal from office

(1) A judge may be deprived of his or her office or of other benefits only if the Presidium decides that that judge no longer fulfils the requisite conditions or meets the obligations arising from his or her office. The judge concerned shall be heard but shall not take part in the deliberations.

(2) The Registrar of the Court shall communicate this decision to the Chairman of the Administrative Committee.

(3) In the case of a decision depriving a judge of his or her office, a vacancy shall arise upon that notification.

Article 11
Training

(1)   Appropriate and regular training of judges shall be provided for within the training framework set up under Article 19 of the Agreement. The Presidium shall adopt Training Regulations ensuring the implementation and overall coherence of the training framework.

(2)   The training framework shall provide a platform for the exchange of expertise and a forum for discussion, in particular by:
  (a)   organising courses, conferences, seminars, workshops and symposia;
  (b)   cooperating with international organisations and education institutes in the field of intellectual property; and
  (c)   promoting and supporting further vocational training.

(3)   An annual work programme and training guidelines shall be drawn up, which shall include for each judge an annual training plan identifying that judge's main training needs in accordance with the Training Regulations.

(4)   The training framework shall in addition:
  (a)   ensure appropriate training for candidate-judges and newly appointed judges of the Court;
  (b)   support projects aimed at facilitating cooperation between representatives, patent attorneys and the Court.

Article 12
Remuneration

The Administrative Committee shall set the remuneration of the President of the Court of Appeal, the President of the Court of First Instance, the judges, the Registrar, the Deputy-Registrar and the staff.

CHAPTER II — ORGANISATIONAL PROVISIONS

Section 1 — Common Provisions

Article 13
President of the Court of Appeal

(1)   The President of the Court of Appeal shall be elected by all judges of the Court   AppG-91
of Appeal for a term of three years, from among their number. The President of the Court of Appeal may be re-elected twice.

(2)   The elections of the President of the Court of Appeal shall be by secret ballot. A judge obtaining an absolute majority shall be elected. If no judge obtains an absolute majority, a second ballot shall be held and the judge obtaining the most votes shall be elected.

(3)   The President of the Court of Appeal shall direct the judicial activities and the administration of the Court of Appeal and chair the Court of Appeal sitting as a full Court.

(4)   If the office of the President of the Court of Appeal falls vacant before the date of expiry of his or her term, a successor shall be elected for the remainder thereof.

Article 14

President of the Court of First Instance

(1) The President of the Court of First Instance shall be elected by all judges of the Court of First Instance who are full-time judges, for a term of three years, from among their number. The President of the Court of First Instance may be re-elected twice.

(2) The first President of the Court of First Instance shall be a national of the Contracting Member State hosting the seat of the central division.

(3) The President of the Court of First Instance shall direct the judicial activities and the administration of the Court of First Instance.

(4) Article 13(2) and (4), shall by analogy apply to the President of the Court of First Instance.

Article 15

Presidium

(1) The Presidium shall be composed of the President of the Court of Appeal, who shall act as chairperson, the President of the Court of First Instance, two judges of the Court of Appeal elected from among their number, three judges of the Court of First Instance who are full-time judges of the Court elected from among their number, and the Registrar as a non-voting member.

(2) The Presidium shall exercise its duties in accordance with this Statute. It may, without prejudice to its own responsibility, delegate certain tasks to one of its members.

(3) The Presidium shall be responsible for the management of the Court and shall in particular:

  (a) draw up proposals for the amendment of the Rules of Procedure in accordance with Article 41 of the Agreement and proposals regarding the Financial Regulations of the Court;

  (b) prepare the annual budget, the annual accounts and the annual report of the Court and submit them to the Budget Committee;

  (c) establish the guidelines for the training programme for judges and supervise the implementation thereof;

  (d) take decisions on the appointment and removal of the Registrar and the Deputy-Registrar;

  (e) lay down the rules governing the Registry including the sub-registries;

  (f) give an opinion in accordance with Article 83(5) of the Agreement.

(4) Decisions of the Presidium referred to in Articles 7, 8, 10 and 22 shall be taken without the participation of the Registrar.

(5) The Presidium can take valid decisions only when all members are present or duly represented. Decisions shall be taken by a majority of the votes.

Article 16

Staff

(1) The officials and other servants of the Court shall have the task of assisting the President of the Court of Appeal, the President of the Court of First Instance, the

judges and the Registrar. They shall be responsible to the Registrar, under the authority of the President of the Court of Appeal and the President of the Court of First Instance.

(2) The Administrative Committee shall establish the Staff Regulations of officials and other servants of the Court.

Article 17

Judicial vacations

(1) After consulting the Presidium, the President of the Court of Appeal shall establish the duration of judicial vacations and the rules on observing official holidays.

(2) During the period of judicial vacations, the functions of the President of the Court of Appeal and of the President of the Court of First Instance may be exercised by any judge invited by the respective President to that effect. In cases of urgency, the President of the Court of Appeal may convene the judges.

(3) The President of the Court of Appeal or the President of the Court of First Instance may, in proper circumstances, grant leave of absence to respectively judges of the Court of Appeal or judges of the Court of First Instance.

Section 2 – The Court of First Instance

Article 18

Setting up and discontinuance of a local or regional division

(1) A request from one or more Contracting Member States for the setting up of a local or regional division shall be addressed to the Chairman of the Administrative Committee. It shall indicate the seat of the local or regional division. AppG-92

(2) The decision of the Administrative Committee setting up a local or regional division shall indicate the number of judges for the division concerned and shall be public.

(3) The Administrative Committee shall decide to discontinue a local or regional division at the request of the Contracting Member State hosting the local division or the Contracting Member States participating in the regional division. The decision to discontinue a local or regional division shall state the date after which no new cases may be brought before the division and the date on which the division will cease to exist.

(4) As from the date on which a local or regional division ceases to exist, the judges assigned to that local or regional division shall be assigned to the central division, and cases still pending before that local or regional division together with the sub-registry and all of its documentation shall be transferred to the central division.

Article 19

Panels

(1) The allocation of judges and the assignment of cases within a division to its panels shall be governed by the Rules of Procedure. One judge of the panel shall be designated as the presiding judge, in accordance with the Rules of Procedure.

(2) The panel may delegate, in accordance with the Rules of Procedure, certain functions to one or more of its judges.

(3) A standing judge for each division to hear urgent cases may be designated in accordance with the Rules of Procedure.

(4) In cases where a single judge in accordance with Article 8(7) of the Agreement, or a standing judge, in accordance with paragraph 3 of this Article, hears a case that judge shall carry out all functions of a panel.

(5) One judge of the panel shall act as Rapporteur, in accordance with the Rules of Procedure.

Article 20

Pool of Judges

(1) A list with the names of the judges included in the Pool of Judges shall be drawn up by the Registrar. In relation to each judge, the list shall at least indicate the linguistic skills, the field of technology and experience of, as well as the cases previously handled by, that judge.

(2) A request addressed to the President of the Court of First Instance to assign a judge from the Pool of Judges shall indicate, in particular, the subject matter of the case, the official language of the European Patent Office used by the judges of the panel, the language of the proceedings and the field of technology required.

Section 3 – The Court of Appeal

Article 21

Panels

AppG-93 **(1)** The allocation of judges and the assignment of cases to panels shall be governed by the Rules of Procedure. One judge of the panel shall be appointed as the presiding judge, in accordance with the Rules of Procedure.

(2) When a case is of exceptional importance, and in particular when the decision may affect the unity and consistency of the case law of the Court, the Court of Appeal may decide, on the basis of a proposal from the presiding judge, to refer the case to the full Court.

(3) The panel may delegate, in accordance with the Rules of Procedure, certain functions to one or more of its judges.

(4) One judge of the panel shall act as Rapporteur, in accordance with the Rules of Procedure.

Section 4 – The Registry

Article 22

Appointment and removal from office of the Registrar

AppG-94 **(1)** The Presidium shall appoint the Registrar of the Court for a term of six years. The Registrar may be re-appointed.

(2) Two weeks before the date fixed for appointing the Registrar, the President of the Court of Appeal shall inform the Presidium of the applications which have been submitted for the post.

(3)   Before taking up his or her duties, the Registrar shall take oath before the Presidium to perform the duties of the Registrar impartially and conscientiously.

(4)   The Registrar may be removed from office only if the Registrar no longer meets the obligations arising from his or her office. The Presidium shall take its decision after having heard the Registrar.

(5)   If the office of the Registrar falls vacant before the date of expiry of the term thereof, the Presidium shall appoint a new Registrar for a term of six years.

(6)   If the Registrar is absent or prevented from attending or where such post is vacant, the President of the Court of Appeal after having consulted the Presidium shall designate a member of the staff of the Court to carry out the duties of the Registrar.

Article 23
Duties of the Registrar

(1)   The Registrar shall assist the Court, the President of the Court of Appeal, the President of the Court of First Instance and the judges in the performance of their functions. The Registrar shall be responsible for the organisation and activities of the Registry under the authority of the President of the Court of Appeal.

(2)   The Registrar shall in particular be responsible for:
   (a)   keeping the register which shall include records of all cases before the Court;
   (b)   keeping and administering lists drawn up in accordance with Articles 18, 48(3) and 57(2) of the Agreement;
   (c)   keeping and publishing a list of notifications and withdrawals of opt-outs in accordance with Article 83 of the Agreement;
   (d)   publishing the decisions of the Court, subject to the protection of confidential information;
   (e)   publishing annual reports with statistical data; and
   (f)   ensuring that the information on opt-outs in accordance with Article 83 of the Agreement is notified to the European Patent Office.

Article 24
Keeping of the register

(1)   Detailed rules for keeping the register of the Court shall be prescribed in the Rules governing the Registry, adopted by the Presidium.

(2)   The rules on access to documents of the Registry shall be provided for in the Rules of Procedure.

Article 25
Sub-registries and Deputy-Registrar

(1)   A Deputy-Registrar shall be appointed for a term of six years by the Presidium. The Deputy-Registrar may be re-appointed.

(2)   Article 22(2) to (6) shall apply by analogy.

(3)   The Deputy-Registrar shall be responsible for the organisation and activities of sub-registries under the authority of the Registrar and the President of the Court of First Instance. The duties of the Deputy-Registrar shall in particular include:

(a)   keeping records of all cases before the Court of First Instance;

(b)   notifying every case before the Court of First Instance to the Registry.

(4)   The Deputy-Registrar shall also provide administrative and secretarial assistance to the divisions of the Court of First Instance.

CHAPTER III – FINANCIAL PROVISIONS

Article 26

Budget

AppG-95 (1)   The budget shall be adopted by the Budget Committee on a proposal from the Presidium. It shall be drawn up in accordance with the generally accepted accounting principles laid down in the Financial Regulations, established in accordance with Article 33.

(2)   Within the budget, the Presidium may, in accordance with the Financial Regulations, transfer funds between the various headings or subheadings.

(3)   The Registrar shall be responsible for the implementation of the budget in accordance with the Financial Regulations.

(4)   The Registrar shall annually make a statement on the accounts of the preceding financial year relating to the implementation of the budget which shall be approved by the Presidium.

Article 27

Authorisation for expenditure

(1)   The expenditure entered in the budget shall be authorised for the duration of one accounting period unless the Financial Regulations provide otherwise.

(2)   In accordance with the Financial Regulations, any appropriations, other than those relating to staff costs, which are unexpended at the end of the accounting period may be carried forward, but not beyond the end of the following accounting period.

(3)   Appropriations shall be set out under different headings according to type and purpose of the expenditure, and subdivided, to the extent necessary, in accordance with the Financial Regulations.

Article 28

Appropriations for unforeseeable expenditure

(1)   The budget of the Court may include appropriations for unforeseeable expenditure.

(2)   The employment of these appropriations by the Court shall be subject to the prior approval of the Budget Committee.

Article 29

Accounting period

The accounting period shall commence on 1 January and end on 31 December.

Article 30

Preparation of the budget

The Presidium shall submit the draft budget of the Court to the Budget Committee no later than the date prescribed in the Financial Regulations.

Article 31

Provisional budget

(1) If, at the beginning of the accounting period, the budget has not been adopted by the Budget Committee, expenditure may be effected on a monthly basis per heading or other division of the budget, in accordance with the Financial Regulations, up to one-twelfth of the budget appropriations for the preceding accounting period, provided that the appropriations thus made available to the Presidium do not exceed one-twelfth of those provided for in the draft budget.

(2) The Budget Committee may, subject to the observance of the other provisions laid down in paragraph 1, authorise expenditure in excess of one-twelfth of the budget appropriations for the preceding accounting period.

Article 32

Auditing of accounts

(1) The annual financial statements of the Court shall be examined by independent auditors. The auditors shall be appointed and if necessary dismissed by the Budget Committee.

(2) The audit, which shall be based on professional auditing standards and shall take place, if necessary, in situ, shall ascertain that the budget has been implemented in a lawful and proper manner and that the financial administration of the Court has been conducted in accordance with the principles of economy and sound financial management. The auditors shall draw up a report after the end of each accounting period containing a signed audit opinion.

(3) The Presidium shall submit to the Budget Committee the annual financial statements of the Court and the annual budget implementation statement for the preceding accounting period, together with the auditors' report.

(4) The Budget Committee shall approve the annual accounts together with the auditors' report and shall discharge the Presidium in respect of the implementation of the budget.

Article 33

Financial Regulations

(1) The Financial Regulations shall be adopted by the Administrative Committee. They shall be amended by the Administrative Committee on a proposal from the Court.

(2) The Financial Regulations shall lay down in particular:
  (a) arrangements relating to the establishment and implementation of the budget and for the rendering and auditing of accounts;
  (b) the method and procedure whereby the payments and contributions, including the initial financial contributions provided for in Article 37 of the Agreement are to be made available to the Court;
  (c) the rules concerning the responsibilities of authorising and accounting officers and the arrangements for their supervision; and
  (d) the generally accepted accounting principles on which the budget and the annual financial statements are to be based.

CHAPTER IV – PROCEDURAL PROVISIONS

Article 34

Secrecy of deliberations

AppG-96 The deliberations of the Court shall be and shall remain secret.

Article 35

Decisions

(1) When a panel sits in composition of an even number of judges, decisions of the Court shall be taken by a majority of the panel. In case of equal vote, the vote of the presiding judge shall prevail.

(2) In the event of one of the judges of a panel being prevented from attending, a judge from another panel may be called upon to sit in accordance with the Rules of Procedure.

(3) In cases where this Statute provides that the Court of Appeal shall take a decision sitting as a full court, such decision shall be valid only if it is taken by at least 3/4 of the judges comprising the full court.

(4) Decisions of the Court shall contain the names of the judges deciding the case.

(5) Decisions shall be signed by the judges deciding the case, by the Registrar for decisions of the Court of Appeal, and by the Deputy-Registrar for decisions of the Court of First Instance. They shall be read in open court.

Article 36

Dissenting opinions

A dissenting opinion expressed separately by a judge of a panel in accordance with Article 78 of the Agreement shall be reasoned, given in writing and shall be signed by the judge expressing this opinion.

Article 37

Decision by default

(1) At the request of a party to an action, a decision by default may be given in accordance with the Rules of Procedure, where the other party, after having been served with a document instituting proceedings or with an equivalent document, fails to file written submissions in defence or fails to appear at the oral hearing. An objection may be lodged against that decision within one month of it being notified to the party against which the default decision has been given.

(2) The objection shall not have the effect of staying enforcement of the decision by default unless the Court decides otherwise.

Article 38

Questions referred to the Court of Justice of the European Union

(1) The procedures established by the Court of Justice of the European Union for referrals for preliminary rulings within the European Union shall apply.

(2) Whenever the Court of First Instance or the Court of Appeal has decided to refer to the Court of Justice of the European Union a question of interpretation of the Treaty on European Union or of the Treaty on the Functioning of the European Union or a question on the validity or interpretation of acts of the institutions of the European Union, it shall stay its proceedings.

ANNEX II

Distribution of cases within the central division[15]   AppG-97

LONDON Section	PARIS Seat	MUNICH Section
	President's Office	
(A) Human necessities	(B) Performing operations, transporting	(F) Mechanical engineering, lighting, heating, weapons, blasting
(C) Chemistry, metallurgy	(D) Textiles, paper	
	(E) Fixed constructions	
	(G) Physics	
	(H) Electricity	

---

[15] The classification into 8 sections (A to H) is based on the International Patent Classification of the World Intellectual Property Organisation (*http://www.wipo.int/classifications/ipc/en*).

INDEX

LEGAL TAXONOMY
FROM SWEET & MAXWELL

This index has been prepared using Sweet and Maxwell's Legal Taxonomy. Main index entries conform to keywords provided by the Legal Taxonomy except where references to specific documents or non-standard terms (denoted by quotation marks) have been included. These keywords provide a means of identifying similar concepts in other Sweet & Maxwell publications and online services to which keywords from the Legal Taxonomy have been applied. Readers may find some minor differences between terms used in the text and those which appear in the index. Suggestions to *sweetandmaxwell.taxonomy@thomson.com*.